International Human Rights

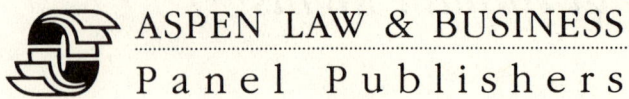

International Human Rights
Problems of Law, Policy, and Practice

Third Edition

Richard B. Lillich
Howard W. Smith Professor of Law
University of Virginia

Hurst Hannum
Associate Professor of International Law
The Fletcher School of Law and Diplomacy
Tufts University

ASPEN LAW & BUSINESS
Aspen Publishers, Inc.

Library of Congress Catalog Card No. 94-74419

ISBN 0-316-52687-8

Third Edition

Second Printing

Published by Aspen Law & Business
Formerly published by Little, Brown & Company

For the poor and the oppressed, for the unemployed and the destitute, for prisoners and captives, and for all who remember and care for them.

The Book of Common Prayer

Summary of Contents

Preface xxxi
Acknowledgments xxxv

Historical Introduction 1

Problem I   The Expulsion of Asians from Uganda
                 *Are States Bound by the Human Rights
                 Clauses of the UN Charter?* 14

Problem II   Fujii, Filartiga, and Beyond
                 *Are States' Courts Bound by the Human
                 Rights Clauses of the UN Charter and the
                 Universal Declaration of Human
                 Rights?* 90

Problem III   Suriname, the United States, and the UN
                 Covenant on Civil and Political Rights
                 *What Obligations Have States Assumed
                 Under the UN Human Rights
                 Treaties?* 178

Problem IV   The "Soft" Law of Principles, Guidelines, and
                 Model Laws
                 *How Does the UN Create New Human
                 Rights Norms Other Than by Treaty?* 276

Problem V   The Greek Case, Resolution 1503, and Other
                 UN Mechanisms
                 *When Does the UN Investigate Human
                 Rights Violations?* 340

Problem VI   The Problem of Fact-Finding and Evidence
                 *How Does the UN Investigate Violations of
                 Human Rights Law?* 408

Problem VII   Sanctions and Southern Africa
                     How Effective in Causing Compliance with
                         Human Rights Law Are Coercive Measures
                         That Do Not Involve the Use of Armed
                         Force?   486

Problem VIII   Bangladesh
                     When May the UN or Its Member States Use
                         Armed Force for Human Rights
                         Purposes?   600

Problem IX   The European Regime for the Protection of
                         Human Rights
                     Can Regional Systems to Protect Human
                         Rights Be More Effective Than UN
                         Mechanisms?   680

Problem X   The Protection of Human Rights in the
                         Americas and Africa
                     Can Regional Systems to Protect Human
                         Rights Be More Effective Than UN
                         Mechanisms?   780

Problem XI   Human Rights in Extremis
                     How Can Human Rights Be Protected in
                         Armed Conflict, Civil Strife, and States of
                         Emergency?   836

Problem XII   International Criminal Law and Procedure and
                         the Domestic Enforcement of "Piecemeal"
                         Conventions
                     Can the Criminal Process Be Used to Help
                         Enforce Human Rights Law?   934

Problem XIII   The Carter Administration's Human Rights
                         Initiatives and Its Legacy
                     How Relevant Are Human Rights Concerns
                         to the Foreign Policy Process?   1026

Index   *1151*

Table of Contents

Summary of Contents		*vii*
Preface		*xxxi*
Acknowledgments		*xxxv*

Historical Introduction   1

Problem I   **14**

The Expulsion of Asians from Uganda

Are States Bound by the Human Rights Clauses of the UN Charter?

I.	*Uganda: The "Pearl of Africa" Despoiled*	*16*
	A. Background: From Stanley to Obote	16
	B. The Role of the Asians and the Rise of Amin	18
	C. The Expulsion of the Asians	19
	Statement by Idi Amin Relating to the Expulsion of Asians from Uganda	19
	The Declaration of Assets (Non-Citizen Asians) Decree, 1972	22
	D. The Response of the World Community	26
	1. Debates in Great Britain	26
	2. Debates at the UN	28
II.	*Human Rights Before the UN Charter*	*32*
	P. Sieghart, The International Law of Human Rights	33
	Farer, Human Rights Before the Second World War	34
III.	*Human Rights After the UN Charter*	*36*
	A. Background and Description of the Human Rights Clauses	36
	Eighteenth Report of the Commission to Study the Organization of Peace, The United Nations and Human Rights	36

J. Brierly, The Law of Nations   38
Comments and Questions   39
B.   Content and Legal Status of the Human Rights
     Clauses   41
     Schachter, The Charter and the Constitution: The
        Human Rights Provisions in American Law   41
     Note: U.S. Recognition of the Legal Status of the
        Human Rights Clauses   46
C.   Invocation of the Human Rights Clauses on the In-
     ternational Level   48
     Legal Consequences for States of the Continued
        Presence of South Africa in Namibia (South
        West Africa)   49
     Schwelb, The International Court of Justice and
        the Human Rights Clauses of the Charter   49
     Comments and Questions   54

IV. *The Relevance of the Human Rights Clauses of the
     UN Charter to the Expulsion of Asians from
     Uganda*   55
     Wooldridge and Sharma, International Law and
        the Expulsion of Ugandan Asians   55
     Plender, The Ugandan Crisis and the Right of Ex-
        pulsion Under International Law   59
     Chhangani, Expulsion of Uganda Asians and In-
        ternational Law   61
     Note: Applying the Human Rights Clauses of the
        UN Charter and Other International Norms to
        the Expulsion of Asians from Uganda   64

V.   *The Response of the International Community to
     Subsequent Human Rights Abuses in Uganda*   66
A.   The Situation Worsens   66
     Uganda — A Lawless State   66
     Mohr, In Amin's Taciturn Uganda, Even Food Is
        Unspeakable   67
     See No Evil   70
B.   UN Action (or Inaction)   71
C.   The U.S. Embargo   73
D.   The Tanzanian Intervention   76

VI. *Concluding Thoughts and Observations*   78
     Bilder, Rethinking International Human Rights:
        Some Basic Questions   79
     Comments and Questions   82

VII. *Final Comments and Questions*   83

Problem II   90

Fujii, Filartiga, and Beyond

Are States' Courts Bound by the Human Rights Clauses of the UN Charter and the Universal Declaration of Human Rights?

I.   *Introduction: The Relationship Between International and Domestic Legal Systems*   *92*
II. *The Status of the Human Rights Clauses in Domestic Law*   *95*
    A.   The Legal Background   95
        Schachter, The Charter and the Constitution: The Human Rights Provisions in American Law   95
    B.   The *Fujii* Case   101
        Note: Mr. Sei Fujii and the California Alien Land Law   101
        Sei Fujii v. State (California District Court of Appeal)   102
        Hudson, Charter Provisions on Human Rights in American Law   104
        Wright, National Courts and Human Rights — The *Fujii* Case   108
        Note: An Unusual Occurrence in the Course of the *Fujii* Appeal   114
        Sei Fujii v. State (California Supreme Court)   115
        Comments and Questions   118
    C.   The Post-*Fujii* Scene: Regrets and Hopes   121
        1.   The Present Status of the UN Charter's Human Rights Clauses   121
        2.   Flashforward: Are Other Human Rights Treaties Self-Executing or Not?   121
III. *The Status of the Universal Declaration in Domestic Law*   *122*
    A.   The Historical Perspective   122
        Kunz, The United Nations Declaration of Human Rights   122
        Schwelb, The Influence of the Universal Declaration of Human Rights on International and National Law   127
        The Universal Declaration of Human Rights at 20   132
    B.   U.S. Case Law Developments   133
        Setting the Stage   133
        Filartiga v. Pena-Irala   137

        Fernandez v. Wilkinson   143
        Forti v. Suarez-Mason   148
        Comments and Questions   154
    C. The Universal Declaration of Human Rights Nears 50   162
        Restatement (Third) of the Foreign Relations Law
            of the United States §702   162
        Lillich, Remarks   162
        International Law Association, Committee on the
            Enforcement of Human Rights Law, Final Report
            on the Status of the Universal Declaration of Hu-
            man Rights in National and International Law   166
IV. Final Comments and Questions   171

Problem III   178

Suriname, the United States, and the UN
Covenant on Civil and Political Rights

What Obligations Have States Assumed Under
the UN Human Rights Treaties?

I.   Suriname: Development, Independence, Repression   181
II. The UN Treaty Approach to Human Rights   183
     A. UN Human Rights Treaties: An Overview   183
         Bilder, Rethinking International Human Rights:
             Some Basic Questions   187
     B. General Human Rights Treaties   189
         Note: Completing the International Bill of Rights   189
         Henkin, Introduction, in The International Bill of
             Rights   191
     C. Specific Human Rights Treaties   193
     D. The Human Rights "Generations"   194
         1. Introductory Note   194
         2. "Second Generation" Human Rights   195
         Prepared Statement of Hon. Roberts B. Owen,
             Legal Adviser, Department of State   198
         3. "Third Generation" Human Rights   201
         Marks, Emerging Human Rights: A New Genera-
             tion for the 1980s?   201
         A. Robertson, Human Rights in the World   202
         Bibliographical Note on the Right to Development   204
     E. UN Human Rights Law-Making: The Need for "Qual-
         ity Control"   206
         UN General Assembly Resolution 41/120 (1987)   207

International League for Human Rights, Human
Rights at the United Nations: New Standard
Setting   208

III. *The Civil and Political Covenant*   209
A. Substantive Provisions   209
B. Implementation Measures   210
    1. State Reporting   211
        Shelton, Compliance Mechanisms [Periodic Re-
        ports]   212
    2. Individual Communications   214
        Lewis-Anthony, Treaty-Based Procedures for Mak-
        ing Human Rights Complaints Within the UN
        System   215
        Report of the Human Rights Committee   220
    3. Interstate Complaints   222
        Leckie, The Inter-State Complaint Procedure in
        International Human Rights Law: Hopeful
        Prospects or Wishful Thinking?   222
    4. General Comments   224

IV. *Suriname Revisited: More Repression in Violation
of the Civil and Political Covenant*   224
        Baboeram Communications   228
        Note: The Aftermath   237

V. *United States Ratification of Human Rights Treaties*   239
A. The U.S. Ratification Record: An Overview   239
    1. Introductory Note   239
    2. The Carter Administration Initiatives   240
        Henkin, The Covenant on Civil and Political Rights   241
        Moore, Statement Before the Senate Committee
        on Foreign Relations   244
        Note: Carter's Legacy   245
    3. Developments During the Reagan and Bush
        Administrations   246
B. U.S. Ratification of the Civil and Political Covenant   248
    1. The Covenant and the U.S. Constitution and
        Laws   248
        Restatement (Third) of the Foreign Relations Law
        of the United States §701   248
    2. The Reservations, Understandings, and Declara-
        tions "Debate"   250
        International Covenant on Civil and Political
        Rights: The Administration's Proposed Reserva-
        tions, Understandings and Declarations   251
        International Human Rights Law Group, Ratifica-
        tion of the International Covenant on Civil and
        Political Rights by the United States   254

Stewart, United States Ratification of the Covenant on Civil and Political Rights: The Signifi-
cance of the Reservations, Understandings, and
Declarations   259
3. Attitudes of the U.S. NGO Community Towards
Ratification Conditioned upon Acceptance of
the Bush Administration "Package"   260
Letter from Lawyers Committee for Human Rights
to Senator Claiborne Pell   261
Letter from Human Rights Watch to Lawyers
Committee for Human Rights   263
Letter from Lawyers Committee for Human Rights
to Human Rights Watch   266
C. U.S. Ratification of the Other Human Rights Treaties:
The "Package" Redux   268
Comments and Questions Concerning U.S. Ratifi-
cation of the Human Rights Treaties   270
VI. *Final Comments and Questions*   *273*

Problem IV   276

The "Soft" Law of Principles, Guidelines, and Model Laws

How Does the UN Create New Human Rights Norms Other Than by Treaty?

I. *The Attica Uprising*   *278*
A. Background and Aftermath   278
B. Current Attitudes Toward Treatment of Prisoners   281
C. International Norms Governing the Treatment of
Prisoners   283
Besharov and Mueller, The Demands of the
Inmates of Attica State Prison and the United
Nations Standard Minimum Rules for the Treat-
ment of Prisoners: A Comparison   285
D. Status of the Standard Minimum Rules   296
The Standard Minimum Rules for the Treatment of
Prisoners in the Light of Recent Developments
in the Correctional Field   296
II. *Applying the "Model Law" or "Soft Law" Approach
to Related Areas*   *300*
A. General Observations   300
Toman, Quasi-Legal Standards and Guidelines for
Protecting Human Rights   300

N. Rodley, The Treatment of Prisoners Under
  International Law   301
Heijder, Codes of Professional Ethics Against
  Torture   302
B. Specific Areas   304
    1. Treatment of Prisoners   305
    2. Juvenile Offenders   305
    3. Standards for the Administration of Justice   306
III. *Implementation of the Standard Minimum Rules
     and Other Criminal Justice Norms*   *306*
     R. Clark, The United Nations Crime Prevention
       and Criminal Justice Program   307
     Report of the Working Group on Arbitrary Deten-
       tion   311
A. Regional Standards: European Prison Rules   313
B. National Standards: United States Federal and State
    Laws and Regulations (and Their Enforcement)   314
C. Non-Governmental and Private Organization Stan-
    dards   317
    Comments and Questions   318
IV. *New Rights for Vulnerable Groups*   *322*
A. General Observations   *322*
B. Minorities   *324*
    Hannum, Contemporary Developments in the In-
      ternational Protection of the Rights of Minorities   324
    Human Rights Committee, General Comment No.
      23(50) (Art. 27)   327
    UN General Assembly Resolution 47/135   329
    Note: Implementation   330
    Note: European Initiatives   331
C. Indigenous Peoples   *332*
D. Self-Determination   *334*
    Comments and Questions   *336*
V. *Final Comments and Questions*   *337*

Problem V   **340**

The Greek Case, Resolution 1503, and Other UN Mechanisms

When Does the UN Investigate Human Rights Violations?

I.   *The Right to Petition as a Human Right*   *342*
II. *The Situation in Greece: The Sub-Commission's First
     Test Case*   *344*

A.   Resolution 1503: High Expectations   344
B.   Historical Note   344
     Note: Greece: Justice in Blinkers   346
     Note: Human Rights Report on Greece   347
C.   Communication Alleging Violation of Human Rights
     in Greece   348
D.   The Sub-Commission's Response to the Communi-
     cation   354
     Note: Disappointing Start to New U.N. Procedure
     on Human Rights   354
E.   The Reaction of the Greek Regime   357
     Letter from the Permanent Representative of
     Greece to the United Nations   357
F.   The Overthrow of the Greek Regime and the Sub-
     Commission's Role Therein   361
     Note: The Overthrow of the Greek Regime   361
     Statement by Amnesty International and the Inter-
     national Student Movement for the UN   362

III. Analyzing the Procedures and Problems of Resolu-
      tion 1503   363
      Newman, The New U.N. Procedures for Human
      Rights Complaints: Reform, Status Quo, or
      Chamber of Horrors?   363
      H. Tolley, Jr., The U.N. Commission on Human
      Rights   366
      Alston, The Commission on Human Rights   379

IV.   Other UN Mechanisms for Investigating Alleged Hu-
      man Rights Abuses   380
A.   Petition Procedures   380
B.   Non-Petition Procedures   382
     J. Carey, UN Protection of Civil and Political Rights   383
     Alston, The Commission on Human Rights   385
     Commission on Human Rights, Torture and Other
     Cruel, Inhuman or Degrading Treatment or
     Punishment   394
     Commission on Human Rights, Question of Arbi-
     trary Detention   394
     Commission on Human Rights, Right to Freedom
     of Opinion and Expression   395
     Report of the Working Group on Arbitrary Deten-
     tion   396
     Commission on Human Rights, Human Rights and
     Thematic Procedures   396
C.   Future Prospects   400
     H. Tolley, Jr., The U.N. Commission on Human
     Rights   400

Farer, The United Nations and Human Rights:
More Than a Whimper, Less Than a Roar   402
V. *Final Comments and Questions*   *405*

Problem VI   **408**

The Problem of Fact-Finding and Evidence

How Does the UN Investigate Violations of Human Rights Law?

I.   *The Challenge: To Find Out What Is Really Happening*   *410*
II. *Gathering the Facts*   *411*
    A. Information Reported by States   411
        Bayefsky, Making the Human Rights Treaties Work   412
    B. Fact-Finding by the UN General Assembly   417
        Rules of Procedure of the Special Committee to
        Investigate Israeli Practices   419
        Report of the Special Committee to Investigate
        Israeli Practices   421
    C. Fact-Finding by the UN Commission on Human Rights 422
        1. Country-Specific Rapporteurs   423
        Consideration of the Report of the Mission Which
        Took Place in Cuba   424
        Jiminez, Report on the Question of Human Rights
        in Chile   427
        Galindo Pohl, Report on the Human Rights Situation in the Islamic Republic of Iran   430
        2. Thematic Mechanisms   431
        Wako, Report [on Summary or Arbitrary Executions]   431
        Kooijmans, Report [on Torture and Other Cruel,
        Inhuman, or Degrading Treatment or Punishment]   436
        Vidal d'Almerida Ribero, Report [on Intolerance
        and Discrimination Based on Religion or Belief]   439
        Report of the Working Group on Arbitrary Detention   441
        Note: The Role of the UN Secretariat   444
        Brody, Improving UN Human Rights Structures   444
        Note: A Rapporteur from the Commission on
        Human Rights Visits Suriname   445
        Wako, Report [on Summary or Arbitrary Executions]   445

D. The Need for General Standards for Fact-Finding by International Organizations   448

Note: Toward a Solution — The Belgrade Rules on Fact-Finding by International Organizations   449

Belgrade Minimal Rules of Procedure for International Human Rights Fact-Finding Missions   449

E. Fact-Finding by Non-Governmental Organizations   452

Orentlicher, Bearing Witness: The Art and Science of Human Rights Fact-Finding   452

H. Thoolen and B. Verstappen, Human Rights Missions: A Study of the Fact-Finding Practice of Non-Governmental Organizations   456

Correspondence: Professor Moore   458

Correspondence: Professor Glennon   461

H. Thoolen and B. Verstappen, Human Rights Missions: A Study of the Fact-Finding Practice of Non-Governmental Organizations   465

Hannum, Fact-Finding by Non-Governmental Human Rights Organizations   468

F. Fact-Finding by Judicial and Quasi-Judicial Bodies   469

T. Buergenthal, R. Norris, and D. Shelton, Protecting Human Rights in the Americas   472

III. *Evaluating the Facts*   475

A. Admissibility of Evidence   475

B. The Burden of Proof   475

Ramcharan, Evidence   476

Bleier v. Uruguay   479

The Velásquez Rodríguez Case   480

The Gangaram Panday Case   481

Weissbrodt, Human Rights Implementation and Fact-Finding by International Organizations   482

IV. *Final Comments and Questions*   483

Problem VII   486

Sanctions and Southern Africa

How Effective in Causing Compliance with Human Rights Law Are Coercive Measures That Do Not Involve the Use of Armed Force?

I. *Rhodesia: The Factual Context*   489

A. The Background   489

B. The Prelude to Independence   490

C. Unilateral Declaration of Independence   491

D.   Initial Attempts at Settlement   493
II.   *UN Economic Sanctions Against Rhodesia: Their
      Legality Under the UN Charter*   495
      Introductory Note   495
      McDougal and Reisman, Rhodesia and the
         United Nations: The Lawfulness of Interna-
         tional Concern   497
      Acheson, The Arrogance of International
         Lawyers   504
III. *A Brief Overview of Economic Sanctions*   509
      A.   International Sanctions   509
      B.   Regional Sanctions   511
      C.   Unilateral Sanctions   513
      D.   Voluntary Sanctions   514
IV.   *U.S. Implementation and Enforcement of UN
      Sanctions Against Rhodesia*   515
      A.   U.S. Implementation of Sanctions   515
           1.   The Legal Framework   515
                Legislative Reference Service, Library of Con-
                gress, The United Nations Participation Act
                Sections Relating to Economic and Military
                Action   515
           2.   Presidential Action: Executive Orders 11,322
                and 11,419   517
                U.S. Extends Program Banning Trade with South-
                ern Rhodesia   518
                Executive Order No. 11,419 (Relating to Trade
                and Other Transactions Involving Southern
                Rhodesia)   518
           3.   The Overlooked (?) Loophole: Rhodesian
                Sanctions Regulation 31 C.F.R. §530.307
                (1969)   520
      B.   U.S. Enforcement of Sanctions   522
           1.   Introduction   522
           2.   Congress Enacts the Byrd Amendment   524
                UN Sanctions Against Rhodesia — Chrome 524
                Hearings on S. 1404, UN Sanctions Against
                Rhodesia — Chrome, Before the Senate Com-
                mittee on Foreign Relations   524
                Note: The Byrd Amendment Becomes Law   531
                Irony in Chrome: The Byrd Amendment Two
                Years Later   532
           3.   Critics Challenge the Byrd Amendment: Diggs
                v. Shultz and the Eventual "Repeal" of the Byrd
                Amendment   535

Diggs v. Shultz   536

The Significance of Diggs v. Shultz   540

Note: Security Council Resolutions in United
States Courts   541

Congress "Repeals" the Byrd Amendment   542

4. The Enforcement of UN Sanctions Under U.S.
Law: At Best, Inconsistent; At Worst, Non-
Existent   543

Carnegie Endowment for International Peace,
Business as Usual: Transactions Violating
Rhodesian Sanctions   544

Lillich, Examining Mobil's Role as Sanctions-
Buster   546

The Treasury Department Investigations   550

Note: Sanctions-Breaking Around the World   554

V. *Rhodesia: The Achievement of Majority Rule*   561

A. The Salisbury Agreement and the Emergence of
Zimbabwe Rhodesia   561

B. The Lancaster House Conference and the Creation
of Zimbabwe   562

Davidow, Dealing with International Crises: Les-
sons from Zimbabwe   563

VI. *Viewpoints on International Economic Sanctions:*
Rhodesia as a Case Study   565

H. Strack, Sanctions: The Case of Rhodesia   565

D. Losman, International Economic Sanctions   567

R. Renwick, Economic Sanctions   568

Auglin, United Nations Sanctions Against South
Africa and Rhodesia   569

M. Doxey, International Sanctions in Contempo-
rary Perspective   571

VII. *Sanctions Against South Africa*   573

A. UN Mandatory Sanctions   573

Security Council Resolution 418   574

Note: Implementation and Enforcement of Reso-
lution 418   575

Note: British and U.S. Vetoes Block Further Man-
datory Sanctions   576

Statement of Mr. Herbert S. Okun, Acting U.S.
Representative to United Nations, February
20, 1987   577

B. UN Voluntary Sanctions   578

1. General Assembly Sanctions   578

2. Security Council Sanctions   578

3. The Intergovernmental Group to Monitor the

Supply and Shipping of Oil and Petroleum Products to South Africa: A Case Study in Implementing UN Voluntary Sanctions 579
C. U.S. Sanctions 580
1. Introduction 580
2. President Reagan's Executive Order: Too Late and Too Little 583
Recent Developments, Economic Sanctions: United States Sanctions Against South Africa 583
3. The Comprehensive Anti-Apartheid Act of 1986 585
Note: The Passage of the Federal Anti-Apartheid Act: The Culmination of Anti-Apartheid Efforts Within the United States 585
Implementation and Enforcement of the Act 587
4. The Rangel Amendment Denies Foreign Tax Credits to U.S. Corporations Doing Business in South Africa 588
5. The End of Sanctions and an Evaluation of Their Effectiveness 589
VIII. *Final Comments and Questions* 590

Problem VIII

600

Bangladesh

When May the UN or Its Member States Use Armed Force for Human Rights Purposes?

I. *Introduction: The Bangladesh Problem* 602
International Commission of Jurists, The Events in East Pakistan, 1971 604
II. *Humanitarian Intervention by States* 613
A. Background and Legal Issues 613
Fonteyne, The Customary International Law Doctrine of Humanitarian Intervention: Its Current Validity Under the U.N. Charter 614
B. The Debate over Humanitarian Intervention 623
Brownlie, Humanitarian Intervention 624
Lillich, Humanitarian Intervention: A Reply to Ian Brownlie and a Plea for Constructive Alternatives 631
Bibliography (Humanitarian Intervention by States) 641

C.   The Aftermath of a Crisis: Bangladesh Since 1971   641
D.   Other Claims of Unilateral Humanitarian Interven-
     tion Since the Bangladesh Crisis   643
E.   Nicaragua v. United States: Delphic Dicta from the
     International Court of Justice   646
        Nicaragua v. United States, Merits   646
        Rodley, Human Rights and Humanitarian Inter-
           vention: The Case Law of the World Court   647
        F. Teson, Humanitarian Intervention: An Inquiry
           into Law and Morality   647
        Comments and Questions on the Court's Dicta   649
III. UN Humanitarian Intervention   651
        Lillich, Humanitarian Intervention Through the
           United Nations: Towards the Development of
           Criteria   652
        Security Council Resolution 940 on Haiti   659
        Note: The Significance of Resolution 940   662
        Bibliography (UN Humanitarian Intervention)   663
IV.   Forcible Protection of Nationals   664
A.   Contrasting Views Regarding Forcible Protection of
     Nationals   665
        Letters to the Editor of the New York Times   665
B.   Reading   667
        Lillich, Forcible Protection of Nationals Abroad:
           The Liberian "Incident" of 1990   667
C.   Forcible Protection of Nationals Abroad: Post-
     Entebbe Case Studies   672
V.   Final Comments and Questions   675

Problem IX   *682-708*   **680**

The European Regime for the Protection of Human Rights

Can Regional Systems to Protect Human Rights Be More Effective Than UN Mechanisms?

I.   The Regional Approach to Human Rights   682
        Weston, Lukes, and Hnatt, Regional Human Rights
           Regimes: A Comparison and Appraisal   682
II.   The Council of Europe   684
A.   The European Convention for the Protection of
     Human Rights and Fundamental Freedoms   684

Council of Europe, Protocol No. 11 to the Conven-
tion for the Protection of Human Rights and
Fundamental Freedoms and Explanatory Report   687
Note: Interstate Complaints   692
Ireland v. United Kingdom   693
Note: "Degrading Treatment or Punishment" vs.
"Cruel and Unusual Punishment"   715
Letters to the Editor   716
Not Sparing the Rod; How Cruel, How Unusual?   721
Soering v. United Kingdom   724
Note: The "Death Row Phenomenon"   760
B.   The European Social Charter   760
C.   The European Convention for the Prevention of
Torture and Inhuman or Degrading Treatment or
Punishment   762
Evans and Morgan, The European Convention for
the Prevention of Torture: Operational Practice   762
Comments and Questions   765
III.   *The Organization on Security and Cooperation in
Europe*   769
Commission on Security and Cooperation in Eu-
rope, Beyond Process: The CSCE's Institutional
Development, 1990-92   769
Helsinki Document 1992, The Challenges of
Change   772
IV.   *The European Community*   775
Boyle, Europe: The Council of Europe, the CSCE,
and the European Community   775
Comments and Questions   777

Problem X   **780**

The Protection of Human Rights in the Americas and Africa

Can Regional Systems to Protect Human Rights Be More Effective Than UN Mechanisms?

I.   *Introduction*   782
II.   *The Inter-American System*   782
A.   The Inter-American Commission and Court   782
Medina, The Inter-American Commission on Hu-
man Rights and the Inter-American Court of
Human Rights: Reflections on a Joint Venture   782

1. Country-Specific Reports   787
Inter-American Commission on Human Rights,
Report on the Situation of Human Rights in
Haiti   788
2. Individual Complaints   793
Association of the Bar of the City of New York,
Committee on International Human Rights,
The Inter-American Commission: A Promise
Unfulfilled   793
Note: The Role of the Court   799
Note: The Velásquez Rodríguez Case   799
Note: The United States Before the Inter-Ameri-
can Commission   802
Inter-American Commission on Human Rights
Resolution 3/87, Case 9647 (United States)   803
3. Advisory Opinions of the Court   804
Compulsory Membership in an Association Pre-
scribed by Law for the Practice of Journalism   805
Note: The U.S. Position on Ratification of the
American Convention on Human Rights   820
Message to the President Transmitting Four Trea-
ties Pertaining to Human Rights   820
B. Other Initiatives   826
III. *The African Charter on Human and Peoples'*
Rights   *826*
Welch, The African Commission on Human and
Peoples' Rights: A Five-Year Report and Assess-
ment   826
International Commission of Jurists, Background
Paper   830
IV. *Final Comments and Questions*   *832*

Problem XI   **836**

Human Rights in Extremis

How Can Human Rights Be Protected in Armed Conflict, Civil Strife, and States of Emergency?

I. *Human Rights in International Armed Conflict:
The Traditional Law of War*   *839*
A. An Eventful Day in My Lai Hamlet, South Vietnam,
March 1968   839

B.   The Development of the Law of War   844
     Note: Historical Roots of the Concern for Human
          Rights in the Law of War   844
     Draper, Human Rights and the Law of War   844
     Note: The Law Protecting Civilians in Time of
          War — International and Domestic   848
C.   Where Does Responsibility Lie for Violations of the
     Law of War?   853
     In re Yamashita   855
     Note: The Treatment of Command Responsibility
          in U.S. Domestic Law   858
D.   Prosecuting Those Persons Responsible for My Lai   859
     1.   The Legal Framework and the Dramatis Per-
          sonae   859
     2.   The Calley Court-Martial   861
          Extracts from the Original Transcript of the
          Court-Martial of Lieutenant William Calley   862
     3.   Lieutenant Calley's Conviction and the Public's
          Response   872
     4.   The Subsequent Fate of Lieutenant Calley   873
     5.   The Courts-Martial of Captain Medina and the
          Other My Lai Defendants   874
     6.   "Orders" from Above: The Experience of Lieu-
          tenant James Duffy   875
          Lieutenant Duffy's Statement   876
          Note: The Gulf War   879
E.   Recent Developments in the Law of War   879
     Baxter, Modernizing the Law of War   880
     Note: Relevant Articles of Protocol I   884
     Roberts, The New Rules for Waging War:
          The Case Against Ratification of Additional Pro-
          tocol I   888
     Aldrich, Progressive Development of the Laws of
          War: A Reply to Criticisms of the 1977 Geneva
          Protocol I   891
     Message from the President Transmitting Proto-
          col II Additional to the 1949 Geneva Conven-
          tions   894
     Comments and Questions   896
II. Human Rights in Internal Armed Conflict: The
     Developing Norms   900
A.   Background   900
B.   Common Article 3: Its Status and Content   901
     Smith, New Protections for Victims of Interna-
          tional Armed Conflicts   901

Case Concerning Military and Paramilitary Activi-
ties in and Against Nicaragua (Nicaragua v.
United States)   903
C. Protocol II: Its Scope and Content   904
Smith, New Protections for Victims of Interna-
tional Armed Conflicts   904
Note: The Content of Protocol II   905
Junod, Additional Protocol II: History and Scope   906
U.S. Position on Protocol II   908
D. Invoking Common Article 3 and Protocol II in Inter-
nal Armed Conflicts   908
Weissbrodt, The Role of International Organiza-
tions in the Implementation of Human Rights
and Humanitarian Law in Situations of Armed
Conflict   909
Comments and Questions   912
III. *Human Rights in Civil Strife and States of Emer-*
gency   *914*
J. Fitzpatrick, Human Rights in Crisis, The Interna-
tional System for Protecting Rights During
States of Emergency   915
Note: Humanitarian Law as a Limitation on the
Right of Derogation: Internal Armed Conflict
and Civil Strife Contrasted   922
Note: Monitoring States of Emergency   924
Habeas Corpus in Emergency
Situations   927
Note: Limitation Clauses   928
IV. *Final Comments and Questions*   *929*

Problem XII   934

International Criminal Law and Procedure and the Domestic Enforcement of "Piecemeal" Conventions

Can the Criminal Process Be Used to Help Enforce Human Rights Law?

I. *Past Efforts to Bring the Criminal Process to Bear*
upon Human Rights Violators   *936*
A. Introduction   936
B. Background and Legal Issues   938

Bridge, The Case for an International Court of
Criminal Justice and the Formulation of International Criminal Law   938

Wise, Codification: Perspectives and Approaches   952

C. The International Criminalization of Human Rights
Violations   954

M. Bassiouni, International Criminal Law: A Draft
International Criminal Code   954

Bassiouni, The Proscribing Function of International Criminal Law in the Processes of International Protection of Human Rights   954

Mueller, Four Decades After Nuremberg: The
Prospect of an International Criminal Code   957

II. *Current Efforts to Draft a Code of Crimes Against
the Peace and Security of Mankind*   *959*

A. Introductory Note   959

B. Readings on the ILC's Draft Code of Crimes Against
the Peace and Security of Mankind   961

Ferencz, An International Criminal Code and
Court: Where They Stand and Where They're
Going   961

Bassiouni, "Crimes Against Humanity": The Need
for a Specialized Convention   963

Note: The ILC's Draft Code: A Prognosis   965

Note: NGO Efforts to Draft an International Criminal Code   966

III. *Toward an International Criminal Court*   *968*

A. An Iraqi War Crimes Tribunal: Proposed But Rejected   968

Moore, War Crimes and the Rule of Law in the
Gulf Crisis   968

O'Brien, The Nuremberg Precedent and the Gulf
War   973

B. The Yugoslav War Crimes Tribunal: The Security
Council Establishes an Ad Hoc International Criminal Court   978

Orentlicher, Yugoslavia War Crimes Tribunal   978

Zagaris, Introductory Note: International Tribunal
for the Prosecution of Persons Responsible for
Serious Violations of International Humanitarian Law Committed in the Territory of the Former Yugoslavia Since 1991: Rules of Procedure
and Evidence   985

Comments and Questions   989

C. The ILC Draft Statute for an International Criminal
Court   993

        D. NGO Efforts to Draft a Statute for an International
            Criminal Court   1001
        E. U.S. Attitudes Toward an International Criminal
            Court   1002
   IV. *The Progressive Development of International
        Criminal Law: The "Piecemeal" Convention Ap-
        proach Coupled with Domestic Enforcement*   *1005*
        A. Transnational Terrorism   1005
                Gross, International Terrorism and International
                    Criminal Jurisdiction   1005
                Murphy, Woetzel, and Lador-Lederer, Correspon-
                    dence [About Professor Gross's Comments]   1006
        B. Apartheid, Torture, Hostage-Taking   1011
    V. *Other Suggested Uses of the International Criminal
        Process*   *1013*
                Mueller, Two Enforcement Models for Interna-
                    tional Criminal Justice   1013
                J. Carey, UN Protection of Civil and Political Rights 1018
   VI. *Final Comments and Questions*   *1022*

Problem XIII   **1026**

The Carter Administration's Human Rights Initiatives and Its Legacy

How Relevant Are Human Rights Concerns to the Foreign Policy Process?

    I. *Human Rights Factors in the Foreign Policy
        Process: A Brief Overview from a Pre-Carter
        Perspective*   *1029*
        A. Lawyers, Human Rights, and the Foreign Policy
            Process   1029
        B. Human Rights and U.S. Foreign Policy   1030
                Bilder, Human Rights and U.S. Foreign Policy:
                    Short-Term Prospects   1031
   II. *The Carter Administration's Attitude Toward Hu-
        man Rights Concerns in the Foreign Policy Process*   *1039*
        A. The Congressional Backdrop: Giving Credit Where
            Credit Is Due   1039
                Lillich, U.S. Foreign Policy, Human Rights, and
                    Foreign Trade and Investment   1039
        B. Defining the Carter Administration's Human Rights
            Policy   1041
                Introduction   1041

Vance, Human Rights and Foreign Policy 1041
Carter, Humane Purpose in Foreign Policy 1047
C. Criticism of the Carter Administration's Human
Rights Policy and Its Response 1048
1. Criticism 1048
Panel, Human Rights: A New Policy by a New
Administration 1048
Hoffman, The Hell of Good Intentions 1052
Kissinger, Continuity and Change in American
Foreign Policy 1053
2. Response 1059
Derian, Human Rights in American Foreign Policy 1059
D. Human Rights and U.S. Foreign Policy: Argentina as
a Case Study: Part I 1064
de Onis, U.S. Denial of Loan Angers Argentines 1065
Evans and Novak, Human-Rights Zeal That Costs
U.S. Jobs 1066
Reagan, Argentina's View on Human Rights 1068
DeYoung and Krause, Our Mixed Signals on Hu-
man Rights in Argentina 1069
Letters to the Editor, When Morality Interferes
with Exports-as-Usual 1075
III. *The Reagan Administration's Attitude Toward Hu-
man Rights Concerns in the Foreign Policy Process* 1077
A. The Initial Reagan Reaction to the Carter Administra-
tion's Rights Policy 1077
1. David Rockefeller: Advance Man in Latin
America 1077
Schumacher, Latins Welcome Word on Reagan by
Rockefeller 1077
Lewis, On Lending Comfort to Evil in Argentina 1079
2. President-Elect Reagan Adopts the Totalitarian/
Authoritarian Distinction 1081
Rosenblum, Reagan and Human Rights: Beyond
Classic Examples 1081
Buchwald, Moderate Repression 1083
3. Downgrading Human Rights: The Reagan Ad-
ministration Takes Office 1084
International Commission of Jurists, Human Rights
and U.S. Foreign Policy 1084
Baker, A Meddling Muddle 1087
4. Human Rights and U.S. Foreign Policy: Argentina
as a Case Study: Part II 1088
de Onis, U.S. Acts to Improve Its Ties with Rightist
Latin Governments 1088
Editorial, Doing Favors for Argentina 1089

        Lewis, U.S. and Argentina: Question of the Soul   1090

        Editorial, Semantics and Human Rights   1093

  B. The Reagan Administration's Human Rights Policy
Falls into Place   1095

        International Commission of Jurists, Human Rights
and U.S. Foreign Policy   1095

        U.S. Department of State, Country Reports on Human Rights Practices for 1982   1097

        U.S. Department of State, Country Reports on Human Rights Practices for 1983   1101

        Note: Two Key Differences in the Reagan Administration's Human Rights Policy   1103

  C. Criticism of the Reagan Administration's Human Rights Policy and Its Response   1105

        Shestack, An Unsteady Focus: The Vulnerabilities of the Reagan Administration's Human Rights Policy   1106

        El Salvador: "The Certification Joke"   1107

        Editorial, The Certification Joke   1108

        Response   1110

        Abrams, Latin America in the Time of Reagan   1110

        Schifter, Building Firm Foundations: The Institutionalization of United States Human Rights Policy in the Reagan Years   1113

        Human Rights and U.S. Foreign Policy: Argentina as a Case Study: Part III   1119

        Editorial, A Toast to Argentina   1120

        Lewis, Lessons from Argentina   1120

        Schell, Carter on Rights — a Re-Evaluation   1122

IV. *The Bush Administration's Attitude Toward Human Rights Concerns in the Foreign Policy Process*   *1124*

V. *The Clinton Administration's Attitude Toward Human Rights Concerns in the Foreign Policy Process*   *1126*

        A Vision for Democracy (Remarks by Governor Bill Clinton)   1127

        Statement of the Honorable Timothy E. Wirth, Counselor, U.S. Department of State   1128

        Shattuck, Human Rights and Democracy in Asia   1131

        President's News Conference (May 26, 1994)   1135

        McGrory, Human Rights Retreat   1139

        Editorial, Speak Louder on Rights in China   1141

VI. *Final Comments and Questions*   *1143*

Index   *1151*

Preface

This coursebook is intended to introduce the student to the established and developing international law rules and procedures governing the protection of basic human rights. Its thesis is that there exists at present a substantial body of substantive and procedural international human rights law, and that lawyers, government officials, and concerned citizens should be familiar with the policies underlying this law and its enforcement as well as with the potential it offers for improving the lives of individuals, even in the United States.

The materials in the coursebook are organized around a series of thirteen Problems, accompanied by selected readings, comments, and questions, designed to raise some of the most significant contemporary issues in this important field. The Problems are intended to serve as a point of departure for the exploration of the relevant principles, procedures, policies, and potentialities for protecting human rights through the international legal process. They are not intended to provide an extensive survey of the subject, although reading through them and the Documentary Supplement will provide a more than adequate grasp of the relevant substantive law norms. Coverage has been limited consciously, however, to concentrate the student's attention on how the international legal process can be invoked to protect the rights of individuals in concrete cases, national as well as international. The coursebook is thus a teaching tool, not an encyclopedia or bibliography.

The thirteen Problems raise some of the most difficult and troublesome issues confronting the international community, including the United States, today. The first four Problems take up the substantive law found in or flowing from the UN Charter; the next four Problems cover the procedural methods by which this body of law is increasingly "enforced" by the UN or other international and national actors; and the final five Problems consider miscellaneous matters — regional human rights regimes, the law of armed conflict, international criminal law, and the relevancy of international human rights law to the foreign policy process. The materials contained in each Problem address topics of great current interest, and they frequently contemplate developments in emerging areas that may become matters of substantial concern in future years.

The coursebook is designed for a three-hour, one-semester course or seminar, at either the law school or the college or university level. With some omissions, a two-hour seminar can be taught from it, while with the addition of one or two Problems, it provides full fare for a four-hour course. Although a background in international law certainly is helpful, with a little help from the instructor it is not required for an adequate appreciation of most of the materials.

The problem-oriented approach, with fact patterns that raise a series of real-life issues and mix substance with procedural considerations, provides a basis for more stimulating classroom sessions than often occur, especially in that vale of ennui, the third year of law school. Also, for the non-law student, whether graduate or undergraduate, such problems place the legal issues in the context of facts with which he or she may have some familiarity, thus enabling the student to come to grips with the relevant legal concepts and their application (or non-application) in concrete cases. Additionally, the coursebook's approach is action-oriented in that it demonstrates repeatedly that international human rights law today is not some high-level abstraction, but a reasonably developed and constantly evolving body of substantive norms and procedural techniques that in many instances can be used to improve the lives of individuals. Hence, the third word in the subtitle.

Pedagogically, some instructors may wish, by student role-playing, to have various Problems (or contemporary versions thereof) presented in a simulated real-life situation (for example, a UN General Assembly session, a U.S. domestic court case, a congressional hearing, an ABA House of Delegates debate, a hearing before the Inter-American Commission on Human Rights, or a foreign policy planners' meeting), with extended analysis, critique, and discussion thereafter. Other instructors, however, may wish to cover the material in the traditional lecture/discussion classroom context. Still other instructors may opt for a mix of both techniques or employ others of their own. In any case, the use of problems as a departure point for discussion rather than the routine coverage of cases and materials has been found to stimulate student interest, as well as to allow the instructor the flexibility to insert his or her own problems, materials, and expertise throughout the course offering — a highly desirable approach in view of the rapid expansion of international human rights law and the role it increasingly has come to play in the foreign policy process.

Finally, it should be recorded that the first edition of this coursebook was a collaborative effort with my long-time colleague and co-worker in the international human rights law field, Frank C. Newman of the University of California (Boalt Hall), while the second edition, following the same format, but completely revised and updated, was entirely my own responsibility. In my Acknowlegments to that edition, however, I gave special thanks to my associate in many joint ventures at the Procedural Aspects of International Law Institute during the 1980s, Hurst Hannum, who had joined the faculty of The Fletcher School of Law and Diplomacy, for producing an excellent draft of one revised

Problem. I also noted that I hoped to have him come aboard as an editor for the third edition. Happily that has come to pass, and the fact that Hurst once was a student of Frank Newman's only underscores the continuing commitment to international human rights law that succeeding classes of students at Berkeley as well as Charlottesville have demonstrated over the past quarter of a century.

Both Hurst and I, as co-editors of this coursebook, hope that it continues in the activist tradition of its predecessors, and we would welcome the comments, corrections, and suggestions from instructors and students alike that would contribute to its improvement as a teaching tool in a contemplated fourth edition.

Richard B. Lillich

March 1995

Acknowledgments

This edition of the coursebook was greatly facilitated by the support that its two editors have had over the past year from the University of Virginia School of Law and The Fletcher School of Law and Diplomacy, Tufts University, respectively. For a summer research grant and a student research assistant, Mark Klupt, Professor Lillich would like to express his appreciation. So, too, would Professor Hannum for the help he received from his research assistants, Jennifer Gergen, Micheline Lévesque, and Linda Maguire, as well as from his administrative assistant, Mary Pyche.

Countless colleagues at other universities, in government, at international organizations, and in private practice and non-governmental organization work have shared their experience with us and helped us to understand (and, we hope, explain) the complexities of several areas of the ever expanding body of international human rights law. Special thanks for their assistance, often beyond the call of duty, go to Elizabeth Abi-Mershed, Christina Cerna, Claudio Grossman, Michael O'Boyle, Elsa Stamatopoulou, David Stewart, and Alfred de Zayas.

Richard B. Lillich
Hurst Hannum

American Bar Association of the City of New York, Committee on Inter-national Human Rights, The Inter-American Commission: A Promise Unfulfilled, 48 The Record 589, 598-602, 603-604, 606-608, 611-613 (1993). Reprinted by permission.

Auglin, United Nations Sanctions Against South Africa and Rhodesia, in The Utility of International Sanctions 34-38 (Layton-Brown ed. 1987). Reprinted by permission of St. Martin's Press.

Bagnell, The Verdict Against Birching, Letter to the Editor, The Times (London), April 28, 1978, at 17, col. 4. Reprinted by permission.

Baker, A Meddling Muddle, International Herald-Tribune, June 5, 1981, at 24, cols. 1-2. Reprinted by permission of The New York Times.

Bassiouni, "Crimes Against Humanity": The Need for a Specialized Con-vention, 31 Columbia Journal of Transnational Law 457, 484-486 (1994). Reprinted by permission.

————, International Criminal Law: A Draft International Criminal Code 1 (1980). Reprinted by permission of Kluwer Academic Publishers.

————, The Proscribing Function of International Criminal Law in the Process of International Protection of Human Rights, 9 Yale Journal of World Public Order 193, 193-197 (1982). Reprinted by permission.

Baxter, Modernizing the Law of War, 78 Military Law Review 165, 168-173 (1978). Reprinted by permission.

Bayefsky, Making the Human Rights Treaties Work 229, 232-236, 238-240, 243, 263-264 (1994). Reproduced with permission from Hu-man Rights: An Agenda for the Next Century (Henkin and Hargrove, eds. 1994) © The American Society of International Law.

Bell, The Verdict Against Birching, Letter to the Editor, The Times (Lon-don), April 28, 1978, at 17, col. 5. Reprinted by permission.

Besharov and Mueller, The Demands of the Inmates of Attica State Prison and the United Nations Standard Minimum Rules for the Treatment of Prisoners: A Comparison, 21 Buffalo Law Review 839 (1972). Reprinted by permission.

Bilder, Human Rights and U.S. Foreign Policy: Short-Term Prospects, 14 Virginia Journal of International Law 597, 597-609 passim (1974). Reprinted by permission.

————, Rethinking International Human Rights: Some Basic Questions, Wisconsin Law Review 171, 187-191. Copyright © 1969 by The Board of Regents of the University of Wisconsin System; Reprinted by permission of the Wisconsin Law Review.

Bourne, The Verdict Against Birching, Letter to the Editor, The Times (London), April 28, 1978, at 17, col. 4. Reprinted by permission.

Boyle, Europe: The Council of Europe, the CSCE, and the European Community in Guide to International Human Rights Practice (2nd ed.) 133, 153-155 (H. Hannum ed. 1992). Reprinted by permission.

Bridge, The Case for an International Court of Criminal Justice and the Formulation of International Criminal Law, 13 International and

Comparative Law Quarterly 1255, 1255-1281 (passim) (1964). This article is reproduced with permission from the publishers, The British Institute of International and Comparative Law, 17 Russell Square, London WC1B 5DR.

Brierly, The Law of Nations (6th ed.) 292-296 (H. Waldock ed. 1963). Reprinted by permission of Oxford University Press.

Brody, Improving UN Human Rights Structures 297, 307-308 (1994). Reproduced with permission from Human Rights: An Agenda for the Next Century (Henkin and Hargrove, eds. 1994) © The American Society of International Law.

Brownlie, Humanitarian Intervention, Law and Civil War in the Modern World 217-288 (J.N. Moore ed. 1974). Reprinted by permission.

Buchwald, Moderate Repression, International Herald-Tribune, Dec. 20-21, 1980, at 16, cols. 1-2. Reprinted by permission.

Buergenthal, Norris and Shelton, Protecting Human Rights in the Americas 299-301 (3d ed. 1990). Reprinted by permission.

Carnegie Endowment for International Peace, Business as Usual: Transactions Violating Rhodesian Sanctions, Interim Report of the Special Rhodesian Project 1, 3-4, 6-9, 12-14 (1973). Reprinted by permission.

Chhangani, Expulsion of Ugandan Asians and Internation Law, 12 Indian Journal of International Law 400, 402, 405-407 (1972). Reprinted by permission.

Davidow, Dealing with International Crises: Lessons from Zimbabwe, Occasional Paper 34, The Stanley Foundation, 9-13 (1983). Reprinted by permission.

de Onis, U.S. Acts to Improve Ties with Rightist Latin Governments, International Herald-Tribune, March 9, 1981, at 2, cols. 1-2. Reprinted by permission of The New York Times.

————, U.S. Denial of Loan Angers Argentines, N.Y. Times, July 21, 1978, at A4, col 3. Copyright © 1978 by The New York Times Company. Reprinted by permission.

Derian, Human Rights in American Foreign Policy, Volume 55, Issue 2 Notre Dame Law Review (1979) 264-280. Reprinted with permission. © by Notre Dame Law Review, University of Notre Dame.

DeYoung and Kranse, Our Mixed Signals on Human Rights in Argentina, Washington Post, October 29, 1978 at C1, col. 5. © 1978 by The Washington Post. Reprinted with permission.

Discussion. Reproduced with permission from 87 American Society of International Law Proceedings 241 (1993), © The American Society of International Law.

Doxey, International Sanctions in Contemporary Perspective 45-46 (1987). Reprinted by permission of St. Martin's Press.

Draper, Human Rights and the Law of War, 12 Virginia Journal of International Law 326, 326-333 (1972). Reprinted by permission.

Frankel, Letter to Human Rights Watch on March 18, 1992, concerning areas of disagreement on U.S. ratification of International Covenant on Civil and Political Rights. Reprinted by permission.

————, Letter to Senator Pell on March 2, 1992, concerning support for U.S. ratification of the International Covenant on Civil and Political Rights. Reprinted by permission.

Glennon, Correspondence in Notes and Comments. Reproduced with permission from 81 American Journal of International Law 393, 397-401 (1987), © The American Society of International Law.

Gross, The Maritime Boundaries of the United States. Reproduced with permission from 67 American Journal of International Law 508 (1973), © The American Society of International Law.

Hannum, Contemporary Developments in the International Protection of the Rights of Minorities, Volume 66, Issue 5 The Notre Dame Law Review (1991) 1431-1448. Reprinted with permission. © by Notre Dame Law Review, University of Notre Dame. The publisher bears responsibility for any errors which have occurred in reprinting or editing.

Harvey, The Verdict Against Birching, Letter to the Editor, The Times (London), April 28, 1978, at 17, col. 5. Reprinted by permission.

Heijder, Codes of Professional Ethics Against Torture, in Codes of Professional Ethics 3, 5-7 (Amnesty International, ACT 07/01/84, 1984). Reprinted by permission.

Henkin, The International Bill of Rights. Copyright © 1981 by Columbia University Press. Reprinted with permission of the publisher.

Hoffman, The Hell of Good Intentions, 29 Foreign Policy 3, 7-9 (1977). Reprinted by permission.

Hudson, Charter Provision on Human Rights in American Law. Reproduced with permission from 44 American Journal of International Law 543, 543-547 (1950), © The American Society of International Law.

International Commission of Jurists, Background Paper for the Brain-Storming Session on the African Charter on Human Peoples' Rights, Dakar (1993). Reprinted by permission.

————, The Events in East Pakistan, 1971, 76-99 (1972). Reprinted by permission.

————, Human Rights and U.S. Foreign Policy 32-35, 35-38 (1984). Reprinted by permission.

————, Note: Disappointing Start to New U.N. Procedure on Human Rights, 9 International Commission of Jurists Review 5, 5-7 (1972). Reprinted by permission.

————, Note: Greece: Justice in Blinkers, 1 International Commission of Jurists Review 6, 6-7 (1969). Reprinted by permission.

————, Note: Human Rights Report on Greece, 7 International Commission of Jurists Review 9, 10 (1971). Reprinted by permission.

_____, Uganda — A Lawless State, The Review No. 7, 18 (Dec. 1972). Reprinted by permission.

International Law Association, The Status of the Universal Declaration of Human Rights in National and International Law, ILA, Report of the Sixty-Sixth Conference (Buenos Aires, 1994). Reprinted by permission.

Junod, Additional Protocol II: History and Scope, 33 American University Law Review 29, 34-37 passim (1983). Reprinted by permission.

Kissinger, Continuity and Change in American Foreign Policy, 15 Society 97, 99-102 (1977). Reprinted by permission.

Kunz, The United Nations Declaration of Human Rights. Reproduced with permission from 43 American Journal of International Law 316, 316-322 (1949), © The American Society of International Law.

Leckie, The Inter-State Complaint Procedure in International Human Rights Law: Hopeful Prospects or Wishful Thinking?, 10 Human Rights Quarterly 249, 266-267 (1988). Reprinted by permission.

Letter to the Editor, N.Y. Times, May 3, 1978, at 32, col. 6.

Letter to the Editor, N.Y. Times, May 9, 1989. Copyright © 1989 by The New York Times Company. Reprinted by permission.

Letter to the Editor, N.Y. Times, July 16, 1976, at 30, col. 3.

Letter to the Editor, N.Y. Times, July 27, 1976, at 28, col. 3.

Lewis, Abroad at Home; Lessons from Argentina, N.Y. Times, January 26, 1984, at A23, cols. 1-3. Copyright © 1984 by The New York Times Company. Reprinted by permission.

Lewis, On Lending Comfort to Evil in Argentina, International Herald-Tribune, November 25, 1980, at 4, cols. 6-7. Reprinted by permission of The New York Times.

Lewis, U.S. and Argentina: Question of the Soul, International Herald-Tribune, May 22, 1981, at 6, cols. 6-7. Reprinted by permission of The New York Times.

Lillich, Forcible Protection of Nationals Abroad: The Liberian "Incident" of 1990, 35 German Yearbook of International Law 205, 213-221 (1993). Reprinted by permission.

_____, Humanitarian Intervention through the United Nations: Towards the Development of Criteria, 53 ZaoRV (Heidelberg Journal of International Law) 557, 563-573 (1993). Reprinted by permission.

_____, Remarks. Reproduced with permission from 79 American Society of International Law Proceedings 84-86 (1985), © The American Society of International Law.

_____, U.S. Foreign Policy, Human Rights, and Foreign Trade and Investment, in Private Investors Abroad — Problems and Solutions in International Business in 1979, at 281, 288-291 (Southwestern Legal Foundation 1979). Reprinted by permission.

Lloyd, Letter to the Editor, N.Y. Times, July 27, 1976, at 28, col. 3. Copyright © 1976 by The New York Times Company. Reprinted by permission.

Losman, International Economic Sanctions 121-123 (1979). Reprinted by permission of University of New Mexico Press.

Marks, Emerging Human Rights: A New Generation for the 1980s?, 33 Rutgers Law Review 434, 451-452 (1981). Reprinted by permission.

McDougal and Reisman, Letter to the Editor, N.Y. Times, July 16, 1976, at 30, col. 3. Copyright © 1976 by The New York Times Company. Reprinted by permission.

————, Rhodesia and the United Nations: The Lawfulness of International Concern. Reproduced with permission from 62 American Journal of International Law 1, 1-19 (1968), © The American Society of International Law.

McGrory, Human Rights Retreat, Washington Post, July 7, 1994, at A1, cols. 1-4. 1994 The Washington Post. Reprinted with permission.

Medina, The Inter-American Commission on Human Rights and the Inter-American Court of Human Rights: Reflections on a Joint Venture, 12 Human Rights Quarterly 439, 440-47 (1990). Reprinted by permission.

Melady, Letter to the Editor, New York Times, August 25, 1984, at 22, cols. 1-3. Reprinted by permission.

Mohr, In Amin's Taciturn Uganda, Even Food is Unspeakable, International Herald-Tribune, Jan. 30, 1975, at 5, cols. 1-4. Reprinted by permission of the New York Times.

Moore, Correspondence in Notes and Comments. Reproduced with permission from 81 American Journal of International Law 186, 192-195 (1987), © The American Society of International Law.

Moore, War Crimes and the Rule of Law in the Gulf Crisis, 31 Virginia Journal of International Law 403, 404-409 (1991). Reprinted by permission.

Mueller, Four Decades after Nuremberg: The Prospect of an International Criminal Code, 2 Connecticut Journal of International Law 499, 501-506 (1987). Reprinted by permission.

Murphy, Woetzel, and Lador-Lederer, Correspondence. Reproduced with permission from 68 American Journal of International Law 306, 719 (1974), © The American Society of International Law.

Murton, The Arkansas Effect, N.Y. Times, February 17, 1978. Copyright © 1978 by The New York Times Company. Reprinted by permission.

Nathan, Letter to the Editor, Deathly Silence on Nigeria, The Times (London), February 4, 1983, at 13, col. 3. Reprinted by permission.

Neir, Letter to Marvin Frankel dated March 5, 1992, concerning U.S. ratification of the Civil and Political Covenant. Reprinted by permission.

Note, The Passage of the Federal Anti-Apartheid Act: The Culmination of Anti-Apartheid Efforts Within the United States, 11 Suffolk Transnational Law Journal 387, 409-413 (1987). Reprinted by permission.

Note, Security Council Resolutions in United States Courts, 50 Indiana Law Journal 83, 92-93 (1974). Reprinted by permission of the Trustees of Indiana University and Fred B. Rothman & Co.

O'Brien, The Nuremberg Precedent and the Gulf War, 31 Virginia Journal of International Law 391, 391-392, 397-401 (1991). Reprinted by permission.

Orentlicher, Bearing Witness: The Art and Science of Human Rights Fact-Finding, 3 Harvard Human Rights Journal 83, 85, 92-108, 135 (1990). Reprinted by permission.

————, Yugoslavia War Crimes Tribunal. Reproduced with permission from ASIL Focus, 1-4, No. 1 (1993), © The American Society of International Law.

Panel, Human Rights: A New Policy by a New Administration. Reproduced with permission from 71 American Society of International Law Proceedings 68, 72-76 (1977), © The American Society of International Law.

Plender, The Ugandan Crisis and the Right of Expulsion Under International Law, International Commission of Jurists, The Review No. 9, 19, 27-30 (Dec. 1972). Reprinted by permission.

Ramcharan, Evidence, in International Law and Fact-finding in the Field of Human Rights 64, 77-80 (1994). Reprinted by permission of Kluwer Academic Publishers.

Reagan, Argentina's Views on Human Rights, The Miami News, October 20, 1978 at 13, col. 1. Reprinted by permission.

Remarks Given by Ambassador Schifter, East Asia Legal Studies, Human Rights and Foreign Policy 13-15 (1994). Reprinted by permission.

Renwick, Economic Sanctions 76-77 (1981). Reprinted by permission of University Press of America.

Restatement of the Law, Third, Foreign Relations Law of the United States, sec. 701, Reporters' Note 8 at 159-160 (1987). Copyright © 1987 by The American Law Institute. Reprinted with the permission of The American Law Institute.

Roberts, The New Rules for Waging War: The Case Against Ratification of Additional Protocol I, 25 Virginia Journal of International Law 109, 124-127, 150-152 (1985). Reprinted by permission.

Robertson, Human Rights in the World: An Introduction to the Study of the International Protection of Human Rights in The Development of the International Law by the European Court 3d. ed. (Copyright © J. Merrills ed. 1989). Reprinted with permission of St. Martin's Press, Incorporated.

Rodley, Human Rights and Humanitarian Intervention: The Case Law of the World Court. This article is reproduced from 1989 38 International and Comparative Law Quarterly 321, 332 with permission from the publishers The British Institute of International and Comparative Law, 17 Russell Square, London WC1B 5DR.

————, The Treatment of Prisoners under International Law (1987), 279. Reprinted by permission of Oxford University Press.

Rosenblum, Reagan and Human Rights: Beyond Classic Examples, International Herald-Tribune, December 30, 1980, at 4, cols. 6-7. Reprinted by permission of The New York Times.

Schachter, The Charter and the Constitution: The Human Rights Provisions in American Law, 4 Vanderbilt Law Review 643, 643-659 (1951). Reprinted by permission.

Schell, Carter on Rights — A Re-evaluation, N.Y. Times, October 25, 1984 at A27, cols. 3-4. Copyright © 1984 by The New York Times Company. Reprinted by permission.

Schifter, Building Firm Foundations: The Institutionalization of United States Human Rights Policy in the Reagan Years, 2 Harvard Human Rights Yearbook 3, 17-24 (1989). Permission granted by the Harvard Human Rights Journal. © 1989 by the President and Fellows of Harvard College.

Schumacher, Latins Welcome Word on Reagan by Rockefeller, N.Y. Times, November 11, 1980, at A10, col. 1. Copyright © 1980 by The New York Times Company. Reprinted by permission.

Schwelb, The Influence of the Universal Declaration of Human Rights. Reproduced with permission from 53 American Society of International Law Proceedings 217 (1959), © The American Society of International Law.

————, The International Court of Justice and the Human Rights Clauses of the Charter. Reproduced with permission from 66 American Journal of International Law 337, 338, 341-350 (1972), © The American Society of International Law.

————, 78 American Society for International Law Proceedings 358 (1984). Reproduced with permission, © The American Society of International Law.

Shelton, Compliance Mechanisms [Periodic Reports] in United States Ratification of the International Covenants on Human Rights 151, 153-155 (H. Hannum and D. Fischer eds. 1993). Reproduced with permission of The American Society of International Law.

Shestack, An Unsteady Focus: The Vulnerabilities of the Reagan Administration's Human Rights Policy, 2 Harvard Human Rights Yearbook 25, 36-39 (1989). Permission granted by the Harvard Human Rights Journal. © 1989 by the President and Fellows of Harvard College.

Sieghart, The International Law of Human Rights 11, 14 (1983). Reprinted by permission of Oxford University Press.

Smith, New Protection for Victims of International Armed Conflicts: The Proposed Ratification of Protocol II by the United States, 120 Military Law Review 59, 63-65, 66-67 (1988). Reprinted by permission.

Stewart, United States Ratification of the Covenant on Civil and Political Rights: The Significance of the Reservations, Understandings, and Declarations, 42 DePaul Law Review 1183, 1205-1207 (1993). Reprinted by permission.

Strack, Sanctions: The Case of Rhodesia 252-253 (1978). Reprinted by permission of Syracuse University Press.

Teson, Humanitarian Intervention: An Inquiry into Law and Morality 232-233, 241-244 passim (1987). Reprinted by permission.

Thoolen and Verstappen, Human Rights Missions: A Study of Fact-finding Practice of Non-Governmental Organizations, 24-26, 31-32, 122-124, 133-135 (1986). Reprinted by permission of Kluwer Academic Publishers.

Tolley, The U.N. Commission on Human Rights 74-82, 125, 127-132, 210-211 (1987). Reprinted by permission.

Umozurike, Tanzania's Intervention in Uganda, 20 Archiv des Völkerrechts 301, 312-313 (1982). Reprinted by permission.

United Nations Human Rights Bodies. The Chart of UN Human Organs reprinted on page 399 has been reprinted by permission of the Minnesota Advocates for Human Rights, which holds the copyright, and with acknowledgment to Professor David Weissbrodt who prepared the chart.

Vannin, Of Birching and Human Rights, Letter to the Editor, New York Times, May 3, 1978, at 32, col. 4. Copyright © 1978 by The New York Times Company. Reprinted by permission.

Wagner, Of Birching and Human Rights, Letter to the Editor, New York Times, May 3, 1978, at 32, col. 4. Copyright © 1978 by The New York Times Company. Reprinted by permission.

Weissbrodt, Human Rights Implementation and Fact-Finding by International Organizations. Reprinted with permission from 74 ASIL Proceedings 17, 19-20 (1980), © The American Society of International Law.

————, The Role of International Organizations in the Implementation of Human Rights and Humanitarian Law in Situation of Armed Conflict, 21 Vanderbilt Journal of Transnational Law 313, 315-317, 331-337, 343-345 (1988). Reprinted by permission.

Welch, The African Commission on Human and Peoples' Rights: A Five-Year Report and Assessment, 14 Human Rights Quarterly 43, 45-49, 53-57 (1992). Reprinted by permission.

Weston, Lukes, and Hnatt, Regional Human Rights Regimes: A Comparison and Appraisal, 20 Vanderbilt Journal of Transnational Law 585, 588-592 (1987). Reprinted by permission.

Wise, Codification: Perspectives and Approaches in 1 M. Bassiouni, International Criminal Law 101, 106-107 (1986). Reprinted by permission.

Wooldridge and Sharma, International Law and the Expulsion of Ugandan Asians, 9 The International Lawyer 30, 48-57 (1975). Reprinted by permission of the American Bar Association.

Wright, National Courts and Human Rights — The Fuji Case. Reproduced with permission from 45 American Journal of International Law 62, 62-66, 68-77 (1951), The American Society of International Law.

Zagaris, Introductory Note to the Rules of Procedure and Evidence of the International Criminal Tribunal for Yugoslavia. Reproduced with permission from 33 I.L.M. 484-490 (1994), The American Society for International Law.

International Human Rights

Historical Introduction

Humphrey,* The International Law of Human Rights in the Middle Twentieth Century
The Present State of International Law and Other Essays 75
(International Law Association 1973)

[Professor Humphrey's essay was a contribution to the centenary celebration of the International Law Association, a non-governmental association comprised of academic scholars, practitioners, and government lawyers.]

I. Traditional Doctrine and Practice

When, a hundred years from now, the International Law Association celebrates its bicentenary, legal historians will surely be saying that one of the chief characteristics of midtwentieth century international law was its sudden interest in and concern with human rights. The founding fathers of the Association had no such special interest. Since human rights were — and indeed still are — essentially a relationship between the State and individuals — usually its own citizens — residing in its territory, they were, in traditional theory and practice, considered to fall within domestic jurisdiction and hence beyond the reach of international law, the norms of which governed the relations of States only. But there were some exceptions or at least it could be argued that there were. . . .

[The author proceeds to discuss the customary rules of international law governing the treatment of aliens and the doctrine of humanitarian intervention, discussed in Problem VIII.]

But if customary international law was only minimally and indirectly concerned with human rights, in the nineteenth and early twentieth centuries an increasing number of treaties were entered into the purpose of which was to protect, if only indirectly, the rights of certain classes of people. The most important of these were the treaties aimed at slavery and the slave trade. By 1885, it was possible to affirm, in the General Act of the Berlin Conference on Central Africa, that "trading in slaves is forbidden in conformity with the principles of international law." And in 1889, the Brussels Conference not only condemned slavery and the slave trade but agreed on measures for their suppression, including the granting of reciprocal rights of search, and the capture and trial of slave ships. This work was continued by both the League of Nations and the United Nations. Steps

---

* John P. Humphrey served as Director of the Division of Human Rights of the UN, 1946-1966.

1

were also taken in the nineteenth century for the relief of sick and wounded soldiers and prisoners of war. By the Geneva Convention of 22 August, 1864, twelve States undertook to respect the immunity of military hospitals and their staffs, to care for wounded and sick soldiers and to respect the emblem of the Red Cross. The Convention was revised in 1929 and has been widely ratified.

In 1906, the second Berne Conference opened two conventions for signature which were forerunners of the many labour conventions which, after the first World War, would be adopted by the International Labour Organization: the International Convention respecting the Prohibition of Night Work for Women in Industrial Employment and the International Convention respecting the Prohibition of the Use of White (Yellow) Phosphorus in the Manufacture of Matches.

II.   THE LEAGUE OF NATIONS

The peace settlement at the end of the First World War brought still more important developments. Attempts were made to enshrine human rights in the Covenant of the League of Nations. President Wilson sponsored an article on religious freedom, but when the Japanese suggested that mention also be made of the equality of nations and the just treatment of their nationals (which frightened some countries the laws of which restricted Asiatic immigration) both suggestions were withdrawn. Wilson put into his second draft an article under which the League would have required all new States to bind themselves, as a condition precedent to their recognition, to accord all racial and national minorities "exactly the same treatment and security, both in law and in fact, that is accorded the racial and national majority of their people." But the Peace Conference decided that the protection of minorities — though only in certain countries — would be dealt with not in the Covenant but by other treaty provisions and by declarations which certain States were required to make on their admission to the League.

Two articles dealing with human rights did find their way into the Covenant. One of these, Article 22, enunciated the principle that colonies and territories which as a consequence of the war had ceased to be under the sovereignty of the States which formerly governed them and which were inhabited by "peoples not yet able to stand by themselves under the strenuous conditions of the modern world," were to be put under the tutelage of advanced nations, who, as mandatories on behalf of the League, would be responsible for their administration under conditions which would guarantee amongst other things freedom of conscience and religion and the prohibition of abuses such as the slave trade. Provision was made for the creation of a permanent mandates commission to receive and examine the reports which the mandatories undertook to make.

The League's mandates system was taken over by the United Nations under a different name and subject to different rules. The Charter expressly says [in Article 76(c)] that one of the purposes of the Trusteeship system is to "encourage respect for human rights and fundamental freedoms for all without distinction as to race, sex, language or religion." The language used in Articles 73 and 74 relating to non-self-governing territories is not so forthright, but at a very early date, the General Assembly invited the administering powers to include, in the information to be transmitted under Article 73(e), a summary of the extent to which the Universal Declaration of Human Rights was being implemented in the non-self-governing territories under their administration. The work of the committee set up to receive reports on the administration of non-self-governing territories has now been taken over by the Special Committee on the Situation with regard to the Implementation of the Declaration on the Granting of Independence to Colonial Countries and Peoples. The Trusteeship Council continues to meet; but only one trust territory remains under its surveillance [the Trust Territory of the Pacific Islands, otherwise known as Micronesia, administered by the United States], all the others having become independent States or parts of independent States.

Human rights were also expressly dealt with in Article 23 of the Covenant. Members of the League, it said, would "endeavour to secure and maintain" fair and humane labour conditions, undertake to secure just treatment for the native inhabitants of territories under their control, and entrust the League with the supervision of agreements relating to the traffic in women and children.

Although President Wilson's suggestion that the Covenant contain a provision protecting minorities was not pursued, the Allied and Associated Powers did require certain newly created States and States, the territory of which had been increased by reason of the war, to grant the enjoyment of certain human rights to all inhabitants of their territories and to protect the rights of their racial, religious and linguistic minorities. These obligations were imposed by treaty and by the declarations which certain States were required to make on their admission to the League — the provisions relating to minorities being put under the guarantee of the League Council.

The elaborate system for the protection of minorities developed by the League — including what was in effect an international right of petition — has not withstood the test of time. Not only did the Charter fail to make any provision for taking over the responsibilities of the League in this matter, but, with one exception, later attempts to cope with the problem — which is certainly as acute now as it was in 1920 — have also failed. The Universal Declaration of Human Rights does not even mention minorities and Article 27 of the Covenant on Civil and Political Rights does not give them the protection that they need, for example in the matter of separate public schools, if they are to retain their distinctive characteristics. The exception was the adoption in 1948 of the widely ratified Convention on the Prevention and Punishment of the Crime of Genocide, which is aimed at the worst kind of treatment that can be meted out to minorities, namely, "acts committed with intent to destroy, in whole or in part, a national, ethnical, racial or religious group as such." There is also a United Nations Sub-Commission on the Prevention of Discrimination and the Protection of Minorities, the members of which are elected to act in their personal capacity. But the history of this body provides perhaps the best evidence that governments are not as interested in protecting minorities as in assimilating them. For although the Sub-Commission tried, in its early years, to work out solutions in respect of both parts of its mandate, its every initiative for the protection of minorities was frustrated by the Human Rights Commission and the Economic and Social Council — both of them bodies consisting of representatives of governments — to the extent indeed that in 1951 the Council decided to liquidate the Sub-Commission, a decision which was reversed only because the more representative General Assembly requested the Council to reconsider the matter. Since then, the Sub-Commission has concentrated on the prevention of discrimination. . . .

The negative attitude in the United Nations towards the protection of minorities is usually rationalized by the argument that, since the Organization is dedicated to obtaining respect for the human rights of everyone without discrimination, no special measures are required to protect minorities — an argument which quite misses the point since minorities, if they are to be protected, need something more than equality.

The League of Nations also did important work on slavery. It created a special committee to study the question, was responsible for the drafting of the Slavery Convention of 1926, and, when Ethiopia applied for admission to the League, it required from her an undertaking to make special efforts to abolish slavery and the slave trade, Ethiopia recognizing that this was not a purely internal matter but one on which the League had a right to intervene.

The work of the League was continued by the United Nations. Slavery and the slave trade in all their forms were prohibited by the Universal Declaration of Human Rights; and, in 1957, the Supplementary Convention on the Abolition of Slavery, the Slave Trade and Institutions similar to Slavery, which had been drafted by a United Nations Conference in 1956, came into force. The United Nations has also published a number of surveys on slavery prepared by special committees and rapporteurs; and now the Sub-Commission on the Prevention of Discrimination and the Protection of Minorities has been given the task of continuing the work. But so far, the Sub-Commission has done very little in the performance of its new mandate. In 1951, a Convention for the Suppression of the Traffic in Persons and the Exploitation of the Prostitution of Others came into force. And in 1957, the International Labour Organization adopted the Abolition of Forced Labour Convention. It came into force in 1959.

Like the League of Nations the International Labour Organization was created by the peace treaties after the First World War. This Specialized

Agency, which now has a history of over half a century of achievement, has adopted well over a hundred conventions which fix international standards many of which deal with human rights and some of which were inspired by the United Nations. It also possesses elaborate systems for the implementation of these standards. Some of them, particularly those relating to reporting, could be well emulated by the United Nations. Other Specialized Agencies, including UNESCO and the World Health Organization have also done important work for the promotion of human rights.

To sum up, international law recognized, by the beginning of the Second World War, a whole series of rules and institutions, as well as some procedures for their implementation, the effect of which was to protect the rights of individuals and groups, even though, in the dominant theory, the individual was neither a subject of international law nor directly protected by it. International law protected the rights of aliens through their States. There may have been a right of humanitarian intervention. Slavery and the slave trade were outlawed. The League of Nations had developed a system for the protection of certain racial, religious and linguistic minorities. There were provisions in the Covenant of the League of Nations for the protection of the rights of the natives of colonial [territories], and the inhabitants of mandated territories and of women and children. And the International Labour Organization had adopted an impressive number of labour conventions, for the enforcement of which it possessed elaborate procedures.

III. The Impact of the Second World War and the United Nations

The Second World War and the events leading up to it was the catalyst that produced the revolutionary developments in the international law of human rights that characterize the middle twentieth century. So potent was this catalyst that it produced not only an unprecedented growth in human rights law, but the very theory of international law had to be adapted to the new circumstances. The individual now becomes a subject of international law which henceforth would more properly be known as "world law." He is directly protected by this law and can even in some cases seek his own remedy. And States can no longer rely on the plea of domestic jurisdiction. It was not only a matter of new norms being added within the confines of an existing order, but the very nature of that order had changed. What had happened was revolutionary.

The Second World War was, as no other war has ever been, a war to vindicate human rights. This was recognized by the leaders of the Grand Alliance and perhaps best expresssed by President Roosevelt when, in January 1941, before the United States entered the war, he defined four freedoms: freedom of speech, freedom of worship, freedom from want, freedom from fear — "everywhere in the world." These he said, were the "necessary conditions of peace and no distant millennium." Yet, when the Dumbarton Oaks Proposals were published in the fall of 1944 they contained only a general reference to human rights. The United Nations would, the Proposals said in a chapter on arrangements for international economic and social cooperation, "promote respect for human rights and fundamental freedoms" — something which considering its context and the generality of the language used hardly met the expectations of a public opinion shocked by the atrocities of the war.

The relatively strong human rights provisions in the Charter through which they run, as someone has said, like a golden thread, were largely, and appropriately, the result of determined lobbying by non-governmental organizations at the San Francisco Conference. Some of the countries represented at San Francisco would have accepted even stronger human rights provisions than found their way into the Charter. There was even an attempt, which failed, to incorporate in the Charter an International Bill of Rights. But the Charter did provide for the creation of a Commission on Human Rights which, as President Truman said in the speech by which he closed the Conference, would, it was generally understood, draft the bill.

This is not the place to analyse the human rights provisions of the Charter. But it should be said that Article One puts the promotion of respect for human rights on the same level as the maintenance of international peace and security as a purpose of the United Nations. And by Articles 55 and 56 member states pledge themselves to take joint and separate action "in cooperation with the Organization" for the promotion and universal respect of human rights, an undertaking which, according to a recent advisory opinion of the International Court of Justice (Advisory Opinion on the Continued Presence of South Africa in Namibia, [1971] I.C.J. 16), binds member states to observe and respect human rights. Reference has already been made to Article 68 which provided for the creation of a Commission on Human Rights.

One of the first acts of the Economic and Social Council was to set up this commission. As first envisaged it was to have three sub-commissions: one on freedom of information and of the press, another on the prevention of discrimination and the protection of minorities, and a third on the status of women. Only one of these has survived, the Sub-Commission on the Prevention of Discrimination and the Protection of Minorities, the mandate of which has been enlarged to include other matters. The Sub-Commission on the Status of Women very quickly became a full commission reporting directly to the Economic and Social Council, and the mandate of the Sub-Commission on Freedom of Information and the Press was brought to an end in 1951.

There are also other organs of the United Nations which are concerned with human rights, including the General Assembly, the International Court of Justice, as its advisory opinion in the Namibian case shows, the Trusteeship Council, the Economic and Social Council and the Security

Council. If violations of human rights give rise to a dispute or situation which threatens international peace and security, the Security Council has at its command the whole arsenal of the United Nations including the application of sanctions. But the Organization will act, as many resolutions — particularly in matters relating to southern Africa — show, even if there is no threat to the peace. In such cases the plea of domestic jurisdiction under Article 2(7) of the Charter has been no obstacle. In the prevailing view, gross violations of human rights are not "essentially within the domestic jurisdiction" of states, nor, it would seem, are the actions which the United Nations has taken intervention in the technical legal sense.

The Commission on Human Rights held its first regular session in February, 1947 and, later in the same year, decided that the International Bill of Human Rights would have three parts: a declaration, a convention or conventions (later called the Covenants) and measures of implementation. Under the chairmanship of the late Eleanor Roosevelt, it worked so efficiently that the first part of the bill was ready for consideration by the General Assembly at its third session and was adopted by it without dissenting vote, on 10 December 1948, as the Universal Declaration of Human Rights.

The Declaration was not meant to be a legally binding instrument. This is apparent from the form in which it was adopted (resolutions of the General Assembly ordinarily have the force of recommendations only), the decision to include substantially the same norms in a convention which would be binding on the states which ratified it, and the many explanations of votes which delegations made when the Declaration was adopted. That was a quarter of a century ago. Many international lawyers now say that, whatever the intentions of its authors may have been, the Declaration is now binding as part of customary law. The point has yet to come squarely before the International Court of Justice although the separate opinion of Judge Fuad Ammoun in the Advisory Opinion mentioned above is indicative. [Judge Ammoun stated that "[a]lthough the affirmations of the Declaration are not binding *qua* international convention . . . , they can bind States on the basis of custom . . . , whether because they constituted a codification of customary law . . . , or because they have acquired the force of custom through a general practice accepted as law. . . ."] But whether the Declaration is now legally binding or not, it has great moral and political authority and its impact on the theory and practice of both international and national law has been profound.

In 1952, the General Assembly decided that there would be not one but two multilateral conventions or covenants on human rights, one on civil and political rights and the other on economic, social and cultural rights — a decision motivated chiefly by ideological considerations which split the United Nations down the middle. The Human Rights Commission completed its work on the two instruments in 1954, but it was only in 1966 that they were approved by the General Assembly and opened for signature. The long delay is partly explained by the fact that the debates on the drafts in the Third Committee were used for the ventilation of political controversies. [The Covenants came into force in 1976.] Apart from the fact that they . . . undoubtedly bind the states which ratify them, the Covenants are distinguished from the Declaration by the procedures which they contemplate for their implementation. If the Universal Declaration of Human Rights is now part of customary law, the chief *raison d'être* of the Covenants . . . is now the presence in them of these enforcement procedures. . . .

[The author proceeds to survey the procedural techniques contained in the two Covenants, which he believes are inadequate, matters to be considered in Problem III.]

In addition to the two Covenants, . . . the United Nations and its specialized agencies had drawn up and opened for signature a large number of other multilateral treaties dealing with specific rights and groups of rights. . . . There is also a growing body of regional law, including the very important European Convention on Human Rights [considered at length in Problem IX] . . . which is the most sophisticated of all contemporary instruments for the international protection of human rights as well as a number of bilateral treaties. So that, including the developments in customary law to which reference has been made, there now exists an impressive body of international law the purpose of which is to protect the rights of individuals and groups. The great task ahead is to reach agreement on procedures for the effective implementation and enforcement of the substantive norms already agreed on, a process to which . . . the Covenants have not made a great contribution.

It is vastly more difficult to obtain international agreement on procedures for implementation than on substantive norms. For, while states with disparate social systems may agree without too much difficulty on objectives, they have radically different methods for translating these objectives into reality. Implementation involves basic philosophical approaches and ultimate social goals. It was, therefore, to be expected that there would be fundamental disagreement in the United Nations on the establishment of international machinery for the enforcement of norms agreed on as expressions of immediate goals. The communist countries and the economically under-developed countries have not been prepared to accept Western proposals for implementation. In the more cohesive European community there has been substantial agreement.

Implementation systems created by treaty have the inherent weakness that they are unlikely to reach those countries where human rights are the least respected and where, therefore, they are most needed. There is no way by which the governments of such countries can be forced to ratify the treaties. Even those governments which are most committed to respecting human rights are cautious about committing themselves in advance to limitations on their discretionary powers; and, in the experience of the United Nations in any event, treaty provisions for implementation have been . . .

extremely limited in their scope and operation. These inherent weaknesses in the treaty method . . . help explain the current interest in the more empirical approach to implementation which seeks to build on powers conferred on the United Nations by the Charter itself. The most promising of these empirical approaches make use of reporting by states and communications addressed to the United Nations by individuals and groups alleging violations of their rights, both of which already have a long and complicated history. . . .

[The author proceeds to review the reporting and communications techniques, matters to be considered in Problems III and V.]

Another interesting development, the future of which is also uncertain, was the proposal made in 1965 by Costa Rica (on the suggestion of an informal group of individuals) that the General Assembly appoint a United Nations Commissioner for Human Rights. As originally conceived, the High Commissioner was to act in an advisory capacity at the request of governments or organs of the United Nations or specialized agencies. It was thought that in a situation such as occurred in Viet-Nam in 1963, for example, when on the request of the Diem government, the United Nations undertook an investigation of charges of discrimination against the Buddhist community, it would have been better both for the government and the United Nations, had the investigation been carried out by an independent officer of the General Assembly rather than by a politically oriented mission of ambassadors.

The Costa Rican proposal was adopted by the Human Rights Commission and the Economic and Social Council in 1967, but only after it had been amended following a study by a working group appointed in 1966. The amendments were aimed at strengthening the powers of the High Commissioner. For not only was he to have access to all communications alleging violations of human rights with the power, when he deemed it appropriate, to bring them to the attention of the governments concerned, but it would be his duty to report to the General Assembly, through the Council, "on developments in the field of human rights, including his observations on the implementation of the relevant declarations and instruments adopted by the United Nations and the Specialized Agencies, and his evaluation of significant progress and problems." Both of these new functions could take the High Commissioner very far indeed, and the adoption of the amendments may have contributed to the reception which the proposal received in the General Assembly. The authors of the Costa Rican proposal had purposely avoided giving any powers to the High Commissioner which might at this stage be unacceptable to a majority of governments. The feeling was that once the institution had been established it would grow under its own momentum, chiefly through the instrumentality of the annual report on his work which the High Commissioner was to make to the General Assembly and the discussions to which it would give rise. In any event, when the proposal reached the General Assembly, governments began to have second thoughts, enthusiasm waned, [and] the item was postponed from year to year. . . .

[The Office of High Commissioner for Human Rights was finally created by the General Assembly in 1994.]

Another technique for the international supervision of human rights standards with which the United Nations has experimented is the series of studies (really surveys) conducted by the Human Rights Commission and its Sub-Commission. The studies were first undertaken by the Sub-Commission at a time when it was under attack in the Commission and Council. In the Sub-Commission, each of the studies is prepared by a rapporteur with the help of the Secretariat on the basis of country monographs which governments have an opportunity to correct and supplement. The studies, particularly when they are read in conjunction with the monographs, throw considerable light on the juridical and factual situations in the countries with which they deal. Some of them have also had fruitful consequences in the development of law. Thus, the report of the late Charles Ammoun on Discrimination in Education both inspired and was the basis for the UNESCO Convention on Discrimination in Education. In the Human Rights Commission the procedure is different. Since its members are governments and not individuals, its studies are prepared by small committees consisting of member governments.

Still another technique is the Advisory Services programme, which was launched at the same time and under the same circumstances as periodic reporting. It was originally meant to provide help to countries seeking assistance in human rights matters, an idea obviously inspired by the technical assistance programme. The idea wasn't too well thought out. Governments were unlikely to seek outside assistance in a politically delicate matter like human rights, because to do so might be interpreted as an admission of weakness. And, as a matter of fact, the technical assistance aspect of the programme has not been important. But the Secretariat was able to put some life into it by subverting its original purpose. One of the methods for extending assistance to countries asking for it was to be the organization of seminars in such countries. When it became apparent that governments would not ask for seminars to be organized as part of a technical assistance programme, the Secretariat adopted the line that to sponsor human rights seminars would be a sign of strength rather than of weakness and began to suggest to certain governments that they sponsor seminars not in matters where they were having difficulties but on subjects where their records were good. On that basis invitations soon began to come in, and the seminars became one of the principal elements of the United Nations human rights programme.

The human rights seminars, of which there have been many, are really informal conferences of individuals who, while they speak in their own names, are appointed by governments. Their purpose is to bring together knowledgeable people to discuss some aspect of human rights without necessarily adopting resolutions, in the hope that an informal exchange of views will not only be valuable for the participants and their governments but will by the publicity given to the discussions — conferences held away from U.N. Headquarters are more likely to be noticed by the press — help create a kind of public opinion which will be conducive to the promotion of respect for human rights. They have been held all over the world, sometimes in countries where there had never been a United Nations conference. Many of the subjects discussed have been juridical in character and many of the participants have been jurists including some holding high judicial office. . . .

[The author next considers regional approaches to the international protection of human rights, a matter to be considered in Problems IX and X.]

V. A NEW CATALOGUE OF RIGHTS

This essay has been chiefly concerned with structural or institutional arrangements for the promotion and protection of human rights. In a sense, we have been discussing Hamlet without the Prince of Denmark. There are two reasons for this. In the first place, there is now relative agreement on the definition of human rights, something which appears most clearly, perhaps, from the fact that the Universal Declaration of Human Rights, which covers the whole gamut of rights, was adopted without dissenting vote. Something must be said, however, about the catalogue and nature of the human rights now recognized by international law.

The principal characteristic of the twentieth century approach to human rights has been its unambiguous recognition of the fact that all human beings are entitled to the enjoyment not only of the traditional civil and political rights but also of the economic, social and cultural rights without which, for most people, the traditional rights have little meaning. One of the chief claims of the Universal Declaration of Human Rights to a place in history is its recognition of this simple truth. The United Nations, however, has always recognized that there is a difference between what can be expected from States in the implementation of economic and social rights and in the enforcement of civil and political rights. The former are looked upon as programme rights, the implementation of which is to be progressive. This is particularly true of economically underdeveloped countries with large populations to feed, which can hardly be expected to guarantee the immediate implementation of all economic and social rights. Even highly industrialized States will hesitate before guaranteeing the right, for example, to work — on any literal interpretation of the meaning of that right. The decision of the General Assembly in 1952 to have two covenants instead of one was rationalized by such considerations; but it is probable that there were also other influences at work, including the fear, in some countries, of socialism. It would have been technically possible to include both categories of rights in the same instrument with different systems for their implementation, and thus to retain the essential unity of the two categories of rights recognized by the Universal Declaration of Human Rights.

Although the two kinds of rights complement each other, they often come into conflict. The dichotomy is closely related to the one between individual and collective rights. In the United Nations, when the Universal Declaration of Human Rights was adopted, first importance was still given to the rights of the individual as such. The present tendency is to give more importance to the rights of groups and of the collectivity, sometimes to the disadvantage of the individual. There have been times, indeed, when it has seemed that member states in their preoccupation with collective rights have had little concern for the traditional civil and political rights of individuals. But the conflict is not often expressed as clearly as an African delegate did when she explained the abstention of her country in the voting on the Optional Protocol to the Covenant on Civil and Political Rights. "Our abstention from the Optional Protocol," she said, "is our manifestation of our apprehension about the utilization of these rights (i.e. civil and political rights) for political ends or propaganda. . . . The young states must guarantee human rights. They also know better than anyone else that there can be no human rights where there is no state. That is why our countries are particularly concerned with the security of the state — in other words the collectivity at the expense of the individual." . . .

[Somewhat depressingly, such arguments continue to be raised today; one might query whether states or individuals are more secure than they were in 1973, when this article was written.]

VI. CONCLUSION

[One comes finally] to the question of the increasing politicization of human rights in the United Nations. Human rights cannot, nor is it desirable that they should, be divorced from politics. To do so would be to divorce them from reality. And as a matter of fact there has always been a good deal of political controversy in the debates on human rights in organs like the Third Committee of the General Assembly, the Human Rights Commission and, regrettably, even in a body of experts acting ostensibly in their individual capacity like the Sub-Commission on the Prevention of Discrimination and the Protection of Minorities. In recent years, however, the debates have become political to the exclusion of almost all constructive work, and one has the impression that governments are chiefly motivated by their conflicts with other countries. This, and the absence of any effective public opinion capable of putting pressure on governments, has resulted in a slowing down, in the United Nations at least, of effective work for the international promotion of respect for human rights.

But there are also some encouraging developments. One of these is the expansion of the concept of human rights to cover new values . . . and new threats to human dignity. The Universal Declaration of Human Rights speaks, for example, of the right to privacy. But privacy was not threatened in 1948 as it now is by new developments in science and technology, including the computer. These and other contemporary challenges to human dignity are aggravated by their increasing trans-national character and national measures will not be able to cope with them. It may be safely predicted, therefore, that, if the international community has a future, the United Nations will have to adjust itself to new circumstances and that the body of international human rights law will continue to grow.

As the middle twentieth century draws to a close, it is still possible, notwithstanding temporary reverses in the United Nations, to speak of an ever growing interest of lawyers in international human rights law. But that interest no longer has as its chief source the war and the events which led up to it, which are already beyond the experience of many international lawyers and other actors. The need to strengthen greatly the guarantees which international law can provide for the rights of individuals and groups is still paramount. More and more the individual stands alone in the face of an all-pervading State. Majorities are still intolerant. People are still discriminated against because of their race, sex, language, religion and other attributes. The great majority of people do not enjoy the economic, social and cultural rights without which there can be little human dignity. And, as the human race moves into the last quarter of the twentieth century, men and women are faced with new threats to their human dignity, including some unexpected byproducts of an advancing and otherwise beneficial technology. One thing is certain. The increasing contemporary interest in, and concern for, human rights does not necessarily mean that the men and women of the middle twentieth century are more enlightened than their ancestors were or their descendants may turn out to be. Concern for the rights of the individual is more likely to be, as it has usually been in history, a sign that his rights are in special jeopardy and of a deep social malaise.

Problem I

The Expulsion of Asians from Uganda

Are States Bound by the Human Rights Clauses of the UN Charter?

I. *Uganda: The "Pearl of Africa" Despoiled*   16
   A.   Background: From Stanley to Obote   16
   B.   The Role of the Asians and the Rise of Amin   18
   C.   The Expulsion of the Asians   19
       Statement by Idi Amin Relating to the Expulsion of Asians from
         Uganda   19
       The Declaration of Assets (Non-Citizen Asians) Decree, 1972   22
   D.   The Response of the World Community   26
      1.   Debates in Great Britain   26
      2.   Debates at the UN   28
II. *Human Rights Before the UN Charter*   32
       P. Sieghart, The International Law of Human Rights   33
       Farer, Human Rights Before the Second World War   34
III. *Human Rights After the UN Charter*   36
   A.   Background and Description of the Human Rights Clauses   36
       Eighteenth Report of the Commission to Study the Organiza-
         tion of Peace, The United Nations and Human Rights   36
       J. Brierly, The Law of Nations   38
       Comments and Questions   39
   B.   Content and Legal Status of the Human Rights Clauses   41
       Schachter, The Charter and the Constitution: The Human
         Rights Provisions in American Law   41
       Note: U.S. Recognition of the Legal Status of the Human
         Rights Clauses   46
   C.   Invocation of the Human Rights Clauses on the International
      Level   48
       Legal Consequences for States of the Continued Presence of
         South Africa in Namibia (South West Africa)   49
       Schwelb, The International Court of Justice and the Human
         Rights Clauses of the Charter   49
       Comments and Questions   54
IV. *The Relevance of the Human Rights Clauses of the UN Charter to the*
    Expulsion of Asians from Uganda   55
       Wooldridge and Sharma, International Law and the Expulsion
         of Ugandan Asians   55

   Plender, The Ugandan Crisis and the Right of Expulsion Un-
    der International Law   59
   Chhangani, Expulsion of Uganda Asians and International Law 61
   Note: Applying the Human Rights Clauses of the UN Charter
    and Other International Norms to the Expulsion of Asians
    from Uganda   64
 V. *The Response of the International Community to Subsequent Human*
  Rights Abuses in Uganda   66
  A. The Situation Worsens   66
   Uganda — A Lawless State   66
   Mohr, In Amin's Taciturn Uganda, Even Food Is Unspeakable 67
   See No Evil   70
  B. UN Action (or Inaction)   71
  C. The U.S. Embargo   73
  D. The Tanzanian Intervention   76
 VI. *Concluding Thoughts and Observations*   78
   Bilder, Rethinking International Human Rights: Some Basic
    Questions   79
   Comments and Questions   82
 VII. *Final Comments and Questions*   83

I. · Uganda: The "Pearl of Africa" Despoiled

A. *Background: From Stanley to Obote*

When Henry Morton Stanley reached Uganda in 1875, he remarked that he had found the Garden of Eden. A generation later Winston Churchill, then Under-Secretary of State for the Colonies, called the Oregon-sized country the "Pearl of Africa." He insisted that the British Empire ought to "concentrate upon Uganda. Nowhere else in Africa will so little go so far. Nowhere else will the results be so brilliant, more substantial, and more readily realized." W. Churchill, My African Journey (1908).

In 1862 J.H. Speke, the first European known to have explored Uganda, discovered a prosperous Bantu-speaking tribal kingdom named Buganda at the site of the present capital of Kampala. The "Kabaka" (king) of the tribe welcomed Speke, as he would the Europeans who followed him, in the hope that they would prove allies against the persistent threat of Arab slavers and ivory merchants.

In 1890 the Kabaka and leading German colonialist Karl Peters signed a treaty intended to establish Germany's rights in the territory. However, that June the British persuaded the Germans to abandon their "exercise of influence" in Buganda in return for, among other things, the cession of the Island of Heligoland in the North Sea. Agreement between

Great Britain and Germany, July 1, 1890, 82 Brit. & Foreign State Papers 35 (1889-1890). By December of that year, Captain F.W. Lugard, a representative of the Imperial British East Africa Company, arrived with an armed force and negotiated a treaty between the Kabaka and Great Britain. Within two years British control extended over most of modern-day Uganda. When the East Africa Company hit financial difficulties, the British government, on 18 June 1894, assumed control of the country by creating the Uganda Protectorate incorporating Buganda and its contiguous territories.

In 1900 Great Britain and Buganda signed a treaty known as the "Ugandan Magna Carta," which established the Protectorate's form of government and remained in effect for over 50 years. The treaty granted rule to the Kabaka, with the assistance of a British Governor, and, in conjunction with similar arrangements with the neighboring kingdoms of Ankole, Toro, and Bunyoro, entrenched the reign of hereditary kings in Uganda.

Initially each semi-independent tribal kingdom legislated local matters, subject to the approval of the Kabaka, in its own "lukiko" or parliament, with the British Governor controlling those portions of the Protectorate not incorporated into the kingdoms through local intermediaries. In 1921 a legislative council was created to assist the governor, and, although Africans were not added to the council until 1945, by 1954 they represented one-half of its membership. As Uganda's first national legislative body, the council proved an effective counterweight to the tribal parliaments and gave rise to national political parties.

Of the African political parties that emerged in the 1950s, the royalist Bugandan Kabaka Yekka and the opposing Ugandan People's Congress Party, led by Lango tribesman Dr. Milton Obote, had the most impact. These two parties laid aside their differences in their joint effort to obtain Ugandan independence from Great Britain, an effort that met with success on 9 October 1962. Upon independence, Obote became the fledgling government's first Prime Minister, while its citizens elected the Kabaka as President.

Friction developed quickly between Dr. Obote and the Kabaka. The latter favored the traditional lukiko form of government, while Obote sought a more unified state. Uganda's 1962 constitution, which had created a federal government in which the four kingdoms enjoyed considerable autonomy, represented a compromise between these approaches. However, Dr. Obote, intent on modernizing Uganda and abolishing the old kingdoms, led a movement that deposed the Kabaka in 1966, forcing him to flee the country. In 1967 a new constitution established Uganda as a republic, with Obote as President, and dissolved the old kingdoms in favor of districts. Obote continued to strengthen the central government by initiating a nationalization campaign in 1970 that took over banks, insurance companies, plantations, and the larger industries, many of which were foreign-owned.

B.   The Role of the Asians and the Rise of Amin

The Ugandan Protectorate established in 1894 witnessed almost no European immigration, primarily because a 1916 law banned non-African land ownership. In spite of this prohibition, however, Asians, mostly from the Indian subcontinent, flocked to Uganda in droves, their journeys facilitated by the British Empire's control over both India and East Africa. The railroad construction projects of the early twentieth century brought the first significant numbers of Asians to Uganda, where they quickly prospered. Many new arrivals became cotton and coffee merchants after their railroad contracts expired, and Asians later introduced and developed Uganda's sugar cane industry. By 1972 Asians owned 90 percent of Uganda's commerce and dominated the country's professional fields. Asians represented 80 percent of the country's doctors, lawyers, teachers, and engineers despite the fact that they constituted only 80,000 of Uganda's 10 million people.

At the same time, the Asians kept their distance from the Africans and remained a discrete and insular minority. They rarely mixed socially with the Africans, who rightly or wrongly believed that the Asians took advantage of them in business. Asians on the legislative council concerned themselves almost exclusively with measures benefitting the Asian community alone, such as relaxed immigration laws and more civil service openings for young Asians. To many young African graduates of Kampala's Makarere University, the Asians, even their classmates at the university, were unwelcome.

During the late 1960s, Dr. Obote's administration claimed that many Asians had acquired Ugandan citizenship improperly following the country's independence, and that therefore they should no longer be considered citizens. Since 23,000 of the Asian population had opted for Ugandan citizenship in 1962 (most, fortunately for them, had elected the status of "British Protected Person" or had sought Indian or Pakistani nationality), Obote's actions left a cloud on the citizenship of many Asians, who without other nationality would become stateless persons. These actions outraged many Ugandan Asians, but they were only a harbinger of what lay ahead for the prosperous Asian minority.

In February 1971, while Obote was at a Commonwealth Conference in Singapore, the Ugandan army commander, General Idi Amin Dada, overthrew the government with little opposition. Independence had been a disappointment thus far for many Ugandans, as Obote's government had failed both to provide its promised strong unified leadership and to manage effectively the country's weakening economy.

Amin, an illiterate ex-enlisted man in the former King's Army Rifles, had built his support by converting to Islam (Uganda has a substantial Muslim population), evoking the traditions of the old kingdoms, and blaming the Asians for the poor status of the economy. Many of his initial acts would have been more widely protested had Amin not placated the majority of his countrymen with popular, high-profile gestures. For instance, while promising free elections, Amin soon proclaimed himself President for life. He also abolished Parliament, packed the civil service and judiciary with his Muslim supporters, and purged his opponents. However, Amin simultaneously won widespread public approval by bringing the remains of the deposed Kabaka of Buganda back into the country. The traditional kingdoms always had been popular with most Ugandans, and, after years of disappointment under Obote, the kingdoms, which the Kabaka had personified, seemed like paradise. Amin also benefitted initially from a warm reception by Great Britain and the United States, both of which had developed an aversion to Obote's policies. They came to dislike Amin's even more.

C.   The Expulsion of the Asians

On 4 August 1972, in a speech to Army troops, General Amin announced the expulsion of all persons of Asian origin who were British citizens. Five days later he explained his action and expanded it to include Asians who were citizens of India, Pakistan, and Bangladesh (Documents, 5 N.Y.U. J. Intl. L. & Pol. 603-605 (1972)).

Statement by Idi Amin Relating to the Expulsion of Asians from Uganda

H.E. The President of Uganda Has Today, August 9, 1972, Issued the Following Statement Concerning the Status of Asian Community in Uganda

[1.] It will be recalled that last Friday, the 4th August, 1972, while addressing Troops at Tororo, I announced the decision of my Government to ask the British Government to take over responsibility for the British citizens of Asian origin living in Uganda who were sabotaging the economy of this country and were practising and encouraging corruption. It will also be remembered that on Saturday, the 5th August, 1972, in my message to the Nation on the occasion of Cooperative International Day, I elaborated on my Friday Statement and made it clear that the British citizens of Asian origin who, it had been established beyond any doubt that their continued presence in Uganda was no longer in the country's best interests, would be given three months within which to leave the country.

2. My Government believes that one of its primary duties is to ensure the welfare of all members of the community. This means, for example, that

no one section of the community can be allowed to dominate, control or monopolize the business life of the nation. No country can tolerate the economy of its nation being so much in the hands of non-citizens as is the case in Uganda today. The Asian community has frustrated attempts by Ugandan Africans to participate in the economic and business life of their country. Asians have used their economic power to ensure that the Ugandan Africans are effectively excluded from participating in the economic life of their own country. They have used their family ties, their languages which are unknown to Ugandans to exclude Ugandan Africans from the business life of their own country. They have refused to identify themselves with Uganda. For instance, at Independence, when they were offered the chance to become Uganda citizens, the majority rejected the offer. Some of the few who became citizens of Uganda did so only half-heartedly as they had no faith in this country and also remained citizens of other countries. Asians have kept themselves apart as a closed community and have refused to integrate with Uganda Africans. They have been milking the economy of the country. They have exported illegally, large sums of money from this country.

3. The Government has an obligation to put the economy of Uganda into the hands of its citizens. It would, therefore, be a futile exercise to request British Asians only to leave Uganda without, at the same time, requiring the nationals of India, Pakistan and Bangladesh also to leave, since their presence is also not in the best interests of the economy of Uganda.

4. I have, therefore, today signed a Decree revoking with effect from today, the 9th August, 1972, all entry permits and certificates of residence which had been granted to the above categories of persons. They are, however, permitted to stay in Uganda for a maximum period of 90 days from today. That means that the persons affected should make arrangements to remove themselves from Uganda during this period. I must emphasise that after the expiry of the 90 days period, any of these people who will still be in Uganda, will be doing so illegally and will face the consequences.

5. Also today, a Statutory Instrument has been signed, exempting certain categories of persons within the nationals affected, allowing them to stay in Uganda in accordance with the provisions of our Immigration Laws. The persons exempted are as follows: —

   (i) All persons in the employment of Government, Government Bodies, Cooperative Movements, East African Community and International Organizations;
   (ii) Professionals such as Teachers, Practising Lawyers, Medical Practitioners, Pharmacists, Dentists, Chemists, Auditors, Architects, Accountants, Surveyors, Quantity Surveyors, Engineers, Technicians in Industries, Commercial and Agricultural Enterprises, Owners of Industrial and Agricultural Enterprises, The Managers

or Owners of Banks and Insurance Companies and Professionals and Technicians engaged in Plant, Animal, Agricultural and Forestry Production, Professing and marketing of the products, and School Owners.

6. It will be recalled that Government organised a census of all Asians in Uganda last year. According to the information gathered from that census, there are 23,242 Asians claiming to be Uganda citizens: of these, 8,791 claimed to be Uganda citizens by registration, while 14,451 claimed to be Uganda citizens by birth. However, records available to Government indicate that the number of Uganda citizens of Asian origin is smaller than 23,242. I have, therefore, directed the Ministry of Internal Affairs to verify the above claims. Each of the persons affected, claiming to be a Uganda citizen, will be called upon to produce documentary proof in support of his claim to Uganda citizenship.

7. It will be appreciated that the above decision and the measures taken to implement them necessitate taking certain security measures. Travellers to or from Uganda are, therefore, requested to cooperate with the Security Forces and Immigration Officers at the points of entry or departure. Travellers leaving Uganda by road are requested to have with them their current motor-vehicle registration books, valid insurance certificates and valid driving permits to establish the ownership of the vehicles and identity of the driver.

8. We are not requesting British citizens of Asian origin and nationals of India, Pakistan and Bangladesh to leave Uganda because of racialism. We are not racists. We have no animosity against Asians or any other foreigners for that matter. The Government took this decision purely in the interests of the economy of this country. The Government has the support of the entire 10 millions in the measures it has taken. Moreover, when the members of the Armed Forces took over the Government and handed power to me on the 25th January, 1971, I was charged with responsibility of ensuring that the economy of this Republic is put into the hands of Ugandans.

In addition to expelling non-Ugandan Asians, which, as will be shown below, provoked the most outrage from the world community, Amin fixed his sights on the 23,000 Asians who considered themselves Ugandan citizens. While nominally avoiding the expulsion of persons with Ugandan citizenship, an act that clearly would have violated international law (see M. Pellonpaa, Expulsion in International Law 20 (1984)), he adopted the practice of the Obote government and began to strip Asians of their citizenship with an eye to their subsequent expulsion. Hundreds of Asians lost their citizenship because their documents contained minor inaccuracies. An unknown additional number lost their status as citizens when government officials destroyed their papers. N.Y. Times, Aug. 13, 1972, at 8, col. 1.

Thus, thousands of Asians were deprived of their Ugandan citizenship and became stateless persons.

Although under general international law a state has the right, absent a contrary treaty obligation, to expel non-citizens from its territory, the state of the expellee also has the right to protest diplomatically if the reasons for the expulsion or the manner in which it was carried out is arbitrary or discriminatory. M. Pellonpaa, supra, at 67, 113, 419. Thus, Great Britain, along with India and to a lesser extent Pakistan and Bangladesh, vehemently protested Amin's expulsion of their nationals, especially its racism and the fact that the departing Asians were given only 90 days to leave the country. Despite such protests, Amin refused to reverse his action or extend the 90-day time period. Indeed, contrary to his assurances to UN Secretary-General Kurt Waldheim that Uganda would not confiscate the property of the departing Asians, on 4 October 1972 Amin issued the decree that follows, retroactive to August, effectively taking their property (11 Intl. Legal Materials 1389-1391 (1972)).

The Declaration of Assets (Non-Citizen Asians) Decree, 1972

A DECREE TO MAKE PROVISION FOR THE DECLARATION OF ASSETS BY NON-CITIZEN ASIANS LEAVING UGANDA AND FOR OTHER PURPOSES CONNECTED THEREWITH

1. No person leaving Uganda by virtue of the provisions of the Immigration (Cancellation of Entry Permits and Certificate of Residence) Decree, 1972 (in this Decree referred to as the departing Asian) may,

(a) transfer any immovable property, bus company, farm, including livestock, or business to any other person;

(b) mortgage his immovable property, bus company, farm, including livestock, or business to any other person;

(c) in the case of a company,

(i) issue new shares;

(ii) change the salaries or terms of employment of staff including terminal benefits; or

(iii) appoint new directors or in any way vary the conditions, terms of service or remuneration payable to the directors.

2. (1) Every departing Asian whether such departing Asian holds any trading licence or a licence to manufacture a scheduled article or not shall declare his assets and liabilities and supply such other particulars and information relating to his property or business, if any, to the Minister on Forms PRO/1 and PRO/2 specified in the Schedule to this Decree.

(2) The forms submitted to the Minister under subsection (1) of this section, shall be accompanied by the following documents, namely,

(a) in the case of a company, a certified copy of the Memorandum of Association and Articles of Association;

(b) copies of the accounts, trading accounts, balance sheets and profit and loss accounts for the last preceding two years;

(c) a list of title deeds, debentures, loan agreements and contracts or other agreements to the like effect; and

(d) a notice in writing nominating a person to act as his agent to sell his property or business.

(3) The agent shall ensure that the property or business of a departing Asian, declared under subsection (1) of this section, is properly looked after until it is transferred by sale to a Uganda citizen.

(4) An agent nominated under subsection (2), of this section, shall have all the powers the principal has over the property or business to be transferred under this Decree, except power to,

(a) make a direct sale or transfer of the property or business to any person;

(b) let any premises;

(c) convey by way of gift to any person, the property or business;

(d) acquire the property or carry on the business himself; or

(e) deal with the property or business in any manner which intends or appears to frustrate the declared policy of the Government to transfer the property or business to a Uganda-citizen.

(5) Every departing Asian shall be given a receipt in Form PRO/3 specified in the Schedule to this Decree, acknowledging receipt of the forms and documents referred to in this section.

3. The Minister shall keep a register of properties and businesses declared under section 2 of this Decree in Form PRO/4 specified in the Schedule to this Decree.

4. (1) An application for the purchase of property or business shall be in Form APP/1 specified in the Schedule to this Decree.

(2) Except where the applicant is the Government or a State Corporation, before any property or business of a departing Asian is sold, the Minister shall advertise the property or business in such manner as he considers appropriate describing the property or business to be sold, and such other particulars relating to the property or business he considers relevant.

(3) Where two or more applications are submitted in respect of the same property or business, the Minister shall refer the applications to an advising committee appointed by him consisting of such number of persons as he thinks fit.

(4) Where there is a dispute as to the price to be paid for the business or property the Minister shall appoint such number of valuers as he thinks fit to determine the value.

(5) No person shall sell or purchase any property or business of a

departing Asian in respect of which no information and documents have not been submitted to the Minister in compliance with the provisions of section 2 of this Decree and henceforth such property or business shall vest in the Government.

5. (1) Any person who fails to comply with any provision of this Decree commits an offence and shall be liable to a fine not exceeding fifty thousand shillings or to imprisonment for a term not exceeding two years or to both.

(2) Where a company is guilty of an offence under this Decree, every director of that company shall be guilty of the same offence and shall be liable to the penalty prescribed under this section unless he proves that the offence was committed without his knowledge or connivance or if he had knowledge of the offence, that he took all reasonable steps to prevent its commission by the company.

6. Where an agent nominated under subsection (2) of section 2 of this Decree,

(a) leaves Uganda for good;

(b) leaves Uganda and fails to return within a period of three months;

(c) is unable to discharge his duties and functions under this Decree, whether arising from infirmity of body or mind or from any other cause, the Minister shall appoint a trustee to perform the duties and functions of an agent under this Decree.

7. The Minister may make regulations,

(a) on any matter connected with the transfer of property or business of a departing Asian to a Uganda citizen; and

(b) prescribing any form which he considers necessary for the proper administration of this Decree.

8. In this Decree unless the context otherwise requires,

"Minister" means the Minister responsible for commerce and industry;

"property" means movable and immovable property including fixtures, fittings and ancillary equipment;

"scheduled article" has the same meaning as in the Industrial Licensing Act, 1969.

9. This Decree shall be deemed to have come into force on the 9th day of August, 1972.

MADE under my hand and the Public Seal, this 4th day of October, 1972.

GENERAL IDI AMIN DADA
President.

To the Asians facing expulsion, the decrees came as a devastating blow. Most of them had been born in Uganda, and a substantial percentage were third-generation residents. They knew little or nothing, therefore, of the language or customs of the countries of which they were nationals. Indeed, most had never even seen "their countries." They faced the prospect of being stripped of their belongings, split off from their communities and, in many cases, their immediate families, and sent to live as strangers in distant lands. Frightened as they were to leave Uganda, however, the Asians were even more frightened of being caught there after the expiration of Amin's deadline. Thus began the exodus.

When the dazed expellees arrived at their destinations, they generally were destitute. Often they claimed that Ugandan army troops had confiscated most of their personal belongings when they arrived at Entebbe Airport. N.Y. Times, Oct. 7, 1972, at 8, col. 5. In addition to such property losses, they reported numerous acts of violence they had experienced or witnessed. The passengers from one flight arriving in Great Britain told horrifying stories: Mr. Charah Singh reported that he fled after seeing soldiers riddle a man with bullets and dump his body in a ditch. Mrs. Kkanalben Vallabh stated that, while she traveled from Kampala to Mbale in compliance with a deportation order, she saw a man stabbed by soldiers at a checkpoint when he said that he was carrying some shillings. Another man said that, when 100 shillings were found in the turban of a Sikh traveling on his train, the latter was stripped and made to crawl naked through the train along with 30 other innocent passengers. Still another man showed bayonet wounds he had gotten from Ugandan soldiers. The Times (London), Oct. 10, 1972, at 8, col. 1.

The destination points of the expellees depended upon their nationality, if they had one, or the good offices of the UN High Commissioner for Refugees, if they were stateless. Official British estimates of the Asian population in Uganda at the time of expulsion were as follows:

Total Asian population	80,000
British passport holders	50,000
Ugandan citizens	23,000
Indian nationals	5,000
Pakistani nationals	2,000

The Times (London), Aug. 30, 1972, at 12, col. 4. Great Britain resettled 27,000 of its nationals, with India taking 8,500 British nationals, all its own nationals, and several thousand stateless persons. N.Y. Times Mag., Dec. 24, 1972, at 11, col. 1. Canada took 1,300 stateless persons while the balance were parceled out to Europe, the United States, and Latin American countries. Note, Asian Ugandans in Europe, 2 New Community (London) No. 3, at 276 (1973). Thus, the exodus ended by the 8 November 1972 deadline with the once insular Ugandan Asian community scattered over much of the globe.

D. The Response of the World Community

1. Debates in Great Britain

The British people and the British Parliament understandably were
shocked by the expulsion of Asians from Uganda. The government reacted
admirably by organizing a massive effort to evacuate them from Uganda
before the expiration of General Amin's 90-day deadline and by accepting
and resettling all expellees with British nationality (interpreted fairly liber-
ally). Nevertheless, a number of questions were raised in the House of
Commons about the British response. Answering them, in the following two
extracts, was Sir Alec Douglas-Home, the Foreign Secretary (843 Parl. Deb.,
H.C. (5th ser.) 770-771 (1972); id. at 164-165 (written answers)).

Sir D. Walker-Smith   asked the Secretary of State for Foreign and Com-
    monwealth Affairs whether he will refer the situation in Uganda to the
    Security Council for a determination under Article [39] of the Charter
    of the United Nations.
Sir Alec Douglas-Home: No. But I must reserve the right to use any part of
    the United Nations machinery if it seems likely to serve the interests of
    the Ugandan Asians or of this country.
Sir D. Walker-Smith: Is not the situation in Uganda a threat to the peace
    within the terms of Article [39] just as much at any rate as was the
    situation six years ago in Rhodesia where the question of domestic
    jurisdiction was not held to invalidate the reference? Does not my right
    hon. Friend agree that not nearly enough is being done in the United
    Nations in regard to what is a clear breach of international law on the
    part of the Ugandan Government?
Sir Alec Douglas-Home: The question of a breach of the peace would first
    arise in relation to a possible conflict with Tanzania. The Tanzanian
    Government have not brought this to the United Nations or requested
    any action under Article 39. It would be difficult to establish in the
    United Nations that this is a breach of the peace under Article 39,
    whatever our opinion may be and notwithstanding the just comparison
    with the Rhodesian situation which my right hon. and learned Friend
    makes.
        As to the action of the United Nations, my right hon. and learned
    Friend is familiar with the speech I made there and knows that the
    Secretary-General and the High Commissioner for Refugees are taking
    action. We had better get this operation over first and get the Asians out
    safely. Then I intend to review the whole of the relationship between
    this country and Uganda. . . .
Mr. Arthur Lewis   asked the Secretary of State for Foreign and Common-
    wealth Affairs whether he will give the reasons for the change in the
    Government's declared policy of only assisting those Ugandan Asians

who can produce British passports to include stateless Asians and others without British passports; how many additional immigrants will be admitted under this new arrangement; and whether all stateless persons with or without British passports will now be able to claim admission into Great Britain.

Sir Alec Douglas-Home: There has been no change of policy. As my right hon. Friend, the Home Secretary, said on 18th October, Her Majesty's Government have made it clear that they do not accept responsibility for stateless Asians in Uganda. The Government have decided that passports may be granted to Asians who had acquired Ugandan citizenship but whose renunciation of United Kingdom citizenship was registered too late for them to retain Ugandan citizenship. It is expected that up to 600 heads of families will be entitled to apply for United Kingdom passports under this arrangement.

Mr. Arthur Lewis   asked the Secretary of State for Foreign and Commonwealth Affairs whether he can give an assurance that the rate he is now applying regarding the admission into Great Britain of Ugandan Asians who failed to apply, or wrongly applied, for their British passports, and therefore became stateless persons or non-British citizens, will apply to all stateless persons or others in a similar situation now, or in the future, so far as these Ugandan citizens are concerned.

Sir Alec Douglas-Home: The Ugandan Asians who acquired Ugandan citizenship after independence and lost it because they failed effectively to renounce their United Kingdom citizenship in time, did not lose their United Kingdom citizenship. They are not stateless, and the procedures regulating their admission into the United Kingdom are not therefore relevant to those governing the admission of stateless persons. My right hon. Friend the Home Secretary made it clear in his statement on 18th October that we cannot and do not intend to admit any stateless Asians from Uganda.

Note Sir Alec's reluctance to invoke the formal machinery of the UN Charter available under Article 39, which permits the Security Council to take action with respect to "any threat to the peace. . . ." Both the question and his response seem to assume that only a clear "breach of the peace" gives the Council jurisdiction over the matter. Read the full text of Article 39 in the Documentary Supplement and ponder whether this assumption is correct. Compare the Council's action in the Rhodesian situation, to which reference is made, set out at pages 495-497 of Problem VII. (Compare also the expansive readings recently given to "any threat to the peace" by the Council in the cases of Iraq, the former Yugoslavia, Sudan, and Haiti, considered at length in the debate over UN humanitarian intervention in Problem VIII.) Is the Rhodesian precedent a valid one for taking similar UN action with respect to Uganda, as the questioner suggests? Does Sir Alec's response indicate a belief that Uganda's conduct, however reprehensible, falls short of a violation of the UN Charter? Of general international law? Compare the extract from his speech to the UN at page 29 infra, which eschews legal arguments in favor of humanitarian concerns. Such concerns, as his answer to the last question reveals, seem less central to British policy when stateless Asians rather than British nationals are involved.

2.   Debates at the UN

The Sub-Commission on the Prevention of Discrimination and the Protection of Minorities, a subsidiary organ of the UN Commission on Human Rights discussed in Problems V and VI, took up the expulsion of Asians from Uganda in late August 1972. Mr. Robert James, a member of the Sub-Commission who happened to be from Great Britain, proposed that the following deferentially worded telegram be sent to General Amin (Report of the Sub-Commission on Prevention of Discrimination and Protection of Minorities on Its Twenty-Fifth Session at 22, U.N. Doc. E/CN.4/1101, E/CN.4/Sub. 2/332 (1972)).

> Your Excellency,
> The United Nations Sub-Commission on Prevention of Discrimination and Protection of Minorities, now meeting in New York, has noted with concern the decision of the Ugandan Government to require all Asians — including those holding Ugandan citizenship — to leave your country.
> The internal affairs of your distinguished country are not a matter for the Sub-Commission, but it does have a particular responsibility in the field of human rights entrusted to it by the United Nations Commission on Human Rights. The Sub-Commission has asked that I communicate to you its serious concern over this situation, and to ask you to give particular attention to the humanitarian aspects of the situation arising out of the decision affecting those Asians living in Uganda who do not have Ugandan citizenship. The Sub-Commission has also expressed its concern over the decision to require Asians holding Ugandan citizenship to leave your country as well.
> The Sub-Commission, fully aware of the magnificent record of your great country in the field of human rights, is convinced that you will give these matters your most careful personal attention.

When several members argued that the Sub-Commission had no mandate to send telegrams to Heads of State, its terms of reference being confined to conducting studies and carrying out other specifically assigned tasks, a motion *not* to send the telegram carried by a 14-1-6 vote. Id. at 23. Ultimately, perhaps as a sop to Mr. James, the Sub-Commission adopted by a 12-1-10 vote his draft resolution recommending that "the Commission on Human Rights should consider the problems of the applicability of the present provisions for the international protection of the human rights of individuals who are not citizens of the country in which they live. . . ." Id. at 60. This decision, hardly of immediate help to the Ugandan Asians, ultimately led to the General Assembly's adoption — some 13 years later — of the Declaration on the Human Rights of Individuals Who Are Not Nationals of the Country in Which They Live, discussed at pages 84-85 infra.

A month later, on 27 September 1972, the British Foreign Secretary, Sir Alec Douglas-Home, addressed the General Assembly and asked it to place the expulsion of Asians from Uganda on its agenda. His appeal, in which he denounced General Amin's treatment of the Asians as "an outrage against standards of human decency, in the face of which this Assembly cannot remain silent," rested upon humanitarian rather than legal concerns. He made two requests of "the world community" (27 U.N. GAOR (2042d plen. mtg.) at 12, U.N. Doc. A/P.V.2042 (1972)).

> The first is to show your good-neighbourliness by sharing some of the practical problems of resettling these unhappy people. I am exceedingly grateful and pay a tribute to all those who have come forward with offers of help. The second is that you should all join in calling upon General Amin to extend his arbitrary and inhumane deadline of 90 days and to allow the Asians expelled to take their belongings with them. These are two simple, humane concepts. My delegation will today request that this question should be added to our agenda as an urgent and important item. We ask that the Assembly debate this matter without delay and we are ready to submit a draft resolution — for this inhumanity which creates refugees is of international concern. I trust that it will be overwhelmingly accepted, because, should this Organization fail to do so, there is no one to whom any person, whatever the colour of his skin, can turn for common justice. This is the basis of my appeal to all of you today.

The following day, 28 September 1972, the British representative to the General Assembly's General Committee responded to the Soviet Union's complaint that the British request to have the matter placed on the Assembly's agenda had been submitted too late. Sir Colin Crowe also suggested a legal as well as a humanitarian basis for UN action, to which the Ugandan representative, Mr. Grace Ibingira, replied as detailed below (27 U.N. GAOR General Comm. (203d mtg.) at 35-37, U.N. Doc. A/BUR/ SR.203 (1972)).

> 6. Sir Colin CROWE (United Kingdom) said that he would try to explain why the matter was so urgent and why it had not been brought to the Committee's attention earlier.
>
> 7. Many of the Asians in Uganda held United Kingdom passports and would come to the United Kingdom, others were citizens of India or Pakistan. Several thousand others among those expelled would be stateless and thus the responsibility of the international community.

8. He wished to make it quite clear that his Government did not wish to intervene in matters which were essentially within the domestic jurisdiction of Uganda; nor did it wish the United Nations or anyone else to do so. Had it been possible to settle the matter in bilateral discussions — and his Government had made every effort to do so — it would not have been necessary to involve the United Nations.

9. However, the case under consideration involved matters that went far beyond domestic jurisdiction: the hardships caused by the collective expulsion of members of an ethnic group raised humanitarian issues germane to the wider purposes of the Charter. Furthermore, Members of the United Nations had an obligation to take joint and separate action in co-operation with the United Nations to promote universal respect for human rights and fundamental freedoms for all. The situation was all the more complicated not only because of the severe restrictions placed on the funds which departing Asians might take with them, but also because inadequate time had been allowed to solve the difficult problem of finding new homes for so many persons, perhaps 80,000 in all.

10. The Secretary-General was already involved, and the United Kingdom welcomed his humanitarian efforts. His delegation had asked for urgent consideration of the matter by the General Assembly in order to secure an immediate expression of the support of the membership as a whole for the Secretary-General's efforts to ease matters, and not least to remove the threat of concentration in military camps and deprivation of property for those unfortunate persons who were to be expelled but who might not succeed in leaving by 8 November.

11. The draft resolution which his delegation would propose would ask for two things. First, it would invite the Secretary-General to continue to use his good offices on behalf of the Asians. Secondly, it would urge the Government of Uganda to respond positively to the Secretary-General's efforts, particularly with reference to the time-limit and the transfer of assets.

12. What he had said about urgency was enough to explain why his delegation sought the earliest possible discussion in the General Assembly. There were only some 40 days left. He therefore asked that the General Committee recommend that the item be added to the agenda of the General Assembly and that it be given the highest priority. In his delegation's view, such a humanitarian issue could not await the conclusion of the general debate.

13. Mr. IBINGIRA (Uganda) said that he had been in consultation with his Government and the points that he would make to the Committee therefore came from the highest authority in his country.

14. It was not correct that the assets of the Asians in Uganda would be confiscated without compensation, as had been stated by the United Kingdom Secretary of State for Foreign and Commonwealth Affairs before the General Assembly, and he challenged the United Kingdom representative to produce evidence that the Government of Uganda had made any such statement. His Government had never, since the issue had arisen, said that it would confiscate the assets of the Asian community; it had, in fact, said that the Asians would receive compensation in due course, but they could not expect to receive it within a week or even a month. His Government had

issued forms, copies of which he would circulate to members of the Committee, requesting details of all the assets, liabilities and property owned by British Asians resident in Uganda, in order that the Ministry of Commerce could assess their value with a view to compensation. He did not believe that such action accorded with his Government's alleged intention to confiscate the property of Asians. He could therefore only express profound surprise that the Foreign Secretary of the United Kingdom had made such an assertion without substantive proof.

15. There were no camps in his country for British citizens of Asian origin who had been requested to leave. There might never be any need to establish such camps, but he wished to make it clear that if it became necessary to make temporary arrangements for Asians in transit, they would be of the highest standard. He pointed out that there were camps for such people in the United Kingdom; there was nothing sinister about them if the amenities were satisfactory.

16. His Government's position was that the matter was of an internal nature and was covered by Article 2, paragraph 7, of the Charter. Although the matter might affect the United Kingdom and other countries as well as his own, it should be pursued through channels other than the United Nations. His Government had not closed the door to negotiations and all other avenues had not yet been explored. Even if they had, the matter was an internal problem for his Government to decide. The problem was, in fact, a result of Uganda's colonial heritage; many countries had been faced with the problem of minorities. Merely because the group under discussion would be going to the United Kingdom, there was no need for the matter to be brought before the United Nations. Many aliens had been expelled previously from other countries without such action being taken. It had been said that the problem indicated that Africans were racist, a factor which could be used to justify the continuation of southern African minority racist régimes. There were countries in Africa which had required black aliens to leave in the past, but the matter had never been brought before the United Nations. It had, for instance, happened in Uganda, when 200,000 alien Africans who were members of the British Commonwealth had been asked to leave. Now, when 55,000 British citizens were asked to leave, it was suggested that the matter should be discussed in the General Assembly. That, in his Government's view, was the greatest evidence of United Kingdom racialism. If anyone was to bring the matter before the United Nations, it should be Uganda, in view of the United Kingdom's reluctance to accept the Asians who had been asked to leave.

17. He wished to make it quite clear that the lives of the Asians in question were not in jeopardy and that the Government would be responsible for their safety and for ultimate compensation for their assets. Therefore, if the United Nations was really seeking a solution to the problem, he requested members not to ask for a debate on it. Such a debate would be used for United Kingdom internal consumption in order to pacify right-wing hardliners such as Enoch Powell, and could only serve to harden the positions of the Governments concerned. If the United Kingdom was seeking a solution, it should explore other avenues. He urged members of the Committee to reject the proposal, since the Secretary-General had already contacted

the Ugandan Government and could pursue his contacts. There was therefore no need for the General Assembly to debate the question or to adopt a resolution on it.

One day later, 29 September 1972, Sir Colin, citing an important development in the Ugandan situation, withdrew the British proposal. This development was an offer by President Mobuto of Zaire to act as an intermediary between the two countries. Although his efforts failed to produce a friendly settlement, Great Britain never reintroduced its proposal, and the United Nations thus never really grappled with the human rights issues raised by Uganda's expulsion of its Asian population.

II. Human Rights Before the UN Charter

Any assessment of the current status of international human rights law and the procedures that have been developed for its enforcement must take into account its relatively recent origins. Traditionally, and even today, international law is primarily a law between states (as its old name, the Law of Nations, made quite clear). States are the subjects and individuals, generally speaking, only the objects of international law. The appallingly low status of the individual in the traditional international legal order is shown by the following extract from the leading treatise only 40 years ago (1 L. Oppenheim, International Law 640-641 (8th ed. H. Lauterpacht ed. 1955) (emphasis added)).

> Writers have occasionally expressed the view that International Law guarantees to individuals, both at home and abroad and whether nationals of a State or stateless, certain fundamental rights usually referred to as rights of mankind. Such rights have been said to comprise the right to life, liberty, freedom of religion and conscience, and the like. It is doubtful whether that view is expressive of the actual practice of States. For it is generally recognized that, apart from obligations undertaken by treaty, *a State is entitled to treat both its own nationals and stateless persons at discretion and that the manner in which it treats them is not a matter with which International Law, as a rule, concerns itself.*

The use in the above extract of the two words, "at discretion" — a "chilling phrase" in the words of one subsequent writer — reveals just how much leeway traditional international law accorded states in the treatment (or mistreatment) of their own nationals and stateless persons. Aliens, for reasons to be developed below, were subject to a different set of international norms that entitled them to far better treatment. In essence, though, from the Peace of Westphalia in 1648 to the adoption of the UN Charter in 1945, the international legal order — built upon the nation-state system — permitted states to treat most individuals as they wished. This unenviable situation and the reasons for the "revolutionary" international human rights regime spawned by the UN Charter, already mentioned in the Humphrey essay (pages 1-13 of the General Introduction), are described and developed in the following two readings.

P. Sieghart, The International Law of Human Rights
11, 14 (1983)

Since the beginnings of the Law of Nations, one of its fundamental principles was that of national sovereignty, which reserves to each sovereign State the exclusive right to take any action it thinks fit, provided only that the action does not interfere with the rights of other States, and is not prohibited by international law on that or any other ground.

According to that principle, a sovereign State has complete freedom of action, in international law, to deal with its own nationals ('personal sovereignty') and with its own territory ('territorial sovereignty'). . . .

It follows from this principle that, in all matters falling within the 'domestic jurisdiction' of any State, international law does not permit any interference, let alone any intervention, by any other State. Such matters do not fall within the concern of international law. Accordingly, so long as 'personal' sovereignty continued to be regarded as falling exclusively within the domestic jurisdiction of sovereign States, 'what a government did to its own citizens was its own affair and beyond the reach of international law or legal intervention by other States'.

[The author describes one exception to this legal regime, the doctrine of humanitarian intervention, taken up in the context of Uganda at pages 76-78 infra and generally in Problem VIII.]

. . . [D]uring the first part of the twentieth century the theory of legal positivism . . . , [c]ombined with a strict application of the doctrine of national sovereignty, . . . effectively excluded the possibility of judging, and therefore criticizing, the treatment of any people by its own government. The apotheosis — and the consequent downfall — of that position came in National Socialist Germany in the late 1930's and early 1940's, where historically unprecedented atrocities were perpetrated by the regime there and then lawfully in power upon some millions of its own citizens. Many of those atrocities were carried out with complete legality under National Socialist legislation: the domestic laws authorized, and paralleled, the pernicious injustice of the acts. Moreover, those laws had been enacted by a legislature lawfully installed under the constitution of a sovereign State.

According to the strict doctrine of national sovereignty, any foreign criticism of those laws was therefore formally illegitimate; according to the strict positivist position, it was also meaningless.

Farer, Human Rights Before the Second World War
in Inter-American Commission on Human Rights: Ten Years
of Activities 1971-1981, at v-vi (1982)

Before the Second World War, scholars and diplomats assumed that international law allowed each equal sovereign an equal right to be monstrous to his subjects. Summary execution, torture, conviction without due process (or any process, for that matter) were legally significant events only if the victim of such official eccentricities were the citizen of another state. In that case, international law treated him as the bearer not of personal rights but of rights belonging to his government, and ultimately to the state for which it temporarily spoke. (In effect, the individual was nothing more than a symbol and a capital asset. Assaults on his person carried out or acquiesced to by representatives of another state were deemed assaults on the dignity and material interests of his state, requiring compensation.)

Guardians of the moral realm were episodically less permissive. Virtually from the start of that bloody enterprise known as the Spanish Empire in the New World, Catholic priests struggled to restrain the awful cupidity and cruder fantasies of the Conquistadors, their secular associates in Spain's civilizing mission. In addition, both Catholic and Protestant missionaries worked to alert decent opinion in Europe to the genocidal trade in African slaves and, thereafter, to such abominations as Belgian King Leopold's personal empire in the Congo.

Even Leopold's fellow monarchs had no stomach for his methods of organizing labor, which included the mutilation of sluggards and drop-outs. And so, while completing the orderly division of Africa at the Congress of Berlin in 1885 and the Congress of Brussels four years later, they announced and Leopold nominally accepted certain standards to be followed in treating the indigenous inhabitants. Since the Conference provided no enforcement machinery, relying on the ineffable Leopold, that noble gentleman carried on business as usual. Nevertheless, the very recognition of limits on Leopold's caprice was a rare early instance of formal concern for and legal restraint on a sovereign's discretion in the disposition of his human assets.

Pogroms in Russia, the massacre of Armenians in Turkey and Maronites in Lebanon, as well as the efforts of governments to wrap coups d'état in a higher morality (as in the Anglo-French effort during the First World War to portray the conflict as a struggle between good and evil, and the half-hearted attempt after the War to prosecute the Kaiser as a war criminal), all helped erode the long-entrenched perception that what went on within a state was not a matter of legitimate international concern unless it affected the interests of aliens. But it was not until the final stage of the Second World War that governments first took the leap from moralizing rhetoric to legal action.

They were driven by popular revulsion over Dachau and the other charnel houses operated by the Nazis, by a surge of idealism sharpened through confrontation with Nazi ideology and, perhaps, by the victors' natural desire to equate success and virtue. In succeeding decades, the community of nations, old and new, established a thicket of legal restraints.

For the first time in history, states assumed obligations to their own citizens as precisely and formally defined in many cases as the legal obligations they had hitherto owed to each other under international law (for example, with respect to the immunity of diplomats). Both through formal treaties and informal practice, they bound themselves not to torture or summarily execute their citizens, or to convict them without due process of law or to dissolve their trade unions or to discriminate among them on the basis of race or religion or to do a great number of other things that in earlier ages were matters entirely at the discretion of sovereigns.

The Charter of the United Nations was the point of departure [for] this unique legal development.

The pre-Charter legal regime that permitted states to treat their nationals "at discretion" recognized several exceptions whereby, under customary or conventional international law, a state's absolute freedom of action supposedly was limited. First and foremost was the doctrine of humanitarian intervention, which permitted a state or group of states to intervene, by force if necessary, to protect the nationals of another state when the latter's treatment of them "shocked the conscience of mankind." See generally Humanitarian Intervention and the United Nations (R. Lillich ed. 1973). The doctrine, then and still controversial, is taken up in the context of Uganda at pages 77-78 infra and generally in Problem VIII. Other exceptions to a state's otherwise unbridled discretion were the abolition of slavery, the development of the law of war (humanitarian law), and the protection of some minorities. See A. Robertson, Human Rights in the World 14-21 (3d ed. J. Merrills ed. 1989). None of these exceptions, however, really addressed what subsequently has emerged as one of the key imperatives of contemporary international law: the need to promote and protect in a comprehensive and systematic fashion the basic human rights of all individuals in all states against abusive state action. As Farer concludes in the reading immediately above, "[t]he Charter of the United Nations was the point of departure [for] this unique legal development."

III. Human Rights After the UN Charter

A. *Background and Description of the Human Rights Clauses*

Eighteenth Report of the Commission to Study the Organization of Peace, The United Nations and Human Rights
1-4 (1968)

1. THE DEVELOPMENT OF THE CONCEPT OF INTERNATIONAL
    PROTECTION OF HUMAN RIGHTS

The idea of international protection of human rights on a universal scale owes its origin to the tragic events accompanying the Second World War and the totalitarian excesses preceding it. . . .

It was during one of the darkest hours of the war, when the Axis powers achieved almost complete control of the European continent, that President Roosevelt provided in his "Four Freedoms" — freedom of speech, freedom of religion, freedom from want and freedom from fear — a rallying cry for all those suffering from the ravages of war and totalitarianism. After another disaster, the Pearl Harbor attack, the Allied Governments agreed in Washington on the "Declaration by United Nations" which named as the basic goal of victory the preservation of "human rights and justice in their own lands as well as in other lands."

Encouraged by this statement, various official and unofficial groups, both in the United States and other countries, started immediately to work on an International Bill of Rights which would be proclaimed by the United Nations after their victory and which would become one of the cornerstones of the new world order to be built after the war. While the official enthusiasm for a codification of the basic principles for the protection of human rights later cooled down, active pressure of non-governmental organizations led to the inclusion in the Charter of the United Nations of several provisions on human rights.

2. THE CHARTER OF THE UNITED NATIONS

In the preamble to the Charter, the peoples of the United Nations have reaffirmed their "faith in fundamental human rights, in the dignity and worth of the human person, in the equal rights of men and women and of nations large and small," and their determination "to promote social progress and better standards of life in larger freedom." Article 1 of the Charter lists among the main purposes of the United Nations the achievement of international cooperation "in promoting and encouraging respect for human rights and for fundamental freedoms for all without distinction as to race, sex, language, or religion." Similarly, in accordance with Article 55 of the Charter, the United Nations has the duty to promote "universal respect for, and observance of, human rights and fundamental freedoms for all without distinction as to race, sex, language, or religion." In Article 56, all Members of the United Nations "pledge themselves to take joint and separate action in cooperation with the Organization for the achievement of the purposes set forth in Article 55."

The Charter of the United Nations contains also significant grants of power to various organs of the United Nations. Thus, under Article 13, the General Assembly has the duty to initiate studies and make recommendations for the purpose of "assisting in the realization of human rights and fundamental freedoms for all without distinction as to race, sex, language, or religion." Responsibility for the discharge of the functions set forth in Chapter IX of the Charter (which includes Articles 55 and 56 mentioned above) is vested by Article 60 in the General Assembly and, "under the authority of the General Assembly in the Economic and Social Council." In discharging this responsibility the Economic and Social Council may, according to Article 62, "make recommendations for the purpose of promoting respect for, and observance of, human rights and fundamental freedoms for all"; under Article 68, it has an obligation to set up a commission "for the promotion of human rights," which is the only functional commission expressly provided for by the Charter itself; and, under Article 64, it may make arrangements with the Members of the United Nations to obtain reports on steps taken by them to give effect to the recommendations of the General Assembly and of the Council. . . .

These provisions define clearly the obligations of all Members and the powers of the Organization in the field of human rights. While the provisions are general, nevertheless they have the force of positive international law and create basic duties which all Members must fulfill in good faith. They must cooperate with the United Nations in promoting both universal respect for and observance of human rights and fundamental freedoms for all without distinction as to race, sex, language, or religion. For this purpose, they have pledged themselves to take such joint and separate action as may be necessary. The General Assembly and, under the Assembly's authority, the Economic and Social Council are responsible, under Article 60 of the Charter, for the discharge of the functions of the United Nations in this area, and for this purpose may initiate such studies and make such recommendations as they may deem necessary. Any refusal to participate in the United Nations program to promote the observance of human rights constitutes a violation of the Charter. The General Assembly may recommend, under Article 14 of the Charter, "measures for the peaceful adjustment of any situation, regardless of origin, which it deems likely to impair the general welfare or friendly relations among nations, including situations resulting from a violation of the provisions of the present Charter setting forth the Purposes and Principles of the United Nations." As the obligation to promote and encourage respect for human rights is set forth in the statement of Purposes in Article 1 of the Charter, the broad powers of the General Assembly under Article 14 clearly apply in case of a violation of the duty to cooperate with the United Nations in this area.

As far as the United States is concerned, the Charter of the United Nations is the only [major] document relating to human rights which has been ratified by the United States since the war. Being embodied in a treaty, the obligations under the Charter form part of the law of the United States. They impose directly an obligation upon the federal government to promote the observance of human rights by all means at its disposal.

J. Brierly, The Law of Nations
292-296 (6th ed. H. Waldock ed. 1963)

The appalling atrocities of the Nazis against the Jews and against other races during the Second World War led to a strong movement for the international protection of fundamental human rights, and the Charter contains numerous references to them. The more important of them are (a) Article 1, which states one of the purposes of the United Nations to be to achieve co-operation in promoting and encouraging respect for human rights and fundamental freedoms for all without distinction as to race, sex, language, or religion; (b) Article 55, which repeats that purpose in the form of an *obligation* upon the United Nations Organization; and (c) Article 56, by which individual members pledge themselves to take "joint and separate action" in co-operation with the Organization to the same ends. The Charter does not, however, define what exactly are the fundamental human rights and freedoms of which it speaks, nor does it make any mention of machinery to secure their observance. On the contrary, it states as a general principle in Article 2(7) that nothing in the Charter is to "authorize the United Nations to intervene in matters which are essentially within the domestic jurisdiction of any State." This provision at once raises the query as to how far, if at all, the Organization is entitled to look into allegations of breaches of human rights by individual members as distinct from trying to encourage respect for human rights generally among members; and some even argue that the Charter clauses only contain a pious injunction to co-operate in promoting respect for human rights and do not impose any legal obligation on members with regard to their own nationals. The latter argument seems in any event to go too far, since a pledge to co-operate in promoting at least implies a negative obligation not so to act as to undermine human rights; for this reason South Africa's racial segregation policies appear to be out of harmony with her obligations under the Charter. But the absence of any definition of human rights and freedoms in the Charter did, of course, greatly weaken the legal content of the Charter clauses, and so an attempt was made to fill them out by drawing up in 1948 the "Universal Declaration of Human Rights and Fundamental Freedoms." This document, which defines in some detail fundamental rights such as the rights to life and liberty of the person, to a fair trial in criminal proceedings, &c., and fundamental freedoms such as freedom of expression, religion, association, &c., is a declaration adopted by resolution, not a treaty; and it was not intended to be a legal instrument binding on members. Nevertheless, it has gained considerable authority as a general guide to the content of fundamental rights and freedoms as understood by members of the United Nations, and it is important as providing a connecting link between different concepts of human rights in different parts of the world. . . .

How far, then, is the United Nations entitled to concern itself with complaints of violations of human rights? Relying on its general power to discuss any matters within the scope of the Charter, the Assembly has asserted the right to discuss such complaints and to make recommendations in regard to them; it has, for example, debated such matters as the Soviet refusal to allow the Russian wives of foreigners to leave with their husbands, the oppression of the religious leaders in Hungary, Bulgaria, and Roumania, the treatment of persons of Indian race in South Africa, South Africa's segregation measures. This interference in the internal jurisdiction of member states with respect to their own nationals has been defended on the basis that mere discussion and recommendation do not amount to "intervention" within the meaning of Article 2(7); according to this doctrine there would only be intervention if the United Nations went further and made recommendations in regard to human rights, with the implication of possible enforcement action if they were not complied with. Although this line of argument presents certain difficulties, the practice of the United Nations makes it clear that the Organization holds itself entitled to "consider," "discuss," and "recommend" with regard to breaches of human rights; on the other hand, it cannot address dictatorial injunctions to the offending state unless the breaches are of such a kind as to endanger peace. Politically, the human rights activities of the United Nations have had a certain importance and the Universal Declaration and other instruments have made a certain contribution to "promoting" the cause of human rights; but the United Nations has not so far proved an effective instrument for remedying flagrant violations of elementary rights and freedoms. . . .

Comments and Questions

1. The human rights clauses in the UN Charter described in the above two readings must be read, as Brierly acknowledges, against Article 2(7) thereof, which provides that "[n]othing contained in the present Charter

shall authorize the United Nations to intervene in matters which are essentially within the domestic jurisdiction of any state or shall require the Members to submit such matters to settlement under the present Charter; but this principle shall not prejudice the application of enforcement measures under Chapter VII." Article 2(7) was intended to ensure that none of the human rights clauses of the Charter should "be construed as giving authority to the Organization to intervene in the domestic affairs of members states." 10 U.N.C.I.O. Docs. 83 (1945) (United States). A vast body of literature exists concerning this "domestic jurisdiction" clause and just what "intervention" by the United Nations it was intended to prohibit. See, e.g., Ermacora, Human Rights and Domestic Jurisdiction (Article 2, §7, of the Charter), 124 Recueil des Cours (Hague Academy of International Law) 371 (1968-II). Suffice it to say that over the years human rights questions — from their placement on the agenda through their investigation and debate to the actual adoption of specific recommendations — have come to be regarded by the United Nations as no longer "essentially within the domestic jurisdiction" of states. Recall, however, that in the UN debates over the expulsion of Asians from Uganda, the representative of that country argued that "the matter was of an internal nature and was covered by Article 2, paragraph 7, of the Charter." See page 31 supra. Was this argument correct then? Would it be given serious consideration today? Why would a state raise it in any event?

2. Brierly states that the United Nations "cannot address dictatorial injunctions to the offending state unless the breaches are of such a kind as to endanger peace." His conclusion rests on language found in Article 39 of the UN Charter, invoked in the debates in the British Parliament and considered above. See pages 26-27 supra. Thus, in those rare cases where the Security Council determines a state's human rights violations to be either a "breach of the peace" or a "threat to the peace" — it made the latter determination in the cases of Rhodesia in 1966 and South Africa in 1977 — Article 2(7) itself renders the "domestic jurisdiction" clause inoperable by specifically authorizing the adoption of economic sanctions or even the use of armed force against the offending state pursuant to Articles 41 and 42 of Chapter VII of the Charter. The issue is considered extensively at pages 495-509 and 573-575 of Problem VII and pages 651-664 of Problem VIII.

3. The Commission to Study the Organization of Peace states that the human rights clauses in the UN Charter "have the force of positive international law and create basic duties which all Members must fulfill in good faith." Moreover, it concludes that "[b]eing embodied in a treaty, the obligations under the Charter form part of the law of the United States. They impose directly an obligation upon the federal government to promote the observance of human rights by all means at its disposal." Since the Charter nowhere defines the scope or content of the "human rights and fundamental freedoms" that the United Nations shall promote and that member states shall help achieve, just what are the "basic duties" assumed by states under

the Charter? Whatever they may be, can they be enforced not only on the international level, but also, as the Commission implies, domestically as well? These issues are considered extensively in Problem II.

B.   Content and Legal Status of the Human Rights Clauses

Schachter, The Charter and the Constitution: The Human Rights Provisions in American Law
4 Vand. L. Rev. 643, 646-653 (1951)

Do the Human Rights Provisions Involve Legal Obligations on the Part of Member States?

As we have seen, unless this question is answered in the affirmative, the human rights provisions cannot be considered as rules of law by American courts. But the question has of course wider significance than its implications for American law; for whether or not the Charter provisions on human rights prescribe legal duties is a matter of considerable importance to all of the Members of the United Nations.

This issue has been a subject of controversy since the establishment of the United Nations. In most cases the discussions have consisted largely of conclusions supported only by fragmentary reference to legislative history. However, it is a problem which warrants the most careful analysis of the language of the Charter and of the intentions of the draftsmen as revealed in the *travaux préparatoires*.

The principal provisions of the Charter involved are Articles 55(c) and 56. . . . [The author quotes the full text of Articles 55 and 56, which may be found in the Documentary Supplement.]

It has been maintained by some authorities that in spite of the "pledge" expressly taken in Article 56, these provisions do not impose upon Members of the United Nations the legal obligation to respect and observe human rights and fundamental freedoms. The provisions of the Charter are characterized as statements of "guiding principles" or "general purposes," or indeed, as "legally meaningless and redundant." In support of this conclusion, the essential argument is that the United Nations has no compulsory powers in regard to human rights; this is an argument based first on the fact that the organs concerned with human rights (i.e. the General Assembly and the Economic and Social Council) may make only recommendations which have no obligatory effect and secondly on Article 2(7), forbidding United Nations intervention in matters of domestic jurisdiction. Kelsen also supports this position with special reference to the language of Article 56. He points out that the pledge is "to take joint and separate action in cooperation with the Organization"; he then states that the only effective way to co-operate with the Organization is by compliance with the recommendations of the appropriate organs; but the Charter does not make such recommendations obligatory; hence (he infers) it is left solely to the Members to decide what kind of action they think appropriate to achieve the co-operation sought by the Organization. Consequently, Kelsen concludes, the pledge does not express a "true obligation." [See H. Kelsen, The Law of the United Nations (1950).]

This brings us to the crux of the problem; Is the pledge to take action in co-operation with the Organization negated by the fact that the Organization admittedly cannot make mandatory decisions in regard to human rights? Or, stated in another way, if it is admitted (as it must be) that an organ may not "order" a Member to take action regarding human rights, does that mean that the Member may act as it deems appropriate, entirely free from legal limitations under Article 56? Is it possible to have [a] legal obligation to act "in co-operation" which does not require full compliance with the recommendations of the Organization?

In considering these questions it is necessary to review briefly the language and history of the human rights provisions. It may be useful to begin with the word "pledge" as used in Article 56. A pledge in its ordinary English meaning is a solemn promise or an undertaking; as used in a legal instrument, the word itself connotes a legal obligation. In the French version "les Membres s'engagent . . . à agir"; this too is the language of legal obligation. The discussions at San Francisco show that this was not accidental; it was stated that "pledge" has been used as a term at least as "strong" as the word "undertake" and that the Technical Committee which drafted the provision attached particular importance to this point. It is therefore difficult to avoid at least a prima facie conclusion that the pledge in Article 56 was intended to constitute a legal commitment on the part of Members.

Now, it is also true that in the course of formulating Article 56 many of the delegations insisted that this provision would not mean that the Organization would have the right to interfere with the internal affairs of Members. It was the understanding that Article 2(7), the "domestic jurisdiction" clause, applied to Articles 55 and 56 and consequently that "intervention" (or enforcement) of human rights by the United Nations was prohibited. But whatever may be the precise meaning of this clause it in no way implies that the pledge in Article 56 is without legal force. It is after all a commonplace in international law that States assume duties of a legal character which are not enforceable by international organs. The Charter itself has many other articles imposing obligations with no provision for enforcement or implementation. Of course, some jurists consider that these are not true legal obligations since they do not involve sanctions for contrary conduct; but this is a specific use of the term obligation which is not generally accepted in international law or in the interpretation of the Charter.

Throughout the Charter it is evident that obligations are imposed upon Members, even though in most cases these obligations do not have sanctions. Indeed, it may even be persuasively argued that the concern of the draftsmen in connection with Article 56 with the prohibition against intervention was based on their understanding and intention that this Article should constitute a legal undertaking, for if it were only a statement of purposes, there would have been little reason to stress noninterference by the Organization.

It is also of considerable significance that in the actual application of the Charter, the Members of the United Nations have found no incompatibility between the principle of nonintervention in Article 2(7) and the position that Members have a definite legal responsibility with respect to human rights by virtue of Article 56. In more than one resolution adopted by the General Assembly, it is clearly stated that Members have made a legal commitment to respect and observe human rights; and in the course of U.N. discussions, numerous representatives including several of legal eminence, have consistently maintained the position that the Charter imposes obligations of a legal character on Member States in regard to the observance of human rights.

This brings us to a further point of controversy; even if it is conceded that there is a legal commitment in Article 56, is it not merely a general duty to co-operate which can be construed by each State as it sees fit, and does this not in effect nullify the notion of a legal obligation? Here again, the *travaux préparatoires* afford some illumination. It appears from the San Francisco records that, at one stage, the pledge in Article 56 was threefold: it called for joint action, for separate action, and for co-operation with the Organization. The U.S. delegation then expressed doubt concerning the pledge to take separate action; it preferred simply a pledge to co-operate. But the Australian delegation, the original sponsor of this provision, continued to urge inclusion of a pledge to take separate action as distinguished from co-operation; this position was supported by the Belgian and British delegations. The final text represented a compromise: the pledge to take separate action was qualified by the phrase "in co-operation with the organization." This compromise text does not seem to have received further clarification in the San Francisco discussions; and no opinions were expressed specifically on what was meant by "co-operation with the Organization." It appears that the U.S. delegation favoured this qualification in order to eliminate the possibility of an interpretation under which the obligation would extend to "internal economic matters . . . and therefore the Organization would be permitted to intervene in them."

The foregoing history seems to bring out several points of significance in connection with this problem. First, it reveals that the draftsmen in San Francisco rejected a text which provided merely for a pledge to co-operate with the Organization and that they attached importance to the words "separate action," although such action was to be "in co-operation with the

Organization." * Secondly, it indicates that this latter expression was mainly intended to avoid the implication that "separate action" would open the door to intervention by the United Nations in domestic affairs. Thirdly, there is no indication that the phrase "co-operation" was intended to confer unlimited discretion on the Member States, a result which would be almost the direct opposite of the normal meaning of co-operation and of the Committee's intentions. † Admittedly, the record also indicates that the obligation is far from precise and leaves considerable latitude to each Member State to carry it out in its own way. But does this mean that it cannot be considered a legal obligation? In view of both the history and the language of this Article, this would certainly be an extreme conclusion; it would, in effect, make a mockery of the efforts of the draftsmen at San Francisco to formulate a pledge which would have legal significance and effectiveness. There is certainly no overriding reason to arrive at this result.

It must be borne in mind, in this respect, that the degree of precision required in a treaty is not the same as that demanded of a criminal statute. Treaty obligations are often expressed in general terms and leave broad discretion to the States which are Parties. But the fact that a State is free to carry out those obligations by its own methods and its own way does not destroy the legal character of this obligation. In the case of Article 56 there is no compelling reason to define a priori and in detail all the implications of the obligation; it is evident that there are large areas where the purposes under Article 55 are as yet so undefined that it is impossible to say what kind of action would be required if a State is to co-operate with the Organization.

However, it is equally evident that in other respects the broad language of Article 55 has specific meaning and effect; this is particularly true of clause (c) relating to human rights and fundamental freedoms. The clause itself contains the significant prohibition against discrimination because of race, sex, language or religion, a theme which is recurrent throughout the Charter and which in itself furnishes considerable content to the notion of human rights. Moreover, it must not be forgotten that the concept of human rights is not an abstract notion introduced for the first time in the Charter; it has had (under various names) a long and rich history in consti-

---

* When the final draft of Article 56 was being considered by the Committee, the Australian representative, Dr. Evatt, moved its adoption with the following statement: "Taking this document as it stands it is a pledge, it is a pledge to take joint action, and is a pledge to take separate action. The Russian colleague said in his language there is no difference between the word 'several' and the word 'separate.' Well, we preferred the word 'separate' and the United States agreed with that. But it is a pledge to take action and take it in co-operation with the Organization, and it is on that point that [the] United States put their view very strongly." U.N.C.I.O. Doc. 747, 11/3/46.

† The legislative history thus offers no support to Kelsen's point (supra) that since "co-operation" could not mean obligatory compliance with the recommendations of the General Assembly, it would have to mean that the states were entirely free to decide what was meant by co-operation. But in fact the Committee inserted the phrase in order to indicate that the separate action being pledged should be in keeping with the basic policies of the Organization. . . .

tutional law, in the practice of states and in the development of the law of nations. Nor is it irrelevant in this connection to consider the wide measure of agreement regarding most specific rights and freedoms which was revealed during the preparation of the Declaration on Human Rights and by the specific resolutions adopted by the General Assembly and other principal organs. Though the outer boundaries of "human rights" remain undefined (perhaps undefinable) it can hardly be denied that the concept has a special core of meaning which is widely recognized and accepted. Certainly an American lawyer familiar with the due process and equal protection clauses and the other broad phrases of the U.S. Constitution is not likely to take the position that a concept such as human rights must be denied legal effect because of its breadth and generality.

There is therefore no sufficient reason to characterize Article 56 as a mere statement of purpose, devoid of legal effect. To do so as we have seen, would be contrary to both the language and the ascertainable intentions of the framers of the Charter. And even if it be granted that there is some obscurity in the text or the intent of the drafters, the choice between alternative interpretations should legitimately be resolved in favour of that construction which best effectuates the major purposes of the provision. In this case, obviously the major purpose is the promotion of human rights;* if a "pledge" to take action to achieve that purpose is interpreted as having no obligatory effect, the whole point of the pledge is lost and it becomes entirely superfluous. A construction which renders an article virtually meaningless is certainly contrary to the principle of effectiveness in the interpretation of treaties.† Undoubtedly, there are occasions when the rule of effectiveness may run counter to the manifest intention of the parties; in this case, however, effectiveness — at least to the extent of a legal commitment — is precisely what most of the drafters desired.**

Thus, both major rules of interpretation — that based on intent and that on effectiveness — reinforce each other and, taken together, practically make inescapable the conclusion that the pledge in Article 56 constitutes a legal commitment on the part of Members to take action in co-operation with the Organization to achieve "respect for and observance of human rights and fundamental freedoms for all. . . ."

---

* It is expressly stated as a purpose in Article 1(3) and recurs as a fundamental theme throughout the Charter. See Preamble and Articles 13, 55, 76. . . .

† The rule of effectiveness may well be deemed to have paramount importance in construing a general international agreement of a constitutional charter, such as the Charter. See the International Court of Justice's advisory opinion, "Reparation for Injuries Suffered in the Service of the United Nations," I.C.J. Rep. 1949, p. 174.

** See for example, Dr. Evatt's statement at Comm. II/3, in connection with the final draft of Article 56: "I don't think any member of the Committee feels we have been fighting merely for words. I think that this pledge means in substance that we not only stamp the objectives stated already with the stamp of an international agreement, but we determine to do our best in co-operation with the Organization not only to preach but to practice what we preach in our own countries in co-operation with the Organization, and I am very pleased to have been associated with the settlement." 17th Meeting, Comm. II/3.

Note: U.S. Recognition of the Legal Status of the
Human Rights Clauses

The United States upon numerous occasions has adopted Professor Schachter's reasoning sub silentio and argued that the human rights clauses of the UN Charter give rise to international legal obligations on the part of member states. Thus, when the revolutionary government of Iraq in early 1969 summarily tried, convicted, and hung in public 14 of its nationals (9 of them Jews) on the ground that they were Israeli spies — their bodies displayed in a grisly carnival atmosphere — the U.S. Ambassador to the United Nations, Charles Yost, raised the matter with the Security Council in the following letter (24 U.N. SCOR Supp. (Jan.-Mar. 1969) at 65, U.N. Doc. S/8987 (1969)).

His Excellency
Mr. Max Jakobson
President of the Security Council

Excellency:

I have been instructed by my Government to draw to your attention the following statement issued by Secretary of State William P. Rogers on 27 January 1969, when he learned of the public execution of fourteen persons convicted for espionage in Iraq:

"We have had no United States representation in Baghdad since the Government of Iraq broke relations in 1967. We are not, therefore, in a position to comment on the facts surrounding the trial. On humanitarian grounds these executions are a matter of deep concern to us. The spectacle of mass public executions is repugnant to the conscience of the world. At my request, Ambassador Yost has called Secretary-General U Thant today to express our deep concern and to tell him that we share the expressions noted in his statement issued earlier today."

The Government of the United States recognizes the legal right of any government to bring to trial and administer justice to any of its citizens. However, *the manner in which these executions and the trials that preceded them were conducted scarcely conforms to normally accepted standards of respect for human rights and human dignity or to the obligations in this regard that the United Nations Charter imposes upon all Members.* [Emphasis added.] Moreover, the spectacular way in which they were carried out seems to have been designed to arouse emotions and to intensify the very explosive atmosphere of suspicion and hostility in the Middle East.

The United States hopes that the worldwide revulsion aroused by the reports of these trials and executions will induce those responsible to carry out their solemn Charter obligations to promote "universal respect for and observance of human rights and fundamental freedoms for all without distinction as to race, sex, language or religion." . . .

If you had been a Department of State lawyer assigned to the U.S. Mission to the United Nations, to which articles would you have referred had Security Council President Max Jakobson's office telephoned for further explanation of "the obligations in this regard that the United Nations Charter imposes upon all Members"? In response to an inquiry by one of our colleagues two years later, the Office of the Legal Adviser of the Department of State, in a letter dated 18 March 1971, explained that "it is the view of the United States Government that the right to a fair trial before an impartial tribunal is a 'fundamental freedom' and that the specific facts in the situation described in [the above letter] justified the statement by Ambassador Yost that the obligations of the Charter had not been met." Is this explanation satisfactory? Does it provide much guidance in identifying other international human rights obligations of states under the UN Charter?

The right to a fair trial is specifically guaranteed by Article 10 of the Universal Declaration of Human Rights and Article 14 of the International Covenant on Civil and Political Rights, both found in the Documentary Supplement. See generally Lillich, Civil Rights, in 1 Human Rights in International Law: Legal and Policy Issues 115, 139-144 (T. Meron ed. 1984). Why did Ambassador Yost not mention these instruments explicitly? Would not his argument have been strengthened by their invocation? Assuming for present purposes that the fair trial norms in these instruments have not achieved the status of customary international law, id., can they not be read back into the UN Charter, as Professor Schachter suggests, to bind states as treaty law? Cf. Henkin, The Constitution at Sea, 36 Me. L. Rev. 201, 209 n.31 (1984) (emphasis added) ("The United States . . . is a party to the UN Charter which includes general human rights obligations, and it may be bound by some of the provisions of the Universal Declaration of Human Rights, either *as elaborations of the Charter obligation* or under customary international law.").

Since the Yost letter, the United States repeatedly has taken the position that the human rights clauses of the UN Charter have legal effect and thus must be observed by all countries, including the United States. Thus, the Acting Legal Adviser of the Department of State, George Aldrich, observed in 1974 that "members of the United Nations have a legal duty to promote respect for and protection of human rights around the world. . . . The Charter of the United Nations and the Universal Declaration of Human Rights are the basic texts in this field. I would point, in particular, to articles 55 and 56 of the United Nations Charter. . . . The United States recognizes these obligations and is determined to live up to them." 1974 Dig. U.S. Prac. in Intl. L. 125 (1975). President Jimmy Carter reaffirmed this position in his March 1977 UN address, declaring that "[t]he solemn commitments of the United Nations Charter, of the United Nations Universal Declaration for Human Rights, of the Helsinki Accords, and of many other international instruments must be taken just as seriously as commercial or security agreements." 1977 Pub. Papers 444, 450-451. Moreover, as is set out immediately below, the United States has invoked the human rights clauses before the International Court of Justice.

C. Invocation of the Human Rights Clauses on the International Level

On the international level, the human rights clauses of the UN Charter have been invoked frequently. Generally, as in the case of the U.S. protest against the Iraqi executions, they are raised in the course of UN debates or other diplomatic exchanges. Occasionally, however, states have been known to argue before international tribunals that the Charter imposes legal obligations upon states that, in the particular case, the respondent state has violated. Thus, in the *Hostages Case*, 1980 I.C.J. 3 (Judgment of May 24, 1980), the United States urged the International Court of Justice (ICJ) to condemn Iran's seizure of 52 U.S. hostages as a violation of fundamental human rights recognized by the international community. "The existence of such fundamental rights for all human beings," the United States contended, "and the existence of a corresponding duty on the part of every State to respect and observe them, are now reflected, inter alia, in the Charter of the United Nations. . . ." Memorial of the United States (U.S. v. Iran), 1980 I.C.J. Pleadings (Case Concerning United States Diplomatic and Consular Staff in Tehran) 182 (Jan. 12, 1980), citing Articles 1, 55, and 56 of the UN Charter.

More significantly, in an earlier Advisory Opinion the ICJ held that the policy of apartheid, as applied by South Africa in Namibia (South West Africa), constituted a violation of the legal obligations South Africa had assumed under the UN Charter. Consider the two relevant paragraphs of the Court's Advisory Opinion and the late Professor Schwelb's exegesis that follow.

Legal Consequences for States of the Continued Presence of South Africa in Namibia (South West Africa)
1971 I.C.J. 16, 57 (Advisory Opinion of June 21, 1971)

130. It is undisputed, and is amply supported by documents annexed to South Africa's written statement in these proceedings, that the official governmental policy pursued by South Africa in Namibia is to achieve a complete physical separation of races and ethnic groups in separate areas within the Territory. The application of this policy has required, as has been conceded by South Africa, restrictive measures of control officially adopted and enforced in the Territory by the coercive power of the former Mandatory. These measures establish limitations, exclusions or restrictions for the members of the indigenous population groups in respect of their participation in certain types of activities, fields of study or of training, labour or employment and also submit them to restrictions or exclusions of residence and movement in large parts of the Territory.

131. Under the Charter of the United Nations, the former Mandatory [South Africa] had pledged itself to observe and respect, in a territory having an international status, human rights and fundamental freedoms for all without distinction as to race. To establish instead, and to enforce, distinctions, exclusions, restrictions and limitations exclusively based on grounds of race, colour, descent or national or ethnic origin which constitute a denial of fundamental human rights is a flagrant violation of the purposes and principles of the Charter.

[Both the Security Council and the General Assembly subsequently adopted resolutions commending the Court's Advisory Opinion. The Security Council noted it "with appreciation" (S.C. Res. 301, 26 U.N. SCOR Res. & Dec. at 7 (1971)), while the General Assembly took similar notice "with satisfaction" (G.A. Res. 2871, 26 U.N. GAOR Supp. (No. 29) at 105, U.N. Doc. A/8429 (1971)).]

Schwelb, The International Court of Justice and the Human Rights Clauses of the Charter
66 Am. J. Intl. L. 337, 338, 341-350 (1972)

I. INTRODUCTORY

The Advisory Opinion on the *Legal Consequences for States of the Continued Presence of South Africa in Namibia (South West Africa), notwithstanding Security Council Resolution 276 (1970)*, contains a veritable *tour d'horizon* of contemporary international law and of the law of international organizations. . . . [This article, however,] is restricted to one particular aspect of the Advisory Opinion, the interpretation by the Court of the human rights clauses of this Charter and Court's answer to the question whether States Members of the United Nations, by becoming parties to the Charter, have undertaken legal obligations in the matter of human rights. . . .

[The author proceeds to discuss scholarly opinions proferred on this subject by Hudson, Kelsen, Lauterpacht, Jessup, and other authorities. See 66 Am. J. Intl. L. at 338-341.]

III.   THE PRACTICE OF THE UNITED NATIONS AND OF MEMBER STATES

In the actual practice of the various organs of the United Nations over the past 25 years the obstacles to taking action based on the human rights provisions of the Charter have proved to be far less formidable than the cleavage of theoretical opinions of scholars and of abstract statements by governments would lead one to assume. In the practice of the United Nations and of its Members neither the vagueness and generality of the human rights clauses of the Charter nor the domestic jurisdiction clause have prevented the United Nations from considering, investigating, and judging concrete human rights situations, provided there was a majority strong enough and wishing strongly enough to attempt to influence the particular development. The cases of action of this type are too well known to require, and too numerous to permit of, listing in the present context. . . .

The question of human rights and discrimination in South Africa has occupied the United Nations since 1946. . . . The concern of the Organization was originally limited to the question of the treatment of Indians . . . in South Africa. Its scope was extended to cover the whole question of race conflict resulting from the policies of apartheid in 1952. In 1953 the General Assembly found that the racial policies of the Government of South Africa and their consequences are contrary to the Charter, a finding that was to be repeated on later occasions with increasing emphasis. In 1962 the General Assembly established a permanent organ, the Special Committee on the policies of apartheid of the Government of South Africa with the mandate to keep the racial policies of South Africa under review when the Assembly is not in session. . . .

[The author discusses in detail the activities of the Security Council and the Commission on Human Rights with regard to South Africa's violation of the human rights clauses in the Charter.]

IV. THE VIEW OF THE COURT

When rendering its opinion on "the legal consequences for States of the continued presence of South Africa in Namibia, notwithstanding Security Council resolution 276 (1970)," the Court divided its reply into three parts dealing with the legal consequences of South Africa's continued presence respectively (1) for South Africa, (2) for other States Members of the United Nations, and (3) for states which are not Members of the United Nations. For the purposes of the present investigation it is necessary to deal only with the first part of the Court's conclusions. In regard to the consequences for South Africa, the Court found, by 13 votes to 2, that "the continued presence of South Africa in Namibia being illegal, South Africa is under obligation to withdraw its administration from Namibia immediately and thus put an end to its occupation of the Territory."

In Resolution 2145 (XXI) of October 27, 1966, the General Assembly, "convinced that the administration of the Mandated Territory [of South West Africa] by South Africa has been conducted in a manner contrary to the Mandate, the Charter of the United Nations and the Universal Declaration of Human Rights," had inter alia declared "that South Africa has failed to fulfil its obligations in respect of the administration of the Mandated Territory and to ensure the moral and material well-being and security of the indigenous inhabitants of South West Africa and has, in fact, disavowed the Mandate." The General Assembly had further decided that the Mandate conferred upon South Africa "is therefore terminated" and "that South Africa has no other right to administer the Territory."

In examining this action of the General Assembly which had been alleged to be ultra vires, the Court found that a material breach of its obligations had been committed by South Africa, that the supervisory powers of the Council of the League of Nations had passed to the General Assembly and that the latter in terminating the Mandate had acted within the framework of its competence.

Among very many other objections against Resolution 2145 (XXI) of the General Assembly it was argued on behalf of South Africa that the consideration set forth in the resolution, "relating to the failure of South Africa to fulfil its obligations in respect of the administration of the mandated territory, called for a detailed factual investigation before the General Assembly could adopt resolution 2145 (XXI) or the Court pronounce upon its validity." In its oral statement and in written communications to the Court, the Government of South Africa

> expressed the desire to supply the Court with further factual information concerning the purposes and objectives of South Africa's policy of separate

development or apartheid, contending that to establish a breach of South Africa's substantive international obligations under the Mandate it would be necessary to prove that a particular exercise of South Africa's legislative or administrative powers was not directed in good faith towards the purpose of promoting to the utmost the well-being and progress of the inhabitants. It is claimed by the Government of South Africa that no act or omission on its part would constitute a violation of its international obligations unless it is shown that such act or omission was actuated by a motive, or directed towards a purpose other than one to promote the interests of the inhabitants of the Territory.

In regard to this request made by South Africa, the Court found that

. . . no factual evidence is needed for the purpose of determining whether the policy of *apartheid* as applied by South Africa in Namibia *is in conformity with the international obligations assumed by South Africa under the Charter of the United Nations.* In order to determine whether the laws and decrees applied by South Africa in Namibia, which are a matter of public record, *constitute a violation of the purposes and principles of the Charter of the United Nations*, the question of intent or governmental discretion is not relevant; nor is it necessary to investigate or determine the effects of those measures upon the welfare of the inhabitants. . . . [Here the Court cites paragraphs 130 and 131, quoted on page 49 supra.]

When the Court speaks of "conformity with the international obligations assumed . . . under the Charter," of "a violation of the purposes and principles of the Charter," of the pledge to observe and respect human rights and fundamental freedoms for all, when it finds that certain actions "constitute a denial of fundamental human rights," and classifies them as "a flagrant violation of the purposes and principles of the Charter," it leaves no doubt that, in its view, the Charter does impose on the Members of the United Nations legal obligations in the human rights field.

The Court says that the former Mandatory had pledged itself to observe and respect, *in a territory having an international status*, human rights and fundamental freedoms for all without distinction as to race. The italicized words indicate that the Court was dealing with a territory having an international status, a fact which was instrumental in the matter's having been brought before the General Assembly and the Security Council. If Namibia (South West Africa) had not been a territory having an international status, the question would not have been submitted to the Court. Moreover, the location of the acts constituting a violation of the Charter in such a territory might, the Court could be understood to say, be an aggravating circumstance, as it were. The inclusion of the words "in a territory having an international status" cannot be interpreted to mean that, in the view of the Court, to establish and to enforce distinctions, exclusions, restrictions and limitations exclusively based on grounds of race, color, descent or national or ethnic origin which constitute a denial of fundamental human rights is *not* a flagrant violation of the purposes and principles of the Charter, if committed elsewhere than in an international territory. The pledge (Articles 55 and 56) which the Court invokes[, however,] is not a pledge to promote universal respect for, and observance of, human rights and fundamental freedoms in international territories only, but "for all without distinction as to race, sex, language, or religion." What is a flagrant violation of the purposes and principles of the Charter when committed in Namibia, is also such a violation when committed in South Africa proper or, for that matter, in any other sovereign Member State or in a non-self-governing or Trust Territory.

The Court speaks of a violation of the purposes and principles of the Charter. These are set forth in Chapter I of the Charter, Article 1 setting forth the purposes and Article 2 the principles. The purpose of the Organization consisting in promoting and encouraging respect for human rights and for fundamental freedoms for all is set forth in Article 1(3). When the Court finds that South Africa's policy constitutes a flagrant violation of the purposes and principles of the Charter, it clearly does not intend to convey the idea that only Article 1(3) has been violated. This follows from the fact that the Court refers to the pledge of Member States which is contained in Chapter IX (Article 56) of the Charter. What is meant is a violation of the relevant provisions of the Charter, i.e., its human rights clauses, as a whole.

As already indicated, the Court's reply that, the continued presence of South Africa in Namibia being illegal, South Africa is under obligation to withdraw its administration from Namibia and to put an end to its occupation of the Territory, was adopted by 13 votes to 2. . . . Both dissenting opinions were based on considerations unconnected with the argument set forth in paragraph 131 of the Opinion. . . .

It can therefore be said that the interpretation of the human rights clauses contained in the Advisory Opinion is backed by the authority of the Court as a body and the thirteen Judges who voted for it and that it is not challenged by [either] of the two dissenting Judges. . . .

The statement in paragraphs 130 and 131 of the Advisory Opinion is not, if it is permissible to use a common law term in an international law context and in regard to an Advisory Opinion, an obiter dictum. It is an essential part of the ratio decidendi. The qualification as a flagrant violation of the purposes and principles of the Charter of the restrictive measures of control officially adopted and enforced in the Territory by the coercive power of South Africa was the justification for the Court's rejection of South Africa's desire to supply further factual information. It was the basis for the Court's decision that no factual evidence, additional to the documents annexed to South Africa's written statements, was needed for determining that the policy of separate development or apartheid in Namibia was not in conformity with the international obligations of South Africa. . . .

To sum up, it is submitted that the authority of the Court is now clearly behind the interpretation of the human rights clauses of the Charter as presented almost a generation ago by Lauterpacht and others. . . .

[The author again refers to the works of Jessup, Wright, Scelle, Sloan, and Guradze. See 66 Am. J. Intl. L. at 339-341.]

Comments and Questions

1. Although the Court clearly holds that the human rights clauses of the UN Charter create legal obligations for states "in a territory having an international status," do you agree with Schwelb's conclusion that these obligations also extend to state actions taken "elsewhere than in an international territory"? Note that the late Judge Dillard in his Separate Opinion cautioned that the Court was dealing with "a very specific and unique situation concerning a territory with *international status*, the administration of which engaged the supervisory authority of the United Nations." 1971 I.C.J. at 138. Should the Court's holding be so limited?

2. The Court in the *Namibia Case* specifically held that South Africa's imposition of the policy of apartheid in Namibia constituted a "flagrant violation" of the human rights clauses of the UN Charter. Since apartheid is one of a small but growing number of actions that, when undertaken by a state, violate the customary international law of human rights (see page 162 of Problem II), this holding was relatively easy to reach. What about other state actions that infringe on human rights but do not rise to the level of customary international law violations? Are such "non-flagrant" human rights violations within the Court's rationale? If so, why? If not, how can one justify the U.S. assertion (see page 46 supra) that the UN Charter imposed a legal obligation on Iraq to accord criminal defendants a fair trial?

3. Whether and to what extent human rights norms can be read back into the Charter to create legal obligations binding upon states (see page 47 supra) was a hotly debated question well before the Court rendered its Advisory Opinion in the *Namibia Case*. Since 1971, however, the incorporation argument has gathered numerous adherents. It has been raised in several U.S. domestic court cases in recent years, although to date no court has endorsed it. Cf. Filartiga v. Pena-Irala, 630 F.2d 876, 880 n.7 (2d Cir. 1980). See Lillich, Invoking International Human Rights Law in Domestic Courts, 54 U. Cin. L. Rev. 367, 378 n.54 (1985). The question is explored more fully at pages 119-120 of Problem II.

IV. The Relevance of the Human Rights Clauses of the UN Charter to the Expulsion of Asians from Uganda

Wooldridge and Sharma, International Law and the Expulsion of Ugandan Asians
9 Intl. Law. 30, 48-57 (1975)

THE INTERNATIONAL LEGALITY OF THE UGANDAN EXPULSIONS

GENERAL CONSIDERATIONS

Collective expulsions of aliens in peacetime have taken place on a number of occasions since the war. It is doubtful what the precise rules of international law concerning collective expulsions are, and what effect, if any, the Charter of the United Nations, the Universal Declaration of Human Rights, and General Assembly resolutions concerning discrimination, have had in this area. Most international arbitral awards concerning expulsions are concerned with individual expulsions. . . .

Despite the paucity of directly relevant material, it is thought that the collective expulsion of Asians from Uganda may have been unlawful on several grounds. The Ugandan Asians were not allowed to submit reasons against their expulsion, or to have their cases reviewed by any competent authority. General Amin, as has been pointed out, attempted to justify the expulsions on economic grounds, but the relevance of these grounds in all cases, and whether such grounds are sufficient to justify mass expulsions, may be doubted. The Asians had been mostly resident for a long time, and perhaps compelling reasons were required for their expulsion. The expulsions were prima facie discriminatory, and in breach of the Charter of the United Nations concerning racial discrimination.

Although certain professional persons, and other categories of persons were exempted from the operation of the expelling decrees, they were applicable to the large majority of persons of certain racial origins irrespective of their character or conduct. The expulsions may also have been in breach of the Universal Declaration of Human Rights. The Asians were required to leave without being granted an adequate time limit and on occasions seem to have been subjected to brutal treatment. The expulsion of the stateless Asians appears to have been in breach of the United Nations Convention Relating to the Status of Stateless Persons.

THE EXPELLEES' RIGHT TO MAKE REPRESENTATIONS, AND TO
HAVE THEIR CASES REVIEWED

In the *Chevreau* case, which concerned the deportation of a French-
man by the British authorities from an area in Persia occupied by them in
the belief that he was a spy, the sole arbitrator, Beichmann, stated that: "In
cases of arrests, suspicions must be verified by a serious enquiry, in which
the arrested person is given opportunity to defend himself against the suspicions directed against him."

Similar principles are thought to apply to deportations, even though
deporting states may not be signatories of the United Nations Covenant on
Civil and Political Rights. Article 13 of this covenant provides that aliens
shall be allowed to submit reasons against their expulsion, and have their
cases reviewed by, and be represented before, the competent authority for
this purpose, unless compelling reasons of national security otherwise require.

International customary law may possibly now contain principles
similar to that of article 13. The law of many countries provides for representations to be made against deportation orders, and for their review by
courts and tribunals. The making of a deportation order without granting
such safeguards may be contrary to international law except in cases of
urgency. . . .

It might be argued that no such principle of international customary
law, as the one contended for exists, or if it does, there were special circumstances, given the number of persons involved, and the possible urgency of
the matter, rendering it inoperative in the present case.

THE ADEQUACY OF THE POSSIBLE REASONS
FOR THE EXPULSIONS

Even if these doubtful contentions be accepted it remains that General
Amin apparently had no adequate grounds for expelling the non-citizen
Asian community. The expulsion may thus be unlawful abuse of Uganda's
rights even if no account be taken of their discriminatory nature.

It appears that the British government never formally asked General
Amin the reason for his expulsion of the Asians, nor did it formally protest
the expulsion itself, but contented itself with endeavouring to obtain an
extension of time for the departing Asians. It also tried to ensure that they
could take certain of their property with them. The absence of such a
British protest did not mean that Britain has conceded that Uganda has an
unlimited right of expulsion.

It may have been thought that a formal protest would exacerbate matters, and lead to further expulsions, or to increased hardships for those
already the subject of deportation orders. Britain, and other states, have
demanded reasons for collective expulsions in the past, and have protested

about them. Expulsions have often been the subject of international arbitrations. Although the large majority of international arbitral awards relating to expulsions have concerned the expulsion of individuals, the principles enunciated in them are perhaps applicable a fortiori to the case of collective expulsions.

As already stated, the authority of certain of the older awards has been questioned, but it is thought that the legal principles stated in them can still be upheld. It appears that, when an international tribunal is presented with serious reasons for the expulsion of an alien, it will normally treat them as conclusive. A considerable margin of appreciation must be granted to a state in matters appertaining to its sovereignty.

However, where an unusual or unexpected use is made of the power of expulsion, as has the collective and apparently discriminatory expulsion of thousands of established aliens which use is detrimental to the interests of the expellees and their receiving states, it is thought that the principle stated in *Boffolo*'s case that an international tribunal may consider whether the reasons advanced for an expulsion are adequate is still applicable. Under the circumstances of the present case, the expulsions may have been an abuse of Uganda's rights. It is possible that the prohibition of the abuse of rights is a general principle of law recognized by civilised nations: the principle has sometimes been applied by the International Court of Justice.

If the principles applied in the pre-1914 cases concerning expulsions are no longer applicable, then it appears that the human rights provisions of the United Nations Charter, possibly the Universal Declaration of Human Rights, which according to some has attained the force of international customary law, and the norm of international law which seems to have crystallised recently, prohibiting racial discrimination, all have the effect of making discriminatory expulsions contrary to international law.

The norm is based on articles 55 and 56 of the United Nations Charter, the many resolutions of the General Assembly condemning apartheid, the International Covenants on Human Rights, the regional instruments relating thereto, the Convention on the Elimination of All Forms of Racial Discrimination, and also on the provisions of many national constitutions. . . .

States rarely engage in the collective and discriminatory expulsion of aliens, and when they do, protests often occur. This fact, added to the general state of *opinio juris* and state practice in the area of racial discrimination, suggests that such expulsions are contrary to customary law if affected on a racial basis.

The suggestion that discriminatory collective expulsions are contrary to the United Nations Charter and the Universal Declaration of Human Rights has already been put forward by Egypt and France in the General Assembly. The Universal Declaration of Human Rights has been thought by many publicists to be relevant to the question of collective expulsions; thus Max Huber, George Scelle and Belladore Pallieri all regarded transfers of population as contrary to certain of the provisions of the Declaration. It is thought that, where discriminatory expulsions have some objective basis, and are not a disproportionate measure in the given circumstances, they are not contrary to the Declaration. This follows from article 29(2) of the Universal Declaration.

The expulsions from Uganda appear to be contrary to the norm of international customary law prohibiting racial discrimination, which has evolved from the sources already mentioned, which include the Declaration. Insofar as the expulsions are contrary to the Charter, the Universal Declaration, and to this newly emergent rule of international customary law, it would apparently be necessary in order to validate them for Uganda, to show that the distinction made between the aliens who were allowed to remain and those expelled, which had an objective justification, and the means employed, namely, the expulsion was proportional to the justification for the differentiation.

The burden of proving these matters would, it seems, be on Uganda. In the unlikely event of Uganda agreeing to international arbitration in respect of the collective expulsions, or in the event of their legality being referred to the International Court of Justice for its decision, it seems unlikely that Uganda would succeed in establishing that there were adequate grounds for expelling the Asians, who were treated differently from other categories of aliens.

As already pointed out, the justification put forward by General Amin for expelling the Asians was mainly economic in character. There seem to have been three economic reasons for his expulsion of the Asians. They were sometimes guilty of economic crimes, such as tax evasion and evasion of exchange control regulations; they also were sometimes guilty of exploitation of Africans, and occupied too prominent a position in Ugandan economy.

Although it is true that certain categories of professional persons were exempted from General Amin's decrees expelling the Asians, it can scarcely be that all non-citizen Asians resident in Uganda came within the ambit of the three reasons mentioned. The objective justification for the differentiation between the non-citizen Asians and the other categories of aliens seems to have been lacking. Even if one assumes there was such a justification, the expulsion of all the non-citizen Asians, was utterly disproportionate to the economic reasons advanced for it.

It would have been possible for the Ugandan authorities instead of embarking on their programme of mass expulsions, to have prosecuted individuals who were guilty of economic crimes. Further programmes of nationalisation, or of Africanisation, extending to smaller business, would have diminished the importance of the Asians in the commercial sector. The expulsion of the Asians seems a specially indefensible action when it is remembered that many of them had been resident for generations in Uganda. . . .

It is doubtful whether any other reasons which General Amin could advance for the expulsions would be regarded as adequate by an international tribunal, or sufficient to rebut the presumption that racial discrimination, as opposed to permissible discrimination, has occurred, when a whole community of a given race has been expelled. Clearly it could not be argued that all the members of the community had been involved in political conspiracy.

It seems that the expulsion of the Ugandan Asians was an act of racial discrimination, as such contrary to international law, and that no adequate reasons have been, or can be advanced, which would enable it to be treated as a permissible differentiation. . . .

Plender, The Ugandan Crisis and the Right of Expulsion Under International Law
Intl. Comm. Jurists, The Review No. 9, at 19, 27-30 (Dec. 1972)

[The author first considers international law limitations on a state's power to expel individuals. He concludes that there must be reasonable cause for the expulsion; that it must be conducted with proper regard for the safety and well-being of the expellee; and that it must be carried out so as not to deprive the expellee of his or her acquired rights.]

V.   MASS EXPULSION

It is patent that those factors which limit a state's competence to expel aliens individually must, where appropriate, limit its competence to expel aliens *en masse*. If this were not so a state could, by compounding its crime, absolve itself from liability. There are, however, certain additional considerations which apply exclusively to mass expulsion.

As a general rule, a state is competent under international law to expel aliens *en masse*, but it follows from our remarks in the previous paragraph that the expulsion may be delictual if it is not justified in the national interest. When in 1934 Yugoslavia expelled a great number of Hungarian subjects as a reprisal against the alleged complicity of the Hungarian authorities in terrorist acts, she purported to justify the expulsion by reference to the widespread unemployment in Yugoslavia and the consequential need to take drastic action for the public welfare. If the justification for the expulsion is disputed, the disagreement must be settled by negotiation between the expelling state and the foreign country; if such negotiations fail, the dispute is to be determined by the umpire or other arbitral or judicial body to which it may be referred. In such cases the expelling state may not claim the *exclusive* right to determine its own national interests, although a margin of appreciation would probably be permitted.

Mass expulsions are now very uncommon. Professor Agrawalla, adapting the words of Professor Oppenheim explained the decreasing use of expulsion by reference to "the gradual disappearance of totalitarian ideologies and . . . the advent of true constitutionalism." This analysis seems unduly optimistic, but there are now some principles of international law which militate against resort to expulsion *en masse*.

Firstly, the expulsion of large numbers of foreign nationals constitutes a breach of the principles of good neighbourliness, enshrined in the Charter of the United Nations. These principles are justiciable, except to the extent that their breach demonstrates an inability or unwillingness to accept Charter obligations and might possibly justify expulsion from the Organization. Nevertheless it may be presumed that the inclusion of these principles in the U.N. Charter exerts some influence on all but the most recalcitrant members. The Universal Declaration of Human Rights does not prohibit mass expulsions, although it does proscribe arbitrary arrest, detention and exile, arbitrary deprivation of nationality, arbitrary interference with the family, and arbitrary deprivation of property. It is possible that the prestige which this Declaration enjoys occasionally inhibits states from violating its provisions.

Secondly, an unprovoked mass expulsion is an unfriendly act, especially if it discriminates against the nationals of one state. According to Amerasinghe, 'the principle of non-discrimination is in general a sound one, for it rests on a fundamental principle of justice and is vital to ordered relations based on mutual respects as between all States.' The expulsion may be considered particularly obnoxious if it is based on a racially discriminatory policy. . . . Although the mere adoption of a racially discriminatory policy in regard to the conduct of foreign affairs may not necessarily amount to a justiciable wrong, there is an international norm or climate of opinion in which such policies are regarded with particular distaste. Moreover, while this climate of opinion is current, it is not exclusively modern. A century ago the United States resolved to remonstrate vigorously if Spain should introduce in Cuba racially discriminatory expulsion laws.

VI.   Expulsion of Former Citizens

President Amin announced on August 9th that he had directed his Ministry of Internal Affairs to verify the claims to Ugandan citizenship made by Asians resident in that country. In the course of this policy of verification, the Ugandan authorities claim to have found defects in the titles of many thousands of Asians. The Ugandan authorities declare that such persons will no longer be regarded as citizens of Uganda, but will be liable to be expelled.

Only a factual examination can determine in each case the national status of an Asian whose claim to Ugandan citizenship is rejected by the Ministry of Internal Affairs in Kampala. It is difficult to envisage a situation in which a formal defect may have arisen so as to vitiate the automatic acquisition of Ugandan citizenship by an Asian who has been born in the Protectorate of parents born there. On the other hand, it is less difficult to conceive of formal defects which may have invalidated a claim to citizenship by registration. . . .

For present purposes we may assume that there have been cases in which former Ugandan citizens have been rendered stateless by the revocation of their former citizenship. We must ask whether any special principles govern the expulsion of such persons. Some writers argue that a deprivation of nationality will not be recognized if it imposes statelessness on a racial minority group and so prevents members of the group from returning home. Professor O'Connell has cast doubt upon this proposition, and on the equally popular proposition that the denaturalizing state must admit its former nationals. The uncertainty about a general rule of international law on this point is mitigated by the Convention Relating to the Status of Stateless Persons, adopted at a Conference convened by E.C.O.S.O.C. in 1954. By article 31 of that Convention it is agreed that

> Contracting states shall not expel a stateless person lawfully in their territory save on grounds of national security or public order. The expulsion of such a stateless person shall be only in pursuance of a decision reached in accordance with due process of law. . . . The contracting states shall allow such a stateless person a reasonable period within which to seek legal admission into another country.

By article 3 parties undertake to apply the terms of the Convention without discrimination on grounds of race. Uganda is a party to the Convention.

VII. Conclusions

The foregoing brief summary demonstrates, at least, the existence of a corpus of existing laws limiting a state's right under international law to expel aliens from its territory. It is hoped that the codification of these laws will be one of the functions undertaken by the United Nations Human Rights Commission when it considers the international legal protection of human rights of non-citizens. . . .

Chhangani, Expulsion of Uganda Asians and International Law
12 Indian J. Intl. L. 400, 402, 405-407 (1972)

. . . The decree of en masse expulsion within ninety days of the Uganda Asians is without any parallel in human history. The decree which is but an offspring of prejudice is arbitrary, illegal and inhuman and can scarcely be justified under international law. . . .

B. RACIAL DISCRIMINATION

The principle that "all beings are born free and equal in dignity and rights" has now been universally accepted. The principle of "equality" moreover implies that there should be no differentiation based upon factors over which the individual has no control, such as his race, his colour, his descent, and his national or ethnic origin. The broad and comprehensive definition of this principle has been incorporated in Article 1 of the International Convention on the Elimination of all forms of Racial Discrimination, 1965.

General Amin's decision to expel the Asians alone conclusively demonstrates differentiation in treatment of individuals on the basis of race as such. Such a discriminatory treatment clearly contravenes the provision of the Universal Declaration of Human Rights. It also amounts to a negation of the principle of equality and an affront to human dignity. As the African countries are in the forefront of the movement against racial discrimination it is but apt to expect from an African country equality of all races. President Nyerere of Tanzania, rightly inveighed against General Amin for his conduct and characterised his act as "clearly racism, representative of the same thing that Africans deplored, when it was practised against them." Such an exercise of racialism by the Ugandan Government is bound to have repercussions on the friendly and peaceful relations among nations generally and the African-Asian countries in particular.

III

A. CONCEPT OF STATE RESPONSIBILITY

Every State has the responsibility to protect the life, liberty and property of individuals residing within its territory. This means all individuals are protected by the State. In case of infringement of their rights either by acts of private persons or by acts of State Officials, they can seek a remedy under municipal law. It is, of course, after they have exhausted the "local remedies" that they can have a recourse to international remedies through their own States.

Thus, so long as the Uganda Asians are in Uganda, it is the principal responsibility of that Government to protect their rights. If Uganda fails to discharge this elemental duty then it would incur international responsibility for denial of justice. As Swaran Singh, the Minister of External Affairs of India said: "As long as Indian nationals remain in Uganda, their honour and the safety and security of their property are a responsibility of the Uganda Government."

B. UNITED NATIONS

As has been set out earlier, it is normally the duty of Uganda to protect the rights and interests of persons living there. The domestic jurisdiction clause contained in Article 2, paragraph 7, cannot be invoked in the case of racial discrimination, and mass expulsion of Uganda Asians by Uganda, as the latter fall outside the constraint of the domestic jurisdiction clause. As a result, the United Nations, *i.e.*, the General Assembly, Security Council, Economic and Social Council, Human Rights Commission, etc., are entitled to secure to the Asians in Uganda adequate *compensation for their assets*, or alternatively, permission to carry with them their assets and/or to ensure that humane treatment is meted out to them and to get the deadline of ninety days extended.

CONCLUSIONS

From the foregoing review of the facts and law pertaining to the mass expulsion of Uganda Asians, the following conclusions can be drawn:

First, General Amin's *en masse* expulsion of Uganda Asians is arbitrary insofar as it is aimed only against one particular racial community, that is, of Asian origin.

Second, the Uganda decree of expulsion is inconsistent with the principle of equality of races and peoples which is a basic tenet of the United Nations. The principle of equality of races cannot be derogated from on the ground of "Africanization" which is probably the motive for the mass expulsion.

Third, the British Government is obligated by international law to render protection to all British passport holders.

Fourth, every State is under an obligation to afford protection to all persons in its territory in accordance with the general principles of international law, the Universal Declaration of Human Rights and all other U.N. international instruments ensuring human dignity to person and protection of his property.

Fifth, when States, particularly Member States of the United Nations, fail to discharge the elemental principles of ensuring equality and human dignity to persons of all races, the United Nations through all its instrumentalities is entitled to redress the situation.

Sixth, the measures and methods to be employed by the United Nations in any case, involving gross violation of human rights naturally depend upon the kind of results sought to be accomplished. The case of expulsion of Uganda Asians calls for the adoption of a range of measures from the United Nations. At the minimum the last date for the expulsion of Uganda Asians — which is 7 November 1972 — should be extended so as to enable the British Government, which is responsible for the repatriation of Uganda Asians, to take this massive problem without infringing the rights of the British passport holders. At the maximum the United Nations can persuade the Government of Uganda to rescind the decree of expulsion of Uganda Asians, as it is inconsistent with the principle of racial equality which is a peremptory norm under general international law and multilateral treaties. There are several other possible actions that can be taken by the United Nations. For example, Member States of the United Nations may be called upon to contribute to a fund to redress the injuries sustained by Uganda Asians, as also to grant asylum to them in accordance with the wishes of the "expellees."

Note: Applying the Human Rights Clauses of the UN Charter and Other International Norms to the Expulsion of Asians from Uganda

The above three readings assess whether Uganda's expulsion of its Asian population violated international law — which includes the human rights clauses of the UN Charter and a variety of other international norms — and they unanimously conclude that it did. What is remarkable in this collective assessment is not only how far the international community has come in this regard since the adoption of the Charter in 1945, but also the extent to which pre-Charter rules governing the treatment of aliens are used to clarify the obligations that states have assumed under contemporary international human rights law. Note, too, that the latter may contribute to the progressive development of the former. See, e.g., Lillich, The Current Status of the Law of State Responsibility for Injuries to Aliens, in International Law of State Responsibility for Injuries to Aliens 1, 26-29 (R. Lillich ed. & contrib. 1983).

How a state treats individuals — whether aliens, stateless persons, or its own citizens — has now become a matter of international concern. States have legal obligations under the human rights clauses of the UN Charter, obligations that no longer can be avoided by invoking the concept of domestic jurisdiction embodied in Article 2(7). Indeed, as has been noted above (see page 27 supra) and will be considered extensively at pages 495-509 and 573-575 of Problem VII, should the Security Council find that a state's human rights violations constitute a "threat to the peace" or a "breach of the peace," it can authorize enforcement action under Chapter VII of the Charter with the objective of terminating such violations and rectifying the situation. While Great Britain chose not to raise the question of mandatory sanctions before the Security Council (see page 29 supra), that option clearly was available to it (see Wooldridge and Sharma, supra page 55, at 47).

Given that states have obligations under the human rights clauses of the Charter, just what are those obligations? Specifically, what legal obligations governed Uganda's expulsion of its Asian population? According to two scholars, Sir Colin Crowe's statement at the United Nations (see pages 29-30 supra) did not "make it clear whether he considered all collective expulsion as being contrary to the human rights provisions of the Charter, or merely expulsions accompanied by special hardships." Wooldridge and Sharma, supra, at 47. However, the fact that "the British government never formally asked General Amin the reasons for his expulsion of the Asians, nor did it formally protest the expulsion itself" (see page 56 supra), suggests that Great Britain regarded only the manner in which the expulsions were carried out, not the expulsions themselves, as giving rise to international responsibility on Uganda's part.

Under the traditional Law of State Responsibility for Injuries to Aliens, which Great Britain with its near-exclusive focus on the plight of those Asians who held British passports obviously had in mind, aliens had no right to remain in a state. Hence, their expulsion engaged an expelling state's international responsibility only to the extent that the manner in which the expulsion took place fell below the international minimum standard of treatment that aliens were guaranteed by customary international law. This standard, then, Great Britain implies and the above three readings make explicit, helps define a state's legal obligations under the human rights clauses of the UN Charter.

A state's human rights obligations under the Charter, however, go well beyond traditional international law in at least two important ways. First, the Charter extends its protection to all individuals, not just aliens. Thus, Uganda was violating its Charter obligations by the manner in which it expelled stateless persons and its own citizens, as well as nationals of Great Britain and other states. Second, the Charter gives rise to new norms, again applicable to all individuals, that limit a state's right to engage in certain acts that historically it was free to undertake "at discretion." Thus, as the above three readings, if not the British protestations, make clear, Uganda's expulsion of Asians in and of itself violated the UN Charter because it was racially discriminatory in nature. This norm against racial discrimination, found in Article 55(c) of the Charter itself, draws support from the Universal Declaration of Human Rights and from other contemporary sources of customary international law. See Restatement (Third) of the Foreign Relations Law of the United States §702(f) (1987).

As has been pointed out, the human rights clauses of the UN Charter have been recognized by the United States as giving rise to international legal obligations (see pages 46-48 supra). Moreover, they have been invoked on the international level repeatedly and endorsed and given legal weight by the International Court of Justice in the *Namibia Case* (see pages 49-54 supra). Certainly they were key in shaping the consensus of the international community that Uganda's expulsion of its Asian population violated international law.

Finally, it should be noted that the above three readings invoke various international law norms not only to provide content to the legal obligations of Uganda under the UN Charter as of 1972, but also to serve as freestanding, independent norms with which Uganda had to demonstrate compliance or be found in violation of international law. Specifically, mention was made of (1) the Universal Declaration of Human Rights (see the Documentary Supplement) and the customary international law of human rights (see Part III of Problem II); (2) the International Convention on the Elimination of All Forms of Racial Discrimination (see the Documentary Supplement); and (3) the Convention Relating to the Status of Stateless Persons, Sept. 28, 1954, 360 U.N.T.S. 117 (entered into force June 6, 1960).

The interrelated status of the Universal Declaration and customary international human rights law will be taken up at length in Problem II. A word of caution should be introduced here, however, about the somewhat loose use of the two conventions in the above readings. First, they do not mention that in 1972 Uganda had not yet become a party to the Racial Discrimination Convention, and, hence, its provisions were not then binding upon Uganda as a matter of treaty law. Second, while at the time Uganda had been a party to the Stateless Persons Convention for seven years and, thus, as Professor Plender points out, clearly was in violation of Article 31 thereof (see page 61 supra), that Convention applied only to a relatively small number of the Asians who were expelled by Uganda. Hence, it could not serve, independently, as a legal basis to condemn the expulsions en masse.

The lesson to be learned here is obvious but most important: while multilateral treaties may create independent legal obligations or provide evidence of the content of the human rights clauses of the UN Charter, or both, careful scholarship as well as effective advocacy mandates that care should be used to identify for what particular purpose or purposes they are being invoked. Additionally, as will be seen at pages 172-173 of Problem II, multilateral treaties also may play an important role in the creation or clarification of customary international human rights norms, which underscores the need to identify the reason for their invocation.

V.   The Response of the International Community to Subsequent Human Rights Abuses in Uganda

A.   *The Situation Worsens*

Uganda — A Lawless State
Intl. Comm. Jurists, The Review No. 9, at 18 (Dec. 1972).

The wholesale expulsion of Asians from Uganda, with expropriation of their property, has profoundly shocked world opinion. . . . The expulsions are bound to do substantial and lasting damage to the economy of East Africa. The damage will not be confined to Uganda. The vigorous denunciations of General Amin's racialism by African leaders in Kenya, Tanzania, Zambia and elsewhere are no doubt in part an expression of their concern at its effects upon the future of the area as a whole.

Evil as are these expulsions, they have served to distract attention from the lawlessness and brutality with which the Ugandan Government and armed forces have been acting towards their fellow-Africans. The arrest by soldiers of Chief Justice Benedicto Kiwanuka in the Supreme Court building at Kampala was an outrage against the Rule of Law. There are persistent reports that he was beheaded within two hours of his illegal arrest. No reasons have been given for his arrest. It may be that as a former Prime Minister and as a person of stature and recognised integrity, he was thought to be a possible alternative head of state. It may be that his independent judgment in a habeas corpus application shortly before he was seized incurred the wrath of the authorities.

In addition to the Chief Justice, other prominent personalities have simply disappeared and are believed to have been murdered by army personnel immediately after their detention. President Amin's standard explanation for such disappearances is that the persons concerned have fled to Tanzania. In addition to prominent personalities, hundreds of suspected opponents of the regime have disappeared and are believed to have been murdered in all parts of the country, especially in the northern districts of Acholi and Lango, as well as in Buganda.

This defiance of the Rule of Law extends to the treatment of common criminals. On July 28, 1972, three suspected thieves, known locally as 'kondos,' were publicly executed in a field at Lugazi, a small town near Kampala. The executions were carried out by members of the so-called Public Safety Unit, comprised of selected police officers. There was no trial, no conviction and no sentence. This is but one example of a practice that has been continuing indiscriminately elsewhere.

Mohr, In Amin's Taciturn Uganda, Even Food Is Unspeakable
Intl. Herald-Tribune, Jan. 30, 1975, at 5, cols. 1-4

KAMPALA, Jan. 29 (NYT) — At a garden party celebrating the fourth anniversary of Maj. Gen. Idi Amin's seizure of power in this East African nation, a Ugandan major wearing a kilt of the Royal Stewart tartan and a cap resembling that of the Gordon Highlanders strolled across the lawn carrying a bottle of beer.

A visitor asked him the name of Gen. Amin's new kilted regiment. The major looked at his interrogator suspiciously for a moment and then said, "the Black Watch." Laughing uproariously at his own joke, he wandered away. That was one of the few interviews possible during the celebration last weekend of President Amin's 1971 coup d'etat. In the atmosphere that the towering, muscular 49-year-old general has created, people do not care to talk. Reliable statistics are nonexistent.

A visit to Uganda these days is much like a visit to a medieval court — a matter of impressions, sounds, sights and smells.

The International Commission of Jurists has accused Gen. Amin of instituting a reign of terror in this nation of more than 10 million persons. A former U.S. ambassador said that a minimum of 50,000 persons had been killed.

In September, 1972, the President expelled the large Asian community of Indian and Pakistani background, many of whom had British passports and had been important in trade and technology. There followed an exodus of most of the British expatriate community. At the same time, Gen. Amin began a program of heavy spending on military equipment and other items that a demoralised civil service could do little to curb.

In early January, Gen. Amin's finance minister, Emmanuel Wakhweya, defected in London, saying that the economy was in chaos. Little is known about the foreign-exchange reserves, but there are hints that they are low.

When the food in restaurants is served it is unspeakable, and there is a shortage of implements with which to eat it. There is also a severe shortage of glasses, so most persons drink their Source of the Nile lager beer from the bottle. The Kampala International Hotel had no ice, no ashtrays and, for two days, no cigarettes.

HOARDERS THREATENED

In January, sugar and other staples almost disappeared, but Gen. Amin threatened to have what he termed hoarding merchants shot. The situation is now said to be better.

The streets are dark and ghostly at night because of a shortage of components for streetlamps. Taxis have almost disappeared — Ugandans say that parts are scarce or too expensive.

SOVIET ARMS

Gen. Amin is believed to have bought a good deal of new military equipment from the Soviet Union, including armored vehicles and possibly ground-to-air anti-aircraft missiles. He had promised to put the equipment on display during the celebration but did not.

Soviet military air and naval attaches were prominent in the crowds at the celebration, which relatively few African dignitaries attended.

Although Gen. Amin expelled the Asians, he is importing about 200

Pakistanis to fill technical and administrative jobs. With their children, they are in the International Hotel, signing checks for what they eat and drink.

The anniversary celebration got off to an unusual start when the newspaper Voice of Uganda printed a half-length nude picture of former Foreign Minister Elizabeth Bagaya, a princess of the royal house of Toro. Last November, Gen. Amin dismissed Miss Bagaya on charges that she had been in contact with Western intelligence agents and had had sexual intercourse with a white man in a rest room at Orly Airport, Paris.

Example for Girls

The picture was sent from abroad, the newspaper said, and was taken when Miss Bagaya was a model and "plunged into an abyss of immorality." The paper said the incident should serve as an example for girls not to sell themselves.

Gen. Amin has promised to release her from house arrest in December, but she apparently is still there. She is described as alive and well.

As for the celebration, the main events in a football stadium were colorful and bore the distinctive stamp of Gen. Amin. His wife, Madina, arrived in a Lincoln, while the President drove his camouflaged jeep.

There was scattered applause as he inspected the ranks of civilian delegations. A parade began with civilians, some of them in tribal dress. There was also a delegation of "economic warriors" — black businessmen who had taken over Asian property. One carried a placard advertising corn plasters.

Tourists Invited

After a salute by a Baganda drummer who struck his great drum 21 times, Gen. Amin invited the people of the world to come to Uganda for their holidays.

Large police contingents then paraded, followed by air force pilots, one group of which carried a placard reading "Suicide Strike Command." Among the army units was one called the Suicide Regiment. There were also high-kicking, dog-trotting men of the airborne, soldiers with kilts and frogmen in wet suits.

The only military equipment to be seen was a small model of an airplane, its propeller powered by what seemed to be a lawn-mower engine, that was pushed across the grass by civilians.

In a speech read for him at midnight the night before the President told the nation that he could not return it to civilian rule because civilian politicians were still corrupt.

WAR SCARES

He warned that any war with neighbors would not be fought on Ugandan soil but on theirs. Last summer, he caused one of several war scares in East Africa by saying that his defense council had "considered the possibility" of extending Uganda's border to the Kagera River, 20 miles inside Tanzania.

At the garden party, hundreds of Ugandans and foreigners mingled on the lawn of the former residence of President Milton Obote. Gen. Amin, in a business suit, shook hands with Arab sheikins and diplomats.

In a corner a band wearing frilled fuchsia shirts played Congolese jazz. A sign proclaimed that they were members of the Suicide Command Dance Band.

See No Evil
The Economist, May 21, 1977, at 76, cols. 2-3

That Uganda has been in the grip of a brutal tyranny since Idi Amin seized power in 1971 is news to nobody. But a report by the International Commission of Jurists, in Geneva, published on Tuesday, has now quanti-

fied the brutality. Between 80,000 and 90,000 people are said to have been killed in 1971-73; since then murders have been more discreet and selective, but probably bring the total to more than 100,000.

The report cites evidence that President Amin, who has direct control over one of the main agents for the slaughter, the so-called State Research Department, himself ordered some of the killings. In other instances he took no action to prevent murders, or to punish the perpetrators.

An outrage behind an atrocity is revealed in the introduction to the report, written by the ICJ's secretary-general, Mr. Niall MacDermot. All the ICJ's evidence has been presented to the United Nations Commission on Human Rights, but "as yet that commission has taken no action." Uganda was considered by the commission in 1975, 1976 and, at Britain's request, again this year. It was decided that the matter should "be kept under review." The commission, of which Uganda has been a member since 1975, has found it possible to recommend immediate action against a few other violators of human freedoms. But then South Africa, Israel and Chile are not members of the third-world club.

B. UN Action (or Inaction)

After the initial flurry of concern over the expulsion of Asians from Uganda, the United Nations dropped the matter completely, save for the resettlement and other related activities of the UN High Commissioner for Refugees (see page 84 infra) and the somewhat academic (albeit highly praiseworthy) efforts of the UN Sub-Commission on the Prevention of Discrimination and the Protection of Minorities to draft a Declaration on the Human Rights of Individuals Who Are Not Nationals of the Country in Which They Live (see pages 84-85 infra). Thus, Uganda successfully escaped UN censure for what clearly was a violation of its human rights obligations under the UN Charter.

The deteriorating human rights situation in Uganda described in the readings in the previous section offered the United Nations repeated opportunities to take remedial action during the 1970s, opportunities that it uniformly avoided or otherwise failed to follow up. Petitions filed with the UN Sub-Commission pursuant to ECOSOC Resolution 1503 (found in the Documentary Supplement and considered at length in Problem V) revealed a "consistent pattern of gross and reliably attested violations of human rights and fundamental freedoms" by General Amin's regime, but when forwarded by the Sub-Commission to its parent body, the Commission on Human Rights, in 1974, 1976, and 1977, led to no action by the latter. H. Tolley, Jr., The U.N. Commission on Human Rights 77 (1987). In 1978 the Commission finally authorized a confidential "thorough study" of the situation in Uganda by former International Court of Justice Judge

Onyeama, id. at 131, a modest response to say the least when one considers that it occurred "several years after the International Commission of Jurists and, subsequently, Amnesty International, had submitted voluminous dossiers on the atrocities in that country." Rodley, The Development of United Nations Activities in the Field of Human Rights and the Role of Non-Governmental Organizations, in The U.S., the U.N., and the Management of Global Change 263, 281 n.28 (T. Gati ed. 1983). Even then, as Rodley points out, "Uganda was able to stall so long that the thorough study was not undertaken within the 15 months or so between the time it was authorized and the rather more radical remedy administered by the Tanzanian army." Id. Hence, the United Nations never even conducted a formal investigation of non-governmental organization (NGO) charges against Uganda, much less pass a resolution condemning it, despite the fact that nearly 300,000 people were brutally killed during the eight years that General Amin reigned in terror. Amnesty International, 1979 Ann. Rep. 38 (1980). In short, to quote one prominent scholar, "Idi Amin was immunized from UN criticism." Franck, Of Gnats and Camels: Is There a Double Standard at the United Nations?, 78 Am. J. Int. L. 811, 828 (1984).

Franck's observations about a UN double standard in the field of human rights amplify the cryptic comments of The Economist (see page 70 supra) and reflected the views held by most "UN watchers" at the time. See, e.g., Kotecha, The Shortchanged: Uganda Citizenship Laws and How They Were Applied to Its Asian Minority, 9 Intl. Law. 1, 28 (1975), noting "the different measuring sticks that are used today, especially in the United Nations, to evaluate the policies and practices of South Africa and Rhodesia, on the one hand, and of some of the black African states on the other." That such views were not the exclusive province of Western observers was underlined in dramatic fashion by the remarkable address made to the UN General Assembly by Mr. Godfrey Binaisa,* the newly installed President of Uganda, shortly after General Amin's ouster (34 U.N. GAOR (14th plen. mtg.) at 269-270, U.N. Doc. A/34/P.V. 14 (1979)).

> 7. This is no ordinary occasion for the people of Uganda. This session of the General Assembly holds special significance for us. As representatives are aware, the people of Uganda have just emerged from a most harrowing nightmare. We have just broken free from the yoke of one of the most vicious dictatorships of modern times. For the first time in eight years we are able to raise our voice in the community of nations as a free people.
>
> 8. Under the Amin dictatorship our people suffered untold indignities, torture and death. At least half a million people were murdered in cold blood.

---

* For a brief biographical portrait of this fascinating man — a London-trained lawyer who became Uganda's first Attorney General after independence, sought and received asylum in the United States after Amin's takeover, returned to Uganda after the dictator's ouster to be named President, was deposed in a coup, and returned to the United States, where until recently he served as a lawyer in New York City's Law Department — see Martin, About New York, June 29, 1991, at 26, cols. 5-6.

However, the purpose of my address today is not to catalogue the atrocities of the Amin régime.

9. Let me, however, touch briefly on the attitude of the United Nations with regard to events in Uganda during that period. In our struggle against the Fascist dictatorship we were inspired by the commitment of the international community to human rights. That commitment is clearly set out in the Charter of this Organization. [The speaker cites and quotes from the Preamble and Articles 1, 55, and 56 of the Charter.]

12. In the light of the clear commitment set out in those provisions of the Charter, our people naturally looked to the United Nations for solidarity and support in their struggle against the Fascist dictatorship. For eight years they cried out in the wilderness for help; unfortunately, their cries seemed to have fallen on deaf ears.

13. The United Nations looked on with embarrassed silence as the Uganda tragedy unfolded. Meanwhile, the Amin régime continued with impunity to commit genocide against our people. We would be less than honest if we did not say openly and clearly that the people of Uganda were deeply disappointed by the silence of this Organization at the time of their greatest need.

14. The Uganda situation is merely one example of a very serious global problem involving extensive violations of human rights. The increasing number of refugees and displaced persons is sufficient testimony to the gravity of the situation. Yet, somehow, it is thought to be in bad taste or contrary to diplomatic etiquette to raise matters of violations of human rights by Member States within the forums of the United Nations.

15. For how long will the United Nations remain silent while Governments represented within this Organization continue to perpetrate atrocities against their own people? Governments come and go, but the peoples of the world remain a permanent constituency of the United Nations. It was for the well-being of the peoples of the world that the United Nations was founded in the first instance. Indeed, it is for their welfare that the United Nations must continue to work. It would be unfortunate if this Organization were reduced to a club of governments afraid to speak out boldly for the rights of the citizens of the world.

16. I find it difficult to embrace the view that matters concerning human rights lie exclusively within the domain of the domestic jurisdiction of the States concerned. Such a view renders meaningless the human rights provisions of the Charter of this Organization. . . .

For similar criticism of the Organization of African Unity's failure to address the human rights situation in Uganda, see Umozurike, pages 77-78 infra.

C. The U.S. Embargo

Although the United Nations never came near adopting economic sanctions against Uganda, in late 1978 the U.S. Congress enacted its own comprehensive trade embargo. This action, taken over the objections of the

Carter Administration, was the first time the United States unilaterally resorted to the use of a trade ban for the sole purpose of attempting to improve the human rights situation in another country. Previous U.S. embargoes had been imposed either for reasons of national security, as in the cases of North Korea and Cuba, or pursuant to mandatory UN Security Council resolutions, as in the cases of Rhodesia and South Africa, considered in Problem VII.

Congress regarded the embargo as a necessary and proper response to General Amin's brutal seven-year reign of terror, during which time an estimated 100,000 to 300,000 Ugandans were murdered by his death squads. Uganda: The Human Rights Situation, 1978: Hearings Before the Subcomm. on Foreign Economic Policy of the Senate Comm. on Foreign Relations, 95th Cong., 2d Sess. 80 (1978) (testimony of Hon. Lowell P. Weicker).

Enactment of the embargo also reflected Congress's displeasure at the limited measures adopted by the Executive Branch to express U.S. disapproval of the Amin regime. The Nixon Administration had closed down the U.S. Embassy in Kampala in 1973 and had terminated the Peace Corps and AID assistance programs. In March of 1977, the Carter Administration had supported efforts to have the UN Commission on Human Rights take action with respect to the human rights situation in Uganda and in October of the same year had adopted a policy requiring all U.S. representatives to international development banks to vote against loans to it. In addition, pursuant to existing statutory authority under the Export Administration Act, the Departments of State and Commerce during the Carter Administration had barred exports to Uganda of certain military items deemed capable of contributing to human rights violations. United States-Uganda Relations, 1978: Hearings Before the Subcomms. on Africa, International Organizations, and International Economic Policy and Trade of the House Comm. on International Relations, 95th Cong., 2d Sess. 59-61, 86-87 (1987). When these actions produced no change in Uganda's policies, however, Congress decided to take a stronger stand.

Support for a trade embargo, despite the absence of UN authorization, was first advocated by Professor Richard H. Ullman of Princeton who, in an article on the use of economic sanctions in international affairs, argued that the total dependence of the Ugandan economy on coffee exports offered a unique opportunity to use economic pressure to pursue human rights objectives. Ullman, Human Rights and Economic Power: The United States Versus Idi Amin, 56 Foreign Aff. 529 (1978). Such an embargo, Ullman contended, would put pressure directly on General Amin, who relied upon the foreign earnings from domestic coffee production to pay and equip his army.

Congressional hearings bore out Ullman's assertions about the vulnerability of the Amin regime to a trade embargo. Uganda's economy was almost entirely dependent upon coffee production, with such exports accounting for one-half of its GNP and 90 percent of government revenues. Moreover, the United States, Uganda's largest trading partner, regularly purchased more than one-third of all Ugandan coffee. At the same time, such a trade embargo would have marginal impact on the U.S. market, since Ugandan coffee accounted for only 6 percent of total coffee imports. In fact, so minimal was the effect of Ugandan coffee supplies on the U.S. market that most major coffee producers supported Congress's initiative.

Despite strong congressional and even industry support, however, the Carter Administration remained opposed to any effort to embargo trade with Uganda, maintaining that such a unilateral embargo would be ineffective without the support of major U.S. trading partners. It argued that Uganda would merely shift exports to other markets, particularly Great Britain, Germany, France, and Japan. Moreover, the administration contended, somewhat fancifully, that an embargo might violate U.S. obligations under the GATT, to which Uganda was also a party. General Agreements on Tariffs and Trade, opened for signature Oct. 30, 1947, 61 Stat. A3, T.I.A.S. No. 1700, 55 U.N.T.S. 187. The Carter Administration's strong opposition to the embargo legislation apparently was rooted in traditional Executive Branch concern to preserve "flexibility" in diplomatic relations.

Despite the Administration's opposition, Congress was determined to take concrete steps to oppose the regime in Kampala. Aside from its belief that a trade embargo would hasten Amin's downfall, Congress also wanted to go on record as opposing his regime in any event. It hoped that such strong action would catalyze world opinion against Amin and encourage other states to adopt similar economic sanctions.

The House of Representatives first passed a resolution on 12 June 1978, calling on President Carter to implement a trade embargo against Uganda. When no Administration action was forthcoming, Congress enacted the embargo's sweeping restrictions into law on 10 October 1978. Bretton Woods Agreement Act, Pub. L. No. 95-435, §5, 92 Stat. 1051 (1978). The new statute provided that "no corporation, institution, group or individual may import directly or indirectly, into the United States . . . any article grown, produced or manufactured in Uganda until the President determines and certifies to the Congress that the Government of Uganda is no longer committing a consistent pattern of gross violations of human rights." It further prohibited the export of any product or technical data to Uganda from the United States. Thus, the statute imposed what amounted to a total ban on trade between the two countries.

Several months after implementation of the statute, General Amin's reign came to an end, toppled by invading Tanzanian troops. Although contemporary press reports gave little credit to the embargo as a factor in Amin's downfall, Congress was quick to cite it as contributing to the end of his regime. 125 Cong. Rec. 8768 (1979); U.S. Policy Toward Uganda, 1979: Hearings Before the Subcomm. on Africa of the House Comm. on Foreign Affairs, 96th Cong., 1st Sess. (1979).

While the Tanzanian military action certainly precipitated Amin's downfall, considerable evidence supports the view that the trade embargo, at the very least, had set in motion the events leading up to his removal. Aside from the fact that Ugandan coffee was "piling up and rotting on the docks," within weeks after the embargo took effect (125 Cong. Rec. 8768 (1979)), the trade ban had several other effects. It not only deprived the Ugandan economy of critical spare parts needed for U.S.-manufactured products, but also curtailed Ugandan access to imported oil. Taken together, these factors disrupted many sectors of the Ugandan economy.

Moreover, the clash between Tanzania and Uganda that caused General Amin's abrupt departure may have been motivated, in large part, by the trade embargo's psychological impact. Some commentators have asserted that Amin instigated the attack upon Tanzania that provoked the Tanzanian invasion to show the Ugandan people that he remained in a strong position despite U.S. economic sanctions. Miller, When Sanctions Worked, 39 Foreign Pol. 118, 125-126 (1980).

Immediately following the flight of Amin, Congress sought to normalize relations with the new Ugandan government, repealing the trade embargo in September 1979. Act to Amend the International Development and Food Assistance Act, Pub. L. No. 96-67, 93 Stat. 415 (1979). Most commentators who have subsequently studied events in Uganda believe the U.S. economic sanctions were a significant factor in Amin's fall. See M. Daoudi and M. Dajani, Economic Sanctions 169 (1983); G. Hufbauer and J. Schott, Economic Sanctions Reconsidered: History and Current Policy 455-460 (1985). See generally Miller, supra; Comment, U.S. Trade Sanctions Against Uganda: Legality Under International Law, 11 Law & Poly. Intl. Bus. 1149 (1979); Note, The Legitimacy of the United States Embargo of Uganda, 13 J. Intl. L. & Econ. 651 (1979); Recent Developments, International Trade: Uganda Trade Embargo, 20 Harv. Intl. L.J. 206 (1979).

D. The Tanzanian Intervention

The above two sections have surveyed the UN and U.S. responses to General Amin's massive human rights violations in Uganda. It was Tanzania, however, that played the key role in bringing about the end of the Amin regime.

Action inside Uganda by groups opposed to General Amin had increased during the latter half of 1978. In October 1978, Amin's troops invaded and occupied the Kagera region of Tanzania. The General justified this invasion on two grounds: (1) as a response to prior incursions into Uganda by Ugandan exiles operating out of Kagera; and (2) as a rectification of an alleged error by the colonial powers in drawing the boundary between Uganda and Tanzania. He also announced that the map of Uganda would be redrawn to include 710 square miles of Tanzanian territory. After 15 days Amin elected to withdraw from Tanzania, apparently wary about reprisals from that country's forces. The pullout was too little, too late. Tanzania, enraged by the haphazard destruction of life and property by the Ugandan Army during its 15-day occupation, declared itself in a state of war with Uganda.

In March 1979, a Tanzanian force of 4,000 troops joined with 1,000 Ugandan exiles to launch a two-pronged attack using long-range artillery. Tanzanian President Julius Nyerere announced that the offensive was actually two separate wars, with Tanzania defending its territorial integrity while the Ugandan exiles were battling to liberate their country. In any event the joint expedition made swift progress as the Ugandan Army crumbled. On 10 April 1979, Kampala fell, and three days later, on Good Friday, a new coalition government took office. By the end of May, it controlled most of Uganda and had received diplomatic recognition from most of the world's states. General Amin fled the country and reportedly moved between a number of Arab states before settling down somewhere in Saudi Arabia.

Although Tanzania justified its going into Uganda on grounds of self-defense, the factual basis for such an argument, as the following reading shows, is doubtful at best. On the other hand, the doctrine of humanitarian intervention, the subject of Problem VIII, although not invoked by Tanzania, arguably provides more than adequate justification for its actions (Umozurike, Tanzania's Intervention in Uganda, 20 Archiv des Volkerrecht 301, 312-313 (1982)).

> Tanzania's military intervention in Uganda cannot be justified as an act of self-defence. It might have been so justified if Tanzania merely cleared the Ugandans from the Kagera region. The flagrant violation of the rights of Ugandans, especially the casual killings of a large number of people, provided the justification for humanitarian intervention: Amin's treatment of his subjects was revolting to the human conscience and the efficiency of the state's representative machinery made action by the people ineffective. The state machinery had become destructive of human rights, indeed of human life and deserved to be removed by appropriate means. Tanzania used proportionate force, i.e., the physical occupation of the whole of Uganda with the support of Ugandan exiles and deserters from [the] Ugandan army. Nothing less could have removed the boisterous and obstreperous dictator from power.
>
> It is true that President Nyerere would not have committed the human and material resources of his country if he had anticipated that the new regime would be hostile to Tanzania or suppress human rights like its predecessor. These are legitimate interests. Long after the event, it has not been possible to decipher imperialistic or economic motives. It was indeed an expensive venture that complicated the economic problems of Tanzania. The humanitarian intervention is a splendid example especially for nations that have the means and yet connive at flagrant abuses of human rights. The reasons for the tolerance have ranged from political, economic to racial.

South Africa and Namibia now stand as the shame of the world. A regime is being propped up by external powers to abuse the rights of the non-white population. The external powers have economic interests in the status quo; they connive at the system because the victims are non-white, a flagrant example of racial discrimination. The cry is loud in Southern Africa for a Tanzanian type or humanitarian intervention to restore human rights and dignity to the people of all races.

The right to intervene on humanitarian grounds is one that must be exercised with the greatest caution. The principle of territorial integrity is so basic that nothing but a flagrant abuse or misuse could justify its contravention. Intervention necessarily involves the destruction of lives and property. The manner of intervention and its cost in terms of lives and property should be commensurate with the evil that it is sought to avert. It follows that collective action by a regional organisation may be preferable to individual state action. The OAU had in the past been apathetic to breaches of human rights by some of its members. Far from condemning the excesses and abuses of President Amin, it honoured him as Chairman of the organisation for 1976-1977. The impossibility of getting the OAU to act, or even to condemn the invasion of Kagera, left Tanzania, revolted by the atrocities, no option but to act unilaterally. It is to be hoped that other African states will share this concern for human rights as a regional strategy.

Compare F. Teson, Humanitarian Intervention: An Inquiry into Law and Morality 159-174 (1988) with N. Ronzitti, Rescuing Nationals Abroad Through Military Coercion and Intervention on Grounds of Humanity 102-108 (1985). See also Chatterjee, Some Legal Problems of Support Role in International Law: Tanzania and Uganda, 30 Intl. & Comp. L.Q. 755 (1981); Hassan, Realpolitik in International Law: After Tanzanian-Ugandan Conflict "Humanitarian Intervention" Reexamined, 17 Willamette L. Rev. 859 (1981). "The defeat of Amin and the liberation of Uganda by Nyerere's Tanzania is the most significant African event of the last decade. With it Africa came of age, able to criticise itself, no longer determined to support the honour of corrupt rulers against the world simply because they are black." Wani, Humanitarian Intervention and the Tanzania-Uganda War, 3 Horn of Africa 18, 24 (1980).

VI.   Concluding Thoughts and Observations

The insertion of the human rights clauses in the UN Charter and the development of other norms and procedures since 1945 to protect the basic human rights of individuals illustrate the assumption — often stated but rarely substantiated — that every individual, as well as his or her government, has a compelling interest in seeing such rights observed throughout the world. This assumption and other conventional wisdom about international human rights are challenged in the provocative reading that follows.

Bilder, Rethinking International Human Rights: Some Basic Questions
1969 Wis. L. Rev. 171, 187-191

C.   SHOULD PEOPLES AND GOVERNMENTS BE CONCERNED WITH
     DENIALS OF HUMAN RIGHTS IN OTHER COUNTRIES?

A basic assumption of international human rights is that every people and government has a direct stake in their observance in other countries. This stake is sufficiently important, it is argued, that all should be willing to accept international limitations on their own freedom of action in order to advance this cause abroad. However, part of the weakness of international efforts seems to be that peoples and governments have not yet been persuaded that they have this stake in international human rights. Can convincing reasons be given?

1.   ARE DENIALS OF HUMAN RIGHTS IN ONE COUNTRY LIKELY
     TO THREATEN WORLD PEACE AND SECURITY?

A major argument advanced in support of international human rights efforts is that such efforts are essential to the search for world peace. The theory seems to be that governments that are permitted to suppress human rights at home will tend to develop aggressive foreign policies, while states in which human rights are widely recognized will tend to live peacefully with their neighbors. Thus, any step toward wider recognition of human rights is argued to be also a step toward ending war. President Kennedy's remark, "Is not peace, in the last analysis, basically a matter of human rights?" is often quoted in this context, along with the example of Nazi Germany. There is an intuitive appeal in this argument, for we would like to think that a free people will choose to live justly and peacefully with their neighbors. But at some point we have to ask whether history supports this assumption. For example, is it entirely clear that the Soviet Union is more inclined to the international use of force than the United States, or Haiti than Israel? If human rights have some direct relation to peace, this is indeed significant for the national interest, and it is important to spell out the linkage quite carefully and persuasively.

It seems reasonable to assume that internal structures of power do affect the willingness of government elites to use force to secure foreign policy objectives, and that the more concentrated and unchecked such internal power is, the more likely that elites will feel free to engage in aggression. Sustained internal denials of human rights may also create widespread internal frustration. Governing elites may seek to discharge this frustration through aggressive foreign policies, and such frustration may at the same time make such policies psychologically more palatable to the internal populace. Moreover, human rights denials may lead to internal turmoil and rebellion. Today such disturbances have a tendency to spill-over and escalate into involvement or attempted humanitarian intervention by other countries. This may be particularly true where the alleged human rights denials occasioning the disturbance involve substantial foreign ethnic minorities, as in Cyprus, Southern Africa, the Near East, and India and Pakistan.

On the other hand, we must recognize that international human rights efforts in themselves contain potential dangers for peace. The concept of wars of liberation and widespread current demands for coercive action to end discrimination in Southern Africa suggest that, at least in the short term, the objectives of human rights and peace may in some cases conflict. Such militant demands raise dramatically the question whether, in a nuclear age, we are prepared to agree with Woodrow Wilson that "the right is more precious than peace."

In any event, it seems clear that the causes of international conflict are deep-rooted and complex and cannot be encompassed in any simple formula. Indeed, the real relation of human rights and peace may exist only at a deeper level, in the dependence of each of the objectives on our ultimate achievement of some rational world order based on respect for human dignity and the peaceful resolution of social differences.

Perhaps a more important truth lies in President Kennedy's statement as read the other way around: "Isn't human rights, in the last analysis, basically a matter of peace?" It is a cliché, but no less valid, to say that human rights and dignity are frequently among the first casualties of war or even the threat of war. Indeed, some of the most dramatic issues of current international human rights concern arise out of the extreme denials of human rights experienced by the civilian victims of present armed conflicts in Asia, the Near East, and Africa. No single development would be more important in creating an environment favorable to human rights than the establishment of a stable and general peace.

2.   DO HUMAN RIGHTS DENIALS TEND TO SPREAD?

If denials of human rights in one country are in some sense contagious and tend to induce similar denials in other countries, freer societies have an obvious interest in taking steps to eradicate the source of infection. But there seems little solid evidence to support such a theory or to explain just how it would work. Of course, if it is true that repressive regimes are more aggressive and expansionist, they may spread their repression through conquest or internal subversion. More subtly, the constant threat of aggression by a totalitarian regime may tempt more liberal governments to adopt increasingly totalitarian controls over their own people as a more efficient means of organizing for defense. The pressures toward a garrison state are very real in such circumstances. Perhaps the mere existence of repressive regimes abroad may encourage adoption of similar repressive measures by domestic elites, particularly if the foreign system has had economic or foreign policy successes. History suggests, however, that any contamination probably tends to run the other way, from more free to less free societies — that it is human rights ideas that typically pose the threat to maintenance of repressive societies rather than the other way around.

3. CAN HUMAN RIGHTS DENIALS HAVE AN ECONOMIC IMPACT
    ON OTHER COUNTRIES?

There has been a traditional fear that slave labor or analogous labor market conditions in foreign countries might permit the production of goods or services for export at prices which seriously threaten or destroy domestic industries in other countries, thus affecting their local wages, prices, and labor conditions. One can argue that a greater recognition of human rights, by increasing labor costs, encourages greater use of machinery, and that it is the substitution of machinery for human labor that has the principal impact on lowering costs of production. But, in any case, it is worth noting that the most widely supported, successful, and sophisticated international human rights programs have involved the International Labor Organization and its efforts to promote international labor standards.

4. ARE MORAL AND HUMANITARIAN CONSIDERATIONS
    SUFFICIENT REASONS FOR CONCERN?

The difficulties in constructing a wholly satisfying selfish rationale for major national commitments to promote the human rights of foreigners seem apparent. In the last analysis we may be driven back to more emotional reasons. Perhaps governments should be concerned with expression, human misery, and denials of human rights in other countries simply because these are wrong. Perhaps any civilized society has an obligation to recognize man's common humanity and its own responsibility to promote dignity everywhere, even at some cost to itself. Perhaps we must accept that the practical rewards for such efforts will be intangible — the improved quality of life and satisfaction from living in a world where men are generally more free and the morning's newspapers less depressing.

But if these are the best reasons that can be given for national concern with international human rights issues, we must recognize the implications. Officials are rarely moved by such intangible considerations. They feel called upon to justify their actions and decisions by more practical criteria which are closely related to immediate and obvious interests of the state. If national dividends from the international promotion of human rights are so indirect and speculative, one cannot expect officials to give them high priority or consider them worth substantial policy risks. . . .

Comments and Questions

1. Bilder, a quarter of a century ago, took a rather gloomy view of the prospects of human rights efforts, largely because he failed to find a "selfish rationale for major national commitments" in the area. Would he be able to find one more, or less, easily today? How necessary do you think such a self-interest component really is to activate a state's human rights concerns? Specifically, how direct and immediate must the payoffs be before a state will take action to attempt to improve human rights conditions in another state? In considering your response, take into account the views and positions of the U.S. government and body politic in regard to events in the former Yugoslavia, Somalia, Haiti, and Rwanda.

2. Even if states fail to make the human rights efforts he obviously believes they should, Bilder offers some consolation by suggesting that over the long run the "contamination probably tends to run . . . from more free to less free societies. . . ." The coming down of the Berlin Wall, the coming apart of the Soviet Union, and the momentous changes that have taken place not only in Eastern Europe, but also in numerous other areas (Southern Africa being a prime example) all seem to bear out this proposition. Or do they?

3. Bilder, who suggests that "national dividends from the international promotion of human rights are . . . indirect and speculative," concludes that such being the case "one cannot expect officials to give them high priority or consider them worth substantial policy risks. . . ." Assuming this view accurately described the foreign policy establishment a quarter of a century ago, is it still true today? Do the initiatives taken during the Carter Administration and, at least to an extent, now built into the foreign policy process not require some reassessment of this view? If so, to what extent? Has any President, from Carter to Bill Clinton, ever advanced "convincing reasons" to persuade U.S. government officials and the body politic that "peoples and governments . . . have [a] stake in international human rights"? If so, when? If not, why?

4. For an excellent collection of articles by Professors Bilder, Buergenthal, Farer, Henkin, and other contributors on the extent to which the United States took into account human rights considerations in foreign policy decision-making up to 1974, see Symposium, 14 Va. J. Intl. L. 591-701 (1974). For an assessment by these and other authors of the significant

developments that took place in the subsequent 14 years, see Symposium on Human Rights: An Agenda for the New Administration, 28 Va. J. Intl. L. 827-917 (1988). More recent developments are considered in Problem XIII.

VII. Final Comments and Questions

1. Although General Amin had assured the United Nations that Uganda would not take the property of the expelled Asians, the Declarations of Assets (Non-Citizen Asians) Decree, 1972, had just that effect. See pages 22-24 supra. Thus, after they were safely out of the country, the Asians were faced with the problem of obtaining compensation for their property losses. While international law requires a state to pay just compensation for the taking of an alien's property, Restatement (Third) of the Foreign Relations Law of the United States §712(1)(c)(1987), it affords the alien himself no direct remedy on the international level. Rather, it requires him to seek redress indirectly by convincing his state to "espouse" his claim against the taking state. Stateless persons — persons without a nationality — are left without even this often ineffective remedy. Id. §713, comment d at 218. See P. Jessup, A Modern Law of Nations, 69, 100 (1948). So, too, are nationals of the state taking the property, who obviously cannot obtain espousal by their state of claims against itself. Thus, most persons of Asian descent who had opted for Ugandan nationality but nevertheless were expelled by General Amin still await compensation or the return of their properties. See Perez, The Land Amin Seized Now Preoccupies Uganda, N.Y. Times, June 12, 1990, at A4, cols. 3-6; Lorch, A Bittersweet Homecoming in Uganda, Intl. Herald-Tribune, Mar. 23, 1993, at 1, cols. 4-6.

Those Asians expelled from Uganda with Indian nationality, however, have received some compensation under a January 1976 lump-sum agreement, which saw Uganda pay India $1,627,115 in settlement of the claims of its citizens. G. Goodwin-Gill, International Law and the Movement of Persons Between States 216 n.1 (1978). On the other hand, Asian expellees with British nationality have been less fortunate. The British government, having broken diplomatic relations with Amin's regime, was unable to achieve such a settlement. Moreover, after Amin's ouster and the passage by Uganda of the Expropriated Properties Act, 1982, the British government has taken the position that remedies under this legislation must be exhausted (and prove ineffective) before it can espouse such claims. Letter to the Editor from Lord Belstead, Minister of State, Foreign and Commonwealth Office, The Economist, May 7, 1983, at 6, cols. 1-2. See Dowden, Uganda Asians Seek Fair Compensation, The Times (London), Apr. 5, 1983, at 4, cols. 7-8. Although no compensation had been paid to the expellees, a lawsuit brought to compel the British government to espouse their claims was dismissed. R. v. Secretary of State for Foreign and Commonwealth Affairs, ex parte Pirbai, The Times (London), Oct. 17, 1985, at 4, cols. 6-8 (C.A. Oct. 15, 1985). The Court of Appeal's reasoning is criticized by F. Mann in Foreign Affairs in English Courts 20-21 (1986).

Surprisingly, the Asians who were stateless persons and, hence, without a government to espouse their claims have fared better than their British counterparts. In an innovative development, the UN High Commissioner for Refugees took up their claims and secured the agreement of the Ugandan government to be "the channel for claims lodged by Asians of undetermined nationality who had left Uganda." Report of the High Commissioner for Refugees, 29 U.N. GAOR Supp. (No. 12A) at 9, U.N. Doc. A/9612/Add. 1 (1974). Eventually, 2,360 claims were registered with the High Commissioner, of which over 1,700 were submitted to Uganda and 959 accepted by it as qualifying for some measure of compensation. Report of the High Commissioner for Refugees, 32 U.N. GAOR Supp. (No. 12) at 15, U.N. Doc. A/32/12 (1977); Report of the High Commissioner for Refugees, 33 U.N. GAOR Supp. (No. 12) at 16, U.N. Doc. A/33/12 (1978). In August 1977, Uganda and the High Commissioner concluded a lump-sum agreement settling the claims for $4,868,416, of which $662,181 was paid immediately and the balance of which was to be paid, also in convertible currency, by semi-annual installments without interest over a 10-year period. Id. See G. Goodwin-Gill, supra. Thus, the stateless Asians, unlike Asians who held British passports, have received some compensation, albeit inadequate and delayed, for their property losses.

2. Recall that, after deciding not to send a telegram to General Amin in August 1972, the UN Sub-Commission adopted a resolution recommending that the Commission on Human Rights study the problem of the application of international human rights instruments to "individuals who are not citizens of the country in which they live," i.e., aliens, including both foreign nationals and stateless persons. See pages 28-29 supra. The Commission, in turn, requested its parent body, the Economic and Social Council, to return the matter to the Sub-Commission for further study. In 1974 the latter appointed one of its members, Baroness Elles of Great Britain, as Special Rapporteur, with the task of preparing a report on the applicability of existing international human rights instruments to "non-citizens."

After submitting several preliminary reports, the Special Rapporteur completed her study in 1980. Elles, International Provisions Protecting the Human Rights of Non-Citizens, U.N. Doc. E/CN.4/Sub.2/392/Rev. 1 (1980). See R. Lillich, The Human Rights of Aliens in Contemporary International Law 51-56 (1984). Attached to it was a Draft Declaration on the Human Rights of Individuals Who Are Not Citizens of the Country in Which They Live. Id. at 127-130. Several years and some revisions later, the UN General Assembly approved the Declaration by consensus on 13 December 1985. G.A. Res. 40/144, 40 U.N. GAOR Supp. (No. 53) at 252, U.N. Doc. A/40/53 (1985).

Although the Declaration has received little scholarly attention, it is well worth careful examination and can be selectively used by international human rights lawyers. For present purposes Article 7 is particularly relevant:

> An alien lawfully in the territory of a State may be expelled therefrom only in pursuance of a decision reached in accordance with law and shall, except where compelling reasons of national security otherwise require, be allowed to submit the reasons why he or she should not be expelled and to have the case reviewed by, and be represented for the purpose before, the competent authority or a person or persons specifically designated by the competent authority. Individual or collective expulsion of such aliens on grounds of race, colour, religion, culture, descent or national or ethnic origin is prohibited.

See also Article 9: "[n]o alien shall be arbitrarily deprived of his or her lawfully acquired assets."

Consider the relevance of the above articles to the expulsion of Asians from Uganda. Do they presently constitute international legal obligations binding upon states? If so, to what extent and under what theory? See generally Problem IV.

3. The refusal of the United Nations, the Organization for African Unity (OAU), and most African states to condemn Uganda's expulsion of its Asian population certainly did nothing to discourage General Amin from his subsequent gross violations of the human rights of Ugandan citizens between 1972 and 1979. Moreover, it also sent a signal to other African states that the international community would tolerate, if not condone, the massive expulsion of aliens. Thus, when Nigeria brutally expelled thousands of Ghanaian migrant workers in early 1983, Ghana itself registered only feeble protests, the United Nations did not debate the matter, and not even one law review article on the expulsion appeared. Consider the following remarks by a speaker at the 78th Annual Meeting of the American Society of International Law (1984 Am. Socy. Intl. L. Proceedings 358).

> I am quite depressed by the lack of any attention in the United Nations, or so far in the scholarly community, with respect to the expulsion of Ghanaian workers by Nigeria last year. When Idi Amin expelled Ugandan Asians in 1972, his action resulted in a major crisis in the United Nations, many published articles and, in effect, a restudy of the norms of expulsion. When the Ghanaians were expelled under conditions equally if not more savage than the Asians from Uganda, there was not a ripple in the United Nations. The only U.N. document I have found which discusses this refers to the Ghanaians as "returnees." I think this particular topic and the U.N. attitude toward it deserve far greater consideration.

Consider also the following more acerbic comments on the Nigerian expulsions (Letter to the Editor from David Nathan, The Times (London), Feb. 4, 1983, at 13, col. 3).

Deathly Silence on Nigeria

From Mr. David Nathan

Sir, the voice of the liberal conscience is suddenly silent and protest is mute. Two million people are being peremptorily thrown out of Nigeria to the accompaniment of such racial commentary as that they were largely responsible for crime (in a population of 80 million) and were the main frequenters of brothels.

Kevin Livingstone has not invited even one of the two million to come to London to explain his dire situation, and Dundee has not twinned with Accra as a gesture of protest against the oppressors.

The Foreign Office has not issued a measured condemnation and Mrs. Thatcher has not been asked by Mr. Andrew Faulds to find time during her day to admonish the Nigerian High Commissioner. The EEC Council of Foreign Ministers has not intervened and the United Nations has not even scheduled the event for debate.

The Soviet Union, the revolutionary parties of the left, even, for that matter, the European Communists, have not condemned the action of the Nigerian Government, and neither the Red Brigades nor any other terrorist group has killed anybody in a fit of righteous indignation on behalf of the victims.

There are no graffiti on the walls and no demonstrations in the streets and the churches, here and in Rome, are as quiet as they were over the Chatila and Sabra massacres carried out by their fellow Christians.

Home Office immigration officials who have been called inhuman fascists for seeking to deport one illegal immigrant [from] this country; supporters of Israel who have endured thousands of words of condemnation over Israel's actions in the West Bank (which it is not the purpose of this letter to defend) and, above all, the two million people who are suffering hardship and are in danger of much worse, are entitled to ask why there is such a deathly silence.

Is it Nigerian oil? Is it the international left-wing consensus that only white states are racist? Or is there a deep-rooted racism in the more vociferous of the anti-racists that causes them to keep silent because they expect no better of Africans? Where, for that matter, are the voices of the other African governments?

Yours faithfully,

David Nathan
20 The Mount,
Wembley Park, Middlesex
February 2.

Assuming that there were good and sufficient grounds to protest Nigeria's expulsion of the Ghanaians, why was no action taken? Were the reasons behind the failure to protest legal or, as the above letter suggests, political, economic, or even racist? With respect to the United Nations, how can one reconcile its "deathly silence" in 1983 with its adoption two years later of the Elles Declaration (see pages 84-85 supra)? Does its second failure in 12 years to condemn a flagrant mass expulsion weaken the argument that the human rights clauses of the UN Charter constitute legal obligations binding upon states? If not, why not?

4. Unhappily, human rights violations in Uganda did not cease with the departure of General Amin and the subsequent return of Dr. Obote. The following letter, written by a former U.S. Ambassador, describes the dilemma that continued to face the United States and the United Nations (Letter to the Editor from Thomas Patrick Melady, N.Y. Times, Aug. 25, 1984, at 22, cols. 1-3).

Saving a People from Its Leaders

To the Editor:

Your Aug. 11 editorial "What Uganda's Flag Is Hiding" raises some disturbing and complex issues, which I know from personal experiences. When I reported to Kampala in June 1972 as the U.S. Ambassador, Idi Amin was classified as one of the many dictators in the world. Within a few months I knew that he was a murderous tyrant and so advised Washington.

But the dilemma that is true today was true then. When the butchery is only against the country's people, what does an external sovereign power do?

While the torture and killings in Uganda were horrendous under the dictatorship of Amin and while the present ruler, Dr. Obote, is no villainous tyrant, he seems unable to curb the massacres now going on. Despite this, any unilateral interference by any power would be ill advised; it would only cause greater problems.

But as a major power, we should say what is fact, and we can consequently be indebted to the U.S. Department of State for reporting these conditions in Uganda.

The one body empowered by its charter to assure the noble mission of intervening to save a people from its own tyrannical government is the United Nations. The tragedy is that in the past decade there have been several cases where that body could have taken action as the conscience of the world but did not.

World opinion about the efficacy of the United Nations is at an all-time low. Instead of useless debate, where several nations are the constant victims of selective outrage in U.N. resolutions, the U.N. should look for ways to improve its ability to take some kind of action in these obvious cases of human suffering, as in Uganda today. This would be good for the people suffering in these areas. It would also help restore the United Nations to the higher level of respect it once had.

Thomas Patrick Melady
Fairfield, Conn.
Aug. 13, 1984.

The writer is president of Sacred Heart University.

5. Although many problems remain, the National Resistance Army (NRA) that took power in Uganda in 1986, led by current President Yoweri Museveni, has sought to end the ethnic and regional hostilities that have troubled the country since its independence. Currently commissions of inquiry are conducting investigations of human rights violations committed not only by the Amin and Obote regimes, but also by the NRA itself. Nevertheless, human rights violations continue to occur with alarming regularity, albeit at a much lower level than during Amin's regime. See Report of the Committee on International Human Rights of the Association of the Bar of the City of New York, Uganda at the Crossroads: A Report on Current Human Rights Conditions, 46 The Record 598 (1991); Amnesty International, 1994 Ann. Rep. 299 (1994); U.S. Department of State, Country Reports on Human Rights Practices for 1993, at 308 (1994). There have, however, been some substantial improvements, and free elections leading to the adoption of a new constitution have been scheduled for late 1994. The latter will include an entire chapter on "Fundamental Human Rights and Freedoms." Thus, one hopes that better days are ahead for the former "Pearl of Africa."

Problem II

Fujii, Filartiga, and Beyond

Are States' Courts Bound by the Human Rights Clauses of the UN Charter and the Universal Declaration of Human Rights?

I. Introduction: The Relationship Between International and Domestic
    Legal Systems   92
II. The Status of the Human Rights Clauses in Domestic Law   95
    A. The Legal Background   95
            Schachter, The Charter and the Constitution: The Human
            Rights Provisions in American Law   95
    B. The *Fujii* Case   101
            Note: Mr. Sei Fujii and the California Alien Land Law   101
            Sei Fujii v. State (California District Court of Appeal)   102
            Hudson, Charter Provisions on Human Rights in American Law   104
            Wright, National Courts and Human Rights — The *Fujii* Case   108
            Note: An Unusual Occurrence in the Course of the *Fujii* Appeal   114
            Sei Fujii v. State (California Supreme Court)   115
            Comments and Questions   118
    C. The Post-*Fujii* Scene: Regrets and Hopes   121
            1. The Present Status of the UN Charter's Human Rights
               Clauses   121
            2. Flashforward: Are Other Human Rights Treaties Self-Executing
               or Not?   121
III. The Status of the Universal Declaration in Domestic Law   122
    A. The Historical Perspective   122
            Kunz, The United Nations Declaration of Human Rights   122
            Schwelb, The Influence of the Universal Declaration of Human
               Rights on International and National Law   127
            The Universal Declaration of Human Rights at 20   132
    B. U.S. Case Law Developments   133
            Setting the Stage   133
            Filartiga v. Pena-Irala   137
            Fernandez v. Wilkinson   143
            Forti, v. Suarez-Mason   148
            Comments and Questions   154

    C.   The Universal Declaration of Human Rights Nears 50   162
           Restatement (Third) of the Foreign Relations Law of the United
              States §702   162
           Lillich, Remarks   162
           International Law Association, Committee on the Enforcement
              of Human Rights Law, Final Report on the Status of
              the Universal Declaration of Human Rights in National and
              International Law   166
IV.   *Final Comments and Questions*   *171*

I.   Introduction: The Relationship Between International and Domestic Legal Systems

Problem I considered the issue of whether or not the human rights clauses of the UN Charter are binding international obligations upon member states. Assuming that the answer to that question is affirmative, there still remains the important issue of whether, and to what extent, the courts and other tribunals of such states are bound to give effect domestically to such obligations. This issue is the subject of Problem II.

To help understand the difficulties of incorporating international obligations within the framework of domestic law, it is useful to review the basic distinctions between international and domestic law. Traditionally, the two systems were quite separate: the international legal system was a law of nations, that is, concerned only with the rights and duties of states, not of individuals; each of the various domestic legal systems, therefore, remained completely free to regulate the lives of its own citizens. See 1 L. Oppenheim, International Law: A Treatise 362-369 (2d ed. 1912).

Furthermore, while domestic legal systems were and generally still are organized in a hierarchical fashion, with laws flowing from a constitution and being laid down by court decisions, statutes, decrees, and administrative regulations, in the international community there exists no sovereign body whose law-making or conflict-resolving authority is accepted universally. The UN may have the functional capacity to fulfill these roles — indeed, the second of these functions, conflict resolution through its political organs or its principal judicial organ, the International Court of Justice, is one reason for its very existence — but the UN is not a sovereign body in the sense that nation states are. Its decisions, generally expressed in the form of resolutions, derive their legal force more from the voluntary consensus of member states than from any sense of legal obligation under the Charter. (But see the legal effects of Security Council resolutions under Article 25, considered in Problem VII.)

What are the sources, then, of international law? Much ink has been spilled on this subject. A brief though hardy dispositive answer can be found in Article 38 of the Statute of the International Court of Justice, which sets down three major and two subsidiary sources of international law. The three major sources are (1) "international conventions" (that is, treaties, which in domestic law terms are more analogous to contracts than to statutes, since adherence is voluntary rather than compulsory); (2) "international custom, as evidence of a general practice accepted as law"; and (3) "the general principles of law recognized by civilized nations." These last two concepts may be distinguished by the fact that, while "international custom" (commonly called customary international law) evolves from the actual day-to-day practice of states, "general principles" embraces the principles of private law administered in domestic courts where such principles are applicable to international relations. See J. Brierly, The Law of Nations 57-63 (6th ed. H. Waldock ed. 1963). Finally, according to Article 38, subsidiary sources of international law are "judicial decisions and the teachings of the most highly qualified publicists of the various nations." For U.S. attitudes toward the sources of international law, see Restatement (Third) of the Foreign Relations Law of the United States §102 (1987).

With respect to content as opposed to sources, it is convenient to classify international law norms into two groups: the written and the unwritten. The latter category, which resembles the unwritten common law of the Anglo-American legal tradition, consists of the customary rules and general principles mentioned above. Together these concepts comprise customary international law. Written rules, known as conventional international law, consist of treaties, conventions, and other international agreements, including, of course, the UN Charter. An important distinction between these two categories is that customary international law is binding upon all states, even though its content is uncodified and, therefore, often is more difficult to ascertain. Treaties, however, bind only those states that choose to adhere to them.

One exception to this last statement, considered in this Problem, arises when a given treaty either restates or incorporates a rule of customary international law. In such a case, the treaty may be said to bind even those states that do not ratify or accede to it. A more accurate way of stating the point, however, would be to say that non-signatory states are bound not by the treaty itself, but rather by the underlying customary international law rule that the treaty restates or embodies. Additionally, it has been argued that certain treaties are normative in character, in that over a period of time they may create, as opposed to restate, rules of customary international law, which then bind non-signatory states.

The distinctions between the international legal system and domestic legal systems have important ramifications. Since the two types of systems are relatively separate, it is possible for a state's actions to contravene international law while at the same time conforming with its own domestic law. Therefore, if a state violates an obligation to which it freely had committed itself by treaty — for example, not to permit racial discrimination — its citizens may be unable to challenge such violations under international law in its domestic courts. The state's domestic law generally will hold that the treaty obligation runs only to other states' parties to the agreement, not to the state's own citizens. Alternatively, it may provide that the state's domestic law simply prevails over the treaty obligation in case of conflict. Individual citizens, thus, remain only the objects, not the subjects, of international law, even when the subject matter of the treaty is of great concern to them. They have only those rights that their domestic legal system accords them. That this traditional view of the relationship between international law and domestic law still holds sway in the United States was illustrated graphically by the case of Committee of U.S. Citizens in Nicaragua v. Reagan, 859 F.2d 929, 935-939 (D.C. Cir. 1988).

The extent to which the traditional view subordinates both conventional and customary international law to domestic legal norms remains a significant problem in the field of international human rights. Jurisprudentially, it conflicts with the major purpose of the post-World War II international human rights movement, namely, to establish that the individual is, at least to some extent, a subject of international law and the possessor of certain basic human rights that are not dependent for their validity upon citizenship of a particular state.

The first developments in this direction came immediately after World War II, in the wake of the unprecedented human rights violations that had taken place before and during that conflict. The universal outrage and indignation over the barbarism that had occurred was institutionalized in the UN Charter clauses concerning human rights. It is interesting to note that the Charter itself begins with words of solidarity and conviction: "We the peoples of the United Nations. . . ."

A next important step in the recognition of specific human rights by the international legal system came on 10 December 1948 with the adoption by the UN General Assembly of Resolution 217A, the Universal Declaration of Human Rights (see the Documentary Supplement), with its stress on "the inherent dignity and . . . the equal and inalienable rights of all members of the human family. . . ." The great, and ever increasing, importance of the Universal Declaration lay in its extensive list of particular human rights to which every person in the world is entitled. Whatever the precise legal status of the Universal Declaration (a question to be considered below), it is clear that its adoption was a seminal event in the history of international human rights law.

Important as both the above developments were on the international plane, their potential domestic impact was of equal significance "in promoting and encouraging respect for human rights," a major purpose of the United Nations set out in Article 1(3) of its Charter. The materials in this Problem first consider whether the Charter's human rights clauses, either in and of themselves or through the incorporation of the norms found in the Universal Declaration and other international human rights instruments, constitute or embody rules of decision binding upon domestic courts (for use of the incorporation argument on the international plane, see pages 48-54 of Problem I). This question — essentially one of treaty law — leads logically to the question of whether the Declaration, once again either in and of itself or in conjunction with other international human rights instruments, constitutes or reflects customary international law furnishing rules of decision for domestic courts.

II. The Status of the Human Rights Clauses in Domestic Law

A. The Legal Background

Under the Supremacy Clause of the U.S. Constitution, "all Treaties made or which shall be made, under the Authority of the United States, shall be the supreme Law of the Land; and the judges in every State shall be bound thereby, any Thing in the Constitution or Laws of any State to the contrary Notwithstanding." U.S. Const. art. VI, §2. However, under principles first enunciated by Chief Justice Marshall in Foster v. Nielson, 27 U.S. (2 Pet.) 253, 314 (1829), the status in U.S. law of treaty provisions like the Charter's human rights clauses turns upon whether or not they are considered to be self-executing, since "[i]t is only when a treaty is self-executing, when it prescribes rules by which private rights may be determined, that it may be relied upon for the enforcement of such rights." Dreyfus v. Von Finck, 534 F.2d 24, 30 (2d Cir.), cert. denied, 429 U.S. 835 (1976). The following reading, one of the earliest on the subject and still one of the best, addresses the question of whether or not the human rights clauses of the UN Charter are self-executing.

Schachter, The Charter and the Constitution: The Human Rights Provisions in American Law
4 Vand. L. Rev. 643, 643-659 (1951)

In the courts of the United States, the problem of the effect of treaties on domestic law has been raised in regard to the United Nations Charter itself and in particular with respect to the question of whether the human rights provisions have become, by virtue of the supremacy clause of the constitution, part of the law of the land, directly binding on the courts. It is this problem — one that has divided the courts — that is the subject of the present article. In dealing with it we shall have to consider three controversial issues: (1) when a treaty is self-operative under the constitution; (2) whether the Charter provisions on human rights impose legal obligations on member States; and, (3) whether, granting the obligatory effect of the Charter provisions, they are capable of constituting a rule of law for the courts notwithstanding the absence of the legislative implementation.

WHEN IS A TREATY SELF-EXECUTING?

The Charter is of course the supreme law of the land by virtue of the Constitution; but it does not follow from this that all of its provisions are automatically operative as domestic law. It is obvious that if a treaty provision by its own terms or nature requires subsequent legislation before it can be made effective, then it cannot be "self-executing" — that is, it cannot, by itself, be a rule of law binding upon a court.

While this statement is a truism — one might even say a tautology — it is by no means always clear just when the "terms of nature" of a treaty require legislative action. Courts and commentators sometimes suggest that the test has been laid down in an oft-quoted statement of Chief Justice Marshall in the case of Foster v. Neilson:

> In the United States a different principle is established. Our constitution declares a treaty to be the law of the land. It is, consequently, to be regarded in courts of justice as equivalent to an act of the legislature, whenever it operates of itself without the aid of any legislative provision. But when the terms of the stipulation import a contract, when either of the parties engages to perform a particular act, the treaty addresses itself to the political, not the judicial department; and the legislature must execute the contract before it can become a rule for the Court.

It is, however, evident that this statement does not in itself provide a workable test to determine whether a provision in a treaty requires legislative action. In almost all treaties one of the "parties engages to perform a particular act" but in many of these treaties the particular acts can be performed by judicial or administrative officers without the aid of legislative action. On occasion, a court has construed the Marshall statement to mean that a treaty is not to be considered self-operative if its language is cast in the future tense. But to take "futurity of language" as the test makes little sense since the future tense is often used in treaties when they are intended to operate in the future and it in no way indicates that legislation is necessary. The Supreme Court certainly does not consider either the use of future language or the agreement of a party to perform a particular act as an indication that a treaty is not self-executing.

An examination of the cases reveals that there are only two clear situations where a treaty provision requires legislative action before it can become effective: (1) where the treaty has an explicit provision to this effect and (2) where the power to deal with the subject of the treaty is vested solely in the legislature, as for example a provision calling for criminal penalties or requiring a direct appropriation of money. Outside of these two categories it does not seem possible to generalize regarding the kind of treaties which require legislative implementation; each case must be examined on its own merits in order to determine whether the treaty provision may become presently effective without awaiting further legislation.

In the case of the human rights provisions of the Charter this involves two principle questions. First, do the Charter provisions impose upon Members a legal obligation with respect to the observance of human rights? Obviously, if the provisions of the Charter express general principles or purposes rather than legal norms, they cannot, by their own terms, be considered as part of domestic law. Second, even if the provisions impose legal obligations, are these obligations capable of execution by the courts without further action by the legislature? In particular, are they sufficiently clear and definite to constitute a rule of law which can be given practical effect by the courts in specific cases?

Do the Human Rights Provisions Involve Legal Obligations on the Part of Member States?

[This portion of the article appears in Problem I, at pages 41-45 supra.]

Is the Legal Obligation Regarding Human Rights a Rule for the Courts?

Having ascertained that Article 56 imposes a legal duty on Member States in regard to human rights, we must consider whether that obligation may under the Constitution be a direct source of law for the courts, notwithstanding the absence of legislative implementation. In Chief Justice Marshall's language the question would be whether the pledge in Article 56 addressed itself solely to the "political, not to the judicial department" and whether "the legislature must execute the contract before it can become a rule for the court."

This question is primarily one of domestic law, since in the absence of any contrary provision in the treaty it is left to the parties to carry out their obligations in accordance with their own constitutional processes. From the standpoint of international law all parties are equally bound by the treaties although their constitutional systems may in some cases provide for self-operative effect of the obligations, in other cases for legislative or executive action. In the United States, the question of whether legislative enactment is necessary in order to make a treaty provision effective in domestic law is in the final analysis left to the courts to determine. As Hyde has stated, "whether a domestic court whose aid is invoked for the purpose of invoking a treaty should conclude that in the circumstances it must await the enactment of a law purporting to render judicially operative what has been agreed upon, is a matter that calls for a judicial conclusion touching both the design and fundamental laws of its own sovereign."

The foregoing observations also suggest why it is not possible to find in the history of the preparation of the Charter evidence regarding the "intent" of the parties in regard to the self-operative effect of Article 56. For it was clear to the representatives at San Francisco that the methods and procedures for carrying out the Charter obligations in municipal law had to be left to the varying constitutional systems of Member States. There is therefore no point in seeking or attempting to postulate a specific legislative intent on the question of whether Article 56 was or was not to be automatically operative in municipal law.

Similarly, no inferences regarding this question can reasonably be drawn from the circumstances that some governments at San Francisco contemplated implementation of the human rights provisions through an international bill of rights which would constitute a new multilateral convention. The fact that it was considered desirable by delegations to have a more detailed and precise statement of human rights in the future possibly with enforcement provisions, surely does not indicate any intention to detract from the present legal effect of the carefully worded obligation in Article 56. One might note in this connection that Articles 104 and 105 of the Charter have been held to have self-executing effect in American law, even though it was contemplated by the draftsmen of the Charter (and, indeed, by Article 105 itself) that there would be a separate convention setting out in greater detail the provisions on privileges and immunities. *

As there is no explicit provision in the Charter itself, or any evidence of legislative intent, which would deprive Article 56 of self-operative effect, we are left with the question of whether the obligation is by its "nature" capable of execution by the courts. For it has been asserted that the pledge to take action to promote respect for and observation of human rights is too vague and indefinite to enable a court to give it practical effect in a concrete situation; and, hence, that legislative measures are required in order that the obligation might have the degree of precision and clarity necessary for judicial action.

This point requires careful consideration. It is, of course, true that the supremacy clause of the Constitution does not compel a court to enforce a treaty provision which is so incomplete or indefinite that it cannot be applied in a particular case. It must also be granted that the meaning of human rights and fundamental freedoms is in many respects a subject of

---

* Such a convention actually exists. See Convention on the Privileges and Immunities of the United Nations, Feb. 13, 1946, 21 U.S.T. 1418, T.I.A.S. No. 6900, 1 U.N.T.S. 15 (entered into force for U.S. Apr. 29, 1970). — Eds.

controversy and that even where a particular right has been generally agreed upon, it is by no means clear just how far a court may go to promote its observance.

These are certainly important considerations in determining the extent to which the Charter obligation may be deemed self-operative; but it does not follow from them that there are no cases at all in which the courts may give effect to this obligation. There is, in the first place, no ground for assuming that because "human rights and fundamental freedoms" are broad and elastic concepts, American courts are for that reason unable to apply them in the absence of legislative definition. These concepts, as we have shown above, do have specific content based on the Charter itself and on precedent and practice; the important and recognized rights and freedoms are no vaguer than any number of well-known constitutional and statutory expressions which have been left to the courts to apply. Probably even more pertinent is the fact that the concepts of human rights and fundamental freedoms are closely akin to the basic rights and freedoms which American courts have traditionally been required to define, in varying circumstances, for the purpose of determining the scope of constitutional protection.

Moreover, it should be borne in mind that the supremacy clause of the constitution does not require an "all or nothing" position in regard to the self-executory effect of a treaty provision. It may well be that the obligation regarding human rights must, for the most part, be acted on by the legislature before it can become a rule for the courts, but this surely does not mean that the courts cannot act in those cases which involve a specific and clearly recognized right or freedom. Similarly, the supremacy clause is not rendered nugatory because the treaty provision does not specify the type of action which the courts may take in carrying out the obligation. Admittedly, the courts do not have *carte blanche* in regard to enforcement or judicial remedies, but again, this does not mean that a court would be entitled to ignore completely the duty to act so as to promote respect for and observance of human rights. One illustration of practical judicial action can be found in the cases involving the Alien Land Law of California[, notably the case of Sei Fujii v. State, which appears at pages 102-104 infra]. In these cases the statute denying persons the right to own land because of race was held to be inconsistent with the pledge undertaken in the Charter; it obviously followed that, under the supremacy clause, the statute would have to yield to the treaty and hence be declared invalid. Another compelling example would be presented where a court is requested to enforce a private agreement which it clearly considers contrary to recognized rights and freedoms; in that case, the Charter provision would reasonably include the duty to withhold the judicial action requested. (It need hardly be argued at this late date — although the error persists in some state court decisions — that a treaty, like a law, is binding on individual citizens and determinative of contractual rights.) Finally, it should be observed that even where there may be doubts or difficulties regarding the precise manner of judicial implementation in a particular case, the courts would be bound at least to consider the human rights commitment as an ingredient in the public policy of the United States in the same way as the laws and applicable legal precedents, and to the extent appropriate, give such policy judicial effect.

For these various reasons, all well supported by judicial precedent, it would be most difficult to conclude that the Charter provisions on human rights cannot legitimately be given effect by the courts in appropriate cases. Indeed, it would be contrary to the letter and the spirit of the supremacy clause of the Constitution if the courts did not attempt to carry out a treaty provision to the fullest extent possible. Nor would it be in consonance with the established principles of interpretation in the United States for a court to rely on the ambiguity of a treaty provision in order to restrict its application. "If a treaty fairly admits of two constructions, one restricting rights which may be claimed under it, and the other enlarging it, a more liberal construction is to be preferred." This rule, it has been observed, is but another form of the general principle long recognized by American courts that treaties are to be construed so as to be more effective rather than less effective.

The constitutional principles and precedents relating to treaties — which have been set forth above — have a special relevance to the human rights provision[s] in the light of the position taken by the United States delegation at San Francisco and before the United States Congress. For, at that time it was made clear that in the view of the United States the pledge on human rights is to be carried out by the Member States "according to their own best ability, in their own way, and in accordance with their own political and economic institutions and processes." In the case of the United States "its own way" has been defined, as it must be, by the Constitution itself and the interpretations of the Supreme Court; and these, as we have seen, indicate that the obligations of the Charter regarding human rights should properly be carried out in certain respects by the courts in the same way as any other treaty which is the supreme law of the land.

Would the practical consequences of such judicial action be "revolutionary" or even "far-reaching" in their impact on domestic law? There appears to be little basis for so extreme a prediction. American courts are not likely to conclude that the Charter concepts of human rights and fundamental freedoms in their generally accepted meaning differ substantially from the basic rights and freedoms embodied in the United States constitution; nor are the courts likely to be unmindful of the necessity of judicial restraint in applying the broad concepts of the Charter. The cases which have thus far arisen would seem to bear this out.

But while such judicial action may not be "far-reaching" in its effect on domestic law, it must not, on the other hand, be considered as without significance. It would be unrealistic to ignore the influence — already evidenced in several cases — of the Charter as a factor in resolving constitutional issues which have hitherto been in doubt. Only rarely in our view will a court's decision be based on the Charter alone, as in the *Fujii* case; more often it might be expected that the Charter provision will be cited as an added reason for extending constitutional liberties; in other constitutional cases there may be only a general reference to treaties as a source of public policy though in fact it would be likely that the Charter provision is the important new element in the situation. Nor will the influence of such decisions be limited to the judicial field alone. By affirming the legal effectiveness of the Charter provision, the courts focus attention on the authoritative character of the obligation undertaken by the United States and on the necessity for its fulfillment; in this sense, they contribute not only to better understanding but also to efforts for implementation which extend beyond the scope of the judiciary.

There are other implications of judicial action, less tangible perhaps, but which it would be myopic to overlook. Much has been said — with obvious justification — regarding the practical importance in present-day international relations of our observance of human rights; at least equally evident has been the importance to ourselves of narrowing the gap between democratic ideals and actual practice. In both respects, the courts can play a significant role; when they act to carry out the human rights provisions of the Charter they necessarily do so in specific cases which have a direct impact on individuals; for that very reason they demonstrate more forcefully than any verbal generality or law-on-the-books ever can that practical effect is being given to the principles we have proclaimed. Moreover, there is an added degree of cogency in the fact that the Charter and not the Constitution alone, is being applied; for that shows that the United States is effectively carrying out its external obligations and particularly that obligation which more than any other involves a limitation of traditional rights of sovereignty.

For these reasons, the decisions which recognize the Charter provisions on human rights as self-executing — though probably modest in their actual effect on American law — have more than slight significance in regard to the crucial problems of our time.

B. The Fujii Case

Note: Mr. Sei Fujii and the California Alien Land Law

The California Alien Property Initiative Act of 1920 (better known as the Alien Land Law) had a long and infamous life. Enacted in the xenophobic atmosphere that prevailed in the United States after World War I, the Alien Land Law distinguished the right to own real property based on class of alienage: aliens who were eligible for U.S. citizenship were permitted to hold title to real property; aliens ineligible for citizenship (principally Chinese and Japanese, although not specifically designated by the statute) were not permitted to own land. Land acquired by those aliens escheated to the state.

The Alien Land Law made a second distinction of historic interest. If an alien purchased land with consideration supplied by another alien, the law would make different presumptions about the nature of the transaction depending upon whether the alien supplying the consideration was eligible for citizenship (and hence eligible to own land). If he was not eligible, the law presumed that the transaction was made with the intention to circumvent the substantive policy behind the statute by setting up an alien eligible to own land as a mere cover for de facto ownership by the ineligible alien. The burden of proof was placed on the party who took title to the land to show that the conveyance was not made simply to avoid the escheat penalty.

The U.S. Supreme Court struck down this second distinction, in Oyama v. California, 332 U.S. 633 (1948), as being violative of the equal protection clause of the Fourteenth Amendment. Two points are noteworthy about this decision. First, four of the nine justices ventured the opinion that the provision violated not only the Fourteenth Amendment, but also the United States' obligations under the UN Charter. The second point that should be remembered is that the decision was cast very narrowly; the substantive policy behind the statute — the disqualification of certain aliens from owning land — was not struck down.

Such was the status of the California Alien Land Law at the time that Mr. Sei Fujii entered the drama. Mr. Fujii, who was not eligible for U.S. citizenship under the prevailing federal naturalization laws, purchased and acquired some real property in 1948. He then made use of a provision of California law that entitled him to apply to the District Court of Los Angeles County (where the land was situated) for a determination of whether or not an escheat had occurred under the Alien Land Law. The court held that it had, whereupon Mr. Fujii appealed that ruling to California's District Court of Appeal. The result, along with commentary both con and pro, was as follows.

Sei Fujii v. State
97 A.C.A. 154, 217 P.2d 481 (1950)

WILSON, J. The sole question on this appeal is the validity and enforceability of the Alien Land Law. . . .

The successive amendments to the naturalization law expanding the class of persons entitled to citizenship and therefore entitled to own land in California, have, by the process of congressional erosion, left only the natives of Japan and an insignificant number of nationals of other countries who remain ineligible to citizenship and hence ineligible under the terms of the statute to own real property.

In the period of thirty years since the Alien Land Law was adopted we have revised our opinions concerning the rights of other peoples. Out of the travail of World War II came the concept of "respect for human rights and for fundamental freedoms for all without distinction as to race, sex, language, or religion" as expressed in the Charter of the United Nations. . . .

The government of the United States has traditionally been the leader in espousing the rights of man and has championed the cause of the smaller and less privileged nations. The war of 1898 was fought in support of an oppressed country. The efforts of our government in this regard reached fruition in the convention of representatives of the nations of the earth at which the Charter of the United Nations was adopted. It was promptly ratified by the Senate of the United States, thereby proclaiming allegiance to its principles and providing precedent and example for other countries. The United States has consistently regarded its treaties with other nations as inviolate.

The Charter has become "the supreme Law of the Land; and the Judges in every State shall be bound thereby, any Thing in the Constitution or Laws of any State to the Contrary notwithstanding." U.S. Const., Art. VI, sec. 2. The position of this country in the family of nations forbids trafficking in innocuous generalities but demands that every State in the Union accept and act upon the Charter according to its plain language and its unmistakable purpose and intent.

Since the Charter is now the supreme law of the land it becomes necessary to examine its provisions and guarantees and to interpret it in the light in which it was adopted by the participating nations. [The Court thereupon discusses, inter alia, Articles 1, 55, and 56 of the Charter.]

On December 10, 1948, the General Assembly of the United Nations passed and proclaimed and called upon all member countries to publicize, disseminate and expound in schools and elsewhere, a "Universal Declaration of Human Rights" affirming among other things that "All human beings are born free and equal in dignity and rights. They . . . should act toward one another in a spirit of brotherhood. [Art. 1.] Everyone is entitled to all the rights and freedoms set forth in this Declaration, without distinction of any kind, such as race, color, sex, language, religion, political or other opinion, national or social origin, property, birth or other status. [Art. 2.] . . . Everyone has the right to own property alone as well as in association with others." [Art. 17.] This Declaration implements and emphasizes the purposes and aims of the United Nations and its Charter.

Democracy provides a way of life that is helpful; however its promises of human betterment are but vain expressions of hope unless ideals of justice and equity are put into practice among governments, and as well between government and citizen, and are held to be paramount. The integrity and vitality of the Charter and the confidence which it inspires would wane and eventually be brought to naught by failure to act according to its announced purposes. Its survival is contingent upon the degree of reverence shown for it by the contracting nations, their governmental subdivisions and their citizens as well.

This nation can be true to its pledge to the other signatories to the Charter only by cooperating in the purposes that are so plainly expressed in it and by removing every obstacle to the fulfillment of such purposes.

A perusal of the Charter renders it manifest that restrictions contained in the Alien Land Law are in direct conflict with the plain terms of the Charter above quoted and with the purposes announced therein by its framers. It is incompatible with Article 17 of the Declaration of Human Rights which proclaims the right of everyone to own property. We have shown that the expansion by the Congress of the classes of nationals eligible to citizenship has correspondingly shrunk the group ineligible under the provisions of the Alien Land Law to own or lease land in California until the latter now consists in reality of a very small number of Japanese. The other Asiatics who still remain on the proscribed list are so few that they need not be considered.

Clearly such a discrimination against a people of one race is contrary both to the letter and to the spirit of the Charter which, as a treaty, is paramount to every law of every state in conflict with it. The Alien Land Law must therefore yield to the treaty as the superior authority. The restrictions of the statute based on eligibility to citizenship, but which ultimately and actually are referable to race or color, must be and are therefore declared untenable and unenforceable.

Judgment reversed with directions to enter a decree in favor of plaintiff in accord with the prayer of his complaint.

Moore, P.J., and McComb, J., concur.

Hudson, Charter Provisions on Human Rights in American Law
44 Am. J. Intl. L. 543, 543-547 (1950)

In Fujii v. California, decided on April 24, 1950, the District Court of Appeal of the second appellate district of California held that the Alien Land Law of California must yield to the Charter of the United Nations as the superior authority, and was therefore unenforceable. As this holding was based upon a misconception of the human rights provisions of the Charter, it seems to call for some comment. . . .

The Human Rights Provisions in the Charter

The Preamble of the United Nations Charter states that "We the peoples of the United Nations" are determined "to reaffirm faith in fundamental human rights." Article 1(3) of the Charter states as one of the purposes of the United Nations:

> To achieve international cooperation in solving international problems of an economic, social, cultural, or humanitarian character, and in promoting and encouraging respect for human rights and for fundamental freedoms for all without distinction as to race, sex, language, or religion; . . .

This statement of a general purpose of the Organization does not impose an obligation on the United States as a Member of the United Nations to take any specific action.

Article 13(1) provides that the General Assembly shall initiate studies and make recommendations for the purpose of

> b. promoting international cooperation in the economic, social, cultural, educational, and health fields, and assisting in the realization of human rights and fundamental freedoms for all without distinction as to race, sex, language, or religion.

This article relates entirely to the powers of the Assembly rather than to obligations of Members, and recommendations by the General Assembly do not have a binding character.

Article 55 provides:

> With a view to the creation of conditions of stability and well-being which are necessary for peaceful and friendly relations among nations based on respect for the principle of equal rights and self-determination of peoples, the United Nations shall promote: . . .
>
> c. universal respect for, and observance of, human rights and fundamental freedoms for all without distinction as to race, sex, language or religion.

This statement of the ends to be "promoted" by the United Nations does not create any specific obligation for a Member of the Organization.

In Article 56, the Members "pledge themselves to take joint and separate action in cooperation with the Organization for the achievement of the purposes set forth in Article 55." The French text, which gives a slightly varied emphasis, provides: "*Les Membres s'engagent, en vue d'atteindre les buts énoncés à l'article 55, à agir, tant conjointement que séparément, en coopération avec l'Organisation.*" The obligation imposed by Article 56 is limited to coöperation with the United Nations. The extent and form of its coöperation are to be determined by the government of each Member. . . .

THE CHARTER PROVISIONS IN AMERICAN LAW

The Constitution of the United States provides in Article 6(2) that treaties made under the authority of the United States shall be "the supreme law of the land; and the judges in every State shall be bound thereby." In consequence, a provision in a treaty may be incorporated in the national law of the United States, so as to supersede inconsistent earlier acts of Congress and inconsistent State legislation (Bacardi Corporation of America v. Domenech (1940), 311 U.S. 150; Clark v. Allen (1947), 331 U.S. 503).

It has long been established, however, that this is true only of self-executing treaty provisions, and that the result does not follow when the treaty provisions merely obligate the United States to take certain action. The classic statement of this principle was made by Chief Justice Marshall many decades ago in Foster v. Neilson (1829), 2 Peters 253, 314, as follows:

> Our Constitution declares a treaty to be the law of the land. It is, conse-quently, to be regarded in Courts of justice as equivalent to an act of the legislature, whenever it operates of itself without the aid of any legislative provision. But when the terms of the stipulation import a contract, when either of the parties engages to perform a particular act, the treaty addresses itself to the political, not the judicial department; and the legislature must execute the contract before it can become a rule for the Court.

Of course a single treaty may contain both kinds of provisions — some which are, and some which are not, self-executing. This view was taken by Chief Justice Stone in Aguilar v. Standard Oil Co. (New Jersey) (1943), 318 U.S. 724, 738.

The Charter is a treaty to which the United States is a party; it is "made under the authority of the United States," within the provision of Article 6(2) of the Constitution. Some of its provisions may have been incorporated into the municipal law of the United States as self-executing provisions; this has been thought to be true, for example, of provisions in Articles 104 and 105 concerning the legal capacity of the Organization and its privileges and immunities (Curran v. City of New York (1947), 77 N.Y.S.(2d), 206, 212).

Clearly, however the Charter's provisions on human rights have not been incorporated into the municipal law of the United States so as to supersede inconsistent State legislation, because they are not self-executing. They state general purposes and create for the United States only obliga-tions to coöperate in promoting certain ends. Insofar as the United States is concerned, they address themselves "to the political, not to the judicial department; and the legislature must execute the contract before it can become a rule for the Court." Apart from action taken by Congress to implement them, the application of the Charter's human rights provisions is not for a court to undertake. . . .

The Universal Declaration of Human Rights

Acting under Article 68 of the Charter, the Economic and Social Council created a commission "for the promotion of human rights." This

Commission drafted the Universal Declaration of Human Rights which was adopted by the General Assembly on December 10, 1948. . . . This Declaration was proclaimed by the General Assembly

> as a common standard of achievement for all peoples and all nations, to the end that every individual and every organ of society, keeping this declaration constantly in mind, shall strive by teaching and education to promote respect for these rights and freedoms and by progressive measures, national and international, to secure their universal and effective recognition and observance, both among the peoples of member states themselves and among the peoples of territories under their jurisdiction.

On the day before the adoption of the Declaration, the representative of the United States, Mrs. Franklin D. Roosevelt, made the following statement concerning the Declaration. . . :

> . . . my Government has made it clear in the course of the development of the declaration that it does not consider that the economic and social and cultural rights stated in the declaration imply an obligation on governments to assure the enjoyment of these rights by direct governmental action. . . .

Speaking in the Third Committee of the General Assembly, Mrs. Roosevelt had previously stated that "the draft Declaration was not a treaty or international agreement," and that if it was adopted it would not be "legally binding." . . .

After these official statements, no doubt can exist as to the character of the Declaration. It is in no sense binding on the Government of the United States, and its provisions have not been incorporated in our national law.

In its opinion the California District Court of Appeal invoked Article 17 of the Universal Declaration, but it did not refer to the limited purpose for which the Declaration was proclaimed by the General Assembly. The provision in Article 17 that "everyone has the right to own property alone as well as in association with others," is so general that it could not sustain the result of the court's decision, even if it were incorporated into American law.

The Human Rights Commission of the United Nations is now engaged in drafting a second instrument — a Covenant on Human Rights. If this Covenant is signed and ratified by the United States, and if it is brought into force by a sufficient number of nations, it will be on a wholly different basis from that of the Declaration. It is designed to be a treaty between various nations. As such, depending on a text which has not yet been finalized, its self-executing provisions might be incorporated into American law; the United States is currently insisting that its provisions should not be self-executing. The California court would seem to have anticipated events which may or may not transpire in the future. . . .

Wright, National Courts and Human Rights — The *Fujii* Case
45 Am. J. Intl. L. 62, 62-66, 68-77 (1951)

. . . THE CONSTITUTIONAL LAW ISSUE

On the issue of constitutional law the opinion follows a long and un-broken tradition that if State legislation conflicts with obligations under-taken by the United States in a treaty, the legislation will not be applied by the courts. The terms of Article 6, paragraph 2, of the Constitution are unambiguous:

> . . . all treaties made, or which shall be made, under the authority of the United States, shall be the supreme law of the land; and the judges in every State shall be bound thereby, anything in the Constitution or laws of any State to the contrary notwithstanding.

This clause came before the Supreme Court for interpretation in 1796 and the Court did not hesitate to hold that Virginia legislation of 1777 confiscating debts owed to British subjects was null and void because in conflict with Article 4 of the Treaty of Peace with Great Britain of 1783 [Ware v. Hylton, 3 U.S. (3 Dall.) 199 (1796)].

In the same spirit the Supreme Court held unanimously a hundred and fifty years later that California inheritance laws which passed by the claims of German beneficiaries could not override the provisions of the treaty of 1923 between the United States and Germany. Justice Douglas held for the Court [Clark v. Allen, 331 U.S. 503, 508 (1947)] that, in spite of the war and the unconditional surrender of Germany, clauses of that treaty protecting private rights continued:

> If, therefore, the provisions of the treaty have not been superseded or abro-gated, they prevail over any requirements of California law which conflict with them.

Scores of opinions of both Federal and State courts have affirmed this stand. Question has been raised, however, in connection with the *Fujii* case, because it is said this principle is not applicable in the case of "non-self-executing treaties." A self-executing treaty refers in American constitu-tional law to a treaty provision which imposes an obligation upon the United States of such character as to be applied by the courts. Many treaty obligations are, however, of such character that execution belongs not to the courts but to the Congress, the President, or the treaty-making authority. Such treaties have been called "non-self-executing." It is conceivable that a treaty might impose an obligation upon a federal state which could be executed only by action of the legislatures of the member states. This seems to be the case in Canada. In the United States, however, the principle of Federal supremacy has been held to mean that the Constitution always confers adequate authority upon Federal agencies to enforce treaties which impose obligations upon the United States. Congress always has power under the "necessary and proper" clause to provide for such enforcement, even though the subject-matter of the treaty is outside the explicit delegation of power to Congress by the Constitution. This position was affirmed by the Supreme Court, speaking through Justice Holmes, in the case of Missouri v. Holland [252 U.S. 416 (1920)]. The Court held that Congress had power to enact criminal laws to enforce a treaty between the United States and Canada for the protection of migratory birds, although the matter was not within the powers expressly delegated to it. The United States is, therefore, never dependent for fulfillment of its treaty obligations upon action by the States. Consequently, the distinction between self-executing and non-self-executing treaties has been used in American constitutional law only with reference to the agency of the Federal Government competent to execute the treaty and has had no reference to the relations between the Federal Government and the States, except in those rare instances where the treaty itself makes execution contingent upon State action. One, therefore, finds little judicial discussion of this distinction in cases involving the compatibility of State legislation with treaty provisions.

The doctrine of non-self-executing treaties in American constitutional law is an aspect of the doctrine of "political questions." It affirms that certain treaty provisions, like certain provisions of customary international law and certain provisions of the Constitution, are of such character that the court leaves their interpretation and application to the political organs of the Government — the President or Congress — and applies whatever decisions these organs may make. This doctrine is the basis for Chief Justice Marshall's opinion in the case of Foster v. Neilson [27 U.S. (2 Pet.) 253 (1829)]. Speaking for the Supreme Court, he held that the provision of the Florida Purchase Treaty, which stated that grants of land in the ceded territories "shall be ratified and confirmed to the persons in possession of the lands," was not self-executing because it was in the form of a contract and because the scope of the ceded territory was a political question. Four years later, in the case of United States v. Percheman [33 U.S. (7 Pet.) 51 (1833)], the Chief Justice held, after examining the Spanish text of the treaty, that he had been in error, saying:

> Although the words "shall be ratified and confirmed" are properly the words of contract, stipulating for future legislative act, they are not necessarily so. They may import that they "shall be ratified and confirmed" by force of the instrument itself.

He, therefore, in the later case which, differing from the earlier case, concerned lands clearly within the ceded territory, applied the treaty directly to protect private land titles. . . .

In practice, the doctrine of non-self-executing treaties has been applied only to preserve the constitutional rights of the political organs of the Federal Government — the President, the Congress, and especially the House of Representatives which does not normally participate in treaty-making — in matters which for historical or practical reasons have been considered peculiarly within the competence of these organs. Thus it has been held that treaty provisions which require appropriations can only be executed by Congress. Treaty provisions referring to tariffs, to the use of military forces, to the incorporation and the administration of territories acquired by the United States, to the organization of tribunals, and to the establishment of criminal jurisdiction have usually been regarded as non-self-executing. . . .

The International Law Issue

Treaty provisions which do not impose obligations on the parties or which specify organs of execution other than national courts, can be called non-self-executing, but in a different sense from that just discussed. Critics of the California court's decision in the *Fujii* case seem to imply that the provisions of the Charter of the United Nations dealing with human rights do not impose obligations upon the Members, but merely recommend action by them or by organs of the United Nations, and that consequently they are not self-executing.

This argument involves consideration of the following questions: Does Article 56 of the United Nations Charter impose obligations upon the Members, including the United States? If so, does the Charter provide organs and procedures for interpreting and enforcing these obligations of such a character as to prevent American courts from doing so? If this is answered negatively, it may be asked: Are the obligations of the United States under the article of a character which American courts can apply? These questions suggest that the term "non-self-executing treaties" may have a meaning in international law different from that in American constitutional law. Instead of referring to treaty obligations which are to be enforced by the political organs rather than by the courts, the term may refer to treaty provisions which do not impose obligations upon the parties or which implicitly or explicitly preclude judicial application. Many provisions of the United Nations Charter are of this character. They recommend to organs of the United Nations or to the Members that they consider certain subjects or promote certain purposes. Treaty provisions which define the purposes, procedures or powers of international bodies may imply obligations by the parties not to obstruct the realization of these purposes, to observe these procedures, and to respect the decisions resulting from the exercise of these powers. But normally such provisions are not susceptible of application or enforcement by national courts and may, therefore, be called non-self-executing. United States courts have, for example, refused to pass upon the exercise of their jurisdiction by tribunals established by international agreements to which the United States is a party.

Article 56 of the Charter in form imposes obligations upon the Members of the United Nations. The word "pledge" implies obligation and the reference to "separate" action as distinct from "joint" action indicates that the Members are individually bound to act "for the achievement" of "universal respect for, and the observance of, human rights and fundamental freedoms for all without distinction as to race, sex, language or religion." This construction was accepted without hesitation by the California court in the *Fujii* case. . . . This opinion gains weight from the fact that it was unanimous among the three judges and that it was unanimously reaffirmed on rehearing. The court said after rehearing that its reference to the Universal Declaration of Human Rights did not imply that the instrument was a treaty or that it directly imposed an obligation upon the United States, but that, like the address of the President to the Senate also referred to, "it emphasized the purposes and guarantees of the Charter. . . ."

That Article 56 imposes obligations on the United States appeared equally clear to four Justices of the Supreme Court who, in concurring opinions in the Oyama case, invoked this article. The Court held that the California Alien Land Law was contrary to the 14th Amendment, at least insofar as it forbade American-born children of Japanese parents ineligible to naturalization to hold land purchased for them by the parents. Justice Black, joined by Justice Douglas, said in his concurring opinion:

> There are additional reasons now why that law stands as an obstacle to the free accomplishment of our policy in the international field. One of these reasons is that we have recently pledged ourselves to cooperate with the United Nations to "promote . . . universal respect for, and observance of, human rights and fundamental freedoms for all without distinction as to race, sex, language or religion." How can this nation be faithful to this international pledge if state laws which bar land ownership and occupancy by aliens on account of race are permitted to be enforced?

Justice Murphy, joined by Justice Rutledge, said:

> Moreover, this nation has recently pledged itself, through the United Nations Charter, to promote respect for, and observance of, human rights and fundamental freedoms for all without distinction as to race, sex, language or religion. The Alien Land Law stands as a barrier to the fulfillment of that national pledge. Its inconsistency with the Charter, which has been duly ratified and adopted by the United States, is but one more reason why the statute must be condemned.

The majority of commentators accept this position, but others have objected that the pledge of "separate" action is not "to treat persons under their jurisdiction with respect for human rights" but "to promote international cooperation to that end." With this construction Article 56 adds little, if anything, to Article 55 and is, therefore, "meaningless and redundant." Ordinary canons of interpretation oppose a construction leading to that result, and common sense suggests that "separate action in cooperation with the organization" implies, as a minimum, abstention from separate action, such as enforcement of racially discriminating land laws, which would oppose the purposes of the organization. It is difficult, if not impossible, to say that a Member is acting in coöperation with the United Nations "for the achievement" of "universal respect for, and observance of, human rights and fundamental freedoms for all without distinction as to race, sex, language or religion," if its courts are enforcing in its own jurisdiction laws which make such discriminations in respect to matters described as human rights in a formal declaration by the principal organ of the United Nations. It is reasonable to infer from the phrase "in coöperation with the organization" that the Members, in fulfilling their pledge to take "separate action," shall be guided by the purposes stated in the Charter and by the more detailed interpretation of the meaning of those purposes and the appropriate methods for achieving them, which organs of the United Nations have recommended. Consequently, the terms of Article 56 amply support the opinion of the court in the *Fujii* case that the Universal Declaration of Human Rights, while not a treaty, constitutes an authoritative interpretation of the words "human rights and fundamental freedoms" in Articles 55 and 56 of the Charter.

This construction gains strength from the legislative history of Article 56, an article which had no counterpart in the Dumbarton Oaks Proposals. It originated at San Francisco in a proposal that:

> All members pledge themselves to take separate and joint action and to cooperate with the Organization and with each other to achieve these purposes.

A threefold pledge for separate action, for joint action, and for coöperation with the Organization was, therefore, clearly stated. Some Members objected, however, and a proposal was made eliminating all but the pledge to coöperate:

> All members undertake to cooperate jointly and severally with the Organization for the achievement of these purposes.

This, however, was objected to specifically on the ground that it did not contain the threefold pledge which had been approved in principle. As a result the committee proposed a new draft which was accepted and became Article 56 of the Charter, apparently with the intention of incorporating the threefold pledge, although the draft was less clear than the original proposal:

> All Members pledge themselves to take joint and separate action in cooperation with the Organization for the achievement of the purposes set forth in Article 55.

Interpretation of this article has been discussed in the United Nations International Law Commission and some differences of opinion have emerged. The Chairman (Hudson) expressed the opinion that the Member States "had merely agreed to promote international cooperation" for the ends stated in Article 55. This conclusion may have been arrived at by assuming that the phrase of Article 56 "in cooperation with the Organization" is identical with the phrase "to cooperate with the Organization." It may, however, have been arrived at by assuming that in referring to "the purposes set forth in Article 55" the "pledge" of Article 56 was "for the achievement" not of "universal respect for, and observance of, human rights," etc., but of "promotion by the United Nations of universal respect for, and observance of, human rights," etc. This interpretation, however, not only makes Article 56 verbally repetitive, but it makes it add nothing to Article 55. The text itself and the history of its drafting suggest an intention to differentiate the two articles. Article 55 imposes an obligation upon the United Nations as a collective entity to promote universal respect for, and observance of, human rights, while Article 56 imposes an obligation upon its Members to take joint or separate action in coöperation with the Organization for the achievement of universal respect for, and observance of, human rights. Certainly, the latter obligation requires Members to see that their organs of government respect and observe human rights in carrying out their normal functions and, therefore, in the United States, where treaties are the supreme law of the land, courts must refuse to apply State or earlier Federal laws which fail to respect or observe these rights and freedoms. . . .

If, as here contended, Article 56 imposes a "separate" obligation upon the United States, there can be no doubt of the capacity of United States courts to interpret and apply it in first instance. Undoubtedly, the organs of the United Nations are also entitled to interpret the duties of the Members of the United Nations, to define the meaning of human rights and fundamental freedoms, and to establish procedures for promoting universal respect for those rights and freedoms. Such action in some cases, may be obligatory upon, and, in some cases, only recommendatory to, the Members. Insofar as organs of the United Nations have acted, whether by interpretative resolutions, by implementation of procedures of the Charter, or by achieving acceptance by states of concrete obligations as proposed in the so-called Covenant of Human Rights, the Members, pledged to act in coöperation with the United Nations, are bound to be guided by, or at least to consider, this action. Within that limitation, however, their own national organs, including their courts, are free and, in the case of the United States, because of the constitutional powers of courts already discussed, obliged to construe and apply Article 56 in the normal exercise of their jurisdiction. No provision of the Charter gives United Nations organs an exclusive competence in this field. Members are, therefore, free to follow their normal constitutional practices in regard to the interpretation, application and enforcement of the Charter as a treaty to which they are parties. . . .

. . . [C]ourts have sometimes given a narrow construction to treaty provisions in order to permit the operation of State laws favoring American nationals in the enjoyment of special privileges deemed to be within the

States' "police power." Fishing, hunting, mining and other utilization of the States' natural resources, employment on public works, engaging in activities affecting public health and security, attendance at public schools, and acquisition of land for agricultural purposes, have sometimes been considered privileges which need not be extended to aliens under national-treatment treaty clauses. This distinction of certain "privileges," which the States of the Union may regulate at discretion, from the "rights" which nationals of foreign states are entitled to enjoy under the treaties has been ostensibly based on the terms of the treaty, but has sometimes seemed rather arbitrary; and the line of distinction built up by judicial interpretation has been by no means certain. Agricultural landholding, for example, was in 1923 held not to be included among the rights of residence assured by the Japanese treaty of 1911; but more recent opinions have tended to consider it a "right" in the enjoyment of which racial discrimination is forbidden both by the 14th Amendment and by relevant treaty provisions. Undoubtedly, however, certain advantages such as immigration, naturalization, voting, and holding public office can properly be considered "privileges" which no principle of non-discrimination in the enjoyment of human rights has extended to all persons equally. It has been said that "the modern tendency has been to bring about an approximation of the Alien to the citizen in the enjoyment of civil as contrasted with political rights," the latter being regarded as privileges.

In view of these divergencies in American practice, it is fortunate that the courts have before them the Universal Declaration of Human Rights as a guide to the interpretation of Article 56 in the Charter. While not a treaty, the Declaration is of great interpretative value, manifesting the opinion of the United Nations as to the scope of human rights and fundamental freedoms. It is to be observed, however, that some of the human rights defined in the Declaration are not susceptible of judicial cognizance until they are implemented by legislation. . . .

Note: An Unusual Occurrence in the Course of the Fujii *Appeal*

Judge Manley Hudson, the author of the first of the two preceding articles, was not content merely to comment negatively on the holding of the district court of appeal. He took the further, and somewhat unusual, step of intruding into the later stages of the litigation. Specifically he addressed the following telegram to the counsel for the State of California, which had appealed the district court of appeal's decision:

> I am astonished by the decision of the District Court of Appeal in Fujii
> vs. California. In holding that the California Alien Land Law must yield
> to the Charter of the United Nations as the superior authority, the court failed

to take account of the established law of the United States that only the self-executing provisions of a treaty are automatically incorporated into the supreme law of the land of the United States so as to supersede previous national or state legislation. Articles 55 and 56 and the other provisions of the Charter cited by the court are in no sense self-executing, and they are not operative as a part of our local law. Apart from legislation enacted by Congress the provisions of the Charter on Human Rights cannot properly be said to have any effect on the Alien Land Law of California. Even less defensible is the court's reliance on Article 17 of the Declaration of Human Rights promulgated by the General Assembly of the United Nations in 1948. That declaration does not have the force of a treaty, and its preamble shows clearly that the declaration was not intended to have any binding effect on the members of the organization. Even if Article 17 of the declaration were operative in American law, its terms are too general for the conclusion to be drawn that the Alien Land Law of California is in conflict with it.

Judge Hudson's motives for minimizing the legal impact of the Charter and of the Universal Declaration in so dramatic a style are unclear. A magnanimous but unpersuasive explanation is found in Oliver, The Treaty Power and National Foreign Policy as Vehicles for the Enforcement of Human Rights in the United States, 9 Hofstra L. Rev. 411, 417 (1981), who suggests that Judge Hudson intervened because he "undoubtedly feared a strong counterreaction against the existing treaty power through the [then-pending Bricker amendment] should the higher court hold that a treaty could invalidate a state act that the Federal Constitution did not."

In any event, the California Supreme Court, apprised of Judge Hudson's sentiments, heard the appeal in the case and gave the following judgment in line with them.

Sei Fujii v. State
38 Cal. 2d 713, 242 P.2d 617 (1952)

GIBSON, C.J. . . . [T]he sole question presented on this appeal is the validity of the California alien land law.

It is first contended that the land law has been invalidated and superseded by the provisions of the United Nations Charter pledging the member nations to promote the observance of human rights and fundamental freedoms without distinction as to race. Plaintiff relies on statements in the preamble and in Articles 1, 55 and 56 of the Charter. . . .

It is not disputed that the charter is a treaty and our federal Constitution provides that treaties made under the authority of the United States are part of the supreme law of the land and that the judges in every state are bound thereby. U.S. Const., art. VI. A treaty, however, does not automatically supersede local laws which are inconsistent with it unless the treaty provisions are self-executing. In the words of Chief Justice Marshall: A treaty is "to be regarded in courts of justice as equivalent to an act of the Legislature, whenever it operates of itself, without the aid of any legislative provision. But when the terms of the stipulation import a contract — when either of the parties engages to perform a particular act, the treaty addresses itself to the political not the judicial department; and the Legislature must execute the contract, before it can become a rule for the court." Foster v. Neilson, 1829, 2 Pet. 253, 314, 7 L. Ed. 415.

In determining whether a treaty is self-executing courts look to the intent of the signatory parties as manifested by the language of the instrument, and, if the instrument is uncertain, recourse may be had to the circumstances surrounding its execution. . . . In order for a treaty provision to be operative without the aid of implementing legislation and to have the force and effect of a statute, it must appear that the framers of the treaty intended to prescribe a rule that, standing alone, would be enforceable in the courts. . . .

It is clear that the provisions of the preamble and of Article 1 of the charter which are claimed to be in conflict with the alien land law are not self-executing. They state general purposes and objectives of the United Nations Organization and do not purport to impose legal obligations on the individual member nations or to create rights in private persons. It is equally clear that none of the other provisions relied on by plaintiff is self-executing. Article 55 declares that the United Nations "shall promote: . . . universal respect for, and observance of, human rights and fundamental freedoms for all without distinction as to race, sex, language, or religion," and in Article 56, the member nations "pledge themselves to take joint and separate action in cooperation with the Organization for the achievement of the purposes set forth in Article 55." Although the member nations have obligated themselves to cooperate with the international organization in promoting respect for, and observance of human rights, it is plain that it was contemplated that future legislative action by the several nations would be required to accomplish the declared objectives, and there is nothing to indicate that these provisions were intended to become rules of law for the courts of this country upon the ratification of the charter.

The language used in Articles 55 and 56 is not the type customarily employed in treaties which have been held to be self-executing and to create rights and duties in individuals. For example, the treaty involved in Clark v. Allen, 331 U.S. 503, 507-508, 67 S. Ct. 1431, 1434, 91 L. Ed. 1633, relating to the rights of a national of one country to inherit real property located in another country, specifically provided that "such national shall be allowed a term of three years in which to sell the [property] . . . and withdraw the proceeds . . ." free from any discriminatory taxation. . . . In Nielsen v. Johnson, 279 U.S. 47, 50, 49 S. Ct. 223, 73 L. Ed. 607, the provision treated as being self-executing was equally definite. There each of the signatory parties agreed that "no higher or other duties, charges, or taxes of any kind, shall be levied" by one country on removal of property therefrom by citizens of the other country "than are or shall be payable in each state, upon the same, when removed by a citizen or subject of such state respectively." In other instances treaty provisions were enforced without implementing legislation where they prescribed in detail the rules governing rights and obligations of individuals or specifically provided that citizens of one nation shall have the same rights while in the other country as are enjoyed by that country's own citizens. . . .

It is significant to note that when the framers of the charter intended to make certain provisions effective without the aid of implementing legislation they employed language which is clear and definite and manifests that intention. For example, Article 104 provides: "The Organization shall enjoy in the territory of each of its Members such legal capacity as may be necessary for the exercise of its functions and the fulfillment of its purposes." Article 105 provides: "1. The Organization shall enjoy in the territory of each of its Members such privileges and immunities as are necessary for the fulfillment of its purposes. 2. Representatives of the Members of the United Nations and officials of the Organization shall similarly enjoy such privileges and immunities as are necessary for the independent exercise of their functions in connection with the Organization." In Curran v. City of New York, 191 Misc. 229, 77 N.Y.S.2d 206, 212, these articles were treated as being self-executory. . . .

The provisions in the charter pledging cooperation in promoting observance of fundamental freedoms lack the mandatory quality and definiteness which would indicate an intent to create justiciable rights in private persons immediately upon ratification. Instead, they are framed as a promise of future action by the member nations. Secretary of State Stettinius, Chairman of the United States delegation at the San Francisco Conference where the charter was drafted, stated in his report to President Truman that Article 56 "pledges the various countries to cooperate with the organization by joint and separate action in the achievement of the economic and social objectives of the organization without infringing upon their right to order their national affairs according to their own best ability, in their own way, and in accordance with their own political and economic institutions and processes." Report to the President on the Results of the San Francisco Conference by the Chairman of the United States Delegation, the Secretary of State, Department of State Publication 2349, Conference Series 71, p. 115; Hearings before the Committee on Foreign Relations, United States Senate [Revised] July 9-13, 1945, p. 106. The same view was repeatedly expressed by delegates of other nations in the debates attending the drafting of article 56. See U.N.C.I.O. Doc. 699 II/3/40, May 30, 1945, pp. 1-3; U.N.C.I.O. Doc. 684, II/3/38, May 29, 1945, p. 4; Kelsen, The Law of the United Nations [1950], footnote 9, pp. 100-102.

The humane and enlightened objectives of the United Nations Charter are, of course, entitled to respectful consideration by the courts and Legislatures of every member nation, since that document expresses the universal desire of thinking men for peace and for equality of rights and opportunities. The charter represents a moral commitment of foremost importance, and we must not permit the spirit of our pledge to be compromised or disparaged in either our domestic or foreign affairs. We are satisfied, however, that the charter provisions relied on by plaintiff were not intended to supersede existing domestic legislation, and we cannot hold that they operate to invalidate the alien land law. . . .

[Having thus disposed of the issues relating to the UN Charter, the court proceeded to hold the Alien Land Law invalid on the ground that it violated the equal protection clause of the Fourteenth Amendment.]

Comments and Questions

1. The California Supreme Court in *Fujii* concluded that it was "clear" that the human rights clauses of the UN Charter were non-self-executing. As all readers of law review articles know, this word frequently is invoked to accord a patina of plausibility to controversial arguments and debatable conclusions. Here the court's judgment ignored both U.S. Supreme Court precedents on self-executing treaties in general and scholarly views on whether the Charter's human rights clauses were self-executing in particular. On the former, the court failed to mention, much less follow, the authoritative case of Asakura v. Seattle, 265 U.S. 332 (1924), where the U.S. Supreme Court, holding that a treaty was self-executing and created enforceable rights in individuals, opined that "[t]reaties are to be construed in a broad and liberal spirit, and, when two constructions are possible, one restrictive of rights which may be claimed under it, and the other favorable to them, the latter is preferred." Id. at 342. On the latter, the court in support of its position cited only H. Kelsen, The Law of Nations 100-102 (1950), although it hardly could have been unaware of Judge Hudson's strong views (see pages 114-115 supra). The scholarly analyses of Schachter (pages 95-101 supra) and Wright (pages 108-114 supra), on the other hand, were either overlooked or thought unworthy even of refutation. Numerous other articles, comments, and notes commending the district court of appeal's decision, all also ignored by the California Supreme Court, are collected in Lockwood, The United Nations Charter and United States Civil Rights Litigation: 1946-1955, 69 Iowa L. Rev. 901, 925 n.161 (1984).

2. Does the non-discrimination norm found in Article 55(c) of the Charter lack the "definiteness" to be self-executing, as the California Supreme Court concludes, or, as most commentators have suggested, does it not constitute "a self-sustaining and definite rule of law even if other human rights are not specified clearly enough to be protected on the basis of the Charter provisions"? Schluter, The Domestic Status of the Human Rights Clauses of the United Nations Charter, 61 Calif. L. Rev. 110, 148 (1973). For data revealing the widespread — indeed, universal — support for the

non-discrimination norm, at least insofar as racial discrimination is concerned, see I. Brownlie, Principles of Public International Law 598-599 (4th ed. 1990); M. McDougal, H. Lasswell, and L. Chen, Human Rights and World Public Order 581-611 passim (1980); and W. McKean, Equality and Discrimination Under International Law 264-288 (1983). See also Section 702(f) of Restatement (Third) of the Foreign Relations Law of the United States (page 162 infra), which takes the position not only that "systematic racial discrimination" violates the customary international law of human rights, but also that its prohibition is a peremptory norm (jus cogens). Accord, *Barcelona Traction, Light & Power Co., Ltd. Case*, 1970 I.C.J. 3, 32 (International Court of Justice states that discrimination on the ground of race violates customary international law, since "the principles and rules concerning the basic rights of the human person, including protection from . . . racial discrimination," constitute obligations erga omnes). See also the *Namibia Case*, page 49 of Problem I. In view of this universal consensus against racial discrimination, "clearly" manifested in Article 55(c), how can one justify *Fujii*'s dictum today?

3. Underlying *Fujii* is the unstated assumption that the "definiteness" standard is higher in human rights than in other cases. Cf. Asakura v. Seattle, page 118 supra. That the standard should be the same regardless of the nature of the case seems the preferable approach, and the one taken by the Court of Appeals for the Ninth Circuit in People of Saipan ex rel. Guerrero v. U.S. Dept. of Interior, 502 F.2d 90 (9th Cir.), cert. denied, 420 U.S. 1003 (1974), where citizens of Micronesia sued to enforce the Trusteeship Agreement that the United States had entered into governing its administration of the Trust Territory of the Pacific Islands. In finding that international instrument to be self-executing, the court of appeals acknowledged that "the substantive rights guaranteed through the Trusteeship Agreement are not precisely defined. However, we do not believe that the agreement is too vague for judicial enforcement. Its language is no more general than such terms as 'due process of law,' 'seaworthiness,' 'equal protection of the law,' 'good faith,' or 'restraint of trade,' which courts interpret every day. . . ." 502 F.2d at 99. Is there a distinction between U.S. courts interpreting vague constitutional or statutory language and these same courts construing similarly vague treaty provisions? Should there be? If so, justify it.

4. Can, as Professor Wright suggested (see page 114 supra), the human rights norms found in the Universal Declaration (and further developed in various international human rights instruments concluded in the post-*Fujii* years) be read back into the Charter to create obligations that are binding on states internationally and also enforceable domestically? Can the Charter's human rights clauses, in effect, draw content and "definiteness" from subsequently developed norms to the extent necessary to overcome the courts' predilection against according them self-executing status? Assuming that this incorporation thesis might have some

appeal to certain contemporary judges, to what extent does the status of the right in question strengthen or weaken any argument based upon it? On a continuum from the norm against racial discrimination through the state actions proscribed by Section 702 of the Restatement (Third) of the Foreign Relations Law of the United States (page 162 infra) to the panoply of rights set out in the Universal Declaration, where would you recommend that a judge draw the line in this incorporation-by-reference process?

5. In considering whether the human rights clauses of the Charter (or particular articles of other international human rights treaties) are self-executing today, it should be noted that most contemporary scholarship supports a general presumption that treaties are self-executing. See, e.g., Paust, Self-Executing Treaties, 82 Am J. Intl. L. 760 (1988). Of particular importance is the fact that Section 111 (3) and (4) of the Restatement (Third) of the Foreign Relations Law of the United States and its accompanying commentary point toward a strong presumption that treaties are self-executing. Restatement (Third) of the Foreign Relations Law of the United States §111 (3) and (4) comment h at 46-47 and Reporters' Note 5 at 53-56 (1987). But see Buergenthal, Self-Executing and Non-Self-Executing Treaties in National and International Law, 235 Recueil des Cours (Hague Academy of International Law) 303, 382 (1992-IV):

> Despite the fact that some have argued that there exists a presumption in the United States in favour of holding treaties to be self-executing, this may well be true only as far as bilateral treaties are concerned. In recent years, a contrary presumption appears to be emerging with regard to multilateral treaties. This may be so because these treaties tend to be invoked more frequently in cases that challenge executive or legislative policies of the United States Government, thus raising issues the courts consider political in character. By holding these treaties to be non-self-executing, American courts resort to this label as a stand-in for the "political question" doctrine, which has traditionally enabled them to avoid deciding issues they consider to be the proper province of the political branches of Government.

6. Although a growing number of other states have adopted the doctrine of self-executing treaties, they still are relatively few in number, and their courts apparently have not generated cases squarely ruling on the domestic status — self-executing or not — of the Charter's human rights clauses. Cf. Iwasawa, The Doctrine of Self-Executing Treaties in the United States: A Critical Analysis, 26 Va. J. Intl. L. 627, 639 n.57 (1986). Persons contemplating a test case in such a state should consider the advice of one commentator that "the nondiscrimination rule in articles 55 and 56 may be said to have the greatest chance to meet the various precision standards of the national legal orders, and thus the greatest chance to be applied directly by national courts." Schluter, supra page 118, at 149. See also Comment 2 supra.

C. The Post-Fujii Scene: Regrets and Hopes

1. The Present Status of the UN Charter's Human Rights Clauses

There is no doubt that the good start that international human rights jurisprudence got off to in the United States came to an abrupt halt when the California Supreme Court in *Fujii* rejected the district court of appeal's holding that the UN Charter's human rights clauses were self-executing. It should be noted, though, that "[t]he decision [in *Fujii*] was not appealed to the Supreme Court of the United States, so the point remains unsettled for the country as a whole." Finch, The Need to Restrain the Treaty-Making Power of the United States Within Constitutional Limits, 48 Am. J. Intl. L. 57, 72 (1954).

While this statement remains technically true today, it also must be noted that no federal or state court that has addressed the question during the past 50 years has held that the Charter's human rights clauses are self-executing; indeed, many courts have held specifically that they are *not*. See, e.g., Frolova v. U.S.S.R., 761 F.2d 370, 374 (7th Cir. 1985). For a compilation of such cases, see R. Lillich, International Human Rights Instruments 10.9-10.11 (2d ed. rev. 1995). In view of this weight of authority, is it still realistic to assert that *Fujii* may be "ripe for overruling"? Note, Individual Enforcement of Obligations Arising Under the United Nations Charter, 19 Santa Clara L. Rev. 195, 209 (1979).

If you were asked to argue before the Supreme Court next Term that Articles 55 and 56 were self-executing, what arguments would you make? (For some possible ones, in addition to those arguments suggested by the above readings, see Lillich, Invoking International Human Rights Law in Domestic Courts, 54 U. Cin. L. Rev. 367, 377-385 (1985).) How do you think the Court — as presently constituted — would rule? Pragmatically, is it not too late for the Court to reject the *Fujii* rationale? Or is *Fujii* the present-day equivalent of Plessy v. Ferguson, waiting for its Brown v. Board of Education?

2. Flashforward: Are Other Human Rights Treaties Self-Executing or Not?

As will become apparent from the materials presented in Problem III, until recently the United States had an exceptionally poor ratification record insofar as other international human rights treaties are concerned. Yet, to the extent that those treaties that the United States has ratified have been invoked in U.S. courts, the *Fujii* rationale has been transposed, and they, too, uniformly have been held to be non-self-executing. See In re Alien Children Educ. Litig., 501 F. Supp. 544, 590 (S.D. Tex. 1980), aff'd unreported mem. (5th Cir. 1981), aff'd sub nom. Plyler v. Doe, 457 U.S. 202 (1982) (OAS Charter non-self-executing); Bertrand v. Sava, 684 F.2d 204, 218-219 (2d Cir. 1982) (Refugees Protocol non-self-executing). See generally Lillich, supra, at 385-393.

The outlook with respect to other international human rights treaties that the United States has now ratified or may someday ratify is scarcely more encouraging. Consider the following extract from Lillich, the U.S. Constitution and International Human Rights Law, 83 Am. J. Intl. L. 851, 855-856 (1989):

> As for those treaties that may be ratified in the future, all six treaties now pending before the Senate — five sent up by President Carter and one by President Reagan — were submitted with the recommendation that the Senate, in giving its advice and consent to the particular treaty, adopt a declaration stating that the substantive provisions are non-self-executing. As many of the provisions in these treaties, especially the International Covenant on Civil and Political Rights, appear to be self-executing in character, this attempt to insulate the American legal system from their potential impact is most unfortunate. While the legal effect of such declarations has been questioned, at the very least they would be accorded "great weight" — in all likelihood nearly conclusive weight — by U.S. courts. Thus, unless the Executive Branch withdraws these recommended declarations, an unlikely event, or the Senate in the process of giving its advice and consent rejects them, an equally doubtful prospect, international human rights law flowing from treaties seems destined to have relatively little *direct* impact upon American constitutionalism.

Of the six treaties mentioned in the above extract, the Civil and Political Covenant and two others have now been ratified, each with a non-self-executing declaration attached to its notice of ratification. For further consideration of the status and impact of such declarations, see pages 242-244, 258, and 271-272 of Problem III.

III.   The Status of the Universal Declaration in Domestic Law

A.   The Historical Perspective

Kunz, The United Nations Declaration of Human Rights
43 Am. J. Intl. L. 316, 316-322 (1949)

At midnight of December 10, 1948, the General Assembly of the United Nations adopted at its Paris Session the Declaration of Human Rights. Now that the first achievement in this field has been reached, it is time to consider the legal situation theoretically, historically, critically, and to look at the more important and more difficult task that remains to be done.

The struggle for the "rights of man" was first waged within the states. The democratic Greek city-state, which was at the same time the Church, knew no rights even of the full citizens as against the state. Even less were there rights for all men. Even Aristotle speaks of men who are by nature slaves. True, the Stoics opposed slavery, and Roman jurists later took over the Stoic natural law; but they never doubted that the positive law of slavery prevailed.

In the "age of reason" the struggle for the rights of man was based on a natural law of revolutionary character. To say that the "rights of man" are inherent, inalienable, preëxisting to the state which the state has to protect, but cannot bestow, was a formidable weapon in the political battle against tyranny. There is no doubt that many formulations of the "Bill of Rights" are drawn in the ideological language of the eighteenth century.

But however great the influence of the "age of reason" was in this respect, it would be a mistake to believe that the idea of "rights of man" was unknown to the Middle Ages. Two more sources must not be forgotten. First, Christianity . . . brought this idea. The Catholic natural law as expressed by St. Thomas of Aquinas and by the Spaniards, Francisco de Vitoria and Suárez, teaches the equality of all men. It is the Catholic natural law which emphasizes the dignity of man as a rational creature, participating in the lex aeterna. . . . It is the Catholic natural law which knows no discriminations as to race and color. . . .

Second, the "rights of man" have a history in positive law. The "rights of Englishmen" are positive law which has historically come into existence in political struggles against the King. And the English settlers brought their "rights of Englishmen" with them to North America; these rights were guaranteed in the colonies, in the charters of the settlements, as early as 1606 in Virginia, 1629 in Massachusetts. From the time of the French Revolution on, the "Bill of Rights" has become a standard part in most constitutions. But long ago attempts were also made to protect the individual against tyranny by international law. The experience of two world wars, the appearance of the totalitarian régimes, the unheard-of cruelties of the National Socialist dictatorship have rendered these endeavors more urgent. During the whole second World War proposals were made in this field. It was only natural that this problem should be taken up by international organizations.

. . . The Charter of the United Nations deals with human rights seven times. The Peace Treaties of 1947 impose upon the ex-enemies the legal obligation to take all measures to secure to all persons under their jurisdiction the enjoyment of human rights and of fundamental freedoms. Analogous norms are contained in the Organic Statute of the Free Territory of Trieste. Here we have norms of positive law. True, the obligation consists in corresponding municipal legislation, administration and justice; but this municipal law is ordered by international law. Any failure in municipal law constitutes a treaty violation.

Entirely different is the character of the corresponding articles in the United Nations Charter. They do not constitute legal norms, but only guiding principles. The United Nations "shall promote and encourage," "assist in the realization," "make recommendations," "promote universal respect and observance" of human rights; it cannot protect them, it cannot take action, apart from the case that the violation of human rights constitutes a danger to peace. Further, under Article 2, paragraph 7, which contains the prohibition to intervene in matters which are essentially within the domestic jurisdiction of any state (Member or not), any action by the United Nations is precluded, for, under positive international law, these matters undoubtedly fall under domestic jurisdiction. When the treatment of the Hindus in the Union of South Africa came up, even a man like Smuts immediately raised the barrier of lack of jurisdiction. . . . [W]e have the authority of the Director of the Division of Human Rights in the United Nations Secretariat that it was primarily on account of the alleged violation of an agreement, not on account of the alleged violation of human rights, that the Assembly accepted jurisdiction. In any event, the result up to now has been nil.

As the corresponding articles of the United Nations Charter contain only a program of principles, not legal norms, and as they do not define these rights and fundamental freedoms, it is obviously necessary to create legally binding norms, defining these rights. . . .

As an amendment to the Charter has no chance and as Article 68 envisages a special Commission of Human Rights, the way of resolutions and draft treaties has been chosen. In nearly three years of work this Commission, under the chairmanship of Mrs. Franklin D. Roosevelt, has elaborated the Declaration of Human Rights which now has been adopted, and is working on a Covenant on Human Rights and a Protocol of Implementation. All three documents together will constitute the "International Bill of Rights." . . .

The Declaration now adopted constitutes obviously a maximum program. The [30] articles of the Declaration proclaim the political rights, then the traditional human rights of liberal democracy, the intellectual rights and finally the economic rights. All the rights stem from the cardinal axiom that all human beings are born free and equal, in dignity and rights, and are endowed with reason and conscience. All the rights and freedoms belong to everybody, without distinction of any kind, such as race, color, sex, language, religion, political or other opinion, national or social origin, property, birth or other status.

The Declaration of Human Rights raises many philosophical, theoretical, legal and political problems. Human rights have played a great rôle in natural law, both the Scholastic natural law and the "law of reason." On the other hand, since we have a genuine science of law, it has been shown that human rights are rights legally only because they have been granted by positive law. Against positivism a new renaissance of natural law, born out of the crisis of our Western-European culture, has set in, and particularly in the field of human rights. Lauterpacht has had recourse to natural law, and Verdross stated recently that human rights "stand and fall with the recognition of natural law." But it seems to us that they, exactly to the contrary, stand and fall with positive law guaranteeing them and giving an effective remedy against their violation in independent and impartial courts. No talk about natural law has saved the Jews from Hitler. What Lauterpacht and Verdross themselves want, is not mere natural law, but positive norms of municipal and international law. The whole dispute about "natural law" seems to this writer to be only a terminological quarrel. We men of the Christian Western culture firmly believe in the basic dignity of the human person. These ethical and religious convictions are sources which contribute to the contents of the positive, man-made law; but "natural law" is not law, but ethics. The Declaration, it is true, is couched in some places in terms of natural law, but the whole contents of the Declaration tend toward the "rule of law," i.e., of positive law. And the proposed Covenant and the Protocol of Implementation make this tendency crystal clear.

The Declaration also raises legal and political problems. The rights referred to in this Declaration are conceived out of the spirit of Western democracy. But a growing part of the world is not democratic in this sense. Every "transpersonalist" conception, and, especially every totalitarian régime, whether Fascist, National Socialist or Bolshevist, is incompatible with "human rights"; the latter necessarily presuppose exactly a non-totalitarian régime. . . . The Soviet Union, therefore, abstained from voting and did not accept the Declaration and was followed by all the states of the Soviet Bloc.

In the field of human rights as in other actual problems of international law it is necessary to avoid the Scylla of a pessimistic cynicism and the Charybdis of mere wishful thinking and superficial optimism. The regrettable fact that a growing part of the world has replaced the legal individualism of nineteenth-century liberalism with collectivistic-totalitarian legal orders cannot be simply ignored. There are, apart from National Socialist cruelties and sufferings brought about by the war, international and national developments even since the end of actual fighting, which are in no way compatible with the concern for human rights. . . .

That human rights are enumerated in a constitution is no proof in itself that they exist. There are cases where such articles remain only on paper. And in all cases it is superficial to quote only the corresponding articles of the constitutions; it is necessary to investigate how these general, abstract norms are being made concrete in simple statutes, administrative ordinances, regulations and decisions, judicial decisions and even private contracts. There is often a remarkable discrepancy between constitution and practice. . . .

In general, the human rights proclaimed in the Declaration correspond broadly to those enumerated in our own First, Fourth, Fifth, Sixth,

Seventh and Eighth Constitutional Amendments. Human rights, as they were understood in English historical development, in natural law and in political development since the French Revolution, were directed against political tyranny: hence, political rights and human rights to secure the person from political oppression dominated. Human rights were the expression of nineteenth-century liberalism, of political democracy; the right to vote was considered the most important right. In the economic field free competition seemed to be the ideal. Economic inequality seemed fully compatible with the *égalité* of the *droits de l'homme*. But here a new, socialistic trend has recently entered into the doctrine of human rights, not only under Communist or socialist, but also under democratic régimes: the tendency to "socialize" the law, the idea of the "century of the common man" have led to economic human rights which also occupy an important place in the United Nations Declaration. Here new problems arise: How to reconcile liberty with a state which shall guarantee to every one social security "from the cradle to the grave," not to speak of the practical problem of how it can be done; how, for instance, to guarantee the fundamental rights to rest and leisure to the more than one billion Asiatics and many others.

. . . [T]he United Nations Declaration is in its basic character

> not a treaty; it is not an international agreement. It is not and does not purport to be a statement of law or of legal obligation. It is a declaration of basic principles of human rights and freedoms to serve as a common standard of achievement for all peoples of all nations.

It is only a resolution, needs no ratification; it may have the effect of moral persuasion, but it is not law, has no legally binding effect. Consequently its non-binding quality explains the maximum program proclaimed. . . . Notwithstanding its legally non-binding character, Mrs. Franklin D. Roosevelt emphasized that certain provisions are stated in such broad terms as to be acceptable only because of the limitations of Article 29. This article allows only such limitations "as are determined by law solely for the purpose of securing due recognition and respect for the rights and freedoms of others and of meeting the just requirements of morality, public order and the general welfare in a democratic society." This latter phrase is an elastic one and subject to interpretation by each state. Mrs. Roosevelt gave an example by stating that, under Article 29, the exclusion from public employment of persons holding subversive political beliefs and not loyal to the basic principles and practices of the Constitution, would in no way infringe upon the right of equal access to the public service. Mrs. Roosevelt made another interpretative reservation: The United States Government does not consider that economic, social and cultural rights imply an obligation on governments to assure the enjoyment of these rights by direct governmental action.

The United Nations Declaration is the first and easiest step leading to the International Bill of Rights. It implements the Charter by defining human rights in a maximum program of a legally non-binding character. . . .

Schwelb, The Influence of the Universal Declaration of Human Rights on International and National Law
1959 Am. Socy. Intl. Law Proceedings 217

Mr. Alejandro Alvarez, the former Judge of the International Court of Justice, said in his dissenting opinion on Competence of the Assembly for the Admission of a State to the United Nations that

> a treaty or a text that has once been established acquires a life of its own. Consequently, in interpreting it, we must have regard to the exigencies of contemporary life rather than to the intentions of those who framed it.

This dictum can hardly be said to be an accepted statement of present-day international law. One is, however, tempted to add that if there ever has been a development which would induce the student to accept it, it has been the fate of the Universal Declaration of Human Rights in the ten years which followed upon its proclamation by the General Assembly of the United Nations on December 10, 1948.

The *travaux préparatoires* make it clear that the overwhelming majority of the speakers in the various organs of the United Nations did not intend the Declaration to become a statement of law or of legal obligations, but a statement of principles devoid of any obligatory character, and which would have moral force "only." One finds in the debates statements which suggest that the Declaration might be considered a complement to the Charter, as its authoritative or "authentic" interpretation, or a formulation of "the general principles of law recognized by civilized nations" within the meaning of Article 38, paragraph 1(c), of the Statute of the Court. Now the difficulty with these suggestions is that the General Assembly, which adopted the Declaration, does not have the constitutional authority to give an authentic interpretation of the Charter. And as to the question of the "general principles of law," the correct answer is, perhaps, this: that while the substance of most, though by no means all, of the provisions of the Declaration may well be said to be identical with general principles of law recognized by civilized nations, the proposition that the Declaration is a codification of these general principles is not warranted.

With a few exceptions, publicists also agree that the Declaration is a "non-binding pronouncement." Nevertheless, a complete denial of the legal relevance of the Universal Declaration does not do justice to a document which was adopted — without a dissenting vote — by the governments forming the most representative body of the international community. The General Assembly adopted the Declaration not only as "a common standard of achievement," but also stressed that a "common understanding" of rights and freedoms, to which the pledge of Member States expressed in Article 56 of the Charter applies, was of the greatest importance. Nor can the developments be disregarded which have taken place since December 10, 1948. . . .

There are three main areas in which the influence of the Declaration can be traced.

The first such area comes . . . under the term "invocation" which . . . consists of "making a preliminary appeal to a prescription in the hope of influencing results," if it is admissible, that is, to apply the term "invocation" in connection with an instrument like the Declaration. There are innumerable instances of the use of the Declaration as a yardstick to measure the degree of respect for human rights: by governments, by international conferences, by regional inter-governmental organizations, by specialized agencies and by the United Nations, or as a basis for action or exhortation. . . .

The second area of influence of the Declaration is international treaties and conventions. In this regard we must distinguish between various types of agreements. Some instruments have simply made the Universal Declaration part and parcel of their substantive and immediately applicable law. The earliest and best-known example is the Special Statute for Trieste of 1954. Another example of full incorporation may be found in the Franco-Tunisian Conventions of 1955, in which Tunisia undertook to grant all persons resident in its territory the rights and personal guarantees proclaimed in the Declaration. . . .

An interesting feature of these conventions is the fact that in one form or another, in their preambles they quote from, or expressly refer to, the Universal Declaration of Human Rights. What is the legal relevance of these references to the Declaration? This is a problem which calls for [a more] thorough examination [than can be undertaken here]. The following may be said, however: It is a well-established rule of interpretation, supported by a long line of decisions and advisory opinions of both the Permanent Court and the International Court of Justice, that every word and part of a treaty is presumed to have a meaning and to produce some legal effect. It is the normal function of a preamble to provide an expression of the objectives of a treaty. . . .

There are many instances on record, however, where a preamble, in addition to being an aid in interpreting a treaty, is a direct source of legal obligations not otherwise set forth in the so-called operative articles. . . .

It is impossible to be dogmatic about the effect which the references to the Declaration contained in the preambles to these various conventions may have upon the municipal legal system of states which become parties to them. By necessity, it varies from country to country and from convention to convention. The ratification of these conventions and their becoming part of the municipal law of states parties either ipso facto or by way of transforming legislation, introduces the provisions of the Declaration into the national legal systems with consequences the consideration of which would carry us too far. It can be assumed, for instance, that these principles might achieve relevance, among others, in situations where public policy or *ordre public* governs legal relations.

This brings me to the third area of the impact of the Declaration, i.e., its direct influence on national constitutions and on municipal legislation and, in some instances, on court decisions. It may be objected that the fact that a constitution or municipal enactment uses the phraseology of the Declaration is by no means proof that the rights thereby proclaimed or defined are in fact respected. This, of course, is true. . . . An audience of American lawyers will perhaps respond with greater understanding than any other to the suggestion that general principles embodied, and general phraseology used, in a basic document sometimes have a decisive effect on subsequent legal history. The Constitutional law of the United States might be different if the Fifth and Fourteenth Amendments had not prohibited deprivation of life, liberty, or property "without due process of law," or if general expressions such as "the privileges and immunities of citizens" and "equal protection of the laws" had not been used. There are already cases on record where the general language of the Universal Declaration has tended to encourage similar developments.

It is not surprising that constitutions drafted in co-operation with the United Nations, such as those of Libya and Eritrea, show the marked influence of the Universal Declaration, although they fall short of its provisions in one important respect, viz., the right of women to vote. It can be seen from express references to the Declaration in many other constitutions and statutes from various regions of the world, and, in the absence of such express references, from extraneous evidence, that the influence of the Declaration is also reflected in many instruments not written under United Nations sponsorship. . . .

The influence of the Universal Declaration is also reflected in the constitutional law of two great European states, the Federal Republic of Germany and France.

The Declaration provides that the family is the natural and fundamental group unit of society and is entitled to protection by society and the state. In the debates of the Commission on Human Rights, this sentence was criticized as being a "sociological concept" and not a legal norm. The idea was taken over, however, by the authors of the Basic Law of the Federal Republic of Germany, which provides in Article 6 that marriage and the family are under the special protection of the state. On the basis of this provision, the Federal Constitutional Court, in a decision of January 17, 1957, in which it traced the provision back to the Universal Declaration, declared unconstitutional and therefore void the provisions of the German Income Tax Act which provided for the joint assessment of the income of husband and wife. The fact that by this assessment married persons were in a less favorable position than unmarried persons, led the Court to the conclusion that such an arrangement amounted to a disturbing interference of the state with marriage and the family and was therefore violative of the constitutional provision. It is not for me to say whether the joint assessment of husband and wife is a good or bad idea. I merely quote this as an example of the influence general provisions and "sociological formulae" may have upon the law in the hands of judges who are ready to exhaust all possibilities to protect the rights of the individual.

The provision of Article 12 of the Universal Declaration that no one shall be subjected to arbitrary interference with his privacy, family, home or correspondence also found its way into the municipal law of the Federal Republic of Germany, this time via Article 8 of the European Convention of Human Rights. The effect of this was illustrated by a judgment of the Federal Court of Administration in 1956. The Court quashed an administrative decision expelling an alien who had a criminal record. It held that the expulsion of the alien, who had a German wife, would interfere with the family life of the alien, his German wife and the wife's illegitimate children.

The Declaration provides that "no one shall be arbitrarily deprived of his nationality." This provision, in a strengthened wording, became Article 16 of the German Basic Law, which is to the effect that no one may be deprived of his German citizenship. . . .

In the preamble to the new French Constitution of 1958 "the French people solemnly proclaims its attachment to the rights of man as defined by the Declaration of 1789, confirmed and complemented by the Preamble of the French Constitution of 1946." In the draft of the preamble as recommended by the Consultative Constitutional Committee, it was proposed that the words "and of the Universal Declaration of Human Rights" be added after the reference to the preamble to the French Constitution of 1946. It is unnecessary to stress the great importance which such reference to the Universal Declaration in the Constitution of a country of the standing of France would have had. In the final text of the Constitution, however, the reference to the Universal Declaration does not appear. Contrary to its predecessor of 1946, the new French Constitution does contain a series of provisions guaranteeing human rights, including at least one which uses the same language as the corresponding provision of the Universal Declaration. This is Article 66 which, in the language of Article 9 of the Universal Declaration, provides that "no one shall be subjected to arbitrary detention." The Constitution further provides that the judicial power, the guardian of individual liberty, shall insure respect for this principle under the conditions provided for by law. . . .

Now a few examples of the Declaration having influenced or having at least been quoted in judicial decisions: There is first the well-known California case of Fujii v. State of California [discussed in detail at pages 101-120 supra].

American Federation of Labor v. American Sash and Door Company involved the constitutionality of an Arizona Constitutional Amendment which prohibited union security arrangements (the closed shop). Mr. Justice Frankfurter, in concurring with the decision of the Court which upheld the Arizona Constitutional Amendment, referred to Article 20(2) of the Universal Declaration providing that "No one may be compelled to belong to an association." Again, it is not for me to say whether this provision of the Declaration applies to trade unions, a matter which is controversial. What we are interested in in this connection is the fact that the Declaration was invoked by one of the Justices of the Supreme Court.

In a case which also dealt with trade union matters, the New York Supreme Court, in Wilson v. Hacker, considered whether it may condemn discrimination based upon sex "as a violation of fundamental principle and judge the legitimacy of union activities in the light of the principle." In this connection, the court stated: "Indicative of the spirit of our times are the provisions of the Universal Declaration," and went on to quote the nondiscrimination provision of Article 2 and also Article 23, which provides that everyone has the right to work, to free choice of employment, to just and favorable conditions of work and to protection against unemployment.

The influence of the Declaration is not limited to cases in this country. The Penal Chamber of the Supreme Court of The Netherlands, in a freedom of the press case, dealt with the proposition of the Prosecutor that it had always been the spirit of the Netherlands Constitution that constitutional rights, including the freedom of the press, were not absolute rights and that the modern tendency was to give greater prominence to the public interest. The Supreme Court of The Netherlands held that this contention was disproved by the adoption and proclamation of the Universal Declaration of Human Rights by the General Assembly of the United Nations. Here the Supreme Court interpreted the Constitution by reference to the Declaration.

Belgian and Italian Courts have invoked the provision of the Universal Declaration that no one shall be arbitrarily denied the right to change his nationality, and decided accordingly. The Italian court stated:

> Though not having the force of a binding rule of law, the provisions of the Declaration nevertheless constitute guiding principles of the highest moral value.

The theoretical difference between a rule of law and a rule of morality becomes of little practical importance when the court accepts the latter as a guide for its decision.

A Belgian court in a case concerning the placing of a person in a mental institution, requested an expert opinion on her state of health, giving as the first ground for its decision Article 3 of the Universal Declaration, which states that everyone has the right to life, liberty and security of person.

The Supreme Court of the Philippines ordered the release from custody of a stateless person about to be deported, and placed him under the surveillance of the immigration authorities on the basis, inter alia, that the Universal Declaration proclaimed the right of everyone to life and liberty, to the rights and freedoms set forth in the Declaration without distinction, the right of everyone to an effective remedy and the prohibition of arbitrary arrest, detention and exile.

There are also a few instances in which the Universal Declaration has been referred to by judges of the International Court of Justice, albeit in dissenting opinions:

Judge Azevedo stated in the *Asylum* Case that the new Declaration of Human Rights should not remain a dead letter. Judge Levi Carneiro, in the *Anglo-Iranian Oil Company* Case, invoked Article 17 of the Declaration, which deals with the right to own property, and provides that no one shall be arbitrarily deprived of his property. Judge Ad Hoc Guggenheim stressed in the *Nottebohm* Case that to dissociate diplomatic protection from nationality will weaken even further the protection of the individual, which is so precarious under existing international law. He considered that this would be contrary to the basic principle embodied in Article 15(1) of the Declaration, according to which everyone has a right to a nationality.

The state of affairs which has been created by all these developments is certainly not neat or logical. We are faced with a haphazard growth, not with a methodical legislative process. International legislation on human rights has been attempted on a grand scale by the ambitious project of the draft International Covenants on Human Rights [which came into force in 1976. For an analysis of the problems and issues involved in the promotion of human rights by use of multilateral treaties, see Problem III]. . . .

The Universal Declaration of Human Rights at 20

After the delivery of the preceding paper in 1959, the evolution of the status of the Universal Declaration in international law continued apace. Even by 1968, the twentieth anniversary of its adoption, arguments were being made that it had become part of customary international law. The non-governmental Assembly for Human Rights meeting in Montreal that year adopted what has become known as the Montreal Statement, which included the assertion that the "Universal Declaration of Human Rights . . . has over the years become a part of customary international law." (9 J. Int. Commn. Jurists 94, 95 (1968).) Also in 1968, the year designated by the UN as Human Rights Year, came a similar statement by the UN-sponsored International Conference on Human Rights meeting in Teheran. The Proclamation of Teheran stated that "[t]he Universal Declaration of Human Rights . . . constitutes an obligation for members of the international community." (For the complete text, see 23 U.N. GAOR, U.N. Doc. A/CONF. 32/41 (1968).)

Merely stating that the Universal Declaration is legally binding as customary international law, of course, does not make it so. Although the views of "highly qualified publicists" are a subsidiary source of customary international law, what counts primarily is the actual day-to-day practice of states or their recognition that the Declaration's norms reflect general principles of law (see page 93 supra). At the very least, however, the Montreal Statement and the Proclamation of Teheran constituted important indications that a law-making consensus as to the Declaration's legal status was evolving.

Whether the Universal Declaration comprises a part of customary international law, as the Montreal Statement explicitly maintains, or constitutes an authoritative interpretation of the UN Charter's human rights clauses for treaty law purposes, as the Statement also contends and the Proclamation of Teheran seems to suggest, makes relatively little difference on the international plane, since all states are bound by customary international law and nearly all states are parties to the UN Charter and hence subject to the legal obligations that flow from its human rights clauses. The distinction between the bases of obligation — whether customary or conventional international law — takes on greater importance in the context of domestic legal systems. Thus, as long as the *Fujii* rationale prevails, the Universal Declaration's significance within the United States is restricted to the impact it may have on the customary international law of human rights. This impact is explored by an examination of three recent U.S. court cases later in this Problem (see pages 137-154 infra).

B. U.S. Case Law Developments

Setting the Stage

Professor Humphrey, whose insider's account of the adoption of the Universal Declaration makes fascinating reading, concludes with the observation that "[i]ts impact on world public opinion has been as great as if not greater than that of any contemporary international instrument, including the Charter of the United Nations." J. Humphrey, Human Rights and the United Nations: A Great Adventure 76 (1984). The Declaration, the complete text of which is found in the Document Supplement, consists of 30 articles, which, as Professor Henkin correctly notes, "are in their essence American constitutional rights projected around the world." Henkin, International Human Rights and Rights in the United States, in 1 Human Rights in International Law: Legal and Policy Issues 25, 39 (T. Meron ed. 1984). Take this opportunity, before proceeding to the materials and cases that follow, to read the Declaration in its entirety.

Over one-half of the articles in the Universal Declaration (Articles 3-18) guarantee the civil rights of individuals. See Lillich, Civil Rights, in 1 Human Rights in International Law, supra, at 115. Another three articles (Articles 19-21) protect their political rights. See Humphrey, Political and Related Rights, in 1 Human Rights in International Law, supra, at 171. Finally, six articles (Articles 22-27) purport to grant individuals certain minimal economic, social, and cultural rights. Since the Declaration was considered by all its drafters to be a standard-setting exercise rather than an instrument with binding legal character, no measures of implementation are included. How the normative impact of its standards has evolved over the years, already suggested by previous readings (see pages 127-133 supra), is demonstrated in graphic fashion by the following brief extracts.

> In giving our approval to the declaration today, it is of primary importance that we keep clearly in mind the basic character of the document. It is not a treaty; it is not an international agreement. It is not and does not purport to be a statement of law or of legal obligation. It is a declaration of basic principles of human rights and freedoms, to be stamped with the approval of the General Assembly by formal vote of its members, and to serve as a common standard of achievement for all peoples of all nations.

Statement of Mrs. Eleanor Roosevelt, Chairman of the Commission on Human Rights, immediately preceding the General Assembly's vote on the Universal Declaration, in 5 M. Whiteman, Digest of International Law 243 (1965).

> Although the affirmations of the Declaration are not binding qua international convention within the meaning of Article 38, paragraph 1(a), of the Statute of the Court, they can bind States on the basis of custom within the meaning of paragraph 1(b) of the same Article, whether because they constituted a codification of customary law as was said in respect of Article 6 of the Vienna Convention on the Law of Treaties, or because they have acquired the force of custom through a general practice accepted as law, in the words of Article 38, paragraph 1(b), of the Statute. One right which must certainly be considered a preexisting binding customary norm which the Universal Declaration of Human Rights codified is the right to equality, which by common consent has ever since the remotest times been deemed inherent in human nature.

Separate Opinion of Judge Ammoun in the *Namibia Case*, 1971 I.C.J. 16, 76.

> The Universal Declaration of Human Rights was not intended to be binding on states as part of positive international law; not only are resolutions of the General Assembly ordinarily not binding, but the Declaration was to be only one part of the International Bill of Rights which was to include a covenant having substantially the same content as the Declaration and which would be binding on those states that ratified it. If the Declaration had been intended to be binding, a covenant would have been unnecessary. Further, though some delegations attempted to breathe legal life into the Declaration by asserting that it was an authentic interpretation of the human rights provisions of the Charter or that it set forth general principles of law, others insisted more convincingly that it was not binding. In the more than a quarter of a century since its adoption, however, the Declaration has been invoked so many times both within and without the United Nations that lawyers now are saying that, whatever the intention of its authors may have been, the Declaration is now part of the customary law of nations and therefore is binding on all

states. The Declaration has become what some nations wished it to be in 1948: the universally accepted interpretation and definition of the human rights left undefined by the Charter.

Humphrey, The International Bill of Rights: Scope and Implementation, 17 Wm. & Mary L. Rev. 527, 529 (1976).

> [Professor Humphrey's] view, first advanced solely by legal scholars but subsequently supported by the resolutions of international conferences, state practice, and even court decisions, now appears to have achieved widespread acceptance. Indeed, the suggestion has been made that the Declaration has "the attributes of jus cogens," * surely an overly enthusiastic assertion in the opinion of the present writer if it is intended to imply that *all* the rights enumerated in the Declaration now constitute peremptory norms of international law.

Lillich, Invoking International Human Rights Law in Domestic Courts, 54 U. Cin. L. Rev. 367, 394-395 (1985).

In addition to Professor Humphrey, the group of legal scholars who have argued that the Universal Declaration now constitutes part of customary international law includes Professor Sohn, who believes it to be not only "an authoritative interpretation of the Charter obligations but also a binding instrument in its own right. . . ." Sohn, The Human Rights Law of the Charter, 12 Tex. Intl. L.J. 129, 133 (1977). While the Declaration has been invoked repeatedly by states in quasi-legal fashion, at the United Nations, before international tribunals, and in the diplomatic context, a recent report by the Committee on the Enforcement of Human Rights Law of the International Law Association (ILA), Final Report on the Status of the Universal Declaration of Human Rights in National and International Law, concludes that persons "who urge acceptance of the Declaration *in toto* as customary law are in a clear minority, and there is insufficient state practice to support such a wide-ranging proposition at present." ILA, Report of the Sixty-Sixth Conference 525, 544 (Buenos Aires 1994). Nevertheless, the report also concludes that "there would seem to be little argument that many provisions of the Declaration today do reflect customary international law." Id. The ILA has adopted a resolution confirming the Committee's views. Id. at 29.

Indeed, in the relatively few instances where states have expressed their views regarding the basis of the obligation to observe human rights under international law, they either have mentioned the provisions of one or more of the human rights treaties or have relied upon the incorporation of the Declaration's articles into the human rights clauses of the UN Charter. See, for example, Legault (ed.), Canadian Practice in International Law During 1979 as Reflected Mainly in Public Correspondence and Statements of the Department of External Affairs, 18 Canadian Y.B. Intl. L. 301 (1980).

---

* M. McDougal, H. Lasswell, and L. Chen, Human Rights and World Public Order 274 (1980).

> It is the view of the Canadian Government that the observance of human
> rights is obligatory under international law. The Canadian Government views
> the Universal Declaration of Human Rights as a valid interpretation and elabo-
> ration of the references to human rights and fundamental freedoms in the
> Charter of the United Nations. Consequently, the obligation on states to ob-
> serve the human rights and fundamental freedoms enunciated in the Universal
> Declaration derives from their adherence to the Charter of the United Nations.

Id. at 326. Thus, the latter half of Professor Sohn's statement — that the
Declaration is "a binding instrument in its own right" — seems to be less a
statement of law than an example of the wish being the parent of the
thought. Compare text at page 155 infra.

Insofar as the Executive Branch of the U.S. government is concerned,
perhaps the most explicit recognition that at least *some* articles of the Universal Declaration now *reflect* customary international law is found in the
U.S. Memorial to the International Court of Justice in the *Hostages Case*,
1980 I.C.J. 3, where, after marshalling traditional international law precedents to demonstrate "that States have an international legal obligation to
observe certain minimum standards in their treatment of aliens," the government added the following brief passage about the nature and scope of
fundamental human rights:

> It has been argued that no such standard can or should exist, but such force
> as that position may have had has gradually diminished as *recognition of the
> existence of certain fundamental human rights has spread throughout the inter-
> national community*. The existence of such fundamental rights for all human
> beings, nationals and aliens alike, and the existence of a *corresponding duty
> on the part of every State to respect and observe them, are now reflected, inter
> alia, in the Charter of the United Nations, the Universal Declaration of Hu-
> man Rights and corresponding portions of the International Covenant on Civil
> and Political Rights*. . . .
>
> In view of the *universal contemporary recognition that such fundamental
> human rights exist* . . . Iran's obligation to provide "the most constant protec-
> tion and security" to United States nationals in Iran includes *an obligation to
> observe those rights*. . . .

Memorial of the United States (U.S. v. Iran), 1980 I.C.J. Pleadings (Case
Concerning United States Diplomatic and Consular Staff in Tehran) 182
(Jan. 12, 1980) (emphasis added). As evidence of the fundamental human
rights to which all individuals are entitled and which all states must guarantee, the Memorial cited Articles 3, 5, 7, 9, 12, and 13 of the Declaration, id.
at 182 n.36, which cover, respectively, the right to life, liberty, and security
of person; the prohibition of torture and cruel, inhuman, or degrading
treatment or punishment; the right to equality before the law and to non-
discrimination in its application; the prohibition of arbitrary arrest or detention; the right to privacy; and the right to freedom of movement. Many of
these "fundamental human rights" were invoked — with some being accepted and a few rejected — in a series of U.S. court cases during the
1980s. Three of the most important of these cases follow.

Filartiga v. Pena-Irala
630 F.2d 876 (Cir. 1980)

[Dr. Joel Filartiga and his daughter Dolly, both citizens of Paraguay who were living in the United States and had applied for political asylum, brought this action in the Eastern District of New York against Americo Noberto Pena-Irala (Pena), also a citizen of Paraguay, for wrongfully causing the death of Dr. Filartiga's 17-year-old son, Joelito. The Filartigas contended that Joelito had been kidnapped and tortured to death by Pena, who was then Inspector General of Police in Asuncion, Paraguay, in retaliation for Dr. Filartiga's political activities and beliefs.

The Filartigas brought their action under the Alien Tort Statute, 28 U.S.C. §1350 (1988), a little-known federal law dating back to the original Judiciary Act of 1789, which provides: "[T]he district courts shall have original jurisdiction of any civil action by an alien for a tort only, committed in violation of the law of nations or a treaty of the United States." The United States at the time not being a party to a treaty proscribing torture, jurisdiction under the statute turned upon whether or not torture now violated "the law of nations," i.e., customary international law. The district court, in an unreported decision, felt constrained by precedent to dismiss the complaint on the ground that " 'the law of nations,' as employed in Section 1350, [excludes] that law which governs a state's treatment of its own citizens." In short, it ruled that torture of a Paraguayan in Paraguay by a Paraguayan official did not violate customary international law. This appeal followed.]

IRVING R. KAUFMAN, Circuit Judge:

Upon ratification of the Constitution, the thirteen former colonies were fused into a single nation, one which, in its relations with foreign states, is bound both to observe and construe the accepted norms of international law, formerly known as the law of nations. Under the Articles of Confederation, the several states had interpreted and applied this body of doctrine as a part of their common law, but with the founding of a "more perfect Union" of 1789, the law of nations became preeminently a federal concern.

Implementing the constitutional mandate for national control over foreign relations, the First Congress established original district court jurisdiction over "all causes where an alien sues for a tort only [committed] in violation of the law of nations." Judiciary Act of 1789, ch. 20, §9(b), 1 Stat. 73, 77 (1789), codified at 28 U.S.C. §1350. Construing this rarely-invoked provision, we hold that deliberate torture perpetrated under color of official authority violates universally accepted norms of the international law of human rights, regardless of the nationality of the parties. Thus, whenever an alleged torturer is found and served with process by an alien within our borders, §1350 provides federal jurisdiction. Accordingly, we reverse the judgment of the district court dismissing the complaint for want of federal jurisdiction. . . .

Appellants rest their principal argument in support of federal jurisdiction upon the Alien Tort Statute, 28 U.S.C. §1350, which provides: "The district courts shall have original jurisdiction of any civil action by an alien for a tort only, committed in violation of the law of nations or a treaty of the United States." Since appellants do not contend that their action arises directly under a treaty of the United States,* a threshold question on the jurisdictional issue is whether the conduct alleged violates the law of nations. In light of the universal condemnation of torture in numerous international agreements, and the renunciation of torture as an instrument of official policy by virtually all of the nations of the world (in principle if not in practice), we find that an act of torture committed by a state official against one held in detention violates established norms of the international law of human rights, and hence the law of nations.

The Supreme Court has enumerated the appropriate sources of international law. The law of nations "may be ascertained by consulting the works of jurists, writing professedly on public law; or by the general usage and practice of nations; or by judicial decisions recognizing and enforcing that law," United States v. Smith, 18 U.S. (5 Wheat.) 153, 160-61, 5 L. Ed. 57 (1820); Lopes v. Reederei Richard Schroder, 225 F. Supp. 292, 295 (E. D. Pa. 1963). In *Smith*, a statute proscribing "the crime of piracy [on the high seas] as defined by the law of nations," 3 Stat. 510(a) (1819), was held sufficiently determinate in meaning to afford the basis for a death sentence. The *Smith* Court discovered among the works of Lord Bacon, Grotius, Bochard and other commentators a genuine consensus that rendered the crime "sufficiently and constitutionally defined." *Smith*, supra, 18 U.S. (5 Wheat.) at 162, 5 L. Ed. 57.

The Paquete Habana, 175 U.S. 677, 20 S. Ct. 290, 44 L. Ed. 320 (1900), reaffirmed that

> where there is no treaty, and no controlling executive or legislative act or judicial decision, resort must be had to the customs and usages of civilized nations; and, as evidence of these, to the works of jurists and commentators, who by years of labor, research and experience, have made themselves peculiarly well acquainted with the subjects of which they treat. Such works are resorted to by judicial tribunals, not for the speculations of their authors concerning what the law ought to be, but for trustworthy evidence of what the law really is.

Id. at 700, 20 S. Ct. at 299. Modern international sources confirm the propriety of this approach.

Habana is particularly instructive for present purposes, for it held that the traditional prohibition against seizure of an enemy's coastal fishing ves-

---

* Appellants "associate themselves with" the argument of some of the amici curiae that their claim arises directly under a treaty of the United States, Brief for Appellants at 23 n.*, but nonetheless primarily rely upon treaties and other international instruments as evidence of an emerging norm of customary international law, rather than independent sources of law.

sels during war-time, a standard that began as one of comity only, had ripened over the preceding century into "a settled rule of international law" by "the general assent of civilized nations." Id. at 694, 20 S. Ct. at 297; accord, id. at 686, 20 S. Ct. at 297. Thus it is clear that courts must interpret international law not as it was in 1789, but as it has evolved and exists among the nations of the world today. See Ware v. Hylton, 3 U.S. (3 Dall.) 198, 1 L. Ed. 568 (1796) (distinguishing between "ancient" and "modern" law of nations).

The requirement that a rule command the "general assent of civilized nations" to become binding upon them all is a stringent one. Were this not so, the courts of one nation might feel free to impose idiosyncratic legal rules upon others, in the name of applying international law. Thus, in Banco Nacional de Cuba v. Sabbatino, 376 U.S. 398, 84 S. Ct. 923, 11 L. Ed. 2d 804 (1964), the Court declined to pass on the validity of the Cuban government's expropriation of a foreign-owned corporation's assets, noting the sharply conflicting views on the issue propounded by the capital-exporting, capital-importing, socialist and capitalist nations. Id. at 428-30, 84 S. Ct. at 940-41.

The case at bar presents us with a situation diametrically opposed to the conflicted state of law that confronted the *Sabbatino* Court. Indeed, to paraphrase that Court's statement, id. at 428, 84 S. Ct. at 940, there are few, if any, issues in international law today on which opinion seems to be so united as the limitations on a state's power to torture persons held in its custody.

The United Nations Charter (a treaty of the United States, see 59 Stat. 1033 (1945)) makes it clear that in this modern age a state's treatment of its own citizens is a matter of international concern. [The Court quotes Articles 55 and 56.]

While this broad mandate has been held not to be wholly self-executing, Hitai v. Immigration and Naturalization Service, 343 F.2d 466, 468 (2d Cir. 1965), this observation alone does not end our inquiry.* For although there is no universal agreement as to the precise extent of the "human rights and fundamental freedoms" guaranteed to all by the Charter, there is at present no dissent from the view that the guaranties include, at a bare minimum, the right to be free from torture. This prohibition has become part of customary international law, as evidenced and defined by the Universal Declaration of Human Rights, General Assembly Resolution 217 (III)(A) (Dec. 10, 1948) which states, in the plainest of terms, "no one shall

---

* We observe that this Court has previously utilized the U.N. Charter and the Charter of the Organization of American States, another non-self-executing agreement, as evidence of binding principles of international law. United States v. Toscanino, 500 F.2d 267 (2d Cir. 1974). In that case, our government's duty under international law to refrain from kidnapping a criminal defendant from within the borders of another nation, where formal extradition procedures existed, infringed the personal rights of the defendant, whose international law claims were thereupon remanded for a hearing in the district court.

be subjected to torture."* The General Assembly has declared that the Charter precepts embodied in this Universal Declaration "constitute basic principles of international law." G.A.Res. 2625 (XXV) (Oct. 24, 1970).

Particularly relevant is the Declaration on the Protection of All Persons from Being Subjected to Torture, General Assembly Resolution 3452, 30 U.N. GAOR Supp. (No. 34) 91, U.N. Doc. A/1034 (1975). . . . The Declaration expressly prohibits any state from permitting the dastardly and totally inhuman act of torture. Torture, in turn, is defined as "any act by which severe pain and suffering, whether physical or mental, is intentionally inflicted by or at the instigation of a public official on a person for such purposes as . . . intimidating him or other persons." The Declaration goes on to provide that "[w]here it is proved that an act of torture or other cruel, inhuman or degrading treatment or punishment has been committed by or at the instigation of a public official, the victim shall be afforded redress and compensation, in accordance with national law." This Declaration, like the Declaration of Human Rights before it, was adopted without dissent by the General Assembly. Nayar, "Human Rights: The United Nations and United States Foreign Policy," 19 Harv. Intl. L.J. 813, 816 n.18 (1978).

These U.N. declarations are significant because they specify with great precision the obligations of member nations under the Charter. Since their adoption, "[m]embers can no longer contend that they do not know what human rights they promised in the Charter to promote." Sohn, A Short History of United Nations Documents on Human Rights, in The United Nations and Human Rights, 18th Report of the Commission (Commission to Study the Organization of Peace ed. 1968). Moreover, a U.N. Declaration is, according to one authoritative definition, "a formal and solemn instrument, suitable for rare occasions when principles of great and lasting importance are being enunciated." 34 U.N. ESCOR, Supp. (No. 8) 15, U.N. Doc. E/CN.4/1/610 (1962) (memorandum of Office of Legal Affairs, U.N. Secretariat). Accordingly, it has been observed that the Universal Declaration of Human Rights "no longer fits into the dichotomy of 'binding treaty' against 'nonbinding pronouncement,' but is rather an authoritative statement of the international community." E. Schwelb, Human Rights and the International Community 70 (1964). Thus, a Declaration creates an expectation of adherence, and "insofar as the expectation is gradually justified by State practice, a declaration may by custom become recognized as laying down rules binding upon the States." 34 U.N. ESCOR supra. Indeed, several commentators have concluded that the Universal Declaration has become, in toto, a part of binding, customary international law. Nayar, supra, at 816-17; Waldlock, Human Rights in Contemporary International Law and the Significance of the European Convention, Intl. & Comp. L.Q., Supp. Publ. No. 11 at 15 (1965).

* Eighteen nations have incorporated the Universal Declaration into their own constitutions. 48 Revue Internationale de Droit Penal Nos. 3 & 4, at 211 (1977).

Turning to the act of torture, we have little difficulty discerning its universal renunciation in the modern usage and practice of nations. *Smith*, supra, 18 U.S. (5 Wheat.) at 160-61, 5 L. Ed. 57. The international consensus surrounding torture has found expression in numerous international treaties and accords. E.g., American Convention on Human Rights, Art. 5, OAS Treaty Series No. 36 at 1, OAS Off. Rec. OEA/Ser 4 v/II 23, doc. 21, rev. 2 (English ed., 1975) ("No one shall be subjected to torture or to cruel, inhuman or degrading punishment or treatment"); International Covenant on Civil and Political Rights, U.N. General Assembly Res. 2200 (XXI)A, U.N. Doc. A/6316 (Dec. 16, 1966) (identical language); European Convention for the Protection of Human Rights and Fundamental Freedoms, Art. 3, Council of Europe, European Treaty Series No. 5 (1968), 213 U.N. T.S. 211 (semble). The substance of these international agreements is reflected in modern municipal — i.e., national — law as well. Although torture was once a routine concomitant of criminal interrogations in many nations, during the modern and hopefully more enlightened era it has been universally renounced. According to one survey, torture is prohibited, expressly or implicitly, by the constitutions of over fifty-five nations, including both the United States and Paraguay. Our State Department reports a general recognition of this principle:

> There now exists an international consensus that recognizes basic human rights and obligations owed by all governments to their citizens. . . . There is no doubt that these rights are often violated; but virtually all governments acknowledge their validity.

Department of State, Country Reports on Human Rights for 1979, published as Joint Comm. Print, House Comm. on Foreign Affairs, and Senate Comm. on Foreign Relations, 96th Cong., 2d Sess. (Feb. 4, 1980), Introduction at 1. We have been directed to no assertion by any contemporary state of a right to torture its own or another nation's citizens. Indeed, United States diplomatic contacts confirm the universal abhorrence with which torture is viewed:

> In exchanges between United States embassies and all foreign states with which the United States maintains relations, it has been the Department of State's general experience that no government has asserted a right to torture its own nationals. Where reports of torture elicit some credence, a state usually responds by denial or, less frequently, by asserting that the conduct was unauthorized or constituted rough treatment short of torture. *

Memorandum of the United States as *Amicus Curiae* at 16 n.34.

---

* The fact that the prohibition of torture is often honored in the breach does not diminish its binding effect as a norm of international law. As one commentator has put it, "The best evidence for the existence of international law is that every actual State recognizes that it does exist and that it is itself under an obligation to observe it. States often violate international law, just as individuals often violate municipal law; but no more than individuals do States defend their violations by claiming that they are above the law." J. Brierly, *The Outlook for International Law* 4-5 (Oxford 1944).

Having examined the sources from which customary international law is derived — the usage of nations, judicial opinions and the works of jurists * — we conclude that official torture is now prohibited by the law of nations. The prohibition is clear and unambiguous, and admits of no distinction between treatment of aliens and citizens. Accordingly, we must conclude that the dictum in Dreyfus v. von Finck, supra, 534 F.2d at 31, to the effect that "violations of international law do not occur when the aggrieved parties are nationals of the acting state," is clearly out of tune with the current usage and practice of international law. The treaties and accords cited above, as well as the express foreign policy of our own government, all make it clear that international law confers fundamental rights upon all people vis-a-vis their own governments. While the ultimate scope of those rights will be a subject for continuing refinement and elaboration, we hold that the right to be free from torture is now among them. . . .

In the twentieth century the international community has come to recognize the common danger posed by the flagrant disregard of basic human rights and particularly the right to be free of torture. Spurred first by the Great War, and then the Second, civilized nations have banded together to prescribe acceptable norms of international behavior. From the ashes of the Second World War arose the United Nations Organization, amid hopes that an era of peace and cooperation had at last begun. Though many of these aspirations have remained elusive goals, that circumstance cannot diminish the true progress that has been made. In the modern age, humanitarian and practical considerations have combined to lead the nations of the world to recognize that respect for fundamental human rights is in their individual and collective interest. Among the rights universally proclaimed by all nations, as we have noted, is the right to be free of physical torture. Indeed, for purposes of civil liability, the torturer has become —

* Earlier in its opinion the court had noted that "[t]he Filartigas submitted the affidavits of a number of distinguished legal scholars, who stated unanimously that the law of nations prohibits absolutely the use of torture as alleged in the complaint." 630 F.2d at 879. Here the court cites the footnote supporting this statement, which in its entirety reads as follows:

> Richard Falk, the Albert G. Milbank Professor of International Law and Practice at Princeton University, and a former Vice President of the American Society of International Law, avers that, in his judgment, "it is now beyond reasonable doubt that torture of a person held in detention that results in severe harm or death is a violation of the law of nations." Thomas Franck, professor of international law at New York University and Director of the New York University Center for International Studies offers his opinion that torture has now been rejected by virtually all nations, although it was once commonly used to extract confessions. Richard Lillich, the Howard W. Smith Professor of Law at the University of Virginia School of Law, concludes, after a lengthy review of the authorities, that officially perpetrated torture is "a violation of international law (formerly called the law of nations)." Finally, Myres MacDougal, a former Sterling Professor of Law at the Yale Law School, and a past President of the American Society of International Law, states that torture is an offense against the law of nations, and that "it has long been recognized that such offenses vitally affect relations between states."

Id. n.4 — Eds.

like the pirate and slave trader before him — hostis humani generis, an enemy of all mankind. Our holding today, giving effect to a jurisdictional provision enacted by our First Congress, is a small but important step in the fulfillment of the ageless dream to free all people from brutal violence.*

Fernandez v. Wilkinson
505 F. Supp. 787 (D. Kan. 1980), aff'd on other grounds sub nom. Rodriguez-Fernandez v. Wilkinson, 654 F.2d 1382 (10th Cir. 1981)

[Pedro Rodriguez-Fernandez, a citizen of Cuba serving time in a Cuban prison, came to the United States by boat along with approximately 130,000 other Cuban nationals in June 1980, seeking admission to the United States. An examining immigration officer determined that Fernandez was not entitled to land, having been convicted of a crime involving moral turpitude, and recommended that he be detained pending an exclusion hearing. During this hearing, which commenced July 21, 1980, an immigration judge determined that Fernandez was excludable from the United States under U.S. law and accordingly entered an order of deportation.

Fernandez, who on June 16, 1980, had been removed from a processing camp and transferred to the U.S. Penitentiary in Leavenworth, Kansas, remained confined in this maximum security institution for the rest of 1980. During this time the Immigration and Naturalization Service and the Department of State attempted to arrange his return to Cuba. However, Cuba either failed to respond or responded negatively to six diplomatic notes. Thus, the United States was unable to carry out the order of deportation expeditiously. Indeed, it was unable even to speculate as to the date of Fernandez's departure.

Fernandez then sought a writ of habeas corpus, contending that his continued confinement without bail and without having been charged with or convicted of a crime in the United States constituted cruel and unusual punishment in contravention of the Eighth Amendment to the U.S. Constitution and a violation of the Fifth Amendment due process clause. The district court, constrained by precedent, rejected these constitutional arguments. It then turned to the contention, raised by an amicus curiae, that Fernandez's continued detention violated "fundamental human justice as embodied in established principles of international law."]

ROGERS, District Judge.

. . . International rules are generally binding upon nations only in cases where either: (1) the nation concerned has expressly consented to be

---

* On remand, Pena-Irala took no further part in the action, and the district court entered a default judgment against him in the amount of $10,385,364. Filartiga v. Pena-Irala, 577 F. Supp. 860 (E.D.N.Y. 1984). It remains uncollected. See Lillich, Damages for Gross Violations of International Human Rights Awarded by US Courts, 15 Human Rts. Q. 207, 217-218 (1993). — EDS.

bound by such rules, as by ratification of a treaty containing the rules; or (2) where it can be established through evidence of a wide practice by states that a customary rule of international law exists.

The most important source of international law is international treaties. At present, the United States has ratified and is a party to only a few human rights treaties. Petitioner does not assert that his detention is in direct violation of any treaty to which the United States is a party. . . .

The difficulty with international agreements as a legal source is that the courts are simply not bound by these documents unless they have been ratified by the United States. And we are signatory to very few international human rights agreements and ratifying state to even fewer such agreements.

One important document by which the United States is bound is the United Nations Charter. 1970 Yearbook of the U.N. 1001, 59 Stat. 1033 (1945). This document "stands as the symbol of human rights on an international scale." [Stotzky, Book Review, 11 Miami J. Intl. L. 229, 237 (1979).] The Charter entered into force on October 24, 1945, and resolves to reaffirm faith in fundamental human rights and in the dignity of the human person. Almost all nations in the world are now parties to the U.N. Charter.

There are a great number of other international declarations, resolutions, and recommendations. While not technically binding, these documents establish broadly recognized standards. The most important of these is the Universal Declaration of Human Rights, adopted by the U.N. General Assembly in 1948. Mrs. Franklin D. Roosevelt, as Chairman of the Commission on Human Rights and a representative of the United States, explained the force and effect of the Declaration before the General Assembly of the U.N. preceding its final vote:

> In giving our approval to the declaration today, it is of primary importance that we keep clearly in mind the basic character of the document. It is not a treaty; it is not an international agreement. It is not and does not purport to be a statement of law or of legal obligation. It is a declaration of basic principles of human rights and freedoms, to be stamped with the approval of the General Assembly by formal vote of its members, and to serve as a common standard of achievement for all peoples of all nations.

5 Whiteman, Digest of International Law 623 (1965).

Richard Bilder, an international legal scholar, has suggested it may currently be argued that

> standards set by the Universal Declaration of Human Rights, although initially only declaratory and non-binding, have by now, through wide acceptance and recitation by nations as having normative effect, become binding customary law. Whatever may be the weight of this argument, it is certainly true that the Declaration is in practice frequently invoked as if it were legally binding, both by nations and by private individuals and groups.

Bilder, R., The Status of International Human Rights Law: An Overview, 1978 International Law and Practice 1, 8.

It is a jurist's opinion that

> although the affirmations of the Declaration are not binding qua international convention within the meaning of Article 38, paragraph 1(a) of the Statute of the Court, they can bind states on the basis of custom within the meaning of the same Article, whether because they constitute a codification of customary law as was said in respect of Article 6 of the Vienna Convention on the Law of Treaties, or because they have acquired the force of custom through a general practice accepted as law, in the words of Article 38, paragraph 1(b), of the Statute.

Separate Opinion of Vice-President Ammoun in Advisory Opinion on the continued presence of South Africa in Namibia (S.W. Africa) 1971 I.C.J. Reports 16, 76. Thus, it appears that the Declaration has evolved into an important source of international human rights law.

Articles 3 and 9 of the Declaration provide that "everyone has the right to life, liberty, and the security of person," and that "no one shall be subjected to arbitrary arrest, detention or exile."

The American Convention on Human Rights, cited by the Amicus Curiae, pertinently declares in Article 5 that "punishment shall not be extended to any person other than the criminal," and "all persons deprived of their liberty shall be treated with respect for the inherent dignity of the human person." In Article 7 of the Convention it is agreed:

> 1. Every person has the right to personal liberty and security.
> 2. No one shall be deprived of his physical liberty except for the reasons and under the conditions established beforehand by the Constitution of the State Party concerned or by a law established pursuant thereto.
> 3. No one shall be subject to arbitrary arrest or imprisonment.

Two other principle [sic] sources of fundamental human rights are the European Convention for the Protection of Human Rights and Fundamental Freedoms (Rome 1950), and the International Covenant on Civil and Political Rights, G. A. Res. 2200A(XXI) Dec. 16, 1966, U.N. Gen. Ass. Off. Rec., 21st Sess., Supp. No. 16(A/6316) p. 52. Although the United States is not bound by either of these documents, they are indicative of the customs and usages of civilized nations.

The European Convention, brought into force in 1953 (213 U.N.T.S. 221) provides that everyone has the right to liberty and security of person and may not be deprived of liberty except in the specified cases and in accordance with a procedure prescribed by law. Section 4 further provides:

> Everyone who is deprived of his liberty by arrest or detention shall be entitled to take proceedings by which the lawfulness of his detention shall be decided speedily by a court and his release ordered if the detention is not lawful.

The International Covenant on Civil and Political Rights contains several apposite paragraphs. [The Court quotes several articles of the Covenant, including Article 9(1), which provides, inter alia, that "[n]o one shall be subjected to arbitrary arrest or detention."]

Members of our Congress and executive department have also recognized an international legal right to freedom from arbitrary detention. Congressman Donald M. Frasier as Chairman of the Subcommittee on International Organizations and the Commission [sic] on International Relations, House of Representatives, described prolonged detention without charges or trial as a gross violation of human rights:

> Congress has sought to write some general laws establishing standards for the granting or withholding of military and economic aid to nations in relation to the human rights issue. Generally we have said the military aid should be reduced or terminated to a country guilty of a consistent pattern of gross violations of internationally recognized human rights. We define gross violations as those involving the integrity of the person: torture, prolonged detention without charges or trial, and other cruel and inhuman treatment.

Frasier D., Human Rights and U.S. Foreign Policy — The Congressional Perspective, 1978 International Human Rights Law and Practice, 171, 178. Patricia M. Derian, Assistant Secretary of State for Human Rights and Humanitarian Affairs, in discussing President Carter's policy on human rights stated:

> Our human rights concerns embrace those internationally recognized rights found in the United Nations Declaration of Human Rights. The specific focus of our policy is to seek greater observance by all governments of the rights of the person including freedom from torture and cruel and inhuman treatment, freedom from the fear of security forces breaking down doors and kidnapping citizens from their homes, and freedom from arbitrary detention.

Derian, P., Human Rights in U.S. Foreign Policy — The Executive Perspective, 1978; International Human Rights Law and Practice 183.

Tribunals enforcing international law have also recognized arbitrary detention as giving rise to a legal claim. The arbitrator in France ex rel. Madame Julien Chevreau, opined that the arbitrary arrest, detention or deportation of a foreigner may give rise to a claim under international law and that if detention is unnecessarily prolonged, a claim is justified. The arbitrator further stated that a claim is justified if the rule is not observed that the prisoner should be treated in a manner appropriate to his situation, and corresponding to the standard customarily accepted among civilized nations. M.S. Dept. of State, file no. 500. AIA/1197, cited in Whiteman, M., Damages in International Law (Washington 1937). . . .

Principles of customary international law may be discerned from an overview of express international conventions, the teachings of legal scholars, the general custom and practice of nations and relevant judicial decisions. Filartiga v. Pena-Irala, 630 F.2d 876 (2d Cir. 1980). When, from this overview a wrong is found to be of mutual, and not merely several, concern among nations, it may be termed an international law violation, id.

International law is a part of the laws of the United States which federal courts are bound to ascertain and administer in an appropriate case. The Nereide, 13 U.S. (9 Cranch) 388, 422, 3 L. Ed. 769 (1815); The Pacquete Habana, 175 U.S. 677, 20 S. Ct. 290, 44 L. Ed. 320 (1900); Filartiga v. Pena-Irala, supra. Our review of the sources from which customary international law is derived clearly demonstrates that arbitrary detention is prohibited by customary international law. Therefore, even though the indeterminate detention of an excluded alien cannot be said to violate the United States Constitution or our statutory laws, it is judicially remedial as a violation of international law. Petitioner's continued, indeterminate detention on restrictive status in a maximum security prison, without having been convicted of a crime in this country or a determination having been made that he is a risk to security or likely to abscond, is unlawful; and as such amounts to an abuse of discretion on the part of the Attorney General and his delegates. . . . We can only speculate that the INS and the State Department have been so overwhelmed handling the extraordinary assimilation of over 100,000 Cuban nationals into this country, not to mention pressing situations involving Iranian and Haitian aliens, as to have not had the available span of attention to perceive or counteract the possible violation of the fundamental human rights of less than two percent of the Cuban influx.

These rationalizations do not, however, assuage the extant violation of petitioner's fundamental human rights. Perpetuating a state of affairs which results in the violation of an alien's fundamental human rights is clearly an abuse of discretion on the part of the responsible agency officials. This Court is bound to declare such an abuse and to order its cessation. When Congress and the executive department decided to exclude certain aliens from entry into this country and thereafter allowed thousands to arrive upon our shores at once, it was their corollary responsibility to develop methods for processing this large influx of admissible and excludable aliens without offending any of their fundamental human rights. If, due solely to the morass created by these official decisions, some aliens who may not seem desirable have been caused to remain in the United States for attenuated periods of time, the courts cannot deny them protection from arbitrary governmental action. . . .

In sum, we hold that the indeterminate detention of petitioner in a maximum security federal prison under conditions providing less freedom than that granted to ordinary inmates constitutes arbitrary detention and is a violation of customary international law; and that the continuation of such detention is an abuse of discretion on the part of the Attorney General and his delegates.

Forti v. Suarez-Mason
694 F. Supp. 707 (N.D. Cal. 1988)

[Alfredo Forti and Deborah Benchoam, both citizens of Argentina who were living in the United States, brought this action in the Northern District of California against Carlos Guillermo Suarez-Mason, also a citizen of Argentina, to recover damages on their own behalf and on behalf of family members for various acts allegedly committed by Argentine military and police personnel under Suarez-Mason's authority and control. The action, brought under the Alien Tort Statute, arose out of events alleged to have occurred in the mid- to late 1970s during Argentina's "dirty war" against suspected subversives.

Suarez-Mason, a general in the Argentine army, was Commander of the First Army Corps from January 1976 until January 1979. The responsibility of this army corps for suppressing terrorism, under a "state of siege" and pursuant to legislation providing that civilians accused of crimes of subversion would be judged by military law, extended to most of the Province of Buenos Aires, including the national capital, where the acts giving rise to the action were alleged to have occurred.

The district court issued an order denying Suarez-Mason's motion to dismiss the plaintiffs' claims for "official torture" and "prolonged arbitrary detention," citing *Filartiga* and Fernandez v. Wilkinson respectively. Forti v. Suarez-Mason, 672 F. Supp. 1531, 1541-1542 (N.D. Cal. 1987). Relying, inter alia, on Article 3 of the Universal Declaration, it also denied defendant's motion to dismiss a claim for "summary execution or murder," holding that such an act constituted a cognizable violation of customary international law under Section 1350. Id. at 1542. However, it granted defendant's motion to dismiss plaintiffs' claims for "causing the disappearance" of Forti's mother and for various acts amounting to "cruel, inhuman or degrading treatment." Id. at 1542-1543.

Plaintiffs then filed a motion to reconsider the court's Order, supported by a memorandum and numerous legal authorities. After reviewing these materials, the court handed down this opinion.]

JENSEN, District Judge.

On October 6, 1987 this Court issued an Order which, in part, denied defendant's Motion to Dismiss plaintiffs' claims for "Official Torture," "Prolonged Arbitrary Detention," and "Summary Execution." The Court granted the Motion to Dismiss the claims for "Disappearance" and for "Cruel, Inhuman or Degrading Treatment." See, e.g., Forti v. Suarez-Mason, 672 F. Supp. 1531, 1540-43 (N.D. Cal. 1987). On November 18, 1987 plaintiffs filed a Motion for Reconsideration of that Order through counsel Thomas J. Long and Jordan Eth, et al. Defendant has filed no opposition to the Motion. The Court has considered the memoranda and numerous legal authorities submitted for the first time on this Motion, and the Motion is GRANTED in part and DENIED in part.

I

Plaintiffs are two Argentine citizens currently residing in the United States. Their initial complaint in this action alleged numerous causes of action against defendant, a former Argentine general, growing out of events which allegedly occurred in the mid to late 1970s during the Argentine military's so-called "dirty war" against suspected subversion. The factual allegations of that complaint are detailed in this Court's October, 1987 Order, published at 672 F. Supp. 1531, 1537-1538. Plaintiffs predicated federal jurisdiction under 28 U.S.C. §1350 (the "Alien Tort Statute"). The Court's previous Order held that the Alien Tort Statute provides a cause of action for "international torts," which the Court defined as follows:

> [V]iolations of current customary international law, [which] are characterized by universal consensus in the international community as to their binding status and their content. That is, they are universal, definable, and obligatory international norms.

672 F. Supp. at 1541.

The Court went on to hold that "on the basis of the evidence submitted" plaintiff Forti had failed to establish "the requisite degree of international consensus which demonstrates a customary international norm" in regard to his claim for causing the disappearance of his mother. The Court also dismissed both plaintiffs' claims for "cruel, inhuman or degrading treatment," holding that plaintiffs had failed to bring forth sufficient evidence of international consensus, and moreover that the tort "lacks readily ascertainable parameters." Id. at 1542-1543.

Plaintiffs subsequently filed this Motion, supported by numerous international legal authorities, as well as affidavits from eight renowned international law scholars.* The Court has reviewed these materials and concludes that plaintiffs have met their burden of showing an international consensus as to the status and content of the international tort of "causing disappearance." Accordingly, the motion to reconsider is GRANTED in this regard and the claim is reinstated. The Court also concludes that plaintiffs have again failed to establish that there is any international consensus as to what conduct falls within the category of "cruel, inhuman or degrading treatment." Absent such consensus as to the content of this alleged tort, it is not cognizable under the Alien Tort Statute. Therefore, the Motion to Reconsider dismissal of this claim is DENIED.

---

* These include Richard Anderson Falk of Princeton University, Thomas Franck of New York University, Louis Henkin of Columbia University, Richard B. Lillich of the University of Virginia, Phillipe Sands of Cambridge University and Boston College Law School, Henry J. Steiner of Harvard Law School, David Weissbrodt of the University of Minnesota Law School, and Burns H. Weston of the University of Iowa College of Law.

II

As stated above and in the October, 1987 Order, the Court interprets the Alien Tort Statute as providing a cause of action for "international torts." 672 F.2d at 1540. The plaintiff's burden in stating a claim is to establish the existence of a "universal, definable, and obligatory international norm[]." Id. To meet this burden plaintiffs need not establish unanimity among nations. Rather, they must show a general recognition among states that a specific practice is prohibited. It is with this standard in mind that the Court examines the evidence presented by plaintiffs.

A

In the Second Amended Complaint, plaintiff Forti alleges a claim for the "Disappearance and Presumed Summary Execution" of his mother. Second Amended Complaint, ¶63-67. Specifically, he alleges that his mother, along with he and his brothers, were seized from an airplane on February 18, 1977 "by police and military officials acting under the direction and control of defendant Suarez-Mason." Id. ¶3. The family was then taken to a detention center where they were held for several days.

On the sixth day of their detention they were bound, blindfolded and taken outside. The five boys, aged 8-16, were put in one car, while Mrs. Forti was put in another. The boys were then released on a Buenos Aires street. Id. ¶10-17. Mrs. Forti was not released, and has not been seen to this day. Forti alleges that he and his brothers tried through all available channels to get their mother released. However, "[t]he Argentine government's response to all of these efforts was always the same — it refused to confirm or deny that Mrs. Forti has been abducted or was being detained." Id. ¶18-20.

The legal scholars whose declarations have been submitted in connection with this Motion are in agreement that there is universal consensus as to the two essential elements of a claim for "disappearance." In Professor Franck's words:

> The international community has also reached a consensus on the definition of a "disappearance." It has two essential elements: (a) abduction by a state official or by persons acting under state approval or authority; and (b) refusal by the state to acknowledge the abduction and detention.

Franck Declaration, ¶7. See also Falk Declaration, at 3; Henkin Declaration, ¶9; Steiner Declaration, ¶3, 5; Weissbrodt Declaration, ¶8(b); Weston Declaration, ¶5.

Plaintiffs cite numerous international legal authorities which support the assertion that "disappearance" is a universally recognized wrong under the law of nations. For example, United Nations General Assembly Resolution 33/173 recognizes "disappearance" as violative of many of the rights recognized in the Universal Declaration of Human Rights, G.A. Res. 217 A (III), adopted by the United Nations General Assembly, Dec. 10, 1948, U.N. Doc. A/810 (1948) [hereinafter Universal Declaration of Human Rights]. These rights include: (1) the right to life; (2) the right to liberty and security of the person; (3) the right to freedom from torture; (4) the right to freedom from arbitrary arrest and detention; and (5) the right to a fair and public trial. Id., articles 3, 5, 9, 10, 11. See also International Covenant on Political and Civil Rights, G.A. Res. 2200 (XXI), adopted by the United Nations General Assembly, December 16, 1966, U.N. Doc. A/6316 (1966), articles, 6, 7, 9, 10, 14, 15, 17.

Other documents support this characterization of "disappearance" as violative of universally recognized human rights. The United States Congress has denounced "prolonged detention without charges and trial" along with other "flagrant denial[s] of the right to life, liberty, or the security of person." 22 U.S.C. §2304(d)(1). The recently published Restatement (Third) of the Foreign Relations Law of the United States §702 includes "disappearance" as a violation of the international law of human rights. The Organization of American States has also denounced "disappearance" as "an affront to the conscience of the hemisphere and . . . a crime against humanity." Organization of American States, Inter-American Commission on Human Rights, General Assembly Resolution 666 (November 18, 1983).

Of equal importance, plaintiffs' submissions support their assertion that there is a universally recognized legal definition of what constitutes the tort of "causing disappearance." The Court's earlier order expressed concern that "the sole act of taking an individual into custody does not suffice to prove conduct which the international community proscribes." 672 F. Supp. at 1543. Plaintiffs' submissions on this Motion, however, establish recognition of a second essential element — official refusal to acknowledge that the individual has been taken into custody. For example, the United Nations General Assembly has expressed concern at the

> difficulties in obtaining reliable information from competent authorities as to the circumstances of such persons, including reports of the persistent refusal of such authorities or organizations to acknowledge that they hold such persons in custody or otherwise to account for them.

U.N. General Assembly Resolution 33/173 (December 20, 1978).

Likewise, the Organization of American States has recognized the importance of this element, commenting on the

> numerous cases wherein the government systematically denies the detention of individuals, despite the convincing evidence that the claimants provide to verify their allegations that such persons have been detained by policy or military authorities and, in some cases, that those persons are, or have been, confined in specified detention centers.

Organization of American States, Inter-American Commission on Human Rights, 1977 Annual Report, at 26. See also M. Berman & R. Clark, State

Terrorism: Disappearances, 13 Rutgers L.J. 531, 533 (1982). ("The denial of accountability is the factor which makes disappearance unique among human rights violations.")

In the Court's view, the submitted materials are sufficient to establish the existence of a universal and obligatory international proscription of the tort of "causing disappearance." This tort is characterized by the following two essential elements: (1) abduction by state officials or their agents; followed by (2) official refusals to acknowledge the abduction or to disclose the detainee's fate. Upon review of the Second Amended Complaint it is clear that plaintiff Forti has sufficiently pled both these elements. See Second Amended Complaint, ¶3, 18. Therefore, the Motion to Reconsider is GRANTED in part and plaintiff Forti's claim is reinstated.

B

In its October, 1987 Order the Court found that plaintiffs had stated claims under the Alien Tort Statute for "official torture," 672 F. Supp. at 1541, but had failed to state claims for "cruel, inhuman and degrading treatment." Id. at 1543. Plaintiffs have now combined their two previous claims to allege "torture or other cruel, inhuman or degrading treatment or punishment. Second Amended Complaint, ¶53-56. The Second Amended Complaint does not state precisely what alleged actions constitute the proposed tort. Rather, it merely incorporates all the factual allegations and alleges that these acts constitute "torture or other cruel, inhuman or degrading treatment or punishment in violation of customary international law." Id., ¶54.

In dismissing plaintiff's earlier "cruel, inhuman or degrading treatment" claim this Court found that the proposed tort lacked "the requisite elements of universality and definability." 672 F. Supp. at 1543. Plaintiffs now submit the aforementioned declarations, see supra note[*], and several international legal authorities in support of their argument that "[t]he definition of cruel, inhuman or degrading treatment or punishment is inextricably related to that for torture." Plaintiff's Memorandum, at 20. Specifically, plaintiffs argue that the two are properly viewed on a continuum, and that "torture and cruel, inhuman or degrading treatment differ essentially in the degree of ill treatment suffered." Id. Thus while the latter treatment is not torture it is an analytically distinct tort which, in plaintiffs' view, is actionable under the Alien Tort Statute.

Plaintiffs emphasize that virtually all international legal authorities which prohibit torture also prohibit cruel, inhuman or degrading treatment. For example, §702 of the Restatement (Third) of the Foreign Relations Law of the United States: "A state violates international law if, as a matter of state policy, it practices, encourages, or condones . . . torture or other cruel, inhuman or degrading treatment or punishment. Likewise, 22 U.S.C. §2304(d)(1) lists "torture or cruel, inhuman or degrading treatment or punishment" among "gross violations of internationally recognized human rights." Article 5 of the Universal Declaration of Human Rights, supra, states that "[n]o one shall be subjected to torture or to cruel, inhuman or degrading treatment." See also De Sanchez v. Banco Central De Nicaragua, 770 F.2d 1385, 1397 (5th Cir. 1985) (recognizing "right not to be . . . tortured, or otherwise subjected to cruel, inhuman or degrading treatment").

While these and other materials establish a recognized proscription of "cruel, inhuman or degrading treatment," they offer no guidance as to what constitutes such treatment. The Restatement does not define the term. The cited statute (22 U.S.C. §2304) and the Universal Declaration of Human Rights also both fail to offer a definition. The scholars whose declarations have been submitted likewise decline to offer any definition of the proposed tort. In fact, one of the declarations appears to concede the lack of a universally recognized definition. See Lillich Declaration, at 8 ("only the contours of the prohibition, not its existence as a norm of customary international law, are the subject of legitimate debate").

This problem of definability is evidenced by the Second Amended Complaint. Plaintiffs simply incorporate all the factual allegations and without elaboration, allege that these constitute the alleged cruel, inhuman or degrading treatment. Second Amended Complaint, ¶53-56. However, the complaint alleges a wide range of discrete acts associated with the detentions. Some of the acts result in physical injury, some do not. Does the proposed tort require physical injury? If purely psychological harm is cognizable, as it would appear to be, is it actionable when caused by purely verbal conduct? Was it "cruel, inhuman and degrading treatment" for the military officials to threaten Mrs. Forti if she did not leave the airplane voluntarily? Second Amended Complaint, ¶11. Was it actionable conduct not to allow Mrs. Forti to talk to the commander of the detention center? Id. ¶13. Absent some definition of what constitutes "cruel, inhuman or degrading treatment" this Court has no way of determining what alleged treatment is actionable, and what is not.

Plaintiffs cite The Greek Case, 12 Y.B. Eur. Conv. on Human Rights 186 (1969), for a definition of "degrading treatment" as that which "grossly humiliates [the victim] before others or drives him to act against his will or conscience." Plaintiffs' Memorandum, at 22. But this definitional gloss is of no help. From our necessarily global perspective, conduct, particularly verbal conduct, which is humiliating or even grossly humiliating in one cultural context is of no moment in another. An international tort which appears and disappears as one travels around the world is clearly lacking in that level of common understanding necessary to create universal consensus. Likewise, the term "against his will or conscience" is too abstract to be of help. For example, a pacifist who is conscripted to serve in his country's military has arguably been forced to act "against his will or conscience." Would he thus have a claim for degrading treatment?

To be actionable under the Alien Tort Statute the proposed tort must be characterized by universal consensus in the international community as to its binding status *and its content*. In short, it must be a "universal, *definable*, and obligatory international norm[]." *Forti*, 672 F. Supp. at 1541 (emphasis added). Plaintiffs' submissions fail to establish that there is anything even remotely approaching universal consensus as to what constitutes "cruel, inhuman or degrading treatment." Absent this consensus in the internal community as to the tort's content it is not actionable under the Alien Tort Statute. Therefore, the Motion to Reconsider the Dismissal of this claim is DENIED. *

Comments and Questions

1. What use, if any, was made of the UN Charter's human rights clauses in the above three cases? Note that Judge Kaufman, in a footnote, indicates that some amici curiae in *Filartiga* did argue that the claim arose "under a treaty of the United States," but that the appellants themselves primarily relied upon "treaties and other international instruments as evidence of an emerging norm of customary international law, rather than independent sources of law." For comment on this use of the Charter and other international human rights treaties, see pages 172-173 infra.

Actually, the appellants themselves had argued that "with respect to torture, Article 55 of the UN Charter, as interpreted in the Universal Declaration . . . , should be viewed as self executing. . . ." Appellants' Reply Brief at 16, Filartiga v. Pena-Irala. They specifically emphasized that the Declaration was "not simply a source from which to infer customary international law," but also a demonstration of "[t]he enforceable nature of the right not to be tortured flowing from the Charter. . . ." Id. See also Brief of the International Human Rights Law Group, the Council on Hemispheric Affairs, and the Washington Office on Latin America as Amicus Curiae at 10-13, Filartiga v. Pena-Irala; Brief for Amnesty International-U.S.A., the International League for Human Rights, and the Lawyers' Committee for International Human Rights as Amicus Curiae at 6-10, Filartiga v. Pena-Irala.

Does the fact that Judge Kaufman passed over these Charter arguments, plus the fact that the Charter apparently was not argued and certainly not considered in Fernandez v. Wilkinson or *Forti*, suggest that attempts today to read the Universal Declaration's norms back into the Charter's human rights clauses to render the latter self-executing would

---

* Judge Jensen later found for the plaintiffs on their other claims and ordered Suarez-Mason to pay them $8 million. N.Y. Times, May 2, 1990 at A12, col. 1. So far the judgment remains uncollected. See Lillich, Damages for Gross Violations of International Human Rights Awarded by US Courts, 15 Human Rts. Q. 207, 218-219 (1993). — Eds.

prove futile? In this regard, reflect again upon the comments and questions at pages 119-120 and 135-136 supra.

2. Note, in contrast to the lack of use of the UN Charter's human rights clauses in the above three cases, the extensive reliance by all three courts upon the relevant articles of the Universal Declaration. Is the Declaration being used, however, because it is customary international law per se, because it reflects customary international law, or because it contributes to the emergence of customary international law? With respect to the first alternative, which would support the position taken by Professor Sohn (page 135 supra), what portions of the opinions in *Filartiga* and Fernandez v. Wilkinson suggest that the courts were of this mind? Does Judge Jensen's holding that "cruel, inhuman or degrading treatment" (as opposed to torture) is not a violation of customary international law for Alien Tort Statute purposes, despite the fact that he notes its prohibition by Article 5 of the Declaration, constitute a rejection of this approach? For other cases holding that various human rights mentioned in the Declaration have not yet achieved customary international law status, see In re Alien Children Educ. Litig., 501 F. Supp. 544, 593 (S.D. Tex. 1980), aff'd unreported mem., (5th Cir. 1981), aff'd sub nom. Plyler v. Doe, 457 U.S. 202 (1982) (right to education: Art. 26); De Sanchez v. Banco Central de Nicaragua, 770 F.2d 1385, 1397 (5th Cir. 1985) (right to property: Art. 17); Guinto v. Marcos, 654 F. Supp. 276, 280 (S.D. Cal. 1986) (right of free speech: Art. 19).

3. Of *Filartiga*, one may say, as Professor Lockwood has of *Fujii*, that "the decision was the legal shot heard around the nation." Lockwood, The United Nations Charter and United States Civil Rights Litigation: 1946-1955, 69 Iowa L. Rev. 901, 925 (1984). It has generated considerable international human rights law litigation, as the *Forti* case attests, and has been highly praised by the vast majority of legal commentators. See, e.g., Blum and Steinhardt, Federal Jurisdiction over International Human Rights Claims: The Alien Tort Claims Act After Filartiga v. Pena-Irala, 22 Harv. Intl. L.J. 53 (1981); Human Rights Symposium, 4 Hous. J. Intl. L. 1 (1981); Symposium, Federal Jurisdiction, Human Rights and the Law of Nations: Essays on Filartiga v. Pena-Irala, 11 Ga. J. Intl. & Comp. L. 305 (1981); and the articles cited in Lockwood, supra, at 901 n.1. Cf. Comment, Torture as a Tort in Violation of International Law: Filartiga v. Pena-Irala, 33 Stan. L. Rev. 353 (1981). For an account by the author of the opinion, see Kaufman, A Legal Remedy for International Torture?, N.Y. Times, Nov. 9, 1980, §6 (Magazine), at 44.

For a recent compilation of all cases that have arisen under the Alien Tort Statute, a majority of them since *Filartiga*, see Donaldson, Annotation, Construction and Application of Alien Tort Statute (28 U.S.C. §1350), Providing for Federal Jurisdiction over Alien's Action for Tort Committed in Violation of Law of Nations or Treaty of the United States, 116 A.L.R. Fed. 387 (1993).

4. For a misguided attempt to establish that acts of "international terror-

ism" violate customary international law and hence are actionable under the Alien Tort Statute, see Hanoch Tel-Oren v. Libyan Arab Republic, 517 F. Supp. 542 (D.D.C. 1981), aff'd per curiam, 726 F.2d 774 (D.C. Cir. 1984), cert. denied, 470 U.S. 1003 (1985). Since even cursory research by counsel would have revealed that customary international law as yet contains no general prohibition of terrorism, compare R. Lillich and L. Wenger, Transnational Terrorism: Conventions and Commentary (2d ed. 1995) with Note, Terrorism as a Tort in Violation of the Law of Nations, 6 Fordham Intl. L.J. 236 (1982), plaintiffs would have been better advised not to have initiated the action, which afforded the district court and two judges on the court of appeals the opportunity to attack the fundamental premises of *Filartiga*.

The leading protagonist in this attack was former Judge Bork, who in a concurring opinion contended, inter alia, that international human rights law could be invoked under the Alien Tort Statute only in those (rare) instances where the treaty provision or customary international law norm in question *explicitly* grants individuals a "cause of action." 726 F.2d at 801. For criticism of this approach, which as a practical matter would restrict such lawsuits to situations involving a handful of self-executing treaties at best, see D'Amato, What Does Tel-Oren Tell Lawyers? Judge Bork's Concept of the Law of Nations Is Seriously Mistaken, 79 Am. J. Intl. L. 92 (1985). See also Schneebaum, The Enforceability of Customary Norms of Public International Law, 8 Brooklyn J. Intl. L. 289 (1982).

Unhappily, and contrary to the position it and the Department of State had taken in *Filartiga* (see Memorandum for the United States as Amicus Curiae, Filartiga v. Pena-Irala, reprinted in 12 Hastings Intl. & Comp. L. Rev. 34 (1988)), the Department of Justice adopted Judge Bork's "cause of action" approach in its Memorandum for the United States as Amicus Curiae, Trajano v. Marcos, No. 86-207, slip op. (D. Haw. July 18, 1986), appeal docketed No. 86-2448 (9th Cir. Aug. 20, 1986), in which it urged the Court of Appeals for the Ninth Circuit to reject *Filartiga*'s teachings and adopt an extremely restrictive interpretation of the Alien Tort Statute. A group of international human rights lawyers filed an amicus curiae brief in reply, pointing out that the Department's new position was contrary to established judicial precedent as well as to basic principles of international law. See Amicus Curiae Memorandum on behalf of International Law Scholars and Practitioners in support of Plaintiffs in Trajano v. Marcos, reprinted in 12 Hastings Intl. & Comp. L. Rev. 4 (1988). The Ninth Circuit did not accept the Department of Justice's invitation to dismantle *Filartiga*. Trajano v. Marcos, No. 86-2448, 1989 WL 76894 (9th Cir. July 10, 1989).

More recently, specifically rejecting the Bork-Justice approach, the Ninth Circuit has joined "the Second Circuit in concluding that the Alien Tort Act . . . creates a cause of action for violations of specific, universal and obligatory international human rights standards which 'confer fundamental rights upon all people vis-a-vis their own governments.' *Filartiga*,

630 F.2d at 885-887." Hilao v. Marcos, 25 F.3d 1467, 1475-1476 (9th Cir. 1994). Furthermore, the Eleventh Circuit currently is addressing the question on an appeal from Abebe-Jiri v. Negewo, No. 90-2010, slip op. (N.D. Ga. Aug. 20, 1993), where one Ethiopian and two Canadian plaintiffs obtained judgments totaling $1.5 million from an Ethiopian defendant who during 1977-1981 had subjected them to prolonged arbitrary detention, torture, and (contrary to the *Forti* holding) cruel, inhuman, and degrading treatment.

For an article by a former member of the Department of Justice supporting its new position, see Rogers, The Alien Tort Statute and How Individuals "Violate" International Law, 21 Vand. J. Transnatl. L. 47 (1988). Another former member of the Department not only endorsed the new position, but also actually advocated the repeal of the Alien Tort Statute. Goldklang, What Time Does the Next Swan Boat Leave?, 40 Intl. Practitioners Notebook 6 (Sept. 1988). Compare the Torture Victims Protection Act discussed in Comment 9 infra.

5. Note that while *Filartiga* and *Forti* involved suits against individuals, nothing in the Alien Tort Statute prohibits suits against foreign states. In such a suit, however, should the state be able to claim sovereign immunity? Compare Frolova v. U.S.S.R., 761 F.2d 370 (7th Cir. 1985) (immunity) with Von Dardel v. U.S.S.R., 623 F. Supp. 246 (D.D.C. 1985) (no immunity), judgment vacated and complaint dismissed, 736 F. Supp. 1 (D.D.C. 1990) (immunity).

The Supreme Court has resolved the question, at least with respect to suits that, as in *Filartiga* and *Forti*, are based on tortious acts occurring outside the United States, by holding that the Alien Tort Statute does not constitute an exception to the Foreign Sovereign Immunities Act (FSIA), which remains the sole basis for obtaining jurisdiction over foreign states in U.S. courts. Argentine Republic v. Amerada Hess Shipping Corp., 488 U.S. 428 (1989). The Court specifically ruled that the "tort exception" contained in Section 1605(a)(5) of the FSIA was inapplicable in *Amerada Hess*, since it was limited by its very terms to cases where the tortious acts occurred within the United States. Id. at 439.

For such a case, see Letelier v. Republic of Chile, 488 F. Supp. 665 (D.D.C. 1980). The enforcement of the judgment in *Letelier* having become a diplomatic matter, it was referred to a five-member arbitral commission of the Organization of American States (OAS), which ordered Chile to pay the plaintiffs just over $2.6 million. Decision with Regard to the Dispute Concerning Responsibility for the Deaths of Letelier and Moffitt, 31 I.L.M. 1 (1992). See Lillich, Damages for Gross Violations of International Human Rights Awarded by US Courts, 15 Human Rts. Q. 207, 226-227 (1993). Postscript: the former head of Chile's military secret police and his deputy, who masterminded Letelier's assassination, recently were sentenced to seven and six years in prison, respectively. They currently remain free pending their appeals. Boston Globe, Nov. 13, 1993, at 2, cols. 4-5.

6. The thesis has been advanced that, when a foreign state's act violates a *jus cogens* norm, that is, a rule of customary international law of such high status that it prevails over other rules of international law in conflict with it (Restatement (Third) of the Foreign Relations Law of the United States §102 comment k at 28 (1987)), the state is not entitled to claim sovereign immunity with respect to that act. See Belsky, Merva, and Roht-Arriaza, Implied Waiver Under the FSIA: A Proposed Exception to Immunity for Violations of Peremptory Norms of International Law, 77 Calif. L. Rev. 365 (1989). This *"jus cogens* exception" to the FSIA was rejected by the Ninth Circuit, however, which noted that "the FSIA does not specifically provide for an exception to sovereign immunity based on *jus cogens*," and concluded that "if violations of *jus cogens* committed outside the United States are to be exceptions to immunity, Congress must make them so. The fact that there has been a violation of *jus cogens* does not confer jurisdiction under the FSIA." Siderman de Blake v. Republic of Argentina, 965 F.2d 699, 718, 719 (9th Cir. 1992) (finding implied waiver of sovereign immunity on other grounds, id. at 720-723), cert. denied, 113 S. Ct. 1812 (1993). The Court of Appeals for the D.C. Circuit recently reached the same conclusion. See Princz v. Federal Republic of Germany, 26 F.3d 1166, 1173-1174 (D.C. Cir. 1994) (2-1), reversing 813 F. Supp. 22, 26, 27 (D.D.C. 1994).

For a perceptive critique of *Siderman*, arguing that a *"jus cogens* exception" should be read into the implied waiver provision of the FSIA, see Comment, *Siderman de Blake v. Republic of Argentina*: Can the FSIA Grant Immunity for Violations of *Jus Cogens*?, 19 Brook. J. Intl. L. 967 (1993). See also Fitzpatrick, Reducing the FSIA Barrier to Human Rights Litigation — Is Amendment Necessary and Possible?, 1992 Am. Socy. Intl. L. Proceedings 338, 345-346 (supporting legislation that would add a "human rights exception" to the FSIA).

Finally, the distinction between sovereign immunity, now apparently governed exclusively by the FSIA, and head-of-state immunity, governed by customary international law, should be kept in mind. The latter doctrine has been held to have survived the enactment of both the FSIA and the Torture Victims Protection Act (see Comment 9 infra), thus assuring official Heads of State continued absolute immunity from human rights lawsuits brought against them in the United States. Lafontant v. Aristide, 844 F. Supp. 128 (E.D.N.Y. 1994).

7. Great Britain has adopted a statute similar to the FSIA. State Immunity Act, 1978, ch. 33 (Eng.). In a recent case brought by a British national against the Government of Kuwait for torture it allegedly inflicted upon him in Kuwait on two occasions in 1991, the court of appeal — reading a "human rights exception" into that statute — held that "no state or sovereign immunity should be accorded even under the State Immunity Act 1978 in respect of acts which it is alleged are properly to be described as torture in contravention of public international law." al-Adsani v. Kuwait, slip op., Q.B. (1994) (Eng. C.A.). See Bindman, Bringing Torturers Before

the Courts, The Times (London), May 31, 1994, at 28, cols. 1-2. How helpful would this precedent be in attempting to convince a U.S. court that a similar exception to the FSIA exists?

8. Both *Filartiga* and *Forti* saw the defendants arguing that the act of state doctrine barred suits against them. In *Filartiga*, Judge Kaufman found it unnecessary to decide the question, although in dictum he expressed doubt "whether action by a state official in violation of the Constitution and laws of the Republic of Paraguay, and wholly unratified by that nation's government, could properly be characterized as an act of state." 630 F.2d at 889. In *Forti*, Judge Jensen, after noting that the defendant's alleged acts violated "fundamental human rights lying at the very heart of the individual's existence," rejected his act of state argument largely for procedural reasons, that is because it was uncertain "at this stage of the proceedings that adjudication of plaintiff's claims [would] necessarily entail considering the legality of the official acts of a foreign sovereign." 672 F.2d at 1546. For an excellent student critique of this aspect of *Forti*, see Comment, Remedying Foreign Repression Through U.S. Courts: Forti v. Suarez-Mason, 20 N.Y.U. J. Intl. L. & Pol. 405, 446-458 (1988).

While the result in these cases may be correct, does the reasoning go far enough? Does the rationale underlying the act of state doctrine, as formulated in the Supreme Court's seminal decision Banco Nacional de Cuba v. Sabbatino, 376 U.S. 398, 428, 430 n.34 (1964), preclude courts from adjudicating cases involving serious human rights violations by foreign government officials? For negative answers, see R. Falk, The Role of Domestic Courts in the International Legal Order 9-10, 72 (1964); Halberstam, Sabbatino Resurrected: The Act of State Doctrine in the Revised Restatement of U.S. Foreign Relations Law, 79 Am. J. Intl. L. 68, 86-87 (1985); Lillich, The Role of Domestic Courts in Promoting Human Rights Norms, 24 N.Y.L. Sch. L. Rev. 153, 159-162 (1978).

The Restatement acknowledges this rationale and correctly, if somewhat timidly, applies it to human rights cases. "A claim arising out of an alleged violation of fundamental human rights — for instance, a claim on behalf of a victim of torture or genocide — would (if otherwise sustainable) probably not be defeated by the act of state doctrine, since the accepted international law of human rights is well established and contemplates external scrutiny of such acts." Restatement (Third) of the Foreign Relations Law of the United States §443 comment c at 370 (1987). Two Ninth Circuit decisions have refused to apply the act of state doctrine in human rights cases. See Republic of the Philippines v. Marcos, 862 F.2d 1355, 1360-1361 (9th Cir. 1988), cert. denied, 490 U.S. 1035 (1989); Liu v. Republic of China, 892 F.2d 1419, 1431-1434 (9th Cir. 1989), cert. denied, 497 U.S. 1058 (1990). The Supreme Court has not yet adopted this commonly called "human rights exception" to the act of state doctrine. Do you think that it eventually will?

9. Its very name indicates that U.S. citizens cannot avail themselves of the Alien Tort Statute. For an excellent suggestion that "Congress should

consider amending [Section 1350] to allow lawsuits brought by U.S. citizens as well as aliens," see The Phenomenon of Torture: Hearings on H.J. Res. 605 Before the House Comm. on Foreign Affairs and Its Subcomm. on Human Rights and International Organizations, 98th Cong., 2d Sess. 247 (1984) (statement of Michael H. Posner, Esq., Exec. Dir., Lawyers Committee for Human Rights). Other amendments to clarify Section 1350 also have been recommended. See Randall, Further Inquiries into the Alien Tort Statute and a Recommendation, 18 N.Y.U. J. Intl. L. & Pol. 473, 511-532 (1986).

While efforts to amend the Alien Tort Statute proved unsuccessful, Congress, over the opposition of the Reagan and Bush Administrations, did enact the Torture Victim Protection Act (TVPA), Pub. L. No. 102-256, 106 Stat. 73, codified at 28 U.S.C. §1350 (1988 & Supp. V 1993), which permits U.S. citizens as well as aliens to sue for recovery of damages from individuals who, under actual or apparent authority or color of law of any foreign nation, have engaged in torture or extrajudicial killing. See Drinan and Kuo, Putting the World's Oppressors on Trial: The Torture Victim Protection Act, 15 Human Rts. Q. 605 (1993). See also Torture Victim Protection Act of 1989: Hearing on S. 1689 and H.R. 1662 Before the Subcomm. on Immigration and Refugee Affairs of the Senate Comm. on the Judiciary, 101st Cong., 2d Sess. (1990).

The TVPA is a welcome, albeit exceptionally limited, effort to accord U.S. citizens equal remedies with aliens in the enforcement of international human rights in U.S. courts. Unfortunately, as Professor Fitzpatrick has observed, it "comes encumbered with three limitations that are not contained in the Alien Tort Claims Act: (1) a specific requirement that 'adequate and available remedies' be exhausted in the state where the violation occurred (section 2(b)); (2) a ten-year statute of limitations on claims (section 2(c)); and (3) a restriction of jurisdiction to individual defendants (section 2(a)), thus excluding foreign states." Fitzpatrick, Reducing the FSIA Barrier to Human Rights Litigation — Is Amendment Necessary and Possible?, 1992 Am. Socy. Intl. L. Proceedings 338, 346. Additionally, it has been held that "the Act was not intended to trump diplomatic and head-of-state immunities." Lafontant v. Aristide, 844 F. Supp. 128, 138 (E.D.N.Y. 1994) (extrajudicial killing action against exiled president of Haiti dismissed on head-of-state immunity grounds).

In cases not involving torture or extrajudicial killing, U.S. citizens presumably can obtain jurisdiction under 28 U.S.C. §1331 (1988), the federal question statute, since as Judge Jensen rightly remarks in Forti "a case presenting claims arising under customary international law arises under the laws of the United States for purposes of federal question jurisdiction." 672 F. Supp. at 1544. Cf. Judge Kaufman in Filartiga, 630 F.2d at 887 n.22. For a persuasive demonstration that federal question jurisdiction exists over international human rights law claims, see Randall, Federal Questions and the Human Rights Paradigm, 73 Minn. L. Rev. 349, 386-424 (1988).

10. As its headnote indicates, the United States appealed Fernandez v. Wilkinson (page 143 supra). On appeal, the U.S. Court of Appeals for the Tenth Circuit neither adopted nor disowned Judge Rogers's holding, but instead construed the relevant statutory provisions to require Fernandez's release from continued detention. 654 F.2d at 1386. In dictum, however, it considered at length "the serious constitutional questions involved if the statute were construed differently." Id. Noting that "[d]ue process is not a static concept," the Court of Appeals thought it proper "to consider international law principles for notions of fairness as to [the] propriety of holding aliens in detention. No principle of international law is more fundamental than the concept that human beings should be free from arbitrary imprisonment." Id. at 1388. Citing the Universal Declaration and the American Convention on Human Rights, it concluded that its construction of the statute was "consistent with accepted international law principles that individuals are entitled to be free of arbitrary imprisonment." Id. at 1390. Thus, while not applying customary international law directly, the Court of Appeals invoked it indirectly in determining the protection afforded by U.S. law. For an excellent essay contrasting the District Court's approach with that of the court of appeals, see Martineau, Interpreting the Constitution: The Use of International Human Rights Norms, 5 Human Rts. Q. 87 (1983). Further comment on this indirect use of international human rights norms may be found in the Comment on pages 174-175 infra.

11. The District Court holding in Fernandez v. Wilkinson that prolonged arbitrary detention violates customary international law was relied upon by Judge Jensen in *Forti*. Compare the various holdings in Garcia-Mir v. Meese, 622 F. Supp. 887 (N.D. Ga. 1985), rev'd in part & aff'd in part & dismissed as moot in part, 788 F.2d 1446 (11th Cir.), cert. denied, 479 U.S. 889 (1986), another case involving excludable Cuban aliens, where the District Court for the Northern District of Georgia observed that "[e]ven the government admits that [the] customary international law of human rights contains at least a general principle prohibiting prolonged arbitrary detention." 622 F. Supp. at 902. (It should be noted that the government maintained that this general principle was "not a rule of law. . . ." Supplemental Brief in Support of Motion for Denial of Habeas Corpus on the Issues of International Law at 3.)

The government, however, proceeded to argue that, under the Supreme Court's caveats to its oft-quoted holding in The Paquete Habana (see page 138 supra), there existed a "controlling executive act" that provided a rule of decision, making resort to customary international law inappropriate. Defendants' Reply Memorandum in Opposition to Habeas Corpus Petition at 17-20. The district court accepted this contention that a controlling executive act effectively preempts customary international law, holding that under the Constitution "the President has the authority to ignore our country's obligations arising under customary international law, and plaintiffs have failed to establish that the Attorney General does not share in that power when he directs the detention of unadmitted aliens. Accordingly, customary international law offers plaintiffs no relief in this forum." 622 F. Supp. at 903-904.

On appeal, the U.S. Court of Appeals for the Eleventh Circuit, after advancing the extraordinary view that the President possesses the power "to disregard international law in service of domestic needs," concluded that the Attorney General's "executive acts here evident constitute a sufficient basis for affirming the trial court's finding that international law does not control." 788 F.2d at 1455. This decision, were it to be followed by other federal courts, would put a severe restraint upon the use of customary international human rights law, at least in those (rare, one hopes) cases where the Executive Branch is willing to take and rely upon acts contrary thereto. The decision has been severely criticized for misreading The Paquete Habana. See, for example, Henkin, The President and International Law, 80 Am. J. Intl. 930 (1986). See generally Panel, The Authority of the United States Executive to Interpret, Articulate or Violate the Norms of International Law, 1986 Am. Socy. Intl. L. Proceedings 297.

C.   The Universal Declaration of Human Rights Nears 50

Restatement (Third) of the Foreign Relations Law of the United States
§702 (1987)

§702.   Customary International Law of Human Rights

A state violates international law if, as a matter of state policy, it practices, encourages, or condones

  (a)   genocide,
  (b)   slavery or slave trade,
  (c)   the murder or causing the disappearance of individuals,
  (d)   torture or other cruel, inhuman, or degrading treatment or punishment,
  (e)   prolonged arbitrary detention,
  (f)   systematic racial discrimination, or
  (g)   a consistent pattern of gross violations of internationally recognized human rights.

Lillich, Remarks
1985 Am. Socy. Intl. L. Proceedings 84, 84-86

My assignment is to discuss the customary international law of human rights in the Revised Restatement. This newly emerging body of law impacts upon various provisions of Tentative Draft No. 6 of the Restatement, for instance, section 469 [now 443] (where it supports a "human rights exception" to the act of state doctrine) and section 711 (where it furnishes a minimum standard of protection for state responsibility for injuries to aliens' purposes). The cornerstone provision upon which I shall focus today, however, is section 702, taken in haec verba from its 1982 predecessor contained in Tentative Draft No. 3. [The text, which was not changed after these remarks, is set out immediately above.]

Section 702, which has no counterpart in the "old" Restatement of 1965, is an exceptionally innovative effort. It is the first time, as the Chief Reporter, Professor Henkin, has stated, that a serious attempt has been made to formulate and restate the customary international law of human rights. For taking this step, he, his fellow Reporters and the American Law Institute (ALI) deserve high marks. While the Chief Reporter has downplayed the section's significance — three years ago he remarked that "[i]n Section 702 we were on new ground and we were trying to be modest and conservative because we don't want to push the Institute to take too far-reaching positions" — the section unquestionably will have considerable impact upon the development and use of customary international human rights law, both within the United States and internationally. Insofar as the former is concerned, one need only refer to section 131(1) [now 111(1)], which provides that customary international law is law of the United States, and to Reporters' Note 4 to section 135 [now 115], which suggests that "arguably later customary law should be given effect as law of the United States, even in the face of an earlier [federal] law or [international] agreement," to see section 702's potential effect in U.S. domestic litigation.

In making their laundry list of human rights protected by customary international law, the Reporters wisely have selected only those rights, as recognized in the Universal Declaration of Human Rights, "whose status as customary law is generally accepted at this time and whose scope and content are generally agreed." Since — pace some overly enthusiastic scholars — not all of the rights set out in the declaration now reflect customary international law, their list necessarily is a "quite cautious" one, provoking comments in some quarters that it does not go far enough in enumerating those rights that international law now guarantees to individuals. Specifically, the right to own property, the right not to suffer sexual discrimination, various civil and political rights (including the right to leave one's country) and the right to join free trade unions have been urged — all unsuccessfully — as candidates for inclusion.

While generally supportive of the Reporters' reluctance to add additional rights to section 702 — indeed, one might question whether "cruel, inhuman or degrading treatment or punishment," as contrasted with torture, currently is prohibited by customary international law as section 702(d) declares (little recognition of the important distinction appears in Comment g and Reporters' Note 5) — I nevertheless am concerned about the seemingly closed nature of the list of rights contained in the section. Moreover, I am not convinced by the Chief Reporter's argument, made during debates on Tentative Draft No. 3 in 1982, that as support for additional rights emerges internationally they can be shoehorned into section 702(g)'s prohibition of "consistent patterns of gross violations of internationally recognized human rights," a phrase developed by the United Nations for altogether different purposes.

As far back as the ALI's 1982 annual meeting, I suggested that section 702 be revised: (1) to add a catchall clause introducing some flexibility into what, as it now stands, is an unnecessarily closed and potentially restrictive list of six specific state acts that constitute violations of customary international human rights law; and (2) to bifurcate the section so as to distinguish such specific state acts from "consistent patterns of gross violations of internationally recognized human rights," currently equated to the other specific acts but in reality a completely different category of human rights violation (involving not only these specific but also other potential acts that, over a period of time and as a result of their severity, may — cumulatively — violate customary international law).

Other supporters of the Revised Restatement have made similar suggestions. Thus Dean Gordon A. Christenson, in a recent memorandum to the ALI Council, while generally agreeing with the thrust of section 702, observed that as presently drafted

> a serious problem of construction will inevitably arise. By specifically limiting the number of categories enumerated as falling within the customary international law of human rights, the Draft might unwittingly limit the emergence or growth of other categories of presently enumerated rights, or of those in the various human rights documents or conventions that have not risen to the level of accepted state practice in respect to their violations. To cure this problem so that it does not deter the emergence of additional customary principles of human rights norms by its provisions, the drafters should consider adding a savings clause such as "among others that may emerge" in the introductory sentence of the black letter in §702.

Dean Christenson's memorandum ends by reiterating what I should like to underscore is my main concern with section 702, namely, that "[t]he black letter should not foreclose the process of emergence of new customary norms as they occur." *

Another change, this one not in the black letter but in a comment, also should be made to assure that section 702 contributes to the proper future

---

* After the delivery of this paper, at the ALI's annual meeting on May 17, 1985, the Chief Reporter proposed, and the Institute endorsed, adding a separate paragraph at the end of Comment a to section 702:

> This section (clauses *a* to *f*) lists those rights as to which there is virtually universal agreement as of 1985 that they have become part of customary international law. This list is not necessarily complete, and is not closed. Human rights not listed in this section might also be found to have achieved that status of customary international law or might achieve that status in the future.

development of the customary international law of human rights. As it now reads, Comment 1 [now n] on "Customary law of human rights and jus cogens" states that "[t]he rules of this section are peremptory norms (jus cogens), and an international agreement that would violate them would be void." This observation may be descriptively correct — save perhaps for its embracing "cruel, inhuman or degrading treatment or punishment," a prohibition that as I mentioned earlier some commentators might consider not even a violation of customary international law, much less of jus cogens — but it is open to the interpretation, surely not the intention of the Reporters, that only peremptory norms (jus cogens) can qualify under section 702 as customary international human right law rules. I would hope that the Reporters would eliminate any possible ambiguity by adding a sentence to Comment 1 [now n] stating explicitly that not all rules need rise to the level of peremptory norms (jus cogens) to find their place, now or in the future, in section 702. †

Despite these important reservations, I believe the Revised Restatement, a pioneering attempt to formulate and restate the customary international law of human rights, is a remarkable accomplishment and deserves the support of all international lawyers, especially ones specializing in human rights. With the prospects for U.S. ratification of the major international human rights instruments at a dead end, at least for the immediate future, the need to develop a body of customary — as contrasted with conventional — international human rights law becomes ever more important. U.S. courts have attached considerable importance to the "old" Restatement in the past, and they already have relied upon numerous provisions in Tentative Drafts of the Revised Restatement in reaching decisions in recent years. Let us hope that the final version of the Revised Restatement, including a modified version of section 702 along the lines I have suggested, will contribute to the use and development of customary international human rights law within the United States as well as on the international level in the years to come.

Although the blackletter of Section 702 remained unchanged from the initial draft in 1982 through the final version in 1987, the Reporters did add a comment that "[t]he list is not necessarily complete, and is not closed: human rights not listed in this section may have achieved the status of customary international law, and some rights might achieve that status in the future." Restatement (Third) of the Foreign Relations Law of the United States §702 comment a at 162 (1987). Possible candidates for customary international law status listed are systematic religious discrimination, the

---

† At the ALI's annual meeting mentioned [in the previous note], the Chief Reporter agreed to add to the end of Comment 1 [now n] the following: "A rule need not be a peremptory norm (*jus cogens*), however, to be part of the customary international law of human rights."

right to property, and gender discrimination (id. at 165-166), all rights guaranteed by the Universal Declaration. To date no U.S. court has found these rights (or, indeed, any other right not contained in Section 702's blackletter) to be part of customary international law. Indeed, inclusion in the blackletter of a right guaranteed by the Universal Declaration is no guarantee of its customary international law status, as *Forti*'s holding with respect to "cruel, inhuman or degrading treatment" demonstrates.

United States courts, of course, are not the sole custodians and expositors of the Universal Declaration's status. Executive Branch practice, as noted previously (see page 136 supra) obviously has considerable impact, as increasingly have acts of Congress (see International Human Rights Law Group, U.S. Legislation Relating Human Rights to U.S. Foreign Policy (4th ed. 1991)). Moreover, U.S. government attitudes, while important and, indeed, perhaps controlling domestically, are only the views of one state and, thus, not necessarily determinative internationally. Cf. generally Simma and Alston, The Sources of Human Rights Law: Custom, Jus Cogens, and General Principles, 12 Austl. Y.B. Intl. L. 82 (1992). The following extract, based upon a six-year study of the practice of numerous UN member states with respect to the Universal Declaration, reveals widespread support for the proposition that a substantial number of the rights contained therein now reflect customary international law.

International Law Association, Committee on the Enforcement of Human Rights Law, Final Report on the Status of the Universal Declaration of Human Rights in National and International Law
ILA, Report of the Sixty-Sixth Conference 525, 544-549
(Buenos Aires 1994)*

THE CONTENT OF CUSTOMARY LAW EVIDENCED IN THE DECLARATION

Those who urge acceptance of the Declaration *in toto* as customary law are in a clear minority, and there is insufficient state practice to support such a wide-ranging proposition at present. Unless one wishes to interpret the proposed customary international law norm as merely expressing general agreement with the desirability of the principles in the Declaration, it would appear difficult to make the case that states recognize an international legal obligation to guarantee, e.g., periodic holidays with pay, full equality of rights upon dissolution of a marriage, or protection against unemployment.

---

* The Editors served as Chairman and Rapporteur of the Committee and were primarily responsible for the preparation of this report. — EDS.

However, there would seem to be little argument that many provisions of the Declaration today do reflect customary international law. "Few claim that any state that violates any provision of the Declaration has violated international law. Almost all would agree that some violations of the Declaration are violations of international law." Almost no state has specifically rejected the principles proclaimed in the Universal Declaration, and it constitutes a fundamental part of what has become known as the Universal Bill of Human Rights.

The American Law Institute's *Restatement* . . . offers one of the most explicit and authoritative opinions as to the content of the customary international law of human rights, at least as of 1987. [The report quotes Section 702, set out at page 162 supra.] The prohibitions against slavery, arbitrary deprivation of life, torture, arbitrary detention, and racial discrimination are explicitly included in the Universal Declaration, as well as other international instruments, and the prohibitions against genocide and gross violations of human rights are certainly implicit in the Declaration's provisions.

It would be presumptuous for the present report to pretend to analyse comprehensively each of the rights set forth in the Universal Declaration. Nevertheless, the evidence of state practice identified by the rapporteur suggests the following tentative conclusions with respect to the various articles of the Declaration.

Articles 1, 2, and 7 express the fundamental right of equal treatment and non-discrimination *with respect to guaranteed human rights* "without distinction of any kind." It would seem difficult to deny the widespread acceptance of such a right to equal treatment under the law, subject to the caveats below.

Of course, even with respect to protected rights, state practice does not support a conclusion that there is full compliance with the principle of equality. Women are prevented from exercising their human rights on an equal footing with men in many states; distinctions based on religious and political beliefs are found in many constitutions; and the effective guarantee of respective rights and obligations to the wealthy and the poor is often quite different.

One specific kind of discrimination, that based on race, is held by all commentators to be prohibited under customary international law, at least when it is pervasive.

Article 3, guaranteeing "the right to life, liberty and security of person," may be too general to be a useful international norm, although protection of the right to life has been cited frequently as falling within customary international law. The prohibition against murder and causing "disappearances" is included in the *Restatement*'s list, and the prohibition against the arbitrary deprivation of life has been referred to by many other commentators.

The prohibition against slavery in *article 4* is also universally held to form part of customary law; it is further prohibited by a series of widely ratified conventions.

Article 5's prohibition against "torture or . . . cruel, inhuman or degrading treatment or punishment" is perhaps the most widely commented upon right in the Declaration (with the possible exception of the prohibition against racial discrimination). Its place in customary international law is confirmed by the *Restatement*, and many other sources could be cited. The Vienna World Conference on Human Rights "reaffirm[ed] that under human rights law and international humanitarian law, freedom from torture is a right which must be protected under all circumstances."

One of the most comprehensive examinations of the evidence of the status of the prohibition against torture in customary international law is the U.S. case of *Filartiga* v. *Peña-Irala*, in which the Court of Appeals for the Second Circuit found that the right to be free from torture is one of the rights conferred by international law "upon all people vis-a-vis their own governments." It relied for its conclusion on provisions of the Universal Declaration and a number of other international instruments (most unratified by the United States), national statutes, U.S. government statements, and the opinions of legal experts.

Article 6 states simply that "[e]veryone has the right to recognition everywhere as a person before the law." Although no direct support for this principle is found in scholarly literature, it would seem impossible to deny the status of custom to such a fundamental expression of the essential equality and value of natural persons. The relegation of certain categories of individuals to the status of "non-persons" without rights may unfortunately exist in practice, but no state publicly adheres to such a view.

Article 8's guarantee of an effective remedy before domestic courts for violations of human rights would seem to be an essential prerequisite to ensure the enjoyment of other human rights, but it is not generally included in lists of customary human rights and has not been the subject of significant domestic jurisprudence.

The prohibition in *article 9* against arbitrary arrest, detention, or exile is included in the *Restatement* list only if it is "prolonged;" other commentators have not made such a fine distinction, although the definition of what is "arbitrary" obviously limits the norm's usefulness in all but the most blatant cases. The International Court of Justice has stated:

> Wrongfully to deprive human beings of their freedom and to subject them to the physical constraint in conditions of hardship is in itself manifestly incompatible with the principles of the Charter of the United Nations, as well as with the fundamental principles enunciated in the Universal Declaration of Human Rights.

The prohibition against arbitrary detention is closely linked to provisions relating to the right to a fair trial, found in *articles 10 and 11*. A comprehensive survey of provisions relating to criminal justice recently concluded that "at times there seems to be an uncanny resemblance between the terminology of more recent constitutions and that of the Universal Declaration and the ICCPR [International Covenant on Civil and Political Rights]," and many observers include the right to a fair trial (without more specific examination of the components of the right) among those now guaranteed under customary law.

Article 12, which deals, inter alia, with the right to privacy, was cited by the U.S. Government in the *Hostages* case as being encompassed in customary law and is included in other major human rights treaties. However, the content of the right varies considerably among states, and the contours of that realm of personal privacy which is beyond the reach of government is perhaps too vague to be deemed a useful part of customary law at present.

Article 13, which is concerned with freedom of movement and the right to leave and return, also was cited by the United States in the *Hostages* case. Meron believes that these rights should be added to those considered to be part of customary law, but there does not seem to be sufficient consensus on this point at present to draw firm conclusions.

Despite widespread acceptance of the 1951 Convention on the Status of Refugees and the 1967 Protocol thereto, the right to seek (not to receive) asylum set forth in *article 14* has not been identified by commentators or states as falling within customary international law. However, returning a person to a country where he would be tortured or persecuted might well violate a developing customary norm against the *refoulement* of refugees.

German courts have recognized that the right to a nationality set forth in *article 15* is "the expression of customary international law in the sense of article 25 of the Basic Law [German Constitution]." The Inter-American Court of Human Rights referred to article 15 of the Declaration as supporting its conclusion that "[t]he right of every human being to a nationality has been recognized as such by international law." However, no other source for including this specific right within customary law has been found.

A German court has likewise found that "there is a consensus under international law that freedom of marriage is one of the fundamental human rights," citing the European Convention of Human Rights and *article 16* of the Universal Declaration.

The right to property, included in *article 17* of the Universal Declaration, was omitted from both of the two human rights Covenants. However, a recent UN study on the right to property concludes that the Declaration's standards "became rules of customary international law and which as such were regarded as mandatory in the doctrine and practice of international law." One must assume that the right to property would be included as one of these "mandatory" rules, so long as one excludes from the right broader issues such as the international norms governing expropriation and other controversial topics. The rapporteur did observe that the right to property is not universally recognized, thus casting some doubt on its status or scope as a customary norm. Nonetheless, it would seem difficult to maintain that a state's power to expropriate or seize individual property is wholly unlimited.

Article 18 guarantees the right to freedom of thought, conscience, and religion; its provisions were expanded upon in the 1981 Declaration on the Elimination of All Forms of Intolerance and of Discrimination Based on Religion or Belief adopted by the UN General Assembly. The Declaration's Preamble considers that "religion or belief, for anyone who professes either, is one of the fundamental elements in his conception of life and that freedom of religion or belief should be fully respected and guaranteed." Although the Special Rapporteur on Iran of the UN Commission on Human Rights has stated that freedom of thought, conscience, and religion has "the character of *jus cogens*," the degree of de facto and de jure suppression of the practice of certain religions makes acceptance of such an assertion problematic. In addition, some Islamic countries have denied that Muslims have a right to change their religion.

Similarly, the widespread restrictions on freedom of opinion and expression, set forth in *article 19* of the Declaration, make it difficult to conclude that this provision is now part of customary international law, unless one accepts that the restrictions to freedom of expression which states believe are permissible can be so broad as to swallow the right itself. Similar observations might be made with respect to *article 20*'s guarantee of the right of peaceful assembly.

Despite the arguments of some that a "right to democracy" may be emerging as a norm of international customary law, it is apparent that many states have not accepted *article 21*'s guarantee of the right to participate in the political life of one's country.

Articles 22 through 27 deal primarily with economic, social, and cultural rights, including social security, the right to work, the right to rest and leisure, the right to an adequate standard of living, the right to education, and the right to participate in cultural life. Despite the fact that the United States, in particular, has often denied the status of "rights" to these norms, they may enjoy wider international support than some of the civil and political rights traditionally emphasized in U.S. jurisprudence. However, they are rarely referred [to] by either commentators or courts in discussions of the content of customary international human rights law.

The following rights would seem to enjoy sufficiently widespread support as to be at least potential candidates for rights recognized under customary international law: the right to free choice of employment; the right to form and join trade unions; and the right to free primary education, subject to a state's available resources. Many rights included within these articles are closely related to other rights, such as the right to life and the prohibition against arbitrary discrimination. The Appeals Board of the Council of Europe has found that "[t]he absence of discrimination based on sex, and equal pay for workers of either sex constitute, at the present time, one of the general principles of law."

Article 28, which calls for "a social and international order" in which the Declaration's rights can be realized is clearly hortatory and insufficiently precise to constitute an international legal norm.

Although it does not set forth a substantive right, *article 29*'s reference to permissible restrictions on rights might be considered as a general principle of international law, if it is interpreted to mean that international human rights may not be restricted arbitrarily. On the other hand, human rights treaties do permit limitations or restrictions on rights to be imposed on grounds other than those specified in article 29, which suggests that the literal terms of the article cannot be taken to represent international custom.

Finally, the savings clause in *article 30* is found in essentially all subsequent human rights treaties and may be seen as an admonition that the Declaration's provisions must be implemented in good faith, so as not to undermine its very purpose. This may simply reflect the general principle of international law which does not allow a treaty party to act in a way which would defeat the object and purpose of the treaty while purporting to rely on its provisions.

Firm conclusions as to the status of any of the provisions of the Universal Declaration of Human Rights in customary international law cannot be drawn without a much more thorough and comprehensive survey of state practice than is possible in the present report. However, these cursory observations may suggest the rights with respect to which such a survey might be most productive.

IV. Final Comments and Questions

1. Do you think that the California Supreme Court would have come to a different conclusion in *Fujii* had Professor Schachter's article, like Judge Hudson's telegram, come to its attention? Note that Professor Kelsen is the only writer cited by the court, lending support to Judge Newman's observation that "the holding was wrong and the briefing was poor." Newman, Important International Human Rights Documents, Cases, and Materials, 17 U.S.F.L. Rev. 2, 5 (1982). Do you think that Professor Schachter altered his views after he saw the Supreme Court's opinion?

2. In Rice v. Sioux City Cemetery, Inc., 245 Iowa 147, 60 N.W.2d 110 (1953), aff'd, 348 U.S. 880 (1954), vacated, 349 U.S. 70 (1955), plaintiff had entered into a contract with the defendant cemetery for the burial of her husband, the contract stipulating that "burial privileges accrue only to members of the Caucasian race." After the ceremonies at the graveside, the defendant removed the body from the site on the ground that the decedent was not Caucasian. The plaintiff sued for breach of contract, one of her claims being that the racially restrictive contract provision was void in that it constituted a violation of the UN Charter's human rights clauses. The Iowa

Supreme Court held that the Charter had no application to contracts between private parties. The U.S. Supreme Court affirmed in a per curiam
opinion by an evenly divided court. Upon rehearing, the Court vacated this
order, dismissing the writ of certiorari as having been improvidently
granted, since Iowa had passed legislation addressing the problem. Thus,
the Court never squarely considered the issue of the relevance of the UN
Charter.

In dismissing the writ, however, Justice Frankfurter, speaking for the
Supreme Court, made the following statement:

> The Iowa courts dismissed summarily the claim that some of the general and
> hortatory language of [the UN Charter] . . . constituted a limitation on the
> rights of the states and of persons otherwise reserved to them under the
> Constitution. . . . [T]here is . . . no basis for any inference that the division
> of this Court [on the case at land] reflected any diversity of opinion on this
> [particular] question.

Does this statement justify the following conclusion by McLaughlin, The
Scope of the Treaty Power in the United States, 42 Minn. L. Rev. 709, 751
(1958):

> This seems to mean that the [U.S. Supreme] Court agreed with the Iowa
> courts that the human rights clauses were inapplicable, presumably because
> non-self-executing but perhaps because merely "general and hortatory."

3. On the domestic legal effect of the human rights clauses of the UN
Charter, a number of writers are cited in Schachter, The Charter and the
Constitution: The Human Rights Provisions in American Law, 4 Vand. L.
Rev. 643 (1951), excerpts from which appear in both Problem I and this
Problem. In addition to these writers, see Schwelb, The International Court
of Justice and the Human Rights Clauses of the Charter, 66 Am. J. Intl. L.
337, 338 (1972) ("The Views of Publicists," particularly page 340 n.9);
Sohn, The Human Rights Law of the Charter, 12 Texas Intl. L.J. 129, 132
(1977) ("Should a state conclude a treaty or issue a legislative act or regula-
tion which constitutes a gross violation of human rights, such a treaty or act
would be clearly invalid as contrary to a basic and overriding norm of the
Charter, and any tribunal, international or domestic, which might be asked
to apply such a treaty, or act as regulation, should refuse to do so."); and
Note, Individual Enforcement of Obligations Arising Under the United
Nations Charter, 19 Santa Clara L. Rev. 195 (1979). See generally Iwasawa,
The Doctrine of Self-Executing Treaties in the United States: A Critical
Analysis, 26 Va. J. Intl. L. 627 (1986); Paust, Self-Executing Treaties, 82
Am. J. Intl. L. 760 (1988); Riesenfeld, The Doctrine of Self-Executing
Treaties and U.S. v. Postal: Win at Any Price?, 74 Am. J. Intl. L. 892 (1980).

4. With respect to the other international human rights treaties that the
United States has ratified, it has been noted that none has been held to be
self-executing (see pages 121-122 supra). Yet such treaties — and, indeed,
even treaties that the United States has signed but not ratified — may con-

tribute to the development of customary international human rights law. Recall that Judge Kaufman in *Filartiga* found evidence that state practice proscribes official torture in "numerous international treaties and accords," including, inter alia, the American Convention on Human Rights and the UN Covenant on Civil and Political Rights (see page 141 supra).

There is ample language in the decisions of the International Court of Justice to support this approach and the late Judge Baxter's observation that "[t]reaties that do not purport to be declaratory of customary international law at the time they enter into force may nevertheless with the passage of time pass into customary international law." Baxter, Treaties and Custom, 129 Recueil des Cours (Hague Academy of International Law) 25, 57 (1970-I). Accord, Restatement (Third) of the Foreign Relations Law of the United States §102 comment i at 27 and Reporters' Note 5 at 33-34 (1987). For the application of this principle to international human rights treaties, see Lillich, Duties of States Regarding the Civil Rights of Aliens, 161 Recueil des Cours (Hague Academy of International Law) 329, 397-399 (1978-III).

Recall also that the U.S. Memorial to the International Court of Justice in the *Hostages Case*, 1980 I.C.J. 3, cited Articles 7, 9, 10, and 12 of the UN Covenant on Civil and Political Rights, which cover, respectively, the prohibition of torture and cruel, inhuman, or degrading treatment or punishment; the right to liberty and security of person and the prohibition of arbitrary arrest or detention; the right to be treated with humanity during detention; and the right to freedom of movement. U.S. Memorial, page 136 supra, at 182 n.37, 183 n.42. See also Memorandum for the United States as Amicus Curiae at 13, Filartiga v. Pena-Irala, page 156 supra, where after citing the two international human rights treaties mentioned in this Comment the United States concluded that "[t]hese treaty provisions, in conjunction with other evidence, are persuasive of the existence of an international norm that is binding as a matter of customary law on all nations, not merely those that are parties to the treaties." Id. at 13 n.28, citing A. D'Amato, The Concept of Custom in International Law 103, 124-128 (1971). For an exchange of views on the role of treaties in the creation of the customary international law of human rights, compare Weisburd, Customary International Law: The Problem of Treaties, 21 Vand. J. Transnatl. L. 1 (1988) (treaties relatively unimportant) with D'Amato, Custom and Treaty: A Response to Professor Weisburd, 21 id. 459 (1988) (treaties exceptionally important).

5. As the extract from Professor Schwelb's remarks indicates (see page 128-132 supra), the Universal Declaration has had substantial impact on the national as well as the international plane. It has been incorporated, for instance, in whole or in part, into a goodly number of African constitutions. See Read, Human Rights Protection in Municipal Law, in Human Rights: The Cape Town Conference 156 (C. Forsyth and J. Schiller eds. 1979). See also Lillich, The Promotion of Human Rights by Domestic Courts: A Com-

parative Approach, in The Individual Under African Law: Proceedings of the First All-Africa Law Conference 160 (P. Takirambudde ed. 1982).

> No legal anthropologist has yet collected and compared the many provisions scattered throughout the constitutions which often are taken in haec verba from provisions found in [the Universal Declaration] and other international human rights instruments, although several studies of individual constitutions do emphasize this transplantation process. What is clear beyond doubt is that the provisions in many African constitutions replicate international human rights law standards found in one or more of the international instruments, allowing domestic courts to apply international law indirectly when construing and applying constitutional standards.

Id. at 166. For an excellent example of a case that supports the above argument, see State v. Ncube, [1987] 2 Zimb. L. Rep. 246, [1988] L.R.C. (Const.) 442 (Sup. Ct. of Zimbabwe).

As Lord Lester has pointed out, after a comprehensive review of Commonwealth constitutions, the constitutions of many Asian, Caribbean, and Pacific states also contain provisions taken from the Universal Declaration, thus permitting their courts to apply it indirectly on the domestic level as well. Lester, The Overseas Trade in the American Bill of Rights, 88 Colum. L. Rev. 537, 541 (1988). See, for example, Constitutional Reference by the Morobe Provincial Govt., [1985] L.R.C. (Const.) 642 (Sup. Ct. of Papua New Guinea). Moreover, both the Canadian Charter of Rights and Freedoms adopted in 1982 and the Hong Kong Bill of Rights Ordinance of 1991 in essence incorporate by reference the provisions of the International Covenant on Civil and Political Rights, which constitutes a restatement and elaboration of the rights found in the Universal Declaration. See A. Bayefsky, International Human Rights Law: Use in Canadian Charter of Rights and Freedoms Litigation (1992); Lillich, Sources of Human Rights Law and the Hong Kong Bill of Rights, in The Hong Kong Bill of Rights: A Comparative Approach 109 (J. Chan and Y. Ghai eds. 1993). The same approach has been taken by the drafters of many of the new constitutions in Eastern European countries, in the former Soviet Republics, and most recently in South Africa. Thus, the basic international human rights norms and standards contained in the Universal Declaration increasingly are finding their way into national constitutions and laws.

6. With prospects for the successful direct invocation of human rights treaties or customary international human rights law before U.S. courts mixed at best, considerable attention has been paid recently to the argument that international human rights law can be used most effectively to infuse U.S. constitutional and statutory standards with its normative content. Indeed, a growing number of U.S. courts have referred explicitly to the UN Charter, the Universal Declaration, or other international human rights instruments to determine the content and contours of various rights guaranteed by U.S. law.

This "indirect incorporation" of both conventional and customary human rights law is an exceptionally promising approach warranting even greater attention and increased use in the future. Scholarly support for it is found in the numerous articles gathered in Lockwood, The United Nations Charter and United States Civil Rights Litigation: 1946-1955, 69 Iowa L. Rev. 901, 901 n.1 (1984); Report of the Committee on Human Rights Law, the U.S. Constitution and Methods of Judicial Incorporation, in Proceedings and Committee Reports of the American Branch of the International Law Association 1983-84, at 59 n.8; and Coliver and Newman, Using International Human Rights Law to Influence United States Foreign Population Policy: Resort to Courts or Congress?, 20 N.Y.U. J. Intl. L. & Pol. 53, 75-84 passim (1987). For a thoughtful attempt to develop a theory of indirect incorporation of international human rights norms into the process of constitutional interpretation, see Christenson, Using Human Rights Law to Inform Due Process and Equal Protection Analyses, 52 U. Cin. L. Rev. 3 (1983). For an excellent article supporting this approach by the president of the American Civil Liberties Union, see Strossen, Recent U.S. and International Judicial Protection of Individual Rights: A Comparative Legal Process Analysis and Proposed Synthesis, 41 Hastings L.J. 805 (1990).

7. Efforts have been made to convince U.S. constitutional law experts that international human rights norms should become a significant factor in constitutional decision-making. See Lillich and Hannum, Linkages Between International Human Rights and U.S. Constitutional Law, 79 Am. J. Intl. L. 158 (1985). Indeed, teaching materials designed to supplement leading U.S. constitutional and criminal law and procedure casebooks have been prepared. See Materials on International Human Rights and U.S. Constitutional Law (H. Hannum ed. 1985); Materials on International Human Rights and U.S. Criminal Law and Procedure (H. Hannum ed. 1989). Were they used or referred to in your basic constitutional law and criminal law classes? If not, why not, in view of the fact that the U.S. Supreme Court, in applying its "evolving standards of decency" test to ascertain the contemporary level of human rights protection afforded by the Constitution's various amendments, utilizes international human rights law standards? See, for example, Thompson v. Oklahoma, 487 U.S. 815, 831 n.34, 851-852 (1988).

At the very least, through the invocation of the established principle of statutory interpretation that "an Act of Congress ought never to be construed to violate the law of nations if any other possible construction remains," Murray v. Schooner Charming Betsy, 6 U.S. (2 Cranch) 64, 118 (1804), international human rights norms should have some impact in statutory construction cases. See Restatement (Third) of the Foreign Relations Law of the United States §114 (1987). Courts in Great Britain have followed this rule of construction when faced with arguments based upon the European Convention. See McBride and Brown, The United Kingdom, the European Community and the European Convention on Human Rights, 1981 Y.B. Eur. L. 167, 177. See also Derbyshire County Council v. Times

Newspapers Ltd., 1992 Q.B. 770, 810-817 (European Convention and Civil and Political Covenant relevant in determining scope of common law free speech).

8. Finally, remember that international human rights norms may be invoked in state as well as federal courts. What additional advantages might the selection of a state court afford? More liberal state law to interpret? A decision based on state law and hence not subject to appeal to the Supreme Court? Others? For a number of articles canvassing the advantages of resorting to state courts in an appropriate case, see Proceedings: Conference on International Human Rights Law in State and Federal Courts, 17 U.S.F.L. Rev. 1 (1982); Burke, Coliver, de la Vega, and Rosenbaum, Application of International Human Rights Law in State and Federal Courts, 18 Tex. Intl. L.J. 291 (1983); and Symposium on International Human Rights Law in State Courts, 18 Intl. Law. 58 (1984). For a state court decision taking international human rights norms into account, see Sterling v. Cupp, 290 Or. 611, 623 n.21, 625 P.2d 123, 131 n.21 (1981).

Problem III

Suriname, the United States, and the UN Covenant on Civil and Political Rights

What Obligations Have States Assumed Under the UN Human Rights Treaties?

I.   Suriname: Development, Independence, Repression   181
II. The UN Treaty Approach to Human Rights   183
     A. UN Human Rights Treaties: An Overview   183
         Bilder, Rethinking International Human Rights: Some Basic
         Questions   187
     B. General Human Rights Treaties   189
         Note: Completing the International Bill of Rights   189
         Henkin, Introduction, in The International Bill of Rights   191
     C. Specific Human Rights Treaties   193
     D. The Human Rights "Generations"   194
         1. Introductory Note   194
         2. "Second Generation" Human Rights   195
         Prepared Statement of Hon. Roberts B. Owen, Legal Adviser,
         Department of State   198
         3. "Third Generation" Human Rights   201
         Marks, Emerging Human Rights: A New Generation for the
         1980s?   201
         A. Robertson, Human Rights in the World   202
         Bibliographical Note on the Right to Development   204
     E. UN Human Rights Law-Making: The Need for "Quality Con-
         trol"   206
         UN General Assembly Resolution 41/120 (1987)   207
         International League for Human Rights, Human Rights at the
         United Nations: New Standard Setting   208
III. The Civil and Political Covenant   209
     A. Substantive Provisions   209
     B. Implementation Measures   210
         1. State Reporting   211
         Shelton, Compliance Mechanisms [Periodic Reports]   212
         2. Individual Communications   214
         Lewis-Anthony, Treaty-Based Procedures for Making Human
         Rights Complaints Within the UN System   215
         Report of the Human Rights Committee   220

         3. Interstate Complaints   222

Leckie, The Inter-State Complaint Procedure in International Human Rights Law: Hopeful Prospects or Wishful Thinking?   222

         4. General Comments   224

IV. *Suriname Revisited: More Repression in Violation of the Civil and Political Covenant*   224

        Baboeram Communications   228

        Note: The Aftermath   237

V. *United States Ratification of Human Rights Treaties*   239

    A. The U.S. Ratification Record: An Overview   239

         1. Introductory Note   239

         2. The Carter Administration Initiatives   240

        Henkin, The Covenant on Civil and Political Rights   241

        Moore, Statement Before the Senate Committee on Foreign Relations   244

        Note: Carter's Legacy   245

         3. Developments During the Reagan and Bush Administrations   246

    B. U.S. Ratification of the Civil and Political Covenant   248

         1. The Covenant and the U.S. Constitution and Laws Restatement (Third) of the Foreign Relations Law of the United States §701   248

         2. The Reservations, Understandings, and Declarations "Debate"   250

        International Covenant on Civil and Political Rights: The Administration's Proposed Reservations, Understandings and Declarations   251

        International Human Rights Law Group, Ratification of the International Covenant on Civil and Political Rights by the United States   254

        Stewart, United States Ratification of the Covenant on Civil and Political Rights: The Significance of the Reservations, Understandings, and Declarations   259

         3. Attitudes of the U.S. NGO Community Towards Ratification Conditioned upon Acceptance of the Bush Administration "Package"   260

        Letter from Lawyers Committee for Human Rights to Senator Claiborne Pell   261

        Letter from Human Rights Watch to Lawyers Committee for Human Rights   263

        Letter from Lawyers Committee for Human Rights to Human Rights Watch   266

    C. U.S. Ratification of the Other Human Rights Treaties: The "Package" Redux   268

        Comments and Questions Concerning U.S. Ratification of the Human Rights Treaties   270

VI. *Final Comments and Questions*   273

I. Suriname: Development, Independence, Repression

In 1499 the Spanish explorer Alonso de Ojeda discovered the coast of Guiana in South America. He began to map some of the inland rivers but gave up when he encountered the difficult terrain and hostile natives. The waves of settlers that followed bypassed Guiana and instead headed for Mexico. Fifty years after its discovery, the so-called Wild Coast was reduced to secondary status by the exploits of the conquistadors and tales of fabulous riches to be gained from the conquered native empires of Mesoamerica.

Throughout the sixteenth century, the Wild Coast was merely a haven for pirates and a few traders and missionaries. By the mid-seventeenth century, however, the Dutch had founded several settlements on the coast. In 1651 the English made the first major impact on the colonial development of Guiana by establishing several large sugar plantations with labor imported from Barbados. These plantations proved to be a successful enterprise, and sugar became the most important colonial resource produced by the area for the next several centuries.

In 1667, following one of the Anglo-Dutch wars, the Treaty of Breda established full Dutch control over the present territory of Suriname. Dutch entrepreneurs took over the sugar business and continued to profit from it. They increased the importation of slaves as plantation laborers, making the plantations even more profitable. Between 1650 and 1820, about 300,000 West Africans were brought into the colony, helping the plantation economy to flourish throughout this period. During the Napoleonic Wars (1799-1815), Suriname again fell under English control, but in the series of treaties that followed that conflict the Dutch regained control of the territory.

During the nineteenth century, the colony suffered from the concentration of Dutch energies on the East Indies and underwent little real development. The sugar economy had been adversely affected by the emancipation of the slaves in 1863. In 1873 the colonial government allowed freedmen to own land, and large plantations were parceled out to independent farmers. However, a lack of central control rapidly led to a breakdown of irrigation and drainage. This development drove many former slaves into the towns along the coast, as well as into the developing bauxite mining industry, which seemed to be the only evidence of the impact of the Industrial Revolution on the colony.

Following an agreement between the government and Great Britain for the importation of immigrants from India, the first of 34,000 indentured servants from the subcontinent arrived in 1873. After 1895 the government allowed the Indian immigrants to own land, creating greater incentives for them to remain. Small farmers from Java imported after 1890 became the catalyst for a sweeping change in the agricultural economy during the early twentieth century. In 1913 rice was introduced, soon replacing the plantation crops as the agricultural staple.

The first effects of post-World War II decolonization were generally salutary for Suriname. After 1945 the colony benefitted from the influx of financial and technical resources diverted from the East Indies. They went mainly to improvements in the bauxite mining industry, although resources were also committed to the modernization of the country's infrastructure.

In 1948 Suriname became a part of the Kingdom of the Netherlands. Six years later it was granted autonomy in all areas except foreign policy and defense. Suriname also joined the EEC as an Associated Overseas Territory. On 25 November 1975, Suriname became an independent republic. The 1975 constitution provided for a president and vice president elected by the Legislative Assembly, which in turn was elected by universal suffrage. A council of ministers, headed by the prime minister and responsible to the Legislative Assembly, held executive authority. In 1975 Prime Minister Henck Arron endorsed the new form of government, and the broadly popular Dr. Johan Ferrier was elected the first president.

For five years Suriname was a functioning democracy, with a good record on human rights. On 28 December 1976, the government acceded to the International Covenant on Civil and Political Rights, that Covenant's Optional Protocol, and several other international human rights instruments. It ratified several more such instruments between 1976 and 1980.

On 25 February 1980, a band of military men led by Sergeant Desi Bouterse overthrew the elected government in an almost bloodless coup, forming the National Military Council (NMR). The NMR proceeded to take over most aspects of civilian government during the next two years. Dr. Ferrier was ousted on 13 August 1980, at which time the Legislative Assembly was dissolved. He was succeeded by Dr. Hendrik Sen. Initially enjoying some popular support, the NMR and its civilian counterpart attempted to appease the democratic opposition with promises of local elections and Marxist rhetoric espousing a program of "renewal" for the people of Suriname. However, political unrest in 1981 brought about increased repression.

On 4 February 1982, President Sen resigned at the behest of the NMR, leaving that body's four military officers, led by Lieutenant Colonel Bouterse, in charge of all civilian affairs as members of the new "Policy Centre." Several opposition journalists reported increased incidents of human rights violations by the military police, including torture and isolated killings among peasant families. The government's efforts to address this conduct did little to satisfy the increasing outrage expressed by a growing segment of Suriname's population.

An attempted coup led by Lieutenant Rambocus and Sergeant Major Hawker failed on 12 March 1982. On 18 March Bouterse responded by declaring a state of war, retroactive to 11 March, and then publicly executing Sergeant Major Hawker. The military police arrested over 50 people in connection with the coup attempt, including several prominent members of the two political parties that had existed before the 1980 coup. Some of them were severely beaten, and one leader allegedly was killed while in military custody. Rising protests were stemmed neither by Bouterse's decree of 30 March 1982, which provided for "rights and duties of the people of Suriname," nor by the formation of a new civilian government under Prime Minister Neyhorst the next day. The Policy Centre, which now included Neyhorst, began to label all opposition as "counter-revolutionary" and dangerous.

The trial of Lieutenant Rambocus began on 13 October 1982. Four lawyers, including John Baboeram, acted in his defense. A military tribunal sentenced Rambocus to 12 years' imprisonment on 3 December 1982. The trial coincided with increasingly organized pressure from social organizations, including the main trade union federation, calling for free elections and a return to constitutional government. Several strikes were held, both by the unions and by the university in Paramaribo. On 31 October 1982, an opposition rally attracted 15,000 persons, while only 1,500 attended a mass meeting held by Bouterse for Grenadan leader Maurice Bishop.

On 17 November 1982, an "Association for Democracy" was established by 13 organizations, including unions, religious groups, and the bar and press associations. The Association sent an open letter to the NMR calling for free elections, the withdrawal of the military from active politics, and an end to totalitarian government. It stated that the majority of the country's population rejected Bouterse's policies as outlined in a speech he had given on 15 November 1982, and that the only way the government could carry out such policies would be to resort to repressive acts previously unknown in Suriname. Events of the following months would prove the latter prediction all too true.

II.   The UN Treaty Approach to Human Rights

A.   UN *Human Rights Treaties: An Overview*

The previous two Problems have examined the meaning and effect of the human rights clauses of the UN Charter, a treaty binding the organization's member states, and the impact of the Universal Declaration of Human Rights upon the human rights obligations of all states. The present Problem is an analysis of what traditionally has been regarded as the UN's principal means of achieving universal respect for human rights — the sponsoring of multilateral treaties for the protection of specifically enumerated human rights.

The use of treaties for such a purpose is not new. Coordinated multi-state action was taken as early as the nineteenth century to combat the problem of slavery, even to the point of establishing international tribunals for the suppression of the slave trade. The Act of Brussels of 1890 marked the culmination of these efforts, committing the signatory parties (the United States among them) to the reciprocal right of on-board search and seizure. Since World War I multilateral action for the protection of human rights increasingly has been funnelled through international organizations. The International Labor Organization (ILO), for example, has adopted numerous conventions (numbering 175 as of 1 July 1994) and recommendations (182 as of 1 July 1994) that seek to promote and protect the human rights of individuals.

The UN treaties have gone much further than most of their predecessors, however, in that they have obligated signatory states to make changes — sometimes drastic changes — in their own domestic legal regimes to bring them into conformity with international law norms. It is one thing for a state to agree to eradicate a practice that takes place on faraway continents or on the high seas; it is quite another to agree to take affirmative steps for the protection of oppressed individuals at home. In this respect, to the extent that states have ratified them, the UN treaties represent a great advance in international human rights law.

Before examining specific human rights treaties of the UN, consider the diversity of human rights problems encompassed in Table 3-1, listing the UN human rights treaties in force as of 1 July 1994. The large time gap between date of signing and date of entry into force of some treaties underscores the reluctance of states to adopt rather than merely to debate protective human rights measures. The limited number of states that are parties to many of the treaties is further evidence of this reluctance. The United States, for instance, has ratified only 8 of the 24 treaties on the list (2 of the 8 prohibit slavery, hardly a controversial topic these days!).

Table 3-1 demonstrates that the UN, in addition to promulgating general human rights treaties containing numerous articles covering a wide variety of individual rights (e.g., No. 2, the International Covenant on Civil and Political Rights), has used treaties to combat specific human rights problems (e.g., No. 22, the International Convention against Apartheid in Sports). Obviously this Problem — or even this coursebook — cannot begin to survey all the substantive provisions of the above-listed treaties. Much like a course in Administrative Law, which covers the administrative process rather than substantive administrative law like the Agricultural Adjustment Act, the course for which this coursebook is designed necessarily must focus primarily on the process of implementing substantive international human rights law, whether found in the UN Charter, the Universal Declaration of Human Rights, or UN (or other) international human rights instruments.

This particular Problem is designed to demonstrate how the UN, by use of the treaty-making process, has encouraged member states over the

TABLE 3-1 UN Conventions in the Field of Human Rights as of 1 July 1994

		Date of signing/ adoption	*Entry into force*
1.	International Covenant on Economic, Social, and Cultural Rights, 993 U.N.T.S. 3 (129 states parties)	19 Dec. 1966	3 Jan. 1976
2.	International Covenant on Civil and Political Rights, 999 U.N.T.S. 171 (127 states parties)	19 Dec. 1966	23 Mar. 1976
3.	Optional Protocol to the International Covenant on Civil and Political Rights, 999 U.N.T.S. 171 (76 states parties)	19 Dec. 1966	23 Mar. 1976
4.	Convention on the Prevention and Punishment of the Crime of Genocide, 78 U.N.T.S. 277 (113 states parties)	9 Dec. 1948	12 Jan. 1951
5.	Convention on the Non-Applicability of Statutory Limitations to War Crimes and Crimes Against Humanity, 754 U.N.T.S. 73 (39 states parties)	26 Nov. 1968	11 Nov. 1970
6.	International Convention on the Elimination of All Forms of Racial Discrimination, 660 U.N.T.S. 195 (139 states parties)	7 Mar. 1966	4 Jan. 1969
7.	Convention relating to the Status of Refugees, 189 U.N.T.S. 137 (122 states parties)	28 July 1951	22 Apr. 1954
8.	Protocol relating to the Status of Refugees, 606 U.N.T.S. 267 (119 states parties)	31 Jan. 1967	4 Oct. 1967
9.	Convention relating to the Status of Stateless Persons, 360 U.N.T.S. 117 (42 states parties)	28 Sept. 1954	6 June 1960
10.	Convention on the Reduction of Statelessness, 989 U.N.T.S. 175 (18 states parties)	30 Aug. 1961	13 Dec. 1975
11.	Convention on the Elimination of All Forms of Discrimination Against Women, 1249 U.N.T.S. 13 (131 states parties)	18 Dec. 1979	3 Sept. 1981

		Date of signing/ adoption	*Entry into force*
12.	Convention on the Political Rights of Women, 193 U.N.T.S. 135 (104 states parties)	31 Mar. 1953	7 July 1954
13.	Convention on the Nationality of Married Women, 309 U.N.T.S. 65 (64 states parties)	20 Feb. 1957	11 Aug. 1958
14.	Convention on Consent to Marriage, Minimum Age for Marriage, and Registration of Marriages, 521 U.N.T.S. 231 (41 states parties)	10 Dec. 1962	9 Dec. 1964
15.	Convention on the International Right of Correction, 435 U.N.T.S. 191 (13 states parties)	31 Mar. 1953	24 Aug. 1962
16.	Protocol amending Slavery Convention, 182 U.N.T.S. 51 (56 states parties)	7 Dec. 1953	7 Dec. 1953
17.	Slavery Convention, as amended, 212 U.N.T.S. 51 (90 states parties)	7 Dec. 1953	7 July 1955
18.	Supplementary Convention on the Abolition of Slavery, the Slave Trade, and Institutions and Practices Similar to Slavery, 266 U.N.T.S. 3 (112 states parties)	7 Sept. 1956	30 Apr. 1957
19.	Convention for the Suppression of the Traffic in Persons and of the Exploitation of the Prostitution of Others, 96 U.N.T.S. 271 (70 states parties)	21 Mar. 1950	25 July 1951
20.	International Convention on the Suppression and Punishment of the Crime of Apartheid, 1015 U.N.T.S. 243 (99 states parties)	30 Nov. 1973	18 July 1976
21.	Convention against Torture and Other Cruel, Inhuman, or Degrading Treatment or Punishment, G.A. Res. 39/46, 39 U.N. GAOR Supp. (No. 51) at 197, U.N. Doc. A/RES/ 39/46 (1984) (82 states parties)	10 Dec. 1984	26 June 1987
22.	International Convention against Apartheid in Sports, G.A. Res. 40/64, 40 U.N. GAOR Supp. (No. 51) at 37, U.N. Doc. A/RES/40/64 (1985) (57 states parties)	10 Dec. 1985	3 Apr. 1988

	Date of signing/ adoption	Entry into force
23. Convention on the Rights of the Child, G.A. Res. 44/25, 44 U.N. GAOR Supp. (No. 49) at 16, U.N. Doc. A/RES/44/25 (1989) (160 states parties)	20 Nov. 1989	2 Sept. 1990
24. Second Optional Protocol to the International Covenant on Civil and Political Rights Aiming at the Abolition of the Death Penalty, G.A. Res. 44/128, 44 U.N. GAOR Supp. (No. 49) at 206, U.N. Doc. A/RES/44/128 (1989) (22 states parties)	15 Dec. 1989	11 July 1991

years to assume international legal obligations in an increasing number of human rights areas. To do so, it uses as a case study one particular human rights treaty, perhaps the most significant product of the UN's treaty-making process, the Civil and Political Covenant (which the United States finally ratified in 1992). You will want to read this treaty, found in the Documentary Supplement, from beginning to end. A half dozen other treaties on the above list are also found in the Documentary Appendix and warrant reading in full. The remaining ones, for persons interested in sampling the wide range of human rights protected by UN treaties, may be found conveniently reprinted in R. Lillich, International Human Rights Instruments (2d ed. updated 1995).

Before turning to the Civil and Political Covenant, though, it is useful to reconsider the conventional wisdom that holds that the treaty (and even the declaration) approach to human rights problems is important and worthwhile enough to warrant the extensive efforts the UN (and other international organizations) has put and continues to put into it. The following brief reading takes up this threshold issue.

Bilder, Rethinking International Human Rights: Some Basic Questions
1969 Wis. L. Rev. 171, 205-207

A. How Useful Are Declarations and Conventions?

Arguments favoring reliance on declarations and conventions emphasize that they define the content of human rights concepts and establish clearer standards of governmental conduct. They educate both officials and the general public in these norms, place governments failing to respect human rights on the defensive, and help create and legitimate internal and external pressures for human rights improvement. Conventions lift general standards to the level of concrete binding rules. Perhaps most important, declarations may stimulate, and conventions require, enactment of internal legislation to implement applicable human rights standards. For example, the provisions of the Universal Declaration have been drawn on by over a score of new nations in drafting their constitutions. In some cases they may help a government to legitimate reforms it itself wishes to undertake. Even where such legislation is initially pro forma, it tends over time to have a growing normative impact.

However there are limitations to such documents. . . . [T]hey may foster a harmful illusion of accomplishment and serve as an excuse for failure to pursue more practical, if more difficult, courses of action.

International human rights declarations, some argue, are of little real significance. Since they are only recommendations without binding legal effect, few governments may take them seriously. . . . Moreover, norms spelled out in declarations are frequently later reflected in conventions; where these conventions subsequently gain only limited acceptance, any normative value the declaration might have may be further diluted.

Conventions similarly may have many weaknesses. First they are legally binding only on states which accept them, and governments with human rights problems within the scope of the convention may simply not become parties. . . .

Second, the provisions of such conventions often reflect agreement only at the lowest common level. Even at this level, a basic lack of agreement or willingness to be committed may be reflected in deliberately vague standards, crippling exceptions, and numerous escape hatches.

Third, even ratification of conventions may have little relation to their observance. Outside (and some would say even within) the small circle of Western countries, the sense of obligation to international legal commitments may be weak, particularly with instruments such as human rights conventions where expectations of compliance are small. Absent effective procedures for authoritative interpretation and implementation, all governments know that the likelihood of being held to such promises is remote; lip-service can be paid and propaganda gains achieved at little risk.

Finally, the implicit faith that such international instruments place in internal law as a way of attaining human rights objectives may itself be over-optimistic. Even where governments do ratify and enact internal implementing legislation, the practical effect of such measures may be slight. Law on the books, without vigorous enforcement, may have little relation to actual conduct. In many cases social problems underlying human rights denials may be hard for law to reach in any case. Unfortunately, we still know very little about the relation between legal norms and structural and cultural factors in a society, of the ways law can be used to effect social change, or about how declared law actually penetrates into the attitudes, propensities and actions of officials and ordinary people. In less developed societies, the general population — and even officials — may not know or care about the written law. Law may even be regarded with hostility as traditionally an instrument of oppression. In other cases enforcement may require economic or political resources beyond a government's means. Thus, internal legislation protecting human rights may often prove only a beginning step in achieving solutions to human rights problems.

Of course, the truth may lie in between. Despite evident weaknesses, international instruments seem in fact to accomplish more than we might expect. Inevitably they legitimate human rights objectives and create some pressures for observance. That governments create obstacles in their drafting, refuse to ratify them, and constantly invoke their provisions in international debate show that they are regarded as of at least some significance. Over time their normative impact may grow as the standards they set are incorporated in their national constitutions and legislation and gradually permeate various societies. Even governments ratifying what they believe are innocuous conventions with which they were already in full compliance may discover that they have more human rights problems than they thought. Thus, the parties to the European Convention are now becoming aware of hitherto unrecognized deficiencies in their criminal procedures and guarantees of due process.

Moreover, any doubts we may feel as to the effectiveness of conventions as an instrument of change should not blind us to their important role as an obstacle to retrogression. Conditions change and seemingly unimportant ratifications today may become significant tomorrow. For example, African governments may endorse the Race Convention as a weapon against antiblack racism, believing they incur no real commitments; but the problem of the future may be antiwhite racism. The European Human Rights Convention . . . proved an embarrassment to the Greek military junta and constitutes a continuing obstacle to any resurgent Nazism.

The problem may be less that international declarations and conventions accomplish too little than that we expect too much. If we recognize that they are only limited tools, we may see their contributions in better perspective. Most important, the dynamics of international organization make such instruments relatively easy to obtain, and we must do what we can. . . .

B.   General Human Rights Treaties

Note: Completing the International Bill of Rights

The UN effort to protect human rights by treaty began with proposals for the enactment of an International Bill of Rights. The first fruit of this campaign was the adoption by the General Assembly in 1948 of the Universal Declaration of Human Rights (the Universal Declaration). (G.A. Res. 217A [III], U.N. Doc. A/810, at 71 (1948).) The Universal Declaration was just a first step, however, since it was "only" a UN resolution, supposedly having no binding effect on member states. As Problem II revealed, a good argument now can be made that, after nearly 50 years, the Universal Declaration, or at least substantial parts of it, has become part of customary international law. Even so, it contains no enforcement provisions, thus rendering important the drafting of binding conventions committing signatory states to concrete enforcement procedures.

At first, it was envisioned that the Universal Declaration would be followed immediately by such a universal convention; political developments, however, dictated otherwise. A draft convention (labeled a covenant by its drafters) was prepared simultaneously with the Universal Declaration and submitted to the General Assembly at its 1948 session. The draft covenant underwent some revisions over the next two years before being submitted again for "basic policy decisions." One of these decisions concerned whether the covenant would provide for economic, social, and cultural rights, in addition to the civil and political rights already contained in it. Some states, however, were reluctant to commit themselves to undertaking economic, social, and cultural obligations on the ground that assuring such rights was more a function of a state's economic health than of its juridical norms.

The General Assembly accepted the force of this position and requested, in 1952 (G.A. Res. 543 (VI), 6 U.N. GAOR Supp. (No. 20) at 36, U.N. Doc. A/2119 (1952)), that two covenants — one on economic, social, and cultural rights and another on civil and political rights — be drafted simultaneously. It ultimately required fully 14 years of painstaking effort for the Third Committee (the General Assembly's committee on human rights) to consider and pass upon all of the various articles of the two covenants. In 1966 the two documents — along with an Optional Protocol to the Civil and Political Covenant allowing states to permit petitions to be lodged against them by their own nationals — finally were ready for submission to the General Assembly for its approval. They were duly approved (G.A. Res. 2200A, 21 U.N. GAOR Supp. (No. 16) at 49, U.N. Doc. A/6316 (1966)) and opened for signature. The International Covenant on Economic, Social, and Cultural Rights, the International Covenant on Civil and Political Rights, and the Optional Protocol to the Civil and Political Covenant — which together with the Universal Declaration of Human Rights are collectively known as the International Bill of Rights — all took effect in 1976. For an extensive discussion of the history of the International Bill of Rights, see the United Nations and Human Rights, Eighteenth Report of the Commission to Study the Organization of Peace 59-169 (1968). A briefer treatment of the problems that arose during the drafting of the two covenants is found in the following extract from Professor Henkin's book on the International Bill of Rights.

Henkin, Introduction
in The International Bill of Rights 9-11 (L. Henkin ed. 1981)

The Universal Declaration was not generally conceived as law but as "a common standard of achievement" for all to aspire to; hence its approval without dissent. Some thought that the United Nations should rest on the Declaration and concentrate on encouraging states to raise their national norms and conform their national behavior to its standards. Instead, governments moved to convert the Declaration into binding legal norms.

The process was very, very long. In some part this was due to the ever-increasing number of states, all of which joined in the process and slowed the negotiations. In part, delay was due to the differences between a declaration and a binding covenant. Some states that had been prepared to declare a general principle wished it carefully defined and circumscribed if it were to be clearly a legal obligation with legal consequences, for though no state was compelled to adhere to any draft covenant that might emerge, most states wanted something they might be able to adopt if it became desirable; they were reluctant, moreover, to have a covenant adopted as the international norm in whose light their behavior would appear to be wanting. The process was also extended because there were strong pressures on the other hand to develop and elaborate the generalities of the Declaration and give them more specific content so that they would afford greater protection. The Declaration, moreover, had not provided for its implementation, while many sessions were spent debating and elaborating means to enforce the new emerging legal undertakings.

In substantial part, it took eighteen years to convert the Declaration into convention because it was necessary to accommodate, bridge, submerge, and conceal deep divisions and differences, especially between democratic-libertarian and socialist-revolutionary states — differences in fundamental conceptions about the relation of society to the individual, about his rights and duties, about priorities and preferences among them.

Western states fought for, and obtained, a division into two covenants, the Covenant on Civil and Political Rights and the Covenant on Economic, Social, and Cultural Rights. The two covenants recognize the difference in the character of rights in various subtle ways. For example, the Covenant on Civil and Political Rights is drafted in terms of the individual's rights: e.g., "Every human being has the inherent right to life"; "No one shall be held in slavery"; "All persons shall be equal before the courts and tribunals." The Covenant on Economic, Social, and Cultural Rights, on the other hand, speaks only to the states, not the individual: "The States Parties to the present Covenant recognize the right to work"; "The States Parties . . . undertake to ensure . . . the right of everyone to form trade unions"; "The States Parties . . . recognize the right of everyone to education." There was wide agreement and clear recognition that the means required to induce compliance with social-economic undertakings were different from those required for civil-political rights. But the Covenant on Economic, Social, and Cultural Rights is law, not merely exhortation and aspiration. The rights it recognizes are as "human," universal, and fundamental as are those of the Civil and Political Rights Covenant. The obligation for a state party is "to take steps . . . to the maximum of its available resources, with a view to achieving progressively the full realization" of these rights, and fulfillment may require national planning and major programs, and international assistance. But these limitations do not derogate from the legal character of the obligations.

Other delays resulted from sharp differences over the inclusion or scope of particular rights. Most of the states were concerned, or were more concerned, with values reflecting their struggle against colonialism but not included in the Universal Declaration and not previously part of the accepted human rights ideology. They insisted that both Covenants include the right of all peoples to self-determination as well as to "economic self-determination," to "sovereignty" over their resources. Western states resisted, arguing that both are at best rights of a "people," not of any individual, and surely not — like human rights generally — rights of individuals against their own society. They argued, too, that the content of these norms was highly uncertain and controversial. The argument did not prevail, and identical provisions on self-determination now head both covenants. Also included in the Covenant on Civil and Political Rights were other, less controversial, rights not mentioned in the Declaration — freedom from imprisonment for debt, rights of children, and rights of minorities (Articles 11, 24, 27). That Covenant also prohibits propaganda for war and incitement to national, racial, or religious hatred (Article 20). Some rights included in the Declaration were substantially elaborated. On the other hand, the right to enjoy private property, included in the Declaration, was finally omitted from the covenants. Much time was also spent in the attempt to bridge the demand of some states for effective means to enforce the covenants and the insistence of others on the "sovereignty" of states and resistance to international scrutiny and "intrusion."

In sum, the international law of human rights developed by the two covenants parallels the Universal Declaration. It provides protections like those in the constitutions and laws of enlightened democratic-liberal countries as well as the promises of socialist and "welfare" constitutions. Before, during, and since the negotiation of these two major covenants, the UN system also promoted specialized declarations and conventions — on genocide, on the status of refugees and stateless persons, on the rights of women, and on the elimination of all forms of racial discrimination. These emphasize, extend, and supplement the protections afforded by the principal covenants. They have also made it possible to "extract" legal obligations on these particular subjects from governments not prepared to adhere to all the obligations of the general covenants.

C.   Specific Human Rights Treaties

Concurrent with its effort to promulgate general human rights norms and necessary enforcement procedures through an International Bill of Rights, the UN began to use the treaty approach to combat human rights violations in specific problem areas. The first such treaty was the Convention on the Prevention and Punishment of the Crime of Genocide (the Genocide Convention). Drafted in 1948, the same year as the Universal Declaration, it came into force in 1951. Since the concept of advancing human rights by means of treaty law was still relatively new, it was deemed advisable to forestall potential state opposition by choosing for attack at the outset the most odious crime ever committed. A second aspect of the Genocide Convention thought to make it particularly acceptable to states was the somewhat ironic fact that it contained no enforcement provisions. Despite its taking the lead in drafting and signing the Convention, the United States failed to ratify it for 40 years, ostensibly for constitutional reasons. That these reasons are without merit is clear from the remarks of Professor Henkin at page 241 of this Problem.

The International Convention on the Elimination of All Forms of Racial Discrimination (the Racial Discrimination Convention) marked a significant advance over the Genocide Convention in that it contains enforcement provisions similar to the type found in the Civil and Political Covenant (see pages 210-224 infra). Racial discrimination, of course, had been condemned in Article 55(c) of the UN Charter, as well as in Article 2 of the Universal Declaration, but the Convention had its immediate origins in a General Assembly Declaration on the Elimination of All Forms of Racial Discrimination (G.A. Res. 1904, 18 U.N. GAOR Supp. (No. 15) at 35, U.N. Doc. A/5515 (1963)), adopted as an expression of international concern over outbursts of swastika painting around the world in 1959-1960. With active U.S. support, the UN completed the drafting of the Racial Discrimination Convention in 1965, and it came into force in 1969. The United States finally ratified it in 1994.

Among the UN human rights treaties listed in Table 3-1, three other specific ones stand out: the Convention on the Elimination of All Forms of Discrimination Against Women (CEDAW) (No. 11), signed in 1979 and in force since 1981, which the United States has not yet ratified; the Convention against Torture and Other Cruel, Inhuman, or Degrading Treatment or Punishment (the Torture Convention) (No. 16), signed in 1984 and in force since 1987, which the United States ratified in 1994; and the Convention on the Rights of the Child (the Children's Rights Convention) (No. 23), signed in 1989 and in force since 1990, which the United States signed in 1995.

Sex discrimination, like racial discrimination, is prohibited by Article 55(c) of the UN Charter and Article 2 of the Universal Declaration. This prohibition is reiterated in Article 2(1) of the Civil and Political Covenant,

Article 3 of which obligates states parties "to ensure the equal rights of men and women to the enjoyment of all civil and political rights set forth in the present Covenant." Torture, moreover, is condemned by Article 5 of the Universal Declaration and also prohibited by Article 7 of the Civil and Political Covenant. Children not only are covered by the all-inclusive language of the Universal Declaration and the Civil and Political Covenant (e.g., "everyone"), but also "are entitled to special care and assistance" under Article 25(2) of the former and are singled out for special protection by Articles 23(3) and 24 of the latter. The question, thus, has been raised whether specific human rights treaties dealing with these three areas really were needed, and if so, whether they are worth the difficulties and costs caused and incurred by overlapping or conflicting norms and systems of supervision.

In any event, with the signing of the International Convention on the Protection of the Rights of All Migrant Workers and Members of Their Families (G.A. Res. 45/158, 45 U.N. GAOR Supp. (No. 49A) at 261, U.N. Doc. A/45/49 (1990)) in December 1990, specific human rights treaty-making by the UN seems to have run its course. At present, UN efforts are limited to drafting optional protocols to human rights instruments already in force, such as the draft optional protocol to the Torture Convention intended to establish a preventive system of visits to places of detention (U.N. Doc. E/CN.4/1994/25, at 17-19 (1993)) and the draft optional protocol to the Children's Rights Convention on the involvement of children in armed conflicts (U.N. Doc. E/CN.4/1994/91, at 2-4 (1993)). Thus, Professor Meron surely was correct when he tentatively concluded over a decade ago that "the international community may have passed the zenith of its legislative activity in the area of human rights, at least as broadly oriented global instruments are concerned." Meron, Norm Making and Supervision in International Human Rights: Reflections on Institutional Order, 76 Am. J. Intl. L. 754, 771 (1982). Continued incremental and upgrading "legislative" activity can be expected, however, not only from the UN, but also from the International Labor Organization (see page 184 supra) and from regional human rights regimes (see Problems IX and X).

D. The Human Rights "Generations"

1. Introductory Note

Civil and political rights, which make up the bulk of the rights mentioned in the Universal Declaration (Arts. 3-21) and are the sole province of the Civil and Political Covenant, traditionally have been the core of international human rights law and hence are often called the "first generation" of human rights. See, e.g., Sohn, The New International Law: Protection of the Rights of Individuals Rather than States, 32 Am U. L. Rev. 1, 17-32

(1982). Economic, social, and cultural rights, also found in the Universal Declaration (Arts. 22-27), received recognition in the Economic, Social, and Cultural Covenant and have become known as "second generation" human rights. See, e.g., Sohn, supra, at 32-48. Although a good number of observers still consider only the former to be true "rights," viewing the latter as mere "goals," the international community today, if not the Reagan and Bush Administrations during 1981-1993 (see pages 199-200 infra), regards both categories as interdependent and possessed of equal status. G.A. Res. 32/130, 32 U.N. GAOR Supp. (No. 45) at 150, U.N. Doc. A/32/45 (1977). The UN recently reiterated this position in the Vienna Declaration and Programme of Action, U.N. Doc. A/CONF. 157/23, at 5 (1993), Part I, Paragraph 5 of which provides, inter alia, that "[a]ll human rights are universal, indivisible and interdependent and interrelated."

Actually, it is technically incorrect as well as confusing to describe economic, social, and cultural rights as "second generation" human rights, since they were "present at the creation," so to speak, in Articles 22-27 of the Universal Declaration. Moreover, these rights have been elaborated in great detail in the Covenant on Economic, Social, and Cultural Rights, a treaty of equal status with the Civil and Political Covenant and, with it, an important component of the International Bill of Rights. Indeed, it even has been suggested that the UN and most governments accord the former Covenant priority status. See Newman, United Nations Human Rights Covenants and the United States Government: Diluted Promises, Foreseeable Futures, 42 DePaul L. Rev. 1241, 1242 (1993). However, since most commentary uses "second generation" language to describe economic, social, and cultural rights, the appellation will be employed here, too, with the caveat that it does not connote second-class status.

2. "Second Generation" Human Rights

United States constitutional law has had a profound impact upon the development of the "first generation" of international human rights. It has helped to shape the norms found in the Universal Declaration and the Civil and Political Covenant and to assist in their clarification and application. As Professor Henkin rightly observes:

> Americans were prominent among the architects and builders of international human rights, and American constitutionalism was a principal inspiration and model for them. As a result, most of the Universal Declaration of Human Rights, and later the International Covenant on Civil and Political Rights, are in their essence American constitutional rights projected around the world.

Henkin, Rights: American and Human, 79 Colum. L. Rev. 405, 415 (1979). See also Lester, The Overseas Trade in the American Bill of Rights, 88

Colum. L. Rev. 537, 538 (1988). Yet, "since the United States has become a quasi-welfare state by popular will rather than constitutional compulsion, its Constitution has contributed little to the 'galaxy of rights' found in the International Covenant on Economic, Social and Cultural Rights." Lillich, The Constitution and International Human Rights, 83 Am. J. Intl. L. 851, 852-853 (1989).

Nevertheless, until relatively recently U.S. support for the development and assurance of such rights — domestically and internationally — has been strong, dating back to President Franklin Roosevelt's State of the Union speech in 1941, when he set out his vision of a world order guaranteeing four essential human freedoms, including freedom from want. 9 The Public Papers and Addresses of Franklin D. Roosevelt, 1940, at 663, 672 (1941). Often overlooked is the fact that, immediately preceding his proclamation of the Four Freedoms, he listed a number of economic and social rights he considered "the foundations of a healthy and strong democracy," including, inter alia, old-age pensions and unemployment insurance, adequate medical care, and the opportunity for gainful employment. Id. at 671.

Three years later, in his State of the Union speech of 1944, the President unveiled his postwar plans for an "Economic Bill of Rights," which he thought was the responsibility of Congress to implement (13 The Public Papers and Addresses of Franklin D. Roosevelt, 1944-1945, at 32, 40-41 (1950)).

> This Republic had its beginning, and grew to its present strength, under the protection of certain inalienable political rights — among them the right of free speech, free press, free worship, trial by jury, freedom from unreasonable searches and seizures. They were our rights to life and liberty.
>
> As our Nation has grown in size and stature, however — as our industrial economy expanded — these political rights proved inadequate to assure us equality in the pursuit of happiness.
>
> We have come to a clear realization of the fact that true individual freedom cannot exist without economic security and independence. "Necessitous men are not free men." People who are hungry and out of a job are the stuff of which dictatorships are made.
>
> In our day these economic truths have become accepted as self-evident. We have accepted, so to speak, a second Bill of Rights under which a new basis of security and prosperity can be established for all — regardless of station, race, or creed.
>
> Among these are:
>
> The right to a useful and remunerative job in the industries or shops or farms or mines of the Nation;
>
> The right to earn enough to provide adequate food and clothing and recreation;
>
> The right of every farmer to raise and sell his products at a return which will give him and his family a decent living;
>
> The right of every businessman, large and small, to trade in an atmosphere of freedom from unfair competition and domination by monopolies at home or abroad;

> The right of every family to a decent home;
>
> The right to adequate medical care and the opportunity to achieve and enjoy good health;
>
> The right to adequate protection from the economic fears of old age, sickness, accident, and unemployment;
>
> The right to a good education.
>
> All of these rights spell security. And after this war is won we must be prepared to move forward, in the implementation of these rights, to new goals of human happiness and well-being.
>
> America's own rightful place in the world depends in large part upon how fully these and similar rights have been carried into practice for our citizens. For unless there is security here at home there cannot be lasting peace in the world.

Ultimately, most of the rights enumerated by President Roosevelt found their expression in the Covenant on Economic, Social, and Cultural Rights.* "Thus that Covenant deals with the right to freely chosen gainful employment and to the enjoyment of just conditions of work, trade union rights, right to social security, protection of the family and of children and young persons, right to an adequate standard of living and freedom from hunger, right to the highest attainable standard of physical and mental health, right to education, and the right to enjoy cultural and scientific freedom." Eighteenth Report of the Commission to Study the Organization of Peace, The United Nations and Human Rights 12 (1968). In recognition of the fact that many states, especially developing ones, would find it difficult, if not impossible, to provide for the enjoyment of all these rights, a state party to the Covenant is obligated only "to take steps, individually and through international assistance and co-operation, especially economic and technical, *to the maximum of its available resources, with a view to achieving progressively* the full realization of the rights recognized in the present Covenant. . . ." (Article 2(1)) (emphasis added). Furthermore, implementation measures under the Covenant were limited to an initially weak reporting system. (Article 16(1).)**

Although the Covenant was concluded in 1966 and came into force in 1976, it was not until 1977 that it was signed by President Jimmy Carter,

---

* "While the rights protected by this Covenant are not among the civil liberties traditionally guaranteed by the United States Constitution, they are entirely consistent with the progress of social concern in this country since the 1930's." Association of the Bar of the City of New York, Committee on International Human Rights, United Nations Human Rights Covenants, 36 The Record 217, 221 (1981).

** See Fischer, International Reporting Procedures, in Guide to International Human Rights Practice 165, 176 (1st ed. H. Hannum ed. 1984) ("[R]eview of the first two years' efforts to implement the Covenant leads to the rather dismal conclusion that the reporting procedure is seriously and probably irreparably flawed."). After the Economic and Social Council's creation in 1986 of an expert Committee on Economic, Social, and Cultural Rights to monitor states parties' compliance with their reporting obligations, this evaluation may need reassessment. See Alston, Out of the Abyss: The Challenges Confronting the New U.N. Committee on Economic, Social and Cultural Rights, 9 Human Rts. Q. 332 (1987). See also Hannum, Compliance Mechanisms, in United States Ratification of the International Covenants on Human Rights 261-265 (H. Hannum and D. Fischer eds. 1993).

who the following year transmitted it to the Senate for its advice and consent. Message of the President Transmitting Four Treaties Pertaining to Human Rights, S. Exec. Doc. Nos. C, D, E, & F, 95th Cong., 2d Sess. viii-xi (1978), reprinted in U.S. Ratification of the Human Rights Treaties: With or Without Reservations?, at 93-97 (R. Lillich ed. 1981). At hearings before the Senate Committee on Foreign Relations the following year, the Department of State's Legal Adviser introduced the Carter Administration's case for the Covenant's approval with the following remarks.

Prepared Statement of Hon. Roberts B. Owen, Legal Adviser, Department of State
in International Human Rights Treaties: Hearings Before the Senate Comm. on Foreign Relations, 96th Cong., 2d Sess. 27, 28 (1979)

Unlike its partner covenant, the International Covenant on Economic, Social and Cultural Rights looks not to the recognition of present rights, but to the future. It commits States to take steps towards the future realization of certain economic, social and cultural goals for the individual, much as many of our domestic enactments and policy statements look towards aspirational goals of full employment, universal health care, and the like. Article 2 requires that ratifying States undertake "to take steps . . . with a view to achieving progressively the full realization of the rights recognized in the present Covenant." These rights include the right to work, and to enjoy just and fair conditions of work; the right of social security, to the enjoyment of a high standard of health, and to an adequate standard of living; the right to the protection of the family and of children; and the right to primary education.

The desirability of realizing these rights is clear, and in keeping with policies fostered in the United States for some fifty years at least. It is worth reiterating that no ratifying party thereby commits itself to the present implementation of these rights. Nor does any party commit itself to distribute the benefits foreseen by the Covenant to individuals directly. Rather, the Covenant obliges governments to work towards the eventual achievement of the minimum standards it sets out. To emphasize that this constitutes an obligation to promote rather than an immediate legal commitment to perform, the Administration has suggested appending a declaration to this effect.

As the Lawyers Committee for International Human Rights observed at the time, the language used in the above-mentioned "declaration" (called a "statement" in the President's Message, but really an understanding) regarding Article 2(1) "undercuts the basic character of the Covenant: it [the

Covenant] does not merely establish goals; it also creates legal obligations, even if they are to be carried out 'progressively' and within the limits of available resources." Hearings, supra, at 54. See also Alston and Quinn, The Nature and Scope of States Parties' Obligations Under the International Covenant on Economic, Social and Cultural Rights, 9 Human Rts. Q. 156 (1987). Thus, as the Chairman of the Committee on Economic, Social, and Cultural Rights has pointed out in his usual trenchant fashion,

> the understanding proposed by the Carter administration to the effect that *all* of the substantive provisions of the Covenant "describe goals to be achieved progressively rather than through immediate implementation" is manifestly incorrect and would be incompatible with the basic object and purpose of the Covenant. Accordingly, it cannot serve as an appropriate basis for future public or congressional debate over ratification of the Covenant. Rather, the starting point for such a debate in the 1990s must be recognition of the fact that a significant range of obligations would flow from ratification.

Alston, U.S. Ratification of the Covenant on Economic, Social and Cultural Rights: The Need for an Entirely New Strategy, 84 Am. J. Intl. L. 365 (1990) (emphasis in original). The nature of the states parties' obligations under Article 2(1) has been authoritatively determined by the Committee on Economic, Social, and Cultural Rights in its General Comment No. 3. See Committee on Economic, Social, and Cultural Rights, Report on the Fifth Session, U.N. ESCOR Supp. (No. 3) at 83-87, U.N. Doc. E/1991/23 (1991). For the other reservations, understandings, and declarations proposed by the Carter Administration, see Message of the President Transmitting Four Treaties Pertaining to Human Rights, supra page 198. They are critiqued by Weston, U.S. Ratification of the International Covenant on Economic, Social and Cultural Rights: With or Without Qualifications, in U.S. Ratification of the Human Rights Treaties, supra page 198, at 27, who concludes that "most, if not all, the reservations, understandings, and declarations . . . can be seen to be either superfluous, churlish, violative of international law, contrary to enlightened self-interest, or a combination of all." Id. at 38.

The Senate took no action with respect to the Covenant during the Carter Administration. Nor, in view of the Reagan Administration's attempt to eliminate economic, social, and cultural rights from the human rights lexicon, did it address the Covenant again during the Reagan-Bush years. As described by the former U.S. Representative to the UN Commission on Human Rights:

> Soon after taking office . . . the Reagan Administration took unilateral steps to eliminate economic and social rights from the United States' definition of human rights and foreign policy concerns. A 1981 State Department memorandum limited the definition of human rights to political and civil rights. And in the 1981 *Country Reports*, the State Department stated that, for the most part, economic and social rights were not used in the *Country Reports*.

At about the same time, Ambassador Kirkpatrick launched a vitriolic attack on the concept of economic and social rights, asserting that "no great reflection produced them" and that they were like a "letter to Santa Claus," grounded in the concept of utopian expectation and "a vague sense that Utopia is one's due." Subsequent *Country Reports* and State Department statements continued to exclude economic and social rights from the term "internationally recognized human rights."

Shestack, An Unsteady Focus: The Vulnerabilities of the Reagan Administration's Human Rights Policy, 2 Harv. Human Rts. Y.B. 25, 40-41 (1989). According to another informed observer, "This process of reinventing the concept of human rights to make it resemble more closely the ideological predilections of the U.S. Government reached a high point in a June 1988 statement by the Deputy Assistant Secretary of State for Human Rights and Humanitarian Affairs [Ms. Paula Dobriansky], in which she sought to dispell a number of 'myths' about human rights, the first of which was that ' "economic and social rights" constitute human rights.' " Alston, supra page 199, at 374.

The Clinton Administration, within six months after coming into office, repudiated the Reagan-Bush approach to economic, social, and cultural rights. Secretary of State Warren Christopher, in his speech to the World Conference on Human Rights in Vienna in June 1993, announced that the President would move promptly to obtain Senate advice and consent to the ratification, inter alia, of the Covenant. Christopher, Democracy and Human Rights: Where America Stands, 4 U.S. Dept. of State Dispatch No. 25, at 1, 3 (1993). Assistant Secretary of State Shattuck, in a speech about the Conference, reported that the U.S. delegation had "acknowledged that the economic, social and cultural rights identified in the UN's Universal Declaration are indeed rights — contrary to the Bush and Reagan Administrations." Shattuck, Vienna and Beyond: U.S. Human Rights Diplomacy in the Post-Cold War World, Address Before the Union Internationale des Avocats, San Francisco, at 3 (Aug. 29, 1993). He added that "[o]ur new position emphasizes our view that *both* types of rights involve restraints and obligations placed on governments to protect the integrity and dignity of individuals, and promote economic and social development." Id. (emphasis added). While this reaffirmation that "second generation" human rights *are* human rights represents a welcome return to the fold on the part of the Clinton Administration, just as the proof of the pudding is in the taste, the sincerity of this commitment depends upon whether the United States actually moves promptly to ratify the Covenant. To date it has taken no steps in this direction. Of the 127 states that have ratified the Civil and Political Covenant, only the United States, Haiti, and Mozambique have not ratified the Economic, Social, and Cultural Covenant. Perhaps more relevant, of all the Western (WEO) states, only the United States, Liechtenstein, and Turkey are not parties to it. The international community awaits, one hopes not in vain, for the United States to assume a leadership role with respect to "second generation" human rights.*

3. "Third Generation" Human Rights

During the past two decades, claims have been advanced for the existence (or development) of a "third generation" of so-called solidarity rights, including the right to development, the right to peace, and the right to a healthy environment. See, e.g., Sohn, supra page 194, at 48-62. While two of these claimed rights — the right to development (G.A. Res. 41/128, 41 U.N. GAOR Supp. (No. 53) at 186, U.N. Doc. A/41/53 (1986)) and the right to peace (G.A. Res. 39/11, 39 U.N. GAOR Supp. (No. 51) at 22, U.N. Doc. A/39/51 (1984)) — have found their way into UN General Assembly resolutions and other documents, to date no discernable effort has been mounted to transfer them into binding treaty obligations. Consider the contrasting views of the following writers on the desirability of attempts to establish "third generation" human rights.

Marks, Emerging Human Rights: A New Generation for the 1980s?
33 Rutgers L. Rev. 435, 451-452 (1981)

Much hostility has been voiced against the idea of a new generation of human rights. Not only is proliferation of rights considered to be dangerous, but also the use of the term "generation" implies, the detractors say, that the rights belonging to earlier generations are outdated. It is also frequently said that the rights of the new generation are too vague to be justiciable and are no more than slogans, at best useful for advancing laudable goals of the U.N., at worst useful for the propaganda of certain countries.

Indeed, it would weaken the idea of human rights in general if numerous claims or values were indiscriminately proclaimed as human rights. It is

---

* That the Clinton Administration is less than fully committed to the entire panoply of economic, social, and cultural rights seems evident from its first round of Country Reports, which fail to survey the status of all such rights in foreign countries, but cover only "key internationally recognized worker rights, including the right of association; the right to organize and bargain collectively; prohibition of forced or compulsory labor; minimum age for employment of children; and acceptable conditions of work." U.S. Dept. of State, Country Reports on Human Rights Practices for 1993, at xii (1994). This focus on workers' rights, to the exclusion of other "second generation" rights, seems to have been motivated less by the plight of foreign workers than by the impact of their low wages and poor working conditions on the U.S. economy. Indeed, the report frankly cites "the rising concern about the impact of international trade on worker rights standards" to justify its selective approach to economic, social, and cultural rights. Id. at xvii.

also true that the essential normative task in the field of human rights was accomplished during the first three decades after the founding of the U.N., and that the more urgent task now is implementation. Nevertheless, I have tried to stress the dynamic nature of the process by which these rights are recognized and the consequent emergence of new human rights in the 1980s.

As the 1980s begin, the human rights specialist is, to a certain extent, faced with the choice of resisting the rights which, whether he likes it or not, are emerging, or understanding and contributing to the process by which a limited number of new rights will succeed in attaining international recognition because (a) the need for them is sufficiently great and (b) the international community is ready to recognize them as human rights. He should seek to apply rigorous standards to the definition of new rights, and in particular, as Professor Rivero of France has insisted, see that they have a clearly defined object and an identifiable subject and can be reasonably expected to be enforced. Many human rights already recognized for several decades fall short of these standards. The proclamation of these rights nevertheless increased the likelihood that they would be translated into law and practice. As long as emerging rights are not so unrealistic or trivial as to be treated with mockery, their recognition does serve the advancement of the cause of human rights without endangering the rights of earlier generations. John Humphrey, Director of the U.N. Division of Human Rights for its first two decades, has written that "there are encouraging developments. One of these is *the expansion of the concept of human rights to cover new values* . . . and new threats to human rights." Although he was referring to the right to privacy, the statement is valid for the new generation of human rights for the 1980s. If we are vigilant and require that proposed new rights be relevant to basic concerns of mankind, do not impinge upon existing rights, and may be followed up through an appropriate implementation machinery, there should be no reason to resist a new generation of human rights.

A. Robertson, Human Rights in the World
255-259 (3d ed. J. Merrills ed. 1989)

SOME OTHER PROPOSALS: 'NEW HUMAN RIGHTS'

In recent years a good deal of thought has been given to the question of extending the scope of human rights beyond those to be found in the Universal Declaration and the two international Covenants. An early indication of this tendency was the proclamation of a 'right to development'. . . . The thinking here is that, quite apart from moral considerations, the economic development of the poorer countries of the world is essential to their social well being and political stability and that without it they are in no position to guarantee the civil, political, economic, social and cultural rights prescribed in the major international texts. As a consequence, the 'right to development' is asserted as a human right.

In a similar way, the concern felt in many countries and international organisations about the need for the protection of the environment, particularly against the pollution generated by modern industrial societies, has led some to the conclusion that there is a human right to a clean and healthy environment.

Then there are those who go further and consider that there is a human right to peace and a human right to share in the 'common heritage of mankind', that is the natural resources of the deep sea bed and other areas not subject to territorial sovereignty. Indeed, some have suggested that the so-called 'new human rights', including the four just mentioned, constitute the 'third generation of human rights' which should receive international recognition after the two first 'generations' or categories protected by the UN Covenants of 1966.

A distinct but related question, which has been much discussed in the United Nations in recent years, is the establishment of a new international economic order. [The author devotes four paragraphs to describing the rise (but not the fall) of the new international economic order (NIEO).]

This brings us back to the so-called 'new rights': the right to development, the right to the environment, the right to share in the common heritage of mankind, the right to peace, and so on. Are these concepts human rights in any meaningful sense of that term? In trying to answer this question, there are several factors to be borne in mind.

In the first place, the word 'human' in the expression 'human rights' has a specific meaning. It indicates that the rights under consideration are rights pertaining to human beings by virtue of their humanity. As stated in both the UN Covenants, 'these rights derive from the inherent dignity of the human person'. In our view this means that the rights which can properly be called 'human rights' are rights of individual human beings stemming from their nature as human beings, and not rights of groups, associations, or other collectivities. This is borne out of the wording repeatedly used in the Universal Declaration and in the Covenant on Civil and Political Rights, 'Everyone has the right . . .'; while the Covenant on Economic, Social and Cultural Rights repeatedly stipulates that 'the States Parties . . . recognise the right of everyone to . . .' the different rights protected. It is quite clear from this language that what the Universal Declaration and the Covenants are concerned with is the rights of individual human beings. True, there is an exception in Article 1 of both Covenants, which states, 'All peoples have the right of self-determination'. But it is clear from the *travaux* that this was regarded as a special provision, and its exceptional character is underlined by the fact that [it] is placed in a distinct chapter of each Covenant, and separated from the articles relating to individual human rights.

This being so, is it accurate to designate as 'human-rights' so-called rights which pertain not to individuals but to groups or collectivities? Usage, of course, is a matter of convention and there is room for more than one view as to what is appropriate here. In our view, however, language and thinking will be clearer if we use the expression 'human rights' to designate individual rights and 'collective rights' to designate the rights of groups and collectivities, a distinction which also has the advantage of being consistent with much generally accepted practice.

The second consideration relates to the use of the word 'rights' in the expression 'new human rights.' Economic development, the protection of the environment, the common heritage of mankind and peace: are these concepts 'rights' in any meaningful sense? They can, and should, be objectives of social policy. They may be items in a political programme. However, they are certainly not legally enforceable claims. Most people no doubt prefer peace. But if one's country is at war, it is certain that there is no legally enforceable 'right to peace'. Naturally, it would be possible to define 'rights' in such a way as to include all desirable objectives of social policy, and in that event, the 'new human rights' would become 'rights' by virtue of the definition. But this would be to distort the ordinary meaning given to the term 'human rights' and, more seriously, would run together goals which enlightened humanity ought to pursue with claims which are already protected by international law. The trouble arises, then, because advocates of the 'new human rights' are confusing objectives of social policy with rights in the lawyers' sense. If one wishes to see some objective achieved — a clean and healthy environment, for example — it is tempting to say that this is a right to which we are all entitled. But it is not a good idea to take wishes for reality.

The last point to be borne in mind is that there is a crucial distinction between legal rights and moral rights. We may consider that we have a moral right to something — consideration from others, perhaps — when we have no legal right to it at all. Countless examples could be given. If advocates of the 'new human rights' assert that we have a moral right to peace, to the environment, and so on, then many will be inclined to agree. But there is all the difference in the world between these and other moral rights, on the one hand, and, on the other, rights, whether civil and political or economic and social, which have been incorporated in international treaties. While it is true that moral ideas provide both an incentive to create new law and a yardstick for its interpretation, until the process of law-making has taken place, 'new human rights' must remain in the realm of speculation.

Bibliographical Note on the Right to Development

There is a substantial body of literature, much of it polemical in nature, concerning "third generation" human rights. Among the best overview studies is Alston, A Third Generation of Solidarity Rights: Progressive Development or Obfuscation of International Human Rights Law?, 29 Neth. Intl. L. Rev. 307, 322 (1982), who concludes that "the concept of third generation solidarity rights would seem to contribute more obfuscation than clarification in an area which can ill afford to be made less accessible to the masses than it already is." But compare Alston, Making Space for New Human Rights: The Case of the Right to Development, 1 Harv. Human Rts. Y.B. 3 (1988), where the author appears to have changed his mind, at least with respect to the principal "third generation" human right. See also Donnelly, In Search of the Unicorn: The Jurisprudence and Politics of the Right to Development, 15 Cal. West. Intl. L.J. 473, 508 (1985), who calls the right to development "not just a charming delusion, but a threat to human rights, and a particularly insidious threat because it plays upon our fondest hopes and best desires, and diverts attention from more productive ways of linking human rights and development." For a recent, more general treatment of the topic from the same perspective, see Donnelly, Third Generation Rights, in Peoples and Minorities in International Law 119 (C. Brölmann, R. Lefeber, and M. Zieck eds. 1993). That criticism of "third generation" human rights is not limited to U.S. and other Western writers, see Dimitrijevic, Peace and Human Rights — Do We Really Need a Right to Peace?, 35 Jugoslovenska Revija Za Medjunarodno Pravo 31 (1988) (answers his title's question in the negative).

Of all proposed "third generation" human rights, only the right to development has received substantial support within the UN system, among states, and from writers. Not only has it been the subject of a UN General Assembly resolution (with the United States casting the sole dissenting vote), but also the UN Commission on Human Rights recently created a working group to "identify obstacles" and "recommend ways and means" to realize the right. Commn. H.R. Res. 1993/22, U.N. ESCOR Supp. (No. 3) at 105, U.N. Doc. E/1993/23 (1993). The right to development was reaffirmed by the World Conference on Human Rights "as a universal and inalienable right and an integral part of fundamental human rights." Vienna Declaration and Programme of Action, U.N. Doc. A/CONF. 157/23, at 5 (1993), reprinted in 32 Intl. Legal Materials at 1666 (1993). Moreover, in its resolution establishing a UN High Commissioner for Human Rights, the General Assembly emphasized the need to observe not only the International Bill of Rights and other human rights instruments, but also its Declaration on the Right to Development, specifically instructing the High Commissioner to "[r]ecognize the importance of promoting a balanced and sustainable development for all people and of ensuring realization of the right to development, as established in the Declaration on the Right to Development. . . ." G.A. Res. 48/141, 48 U.N. GAOR Supp. (No. 49) at 261, 262.

With respect to the legal status of the right to development, "it is clear that very considerable work of a multi-disciplinary nature will be required in order to translate the basic demand into a meaningful set of general legal principles let alone specific, binding legal rules." Alston, supra page 205, at 14. Erstwhile proponents of the NIEO currently seek to achieve many of its purported redistributive benefits through invocation of the right to development, which "can generally be boiled down to a demand for the establishment of a new international economic order which is structurally conducive to the 'development' of the poorer countries and of their more disadvantaged inhabitants." Id. That an attempt to "recycle" NIEO claims into binding legal obligations under Article 2(1) of the Covenant on Economic, Social, and Cultural Rights is afoot seems apparent from Paragraph 14 of General Comment No. 3 of the Committee on Economic, Social, and Cultural Rights.* Whether this linkage of human rights and development will be a productive one remains to be seen. Certainly it will become a matter of great debate.

E.   UN Human Rights Law-Making: The Need for "Quality Control"

In 1986, responding to scholarly criticism by Professor Alston (Alston, Conjuring Up New Human Rights: A Proposal for Quality Control, 78 Am. J. Intl. L. 607 (1984)) and Professor Meron (T. Meron, Human Rights Law-Making in the United Nations (1986)), plus the growing realization by many of its member states that its human rights "legislative" agenda was in chaos, the United Nations took an important initial step towards systematizing its development of new international human rights standards. The General Assembly responded to widespread concerns that proliferating claims for the recognition of additional specific or "third generation" human rights could threaten the integrity of the existing body of international human rights law by adopting Resolution 41/120 on "Setting International Standards in the Field of Human Rights." Read that Resolution and the commentary on it by the International League for Human Rights that follows. There seems little doubt that since 1990 specific human rights treaty-

---

* "The Committee wishes to emphasize that in accordance with Articles 55 and 56 of the Charter of the United Nations, with well-established principles of international law, and with the provisions of the Covenant itself, international cooperation for development and thus for the realization of economic, social and cultural rights is an obligation of all States. It is particularly incumbent upon those States which are in a position to assist others in this regard. The Committee notes in particular the importance of the Declaration on the Right to Development adopted by the General Assembly in its resolution 41/128 of 4 December 1986 and the need for States parties to take full account of all of the principles recognized therein. It emphasizes that, in the absence of an active programme of international assistance and cooperation on the part of all those States that are in a position to undertake one, the full realization of economic, social and cultural rights will remain an unfulfilled aspiration in many countries. . . ." Report on the Fifth Session, U.N. ESCOR Supp. (No. 3) at 87, U.N. Doc. E/1991/23 (1991).

making by the UN almost has come to a halt (see page 194 supra). Is that because the Resolution has been taken seriously, because the UN increasingly has opted for "soft law" standards (see Problem IV), or because a combination of these and perhaps other reasons has affected treaty-making efforts?

United Nations General Assembly Resolution 41/120
U.N. GAOR Supp. (No. 53) at 178-179, U.N. Doc. A/41/53
(1987)

41/120.   SETTING INTERNATIONAL STANDARDS IN THE FIELD OF
HUMAN RIGHTS

The General Assembly,

Recalling the extensive network of international standards in the field of human rights, which it, other United Nations bodies and the specialized agencies, have established,

Emphasizing the primacy of the Universal Declaration of Human Rights, the International Covenant on Civil and Political Rights and the International Covenant on Economic, Social and Cultural Rights in this network,

Reaffirming that effective implementation of these international standards is of fundamental importance,

Recognizing the value of continuing efforts to identify specific areas where further international action is required to develop the existing international legal framework in the field of human rights pursuant to Article 13, paragraph 1 a, of the Charter of the United Nations,

Recognizing also that standard setting should proceed with adequate preparation,

Emphasizing that the standard setting activities of the United Nations should be as effective and efficient as possible,

1. *Calls upon* Member States and United Nations bodies to accord priority to the implementation of existing international standards in the field of human rights and urges broad ratification of, or accession to, existing treaties in this field;

2. *Urges* Member States and United Nations bodies engaged in developing new international human rights standards to give due consideration in this work to the established international legal framework;

3. *Reaffirms* the important role of the Commission on Human Rights, among other appropriate United Nations bodies, in the development of international instruments in the field of human rights;

4. *Invites* Member States and United Nations bodies to bear in mind the following guidelines in developing international instruments in the field of human rights; such instruments should, *inter alia:*

(*a*) Be consistent with the existing body of international human rights law:

(*b*) Be of fundamental character and derive from the inherent dignity and worth of the human person;

(*c*) Be sufficiently precise to give rise to identifiable and practicable rights and obligations;

(*d*) Provide, where appropriate, realistic and effective implementation machinery, including reporting systems;

(*e*) Attract broad international support;

5. *Requests* the Secretary-General to provide appropriate specialized support to United Nations bodies working on standard setting in the field of human rights.

International League for Human Rights, Human Rights at the United Nations: New Standard Setting
Brief No. 10, at 2 (Oct. 1988)

[After summarizing the Resolution, the article states that it articulates several principles with significant implications for future UN human rights standard setting.]

First, the GA emphasized the "primacy" of the Universal Declaration and the two Covenants. At a minimum, this insistence on the primacy of the Universal Declaration and the Covenants requires that standards stated in new declarations or conventions not conflict with norms contained in those instruments.

Second, resolution 41/120 recognizes the value of additional standard setting in human rights, but calls for the UN and member states to give priority to the implementation of existing standards. Although the resolution highlights guidelines for standard setting, it advocates restraint in, if not abstention from, further law-making efforts until established norms have been transformed into practice. This emphasis on realization of existing human rights guarantees is reflected in the GA's reaffirmation of the "fundamental importance" of effective implementation of the Declaration and the Covenants and its reference to the "extensive network" of established human rights standards. In addition, the GA urged that the established legal framework be given "due regard" in developing new standards.

Third, law-making processes should be "as effective and efficient as possible." In this connection, the GA recognized the need for "adequate preparation" in the standard setting activities. Resolution 41/120 reaffirms the "important role" of the Commission on Human Rights (the Commission) in that process but does not elaborate on the nature of that role. The Secretary-General is requested to assist in the process by providing "appropriate specialized support" to bodies engaged in standard setting.

III. The Civil and Political Covenant

A. *Substantive Provisions*

Although ideological and political differences were behind the UN's decision in 1952 to draft two separate covenants, "[t]he division has also been supported by the argument that the grant or concession of most of the rights defined in [the Civil and Political Covenant] lies in the simple power of national governments, which are able if they wish to protect or guarantee them by legislation or administrative action, whereas most of the rights described in [the Economic, Social, and Cultural Covenant] are said to depend for their realization on the progressive economic development of a country, which may take many years and does not lie exclusively within the power of its government. . . ." P. Sieghart, The International Law of Human Rights 25 (1983). The different phraseology used in Articles 2(1) of the two covenants also suggests, in the view of most observers, that under the former a state must ensure the rights recognized immediately while under the latter its obligation is only to achieve the rights recognized progressively, taking into account its available resources.

You already have been asked to read the Civil and Political Covenant and have been introduced to its drafting history and basic coverage (pages 189-192 supra). Now take the opportunity to compare the rights set forth in Articles 3-21 of the Universal Declaration with the rights that are restated, in greater detail and with more legal precision, in Articles 6-27 of the Covenant. You will find that the Covenant contains a number of rights not found in the Declaration; the right of detained persons to be treated with humanity (Art. 10); freedom from imprisonment for debt (Art. 11); prohibition of propaganda for war and advocacy of hatred that constitutes incitement to discrimination, hostility, or violence (Art. 20); the rights of the child (Art. 24); and the rights of minorities (Art. 27). On the other hand, the right to own property and not to be arbitrarily deprived of it, guaranteed by Article 17 of the Declaration, is not expressly mentioned in the Covenant. This omission was thought serious enough to necessitate a declaration by the United States when it ratified the Covenant in 1992. (See page 254 infra.)

It is unnecessary to describe all the rights that an individual enjoys under the Covenant, but it is important to underscore the fact that they are not all absolute: as developed in greater detail at pages 914-929 of Problem XI, the Covenant allows a state to impose two types of restrictions upon an individual's rights. The first type consists of "claw-back" clauses contained in particular articles that permit the state to limit the rights guaranteed in those articles. Article 12(3), for instance, sanctions state restrictions on the freedom of movement when "necessary to protect national security, public order (*ordre public*), public health or morals or the rights and freedoms of others. . . ." The second type, authorized by Article 4(1), permits states to derogate from, that is, suspend, certain rights "[i]n time of public emergency which threatens the life of the nation. . . ." While no derogation may be made from the rights guaranteed by Articles 6, 7, 8(1), 11, 15, 16, and 18, the fact that a wide variety of important rights — for example, the right to liberty and security of person guaranteed by Article 9(1) — may be rendered temporarily "inoperative" by means of derogation greatly weakens the protections of the Covenant.

We shall have the opportunity to compare some of the rights guaranteed by the Covenant with rights found in the U.S. Constitution later in this Problem (see pages 241-244 infra). We also shall see how the Covenant (and its Optional Protocol) was invoked following severe human rights abuses in Suriname (see pages 224-239 infra). As a prelude to the latter, one must first study the various techniques by which the Covenant — and other such human rights treaties as the Racial Discrimination Convention — is implemented.

B.   Implementation Measures

Rights without remedies, Justice Holmes is purported to have remarked, are no rights at all, and in the area of international human rights, states unfortunately have shown a marked reluctance — witness the Genocide Convention mentioned at page 193 supra — to devise and adopt implementation measures that would ensure the effective enforcement of the substantive rights guaranteed by the various human rights treaties. Generally speaking, as Professor Shelton reminds us, "[w]e may distinguish four types of procedures, based upon the character of the instigating party: self-reporting by the state, interstate complaint procedures, individual petition procedures, and ad hoc investigations launched by organs of international organizations." Shelton, International Enforcement of Human Rights: Effectiveness and Alternatives, 1980 Am. Socy. Intl. L. Proceedings 6, 7. She adds the obvious: "[a]ll of these procedures should be viewed as supplementary and supervisory, since primary responsibility for enforcing international human rights norms continues to rest with each state." Id. at 7-8.

Of the four types of procedures, the last — ad hoc (or other) investigations by international organizations — is taken up at pages 417-448 of Problem VI. The other three types — state reporting, individual petitions, and interstate complaints — all may be available to enforce a state's obligations under the Civil and Political Covenant.

1. State Reporting

Article 40 of the Covenant creates a mandatory reporting system under which every state party must submit reports to the Human Rights Committee on the measures it has adopted that give effect to the rights protected by the Covenant and on the progress made in the enjoyment of those rights. The reports also are to include factors and difficulties, if any, that affect the state's implementation of the Covenant. An initial report is due one year after the Covenant enters into force for a state, with subsequent reports due at five-year intervals. Supplementary reports also may be requested by the Committee if a state report does not contain sufficient information or if, in the Committee's opinion, human rights protected under the Covenant had been affected in the state party.

The Committee over the years has formulated general guidelines on the form and content of such reports. They may be found in the UN's Manual on Human Rights Reporting, U.N. Doc. HR/PUB/91/1, at 79-125 (1991).* Before the Committee meets, an ad hoc working group reviews the report to be examined, identifies the issues to be raised with the representative of the state, and prepares a list of questions where further information is sought. Normally it takes two days for the Committee to examine a report. It is introduced by the representative of the state, after which Committee members put questions to him or her and engage in what aims to be a "constructive dialogue." Here it is important to note the commentary of a prominent member of the Committee on the nature of this dialogue (Manual, supra, at 121):

> [I]t has to be underlined that the Committee in its consideration of States reports is neither a judicial nor even a quasi-judicial body. Its role is not to pass judgement on the implementation of the provisions of the Covenant in any given State. The main function of the Committee is to assist States parties in fulfilling their obligations under the Covenant, to make available to them the experience the Committee has acquired in its examination of other reports and to discuss with them any issue related to the enjoyment of the rights enshrined in the Covenant in a particular country.

Other aspects of the Committee's review process, as well as the status of its general comments on particular reports, are taken up in the following extract.

---

* The Manual also includes guidelines for reports to the Committee on Economic, Social, and Cultural Rights under its covenant (pages 39-77); the Committee on the Elimination of Racial Discrimination under its convention (pages 127-142); the Group of Three (members of the Commission on Human Rights) under the Convention on the Suppression and Punishment of the Crime of Apartheid (pages 143-152); the Committee on the Elimination of Discrimination Against Women under its convention (pages 153-176); and the Committee against Torture under its convention (pages 177-189). Guidelines for reports to the Committee on the Rights of the Child under its convention may be found in U.N. Doc. CRC/C/5 (1991).

Shelton, Compliance Mechanisms [Periodic Reports]
in United States Ratification of the International Covenants on Human Rights 151, 153-155 (H. Hannum and D. Fischer eds. 1993)

There is no explicit provision in the Covenant for consideration of outside information by the Committee in reviewing State reports, which has resulted in some dispute within the Committee on the role of specialized agencies and non-governmental organizations. In practice, the specialized agencies have been invited to attend public meetings of the Committee where State reports are considered and to address the Committee on any matter on which it might require information. In addition, the Committee has agreed in rule 67 of its rules of procedure to have the Secretary-General transmit relevant parts of reports to the specialized agencies. It should be noted, however, that the specialized agencies have no right under the Covenant to comment on State reports and may do so only if specifically requested by the Committee. The Committee has not formalized any procedure by which the specialized agencies may present information on their practice in relation to the application of provisions similar to those of the Covenant.

Although specialized agencies have not presented formal reports, the Committee has made use of the work of other organs of the United Nations. In the case of Chile, it took official notice of General Assembly resolutions and the work of the United Nations' Ad Hoc Working Group on Chile. The result was a request of Chile to file a new report, based on the view that the first report did not reflect the realities of the human rights situation in that country.

There is no provision in either the Covenant or the rules of procedure which would permit formal presentation of information to the Committee by non-governmental organizations (NGOs). This does not prevent NGOs from supplying information to members of the Committee individually, but use of such information was questioned by at least one State in the Committee's early deliberations. Now, however, Committee members have frequently referred directly to information provided by NGOs. . . .*

The power of the Committee is limited in respect to making recommendations. The Committee's mandate is to "study" the reports submitted and then to "transmit its reports" on them, together with such "general

* Note that the Committee still has not adopted procedures for the direct receipt of information from NGOs. "Three committees, CESCR, CRC, and CAT [Committee on Economic, Social, and Cultural Rights, Committee on the Rights of the Child, and Committee Against Torture], currently permit NGOs to make formal written interventions. CESCR permits NGO representatives to make oral interventions, on all matters, and CRC permits oral statements on matters other than the examination of state reports." Coliver, International Reporting Procedures, in Guide to International Human Rights Practice 173, 189 (2d ed. H. Hannum ed. 1992). Some time may pass before the Human Rights Committee permits NGOs to make such information directly available to it. — EDs.

comments" that it considers appropriate. These comments are also transmitted to the States Parties and may be sent to the Economic and Social Council. States Parties may submit to the Committee their observations on the latter's comments on their reports. The only publication requirement is that the Committee submit an annual report on its activities through ECOSOC to the General Assembly.

Committee members have not been able to agree fully on the scope of the "general comments" it is permitted to make under article 40(4) of the Covenant. While the Committee has adopted a number of comments on the substantive content of particular rights or procedural matters to guide reporting states,* it has not directly addressed the issue of any specific State's compliance or non-compliance with its obligations. However, several individual members have adopted the practice of offering their own opinions on the adequacy of a State's report or its guarantee of Covenant rights as part of their final comments during consideration of Article 40 reports. These comments are reflected in the Committee's summary records and also are summarized in the Committee's annual report to the General Assembly.**

In general, although it appears that some States have been delinquent in presenting their reports, compliance with the reporting requirement has been extensive. Most reports contain detailed information on measures taken to implement the Covenant, and every State has sent a representative to the proceedings to introduce the State report and answer questions. The Committee has begun to develop links with specialized agencies and other bodies, as well as informal contacts from NGOs, from whom independent information can be obtained.

Thus, while State reporting as an effective measure of implementation

---

* See Table 3-2, infra pages 225-226. — EDS.
** In 1992 the Committee broke with past precedents and decided

> that comments would be adopted reflecting the views of the Committee as a whole at the end of the consideration of each State party report. That would be in addition to, and would not replace, comments made by members, at the end of the consideration of each State party report. A rapporteur would be selected in each case to draft a text, in consultation with the Chairman and other members, for adoption by the Committee. Such comments were to be embodied in a written text and dispatched to the State party concerned as soon as practicable before being publicized and included in the annual report of the Committee. They were to provide a general evaluation of the State party report and of the dialogue with the delegation and to underline positive developments that had been noted during the period under review, factors and difficulties affecting the implementation of the Covenant, as well as specific issues of concern regarding the application of the provisions of the Covenant. Comments were also to include suggestions and recommendations formulated by the Committee to the attention of the State party concerned.

Report of the Human Rights Committee, 47 U.N. GAOR Supp. (No. 40) at 10, U.N. Doc. A/47/40 (1994). For such country-related "Comments of the Committee," see id. at 67-69 (Algeria); id. at 80-83 (Peru); id. at 92-94 (Colombia); id. at 101-102 (Belgium); id. at 111-112 (Yugoslavia); id. at 122-124 (Korea); id. at 132-134 (Belarus); and id. at 142-143 (Mongolia). — EDS.

has been criticized, the Committee appears to be making reasonably full use of its authority to assess impartially the efforts of States Parties to implement the Covenant. When such critical appraisal is permitted and made, including obtaining supplemental information, using outside sources, and commenting on inadequate or inaccurate reporting, a reporting mechanism can be an effective, if limited, enforcement measure. *

For additional detailed analyses of state reporting under the Covenant, see pages 411-417 of Problem VI; M. Nowak, U.N. Covenant on Civil and Political Rights: CCPR Commentary 545-579 (1993); D. McGoldrick, The Human Rights Committee 62-119 (1991); Shelton, Compliance Mechanisms [Periodic Reports], in United States Ratification of the International Covenants on Human Rights 151-155 (H. Hannum and D. Fischer eds. 1993); and Coliver, International Reporting, in Guide to International Human Rights Practice 173-191 (2d ed. H. Hannum ed. 1992).

2. Individual Communications

The right of individual petition has long been considered the key to effective enforcement of international human rights law. Occasionally it is made mandatory by a human rights instrument, as in the case of the American Convention on Human Rights (Art. 44), but more frequently it is made optional, the Racial Discrimination Convention (Art. 14) being a leading example. In the case of the Civil and Political Covenant, neither approach was taken. Instead, by a very close vote it was decided to relegate the right of individual petition to a separate legal text, straightforwardly called the Optional Protocol to the International Covenant on Civil and Political Rights (Documentary Supplement). As of 1 July 1994, it has been ratified by 76 of the 127 states parties to the Covenant (60 percent thereof). The United States, which ratified the Covenant in 1992, has not yet ratified the Optional Protocol. Indeed, it has not even signed it.

One commentator, giving state reporting short shrift, opines that "given the likely continued non-invocation of the Covenant's inter-State dispute settlement procedure, the success of the international measures of protection will be gauged by whether or not the individual communication procedure, in which the Committee plays the fundamental role, will provide an effective international remedy to an individual whose rights under the Covenant have been violated," Ghandi, The Human Rights Committee and the Right of Individual Communication, 57 Brit. Y.B. Intl. L. 201, 205 (1986).

---

* For a case study of how the Committee's use of the reporting system has encouraged states to bring their laws into compliance with the Covenant, see Cohn, The Early Harvest: Domestic Legal Changes Related to the Human Rights Committee and the Covenant on Civil and Political Rights, 13 Human Rts. Q. 295 (1991). — Eds.

In any event, it warrants the extended treatment that it is accorded in the following extract.*

Lewis-Anthony, Treaty-Based Procedures for Making Human Rights Complaints Within the UN System
In Guide to International Human Rights Practice 41, 42-49 passim (2d ed. H. Hannum Ed. 1992)

SUBSTANTIVE REQUIREMENTS FOR COMPLAINTS

WHO MAY FILE

Article 1 of the Optional Protocol provides that the Committee may receive communications from "individuals subject to [the State Party's] jurisdiction who claim to be victims of a violation by that State Party of any of the rights set forth in the Covenant." The rules of procedure provide that communications may be submitted by the victim directly or by his or her representative. In circumstances in which the victim is unable to submit an application (for example, when it is alleged that the state is responsible for the victim's disappearance), applications may be submitted by a close relative on behalf of the victim. The burden rests with the author of a complaint to show that there is a sufficiently close connection to entitle the representative to act on the victim's behalf. Failure to do so renders the application inadmissible.

The Committee has stated that a person can only claim to be a "victim" in the sense of article 1 of the Protocol if he or she is personally affected by a violation of the Covenant. Thus, an individual cannot challenge a law in the abstract by way of an *actio popularis* or a request for a declaratory judgment.

STATES AGAINST WHICH COMPLAINTS MAY BE LODGED

Only states which have ratified the Optional Protocol may be the subject of a complaint to the Human Rights Committee. An individual need

* Article 14 of the Racial Discrimination Convention provides for complaints from individuals and groups of individuals; Article 22 of the Torture Convention provides for complaints from individuals. Both conventions, however, require states parties to recognize the competence of their committees to receive such complaints before the procedure becomes operative. As of 14 February 1994, 19 parties to the Racial Discrimination Convention and 34 parties to the Torture Convention had done so. Report of the Secretary-General, Effective Functioning of the Various Mechanisms Established for Supervision, Investigation and Monitoring of the Implementation of the Treaty Obligations Entered into by States in Regard to Human Rights and of the Existing International Standards in This Regard, U.N. Doc. E/CN.4/1994/42, at 9 (1994). The United States, which has now ratified both conventions, is not among them. For a brief treatment of these complaint procedures, see Lewis-Anthony, infra, at 49-57. — EDS.

not be a citizen or a resident of the state concerned as long as he or she was subject to the jurisdiction of a state party to the Protocol at the time of the complaint.

The phrase "subject to the jurisdiction of" has been considered by the Committee in a number of cases. Normally, the individual must have been present within the territory of the state concerned at the time of the alleged violation. . . .

SUBJECT MATTER

All complaints submitted under the Optional Protocol must allege a violation of one or more rights contained in Parts II and III of the Covenant. These include the rights not to be tortured or subjected to cruel, inhuman, or degrading treatment or punishment; to life; to liberty and security; to a fair trial; to freedom of expression; to freedom of thought and religion; to freedom of peaceful assembly; to freedom of association; to participation in political life; not to be discriminated against; and to equality before the law and equal protection of the law. In addition, the Second Optional Protocol, which entered into force on 11 July 1991, prohibits capital punishment. . . .

The Covenant does not have retroactive effect. Thus, a communication will be declared inadmissible if it alleges a violation of the Covenant which took place prior to the entry into force of the Covenant and the Protocol for the state concerned. However, if a violation appears to have continued or has had continuing effects after the Covenant and Protocol have entered into force for the state concerned, the Committee will consider the complaint. For example, the Committee has found a violation when a person was tried under conditions in which due process was denied after the entry into force of the Covenant, although he had been detained and tortured prior to its entry into force. . . .

Article 5(2)(a) of the Protocol provides that the Committee cannot consider a communication if the same matter is simultaneously being examined under another procedure of international investigation or settlement. Unless a state has entered a reservation to the contrary, there is nothing to prevent an applicant from using another procedure first and then, upon the termination of those proceedings, bringing the case before the Human Rights Committee. However, several countries have filed reservations to bar consideration of a communication that is being or has been considered in another international forum, thus preventing an "appeal" to the Committee.

The concept of "the same matter" refers to "identical parties, to the complaints advanced and the facts adduced in support of them." A two-line reference to the person concerned in a case before the Inter-American Commission on Human Rights which listed, in a similar manner, the names of hundreds of other persons allegedly detained in Uruguay was found not to constitute "the same matter" as that described in detail by the same author in a communication to the Human Rights Committee. Consideration by UN bodies of a country under the "1503 procedure," which governs the examination of communications which appear to reveal a consistent pattern of gross violations of human rights, does not prevent an individual complaint under the Protocol, since the former procedure is concerned with a "situation" rather than an individual communication.

Like other international human rights bodies, the Committee may not consider communications unless all domestic remedies have been exhausted, although exhaustion of domestic remedies is required only to the extent that the remedies are effective, available, and not unreasonably prolonged. The burden is upon the complainant to show that all domestic remedies have been exhausted or that no effective remedies exist. If the state concerned disputes the assertion that all remedies have been exhausted, the state must give details of the particular remedies available to the alleged victim and proof of their effectiveness. A general description of remedies provided under the law, without linking them to the specific circumstances of the complaint, has been deemed insufficient.

FORMAL OR PROCEDURAL REQUIREMENTS

The Human Rights Committee has produced a model communication to assist complainants, but it is not compulsory to use the model form. The essential information for inclusion in a petition consists of the following: name, address, and nationality of the victim and the author, if different; justification for acting on behalf of the victim; identification of the state against which the complaint is being made; the articles of the Covenant allegedly violated; steps taken to exhaust domestic remedies; a statement whether the same matter is being dealt with by another international procedure of investigation or settlement; and a detailed description of the facts substantiating the allegations, including relevant dates. The more complete the information given in the original application, the faster it will be processed — although it is not uncommon for three or four years to elapse before the Committee finishes its consideration. The communication must not be anonymous, but it is possible to request the Committee not to reveal the name of the author and/or victim when it publishes its decision. All documents relating to the consideration of communications under the Protocol are confidential. Communications must be signed and dated.

There is no time limit for the submission of applications under the Optional Protocol, although it is generally in the interests of the complainant to submit a communication in a timely fashion. Unfortunately, there is no provision for legal aid, whether the victim is the author or is represented by legal counsel. . . .

MEANS OF INVESTIGATION

Once a communication has been received by the Human Rights Committee, it is screened by a member of the secretariat of the UN Centre for Human Rights, who may contact the author for additional information. The secretariat registers applications and forwards them to the Committee's Special Rapporteur on New Applications. The rapporteur is a member of the Committee designated to act on communications received between sessions. The rapporteur's first task is to ensure that sufficient information is obtained from the parties to enable the Committee to rule on the question of admissibility. When the rapporteur is satisfied that the communication complies with preliminary admissibility requirements (i.e., that the communication is not anonymous, an abuse of the right of submission, or incompatible with the Covenant), then he or she may transmit the communication to the state concerned, with a request for observations as to its admissibility. The state is usually given two months in which to respond, and the author is given an opportunity to comment on the state's response.

In cases involving the death penalty, the rapporteur may communicate to the state the Committee's "views on whether interim measures may be desirable to avoid irreparable damage to the victim of the alleged violation." In all other cases, the Committee as a whole looks at the issue of interim measures. Requests for interim measures can be made within a short time after the communication is filed, even when the Committee needs further information from the author on the question of admissibility. In such circumstances, the Committee requests the state concerned not to carry out the death penalty before the Committee considers the question of admissibility. Requests for interim measures clearly do not bind a state; they have moral force only, and the power to suggest interim measures is most frequently used in cases involving persons under sentence of death who are challenging a violation of their right to a fair trial.

A working group of not less than five members of the Committee meets for one week prior to each session and can declare a case admissible as long as the group is unanimous. Otherwise, admissibility is decided upon by the whole Committee. Only the entire Committee can declare a case inadmissible, although it considers advice given by the rapporteur and working group. It is possible for the author of a communication to request, in writing, a review of an inadmissibility decision, for instance, on the grounds that the matter is no longer being examined by another international procedure or that all domestic remedies have been exhausted.

Once a case has been declared admissible, article 4(2) of the Protocol allows the state six months in which to "submit written explanations, or statements clarifying the matter, and the remedy, if any, that may have been taken." Any statement or explanation received is communicated to the author who, in turn, is usually given six weeks to submit additional written information or observations.

The Committee is directed by article 5 of the Protocol to consider the communications it receives "in the light of all written information made available to it by the individual and by the State Party concerned." There is no provision for oral hearings or on-site investigation of complaints. Unlike many other international procedures, the Committee is not mandated to facilitate a friendly settlement between the parties.

DECISIONS AND IMPLEMENTATION

The Covenant stipulates that all decisions of the Committee are to be made by majority vote of the members present, but efforts are normally made to arrive at decisions by consensus. Upon receiving all relevant information on the merits of the case, the Committee adopts what are known as its "views," which it forwards to both the complainant and the state concerned. The views take the form of a collegiate opinion, but any member of the Committee may request that a summary of his or her individual opinion be appended to the views of the Committee. The Committee's views are made public in communiques issued at the end of each session and are published in the Committee's Annual Reports to the General Assembly. . . .

The Committee normally goes beyond merely stating its views as to whether there has been a violation; it will usually offer its opinion on the obligation of the state in light of the Committee's findings. For example, it has called upon states to take immediate steps to ensure strict observance of the Covenant; to release a victim from detention and ensure that similar violations do not occur in the future; to commute a sentence of death imposed in circumstances in which there have been violations of the Covenant; and to provide a victim with effective remedies, including compensation, for the violations suffered.

The views of the Committee are not legally binding and, until recently, no sanction was available for noncompliance by states found to have violated the Covenant. In the majority of cases, states have failed to heed the Committee's views. As a result, there has been much debate over the extent of the Committee's powers once its views have been transmitted to the state concerned. Since 1982, the practice of the Committee has been to send a letter setting forth its views and inviting the state to inform the Committee of any action taken in light of those views. A few states have responded positively to this invitation and have informed the Committee of steps they have taken to remedy the situation.

As a result of pressure from victims, the Committee finally adopted a series of measures in 1990 to monitor compliance with its views. Under the new measures, whenever the Committee finds a violation of the Covenant, it now asks the state concerned to inform the Committee of any action it has taken in relation to the case, within a period of up to 180 days. Beginning in 1991, the Committee's Annual Report will indicate those states which fail to respond to the request or fail to provide a remedy, as well as those states which have cooperated with the Committee's request. In addition, information concerning measures taken to redress a violation now must be given by states when submitting their periodic reports under article 40 of the Covenant. The Committee has also appointed a "Special Rapporteur for the Follow-Up of Views," to recommend action which might be taken in respect of victims who claim that no appropriate remedy has been provided. The rapporteur may communicate directly with governments and victims, which may prove to be an effective tool. The Committee's follow-up plan does represent an imaginative attempt to monitor implementation of the Covenant and one can only hope that the effort will be successful. *

With 60 percent of the states parties to the Civil and Political Covenant now having ratified or acceded to the Optional Protocol, individual communications under the latter have been increasing in popularity, number, and perhaps effectiveness, as the following extract from the latest report of the Human Rights Committee indicates.

Report of the Human Rights Committee
47 U.N. GAOR Supp. (No. 40) at 145-147, U.N. Doc. A/47/40
(1994)

A.   PROGRESS OF WORK

608. The Committee started its work under the Optional Protocol at its second session in 1977. Since then, 514 communications concerning 42 States parties have been registered for consideration by the Committee, including 46 placed before it at its forty-third to forty-fifth sessions, covered by the present report.
609. The status of the 514 communications registered for consideration by the Human Rights Committee so far is as follows:
(a) Concluded by views under article 5, paragraph 4, of the Optional Protocol: 138;
(b) Declared inadmissible: 155;

---

* See de Zayas, The Follow-Up Procedure of the UN Human Rights Committee, Intl. Comm. Jurists, The Review No. 47, at 28 (Dec. 1991). For additional detailed analyses of individual communications under the Optional Protocol, see M. Nowak, supra page 214, at 647-723; M. McGoldrick, supra page 214, at 120-246; Shelton, Compliance Mechanisms [Individual Communications], in United States Ratification of the International Covenants on Human Rights 157-160 (H. Hannam and D. Fischer eds. 1993); Schmidt, Individual Human Rights Complaint Procedures Based on United Nations Treaties and the Need for Reform, 41 Intl. & Comp. L.Q. 645 (1992); and Davidson, The Procedure and Practice of the Human Rights Committee Under the First Optional Protocol to the International Covenant on Civil and Political Rights, 4 Canterbury L. Rev. 357 (1991). — EDS.

(c) Discontinued or withdrawn: 80;

(d) Declared admissible, but not yet concluded: 49;

(e) Pending at the pre-admissibility stage: 92.

610. In addition, the secretariat of the Committee has several hundred communications on file, in respect of which the authors have been advised that further information would be needed before their communications could be registered for consideration by the Committee. The authors of some 100 further communications have been informed that the Committee does not intend to consider their cases, as they fall clearly outside the scope of the Covenant or appear to be frivolous.

611. Two volumes containing selected decisions of the Human Rights Committee under the Optional Protocol, from the second to the sixteenth sessions and from the seventeenth to the thirty-second sessions, respectively, have been issued. . . . .*

612. During the forty-third to forty-fifth sessions, the Committee concluded consideration of 19 cases by adopting its views thereon. . . .

613. The Committee also concluded consideration of 31 cases by declaring them inadmissible. . . .

614. During the period under review, 24 communications were declared admissible for examination on the merits; decisions declaring communications admissible are not made public. Consideration of seven cases was discontinued. Procedural decisions were adopted in a number of pending cases (under rules 86 and 91 of the Committee's rules of procedure or under article 4 of the Optional Protocol). Secretariat action was requested on other pending cases.

B. Growth of the Committee's Case-Load Under the Optional Protocol

615. As the Committee has already stated in previous annual reports, . . . the increased number of States parties to the Optional Protocol and increased public awareness of the Committee's work under the Optional Protocol have led to a substantial growth in the number of communications submitted to it. At the opening of the Committee's forty-fifth session, there were 153 cases pending. This increased workload means that the Committee can no longer examine communications as expeditiously as hitherto and highlights the urgent need to reinforce the Secretariat staff. The Human Rights Committee reiterates its request to the Secretary-General to take the necessary steps to ensure a substantial increase in the number of staff,

---

* Human Rights Committee, Selected Decisions Under the Optional Protocol (Second to Sixteenth Sessions), U.N. Doc. CCPR/C/OP/1 (1985); Human Rights Committee, Selected Decisions Under the Optional Protocol (Seventeenth to Thirty-Second Sessions), Vol. 2, U.N. Doc. CCPR/C/OP/2 (1990). — Eds.

specialized in the various legal systems, assigned to service the Committee, and wishes to record that the work under the Optional Protocol continues to suffer as a result of insufficient secretariat resources.

3. Interstate Complaints

Article 41 of the Covenant permits a states party to file a formal complaint respecting the nonfulfillment of human rights obligations by another states party. This procedure is optional, applying only to those situations where both states have declared that they recognize the competence of the Human Rights Committee to receive and consider such formal complaints. As of 1 July 1994, only 44 states had made the requisite declaration. The United States is one of them. However, to date no interstate complaint has been filed. How one would be handled and whether the procedure eventually will turn out to be worthwhile are the subject of the following reading.

Leckie, The Inter-State Complaint Procedure in International Human Rights Law: Hopeful Prospects or Wishful Thinking?
10 Human Rts. Q. 249, 266-267 (1988)

Under the ICCPR, if a state party that has made the necessary declaration believes that another state party, which has also made the declaration, is not giving effect to the provision of the Covenant, it may bring the matter directly to the attention of that state party. The state receiving the communication is then obliged to explain or clarify the matter to the state that sent the communication, with reference to domestic procedures and remedies taken, pending, or available in the matter, within three months time. If the matter is not resolved to the satisfaction of both parties within six months of the initial communication, either state may then refer the matter to the Human Rights Committee by giving notice directly to the Committee and to the other state. Once the Committee has discerned that all available domestic remedies have been exhausted in accordance with the generally recognized principles of international law, it begins its work.

From the moment that the Committee becomes involved in the process, there is a strong emphasis upon reaching an amicable solution to the matter. The Committee is to make available to the parties its good offices in order to create conditions conducive to resolving the matter. During its closed sessions while examining the communication, the Committee may call upon the states parties concerned to supply any relevant information on the issue under consideration. Accordingly, these states "shall have the right to be represented when the matter is being considered and to make submissions orally and/or in writing."

The Committee is to submit a report within twelve months of its initial involvement. "If a [friendly] solution . . . is reached," the Committee shall confine its report to a brief statement of the facts and of the solution reached. . . ." If no solution is arrived at, the Committee may, with the prior consent of the states parties concerned, appoint an ad hoc Conciliation Commission.

The Commission, which is to be composed of five independent persons acceptable to both states parties, will lay considerable emphasis on arriving at a mutually agreed upon reconciliation of the matter in contention. For example, Article 42(1)(a) states, inter alia, "the good offices of the Commission shall be made available to the States Parties concerned with a view to an amicable solution of the matter on the basis of respect for the present Covenant." The Commission has twelve months to fully consider the matter. Within this period of time it shall submit to the chairman of the Committee a report for communication to the states parties concerned. If an amicable solution is found, the Commission, like the Committee, shall confine its report to a brief statement of the facts and the solution reached. More importantly, if no solution is reached, the Conciliation Commission's final involvement with the complaint will involve the issuance of a report embodying its findings on all questions of fact relevant to the issues between the states parties concerned, and its views on the possibilities of an amicable solution of the matter.

Several points are worth mentioning with respect to the ICCPR in the overall consideration of inter-state complaints.

1. Most of the eighteen states that have made formal declarations have very good domestic human rights records, thereby decreasing the probability of its use among these states.

2. The lack of stringent time limits may act as a prohibitive factor in the use of this procedure. Should the entire process be carried out it could take up to thirty-three months or longer. Certainly states that are already hesitant to tarnish political relations and images may find this period of time too long to sustain the necessary support to complete the process in a productive way.

3. The ability of individuals to make complaints to the Human Rights Committee, the detailed scrutiny of such complaints by the Committee, and the detailed nature of state reports forwarded by states parties and analyzed by the Committee all constitute less drastic and, hence, more frequently considered methods of ensuring compliance with the Covenant.

This is not to say that this procedure will never be used, but rather that the breadth of scope of the ICCPR, several procedural hurdles, and other contemporary dilemmas continue to make this procedure less appealing to those states that might implement it successfully. *

---

* For additional commentary on interstate complaints, see M. Nowak, supra page 214, at 580-614. See also Shelton, Compliance Mechanisms [Inter-State Communications], in United States Ratification of the International Covenants on Human Rights 155-157 (H. Hannum and D. Fischer eds. 1993). — Eds.

4. General Comments

Beginning in the 1980s, to assist states parties in fulfilling their reporting obligations, the Human Rights Committee from time to time has issued
general comments about the nature of the obligations states have assumed
under particular articles of the Covenant. Obviously, these comments also
are relevant to individual communications and, should they ever be invoked, interstate complaints as well. Strictly speaking, of course, they are
not an implementation measure, but the gloss they put on the Covenant's
substantive provisions may make it easier to determine a state's obligations
thereunder and, if the facts warrant, hold it accountable for any violations
thereof. Table 3-2, found on pages 225-226, is a summary of the general
comments, their relationship to particular articles of the Covenant, and
their substance.

IV. Suriname Revisited: More Repression in Violation of the Civil and Political Covenant

The almost bloodless coup of February 1980 that had ousted the democratically elected government of Suriname attracted relatively little international attention. Recall that the country had acceded to the Civil and
Political Covenant in December 1976, and by a remarkable coincidence its
initial report, submitted by the pre-coup government, came before the Human Rights Committee in July 1980. Members of the Committee, after
laconically remarking "that the report had been transmitted by a Government that had been repudiated and overthrown and that the report might
not, in many respects, reflect the present situation in Suriname," expressed
the hope "that a new report be submitted at a future date containing information on the measures taken to implement the rights provided for in the
Covenant in the new political context." Report of the Human Rights Committee, 35 U.N. GAOR Supp. (No. 40) at 62, 63, U.N. Doc. A/35/40 (1980).
After noting, somewhat mystifyingly, that the fact that Suriname was a very
young country, and a former colony to boot, "had to be taken into consideration when examining the human rights situation" there, id., the Committee members engaged in a lengthy dialogue over three meetings with the
government representative, which ended with the latter's inviting them to
visit his country and promising that "an additional report would be transmitted to the Committee when a measure of stability had been achieved in
Suriname." Id. at 68. (For whatever reason, no further reports have been
forthcoming from Suriname. See Note by the Secretary-General, Provisional Agenda and Annotations [Human Rights Committee], U.N. Doc.
CCPR/C/97, at 4-5 (1994) (second periodic report of Suriname due in 1985

TABLE 3-2 Summary of General Comments (1981-1994)*

General Comment	Relates to	Substance
General comment 1/13, 36 U.N. GAOR Supp. (No. 40), Annex VII at 107, U.N. Doc. A/36/40 (1981)	Article 40	Delays in submission of initial reports
General comment 2/13, 36 U.N. GAOR Supp. (No. 40), Annex VII at 108, U.N. Doc. A/36/40 (1981)	Article 40	Form and content of initial reports
General comment 3/13, 36 U.N. GAOR Supp. (No. 40), Annex VII at 109, U.N. Doc. A/36/40 (1981)	Article 2	States parties' obligations and publicity for the Covenant
General comment 4/13, 36 U.N. GAOR Supp. (No. 40), Annex VII at 109, U.N. Doc. A/36/40 (1981)	Article 3	Assurance of equal rights for men and women
General comment 5/13, 36 U.N. GAOR Supp. (No. 40), Annex VII at 110, U.N. Doc. A/36/40 (1981)	Article 4	Extent and nature of derogations from articles of the Covenant under states of emergency
General comment 6/16, 37 U.N. GAOR Supp. (No. 40), Annex V at 93, U.N. Doc. A/37/40 (1982)	Article 6	No derogation from right to life; war prevention; measures to reduce mortality rates; abolition of death penalty
General comment 7/16, 37 U.N. GAOR Supp. (No. 40), Annex V at 94, U.N. Doc. A/37/40 (1982)	Article 7	Effective protection against torture or forced medical or scientific experimentation
General comment 8/16, 37 U.N. GAOR Supp. (No. 40), Annex V at 95, U.N. Doc. A/37/40 (1982)	Article 9	Deprivation of liberty and rules regarding treatment of detainees
General comment 9/16, 37 U.N. GAOR Supp. (No. 40), Annex V at 96, U.N. Doc. A/37/40 (1982)	Article 10	Humane treatment of persons deprived of their liberty; treatment of juvenile offenders
General comment 10/19, 38 U.N. GAOR Supp. (No. 40), Annex VI at 109, U.N. Doc. A/38/40 (1983)	Article 19	Right to freedom of opinion
General comment 11/19, 38 U.N. GAOR Supp. (No. 40), Annex VI at 109, U.N. Doc. A/38/40 (1983)	Article 20	Banning of advocacy or war propaganda inciting racial or religious hatred or violence

*The first 21 general comments are collected in Note by the Secretariat, Compilation of General Comments and General Recommendations Adopted by Human Rights Treaty Bodies, U.N. Doc. HRI/GEN/1, at 1-34 (1992), reprinted in M. Nowak, supra page 214, at 847-875.

General Comment	Relates to	Substance
General comment 12/21, 39 U.N. GAOR Supp. (No. 40), Annex VI at 142, U.N. Doc. A/39/40 (1984)	Article 1	Process allowing exercise of the rights of self-determination and use of national resources
General comment 13/21, 39 U.N. GAOR Supp. (No. 40), Annex VI at 143, U.N. Doc. A/39/40 (1984)	Article 14	Right to fair and public hearing before an impartial and independent tribunal under law
General comment 14/23, 40 U.N. GAOR Supp. (No. 40), Annex VI at 162, U.N. Doc. A/40/40 (1985)	Article 6	Production, testing, deployment, and use of nuclear weapons is a crime against humanity
General comment 15/28, 41 U.N. GAOR Supp. (No. 40), Annex VI at 117, U.N. Doc. A/41/40 (1986)	— —	Position of aliens under the Covenant
General comment 16/32, 43 U.N. GAOR Supp. (No. 40), Annex VI at 181, U.N. Doc. A/43/40 (1988)	Article 17	Prohibition of government interference with privacy, home, or correspondence
General comment 17/35, 44 U.N. GAOR Supp. (No. 40), Annex VI at 173, U.N. Doc. A/44/40 (1989)	Article 24	Rights of the child
General comment 18/37, 45 U.N. GAOR Supp. (No. 40), Annex VI at 173, U.N. Doc. A/45/40 (1990)	— —	Assurance of non-discrimination
General comment 19/39, 45 U.N. GAOR Supp. (No. 40), Annex VI at 175, U.N. Doc. A/45/40 (1990)	Article 23	Protection of the family
General comment 20/44, 47 U.N. GAOR Supp. (No. 40), Annex VI at 193, U.N. Doc. A/47/40 (1992)	Article 7	Replaces General Comment No. 7 dealing with protection against torture or forced medical or scientific experimentation
General comment 21/44, 47 U.N. GAOR Supp. (No. 40), Annex VI at 193, U.N. Doc. A/47/40 (1992)	Article 10	Replaces General Comment No. 9 dealing with deprivation of liberty and rules regarding treatment of detainees
General comment 22/48, U.N. Doc. E/1994/107, at 2 (1994)	Article 18	Right to freedom of thought, conscience, and religion
General comment 23/50, U.N. Doc. E/1994/107, at 5 (1994)	Article 27	Rights of individuals belonging to minorities

not yet received, after 17 reminders) (third periodic report of Suriname due in 1990 not yet received, after seven reminders).)*

The situation in Suriname, as we have seen (see pages 182-183 supra), continued to worsen over the next two years and had come to flashpoint proportions in mid-November 1982. Ignition occurred early in the morning of 8 December 1982, when 16 persons were arrested and taken to the military base at Fort Zeelandia. In this group were four journalists, four lawyers, including John Baboeram and the dean of the bar association, two university professors, the leader of the main trade union, two businessmen, and two army officers. Most of this group were leading members of the Association for Democracy, and several had been linked to the failed March 1982 coup. Simultaneously, several radio stations, newspaper headquarters, and the headquarters of the main trade union were burned. On the morning of 9 December 1982, the corpses of 15 of those persons arrested the day before were delivered to the morgue at the University Hospital. It was evident to many observers that the victims had been tortured and deliberately killed. For a detailed account of the victims' condition and the events of 8-9 December 1982, see Report of the Dutch Lawyers Committee for Human Rights, Annex to Letter dated 23 February 1983 from the Representative of the Netherlands to the Thirty-Ninth Session of the Commission on Human Rights, U.N. Doc. E/CN.4/1983/55 (1983).

Military Commander Bouterse appeared on television that evening and announced that a number of those persons arrested had been killed in an escape attempt following an abortive coup. The government, however, made no effort to perform autopsies, nor did the new government that took over following Prime Minister Neyhorst's resignation undertake any investigation of the deaths or the events that had precipitated them. Finally, on 28 February 1983, the International Commission of Jurists sent a mission to Suriname to investigate the incident and the human rights situation in general. Their report raised a "number of serious questions concerning respect for internationally respected standards, as formulated in the International Covenant on Civil and Political Rights." Bossuyt and Griffiths, Human Rights in Suriname, 30 Intl. Comm. Jurists, The Review 52, 58 (July 1983). Although the report called for an investigation of the incident, the Policy Centre was unresponsive.

---

* In its Core Document Forming Part of the Report of States Parties, U.N. Doc. HRI/CORE/1/Add. 39, at 19 (1994),

[t]he Suriname Government recognizes the need to fulfill its reporting obligations, based on the importance it attributes to the promotion of and respect for human rights. Thus, the fact that the Government has not been able to present the required reports should not be attributed to a neglect of its responsibilities, but merely to a lack of trained and experienced reporting officers in the country. In order to solve this problem and guarantee continuous reporting, initiatives have been taken by the Government to organize on short term — with external assistance — a training course for reporting officers in the field of human rights.

Both the Inter-American Commission on Human Rights (see Report on the Situation of Human Rights in Suriname, OAS Doc. OAS/Ser. L/II.61, doc. 6, rev. 1 (1983)) and the International Labor Office (see Annex, Report on the Direct Contacts Mission to Suriname, Case No. 1160, 230th Report of the Committee on Freedom of Association 117-131 (GB.224/97)) conducted investigations of the incident, as did Amnesty International (see Amnesty International, 1982 Ann. Rep. 171 (1983); Amnesty International, 1983 Ann. Rep. 192 (1984)). All of these reports concluded that an official investigation by the NMR was necessary, and most carried at least an implicit condemnation of the incident.

On 5 July 1983, Kanta Baboeram-Adhin, the wife of John Baboeram, one of the 15 men killed in the December 1982 incident, submitted a letter to the Human Rights Committee under Article 5(4) of the Optional Protocol to the International Covenant on Civil and Political Rights, alleging violations of Articles 6, 7, 9, 10, 14, and 17 of the Covenant. This letter, officially labelled Communication No. 146/1983, initiated the procedures for the handling of individual communications by the Committee under the Optional Protocol.

Communications Nos. 146/1983 and 148 to 154/ 1983, John Baboeram et al. v. Suriname
40 U.N. GAOR Supp. (No. 40) at 187, 187-194, U.N. Doc. A/40/40 (1985)

Views of the Human Rights Committee Under Article 5, Paragraph 4, of the Optional Protocol to the International Covenant on Civil and Political Rights – Twenty-Fourth Session Concerning Communications Nos. 146/1983 and 148 to 154/1983

Submitted by: — Kanta Baboeram-Adhin on behalf of her deceased husband, John Khemraadi Baboeram (146/1983)

— Johnny Kamperveen on behalf of his deceased father, André Kamperveen (148/1983)

— Jenny Jamila Rehnuma Karamat Ali on behalf of her deceased husband, Cornelis Harold Riedewald (149/1983)

— Henry François Leckie on behalf of his deceased brother, Gerald Leckie (150/1983)

— Vidya Satyavati Oemrawsingh-Adhin on behalf of her deceased husband, Harry Sugrim Oemrawsingh (151/1983)

— Astrid Sila Bhamini-Devi Sohansingh-Kanhai on behalf of her deceased husband, Somradj Robby Sohansingh (152/1983)

— Rita Dulci Imanuel-Rahman on behalf of her deceased brother, Lesley Paul Rahman (153/1983)

— Irma Soeinem Hoost-Boldwijn on behalf of her deceased husband, Edmund Alexander Hoost (154/1983)

Alleged victims: John Khemraadi *Baboeram*, André *Kamperveen*, Cornelis Harold *Riedewald*, Gerald *Leckie*, Harry Sugrim *Oemrawsingh*, Somradj Robby *Sohansingh*, Lesley Paul *Rahman* and Edmund Alexander *Hoost*.

State party concerned: Suriname

Date of communications: 5 July 1983, 31 July and 4 August 1983

Date of decision on admissibility: 10 April 1984

The Human Rights Committee established under Article 28 of the International Covenant on Civil and Political Rights:

Meeting on 4 April 1985;

Having concluded its consideration of communications Nos. 146/1983 and 148-154/1983 submitted to the Committee under the Optional Protocol to the International Covenant on Civil and Political Rights;

Having taken into account all written information made available to it by the authors of the communications and by the State party concerned;

adopts the following:

Views Under Article 5, Paragraph 4, of the Optional Protocol

COMMUNICATION NO. 146/1983

1.1 The author of communication No. 146/1983 (initial letter dated 5 July 1983 and further letters of 4 November 1983 and 3 January 1985) is Kanta Baboeram-Adhin, a Surinamese national, at present residing in the Netherlands. She submits the communication on behalf of her deceased husband, John Khemraadi Baboeram, a Surinamese lawyer who was allegedly arrested by Surinamese military authorities on 8 December 1982 and whose corpse was delivered to the mortuary on 9 December 1982 showing signs of severe maltreatment and numerous bullet wounds.

1.2 It is stated that on 8 December 1982 at around 2 A.M. a number of persons in Paramaribo, Suriname, were taken from their beds and arrested, including John Baboeram, whose corpse along with the corpses of 14 other persons was identified on 10 December 1982 and was described in the "Report of the Dutch Lawyers Committee for Human Rights" (United Nations Commission on Human Rights document E/CN.4/1983/55, submitted by the author as an annex to her communication) as "heavily and brutally maltreated in the face. He for instance had a broken upper jaw. Almost all his teeth, except for one, on the upper right hand side, were beaten inwards and his lips were pulped. He had a horizontal gash on his forehead. In addition he had a bullet wound on the left side of his nose, which was later covered by a plaster. Further he had wounds, cuts on the cheeks and internal haemorrhages."

1.3 The persons arrested and allegedly killed were four journalists, four lawyers, amongst whom was the Dean of the Bar Association, two professors, two businessmen, two army officers and one trade union leader. The names of the victims are John Baboeram, Bram Behr, Cyrill Daal, Kenneth Gonçalves, Eddy Hoost, André Kamperveen, Gerald Leckie, Sugrim Oemrawsingh, Lesley Rahman, Soerindre Rambocus, Harold Riedewald, Jiwansingh Sheombar, Jozef Slagveer, Somradj Sohansingh and Frank Winjngaarde. The executions are said to have taken place at Fort Zeelandia.

2.1 The author of the communication states that she has not submitted the matter to any other procedure of international investigation.

2.2 With respect to the exhaustion of domestic remedies, the author states that no recourse has been made to any court in Suriname because "it became obvious from different sources that the highest military authority . . . was involved in the killing," because the official judicial investigation required in such a case of violent death had not taken place, and "because of the atmosphere of fear one would find no lawyer prepared to [plead] such a case, considering the fact that three lawyers have been killed, apparently because of their concern with human rights and democratic principles." The author also refers to the report of the International Commission of Jurists' mission to Suriname, dated 21 March 1983, which, inter alia, surveys the situation in Suriname with respect to freedom of the press, freedom of association, freedom from arbitrary arrest, the right to protection of life and bodily integrity and the right of recourse to effective legal remedies. The report confirms the author's contention that there are no effective legal remedies.

2.3 The author claims that her husband was a victim of violations of articles 6, 7, 9, 10, 14 and 17 of the International Covenant on Civil and Political Rights.

3. By its decision of 27 July 1983, the Working Group of the Human Rights Committee transmitted communication No. 146/1983 under rule 91 of the provisional rules of procedure to the State party concerned, requesting information and observations relevant to the question of admissibility of the communication. The Working Group also requested the State party to transmit to the Committee copies of the death certificate and medical report and of a report on whatever inquiry has been held in connection with the death of John Khemraadi Baboeram.

4. In a submission dated 5 October 1983, the State party objected against the admissibility of communication No. 146/1983 on the ground that the same matter had already been submitted to and was "being examined under another procedure of international investigation or settlement," referring in this connection to "investigations regarding the human rights situation in Suriname by international organizations dealing with human rights such as the Inter-American Commission on Human Rights and the International Committee of the Red Cross." The State party also mentioned that "the Special Rapporteur on summary or arbitrary executions of the United Nations Commission on Human Rights, Mr. Amos Wako," would pay a visit to Suriname during the week beginning 31 October 1983.

5. In her comments dated 4 November 1983, the author of communication No. 146/1983 rejected the State party's contention that "the same matter" had been submitted to another procedure of international investigation or settlement. She submitted that the procedures mentioned by the Government of Suriname for the study of the human rights situation in that country were not comparable with the procedure for the examination of individual cases under the Optional Protocol to the International Covenant on Civil and Political Rights.

COMMUNICATIONS NOS. 148 TO 154/1983

6.1 Five communications Nos. 148/1983, 149/1983, 150/1983, 151/1983 and 152/1983 dated 31 July 1983 and two communications Nos. 153/1983 and 154/1983 dated 4 August 1983 were submitted by close relatives of 7 of the 15 persons allegedly killed in Suriname on 8/9 December 1982. All seven authors, at present residing in the Netherlands, allege that the deceased were victims of violations by the Government of Suriname of articles 6, 7, 9, 10, 14, 17 and 19 of the International Covenant on Civil and Political Rights. The facts of these cases are similar to those of communication No. 146/1983 concerning John Khemraadi Baboeram.

6.2 The authors of these seven cases are Johnny Kamperveen, on behalf of his late father, André Kamperveen, formerly a businessman in Paramaribo (No. 148/1983); Jenny Jamila Rehnuma Karamat Ali, on behalf of her late husband Cornelis Harold Riedewald, formerly a lawyer in Paramaribo (No. 149/1983); Henry François Leckie, on behalf of his late brother Gerald Leckie, formerly a professor at the Faculty of Social Sciences of the

University of Suriname (No. 150/1983); Vidya Satyavati Oemrawsingh-Adhin, on behalf of her late husband Harry Sugrim Oemrawsingh, formerly a professor at the Technical Faculty of the University of Suriname (No. 151/1983); Astrid Sila Bhamini-Devi Sohansingh-Kanhai, on behalf of her late husband Somradj Robby Sohansingh, formerly a businessman in Paramaribo (No. 152/1983); Rita Dulci Imanuel-Rahman, on behalf of her late brother Lesley Paul Rahman, formerly a journalist and trade union leader from Aruba, Netherlands Antilles (No. 153/1983); and Irma Soeinem Hoost-Boldewijn, on behalf of her late husband Edmund Alexander Hoost, formerly a lawyer in Paramaribo (No. 154/1983).

6.3 Common to all of these communications are the following allegations: the alleged victims were arrested at their respective homes in the early morning hours of 8 December 1982; in the evening of the same day it was declared by the Surinamese authorities that a coup attempt had been foiled and in the evening of 9 December 1982 it was declared that a number of arrested persons had been killed during an attempt to escape; the bodies of the 15 persons lay from 10 to 13 December 1982 in the mortuary of the Academic Hospital and were seen by family members and other persons; the bodies showed numerous wounds, apparently inflicted from the front side. Neither autopsies nor official investigations of the killings have taken place. The relevant facts are also described in United Nations Commission on Human Rights document E/CN.4/1983/55, which some of the authors incorporate by reference.

6.4 A summary of the specific allegations in the individual cases follows:

André Kamperveen was allegedly subjected to violence upon his arrest. Much damage was done to his house through fire arms and handgrenades; his radio station ABC was burned down. His body reportedly showed injuries to the jaw and a swollen face, 18 bullet wounds in the chest, a shot wound in the right temple, a fractured femur and a fractured arm.

Cornelis Harold Riedewald was arrested by military police who allegedly did not show a warrant. His body showed a bullet wound through the right temple, severe injuries on the left side of the neck and numerous bullet wounds in the chest.

Gerald Leckie was arrested by military police who allegedly did not show a warrant. His body had internal haemorrhages in the face and bullet holes in the chest.

Harry Sugrim Oemrawsingh was arrested by military police who allegedly did not show a warrant. His body had a wound in the right cheek and a bigger wound on the left temple.

Somradj Robby Sohansingh had already been detained seven months and allegedly subjected to mistreatment, but had been released pending trial for his alleged participation in the coup attempt of 13 March 1982. He was rearrested by military police on 8 December 1982. His body had wounds on the face, his teeth were beaten inwards and one of his cheekbones was fractured. He had six bullet wounds in the chest and abdominal area.

Lesley Paul Rahman was arrested by military police who allegedly did not show a warrant. His body had lumps on the forehead and parts of the skin of the upper thigh were torn off.

Edmund Alexander Hoost was arrested by military police who allegedly did not show a warrant. His body had several bullet wounds which had entered the body from the front side.

6.5 The authors of the seven communications state that they have not submitted the same matter to any other procedure of international investigation or settlement.

6.6 With respect to exhaustion of domestic remedies, the authors explain in an annex common to all seven communications that no recourse has been made to any court in Suriname because, inter alia:

> 1. The highest military and civilian authorities were involved in planning and carrying out the murders. 2. Taking into account the general atmosphere of fear and the fact that three lawyers were killed apparently because of their involvement in defending opponents of the régime one would find no lawyer prepared to defend such a case. 3. From official side there was neither an autopsy, nor an investigation of the death of the 15 victims as is required in such a case of violent death. . . .

7. By decisions of 20 October 1983, the Working Group of the Human Rights Committee transmitted communications Nos. 148/1983 to 154/1983 to the State party concerned under rule 91 of the Committee's provisional rules of procedure, requesting information and observations relevant to the question of admissibility of the communications. The Working Group also requested the State party to provide the Committee with copies of the death certificates and medical reports and reports of whatever inquiry has been held in connection with the death of the alleged victims.

8. In a submission dated 6 April 1984 the State party objected against the admissibility of communications Nos. 148/1983 to 154/1983 on the grounds already set out in its submission of 5 October 1983 in respect of communication No. 146/1983 (see para. 4 above), namely, that the matter had already been submitted to and is "being examined under another procedure of international investigation or settlement". The State party added the following:

> In this regard, the Government of the Republic of Suriname wishes to refer once more to investigations regarding the human rights situation in Suriname by international organizations dealing with human rights, such as the Inter-American Commission on Human Rights of the Organization of American States, the International Committee of the Red Cross, the International Labour Organisation, the International Commission of Jurists, Amnesty International, as well as the proposed visit to Suriname of the United Nations Special Rapporteur on summary or arbitrary executions. . . .

9.1 With respect to the admissibility of the communications the Human Rights Committee observed firstly that a study by an intergovernmental organization either of the human rights situation in a given country (such as that by IACHR in respect of Suriname) or a study of the trade union rights situation in a given country (such as the issues examined by the Committee on Freedom of Association of the ILO in respect of Suriname), or of a human rights problem of a more global character (such as that of the Special Rapporteur of the Commission on Human Rights on summary or arbitrary executions), although such studies might refer to or draw on information concerning individuals, cannot be seen as being the same matter as the examination of individual cases within the meaning of article 5, paragraph 2 (a), of the Optional Protocol. Secondly, a procedure established by non-governmental organizations (such as Amnesty International, the International Commission of Jurists or the ICRC, irrespective of the latter's standing in international law) does not constitute a procedure of international investigation or settlement within the meaning of article 5, paragraph 2 (a), of the Optional Protocol. Thirdly, the Human Rights Committee ascertained that, although the individual cases of the alleged victims had been submitted to IACHR (by an unrelated third party) and registered before that body, collectively, as case No. 9015, that case was no longer under consideration. Accordingly, the Human Rights Committee concluded that it was not barred by the provisions of article 5, paragraph 2 (a), of the Optional Protocol from considering the communications.

9.2 With regard to article 5, paragraph 2 (b), of the Optional Protocol, the Committee noted that the State party did not challenge the author's contention that there were no effective legal remedies to exhaust. The Committee recalled that it had already established in numerous other cases that exhaustion of domestic remedies could be required only to the extent that these remedies were effective and available within the meaning of article 5, paragraph 2 (b), of the Optional Protocol. Accordingly, the Human Rights Committee concluded that it was not barred by the provisions of article 5, paragraph 2 (b), of the Optional Protocol from considering the communications.

10.1 On 10 April 1984, the Human Rights Committee therefore *decided*:

1. That the communications were admissible;

2. That, in accordance with article 4, paragraph 2, of the Optional Protocol, the State party be requested to submit to the Committee, within six months of the date of the transmittal to it of this decision, written explanations or statements clarifying the matter and the remedy, if any, that may have been taken by it. These should include copies of the death certificates and medical reports and of reports of whatever inquiry has been held in connection with the death of John Khemraadi Baboeram, André Kamperveen, Cornelis Harold Riedewald, Gerald Leckie, Harry Sugrim Oemrawsingh, Somradj Robby Sohansingh, Lesley Paul Rahman and Edmund Alexander Hoost.

10.2 The Committee also decided, pursuant to rule 88 (2) of its provisional rules of procedure, to deal jointly with all eight communications, i.e., communications Nos. 146/1983 and 148/1983 to 154/1983.

11.1 In response to the Committee's request for explanations or statements in accordance with article 4, paragraph 2, of the Optional Protocol the State party submitted a note, dated 12 November 1984, a death certificate, issued by the medical staff of the University Hospital in Suriname on 25 October 1984, and a copy of Suriname's observations dated September 1983, on a report prepared by the Inter-American Commission on Human Rights on the human rights situation in Suriname, following an IACHR visit to Suriname from 20 to 24 June 1983.

11.2 In its note of 12 November 1984, the State party indicates that the investigation of the Special Rapporteur on summary or arbitrary executions, Mr. Amos Wako, temporarily deferred in 1983, was finalized during the period of 17 to 21 July 1984. "[T]his important investigation concentrated on the unfortunate occurrences of 8 and 9 December 1982, the causes of these occurrences, the plans to promote democratization of the Surinamese society, as well as the maintenance of the constitutional state in our society and the measures taken to prevent a repetition of the occurrences referred to before."

11.3 In the relevant parts of Suriname's observations on the IACHR report the State party notes:

> The right to life is only being discussed in connection with the death of 15 persons early in December 1982, whereas this right comprises much more. The Surinamese authorities deeply regret the death of these persons not because they are said to be of 'National Stature' but because they were citizens of this country. . . .
>
> It is regretted that the IACHR hardly pays any attention to the information supplied on the Surinamese side concerning the developments of Suriname regarding the occurrences of early December 1982. Beforehand, the reply of the Surinamese authorities seems to be regarded as of no importance, whereas great value is attached to information of the 'responsible sources.' . . .
>
> Again and again the oppositional view is being given which leads to the Committee's conclusion that 15 prominent Surinamese citizens have been eliminated because they led a critical movement for the return to democracy. Nowhere is the analysis objectively and systematically entertained which has been expressed in official talks, about the part which the deceased played in the planning of the overthrow of the legal authority.
>
> See . . . the intensified continuation of these attempts with mercenaries after 8 December 1982 as well as the CIA disclosures about this matter.

12.1 On 3 January 1985, the author of communication No. 146/1983, Kanta Baboeram-Adhin submitted her comments on the State party's submission under article 4, paragraph 2, of the Optional Protocol. Identical comments were submitted by the author of communication No. 151/1983, Vidya S. Oemrawsingh-Adhin, on 5 January 1985.

12.2 In their comments the authors claim that the State party has failed to clarify the matters placed before the Human Rights Committee by the authors and that no information has been given about measures taken to remedy the alleged violations. The authors further point out that the official version of the killings had maintained that the victims had been shot while trying to escape. However, "in a recent interview with a well-known Dutch Magazine 'Elsevier' the military leader, also the highest authority in Suriname, admits that the victims were executed and that it was a matter of 'their lives or ours' and that 'we killed them first before they could kill us.' "

13.1 The Human Rights Committee has considered the present communications in the light of all information made available to it by the parties, as provided in article 5, paragraph 1, of the Optional Protocol. The Committee bases its views on the following facts, which are not in dispute or which are unrefuted by the State party.

13.2 In the early hours of 8 December 1982, 15 prominent persons in Paramaribo, Suriname, including journalists, lawyers, professors and businessmen, were arrested in their respective homes by Surinamese military police and subjected to violence. The bodies of these 15 persons, among them eight persons whose close relatives are the authors of the present communications, were delivered to the mortuary of the Academic Hospital, following an announcement by Surinamese authorities that a coup attempt had been foiled and that a number of arrested persons had been killed while trying to escape. The bodies were seen by family members and other persons who have testified that they showed numerous wounds. Neither autopsies nor official investigations of the killings have taken place.

14.1 In formulating its views, the Human Rights Committee also takes into account the following considerations, which reflect a failure by the State party to furnish the information and clarifications requested by the Committee. The Committee notes that the death certificate submitted by the State party is dated nearly two years after the killings and does not indicate whether the medical doctors who signed the certificate had carried out any autopsies or whether they had actually seen the bodies. The death certificate merely confirms that "on 9 December 1982 the following persons died, probably as a result of gunshot wounds. . . ."

14.2 In operative paragraph 2 of its decision on admissibility of 10 April 1984, the Committee requested the State party to forward copies of medical reports and of reports of whatever inquiry has been held in connection with the deaths of the eight named victims. No such reports have been received by the Committee. In this connection, the Committee stresses, as it has done in a number of other cases (e.g. Nos. 30/1978, 84/1981) that it is implicit in article 4 (2) of the Optional Protocol that the State party has the duty to investigate in good faith all allegations of violation of the Covenant made against it and its authorities and to furnish to the Committee the information available to it. In cases where the allegations are corroborated by evidence submitted by the authors and where further clarification of the cases depends on information exclusively in the hands of the State party, the Committee may consider the authors' allegations as substantiated in the absence of satisfactory evidence and explanations to the contrary submitted by the State party.

14.3 Article 6 (1) of the Covenant provides: "Every human being has the inherent right to life. This right shall be protected by law. No one shall be arbitrarily deprived of his life." The right enshrined in this article is the supreme right of the human being. It follows that the deprivation of life by the authorities of the State is a matter of the utmost gravity. This follows from the article as a whole and in particular is the reason why paragraph 2 of the article lays down that the death penalty may be imposed only for the most serious crimes. The requirements that the right shall be protected by law and that no one shall be arbitrarily deprived of his life mean that the law must strictly control and limit the circumstances in which a person may be deprived of his life by the authorities of a State. In the present case it is evident from the fact that 15 prominent persons lost their lives as a result of the deliberate action of the military police that the deprivation of life was intentional. The State party has failed to submit any evidence proving that these persons were shot while trying to escape.

15. The Human Rights Committee, acting under article 5, paragraph 4, of the Optional Protocol to the International Covenant on Civil and Political Rights, is of the view that the victims were arbitrarily deprived of their lives contrary to article 6 (1) of the International Covenant on Civil and Political Rights. In the circumstances, the Committee does not find it necessary to consider assertions that other provisions of the covenant were violated.

16. The Committee therefore urges the State party to take effective steps (i) to investigate the killings of December 1982; (ii) to bring to justice any persons found to be responsible for the death of the victims; (iii) to pay compensation to the surviving families; and (iv) to ensure that the right to life is duly protected in Suriname.

Note: *The Aftermath*

The political climate in Suriname improved somewhat in the years following the Human Rights Committee's report of its views on the Baboeram communication. Obviously its stance, and that of the other IGOs and NGOs who unanimously condemned or at least questioned the 8-9 December 1982 incident, brought considerable pressure to bear against Suriname. So, too, did the report of the Special Rapporteur on Summary or Arbitrary Executions of the UN Commission on Human Rights, who visited the country on 22-27 July 1984 and concluded that "in view of the fact that there can be no derogation from article 6 of the International Covenant on Civil and Political Rights, . . . the executions of 8-9 December 1982 cannot be justified [and] the right to life cannot be effectively protected unless an independent inquiry is conducted . . . and the persons who planned and carried out these executions are . . . convicted." See Wako, Visit by the Special Rapporteur to Suriname, Report [on Summary or Arbitrary Executions] at 16, U.N. Doc. E/CN.4/1985/17 (1985).

Other factors, of course, were also at play. As far back as 1982, the Netherlands, the former colonial power, suspended development aid to Suriname, citing human rights violations by the NMR regime. This suspension, combined with increased foreign reluctance to invest in the country after international attention created by the December 1982 killings and the international reaction thereto, caused economic deterioration. Pressure from both within and without Suriname for improved civil and political conditions increased dramatically.

In response, Military Commander Bouterse announced in January 1985 a timetable for a "planned return to democracy" and organized an appointed National Assembly to draft a new constitution by 1987. In July 1986, representatives of the principal political parties, business, and labor joined the ruling Council of Ministers to administer the government. The first step toward a return to democracy occurred on 30 September 1987, when over 95 percent of the population approved the drafted constitution. On 25 November 1987, in elections observed by a U.S. presidential delegation, the population voted overwhelmingly to return to democracy and elected a new civilian government. This government, however, had difficulty restraining the military and paramilitary forces, which remained under the control of Commander Bouterse. Repression remained a fact of life, and massacres occurred from time to time throughout the country. One particularly egregious incident, when a group of soldiers attacked unarmed civilians, ordered them to dig their own graves, summarily executed six, and mortally wounded a seventh, resulted in a recent judgment of the Inter-American Court of Human Rights awarding the victims' families $450,000 in damages. *

Commander Bouterse again seized power in a bloodless coup in late 1990, but new elections, held on 25 May 1991 and monitored by a 100-person OAS observer team from 16 different member states, produced a freely elected government still in power. The Inter-American Commission has noted the absence of complaints of human rights violations since the

---

* The Court had jurisdiction to hear the case, referred to it by the Inter-American Commission on Human Rights, because six weeks before the incident, on 12 November 1987, Suriname had ratified the American Convention on Human Rights, at which time it also recognized the contentious jurisdiction of the Court pursuant to Article 62 thereof. See generally pages 799-802 of Problem X. At a hearing, convened on 2 December 1991, Suriname acknowledged its responsibility in the case. Aloeboetoe v. Suriname, 13 Human Rts. L.J. 140 (1992). On 10 September 1993, the Court awarded damages, required Suriname to compensate the victims' families for certain expenses, and — determining that financial reparations were not sufficient redress — ordered the state to reopen and staff a medical dispensary and school in the victims' village. Aloeboetoe v. Suriname, 14 Hum. Rts. L.J. 413 (1993).

new government assumed office. "On the other hand," it has pointed out, "nothing has been done to investigate and punish Army officers responsible for the most notorious violations in Suriname's history, namely the killing of 15 prominent Surinamese citizens in December of 1982. The Commission has and continues to insist that a full accounting of this incident must be made." Inter-American Commission on Human Rights, Ann. Rep. 1991, OAS Doc. OEA/Ser.L/V/II.81, doc. 6, rev. 1 at 252 (1992). See also U.S. Department of State, Country Reports on Human Rights Practices for 1993, at 551, 552 (1994).

V. United States Ratification of Human Rights Treaties

A.   *The U.S. Ratification Record: An Overview*

1.   Introductory Note

Although the United States played a leading role in the immediate post-World War II period in the drafting of, first, the Genocide Convention and, second, the Covenants on Civil and Political Rights and on Economic, Social, and Cultural Rights, its ratification record until the last few years has been exceptionally poor. Of the 39 such treaties and agreements of especial interest to the United States, aside from International Labor Organization (ILO) conventions, it is now a party to only 16. While it has signed another six, all but one of which have been submitted to the Senate for its advice and consent, in 17 instances the United States has not even signed the international instrument in question. See generally R. Lillich, International Human Rights Instruments (2d ed. updated 1995). The most charitable reason for this sad record, as Professor Henkin noted two decades ago, is that "[t]he United States has seen international human rights as designed for others only. Our respect for human rights, we believe, already surpasses any foreseeable, acceptable international standard; the need is to bring the blessings of liberty to others." Henkin, The United States and the Crisis in Human Rights, 14 Va. J. Intl. L. 653, 663 (1974).

The late Professor Ferguson, who helped draft both the Civil Rights Acts of the 1960s and the Racial Discrimination Convention, after noting the lack of "political will" to ratify the human rights treaties, was characteristically even more outspoken. "The major problem of ratification of the Covenants is precisely the fact that the Covenants relate to human rights." Ferguson, The United Nations Human Rights Covenants: Problems of Ratification and Implementation, 1968 Am. Socy. Intl. L. Proceedings 83, 91. He explained:

Certainly one of the major forces present in the Bricker Amendment episode was that of a hostility toward dealing with the matter of human rights through law. In fact, there is considerable evidence, then and now, that resistance to human rights treaties in general arises from a fear that eventually such treaties would touch upon and deal with the condition of blacks in the United States. In discussing the three human rights conventions now pending before the Senate, for example, Mr. Eberhard P. Deutsch expresses the fear that ratification of any human rights treaty might serve as a precedent for ratification of treaties which have been concluded and signed by the United States, but not yet submitted to the Senate. The fear is clearly that of a treaty which relates to race. Such a treaty has been concluded and signed by the United States. . . . The treaty is the Convention on the Elimination of All Forms of Racial Discrimination. There is some evidence that it was precisely the fear of a treaty such as the Race Convention that generated support for the Bricker Amendment in the Senate. *

Id. He concluded that "in the political context extant in the United States today . . . there is a serious question of the existence of a national will to deal affirmatively with human rights in either the domestic or international context." Id. at 92. His remarks retain much of their relevancy today.

2.   The Carter Administration Initiatives

As part of the Carter Administration's human rights policy (see pages 1039-1077 of Problem XIII), the President signed the two covenants as well as the American Convention on Human Rights in 1977 and the following year sent them, along with the Racial Discrimination Convention, signed by President Lyndon Johnson in 1966, to the Senate for its advice and consent. See Message of the President Transmitting Four Treaties Pertaining to Human Rights, S. Exec. Doc. Nos. C, D, E, & F, 95th Cong., 2d Sess. (1978), reprinted in U.S. Ratification of the Human Rights Treaties: With or Without Reservations? (R. Lillich ed. 1981). Although the Committee on Foreign Relations held four days of hearings on the treaties in 1979, it took no action on them during President Carter's term in office. Nevertheless, in debates over the treaties and in the Senate hearings both the political wisdom and the legal rationale of Carter's approach to the ratification process were called into question, as the first of two statements by supporters of the treaties demonstrates.

* Subsequent research provides ample evidence that proponents of the Bricker Amendment were primarily interested in blocking possible efforts to dismantle racial segregation within the states by use of the international agreement-making powers. Kaufman and Whiteman, Opposition to Human Rights Treaties in the United States Senate: The Legacy of the Bricker Amendment, 10 Human Rts. Q. 309 (1988). See generally N. Hevener, Human Rights Treaties and the Senate: A History of Opposition (1990); L. Le Blanc, The United States and the Genocide Treaty (1991). — Eds.

Henkin, The Covenant on Civil and Political Rights
in U.S. Ratification of the Human Rights Treaties: With or Without Reservations? 20, 20-25 passim (R. Lillich ed. 1981)

A full discussion of our subject might address a number of questions: Is ratification in the national interest? Are there any constitutional obstacles to ratification? Should we attach reservations, and if so, is there some principle of reservation to apply, or are there particular reservations we should impose? . . .

Some of the questions need not detain us long. I have little to add to what [has been] said about why it is in the interest of the U.S. to adhere. I would only stress that I have heard no reason for not adhering and that perhaps the strongest argument for adhering is that it will bring benefits and will cost nothing. The argument that adherence is undesirable because it would subject the U.S. to scrutiny, and to false accusations and distortions, is wholly unpersuasive. Our human rights record is subject to scrutiny whether we adhere or not. If there is valid criticism of us, we deserve it and should welcome it. False accusations and distortions may come and will have to be met whether or not we are a party. The Covenant on Civil and Political Rights, moreover, contains values with which we identify, and by which we try to live, and which are our most effective weapon in continuing ideological competition; it is particularly ironical that we have refused to adhere to it and that we now insist on attaching so many reservations to it.

I. CONSTITUTIONAL OBJECTIONS

I can also dispose quickly of constitutional objections to ratification. In principle, there are no constitutional objections. The treaty makers can adhere to the human rights covenants. There are no constitutional objections based on federalism or the separation of powers or on some notion that the subject is not of international concern. Even Senator Bricker knew that 25 years ago; that is why he tried to amend the Constitution to make it impossible for us to adhere to such covenants. He knew that, if the Constitution were not amended, we could adhere to them. And the Constitution was not amended. . . . [T]he objections to ratification, then, are not constitutional but political, and even constitutional arguments are made principally for their political influence. The obstacle is an abiding and deep isolationism, and I am afraid that no reservations will meet that particular problem.

II. RESERVATIONS

As for the reservations proposed by the executive branch, I said that there were no constitutional obstacles to adherence in principle. It may be necessary to enter a reservation or to express an understanding as regards Article 20, which provides that a state must forbid war propaganda and advocacy of racial hatred. Under our constitutional jurisprudence the U.S. could prohibit such propaganda only if it incites to violence or other unlawful action. A reservation or understanding to that article just about disposes of constitutional problems.

The other proposed reservations are of a different character. They do not reflect constitutional or other objections to the substance of some article in the covenant. Rather, they represent three principles to which the executive branch is committing itself for political reasons. And the three principles cumulate, overlap, and supplement each other. Any of them would just about achieve the desired end, but the executive branch suggests a triple approach.

What are these three principles? The first is that, while the U.S. will adhere to this covenant, it will not agree to any change in U.S. law as it is today. Mr. Rodley [On the Necessity of United States Ratification of the International Human Rights Conventions, in U.S. Ratification of the Human Rights Treaties: With or Without Reservations? 3 (R. Lillich ed. 1981)] referred to this as unseemly; I have called it ignoble and have sometimes thought of it as outrageous. The purpose of adhering to a treaty is to undertake obligations, in this case to adhere to a common international standard. What sort of convention would you have if every country adhered subject to the reservation that it would not make any changes in its laws? If the Soviet Union made such a reservation, we would, rightly, reject its adherence as fraudulent.

Some apparently support such a reservation with the argument that it is necessary because it is unconstitutional or undesirable to make changes in domestic law by treaty. That is plain nonsense. We always have made changes in domestic law by treaty. In fact, the framers of the Constitution contemplated and desired that. If one did not make domestic law by treaty, there would be no sense in, no need for, a clause that declares treaties to be the supreme law of the land.

That first principle of reservation is, to put it mildly, undesirable. What is more, the second reservation, that these conventions shall not be self-executing, makes the first unnecessary. If the covenant will require legislation to give it effect, we would not be making law by treaty: all the changes made in the law would be made by the implementing legislation. ✻

I am not insisting that one must accept every change the covenant would make in our law. I do say that we cannot refuse in principle to make any change. We should look at every change on its merits. I should add that, in fact, the covenant would make very few changes in U.S. law if we adhered without this first reservation. In most respects the covenant spells out what American rights are now and makes some others explicit. Students of constitutional law are always surprised to realize that there is no right to vote in the American Constitution, that there is no presumption of innocence, *racog*

and that, looking at the text of the Constitution, the equal protection of the laws and freedom from racial and other invidious discrimination is required only of the states, not of the U.S. The U.S. cannot object to a document that says that it is also committed to equality. It would be nice to have a document that says we do not believe in torture; we do not have that in our Constitution — the Constitution forbids only cruel and unusual punishment, not torture or other forms of inhuman treatment not used as criminal punishment. The covenant forbids double jeopardy. In the U.S. we have a constitutional prohibition of double jeopardy, but it is not applicable when one of the "jeopardies" is by the state and one by the federal government. That was the result of a 5-4 decision by the Supreme Court [Bartkus v. Illinois, 359 U.S. 121 (1959)], but one could hardly insist that the opposite view, the one that the covenant would presumably take, goes against the grain of our Constitution. If Congress or a treaty decided to accept the dissenting point of view in that case, I should have thought most of us would be happy about it. This reservation is designed to prevent that. Noting another proposed reservation, it certainly appears ludicrous for the U.S. to reserve, in effect, the right to execute children and pregnant women.

Although we have lived with self-executing treaties at least since John Marshall, the concept is still confused in many minds, and it is not clear what making these covenants non-self-executing will mean. Probably, it will mean that the courts will not look to the treaties at all. They will look only at any implementing legislation that might be adopted. Of course, since — under the first principle of reservation — the U.S. would refuse any obligation to make any change in the current law, why do you need to insist that the treaty is not self-executing? There is nothing new to execute; no changes are being made. If you should somehow wish to conform to the international standard in some respect, you would have to repeat in both Houses the political controversy that we anticipate in the Senate to enact legislation to execute the covenant. And then, by the way, if you have in mind the third reservation, to which I am coming — the federal-state clause — you might have to repeat that struggle fifty times more in 50 state legislatures. Again, it should be clear, I am not objecting to having some particular clauses in the covenant left for legislative implementation, but why a blanket reservation requiring legislative implementation of every clause?

The third reservation, as I have mentioned, is the so-called federal-state clause. Again, unlike in Senator Bricker days, nobody is prepared to argue today that such a clause is constitutionally necessary. It is also unnecessary and undesirable for other reasons. The efforts to draft federal-state clauses during the past 25 years have produced a dozen different versions. (The present one, I think, is the same as in the American Convention.) One of my objections to this reservation is that I simply do not understand it, and I must assume that the courts will have a little trouble with it too. On the one hand, it may have no effect and serve no purpose, in which case nothing will come of it. Or, if it serves a purpose, it will require implementation by fifty states and will presumably leave the U.S. in default unless these fifty states execute the obligations assumed by the U.S. Again, if there were some particular problem in which state autonomy is important, we ought to be willing to examine it. But this blanket obeisance to states' rights, or whatever one wishes to call it, seems to me an unnecessary confusion.

The executive branch, I am confident, has acted with great good will and tried to make the covenant palatable to Senators. Perhaps the Executive thought that one could split the opposition: if you take on all of them and give something to the states' rights people, something to those who believe laws should be made only by Congress, and something to those who insist we should not change American law to suit international standards, then you might get enough votes detached from that one-third opposition which could defeat ratification. My own view is that we ought to fight the opposition, not join them. I still hope we can persuade the Executive to move from these blanket reservations to a few precise ones, if any.

Statement of Prof. John Norton Moore
in International Human Rights Treaties: Hearings Before the Senate Comm. on Foreign Relations, 96th Cong., 2d Sess. 66-68 passim (1979)

Mr. Chairman, it is a . . . special honor this morning to be testifying on behalf of the American Bar Association in support of ratification of the . . . human rights treaties which are before the committee.

The American Bar Association strongly supports ratification of these . . . treaties with the reservations, understandings, and declarations that have been proposed by the administration. . . .

The points I would like briefly to discuss are these: Why the United States should ratify the . . . human rights treaties: [and] why this ratification would be fully consistent with the Constitution of the United States, the Federal system and the laws of the United States. . . .

Mr. Chairman, ratification of these treaties will be fully consistent with an important goal of the United States in promoting human rights in the world, and failure to ratify these treaties will be inconsistent with that important foreign policy goal.

I think it is important to achieve that goal for a number of reasons.

First, we want to promote minimum standards embodied in international law and it is very important to develop these uniform standards in international law guaranteeing minimum human rights. As a vice chairman of the section of international law of the American Bar Association, I would like to emphasize the importance of the development of international law in this area.

Second, as a leader in the movement to promote human rights in the world, it certainly would be inconsistent for the United States not to adhere to these agreements and it will continue to undermine the effectiveness of the United States in achieving human rights goals in failing to adhere to these treaties.

As you know, the United States has taken an active role in the past in the negotiations leading to these agreements and certainly even in the charter of the United Nations in seeking to promote respect for human rights.

In addition to that, the ratification of these . . . treaties would encourage the progressive development of a variety of institutional mechanisms which would seek to protect human rights around the world. In this connection I particularly would emphasize that if we become a treaty party to the Civil and Political Covenant, we would be entitled to participate in the Human Rights Committee, and we could file state-to-state complaints in the human rights area. . . .

Mr. Chairman, . . . the American Bar Association believes that the ratification of these four treaties, with the understandings, reservations, and declarations recommended, would be fully consistent with the Constitution of the United States, would be fully consistent with the State-Federal system, and would be something that would be consistent with the overall domestic law of the United States.

From time to time arguments have been raised that perhaps we ought not adhere to these treaties because of some legalism or some supposed inconsistency with the U.S. Constitution, and, provided that there is a clear understanding and reservation in those areas where there may be inconsistency, we feel that certainly there is no valid reason whatsoever not to sign the treaties on that basis. I might add that this is an area where the American Bar Association can speak with particular authority that with these understandings and reservations it is our judgment that there is no inconsistency with the Constitution of the United States or the principle of federalism.

Note: Carter's Legacy

As the above extracts indicate, in an attempt to disarm opponents of the treaties in advance, the Carter Administration — without consulting treaty supporters or the NGO community — took the same three-prong approach to the ratification of each one: (1) it recommended the adoption of a reservation or other qualifying proviso whenever the treaty standard was thought to require some modification of U.S. law (the President's Message, supra page 240, at xii-xv, suggested that in approving the Civil and Political Covenant the Senate adopt four reservations, one understanding, one statement, and two declarations); (2) it recommended the adoption of a non-self-executing declaration in an attempt to render all the treaties' substantive standards unenforceable in U.S. courts; and (3) it refused to recommend adoption of the most effective international remedy for the enforcement of each of the particular treaties (manifested in the case of the Civil and Political Covenant by the refusal to sign and seek ratification of the Optional Protocol, which would have made the individual communication procedure therein available to persons claiming that their rights under the Covenant had been infringed). It should be noted that no state that has ratified the Covenant to date — including Suriname — has sought so frankly to immunize itself, substantively and procedurally, from so many of the Covenant's legal obligations.

At the Senate hearings on the four treaties, Senator Claiborne Pell asked the Department of State's Legal Adviser, Roberts Owen, whether "by affixing reservations we may be making an error in that we would be permitting other nations also to affix reservations and reinterpret the covenants according to their own ideologies?" He replied that, should the Senate decide that some of the reservations were unnecessary, "I think that the administration would be willing to dispense with them. Then we would be, in effect, bringing about a more rigorous civil rights regime and there would be no possible criticism that we were not fulfilling the treaties as a whole." Hearings, supra page 244, at 42. This response turned out to be wishful thinking, to say the least. As one of the editors of this coursebook remarked at the time, "I don't think that you are going to find any Senators who are going to propose the elimination of any of these reservations. I think we are stuck. . . . I think it will eventually come down, perhaps, not even to, Do we take them warts and all? but Do we take them with all these warts plus a lot of other things that may be tacked on as they sail through the Senate?" U.S. Ratification of the Human Rights Treaties: With or Without Reservations?, supra page 240, at 78-79. Unhappily, like one of Cassandra's predictions, this one turned out to be all too true.

3.   Developments During the Reagan and Bush Administrations

After the Senate hearings on the Civil and Political Covenant and the other three human rights treaties, the Senate Foreign Relations Committee took no further action with respect to them. The Carter Administration, preoccupied by the seizure of the U.S. hostages in Iran and other concerns, did not press the matter. So, too, the Reagan Administration, which, after taking office in 1981, evinced no interest in securing the treaties' ratification, seemingly content "to let sleeping dogs lie." See Letter from Robert E. Dalton, Assistant Legal Adviser for Treaty Affairs, U.S. Department of State, to Richard B. Lillich, Apr. 4, 1986, stating that, in a ranking of unratified treaties then pending before the Senate, the human rights treaties were next to the bottom of a six-category list insofar as importance was concerned. See also the testimony of Assistant Secretary of State for Human Rights and Humanitarian Affairs Schifter, who during the 1980s was initially a "closet" and later an outright opponent of ratification. Implementation of the Helsinki Accords: Hearing Before the Comm. on Security and Cooperation in Europe, 100th Cong., 2d Sess. 9-12 (1988). Surprisingly, too, no NGO, much less a U.S. senator, took the lead to get one or more of the treaties ratified. See Lillich, U.S. Ratification of the Human Rights Covenants: Now or Ever?, 1986 Am. Socy. Intl. L. Proceedings 419.

The logjam preventing ratification of the treaties first showed signs of breaking up when President Ronald Reagan, in a campaign speech before an International Convention of B'nai B'rith on 6 September 1984, announced that he supported ratification of the Genocide Convention, which at the time had been pending before the Senate for 35 years. Pub. Papers of the Presidents, Ronald Reagan, 1984, Bk. II, at 1244 (1987). The Senate finally gave its advice and consent to its ratification on 19 February 1986, subject to two reservations, five understandings, and a proviso that the President would not ratify the Convention until Congress had enacted implementing legislation. 132 Cong. Rec. S1377-1378 (daily ed. Feb. 19, 1986). President Reagan signed such legislation into law on 4 November 1988 in a hangar at O'Hare International Airport while on a campaign trip. Remarks on Signing the Genocide Convention Implementation Act of 1987 (the Proxmire Act) in Chicago, Illinois, Pub. Papers of the Presidents, Ronald Reagan, 1988-89, Bk. II, at 1443-1444 (1991). See 18 U.S.C.A. §§1091-1093 (Supp. 1994). The Genocide Convention came into force for the United States on 23 February 1989, 90 days after the deposit of the instrument of ratification by President Reagan.

A further breakup of the logjam occurred when President Reagan signed the Torture Convention and submitted it to the Senate on 20 May 1988. Message of the President Transmitting the Convention Against Torture and Other Inhuman Treatment or Punishment, Treaty Doc. No. 20, 100th Cong., 2d Sess. (1988). After extensive consultations within the Executive Branch and with NGOs, the initial package of reservations, understandings, and declarations proposed by President Reagan was scaled back somewhat by the Bush Administration, which submitted a revised package of three reservations, four understandings, two declarations, and an implementing legislation proviso that — after a proposed federal-state reservation was rewritten and recast as an understanding — was approved by the Senate on 27 October 1990. 136 Cong. Rec. S17491-17492 (daily ed. Oct. 27, 1990). Following the enactment of the implementing legislation (Foreign Relations Authorization Act, Fiscal Years 1994 and 1995, Pub. L. No. 103-236, §506, 108 Stat. 382, 463 (1994) (to be codified at 18 U.S.C. §§2340-2340B)), the Torture Convention came into force for the United States on 20 November 1994, after the deposit of the instrument of ratification by President Clinton.

As the Department of State's Assistant Legal Adviser for Democracy, Human Rights, and Labor, David Stewart, has observed, "[w]ith approval of

the Genocide Convention . . . and the Senate's subsequent advice and consent to ratification of the United Nations Torture Convention, the groundwork had been prepared for resolving the various issues which had stood for many years in the way of ratification of the [Civil and Political] Covenant." Stewart, United States Ratification of the Covenant on Civil and Political Rights: The Significance of the Reservations, Understandings, and Declarations, 42 DePaul L. Rev. 1183, 1185 (1993). Compare Lillich, United States Ratification of the United Nations Covenants, 20 Ga. J. Intl. & Comp. L. 279 (1990). How the issues were resolved, and whether they were resolved satisfactorily, will be considered in the next section. For, on 8 August 1991, in the bicentennial year of the ratification of the U.S. Bill of Rights, President George Bush wrote to Senator Pell, the Chairman of the Foreign Relations Committee, "to urge the Senate to renew its consideration of the International Covenant on Civil and Political Rights with a view to providing ["[s]ubject to a few essential reservations and understandings"] advice and consent to ratification." Senate Comm. on Foreign Relations, International Covenant on Civil and Political Rights, S. Exec. Rep. No. 23, 102d Cong., 2d Sess., App. A at 25 (1992).

B.   U.S. Ratification of the Civil and Political Covenant

In his letter to Senator Pell, President Bush stated that "[t]he Covenant codifies the essential freedoms people must enjoy in a democratic society. . . ." With few exceptions, he added, "it is entirely consonant with the fundamental principles incorporated in our own Bill of Rights. . . ." Id. The latter statement tracks that of President Carter in his original Letter of Transmittal, supra page 240, at iii, where he remarked that "[t]he great majority of the substantive provisions of [the Covenant] are entirely consistent with the letter and spirit of the United States Constitution and laws." The soundness of these assertions is demonstrated in the following extract from the American Law Institute's Restatement.

1.   The Covenant and the U.S. Constitution and Laws

Restatement (Third) of the Foreign Relations Law of the United States, §701
Reporters' Note 8 at 159-160 (1987)

8. *Effect of future United States ratification of principal international covenants.* Adherence by the United States to the principal international

covenants would not effect any major change in the rights enjoyed by inhabitants of the United States under the United States and State constitutions and laws. The International Covenant on Civil and Political Rights requires states parties to the Covenant to respect and ensure rights generally similar to those protected by the United States Constitution. Some provisions in the Covenant parallel express constitutional provisions, for example, the freedoms protected by the First Amendment, and the prohibition on double jeopardy. Other provisions in the Covenant parallel rights that the Supreme Court has found to be constitutionally protected, e.g., the right to vote, Harper v. Virginia Bd. of Elections, 383 U.S. 663, 86 S. Ct. 1079, 16 L. Ed. 2d 169 (1966); Wesberry v. Sanders, 376 U.S. 1, 84 S. Ct. 526, 11 L. Ed. 2d 481 (1964); Reynolds v. Sims, 377 U.S. 533, 84 S. Ct. 1362, 12 L. Ed. 2d 506 (1964); the presumption of innocence, In re Winship, 397 U.S. 358, 90 S. Ct. 1068, 25 L. Ed. 2d 368 (1970); the right to travel, Edwards v. California, 314 U.S. 160, 62 S. Ct. 164, 86 L. Ed. 119 (1941); Shapiro v. Thompson, 394 U.S. 618, 629-31, 89 S. Ct. 1322, 1328-30, 22 L. Ed. 2d 600 (1969); Oregon v. Mitchell, 400 U.S. 112, 91 S. Ct. 260, 27 L. Ed. 2d 272 (1970); Kent v. Dulles, 357 U.S. 116, 78 S. Ct. 1113, 2 L. Ed. 2d 1204 (1958); but cf. Haig v. Agee, 453 U.S. 280, 101 S. Ct. 2766, 69 L. Ed. 2d 640 (1981) . . . ; the right to marry and have a family, Loving v. Virginia, 388 U.S. 1, 87 S. Ct. 1817, 18 L. Ed. 2d 1010 (1967); Zablocki v. Redhail, 434 U.S. 374, 98 S. Ct. 673, 54 L. Ed. 2d 618 (1978); the right of parents to control the moral and religious education of their children, Pierce v. Society of Sisters, 268 U.S. 510, 45 S. Ct. 571, 69 L. Ed. 1070 (1925); Meyer v. Nebraska, 262 U.S. 390, 43 S. Ct. 625, 67 L. Ed. 1042 (1923); cultural and linguistic rights for minority groups, Wisconsin v. Yoder, 406 U.S. 205, 92 S. Ct. 1526, 32 L. Ed. 2d 15 (1972). Protection under the Covenant, however, may not be congruent in all respects with that provided by the Constitution. In some respects, United States adherence to the Covenant without material reservations might add somewhat to the rights enjoyed by individuals under the Constitution. E.g., Article 6 of the Covenant outlaws capital punishment for pregnant women and for crimes committed by persons under 18 years of age, which has not been held to be a violation of the United States Constitution. Article 7 would forbid not only cruel and unusual punishment for crime, but all torture, and any cruel, inhuman or degrading treatment in any circumstances. Compare Ingraham v. Wright, 430 U.S. 651, 97 S. Ct. 1401, 51 L. Ed. 2d 711 (1977) (corporal punishment in schools not "punishment" within Eighth Amendment). Under Article 14(7) of the Covenant, individuals accused of crime would apparently be protected against trial by both State and federal authorities for offenses arising out of the same act. Compare Abbate v. United States, 359 U.S. 187, 79 S. Ct. 666, 3 L. Ed. 2d 729 (1959); Bartkus v. Illinois, 359 U.S. 121, 79 S. Ct. 676, 3 L. Ed. 2d 684 (1959). Some of the rights recognized by the Covenant are given effect in the United States by federal or State law, notably the civil rights laws. For example, honor and reputation, protected by Article 17 of the Covenant, held not "liberty" or "property" within the protection of the due process clause of the Constitution, Paul v. Davis, 424 U.S. 693, 96 S. Ct. 1155, 47 L. Ed. 2d 405 (1976), are accorded substantial protection by State libel laws. The right of every child "to such measures of protection as are required by his status as a minor, on the part of his family, society and the State," Art. 24, is also largely given effect by State law. On the other hand, compensation for persons who have suffered punishment as a result of miscarriage of justice, Art. 14(6), is generally given effect in the United States only ad hoc as a matter of legislative grace.

Article 20 of the Covenant on Civil and Political Rights requires states to prohibit "propaganda for war" and "advocacy of national, racial or religious hatred that constitutes incitement to discrimination, hostility or violence." The United States would have to enter a reservation to or understanding of this article, since, under the Constitution, the United States (or a State) cannot prohibit "propaganda" and can prohibit incitement to unlawful action but not mere advocacy of it. See Yates v. United States, 354 U.S. 298, 77 S. Ct. 1064, 1 L. Ed. 2d 1356 (1957), overruled on other grounds, Burks v. United States, 437 U.S. 1, 98 S. Ct. 2141, 57 L. Ed. 2d 1 (1978); cf. Scales v. United States, 367 U.S. 203, 81 S. Ct. 1469, 6 L. Ed. 2d 782 (1961); Brandenburg v. Ohio, 395 U.S. 444, 89 S. Ct. 1827, 23 L. Ed. 2d 430 (1969).

2. The Reservations, Understandings, and Declarations "Debate"

Despite the similarity of the Covenant to the U.S. Constitution and laws, one of President Carter's legacies to the ratification process, it will be recalled (see page 245 supra), was the precedent he created of recommending a reservation or other qualifying proviso not only in cases where the Covenant actually might conflict with the Constitution's guarantees (e.g., Article 20's restrictions on incitement to war and "hate speech" that might run afoul of the First Amendment), but also in *any* case where the Covenant, by setting a more humane standard than the Constitution, would require a modification of U.S. law (e.g., Article 6's prohibition of capital punishment in the case of crimes committed by persons below 18 years of age, which would necessitate the enactment of legislation to this effect).

Consistent with this approach, President Carter had recommended the adoption of four reservations, one understanding, one statement, and two declarations. President Bush, following President Carter's path, went several steps further; his promised "few essential reservations and understandings" turned out to include a "package" of five reservations, five understandings, and four declarations. They are set out and then assessed in the following three extracts.

International Covenant on Civil and Political Rights:
The Administration's Proposed Reservations,
Understandings and Declarations
in International Covenant on Civil and Political Rights:
Hearing Before the Senate Comm. on Foreign Relations,
102d Cong., 1st Sess. 8-9 (1991)

A. RESERVATIONS

1. FREE SPEECH

Article 20 does not authorize or require legislation or other action by the United States that would restrict the right of free speech and association protected by the Constitution and laws of the United States.

2. CAPITAL PUNISHMENT

The United States reserves the right, subject to its Constitutional constraints, to impose capital punishment on any person (other than a pregnant woman) duly convicted under existing or future laws permitting the imposition of capital punishment, including such punishment for crimes committed by persons below eighteen years of age.

3. CRUEL, INHUMAN OR DEGRADING TREATMENT
OR PUNISHMENT

The United States considers itself bound by Article 7 to the extent that "cruel, inhuman or degrading treatment or punishment" means the cruel and unusual treatment or punishment prohibited by the Fifth, Eighth and/or Fourteenth Amendments to the Constitution of the United States.

4. CRIMINAL PENALTIES

Because U.S. law generally applies to an offender the penalty in force at the time the offense was committed, the United States does not adhere to the third clause of paragraph 1 of Article 15.

5. JUVENILES

The policy and practice of the United States are generally in compliance with and supportive of the Covenant's provisions regarding treatment of juveniles in the criminal justice system. Nevertheless, the United States reserves the right, in exceptional circumstances, to treat juveniles as adults, notwithstanding paragraphs 2(b) and 3 of Article 10 and paragraph

4 of Article 14. The United States further reserves to these provisions with respect to individuals who volunteer for military service prior to age 18.

B.   UNDERSTANDINGS

1.   NON-DISCRIMINATION AND EQUAL PROTECTION

The Constitution and laws of the United States guarantee all persons equal protection of the law and provide extensive protections against discrimination. The United States understands distinctions based upon race, colour, sex, language, religion, political or other opinion, national or social origin, property, birth or any other status — as those terms are used in Article 2, paragraph 1 and Article 26 — to be permitted when such distinctions are, at minimum, rationally related to a legitimate governmental objective. The United States further understands the prohibition in paragraph 1 of Article 4 upon discrimination, in time of public emergency, based "solely" on the status of race, colour, sex, language, religion or social origin not to bar distinctions that may have a disproportionate effect upon persons of a particular status.

2.   RIGHT TO COMPENSATION FOR ILLEGAL ARREST AND MISCARRIAGE OF JUSTICE

The United States understands the right to compensation referred to in Articles 9(5) and 14(6) to require the provision of effective and enforceable mechanisms by which a victim of an unlawful arrest or detention or a miscarriage of justice may seek and, where justified, obtain compensation from either the responsible individual or the appropriate governmental entity. Entitlement to compensation may be subject to the reasonable requirements of domestic law.

3.   SEPARATE TREATMENT OF THE ACCUSED AND JUVENILES

The United States understands the reference to "exceptional circumstances" in paragraph 2(a) of Article 10 to permit the imprisonment of an accused person with convicted persons where appropriate in light of an individual's overall dangerousness, and to permit accused persons to waive their right to segregation from convicted persons. The United States further understands that paragraph 3 of Article 10 does not diminish the goals of punishment, deterrence, and incapacitation as additional legitimate purposes for a penitentiary system.

4.   RIGHT TO COUNSEL, COMPELLED WITNESSES, DOUBLE JEOPARDY

The United States understands that subparagraphs 3(b) and (d) of Article 14 do not require the provision of a criminal defendant's counsel of choice when the defendant is provided with court-appointed counsel on grounds of indigence, when the defendant is financially able to retain alternative counsel, or when imprisonment is not imposed. The United States further understands that paragraph 3(e) does not prohibit a requirement that the defendant make a showing that any witness whose attendance he seeks to compel is necessary for his defense. The United States understands the prohibition upon double jeopardy in paragraph 7 to apply only when the judgment of acquittal has been rendered by a court of the same governmental unit, whether the Federal Government or a constituent unit, as is seeking a new trial for the same cause.

5.   FEDERALISM

The United States understands that this Convention shall be implemented by the Federal Government to the extent that it exercises legislative and judicial jurisdiction over the matters covered therein, and otherwise by the state and local governments; to the extent that state and local governments exercise jurisdiction over such matters, the Federal Government shall take measures appropriate to the Federal system to the end that the competent authorities of the state or local governments may take appropriate measures for the fulfillment of the Convention.

C.   DECLARATIONS

1.   NON-SELF-EXECUTING

The United States declares that the provisions of Articles 1 through 27 of the Covenant are not self-executing.

2.   LIMITATIONS ON RIGHTS

It is the view of the United States that States Party to the Covenant should wherever possible refrain from imposing any restrictions or limitations on the exercise of the rights recognized and protected by the Covenant, even when such restrictions and limitations are permissible under the terms of the Covenant. For the United States, Article 5, paragraph 2, which provides that fundamental human rights existing in any State Party may not be diminished on the pretext that the Covenant recognizes them to a lesser extent, has particular relevance to Article 19, paragraph 3, which would permit certain restrictions on the freedom of expression. The United States declares that it will continue to adhere to the requirements and constraints of its Constitution in respect of all such restrictions and limitations.

3.   COMPETENCE OF THE HUMAN RIGHTS COMMITTEE

The United States declares that it accepts the competence of the Human Rights Committee to receive and consider communications under Article 41 in which a State Party claims that another State Party is not fulfilling its obligations under the Covenant.

4.   NATURAL WEALTH AND RESOURCES

The United States declares that the right referred to in Article 47 may be exercised only in accordance with international law.

International Human Rights Law Group, Ratification of the International Covenant on Civil and Political Rights by the United States
in International Covenant on Civil and Political Rights: Hearing Before the Senate Comm. on Foreign Relations, 102d Cong., 1st Sess. 101-104 (1991)

EXECUTIVE SUMMARY

NECESSITY OF UNITED STATES RATIFICATION OF THE COVENANT

The International Human Rights Law Group (the "Law Group") is of the opinion that United States ratification of the Covenant on Civil and Political Rights will be highly desirable to the interests of the United States. There are a number of reasons:

(i) Ratification of the Covenant will strengthen United States credibility as a proponent of international concern for human rights. Continued failure to ratify the Covenant would allow the United States to be portrayed as applying a double standard. The fact that most of the rights embodied in the Covenant are already recognized in the Bill of Rights and laws passed by the United States Congress makes nonratification of the Covenant particularly inconsistent with United States foreign policy positions.

(ii) Ratification of the Covenant also will help the United States to fulfill its Helsinki commitments. Although the Helsinki Final Act does not in terms require ratification of the Covenant, its spirit certainly favors ratification. By signing the Concluding Document of the Vienna Meeting of the

Conference on Security and Co-operation in Europe ("CSCE") in 1989, the United States committed itself to develop its laws and policies in the field of civil, political, economic, social, cultural and other human rights and fundamental freedoms and to put them into practice in order to guarantee their effective exercise.

(iii) Ratification of the Covenant will promote the increased recognition of an international standard of human rights. The United States was instrumental in the initial drafting of the Covenant. Its subsequent failure to participate as one of the guarantors of the interpretation and implementation of the Covenant has weakened the international consensus on standards and enforcement mechanisms for the protection of human rights.

(iv) Ratification of the Covenant will enable the United States to actively influence the further development of the international law of human rights. Participation in the various international institutions and structures created by the human rights instruments, in particular the Human Rights Committee, will permit the United States to monitor compliance with international human rights at the international level, and to influence the evolution of human rights norms in ways acceptable to the United States.

(v) Ratification of the Covenant will encourage other countries to ratify the Covenant and thereby increase the overall effectiveness of the international human rights structure.

(vi) Ratification of the Covenant will strengthen the effectiveness of the United States domestic human rights policy in areas where the Covenant goes beyond existing protections.

RATIFICATION SHOULD OCCUR WITH AS FEW RESERVATIONS,
DECLARATIONS, AND UNDERSTANDINGS AS POSSIBLE

The Law Group believes that United States ratification of the Covenant should occur with as few as possible reservations, declarations, and understandings. While it is well recognized in international treaty law that a state may, by use of a reservation, accede to a treaty on the condition that a specific provision shall not apply to it, excessive use of reservations may be viewed as incompatible with the object and purpose of the Covenant and as a breach of international norms.

POSITION ON THE BUSH ADMINISTRATION'S PROPOSED
RESERVATIONS, UNDERSTANDINGS, AND DECLARATIONS

A. *Freedom of Speech and Expression (Art. 20)*

The Law Group *supports the adoption of the Administration's proposed reservation* with respect to Article 20 of the Covenant. This will make certain that ratification of the Covenant will not reduce the protection of freedom of expressions in the United States.

B.   The Capital Punishment Reservation (Art. 6)

The Law Group supports the Administration's proposal to accept the prohibition against executing pregnant women as an international obligation. The Law Group, however, *opposes the adoption of the proposed reservation* with respect to the execution of minors. Although ratification of the Covenant without reserving to Article 6 would require a change in current United States law, the Law Group is of the opinion that the prohibition against the imposition of capital punishment on minors would be a *desirable change.*

C.   Cruel, Inhuman or Degrading Treatment or Punishment (Art. 7)

The Law Group *opposes the adoption of the proposed reservation.* If, however, it is felt necessary to reiterate the United States' position adopted in the instrument of ratification of the Convention Against Torture and Other Cruel, Inhuman or Degrading Treatment or Punishment ("Torture Convention"), the Law Group *recommends that the proposed reservation be changed into a declaration.*

D.   Retroactive Imposition of Reduced Penalties (Art. 15(1))

The Law Group *opposes the adoption of the proposed reservation.* Although Article 15(1) requires a change, at least as a matter of degree, in both federal and state practice, the Law Group is of the opinion that such a change would be desirable and consistent with the concepts of American criminal justice. Should it be felt necessary to adopt a reservation with respect to Article 15(1), the Law Group *recommends* that it be *narrowed to persons already convicted,* thus maintaining the benefit of a lighter sentence for cases still pending.

E.   Segregation of Juveniles and Adults (Arts. 10(2) (b), (3), and 14(4))

While the Law Group *does not oppose the adoption of the proposed reservation,* it believes that, as a strict legal matter, it is not necessary. The negotiating history of the Covenant seems to indicate that the obligations concerning the separate treatment of juveniles are not absolute and leave the States parties to the Covenant with a considerable degree of flexibility in the execution of these obligations. As a result, a reservation seems merely to reiterate the margin of discretion already provided for by the Covenant itself.

F. Nondiscrimination and Equal Protection (Arts. 2(1), 4(1), and 26)

The Law Group *does not oppose the adoption of the proposed under-standing*, although the understanding is not necessary. Given the very extensive protection already provided under United States law, the intention of the drafters, and the Committee's views on the issue, there seems to be no need for the United States to introduce the proposed understanding. If, however, the United States believes it is necessary to articulate its interpretation of what constitutes acceptable differentiation, the Law Group does not oppose adoption of an understanding.

G. Right to Compensation for Unlawful Arrest or Detention (Art. 9(5)) and Right to Compensation for Miscarriage of Justice (Art. 14(6))

The Law Group *does not oppose the adoption of the proposed under-standing* with respect to Article[s] 9(5) and 14(6) of the Covenant. From the negotiating history and the wording of Article 14(6) it seems clear that current United States practice is in compliance with Article 14(6). The proposed understanding thus does not seem to be necessary. However, as an understanding it is not objectionable, as it would not derogate from the international obligation of the United States.

H. Separate Treatment of the Accused and Convicted (Art. 10(2)(a) and (3))

The Law Group *accepts the adoption of the proposed understanding.* The segregation of accused and convicted prisoners depends for its implementation on the facilities and resources of each community; and small towns and counties with limited prison facilities and resources may be unable to comply. It may also be unwise to accept reformation and rehabilitation unqualifiedly as the "essential aim" of the United States prison system, since this is a philosophy of punishment that is not fully accepted in the United States.

I. Standard for the Conduct of Trials (Art. 14)

The Law Group *does not oppose the adoption of the proposed under-standing* with respect to Article 14(3)(b), (d), and (e) of the Covenant, although the understanding does not appear to be strictly necessary. However, with respect to double jeopardy (Article 14(7)), the Law Group *recommends the adoption of an understanding only with respect to multiple prosecutions on a state/federal level.* A change in United States law might be welcome with respect to current practices of state/state double jeopardy, in view of the disfavor in which successive prosecutions are generally viewed today.

J. Federalism (Art. 50)

The Law Group *does not oppose the adoption of the proposed understanding* with respect to Article 50, although the understanding does not seem to be strictly necessary. If an understanding is adopted, we believe it should be rephrased. In any event, there is no need to adopt a reservation similar to the one proposed by the Carter Administration in 1979.

K. The Issue of Self-Execution (Arts. 1-27)

The Law Group *opposes the adoption of the proposed declaration* for the following reasons: (a) rendering all the substantive provisions of the Covenant non-self-executing may be so inconsistent with the language of the Covenant as to violate the principle embodied in Article 19 of the Vienna Convention on the Law of Treaties; (b) a declaration of the non-self-executing nature of the Covenant would not, in any event, absolve the United States from its international obligations under the Covenant; (c) many of the substantive provisions of the Covenant are undoubtedly capable of immediate judicial application; (d) self-execution is a very effective mechanism of enforcement of treaties; (e) the declaration would exclude the judiciary from participating in the analysis of the Covenant, and thereby also deprive United States courts of the unique opportunity to influence subsequent interpretations by international and foreign courts; and (f) it is not clear that such a declaration would be binding on the judiciary.

L. Limitations on Rights

The Law Group *supports the adoption of the proposed declaration.* The proposed declaration in no way derogates from the United States' international obligations. The concerns raised by the representatives of the media in the United States over restrictions placed by some governments on the free flow of information or ideas provide adequate justification for adoption of the proposed declaration.

M. Competence of the Human Rights Committee (Art. 41)

The Law Group *supports the adoption of the proposed declaration* to accept the competence of the Human Rights Committee to receive and consider state-to-state complaints under Article 41. This step will give the United States the right to participate in the work of the Human Rights Committee. This in turn will give the United States the opportunity to bring its human rights standards to bear in the international human rights arena, as well as the opportunity to counter any unfair criticism of domestic United States practices.

N.   Right to Private Property (Art. 47)

The Law Group *opposes the adoption of the proposed declaration* because it is an unnecessary political statement, and because it is not an appropriate subject of a declaration as a matter of international law. The reasoning offered in support of such a declaration is unconvincing. Considering the fact that a declaration or even a reservation by a party to an international treaty does not in any way obligate other signatory parties, the proposed declaration would be merely a unilateral assertion of United States views on an issue that arises outside the scope of the Covenant.

Stewart, United States Ratification of the Covenant on Civil and Political Rights: The Significance of the Reservations, Understandings, and Declarations
42 DePaul L. Rev. 1183, 1205-1207 (1993)

The debate over ratification of the Covenant, and more importantly the forthcoming debate over whether the United States should proceed to ratify other pending human rights treaties and on what terms, turns in large part on whether, taken individually and collectively, the reservations, understandings, and declarations were necessary and, even if warranted, whether they represented too high a price to pay to obtain Senate approval.

The above analysis indicates that the most common criticisms of the specific elements of the package have been that they were not legally necessary and that the United States should have conformed its laws and practices to the international standards reflected in the Covenant. There seems to be general agreement that only one reservation, interposing the First Amendment as a bar to Article 20, is constitutionally required. As the Lawyers Committee on Human Rights has contended, the others appear to reflect three operative principles: (1) that the United States would not commit itself to do anything that would require a change in present U.S. law or practice; (2) that the treaty should not be self-executing but should require implementation by legislation; and (3) that subjects within the jurisdiction of the states might be excluded from the obligation of the treaty or left exclusively to implementation by legislation by the states.

The response to these objections is straightforward. The premise underlying most of the reservations, understandings, and declarations was the conclusion that existing U.S. law, even if not strictly in conformity with the precise language of the Covenant, was acceptable and indeed preferable. A subsidiary concern was a desire not to effectuate changes to domestic law by means of the treaty-making power. There is little question that under Article VI of the Constitution, the federal government could in fact have made necessary changes to federal law and required parallel changes in state and local law to give effect to the Covenant's provisions. For many reasons, including those rooted in respect for our federal system of government, there was substantial resistance in both the Executive branch and the Senate to exercising that authority. But the principal conclusion was, as a policy matter, not to seek changes to U.S. law at those relatively minor points at which it diverged from the Covenant.

The experience gained in obtaining advice and consent to ratification of the Covenant suggests strongly that, in pursuing ratification of additional human rights treaties, serious consideration should be given to the simultaneous submission of proposed implementing legislation wherever U.S. law differs from the treaty requirements *and* it is determined that conforming changes to that U.S. law are desirable. As a general matter, conformity with widely accepted international human rights standards is a worthy and achievable goal, and it should be U.S. policy to adopt as few reservations, understandings, and declarations as possible. Modification of U.S. law through the legislative process would eliminate the need for provisos in many instances.

In their details, however, not all internationally recognized human rights treaties are in fact superior to established U.S. principles and practices. By definition, the negotiation of multilateral treaties between states with widely differing legal systems produces compromises and ambiguities. Where the treaty provision is inferior, there is no reason for the United States to adhere to it, even if that could be done constitutionally.

The task, therefore, is, first, to identify any provisions of the treaty which conflict with or raise significant questions about U.S. law, and, second, to determine whether a change to the relevant U.S. law is possible and desirable or whether an appropriate reservation, understanding, or declaration must be taken to condition U.S. obligations under the instrument. Proposed changes to U.S. law should be presented in the form of draft legislation at the time the Senate considers the question of advice and consent to ratification. Where changes are not desirable, ratification should be conditioned upon an appropriate caveat. Ideally, both the Executive Branch and the Congress would work in open partnership with each other in this process, together with interested nongovernmental organizations and knowledgeable individuals.

3. Attitudes of the U.S. NGO Community Towards Ratification Conditioned upon Acceptance of the Bush Administration "Package"

The Bush Administration, building upon the Carter legacy and its own experience in obtaining Senate advice and consent to the Torture Convention, presented the Senate Foreign Relations Committee with its "package" of reservations, understandings, and declarations to the Covenant on what might be called a *fait accompli* basis. On the very morning the Administration delivered the final text of the package to the Senate Committee, the latter, without having had "a chance to examine the specific language," held its one and only hearing on the Covenant, a 129-minute session attended by three senators who heard the testimony of 10 witnesses. International Covenant on Civil and Political Rights: Hearing Before the Senate Comm. on Foreign Relations, 102d Cong., 1st Sess. 4 (1991). Thus, although the Committee kept the record open "to enable committee members to submit additional questions, and our public witnesses to provide written, detailed comments on the specific language of the administration's package now that it has become available," it made no real effort to generate a serious and informed debate over the package and the need for or desirability of its various components. This "take it or leave it" approach received the tacit endorsement of the Committee in its brief, conclusory report recommending that the full Senate give its advice and consent to ratification. S. Exec. Rep. No. 23, 102d Cong., 2d Sess. (1992). Therefore, it is not surprising that the package, as has been pointed out, ultimately "was accepted without change, or even significant debate, by the Senate." Stewart, supra page 259, at 1186. See 138 Cong. Rec. S4781-4784 (daily ed. Apr. 2, 1992). The Covenant eventually came into force for the United States on 8 September 1992 after the deposit of the instrument of ratification by President Bush.

The lack of serious debate by the Senate, however, did not preclude the airing of different views and the taking of different stands by various members of the U.S. NGO community. The differences of opinion expressed by the spokesmen for two leading NGOs in the exchange of letters that follows should not surprise anyone, since, as one of the editors of this coursebook suggested during the Carter years, "[i]f these treaties are presented for final vote in the Senate with all of the reservations that are attached now, all of us . . . must question whether the treaties should be approved at all . . . ; it is a dangerous position to take that these treaties should be ratified under any circumstances." U.S. Ratification of the Human Rights Treaties: With or Without Reservations?, supra page 240, at 40.

Lawyers Committee   March 2, 1992
for Human Rights

Senator Claiborne Pell
Chairman
Senate Foreign Relations Committee
United States Senate
Washington, D.C. 20510-3901

Dear Senator Pell:

We are writing to you, and other members of the Foreign Relations Committee, to express our concerns about the approach the Administration is now taking with respect to the International Covenant on Civil and Political Rights.

At the outset, we wish to reiterate our continued appreciation to you for your long-standing support for international human rights. As the Lawyers Committee testified in November, we strongly support U.S. ratification of the Covenant.

Since the end of the Second World War, the U.S. government and the American people have been deeply involved in the development of international human rights laws and enforcement practices. United States diplomats helped draft the basic international treaties, including the Covenant on Civil and Political Rights. The Lawyers Committee emphatically endorses the view that ratification of the Covenant would underscore our national commitment to promoting human rights in U.S. foreign policy.

We are deeply concerned, however, by the reservations, declarations and understandings proposed by the Administration. We believe that only one reservation, relating to limitations on free speech in Article 20 of the Covenant, is constitutionally required. The other qualifications proposed by the Administration are all designed to support the Administration's view that this treaty should not, in any way, change or commit us to change anything in U.S. law or practice, now or in the future. It is this principle that we strongly oppose. Ratification, subject to the reservations proposed by the Administration, would render the treaty forever useless as a tool to improve human rights in the United States.

The Administration's qualifying language applies one set of rules to the United States and another set of rules to the rest of the world. No other nation, including our closest allies, has taken this view. We believe it is wrong; it undermines the basic purpose of the treaty.

The Administration's position is that the Senate must either accept ratification subject to this principle or not ratify the treaty at all. We oppose the Administration's approach on three grounds. First, we believe that other countries, including our closest allies, will view ratification in this manner as hypocritical. They will see it as an attempt by the Executive Branch to obtain the benefit of being a party to the treaty, and being able to say that we are, without undertaking any of the obligations that accompany that status. Second, our ratification subject to the principle of "no domestic application" may be imitated cynically by other states, such as China or Cuba, which seek the diplomatic benefits of ratification but cling to the view that adherence to international human rights standards violates their sovereignty. We would scorn any ratification by other countries, such as China, if they included reservations identical to those proposed by the Administration. Finally, we question what advantage there is to the cause of human rights, either internationally or in the U.S., if we ratify in this manner.

The decision to write this letter reflects an evolution in the Lawyers Committee's position and our participation in numerous discussions with Senate staff, NGOs and representatives of the Executive Branch in the last several months. Reluctantly, we have come to conclude that if the choice before the Senate is now between ratifying the Covenant subject to the Administration's misguided principle or delaying ratification until the most objectionable reservations are removed, we support delay.

Ratification now in a manner which sets us apart from the rest of the world, and which says that international human rights treaties do not apply to the United States, would not serve the advancement of human rights here or elsewhere.

Sincerely,
MARVIN E. FRANKEL
Chairman

Human Rights Watch   March 5, 1992

Judge Marvin Frankel
Kramer, Levin, Nessen, Kamin
    & Frankel
919 Third Avenue
New York, NY 10022

Dear Marvin:

I am writing to you because I am disturbed by your letter of March 2 to Senator Pell in which you oppose ratification of the International Covenant on Civil and Political Rights in the manner in which it has been presented to the Senate by the Bush Administration. Though like you, I would have preferred it if the Administration had not included most of the reservations, declarations and understandings which are part of the package going to the Senate, it seems to me nevertheless that the case for ratification is overwhelming. Moreover, it seems to me that a number of the assertions in your letter are mistaken.

In essence, your letter says that ratification in this form means "no domestic application" (the quotes appear in your letter, but I am not able to determine what you are quoting); that other countries will see ratification in this form, in your words, "as hypocritical"; and that, again in your words, you "question what advantage there is to the cause of human rights, either internationally or in the U.S., if we ratify in this manner." I will deal with each of these objections.

The assertion that ratification of the treaty in this manner will have "no domestic application" seems to me flatly wrong. Here are the reasons.

First, as you know well, the foremost means that the international human rights movement has developed to promote human rights worldwide has been to document the discrepancies between the international commitments that governments have made to respect rights and their actual practices. By and large, that means has not been used with respect to the United States. There are several reasons for this, but surely one of them is that the United States has undertaken relatively few international commitments. By ratifying the treaty in this form, the United States would assume international obligations and explicitly invite international assessment of its performance. In and of itself, I believe this would promote the cause of human rights in the United States as it has throughout the world. Moreover, I believe this will be more important in the years ahead as litigation within the United States is less and less useful in protecting rights.

Second, in contending that ratification would have "no domestic application," you say that the reservations "would render the treaty forever useless as a tool to improve human rights in the United States." One of my difficulties with this assertion is that it seems to misapprehend our current historical circumstances. In my view, there is little prospect of improving human rights in the United States in the next ten or twenty years or, in other words, in the foreseeable future. I believe that the recasting of the federal judiciary, and especially of the Supreme Court, in the Reagan-Bush years largely precludes this. The task in my view, will be to preserve the rights we now enjoy. This will not be easy, and I am certain we will suffer severe setbacks.

Under these circumstances, I believe it is extremely valuable to have the Administration and the Senate adopt an international treaty which will have the force of law that commits the United States internationally to respect many rights which are vulnerable to erosion or reversal. I refer to rights which are explicitly provided in the Covenant but which are only available to Americans either as a consequence of judicial decisions interpreting the United States Constitution but which are not explicitly protected in our Constitution or, less frequently, as a result of state constitutional or federal or state statutory provisions. [Eleven such rights then are listed.]

I could continue, but I think the point has been made. As one who is deeply pessimistic about the possibility that we will preserve all these rights, or that we will obtain some of these rights not now provided in practice, I welcome the decision of our government to accept their protection as an international obligation.

Moreover, despite the Administration's submission of the treaty in a form that is not self-executing, it seems to me that litigants will cite this international obligation. Also, judges and legislators will look to this international obligation to buttress their own efforts to safeguard these rights. Similarly, the press and voluntary organizations within the United States will be able to point out that efforts to erode or reverse such protections violate international obligations. Under the circumstances, I find it simply incomprehensible that you assert that the treaty has "no domestic application" or is "useless" in the United States.

Let me now turn to your objection that ratification in this form would be "hypocritical." I think the term is inapposite.

Rather, I believe that the term hypocritical is properly applied to those states that ratified without substantive reservations but have then completely disregarded the rights set forth in the Covenant. I have in mind states such as Syria, Iraq, Iran, El Salvador and Vietnam. Frankly, though I object to most of the reservations by the United States, it seems to me far less hypocritical to engage in a careful exercise such as the Administration has done in which it says it will honor the great majority of the provisions of the Covenant but that it will not accept a few provisions. In general, it has been the governments that have taken their obligations seriously that have entered substantive reservations. The fact that the Administration has not provided litigants with a new cause of action by making the treaty self-executing does not seem to me to render ratification hypocritical. Without having done a survey, I think it is safe to say that citizens in the majority of the countries that have ratified the Covenant have no cause of action under the Covenant. That hardly negates the value of the Covenant in holding those governments to account internationally for their failures to live up to their commitments.

Your final point — that you question the value of ratification in this form internationally or in the U.S. — sums up the other two points. To my comments above, I want to add the following in commenting on your conclusion.

As I am sure you agree, there are great benefits to be gained internationally and in the United States from adherence by the United States to the international system of protecting rights. In my view, ratification of the Covenant in this form would be an important step in that direction. Its importance is especially great at a time when there is a significant prospect of retrenchment in U.S. law and when ratification would commit the United States to oppose such retrenchment and, if it takes place, to bring the United States back into compliance with the standards of the Covenant. It also means that if international interpretations of the provisions of the Covenant are more generous towards rights than U.S. Supreme Court interpretations of analogous rights that are available under the U.S. Constitution — which seems likely — there would be a basis for arguing that the United States has obligated itself internationally to bring its practices into line with international standards. . . .

Best regards.

Sincerely,
ARYEH NEIER

266 International Human Rights

Lawyers Committee · March 18, 1992
for Human Rights

Aryeh Neier
Executive Director
Human Rights Watch
485 Fifth Avenue
New York, NY 10017

Dear Aryeh,

I have given some thought to your letter of March 5. Let me attempt to identify our areas of agreement and our points of disagreement.

1. Both of us would like to see the U.S. ratify the Covenant. Both of us wish that the Bush Administration had not included the package of reservations, understandings, etc. You think that even with all the reservations "the case for ratification is overwhelming." We think the reservations seriously undermine the benefits of ratification. Therefore, we think that the human rights organizations should seek to persuade the Senate not to include them in its consent to ratification; after agonizing about it, we have concluded also that we should seek to build up Senate resistance to the reservations even at the risk that we might succeed only in derailing the present Bush initiative and delay U.S. ratification for some years more.

2. In our view, the principal purpose of U.S. ratification is to strengthen evolving international human rights standards. U.S. participation in this process reinforces the requirement that all governments, including our own, accept these universal minimal standards of behavior. In our view, ratification with the reservations would not further, and might even set back, the international human rights effort and our human rights policy; and ratification with the reservations would reduce the domestic benefits to virtually nil.

3. The pressures for U.S. ratification have been wholly on international grounds and for international reasons. We have been the major international "delinquent," while a hundred states, including all our friends and even our erstwhile enemies (the U.S.S.R. et al.) have adhered long ago. Our failure to ratify the Covenants is thrown up at us at every human rights occasion, in every human rights context, by every state (including China!). All would welcome our ratification (though they would note that we are not ratifying the Covenant on Economic, Social and Cultural Rights).

By ratifying with the reservations, however, the U.S. would be saying clearly that we will ratify only if doing so makes no change in our internal law. The world thinks that adhering to the Covenant means accepting international standards, bringing national standards up to those international standards, and submitting to scrutiny; with the Bush package ratification by the United States will do none of that. Some will say that such reservations are unacceptable because together they are incompatible with the object and purpose of the Treaty. (See Vienna Convention on the Law of Treaties, Art. 19.) Ratification by the United States with these reservations will be seen as "hypocritical" (the word I used in my letter) because it seeks to avoid any international obligations yet claims to have ratified and claims the benefits of ratification. We, I think, would scorn ratification by other countries (such as China or Cuba) if they made similar reservations.

One of the purposes of our ratification is to enable us to participate in the work of the Human Rights Committee and thus further the cause of human rights. This would require the U.S. to submit reports to the Committee and discuss their content with Committee members. It would also create the opportunity for the U.S. to nominate and elect a U.S. expert to the Committee. Yet if we become a part of this process following ratification with the Bush reservations, we will not do much for the cause of human rights and may even damage it. This is a view that we know is shared by some members of the Human Rights Committee.

4. Your emphasis on the domestic consequences of U.S. ratification suggests that in your opinion, even if the international consequences were negative, we should ratify because of the domestic benefits of ratification. You seem to see in the Covenant important support for human rights in the United States, especially in view of our increasingly conservative federal judiciary. We disagree.

If the Covenant were ratified without any reservations (other than the one on propaganda for war and "racial speech," presumably required by the Constitution as now interpreted), its support for human rights in the United States would be modest. That makes the Administration's reservations even more difficult to accept. With the reservations, the effect in the United States is designed to be — and will be — virtually zero. The Covenant will not be self-executing. And the Administration has indicated that it will not seek Congressional implementation. The courts — the conservative courts from which you expect nothing but erosion of our constitutional rights — will hardly find a basis for preventing such erosion in a non-self-executing treaty that Congress has not implemented and that the record shows was not intended to be implemented.

5. You seem to recognize that, but apparently expect that even if ratified with the reservations, the Covenant will serve as a "floor" so that the United States will be internationally committed not to fall below that floor. But with the reservations and understandings we will

have entered there is no commitment to accept the international standard where it might improve human rights in the United States, *e.g.* on juvenile execution, or on cruel and inhuman treatment. I share your concern about the conservative judiciary. I do not share your apparent fear that gender equality, or the right of privacy in the family or correspondence or liberty of movement, or involuntary medical or scientific experiments, or the right to educate one's children are in jeopardy because they are not explicit in the Constitution. The jurisprudence on such matters is deeply rooted. If these were eroded, so could all the explicit protections be eroded. In that case, explicit phrases in a treaty would not save them, surely not in a non-self-executing treaty not implemented by Congress as read by the same conservative judiciary.

6. By my letter to Senator Pell we hoped to call attention to the import and consequences of the package of reservations. We hoped to strengthen the backbone of the Senate to resist the reservations. All of us tillers in the human rights vineyard ought to be pressing together for Senate hearings on the reservations and for ratification without them. If we cannot eliminate most of the Bush package and the Senate puts the Covenant back on the shelf, we ought to gird ourselves for the next opportunity. We have waited twenty-six years; we can wait a few years more — rather than settle for approximately nothing (or less). And if the Senate were to give its consent subject to the Bush package, we ought to be together pressing Congress hard to make our ratification significant and honest by implementing the treaty in every respect despite reservations and declarations.

All good wishes.

Sincerely,
MARVIN E. FRANKEL
Chairman

C. U.S. Ratification of the Other Human Rights Treaties: The "Package" Redux

On 26 April 1994, the Acting Secretary of State wrote to Senator Pell urging "the Senate Foreign Relations Committee to give its prompt attention to and approval of the Racial Discrimination Convention." Senate Comm. on Foreign Relations, International Convention on the Elimination of All Forms of Racial Discrimination, S. Exec. Rep. No. 29, 103d Cong., 2d Sess. 9 (1994). As the Committee subsequently noted, the Clinton Administration submitted a proposed package of five conditions — three reservations, one understanding, and one declaration — that was similar to the one submitted by the Carter Administration, but went beyond it in some areas. Id. at 7. Notably, it recommended a reservation to Article 22, which permits the referral of disputes under the Convention to the International Court of Justice at the request of any party to the dispute. Id. at 26-27.*

While a "free speech" reservation to Articles 4 and 7 clearly was required, as was a similar reservation to Article 20 of the Civil and Political Covenant, all the other recommended conditions were unnecessary, as amply demonstrated in a report submitted to the Committee by the International Human Rights Law Group. See International Human Rights Law Group, U.S. Ratification of the International Convention on the Elimination of All Forms of Racial Discrimination (May 1994). As in the case of the Civil and Political Covenant, the Clinton Administration recommended a non-self-executing declaration and indicated that it would not accept the right of individual petition (by making a declaration under Article 14), thus rendering individuals unable to enforce their rights under the Convention directly in U.S. courts or before the Committee on the Elimination of All Forms of Racial Discrimination.

The Foreign Relations Committee held a hearing on the Convention on 11 May 1994 and on 2 June 1994 issued a report recommending that the Senate give its advice and consent to the Convention conditioned upon the adoption in haec verba of the Administration's package. The Senate did so on 21 June 1994 (140 Cong. Rec. S7634 (daily ed. June 24, 1994), and the Convention came into force on 20 November 1994 after the deposit of the instrument of ratification by President Clinton.

From the above materials it appears that, while the logjam blocking the ratification of human rights treaties finally has been broken up, the price that has been paid by the use of the "package" approach to obtain Senate advice and consent has been great. It now seems a given that U.S. ratification of other human rights treaties will be subject to (1) the uniform adoption of reservations, understandings, and declarations whenever an international standard appears to be more humane than that required by the U.S. Constitution or laws; (2) the uniform adoption of non-self-executing declarations that attempt to prevent individuals from enforcing their international rights in U.S. courts; and (3) the uniform refusal to opt for the right of individual petition, thus denying individuals access to international committees to enforce their rights.

---

* The United States had adopted a similar reservation to Article 9 of the Genocide Convention. 132 Cong. Rec. S1377 (daily ed. Feb. 19, 1986). To date, at least five countries — Great Britain, Greece, Italy, Mexico, and The Netherlands — have objected to this reservation on the ground that it is incompatible with the object and purpose of the Convention. United Nations, Multilateral Treaties Deposited with the Secretary-General: Status as at 31 December 1992, at 95-97 (1993). The Netherlands has even stated that it does not consider the United States to be a party to the Convention. Id. at 96. Similar objections presumably will be raised regarding the U.S. reservation to Article 22 of the Racial Discrimination Convention.

Comments and Questions Concerning U.S. Ratification of Human Rights Treaties

1. As Professor Henkin's extract (see page 241 supra) and the other readings make clear, one matter at least now is beyond debate: there are no constitutional objections, in principle, to U.S. ratification of international human rights treaties. See the definitive treatment of this issue in Henkin, The Constitution, Treaties, and International Human Rights, 116 U. Pa. L. Rev. 1012 (1968). Constitutional problems, of course, may arise with respect to particular provisions of a particular treaty, which is the reason for the "free speech" reservations to the Civil and Political Covenant and the Racial Discrimination Convention. Absent a reservation in such a case, the courts, should they find a conflict between a treaty provision and the U.S. Constitution, of course, would hold the latter to prevail. Reid v. Covert, 354 U.S. 1 (1957). Thus, fears that human rights treaties might deprive persons in the United States of their constitutional rights are groundless.

2. Since, as Mr. Stewart acknowledges, "[t]here is little question that under Article VI of the Constitution, the federal government could in fact have made necessary changes to federal law and required parallel changes in state and local law to give effect to the Covenant's provisions," supra page 259, why was this approach not taken? Why was there "substantial resistance in both the Executive branch and the Senate to exercising that authority"? Among the "many reasons," Stewart mentions "respect for our federal system of government," a factor not noticeably present when the international agreement-making power is used in the business and trade areas (compare the North American Free Trade Agreement (NAFTA) negotiations), and "the conclusion that existing U.S. law, even if not strictly in conformity with the precise language of the Covenant, was acceptable and indeed preferable." True, "[w]here the treaty provision is inferior, there is no reason for the United States to adhere to it, even if that could be done constitutionally." However, is the Covenant law prohibiting the execution of juveniles and cruel, inhuman, or degrading treatment or punishment really "inferior" to U.S. law, or is this argument really a case of "everyone is out of step but Johnny"? Apparently Belgium, Denmark, Finland, Germany, Italy, The Netherlands, Norway, Portugal, and Spain — all states parties to the Covenant and all objectors to the U.S. reservations in this regard — believe the latter.

3. Another reason for the resistance to international human rights treaties that might be considered self-executing is the mistaken belief that *any* changes in U.S. law should be made through "the normal legislative process." S. Exec. Rep. No. 23, 102d Cong., 2d Sess. 25 (1992). To accommodate such concerns, Mr. Stewart "suggests strongly [and imaginatively] that, in pursuing ratification of additional human rights treaties, serious consideration should be given to the simultaneous submission of proposed implementing legislation wherever U.S. law differs from the treaty requirements

and it is determined that conforming changes to that U.S. law are desirable." Stewart, supra page 260 (emphasis in original). "Modification of U.S. law through the legislative process," he adds, "would eliminate the need for provisos in many instances." Whether Stewart's suggestion will be adopted as Executive Branch policy is problematic.

Despite the fact that the above approach is "water under the bridge" as far as the Civil and Political Covenant is concerned, a group of U.S. civil and human rights organizations has proposed legislation addressing "the most important respects in which U.S. reservations to the Covenant will otherwise entrench disparities between U.S. law and that of other parties to the accord." Posner and Spiro, Adding Teeth to United States Ratification of the Covenant on Civil and Political Rights: The International Human Rights Conformity Act of 1993, 42 DePaul L. Rev. 1209, 1214 (1993). Whether Congress will demonstrate much enthusiasm for such legislation also is problematic.

4. Review the arguments for and against U.S. ratification of the Civil and Political Covenant, "warts and all," raised by the representatives of Human Rights Watch and the Lawyers Committee for Human Rights (see pages 261-268 supra). If you had been a legislative staff member to a U.S. Senator otherwise disposed to vote for the Covenant, how would you have recommended that he or she vote, given the nature of the "package"? Why? Would the fact that the American Bar Association, as exemplified by the testimony of Professor Moore at page 244 supra, had accepted the conditions without serious question have influenced your recommendation?

5. During the ratification process, probably nothing attracted the criticism of NGOs and other supporters of the Covenant's ratification more than the proposed non-self-executing declaration. Reread the substantive articles of the Covenant (Arts. 6-27) and decide just what provisions in them might be held self-executing. Does this possibility warrant the declaration, not only in this, but also in the case of other international human rights treaties, that the treaty is non-self-executing? Would you agree or disagree with Professor Weissbrodt's assessment that "[t]he effect of this declaration is to deprive American courts of their most potent technique for contributing meaningfully to the interpretation of the [Covenant]"? Weissbrodt, United States Ratification of the Human Rights Covenants, 63 Minn. L. Rev. 35, 67-68 (1978).

Now that the Covenant has been ratified with the non-self-executing declaration attached, does that necessarily mean that its provisions will have no domestic effect? Could not U.S. courts, as several writers cited in Comment 6 contend, just ignore the declaration, since it is technically not part of the treaty and, hence, not the supreme law of the land? Would they, as a practical matter? Even assuming the courts do consider themselves bound by the declaration's determination that the Covenant is non-self-executing, might they not refer to its provisions in determining whether a particular norm has acquired customary international law status or infuse its provisions into U.S. constitutional and statutory standards? See pages 172-173 and 174-175 of Problem II for arguments along these lines. See also Quigley, Judge Bork Is Wrong: The Covenant Is the Law, 71 Wash. U. L.Q. 1087, 1100-1104 (1993).

Note, too, that the Alien Tort Statute gives U.S. courts jurisdiction over "any civil action by an alien for a tort only, committed in violation of the law of nations or *a treaty of the United States.*" (Emphasis added.) Arguably this language, which makes no mention of self-execution, permits the invocation of the statute whenever a tort has been committed in violation of any provision in the Covenant (or the Torture Convention or the Racial Discrimination Convention), thus often obviating the necessity, as in all past cases, of having to establish that the tort violates customary international law. If this reading of the interaction of the Covenant and the Alien Tort Statute is correct, one may expect to see a great increase in the number of such cases.

6. Until recently, non-self-executing declarations were a rare phenomenon in the treaty-making process, and no U.S. court has yet ruled on their legal effect. At the 1979 Senate hearings on the four treaties, it was generally agreed that, while not legally binding upon the courts, in all likelihood they would be given great, and perhaps dispositive, weight by the Judicial Branch. See International Human Rights Treaties: Hearings Before the Senate Comm. on Foreign Relations, 96th Cong., 1st Sess. 278 (1979) (Schachter), id. at 288 (Henkin), id. at 294 (Redlich), id. at 315 (Owen), and id. at 348-349 (Lillich). More recently, sparked by the U.S. ratification of the Civil and Political Covenant, several scholars have questioned the legal effect as well as the wisdom of such declarations. See, e.g., Damrosch, The Role of the United States Senate Concerning "Self-Executing" and "Non-Self-Executing" Treaties, 67 Chi.-Kent L. Rev. 515, 526-532 (1991); Riesenfeld and Abbott, The Scope of U.S. Senate Control over the Conclusion and Operation of Treaties, 67 Chi.-Kent L. Rev. 571, 603-609, 631-632 (1991); Paust, Avoiding "Fraudulent" Executive Policy: Analysis of Non-Self-Execution of the Covenant on Civil and Political Rights, 42 DePaul L. Rev. 1257 (1993).

7. United States constitutional lawyers, both academics and practitioners, frequently fail to pay much attention to international human rights law, believing that the Constitution itself, coupled with what Professor Henkin has called "American constitutionalism" (Henkin, Rights: American and Human, 79 Colum. L. Rev. 405, 407 (1979)), provides all the basis necessary for the progressive development of enlightened jurisprudential standards. Is this belief still correct (or was it ever)? See Lillich, The Constitution and International Human Rights, 83 Am. J. Intl. L. 851, 860-862 (1989). For interesting comparisons of U.S. constitutional and criminal law with its international human rights law counterparts, see Materials on International Human Rights and U.S. Constitutional Law (H. Hannum ed. 1985); and Materials on International Human Rights and U.S. Criminal Law and Procedure (H. Hannum ed. 1989).

VI. Final Comments and Questions

1. No international human rights norm is more clearly established by the UN Charter than the one against discrimination. (Arts. 1(3) and 55(c).) See also Article 2 of the Universal Declaration of Human Rights. As the International Court of Justice's Advisory Opinion on Namibia (see page 49 of Problem I) demonstrates, states have an international legal obligation not to violate the non-discrimination norm. Moreover, as the material in Problem II reveals, respectable arguments can be advanced that the Charter's human rights clauses are now binding on the domestic courts of member states. Why, then, were the Racial Discrimination Convention and the Discrimination Against Women Conventions thought necessary? For standard-setting reasons? For purposes of easier enforcement? What other factors may have been at work?

2. The non-discrimination norm contained in the Charter and Declaration also embraces discrimination based on language and religion. Yet efforts to marshall support for conventions in these two areas have been met with considerably less support at the UN. See generally M. McDougal, H. Lasswell, and L. Chen, Human Rights and World Public Order chs. 11, 13 (1980). What factors do you think account for this lack of enthusiasm?

3. For the past quarter of a century, but especially since the coming into force of the two covenants in 1976, many observers have made the point that the "stage of definition" is nearly over while the "stage of implementation" has just begun. See, e.g., Korey, The Key to Human Rights — Implementation, International Conciliation (Nov. 1968). At present, the conventional approach to standard-setting by the UN appears to have lost some steam. See page 194 supra. Compare the "model law" approach considered in Problem IV.

Assume that you were asked — by the UN High Commissioner for Human Rights, the U.S. Assistant Secretary of State for Democracy, Human Rights, and Labor, or a prominent international NGO — to draft a memorandum outlining those areas where international human rights norms need development or clarification. What areas would you suggest? Electronic or other invasions of privacy? The right to die? Eugenic engineering? Organ transplants? The rights of indigenous peoples? Would you recommend the drafting of conventions in all, some, or none of the areas you suggest? (After reading Problem IV, return and reassess your answer to the last question.)

4. Professors McDougal and Arens, writing in support of U.S. ratification of the Genocide Convention in 1950, correctly predicted that it was but the first of many international human rights treaties to follow. See McDougal and Arens, The Genocide Convention and the Constitution, 3 Vand. L. Rev. 683 (1950). See also the list of UN treaties on pages 185-187 supra. Is it just a matter of time before constitutional and other objections to

full U.S. participation in these treaty regimes must give way to a broader national public policy that reflects the sense of the international community? McDougal and Arens correctly envisioned that the Fourteenth Amendment would play a key role in widening the scope of federally secured individual rights in the United States, noting that "[t]he same forces that are operating on a global scale to make the world one for . . . human rights . . . are operating even more intensely to make the nation one for these same values, and constitutional interpretation and practice move . . . at an accelerating tempo toward a structure rationally designed to secure the national interest." Id. at 708. Presumably they thought that the Senate as well as the judiciary would benefit from such an enlightened view. But compare it with the later opinion of Ambassador Hauser, the U.S. representative to the Commission on Human Rights in the early 1970s: "[O]ur Senators, unlike legislators in other countries, feel there is no need for American citizens to turn outside of the United States for protection and remedies." Hauser, United Nations Law on Racial Discrimination, 1970 Am. Socy. Intl. L. Proceedings 114, 118. With whose view do you agree? Why? What does the recent ratification of the Covenant and other human rights treaties tell us in this regard?

5. In the Baboeram communication, the Human Rights Committee found that Suriname had violated Article 6(1) of the Civil and Political Covenant and urged it to take four specific steps to remedy the situation and redress the violations. See page 237 supra. The communication also alleged violations of Articles 7, 9, 10, 14, and 17. Reread these articles and decide, on the basis of the facts set out in the communication, whether they, too, were violated. The Committee sidestepped the issue by stating that, in the circumstances, it found it unnecessary "to consider assertions that other provisions of the Covenant were violated." Why did the Committee not decide? If you had been a member, what would have been your view? Recall that Suriname's initial report was submitted before the incident that gave rise to the communication, and that it has filed no subsequent report. In evaluating the respective importance of state reporting and individual petitions, is not this fact an exceptionally persuasive argument in favor of ratification of the Optional Protocol?

6. As noted earlier in this Problem (see page 214 supra), 76 of the 127 states parties to the Civil and Political Covenant also have ratified the Optional Protocol. Nearly one-half are from Europe (Western and Eastern), few are from Africa or Asia, and none is from the Middle East. What can be done to bring about wider ratification of the Protocol? Is the United States, not having ratified the Protocol itself, in any position to point the finger at other states?

7. Despite U.S. ratification of the Civil and Political Covenant "warts and all," including a declaration that purports to deny the treaty legal effect within the country, the United States still remains legally obligated on the international plane to guarantee that non-reserved rights are respected.

True, individuals cannot raise questions about the fulfillment of such obligations before the Human Rights Committee, since the United States has not ratified the Optional Protocol, and it is highly unlikely that they will be raised via the interstate complaint procedure, at least in the near future. However, the United States still is subject to the periodic reporting requirement, and it can expect a comprehensive and thorough ventilation of its first and subsequent reports by the Committee. Indeed, two U.S. NGOs already have provided detailed information alleging U.S. violations of its legal obligations in the following areas: race discrimination, sex discrimination, language rights, immigrants and refugees, prison conditions, police brutality, the death penalty, freedom of expression, and religious liberty. See Human Rights Watch and American Civil Liberties Union, Human Rights Violations in the United States: A Report on U.S. Compliance with the International Covenant on Civil and Political Rights (Dec. 1993). For other ways in which ratification of the Covenant may have a positive and progressive impact upon the United States, see Neier, Political Consequences of the United States Ratification of the International Covenant on Civil and Political Rights, 42 DePaul L. Rev. 1233 (1993); Ginger, The Energizing Effect of Enforcing a Human Rights Treaty, id. at 1341.

8. Finally, while this Problem has shown that there is a great body of UN-sponsored human rights treaty law extant, it by no means has exposed the reader to the full range of treaty and other standards that now exist and are growing apace. Problem IV considers the "soft law" approach to establishing human rights norms; Problem IX and X take up the growing body of regional human rights law; Problem XI explores the often-overlooked importance of the law of war (or humanitarian law) and its relation to human rights law; and Problem XII introduces the subject of international criminal law and how it might be used to protect the rights of individuals and groups. In short, there is plenty of international human rights law available in the world today; the task of the international human rights lawyer is to identify what the relevant law is and, far more difficult in most instances, to find a forum for enforcing it.

A note of caution, however, is advisable. As the table on pages 185-187 supra shows, not all human rights treaties, UN or otherwise, are widely ratified. Moreover, even when ratified, their full impact often cannot be brought to bear upon a state's conduct because it has made reservations, declarations, understandings, and other statements at the time it ratified the instrument in question. Even absent reservations or the like, the treaties themselves, as we have seen, generally contain limitation and derogation clauses that can be invoked to restrict the rights guaranteed by the treaty. Thus, even if one assumes that the major effort to codify the substance of international human rights law is nearly complete, much remains to be done to make that law truly applicable to more states and in more situations, extending what too often today are mere textual protections to human beings.

Problem IV

The "Soft" Law
of Principles, Guidelines,
and Model Laws

How Does the UN Create New Human Rights Norms Other Than by Treaty?

I.	*The Attica Uprising*	278
	A. Background and Aftermath	278
	B. Current Attitudes Toward Treatment of Prisoners	281
	C. International Norms Governing the Treatment of Prisoners	283
	Besharov and Mueller, The Demands of the Inmates of Attica State Prison and the United Nations Standard Minimum Rules for the Treatment of Prisoners: A Comparison	285
	D. Status of the Standard Minimum Rules	296
	The Standard Minimum Rules for the Treatment of Prisoners in the Light of Recent Developments in the Correctional Field	296
II.	*Applying the "Model Law" or "Soft Law" Approach to Related Areas*	300
	A. General Observations	300
	Toman, Quasi-Legal Standards and Guidelines for Protecting Human Rights	300
	N. Rodley, The Treatment of Prisoners Under International Law	301
	Heijder, Codes of Professional Ethics Against Torture	302
	B. Specific Areas	304
	1. Treatment of Prisoners	305
	2. Juvenile Offenders	305
	3. Standards for the Administration of Justice	306
III.	*Implementation of the Standard Minimum Rules and Other Criminal Justice Norms*	306
	R.S. Clark, The United Nations Crime Prevention and Criminal Justice Program	307
	Report of the Working Group on Arbitrary Detention	311
	A. Regional Standards: European Prison Rules	313
	B. National Standards: United States Federal and State Laws and Regulations (and Their Enforcement)	314
	C. Non-Governmental and Private Organization Standards	317
	Comments and Questions	318
IV.	*New Rights for Vulnerable Groups*	322
	A. General Observations	322
	B. Minorities	324
	Hannum, Contemporary Developments in the International Protection of the Rights of Minorities	324

Human Rights Committee, General Comment No. 23(50)
(Art. 27)   327
UN General Assembly Resolution 47/135   329
Note: Implementation   330
Note: European Initiatives   331
C.   Indigenous Peoples   332
D.   Self-Determination   334
Comments and Questions   336
V.   Final Comments and Questions   337

I.   The Attica Uprising

A.   *Background and Aftermath*

In the fall of 1971, New York State Commissioner of Corrections Russell G. Oswald attempted to defuse prisoner unrest by promising certain reforms in the state prison system. In a message broadcast to inmates on September 3 (N.Y. Times, Sept. 16, 1971, at 43, col. 4), he stated:

> We will install full law libraries in six of our major institutions. These libraries will be for the use of inmates who need and desire access to legal reference materials.
>
> We'll conduct a program for training in meaningful rehabilitative methods of all institutional and parole personnel. . . . Academic and vocational programs will be extended into the evening hours in four of the major facilities on an experimental basis. . . . We are concerned with the quality of living in our facilities . . . [and with the] inconsistencies between institutions.
>
> These fall in the following areas: authorized personal possessions; personal state-issued items; problems relating to food service; standardized cell furnishings; health and dental service; standardization of a code of personal appearance; issues relative to recreation, sports activity and visiting, and issues relating to recognition of mutual rights and responsibilities of both staff and inmates. . . . I appreciate your patience, trust and confidence in what we are trying to do together.

On September 13, an assault force consisting of 211 State Troopers, backed by hundreds of National Guardsmen, correction officers, and sheriff's deputies, stormed the Attica State Correctional Facility in Attica, New York, where 1,281 rebel inmates had held over three dozen prison guards and civilian employees as hostages for four days. Thirty-two inmates and 11 guards died, and many more were injured. The assault by the forces of law was labelled by then-Newark Mayor Kenneth Gibson as "one of the most callous and blatantly repressive acts ever carried out by a supposedly civilized society. . . ." (N.Y. Times, Sept. 17, 1971, at 43, col. 2).

At the time of the uprising, about two-thirds of the 2,243 prisoners in

Attica were black or Puerto Rican. All 383 guards were white. Among the grievances voiced by the inmates were the following: little useful vocational training; solitary confinement often imposed for minor infractions; inmates allowed only one shower per week — although many worked for 30-50 cents per day in the metal shop, where the temperature apparently exceeded 100 degrees; one bar of soap and one roll of toilet paper as the maximum monthly allotment.

During negotiations that preceded the storming of the prison, authorities offered inmates 28 "concessions" in exchange for a peaceful end to the uprising. The refusal of inmate leaders to accept the proposed terms contributed to public outrage. The general tendency to lay blame for the Attica slaughter on the prisoners themselves was reflected in the remarks of then-Vice President Spiro Agnew following the incident (N.Y. Times, Sept. 17, 1971, at 43, col. 5).

> To position the "demands" of convicted felons in a place of equal dignity with the legitimate aspirations of law-abiding American citizens — or to compare the loss of life by those who violate the society's law with a loss of life of those whose job it is to uphold it — represents not simply an assault on human sensibility, but an insult to reason. . . . What happened at Attica proves once again that when the responsible voices of society remain mute, the forces of violence and crime grow arrogant. One need only recall the era of Hitler's Storm Troopers to realize what can happen to the most civilized of societies when such a cloak of respectability is provided thugs and criminals. . . .

In a revealing New York Times column responding to this public indignation (N.Y. Times, Sept. 19, 1971, §IV, at 15, col. 1), Tom Wicker* analyzed the proposed "concessions" and concluded that they represented little more than a grant of the most basic human necessities. Four points involved only the procedural arrangements for ending the inmate occupation. Nine points were mere recommendations to be made to the state legislature; no substantive change was promised. Twelve of the remaining points "represent 'concessions' of things that a decent and humane and sensible penal system ought to have been doing or permitting all along — for instance, religious freedom, allowing inmates to telephone relatives and friends at their own expense, providing a Spanish-speaking doctor or a medical interpreter and employing black and Puerto Rican guards. . . ." Wicker concluded that "only three points represent real 'steps forward' past a standard of bare minimum decency in the treatment of prisoners.

"These would have instituted an ombudsman program for prisoners, allowed them to be politically active and established regular inmate grievance procedures and some inmate voice in prison operations. . . ." Thus, the proffered settlement hardly would have responded to the Attica inmates' demands for a humane environment.

---

* Mr. Wicker served as one of the intermediaries between prisoners and prison officials during the uprising.

Conditions did not change after the uprising. The New York Times reported in the aftermath of the tragedy (N.Y. Times, Sept. 20, 1971, at 29, col. 1) that

> [m]embers of the Committee formed by Governor Rockefeller to safe-guard the rights of Attica prisoners reported today that 600 of them had been moved in the last week and that some had been interrogated by State investigators without having been advised of their legal rights.
>
> Inmates' lawyers who went inside the prison today said that prisoners they saw were still "terrified," unshaved, unbathed, without underwear and often without shoes.
>
> They said that their clients told them that some prisoners were being awakened at 3 A.M. for interrogation, and others had pistols held to their heads, or were threatened with castration. . . . "We're extremely distressed by this," said William E. Hellerstein, chief Appellate Counsel for the Legal Aid Society. "We've learned there have been persistent, round-the-clock interrogations of inmates, and they are not being warned of their constitutional right to remain silent and to have the assistance of counsel at an interrogation. . . ."
>
> Mr. Hellerstein said, "The rights of a prisoner with respect to questions of custodial interrogation, within the confines of prison walls, are certainly equal, and we believe, even greater under the law" than those of free men.

In fact, despite official attempts to ameliorate conditions after the 1971 uprising (see N.Y. Times, Dec. 15, 1974, at 70, col. 4), so little real improvement resulted that a similar, though less dramatic, outbreak of violence occurred on July 11, 1976, in which eight guards were injured and one inmate severely beaten. The chief of a State Commission of Correction team sent into Attica following the violence described conditions in the prison as "just as bad, perhaps worse" than prior to the September 1971 uprising (N.Y. Times, July 21, 1976, at 1, col. 3).

The situation has changed only gradually in the past two decades, and improvement has been only partial. In 1982 a report by the Correctional Association of New York, an independent prison study group formed in 1844, concluded that conditions at Attica were little different than they were before the 1971 riot. Correctional Association of New York, Attica 1982: An Analysis of Current Conditions in New York State Prisons 4 (1982). Another report the following year contended that racism, administrative indifference toward inmate grievances, physical abuse, and the lack of meaningful programs for most inmates, as well as inadequate medical care, poor visitation policies, and law library deficiencies, made conditions at Attica so "odious" that "only substantial, immediate changes will prevent more drastic [prisoners'] actions in the future." Prisoners' Legal Services of New York, Attica: A Report on Conditions, 1983, at 4 (1983).

Throughout the 1980s education and job-training programs were expanded, and legal services and grievance procedures were improved (Mangels, Prison Upheavals Usher in Changes, Cleveland Plain Dealer, Apr. 25, 1993, at 12C). Nevertheless, problems of racism and guard brutality remain. See Embers of the Attica Uprising Still Smolder, Newsday, Sept. 13, 1991, at 72 (Attica's corrections staff was more than 98 percent white, while over 80 percent of the inmates were non-white); Leven, Attica Remembered, N.Y.L.J., Aug. 29, 1991, at 2 (reporting an award of $65,000 to an Attica inmate who had been beaten).

Of course, the Attica riot was not the only U.S. prison riot in recent years. In 1980, 33 inmates were killed by other inmates in New Mexico's only maximum security facility during the 36 hours in which the prison was under their control. Although it has been suggested that corruption, the use of inmate "snitches," and poor administration were major factors in the riot, so were abysmal living conditions. "By the mid-seventies the New Mexico penitentiary was a physical as well as psychological horror. Rats and roaches infested the building. . . . Food practices were primitive and unsanitary. . . . With exposed and frayed wiring everywhere, successive fire marshals' reports warned of potential holocaust. On seeing the pen for the first time, a visiting warden thought it 'a national disgrace' and 'the filthiest institution I'd ever seen.' " Morris, The Devil's Butcher Shop: The New Mexico Prison Uprising 47 (1983), quoted in B. Useem and P. Kimball, States of Siege, U.S. Prison Riots, 1971-1986, at 96 (1989). In 1993 seven inmates and one guard were killed during an 11-day insurrection at Ohio's maximum security prison in Lucasville; again, prison conditions were at least partly to blame, and the emphasis had been decidedly on security and not on rehabilitation (Sharkey, Lucasville Was Easy to Predict, Cleveland Plain Dealer, Apr. 14, 1993, at 7B).

B.   Current Attitudes Toward Treatment of Prisoners

The Attica uprising and its aftermath raise the perennial question: what legal rights should prisoners have? The present legal status of a prisoner has been described by two authorities to "lie in the gray area between slaves and citizens." J. Gobert and N. Cohen, Rights of Prisoners 13 (1981). In many states in the United States, a convicted felon permanently loses the right to vote, the right to hold public office, and the right to serve on a jury. Prisoners have minimal rights to freedom of speech and assembly. No laws (either federal or state) provide an adequate minimum wage for work done by prisoners, and no system grants prisoners compensation for injuries suffered on the job. Compensation for prison labor is frequently below $1 a day for work that often is, in effect, compulsory. Id. at 196. There is no right to counsel in prison disciplinary proceedings. Moreover, an inmate bringing an action outside prison (with regard to an alleged violation of his rights while incarcerated) assumes a heavier than normal burden of proof. Thus, as the above authorities remark, "no necessary correlation exists between the status of a constitutional right inside and out of prison." Id. at 14. Or, put more graphically, "[p]risons have been such a garbage can of society that they have been a garbage can of the law as well." *

Before examining the issue of how the imprisoned should be treated, one must understand the development of society's views as to the purpose of criminal incarceration. Are prisons meant to punish, to deter, or to rehabilitate? Should they inflict the maximum suffering on the offender or offer him the maximum opportunity for readjustment and self-improvement? Is the grim correctional facility a deterrent to crime or a breeding ground for more experienced and embittered offenders? Is "rehabilitation" possible at all, and if so, is it really best accomplished by humane treatment?

The answers to these questions — indeed, the questions themselves — have changed radically in recent decades. One scholar has compared succinctly the three major divergent views. H. Packer, The Limits of the Criminal Sanction 9-12 (1968). Traditionalists still view the correctional system in a retributive framework; according to this view, the oldest penological perspective,

> man is a responsible moral agent to whom rewards are due when he makes right moral choices and to whom punishment is due when he makes wrong ones. . . . There is a perceived sense of fitness in the sight of wrongdoers being made to suffer for their misdeeds. As individuals we have a wholly proper desire to seek revenge when wrongs are inflicted on us; as a society we demand that constituted authority punish those who unjustifiably inflict injury on others or otherwise act in ways we think are wrong. . . . The purpose of punishment is to inflict deserved suffering. . . .

More moderate observers of the correctional process see its purpose as essentially deterrent: first, the criminal is removed from society, thereby deprived (at least for a time) of opportunity to commit further offenses; second, the unpleasant prospect of such confinement serves to discourage potential offenders on the outside. In Packer's words:

> This view rejects retribution as a basis for punishment on the ground that suffering is always an evil and that there is no justification for making people suffer unless some secular good can be shown to flow from doing so.

In recent years the deterrent position has evolved toward what is characterized as a "behavioral" perspective. Packer identifies four principles on which behaviorists premise their correctional philosophy:

> First, free will is an illusion, because human conduct is determined by forces that lie beyond the power of the individual to modify. Second, moral responsibility . . . is an illusion, because blame cannot be ascribed for behavior that is ineluctably conditioned. Third, human conduct, being causally determined,

---

* Unpublished remarks of Professor Herman Schwartz, now Professor of Law at the Washington College of Law, American University, and one of the intermediaries between prisoners and prison officials during the Attica uprising.

can and should be scientifically . . . controlled. Fourth, the function of the criminal law should be purely and simply to bring into play processes for modifying the personality and hence the behavior, of people who commit antisocial acts, so that they will not commit them in the future; or, if all else fails, to restrain them from committing offenses by the use of external compulsion (e.g., confinement).

Taking its cue from the scientific community, which has altered its own perspective on the purposes and practices of incarceration, the lay public now at least pays lip service to the proposition that decent prison conditions certainly will not detract from the deterrent function of the penal sanction, and that indeed such conditions, in some cases, even may contribute to the "rehabilitation" of the offender. Voices embodying the retributive position continue to be raised, however, and, in a world where both the number and the seriousness of crimes are rising, public outrage against the criminal tends to weigh heavily against whatever concern may be felt for his lot after he is imprisoned.

There also is a growing emphasis on security over rehabilitation in the U.S. prison system, at both federal and state levels. According to Human Rights Watch, the federal super-maximum security (or "maxi-maxi") prison in Marion, Illinois, has served as a model for similar institutions designed by 36 states. Human Rights Watch, Prison Conditions in the United States 3 (1991). Such prisons typically house inmates who have committed serious crimes while incarcerated; they normally spend up to 23 hours a day in their cells. Security has been taken to new technological heights in the California state prison at Pelican Bay, where there are no windows and electronic monitoring records all conversations and even footsteps. See White, Inside the Alcatraz of the '90s, Cal. Law. 42 (Apr. 1992). However, "the increasing use of 'prisons within prisons,' that is, special wards or separate institutions with much harsher regimes, leads to numerous human rights abuses and frequent violations of the U.N. Standard Minimum Rules." Human Rights Watch, Prison Conditions in the United States 3-4 (1991).

C. International Norms Governing the Treatment of Prisoners

The attitude of the international community toward the treatment of prisoners also has evolved in recent years. Article 5 of the Universal Declaration of Human Rights states a broad, general norm:

No one shall be subjected to torture or to cruel, inhuman or degrading treatment or punishment.

Article 10(1) of the International Covenant on Civil and Political Rights applies this norm specifically to the treatment of prisoners, while Article

10(3) adopts the behavioral view that prisoners can be rehabilitated if treated humanely:

> 1. All persons deprived of their liberty shall be treated with humanity and with respect for the inherent dignity of the human person. . . .
>
> 3. The penitentiary system shall comprise treatment of prisoners the essential aim of which shall be their reformation and social rehabilitation.

While the rehabilitative approach has influenced most recent attempts to codify minimum standards of humane treatment for prisoners on the international and regional levels, it appears to have become less important in the eyes of the U.S. government. In an "understanding" filed at the time it ratified the Civil and Political Covenant, for example, the United States stated that "paragraph 3 of Article 10 does not diminish the goals of punishment, deterrence, and incapacitation as additional legitimate purposes for a penitentiary system." 138 Cong. Rec. S4783 (daily ed. Apr. 2, 1992).

Rather than being adopted through internationally binding treaties, most new norms in the areas of criminal justice and treatment of prisoners have taken the form of "soft law," that is, principles, guidelines, and model laws designed to encourage the adoption of comparable national standards. As noted by Toman, infra at pages 300-301, the widespread acceptance of "soft" norms also may play an important role in providing persuasive interpretations of domestic and international law, as well as eventually contributing to the development of new customary international law.

While this approach probably has been applied more widely in the area of prisoners' rights than in any other human rights context, it has subsequently been applied to issues as varied as religious discrimination, self-determination, minority rights, development, the rights of disabled or mentally ill persons, and the rights of non-citizens. This Problem will first consider the development of norms in the field of criminal justice and will then discuss similar approaches utilized in other illustrative areas in which the adoption of norms through treaties was not feasible or desirable.

The basic international prison regulations are the Standard Minimum Rules for the Treatment of Prisoners (Documentary Supplement). The Rules were first drawn up in 1933 by the International Penal and Penitentiary Commission and approved by the Assembly of the League of Nations in 1934. After World War II the Rules were revised by the Secretariat of the United Nations and endorsed by the UN's First Congress on the Prevention of Crime and the Treatment of Offenders in 1955. For a historical perspective on the Rules, see Clifford, The Standard Minimum Rules for the Treatment of Prisoners, 66 Am. Socy. Intl. L. Proceedings 232 (1972). In 1957 the UN Economic and Social Council formally approved the Rules. E.S.C. Res. 663 (XXIV)C, 24 U.N. ESCOR Supp. (No. 1) at 11, U.N. Doc. E/3048 (1957). Drawing the attention of all governments to them, the Council recommended:

(a) That favourable consideration be given to their adoption and application in the administration of penal and correctional institutions.
(b) That the Secretary-General be informed every five years of the
progress made with regard to their application.

The following analysis of the Attica inmates' demands gives some sense
of how the adoption and implementation of the Rules might alter present
conditions in U.S. correctional facilities.

Besharov and Mueller, The Demands of the Inmates of Attica State Prison and the United Nations Standard Minimum Rules for the Treatment of Prisoners: A Comparison
21 Buff. L. Rev. 839, 839-854 (1972)

The recent tragic disturbances in various American and foreign prisons
have dramatized anew the enduring and painful questions concerning the
treatment of those of our fellow citizens who, by operation of law, have been
temporarily or permanently removed from free society and confined into
institutions called prisons. Almost without exception, the inmates who participate in such disturbances make a series of "demands" on the authorities
regarding the nature of their confinement and management. Much has and
more will be written about the reasons for the outbreaks and the reasonableness of the demands made. This article is limited to one small, but we
think not insignificant issue, namely, the similarity of the Attica demands
to the United Nations Standard Minimum Rules for the Treatment of Prisoners. . . .

The Rules are not a part of international criminal law in the strict
sense, and thus, are "not binding" in the sense of enforceability. In their
own words, the Rules "seek only . . . to set out what is generally accepted as
being good principle and practice in the treatment of prisoners and the
management of institutions." In that light, the Rules are meant to be binding on the conscience of Nations.

Although, thus, not "international law," the Rules demonstrate and
voice the international concern for the recognition and protection of prisoners' rights. They describe the "minimum conditions which are accepted as
suitable by the United Nations." Basically, "the Rules inject the humanitarian spirit of the Universal Declaration of Human Rights into the correctional system without compromising public safety or prison security."

Specifically, the Rules deal with such issues as a register of inmates,
separation of categories of prisoners, accommodations, personal hygiene,
clothing and bedding, food, exercise and sport, medical services, discipline
and punishment, instruments of restraint, information to and complaints by
prisoners, contact with outside, books, religion, retention of prisoners' prop-

erty, notification of death, illness, transfer, etc., institutional personnel, inspection, treatment, classification and individuation, privileges, work, education and recreation, social relations and after care, insane and mentally abnormal prisoners, prisoners under arrest or awaiting trial, and civil prisoners.

Due to the lack of any governmental machinery capable of properly receiving and recording the prisoners' demands at the time of the Attica rebellion . . . there remains a dispute as to what and how many demands were actually made on the authorities. While according to one source, the Attica prisoners, at least initially, made only a few but politically pungent demands, all newspaper accounts reported that, through the committee of observers, they made thirty demands on the prison authorities. The demands covered the issues of food, shelter, return to cells and amnesty, work, complaints and ombudsman, political action, religious freedom, contact with outside world, treatment and education, narcotics treatment, legal assistance, recreation, medical treatment, minority personnel, inmate funds, resentencing and parole, discipline, implementation, complete amnesty from criminal prosecution for the uprising itself and for any incidents arising therefrom and the dismissal of the Warden. All but the last two demands were "accepted" by the State Commissioner of Correctional Services.

The Attica demands were striking in their similarity to the United Nations Standard Minimum Rules for the Treatment of Prisoners. With few exceptions, each Attica demand has a parallel if not identical counterpart in the Rules.

Food

The inmates' first Demand was for adequate food and water; Demand #15 is even more specific: "Provide a healthy diet, reduce the number of pork dishes, increase fresh fruit daily." The parallel provision in the United Nations Standard Minimum Rules is Rule 20 (1):

> Every prisoner shall be provided by the administration at the usual hours with food of nutritional value adequate for health and strength, of wholesome quality and well prepared and served.

Return to Cells and Amnesty

Demands #2 and #3 refer to the manner in which the rebelling inmates were to be permitted to return to their cells, at the end of the uprising, and their protection against administrative reprisals, and their subsequent amnesty. While prison uprisings, as such, are not dealt with in the Rules, in light of the charges that have been brought by Attica prisoners in federal court, alleging brutality by state police and prison guards, the following two rules come into play:

> 31. Corporal punishment . . . shall be completely prohibited as punishments for disciplinary offenses.
> 54. (1) Officers of the institutions shall not, in their relations with prisoners, use force except in self-defense or in cases of attempted escape, or active or passive physical resistance. . . .

The issue of amnesty does not arise under the Rules, and American law on the issue of amnesty is extremely undeveloped.

WORK

In Demand #4 the inmates requested "the application of the New York State Minimum Wage Law standards to all work done by inmates." The Rules require:

> 76. (1) There shall be a system of equitable remuneration of the work of prisoners.

The duty to remunerate equitably would seem equivalent or nearly equivalent to the wage set by the state legislature as the minimum required. Such a system of full remuneration has indeed developed in some of the more advanced countries, e.g., Sweden. New York State, on the other hand, seems to authorize payment of 10¢ per day for inmate labor. *

Of course, if inmates are being paid minimum wages, they must expect to contribute to their living expenses, as do those on the outside who are paid the same wages.

COMPLAINTS AND OMBUDSMAN

Demand #5 and Demand #18 call for the establishment of an Ombudsman and an inmate grievance commission, respectively. In our view, these Demands are not only in accord with the spirit of the United Nations Standard Minimum Rules, but, in fact, go to their very heart. By providing elaborate complaint and inspection procedures, the Rules codify a complaint and inspection system in the tradition of continental law which has long utilized a special judge, called in the Italian system the "Surveillance Judge," who has the exclusive jurisdiction over the proper, lawful and hu-

---

* As of April 1994, New York state prison inmates who are non-industrial workers are paid at a beginning rate of $.10 an hour and may make up to $2 a day. Industrial workers are paid at a beginning rate of $.16 an hour and may make up to $.65 an hour. Inmates who are willing to work when jobs are not available are paid $.45 a day. Inmates are normally paid once a week, based upon a six-hour, five-day week. Source: Robert Cavosie of the Department of Correctional Services in Albany, New York. — EDS.

mane execution of prison sentences, which after all are court orders. (By contrast, the American judiciary has until recently adhered strictly to a judicial "hands-off" doctrine under which they refused "to enter the domain of penology.") In terms of preventing future prison disturbances, this may be the most far-reaching aspect of both the Rules and the Demands. For elementary psychology is cognizant of the fact that whenever large numbers of human beings are confined in close quarters, frictions increase to potentially explosive effect. The cathartic effect of an authentic governmental grievance machinery which would provide an outlet for complaints and dissatisfaction is self-evident.

The Rules provide:

> 55. There shall be regular inspection of penal institutions and services by qualified and experienced inspectors appointed by a competent authority. Their task shall be in particular to ensure that these institutions are administered in accordance with existing laws and regulations and with a view to bringing about the objectives of penal and correctional services.
> 36.   (1) Every prisoner shall have the opportunity each weekday of making requests or complaints to the director of the institution or the officer authorized to represent him.
> (2) It shall be possible to make requests or complaints to the inspector of prisons during his inspection. The prisoner shall have the opportunity to talk to the inspector or to any other inspecting officer without the director or other members of the staff being present.
> (3) Every prisoner shall be allowed to make a request or complaint, without censorship as to substance but in proper form, to the central prison administration, the judicial authority or other proper authorities through approved channels.
> (4) Unless it is evidently frivolous or groundless, every request or complaint shall be promptly dealt with and replied to without undue delay.

As part of the complaints and inspection mechanism, the Rules require regular inspections by the medical doctor permanently assigned to the prison. The medical officer is expected to review such things as (1) the inmates' food, (2) the hygiene and cleanliness of the institution and of prisoners, (3) living conditions, (4) prisoners' clothing, and (5) the rules concerning physical education and sports. The doctor reports to the prison director who must act on the doctor's findings unless he does not concur, in which case he must submit them along with his own report to higher authorities.

POLITICAL ACTION

The sixth Demand was for the right to be politically active. The Rules do not deal specifically with this issue. However, it is a "guiding principle" of the Rules that "the treatment of prisoners should emphasize not their exclusion from the community, but their continuing part in it." Sub silentio, therefore, the Rules extend the correctional process to civic, and thus, political activity, for purposes of enhancing a prisoner's resocialization.

Religious Freedom

Demand #7 simply states: "Allow true religious freedom." One would suspect that this demand arises, at least in part, from the difficulties the establishment — any establishment — has in accepting and dealing with an unusual religion or sect, in this case that of the Black Muslims. The Rules deal very specifically with such questions as access to representatives of one's religion, regular services, pastoral visits and freedom of having no religion. For example, Rule 41 (3) provides:

> Access to a qualified representative of any religion shall not be refused to any prisoner. On the other hand, if any prisoner should object to a visit of any religious representative, his attitude shall be fully respected.

Although the Rules do not deal with such specifics as unusual religious observances, e.g., a different sabbath or special diet, Rule 42 provides:

> So far as practicable, every prisoner shall be allowed to satisfy the needs of his religious life by attending the services provided in the institution and having in his possession the books of religious observance and instruction of his denomination.

Contact with the Outside World

Another aspect of maintaining a prisoner's sense of being part of the community is the nature and quality of his contact with the outside world. Once again, the Rules and the Demands are substantially alike.

An important bridge between the outside world and the prison is formed by books and periodicals. In Demand #8, the inmates postulated:

> End all censorship of newspapers, magazines and other publications from publishers, unless it is determined by qualified authority, which includes the ombudsman, that the literature presents a clear and present danger to the safety and security of the institution.

Rule 90 takes this position precisely:

> An untried prisoner shall be allowed to procure at his own expense or at the expense of a third party such books, newspapers, writing materials and other means of occupation as are compatible with the interests of the administration of justice and the security and good order of the institution.

Although this Rule has been placed in the section dealing with prisoners awaiting trial, there is no reason to limit its application to pretrial detainees. However, Rule 39, in the section of Rules of general applicability, is more limiting:

> Prisoners shall be kept informed regularly of the more important items of news by the reading of newspapers, periodicals or special institutional publications, by hearing wireless transmissions, by lectures or by any similar means as authorized or controlled by the administration.

This is the first of the very few instances where the prisoners' demands reflect a more liberal standard than the Rules provide.

The most important contact with the outside world is, of course, personal contact. Thus, Demand #9 provided that inmates be allowed "at their own expense to communicate with anyone they please," and Demand #23 called for the "end [of] approved lists for correspondents and visitors." Demand #24 was for the removal of "visitation screens as soon as possible." The applicable provision in the Rules is Rule 37, which provides:

> Prisoners shall be allowed under necessary supervision to communicate with their family and reputable friends at regular intervals both by correspondence and by receiving visits.

Rule 37 limits correspondence and visits to "family and reputable friends." The determination of reputability is presumably left to the authorities. Hence, on the issue of freedom to correspond and receive visitors, the Attica prisoners again, as in the area of receipt of publications, seemed to have asked for freer contact with the outside world than the Rules would appear to allow.

TREATMENT

The institution of "realistic, effective rehabilitation programs for all inmates according to their offense and personal needs" was the inmates' tenth Demand. Demand #22 requested, in particular, the necessary legislation and appropriations for expanded work release programs. The theme of rehabilitation through treatment resounds throughout the Rules, both explicitly and implicitly. Rule 59 is the most concise statement of this theme:

> To this end, the institution should utilize all the remedial, educational, moral, spiritual and other forces and forms of assistance which are appropriate and available, and should seek to apply them according to the individual treatment needs of the prisoners.

In addition, the Rules prescribe the kind of work to which prisoners should be assigned. Among other requirements, the Rules mandate that the work provided be such as will maintain and increase the prisoners' "ability to earn an honest living after release," that vocational training be provided and that, as much as possible, the prisoners be "able to choose the type of work they wish to perform." These provisions lend support, albeit inferentially, to the demand concerning work release programs.

During the discussions of the Standard Minimum Rules at the Fourth United Nations Congress on the Prevention of Crime and the Treatment of Offenders in 1970 [Kyoto Congress], extension of the Rules to work release programs and similar non-institutional treatment modes was recommended to the Economic and Social Council for inclusion in the contemplated redraft of the Minimum Rules.

EDUCATION

The eleventh Demand was for the "modernization" of the "inmate education system, including the establishment of a [Spanish-language] library." Rule 77 reads, in part:

> (1) provision shall be made for the further education of all prisoners capable of profiting thereby. . . .
> (2) So far as practicable, the education of prisoners shall be integrated with the educational system of the country so that after their release they may continue their education without difficulty.

In addition, Rule 40 provides:

> Every institution shall have a library for the use of all categories of prisoners, adequately stocked with both recreational and instructional books, and prisoners shall be encouraged to make full use of it.

Making "full use" of a library would seem to imply that at least some of the books be in the language of substantial numbers of prisoners. The need to deal with languages other than that of the majority is dealt with in, for example, Rule 51 which provides for the use of interpreters where necessary.

LEGAL ASSISTANCE

Demand #13 was for "adequate legal assistance. . . ." Rule 93 provides for the availability of legal assistance, although in the context of prisoners awaiting trial.

> For the purposes of his defense, an untried prisoner shall be allowed to apply for free legal aid where such aid is available, and to receive visits from his legal advisor with a view to his defense. . . .

While the drafters of the Rules clearly did not contemplate the elaborate post-conviction remedies that have developed during the past decade in American jurisprudence, it might be said in their defense, that had they anticipated it, they would probably have included provisions for assistance of counsel in actions seeking post-conviction relief.

RECREATION

The fourteenth Demand is to "[r]educe cell time, increase recreation time and provide better recreational facilities. . . ." Throughout, the Rules set a high priority on the physical and mental well-being of prisoners. On this specific topic, they provide:

> 21. (1) Every prisoner who is not employed in outdoor work shall have at least one hour of suitable exercise in the open air daily if the weather permits.
> 21. (2) Young prisoners, and others of suitable age and physique, shall receive physical and recreational training during the period of exercise. To this end space, [sic] installations and equipment should be provided.

MEDICAL TREATMENT

Demand #12, reflecting the needs of inmates who were narcotics addicts, asked for "an effective treatment program for all prisoners requesting such treatment." Demand #16 called for "adequate medical treatment for every inmate" and Spanish speaking doctors or interpreters. Demand #27 was to "[p]ermit access to outside dentists and doctors at the inmates own expense within the institution where possible and consistent with scheduling problems, medical diagnosis and health needs." The Rules place greater importance on the need for medical services and the role of prison medical personnel in both providing medical service and performing inspections. Rule 22(1) requires that every institution have available the services of at least one "qualified" medical officer. Rule 24 provides, in part:

> The medical officer shall see and examine every prisoner as soon as possible after his admission and thereafter as necessary, with a view particularly to the discovery of physical or mental illness and the taking of all necessary measures. . . .

Rule 51(2) provides for the use of interpreters "wherever necessary" and this would apply for medical personnel as well. The only provision in the Rules for prisoner treatment by outside doctors or dentists is found in Rule 91, which applies only to prisoners awaiting trial. It provides:

> An untried prisoner shall be allowed to be visited and treated by his own doctor or dentist if there is reasonable ground for his application and he is able to pay any expenses incurred.

No reason is given why this provision does not also apply to prisoners under sentence.

Minority Personnel

Institution of "a program for the recruitment and employment of a significant number of black and Spanish-speaking officers" was the prisoners' seventeenth Demand. As envisioned by the Rules, prison staff should be professional, capable and fully trained in a variety of areas. Except for Rule 51, no reference is made to language differences and in no Rule is nationality or racial difference mentioned. The Rules simply do not contemplate different nationalities or races within one country, or at least they do not contemplate this to be an aspect of prison life which must be dealt with. Nevertheless, the general intent of the Rules is evident in Rule 51, which reads as follows:

> (1) The director, his deputy, and the majority of the other personnel of the institution shall be able to speak the language of the greatest number of prisoners, or a language understood by the greatest number of them.
> (2) Whenever necessary, the services of an interpreter shall be used.

Inmate Funds

Two Demands concern inmate funds. Demand #19 asks for an investigation of "the alleged expropriation of inmate funds and the use of profits from the metal and other shops." In relation to requested minimum wage payments for prisoners' work, Demand #4 calls for "[e]very effort . . . to make the records of payments available to inmates." Two provisions in the Rules apply to these Demands.

> 43. (1) All money, valuables, clothing and other effects belonging to a prisoner which under the regulations of the institution he is not allowed to retain shall on his admission to the institution be placed in safe custody. . . .
> 76. (1) There shall be a system of equitable remuneration of the work of prisoners.
> 76. (3) The system should also provide that a part of the earnings should be set aside by the administration so as to constitute a savings fund to be handed over to the prisoner on his release.

Resentencing and Parole

The inmates made a series of demands concerning the administrative resentencing of inmates returning for parole violation, the prompt and fair holding of Menechino hearings, and the ending of charges of parole violation for moving traffic violations or driving without a license. There are no direct or parallel provisions in the Rules, it being customary for most foreign legal systems to properly regulate such matters through their codes of criminal procedure.

Discipline

Demand #25 was for a "30-day maximum for segregation arising out of any one offense." Although the Rules do not deal with such specificity with the question of segregation, Rules 27-32 present a standard for discipline of "firmness, but with no more restriction than is necessary for safe custody and well-ordered community life." "Segregation" can mean different things in different institutions and contexts, and therefore, the general proscription of Rule 31 would be applicable, particularly if "segregation" refers to the practice of caging a prisoner in a dark cell. Rule 31 outlaws such practices as follows:

> Corporal punishment, punishment by placing in a dark cell, and all cruel, inhuman and degrading punishments shall be completely prohibited as punishments for disciplinary offences.

Implementation

The final one of the roster of Demands "accepted" by the Commissioner of Corrections, Demand #28, concerns inspections by members of the observer committee to monitor the implementation of the Demands. It provides that if they are not satisfied with the implementation of the accepted demands, they are to bring the matter to the attention of Correctional Services. It can be assumed that should the Committee have been dissatisfied with the Commissioner's determination, it would have brought the matter to the attention of the public. Thus, even as to method of implementation, the Rules and the Demands are in accord. For, as recognized by a Working Paper of the United Nations Secretariat for the Kyoto Congress, the effectiveness of the United Nations Standard Minimum Rules largely depends upon "the extent to which they are publicized, propagated and understood by everyone likely to be concerned with or interested in the subject matter."

Conclusion

This comparison between the Rules and the Demands has been somewhat mechanical because it was not our purpose to comment on the propriety of either the Demands or the Rules. Our attitudes with respect to the policies embodied in the Rules and our views on humanitarian correctional policies have been dealt with extensively elsewhere. In this brief study, it has been solely our purpose to demonstrate the remarkable fact that almost every one of the Demands of the rebelling Attica inmates has a corollary in the United Nations Standard Minimum Rules for the Treatment of Prisoners. Hence, the prisoners demanded their putative rights as world citizens.

Furthermore, the basic elements of both the Minimum Rules and the Demands are accepted within the American corrections profession. The Manual of Corrections Standards, issued by the American Correction Association which represents American professional opinion on the subject has identical or parallel standards to both the Demands and the Rules. Indeed, the "Correctional Standards" have been considerably influenced by the United Nations Rules.

Up to this point in history, both the United Nations Standard Minimum Rules and the Correctional Standards of the American Correctional Association have rested in obscurity just as the entire area of prisoners' rights and correction reform has lain dormant. But all evidence now points to an awakened interest in and possible reform of American correctional processes and standards. . . .

Prisoners' rights litigation is pending in courts across the country. The traditional "hands-off" doctrine has at last been . . . curtailed in this area. In doing so, courts have ruled favorably on such topics covered by the Attica demands as medical care, discipline, work and wages, access to books, and freedom of religion.

Since we as a nation are clearly on the way toward recognizing and elaborating prisoners' rights as legally enforceable, we should accept and adopt the United Nations Standard Minimum Rules as a code of rights which already enjoys world recognition. Such a general acceptance of the Rules would be preferable to the route of unpredictable and expensive court litigation, point by point, standard by standard.

No one should deceive himself into thinking that the millennium of correctional justice will have arrived with successful prisoner's rights litigation. Even legislation will not be fully successful unless it is accompanied by public understanding and support. True reform can occur only if the hearts and minds are changed as well as the law. . . .

We cannot conclude without noting that much of the impetus for correctional law reform has come from the consumers of our corrections policy, the inmates of our prisons. Some of this impetus has come through litigation and court process. But it cannot be denied that a substantial amount of the current impetus for change has come from prison "disturbances" such as the one at Attica. And we acknowledge and respect the fact that the inmates who put their demands before the authorities, under the pressure of time and circumstance, demanded the same minimum standards which the world's correctional policy makers have agreed upon after years of study and deliberation. In fact, where the prisoners demanded more than the policy makers and theoreticians had granted them — especially the area of contact with the outside world — it may well be theory that needs adjustment to the demands coming from experience. We can in no

way condone violence and useless lawlessness that may have occurred in
some of the prison disturbances. On the other hand, we feel obliged to state
that any correctional law policy must comport at least with the United
Nations Standard Minimum Rules which are accepted by all mankind. It is
that which the prisoners demand.

D.   Status of the Standard Minimum Rules

Professors Besharov and Mueller close their excellent survey of the
relevance of the Standard Minimum Rules to the Attica uprising by stating
that they are "accepted by all mankind." While the Rules have been formally approved by the UN Economic and Social Council, they obviously
do not have the status of a General Assembly resolution such as the Universal Declaration of Human Rights (see pages 122-171 of Problem II), much
less that of a multilateral treaty (see generally Problem III). What, then, is
their precise legal status? What impact have they had on the prison systems
of the UN's member states? What steps have been taken to achieve their
implementation? What problems have yet to be solved, and what prospects
exist for future progress?

Over the years, the UN has addressed — and is still addressing — the
above questions. It continually reviews the Standard Minimum Rules in
light of current penological thinking in an effort to achieve greater success
with respect to their adoption and implementation. This duty is shared by
two components of the UN system little known even to most international
human rights lawyers: the Commission on Crime Prevention and Criminal
Justice of the Economic and Social Council (which was created in 1991 to
replace the former Committee on Crime Prevention and Control) and the
periodic (every five years) Congresses on the Prevention of Crime and the
Treatment of Offenders. The question of the legal status of the Rules is
considered in the following extract from a working paper prepared by the
Secretariat for the Fourth U.N. Congress.

The Standard Minimum Rules for the Treatment of Prisoners in the Light of Recent Developments in the Correctional Field

Working Paper by the Secretariat, 4 U.N. Congress on the
Prevention of Crime and the Treatment of Offenders 1, 13-18,
U.N. Doc. A/CONF.43/3 (1970)

IV.   LEGAL STATUS OF THE RULES

40. Acceptance by the United Nations and approval by the Economic
and Social Council, however important, are still not sufficient to invest the

Standard Minimum Rules with the force of international law. Nevertheless, the fact of this acceptance and adoption does serve to lend an international significance to the Rules superior by far to that enjoyed by international practices and standards which have not been so endorsed. The Secretary-General's request for periodic reporting, moreover, gives to the Rules an official status enjoyed by few matters under the jurisdiction of the United Nations. Through the periodic reports, the Secretary-General wishes to be kept informed about the progress of implementation, so that he will be in a position to inform the world of the status of enlightened correctional practice and the extension of the minimum conditions agreed upon by Member States. It has been widely recognized that the exercise of such a reporting power by the Secretary-General amounts, in itself, to a powerful incentive for nations to compete in improving the circumstances of those protected by the Rules.

41. There has always been a body of opinion advocating the raising of the Rules to a higher level of authority. As guidelines, the Rules depend for their effect upon their adoption by local, that is national or municipal, law. Such incorporation of the principles can be regarded either as local law embracing and giving formal authority to precepts which otherwise are not binding and have no more than a mild ethical validity or justification, or as local law recognizing standards of a higher moral and international authority which have a binding effect. . . .

A.   RULES AND CONVENTIONS

44. The fact that the Rules do not have the legal status of an international convention has frequently been raised and is a matter of concern to a number of organizations and countries which would prefer to see them given a more formal legal status and greater international significance. The Consultative Group felt that further consideration might be given to whether it would be both appropriate and feasible to embody certain of the Rules in a convention. . . . Others, too, have stressed the importance of imparting legal as well as moral force to the guidelines. . . .

47. It is important to observe here that, quite apart from the Rules, there is the Universal Declaration of Human Rights which applies to everyone, that is, to prisoners as well as to persons who have not been convicted. The right to life, liberty, education, work and a degree of leisure are all rights which are not always wholly (nor necessarily partially) abrogated by the commission of a crime. Logically, then it should not be necessary to spell out such basic rights separately for the benefit of any one group of persons in the population.

48. This is not the whole picture, however. It has to be remembered that not all nations have endorsed the Universal Declaration and that it, too, has its problems of implementation; and finally, that conviction followed by imprisonment is a special case involving a legal loss of personal liberty. The prisoner may not only be in danger of losing recognition of

his basic rights but also of not being able to protest effectively. It is often argued, therefore, that there is a special need for a convention to protect rights in the case of prisoners, and that if the Rules eventually became a convention there need be no difficulty in adjusting them to their special purpose. Such a convention or conventions could, in fact, have optional protocols dealing with additional methods of implementation and enforcement, as does the International Covenant on Civil and Political Rights.

49. The increased number of international conventions in recent years has been matched by a concern for their endorsement and implementation on a national scale. Not all countries are prepared to go through the local legislative process even when in principle they do not object to the terms of a convention. Many of the well-established conventions on human rights have not yet been accepted by some of the States which helped to draft them. Moreover, it has been pointed out at recent United Nations meetings that not all Governments which ratified a given convention necessarily implemented it fully, and obligations undertaken were being violated. It might just be possible that in some parts of the world the Rules already operate as effectively as certain types of conventions. If they are indeed widely accepted, the real question is not so much the prestige or authority of a translation into a convention, but the effect this would have on actual practice. One point of view, therefore, is that the Rules as they stand can be implemented in any country without any necessary formality, whereas the formal acceptance of a convention is sometimes technically difficult because of the need to pass through the usual formal channels of legislation, and resistance is greater. The opposite argument is that for the Rules to become a convention greater governmental activity is needed to initiate this, and to take a position on endorsement. Thus the pressure to conform to international standards is greater.

50. It is clear that the Rules already have considerable moral force and are beginning to acquire even greater international standing especially as they become the subject of reports to the Secretary-General, the focus of a number of different studies and the occasion for the results and findings of inquiries and studies to be submitted to an international Congress, as now. To convert the Rules into a convention or a series of conventions would certainly further enhance their international status. It would have the value of changing a set of moral obligations into a set of voluntarily accepted contractual obligations. Perhaps it might lead eventually to the adoption of international sanctions for non-compliance. It is difficult to escape the conclusion that this change would serve to emphasize their importance and bring them more forcibly to the attention of administrators and government officials who might not otherwise have known of their existence, and could thereby increase pressure towards conformity and implementation.

B.   THE EFFECT OF STATUS ON RECEPTION

51. The issue of the status of the Rules really emerges from the need to promote their recognition and implementation as effectively as possible. Clearly, they can and have inspired better prison regulations and have also improved practice but, ultimately, the Rules are effectively implemented, as indicated already, when they are incorporated into national or municipal law. It may be expected that this process will become more extensive with the increasing support which the Rules are receiving internationally, regionally and municipally. The underlying question which has not been answered is whether the Rules, becoming a convention and therefore more formally based in international law, will encourage or discourage this process of their reception into national law. One difficulty about seeking a solution now by trying a formal convention is that this is a step it will not be easy to retrace. There is undoubtedly a great deal of impatience in professional, academic and administrative circles at the slowness of the process by which the Rules become locally effective. Acceptance of the moral rightness of a set of principles is sometimes mocked by their complete or near complete disregard in practice. The strength of the demand for the Rules to be embodied in a convention derives largely from this impatience with the shortcomings of practice. It is argued that a convention, even if no more effective than the Rules are now, is at least the next logical step to international standards which will be binding and enforceable.

52. Another aspect of the same problem is the enforcement by national tribunals of the precepts of positive international law. Municipal court enforcement of international conventions in human rights, whether for prisoners or unconvicted persons would appear to present no insurmountable problems, but it is a very delicate procedure which has yet to be developed within the family of nations. It would certainly strengthen the movement for local adoption and enforcement to have international standards formally embodied in local laws and regulations. This process too would presumably be promoted by the Rules becoming a convention and therefore having a more accepted significance in international law. On the other hand, if the Rules are already so recognized as international standards, and if, as it appears, most nations are making bona fide attempts to live up to the standards espoused by the Rules, then they may not need to become a convention to achieve informal but effective local judicial recognition. There is a well-defined area of law which has been set up by judicial interpretation, whose scope in a given country depends largely upon precedent; but it also depends upon the individual lawyer's concept of standards. It is difficult to estimate for example the extent to which the interest and preoccupation with human rights in the past twenty years has affected conditions within countries by means of judicial interpretation.

53. There is, therefore, much to be said for both points of view. It seems that a convention could either help or hinder, but the weight of

opinion so far appears to favour a strengthening of the international status of the Rules. No doubt the issue can be resolved only by a major policy decision; it is, among other reasons, to consider whether a move towards such a decision should be made that this subject has been placed on the Congress agenda.

II. Applying the "Model Law" or "Soft Law" Approach to Related Areas

A. General Observations

Toman, Quasi-Legal Standards and Guidelines for Protecting Human Rights
in Guide to International Human Rights Practice 192, 208-209 (2d ed. H. Hannum ed. 1992)

Standards, guidelines, and principles constitute a form of "soft" law with notable influence and utility in protecting human rights. As an expression of policy and ideals rather than binding or "hard" law, standards set forth basic principles which have been agreed upon and elaborated by the United Nations or other organizations in the form of guidelines for international action and national legislation. While these instruments are not directly legally binding, they are more appropriately considered to be quasi-legal rather than nonlegal in their effect.

Standards provide recommendations and guidance for governments in developing national legislation. They also constitute important interpretive tools, for they are often based on or lead to the adoption of other internationally binding instruments.

International human rights standards may constitute elements of state practice and thus contribute to the formation of customary international law, although they are insufficient by themselves to create binding legal obligations. The cumulative enunciation of the same guideline in numerous non-binding texts may also contribute to expressing the *opinio juris* of the world community which is necessary to the development of customary law.

For decades, the only example of this "soft" law was the Standard Minimum Rules for the Treatment of Prisoners, adopted first by the League of Nations and later by the United Nations. In the mid-1970s, new standards began to appear, and since the 1980s they have proliferated, particularly in the field of criminal justice. . . .

The value of international standard-setting instruments varies in direct proportion to the extent they are publicized, utilized, and taken seriously by those affected by them. Much of human rights practice consists of persuasion rather than coercion, and the existence of agreed-upon international norms can assist that process of persuasion while avoiding (where appropriate) the adversary situation created where "violations" of human rights are alleged.

The quasi-legal nature of these international standards should not obscure the fact that they often interpret and implement fundamental human rights — the right to be free from torture, to receive a fair trial, to have the assistance of legal counsel, and other related rights. In this sense, they might be viewed as the international equivalent of administrative regulations, whose implementation will ensure that basic rights are effectively guaranteed.

N. Rodley, The Treatment of Prisoners Under International Law
279 (1987)

INTERNATIONAL CODES OF ETHICS FOR PROFESSIONALS

INTRODUCTION

One of the legacies of the Nuremberg and Tokyo war crimes trials was the recognition that, while the organs of the state may be responsible for the most appalling atrocities against those they are supposed to serve and protect, the evil acts themselves are committed not by abstract entities (the police, the judiciary, the military) against other abstract entities (the enemy within or without) but by individual men and women against other men and women. One result of this recognition has been the attribution of individual criminal responsibility to those guilty of some of the more egregious excesses with which this text is concerned [see Problems XI and XII].

Important as this formal legal response may be, it cannot be the sole solution to the problem. To paraphrase the Constitution of Unesco: since human rights violations begin in the minds of men, it is in the minds of men that the defenses of human rights must be constructed. The purpose of a code of ethics is to create a set of desired responses in each individual member of the group or profession to which the code is addressed. Since certain groups may be seen to be more vulnerable to, or more exposed to, demands that they (for example) inflict torture on perceived enemies of society, it is clearly necessary to create within such groups an ethos conducive to the rejection of such demands. The groups most directly concerned with torture and other violations of human rights are the police and other law enforcement officials, including the military, but doctors and other health personnel are also often affected, as too may be members of the legal profession.

Heijder, Codes of Professional Ethics
Against Torture
in Codes of Professional Ethics 3, 5-7 (Amnesty International, ACT 07/01/84, 1984)

FUNCTIONS OF CODES OF PROFESSIONAL CONDUCT

The regulation of professional behaviour has many sources. Most of these sources can be located in four different fields.

First, all professional bodies, and thus each individual member of the professions, work in the context of a given *political system*. This simple observation has disturbing implications in the case of professionals working in or connected with the service of the state. The values, goals and accepted means of the general political system are an important regulating force for professional behaviour. In an official document of the United Nations (A/CONF. 56/5, page 36) it is said that corruption within the police depends largely upon the influence, guidance and interest of the total society in the police. Such a statement also holds true for the attitude towards torture. The connivance of other significant persons in the political system is of crucial importance.

Second, within such an overall political system, no one works alone. The work is mostly done in *organizations and functional units*. Every professional has colleagues who exert influence by their opinion on his or her attitudes, behaviour and performance. The influence of social interaction in the professional group is pervasive and omnipresent.

Third, in general, and given certain conditions of information and publicity, *public opinion* is a regulating force too, either in a direct way or via the political system or the opinions of colleagues. In a way and to a certain degree, public opinion sets the boundaries for professional conduct. Hence the strenuous attempts to modify or manipulate public opinion.

Fourth, there are of course the *individual values*, which the professional expresses to a certain degree in his professional behaviour, too.

Each of these four fields — the political system, the professional group, public and individual opinion — can have its own value orientation and its different sets of rules of conduct. The question whether these four fields constitute a hierarchy of values is relevant only in case of conflicting values.

There are two categories of conflicts. First, there may be different values *in one field*, which under certain conditions may conflict. Thus we find in the general political system conflicts between the *raison d'Etat* and morality or between the concept of national sovereignty and individual human rights. Second, conflicts may arise between values not in one field alone but in different fields. Thus the general political system will find the preservation of national security an overriding consideration, while professionals such as doctors or lawyers defend human lives and human rights irrespective of the issue of security. In many situations the doctor, lawyer or police-man has to choose among competing values in the face of a variety of situations.

It is obvious that the professionals who are in the service of the state are most exposed to conflicting demands of allegiance. For their skills and expert knowledge are most easily perverted against their original intentions. In cases where such conflicts become manifest and a choice must be made, the individual will look for concrete orientation points to guide his behaviour.

When the individual is part of a professional group, he will be aware of what his colleagues do in the same situation. Since not only general recognition but a prolonged specialized training is a precondition for an occupation being recognized as a profession, he will have undergone during that training a process of anticipatory socialization. He is taught not only the skills of the job but also is oriented to the professional values and norms. The generative traits of a profession call for a measure of professional autonomy against the pressures of the general political system, public opinion and sometimes even one's own value orientation. Codes of professional conduct can be seen as a formalization of the more or less diffuse colleague opinion in the professional field. Sometimes the existence of a full-fledged code is even mentioned as one of the main traits of a profession. A code of professional conduct will help the individual to cope with the problems arising from the different demands of a situation. Its influence may even reach beyond that.

Preliminary to any self-determined act of behavior there is always a stage of examination and deliberation which we may call the definition of the situation. In many instances there is rivalry between the spontaneous definition of the situation made by someone and the definitions which others provide. The prison doctor should not see an enemy of the state on hunger-strike, he should see a patient. The defense lawyer should see a client entitled to a fair trial, not a security risk to be eliminated by judicial means. One aspect of morality is that it provides a generally accepted definition of the situation, expressed in some socially visible form.

There are several defining agencies in society. In fact, the four fields we referred to as sources for rules can be seen as harbouring several defining agencies. Institutions and professional groups offer standardized definitions of the situation, implying that the standard reaction of the individual is not only the expected, reasonable one, but the safe one too. That is why it is so important for doctors, lawyers and law enforcement personnel that their codes of professional conduct should enlarge upon the implications of Article 5 of the Universal Declaration of Human Rights, which addresses itself to "all people and all nations, every individual and every organ of society."

But will a code be an effective force? From a sociological point of view we can say that the reaction to an induced force will vary, depending, among other things, on the person's relation to the inducing agent. Rules and pressure to conform, coming from a friend or colleague, may be accepted in such a way that it acts more like one's own force. A force induced by a stranger or an enemy may be resisted and compliance may arouse conflicts and tensions. Thus a code of professional ethics can be a strong force since it is an acceptable induced force. The acceptance of an induced force sets up additional personal forces in the same direction, while rejection does the same in the opposite direction.

Once a code is established, we can expect — since attitudes and group affiliation are closely connected — that it will play its part in the process of shaping professional attitudes. In this way a code of professional ethics, as a model pattern of behaviour, exerts influence first of all on a conceptual level and only after some time and after some enforcement mechanisms are set in motion, on an operational level. So we can be modestly optimistic about the effectiveness of such codes.

From this general and not exhaustive survey we come to the criteria on which the merits of different proposals should be judged. There are, I suggest, three points on which to focus attention.

1.   Is the code more than a declaration of good intentions? Does it formulate real and detailed norms of conduct?
2.   Does the code provide for the mechanisms necessary for its implementation and enforcement?
3.   Does the code provide for freedom of information about its norms, reports on deviance and efforts to enforce its rules?

B.   Specific Areas

The "model law" approach of the Standard Minimum Rules or the "soft law" of principles and guidelines has been utilized frequently to develop international norms that protect, directly or indirectly, the rights of prisoners and detainees. The Compendium of United Nations Standards and Norms in Crime Prevention and Criminal Justice, published by the United Nations in 1992, UN Sales No. E.92.IV.1, includes 48 instruments that set international standards on issues ranging from international cooperation in combating crime and suppression of prostitution to codes of conduct or principles concerning law enforcement officials, judges, prosecutors, lawyers, and health personnel. Forty of these instruments, including four resolutions adopted in 1989 to implement substantive norms, have been adopted since 1980. Following the extraordinarily productive Eighth

UN Congress on the Prevention of Crime and the Treatment of Offenders in 1990, the UN General Assembly adopted eight resolutions on crime prevention and criminal justice; an additional 10 resolutions were adopted by the Congress itself or the 1990 session of the Economic and Social Council.

Space constraints prohibit more than a simple listing of some of the most important of these instruments, but their titles indicate the range of issues they address. For convenience, they are grouped under three major headings; the text of each document may be found in United Nations, Compendium of United Nations Standards and Norms in Crime Prevention and Criminal Justice, cited supra.

1. Treatment of Prisoners

Principles of Medical Ethics, G.A. Res. 37/194, 37 U.N. GAOR Supp. (No. 51) at 210, U.N. Doc. A/37/51 (1982)

Body of Principles for the Protection of All Persons Under Any Form of Detention or Imprisonment, G.A. Res. 43/173, 43 U.N. GAOR Supp. (No. 49) at 297, U.N. Doc. A/43/49 (1988)

Standard Minimum Rules for Non-Custodial Measures (The Tokyo Rules), G.A. Res. 45/110, 45 U.N. GAOR Supp. (No. 49) at 195, U.N. Doc. A/45/49 (1990)

Basic Principles for the Treatment of Prisoners, G.A. Res. 45/111, 45 U.N. GAOR Supp. (No. 49) at 199, U.N. Doc. A/45/49 (1990)

Safeguards Guaranteeing Protection of the Rights of Those Facing the Death Penalty, E.S.C. Res. 1984/50, U.N. ESCOR Supp. (No. 1) at 33, U.N. Doc. E/1984/92 (1984), Annex

Effective Prevention and Investigation of Extra-Legal, Arbitrary, and Summary Executions, E.S.C. Res. 1989/65, U.N. ESCOR Supp. (No. 1) at 52, U.N. Doc. E/1989/91 (1989), Annex

Declaration of Basic Principles of Justice for Victims of Crime and Abuse of Power, G.A. Res. 40/34, 40 U.N. GAOR Supp. (No. 53) at 213, U.N. Doc. A/40/53 (1985)

2. Juvenile Offenders

Standard Minimum Rules for the Administration of Juvenile Justice (The Beijing Rules), G.A. Res. 40/33, 40 U.N. GAOR Supp. (No. 53) at 206, U.N. Doc. A/40/53 (1985)

United Nations Rules for the Protection of Juveniles Deprived of Their

Liberty, G.A. Res. 45/113, 45 U.N. GAOR Supp. (No. 49) at 204, U.N. Doc. A/45/49 (1990)

Guidelines for the Prevention of Juvenile Delinquency (The Riyadh Guidelines), G.A. Res. 45/112, 45 U.N. GAOR Supp. (No. 49) at 200, U.N. Doc. A/45/49 (1990)

3. Standards for the Administration of Justice

Code of Conduct for Law Enforcement Officials, G.A. Res. 34/169, 34 U.N. GAOR Supp. (No. 46) at 185, U.N. Doc. A/34/46 (1979)

Basic Principles on the Independence of the Judiciary, Seventh U.N. Congress on the Prevention of Crime and the Treatment of Offenders, Report Prepared by the Secretariat, U.N. Doc. A/CONF. 121/22/Rev.1, at 58 (1985)

Basic Principles on the Use of Force and Firearms by Law Enforcement Officials, Eighth U.N. Congress on the Prevention of Crime and the Treatment of Offenders, Report Prepared by the Secretariat, U.N. Doc. A/CONF.144/28, at 110 (1990)

Basic Principles on the Role of Lawyers, Eighth U.N. Congress on the Prevention of Crime and the Treatment of Offenders, Report Prepared by the Secretariat, U.N. Doc. A/CONF.144/28, at 117 (1990)

Guidelines on the Role of Prosecutors, Eighth U.N. Congress on the Prevention of Crime and the Treatment of Offenders, Report Prepared by the Secretariat, U.N. Doc. A/CONF.144/28, at 188 (1990)

III. Implementation of the Standard Minimum Rules and Other Criminal Justice Norms

UN efforts with respect to prisoners' rights have combined the standard-setting activities outlined immediately above with varying attempts to monitor implementation of those standards. At first, efforts were directed primarily to the Standard Minimum Rules and consisted of surveys of national practice conducted by the Secretary-General. The results of these surveys (which depended entirely on the cooperation of states) were then communicated to the quinquennial Crime Congresses. The following reading outlines subsequent efforts at the international level to promote the Rules and related norms.

R. Clark, The United Nations Crime Prevention and Criminal Justice Program
238-242, 255, 259-260, 282-283 (1994)

It was not until 1984 that the Economic and Social Council, acting on a new recommendation of the Committee on Crime Prevention and Control, was moved to try harder and ultimately approved the so-called Procedures for the Effective Implementation of the Standard Minimum Rules for the Treatment of Prisoners (Procedures). . . .

The Procedures established a somewhat more precise reporting requirement than that in the earlier 1957 resolution. States were required to inform the Secretary-General every five years of the extent of the implementation, the progress made with regard to the application of the Rules, and the factors and difficulties, if any, affecting their implementation. This information would be conveyed mainly by responding to the Secretary-General's questionnaire. Taking into account these reports, as well as other relevant material available within the United Nations system, the Secretary-General was required to prepare independent periodic reports on progress made and to submit them to the Committee on Crime Prevention and Control. In preparing the independent reports, the Secretary-General was authorized to enlist the cooperation of the specialized agencies and of relevant intergovernmental organizations and non-governmental organizations in consultative status with ECOSOC.

In order to increase awareness of these standards, the Secretary-General was required to disseminate the Rules, implementing procedures and reports on the subject to as wide an audience as possible. In a further effort to have knowledge of the Rules permeate national and international administrations, the Secretary-General was also required to ensure the widest possible reference to and use of the text of the Rules by the organization in all its relevant programs, including technical assistance activities. . . .

For its part, the Committee on Crime Prevention and Control was instructed to keep the Rules under review with an aim of elaborating new rules, standards and procedures and following up the implementing procedures, including periodic reporting. Moreover, the Crime Prevention Committee was instructed to assist the General Assembly, the Economic and Social Council and any other United Nations human rights bodies, as appropriate, in developing recommendations relating to reports of *ad hoc* inquiry commissions on matters pertaining to the application and implementation of the Standard Minimum Rules. This power remained dormant as nothing "appropriate" emerged.

A final provision in the Procedures asserted that nothing in their content should be construed as precluding resort to any other means or remedies available under international law or set forth by other United Nations bodies and agencies for the redress of violations of human rights. This was specifically said to include the procedure on consistent patterns of gross violations of human rights under Economic and Social Council resolution 1503 (XLVIII) of May 27, 1970 [see pages 344-380 of Problem V], the communication procedure under the Optional Protocol to the International Covenant on Civil and Political Rights [see pages 214-222 of Problem III] and the communication procedure under the International Convention on the Elimination of All Forms of Racial Discrimination. This was the only hint of a "violations" approach to implementation and it was, it will be noted, a reference to procedures other than those of the Committee on Crime Prevention and Control itself. . . .

One thing at least was clear with the adoption of the Procedures in 1984: a vision of "implementation" had become a part of the currency of the [UN Criminal Justice] Program. The issue now became how to make it work and how far to expand beyond the area of the Standard Minimum Rules. The impetus to so expand was strengthened by comparable, if not quite so far reaching, efforts that had been occurring in respect of capital punishment. . . .

[In 1990 the] Eighth Congress added significantly to the reporting work-load. Reports were required by the resolutions adopting the Standard Minimum Rules for Non-Custodial Measures (the Tokyo Rules), the Guidelines for the Prevention of Juvenile Delinquency (the Riyadh Guidelines), the Standard Minimum Rules for the Protection of Juveniles Deprived of Their Liberty, the Basic Principles on the Use of Force and Firearms by Law Enforcement Officials, the Basic Principles on the Role of Lawyers, and the Guidelines on the Role of Prosecutors.

Along with adding to the implementation work-load, the Eighth Congress adopted a strong resolution recommending that "the role of the Committee on Crime Prevention and Control should be supported so as to enable it to function more effectively as the monitoring body for United Nations norms and guidelines in the field of criminal justice and to assist the Economic and Social Council with recommendations." The resolution requested that the Secretary-General, subject to the provision of extrabudgetary funds, convene an *ad hoc* group of experts which would submit concrete proposals to the Crime Prevention Committee at its Twelfth Session for (a) promoting the implementation of existing standards; (b) consolidating and rationalizing arrangements for the effective evaluation and monitoring of the standards; and (c) improving the techniques to aid in such evaluations. . . .

[In 1992 the Committee on Crime Prevention and Control, a body of independent experts, was replaced by the intergovernmental Commission on Crime Prevention and Criminal Justice.]

At the 1993 session of the Commission on Crime Prevention and Criminal Justice, it became apparent that the reporting system had ground to a halt and that a decision had been made within the Secretariat simply to devote no resources to it. Accordingly, a decision was made to begin again in a modest way "a process of information-gathering to be undertaken by means of surveys." Since it was not believed to be possible to tackle everything at once, initial efforts would be made in respect of the Standard Minimum Rules for the Treatment of Prisoners, the Code of Conduct for Law Enforcement Officials (together with the Basic Principles on the Use of Force and Firearms by Law Enforcement Officials), the Declaration of Basic Principles of Justice for Victims of Crime and Abuse of Power, and the Basic Principles on the Independence of the Judiciary. Underlying all of the discussion on the process was an appreciation that, in a world of limited resources, not everything can be done at once by any international implementation system. . . .

Above and beyond the question of priorities, . . . the discussion in 1992 and 1993 suggests that future efforts at implementation might be considered broadly under four categories: efforts involving reporting and monitoring; efforts at encouraging the use by the human rights organs of the United Nations system of the norms and standards created in the crime and criminal justice part; advisory services and other kinds of technical assistance; and the creation of other implementation mechanisms. . . .

It is hard to be very sanguine about the prospects for an ambitious "implementation" program under the auspices of the Commission on Crime Prevention and Criminal Justice. It has limited Secretariat resources available to it and there is serious apathy even among vocal supporters of the criminal justice program when it comes to delivering reports or agreeing to the provision of budgetary funds. Despite this, there is some disposition to press on.

In the final years of the Committee on Crime Prevention and Control, the Crime Prevention and Criminal Justice Program was staking its claim to a serious place in the United Nations implementation system by endeavoring to make its reporting system work. By 1993, reporting had simply ceased, although it is now under way again in a limited way in response to a request from ECOSOC. The program is now looking more seriously at the role of technical cooperation. Increasingly, however, with its organs such as the Working Group on Enforced or Involuntary Disappearances and its Special Rapporteurs on particular countries and its "theme" Rapporteurs such as those on Torture and on Summary or Arbitrary Executions, the Geneva-based human rights system has been showing a much greater disposition to go beyond reporting regimes and to deal with the individual problems of individual people [See pages 382-400 of Problem V.] As it moves further on "implementation," the Commission on Crime Prevention and Criminal Justice cannot be unmoved by such developments and no doubt will make sympathetic responses to them, both in its own functions and in working with other parts of the system. In doing so, it will need to be sensitive to questions of turf and comparative advantage. For instance, when should the Crime Prevention Commission encourage the appointment of theme Rapporteurs from its ranks, or of independent individuals or groups reporting to it? When should it acquiesce in having such mechanisms under the auspices of the Commission on Human Rights? When should it defer to the efforts of the Commission on Human Rights or the treaty-based committees? Should it, indeed, go any further down the present route, or should it instead leave the field substantially to the Geneva-based organs, thus avoiding duplication?

In so far as they have been acting as "human rights agencies," the Committee on Crime Prevention and Control, the congresses and the United Nations Crime Prevention and Criminal Justice Program in general have had the advantage over others of the human rights organs in emphasizing "technical" and "professional" aspects of the area. They have thus succeeded in avoiding some of the politicization of the others. If its first two meetings are any indication, the Commission on Crime Prevention and Criminal Justice could easily be mistaken for just another political body where nation states peddle their wares. The challenge to the Crime Prevention Commission and its working groups as they move to consider such implementation strategies as much more vigorous examination of governmental reports, involvement in concrete situations, the appointment of Special Rapporteurs, the creation of an early warning system for victims, or more serious involvement in technical cooperation activities, is to maintain the relatively non-politicized approach of the earlier organs.

As noted in the Clark excerpt, the Commission on Crime Prevention and Criminal Justice in 1993 recommended a new system for monitoring implementation of the wide range of criminal justice norms adopted by the UN and its organs and identified five instruments as initially deserving particular attention. See Report of the Commission on Crime Prevention and Criminal Justice on Its Second Session, Draft Res. VII, U.N. ESCOR Supp. (No. 12) at 21, U.N. Doc. E/1993/32, pt. III, ¶8 (1993). An open-ended sessional working group was to be established beginning at the Commission's 1994 session to discuss, inter alia, the role of the United Nations in promoting the use and application of the above instruments, evaluation of the reporting system, and measures to improve the dissemination of information, education, and technical assistance to enhance application of the norms. Id. The Secretary-General is to "commence without delay a process of information-gathering to be undertaken by means of surveys, such as reporting systems, and contributions from other sources . . . ; the surveys should be conducted over a two-year period . . . [and] should be considered at the earliest possible session of the Commission [on Crime Prevention and Criminal Justice]." Id, ¶7. Although the "other sources" are not specified, an earlier draft of the Commission's resolution referred to regional institutes and non-governmental organizations as among such sources. See Report of the Commission, supra, at 96. The impact of this most recent attempt to implement international norms in the criminal justice area obviously remains to be evaluated.

As mentioned at the end of the Clark excerpt, the "Geneva-based human rights system" of the UN is also active in monitoring the implementation of standards of criminal justice. In response to an inquiry from the Cuban government, the Human Rights Commission's Working Group on Arbitrary Detention adopted the following "deliberation" in its second annual report to the Commission.

Report of the Working Group on Arbitrary Detention
U.N. Doc. E/CN.4/1993/24, at 11-13 (1993)

C.   POSSIBILITY OF THE GROUP'S REFERRING TO INSTRUMENTS OF A PURELY DECLARATORY NATURE

15. The Working Group would point out that resolution 1991/42, which lays down its mandate, refers expressly to "the . . . international legal instruments accepted by the States concerned" as an international reference standard for the Working Group, in addition to the Universal Declaration of Human Rights. Consequently, the specific question raised by the Cuban Government's letter, as applied to the Body of Principles for the Protection of All Persons under Any Form of Detention or Imprisonment (hereinafter referred to as the "Body of Principles"), is to establish (a) whether the Body of Principles is actually an "instrument", (b) whether it is of a "declaratory" nature and, if so, (c) whether it can be regarded as having been "accepted" by Member States.

(A)   LEGAL DEFINITION OF "INSTRUMENT"

16. As interpreted in legal writings generally, the term "legal instruments" covers all legal texts, whether they are conventional, that is to say binding, instruments, such as conventions, covenants, protocols and other treaties or such forms of agreement as resolutions or gentlemen's agreements (for instance, the Final Act of the Conference on the Security and Co-operation in Europe, the Paris Charter). . . .

18. The use of the word "instruments" without further qualification in paragraph 2 of resolution 1991/42 therefore shows that it was not the intention of the Commission on Human Rights to confine the reference standards of the Working Group to treaties and other similar instruments but that it also wished to include in it acts of agreement, such as resolutions.

(B)   "DECLARATORY" NATURE

19. The question put to the Working Group is whether the Body of Principles should be regarded as an "instrument of a purely declaratory

nature", according to the characterization given by the Cuban Government, and, if so, whether the Working Group can still invoke it.

20. The Body of Principles is an instrument declaratory of pre-existing rights, inasmuch as the main purpose of many of its provisions is to set forth, and sometimes develop, principles already recognized under customary law.

21. It should be noted that, in the case of mere acts of agreement (and this applies to General Assembly resolutions), legal writers draw a distinction between those which are declaratory of pre-existing rights (as in the above-mentioned example of most of the provisions of the Body of Principles or the Declaration on Territorial Asylum or the Declaration on Torture, etc.) and those — purely declaratory — instruments whose purpose is not to produce such an effect (for example, resolutions which take note of a report of a working group, or which institute a decade on a given theme).

22. The Working Group also wishes to point out in this connection that, according to legal writers, in the case of a non-party State, the same applies to any convention since it is not an instrument which lays down procedural rules, for instance, and therefore has no declaratory effect (as, for example, the Optional Protocol to the International Covenant on Civil and Political Rights) but is an instrument which lays down principles (such as the Covenant). In other words, and to take the case of the Covenant again, it has a binding effect with respect to States parties and a declaratory effect with respect to non-party States.

23. In the light of the foregoing, the Working Group considers that, when it takes a decision on whether a case of detention is arbitrary, it is justified in referring . . . both to:

> the International Covenant on Civil and Political Rights, even if the Working Group has before it a case concerning a non-party State, in view of the tenacity of the declaratory effect of the quasi-totality of its provisions;
> and the Body of Principles, again on account of the declaratory effect of its substantive provisions.

(C)   THE CONCEPT OF "ACCEPTED" INSTRUMENT

24. When it comes not to treaty instruments having binding force but to acts of agreement, the question is whether they can still be regarded as having been "accepted", inasmuch as resolution 1991/42 setting up the Working Group refers, *inter alia*, to "the relevant international legal instruments accepted by the States concerned" as reference standards for the Working Group.

25. In adopting a position on this point, the Working Group relied on a decision of the International Court of Justice (Judgment of 27 June 1986: *Case concerning Military and Paramilitary Activities in and against Nicaragua — Nicaragua v. United States of America* — Reports 1986, pp. 100 *et seq.*), which held that the "consent" of the States Members of the United

Nations to the text of declaratory resolutions setting forth customary law (particularly where they are adopted by consensus) may "be understood as an *acceptance* of the validity of the rule or set of rules declared by the resolution by themselves" and, in so far as the United States had supported those resolutions, the Court considered that it had "*accepted*" them.

26. In paragraph 1 of the above-mentioned resolution 43/173, however, the General Assembly "approves" the Body of Principles. International legal terminology makes no distinction between "acceptance" and "approval". Approval was given by all States since the resolution was adopted by consensus. By participating in that consensus, the States therefore "accepted" the Body of Principles.

27. This is particularly so since:

> paragraph 4 of General Assembly resolution 43/173 "urges that every effort be made so that the Body of Principles becomes generally known and respected";
>
> the first paragraph of the Body of Principles stipulates: "These principles apply for the protection of all persons . . .".

28. The Working Group therefore considers that the Body of Principles, as an act of agreement, should be regarded as having been "accepted" within the meaning of the paragraph in resolution 1991/42 which lays down its mandate.

Conclusion

29. These are the legal grounds — this being the question posed — which led the Working Group to adopt the term "accepted declaratory instrument":

> for the Body of Principles, on the one hand, in so far as Member States are concerned;
>
> for the International Covenant on Civil and Political Rights, on the other, in so far as States which have yet to ratify it are concerned;

and hence to take it into consideration when determining whether a deprivation of freedom is arbitrary.

A. *Regional Standards: European Prison Rules*

The United Nations is not the only body to have issued a set of "minimum standards" on which to pattern the treatment of prisoners. Rules for the treatment of prisoners have been promulgated on the regional, state, and local levels by governments and by private organizations.

On the regional level, the most progressive prison regulations were prepared by the European Committee on Crime Problems of the Council of Europe. The Council's Standard Minimum Rules for the Treatment of Prisoners were adopted in 1973 by a resolution recommending that all member governments "be guided in their internal legislation and practice" by the European Rules, with a view to their "progressive implementation" over the years. Council of Europe, Resolution 73(5) (1973) Adopted by the Committee of Ministers on 19 January 1973 at the 217th Meeting of the Ministers' Deputies.

The European Rules generally parallel the UN Standard Minimum Rules. They have been adapted, however, to incorporate the philosophy of the European Convention on Human Rights (to be discussed in Problem IX) and the belief that, "in their narrower framework, [the European states could] find a more liberal common denominator than the one established at world level." Council of Europe Activities in the Field of Crime Problems 1956-1976, at 45 (1977).

The Council of Europe, noting that "significant social trends and changes in regard to prison treatment and management have made it desirable to reformulate the [European Rules] so as to support and encourage the best of these developments and offer scope for future progress," revised its Rules extensively in 1987, adopting a 100-Rule version to be known as the European Prison Rules. Council of Europe, Recommendation No. R (87)3 (1987) Adopted by the Committee of Ministers on 12 February 1987 at the 404th Meeting of the Ministers' Deputies.

B. National Standards: United States Federal and State Laws and Regulations (and Their Enforcement)

"The major goal in formulating and approving the Standard Minimum Rules was to encourage their enactment (explicitly or in substance) in national penal codes. However, the record of actual incorporation of the Standard Minimum Rules in legislation and administrative regulations is hazy, not well documented, and largely disappointing. . . . What emerges . . . is a picture of spotty implementation, perhaps optimistic in terms of the true conditions, poor financing, and trained personnel shortages of most prison systems, but nevertheless showing a basic respect for and desire to adhere to the rules." Skoler, World Implementation of the United Nations Standard Minimum Rules for the Treatment of Prisoners, 10 J. Intl. L. & Econ. 453, 459, 467 (1975).

Although written two decades ago, Skoler's conclusion remains largely valid today. Despite five surveys undertaken by the United Nations since 1970, little specific information is available about the number of states that have adopted, in whole or in part, the UN Standard Minimum Rules. There is likewise little information about the status of the many more recent standards listed at pages 305-306 supra.

In the United States, a few states did adopt the Rules, at least "in principle," in the mid-1970s, but the vast majority have not. The most common method of responding to the UN's request that the Rules "be effectively implemented in the administration of penal and correctional institutions" has been through the administrative adoption of the Rules, either in toto or in substance. For example, Connecticut, South Carolina, Pennsylvania, and Illinois have directly or by reference ordered that the Rules be enforced, sometimes subject to specific exceptions or more general subsidiarity to state laws. The governor of Ohio adopted a somewhat more general executive order, declaring that he adopts, "on behalf of the State of Ohio, the philosophy, intent, principle, and purpose of these standards, and hereby direct[s] that the . . . Department of Rehabilitation and Correction . . . adhere to and pursue their spirit and intent." Minnesota adopted a similar order. For the texts of the legal orders adopting the Rules in these states and a history of their adoption, see American Bar Assn. Corrections Commn., The United Nations Standard Minimum Rules for the Treatment of Prisoners, 11 Crim. L. Bull. 637 (1975).

The federal government has not adopted the Standard Minimum Rules, and the possibility of its doing so is remote. See U.S. Dept. of Justice, Federal Standards for Prisons and Jails (1980), for the federal standards, which generally approximate the Rules.

In the meantime the Rules have not been without impact upon prisoners' rights litigation in the United States. Although not legally binding, they have been invoked repeatedly by courts looking for constitutional guidance in particular cases. For cases in which the Rules have been discussed or cited, see R. Lillich, International Human Rights Instruments §450.14 (2d ed. updated 1995). The Supreme Court has cited the Rules as evidence of "contemporary standards of decency" for purposes of the Eighth Amendment. Estelle v. Gamble, 429 U.S. 97, 103-104 & n.8 (1976). Indeed, two lower federal courts in a case arising from Connecticut, which adopted the Rules in 1974, have held that the practice of "double-bunking," when combined with general overcrowding and other inadequate prison conditions, violated prisoners' Eighth Amendment rights, citing Article 9(1) of the Rules, which categorically states that "each prisoner shall occupy by night a cell or room by himself." Lareau v. Manson, 507 F. Supp. 1177, 1187-1189 & n.9, 1192-1193 & nn.18, 19 (D. Conn. 1980), aff'd, 651 F.2d 96, 106-107 (2d Cir. 1981).

The Supreme Court, however, has upheld "double-bunking" twice without mentioning the Rules. In Bell v. Wolfish, 441 U.S. 520, 542 (1979), Justice Rehnquist, reversing lower court decisions that had invoked standards drafted by several professional associations, disagreed with their conclusion "that there is some sort of 'one man, one cell' principle lurking in the Due Process Clause of the Fifth Amendment." Their recommendations, he wrote for the Court in 1979, "may be instructive in certain cases, [but] they simply do not establish the constitutional minima; rather, they establish goals recommended by the organization in question." Id. at 543 n.27.

Two years later, the Court reiterated its view that "double-bunking" was not unconstitutional in Rhodes v. Chapman, 452 U.S. 337 (1981), reversing the finding to the contrary of a district court that had relied upon prohibitions of the practice found in standards drawn up by the American Correctional Association, the National Sheriffs' Association, and the National Council on Crime and Delinquency (Article 9(1) of the Rules apparently had not been argued). Id. at 343 n.7. Justice Powell, writing for the Court, concluded that the district court had "erred in assuming that opinions of experts as to desirable prison conditions suffice to establish contemporary standards of decency." Id. at 348 n.13. Justice Marshall dissented strenuously, especially as to the weight to be accorded expert evidence. Id. at 376 n.8.

Prisoners' rights litigation in the United States has increased tremendously in the past three decades. Most of it has been brought under the Civil Rights Act, 42 U.S.C. §1983 (1994), which gives a private federal court remedy to prisoners when they have been deprived of their constitutionally guaranteed rights by correction personnel. See Turner, When Prisoners Sue: A Study of Prisoner Section 1983 Suits in Federal Courts, 92 Harv. L. Rev. 610 (1979). Such suits — which numbered 33,000 in 1993 — now account for 15 percent of all civil suits filed in the federal courts, and many state attorneys are urging new restrictions to deal with frivolous complaints. See Dunn, Flood of Prisoner Rights Suits Brings Effort to Limit Filings, N.Y. Times, Mar. 21, 1994, at A1, col. 2. However, the need for such suits is demonstrated by the fact that, as of October 1987, 45 states plus the District of Columbia, Puerto Rico, and the U.S. Virgin Islands were under court order or bound by consent decrees to improve prison conditions. *

Judicial review of prison conditions was substantially limited by the Court in Wilson v. Seiter, 501 U.S. 294 (1991), perhaps in response to the great increase in prisoners' rights litigation. In this case the Court held that a prisoner must demonstrate that prison officials acted with "deliberate indifference" in imposing abusive conditions. It appears that no U.S. case has referred specifically to the UN Standard Minimum Rules since 1988.

Until 1980 prisoners' rights litigation was hampered by the average prisoner's physical isolation, lack of resources and access to competent legal counsel, and, perhaps most important, fear of retaliation. In that year Congress enacted the Civil Rights of Institutionalized Persons Act, 42 U.S.C.

---

* Status Report: State Prisons and the Courts, J. Natl. Prison Project 24 (No. 13, Fall 1987). The list included the entire prison or jail systems of Alabama, Alaska, Arkansas, Florida, Mississippi, Oklahoma, Rhode Island, South Carolina, Tennessee, Texas, the District of Columbia, and Puerto Rico.

§1997 (1994), a Carter Administration-supported law authorizing the U.S. Attorney General to initiate or intervene in civil actions when there is reasonable cause to believe that a state's treatment of prisoners (or persons who are mentally ill, disabled, retarded, or chronically ill or handicapped and residing in a state institution) constitutes an "egregious or flagrant" violation of their constitutional rights. Opposed by the governors and attorneys general of 40 states, the Act was called by the American Civil Liberties Union "[t]he first significant civil rights victory of the 1980s." N.Y. Times, Feb. 29, 1980, at A12, cols. 1-2.

The federal government availed itself of the opportunities afforded by the Act to challenge state prison conditions in several cases initially filed in the mid-1980s. See, e.g., United States v. Michigan, 940 F.2d 143 (6th Cir. 1991); United States v. Colorado, 937 F.2d 505 (10th Cir. 1991); United States v. Massachusetts, 890 F.2d 507 (1st Cir. 1989); United States v. Pennsylvania, 832 F. Supp. 122 (E.D. Pa. 1993); United States v. Illinois, 803 F. Supp. 1338 (N.D. Ill. 1992); United States v. Tennessee, 798 F. Supp. 483 (W.D. Tenn. 1992); United States v. County of Crittenden, 1990 U.S. Dist. LEXIS 18112 (E.D. Ark. 1990); United States v. New York, 690 F. Supp. 1201 (W.D.N.Y. 1988); United States v. Oregon, 675 F. Supp. 1249 (D. Or. 1987).

C. Non-Governmental and Private Organization Standards

The impetus for updating the content and monitoring the application of the Rules comes not only from the UN, regional organizations, and some states, but also from many non-governmental and private organizations. (On the role of NGOs in the international legislative process generally, see van Boven, The Role of Non-Governmental Organizations in International Human Rights Standard-Setting: A Prerequisite of Democracy, 20 Cal. W. Intl. L.J. 207 (1990).

For example, Amnesty International launched a post-Attica campaign in 1972 to have the Rules adopted by every UN member state. Its then-Secretary-General, Martin Ennals, emphasized their importance at a UN press conference and called them to the attention of then-UN Secretary-General Waldheim, who, Mr. Ennals said, was "surprised — he had never heard about the rules" (N.Y. Times, Apr. 9, 1972, at 9, col. 1). Amnesty International also played a significant role, along with the International Commission of Jurists, in getting additional Article 95 added to the Rules in 1977. E.S.C. Res. 2076 (LXII), 62 U.N. ESCOR Supp. (No. 1) at 35, U.N. Doc. E/5988 (1977). See Note, Progress Report on United Nations Human Rights Activities to Protect Prisoners, 7 Ga. J. Intl. & Comp. L. 467, 469 (1977). The only amendment to the Rules ever to be adopted, it extends their protection to persons arrested or imprisoned without charge (detainees). Amnesty International was instrumental, too, in getting the UN to adopt, first, a Declaration on the Protection of All Persons from Being Subjected to Torture and Other Cruel, Inhuman, or Degrading Treatment or Punishment, G.A. Res. 3452, 30 U.N. GAOR Supp. (No. 34) at 91, U.N. Doc. A/3452 (1975), and, more recently, the Convention Against Torture and Other Forms of Cruel, Inhuman or Degrading Treatment or Punishment (see page 194 of Problem III). In this case the "model law" approach gave way to the resolution and treaty routes.

Private professional groups in the United States, while not pushing for the adoption of the Rules per se, themselves have developed standards designed to improve the lot of U.S. federal and state prisoners. The American Bar Association's Joint Committee on the Legal Status of Prisoners, for instance, has issued its Standards Relating to the Legal Status of Prisoners (14 Am. Crim. L. Rev. 377 (1977)). Similar model rules, differing in degree of specificity and in points of emphasis, have been drafted by the American Correctional Association, the National Sheriffs' Association, and the National Council on Crime and Delinquency. Only the last acknowledged to the editors that no consideration was taken of the UN Standard Minimum Rules in preparing their model act. See Committee, A Model Act to Provide for Minimum Standards for the Protection of Rights of Prisoners, 18 Crime & Delinq. 4 (1972). Pace Justice Powell in Rhodes v. Chapman, page 316 supra, to the extent to which U.S. courts take these model rules into account in determining constitutional minima, they are indirectly applying the UN Rules.

Comments and Questions

1. Besharov and Mueller state that the UN Standard Minimum Rules "are not a part of international criminal law in the strict sense." See page 285 supra. What do they mean by this statement? How would you characterize the legal status of the Rules? Although, as the UN Secretariat's working paper acknowledges (page 296 supra), they may not have the status of an international convention, might not the Rules, or at least many of them, constitute "international custom" or "general principles of law recognized by civilized nations" within the meaning of Article 38(1)(b)(c) of the Statute of the International Court of Justice? Recall how certain articles of the Universal Declaration of Human Rights now are regarded as reflecting customary international law (see pages 122-171 of Problem II).

2. Rodley distinguishes between specific rules that constitute "legal obligations" and other rules that can be "more easily seen as guidelines only. . . ." N. Rodley, page 301 supra, at 222. "Although not every rule may constitute a legal obligation, it is reasonably clear that the SMR [Standard Minimum Rules] can provide guidance in interpreting the general rule against cruel, inhuman, or degrading treatment or punishment. Thus, serious non-

compliance with some rules or widespread non-compliance with some others may result in a level of ill-treatment sufficient to constitute violation of the general rule." Id. The "general rule," of course, may be one of conventional as well as customary international law; thus, the Rules may assist the Human Rights Committee in interpreting, for example, Article 10(1) of the International Covenant on Civil and Political Rights, just as the European Commission on Human Rights has found the Rules helpful in determining whether detention conditions in certain states meet those states' obligations under the European Convention on Human Rights. Id. at 222-223.

3. Bearing in mind that procedural guarantees are often essential if substantive norms are to be enforced effectively, how would you, as Chairman of the Criminal Law Section of your State Bar Association, charged with initiating a program to have the substance of the Standard Minimum Rules (or the Rules themselves, if you prefer) adopted in your state, go about achieving this end? Would you recommend state legislation? Local legislation? State or local executive action? Consider what strategies and tactics would be most useful to obtain your objective. Would the efforts of NGOs, such as those of Amnesty International mentioned on pages 317-318 supra, be helpful? Counterproductive? Irrelevant?

4. Assume that you are appointed chief of the U.S. or another country's delegation to the Ninth UN Congress on the Prevention of Crime and the Treatment of Offenders. Prepare a 15-minute statement examining the record of your country in incorporating the Code of Conduct for Law Enforcement Officials into domestic law and in implementing it.

5. The following extract is from an article written by a former superintendent of the Arkansas prison system 10 years after the bodies of three unknown prisoners were unearthed at the Tucker State Farm prison.

> . . . The primary effect of the [1968] Arkansas prison scandal was an impetus to reform, worldwide attention on American prisons, and the dismissal of the reform staff.
>
> A secondary effect was to increase national awareness of prison conditions through the Congressional hearings conducted by Senator Thomas J. Dodd in 1969 and 1970.
>
> The Attica riot in New York State in 1971 expanded the movement to examine our penal institutions. A loose coalition of reformers, liberals, prisoners, religious groups and assorted charlatans entered the arena, but by the mid-1970's reform efforts failed to produce substantial results. Prisons across the United States are now more immune to external examination and change than ever.
>
> The law-and-order folks have spawned a new breed of writers who have rushed into print acknowledging the futility of reformation and, instead, have advocated a return to longer sentences, more punishment — consequently, less humanization of the confined. And they shall prevail for a time. Prevail until the cost of new prisons becomes prohibitive, the harshness of the law once again becomes self-defeating, and the cycle of change is complete. On that day, the neophyte reformers will dust off the principles of their prede-

cessors, uncover the atrocities of the prisons, suggest rational reforms, develop a new rhetoric and forge valiantly ahead until a time when they too will be wiped out at the pass, thwarted not by the enemies of reform but by the reformers themselves as they scramble to appease what is assumed to be the will of their constituents.

Winthrop Rockefeller [Governor of Arkansas] is dead. A legion of Arkansas inmates are dead. Prison reform across the country is dead. The Arkansas prison system is the worst-kept secret in the world of penology, yet the inmates' bones lie moulding in the ground 10 years after the discovery and apparently no one cares.

Murton, The Arkansas Effect, N.Y. Times, Feb. 17, 1978, at 27, col. 1.

This pessimistic view of penal reform in the United States is in sharp contrast to the flurry of activity engendered by the UN, the Council of Europe, and NGOs. Does the above article support implementation of the Standard Minimum Rules (or their substance) in the United States? Does the United States, as a member of the UN, have the obligation to ensure the observation of minimum penal standards on the federal or the state levels? Does the United States at least have the obligation to sustain federal and state interest in penal reform? How should the United States do so?

6. The poor conditions prevailing in many federal and state prisons make U.S. protests about the treatment of prisoners in foreign countries seem somewhat hypocritical. Moreover, they weaken the moral credibility and, hence, the potential effectiveness of such protests in the eyes of the international community. In this regard consider the following letter to the editor written by a former U.S. Parole Commissioner (N.Y. Times, Mar. 9, 1989, at A30, cols. 3-4): *

To the Editor:

Early in 1988, the Cuban Government extended an invitation to the United Nations Human Rights Commission, allowing a team to choose the prison it wanted to visit and to conduct confidential interviews with the prisoners.

Before the visit by the United Nations team, the Cubans had invited a group of Americans to visit their prisons and conduct confidential interviews. This was handled by the Institute for Policy Studies in Washington. The Cubans had expected an invitation from the Department of Justice to permit a Cuban team to visit Bureau of Prisons facilities. Nothing doing! The United States Government denied the Cubans visas to this country.

During the summer and fall of 1988, both the American and

---

* Although it does not detract from the general point of the letter that follows, it might be noted that the Commission on Human Rights, the year after the visit described in the letter, expressed its concern at reports "that witnesses who testified before the Working Group of the Commission have since been subject to arrest, harassment, or other forms of reprisals by the Government of Cuba." C.H.R. Res. 1990/48, Report on the Forty-Sixth Session, U.N. ESCOR Supp. (No. 2) at 109, 110, U.N. Doc. E/1990/22 (1990).

United Nations teams were able to go where they wanted and talk with prisoners confidentially. Both the Institute for Policy Studies and the Human Rights Commission teams were favorably impressed with the Cuban openness to inspection.

The reason the United States Government has refused a similar inspection of Bureau of Prisons facilities in this country should be obvious: The bureau would flunk the test.

In 1986 Representative Robert Kastenmeier, chairman of the House Subcommittee on Courts, Civil Liberties and the Administration of Justice, reported to Congress on the conditions under which the Cuban detainees were held. He described the conditions at Atlanta as "brutal and dehumanizing." Mr. Kastenmeier said, "the conditions under which these persons live are worse than those which exist for the most dangerous convicted felons." He added, "The conditions of confinement at Atlanta do not appear to meet minimum standards."

After the prisons at Atlanta and Oakdale, La., exploded in the November 1987 riots, the Bureau of Prisons scattered the Cuban detainees through the country. Yet, reports of brutal treatment continue to pour in: endless hours of "lock-down" confinement; overcrowding; no educational or recreational programs; beatings by prison staff.

Only last month, Sharon Caulum and John Tompos, pro bono lawyers, wrote Representative Kastenmeier: "The most common complaint centers on their lock-down status with no mental stimulation. . . . There are no hobby crafts, table games or cards available. . . . The paint-by-number sets . . . were taken away from them. On Jan. 5, without explanation, their books and all magazines . . . were removed from the cells. There are currently no educational programs available. The metal doors inhibit communication to staff and other detainees. If the detainee needs or wishes to communicate, he must holler loudly. The noise level of the unit is very loud. The officers wear earplugs to deafen the noise. This inhibits legitimate requests for help to staff by detainees. Earplugs are not available for the detainees."

The litany of inhuman treatment has gone on for years. The cruelty and indifference of the Bureau of Prisons are a shame to anyone concerned about fair play.

The Federal prison system was once a model for corrections officials at the state level. Those days are long gone. The obvious proof lies in our Government's resistance to objective assessment of what goes on behind the walls.

The United States Government should be silent about civil rights violations in other countries until it puts its own house in order. Right now, in the world's eye, Fidel Castro has far more credibility.

O.J. KELLER
Atlanta, Feb. 18, 1989

7. "The mills of justice grind slowly, but they grind exceedingly fine." Although federal courts dismissed a class action brought by Attica prisoners under 42 U.S.C. §1983 (1994) against the late Governor Rockefeller, Al-Jundi v. Estate of Nelson Rockefeller, 885 F.2d 1060 (2d Cir. 1989), the New York Court of Claims on 25 October 1989, finding that the state police had used excessive force in retaking the prison, held the state liable and awarded seven prisoners (or their estates) $1.3 million for injuries they had sustained on 13 September 1971 (Kolbert, State Court Awards $1.3 Million for 7 Attica Inmates' Injuries, N.Y. Times, Oct. 26, 1989, at Bl, cols. 2-5). Recall the remarks of a disgraced former Vice President found at page 279 supra. In February 1992, a class action suit claiming $2.5 billion in damages on behalf of 1,281 former Attica inmates ended in a hung jury in a federal district court in Buffalo, New York (Today's News Update, N.Y. L.J., Nov. 3, 1992, at 1). See also Pines, 11-Week Attica Trial Winds Up; Jury to Weigh Evidence in $2.5 Billion Class Action Suit by Inmates, N.Y.L.J., Jan. 9, 1992, at 1.

IV.   New Rights for Vulnerable Groups

A.   General Observations

The "model law" or "soft law" approach to international standard-setting has become more pronounced not only in the area of criminal justice, but also with respect to the protection of other vulnerable groups. In the past two decades, for example, the following declarations have been adopted by the UN General Assembly:

Declaration on the Rights of Mentally Retarded Persons, G.A. Res. 2856, 26 U.N. GAOR Supp. (No. 29) at 93, U.N. Doc. A/8429 (1971)

Declaration on the Rights of Disabled Persons, G.A. Res. 3447, 30 U.N. GAOR Supp. (No. 34) at 88, U.N. Doc. A/10034 (1975)

Declaration on the Elimination of All Forms of Intolerance and of Discrimination Based on Religion or Belief, G.A. Res. 36/55, 36 U.N. GAOR Supp. (No. 51) at 171, U.N. Doc. A/36/51 (1981)

Declaration on the Human Rights of Individuals Who Are Not Nationals of the Country in Which They Live, G.A. Res. 40/144, 40 U.N. GAOR Supp. (No. 53) at 252, U.N. Doc. A/40/53 (1985)

Declaration on Social and Legal Principles Relating to the Protection and Welfare of Children, with Special Reference to Foster Placement and Adoption Nationally and Internationally, G.A. Res. 41/85, 41 U.N. GAOR Supp. (No. 53) at 265, U.N. Doc. A/41/53 (1986)

> *Principles for the Protection of Persons with Mental Illness and for the Improvement of Mental Health Care*, G.A. Res. 46/119, 46 U.N. GAOR Supp. (No. 49) at 188, U.N. Doc. A/46/49 (1991)
>
> *Declaration on the Rights of Persons Belonging to National or Ethnic, Religious or Linguistic Minorities*, G.A. Res. 47/135, 47 U.N. GAOR Supp. (No. 49) at 210, U.N. Doc. A/47/49 (1992)

None of these declarations has been succeeded by binding conventions on the same subject, although UN conventions were adopted after declarations on the rights of the child (declaration 1959, convention 1989) and the prohibition of torture (declaration 1975, convention 1984).

General Assembly resolutions, of course, are only recommendations, although they also may contribute to or reflect a norm of customary international law. See pages 122-171 of Problem II and pages 334-336 infra (concerning self-determination). What do the above "soft law" resolutions by the UN have in common with the declarations and guidelines discussed in the preceding sections concerning the treatment of prisoners and criminal justice?

Two somewhat contradictory propositions might be advanced in response. Many of the codes or guidelines adopted in the criminal justice field are extremely detailed, the international equivalents of administrative regulations designed to implement broader principles, that is, "humane treatment" for prisoners or guarantees of a "fair trial." Given the great variation in national resources and penal systems, it would probably be impossible for such detailed provisions to be applied in the same manner throughout the world. Thus, promulgation of non-binding models or guidelines, which may be adapted by individual states to meet their own circumstances, may be the best means of encouraging domestic compliance with the underlying norms.

On the other hand, political disagreements over the exact scope of the rights of minorities or religious groups, for example, may make it easier to adopt hortatory language in a General Assembly resolution than to agree on more specific provisions in a legally binding treaty. In such cases general principles may set forth only the lowest common denominator of agreement on contentious issues, leaving detailed compliance to the discretion of states.

As seen above in the context of prisoners' rights, even "soft" norms may have a considerable impact on the actual practice of states. Irrespective of their impact on the formation of customary international law, resolutions adopted by consensus by major intergovernmental bodies — such as the UN General Assembly and regional organizations such as the Conference (now Organization) on Security and Cooperation in Europe and the Organization of African Unity — have an undeniable political force that may be as effective in changing government policies as are many treaties. In both cases the political will of states to adopt pro-human rights policies may be more important than the legal status of a particular norm. See generally the discussion of foreign policy in Problem XIII.

Complaints about the alleged violation of minority rights, the rights of indigenous peoples, and self-determination are at the heart of many of the most violent domestic conflicts that have erupted in the 1990s. The remainder of this Problem will consider how new formulations of these rights are being developed and their potential impact.

B. Minorities

Hannum, Contemporary Developments in the International Protection of the Rights of Minorities
66 Notre Dame L. Rev. 1431, 1431-1436 (1991)

One can trace the international protection of minorities at least to the Treaty of Westphalia in 1648, under the terms of which the parties agreed to respect the rights of certain (not all) religious minorities within their jurisdiction. Given the historical congruence of religious and secular authority prior to this period, however, such agreements could just as easily be seen as recognizing the power of certain political groups rather than religious rights per se. Religion was certainly the most significant distinction among most groups until at least the eighteenth century, and most of the early provisions for the protection of minorities were concerned with what today might be viewed as freedom of religion rather than group rights.

The Congress of Vienna, which dismembered the Napoleonic empire in 1815, also considered the rights of national minorities to some extent. The 1876 Treaty of Berlin included protection for the "traditional rights and liberties" enjoyed by the religious community of Mount Athos in Greece. In addition, the Bulgarian constitution of 1879 contained guarantees for its Greek and Turkish minorities.

To date, the most conscious and comprehensive attempt to protect ethnic and other minorities through international legal means was through the so-called minority treaties adopted at the end of the First World War and subsequently overseen by the League of Nations. These treaties fell within three categories, although the substantive protections included in each were relatively similar. The first group of treaties included those imposed upon the defeated states of Austria, Hungary, Bulgaria, and Turkey. The second included either new states created out of the dissolution of the Ottoman Empire or states whose boundaries were altered specifically to respond to what President Wilson referred to as "self-determination"; in this group were Czechoslovakia, Greece, Poland, Romania, and Yugoslavia. Finally, special provisions relating to minorities were included in the international regimes established in Åland, Danzig, the Memel Territory, and Upper Silesia.

Among the protections commonly included in the first two categories of treaties were the right to equality of treatment and nondiscrimination; the right to citizenship, although a minority group member could opt to retain another citizenship if desired; the right to use one's own language; the right of minorities to establish and control their own charitable, religious, and social institutions; a state obligation to provide "equitable" financial support to minority schools (in which instruction at the primary level would be in the minority language) and other institutions; and recognition of the supremacy of laws protecting minority rights over other statutes. A certain degree of territorial autonomy was provided for the Åland Islands, Ruthenia in Czechoslovakia, the Valachs of Pindus in Greece, and the Transylvanian Saxons and Szeklers in Romania.

The minority guarantees built into the various post-1919 treaties were not inserted to redress earlier depredations by empires (despite such atrocities as the Armenian genocide in 1915-16), but rather to assuage and protect those "national" minorities whose claims to self-determination were not recognized by the victorious Great Powers. Extensive critiques of the minority treaties have been written and need not be repeated here; there can be little doubt about their ultimate failure. Nevertheless, the result of the Versailles Treaty was a map of Europe that more closely approached the theoretical goal of a collection of true "nation states" than did pre-war Europe, and often cumbersome supervisory mechanisms adopted by the League of Nations to examine minority questions did, on occasion, serve their intended purposes.

Three aspects of the League of Nations treaties should be underscored. First, the minority protections set forth therein were imposed only on a few selected states; no suggestion was made that the Great Powers should be bound by similar obligations. Secondly, the treaties guaranteed what by that time had come to be viewed as traditional minority rights dealing with religion, language, and cultural activities. They did not imply any broader economic or political autonomy, except in the special cases of Danzig, Memel, and Upper Silesia. Third, the purported "self-determination" of certain nationalities resulted, in fact, from the dictates of the Great Powers; the minorities involved were permitted to lobby in Paris, but not to vote at home. . . .

The new United Nations had little difficulty ignoring the preoccupation with minority issues that was the hallmark of its predecessor. The United Nations Charter contains no provision specifically addressing the issue of minority rights. Instead of adopting the League of Nations approach of attempting to resolve the territorial-political problems posed by the existence of minority groups within a state (particularly those which had linguistic or ethnic ties to neighboring states) by boundary adjustments that might more accurately reflect a true nation state, the drafters of the United Nations Charter seemed to assume: 1) that European and other minorities would be satisfied if their individual rights, particularly those of equality and nondiscrimination, were respected; and 2) that reference to the principle of self-determination would be adequate to resolve the problem of colonialism.

While the Universal Declaration of Human Rights . . . makes no specific mention of minority rights, the United Nations became actively involved in minority issues during the 1950s. The ultimately unimplemented proposal for a Free Territory of Trieste and the United Nations-approved establishment of an autonomous Eritrea federated with Ethiopia both addressed minority situations, although each envisioned a greater degree of political autonomy than would traditionally have been reserved to a minority group. The United Nations Commission on Human Rights soon established a Sub-Commission on Prevention of Discrimination and Protection of Minorities, although early attempts by the Sub-Commission to address minority issues were essentially rebuffed by the Commission.

In 1960, the United Nations Educational, Scientific and Cultural Organization (UNESCO) adopted the Convention Against Discrimination in Education, which generally recognized the right of members of national minorities to carry on their own educational activities, including the maintenance of schools and the use or teaching of their own language. However, the latter right was dependent upon "the educational policy of each State," and the general right to minority education was not to prevent minority group members "from understanding the culture and language of the community as a whole and from participating in its activities, or . . . prejudice[] national sovereignty."

The drafting of binding international agreements to implement the Universal Declaration began soon after the Declaration's adoption, and article 27 of the International Covenant on Civil and Political Rights specifically addresses the issue of minority rights. However, the Covenant addresses only minimal, traditional minority rights, i.e., cultural, religious, and linguistic rights. In addition, rights are granted to "persons belonging to such minorities" rather than to minority groups themselves. While this latter distinction may not be important in practice, it is an indication of the individualistic orientation of the Covenant on Civil and Political Rights, as well as the reluctance to recognize the rights of groups which have not yet been satisfactorily defined.

There have been significant international developments since the above article was written in 1991, but Article 27 of the Civil and Political Covenant remains the only legally binding statement of minority rights applicable to the majority of states. It provides, in its entirety:

> In those States in which ethnic, religious or linguistic minorities exist, persons belonging to such minorities shall not be denied the right, in community with the other members of their group, to enjoy their own culture, to profess and practise their own religion, or to use their own language.

The Human Rights Committee has considered a number of complaints concerning alleged violations of Article 27, brought under the Optional Protocol; it also has raised minority issues in its examination of states' periodic reports. See Spiliopoulou, Protection of Minorities Under Article 27 of the International Covenant on Civil and Political Rights and the Reporting System [of] the Human Rights Committee, in Writings in Human and Minority Rights (F. Horn ed. 1994). After years of debate, the Committee in 1994 adopted a General Comment on Article 27, which addressed at least some of the questions raised by the terse text of the article itself.

Human Rights Committee, General Comment No. 23(50) (Art. 27)
U.N. Doc. CCPR/C/21/Rev.1/Add.5, at 2-4 (1994)

5.1 The terms used in article 27 indicate that the persons designed to be protected are those who belong to a group and who share in common a culture, a religion and/or a language. Those terms also indicate that the individuals designed to be protected need not be citizens of the State party. In this regard, the obligations deriving from article 2(1) are also relevant, since a State party is required under that article to ensure that the rights protected under the Covenant are available to all individuals within its territory and subject to its jurisdiction, except rights which are expressly made to apply to citizens, for example, political rights under article 25. A State party may not, therefore, restrict the rights under article 27 to its citizens alone.

5.2. Article 27 confers rights on persons belonging to minorities which "exist" in a State party. Given the nature and scope of the rights envisaged under that article, it is not relevant to determine the degree of permanence that the term "exist" connotes. Those rights simply are that individuals belonging to those minorities should not be denied the right, in community with members of their group, to enjoy their own culture, to practice their religion and speak their language. Just as they need not be nationals or citizens, they need not be permanent residents. Thus, migrant workers or even visitors in a State party constituting such minorities are entitled not to be denied the exercise of those rights. As any other individual in the territory of the State party, they would, also for this purpose, have the general rights, for example, to freedom of association, of assembly, and of expression. The existence of an ethnic, religious or linguistic minority in a given State party does not depend upon a decision by that State party but requires [the existence of a minority] to be established by objective criteria. . . .

6.1. Although article 27 is expressed in negative terms, that article, nevertheless, does recognize the existence of a "right" and requires that it shall not be denied. Consequently, a State party is under an obligation to ensure that the existence and the exercise of this right are protected against their denial or violation. Positive measures of protection are, therefore, required not only against the acts of the State party itself, whether through its legislative, judicial or administrative authorities, but also against the acts of other persons within the State party.

6.2. Although the rights protected under article 27 are individual rights, they depend in turn on the ability of the minority group to maintain its culture, language or religion. Accordingly, positive measures by States may also be necessary to protect the identity of a minority and the rights of its members to enjoy and develop their culture and language and to practice their religion, in community with the other members of the group. In this connection, it has to be observed that such positive measures must respect the provisions of articles 2(1) and 26 of the Covenant both as regards the treatment between different minorities and the treatment between the persons belonging to them and the remaining part of the population. However, as long as those measures are aimed at correcting conditions which prevent or impair the enjoyment of the rights guaranteed under article 27, they may constitute a legitimate differentiation under the Covenant, provided that they are based on reasonable and objective criteria. . . .

9. The Committee concludes that article 27 relates to rights whose protection imposes specific obligations on States parties. The protection of these rights is directed to ensure the survival and continued development of the cultural, religious and social identity of the minorities concerned, thus enriching the fabric of society as a whole. Accordingly, the Committee observes that these rights must be protected as such and should not be confused with other personal rights conferred on one and all under the Covenant. States parties, therefore, have an obligation to ensure that the exercise of these rights is fully protected and they should indicate in their reports the measures they have adopted to this end.

At the initiative of Yugoslavia, a working group of the Commission on Human Rights began work on a declaration on minority rights in 1979, but a final text could not be adopted until 1992. Among the initial impediments were the issue of defining "minority" and whether the declaration would adopt the individualistic orientation of the Civil and Political Covenant (protecting "individuals belonging to" minority groups) or proclaim more straightforward protections for minority groups.

The final product, adopted without a vote by the General Assembly in December 1992, ducked the first issue and followed the Covenant's precedent on the second. Nevertheless, it did expand upon the rather narrow focus of Article 27 of the Covenant. Among the more significant provisions in the short declaration (nine articles) are the following:

UN General Assembly Resolution 47/135
47 U.N. GAOR Supp. (No. 49) at 210, U.N. Doc. A/47/49
(1992)

ARTICLE 1

1. States shall protect the existence and the national or ethnic, cultural, religious and linguistic identity of minorities within their respective territories, and shall encourage conditions for the promotion of that identity.

2. States shall adopt appropriate legislative and other measures to achieve those ends.

ARTICLE 2

1. Persons belonging to national or ethnic, religious and linguistic minorities (hereinafter referred to as persons belonging to minorities) have the right to enjoy their own culture, to profess and practise their own religion, and to use their own language, in private and in public, freely and without interference or any form of discrimination.

2. Persons belonging to minorities have the right to participate effectively in cultural, religious, social, economic and public life.

3. Persons belonging to minorities have the right to participate effectively in decisions on the national and, where appropriate, regional level concerning the minority to which they belong or the regions in which they live, in a manner not incompatible with national legislation.

4. Persons belonging to minorities have the right to establish and maintain their own associations.

5. Persons belonging to minorities have the right to establish and maintain, without any discrimination, free and peaceful contacts with other members of their group and with persons belonging to other minorities, as well as contacts across frontiers with citizens of other States to whom they are related by national or ethnic, religious or linguistic ties. . . .

ARTICLE 4

1. States shall take measures where required to ensure that persons belonging to minorities may exercise fully and effectively all their human rights and fundamental freedoms without any discrimination and in full equality before the law.

2. States shall take measures to create favourable conditions to enable persons belonging to minorities to express their characteristics and to develop their culture, language, religion, traditions and customs, except where specific practices are in violation of national law and contrary to international standards.

3. States should take appropriate measures so that, wherever possible, persons belonging to minorities have adequate opportunities to learn their mother tongue or to have instruction in their mother tongue.

4. States should, where appropriate, take measures in the field of education, in order to encourage knowledge of the history, traditions, language and culture of the minorities existing within their territory. Persons belonging to minorities should have adequate opportunities to gain knowledge of the society as a whole.

5. States should consider appropriate measures so that persons belonging to minorities may participate fully in the economic progress and development in their country.

ARTICLE 5

1. National policies and programmes shall be planned and implemented with due regard for the legitimate interests of persons belonging to minorities.

2. Programmes of cooperation and assistance among States should be planned and implemented with due regard for the legitimate interests of persons belonging to minorities.

ARTICLE 8 . . .

3. Measures taken by States to ensure the effective enjoyment of the rights set forth in this Declaration shall not *prima facie* be considered contrary to the principle of equality contained in the Universal Declaration of Human Rights.

Note: Implementation

As seen with respect to the Standard Minimum Rules, mere promulgation of norms is unlikely to have much impact unless it is accompanied by some mechanism for monitoring compliance. Unfortunately, the Commission on Human Rights has not yet created any mechanism specifically to oversee compliance with the Declaration on Minorities. It has simply called upon states to adopt national measures "to promote and give effect to" the Declaration on Minorities and urged other UN organs and the High Commissioner for Human Rights "to give due regard" to the Declaration. See C.H.R. Res. 1994/22, U.N. ESCOR Supp. (No. 4) at 88, U.N. Doc E/1994/24, ¶¶2, 4-6 (1994). It is anticipated, however, that other UN organs will begin increasingly to refer to the Declaration when considering allegations of violations of minority rights, just as they now utilize the Standard Minimum Rules and other criminal justice principles.

It would be particularly ironic, given its title, if the UN Sub-Commission on the Prevention of Discrimination and the Protection of Minorities did not adopt a more regular means of monitoring the Declaration, perhaps by creating a pre-sessional working group comparable to the Working Group on Indigenous Populations.

Note: European Initiatives

The European system for protecting human rights is discussed in detail in Problem IX, but it is appropriate to note here that Europe has been in the forefront of international legal developments in the definition and protection of the rights of minorities. Indeed, the concepts of nationalism and national minorities were largely developed by Europeans in the nineteenth century, and the various minorities treaties supervised by the League of Nations applied to European states.

Nonetheless, Europe seemed content to ignore "minority" issues until the collapse of communism in the late 1980s, and neither the European Convention on Human Rights (adopted in 1950) nor any of its 11 additional protocols directly address minority issues. However, a proposed European Convention for the Protection of Minorities was submitted to (but not adopted by) the Council of Europe in 1991, and the Committee of Ministers of the Council did adopt and open for signature a European Charter for Regional or Minority Languages, Europ. T.S. No. 148, in 1992. See H. Hannum, Documents on Autonomy and Minority Rights 66, 86 (1993).

During a remarkable four-week meeting in Copenhagen in 1990, the states participating in the Conference on Security and Cooperation in Europe (CSCE) adopted a final document that set forth a wide range of human rights principles, including several paragraphs that represented, at the time, the most extensive catalog of minority rights since the League of Nations. See Document of the Copenhagen Meeting of the Conference on the Human Dimension of the CSCE, adopted June 29, 1990, reprinted in 29 Intl. Legal Materials 1305 (1990).

In 1992, at its summit meeting in Helsinki, the CSCE created the office of High Commissioner on National Minorities, to be "an instrument of conflict prevention at the earliest possible stage." CSCE Helsinki Doc. 1992, The Challenges of Change, Annex II at 7, ¶2 (1992). Although theoretically subject to close political control by the CSCE's Committee of Senior Officials, the High Commissioner adopted an extremely activist interpretation of his mandate in the first two years and submitted a number of recommendations to individual countries concerning specific minority situations. See, e.g., Recommendations by the CSCE High Commissioner on National Minorities upon His Visits to Estonia, Latvia and Lithuania, 4 Helsinki Monitor 76 (No. 3 1993).

The High Commissioner's work is to be "based on CSCE principles and commitments," which are political rather than legal. CSCE Helsinki Doc. 1992, The Challenges of Change, Annex II at 7, ¶4 (1992). His work is to be confidential, although approval has been given for many of his recommendations subsequently to be made public. The High Commissioner is not authorized to "consider violations of CSCE commitments with regard to an individual person belonging to a national minority," but he is permitted to "collect and receive information . . . from any source, including the media and non-governmental organizations . . . [and] receive specific reports from parties directly involved regarding developments concerning national minority issues. These may include reports on violations of CSCE commitments with respect to national minorities as well as other violations in the context of national minority issues." Id. at 11, ¶23. There also is a clear presumption that the High Commissioner will be permitted to conduct on-site investigations, after prior consultation with the concerned state. See id. at 12, ¶¶27-30.

C. *Indigenous Peoples*

The history of Indians in the Western Hemisphere, aboriginal peoples in Australia and New Zealand, and tribal peoples in Asia and Africa has been one of conflict, conquest, marginalization, and even genocide. In many countries native peoples have been simply treated as impediments to territorial expansion; in others they have been accorded special status, often in order to deny them full participation in the surrounding society.

The status of Indian nations and people was the subject of early discourses by Franciscus de Victoria, Alberico Gentili, and others, and France, England, Canada, the United States, and other states entered into treaties with Indian governments. Nonetheless, the conquering Europeans ultimately refused to recognize that indigenous societies were among the "civilized nations" that participated in the formulation of and enjoyed the benefits of international law. See generally R. Williams, Jr., The American Indian in Western Legal Thought (1990).

In the United States, Chief Justice Marshall's acceptance of the doctrine of discovery in Johnson v. McIntosh, 21 U.S. (8 Wheat.) 543 (1823), and his later characterization of Indian tribes as "domestic dependent nations" in Cherokee Nation v. Georgia, 30 U.S. (5 Pet.) 1 (1831), confirmed that Indian governments were subject to the jurisdiction of the United States. Only a year later, however, Marshall refined his characterization and described Indian tribes as "distinct people, divided into separate nations, independent of each other, and of the rest of the world, having institutions of their own, and governing themselves by their own laws."

Worcester v. Georgia, 21 U.S. (6 Pet.) 515, 542-543 (1832); see R. Barsh and J. Henderson, The Road 50-61 (1980).

As one author has noted, "Indian law is a complex field, and generalizations are subject to exceptions and can be misleading." Suagee, Self-Determination for Indigenous Peoples at the Dawn of the Solar Age, 25 Mich. J. L. Reform 671, 698 (1992). This is not the place to summarize the convoluted history of relations between the federal government and tribal governments, which generally led to the assertion of greater authority by the former over the latter until a change of policy in the 1970s. Congress has assumed plenary power to legislate for Indian tribes, but the latter have always retained residual governmental powers as an aspect of their original or inherent sovereignty. "Within their reservations, tribes generally retain all powers other than those they gave up in treaties, had taken away by an express act of Congress, or had taken away by implicit divestiture as a result of their dependent status." Id. at 699.

At whatever stage of Indian-federal relations one chooses, however, it is abundantly clear that Indians and their right of self-government are quite different from the rights of "national minorities" recognized in Europe and discussed in the immediately preceding section. Indigenous peoples themselves have consistently rejected classification as minorities, and, both conceptually and politically, assertions of indigenous rights have always involved claims to resources, territory, and governmental powers that go far beyond the traditional concerns of minorities for protection of their language, religion, and culture.

The inherent conflict of authority — often debated in terms of sovereignty — between national and indigenous governments led the former to claim that relations with indigenous tribes were purely a matter of domestic jurisdiction. Thus, despite the existence of treaties between some indigenous nations and European settler states, indigenous rights were not recognized as a separate issue of international concern until relatively recently. Although the International Labor Organization (ILO), in particular, had been concerned with the status and condition of indigenous workers since the 1920s, no multilateral treaty addressed the issue of indigenous rights per se until the adoption in 1957 of ILO Convention No. 107 Concerning the Protection and Integration of Indigenous and Other Tribal and Semi-Tribal Populations in Independent Countries, 328 U.N.T.S. 247.

The assimilationist orientation of this treaty was soon challenged and ultimately rejected by the ILO in 1989, when Convention No. 107 was revised by Convention No. 169 Concerning Indigenous and Tribal Peoples in Independent Countries, which entered into force in 1991. Convention No. 169 requires, inter alia, that indigenous peoples be consulted whenever laws or administrative regulations affecting them are considered, and that "special measures" be adopted to safeguard indigenous interests. Article 14 of the Convention recognizes "[t]he rights of ownership and possession of the peoples concerned over the lands which they traditionally occupy," and

Article 8 declares that indigenous peoples "shall have the right to retain their own customs and institutions, where these are not incompatible with fundamental rights defined by the national legal system and with internationally recognized human rights."

Note also should be taken of the shift in terminology from indigenous "populations" to "peoples." However, responding to state fears of indigenous self-determination claims, Article 1(3) superfluously provides that "use of the term 'peoples' in this Convention shall not be construed as having any implications as regards the rights which may attach to the term under international law."

Although no specific mechanism to encourage compliance is created by Convention No. 169, states are obliged to report on their implementation of its provisions through the ILO's regular and comprehensive supervisory machinery. See generally Leary, Lessons from the Experience of the International Labour Organisation, in The United Nations and Human Rights (P. Alston ed. 1992).

A much more ambitious attempt to define internationally recognized rights for indigenous peoples began in 1982, with the establishment of the Working Group on Indigenous Populations of the UN Sub-Commission on the Prevention of Discrimination and the Protection of Minorities. It was not until 1994 that a draft declaration on indigenous rights was forwarded by the Sub-Commission to the Commission on Human Rights for adoption, and many governments and indigenous peoples continue to disagree over provisions in the draft concerning, inter alia, self-determination, the extent of indigenous self-government, and indigenous control over land, resources, and development activities. See Report of the Working Group on Indigenous Populations, U.N. Doc. E/CN.4/Sub.2/1993/29, Annex I at 50 (1993), for the text of the draft declaration.

D. Self-Determination

The only multilateral treaties that formally recognize the right of self-determination are the two covenants on human rights, which contain identical language as their first articles. However, what has become a norm of customary international law in the context of classic decolonization developed initially not through a treaty but as "soft law" proclaimed in General Assembly resolutions, which eventually came to be supported by the practice of states.

Although it was not the first resolution to set forth a right to self-determination, the 1960 Declaration on the Granting of Independence to Colonial Countries and Peoples, G.A. Res. 1514, 15 U.N. GAOR Supp. (No. 16) at 66, U.N. Doc. A/4684 (1960), probably remains the most significant statement on the topic. It sets forth the fundamental principle of self-determination, along with an equally fundamental limitation on its application:

2. All peoples have the right to self-determination; by virtue of that right they freely determine their political status and freely pursue their economic, social and cultural development. . . .

6. Any attempt aimed at the partial or total disruption of the national unity and the territorial integrity of a country is incompatible with the purposes and principles of the Charter of the United Nations.

Since 1960 these principles have been reiterated on numerous occasions, most notably in the authoritative 1970 Declaration on Principles of International Law Concerning Friendly Relations and Co-Operation Among States in Accordance with the Charter of the United Nations, G.A. Res. 2625, 25 U.N. GAOR Supp. (No. 28), Annex at 121, U.N. Doc. A/5217 (1970).

Assertions of a right of self-determination or secession by ethnic and other groups have occurred regularly throughout the twentieth century, and the expansion of these demands outside the colonial context has led increasingly to violent conflict. The post-1989 dissolution of the Soviet Union, Yugoslavia, Czechoslovakia, and Ethiopia has emboldened groups seeking either independence or some form of self-government and, at the same time, has demonstrated the inability of international law to provide persuasive normative criteria for resolving such conflicts.

Despite the fact that the right to self-determination is proclaimed in the Civil and Political Covenant, the Human Rights Committee has refused to consider this highly charged issue in the context of allegations of human rights violations raised under the Optional Protocol. The Committee's General Comment on Article 1 did little more than restate the article itself; see General Comment No. 12/21, Report of the Human Rights Committee, 39 U.N. GAOR Supp. (No. 40), Annex VI at 142, U.N. Doc. A/39/40 (1984). After refusing to consider Article 1 arguments raised in several communications under the Optional Protocol, the Committee restated its position in 1994 in its General Comment on Article 27:

3.1. The Covenant draws a distinction between the right to self-determination and the rights protected under article 27. The former is expressed to be a right belonging to peoples and is dealt with in a separate part (Part I) of the Covenant. Self-determination is not a right cognizable under the Optional Protocol. Article 27, on the other hand, relates to rights conferred on individuals as such and is included, like the articles relating to other personal rights conferred on individuals, in Part III of the Covenant and is cognizable under the Optional Protocol.

3.2. The enjoyment of the rights to which article 27 relates does not prejudice the sovereignty and territorial integrity of a State party. At the same time, one or [the] other aspect of the rights of individuals protected under that article — for example, to enjoy a particular culture — may consist in a way of life which is closely associated with territory and use of its resources. This may particularly be true of members of indigenous communities constituting a minority.

Human Rights Committee, General Comment No. 23(50) (Art. 27), U.N. Doc. CCPR/C/21/Rev.1/Add.5, at 2 (1994). Although the Committee's distinction between Articles 1 and 27 is accurate as far as it goes, it obviously does little to help determine which groups are minorities and which are peoples entitled to self-determination.

It remains to be seen whether self-determination claims, with their potentially profound impact on the very structure of the state, can be better considered from a human rights perspective instead of being subject exclusively to the geopolitical calculations that guide responses to such claims today. For arguments in favor of the human rights approach, see Anaya, A Contemporary Definition of the International Norm of Self-Determination, 3 Transnatl. L. & Contemp. Probs. 131 (1993); Hannum, Rethinking Self-Determination, 34 Va. J. Intl. L. 1 (1993); a more traditional (and less useful) approach is adopted in M. Halperin, D. Scheffer, and P. Small, Self-Determination in the New World Order (1992).

Comments and Questions

1. Is the Committee's General Comment on Article 27, pages 327-328 supra, an expansive or a restrictive interpretation of the language of the article? Do you think states intended to grant minority rights to migrant workers and tourists? Does Paragraph 6.1 mean that private employers cannot prohibit employees from speaking their own language on the job? What kinds of "positive measures . . . may also be necessary to protect the identity of a minority"?

2. Although two UN rapporteurs have proposed definitions that have been generally accepted, states have been unwilling or unable to reach formal agreement on a definition of either minorities or indigenous peoples. See United Nations, Study on the Rights of Persons Belonging to Ethnic, Religious and Linguistic Minorities 96 [F. Capotorti, Special Rapporteur], U.N. Sales No. E.91.XIV.2 (1977, reprinted 1991); United Nations, Study of the Problem of Discrimination Against Indigenous Populations, Conclusions and Recommendations 50, 51 [A. Martinez Cobo, Special Rapporteur], U.N. Sales No. E.86.XIV.3 (1986). Can one develop meaningful norms in this area without defining such essential terms as minority, indigenous, and people?

3. In 1975 Congress adopted the Indian Self-Determination and Education Assistance Act, 25 U.S.C. §§13a, 450-450n, 455-458e, 42 U.S.C. §2004b (1994), which permits tribes to enter into contracts with the federal government and assume responsibility for various federally administered programs. Does this constitute "self-determination" as that term is understood in international law?

4. Are the so-called group rights of minorities, indigenous peoples, and others inherently too political to be usefully considered to be human rights?

Compare the discussion of "third generation" rights at pages 201-206 of Problem III. Are judicial or quasi-judicial forums less well suited to assessing claims of violations of these rights, as opposed to bodies whose purpose is conciliation or mediation?

5. There is an extensive body of literature on all of the topics discussed in this section. On minority rights, particularly in the League of Nations era, see, for example, I. Claude, Jr., National Minorities (1955); C. Macartney, National States and National Minorities (1934). Both historical and contemporary aspects of minority rights are addressed in P. Thornberry, International Law and the Rights of Minorities (1991); J. Sigler, Minority Rights, A Comparative Analysis (1983); the Capotorti study, cited supra in Comment 2; Das Minderheitenrecht europäischer Staaten (J. Frowein, R. Hofmann, and S. Oeter eds. 1993).

Although it is now somewhat dated, one of the most comprehensive comparative studies on indigenous peoples is United Nations, Study of the Problem of Discrimination Against Indigenous Populations [A. Martinez Cobo, Special Rapporteur], U.N. Doc. E/CN.4/Sub.2/1986/7 & Adds. 1-4 (1986); the final addendum, which includes the study's conclusions and recommendations, is published as U.N. Sales No. E.86.XIV.3 (1986). See also Barsh, Indigenous Peoples: An Emerging Object of International Law, 80 Am. J. Intl. L. 369 (1986); Daes, Some Considerations on the Rights of Indigenous Peoples to Self-Determination, 3 Transnatl. L. & Contemp. Probs. 1 (1993); Hannum, New Developments in Indigenous Rights, 28 Va. J. Intl. L. 649 (1988); Sambo, Indigenous Peoples and International Standard-Setting Processes: Are State Governments Listening?, 3 Transnatl. L. & Contemp. Probs. 13 (1993).

Among the many works that address the issue of self-determination from a legal perspective, see H. Hannum, Autonomy, Sovereignty, and Self-Determination, The Accommodation of Conflicting Rights (1990); M. Pomerance, Self-Determination in Law and Practice (1982); A. Rigo Sureda, The Evolution of the Right of Self-Determination (1973); United Nations, The Right to Self-Determination, Historical and Current Developments on the Basis of the United Nations Instruments [A. Cristescu, Special Rapporteur], U.N. Sales No. E.80.XIV.3 (1981); United Nations, The Right to Self-Determination, Implementation of United Nations Resolutions [H. Gros Espiell, Special Rapporteur], U.N. Sales No. E.79.XIV.5 (1980).

V. Final Comments and Questions

1. As noted in Problem III, it appears that standard-setting activities in the UN are increasingly taking the form of non-binding declarations or

guidelines rather than new treaties. Which of the following factors might contribute to this trend?

(a) The general unwillingness of states to subscribe to additional international human rights instruments.
(b) The realization of some states that model laws and guidelines, being just that, carry with them no international legal obligation.
(c) The recognition that, even when an international human rights instrument has been ratified, it has little "legal bite" absent good faith compliance, so why not agree to declarations of "soft law," which implicitly accept that voluntary compliance is the sine qua non of effective international human rights law.

2. What difference does it make, substantively and procedurally, if the United States subscribes to an international human rights norm embodied in:

(a) A self-executing treaty?
(b) A non-self-executing treaty?
(c) A model law or declaration approved in an international forum but not enacted into national legislation?
(d) A model law or declaration subsequently enacted into state or federal law?

3. This Problem has referred to the standards it discusses as "soft law." Would it be appropriate to refer to the implementation procedures it describes as "soft procedures"? What impact can reporting systems such as those discussed herein have if states are under no legal obligation to cooperate with UN requests for information? Keep these issues in mind as you read the next two Problems, which consider in greater detail the issues of UN enforcement of human rights norms and fact-finding.

Problem V

The Greek Case, Resolution 1503, and Other UN Mechanisms

When Does the UN Investigate Human Rights Violations?

I.   The Right to Petition as a Human Right   342
II. The Situation in Greece: The Sub-Commission's First Test Case   344
     A. Resolution 1503: High Expectations   344
     B. Historical Note   344
         Note: Greece: Justice in Blinkers   346
         Note: Human Rights Report on Greece   347
     C. Communication Alleging Violation of Human Rights
         in Greece   348
     D. The Sub-Commission's Response to the Communication   354
         Note: Disappointing Start to New U.N. Procedure on Human
         Rights   354
     E. The Reaction of the Greek Regime   357
         Letter from the Permanent Representative of Greece to the
         United Nations   357
     F. The Overthrow of the Greek Regime and the Sub-Commission's
         Role Therein   361
         Note: The Overthrow of the Greek Regime   361
         Statement by Amnesty International and the International Stu-
         dent Movement for the UN   362
III. Analyzing the Procedures and Problems of Resolution 1503   363
         Newman, The New U.N. Procedures for Human Rights Com-
         plaints: Reform, Status Quo, or Chamber of Horrors?   363
         H. Tolley, Jr., The U.N. Commission on Human Rights   366
         Alston, The Commission on Human Rights   379
IV. Other UN Mechanisms for Investigating Alleged Human
     Rights Abuses   380
     A. Petition Procedures   380
     B. Non-Petition Procedures   382
         J. Carey, UN Protection of Civil and Political Rights   383
         Alston, The Commission on Human Rights   385
         Commission on Human Rights, Torture and Other Cruel, Inhu-
         man or Degrading Treatment or Punishment   394
         Commission on Human Rights, Question of Arbitrary Detention   394
         Commission on Human Rights, Right to Freedom of Opinion
         and Expression   395

Report of the Working Group on Arbitrary Detention   396
Commission on Human Rights, Human Rights and Thematic
   Procedures   396
C. Future Prospects   400
   H. Tolley, Jr., The U.N. Commission on Human Rights   400
   Farer, The United Nations and Human Rights: More Than a
   Whimper Less Than a Roar   402
V. Final Comments and Questions   405

I.   The Right to Petition as a Human Right

The process of enforcing human rights takes many forms, including diplomatic debates in political fora (see Problem I), formal state-to-state complaints under relevant treaties (see pages 222-223 of Problem III and 692-715 of Problem IX), and discussions by expert bodies of reports on human rights implementation submitted by states (see pages 211-214 of Problem III). As discussed in this Problem, attention also may be focused on human rights violations through investigations of particular countries or issues by intergovernmental bodies. All of these techniques, it will be noted, are triggered by the decisions of states — individually and collectively.

Previous Problems have shown that the development of international human rights law closely tracks the recognition of the individual — as distinct from the state — as now being a proper subject of international law. Since states frequently are reluctant to protest human rights violations in other states, it is only logical — and, indeed, absolutely necessary — that not only states, but also individuals be accorded standing to protest such violations. Otherwise, many human rights violations will go without any possible redress, assuredly an anomaly in view of the professed concern with individual rights articulated on all sides today. For this reason it is not surprising that the UN General Assembly, nearly 50 years ago, declared that "the right of petition is an essential human right, as is recognized in the Constitutions of a great number of countries" (G.A. Res. 217B [III], U.N. Doc. A/810, at 77 (1948)).

Several important international agreements, notably the UN Charter and the "Declaration of Santiago" establishing the Inter-American Commission on Human Rights in 1959, have been interpreted to permit the right of petition even in the absence of an express provision to that effect. The right has been codified as well in several other UN treaties, regional conventions, and specialized agreements, and, in more recent years, pro-

Petition

cedures concerning these petitions (or "applications" or "communications," as they are sometimes called) have been established within various international organizations. The following treaty clauses specifically provide that individuals or sometimes NGOs acting on their behalf may complain to an international forum or tribunal directly via the petition route:

1. UN Charter, Art. 87(b) (Trusteeship Council);
2. UN Convention on Racial Discrimination, Art. 14;
3. Optional Protocol to the UN Covenant on Civil and Political Rights;
4. UN Convention Against Torture, Art. 22;
5. ILO treaties;
6. European Convention on Human Rights, Art. 25;
7. American Convention on Human Rights, Art. 44;
8. African Charter on Human and Peoples' Rights, Art. 56.

In addition, the UN Educational, Scientific, and Cultural Organization (UNESCO) has created by resolution of its Executive Board, Decision 104 EX/3.3, a confidential procedure for consideration of petitions alleging violations of human rights within UNESCO's competence. Finally, the UN Commission on the Status of Women is provided an annual list that summarizes communications received alleging violations of human rights that affect the status of women.

Among the treaty-based regimes, acceptance of the right of individual petition is mandatory only under the American Convention (although it also will be mandatory under the European Convention when Protocol No. 11 enters into force). However, all parties to the European Convention have accepted the right under Article 25 (or will do so soon after ratifying the Convention). As of mid-1994, 76 of the 127 parties to the Civil and Political Covenant had accepted the Optional Protocol, but only 18 of the 135 parties to the Convention on Racial Discrimination had accepted its Committee's competence to consider communications under Article 14; 35 of the 82 parties to the Torture Convention had accepted the right of individual petition under Article 22.

Although some of the above treaty clauses will be mentioned again, this Problem will focus primarily on the right of petition and other means of investigating human rights abuses inherent within the UN system. In addition to the confidential "communications" under the Resolution 1503 procedure, we will examine the initiation and scope of investigations by the "thematic" and country-specific rapporteurs of the UN Commission on Human Rights and briefly describe the activities of UNESCO and the International Labor Organization.

II.   The Situation in Greece:
The Sub-Commission's First Test Case

A.   *Resolution 1503: High Expectations*

Despite the fact that the UN received thousands of complaints from individuals about alleged human rights violations throughout the world, for over a decade no UN organ would consider such petitions (except in the context of trust and non-self-governing territories, discussed at pages 380-381 infra). It was only in 1959 that the Commission on Human Rights was authorized to review summaries of communications received by the Secretary-General, but with the caveat that the Commission had "no power to take any action in regard to any complaints concerning human rights" (E.S.C. Res. 728F, 28 U.N. ESCOR Supp. (No. 1) at 19, U.N. Doc. E/3290 (1959)). Eight years later, in 1967, the Commission and its Sub-Commission on Prevention of Discrimination and Protection of Minorities were empowered to make studies "of situations which reveal a consistent pattern of violations of human rights as exemplified by . . . apartheid . . . and racial discrimination" and report and make recommendations to the Economic and Social Council (E.S.C. Res. 1235, Documentary Supplement) (see pages 383-390 infra).

Finally, in 1970, ECOSOC Resolution 1503, entitled "Procedure for Dealing with Communications Relating to Violations of Human Rights and Fundamental Freedoms," was adopted. This landmark resolution, coupled with a subsequent resolution of the Sub-Commission which set out still more specific procedures (Sub-Commission on Prevention of Discrimination and Protection of Minorities Res. 1, Documentary Supplement), broke the logjam at the UN that had until that time prevented it from discussing specific human rights violations, except for those occurring in colonial territories, Southern Africa, and (after 1967) the Israeli-occupied territories in the Middle East. The UN was now in the business (or so it was thought) of enforcing human rights worldwide through individual petitions.

Less than a year after the Sub-Commission had adopted a set of specific procedures for dealing with communications, the first major petition arrived.

B.   *Historical Note*

On 21 April 1967, a military junta of right-wing army colonels successfully seized control of the government of Greece. This coup d'etat was the fifth one in Greece since 1920, revealing the political unrest and volatility that has characterized Greece during its century and a half of independence.

The 1967 upheaval had its roots in a 1965 confrontation between King Constantine II and the popular Center Union party of Premier George Papandreou. The famous Aspida case brought these two powerful figures into combat. King Constantine alleged that the leftist organization Aspida (the Shield) was penetrating the army. An investigation by Papandreou's Center Union government reported that the group was harmless, and that the King's accusations were a red herring. When Papandreou, in retaliation, demanded that King Constantine's right-wing Defense Minister Garoufalias resign, the King refused to comply and demanded and accepted Papandreou's resignation instead.

Popular support for Papandreou escalated into violence and bloodshed over the following months, and for the next two years the country was torn between two extremes, with caretaker governments continually being reshuffled. During this time, the alleged Aspida plotters, including both George Papandreou and his son Andreas, were indicted on charges of conspiracy to seize power and depose the monarchy. Although the Papandreous eventually were released, the trial served to agitate and polarize the nation even further. Most of the 28 defendants refused to defend themselves on the ground that the entire Aspida case rested on trumped-up charges. Fifteen officers finally were convicted on 16 March 1967.

Only a few days before the close of the trial, Andreas Papandreou published an article charging that forces in Greece were conspiring to rig the upcoming May elections, thereby keeping his father from being chosen Premier. The dictatorship that Andreas Papandreou rightly predicted would oust the caretaker government of Premier Panayotis Kanellopoulos by military coup seized power in Athens in April 1967.

The five-officer military junta, led by Colonel George Papadopoulos, immediately occupied all government buildings, commandeered all media operations, and closed all borders. It declared a curfew, and all vehicles and pedestrians were forbidden on the streets. Broadcasts announced that the country was in a state of siege and that many constitutional rights were temporarily suspended, specifically:

(1) Individuals can be apprehended and arrested without charge. They can be detained for any length of time. (2) There is no bail for political crimes. (3) All citizens, independent of position, can be brought before an emergency court-martial. (4) All gatherings, indoors or outdoors, are forbidden. All gatherings will be dissolved by force. (5) It is forbidden to form a syndicate [union] or group with labor union aims. Strikes are completely forbidden. (6) It is permitted to search houses, political premises, public buildings, all buildings, day and night, without special warrant. (7) It is forbidden to announce or publish any kind of information in any way through the press, radio and television without censorship beforehand. (8) Letters, telegrams and all means of communication will be censored. (9) Crimes, political crimes as well as those of the press, whether they have to do with private life or not, as well as the crimes to be judged by the court of appeal, will be judged by

court-martial. (10) Everyone who commits a crime which should be punished by law, even if it is not against the army, will also be judged by court-martial.

Greece Under the Junta 14 (P. Schwab and G. Frangos eds. 1970).

Army patrols reportedly rounded up between 2,500 and 6,000 persons, including all the country's major political figures, within 48 hours of the coup. The most prominent among them were kept under arrest in Athens hotels. Other prisoners were detained in hastily built camps or converted soccer stadiums. Newspapers and other publications were shut down or placed under heavy censorship.

The scheduled May elections thus were preempted by mass arrests, censorship, purges, and the imposition of a state of siege, all executed in the name of freedom from communism. Numerous reports of the barbaric torture of political prisoners, arbitrary arrests, and prolonged detention without charge began filtering through to international human rights organizations. In 1969, and again in 1971, the International Commission of Jurists reported no change in the regime initially imposed by the military junta.

Note: Greece: Justice in Blinkers
1 Intl. Commn. Jurists Rev. 6, 6-7 (1969)

Little has changed in Greece since the Colonels seized power two years ago. The regime is still totalitarian. The old Constitution has been repealed and the main provisions of the new Constitution, those governing the fundamental freedoms of citizens, have been suspended. Despite assurances to the contrary, a return to democracy seems as remote as before; the regime seems even to be tightening its grip on the country as opposition to it becomes more overt. A symptom of the deterioration in the situation is the increase in political trials. Most of the accused are quite clearly being tried for their political opinions. The principal victims of this purge are the liberal intellectuals.

The International Commission of Jurists sent Observers to two of these trials. Mr. Michael Ellman, a solicitor from London, was sent to Athens in July 1968 to observe the trial of *Notaras and others* and Professor Edmond Martin-Achard, former President of the Genevan Bar, attended the trial of *Nestor and others*, held at Salonika in November 1968. The main points that Mr. Ellman made in his report are again to be found in that of Professor Martin-Achard, which . . . gives a good picture of how such trials are conducted.

Perhaps the most characteristic and disturbing feature brought out by these reports is the absence of any real legal basis to support the prosecution or the sentences imposed. The Colonels were not even able to resort to their "Basic Decrees," a device purporting to give their actions legal validity.

They finally fell back on a law dating from the civil war, No. 509 of 1947, which is now their principal instrument for removing opponents under the semblance of legality.

The arbitrary use that is made of this law is indefensible. Acts which are often so innocuous that in a free country they would not even be considered criminal are assimilated to treason. Moreover, Law 509 was an emergency law passed during a civil war to meet a special situation; it should have been repealed long ago. In addition, its purpose was to outlaw communism: the accused must be shown to have committed acts "in implementation of an ideology whose manifest and avowed aim is the forceful overthrow of the established social order and political system." In most of the cases the elements of the offence under Law 509 were not present. But that was no obstacle. The military judges were soldiers not lawyers and saw no reason why they should be prevented by purely legal considerations from convicting the accused and imposing disproportionate sentences upon them.

It is perhaps understandable that the Colonels should be fond of courts martial and should find in martial law a means of acquiring powers which are normally exercised by others. They are enabled to establish an authoritarian government, unembarrassed by opposition from those they rule over. But so long as martial law is in force, it is useless to talk of restoring the proper balance of power and normal political life, and equally useless for the Greeks to expect any guarantee of impartiality from the courts. . . .

Note: Human Rights Report on Greece
7 Intl. Commn. Jurists Rev. 9, 10 (1971)

The International Commission of Jurists is also deeply concerned about the continuing cases of arbitrary arrests and prolonged detentions without trial in Greece. Among the most notorious of these is the detention of Judge Christos Sartzetakis and other members of the legal profession. The case of Judge Sartzetakis has received wide public attention because of his independence and personal courage. His brilliant handling of the Lambrakis case, at the conclusion of which he committed several senior police and gendarmerie officers to the Criminal Court for trial, was portrayed in the French film "Z." In May 1968, the military regime "suspended" for three days the provision of the Constitution guaranteeing the independence of the judiciary, and then dismissed Sartzetakis and a number of other judges for alleged acts "incompatible with the status of the Judiciary" and "political partiality" in the exercise of their functions. An appeal was lodged before the Council of State in July 1968, which led to the crisis between the Government and the highest administrative Tribunal. By annulling the judges' dismissal, the Council of State entered into an open conflict with the military régime who reacted by dismissing the President of the Council and forcing the resignation of its most distinguished members. Judge Sartzetakis was arrested on Christmas Eve, 1970. He was held by the military police, for nearly a year — practically incommunicado — with no date set for his trial. Following many powerful representations by legal professions from all over Europe and the United States and by many organisations including the International Commission of Jurists Judge Sartzetakis was at last released on 19 November 1971.

C.   Communication Alleging Violation of Human Rights in Greece

His Excellency Kurt Waldheim   May 19, 1972
Secretary-General of the United Nations
United Nations
New York, N.Y. 10017

Dear Mr. Secretary-General:

On behalf of [five] individuals and [two non-governmental] organizations, and at their request, I address this letter to you as their Communication Concerning Human Rights in Greece:

You will see that this communication (with its annexes) reveals a consistent pattern of gross violations of human rights and fundamental freedoms by the Greek Government.

Some of the people whom I represent are victims of those violations. All have reliable knowledge that enables them to present clear evidence of the violations.

The object of this communication is to seek implementation of the relevant principles of the United Nations Charter, of the Universal Declaration of Human Rights, and of other applicable instruments in the field of human rights. Among the rights that in Greece have been and are being grossly violated are these:

> The right not to be subjected to torture or to cruel, inhuman or degrading treatment or punishment.
>
> The right to liberty and security of person, and to be free from arbitrary arrest and detention.
>
> The right to a fair and public hearing by an independent and impartial tribunal, and the right when charged with a penal offense to be presumed innocent until proved guilty in a public trial which respects the guarantees necessary for one's defense.

✻ L against torture

The right to freedom of opinion, expression, peaceful assembly and association.

The right to be free from arbitrary deprivation of nationality.

The right to take part in the government of one's country, directly or through freely chosen representatives, and the right of the Greek people to express their will in genuine elections.

The right to equal protection against discrimination that violates the Universal Declaration of Human Rights.

ANNEX I to this communication sets forth the clauses of the Universal Declaration of Human Rights that are pertinent. It also summarizes the discussions regarding Greece that took place in the UN Commission on Human Rights during 1968.

ANNEX II to this communication sets forth evidence of torture and of other gross violations, and it shows that they are part of a consistent pattern. Some of the evidence we set forth was examined formally by the Council of Europe in 1969 and 1970. Those European proceedings and the consequent condemnation of the Greek Government are discussed in ANNEX II. The Greek government rejected that verdict, however; and thus there has not been any settlement in accordance with the principles set forth in the Universal Declaration of Human Rights or other applicable documents in the field of human rights.

ANNEX III [not reprinted here] shows how the torture and other gross violations of human rights in Greece have continued since 1970, notwithstanding the Council of Europe action. Accordingly, the purpose of this letter is to secure, pursuant to ECOSOC Resolutions 728F and 1503, a study or investigation of the pertinent facts.

Therefore, Mr. Secretary-General, we request that you proceed pursuant to ECOSOC Resolutions 728F and 1503, and that you recommend whatever steps may be appropriate to help secure the study or investigation we herein request.

It should be recalled that Greece, as a Member of the United Nations, more than a quarter-century ago pledged itself to take joint and separate action, in cooperation with the Organization, for the achievement of the human rights goals set forth in Article 55 of the United Nations Charter.

Also to be recalled is the awesome pronouncement in the Universal Declaration of Human Rights that ". . . it is essential, if man is not to be compelled to have recourse, as a last resort, to rebellion against tyranny and oppression, that human rights should be protected by the rule of law."

Sincerely,
FRANK C. NEWMAN, Counsel

ANNEX I

This Annex contains first, a chart that shows how violations of human rights in Greece relate to clauses of the Universal Declaration; and second, a summary of a discussion of the Greek situation that took place in the United Nations Commission on Human Rights during February 1968.

Rights violated in Greece	Universal declaration of human rights
The right not to be subjected to torture or to cruel, inhuman or degrading treatment or punishment.	Article 5. No one shall be subjected to torture or to cruel, inhuman degrading treatment or punishment.
The right to liberty and security of person, and to be free from arbitrary arrest and detention.	Article 3. Everyone has the right to life, liberty and security of person.
	Article 9. No one shall be subjected to arbitrary arrest, detention or exile.
The right to a fair and public hearing by an independent and impartial tribunal, and the right when charged with a penal offense to be presumed innocent until proved guilty in a public trial which respects the guarantees necessary for one's defense.	Article 10. Everyone is entitled in full equality to a fair and public hearing by an independent and impartial tribunal, in the determination of his rights and obligations and of any criminal charge against him.
	Article 11. (1) Everyone charged with a penal offence has the right to be presumed innocent until proved guilty according to law in a public trial at which he has had all the guarantees necessary for his defense.
The right to freedom of opinion, expression, peaceful assembly and association.	Article 19. Everyone has the right to freedom of opinion and expression; this right includes freedom to hold opinions without interference and to seek, receive and impart information and ideas through any media and regardless of frontiers.
	Article 20. (1) Everyone has the right to freedom of peaceful assembly and association.
The right to be free from arbitrary deprivation of nationality.	Article 15. (1) Everyone has the right to a nationality. (2) No one shall be arbitrarily deprived of his nationality nor denied the right to change his nationality.
The right to take part in the government of one's country, directly or through freely chosen representatives, and the right of the Greek peo-	Article 21. (1) Everyone has the right to take part in the government of his country, directly or through freely chosen representatives . . . .(3) The

ple to express their will in genuine elections.

The right to equal protection against discrimination that violates the Universal Declaration.

will of the people shall be the basis of the authority of government; this will shall be expressed in periodic and genuine elections which shall be by universal and equal suffrage and shall be held by secret vote or by equivalent free voting procedures.

Article 7. All are equal before the law and are entitled without any discrimination to equal protection of the law. All are entitled to equal protection against any discrimination in violation of this Declaration and against any incitement to such discrimination.

Article 2. Everyone is entitled to all the rights and freedoms set forth in this Declaration, without distinction of any kind, such as race, colour, sex, language, religion, political or other opinion, national or social origin, property, birth or other status.

THE UNITED NATIONS AND HUMAN RIGHTS IN GREECE

Four years ago [1968] the UN Commission on Human Rights discussed Greece, in connection with the "Study of situations which reveal a consistent pattern of violations of human rights." . . . In those discussions the Greek representative argued:

1. That "protests against the situation in Greece . . . were vile fabrications" and that "charges of ill-treatment of political prisoners were entirely false, unfounded and malevolent."

This Annex will demonstrate that charges against the Greek Government are not "vile fabrications" and, specifically, that the charges of torture and other ill-treatment are not "false, unfounded and malevolent."

2. That "the change of Government in Greece on 21 April 1967 was of a purely temporary character," that "certain human rights had been temporarily suspended in time of emergency," and that "[t]here was no consistent pattern of violations of human rights; instead there had been a temporary suspension of certain human rights which were now being gradually restored."

In 1972 the new regime appears entrenched. It recently celebrated the Fifth Anniversary of its seizure of power, which no longer can be described as "of a purely temporary character." The "temporary suspension of certain human rights" unhappily has become long-lived. Promises that continue to be made about rights, "being gradually restored" are infected with knowledge that restorations have been far too gradual.

3. That "article 15, paragraph 1 of the Convention of Rome for the Protection of Human Rights and Fundamental Freedoms, to which his country was party, provided for derogation in case of emergency," that "the Council of Europe had already begun the legal and judicial examination of the question of violations," and that a "report by the Council of Europe on the situation in Greece provided clear proof of the falsity of the accusations. . . . [T]he report stated that it had no direct proof on which it could objectively state that torture was officially used."

In 1970 the Council of Europe concluded its "legal and judicial examination." It held that the Government's "measures and practices were and are not justified under Article 15." On the basis of both direct and indirect proof it held the Government guilty of violating the treaty's Article 3 ("No one shall be subjected to torture or to inhuman or degrading treatment or punishment.").

4. That human rights violations in Greece "could not be compared with consistent violations of human rights based on racist *or dictatorial philosophies* perpetuating themselves to the point of falling within the Commission's terms of reference," [italics added] and that on "16 December 1967, the Chairman of the [Constitutional] Commission has stated officially that the new, democratic draft constitution fully safeguarded human rights and fundamental freedoms. A series of measures had also been taken to guarantee freedom of assembly and by September 1968 that freedom would be completely restored."

It appears that continued, gross violations are "based on . . . dictatorial philosophies." The new constitution does *not* safeguard rights and freedoms. Freedom of assembly was *not* restored in September 1968. It is merely one of the many rights and freedoms that still are denied to the Greek people, grossly.

5. That, regarding the Council of Europe, "[i]t was unfortunate that the United Nations did not yet have similar machinery"; and "his delegation should be given all information relating to the charges made."

It should be noted that procedures similar to the European machinery now have been set up by the UN Economic and Social Council (in its Resolution 1503, 27 May 1970) and by the Sub-Commission on Prevention of Discrimination and Protection of Minorities (in its Resolution 1, 13 August 1971). Those procedures and ECOSOC Resolution 728F, 30 July 1959, ensure that "all information relating to the charges" is made available to the representatives of Greece.

We should presume that, in 1968, the decision of the UN Commission on Human Rights not to take action regarding Greece was appropriate. In the words of the Iranian and Nigerian representatives, who stated a view shared by representatives of India, Italy, and other States, "The Commission did not have the facts to warrant a discussion" and "there was no adequate basis for determining whether the allegations made by the Sub-Commission were true or not."

Now, however, more than four years have passed. Words such as "emergency" and "temporary" have a hollow sound. The Council of Europe has published its findings and made its decisions. Its documents . . . now do provide an adequate basis for inquiry on behalf of the United Nations by the Resolution 1503 Working Group, by the Sub-Commission on Prevention of Discrimination and Protection of Minorities, and by the Commission on Human Rights.

The European documents and the supplementary facts reveal a consistent pattern of gross and reliably attested violations of human rights and fundamental freedoms in Greece.

Annex II

[This annex set forth evidence to show the consistent pattern, since April 1967, of gross violations of human rights and fundamental freedoms in Greece. The statements, some of which are statements on torture, are not reprinted here. Allegations pertaining to the violations considered in proceedings of the Council of Europe are summarized below.]

THE COUNCIL OF EUROPE AND HUMAN RIGHTS IN GREECE

On 18 November 1969 the Greek report of the European Commission of Human Rights was transmitted to the Committee of Ministers of the Council of Europe. [See "The Greek Case," (1969) Y.B. Eur. Conv. on Human Rights (Eur. Comm. on Human Rights).] The Commission expressed the opinion:

"that legislative measures and administrative practices of the respondent Government have contravened Articles 5, 6, 8, 9, 10, 11, 13, and 14 of the Convention [on Human Rights] and Article 3 of the First Protocol;

"that these measures and practices were and are not justified under Article 15 of the Convention; . . .

"that the respondent Government has violated Article 3 of the Convention" [Art. 3 of the Convention reads: "No one shall be subjected to torture or to inhuman or degrading treatment or punishment."] . . .

"Agreeing with the opinion of the Commission," on 15 April 1970 the Committee of Ministers decided "that the Government of Greece has violated Articles 3, 5, 6, 8, 9, 10, 11, 13 and 14 of the Convention and Article 3 of the First Protocol."

Further, "Considering that the Greek Government was given an opportunity to take part in the discussions of the Committee of Ministers when it was examining the Report of the Commission, but in a letter of 19th February 1970 the Government stated that it had no intention whatsoever of doing so and that such a participation would be 'inconsistent with Greece's formal denunciation of both the Commission's Report and the European Convention'; . . . [and] Considering that these circumstances and communications clearly established that the Greek Government is not prepared to comply with its continuing obligations under the Convention and thus with the system of collective protection of human rights established thereby . . .

"Decides to make public forthwith the Report drawn up by the Commission . . . [and] urges the Government of Greece to restore, without delay, human rights and fundamental freedoms in Greece in accordance with the Convention and the First Protocol, taking into account, inter alia, the proposals made by the Commission which are attached hereto; . . . [and] Also urges the Government of Greece, in particular, to abolish immediately torture and other ill-treatment of prisoners and to release immediately persons detained under administrative order. . . ."

[Statements supporting this communication were submitted to the Sub-Commission by the International Association of Democratic Lawyers (Brussels), the International Commission of Jurists (Geneva), the International Federation for the Rights of Man (Paris), the International League for Human Rights (New York), and Amnesty International (London).]

D.   The Sub-Commission's Response to the Communication

Note: Disappointing Start to New U.N. Procedure on Human Rights
9 Intl. Commn. Jurists Rev. 5, 5-7 (1972)

At its forty-eighth session in 1970 the UN Economic and Social Council laid down in Resolution 1503 a new procedure for dealing with communications to the Secretary-General alleging violations of human rights and fundamental freedoms.

Under this new procedure there are three stages. First, the Sub-Commission on Prevention of Discrimination and Protection of Minorities is authorized to appoint a Working Party "to consider all communications, including replies of governments thereon . . . with a view to bringing to the attention of the Sub-Commission those communications, together with the replies of governments, if any, which appear to reveal a consistent pattern of gross and reliably attested violations of human rights and fundamental freedoms." Secondly, the Sub-Commission is requested to consider the communications brought before it by the Working Group, and any replies of governments and any other relevant information, "with a view to determining whether to refer to the Commission on Human Rights particular situations which appear to reveal a consistent pattern of gross and reliably attested violations of human rights requiring consideration by the Commission." Finally, the Commission on Human Rights, after examining any situation referred to it, is asked to determine (a) "whether it requires a thorough study by the Commission and a report and recommendation thereon to the Council," or (b) "whether it may be a subject of an investigation by an ad hoc committee to be appointed by the Commission, which shall be undertaken only with the express consent of the State concerned and shall be conducted in constant cooperation with that State and under conditions determined by agreement with it."

On 14 August 1971 the Sub-Committee adopted Resolution 1 (XXIV) setting out the procedures for dealing with the question of the admissibility of communications, and laying down the standards and criteria, and rulings relating to the sources of communications, the contents and nature of allegations, the existence of other remedies, and their timeliness. Admissible communications may originate from individuals or groups who are victims of violations, persons having direct knowledge of violations, or non-governmental organisations acting in good faith and not politically motivated and having direct and reliable knowledge of such violations.

This new procedure constitutes a landmark in the history of the implementation of human rights. For the first time within the framework of the United Nations there is a procedure under which private individuals and non-governmental organisations, as well as governments, can raise complaints about violations of human rights within a state and have those complaints investigated and reported upon by an impartial international body.

By its constitution the Sub-Commission on Discrimination and Minorities is intended to be a body of independent experts. They are appointed by governments, but to act in their individual capacity and not as representatives of or spokesmen for their governments. Some governments adhere to the spirit of this procedure, but unfortunately in many cases the persons appointed are government employees and even members of official government missions to the U.N. It is inevitable in these circumstances that political considerations will tend to affect unduly the work of the Sub-Commission, thus following the pattern of its parent body, the Commission on Human Rights, whose members are explicitly government representatives.

The new procedure came into operation for the first time in 1972. The Working Group met in New York for the 10 days immediately preceding the meeting of the Sub-Commission in August. According to a report in the New York Times on September 21, 1972, the Working Group singled out for consideration by the Sub-Commission communications relating to three countries, Greece, Iran and Portugal.

The communication concerning Greece was a very complete dossier filed on May 19 and June 20, 1972, by Professor Frank Newman of the University of California as Counsel for the International Commission of Jurists, the International League for the Rights of Man, the Fédération Internationale des Droits de l'Homme, the International Association of Democratic Lawyers, Amnesty International and seven Greek exiles who have personally suffered violations of their human rights; one of them was Lady Amalia Fleming. The communication included a large number of reports and personal affidavits by individuals who had been subjected to arbitrary arrest and detention, torture or cruel or inhuman treatment, persons who had been denied fair trials, who had been denied their right to freedom of opinion, expression, peaceful assembly and association, who had been deprived arbitrarily of their nationality, who had been prevented from expressing their will in genuine elections or in other respects subjected to violation of their human rights.

The Sub-Commission spent two days in private session considering the report of the Working Group and the communications referred to the Sub-Commission. Regrettably they failed to decide whether or not to refer to the Commission on Human Rights the communications brought to their attention by the Working Group. Instead they referred them back to the Working Group for another year. The reason put forward for this was that the Governments of the countries concerned had not replied to the communications. The official report of the Sub-Commission records the decision "that the Working Group shall consider at its next session those communications it was not able to examine at its last session, as well as communications received thereafter, and that *it may reexamine the communications singled out in its report, in the light of replies of governments, if any*" (italics added). The effect of this decision is that the consideration of allegations of gross violations of human rights, involving the liberty, the safety, the freedom from torture and even the lives of many individuals has been shelved for a whole year.

There appears to be no justification for this long delay. The governments concerned had ample opportunity to reply to the communications if they had wished to do so. Under the procedure for dealing with these communications the Secretary-General furnishes each Member State concerned with a copy of any communication concerning human rights which refers explicitly to that state or to territories under its jurisdiction, and the governments are asked when sending replies to say whether they wish their replies to be presented to the Commission in summary form or in full. If the governments concerned had not replied to the communications singled out by the Working Group, the reasonable inference is that they did not wish to do so.

The terms of the resolutions adopted by ECOSOC and by the Sub-Commission also clearly contemplate the reference to the Commission of communications to which there has been no governmental reply. As has been seen, ECOSOC Resolution 1503 (XLVIII) speaks of the Working Group bringing to the attention of the Sub-Commission "those communications, together with the replies of governments, *if any* . . ." and the Sub-Commission are asked to consider those communications "and *any* replies of governments relating thereto." The Sub-Commission's Resolution 1 (XXIV) says that "Communications shall be admissible only if, after consideration thereof, together with the replies, *if any*, of the governments concerned, there are reasonable grounds to believe . . ." (all italics added).

In view of these clear provisions in the Resolutions laying down the procedure, it is difficult to avoid the conclusion that the decision of the Sub-Commission was affected by undue regard for the susceptibilities of governments.

It is to be hoped that the Commission on Human Rights and the ECOSOC will give clear directions to ensure that this new procedure is not brought into contempt by prevarication and delay.

E.   The Reaction of the Greek Regime

Letter Dated 12 August 1973 from the Permanent Representative of Greece to the United Nations Addressed to the Secretary-General
U.N. Doc. E/5415 (1973)

Further to my letter of 9 May 1973, which was circulated as Economic and Social Council document E/5333, I have been instructed to express to you the deep regret of the Greek delegation of the fact that certain Member States are engaging in systematic attacks on Greece and its Government in violation both of the fundamental principles of the Charter and of the Economic and Social Council resolutions concerning the sequential procedure to be followed in considering any communication containing accusations of violations of human rights and fundamental freedoms. . . .

. . . My delegation is obliged to note with regret that since the summer of 1972 [the] procedural principles [of Resolution 1503] seem to have been lost sight of in so far as relates to Greece and that the distressing situation resulting from that fact shows a tendency to continue.

It seems quite probable that delegates of certain Member States, who are instructed by their Governments to support complaints against my country, are not sufficiently familiar with the procedural principles in question;

what is clear, however, is that the competent division of the Secretariat has the responsibility of ensuring that this procedure is observed under all circumstances.

While it is in no sense attempting to assign blame in this matter, my delegation nevertheless hopes that the Division concerned will be instructed to take action henceforth as a *matter of course* to prevent the use of tactics which might detract from the high degree of objectivity and impartiality which must prevail in the consideration of questions of this kind. In that connection, mention should also be made of a specific incident which greatly disturbed my delegation and which I feel I must bring to your attention. On 21 September 1972, The New York Times published an article headed "U.N. Unit Said to Report Greeks Violate Human Rights" which reported allegations brought to the attention of the Sub-Commission by the Working Group and referred to the Sub-Commission's resolution 2(XXV) of 28 August 1972. It has not so far been possible to obtain any concrete information indicating how this indiscretion occurred, but, since questions of this nature are to be kept strictly confidential and their premature disclosure can be extremely harmful both to the countries concerned and to the Secretariat, it is most desirable that strict measures should be taken to ensure that such leaks do not occur again. In addition, my delegation wishes to point out that the provisions of Article 2, paragraphs 1, 4 and 7, of the Charter are violated by the slanderous references to Greece and its Government in paragraph 262 of the report of the Commission on Human Rights. . . . The paragraph in question, which we find it difficult to accept as it stands, grossly distorts the basic facts with which it deals, and this distortion was unfortunately not corrected by the Economic and Social Council at its fifty-fourth session.

In the light of what has been said above, this delegation is certain that, in your wisdom and acumen, you will take the necessary steps to put an end to the prejudiced and discriminatory attitude adopted towards Greece by the Commission on Human Rights, whose very reason for being is the elimination of all discrimination. If this unacceptable state of affairs should continue — and we trust that it will not — my delegation will have no choice but to draw the obvious conclusions and determine its attitude towards the Commission accordingly.

At the same time, wishing to prevent my misinterpretation of the reasons which might dictate a decision to by-pass the machinery of the Commission on Human Rights if the situation should deteriorate, the Government of Greece, which has no cause for self-reproach and nothing to hide, feels it would be useful to bring to the attention of all Member States, for the purpose of refuting the oral and written allegations which have up to now been communicated to the Commission, the following information on the laws and regulations applied in Greece in conformity with the provisions of the Universal Declaration of Human Rights and the relevant articles of the Charter:

1. *Alleged Violation of Articles 2, 3, 5, 7, 9, 13(1),*
   19, 20(1), 21(1) and 23(4) of the Universal
   Declaration of Human Rights

(a) Safeguards against violations of the above articles are provided in the Greek Constitution and the laws in force. Consequently any allegation concerning such so-called violations is devoid of foundation, motivated by considerations of political opportunism, and constitutes an attempt at interference in the domestic affairs of a State which contravenes Article 2(7) of the Charter.

(b) Article 20(1) of the Universal Declaration, referring to freedom of association, is not violated in Greece at all. In fact:

I. Articles 18 and 19 of the Constitution, dealing with the rights of assembly and association, were put into effect under Government Act No. A/16.11.1978.
II. The right of association (covering the establishment of associations and trade unions, elections, etc.) is freely exercised on the basis of the provisions of the Civil Code and the laws relating thereto.
III. The governing bodies of all trade unions and associations are the outcome of free elections.
IV. No trade unionist has been arrested or deported for his trade union activities.
V. The right to strike is recognized and freely exercised.

2. *Political Prisoners and Imprisonment by*
   Administrative Order

(a) There is not a single political prisoner in Greece. All the detention camps have been abolished by orders issued by the Ministries of Public Order and Justice.

(b) All persons arrested in the past have since been gradually released, and this procedure was completed on 18 December 1971.

(c) The number of persons deported on various dates, under earlier laws concerning the security of the State, was very small. The deportations in question, carried out in accordance with decisions, duly accompanied by a statement of reasons, by the special commissions established by law, ended on 16 December 1972, which was the date on which the last deportee was freed.

3. *Arrests and Ill Treatment*

The arrests made after 21 April 1967 were aimed at dismantling cells belonging to terrorist organizations. The members of these organizations were caught in the act of planting bombs, importing explosives from abroad or attempting to arrange for the escape of persons sentenced to terms of imprisonment by Greek courts. Approximately 30 cells were dismantled and several of their members convicted by the courts under earlier laws concerning the security of the State. Furthermore, the allegations concerning torture are totally devoid of foundation, especially as torture is strictly forbidden by article 11, paragraph 2, of the Constitution. In short, these allegations are designed solely to damage Greece's reputation abroad.

4.   Long-Term Detention Without Trial

Allegations of this kind constitute flagrant interference in the domestic affairs of Greece, since detention pending trial is governed by the laws in force, whose provisions are scrupulously applied.

5.   Refusal to Issue Passports

According to article 17 of Act No. 4310/1929 "no one may leave the territory of Greece unless his passport has first been visaed by the police authorities." The competent authorities may therefore refuse to issue a visa, or may cancel a visa that has been issued at any time in the event that the person intending to travel "is in Greek territory and his departure may be considered detrimental to the interests of the State." The competent authorities have, however, frequently granted permission to travel abroad to persons radically opposed to the constitutional order currently in force in the country, taking into account the possibility that the persons in question might act against the interests of the country, which was, in fact, very often the case. Also, the persons concerned shall have the right to appeal to the Council of State against the administration's refusal to issue them a passport or to visa a passport. In fact, on several occasions, the Council of State has actually revoked administrative decisions involving such refusal.

6.   Deprivation of Greek Nationality

This can occur in accordance with following provisions:

(a) According to article 19 of Legislative Decree No. 3370/1955 (Greek Nationality Code), "any Greek citizen of foreign origin who leaves Greek soil without intending to return there, may be deprived of Greek nationality." This is effected by a decision of the Ministry of the Interior, with the concurrence of the Nationality Council.

(b) Legislative Decree No. 4334/62, governing matters affecting the security of the nation, provides for loss of Greek nationality in the case of any person temporarily or permanently domiciled abroad who acts or has acted in an anti-Greek manner, with a view to serving parties or organizations which have been dissolved or are to be dissolved, in accordance with Act No. 509/47. Loss of nationality is effected by a decision of the Minister of the Interior, with the concurrence of the Nationality Council.

(c) Const. Act. No. H/1967, entitled "Deprivation of nationality of persons acting in an anti-Greek manner," makes provision for the "possibility of loss of Greek nationality in the case of persons temporarily or permanently residing abroad, and of persons simultaneously possessing the nationality of a third country and residing abroad, who act or have acted in an anti-Greek manner or commit acts incompatible with Greek citizenship, or work against the interests of Greece or serve the interests of parties or organizations which have been dissolved or are to be dissolved, in accordance with the provisions of Act No. 509/1947." The loss of nationality is effected by a decision of the Ministry of the Interior.

I have the honour to request that this letter should be circulated as a document of the Economic and Social Council.

(*Signed*) C. P. Panayotacos
Ambassador
Permanent Representative of Greece
to the United Nations

While the official reaction of the Greek regime was to counterattack the UN's handling of the 1503 procedure and then to deny any violations of human rights in Greece, a dramatic turnabout occurred not more than two weeks after Ambassador Panayotacos's letter to the Secretary-General. On 20 August 1973, President George Papadopoulos officially ended martial law and declared a general amnesty for all political prisoners, including Alexandros Panagoulis, who had attempted his assassination in 1968. The Sub-Commission thereupon decided to remove Greece from its agenda and turn its attention to other matters.

F.   The Overthrow of the Greek Regime and the Sub-Commission's Role Therein

Note: The Overthrow of the Greek Regime

A little over two months after the release of prisoners and the declaration of amnesty, the Papadopoulos regime was overthrown by yet another military coup. An International Commission of Jurists (ICJ) report four months into the regime of General Phaedon Ghizihis concluded that "the new regime in Greece is showing no greater respect for the principles of the Rule of Law than did its predecessors, and there is even less legal basis for it.

The authority of the government rests on naked force alone" (ICJ Press Release, 25 March 1974).

On 17 May 1974, a communication similar to that of 19 May 1972 was sent to the UN Secretary-General on behalf of numerous human rights groups concerned with the situation in Greece. Again, the procedures that route such petitions to the Sub-Commission and the Commission on Human Rights failed to produce a condemnation of the well-documented violations of human rights by this new Greek regime.

The Ghizihis regime itself finally was toppled, but only because it precipitated the Cyprus crisis, which nearly plunged it into full-scale war with Turkey. Thus, at last, constitutional government returned to Greece on 24 August 1974 when Premier Constantine Caramanlis swore in a civilian cabinet. Several officials in the military regime were subsequently convicted of torture and other human rights violations, and Judge Christos Sartzetakis (see page 348 supra) became President of Greece.

During the final year of the Greek military regime, the Sub-Commission maintained its record of silence, prompting the following comments (made five days before the return of civilian rule) by Amnesty International and the International Student Movement for the UN.

Statement by Amnesty International and the International Student Movement for the UN
57 U.N. ESCOR, Commission on Human Rights (708th mtg.) at 77, U.N. Doc. E/CN.4/Sub.2/SR. 708 (1974)

Mr. Chairman, we suggest that August 1974, the second month of crisis on the Island of Cyprus, hardly seems to be the month for continued silence as to gross violations of human rights in Cyprus and in Greece. Today the Secretariat seems to have forgotten that, seven years ago, this Sub-Commission did report to the Human Rights Commission, under par. 2 of ECOSOC resolution 1235, regarding activities of the Greek militarists. There then were two years of silence, pending the condemnation of the Greek colonels by the Council of Europe. There then were four more years of silence (1970, '71, '72, '73). Many friends of the United Nations wondered *why*, since the evidence of torture and other gross violations seemed so persuasive.

Mr. Smirnov, this morning and again this afternoon, correctly stated that this Sub-Commission can be proud of its fine record as to apartheid, and as to racial discrimination generally, in Southern Africa. But Ms. Gillian Walker last year observed that many students, concerned about the United Nations, were asking whether the Greek Case did not illustrate a basic rule of this Sub-Commission, to hear no evil, see no evil, speak no evil, except as to Southern Africa and (occasionally and appropriately) the Middle East.

Last month the Greek militarists, in their desperate and cynical last act, launched in Cyprus their third coup, thus unleashing greeds and fears and passions that now involve the people of three nations in a brutal war that most of us thought was inconceivable.

We will never know for sure whether that war might have been prevented. If during the last four years, however, available United Nations procedures for protecting human rights had been utilized, can anyone say for sure that the Greek militarists would have retained the awful, minimal strength that enabled them insanely to ignite this current crisis? Rarely do we witness a situation where violations of human rights lead so directly, so indisputably to war. . . .

III. Analyzing the Procedures and Problems of Resolution 1503

Although the Working Group of the UN Sub-Commission had failed to refer the communication concerning the situation in Greece to the Sub-Commission, during 1973 it had referred communications involving eight other countries. The Sub-Commission, after much deliberation, thereupon had referred to the Commission on Human Rights communications describing particular situations in Brazil, Britain, Burundi, Guyana, Indonesia, Iran, Portugal, and Tanzania for consideration at its 1974 session. 11 Intl. Commn. Jurists Rev. 27 (1973). Some observers viewed this development as a noteworthy victory compared with the inertia shown in the case of Greece. However, the Commission refused to initiate either a thorough study or even an ad hoc investigation into any of the eight situations.

Many of the procedural problems in the 1503 process were immediately apparent and are raised in the following reading.

Newman, The New U.N. Procedures for Human Rights Complaints: Reform, Status Quo, or Chamber of Horrors?

Hearings on the International Protection of Human Rights
Before the Subcomm. on International Organizations and
Movements of the House Comm. on Foreign Affairs,
93d Cong., 1st Sess. 715-716 (Comm. Print 1973)

. . . To whom in the UN the communications are sent matters not. He or she is not the official who formally acknowledges receipt. All "communications concerning human rights, however addressed" go to an employee of the Division of Human Rights, who then advises the authors that the communication will be dealt with under relevant UN resolutions, "copies of which are enclosed for your information."

[The relevant resolutions] provide that:

(1) if the communication refers to a Government or to territories under its jurisdiction, it gets a copy and also a chance to reply;

(2) "a brief indication of the substance" of the communication appears on a confidential list prepared for each annual session of the Commission on Human Rights;

(3) that list is accompanied by Governments' replies, "in summary form or in full" as each Government requests;

(4) the list and the replies, including "a brief description" of each communication, are furnished every month to the members of the Sub-Commission.

One also learns from these resolutions that at no time will the author (or lawyer) ever be allowed to see the list or the Government's reply or the brief indication of the substance or the brief description of the communication.

During July/August, "for a period not exceeding ten days immediately before the session of the Sub-Commission [held in August/September]," a 5-person working group elected by the Sub-Commission from its members meets to "consider all communications, including replies of Governments thereon." In 1972 the Secretariat submitted 27,577 communications to the working group; more than 20,000 were considered.

These questions come to mind:

1. May the author (or lawyer) attend those meetings? testify? argue?

2. Will the author be notified if the working group's action is favorable? unfavorable?

3. May the author be told anything about the group's proceedings?

4. May translations be checked, for accuracy and completeness?

The answer to each of those questions is no. The working group's sole function seems to be "bringing to the attention of the Sub-Commission those communications, together with replies of Governments, if any, which appear to reveal a consistent pattern of gross and reliably attested violations of human rights and fundamental freedoms within the terms of reference of the Sub-Commission."

At higher levels is the UN more respectful of authors' concerns? Again the answer is no. After hearing from its working group, the Sub-Commission decides "whether to refer to the Commission on Human Rights particular situations which appear to reveal a consistent pattern of gross and reliably attested violations of human rights requiring consideration by the Commission." The Commission, "after it has examined any situation referred to it," then decides whether (1) to undertake "a thorough study," or (2) to sponsor "an investigation by an ad hoc committee." The governing rule is that "all actions . . . remain confidential until such time as the Commission may decide to make recommendations to the Economic and Social

Council." Further, the Sub-Commission's meetings are "private"; the working group's meetings are both "private" and "closed"; and "the results of the Working Group's work shall be communicated to the Sub-Commission confidentially."

Where does all that leave authors (and their lawyers)? In hopelessly complete ignorance, unhappily. They get absolutely none of the protections that due process, natural justice, and similar concepts rightfully are presumed to ensure.

We must look also at the rights of the accused Government. As we have seen it has a chance to "reply." Yet its representatives have no right to attend meetings, testify, or argue. Unless the rules are breached it has no more access than does the author to information regarding what has happened. Iran, for example, was singled out in the working group's secret 1972 report because of several communications thought to reveal a consistent pattern of gross violations. No Iranian was a member of the Sub-Commission. A representative of the Iranian government was an observer at the Sub-Commission's session, but we may not infer that he or she observed the "private meetings." So far as the record shows, Iran still has no notice as to the present status of those critical communications. . . .

Although there have been no formal amendments to the 1503 procedure since its adoption, a regular practice has developed in ensuing years. Communications are initially received and filed by members of the secretariat of the UN Center for Human Rights in Geneva. Each month, a list of communications, a short summary of each case, and any replies received from governments are sent to each member of the Sub-Commission (and to members of the Commission). A five-member Working Group of the Sub-Commission meets for two weeks immediately prior to the Sub-Commission's annual session in August to determine, by majority vote, which situations should be brought to the attention of the full Sub-Commission. Each member of the Working Group is responsible for preliminary review of a particular group of rights set forth in the Universal Declaration of Human Rights. If the Sub-Commission decides to refer a situation to the Commission on Human Rights, it so informs the government concerned and invites that government to submit its observations in writing to the Commission. A five-member Working Group on Situations meets before the Commission's annual session in February and March and recommends action to be taken by the Commission. The government concerned has the right to be represented during the Commission's confidential debate on the issue. Since 1978, the Chairman of the Commission has announced in public session the names of the countries that have been examined under the 1503 procedure, distinguishing between those countries the Commission has decided to keep under review and those with respect to which it has been decided to take no further action.

The Sub-Commission's Working Group on Communications considered over 350,000 allegations of human rights violations under the 1503 procedure between 1972 and 1988. Except in 1986, when it did not meet, the Sub-Commission has referred at least one situation to the Commission each year; by the mid-1990s, the human rights situations in over 50 countries had been placed before the Commission. The Commission decided in five cases to lift the secrecy of the 1503 discussions and materials (with respect to Equatorial Guinea (1979), Argentina (1985), Uruguay (1985), the Philippines (1986), and Albania (1988)). The three decisions concerning Argentina, Uruguay, and the Philippines followed the restoration of democratic governments in the countries concerned. (The decision to release materials on Albania was not approved by the Economic and Social Council.) In 1987, following the flight of Jean-Claude Duvalier, the Commission decided to make public a confidential report on Haiti prepared by a Special Representative of the Commission. In one case, that of Uganda (see pages 71-72 of Problem I), the Commission decided to undertake a confidential investigation as envisaged under Resolution 1503, but it subsequently canceled the investigation when the Idi Amin regime was overthrown. See generally Rodley, United Nations Non-Treaty Procedures for Dealing with Human Rights Violations, in Guide to International Human Rights Practice 64-70 (2d ed. H. Hannum ed. 1992); Alston, The Commission on Human Rights, in The United Nations and Human Rights 145-155 (P. Alston ed. 1992).

H. Tolley, Jr., The U.N. Commission on Human Rights
74-82, 125, 127-132 (1987)

Despite firm political opposition, a Working Group majority consistently referred situations to the full Sub-Commission each year after 1972. . . . Notwithstanding the political and procedural obstacles, the Working Group apparently forwarded about eight to ten situations annually to the full Sub-Commission.

Sub-Commission Review. After the Working Group identified situations for consideration by the Sub-Commission, the Secretariat translated the original communications referred into the U.N. working languages: English, French, and Spanish. Starting in 1979 the Sub-Commission has taken up the 1503 communications after the general public debate on violations, as a separate agenda item during two to three days of private meetings. In addition to the Working Group's documentation, the experts also considered other available information on the situations identified. Current press accounts, NGO country studies, and global surveys, such as Amnesty's annual report, provide additional material. The experts also had access to records of the Commission's confidential deliberations on prior referrals, including written replies and oral interventions by government representatives. It is conceivable, though not very likely, that the full Sub-Commission might also have identified a situation and reviewed the originals of communications not referred by its Working Group.

Recurrent procedural disputes over secret voting, conflicts of interest, and duplication of public and confidential deliberations reflected the political interests at stake. While government observers cannot attend the private meetings, they can learn from confidential summary records and their own nationals what the experts said and how they voted. Secret voting might provide greater protection against intimidation, but only a few experts believed the Sub-Commission could make that procedural change unilaterally. Despite obvious conflicts of interest, "independent" experts participated in decisions affecting their own countries. In 1978 Halima Warzazi answered at great length a complaint against Morocco; to block action against their governments, H. W. Jawardene of Sri Lanka and Mario Amadeo of Argentina successfully moved to postpone a decision. U.S. Ambassador Beverly Carter actually favored action on communications from the United States in the Working Group, but then changed his decisive vote in the full Sub-Commission; he explained that a late government reply had resolved his concerns. Finally, the experts have repeatedly addressed without resolving the procedural confusion created by simultaneous public and confidential review of the same situations. Normally the Sub-Commission completes the public agenda item on violations before conducting confidential deliberations; after several years of confidential referral under Resolution 1503, at least seven situations have become subject to public recommendations.

In 1979 the twenty-six experts discussed procedure first before reviewing all the situations and accompanying recommendations from the Working Group. The experts concluded by voting on each situation taken in alphabetical order. In addition to referring cases to the Commission, the Sub-Commission may refer situations back to its Working Group, allowing governments an additional year to answer the allegations. The experts may also defer consideration by the full body until the next session, as it did for several years on Sri Lanka.

Neither the Sub-Commission nor the Commission could deal with urgent situations or communications received between sessions. That institutional deficiency contributed to the Sub-Commission's 1973 failure to refer violations by the Greek junta. On August 20, President George Papadopoulos proclaimed an amnesty and released hundreds of political prisoners. While meeting that month in Geneva, the Sub-Commission discontinued its consideration of the Greek situation. Two months later another military coup ended the Papadopoulos regime and reinstituted repressive measures. Despite Sub-Commission concern over the Greek situation dating to 1967, the experts had no opportunity to refer confidential communications in time for the Commission's February 1974 session.

By the time the Sub-Commission reconvened in August 1974, the

Greek military's intervention on Cyprus had triggered a confrontation with Turkey. That crisis, rather than United Nations action, brought a return to constitutional government in August 1974. . . . The Greek situation revealed anew the link between human rights violations and international conflict. Despite, or perhaps because of its failure to refer the Greek situation to the Commission, the Sub-Commission has subsequently identified numerous instances of gross violations that received more serious consideration.

From 1973 to 1979 the Sub-Commission referred to the Commission at least 20 situations, including two complaints against governments not belonging to the United Nations. Unofficial sources identified 18 referrals made before 1978, and starting in that year the Commission Chair has announced the names of governments subject to confidential decisions. [Table 5-1], drawn from both official and unofficial sources, while somewhat speculative and incomplete, presents a reasonably accurate overview of the Sub-Commission's referrals. The comparable totals for Africa, Asia, and Latin America support complaints that regional balance has been sought. Over half the referrals involve NAM [Non-Aligned Movement] members, indicating that the non-aligned majority controlling U.N. policy organs did not block Sub-Commission experts from confidential review of NAM members.

COMMISSION REVIEW

Information Forwarded. When the Sub-Commission referred a documented situation to the Commission, the Secretariat notified the government of its right to make written observations and to appoint a representative. The individual petitioner, however, was never notified of any disposition. The complainant had no opportunity to refute the government response. The Commission, not the victim, had the responsibility to enforce international norms in the ex parte proceedings. The policy of nondisclosure made the Resolution 1503 procedure more of a "petition-information" than a "petition-recourse" system. The ostensible purpose was not to remedy individuals' injuries but to reveal and to stop patterns of gross violations.

That rationale does not explain why supplementary communications from the complaining individual were routed through the Sub-Commission Working Group to be treated like a new situation. Situations referred by the Sub-Commission did not reach the Commission until at least a year after the events reported. Supplemental information sent to the Secretariat after the Sub-Commission's confidential recommendation did not ordinarily become part of the record sent to the Commission. Although the type of situations identified involved ongoing violations, the Commission received only the first materials presented to the Sub-Commission working group.

The prolonged consideration of communications about Equatorial Guinea illustrates the delay. The first complaint of November 14, 1974,

TABLE 5-1
Situations Reportedly Referred to the Commission, 1973-1979

Region	Country	Years
Africa (6)		
	Burundi	1973
	Equatorial Guinea	1975, 1976
	Ethiopia	1977
	Malawi	1976
	Tanzania (Zanzibar)	1973
	Uganda	1974, 1976, 1977
Asia (6)		
	Burma	1979
	Indonesia	1973, 1974, 1977
	Iran	1973
	Israel	1974
	Korea	1976, 1978
	South Vietnam	1974
Latin America (6)		
	Bolivia	1976
	Brazil	1973, 1974
	Chile	1974, 1976, 1977
	Guyana	1973
	Paraguay	1977
	Uruguay	1977
Eastern Europe (0)		
Western Europe and other (2)		
	Portugal (Territories)	1973
	United Kingdom (Northern Ireland)	1973

detailed atrocities which had begun with Macías Nguema's accession to power in 1968. In August 1975, the Sub-Commission reviewed additional allegations from the International Federation for the Rights of Man in letters dated March 28 and April 11, 1975. At its 1976 session, the Commission considered a thirteen-page reply and an oral intervention from the government's representative. The Commission concluded that the evidence forwarded from the Sub-Commission did not reveal systematic and flagrant violations. As a result of procedural obstacles, that decision was taken in March 1976 without knowledge of letters submitted between June 1975 and January 1976. The Commission did not receive those letters from the Sub-Commission until 1977, a full year later, when the members did find a pattern of gross violations.

NGO representatives urged that the Commission allow petitioners the same opportunity afforded governments to update the information submitted. The United States supported that procedural reform in 1976, and in

1977 the Commission reportedly decided to "receive and consider recent communications relating to situations referred by the Sub-Commission." It appears that a December 1978 communication on Equatorial Guinea from the University Exchange Fund did go directly to the Commission's 1979 session without prior consideration by the Sub-Commission. NGO observers, however, continued to object that the Secretariat only provided inadequate summaries of supplemental communications, when the Commission should have received detailed extracts containing additional information.

Working Group.   The Commission designated its own five member, regionally balanced Working Group to make recommendations involving the communications forwarded by the Sub-Commission. The Group met for five days before the Commission convened and considered as many as 17 situations at one session. Normally, the Commission received only two to three new referrals in a year and continued review of four to six situations previously identified. Resolution 1503 does not call for a Commission Working Group, and its members apparently do not screen out any cases referred by the Sub-Commission. The Group makes one of the following recommendations:

1.   to take no action on a new referral;
2.   to continue confidential review at the next session, allowing the government time to report developments;
3.   to initiate direct contacts with the government charged for discussions prior to the next session;
4.   to appoint a rapporteur or investigatory committee to report on the situation;
5.   to discontinue confidential review and undertake a public inquiry;
6.   to take no further action on a situation previously identified.

The Secretariat promptly forwards the group's recommendation to the government affected so that an informed representative may be sent for the full Commission's deliberations.

Deliberations.   Several weeks after the Working Group notified the target governments, the Commission spent three to six days in closed session to review the Group's recommendations. Unlike the Sub-Commission, the Commission began with private deliberations and decisions before a general public debate under the same agenda item on violations. Secretariat staff and the Chairman of the Commission and Sub-Commission Working Groups introduced the item noting any procedural problems. In 1979 Human Rights Division Director Theo van Boven unsuccessfully sought Commission authorization for the Secretariat to direct confidential communications to public procedures whenever possible. The Soviet representative regularly objected for the record, challenging the confidential procedure as a violation of Charter Article 2(7), but he then participated in the decisions. Peru's representative candidly explained that he wanted to delay voting until after discussing all cases "with the specific purpose of ensuring a balance between . . . various decisions."

Following procedural remarks, the Commission took up each situation separately, scheduled either in alphabetical order or for the convenience of government representatives dispatched to Geneva. Commission members being reviewed under the 1503 procedure such as Ethiopia, Uganda, and Uruguay both discussed and voted on their own situations. Nonmember governmental respondents from Bolivia, Equatorial Guinea, Indonesia, Korea, and Paraguay appeared separately and could remain until the final vote on their situation. When a government such as Burma or Malawi failed to appear, the Working Group chairman or an individual designated to contact the government opened the discussion.

When the government charged was represented or was a member of the Commission, the 1503 deliberations resembled a legislative inquiry. The delegate's official response began the discussion. After enumerating statutory rights guarantees, the more persuasive representatives described government justification for and responses to the violations alleged. Commission questioners, both principled members and political antagonists, closely interrogated the representatives about detailed NGO reports of torture, disappearances, and executions. In defense, respondents questioned human rights practices of the critical government and attacked the NGO's partiality. Since complainants do not attend, NGOs cannot respond and remain uninformed of the exchange. Friendly members have sought to protect clients or allies by objecting to probing questions more appropriate for a judicial tribunal than for an inter-governmental Commission. The same rules govern voting in both private and public sessions, except that every situation identified is put to the vote in the confidential proceedings. When a cooperative target acknowledged a problem, the Commission decided by consensus to continue review. When a Soviet bloc client such as Ethiopia was the target, roll call votes revealed predictable cold war competition for the decisive non-aligned vote.

Decisions and Responses. In responding to the confidential communications, the Commission followed Resolution 1503 when it decided to reject some complaints, to treat situations in Chile and Equatorial Guinea under public procedures, and to conduct a confidential study on Uganda. In most of the situations, however, the Commission departed from procedures authorized by Resolution 1503. The Commission requested the Secretary General to designate a representative to visit Equatorial Guinea, Ethiopia, Paraguay, and Uruguay to provide good offices and to obtain information required for future decisions. In many other cases the Commission merely decided to continue reviewing the allegations in confidential sessions year after year.

Even though Burma failed to send a representative, the Commission effectively rejected the complaint against that government by deciding not to respond. The Commission's 1976 resolution on Equatorial Guinea illustrates that type of non-decision:

> the Commission endorsed the conclusions reached by its Working Group . . .
> that the information submitted to the Commission did not seem sufficient to
> justify the conclusion that flagrant and systematic violations had been com-
> mitted in the situation concerned. The Commission therefore decided that
> there was no need to take action under Council Resolution 1503 (XLVIII) on
> the basis of the documents before it.

Subsequent referrals from the Sub-Commission led to further confidential review of Equatorial Guinea, but the government refused to cooperate with the confidential monitoring. The Commission gave the Macías regime a year to accept the Secretary-General's good offices or to face public disclosure of the confidential communications. Equatorial Guinea's recalcitrance provoked the Commission to recommend that ECOSOC authorize disclosure of the 1503 materials. Subsequently, a special rapporteur on Equatorial Guinea appointed under Resolution 1235 prepared a report making other recommendations approved by ECOSOC.

Malawi also refused to cooperate with the confidential procedures. In a 1980 recommendation to ECOSOC the Commission noted Malawi's failure to respond to allegations concerning abuse of Jehovah's Witnesses between 1972-1975, publicly deplored the violations, and urged the government to provide remedies. Since there had been no further reports of violations for several years, the members discontinued consideration under Resolution 1503. As Chile's case revealed, noncooperation was not the only reason for publicizing alleged violations. The Commission immediately took up the complaints about Chile in public proceedings without first undertaking any confidential review.

In other situations, the Commission initiated a more conciliatory response which deferred to cooperative target governments' preference for confidential review. The Commission requested the Secretary-General to designate a representative to establish direct contacts with the target government for discussions between sessions. As a result, Davidson Nicol visited Ethiopia, Javier Perez de Cuellar conducted a mission to Paraguay, and Rivas Poseda met with Uruguayan officials. The appointees conducted discreet missions and then reported to the Commission on their prison visits, official interviews, and general observations. The appointees are expected to provide good offices to mediate a human rights dispute and to obtain information required by the Commission for future decisions. After Ethiopia barred the Secretary-General's representative from visiting an overcrowded prison, cold war partisans disputed whether to discontinue review based on his partial report. Although there is little to report, the [Secretary-General] is expected to inform Commission members each quarter about developments in situations where he has been requested to obtain information or to use his good offices.

Other cooperative governments such as South Korea have simply been requested to return to future sessions as the members keep the situation under review. Three operative paragraphs from the Commission's 1981 confidential resolution on Afghanistan reveal the scope of confidential monitoring.

> The Commission on Human Rights,
>
> 1. *Decides* to keep the alleged human rights violations in Afghanistan under review within the framework of Economic and Social Council resolution 1503 (XLVIII), in the light of any official observations received from Afghanistan or information from other sources, without prejudice to resolution 10 (XXXVII) of the Commission on Human Rights;
>
> 2. *Urges* the Afghanistan authorities to co-operate with the Commission;
>
> 3. *Requests* the Secretary-General to communicate this decision to the Government of Afghanistan.

By deciding to keep a situation "under review," the Commission allowed a government an additional year to respond to the complaint and to report any improvements. After the Commission Chair began announcing the names of governments subject to decisions in 1978, complainants could tell whether to submit additional information during the interval.

In only one case, Uganda, did the Commission approve the type of confidential investigation authorized by Resolution 1503. Before the designated rapporteur, Justice Onyeama of Nigeria, could begin the study, Idi Amin had been overthrown. The successor government argued that the study was no longer required, and the Commission obliged by discontinuing consideration. Five other governments made subject to confidential monitoring in the late 1970s (Ethiopia, Indonesia, Korea, Paraguay, and Uruguay) remained under prolonged review as new complaints documented ongoing violations. . . .

For the 1984-1985 biennium, the United Nations budgeted funds to process 40,000 to 50,000 communications received each year outside the Covenant's optional protocol. The Secretariat referred 25,196 communications concerning 76 countries to the Sub-Commission Working Group in 1980. Communications exceeded 26,000 in each of the following two years, with mass mailings of 10,000 in 1981 and 13,000 in 1982 concerning a single situation. The Working Group could not review any communications in 1986 when the U.N. budgetary crisis forced postponement of the annual Sub-Commission session. . . .

SELECTING SITUATIONS FOR REVIEW

Between 1978 and 1986 the Sub-Commission referred thirty situations to the Commission under the Resolution 1503 procedure. [See Table 5-2.] In seven cases the Commission decided not to keep the case under review;

TABLE 5-2
Thirty Governments Subject to Commission Review Under Resolution 1503 from 1978 to 1986

Commission decisions	Years	Total years	Years observed	Ratified Coven.	Protoc.
Africa (9)					
Benin	1984, 1985	2	0		
Central African Republic	1980, 1981	2	1	Y	Y
Equatorial Guinea	1976-1979	4	2		
Ethiopia	1978-1981	4	4 (M)		
Gabon	1986	1	1		
Malawi	1977-1979	3	0		
Mozambique	1981	1	0		
Uganda	1978-1981	4	2 (M)		
Zaire	1985-1986	2	1	Y	Y
Asia (8)					
Afghanistan	1981-1983	4	4		
Burma	1979	1	0		
Indonesia	1978-1981, 1983-1985	7	6		
Iran	1973, 1983	1	1	Y	
Japan	1981	1	1	Y	
Republic of Korea	1978-1982	5	3	Y	
Malaysia	1984	1	1		
Pakistan	1984, 1985	2	2 (M)		
Philippines	1984-1986	3	3 (M)	S	S
Vietnam	1974				
Latin America (10)					
Argentina	1980-1984	5	5 (M)	S	
Bolivia	1978-1981	4	4		
Brazil	1973, 1974				
Chile	1974, 1976, 1977, 1981	1	0	Y	
El Salvador	1981	1	0	Y	S
Guatemala	1981	1	1		
Haiti	1981-1986	6	5		
Paraguay	1978-1986	9	8		
Uruguay	1978-1984	7	7 (M)	Y	Y
Venezuela	1982	1	1	Y	Y
Eastern Europe (2)					
Albania	1984-1986	3	0		
German Democratic Republic	1981-1983	3	3	Y	
Western Europe and Other (1)					
Turkey	1983-1986	4	4		

(M) denotes member   Y = yes   S = signed but not ratified

the Commission kept most of the remaining twenty-three situations under confidential review for at least a year, initiated private contacts with five governments, and transferred eight cases to the public procedures. By 1986, when the budgetary crisis delayed further Sub-Commission screening, the Commission had discontinued review of twelve situations, and only four governments remained subject to confidential review.

Without access to the confidential communication, it is difficult to tell what differentiates the seven referrals disregarded by the Commission from the twenty-three situations kept under review. [See Table 5-2.] Allegations of arbitrary detention, abductions, and extra-legal killings result in such imprecise and unverifiable tallies that efforts to rank order offending regimes are of dubious value. With the possible exception of Pakistan, the other six situations disregarded appear to have attracted less press and NGO attention than the cases kept under review.

A government's failure to answer the allegations has not uniformly provoked scrutiny. Although Mozambique and Burma failed to send any representative, the Commission rejected those Sub-Commission's referrals after some members supported the governments and criticized the complaints as without foundation. The Commission has kept under review six other governments which failed to send representatives and publicly criticized two regimes for noncooperation. Governments sending representatives, however, have been subjected to review in about the same proportion as nonparticipants, with three Sub-Commission referrals accepted for each one disregarded. Nor has membership resulted in more lenient treatment; four governments represented on the Commission became subjects of review, and Pakistan was the only member referred by the Sub-Commission to escape ongoing scrutiny (despite separate recommendations in two succeeding years).

By deciding to keep a situation under review, the Commission requests the government charged to report at the next session. In most cases, confidential monitoring has never gone beyond annual reports in the closed meetings. In five cases where reports of serious violations continued, the Commission arranged for Secretariat staff or one of its own members to make direct contacts with the accused regime. Some favorable reports from the appointees have sparked skeptical questions and partisan squabbling in the closed sessions. Theo van Boven reportedly challenged then Under Secretary-General Perez de Cuellar's account of an interview conducted with an Argentinian detainee. Skeptical members wondered how Jonas K. D. Foli could conclude after two visits to Haiti that conditions were so much better than those described by a mission from the Inter-American Commission for Human Rights. After Ethiopia barred Davidson Nicol from visiting an overcrowded prison, Western members objected to discontinuing review based on his partial report. Since the "thorough study" authorized for Uganda was never completed, it is unclear how such a report would have differed from the reports of those making direct contacts.

TABLE 5-3
Speculative Overview of the Types of Confidential Decisions Taken with Illustrative Examples of Governments Possibly Affected

I. No action on a new referral. The situation referred need not be subjected to confidential review: (7)
  A. The communications do not reveal a sufficient violation
    Burma 1979
    Mozambique 1981
  B. The Government's response to the communications was adequate
    Gabon 1986
    Japan 1981
    Malaysia 1984
    Pakistan 1984, 1985
    Venezuela 1982

II. The situation should be confidentially monitored (14)
    Afghanistan 1980-83
    Albania 1984-198__
    Argentina 1980-83
    Benin 1984
    Bolivia 1978-83
    Central African Republic 1980
    German Democratic Rep. 1980-82
    Indonesia 1978-81, 1983-84
    Paraguay 1978-198__
    Republic of Korea 1978-81
    Philippines 1984-1985
    Turkey 1983-1985
    Uruguay 1978-1984
    Zaire 1985-198__

III. The violations require a confidential Resolution 1503 inquiry: (6)
  A. Direct contacts by the Secretary-General or a rapporteur
    Equatorial Guinea (Secretary-General)
    Ethiopia (Davidson Nicol)
    Haiti (Jonas K. D. Foli)
    Paraguay (Perez de Cuellar)
    Uruguay (Rivas Poseda)
  B. A confidential "thorough study"
    Uganda 1978 (Judge Onyeama)
  C. A confidential ad hoc committee investigation subject to approval (None ever conducted)

IV. The situation is subject to public procedures (7)
    Afghanistan 1984
    Bolivia 1981
    Chile 1981
    Equatorial Guinea 1979
    El Salvador 1981
    Guatemala 1981
    Iran 1983

V. Confidential review should be discontinued (12)
    Argentina 1984
    Benin 1985
    Central African Republic 1981
    Ethiopia 1981
    German Democratic Republic 1983
    Haiti 1987
    Indonesia 1981, 1985
    Republic of (South) Korea 1980
    Malawi 1980
    Paraguay 1981
    Philippines 1986
    Turkey 1986
    Uruguay 1985

As long as the target government cooperates by responding to the complaint, by accepting direct contacts, and by sending representatives to answer member's questions, the confidential review may continue indefinitely with no apparent deadline for action or a recommendation to ECOSOC. The Commission has monitored the situations in Paraguay for over nine years without a thorough study, investigation, or public disclosure of the evidence presented. The Commission twice discontinued review of Paraguay, but the Sub-Commission referred more communications. Prior to restoration of democratic rule, Uruguay's military cooperated in seven years of confidential review by allowing the de Cuellar visit described above and by releasing a long-term detainee just prior to the Commission's 1984 discussion of its situation. On August 31, 1983 the Sub-Commission had cabled the government urging clemency for Professor José Luis Massera Lerena, a mathematics professor and parliamentary deputy. Uruguay's regime appears to have timed the release to influence the Commission's seventh year of deliberation on its situation. Situations in Haiti and Indonesia also remained on the Commission's confidential agenda for over four years. The Commission has publicly disclosed its recommendation that ECOSOC request assistance for Haiti "to facilitate the realization of full enjoyment of human rights." Indonesia, initially charged with torture and murder of political detainees, has more recently been scrutinized for repression on East Timor.

NGO observers have urged the Commission to assume the truth of unrebutted allegations in order to make a timely decision on the merits. Governments have several months to reply after the Sub-Commission has referred communications and should not require any more time. The NGO proposal notes that The Inter-American Commission on Human Rights and the Human Rights Committee do not defer their decisions to benefit governments which fail to respond.

For the most recalcitrant and politically disfavored offenders, confidential review has merely been the initial stage of a process leading to more embarrassing public scrutiny. In four cases, the Commission never acted on Sub-Commission confidential referrals because public review was already underway. In four other situations several years of confidential review preceded public deliberations or disclosure. A 1980 Bolivian coup d'etat aggravated a situation that had been under confidential review for several years. At the urging of the Sub-Commission and the General Assembly, the Commission appointed a Special Envoy to prepare a report. After four years of monitoring, the Commission discontinued confidential review of Afghanistan in 1984, because a Special Rapporteur had been authorized to study that situation under Resolution 1235. Paraguay, by contrast, came under both procedures — confidential monitoring for the massacre and enslavement of tribal Indians, and a 1984 public resolution concerning a twenty year state of siege.

The Commission has discontinued confidential proceedings against twelve other states without public explanation. In four cases new regimes repudiated past violations. After Tanzania helped overthrow Uganda's Idi Amin and France intervened to topple Bokassa of the Central African Empire, the Commission discontinued review of those situations without any public report. Argentina's new foreign minister reported to the Commission after his democratically elected government began prosecution of past human rights offenders. Uruguay made a similar presentation after a democratically elected government replaced the military. Both Argentina and Uruguay have requested and ECOSOC has agreed to release the confidential materials about the prior violations.

In several other cases, the Commission apparently discontinued confidential review because there had been no recurrence of violations after the offense which gave rise to the initial allegation. The closely contested decisions to end monitoring of Ethiopia and the German Democratic Republic revealed partisan East-West calculations, while the political factions on Indonesia departed from the normal alignments. The Sub-Commission's more independent experts have found ongoing violations in several situations found acceptable by the Commission. When the Commission discontinued review of Indonesia and Paraguay, the Sub-Commission referred further complaints against those governments. NGOs have also continued to publicize violations by other governments relieved of confidential scrutiny by the Commission.

A well-informed observer summarizes the merits and disadvantages of the 1503 procedure in the following excerpt before concluding that it should at least be reformed in a major way.

Alston, The Commission on Human Rights
in The United Nations and Human Rights 139, 152-53
(P. Alston ed. 1992)

Providing a general evaluation of the 1503 procedure is difficult but necessary. The question is whether the procedure provides adequate returns in terms of the investments of faith, time, energy, and media attention that have been made in it; whether, on balance, it succeeds in putting enough pressure on enough countries in ways that could not more effectively be achieved by other means. Some of those means might already be in existence, others might more easily be created if the 1503 procedure were to be eliminated.

The first point to be made is that the historical value of the 1503 procedure cannot be doubted. In many ways it laid the groundwork for the development of the potentially effective public (i.e., resolution 1235-based) response to violations which began to come into its own after 1979. It put paid once and for all to the domestic jurisdiction *canard*; it accustomed States to the need to defend themselves and gave them practice in examining (and prosecuting) the performance of others; it galvanized some of the NGOs at a time when some of the other procedures offered even lower rates of return; and it exposed the Commission and Sub-Commission to the real world of violations more effectively than any earlier exercise had. But a valuable historical role does not of itself justify the procedure's retention in the 1990s. Among commentators, the procedure has had both its defenders and its critics. Among the latter was Amnesty International which, in the mid-1970s, characterized the confidentiality of 1503 as 'an undisguised stratagem for using the United Nations, not as an instrument for promoting and protecting and exposing large-scale violations of human rights, but rather for concealing their occurrence'. . . . Writing a decade later, in 1990, Iain Guest concluded that 'confidentiality has not persuaded governments to cooperate with the United Nations' and that '1503 has become truly dangerous to human rights — and that it offers a useful refuge to repressive regimes'.

While some of the procedure's proponents would disagree strongly with such assessments, their enthusiasm is nevertheless usually rather restrained. Writing in 1980, Tardu was optimistic about the procedure's future while conceding that its past performance had left much to be desired. In 1982 Zuijdwijk, after an exhaustive study of the procedure, damned it with faint praise by concluding that it is 'worth sending a petition to the United Nations under resolution 1503 (XLVIII) but petitioners should limit their expectations'. Tolley is equally sparing in his praise for 1503 although he attaches importance to the fact that most target governments feel threatened by it and that 'only four states have failed to have observers at two consecutive [Commission] sessions when their government was under Reso-

lution 1503 review'. An experienced Sub-Commission member, Marc Bossuyt, has strongly defended the procedure on the grounds that: (1) 1503
review facilitates subsequent consideration of a country under the public
procedures — a hypothesis that would appear to be at least questionable;
and (2) that it enables attention to be paid to situations that would otherwise
be ignored. His views are predicated on the assumptions that a government's
reputation suffers from remaining under 1503 review and that a continuing
dialogue is the key to success in dealing with human rights violations.
While in some instances these may be valid, they would seem to be applicable only with great difficulty to many of the cases in which 1503 has clearly
failed during the 1980s.

IV.   Other UN Mechanisms for Investigating
Alleged Human Rights Abuses

A.   Petition Procedures

The procedure established under ECOSOC Resolution 1503 and discussed in this Problem is the primary, but not the only, direct petition
procedure available to individuals and groups to complain about alleged
human rights violations. It also is important to bear in mind that the 1503
procedure is not available where an individual violation occurs but is limited to *situations* "which appear to reveal a consistent pattern of gross . . .
violations of human rights."

While most of the other petition procedures have been created pursuant to treaties or conventions, four additional UN procedures have been
established pursuant to the inherent authority of the UN Charter. See generally Centre for Human Rights, Communications Procedures (Fact Sheet
No. 7, 1989); M. Tardu, Human Rights: The International Petition System
(1979).

Article 87(b) of the UN Charter provides that the Trusteeship Council
has authority to accept and examine petitions concerning the trust territories. However, with the termination in 1994 of the final trusteeship, the
U.S.-administered Trust Territory of the Pacific Islands, the Trusteeship
Council decided to discontinue its regular meetings, holding open the possibility of meeting in the future if necessary.

The Special Committee on the Situation with regard to the Implemen-
tation of the Declaration on the Granting of Independence to Colonial
Countries and Peoples (commonly known as the Special Committee on
Decolonization or the Committee of 24) was created by the General Assem-

bly in 1961 to oversee implementation of the 1960 Declaration on Decolonization (G.A. Res. 1514, 15 U.N. GAOR Supp. (No. 16) at 66, U.N. Doc. A/4684 (1960)). The Special Committee may receive petitions from individuals and groups and, with the permission of the administering state, conduct on-site visits to territories. In 1994 its mandate extended to 17 non-self-governing territories, ranging from small island possessions of the United Kingdom to the Western Sahara. See generally the annual reports of the Special Committee to the General Assembly, issued as supplements to the General Assembly's Official Records; UN Dept. of Public Information, Decolonization, The Task Ahead, Publication DPI/1109 (1991).

More important from the perspective of individual rights (as opposed to the collective right of self-determination) is the procedure adopted by the UN Economic, Cultural, and Scientific Organization (UNESCO) in 1978. Pursuant to Decision 104 EX/3.3 of the UNESCO Executive Board (Documentary Supplement), UNESCO's Committee on Conventions and Recommendations may consider petitions that allege violations of human rights within UNESCO's competence, that is, in the fields of education, science, culture, and information. While the Committee's deliberations are confidential, the petitioner is informed of any action taken. The Committee does not act as an adjudicative body; its primary goal is to engage in a dialogue with the government concerned, in the hope of resolving the complaint on a humanitarian basis. Its conclusions are not published, and there is no formal enforcement mechanism, but the secrecy of the procedure is less complete than that under Resolution 1503. See Marks, The Complaint Procedure of the United Nations Educational, Scientific and Cultural Organization, in Guide to International Human Rights Practice 86-98 (2d ed. H. Hannum ed. 1992); Weissbrodt and Farley, The UNESCO Human Rights Procedure: An Evaluation, 16 Human Rts. Q. 391 (1994).

The International Labor Organization (ILO) has a fairly comprehensive system of monitoring and supervising implementation of the approximately 170 of its conventions currently in force. In addition, workers' or employers' organizations may file formal "representations" or "complaints" under the ILO constitution, alleging violations by a state of any ILO convention to which that state is a party. The most widely used ILO petition procedure does not even require ratification of an ILO convention, as complaints from a workers' or employers' organization concerning violations of freedom of association by any ILO member are within the competence of the ILO's Committee on Freedom of Association. The various ILO petition procedures and reporting systems are described in Leary, Lessons from the Experience of the International Labour Organisation, in The United Nations and Human Rights (P. Alston ed. 1992); Swepston, Complaints Procedures of the International Labour Organization 99-116 (2d ed. H. Hannum ed. 1992).

In most instances, the most effective forums for filing individual petitions are those created under specific human rights treaties that the concerned state has ratified. Those procedures are discussed in Problems III (Optional Protocol to the Covenant on Civil and Political Rights), IX (European Convention on Human Rights), and X (American Convention on Human Rights and African Charter on Human and Peoples' Rights).

B. Non-Petition Procedures

Formal petition procedures remain the exception rather than the rule, and the limitations of the 1503 and UNESCO procedures may make them inappropriate to redress either notorious cases of massive human rights abuses, where maximum publicity is desired, or little-known individual cases, where the remedy sought is immediate and humanitarian rather than political. As demonstrated by Figure 5-1 (see page 399 infra), the United Nations has developed an impressive array of bodies that deal, in some manner or other, with human rights issues.

The most important procedures have been developed at the initiative of, and are implemented primarily by, the UN Commission on Human Rights. The Commission on Human Rights is a subsidiary body of the Economic and Social Council, composed of 53 state members; it is, therefore, an avowedly political body, unlike the Sub-Commission on the Prevention of Discrimination and the Protection of Minorities, whose members are, in theory, experts independent of any government. The Commission meets annually for six weeks in February-March, and it has become the primary diplomatic forum in which human rights issues are publicly discussed. It adopted over 100 resolutions at its 1994 session, which ranged from relatively innocuous texts adopted without a vote to highly politicized resolutions on the human rights situations in specific countries.

The Commission on Human Rights spent most of its early years engaged in standard-setting activities, which led to adoption by the General Assembly of the Universal Declaration of Human Rights in 1948 and the two covenants in 1966. It also has played a promotional role in calling attention to important human rights issues. The greatest transformation, however, has been in the Commission's ability and willingness to address specific issues of human rights violations, albeit in a highly political context.

The following two readings provide an essential historical overview of the Commission's activities. The second also describes the major mechanisms through which the Commission attempts to address human rights violations, including the general debate and adoption of resolutions authorized under ECOSOC Resolution 1235 and the appointment of various rapporteurs or working groups to consider specific countries or issues.

J. Carey, UN Protection of Civil and Political Rights
84-90, 135-138 (1970)

INVESTIGATION AS A MEANS OF PROTECTION

During the United Nations' first two decades, it seemed to be firmly established that the UN would take no action with respect to the complaints of persons claiming to be oppressed by their own governments. However, towards the end of these two decades . . . a set of practices grew up, applicable only to colonies and to the Republic of South Africa, which took account of individuals' complaints and gave them wide notice. So extensive a set of practices seemed bound in the end to lap over into the broader area of human rights complaints generally.

In the first half of the decade of the 1960's, the Committee on Colonialism of the UN General Assembly, followed shortly thereafter by the Committee on South African Apartheid, began holding hearings for complainants and publishing their written complaints. While some persons felt that this process produced very few results, the mere publication, either in writing or orally, of individuals' complaints was a new field of activity for the UN. As a result of some of the complaints which were brought to the surface by this process in the Colonialism Committee, the General Assembly in October of 1966 by its landmark resolution 2144 invited the Economic and Social Council and the Commission on Human Rights to give urgent consideration to ways and means of improving the capacity of the UN to put a stop to violations of human rights wherever they might occur. The resolution was, in one view, "in accordance with an entirely new doctrine, namely, that it is the right and duty of the United Nations to consider specific violations of human rights and to recommend appropriate measures to halt such violations wherever they may occur." . . .

How far open the door is, and how much effort is necessary to keep it even that far open, can be seen by looking at developments which have occurred since October 1966 when the General Assembly declared the "new doctrine." The UN Human Rights Commission, meeting in early 1967 shortly after Assembly resolution 2144 was adopted, resolved to ask the Sub-Commission on Prevention of Discrimination and Protection of Minorities to bring to the Commission's attention any situation which the Sub-Commission had reasonable cause to believe revealed a consistent pattern of violations of human rights and fundamental freedoms in any country, including policies of racial discrimination, segregation, and apartheid, with particular reference to colonial and dependent territories. . . .

A little later, in June 1967, the ECOSOC [in Resolution 1235, found in the Documentary Supplement] gave its blessing to these arrangements, and in addition took a step of great significance by giving authority to both the Commission and the Sub-Commission to inspect all of the many thousands of written human rights complaints which flow year by year to the UN. . . .

The new procedure approved by ECOSOC, allowing the Commission and Sub-Commission to look at these complaints in the original form instead of in the form of summaries prepared by the Secretariat, first was put into effect at the meeting of the Sub-Commission in Geneva in October 1967. The outcome was a resolution, adopted without any contrary vote, which recommended to the Human Rights Commission further investigation concerning not only those parts of Southern Africa which had become traditional targets of UN investigation, but also two countries elsewhere in the world, Greece and Haiti. It was in this manner that the Sub-Commission complied with the Commission's request that situations revealing consistent patterns of violations be brought to the Commission's attention. The Commission's other request, that the Sub-Commission prepare a report containing information on violations from all available sources, was met by means of a one-page annex to the resolution. As to Southern Africa, this annex cited various documents already published by the UN and therefore fully available to any member of the public. As to Greece and Haiti, however, a new departure was represented in the annex, which referred to communications received by the Sub-Commission pursuant to ECOSOC resolution 1235 and identified at a meeting of the Sub-Commission held in private by virtue of ECOSOC resolution 728F. In the case of Greece, the government's response was also cited. By this kind of coded reference, the secrecy of the communications was retained, while at the same time making clear that definite documents, two in the case of Greece and one in the case of Haiti, were being specified and could be individually identified through reference to the minutes of the private Sub-Commission meeting, which, though unpublished, were available to all Sub-Commission members.

When the matter came before the Human Rights Commission meeting in February and March 1968, an assortment of currents swirled and surged over a period of several days, buffeting but finally leaving intact the flimsy structure created during the previous months for the examination of communications complaining about governmental oppression anywhere in the world. The Commission declined the Sub-Commission's request for further investigation of Greece and Haiti, but did not scold the lower body for requesting it. Representatives of the Greek and Haitian Governments spoke at length before the Human Rights Commission in an effort to vindicate their governments and to defend them against any accusation of human rights violation. . . .

Self-defense by the governments accused was therefore one of the currents surging at the Human Rights Commission meeting in early 1968. Political attacks also were heard. The Soviet Union launched an attack against Greece, also assaulting Israel because of its alleged aggression, and the United States in regard to Vietnam. . . .

By launching its three-pronged attack, the Soviet Union was sanctioning a broad interpretation of the proper scope of the UN's concern with the agenda item on violations of human rights. Its assaults against Greece, Israel, and the United States were inconsistent with the narrower view that only racial discrimination like that in Southern Africa is a proper human rights subject for UN concern. . . .

Tanzania introduced a draft resolution which, while not clearly saying so, was described by its author as having the purpose of cutting down the jurisdiction of the Sub-Commission to limit it in the future to matters of apartheid and similar practices in Southern Africa. . . . However, Austria and the Philippines submitted amendments to the Tanzanian proposal to endorse fully and renew the Sub-Commission's previously wide scope, whereupon Tanzania withdrew its resolution altogether.

This development left no proposal before the Commission under the pending agenda item except an entirely separate UAR draft aimed at Israel. The anti-Israel draft was presented as being humanitarian in purpose, and dealt with persons displaced during hostilities and their right to return to their homes. Compromise on the wording, brought about through lengthy consultations, resulted in language that all members except Israel were able to support, while even Israel did not find it necessary to vote against or even abstain, but simply did not participate in the voting. . . .

The unanimous adoption of the UAR resolution can be said to have confirmed that the UN's geographic capacity to take specific positions with respect to human rights violations was as broad as the whole world. While it is true that the Middle East situation is an international one, an international war in this respect is not far from a war within the borders of one country. This fact is demonstrated in the Geneva Conventions of 1949, which concern themselves with both types of hostility. Once into the sphere of civil war, it is no great step to be concerned also with civil unrest short of war. The UAR resolution, together with the fact that the Commission left undisturbed the broad scope of the Sub-Commission's authority to concern itself with human rights violations the world over, indicated that international human rights protection procedures were evolving apart from those embodied in treaties. . . . [T]he rate of development of such procedures depends on the ingenuity of their proponents.

Alston, The Commission on Human Rights
in The United Nations and Human Rights 139, 155, 158-161, 165, 167-168, 171-173, 175-177, 180-181 (P. Alston ed. 1992)

THE HISTORICAL EVOLUTION: AN OVERVIEW

Although it is tempting to evaluate the Commission's performance solely on the basis of recent developments, any such assessment is likely to be grossly distorted if it is not placed carefully in historical perspective. In brief, there have been three very distinct phases: (1) 1946-66, during which time the Commission was not prepared to address the issue of specific violations at all; (2) 1967-78, when the Commission struggled to evolve procedures which were initially designed to respond only to problems associated with racism and colonialism; and (3) 1979 to the present, when the procedures developed earlier have been applied in an increasingly creative and tailored fashion to an ever-widening range of countries and types of violations. Thus any meaningful evaluation must at least recognize these distinct phases and acknowledge that it is only in the present (third) phase that the member States of the United Nations have made any serious effort to respond to violations in a manner that at all purports to be objective and even-handed. Thus any evaluation of recent actions by comparing them with those of a decade or more ago is the equivalent of seeking to compare apples and oranges. . . .

The 1235 Procedure

Origins   ECOSOC resolution 1235 (XLII) of 6 June 1967 established the procedure on the basis of which the Commission holds an annual public debate focusing on gross violations of human rights. It is in this context that it has developed an array of methods by which to investigate and apply pressure to individual states. The 1235 procedure illustrates, perhaps better than any other single example, the gradual evolutionary manner in which the Commission's mandate has been expanded over the years. The ways in which violations are dealt with by the Commission in the 1990s, always under the rubric of 'the 1235 procedure', bears only a passing resemblance to the actual procedure formally authorized by that resolution. . . .

In the early 1970s the Commission heard many allegations under the 1235 procedure but it remained unmoved by incidents such as the mass killings that accompanied efforts to suppress the secession of East Pakistan (subsequently Bangladesh) and the mass expulsion of Asians from Uganda. The case that finally drew a response was that of Chile. In setting up an *Ad Hoc* Working Group of five of its members to investigate the human rights situation arising out of the military *coup d'état* against President Allende, the Commission was setting another vital precedent. Chile was the first situation, which involved neither colonialism nor racism, to be investigated by the Commission. In principle at least, the door had finally been opened, albeit only a fraction, to permit the effective use of 1235 in virtually any situation, provided only that the political will could be mustered. There are several reasons why Chile was able to play this vital role: it had a long history of democracy; the circumstances of the coup were particularly bloody; the government that had been overthrown was a member of the Non-Aligned Movement and of the Socialist International; the involvement of the United States in the coup was documented; the ILO had already appointed a Commission of Inquiry; and the resulting international campaign was intensive.

It is important to note at this point that each of the three precedent-setting investigations [southern Africa, the Israeli-occupied territories and Chile] (the 'unholy trinity' as South Africa liked to term the trio) had been authorized on the 'understanding' that it would not in fact create a precedent. Rather, each situation was presented as though it were *sui generis*. . . . Between 1975 and 1979 an impressive succession of horror stories was presented to the Commission but none was deemed worthy of an inquiry under the 1235 provisions. Idi Amin's atrocities in Uganda, Emperor Bokassa's barbarisms in the Central African Empire, Pol Pot's genocidal regime in Democratic Kampuchea, the annexation of East Timor and the abuse of its people by Indonesia, the systematic disappearances and the widespread terror that accompanied them in Argentina and Uruguay, the brutality of the military regime in Brazil, and many other comparable situations were all ignored in the 1235 context.

The Opening-Up of the Procedure By 1979, however, the situation had changed. NGOs such as Amnesty International and others had created a far better informed public opinion and governments were beginning to be subjected to domestic pressure to do something about human rights. The United Nations forum provided a convenient setting in which to take a stand. The Carter Administration's heavy-handed but none the less pioneering efforts, building upon continuing Congressional efforts, had dramatically elevated the international profile of human rights issues.

The Commission's first tentative move to open up its procedures came in 1978. It asked the government of Democratic Kampuchea to respond to allegations brought against it and requested the Sub-Commission to consider that response and any other material and report to the Commission. . . . In the same year the Commission . . . condemn[ed] the Somoza regime in Nicaragua for violations and also sent a telegram to the Guatemalan government expressing concern over the 'assassination' of a former Minister for Foreign Affairs. It also took action under resolution 1235 against Equatorial Guinea. . . . Taken together these developments opened the door much wider than before and set the scene for a comparatively rapid development of the means by which the United Nations could use the 1235 procedure to respond to violations. . . .

In 1980, the Assembly requested the Commission to take action in cases concerning Bolivia and El Salvador, which it did the following year. From then on, the 1980s witnessed a steady stream of resolutions under the 1235 procedure calling for a variety of 'special procedures' to be undertaken. As of the end of its 1991 session the Commission had, since 1979, taken the following country-specific actions under the 1235 procedure:*

* At its 1992 through 1994 sessions, the Commission added Cambodia, Indonesia (with respect to East Timor), Myanmar, Papua New Guinea (with respect to Bougainville), Romania, Sudan, Togo, former Yugoslavia, and Zaire to the list of countries with respect to which some form of specific action has been mandated. — EDS.

(a) *Appointment of a special rapporteur*: Afghanistan 1984-present; Chile 1979-90; Equatorial Guinea 1979; Guatemala 1982-5; Romania 1989-present; 'Occupied Kuwait' 1991-present; Iraq 1991-present.

(b) *Appointment of a special representative*: El Salvador 1981-present; Guatemala 1986-7; Iran 1984-present; Cuba 1991-present.

(c) *Appointment of an expert*: Equatorial Guinea 1980, 1984.

(d) *Appointment of an independent expert*: Haiti 1990-present; Guatemala 1990-present.

(e) *Appointment of a working group*: Southern Africa 1967-present; Israeli Occupied Territories 1968-present; Chile 1975-9.

(f) *Appointment of a Commission delegation (6 members)*: Cuba 1988.

(g) *Secretary-General to maintain direct contacts*: Iran 1982; Cuba 1989-91.

(h) *Review of available information by Sub-Commission member*: Democratic Kampuchea 1979-83.

(i) *Report to the Commission by the Secretary-General*: Nicaragua 1979; Albania 1990-present.

(j) *Report to the Commission by the Secretary-General or his designated representative*: Poland 1982-4. . . .

. . . An enormous range of situations has been specifically discussed under the 1235 item, and in some of those cases, the mere expression of serious concern or the threat of a resolution has been sufficient to provoke a constructive response from the government concerned. In addition, the Commission has adopted a number of country-specific resolutions and decisions which stop short of initiating a special procedure. A new technique, pioneered in 1991, is for the Chairman to make a formal (pre-agreed) 'statement' on a specific situation. Moreover, the agenda items on self-determination, advisory services, slavery, and other matters have provided important opportunities for discussing specific violations. . . .

Designation and Selection of Rapporteurs The implementation of special procedures has been entrusted to a wide range of entities. While 'working groups' and 'special rapporteurs' were initially the favoured means of fact-finding, various other designations have been added over the years. They include 'rapporteurs', 'envoys', 'special representatives', 'experts', 'independent experts', 'delegations', etc. The different terminology was originally intended to reflect an unstated hierarchy according to the gravity of the response. But the Commission's creativity, combined with its inconsistency in this regard, has served to blur the significance of these distinctions, at least in the minds of all but those diplomats who continue to fight with such vigour and enthusiasm to secure one designation rather than another. Of much greater importance today is the agenda item under which the appointment is made. If made under the advisory services item it has been presumed to have a far less negative connotation than if made under the violations item. But the significance of this distinction may also disappear in time if the Commission continues to blur the lines between the two items, as has clearly been the case in respect of Haiti and Guatemala. . . .

The Mandate: Prosecutors, Solution Seekers or Fact-finders?   The terms used to describe the formal mandates given to country rapporteurs have varied considerably. But whether they have been asked to 'study', 'inquire into', 'investigate', or 'examine', most rapporteurs have tended to assume considerable flexibility and to approach each situation as they see fit. The Commission, for its part, has generally not sought to impose any procedural straitjackets and has been reluctant to criticize the approach adopted by individual rapporteurs. Not surprisingly, this lack of structure has resulted in enormous disparities of style, methodology, content, and focus from one report to another. It has also enabled individual rapporteurs to assume that they have a *carte blanche* in determining the nature of their reports.

For analytical purposes, three principal approaches to country-reporting may be discerned. The first emphasizes the *fact-finding and documentation function*. In this view the function of reporting is to record the facts, to provide a reliable historical record, and to provide the necessary raw material against the background of which the political organs can determine the best strategy under the circumstances. . . . The second approach assumes that the *prosecutorial/publicity function* is paramount. Thus the rapporteur's role is not to establish whether violations have occurred but to marshal as much evidence as possible to support a condemnation that, in many instances, will already have been made. . . . The third approach is to emphasize the *conciliation function*. The rapporteur's role is not to confront the violators but to seek solutions which will improve, even if not necessarily resolve, the situation. . . .

The Commission's Response to Reports   The Commission's response to a rapporteur's report is dictated in part by the approach adopted in the report itself. If extensive conclusions and recommendations are offered by the rapporteur, as is usually the case whether or not the Commission has specifically requested them, the latter's room for manœuvre is very limited. It cannot readily reach a conclusion which is at odds with that of its fact-finder without putting the government concerned in a strong position to denounce the fairness of the process. . . .

The Commission's debates are rarely the occasion for any serious and sustained analysis of the content of the reports it has commissioned. Delegate's speeches are usually taken up by general justifications of the position which that State proposes to take in response to the report. The real action is in the corridors where the content of the draft resolution is determined. Determined lobbying can also take place in the capitals and the content of the report is at best a minor element in such negotiations. . . .

The Effectiveness of the 1235 Procedure   Evaluating effectiveness of any procedure in the human rights field is a vexing issue. The principal question concerns the criteria to be applied. Objectives range from general consciousness-raising to the actual saving of lives. It would seem difficult to sustain many strong claims on behalf of the 1235 procedure at the latter end of the spectrum. The response time is too great, the potential sanction too distant (or un-immediate), and the range of other relevant pressures in most situations too vast to be able to say with confidence in any given situation that 1235 made the crucial difference. This is borne out by the few studies which have sought to evaluate the United Nations' impact within the context of specific situations. . . .

While an overall assessment cannot be made without taking account of the panoply of other UN techniques and procedures and their complex interaction with 1235, it is difficult to escape the conclusion that the glass is at best half full. Although that is an achievement that should not be underestimated it is nevertheless difficult to accept that, after almost half a century of concerted efforts, the principal UN procedures for responding to violations are quite as embryonic, marginally effective and unevenly applied as they are.

THE THEMATIC PROCEDURES

Just as the reinvigoration of the 1235 procedure resulted in part from the horrors of the 1970s and the accompanying unresponsiveness of the UN's human rights organs, so too did the evolution of various 'thematic' procedures. The first of these procedures, the Working Group on Enforced or Involuntary Disappearances, was established in 1980 in response to developments in Argentina and Chile. . . .

Once again, as with the opening up of the 1235 procedure after 1979, the establishment of the Disappearances Group served as a vital precedent that enabled other comparable initiatives to be taken in later years. . . .

Initially, the thematic procedures might have been seen as being located in-between the 1503 and 1235 procedures. Their work was not to be confidential but nor was it to be country-specific in the full sense. The procedure was more co-operative than adversarial in design and condemnations were neither the goal nor the likely result of the exercise. Indeed the term 'fact-finding' was of dubious application to the procedures that were envisaged. But, despite the procedures' initially very modest aspirations, they have over the course of their first decade proven to be far more flexible, innovative, and persistent than either their original detractors or proponents would have dared to think. . . .

Mandates and Procedures   Each of the procedures has been endowed with slightly different terms of reference, although the resulting differences have gradually been diminished, if not eliminated, over time. The Disappearances Group was empowered to 'examine questions' relating to the problem, to 'bear in mind the need to be able to respond effectively' and to 'work with discretion'. The latter element was reiterated in 1981 when the Commission specified that such discretion was needed to 'protect persons providing information' as well as 'to limit the dissemination of information provided by Governments'. The Commission also characterized the Group's objectives as 'strictly humanitarian'. By 1990, however, the Group's practice had evolved to the point where its mandate 'to examine questions' was the one to which it gave the greatest emphasis, thus playing down many of the constraints implicit in some of the other language used at one time or other by the Commission to describe its mandate. In this context it has worked at three different levels, examining: (1) individual cases; (2) overall country situations; and (3) the 'dynamics' of the phenomenon of disappearances. In the latter context it has focused on systemic factors such as the role of paramilitary groups, harassment of witnesses and relatives, impunity for perpetrators, and the role of military courts and of amnesties. It has also consistently advocated the adoption of a new international instrument dealing with disappearances.

The injunctions to examine or study the relevant phenomenon and to seek to 'respond effectively' is common to the mandates of most of the thematic rapporteurs. The principal exception is the Rapporteur on Mercenaries whose mandate is somewhat different as a result of the nature of the phenomenon with which he is dealing and of its status in international law. Thus his mandate is closely linked to the right to self-determination and he is specifically directed to 'develop further the position that mercenary acts are means of violating human rights and thwarting the self-determination of peoples'. . . .

Sources of Information   Unlike other United Nations efforts to monitor human rights violations, the thematic procedures have never been hobbled in terms of the sources of information on which they are authorized to rely. The Disappearances Group was empowered to make use of information from any 'reliable sources', a term which placed only a minimal limitation upon it. It has sought to develop working relationships with as wide a variety of NGOs and others as possible and in its 1990 report lists ninety-eight different groups with which it has been in contact since its inception. The other thematic rapporteurs have been restricted to seeking or obtaining information from NGOs or even from NGOs in consultative status with ECOSOC. But these restrictions have not been permitted to hinder their activities. Thus, for example, a significant number of on-site visits has been undertaken under each of the thematic procedures. Such visits should, and usually do, provide unrivalled opportunities for the collection of information. In the words of one commentator, 'all procedures appear to have had a healthy disregard for formality and to have employed a wider range of sources than officially permitted'. . . . [See pages 431-443 of Problem VI.]

Means of Pressure   While each of the thematic procedures has experimented with different priorities in terms of the various means by which pressure can be exerted upon governments, the type of approaches used by the Disappearances Working Group have been broadly representative. For analytical purposes, five different techniques may be identified: routine requests for information; urgent action requests; country visits; prompt interventions; and reporting to the Commission. . . .

Evaluating Effectiveness   . . . [I]t would seem that the thematic procedures have, in a number of important respects, been more effective than either the 1235 or 1503 procedures. In terms of the fact-finding function, as narrowly defined, the country visits being undertaken with increasing frequency under the auspices of the thematic procedures may well turn out to be more effective than the country-specific procedures under resolution 1235. Their working methods, while far from uniform across the different mandates, are generally better developed and more sophisticated than those of their 1235 counterparts. Their missions have been generally better prepared, their co-operation with NGOs and other sources more comprehensive and they have demonstrated a greater willingness to tackle some of the structural dimensions of the problems with which they are dealing. Perhaps none of this should be surprising in view of the ability of the thematic rapporteurs to pick and choose their priorities, their greater insulation from political pressures generated by individual governments, and, in most cases, the stronger Secretariat support that they have received.

In terms of the public relations function, the thematic rapporteurs have also been very effective, especially in comparative terms. They have developed and maintained contacts with a wide range of NGOs, they have reached out systematically to the victims and their supporters, and they have succeeded in generating a better informed public debate around the relevant issues. In particular, most of the procedures have played an important role as catalysts to the development of new international instruments. Finally, in terms of the conciliation function, the thematic procedures have often succeeded in producing highly critical analyses while at the same time reassuring the governments concerned that co-operation was all that they sought.

Several criticisms may, however, be levelled at the thematic procedures. In the first place, the range of issues that they cover is clearly skewed. While disappearances, summary executions, torture, religious intolerance, and the use of mercenaries are all issues of the utmost importance, there remain many other important issues that are not being accorded comparable attention, and efforts to reduce and limit the overall number of thematic procedures have already been foreshadowed. Such imbalance risks creating a *de facto* hierarchy of rights within the UN context, despite the inconsistency of such an outcome with the theoretical foundations of international endeavours.

A more telling criticism of the thematic procedures is that they do not succeed in putting much pressure upon individual countries. This is best illustrated by several very serious cases of States that have simultaneously been the subject of major attention by several of the thematic procedures (e.g., Colombia and Iraq) but have still not been given any particular attention by the Commission itself. In this regard, it is clear that the thematic procedures should be given particular weight in the process of identifying countries that deserve to be targeted under the 1235 procedure. Yet no country has so far been graduated in this way. As a result it is feared that the thematic procedures might only make the development of the 1235 procedure even more difficult, thus enabling States to shield behind the less targeted and inevitably much more narrowly focused thematic procedures.

As implied in the Alston reading, the 1235 procedure is not so much a procedure as an authorization for the Commission on Human Rights to call attention to allegations of human rights violations anywhere in the world through debate, the adoption of resolutions, and other actions (such as the appointment of a special rapporteur). Although governments are not required to cooperate with the Commission or even participate in the debates, most defend their records vigorously, and most do cooperate, however reluctantly and incompletely, with investigations by either country-specific or thematic rapporteurs.

The decision to appoint a country-specific rapporteur is always a highly political one, and the mandate of such a rapporteur must be reviewed each year. The thematic rapporteurs and working groups also were subject to annual renewal in their early years, but they have now become an integral part of the Commission's monitoring machinery and are normally appointed for three-year terms.

There are now 13 thematic rapporteurs or working groups operating under the authority of the Commission, and their respective mandates deal with disappearances (1980); extrajudicial, summary, or arbitrary executions (1982); torture (1985); religious intolerance (1986); mercenaries (1987); arbitrary detention (1991); the sale of children and child prostitution and pornography (1992); internally displaced persons (1993); the right to development (1993); racism and xenophobia (1993); freedom of opinion and expression (1993); the independence of the judiciary (1994); and violence against women (1994). Their methods of work are discussed briefly at pages 390-393 infra.

Although all of the above individuals and groups are usefully described as "thematic," their mandates may vary significantly. Compare, for example, the following excerpts from the resolutions creating the respective rapporteurs.

Commission on Human Rights, Torture and Other Cruel, Inhuman or Degrading Treatment or Punishment

Commn. on Human Rights Res. 1985/33, U.N. ESCOR Supp.
(No. 2) at 71, 72, U.N. Doc. E/1985/22 (1985)

2. *Requests* the Chairman of the Commission to appoint, after consultation with the other members of the Bureau, an individual of recognized international standing as special rapporteur;

3. *Decides further* that the special rapporteur, in carrying out his mandate, shall seek and receive credible and reliable information from Governments, as well as specialized agencies, intergovernmental organizations and non-governmental organizations;

4. *Requests* the Secretary-General to appeal to all Governments to cooperate with and assist the special rapporteur in the performance of his tasks and to furnish all information requested;

5. *Further requests* the Secretary-General to provide all necessary assistance to the special rapporteur;

6. *Invites* the special rapporteur, in carrying out his mandate, to bear in mind the need to be able to respond effectively to credible and reliable information that comes before him and to carry out his work with discretion. . . .

Commission on Human Rights, Question of Arbitrary Detention

Commn. on Human Rights Res. 1991/42, U.N. ESCOR Supp.
(No. 2) at 105, 106, U.N. Doc. E/1991/22 (1991)

2. *Decides* to create, for a three-year period, a working group composed of five independent experts, with the task of investigating cases of detention imposed arbitrarily or otherwise inconsistently with the relevant international standards set forth in the Universal Declaration of Human Rights or in the relevant international legal instruments accepted by the States concerned;

3. *Decides* that the working group, in carrying out its mandate, shall seek and receive information from Governments and intergovernmental and non-governmental organizations, and shall receive information from the individuals concerned, their families or their representatives;

4. *Invites* the working group to take account, in fulfilling its mandate, of the need to carry out its task with discretion, objectivity and independence;

5. *Requests* the working group to present a comprehensive report to the Commission at its forty-eighth session;

6. *Requests* the Secretary-General to provide all necessary assistance to the working group to enable it to accomplish its task. . . .

Commission on Human Rights, Right to Freedom of Opinion and Expression
Commn. on Human Rights Res. 1993/45, U.N. ESCOR Supp. (No. 3) at 154, 156-157, U.N. Doc. E/1993/23 (1993)

12. *Requests* the Special Rapporteur to gather all relevant information, wherever it may occur, of discrimination against, threats or use of violence and harassment, including persecution and intimidation, directed at persons seeking to exercise or to promote the exercise of the right to freedom of opinion and expression as affirmed in the Universal Declaration of Human Rights and, where applicable, the International Covenant on Civil and Political Rights, taking into account the work being conducted by other mechanisms of the Commission and Sub-Commission which touches on this right, with a view to avoiding duplication of work;

13. *Also requests* the Special Rapporteur, as a matter of high priority, to gather all relevant information, wherever it may occur, of discrimination against, threats or use of violence and harassment, including persecution and intimidation, against professionals in the field of information seeking to exercise or to promote the exercise of the right to freedom of opinion and expression, as affirmed in the Universal Declaration of Human Rights and, where applicable, the International Covenant on Civil and Political Rights;

14. *Further requests* the Special Rapporteur to seek and receive credible and reliable information from Governments, non-governmental organizations and any other parties who have knowledge of these cases;

15. *Urges* all Governments to cooperate with and assist the Special Rapporteur in the performance of his or her tasks and to furnish all information requested;

16. *Requests* the Secretary-General to provide the Special Rapporteur with all necessary assistance, in particular the staff and resources deemed necessary, within existing overall United Nations resources, to fulfil his or her mandate. . . .

From the cautious beginnings in the early 1980s, the thematic mechanisms have taken an increasingly aggressive approach toward their task of responding effectively to human rights violations. The new attitude is perhaps best exemplified by the Working Group on Arbitrary Detention, which adopts approximately 50 country-specific "decisions" each year during its three weeks of meetings in between the annual sessions of the Commission. A typical example of these formal decisions is the first adopted in 1993, which concerned the Philippines.

Report of the Working Group on Arbitrary Detention
U.N. Doc. E/CN.4/1994/27, at 40-41 (1993)

. . . [T]he Working Group decides:

The detention under a "John Doe" warrant, of Roland Abiog and Antonio Cabardo is declared to be arbitrary despite their release on bail, being in contravention of article 9 of the Universal Declaration of Human Rights, and article 9 of the International Covenant on Civil and Political Rights and falling within category III of the principles applicable in the consideration of the cases submitted to the Working Group [cases in which failure to observe international norms results in arbitrary trial proceedings]. Roland Abiog having been detained for being a member of the Communist Party of the Philippines, his detention is also declared to be in violation of article 19 of the Universal Declaration of Human Rights and article 19 of the International Covenant on Civil and Political Rights and falling within Category II of the principles applicable in the consideration of the cases submitted to the Working Group.

Having declared the detention of Roland Abiog and Antonio Cabardo to be arbitrary, the Working Group requests the Government of the Philippines to take note of its decision and in the light thereof bring its laws into conformity with the norms and principles incorporated in the Universal Declaration of Human Rights and in the International Covenant on Civil and Political Rights.

In view of the expanding substantive range of the rapporteurs' mandates and the generally excellent quality of their annual reports, the Commission has begun increasingly to recognize that the work of the special rapporteurs and thematic working groups constitutes a valuable source of information for human rights bodies throughout the UN system, as implied by the recommendations in the following resolution.

Commission on Human Rights, Human Rights and Thematic Procedures
Commn. on Human Rights Res. 1993/47, U.N. ESCOR Supp. (No. 3) at 159, U.N. Doc E/1993/23 (1993)

The Commission on Human Rights,

Considering that, over the years, thematic procedures established by the Commission with regard to the consideration of questions related to the promotion and protection of civil and political rights have earned an important position among its human rights monitoring mechanisms,

Noting with satisfaction that an increasing number of Governments, as well as non-governmental organizations, have developed a working relationship with one or more of the thematic procedures, . . .

3. *Encourages* Governments to respond expeditiously to requests for information made to them through the procedures, so that the thematic special rapporteurs concerned, the Working Group on Enforced or Involuntary Disappearances and the Working Group on Arbitrary Detention may carry out their mandates effectively;

4. *Also encourages* Governments encountering problems in the field of human rights to cooperate more closely with the Commission through the pertinent thematic procedures, in particular by inviting a thematic special rapporteur or working group to visit their countries;

5. *Invites* the Governments concerned to study carefully the recommendations addressed to them under thematic procedures and to keep the relevant mechanisms informed promptly on the progress made towards their implementation;

6. *Invites* the thematic special rapporteurs and working groups to include in their annual reports information provided by Governments on follow-up action, as well as their own observations thereon;

7. *Invites* non-governmental organizations to continue their cooperation with the thematic procedures;

8. *Encourages* the thematic special rapporteurs and working groups to follow closely the progress made by Governments in their investigations carried out within their respective mandates;

9. *Also encourages* the thematic special rapporteurs and working groups to continue to cooperate closely with relevant treaty bodies and country rapporteurs;

10. *Requests* the thematic special rapporteurs and working groups to include in their reports gender-disaggregated data, as well as comments on problems of responding and the results of analyses, as appropriate, in order to exercise their mandates even more effectively;

11. *Requests* the Secretary-General to consider the possibility of convening a meeting of all the thematic special rapporteurs and the Chairmen of working groups of the Commission on Human Rights in order to enable an exchange of views and closer cooperation;

12. *Also requests* the Secretary-General, in close collaboration with the thematic special rapporteurs and working groups, to issue annually their conclusions and recommendations. . . .

Beginning in 1994, an annual compilation of the conclusions and recommendations of the various rapporteurs and working groups has been issued as a Commission document, thus making it easier for Commission members and NGOs to make use of the rapporteurs' work.

Another example of the increasing use of the thematic rapporteurs is the Commission's recommendation to Indonesia (with respect to East Timor) that it implement the recommendations of the special rapporteur on torture and that it invite the special rapporteurs/working groups on torture, arbitrary executions, arbitrary detention, and disappearances to visit East Timor. See Commn. on Human Rights Res. 1993/97, U.N. ESCOR

Supp. (No. 3) at 277, 278, U.N. Doc. E/1993/23 (1993). At the same session, the Commission also requested the thematic rapporteurs and working groups "to keep a close watch on the situation of human rights in Zaire." Commn. on Human Rights Res. 1993/61, U.N. ESCOR Supp. (No. 3) at 190, 191, U.N. Doc. E/1993/23 (1993).

A major disadvantage to Commission action has been the fact that the Commission meets only once a year. This lacuna was addressed in 1990, when the Economic and Social Council approved a Commission recommendation that the Commission be permitted to convene emergency sessions to address urgent human rights situations when requested by a majority of Commission members. E.S.C. Res. 1990/48, U.N. ESCOR Supp. (No. 1) at 37, U.N. Doc. E/1990/90 (1990). Special sessions were convened three times in the succeeding four years, twice with respect to events in the former Yugoslavia (August and November 1992) and once to consider genocide in Rwanda (1994). However, no action has been taken on a 1992 proposal by the Commission to create an emergency mechanism under which a report would be prepared by a group of experts and sent to all Commission members on any "acute situation arising from a gross violation of human rights." See Commn. on Human Rights Res. 1992/55, U.N. ESCOR Supp. (No. 2) at 131, U.N. Doc. E/1992/22 (1993).

There are many other UN bodies to which information regarding human rights violations may be presented, although most do not have the power to act directly on the information they receive. Among these bodies (in addition to the treaty-based committees discussed in Problem III) are the following:

The *Commission on the Status of Women* receives confidential lists of communications that allege violations of women's rights from the UN Center for Human Rights, but it has never been given investigatory or even discussion authority equivalent to that of the Commission on Human Rights. It also addresses women's rights generally and has attempted to draw the attention of states to particular issues, such as violence against women and the need for equal pay for equal work. See Coliver, United Nations Machineries on Women's Rights: How Might They Better Help Women Whose Rights Are Being Violated?, in New Directions in Human Rights (E. Lutz, H. Hannum, and K. Burke eds. 1989); Galey, International Enforcement of Women's Rights, 6 Hum. Rts. Q. 463 (1984).

The General Assembly's *Special Committee on Colonialism* and *Special Committee to Investigate Israeli Practices Affecting the Human Rights of the Population of the Occupied Territories* may receive information related to their mandates from various sources. Similar General Assembly and Commission bodies concerned with

Figure 5-1
UNITED NATIONS HUMAN RIGHTS BODIES*

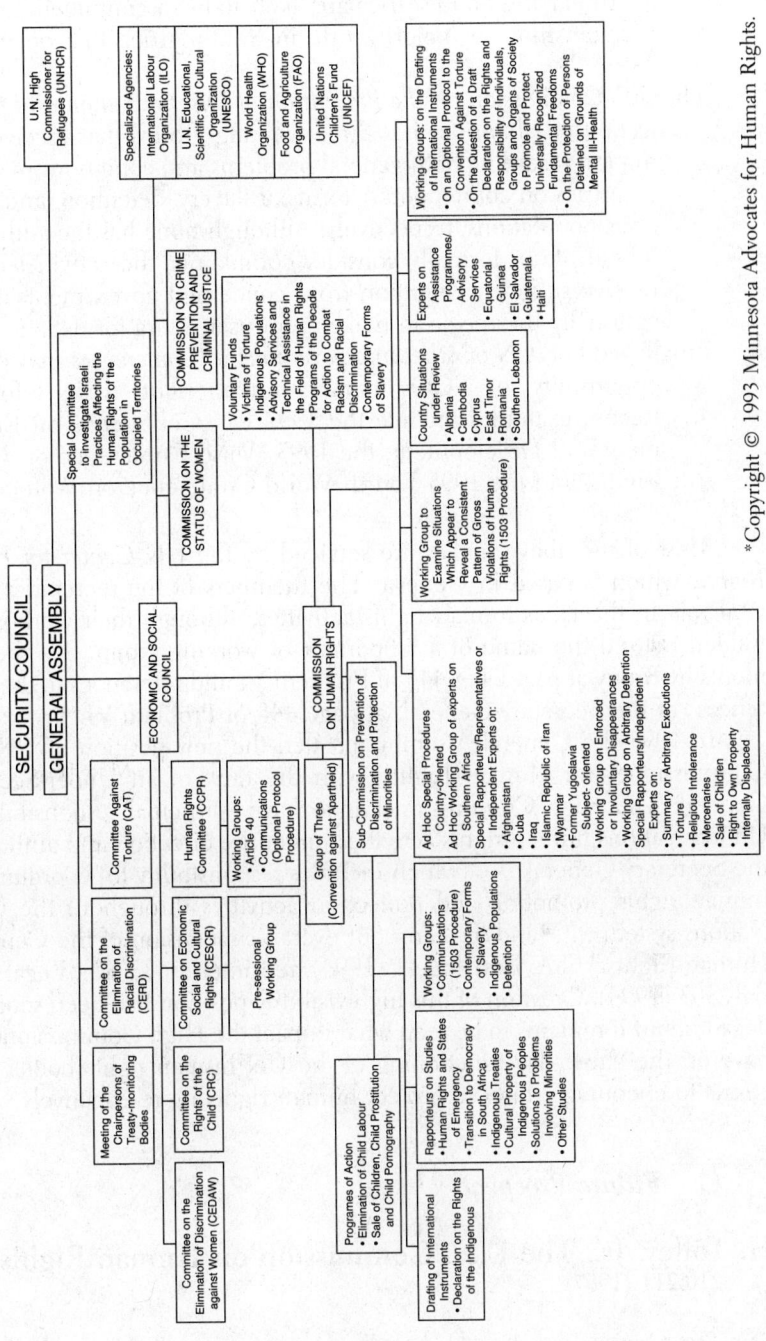

apartheid and South Africa are likely to be discontinued, following the transition to majority rule in South Africa that occurred in 1994.

The *Sub-Commission on the Prevention of Discrimination and the Protection of Minorities* has three working groups that receive information regarding both general problems and conditions in specific countries on contemporary forms of slavery, detention, and indigenous populations, respectively. Although none has the authority to investigate or formally consider complaints, the activities of each receive sufficient attention from concerned governments and occasionally the media to make them useful fora for debate.

Finally, ad-hoc *UN or other intergovernmental conferences* may offer an opportunity for NGOs to raise human rights issues informally. Recent examples include the 1992 UN Conference on Environment and Development, the 1993 World Conference on Human Rights, and the 1995 Fourth World Conference on Women.

Most of the above bodies are serviced by the *UN Center for Human Rights*, which is based in Geneva. The members of the secretariat play a vital role in the UN's human rights activities, although their work is often hidden behind the name of a rapporteur or working group. See the comments by Brody at pages 444-445 of Problem VI and references to the "good offices" of the Secretary-General, at page 445 of Problem VI.

In 1994 the General Assembly created the new position of UN High Commissioner for Human Rights, with the rank of an Under-Secretary-General. The High Commissioner is to have "principal responsibility for United Nations human rights activities under the direction and authority of the Secretary-General . . . [which includes responsibility to] coordinate the human rights promotion and protection activities throughout the United Nations system . . . [and to] carry out overall supervision of the Centre for Human Rights." G.A. Res. 48/141 (1994), reprinted in 33 Intl. Legal Materials 303 (1994). Creation of this high-visibility position had been sought for decades, but it remains to be seen what impact the High Commissioner will have on the day-to-day functioning of the UN human rights bodies or on efforts to encourage states to protect human rights more effectively.

C. Future Prospects

H. Tolley, Jr., The U.N. Commission on Human Rights
210-211 (1987)

The Commission has addressed a few situations that have never been acted on by other, more politicized United Nations organs — Poland, Iran,

Equatorial Guinea. (The Sub-Commission has responded to still more — the Sudan, Suriname, Sri Lanka.) Meeting in mid-winter after the Assembly has adjourned, the Commission provides ongoing review and continuous pressure on regimes that might otherwise enjoy a year long respite. Condemnation by sovereign governments embarrasses in a way that exposure by nongovernmental critics cannot. The Geneva meetings provide a forum where human rights specialists can negotiate understandings that might not be obtainable in the larger, more heavily politicized New York headquarters. The Commission has also provided a needed forum for developing and debating new legal theories and implementation measures to enforce compliance.

In many cases beyond the jurisdiction of the Human Rights Committee and regional bodies, the Commission has had a unique and significant impact. Since 1970 the Commission has fashioned an international complaint procedure that has enabled individual petitioners and nongovernmental organizations to charge any state with violations of human rights. Conceivably, the broad provisions of Resolutions 1235 and 1503 might also support allegations against transnational corporations and other nongovernmental actors. The Commission has successfully subjected to international scrutiny governments that never formally consented to United Nations jurisdiction over domestic human rights practices. . . . So many governments have now been reviewed under Resolutions 1235 and 1503, that ample precedent supports the Commission's quasi-judicial authority to receive complaints.

Governments that rhetorically proclaim that the Charter forbids intervention in their domestic affairs have in practice cooperated with international enforcement measures. Target governments that never formally accepted the International Covenants have in practice responded to complaints alleging violations of those standards. The skeptics are undoubtedly correct that compliance remains an occasional and largely voluntary phenomenon, but by successfully asserting its jurisdiction the Commission has taken a vital first step toward enforcing international norms.

Fewer than half of the thirty states subject to decisions under Resolution 1503 have ratified the International Covenant on Civil and Political Rights, and only three that have ratified allowed an individual right of petition under the optional protocol. When ratifying the covenants, neither Japan nor the German Democratic Republic accepted a right of individual petition under the optional protocol. Yet the Commission has effectively asserted the right to review complaints of covenant violations made against those two states. . . . The Commission has for ten years claimed the authority to review communications charging thirty governments with violations of international human rights law. The governments charged have challenged the Commission's power to act, but have also responded to the allegations. Nineteen of the target governments have had representatives in Geneva the first year their states were subject to confidential decisions; only four states have failed to have observers at two consecutive sessions when their government was under Resolution 1503 review. . . .

However successful in creating the world's most comprehensive international complaint procedure, the Commission has failed to achieve its stated objective — to stop gross violations. At most, the procedures have benefited a few individuals released as a symbolic gesture in response to Commission pressure. Just as the Security Council has exercised jurisdiction over acts of war without maintaining peace, the Commission has taken only the first step toward enforcing international law. NGO activists who initially hoped the 1503 procedure would lead to meaningful international scrutiny have found the procedures manipulated to aid offending governments. * Regimes use the process as a shield against public embarrassment and attempt to muzzle NGOs by using the confidentiality rule to prevent disclosure of documented atrocities. To the extent that an oppressive government feigns cooperation with the Commission's confidential scrutiny, it can escape public inquiry and political shame under the Resolution 1235 procedure. Communications showing government responsibility for thousands of involuntary disappearances were not disclosed while Argentina's situation remained under confidential review; the Commission kept complaints about Paraguay and Uruguay confidential for over seven years.

The first twenty years of serious enforcement efforts have gravely disappointed those seeking effective implementation measures. Although its direct contributions have not been substantial, the Commission has nevertheless added an unquantifiable something to attempts to secure compliance.

Farer, The United Nations and Human Rights: More Than a Whimper Less Than a Roar
9 Hum. Rts. Q. 550, 570, 581-585 (1987)

Attributing any capacity at all to the United Nations requires a certain leap of faith in the efficacy of exposure by a credible fact finder. For other than the unusual case where human rights violations produce a threat to or breach of the peace, thus providing the jurisdictional conditions for mandatory sanctions under Chapter 7 of the Charter, exposure is the principal weapon in the UN armory. . . .

The United Nations is now a participant, however ambivalent, in the defense of human rights. That is indisputable. . . .

The trajectory of political and social development within and among nations will determine the form and vigor of UN-sponsored activity. Predicting that trajectory is work more for the seer than the analyst. One thing that can be said with confidence of its accuracy is that human rights enforcement will remain highly politicized and therefore, intensely controversial. How could it be otherwise? As Stanley Hoffman noted shortly after the inaugura-

---

* For an excellent journalistic account of the efforts of the Argentine junta to manipulate UN consideration of human rights violations in Argentina in the late 1970s, see I. Guest, Behind the Disappearances, Argentina's Dirty "War" Against Human Rights and the United Nations (1990). — Eds.

tion of Jimmy Carter, "[t]he issue of human rights, by definition, breeds confrontation. Raising the issue touches on the very foundations of a regime, on its sources and exercise of power, on its links to its citizens or subjects. It is a dangerous issue. . . ." But the history of the last forty years suggests that, absent a nuclear holocaust, it will remain an unavoidable one. . . .

But surely cultural products spread for much the same reason as material ones, because they serve the consumer's needs. Nationalism helped to mobilize indigenous resistance to colonial rule and to stabilize the post-independence ethnic and tribal mix. Socialism, or at least its harsh communist deviation, has helped to justify concentration of power in the new political elites and to explain economic failure when it occurs.

Liberalism has its problems for non-Western consumers, yet it also has a certain utility, initially as a means for eroding the moral basis of Western hegemony. Now, in the post-imperial era, for the burgeoning middle classes of the Third World, it has the same appeal it had originally for their Western counterparts who had invoked its name and its reasons as they fought to break loose from the suffocating grip of absolute monarchies and narrow aristocracies. Liberalism remains a powerful weapon in the struggle to move from ascriptive to meritocratic criteria for the acquisition of wealth and power. . . .

Despite all the horror that surrounds us, I believe, as I said at the outset, that we are in a new era. At its outset, we had the Word, the Universal Declaration. In the past four decades it has acquired a little flesh. Within its means, means so conspicuously limited by the fact that material sanctions and incentives remain at the discretionary disposition of powerful states, the United Nations organization has helped. Historical perspective eases the pull of cynicism. Having won a revolution in the name of man's inalienable rights, the Founding Fathers of the United States incorporated slavery into the new nation's constitutional foundations. Seventy-six years passed before formal emancipation. And another century passed before blacks in the United States could enjoy the full rights of citizenship.

The distance the United Nations has come in four decades is one ground for optimism about where it will go in the next four. Another is the effort so many governments have made to restrain its forward progress and to evade its primitive machinery of enforcement. By their acts they have recognized the influence the idea of human rights has acquired over the minds of their subjects. Hypocrisy continues to offer credible evidence of the possibility of virtue.

Farer's final point is amply illustrated by the paid announcement on page 404, which was taken from the Washington Post, Mar. 5, 1989, at A26, col. 1, and was placed in major U.S. and European newspapers by the government of Zaire. The announcement obviously ignores the required confidentiality of the 1503 procedure, but it also suggests that governments find even secret UN procedures of some relevance.

UNITED NATIONS REPORT:
HUMAN RIGHTS SITUATION IMPROVES MARKEDLY IN ZAIRE

The Embassy of the Republic of Zaire in Washington, D.C. is pleased to bring to your attention the conclusions of the United Nations Commission on Human Rights, based on our country's accomplishments in promoting and protecting human rights.

Zaire, true to President Mobutu's guidelines and goals, continues to demonstrate the commitment of its government to the principles of Human Rights and Democracy.

We would like to take this opportunity to salute the cordial and long standing relations between the United States of America and the Republic of Zaire.

H.E. Mushobekwa Kalimba wa Katana
Ambassador E. and P.

**OFFICE DES NATIONS
UNIES A GENEVE**

**UNITED NATIONS
OFFICE OF GENEVA**

DECISION CONCERNING ZAIRE ADOPTED WITHOUT A VOTE AT THE 38TH MEETING (CLOSED) OF THE COMMISSION HELD ON 24 FEBRUARY 1989

The Commission on Human Rights,

Having examined the material concerning the human rights situation in Zaire brought before it under Economic and Social Council resolution 1503 (XLVIII), including the report of the Secretary-General on his direct contacts with the government of Zaire (E/CN.4/1989/R.4),

Noting with appreciation the willingness of the Government of Zaire, with the active participation of Maitre Nimy Mayidika Ngimbi, Commissaire d'Etat aux droits et libertes du citoyen, to co-operate with the Commission by furnishing replies and observations relating to the material which the Commission has before it,

1. *Decides* to discontinue consideration of the matter;
2. *Encourages* the Government of Zaire in its efforts to promote and protect human rights;
3. *Requests* the Government of Zaire to inform the Commission at its forty-sixth session, of the results of the action already taken to this and at a special closed meeting;
4. *Requests* the Secretary-General to provide Zaire with all the assistance it desires under the advisory services program in order to help that country in its efforts to strengthen the machinery established for the purpose of protecting and promoting human rights;
5. *Requests* the Secretary-General to communicate this decision to the Government of Zaire.

V. Final Comments and Questions

1. In 1976 John Humphrey, the first Director of the UN's Division of Human Rights, observed, "Human rights cannot and should not be divorced from politics and in a political organization like the United Nations they always will be discussed in political contexts, but there should be an opportunity in the Organization for complaints of individuals protesting the violation of their rights to be considered objectively on their merits, particularly if there are gross violations following consistent patterns. . . . What is needed is some judicial or quasi-judicial body, composed of independent persons acting in their personal capacity, before which individual complaints could be brought with some hope that they would be examined fairly and objectively." Humphrey, The International Bill of Rights: Scope and Implementation, 17 Wm. & Mary L. Rev. 527, 532-533 (1976). Is not the Sub-Commission composed of independent, individual experts? What could be done to improve the Sub-Commission's independence and objectivity?

2. Despite the fact that the Resolution 1503 procedure has not fulfilled the expectations of its most ardent advocates, has it not been a limited success? Consider:

(a)   The fact that, while Greece was able to defeat European Convention procedures (see page 692 of Problem IX) by withdrawing from the Council of Europe, neither Greece nor any other state can escape the potential application of Resolution 1503, which is universal in coverage.

(b)   The fact that, by the practice of publicly naming states being considered under the 1503 procedure, the Commission marshals much-maligned world public opinion against them, which in the case of Greece produced an amnesty for political prisoners literally on the eve of the Working Group's meetings in 1973.

(c)   The fact that the "quiet diplomacy" epitomized by the confidential 1503 procedure may, in some instances, be more effective than public condemnation in encouraging states to reform. For example, a 1503 communication filed against Japan by the International Human Rights Law Group in 1981 alleged widespread official discrimination against members of the Korean minority in Japan and supplied valuable international support for domestic Japanese efforts to remedy the situation.

(d)   The fact that well-known NGOs, such as Amnesty International and the International Commission of Jurists, continue to file communications under Resolution 1503, often in conjunction with more public activity concerning the same situation as part of increasingly sophisticated strategies to improve human rights conditions.

3. The Greek Communication (see pages 348-354 supra), while cut out of whole cloth (no form books then existing), still constitutes an acceptable model for international human rights lawyers "drafting a complaint." Useful suggestions in this regard — not only as to Resolution 1503 communications, but also as to the other UN and regional procedures — are contained in Guide to International Human Rights Practice (2d ed. H. Hannum ed. 1992) (the Model Communication contained in Appendix C of the Guide is included in the Documentary Supplement); see also Minnesota Advocates for Human Rights and International Service for Human Rights, The U.N. Commission on Human Rights, Its Sub-Commission, and Related Procedures: An Orientation Manual (1992).

4. One of the main drawbacks of the Resolution 1503 procedure is that the petitioner must show the existence of "a consistent pattern of gross" human rights violations. What is a non-gross violation? Is there a "consistent pattern" if the kind of violations varies over time? Can the 1503 procedure deal effectively with even gross violations that are not of a continuing nature, such as the armed and poison gas attacks on Kurds in Iraq or the massacre of demonstrators in Beijing's Tiananmen Square?

5. Despite massive human rights violations in countries such as Albania, Argentina, Guatemala, Haiti, Indonesia, Paraguay, Turkey, and Zaire, no "thorough study" as envisaged under Resolution 1503 has ever been undertaken. At the same time, however, country-specific investigations have been carried out by regional bodies or under other UN procedures. NGOs also are much freer than they were in the 1970s to denounce human rights violations publicly during Commission and Sub-Commission debates under Resolution 1235. Do such activities undermine the value of the 1503 procedure? If the 1503 procedure were abandoned, what procedures would petitioners from states not parties to the European or American Conventions on Human Rights or to the Optional Protocol to the Covenant on Civil and Political Rights be able to invoke?

6. In recent years, African-Americans, Native Americans, and other groups have (thus far unsuccessfully) filed complaints against the United States under Resolution 1503. What should the U.S. government's reaction to such complaints be? Can you predict the response based on the consistent U.S. rejection thus far of any individual complaint procedure contained in a human rights treaty? How do you think the general public would react to a UN investigation of human rights in the United States?

7. Running through all the petition procedures is the requirement that the petitioner have exhausted his or her domestic remedies. What relevance does this requirement, which was borrowed from the traditional law governing the Responsibility of States for Injuries to Aliens, have in the human rights context? If the possibility of obtaining compensation for human rights violations exists and is considered — as it normally is — an adequate remedy, does not this allow a state, as the applicant argued before the European Commission of Human Rights in Donnelly v. United Kingdom, to "pay for

the right to torture"? See Boyle and Hannum, Individual Applications Under the European Convention on Human Rights and the Concept of Administrative Practice: The Donnelly Case, 68 Am. J. Intl. L. 440, 447-451 (1974); Hannum and Boyle, The Donnelly Case, Administrative Practice and Domestic Remedies Under the European Convention: One Step Forward and Two Steps Back, 71 Am. J. Intl. L. 316 (1977). See generally A. Cançado Trindade, The Application of the Rule of Exhaustion of Local Remedies in International Law (1983). If compensation is awarded to victims, does this end a government's obligation to protect human rights? See Netherlands Institute of Human Rights, Seminar on the Right to Restitution, Compensation and Rehabilitation for Victims of Gross Violations of Human Rights and Fundamental Freedoms (1992); Orentlicher, Settling Accounts: The Duty to Prosecute Human Rights Violations of a Prior Regime, 100 Yale L.J. 2537 (1991).

8. Do you consider the present practice of the Sub-Commission's Working Group (whereby it "considers" thousands of communications once a year during a two-week session) satisfactory, barely acceptable, or woefully inadequate? What changes in the Sub-Commission's operating procedures would you recommend that the U.S. member of the Sub-Commission support? What chances of success would there be for each of your various recommendations? From whence could you expect opposition to "reform"?

Problem VI

The Problem of Fact-Finding and Evidence

How Does the UN Investigate Violations of Human Rights Law?

I. The Challenge: To Find Out What Is Really Happening   410
II. Gathering the Facts   411
   A. Information Reported by States   411
     Bayefsky, Making the Human Rights Treaties Work   412
   B. Fact-Finding by the UN General Assembly   417
     Rules of Procedure of the Special Committee to Investigate
      Israeli Practices   419
     Report of the Special Committee to Investigate Israeli Practices   421
   C. Fact-Finding by the UN Commission on Human Rights   422
     1. Country-Specific Rapporteurs   423
     Consideration of the Report of the Mission Which Took Place
      in Cuba   424
     Jiminez, Report on the Question of Human Rights in Chile   427
     Galindo Pohl, Report on the Human Rights Situation in the
      Islamic Republic of Iran   430
     2. Thematic Mechanisms   431
     Wako, Report [on Summary or Arbitrary Executions]   431
     Kooijmans, Report [on Torture and Other Cruel, Inhuman, or
      Degrading Treatment or Punishment]   436
     Vidal d'Almerida Ribero, Report [on Intolerance and Discrimi-
      nation Based on Religion or Belief]   439
     Report of the Working Group on Arbitrary Detention   441
     Note: The Role of the UN Secretariat   444
     Brody, Improving UN Human Rights Structures   444
     Note: A Rapporteur from the Commission on Human Rights
      Visits Suriname   445
     Wako, Report [on Summary or Arbitrary Executions]   445
   D. The Need for General Standards for Fact-Finding by International
    Organizations   448
     Note: Toward a Solution — The Belgrade Rules on Fact-
      Finding by International Organizations   449
     Belgrade Minimal Rules of Procedure for International Human
      Rights Fact-Finding Missions   449
   E. Fact-Finding by Non-Governmental Organizations   452
     Orentlicher, Bearing Witness: The Art and Science of Human
      Rights Fact-Finding   452

H. Thoolen and B. Verstappen, Human Rights Missions: A
Study of the Fact-Finding Practice of Non-Governmental
Organizations   456
Correspondence: Professor Moore   458
Correspondence: Professor Glennon   461
H. Thoolen and B. Verstappen, Human Rights Missions: A
Study of the Fact-Finding Practice of Non-Governmental
Organizations   465
Hannum, Fact-Finding by Non-Governmental Human Rights
Organizations   468
F.   Fact-Finding by Judicial and Quasi-Judicial Bodies   469
T. Buergenthal, R. Norris, and D. Shelton, Protecting Human
Rights in the Americas   472
III.   Evaluating the Facts   475
A.   Admissibility of Evidence   475
B.   The Burden of Proof   475
Ramcharan, Evidence   476
Bleier v. Uruguay   479
The Velásquez Rodriguez Case   480
The Gangaram Panday Case   481
Weissbrodt, Human Rights Implementation and Fact-Finding by
International Organizations   482
IV.   Final Comments and Questions   483

I.   The Challenge: To Find Out What Is Really Happening

Problem III demonstrated the way the Human Rights Committee dealt with the incident of the summary executions that took place in Suriname in December 1982. It should be appreciated, however, that, at first instance, there were only *allegations* of violations of international human rights law. Before the Human Rights Committee could reach a conclusion as to whether or not the law had been violated, it had to decide what the facts of the case were. In general, without detailed and reliable knowledge about what is actually happening in countries around the world, there can be no effective protection of human rights.

What are the methods by which the UN discovers what is happening "on the ground" in the various member states? What are the most effective fact-finding techniques in the human rights field? What sorts of bodies are best equipped to conduct accurate fact-finding? To what extent may it be said that there are general standards in this area? What role, if any, can non-governmental organizations play in the UN fact-finding process? How is the reliability of gathered evidence determined? What standards of proof should be applied in human rights investigations? These are some of the questions we shall be exploring in this Problem.

The need for action in this area was recognized as long ago as 1968, when the Montreal Conference on International Human Rights lamented "the absence of effective and impartial fact-finding mechanisms." Montreal Statement of the Assembly for Human Rights, March 22-27, 1968, 9 J. Intl. Commn. Jurists 94, 106 (1968). Since that time, massive strides have been made. New problems, in turn, have arisen. The concern is no longer whether the UN can or should engage in human rights fact-finding. Rather, it is *how* the UN and other bodies can most effectively do so.

Some observers have advocated a strongly centralized system of fact-finding at the UN. A notable proposal along these lines was advanced by the Netherlands in 1964. It suggested that the UN establish a permanent organ for fact-finding activities. It would consist of a standing body of approximately 15 persons, who would have the option of forming chambers. This body would be at the permanent disposal of the UN and its specialized agencies, with a separate mandate for each inquiry that it undertook. Its reports would be adopted by a majority vote, with dissenting opinions permitted.

This proposal was not adopted, and UN fact-finding has taken a much different form. Instead of a single, specialized body, the UN has devised, over the years, a welter of different fact-finding strategies conducted by a variety of different bodies. This fact-finding "system" has grown up over a period of decades in a rather ad hoc, haphazard fashion. As a result, some of the basic questions about effective fact-finding have failed to receive the attention they deserve.

It is impossible, within the compass of a single Problem, to provide anything like a comprehensive survey of human rights fact-finding. Instead, the following readings will identify some of the more important or innovative activities in this area and also point up some of the major legal issues that have arisen in connection with them.

II. Gathering the Facts

A. Information Reported by States

One of the most obvious ways — if not necessarily the most reliable — to discover what is happening in a country is to seek information from the government concerned. Seven major UN-sponsored human rights conventions require states parties to submit periodic reports on matters relevant to the particular treaty: the Convention on Racial Discrimination (1965), the

Covenant on Civil and Political Rights and the Covenant on Economic, Social, and Cultural Rights (1966), the Convention Against Apartheid (1973), the Convention on Discrimination Against Women (1979), the Convention Against Torture (1984), and the Convention on the Rights of the Child (1989).

The weaknesses of relying on state reports for fact-finding are perhaps more obvious than the strengths. It is hardly surprising that state reports tend to express a fairly high degree of satisfaction with the state's efforts in the human rights area. Nor is it surprising that the reports tend to be rather formalistic in character, i.e., to concentrate on the state of the law in the country rather than the state of the facts. Finally, there is the problem that many states are extremely remiss in even submitting their reports as required. The Human Rights Committee, in its consideration of the events in Suriname of December 1982, certainly received no assistance from the reporting procedure of the Covenant on Civil and Political Rights. Suriname was due to submit its second report in June 1985. As of July 1994, it still had not done so, despite no fewer than 17 reminders sent to it by the Human Rights Committee. Nor has it submitted its third report, due in 1990, despite seven reminders. See pages 181-183 and 224-237 of Problem III.

There is no doubt that state-prepared reports contain much useful information, at least about constitutional and legislative schemes. The formal declarations of commitment to human rights proclaimed by governments in their reports also may be used to expose the hypocrisy of those governments that ignore such commitments in practice. Nevertheless, one of the only commentators to evaluate the reporting system in detail concludes with an assessment that is indeed bleak.

Bayefsky, Making the Human Rights Treaties Work
in Human Rights: An Agenda for the Next Century 229, 232-236, 238-240, 243, 263-264 (L. Henkin and J. Hargrove eds. 1994)

When the human rights treaties were first written, enforcement was intended largely to depend on a system of state reporting. According to the original rationale, state reports could further human rights protection in two ways. The process of drafting the state report could serve as an exercise of internal self-analysis and soul-searching, which in itself could prompt improvements in national laws and practices. Secondly, the subsequent scrutiny of those reports by independent expert bodies would expose human rights violations and such exposure would encourage change.

On the first score, the experts say state reports are "quintessentially government reports". Their preparation is a governmental task, and involvement of nongovernmental organizations or members of the public in their preparation is an unreasonable expectation. The role for the national non-governmental organization or individual is in presenting a critique of state reports once written. Governments should *ex post facto* encourage such discussion.

In practice, the process of drafting state reports is almost never conducted in consultation with the individuals or the nongovernmental organizations most closely concerned with the terms of the treaty. Their preparation is generally understood — with some few exceptions — as a bureaucratic exercise or diplomatic chore and not as an opportunity for self-analysis and the amendment of national laws or practices. As for after-the-fact discussion, domestic interest in another self-congratulatory government publication has been, and will continue to be, minimal at best.

But even that assumes the report is available to the public. In some states, it is not translated into the language[s] citizens understand. In others, it is a classified document. In still others, citizens cannot get the report and must obtain it from international sources. And in other states, even copies of the treaties are not available.

The idea that governments will take the opportunity to present their internal human rights situation to international forums in self-critical or negative terms is illusory. The treaty bodies euphemistically refer to the effort to encourage states to expose their shortfalls as reporting on the "factors and difficulties impeding the application of the treaty." The predictable response from so many of the most culpable states, year after year, is to claim that the treaty obligations are all satisfied. For example, the Libyan report to the Human Rights Committee, dated May 4, 1993, states:

> Following the revolution of 1 September 1969, sovereignty has been exercised by the people . . . Libya is a free and democratic Arab republic. . . . Since the revolution . . . [Libya] has shown concern for basic human rights. Its fundamental and supreme objective is to promote the health, social and cultural aspects of human welfare. . . . [T]he . . . law in the Jamahiriya . . . meets the standards set in the most modern and progressive constitutions and laws anywhere in the world.

This is not to say that the treaty bodies themselves fail to perceive either the inadequacies of the preparation, internal distribution, and discussion of state reports, or the close relationship between these procedural inadequacies and the degree of seriousness with which the state takes the substantive terms of the treaty. But it is quite clear that what was supposed to be the secondary role for international monitors has turned out to be the primary hope for the victims of human rights abuses.

On the second score, however, the exposure anticipated from the scrutiny of the treaty bodies, as statistical evidence alone reveals, is grossly inadequate.

There are an extremely large number of overdue reports, specifically 596. Furthermore, these overdue reports emanate from a large percentage of states parties. In the case of four of five human rights treaties, roughly half — or more — states parties have overdue reports. Of those reports that are overdue, many have been outstanding for considerable lengths of time. Significant numbers of even initial reports are overdue. This circumstance cannot be explained by an overloading of the state through some internal backlog. Such an excuse tends to be a favourite alibi of defaulting states. This neglect of the basic obligation to produce state reports clearly indicates that for a large number of states ratification has become an end in itself. It is appearance, rather than compliance, that has become important.

Among those states having the greatest number of overdue reports are some of the world's most notorious human rights violators, such as Zaire. And the statistics indicate that generally, a larger number of overdue reports cannot be accounted for by the fact that the state has ratified a larger number of treaties. . . .

When state parties do produce reports, the treaty bodies spend minimal amounts of time considering them. The time the treaty bodies allot to considering state reports relates to the amount of meeting time that is permitted during the year. This varies widely. The normal number of weeks per year, without budget cuts or additional sessions, is as follows: CERD [Convention on the Elimination of All Forms of Racial Discrimination] — six weeks, the Human Rights Committee — nine weeks, the Economic Rights Committee — three weeks, CEDAW [Committee on the Elimination of All Forms of Discrimination Against Women] — two weeks, CAT [Committee Against Torture] — four weeks, and CRC [Committee on the Rights of the Child] — four weeks. Some of this time is used for activities other than the examination of state reports. In general, a state party will be required to account orally for the implementation of each human rights treaty for roughly two hours minimum to ten hours maximum. This procedure will be repeated in each treaty body every four to five years, and probably even less frequently in light of the backlogs. Obviously this time allotment for public scrutiny is minimal. As one member of the Human Rights Committee has stated, "two hour examinations are simply pointless." This would be true even assuming the treaty bodies were to be organized in such a way as to evenly stagger reports from one state over the five-year time span, which is not currently the case.

If one combines the time each treaty body devotes to the consideration of state reports with the current number of overdue reports, the time it would take to consider all the overdue reports if they were to be submitted can be calculated. In the case of four of five of the human rights treaties, it would take six to nine and one-half years to consider all the overdue reports if submitted, and if considered one by one. These figures will be lower in the case of CERD, CEDAW, and CAT if one takes into account their current practice of attempting to deal with the backlog by considering a single report that is submitted as satisfying the production of all overdue reports of that state party. CERD adopts the pretense, for example, that "the report received from the Government of Viet Nam on 15 April 1993 constitutes the second, third, fourth and fifth periodic reports of Viet Nam, due on 9 July 1985, 1987, 1989 and 1991 respectively." CEDAW engages in the fiction of calling the long-awaited submission a "combined report". CAT "invites" states parties to submit overdue reports "in one document." But even in the case of these treaty bodies, and their dubious practice of essentially foregoing the treaty obligations, the number of states parties with overdue reports is in itself sufficiently large as to make the backlog run into several years. Obviously, this amount of time would simply overrun the proper functioning of the treaty bodies. The degree to which the system provides any exposure from the scrutiny of the treaty bodies for some states depends on the delinquency and resultant nonexposure of large numbers of other states.

The efficacy of the treaty bodies in revealing human rights violations, or disrespect for treaty obligations, through a system of state reports is summed up by the Chair of the Economic Rights Committee:

> [The] fact remains in 1993 that many of the treaty bodies are only able to function within their existing allocations of meeting time because of the enormous rate of overdue and unsubmitted reports, and because they are devoting a clearly inadequate amount of time to the consideration of each report. . . .

The failures of the current mechanisms for implementing the human rights treaties can be attributed to three sources: (1) the states parties, (2) the treaty bodies, and (3) the General Assembly or the larger corpus of states. . . .

The states parties themselves carry primary responsibility for the failures of the largely voluntary state reporting system. In large numbers, they fail to produce timely reports, do not engage in reform activities in the course of producing reports, author inadequate reports, send uninformed representatives to the examination of reports by the treaty bodies, fail to respond to questions during the examinations, discourage greater media attention of the examination of reports, fail to disseminate reports and the results of examinations within the state, elect government employees rather than independent persons to treaty body membership, make reservations that are incompatible with the object and purpose of the treaties, fail to object to reservations, and fail to challenge reservations by additional means. . . .

When states do report, they frequently recite intolerable situations without any recognition of a human rights abuse, or any state responsibility to prevent the violation. To give only two examples, the recent report of the Sudan to CERD states:

> Any Sudanese citizen is free under the law to travel abroad or within the country, without restriction. . . . However, a prerequisite to going abroad is the possession of a return air ticket, in order to avoid unnecessary exposure to suffering away from home.

By virtue of their physiological weaknesses, women do face some additional conditions that have to be met before they are allowed to travel abroad. These restrictions are on religious grounds.

As far as freedom of thought is concerned, the only restriction is that the abandonment of Islam and the embracing of another faith constitutes the crime of apostasy in Islam, which is punishable by death. No one dare change that. There is no discrimination here, however, since this restriction affects only Muslims, regardless of their race, colour or national origin.

The last report of Tanzania submitted to the Human Rights Committee states:

> Other controls in the exercise of the right to free association include the requirement that official permission has to be obtained beforehand from the Government for the holding of any procession, meeting or rally, as well as the requirement that all associations have to be registered with the Ministry of Home Affairs under the Registration of Societies Ordinance. However, these are administrative measures for convenience and are not meant to stifle peoples' freedom to associate with others.

As for the length of reports, the following examples are not uncommon. The tenth, eleventh, and twelfth reports of Spain to CERD, which were due in January 1988, 1990 and 1992 respectively, were "consolidated" into a single document. It was three pages long. The initial report of Niger to the Human Rights Committee due in 1987 was submitted in May of 1991 and was four pages long.

Frequently, reports do little more than recite the laws of the state (contrary to guidelines such as those of the Human Rights Committee) and then often on a selected basis and in the words of the author of the report. The laws themselves, including constitutions, civil codes, and codes of criminal procedure, may be submitted as annexes. But they are submitted in the local language and are not translated. . . .

States that do report and appear before the treaty bodies to engage in what is euphemistically referred to as a "constructive dialogue" often do not anticipate much public interest in the spectacle. Nor do states encourage such interest, either on the part of the international media and international nongovernmental organizations, or on the part of local media and national nongovernmental organizations. One stark example of state expectations is the case of the Moroccan report before the Human Rights Committee. In July 1991, the Moroccan delegation came to their session with the Committee and were surprised to find many television cameras, from France and Switzerland, awaiting them. They then refused to attend the meeting in the presence of the television crews. The Committee decided to postpone the examination of the report until the following session four months later. At that time, the examination was completed in the presence of French television. But most often, no such interest in the proceedings of the treaty bodies exists. There are usually very few outside observers of the treaty body sessions. . . .

The machinery for the implementation of human rights treaties was developed at the time of the Cold War, and was strongly influenced by convictions that international concern over human rights was an intervention in internal affairs or domestic jurisdiction. It must therefore be reconstructed. . . .

The system does not work, at bottom, because it presupposes democratic impulses on the part of states parties that in reality are not shared. The state reporting scheme does not work for states that are subject to no internal scrutiny. Their citizens know nothing of the production of state reports or of the examination of reports. Such states have no independent media covering examinations. Press reports of criticisms do not reach people within such states. In short, the so-called "constructive dialogue" with such states is a hoax. Individual communication schemes also do not work for undemocratic states. Such states rarely ratify individual petition mechanisms. When they ratify, they do not encourage their use. Nor do they feel compelled to implement negative findings. The membership of such states in the treaty regime saps its integrity.

Not all observers are as critical in their appraisals of the value of state reporting, although none would maintain that the present system is satisfactory. For somewhat more positive views and suggestions on how best to utilize the existing system, see Coliver, International Reporting Procedures, in Guide to International Human Rights Practice 173-191 (2d ed. H. Hannum ed. 1992); D. McGoldrick, The Human Rights Committee 62-119 (1994). See generally the discussion at pages 211-214 of Problem III.

B.   Fact-Finding by the UN General Assembly

Several significant initiatives in human rights fact-finding at the UN have been undertaken by the General Assembly. Those bodies, such as the special committees on apartheid and the Israeli-occupied territories, that have become quasi-permanent have frequently been criticized as being political rather than fact-finding bodies, although the failure of the governments in question to cooperate with the committees has necessarily led to one-sided reports. It certainly would be fair to characterize their work as primarily the collecting and disseminating of information rather than truly independent fact-finding.

The earliest fact-finding committee was the Special Committee on the Situation with regard to the Implementation of the Declaration on the Granting of Independence to Colonial Countries and Peoples, established in 1960 and popularly known as the Committee of 24. The Committee is tasked generally with promoting decolonization, and it utilizes publicity, hearings, consideration of petitions, and visiting missions to fulfill its mandate; many of the missions have been for the purpose of observing elections or referenda in non-self-governing territories. The Committee's rules of procedure in examining petitions have been described as "self-created and largely undefined," but since the mid-1970s those countries administering non-self-governing territories within the Committee's mandate have been generally cooperative with the Committee's fact-finding efforts, including requests to conduct on-site missions.

The General Assembly created the Special Committee on the Policies of Apartheid of the Government of the Republic of South Africa in 1962. The Committee against Apartheid, as it was known, was composed of 19 states and reported annually to the General Assembly on conditions in South Africa. The Committee was not able to visit South Africa itself until 1993, one year before the Committee was dissolved following the inauguration of majority rule in South Africa. Its fact-finding activities consisted primarily of following developments in South Africa through hearings, meetings, and consultations with anti-apartheid groups and monitoring press reports. Given the universal condemnation of South Africa's former policy of apartheid by the international community, the Committee served primarily to publicize and support anti-apartheid initiatives rather than to gather information independently.

In 1963 the General Assembly decided to dispatch a fact-finding mission to South Vietnam, in response to a complaint by 14 states of human rights violations there. The mission was composed of representatives from six countries, supported by a staff of four persons from the UN Secretariat. It undertook investigations in the country with the consent of the South Vietnamese government. In immediate terms, nothing came of the effort, since the project was effectively thwarted by the overthrow of the host government. The mission did, however, make a valuable contribution to the methodology of human rights fact-finding by adopting a set of rules of procedure that remains a useful guide. See Violation of Human Rights in South Viet-Nam: Report of the United Nations Fact-Finding Mission to South Viet-Nam, U.N. Doc. A/5630 (1963).

Another continuing effort in the fact-finding area is the Special Committee to Investigate Israeli Practices Affecting the Human Rights of the Palestinian People and Other Arabs of the Occupied Territories, created by the General Assembly in 1968 following Israel's occupation of the Gaza Strip and West Bank after the 1967 Middle East War. Like the Special Committee on Apartheid, this body is composed of member states; it, too, has been barred from entering the territories it is charged with investigating. As a result, its periodic reports are based on press reports and other information submitted to it from various sources, as well as hearings held in nearby states.

In 1987 the General Assembly established another fact-finding body, the Intergovernmental Group to Monitor the Supply and Shipping of Oil and Petroleum Products to South Africa, which consisted of 11 member states (see pages 579-580 of Problem VII). In its seven years, the group relied for its information primarily upon material submitted to it by the non-governmental Shipping Research Bureau. From 1989 until it was discontinued in 1994, the group also held occasional public hearings, at which NGO representatives, academics, and others presented information relevant to the group's mandate.

For many years, Israel was the only other state (in addition to South Africa) singled out by the General Assembly for special attention. The next two readings give an idea of how bodies of this kind function.

Rules of Procedure of the Special Committee to Investigate Israeli Practices
U.N. GAOR Spec. Comm., 25th Sess., at 65, 69-71, U.N. Doc. A/8089, Annex III (1971)

SECTION VII: CO-OPERATION WITH MEMBER STATES

RULE 13

(a) The Special Committee shall be entitled to consult the representative of any State in respect of any matter relevant to its terms of reference.

(b) The Special Committee shall have the right to request in particular the State directly concerned with the subject of the study or investigation to communicate to it such statements and documents as that State may consider to be useful for ascertaining the facts or as relevant to the issues referred to the Special Committee, as well as a list of witnesses and experts whose evidence the Special Committee may desire to hear.

(c) The Special Committee may invite the State directly concerned with the subject of the study or investigation to be represented by an accredited representative at one, several or all meetings of the Special Committee or parts of such meetings.

(d) States directly concerned with the subject of the study or investigation undertaken by the Special Committee may at their request, or at the invitation of the Special Committee, make statements to it, submit such written material as they may deem appropriate, and address to it written or oral evidence. They may, in accordance with procedures adopted by the Special Committee, put questions to witnesses at hearings conducted by the Special Committee.

(e) The Special Committee may, with the consent of the State concerned, move temporarily to any place in the territory of that State where it considers it may be useful to gather information or to hear witnesses or experts on issues arising out of its terms of reference.

Section VIII: Oral and Written Testimony and Other
                Sources of Information

RULE 14

The Special Committee may, as soon as practicable, publicize by all available means its terms of reference, the methods it will adopt for collecting information and receiving documentary and oral testimony, the dates and places of its meetings and details, if any, concerning the particulars to be supplied by those wishing to offer testimony. Failure to adhere to this rule of procedure shall not vitiate any proceedings of the Special Committee.

RULE 15

The Special Committee shall be entitled to receive oral and written testimony. Such testimony:

(a) May be submitted by the State directly concerned with the study or investigation undertaken by the Special Committee or by any of its witnesses and experts;

(b) May be received from any other sources at the invitation or upon the decision of the Special Committee.

RULE 16

(a) The Special Committee shall decide upon the relevance and upon the use which may be made of:

(i)   Anonymous communications;
(ii) Written material and documentary evidence;
(iii) Evidence submitted in the form of sound-recordings, films, photographs, drawings or other objects;
(iv) All legislative and administrative provisions falling within the scope of the terms of reference of the Special Committee;
(v)   Writings and articles published in the press or elsewhere;
(vi) Activities of organizations and reports of activities which are relevant to the terms of reference of the Special Committee;

(b) Written evidence may, at the request of the person submitting it, be presented in such a manner as not to disclose his identity and/or be made available only to the members of the Special Committee and the secretariat.

RULE 17

(a) Requests by the representative of a State for oral hearing shall include an indication of the subject or subjects on which that representative desires to be heard.

(b) Requests by an individual for oral hearing shall contain an indication of the subject or subjects on which the witness desires to testify, his full name, address, age, nationality, occupation and profession or calling.

RULE 18

. . . (d) The Special Committee may decide that a person may not be present at its meeting except when giving evidence and that he may not consult any records of hearings until he himself has given evidence.

(e) The Special Committee may agree to hear a witness in a closed meeting and/or not to disclose his identity.

(f) The Special Committee shall give a witness all reasonable latitude to furnish evidence and information, but statements or questions outside the Special Committee's terms of reference or issues connected therewith shall not be permitted.

(g) All questioning of witnesses shall be subject to the direction of the Chairman acting under the authority of the Special Committee. . . .

SECTION X: REPORTS

RULE 20

(a) After recording such evidence as is available, the Special Committee shall draw up its report in private, including in it its conclusions and recommendations. . . .

Report of the Special Committee to Investigate Israeli Practices
U.N. Doc. A/48/557, at 10-15 (1993)

11. The Special Committee held a series of meetings at Damascus (28-29 April 1993), Amman (30 April-3 May 1993) and Cairo (5-8 May 1993). At these meetings, the Special Committee examined information on developments occurring in the occupied territories between December 1992 and February 1993. It had before it a number of communications addressed to it by Governments, organizations and individuals in connection with its mandate. The Special Committee took note of the letters addressed to it by the Permanent Representative of Jordan to the United Nations Office at Ge-

neva on matters related to its mandate. At Damascus, Amman and Cairo the Special Committee heard testimonies of persons who have just returned from or are living in the West Bank, the Gaza Strip and the occupied Syrian Arab Golan concerning the situation in those territories. . . .

20. The mandate of the Special Committee, as set out in resolution 2443 (XXIII) and subsequent resolutions, was "to investigate Israeli practices affecting the human rights of the population of the occupied territories". . . .

The "human rights" of the population of the occupied territories consisted of two elements, namely, those rights which the Security Council referred to as "essential and inalienable human rights" in its resolution 237 (1967) of 14 June 1967 and, secondly, those rights which found their basis in the protection afforded by international law in particular circumstances such as military occupation and, in the case of prisoners of war, capture. In accordance with General Assembly resolution 3005 (XXVII), the Special Committee was also required to investigate allegations concerning the exploitation and the looting of the resources of the occupied territories, the pillaging of the archaeological and cultural heritage of the occupied territories, and interference in the freedom of worship in the Holy Places of the occupied territories. . . .

24. In the course of carrying out its mandate, the Special Committee has relied on the following sources:

(a) The testimony of persons with first-hand knowledge of the situation of the population in the occupied territories;

(b) Reports in the Israeli press, including of pronouncements by responsible persons in the Government of Israel;

(c) Reports appearing in other news media, including the Arab language press published in the occupied territories, in Israel and the international press.

25. The Special Committee also received written statements from the Governments of Jordan and the Syrian Arab Republic and from the Observer for Palestine. . . .

31. The Special Committee has taken particular care to rely on information appearing in the Israeli press that has not been contradicted by the Government of Israel.

C.   Fact-Finding by the UN Commission on Human Rights

The UN Commission on Human Rights, together with its Sub-Commission, engages in fact-finding in a number of different ways. Sometimes these bodies play a relatively passive role. In the 1503 procedure, for example, the Sub-Commission and the Commission receive information from interested parties and then proceed to determine whether the information appears to merit further investigation. See pages 365-380 of Problem V. For a number of years, the Sub-Commission has also organized sessional working groups in various subject-matter areas, whose basic task is to receive information from a wide array of interested parties. The two most important working groups — on contemporary forms of slavery and indigenous peoples, respectively — meet immediately prior to each session of the Sub-Commission and report annually to it. Their task is to draw attention to problems rather than to act as determinative fact-finding bodies, and their reports generally summarize presentations made by NGOs to the respective working groups, along with any responses and observations by governments. At its 1993 session, for example, the Working Group on Contemporary Forms of Slavery heard from over a dozen NGO representatives who raised country-specific issues, often in highly critical terms, ranging from child prostitution to debt bondage and sex tourism; government observers from Brazil, Japan, North Korea, South Korea, India, and Pakistan also made statements. The Working Group made a number of recommendations, but all were couched in general terms rather than singling out specific countries or situations for comment. See Report of the Working Group on Contemporary Forms of Slavery on Its Eighteenth Session, U.N. Doc. E/CN.4/Sub.2/1993/30 (1993).

More important for present purposes are the various devices that have emerged over the years for independent fact-finding by the Commission itself. The seminal event in this regard was the Chilean revolution of 1973 and the widespread concern over the massive human rights violations that allegedly accompanied it. In response to this concern, the Commission on Human Rights at its 1975 session established a Working Group to Inquire into the Situation of Human Rights in Chile. Numerous ad hoc investigations of specific countries have occurred in the ensuing years, most of which have been undertaken by individual rapporteurs or special representatives. The Commission also may investigate human rights violations by appointing groups rather than individuals, as occurred with respect to Cuba in 1988.

In addition, the use of thematic rapporteurs and working groups has increased dramatically since the appointment of the first such body, the Working Group on Disappearances, in 1980. These developments are discussed at pages 390-398 of Problem V.

1. Country-Specific Rapporteurs

The country-specific rapporteurs are allowed considerable latitude as to the fact-finding methods they employ. Most rapporteurs are appointed for an initial period of one year, but their mandates are frequently renewed on an annual basis. Some of the investigations, accordingly, have gradually taken on the character of continuous monitoring efforts.

Investigations by the Commission on Human Rights are not designed to be adversarial in character. They are not directed toward the bringing of proceedings of any kind against the states in question. They are designed, instead, to be purely informational. It is not surprising, however, that some states fail to see the matter in that light. If a state refuses to cooperate with a special rapporteur or representative or fact-finding group, then there is little that the Commission can do. The Commission possesses no police powers or coercive authority over UN member states. Fact-finders are not even allowed into the territory of the states they are investigating unless the relevant governments give their consent. Sometimes governments avail themselves of this power to block investigations. Chile and Afghanistan, for example, both refused access to their territories to the respective special rapporteurs for a time, although both relented eventually.

The following three readings provide a sample of the experiences of fact-finding on behalf of the Commission on Human Rights in three countries. The first is from the report of the group that undertook a mission to Cuba in September 1988 and reported its results the following year. The group consisted of the chairman of the Commission on Human Rights, together with five Commission members and supporting staff from the UN Secretariat. The extract describes how the group went about its task during the mission to the country. The extracts that follow, concerning Chile and Iran, give an indication of the various fact-finding strategies adopted by special rapporteurs and special representatives and also of some of the problems that they encounter.

Consideration of the Report of the Mission Which Took Place in Cuba
U.N. Doc. E/CN.4/1989/46, at 10-13 (1989)

F.   THE VISIT TO CUBA (16-25 SEPTEMBER 1988)

13. The group, accompanied by five members of the staff of the Centre for Human Rights, six interpreters, two sound engineers and a press officer, arrived at José Marti airport in Havana early in the morning of 16 September 1988 and was met by the Deputy Minister for External Relations of Cuba, Mr. Raúl Roa Kouri. Both the Deputy Minister and the group's Chairman made statements to the press. In the afternoon of the same day the group was received in person by Mr. Isidoro Malmierca, Minister for External Relations who stated that, in the view of Cuban authorities the mandate of the group was to observe the situation of human rights in Cuba. During its stay in Cuba, the group met Dr. Fidel Castro Ruz, President of

the Council of State (25 September). It was also received by Mr. Carlos Rafael Rodríguez, Vice-President of the Council of State (25 September), and other senior government officials, in particular those responsible for sectors directly related to human rights.

14. The group also met officials of the Housing Institute (20 September) and leaders of the following mass organizations: National Co-ordinating Organization for the Committees for the Defence of the Revolution (CDR) (21 September), Federation of Secondary School Students (FEEM), Federation of University Students (FEU), Union of Communist Youth (UJC) and Cuban Union of Journalists (23 September). In addition, the group had the opportunity to hear and talk with the President of the Cuban Radio and Television Institute (23 September).

15. At a meeting held on 18 September the group exchanged views with prominent figures in the world of Cuban arts and culture invited by the Union of Writers and Artists of Cuba. It also met directors of the principal newspapers, periodicals and television and radio stations, namely Granma, Bohemia, Juventud Rebelde, Trabajadora, TeleRebelde and Radio Rebelde (23 September). This meeting was also attended by the Dean of the Faculty of Journalism in the University of Havana and the President of the Cuban Union of Journalists.

16. During its stay in Havana the group visited educational institutions, hospitals, a Committee for the Defence of the Revolution, a detention centre, and a prison. The educational institutions visited included the José Antonio Echeverria Advanced Political Institute, the San Antonio de los Baños Secondary School, the International Cinema School (19 September) and the Casáreo Fernández Díaz Primary School (20 September). The hospitals visited included the Hermanos Ameijeida Hospital and the Psychiatric Hospital (20 September). The group also visited the Armando Parra Committee for the Defence of the Revolution (No. 5) in the municipality of 10 de Octubre, and the Villa Marista (Headquarters of the Department of State Security and Holding Centre for interrogation of State Security prisoners) and the Combinado del Este prison, where it talked with nine prisoners chosen by the group during its visit (21 September).

17. The group travelled outside Havana on two occasions. On the first occasion (17 September), at the suggestion of the Government of Cuba, it visited the Isla de la Juventud, where it was met by local officials and the Minister of Education, who accompanied the group on a visit to a school for Namibian children, where these and children of other nationalities attending other schools on the Isla de la Juventud gave a musical performance. The group also visited the old Isla de Pinos prison now converted into a museum.

18. On the second occasion (24 September) and on its own initiative, the group travelled to the province of Pinar del Río, where it met provincial officials. It visited the provincial prison, known as "Cinco y Medio," where it talked with two common prisoners and one counter-revolutionary prisoner,

and at the República de Chile Agricultural Production Co-operative, where it had a wide-ranging informal talk with the Co-operative's leaders and members, and afterwards visited their premises. On the same day, the group split up for the second and last time during its visit to Cuba. One of the resulting subgroups talked with the Provincial Social Welfare and Assistance Commission, while the other talked with provincial representatives of the Federation of Cuban Women. The other occasion on which the group split up was when Ambassadors Lillis and Dichev were asked by the group to receive communications that some political prisoners wanted to convey to it in Combinado del Este Prison. In the late afternoon, the group received oral testimony from 10 persons from Ciudad Sandino and written testimony from some 40 other persons.

19. In addition to all these activities, and in strict conformity with its earlier decision to divide its time equitably between the governmental and non-governmental sectors, the group received non-governmental organizations at the Hotel Comodoro in Havana, where it was staying. These were the Cuban Committee for Human Rights, represented by its Vice-President, Mr. Gustavo Arcos Bergnes, and by the heads of the sectoral sub-committees on Education, Art and Letters and on Public Health represented by Mr. Sebastián Arcos (son); the Commission for Human Rights and National Reconstruction, headed by Mr. Elizardo Sánchez Santa Cruz (17 September); the Allied Human Rights and National Reconciliation Organizations, headed by Mr. Julio Soto Angurel (17 September); the Asociación Naturista Vida, represented by Mr. Orlando Polo and Mrs. Mercedes Pérez Lorénte (17 September); and the Asociación Pro-Art Libre (Free Arts Association), headed by Mr. Armando Araya García and Ms. Rita Fleitas Fernández (22 September). The group also invited the leaders of the Cuban Ecumenical Council, headed by Reverend Raúl Suárez Ramos (17 September) and the Catholic Episcopal Conference (23 September) to meet with the group, at which the Conference was represented by its President monsignor Jaime Ortega, Archbishop of Havana, Monsignor José Siro Gonzáles, bishop of Pinar de Rio and Monsignor Carlos Manuel de Céspedes, Director of the Secretariat of the Episcopal Conference. In all, the group received testimony from more than 30 official representatives of non-governmental organizations.

20. The group also received oral testimony from approximately 50 persons. The group was obliged to take steps to ensure that, as far as possible, all persons requesting a meeting were duly heard and their cases appropriately recorded. Individual and collective testimony received by mail was also recorded and filed, together with testimony given in person. This was done by organizing a reception system which operated permanently throughout the visit. In addition to direct testimony from the 87 persons it interviewed, more than 30 of whom represented non-governmental organizations, with the co-operation of the United Nations Development Programme office in Havana and the secretariat, the Secretariat on behalf of

the group also received written testimony from approximately 1,600 persons. . . .

21. On 25 September, the day of its departure, the group was received separately by Dr. Fidel Castro Ruz, President of the Council of State, and Mr. Carlos Rafael Rodríguez, Vice President of the Council of State. The latter answered the principal questions which had arisen during the group's visit concerning various aspects of human rights in Cuba and any other questions the group wished to ask him. For his part, President Fidel Castro received the group at the Presidential Palace and, after conversing with the group, entertained it to a working luncheon, in which members of the group exchanged opinions with him and with the Vice-President of the Council of State, other senior Cuban officials present, and intellectuals and leaders of mass organizations the group had met in the course of its visit. . . .

23. At the end of the group's visit and before it returned from Cuba, the Chairman gave a press conference, at which he was accompanied by the other members of the group. The Chairman summarized the group's activities during its visit and answered questions from journalists. Throughout the visit, a member of the secretariat informed the press every day of the group's activities. On his return to Geneva, the Chairman gave a press conference.

24. The logistic preparations requested by the secretariat on behalf of the group were made by the Cuban authorities. Security measures connected with the group's activities in Cuba were handled by the Cuban authorities. The Cuban Government also made itself fully responsible for the group's transport in Cuba. The group itself bore the cost of its travel to Cuba and of its board and lodging.

Jiminez, Report on the Question of Human Rights in Chile
U.N. Doc. E/CN.4/1988/7, at 2-4, 48 (1988)

II.   THIRD VISIT TO CHILE

5. The Special Rapporteur arrived in Santiago (Chile) on his third official visit in the morning of Tuesday, 8 December 1987. He was welcomed at the airport with particular courtesy by senior officials from the Ministry of Foreign Affairs and representatives of the Economic Commission for Latin America and the Caribbean (ECLAC). He then had an initial informal contact with representatives of the media. He stayed in Chile for 14 days, during which he had a very full schedule.

6. As on his previous visits, the Special Rapporteur was afforded full cooperation by the Government and given complete freedom of action; he enjoyed complete independence in drawing up his programme of work. In

carrying out his mandate, he also received the invaluable practical assistance of ECLAC headquarters in Santiago and the precious co-operation of the various Chilean human-rights organizations. He was the subject of keen interest on the part of the media, which followed and reported his activities, enabling him to keep all Chileans and in particular the various sectors concerned informed of his opinions and activities and thus making it easier for them to contact him.

7. Despite the above-mentioned permission and co-operation on the part of the Government, the Special Rapporteur is obliged to mention two incidents which hampered his mission in Chile. Firstly, as he states later, he was granted a hearing by the Minister of Justice, during which he was taken aback by the hostile, discourteous and unco-operative attitude of the Minister, who gave him warnings that were clearly out of place. This incident cast a shadow on the permission for the visit and the co-operative spirit with which the Government had promised to receive the Special Rapporteur. Secondly, several competent representatives of the military courts did not respond promptly or in a proper manner to his request for a hearing; he specifically wanted to discuss with them important questions relating to the performance of their duties in the military courts. In addition, the Special Rapporteur requested, also in good time through diplomatic channels, hearings with the Director-General of the National Information Agency (CNI) and with representatives of the ordinary courts who are investigating important complaints of human rights violations. On this occasion, too, the Special Rapporteur did not receive an affirmative response from any of the parties concerned, with the result that he was obliged to make direct contact, at very short notice, with the various civil judges and magistrates, who gladly allowed the Special Rapporteur to interview them. The content of these interviews will be referred to below.

8. During this third visit to Chile, the Special Rapporteur extended his programme of work to five cities; Santiago, Valparaíso, Concepción, Temuco and Nueva Imperial. He had 26 working meetings with official organizations and interviewed a total of 54 officials, including the Minister of Foreign Affairs (twice), the Deputy Minister for Foreign Affairs, the Minister of the Interior, the Minister of Justice, the Under-Secretary of the Ministry of the Interior, the Director of Electoral Registration, the President of the Ministry of the Interior's Advisory Commission on Human Rights and the plenary Commission, the Director-General of the Police Department and the Director-General of the Indigenous Regional Council in the Ninth Region. He was also received by the Director-General of the Carabineros and by the Carabineros General who is serving as Chief of the Second Zone (Valparaíso). He interviewed the Rector of the University of Chile and visited six prisons in five different cities. As to representatives of the Judiciary, he was received by the President of the Supreme Court, the President of the National Association of Judicial Officers, two inspecting magistrates and two criminal court judges. He also interviewed Cardinal Fresno, Arch-

bishop Santos, two bishops, the Vicar of the Pastoral Obrera and the parish priest at Lo Hermida, all members of the Catholic Church, and a bishop of the Lutheran Evangelical Church. In addition, he interviewed several diplomatic representatives, and the delegates in Santiago of the Intergovernmental Committee for Migration (ICM) and the International Committee of the Red Cross (ICRC). On various occasions the Special Rapporteur met 288 persons representing 83 Chilean human-rights, social, vocational and community organizations. He also received 235 persons who, in an individual capacity, had expressed an interest in meeting him in order to explain their complaints and demands. In addition, he held working meetings with eight representatives of various political organizations. All in all, during this third visit to Chile, he interviewed no less than 580 persons representing a wide social spectrum. . . .

77. As in December 1985 and in March 1987, in this third on-the-spot investigation conducted in Chile in December 1987, the Government gave the Special Rapporteur all necessary facilities for carrying out his mission. The Special Rapporteur himself drew up his programme of work and put it into practice independently, without any interference from the Government.

78. The lack of co-operation on the part of the Minister of Justice is the exception — and an important one — to the rule. His hostility and disrespect towards the Special Rapporteur, together with his dogmatism and his refusal to collaborate with the mission, not only prevented any constructive dialogue, but also spoiled the atmosphere, in which the Special Rapporteur was doing his work. In practice, they also fomented hostility towards him in a sector of public opinion which tends to defend the status quo, giving a misleading impression of the nature and purposes of the visit.

79. On the other hand, during this most recent visit, the Special Rapporteur easily realized that the sector of the Chilean people with the greatest faith in the mission which links him to Chile is constantly growing. His delicate and complex task was also aided by the more open, familiar and frank manner in which he was approached by the various persons and groups interested in human rights and, generally speaking, in the country's political future, in other words, those interested in a deeply desired — by a significant majority — transition to a system of peaceful, representative, democratic Government which respects the rights inherent in every individual.

80. Naturally, there are still people who do not understand the Special Rapporteur's mission and therefore regard him as an intruder, although he has repeatedly told the Chilean media that his mission constitutes a means of assisting the Government and people of Chile in seeking ways of solving the human-rights problems besetting the country. The Special Rapporteur has also stressed that his interest lies only in the well-being of the ordinary Chilean, whom the results of his observations should reach.

Galindo Pohl, Report on the Human Rights Situation in the Islamic Republic of Iran
U.N. Doc. E/CN.4/1987/23, at 2-3 (1987)

III.   INFORMATION AVAILABLE TO THE SPECIAL REPRESENTATIVE

7. In the absence of any formal reply from the Iranian Government regarding the allegations submitted to it, the Special Representative proceeded to analyse the information and material available to him, containing specific allegations of human rights violations in the Islamic Republic of Iran, in the light of the Charter of the United Nations, the Universal Declaration of Human Rights, the International Covenant on Economic, Social and Cultural Rights and the International Covenant on Civil and Political Rights, with special emphasis on the latter instrument.

8. In examining and assessing the information available to him, the Special Representative strove to adhere strictly to the principles of fairness and objectivity, and therefore submitted all the allegations appearing in the present report to the Iranian Government in due time.

A.   WRITTEN INFORMATION

9. The Special Representative had before him the "Report on the performance of the Islamic Republic of Iran in 1985, submitted to the Special Representative by the Ministry of Foreign Affairs of the Islamic Republic of Iran" (A/40/874, annex IV). It may be noted that this document addressed itself to two out of five sets of questions submitted to the Iranian Government by the former Special Representative in his aide-memoire of 15 July 1986 (A/40/874, annex III).

10. The Special Representative also took note, for the preparation of the present report, of various documents published by the Ministry of Foreign Affairs of the Islamic Republic of Iran. In addition, information regarding the human rights situation in the Islamic Republic was provided by various organizations opposing the present régime, and in particular the People's Mojahedin Organization of Iran, Organization of Iranian People's Fedaian and the Tudeh Party of Iran. (A detailed list of the publications taken into account in the preparation of the present report appears in the annex.)

11. Non-governmental organizations enjoying consultative status with the Economic and Social Council, and in particular the Baha'i International Community and Amnesty International, provided information containing both legal and factual elements.

12. Furthermore, the Special Representative received a large number of petitions and letters from various organizations and individuals, concerning the human rights situation in the Islamic Republic of Iran in general, or particular cases of imprisoned groups or individuals.

B.   ORAL INFORMATION

13. The Special Representative noted that numerous persons who alleged that they had been the victims of violations of human rights wished to communicate their experience to him. In the circumstances, and in an effort to obtain as complete a picture as possible of these cases, the Special Representative received 16 persons who approached him in the course of informal hearings conducted on 23-25 September 1986. They claimed to have firsthand knowledge and experience of various aspects of the human rights situation in the Islamic Republic of Iran. Six of these persons described themselves as sympathizers of the People's Mojahedin Organization of Iran. They were: Robabeh Boudaghi, Behzad Naziri, Azame (this person requested that her surname should not be disclosed), Mina Vatani, Ali Hossein-Zadeh and Hossein Hosseini. The other 10 persons were followers of the Baha'i faith (all of them requested that their name should not be disclosed).

14. All persons mentioned above spent periods of various duration in Iranian prisons between the years 1981 and 1985, and all of them subsequently fled the country.

---

2. Thematic Mechanisms

The thematic rapporteurs and working groups may be less vulnerable to accusations of bias against a particular country, since their mandates are global. By the same token, however, it is extremely difficult for single individuals to cover the entire world effectively, a concern expressed clearly in the 1992 report of the Special Rapporteur on Summary or Arbitrary Executions. The subsequent two excerpts from other rapporteurs provide insight into the diverse ways these investigators approach their tasks.

Wako, Report [on Summary or Arbitrary Executions]
U.N. Doc. E/CN.4/1992/30, at 161-167, 171, 172, 175 (1992)

A.   REVIEW OF FIRST DECADE OF ACTIVITIES

1.   THE MANDATE OF THE SPECIAL RAPPORTEUR

605. The mandate of the Special Rapporteur which was established by the Economic and Social Council in its resolution 1982/35 of 7 May 1982, has evolved during the last 10 years. . . .

607. In its resolution 1985/40 of 30 May 1985, the Economic and Social Council requested the Special Rapporteur "to respond effectively to information that comes before him, in particular when a summary or arbi-

trary execution is imminent or threatened". This contributed to an important evolution of the mandate, as the Special Rapporteur began to send appeals for urgent action not only in cases of persons in custody where there was reason to believe execution might be imminent, but also in cases of persons in liberty who receive death threats, as well as in situations in which the fear was expressed that reported excesses by security forces might be repeated. Cases of this kind have become an important part of the caseload in several countries, and in many instances governmental authorities have offered protection to the persons concerned after being contacted by the Special Rapporteur. . . .

610. Over the past 10 years, the Special Rapporteur has sent letters or urgent appeals to over 100 States, many of which concern the application of the death penalty without full compliance with the standards set forth in the International Covenant on Civil and Political Rights. The relevant provisions of the Covenant are cited in all such letters and messages, whether or not the State to whom it is addressed is a State party. . . .

612. . . . The information received during the last decade contain[s] many examples of situations in which individuals or groups operating independently from the Government pose a very serious threat to the right to life, in some cases comparable to the threat which may be posed by a Government. These situations include communal, racial, ethnic, religious and tribal violence, assassinations or massacres committed by revolutionary, counter-revolutionary or separatist movements, assassinations by elements of the police or governmental armed forces or militia which are not under effective governmental control and assassinations by private individuals or groups employed to defend the economic interests of large landowners, drug traffickers or others.

613. In cases such as these, involving not isolated homicides for personal motives, but the deliberate and systematic killing of significant numbers of persons, the Government may be responsible before the international community either because of direct involvement or by tolerance, that is, by wilful failure to prevent the killings or to investigate and punish the responsible parties. This does not mean that the mandate of the Special Rapporteur extends to ordinary crimes. In cases where a government reply indicates that a thorough investigation has led to identification of those responsible for a killing, and that the motives for the crime were purely personal, the Special Rapporteur does not pursue the case further. . . .

614. The situation of executions by opposition forces is a different matter, in that the question of governmental tolerance or acquiescence does not arise. Nevertheless, such groups are an important source of summary and arbitrary killings, and Commission on Human Rights resolution 1990/75 of 7 March 1990 expressly asks the Special Rapporteur to include information on such executions in his Report, as well as information concerning violence by drug traffickers. Considerable information concerning execu-

tions by opposition groups has been received over the years, and special attention was given to this matter in the sixth report of the Special Rapporteur (E/CN.4/1988/22, paras. 182-87). The present report contains information and allegations concerning executions by the National Liberation Army and Revolutionary Armed Forces of Colombia, the Farabundo Marti Liberation Front of El Salvador, the Eritrean People's Liberation Front and Ethiopian People's Revolutionary Front, the Guatemalan National Revolutionary Unity, the National Patriotic Front of Liberia, the "Shining Path" and Tupac Amaru Revolutionary Movement in Peru and the "Liberation Tigers of Eelam Tamil" and Muslim Home Guards in Sri Lanka. . . .

2.   NUMBER AND TYPE OF CASES REPORTED

616. The number of cases reported has grown dramatically, especially during the last few years. . . .

619. The factors which the Special Rapporteur identified as being conducive to summary and arbitrary executions were the absence of a democratic political process, the existence of a state of emergency or equivalent, the existence of special courts, the lack of judicial independence, lack of discipline among law enforcement and military personnel, the existence of secret police or paramilitary groups, ethnic conflicts, religious intolerance and racial discrimination. The Special Rapporteur also emphasized the importance of unequal distribution of wealth as a root cause, generating social struggles by the poor which in some cases meet with a violent response on the part of the State or economically powerful groups.

620. In subsequent reports, the Special Rapporteur analysed many of the above mentioned phenomena in more detail, in some cases proposing new standards or other action, as well as new aspects of the problem which have emerged from the information received. In 1986, special attention was devoted to internal armed conflicts and deaths in custody; in 1988 special attention was given to violations of the right to life by opposition groups and death squads not under government control; and in 1990 the report analysed the problems of death threats and the execution of human rights defenders. . . .

3.   WORKING METHODS

622. Most of the allegations concerning summary and arbitrary executions and death threats received by the Special Rapporteur are presented by non-governmental organizations. Some Governments also present allegations concerning summary or arbitrary executions attributed to opposition forces. In addition, in order to enhance the complementarity, cooperation and effectiveness of the various thematic and country specific procedures existing within the United Nations system, the Special Rapporteur makes an

effort to keep abreast of information being generated within the framework of other mandates or procedures and, when appropriate, takes action on the basis of such information.

623. When allegations indicating that a summary or arbitrary execution may be imminent are received, and in other situations where it appears that urgent measures by the Government might prevent the recurrence of loss of life or repetition of excessive use of force by law enforcement officials, the usual course of action is to send an urgent message to the Government concerned, in keeping with Economic and Social Council resolution 1985/40 which requested the Special Rapporteur to "respond effectively to information that comes before him, in particular when a summary or arbitrary execution is imminent or threatened".

624. Urgent appeals are also sent in response to allegations that individuals or groups who seek to cooperate with the United Nations and representatives of its human rights bodies or who have sought to avail themselves of United Nations human rights procedures are being subjected to intimidations or reprisals involving possible threat to the right to life. . . . During the year covered by the present report, the Special Rapporteur sent urgent appeals under resolution 1991/70 to 49 Governments concerning some 4,200 cases of death threats against persons who seek to cooperate with the United Nations and representatives of its human rights bodies, or who have sought to avail themselves of procedures established under United Nations auspices for the protection of human rights and fundamental freedoms. The Special Rapporteur has also taken urgent steps in cases of reprisals against persons who have been victims, their representatives, family members or witnesses, in relation to cases or incidents falling under the Special Rapporteur's mandate.

625. The precise tenor of the message depends on the nature of the allegations and the amount of information available. In some cases, in particular death threats, the Government is usually requested to provide protection to the person or persons concerned and to investigate the origins of the threat. Where a judicially imposed death sentence is concerned, the Government is usually asked to provide more information in order to help determine whether or not sentence has been imposed in full compliance with relevant international standards; the Special Rapporteur has on occasion requested the Government to suspend the application of the sentence until he has time to evaluate the reply. In some cases, the Special Rapporteur requests that the sentence be commuted on humanitarian grounds, as for example when the information available leaves room for doubt as to whether or not the trial or sentence was fully compatible with international standards. . . .

628. When a communication has been sent to a Government and no reply has been received, the request for information is usually reiterated. When a reply is received, a number of situations may arise. Sometimes, the information provided by the Government demonstrated clearly that the

allegations were unfounded, that the individuals responsible for the executions concerned were duly convicted or sentenced, or that the Government was taking firm measures to prevent the recurrence of summary and arbitrary executions and to investigate those which had occurred.

629. Other times, the reply may reveal that there was little or no discrepancy concerning the facts, but disagreement as to whether or not the situation constituted a summary or arbitrary execution. This situation often occurs in cases concerning the application of the death penalty. . . .

639. Beyond any doubt, missions constitute the most effective method [at] the disposal of the Special Rapporteur for evaluation of the veracity of allegations received, and for arriving at a proper understanding of the social, legal, political and economic context in which executions occur in any given country. When a Government contests the factual aspects of an allegation, or when the question of impunity arises, or the question of whether or not courts operate in accordance with international standards of fairness and due process, it is difficult for the Special Rapporteur to evaluate the allegations properly without the possibility of visiting a country and speaking with the authorities and other concerned persons and organizations. The small number of countries which have invited the Special Rapporteur to undertake missions during the last decade is one of the most important limitations on the effectiveness in fulfilling his mandate, and countries where there are a significant number of cases pending which the Special Rapporteur has been unable to resolve on the basis of written submissions should be strongly encouraged to invite the Special Rapporteur to undertake a mission. It must also be recognized that missions create considerable additional work for the Secretariat, already overburdened by a steadily increasing case-load, which is yet another reason for providing increased support for the Special Rapporteur. . . .

647. Non-governmental organizations are the source of most of the information and allegations concerning arbitrary and illegal executions received by the Special Rapporteur. This information is indispensable to the effective fulfilment of the mandate of the Special Rapporteur, as is the cooperation of Governments. The great majority of information received is objective and reliable, and the Special Rapporteur would like to express his gratitude to the large number of national and international NGOs in all parts of the world who, by providing such information, have made a valuable contribution to the cause of human rights and dignity. . . .

[652.] (b) Responding to such cases more rapidly and frequently has stretched the staff resources of the Centre for Human Rights assigned to the Special Rapporteur to the limit. Yet it is necessary to improve the efficiency of the working methods of the Special Rapporteur in other ways as well. In resolutions 44/159 and 45/162, the General Assembly requested the Special Rapporteur, as indicated above, "to promote exchanges of views between Governments and those who provide reliable information to the Special Rapporteur, where the Special Rapporteur considers that such exchanges of information might be useful." In various resolutions, the Commission on Human Rights has invited governments to keep the Special Rapporteur informed on the progress made towards implementing recommendations he has addressed to them, and has encouraged governments encountering problems in the field of human rights to extend invitations to realize missions. The Special Rapporteur considers that it is essential to improve the effectiveness not only in the first response to imminent executions, but also in improving access to reliable information which is sufficient to allow him to form opinions on a greater number of the cases brought to his attention. He also considers it necessary, at this stage of the development of his mandate, to follow up more effectively in cases where there has been no response, where the reply is not sufficient to allow the allegations to be clarified, and to follow up efforts made by Governments to implement recommendations which have been made, as requested by the Commission on Human Rights;

(c) At present, only one professional staff member is assigned to assist the Special Rapporteur. While the Special Rapporteur is very grateful for the dedication, commitment and ability of the staff who have worked for him throughout these 10 years, it will be materially impossible for him to respond more efficiently to the allegations received unless resources are substantially increased. Indeed, the number of allegations received is steadily increasing as the work of the Special Rapporteur becomes better known. However, his efficiency is likely to deteriorate if resources remain at the present level. There is a compelling need to prevent additional summary or arbitrary executions, and to seek justice for the victims, as well as to deal with allegations concerning matters of great sensitivity for the governments concerned in a thorough, careful and professional manner. This makes it urgent to take steps to increase the resources available for carrying out all aspects of the mandate of the Special Rapporteur.

653. The Special Rapporteur therefore appeals to the Commission on Human Rights, and, through it, to the international community, to take prompt steps to preserve and strengthen this essential mechanism for the protection of human rights.

Kooijmans, Report [on Torture and Other Cruel, Inhuman, or Degrading Treatment or Punishment]
U.N. Doc. E/CN.4/1987/13, at 2-3, 5-6, 8 (1987)

5. On various occasions the Special Rapporteur has been asked to disclose the identity of his sources, as they were considered by the country concerned to be unreliable or biased. He has invariably replied that he is not in a position to do so for several reasons. First, if he provided this information in some cases and refused to do so in others, it would put him

in an awkward position. And in some cases there are very good reasons for not disclosing the identity of the source in order to protect the persons involved or their relatives against retaliatory measures. This is true in particular when the organization which provided the information is either within the country where torture is allegedly practised or received its information directly from persons living in that country. Secondly, the Special Rapporteur feels that it is his responsibility to determine which information is reliable and which is not. It would be wrong to shift that responsibility to the organization which provided the information. Since torture generally takes place in secluded places and often leaves no directly recognizable physical marks, evidence is hardly ever fully conclusive. It is only by carefully evaluating the concrete information against the background of what is known about the general situation in the country concerned that the reliability of the source can be determined. Moreover, as stated in the previous report, torture almost invariably takes place in a political context. Victims of torture are very often opponents of the government in power. First-hand information about torture, therefore, in many cases inevitably comes from groups whose political ideas are at variance with those of the incumbent régime. The fact that allegations of torture are coming from politically motivated sources does not imply, however, that the allegations themselves are politically motivated too. Torture is absolutely forbidden under international law and everybody therefore has the right to bring alleged cases of torture to the attention of the world community. To his regret, the Special Rapporteur has found too often that the alleged unreliability of the sources has been used by governments as an argument for not giving detailed information about the cases brought to their attention. The best way to prove the falseness of the allegations is to provide this detailed information or to invite the Special Rapporteur to visit the country and to see for himself what the situation is.

6. As the Special Rapporteur said in his first report, in view of the fact that all States have unequivocally committed themselves to respect the inherent dignity of man, torture should be seen essentially as a non-political issue. It should, therefore, be a matter of concern that still too often disclosure of the practice of torture is seen as a hostile act against the State and that those who have made such disclosures are in danger of being arrested and, possibly, subjected to torture themselves. Highly detailed information is frequently brought to the attention of the Special Rapporteur with the explicit request that it should not be conveyed to the Government of the country concerned as that could place certain persons or their relatives in great danger.

7. The Special Rapporteur wishes to stress that the identity and character of the source which provides the information is not the only criterion for ascertaining its reliability; other factors, such as its consonance with information from other sources and the general human rights situation in the country concerned, are also taken into account. . . .

II. Activities of the Special Rapporteur

A. CORRESPONDENCE

12. In pursuance of paragraph 3 of resolution 1986/50, the Special Rapporteur addressed notes verbales to Governments and letters to intergovernmental organizations and non-governmental organizations on 17 June 1986 with the request that they provide information on measures taken or envisaged, including legislation, to prevent and/or combat torture and to establish safeguards designed to protect the individual against torture.

13. In a reminder, dated 19 June 1986, the Special Rapporteur reiterated his invitation to Governments to provide him with information on allegations of cases of torture transmitted in 1985. He also stressed the importance of receiving information on legislation aimed at ensuring adequate protection of the right to physical and/or mental integrity of the individual, as well as on training programmes for police and security personnel.

14. In response to his request the following Governments submitted information: Byelorussian Soviet Socialist Republic (23 October 1986), Bolivia (22 June 1986), Congo (17 September 1986), Cuba (16 July 1986), Denmark (23 June 1986), Finland (9 July 1986), German Democratic Republic (26 September 1986), India (18 October 1986), Indonesia (12 August 1986), Italy (5 February 1986), Japan (27 August 1986), Liechtenstein (15 November 1986), Libyan Arab Jamahiriya (2 July 1986), Mexico (15 October 1986), Netherlands (24 July 1986), New Zealand (17 July 1986), Norway (16 January 1986), Nigeria (5 August 1986), Peru (11 August, 10 September 1986), Philippines (15 August 1986), Portugal (30 September 1986), Republic of Korea (6 November 1986), Sweden (11 July, 25 August 1986), Switzerland (2 September 1986), Syrian Arab Republic (14 July 1986), Togo (17 October 1986), Turkey (15 September 1986), Ukrainian Soviet Socialist Republic (2 October 1986), Union of Soviet Socialist Republics (13 October 1986), Zaire (27 August 1986).

15. Information was also provided by the International Labour Organisation (ILO); the United Nations Educational, Scientific and Cultural Organization (UNESCO); the Inter-American Commission on Human Rights; Amnesty International; SOS Torture; the British Medical Association; the Commission on Human Rights of Guatemala; Socorro Jurídico (El Salvador) and the Swiss Committee against Torture.

16. As in 1985, the Special Rapporteur received numerous allegations of the practice of torture from different sources. After analysing them, letters with a brief description of the allegations received were transmitted to 19 countries for clarification. In addition, the Special Rapporteur decided to retransmit, on 19 July 1986, allegations sent to 15 Governments in 1985. At the time of the preparation of this report no replies to specific allegations had been received from the Governments of Afghanistan, the Congo, Egypt, El Salvador, Iran (Islamic Republic of), Iraq, the Libyan Arab

Jamahiriya, Mozambique, South Africa, Suriname, the Syrian Arab Republic, Uganda and Zimbabwe.

B. CONSULTATIONS

17. The Special Rapporteur held consultations in Geneva during visits in June, September and November 1986. Private consultations with those Governments that expressed the wish to meet with him were maintained. He also received non-governmental organizations, private individuals and groups. On 26 November 1986, the Special Rapporteur heard six witnesses, who testified concerning the torture and ill-treatment to which they had been subjected while held in detention. . . .

D. ON-SITE OBSERVATIONS

22. The Special Rapporteur has on several occasions expressed his readiness to travel to the territory of any member State with the consent or at the invitation of the Government concerned for the purpose of carrying out on-site observations. Such visits would enable the Special Rapporteur to assess the allegations transmitted by different sources on concrete cases and verify facts. During such visits the Special Rapporteur in addition to consulting with the authorities, might also hold private interviews with alleged victims of torture, groups, entities or institutions, including persons sentenced or in detention in local prisons.

Vidal d'Almerida Ribero, Report [on Intolerance and Discrimination Based on Religion or Belief]
U.N. Doc. E/CN.4/1987/35, at 8-9 (1987)

III. Organization of Work

20. In conformity with the provisions of paragraph 4 of Commission on Human Rights resolution 1986/20, according to which the Special Rapporteur ". . . shall seek credible and reliable information from Governments, as well as specialized agencies, intergovernmental organizations and non-governmental organizations, including communities of religion or belief", a request for information dated 29 August 1986 was addressed in a note verbale to Governments and in letters to United Nations bodies, specialized agencies, and interested intergovernmental and non-governmental organizations.

21. On 10 December 1986, replies had been received from the following Governments: Belize, Bolivia, Brazil, Colombia, Dominican Republic, Ecuador, Finland, Germany, Federal Republic of, Iraq, Israel, Mauritius,

Mexico, New Zealand, Panama, Peru, Poland, Spain, Sweden, Trinidad and Tobago, Turkey, Uganda, Union of Soviet Socialist Republics and the United States of America.

22. The following United Nations bodies have also replied: United Nations Children's Fund, Office of the United Nations High Commissioner for Refugees, United Nations University.

23. Replies were also received from the following specialized agencies: International Labour Organisation, United Nations Educational, Scientific and Cultural Organization.

24. The Organization of American States also replied.

25. The following non-governmental organizations, in consultative status with the Economic and Social Council or on its Roster, also replied: Amnesty International, Baha'i International Community, Commission of the Churches on International Affairs of the World Council of Churches, Four Directions' Council, Friends World Committee for Consultation, International Association for Religious Freedom, International Commission of Jurists, International Federation for the Protection of the Rights of Ethnic, Religious, Linguistic and Other Minorities, International Humanist and Ethnical Union, International PEN, Inter-Parliamentary Union, Lutheran World Federation, Minority Rights Group, Survival International, World Union for Progressive Judaism.

26. The Special Rapporteur also received information from various other religious or secular sources reporting alleged infringements of the provisions of the Declaration in many countries.

27. In fulfilling his mandate, the Special Rapporteur met members of non-governmental organizations and individuals at Lisbon. He also visited Geneva for consultations at the Centre for Human Rights in July, October and November 1986. During those consultations, he received the Permanent Observer for the Holy See to the United Nations Office at Geneva and representatives of non-governmental organizations, namely, the Lutheran World Federation, the Commission of the Churches on International Affairs of the World Council of Churches, the Baha'i International Community, Pax Romana and the World Union for Progressive Judaism. In his capacity as Special Rapporteur, he participated in a conference on tolerance for differences of religion or belief organized by the University of Minnesota at Minneapolis, from 19-22 October 1986, in which representatives of the main contemporary ideological systems participated. On this occasion, the Special Rapporteur met representatives of the Minnesota Lawyers International Human Rights Committee. He also visited the United States of America in December 1986 at the invitation of American religious and secular associations.

A quasi-judicial "adversarial" approach is taken by the Working Group on Arbitrary Detention, which meets for three week-long sessions throughout the year and issues formal "decisions" in specific cases as to whether the challenged detention is arbitrary. (The working group and other "thematic" mechanisms of the UN Commission on Human Rights are discussed at pages 390-398 of Problem V.)

Report of the Working Group on Arbitrary Detention
U.N. Doc. E/CN.4/1994/27, at 22-24 (1993)

REVISED METHODS OF WORK AS OF DECEMBER 1993

1. The methods of work are largely based on those applied, in the light of 11 years' experience, by the Working Group on Enforced or Involuntary Disappearances, with due regard for the specific features of the Group's terms of reference under Commission on Human Rights resolution 1991/42, whereby it has the duty of informing the Commission by means of a comprehensive report (para. 5), but also of "investigating cases" (para. 2).

2. The Group takes the view that such investigation should be of an adversarial nature so as to assist it in obtaining the cooperation of the State concerned by the case considered.

3. In the opinion of the Working Group, situations of arbitrary detention, in the sense of paragraph 2 of resolution 1991/42, are those described in accordance with the principles set out in annex I of document E/CN.4/1992/20.

4. In the light of resolution 1991/42, the Working Group shall deem admissible communications received from the concerned individuals themselves or their families. Such communications may also be transmitted to the Working Group by representatives of the above-mentioned individuals as well as by Governments and intergovernmental and non-governmental organizations.

5. The communications must be submitted in writing and addressed to the secretariat giving the family name, first name and address of the sender, and (optionally) his telephone, telex and telefax numbers.

6. As far as possible, each case shall form the subject of a specific presentation indicating family name, first name and any other information making it possible to identify the person detained and all elements clarifying the legal status of the person concerned, particularly:

(a) The date, place and the forces presumed to have carried out the arrest or detention together with all other information shedding light on the circumstances in which the person was arrested or detained;

(b) The reasons given by the authorities for the arrest or detention or the offences;

(c) The relevant legislation applied to the case in point;

(d) The internal steps taken, including domestic remedies, especially approaches to the administrative and legal authorities, particularly for verification of the detention and, as appropriate, their results or the reasons why such steps were ineffective or were not taken; and

(e) A short account of the reasons why the deprivation of liberty is regarded as arbitrary.

7. In order to facilitate the Group's work, it is hoped that communications will be submitted taking into account the model questionnaire.

8. Failure to comply with all formalities set forth in paragraphs 6 and 7 shall not directly or indirectly result in the inadmissibility of the communication.

9. The cases notified shall be brought to the attention of the Government concerned by the Chairman of the Group or, if he is not available, by the Vice-Chairman, by means of a letter transmitted through the Permanent Representative to the United Nations asking the Government to reply after having carried out the appropriate inquiries so as to provide the Group with the fullest possible information.

10. The communication shall be transmitted with an indication of the deadline established for receipt of a reply. The deadline may not exceed 90 days. If the reply has not been received by the time the deadline is reached, the Working Group may, on the basis of all data compiled, take a decision.

11. The procedure known as "urgent action" may be resorted to:

(a) In cases in which there are sufficiently reliable allegations that a person is being detained arbitrarily and that the continuation of the detention constitutes a serious danger to that person's health or even life. In such cases, between the sessions of the Working Group, the Working Group authorizes its Chairman or, in his absence, the Vice-Chairman, to transmit the communication by the most rapid means to the Minister for Foreign Affairs of the country concerned, stating that this urgent action in no way prejudges the Working Group's final assessment of whether the detention is arbitrary or not;

(b) In other cases, where the detention may not constitute a danger to a person's health or life, . . . the particular circumstances of the situation [may] warrant urgent action. In such cases, between the sessions of the Working Group, the Chairman or the Vice-Chairman, in consultation with two other members of the Working Group, may also decide to transmit the communication by the most rapid means to the Minister for Foreign Affairs of the country concerned.

However, during sessions, it devolves on the Working Group to take a decision whether to resort to the urgent action procedure.

12. Between the sessions of the Working Group, the Chairman may, either personally or by delegating any of the members of the Group, request an interview with the Permanent Representative to the United Nations of the country in question in order to facilitate mutual cooperation.

13. Any information supplied by the Government concerned on specific cases shall be transmitted to the sources from which the communica-

tions were received, with a request for comments on the subject or additional information.

14. In the light of the information examined during its investigation, the Working Group shall take one of the following decisions:

(a) If the person has been released, for whatever reason, since the Working Group took up the case, the case is filed; nevertheless, the Working Group reserves the right to decide, on a case-by-case basis, whether or not the deprivation of liberty was arbitrary, notwithstanding the release of the person concerned;

(b) If the Working Group determines that it is established that the case is not one of arbitrary detention, the case is also filed;

(c) If the Working Group decides that it does not have enough information to take a decision, the case remains pending for further information;

(d) If the Working Group decides that it does not have enough information to keep the case pending, the case may be filed without further action;

(e) If the Working Group decides that the arbitrary nature of the detention is established, it shall make recommendations to the Government concerned. The recommendations shall also be brought to the attention of the Commission on Human Rights in the annual report of the Working Group to the Commission.

15. When the case under consideration concerns a country of which one of the members of the Working Group is a national, that member shall not, in principle, participate in the discussion because of the possibility of a conflict of interest.

16. The Working Group will not deal with situations of international armed conflict in so far as they are covered by the Geneva Conventions of 12 August 1949 and their Additional Protocols, particularly when the International Committee of the Red Cross (ICRC) has competence.

17. In accordance with the provisions of paragraph 4 of resolution 1993/36, the Working Group may, on its own initiative, take up cases which, in the opinion of any one of its members, might constitute arbitrary detention. If the Group is in session, the decision to communicate the case to the Government concerned shall be taken at that session. Outside the session, the Chairman, or in his absence the Vice-Chairman, may decide on transmittal of the case to the Government, provided at least three members of the Group so agree. When acting on its own initiative, the Working Group shall give preferential consideration to the thematic or geographical subjects to which the Commission on Human Rights has requested it to pay special attention.

18. The Working Group shall also communicate any decision it adopts to the Commission on Human Rights body, whether thematic or country-oriented, or to the body set up by the appropriate treaty for the purpose of proper coordination between all organs of the system.

Note: The Role of the UN Secretariat

As noted at the end of the Wako excerpt, supra page 431, the staff of the UN Center for Human Rights in Geneva play an essential role in providing research assistance, making logistical arrangements, and often drafting the reports prepared by country-specific or thematic rapporteurs. However, the Center's human and financial resources (which have accounted for less than 1 percent of total UN expenditures) have been placed under increasingly severe strains as their obligations to service human rights bodies mounts.

Brody, Improving UN Human Rights Structures
in Human Rights: An Agenda for the Next Century 297, 307-308 (L. Henkin and J. Hargrove eds. 1994)

The UN Centre for Human Rights is shockingly ill-equipped to provide its factfinders with even basic resources. The Special Rapporteur on Summary or Arbitrary Executions, Bacre Waly N'Diaye, has called the human rights program "the UN's third world." Almost every yearly thematic report ends with a plea for more resources. At the heart of the problem is the fact that the Centre's responsibilities have expanded while overall resources have remained stable (and even shrunk) as a result of the zero-growth budget imposed on the UN by governments in the early 1980s. Until 1985 the UN made available extra funds for new mandates when they were created by the Commission. But since 1985 all new funding has come out of a contingency fund (program support cost fund) that is reviewed every two years. At its current level ($300,000 a year) this covers less than half the 1993 budget of the Special Rapporteur for Former Yugoslavia alone, and is clearly inadequate.

Twenty years ago, the forty-three professional staff in the human rights secretariat handled three bodies (the Commission, Commission on the Status of Women, and Sub-Commission) and serviced seventy working days of meetings. Today, with only fifty-four professionals, the secretariat has to service seven hundred days of meetings, thirty-nine special procedures (rapporteurs and working groups), one hundred and fifty thousand individual communications annually, and four thousand pages of reports by states parties to conventions.

All parts of the Centre are hampered by the funding and staffing shortfall, but none more so than the Special Procedures Section, which provides the back-up for factfinding. In 1980, the unit serviced four mandates. The number has now grown to twenty-nine. This includes the nine country rapporteurs and the seven [now 13] thematic working groups or rapporteurs; it does not include another ten [now 11] human rights missions by special representatives of the Secretary-General. The section has to deal with five urgent appeals a day (up from one a week in 1980). Eight thousand cases of disappearances are waiting to be transmitted to governments — not including the fourteen thousand that recently arrived from former Yugoslavia.

Five years ago, the Working Group on Disappearances was serviced by five professionals. Today it has two and a half.

No discussion of the role of the UN Secretariat would be complete without mentioning the office of the Secretary-General. The Secretary-General has long played a role as mediator and informal fact-finder through the exercise of his "good offices." In practice, this often means the appointment of individuals as special representatives or envoys of the Secretary-General, who generally travel to the areas in question and may receive information informally from a wide range of governmental and non-governmental sources. As of June 1994, the Secretary-General was being represented or advised by individuals he had appointed with respect to Afghanistan, Angola, the Baltic states, Burundi, Cambodia, Cyprus, East Timor, El Salvador, Georgia, a dispute between Guyana and Venezuela, Haiti, Liberia, the Middle East, Mozambique, Rwanda, Somalia, Tajikistan, Western Sahara, Yemen, the former Yugoslav Republic of Macedonia, the former Yugoslavia, and Zaire. UN Notes, 5 Intl. Documents Rev. 6. (No. 21, 1994). See generally B. Ramcharan, Humanitarian Good Offices in International Law (1983).

Where the primary issue is human rights, as opposed to larger issues of peace and security, the UN High Commissioner for Human Rights (a post created only in 1994) may take on some of the fact-finding responsibility formerly given to special envoys. See page 400 of Problem V.

Note: A *Rapporteur from the Commission on Human Rights Visits Suriname*

The events in Suriname of December 1982 (see page 227 of Problem III) came to the attention of one of the thematic rapporteurs of the Commission on Human Rights. Amos Wako, rapporteur on the subject of summary or arbitrary executions, took an interest in the incident and even traveled to the country (with its government's consent) to look into the matter. In the following extract from his 1985 annual report to the Commission, Mr. Wako explained what took place during his visit.

Wako, Report [on Summary or Arbitrary Executions]
Annex V, at 1-4, 11-12, 16, U.N. Doc. E/CN.4/1985/17 (1985)

2.   Arrangements

5. Prior to his visit, and by a cable dated 18 June 1984, the Special Rapporteur communicated to the Permanent Representative of Suriname

the names of those persons whom he wished to meet in Suriname. Further-more, on the request of the Special Rapporteur, a public announcement was made in newspapers and other media concerning his visit to Suriname, prior to his arrival as follows:

> By a resolution adopted by the Economic and Social Council on 24 May 1982, the Council appointed Mr. S. Amos Wako as Special Rapporteur of the Commission on Human Rights with a mandate to examine the ques-tion of summary or arbitrary executions. In another resolution adopted on 24 May 1984, the Council decided to continue the mandate of the Special Rapporteur for another year. Mr. Wako presented a report to the Commission on Human Rights at its thirty-ninth session in 1983. The report contained a statement concerning Suriname and, in particular, the events which oc-curred on 8 and 9 December 1982. In that connection, the Government of Suriname extended an invitation to Mr. Wako to visit the Republic of Suri-name. That visit will take place from 23 to 27 July 1984. Mr. Wako will meet Government officials, military and prominent civil leaders. Mr. Wako will also be available to meet any person wishing to provide information concern-ing the events referred to above. The Special Rapporteur has been assured by the Government of Suriname that it shall grant the pertinent guarantees to all those who may provide the Special Rapporteur and his staff with information, testimony or evidence of any kind. Mr. Wako may be contacted at Hotel Krasnapolsky.

3. Schedule

6. With the assistance and co-ordination of the National Commission of Information and Guidance on Human Rights, meetings were arranged with Government officials, military personnel, trade-union leaders, profes-sional and religious groups and the business community. The Special Rap-porteur also met a number of private individuals. . . .

III. Reports by Other International Organizations

11. The Special Rapporteur has taken note of reports prepared on Suriname by the following organizations:

(a) International Commission of Jurists, Human Rights in Suriname, Report of a Mission (February/March 1983) by M. Bossuyt and J. Grif-fiths;

(b) International Labour Office, 230th Report of the Committee on Freedom of Association (GB.224/9/7), Case No. 1160, annex "Report on the direct contacts mission to Suriname carried out by Mr. W.R. Simp-son, Chief of the Freedom of Association Branch, International Labour Standards Department" pp. 117-131;

(c) Organization of American States, Inter-American Commission on Human Rights: Report on the situation of human rights in Suriname (OAS/Ser.L/II.61, Doc.6 Rev.1, October 5, 1983).

12. The Government's observations on the report of the Inter-American Commission on Human Rights submitted to its Chairman in September 1983 were made available to the Special Rapporteur by the Government of Suriname.

13. The Special Rapporteur has taken note of the findings and conclusions of these reports and also the observations by the Government of Suriname as far as they are relevant to his mandate.

IV.   INFORMATION OBTAINED DURING THE VISIT

14. During his visit to Suriname and the Netherlands, the Special Rapporteur did his utmost to inform himself of the events of December 1982 regarding the allegations described above and of the measures taken by the Government to prevent the recurrence of such events. His activities in this respect, however, cannot be considered as a formal investigation which might correspond to or replace the investigations envisaged in criminal procedure in the domestic legal system or an inquest. . . .

E.   QUESTION WHETHER ANY MEASURES WERE TAKEN TO DETERMINE THE FACTS OF THE EVENTS OF DECEMBER 1982

35. The question arises why there was no investigation or inquiry into an incident which, by all accounts, shook the entire country.

36. This question was put by the Special Rapporteur to the military officers whom he met. No official inquiry into the incident of the night of 8-9 December 1982 was conducted. The Special Rapporteur was told by the military officers that Maj. Horb had been entrusted with the preparation of a report on the incident. This was corroborated by Capt. Graanoogst, who was the Minister for Army and Police at the time and who told the Special Rapporteur that the military wanted to clarify these matters. Maj. Horb was found dead in his cell on 3 February 1983; no evidence of his report has been found.

37. This question was put by the Special Rapporteur to the Minister of Justice, Dr. Frank Lefflang:

Special Rapporteur: May I ask if there was an investigation on the events of December 1982?

Minister: This question is difficult as it is impossible to answer if you don't know the Suriname reality. There were no investigations. These were special circumstances. No formal request was made to investigate those facts, therefore, our Government is not able to investigate because it did not know all the facts concerning this matter. The Government is in a very difficult position.

Procurator: The facts were not brought to the Government. Because of that no investigations could be made.

38. The Special Rapporteur also put the same question to the Prime Minister, Mr. Udenhout:

Special Rapporteur: Are there any obstacles to the collection of information on the events by the Government? I assume that [since you became Prime Minister] you have tried to get a correct picture.

Prime Minister: . . . It is a problem of having to ask the question. What will be served by ascertaining the facts and bringing to justice all those responsible, directly or indirectly? What would be served by this kind of justice? It might lead to violence again. . . .

39. At the meeting with Lt. Col. Bouterse the latter confirmed to the Special Rapporteur that "no attempt has been made to set up a body to investigate the events." . . .

H.   CONCLUDING REMARKS

64. On the basis of the information in his possession the Special Rapporteur finds that summary or arbitrary executions took place on the night of 8-9 December in Fort Zeelandia. In view of the fact that there can be no derogation from article 6 of the International Covenant on Civil and Political Rights, that article is binding also "in time of public emergency which threatens the life of the nation and the existence of which is officially proclaimed" (art. 4) and therefore even if such a threat had existed or was presumed to exist, the executions of 8-9 December 1982 cannot be justified and cannot but be considered summary or arbitrary. The executions had a traumatic effect on the population of Suriname in view of the prominence or stature of the victims.

D.   *The Need for General Standards for Fact-Finding by International Organizations*

Considering the wide variety of fact-finding that international organizations undertake, the inherent sensitiveness of most of the investigations, and the high degree of autonomy the fact-finders have in deciding upon their methodology, it can hardly be expected that the fact-finders' activities will please everyone. On the one hand, there is the danger that the fact-finding process might be unfairly biased against the states concerned. On this danger, see Franck and Fairley, Procedural Due Process in Human Rights Fact-Finding by International Agencies, 74 Am. J. Intl. L. 308 (1980), which contains two instructive case studies. On the other hand, there is the opposite danger: that fact-finders will tread too warily or be manipulated or duped by governments into painting too rosy a picture. See, e.g., Peer in

"Whitewash" Row over Guatemala Report, Sunday Times (London), Dec. 2, 1984, at 26, col. 6; UN's Poland Report Considered Timid, The Times (London), Feb. 28, 1983, at 4, col. 6.

Note: *Toward a Solution — The Belgrade Rules on Fact-Finding by International Organizations*

There has been an awareness for some time for the need for general standards on fact-finding. An attempt on the part of the Commission on Human Rights to devise a body of rules on the subject, however, met with scant success. During the late 1960s and early 1970s, a working group of the Commission attempted to devise a set of guidelines on fact-finding, with a view to their being adopted by the Commission by consensus. However, the rules produced by the group had to be seriously watered down in order to muster the necessary consensus in 1974. Even then, the UN took little notice of the effort. The rules were forwarded by the Commission to its parent body, ECOSOC, which simply drew the attention of UN member states to their existence. It did not even go so far as to recommend that UN human rights fact-finding bodies take them into account in their work.

After that chastening experience, the initiative in this area passed to non-UN bodies. The most productive work has been done by the International Law Association (ILA), a group of international lawyers acting in their personal capacities. The Human Rights Committee of the ILA drew up a set of rules for fact-finding by international organizations, which the Association adopted at its meeting in Belgrade in 1980. For the report of the Committee, see Lillich, Human Rights: Report of the Committee, Report of the 59th Conference of the International Law Association 83 (Belgrade 1980). The Belgrade Rules, as they are known, are the principal guidelines in this area.

Belgrade Minimal Rules of Procedure for International Human Rights Fact-Finding Missions
75 Am. J. Intl. L. 163, 163-165 (1981)

I.   Terms of Reference (Mandate)

1. The organ of an organization establishing a fact finding mission should set forth objective terms of reference which do not prejudge the issues to be investigated. These terms should accord with the instrument establishing the organization.

2. The resolution authorizing the mission should not prejudge the mission's work and findings.

3. While terms of reference should not unduly restrict the mission in the investigation of the subject and its context, they should be so specific as to indicate the nature of the subject to be investigated.

II.   Selection of Fact Finders

4. The fact finding mission should be composed of persons who are respected for their integrity, impartiality, competence and objectivity and who are serving in their personal capacities.

5. Where the mandate of the mission concerns one or several specific states, in order to facilitate the task of the mission, the government or governments concerned, whenever possible, should be consulted in regard to the composition of the mission.

6. Any person appointed a member of the fact finding mission should not be removed from membership except for reasons of incapacity or gross misbehaviour.

7. The chairman and the rapporteur of the fact finding mission should not be replaced during the term of the mission except for reasons of incapacity or gross misbehaviour.

8. Once a fact finding mission has been established and its chairman and members appointed, no persons should be added to the mission as members except to fill vacancies in the mission.

III.   Collection of Evidence

9. At the commencement of the mission, all material relevant to the purpose of the mission should be made available to it, with the assistance of the organization concerned.

10. Fact finding missions should operate with staff sufficient to permit the independent collection of data and should be assisted by such independent experts as the mission may deem necessary.

11. Fact finding missions may invite the submission of evidence that is in writing and contains specific statements of fact that are in their nature verifiable.

12. The state concerned should have an opportunity to comment in writing on data referred to in paragraph 10 and statements referred to in paragraph 11.

13. Both the petitioners, such as states, non-governmental organizations, or groups of individuals, and the states concerned may present lists of witnesses to the fact finding mission. The fact finding mission should make its own determination as to which witnesses it will hear.

14. Petitioners ought ordinarily to be heard by the fact finding mission in public session with an opportunity for questioning by the states concerned.

15. The fact finding mission shall in advance require the state concerned to provide adequate guarantee of non-retaliation against individual petitioners, witnesses and their relatives.

16. In case a guarantee, as referred to in paragraph 15, is provided to the satisfaction of the fact finding mission, the latter should, on hearing witnesses, either provide an opportunity for the state concerned to be present and to question witnesses, or make available to the state concerned a record of the witnesses' testimony for comment.

17. The fact finding mission may withhold information which, in its judgment, may jeopardize the safety or well-being of those giving testimony, or of third parties, or which in its opinion is likely to reveal sources.

18. On the basis of data generated by its staff, written statements, and testimony of witnesses, the fact finding mission should make its own determination as to whether it needs to conduct an on-site inspection.

IV. The On-Site Investigation

19. The fact finding mission should draw up its programme of work, including the list of witnesses it wishes to interview at the site of the investigation, places it wishes to visit, and the sequence, timing and location of its activities on the site.

20. The fact finding mission may operate as a whole or in smaller groups assigned to conduct specific parts of the investigation.

21. The fact finding mission should insist on interviewing any persons it deems necessary, even if incarcerated.

V. Final Stage

22. After conclusion of the on-site investigation, members of the fact finding mission should draw up a set of preliminary findings and submit these, together with supplementary questions where appropriate, to the state concerned, giving it an opportunity, within a reasonable time, to present comments and/or to rectify the matter investigated.

23. A final report shall be prepared by the chairman reflecting the consensus of the fact finding mission. In the absence of a consensus, the mission's report should contain the findings of the majority as well as any views of dissenting members.

24. In case a decision is made to publish the report, it should be published in its entirety.

25. The Organization establishing the fact finding mission should keep under review the compliance of states with their undertaking regarding nonreprisal against petitioners, witnesses, their relatives and associates.

E.   Fact-Finding by Non-Governmental
Organizations

It is not merely — or perhaps even primarily — intergovernmental organizations (IGOs) that are engaged in the process of fact-finding in the
human rights field. NGOs are active in this sphere as well — perhaps even
too active for the liking of certain countries. NGOs have so wide a variety of
interests and functions and levels of material resources as nearly to defy
generalization entirely. Even the purposes to which they put the facts they
gather vary enormously. The International Committee of the Red Cross
(ICRC), for example, has extensive experience in investigations of the conditions in which prisoners are held during armed conflicts. This organization resolutely shuns publicity. Its function is essentially to carry on discreet
negotiations with the states immediately concerned. Organizations such as
Amnesty International and Human Rights Watch, on the other hand, do
reports on the human rights situations in various countries and disseminate
those reports to the general public as widely as possible. Still other groups
are engaged in the litigating of human rights issues before international or
domestic courts. They must gather the kind of evidence that will pass the
stern muster of a court of law.

Orentlicher, Bearing Witness: The Art and Science
of Human Rights Fact-Finding
3 Harv. Hum. Rts. J. 83, 85, 92-108, 135 (1990)

As the influence of NGO human rights reporting has grown, NGOs'
underlying research methodology has come under heightened scrutiny and,
at times, pointed attack. In an age when acquiring the status of "human
rights pariah" carries unprecedented costs internationally, governments
whose rights violations are publicized frequently respond by challenging the
credibility of the fact-finding methodology. United States officials, too, have
publicly attacked the credibility of organizations that released reports chron-
icling abuses committed by strategic allies of the United States government.

In this setting, perhaps no asset is more important to a human rights
NGO than the credibility of its fact-finding and, in particular, its reputation
for meticulous methodology. Despite the unprecedented attention to issues of
human rights methodology, however, the leading NGOs have not adopted
uniform methodological standards; most have not even adopted comprehensive, formal standards for use by their own staffs. And while NGO reporting
has drawn the close scrutiny of various parties, critiques of NGO methodology do not reflect a coherent set of commonly accepted standards. . . .

For NGOs, . . . [t]he credibility of their fact-finding is their stock-in-
trade. Broadly stated, the chief objective of human rights NGOs is to

promote compliance with international human rights standards. As self-appointed watchdogs, NGOs have no "authority" to compel governments to bring their practices into compliance with those standards; NGOs can aspire only to *persuade* governments to respect the rights of individuals subject to the governments' jurisdictions. To this end, NGOs appeal to governments believed to be responsible for abuses to cease the violations. NGOs also frequently marshall external sources of pressure, such as the intervention of other governments or intergovernmental bodies. Fact-finding lies at the heart of these efforts, and the fact-finding "works" when it convinces the target audience that the published allegations are well founded.

Although critiques of NGO reporting do not reflect a coherent set of commonly acknowledged standards, it is possible to identify factors that figure prominently in public assessments of NGO fact-finding. The most frequently cited criteria fall into two categories. One relates to the integrity of an NGO's fact-finding methodology; the other takes account of various factors that are thought to indicate whether the NGO has an institutional bias — other than a bias in favor of human rights — that may taint the credibility of its conclusions. . . .

The obstacles to fact-finding posed by the state's nearly exclusive control of essential information are often compounded by other, related circumstances. In a context of widespread state lawlessness, for example, witnesses and victims often are afraid to provide testimony to human rights investigators, fearing retaliation by government forces. Moreover, a substantial number of countries in which gross violations are practiced on a systematic basis are closed to foreign investigators. In many countries, political repression is so severe that independent human rights monitors either cannot operate internally or do so under enormous constraints and at great personal risk. And in countries with serious systematic abuses, a bridled press often does not — because it cannot — provide independent accounts of human rights violations.

Thus, the circumstances in which human rights investigation is undertaken typically place substantial limitations on fact-finding. Though such constraints may be unavoidable, their effect on NGO methodology can invite challenge from a critical audience. . . .

Second, the role of interpretation in the preparation of country reports contributes to their vulnerability to challenge. While it may be a truism that there are no "pure facts" and that any attempt to describe factual conditions entails substantial interpretation, the role of interpretation is particularly large in the context of human rights country reports. Because country reports aspire to describe broad patterns, the finder of fact must attempt not only to verify individual incidents of abuse, but also to reach more sweeping judgments about the extent of the violations, the nature of government (and, where relevant, insurgent) responsibility for the abuses, and the significance of apparent trends. . . .

A third aspect of human rights fact-finding further increases the potential for different conclusions to emerge from the same facts: the investigator must measure facts against an abstract standard. Most NGOs evaluate states' compliance with internationally recognized human rights standards. Some NGOs also assess state practices in light of protections embodied in domestic law. Thus, in seeking to verify a reported violation, NGOs must attempt to determine both what actually happened, and whether the facts, under all the attendant circumstances, constitute a violation of relevant standards. These determinations often require difficult judgment calls, and it is scarcely surprising that different analysts sometimes reach different judgments about the legality of particular conduct. . . .

Recent critiques of NGO fact-finding have focused as much on indicia of institutional credibility as on methodology. Challenges to the institutional credibility of NGOs have focused on two charges in particular. . . .

The first charge is that a survey of an NGO's work betrays a high degree of selectivity in the countries that are monitored, and that the selection is driven by a decided political slant. When applying this measure, critics often make reference to both the range of countries which an NGO has scrutinized and the evenhandedness of the organization's application of international standards to different countries' human rights records. Thus, even NGOs that attempt to monitor countries of every political orientation have been criticized for "going easier" on countries of one political shading than another. Sometimes the apparent disparity has been largely a matter of tone — a difference in the moral fervor of an NGO's respective condemnations of similar violations by different governments. But in human rights reporting, in which shadings of language convey varying levels of opprobrium, tone is substance. . . .

The second charge is that an NGO's work on a particular country betrays a political bias against the government and in favor of its opponents. The criticism often arises with respect to reports that examine countries in which the most serious abuses occur in a context of civil war. In these circumstances, government officials have frequently charged that an NGO report is biased if it criticizes only abuses by government forces, and not those of their armed adversaries.

This charge played a prominent role in the Reagan Administration's efforts to discredit human rights reports that documented gross violations by several strategic allies of the United States. Early in its first term, the Administration began to press the view that, to be credible, NGOs that report on violations in a country in a state of armed conflict must monitor the practices of the rebels as well as the government forces.

There are, however, principled reasons for NGOs to monitor violations attributable only to government forces, and most domestic NGOs, as well as many international NGOs, follow this practice. These organizations base their work on international human rights law, which establishes international responsibility for violations only on the part of governments, in contrast to the laws of war (also known as humanitarian law), which generate international responsibility for violations by all sides to an armed conflict. [See generally Problem XI.] Thus an NGO that bases its mandate exclusively on international human rights law is faithful to the law by focusing on government conduct. . . .

Beyond such considerations as whether NGOs monitor both sides to an armed conflict or whether they monitor governments of the right and left with equal vigor, more subtle factors affect public perceptions of NGOs' credibility. Governments that are the subject of scrutiny as well as other audiences often evaluate NGO reporting according to its "fairness" in a particular sense: whether it acknowledges contextual factors that place violations "in perspective." Thus, for example, the Israeli government is more likely to credit a report describing its violations in the West Bank and Gaza if the report acknowledges that human rights conditions are deplorable in other areas of the Middle East. Similarly, even if a human rights NGO's mandate does not extend to monitoring abuses committed by armed rebels, its account of a government's violations is likely to seem more credible to that government if the report acknowledges in a more-than-perfunctory fashion the threat posed by the insurgents. Indeed, human rights reports that criticize abuses committed by governments responding to an armed insurgency now routinely acknowledge not only the government's right to respond militarily and, under certain circumstances, to derogate from some human rights, but also express opprobrium of violations committed by the insurgents. . . .

A key point to be made here is that human rights reports are not merely abstract factual accounts. The reports are advocacy tools, designed to promote change in government practices. As such, their presentation of facts is designed to respond to factors likely to affect the report's impact. . . .

A variety of factors account for NGOs' general reluctance to develop standardized methodologies. Most importantly, many human rights professionals believe that the nature of the human rights violations they monitor requires broad flexibility in fact-finding strategies. As noted earlier, NGO fact-finding has focused on abuses which governments deliberately cloak in secrecy. Many human rights professionals believe that adopting rigid methodological standards would limit their ability to adapt their fact-finding efforts to the particular constraints of particular circumstances, and could preclude them from undertaking effective advocacy with respect to countries that engage in the most severe and systematic abuses.

In addition, some human rights professionals believe that the articulation of general fact-finding standards inadvertently could increase the risks faced by domestic human rights monitors. Such monitors frequently work under conditions of extreme danger, and government attacks on the credibility of their methodology often heighten those risks, serving in effect as a public "death warrant." In this setting, some human rights professionals fear that governments might cite, with dangerous consequences, a domestic

NGO's failure to adhere to established uniform standards to harm the organization's credibility. . . .

While there are valid reasons for eschewing narrow methodological standards, NGOs should nonetheless aspire to the highest standards possible under prevailing circumstances. Indeed, their institutional objectives would be defeated if their reports failed to persuade their target audiences that the factual conclusions were well-founded. To meet this "burden of persuasion," each report must satisfy a threshold standard of credibility. . . .

. . . While flexible evidentiary standards are appropriate to NGO human rights fact-finding methodology, NGO reports should make out a prima facie case for their factual allegations by developing highly probative — if inconclusive — evidence. If the NGO's methodology is persuasive, the government responsible for alleged violations is likely to face substantial pressure to "answer for itself," while the concerned public is unlikely to accept a bald denial as an adequate response. . . .

[The article then considers in detail various "methodological strategies" that NGOs might adopt to investigate and confirm human rights violations.]

Emerging criteria for judging institutional credibility present especially difficult challenges for NGOs. Their concerns as advocacy organizations may prompt NGOs to take some actions, such as addressing essentially political contextual factors peculiar to a country or pressing for a ban on foreign aid to a government that violates human rights, that might jeopardize the organizations' appearance of political evenhandedness and disinterestedness. While such dilemmas cannot be eliminated — they are inherent in the advocacy nature of human rights organizations — NGOs should be mindful of the trade-offs entailed in some forms of advocacy, and take whatever measures they can to minimize the risks.

In 1986 two Dutch researchers carried out a survey of NGO reporting in the human rights field, based on the consideration of 340 NGO reports of fact-finding missions, of which 187 were studied in greater detail. A sense of the diversity of NGO practices is given in the study's conclusions and recommendations.

H. Thoolen and B. Verstappen, Human Rights Missions: A Study of the Fact-Finding Practice of Non-Governmental Organizations
133-135 (1986)

Only a minority of the reports contain a detailed programme or agenda, without making it clear that the absence of such information is related to security considerations.

In one-third of the reports there are indications that the programme of the mission could not be established or followed without governmental limitations. In 14 cases these restrictions took the form of straightforward interference, sometimes measures against the members of the delegation, sometimes against their contacts.

Information on the place where the records of the findings of the mission are stored, and under which conditions this information is available to those interested, is included in only very few reports.

The holding of preliminary missions seems to be an exceptional practice. Information not collected during the mission concerns mostly written or documentary information. The inclusion of such information (desk research) seems to be connected to the strength of the secretariat of the NGO. Oral information not collected during the mission is not often contained in the report, or is not identified as such.

Neither references to standards to be applied for establishing the facts and checking their veracity nor a description of a systemic practice on these points by the delegation could be deduced from the reports. Where procedural standards exist, it concerns mainly standards of proof applied during medical missions or other standards of a special character, which do not aspire to have general validity. . . .

RECOMMENDATIONS

NGO's have no reason to be reluctant in providing detail, whether it is with regard to the programme (showing the purposefulness of the mission), with regard to the circumstances under which the facts were collected, the sources or the methods of checking which were used.

Omissions of specific information on grounds of security are acceptable if done openly, and without making it a pretext for withholding other source relations.

Desk research forms an important element in a reliable report, and ought to be recognizable as such. NGO's with weak supporting secretarial services should perhaps involve (voluntary) support of more research-oriented institutions. These links, when established, could also provide a solution to the question of how public records of the mission's findings could be maintained.

Almost all reports contain oral information collected during the mission; in about half of the reports, mention is made of obtaining information by on-site visits or by gathering written and documentary evidence. Detailed information with regard to the circumstances under which the information was collected by the delegates is usually not provided.

The variety of the types of information can be considered large, although only about one-fourth of the reports does contain information based upon all types of sources which were distinguished.

The use of a large variety of different sources in the report does not seem to have a negative effect on the attribution of specific information to the sources upon which it is based. Even stronger, the more different sources are used, the more likely the report will provide precise information about those sources.

In a minority of the reports, mention is made of measures which were taken to protect sources which provided information to the mission. It mostly concerns prudence in providing the identities of witnesses and/or victims of human-rights violations.

The taking of such measures does not seem to lead to a general weakening of the attribution of information to sources. It even can be stated that the taking of protection measures goes together with a greater awareness of the importance of linking other information provided in the report to specific sources.

A rather low number of reports contains clear descriptions of the methods used for checking the information collected during on-site investigations. More often, the application of such methods had to be interpreted from the text of the report. The variety of methods used for checking during and after the mission is large; corroboration of sources and cross-checking seems to be practised most often.

That the debate over the NGO fact-finding methodology is no mere academic one is apparent from the following two readings, which are extracts from an exchange of correspondence concerning the methods used by an NGO fact-finding mission to Nicaragua at the height of the civil war between the U.S.-backed *contras* and the Sandinista government. The mission's conclusions were published in D. Fox and M. Glennon, Report to the International Human Rights Law Group and the Washington Office on Latin America Concerning Abuses Against Civilians and Counterrevolutionaries Operating in Nicaragua (1985), referred to in the readings as the Fox-Glennon Report. The fact-finding methods employed by the mission were the subject of a vigorous attack by Professor John Norton Moore and of an equally vigorous defense by Professor Michael Glennon.

Correspondence: Professor Moore
81 Am. J. Intl. L. 186, 192-195 (1987)

. . . [T]he procedures for the selection of persons interviewed about contra abuses do not fill one with confidence in view of the reported tactic of the Sandinistas to field "casual encounter" teams for foreign visitors and the existence of Sandinista-controlled Sandinista Defense Committees (SDCs) at the local level throughout Nicaragua. Apparently, 10 of the "over

36" witnesses were selected from Brody report affidavits already tainted by heavy involvement of the Nicaraguan Government. And unknown numbers of others, according to the Fox-Glennon report, "came to see us because they heard we were there." Although the authors say they did not reveal their itinerary, they do not indicate how it was selected and seem insensitive to the fact that their government driver could certainly know their whereabouts.

. . . [T]he procedures used to conduct the "investigation" were rudimentary at best. The investigators apparently spent no more than 4 days interviewing in the field, and while they say they sought to cross-check where possible, their report does not reveal what percentage of interviews relied on were cross-checked, what percentage of incidents discussed were corroborated through cross-checks, or what techniques were used to verify that those perpetrating incidents were in fact contras. A recent report by investigators at Berkeley who examined North Vietnamese human rights violations provides an instructive contrast in the specificity with which cross-check methodology is developed and discussed. In place of careful investigation techniques, the authors of the report, and Larry Garber in his letter,* rely heavily on an almost mystical assertion of a lawyer's alleged ability to find the facts through cross-examination. But, as any experienced lawyer knows, cross-examination is largely a technique used by an adverse party for impeaching a witness's testimony when contrary facts are known through previous investigation. How witnesses were to be reliably tested by nonadverse interviewers who had not conducted a full investigation of the alleged incidents remains a mystery. Moreover, almost none of the questions asked interviewees in this assertedly tough cross-examination are reproduced in the Fox-Glennon report. Similarly, the investigators apparently felt that they had adequately verified the controversial Brody report by interviewing 10 of some 146 persons interviewed by Brody. Again, the investigators seem unaware that the issue is less one of the existence of persons making statements than the accuracy of those statements and the existence of corroborative evidence of the underlying incidents, including the identity of the perpetrators. The crux of an investigation of human rights abuse in an area of high political controversy surely must be a careful cross-checking of incidents through multiple sources, rather than interviewing and counting of affidavits.

. . . [T]he reporting of the data is poor. As previously mentioned, it does not reveal all the questions asked by the interrogators or anything about the number of affidavits or incidents verified through cross-checks or how any such cross-checks were conducted. Eleven out of 25 of the attached affidavits conclude with a statement roughly to the effect that the

* Garber, Correspondence, 81 Am. J. Intl. L. 185 (1987). — Eds.

interviewee is a good Catholic and not a Communist. Since this is a rather startling coincidence, not only in content but also in location — and one coinciding with an obvious Sandinista public affairs theme — it suggests either an effort to manipulate the authors or a pattern of questioning by them that resembles leading questions more than rigorous cross-examination. Since at least one of the authors of the report in a conversation with me expressed doubts about the questioning of the other (a difference itself suggesting little advance thought or institutional input in critical methodology to the investigation), and since the report itself refers to the team's getting as a response to a question that the witness was Catholic, I will assume that the latter was true. Neither conclusion lends much confidence to the investigative process. Similarly, the report does not fully present to the reader any contrary views heard by the delegation. While the report in passing reveals that some interviewees were inclined to dismiss reports of contra atrocities, no affidavits from any such persons are included except for El Muerto, a contra leader interviewed in Tipitapa at the Modelo Prison who denied contra participation in abuses and whose statement is apparently disregarded by the authors. Although the affidavit of the Nicaraguan Deputy Minister of the Interior, Luis Carrión (accused by Baldizón of authorizing "special operations" to kill dissidents), is included, no affidavit is supplied from Cardinal Obando y Bravo, a leading critic of the Sandinistas with whom the delegation met. Even more significantly, the report only includes 25 affidavits out of "more than 36" interviews. Why some were omitted, and why no full transcripts of the interviews seem to have been made available, is not apparent. The report also does not reveal why no affidavits were included from the field investigations in Esteli and which of the included affidavits were from interviewees of the Brody investigation. A puzzling technical matter is that not all the dates on the affidavits coincide with the reported itinerary. . . .

Additional comparisons with the official U.S. observer mission to the Salvadoran presidential election further demonstrate the shortcomings of the Fox-Glennon report. Since an election observation mission is primarily to monitor the voting, it is not inappropriate for it to remain in the country only for that event and rely on secondary sources for characterization of preelection events. In contrast, there is no apparent reason for a serious investigation of contra human rights abuses that relies exclusively on events not observed by the delegation to confine itself to 4 days of field investigation. Moreover, the U.S. special mission to observe the presidential election in El Salvador did not rely on the Salvadoran Government; rather, it exclusively used transportation and facilities supplied by the United States Government, and arrangements were made through the United States Embassy. It should also be pointed out that the U.S. mission included an internationally known expert on the election process and did not purport to be anything other than an official United States government delegation. Contrary to the suggestion that my *Journal* article relies on questioning of Duarte to reveal his human rights record, the reference to the interview with Duarte appears in a footnote and is clearly cited only for the unexceptional proposition that *the United States delegation* was "impressed with the depth of Duarte's commitment" on human rights. Incidentally, Garber's account of the U.S. observation mission is factually inaccurate in numerous respects, but those inaccuracies, like his use of this very different mission as a comparison, are largely irrelevant. Even if the mission was not perfectly conceived, that would no more justify structural defects in an important human rights investigation than the argument that Sandinista human rights abuses justify contra abuses. That is, this argument of Garber, as all such arguments, is a paradigm of the logical fallacy known as a *non sequitur.*

The Fox-Glennon report cites as a reason the authors did not prepare a report on Sandinista abuses that their "sponsors also have monitored human rights developments in Nicaragua since the 1979 revolution." As far as I can ascertain, this "monitoring" by Larry Garber's International Human Rights Law Group has resulted in only two reports. One is cautiously critical of the Sandinistas for press censorship, while the other proclaims that the Sandinista elections were genuine. That is the same election in which mobs organized by the Government stoned Arturo Cruz, the principal non-Sandinista candidate. It should be recalled that the *New York Times* editorialized about the same elections that "only the naive believe" they were democratic and legitimating.

Most importantly for the future, if independent human rights organizations are effectively to implement their mandate for promoting human rights, they must toughen their standards of independence, evenhandedness, investigation and reporting. The Fox-Glennon report is a flawed report, but in that respect it may not be much different from many current efforts in the difficult Central American setting including, in this author's judgement, some of the Americas Watch reports. It is hoped that rather than seeking to stifle criticism, human rights organizations working on Central America will begin to police one another and to raise the level of independent human rights reporting generally. It is precisely because the stakes for human rights and world order are so high that we must accept no less.

Correspondence: Professor Glennon
81 Am. J. Intl. L. 393, 397-401 (1987)

. . . Moore maintains that the "procedures for the selection of persons interviewed" were unreliable. The problem, it appears, is nothing specific in either our selection criteria or the manner in which they were applied; the problem is that some Nicaraguan defector is reported to have claimed that some foreign visitors were intentionally exposed to certain Nicaraguans. But what exactly were his responsibilities for the Nicaraguan Government and what qualifies him to know this? What foreign visitors were involved? Where? When? Were they told lies? On what subjects? Moore, again, apparently has no idea — indeed, he candidly acknowledges that the fellow's statements "have not been independently cross-checked" by him — or, evidently, by anyone else.

. . . [W]e spent only 4 days in the field; after so little time, how can we really be so sure that the contras are doing these things? The question contains the answer: if in that relatively short period it is possible to encounter credible evidence of 16 murders, 44 kidnappings, one rape, and numerous instances of beatings and destruction of property, there is every reason to believe that those numbers could be extended — and extended substantially — by a longer investigation.

. . . [W]e do not quantify precisely our methodology; we do not, for example, say what percentage of interviews were cross-checked, or what percentage of incidents were cross-checked. Moore provides us with an "instructive" example in the "specificity with which cross-check methodology is developed and discussed": a study purporting to have calculated, through statistical techniques, the number of persons killed in Vietnam after the war ended. In fact, there is *no* quantification of cross-checking described anywhere in that report. The closest that the authors came is to indicate that "a substantial number" of victims were named by more than one person interviewed (all of whom were refugees): "A substantial number of our fully identified victims were named by more than one respondent, and were therefore duplicates. That diverse respondents independently reported the execution of the same individual gave us confidence in the reliability of our data." There is *no* indication as to "what percentage of interviews relied upon were cross-checked." There is *no* indication as to "what percentage of incidents discussed were corroborated through cross-checks." Moreover, there is no indication that any "techniques were used to verify that those perpetrating incidents" were actually officials of the Vietnamese Government. The authors openly admit that they simply *assumed* "that people who reported in convincing detail about persons who were incarcerated or executed were probably telling the truth." So far as I can see, they do not even use the word "cross-check." Although, as noted above, they describe statements that in some respects happened to be duplicative, *they do not claim to have made any special effort to cross-check so much as a single statement or a single incident.* An "instructive" model indeed!

I wish to be clear: I do not fault the "Vietnam blood bath" researchers for failing to quantify cross-checking. Standard human rights fact-finding techniques simply do not lend themselves to mathematically precise quantification of that sort. Statistical methods might provide specious support for a given study, but however easy it would be, such buttressing would be precisely that — specious. Statistics concerning these matters say nothing about the relationship of the persons interviewed to each other, their demeanor or credibility, the extent of their recall or basis of their knowledge. These and multiple other factors affect the weight that can be accorded their statements.

It thus will come as no surprise that none of the developing literature on the subject of on-site human rights investigations recommends such statistical smoke screens. Our report makes clear that we believed that any pretense of mathematical precision would inevitably be misleading — and that analogical verbal formulations were similarly suspect. We rejected, for example, any use of the term "pattern" in reference to violations. It is "unclear," we said, "what level of frequency is required before a high level of frequency is properly called a 'pattern,' or before a pattern is called a 'consistent pattern.'" We acknowledged that the methodology employed could not "provide knowledge to a certainty," but only a "level of probabilit[y]":

> How frequently do such abuses occur? There are in general two methods of seeking to determine whether a "pattern" exists of these sorts of violations. The first is to canvass all available evidence — in this case, to interview everyone alleging some abuse by the Contras, and to delve thoroughly into the facts related by those interviews. This kind of comprehensive review is the only way of knowing with certainty whether an actual pattern exists. It obviously was not possible to conduct such a review in the period of one week we spent in Nicaragua.
>
> The second method is to gather as much information as possible, to make reasonable efforts to distinguish between probative and non-probative evidence, and to draw reasonable inferences from the evidence that appears probative. This method does not produce knowledge to a certainty; it merely alleges varying levels of probabilities, depending upon the care with which each stage of the investigatory process is conducted. The limited time and amount of resources available made it necessary to employ this second, inferential method. *We have framed our conclusions accordingly, using concepts such as the "rebuttable presumption," "prima facie," and "shifting the burden of persuasion" to reflect the measure of reliability we believe those conclusions merit.*

(I comment below on this important element, which Moore understandably ignores altogether; namely, the calibration of the findings to reflect the level of exactness afforded by the methodology. It is worth underscoring that investigatory findings need not be binary, that a report need not be painted only in blacks and whites, and that there are such things as qualification and nuance — with which this particular report happens to be filled.)

. . . Moore faults our questioning of witnesses. One of his criticisms is that our questions are not included in the report. The "instructive" Vietnam blood-bath study from which Moore learned so much contains not a single interviewer's question. We excluded our questions, as well as some statements, because our sponsors did not have the financial resources to reproduce every interview conducted over the course of our investigation.

Moore, however, infers sinister designs and jumps reflexively to a conspiracy theory: statements concerning membership in the Catholic Church or the Communist Party are evidence of manipulation by those orchestrating the "Sandinista public affairs" campaign. The truth is that I asked all the persons we interviewed, or just about all, about their religion and politics, and those comments were their responses.

With respect to the exclusion of witness statements, we applied, as indicated above, a standard of materiality. We included some in the report because the words of the victims seemed to us to have a certain poignancy that would be lost in a sterile summary. Few human rights reports include *any* witness statements, let alone questions; they consist entirely of paraphrases and synopses. The Vietnam blood-bath piece does not set forth a single entire statement. It contains only two- or three-sentence excerpts from about a dozen witness statements — out of a total of 615 refugees interviewed. No "contrary" statement is included. Again, I do not object; I assume that the authors thought, as we did, that the inclusion of a few witness statements would give readers a sense of the horror experienced by real people with real names.

In sum, the growing body of literature on human rights fact-finding is all but devoid of any support for Moore's apparent belief that all witness statements, including questions, should have been included in their entirety. Nor, for that matter, does the literature provide any support for his protests concerning nonquantification. Our report comports fully, for example, with the Belgrade Minimal Rules of Procedure for International Human Rights Fact-finding Missions, which in this regard require only that "the mission's report should contain the findings of the majority as well as any views of dissenting members." The Belgrade Rules do not suggest the desirability of including witness statements, let alone interviewers' questions. Our report also is in complete accord with apposite provisions of the Draft Rules of Procedure Suggested by the UN Secretary-General for *Ad Hoc* bodies of the United Nations Entrusted with Studies of Particular Situations Alleged to Reveal a Consistent Pattern of Violations of Human Rights. In short, our report includes each of the "matters [usually] covered in the reports of fact-finding bodies dealing with [particular] situations."

One means of approaching the problem of identifying standards for NGO fact-finding would be simply to apply the Belgrade Rules (supra at pages 449-451) to NGOs, although the Rules were intended to apply only to the activities of IGOs. However, as the following reading points out, there are important differences between NGO and IGO fact-finding, and it may be difficult to apply the same standards to both. The reading also summarizes the conclusions of a 1983 conference, which remain relevant to contemporary discussions. Some additional recommendations are offered in the second reading.

H. Thoolen and B. Verstappen, Human Rights Missions: A Study of the Fact-Finding Practice of Non-Governmental Organizations
24-26, 31-32 (1986)

1.6 Procedures for Non-Governmental Organizations

INTRODUCTION: NGO VERSUS IGO

The last decade has witnessed an increase in NGO fact-finding activities, including on-site investigations. This increase has not been accompanied by due procedural accounting, contrary to the development of IGO fact-finding, where a substantial number of procedural standards have been elaborated.

This does however not imply that there would be no need for procedural standards for NGO fact-finding missions. By paying more attention to procedural aspects, NGO's should be able to engage themselves in fact-finding which will lead to a higher degree of verifiability and reliability of findings and more objective conclusions. This will enhance the credibility of the NGO. Criticized governments, intergovernmental organizations concerned with human rights and public opinion will take the results of fact-finding efforts more seriously.

To use the words of Franck and Fairley once more: "Since the efficacy of fact-finding rests so largely on credibility, and credibility emanates primarily from manifest integrity of process, sound procedures are not merely desirable but a functional prerequisite."

A central question is whether and to what extent the existing procedural standards for on-site investigations by IGO's can be applied to NGO fact-finding. When taking account of the different contexts in which the fact-finding activities of both types of organizations take place, there seem to be good reasons to be hesitant in doing so.

The mandate of most IGO's covers more than human rights, and the conduct of human-rights fact-finding missions is but a small part of their activities. On the other hand, NGO fact-finding usually is conducted within the framework of an organization that is entirely or to a large degree concerned with the issue of human rights. Generally, in IGO fact-finding the divergence between the fact-finding body and the initiating organization is often somewhat greater.

NGO's lack the resources available to IGO's. It is assumed that they feel stronger financial restraints, are more limited in their staff, mostly have less members on a mission, and usually can't afford to send a mission for several weeks, or provide it with staff for secretarial and interpretation activities. In addition, as NGO's have no diplomatic channels and contacts at their disposal, answers to questions or requests for appointments with the government may suffer considerable delay.

A distinction between IGO and NGO fact-finding, frequently said to be of considerable impact, is that IGO fact-finding emerges within intergovernmental context. IGO fact-finding missions are based on cooperation between governments within the framework of the IGO, and therefore should have less problems in getting access to the territory of a member state. This distinction is correct but does not take into account that NGO's operate on a much more informal basis than IGO's. IGO missions are "heavier" because two entities of a governmental character are meeting. Such missions are conducted at a formal governmental level, official contacts (protocol) are much more preponderant than in NGO fact-finding. NGO's can be more flexible in the conduct of their investigations. They do not have to wait for lengthy diplomatic negotiations, but can send observers in their personal capacity or even "as tourists." Besides, if IGO missions should have less problems in getting access to the territory of a member state, the question can be raised what price had to be paid for that access during preliminary negotiations with the government concerned. Thus, the basic distinction between IGO and NGO fact-finding concerning the cooperation of the government concerned, could be of less importance than one would be inclined to accept at first sight.

Differences between IGO and NGO fact-finding seem to lie in the fields of:

— the difference in the mandate of the sending organization, and, related to this, the difference in objectives for sending a mission.

— the difference in the way in which the decision to send a fact-finding mission is taken. For IGO fact-finding, this is often a lengthy process, in which strong account has to be taken of the extreme sensitivity of governments to foreign intrusion in their internal affairs, especially in the field of human rights. Also NGO's will often establish advance contacts with the government concerned, but in general this is a less complex undertaking.

— the difference in the relationship between the sending organ and the members of the mission.

— the relatively limited availability of expertise, time and financial resources of NGO's.

— the amount of cooperation of the government concerned, and the facilities which it is required or willing to give.

— the formal character of IGO fact-finding versus the informal character of NGO fact-finding. NGO's will often have better opportunities to make use of informal contacts in advance of the mission and in the country to be visited.

— more generally speaking and taking all this into account, there seems to be a strong need for a greater amount of flexibility in NGO fact-finding guidelines.

In general, it does not seem possible for NGO's to simply adopt IGO procedures as a whole. Nevertheless, the considerable fact-finding experience of IGO's should be considered and utilized by NGO's where appropriate. In particular to the extent that NGO's seek to influence government conduct in the area of human rights, IGO procedural rules and guidelines may be instructive and helpful to NGO's. . . .

THE SIM FACT-FINDING CONFERENCE

In June 1983, the Netherlands Institute of Human Rights (SIM), an NGO based in Utrecht, organized a conference on fact-finding and specialized research in the field of human rights. Having in mind the existing lack of procedures for NGO fact-finding missions, the conference focused primarily on fact-finding by NGO's. The above mentioned IGO rules and NGO studies were the main topic of discussion by over 40 participants from all parts of the world, of both intergovernmental and non-governmental organizations.

It was generally accepted that more detailed guidelines could be expected from IGO's than from NGO's. Nevertheless, it was agreed that there existed sufficient resemblance between IGO and NGO fact-finding to identify certain basic principles.

Main conclusion of the conference was that, taking into account the diverse and rich experience of human-rights fact-findings, it will not be easy to establish fixed rules for human-rights fact-finding activities. Therefore, no universally agreed and at the same time precise rules were likely to be established on the short term.

The summary report by David Weissbrodt provides a broad framework within which it is strongly advised that fact-finding is conducted; this framework is based on the experience of both IGO's and NGO's, as well as individual expertise. The main features of this framework are:

— the members of the mission should be independent, objective and impartial.

— guidelines should be established by the sending NGO or the members of the mission.

— the reports should contain terms of reference and a description of working methods.

— the terms of reference should provide a reasonably clear objective for the fact-finding effort, but might also include a catch-all omnibus clause to provide some flexibility.

— mission delegates should be carefully selected, the relevant considerations including capacities and experience of the members and various aspects of the situation and country under investigation.

— organizations should inform the government of the country to be visited of the terms of reference and members of the mission.

— within the framework of its terms of reference and guidelines, fact-finders should be free to receive, test and evaluate evidence from diverse sources available. The way in which this is done must be explained in the report if not otherwise available.

— in evaluating evidence, reference should be made to relevant articles of international human-rights law.

— the sending NGO should give the government concerned a reasonable opportunity to comment upon the substance of the report, or at least the report should be made available to the government concerned just prior to the publication.

— unless otherwise provided in the terms of reference or guidelines, the report might include conclusions, advices, and/or recommendations.

— the organizations should have the responsibility to consider what follow-up is required, including the publicity for the report. The way of presentation of the report and the issuing of a summary or press release might be considered. NGO reports should be distributed broadly to governments, IGO's and NGO's.

Hannum, Fact-Finding by Non-Governmental Human Rights Organizations
in Fact-Finding Before International Tribunals 293, 301-303
(R. Lillich ed. 1992)

As noted above, there has been no consensus among NGOs on the minimum requirements for accurate fact-finding, although most would no doubt share the ideal aspirations expressed in various formulations designed to guide potential fact-finders. Nevertheless, there do seem to be several practices that would enable observers better to judge the reliability and accuracy of NGO press releases, statements, and reports.

First, every comprehensive NGO report on a particular country should include a clear statement both of the scope of the report (human rights in general? only violations of humanitarian law? only violations by the government? only a specific category of violations?) and of its methodology. Beyond the common practice of listing meetings and interviews, a full statement of the sources for other materials and the particular assistance offered by any other NGOs should be offered. If a report is based on an on-site mission, fuller information should be provided about the mission members and their expertise (beyond a mere listing of names and titles). The person who actually prepared the report should be identified, even if it is ultimately the responsibility of the NGO.

Second, particularly in those situations where an NGO is performing a watchdog or early-warning function rather than claiming to present well-documented facts, the source(s) of the information must be clear, unless there is a legitimate fear of reprisals. The distinction between NGOs as watchdogs and NGOs as impartial fact-finders should be maintained with greater clarity, and neither function will necessarily suffer as a result.

Third, the distinction between NGOs as fact-finders and NGOs as political advocates must be deepened. No U.S.-based NGO escaped confusing these issues in dealing with Central America, and each was hurt whenever a political opponent looking for bias could find it. A few organizations successfully manage both functions; Amnesty International, for example, has generally been able to keep its advocacy of fair trials and abolition of the death penalty separate from its more factual conclusions as to the human rights situation of particular persons or countries.

Fourth, NGO fact-finding will continue to be seen as biased against governments unless NGOs are willing, where appropriate, to support unpopular causes, *i.e.*, governments and government supporters. Given its early and vocal criticism of the human rights practices of the South Korean government, for example, the fact that an election observer team of the International Human Rights Law Group found the 1987 South Korean elections to be essentially fair — although the pro-government candidate won — contributed significantly to the recognition of the legitimacy of that election. NGOs may occasionally forget that the protection of human rights is largely concerned with defending the political process or the rights of individuals; it does not legitimize the preference of outside observers for one political or economic system over another.

Despite the lack of common fact-finding procedures, despite the occasional (and unavoidable) confusion of advocacy and reporting, human rights NGOs have, as a group, enjoyed a remarkable degree of credibility and trust. While allegations of political bias or "softness" towards countries of a particular political persuasion continue to be made against human rights groups, there are no important examples of countries being unfairly targeted for attack on human rights grounds. Given the increasing use of the phrase "human rights" by any group that disagrees with government policy, this record is all the more impressive.

F.   Fact-Finding by Judicial and Quasi-Judicial Bodies

In the Anglo-American legal system, judicial bodies typically play only a passive role in fact-finding. It is the task of the parties to a lawsuit to gather the evidence and then present it to the court — often, of course, in contradictory versions — which will then proceed to evaluate it and render a decision. Courts and juries, then, are triers, not finders, of fact. In civil law systems of justice, the position is significantly different. There the judicial authorities participate in the investigation of the facts, by means of such institutions as a body of examining magistrates. Since the judiciary, in this kind of system, does not merely passively receive information presented to it, but actively inquires into the facts itself, the process is said to be "inquisitorial" in character (in contrast to the "adversarial" character of the Anglo-American system).

This civil law approach has exercised an important influence over the international legal system, including the human rights sphere. Accordingly, a number of international bodies of a judicial or quasi-judicial nature possess fact-finding, as well as adjudicatory, functions. The International Court of Justice, for example, is authorized by Article 50 of its Statute to "entrust any individual, body, bureau, commission, or other organization . . . with the task of carrying out an enquiry. . . ." So far, the Court has not had occasion to make use of this fact-finding power in the human rights field, but it is possible that it may find some occasion to do so in the future.

There are many international human rights bodies with fact-finding capabilities, although (with the exception of the two regional courts) most would be described as only quasi-judicial in character. All fact-finding procedures are based on specific grants of authority contained within the treaties establishing the various bodies, but even similar treaty language may lead to quite different practices.

At the universal level, the Human Rights Committee is mandated to "consider communications received under the . . . [Optional] Protocol in the light of all written information made available to it by the individual [submitting the communication] and by the State Party concerned." Thus far, the Committee has relied exclusively on written submissions in determining its "views" on the merits of allegations; it has apparently not attempted to gather facts independently, nor has it held oral hearings on any case.

The Committee Against Torture is authorized under Article 20 of the Convention Against Torture and Other Cruel, Inhuman or Degrading Treatment or Punishment to appoint one of its members to undertake a "confidential inquiry" whenever it "receives reliable information which appears to it to contain well-founded indications that torture is being systematically practised." The Committee "shall seek the co-operation of the State Party concerned," but no on-site visit may be undertaken without the specific consent of the state. Such a visit to Turkey was made in 1992.

The fact-finding practices of regional human rights bodies vary considerably and are discussed in greater detail in Problems IX and X, but a brief summary may be appropriate here. The European Commission on Human Rights may "take any action which it considers expedient or necessary for the proper performance of its duties," and it has conducted on-site investigations, heard witnesses both at the Commission's seat in Strasbourg and elsewhere, and invited individuals and states to participate in oral arguments. States "shall furnish all necessary facilities" for the Commission's investigation. The European Court of Human Rights does not seem to be prohibited from independent fact-finding, but, in practice, it has limited itself to reviewing documentary evidence and considering oral and written submissions by the parties and amici curiae. As it stated in a recent case, "[u]nder the Convention system, the establishment and verification of the facts is primarily a matter for the Commission. Accordingly, it is only in exceptional circumstances that the Court will use its powers in this area." Stocké v. Germany, Judgment of 19 Mar. 1991, Ser. A No. 199, slip op. at 14 (1991).

The oversight committee established by the European Convention on the Protection of Detainees from Torture and from Cruel, Inhuman or Degrading Treatment or Punishment is entitled to visit places of detention in the member states on both a periodic and an ad hoc basis. The general rule is that states parties have no right to prevent such visits, although in certain exceptional cases the state concerned may consult with the committee "in order to clarify the situation and seek agreement on arrangements to enable the Committee to exercise its functions expeditiously." (The Convention does not specify what happens if such an agreement is not reached.) The normal procedure, however, is that the committee simply notifies the state of its intention to carry out a visit, during which it is to have unlimited access to places of detention and detained persons. See Cassese, A New Approach to Human Rights: The European Convention for the Prevention of Torture, 83 Am. J. Intl. L. 128 (1989); pages 762-765 of Problem IX.

The Inter-American Commission on Human Rights has a broad mandate to investigate individual complaints as well as human rights conditions in a particular country, and it has engaged in a wide range of fact-finding activities. Article 66 of the Commission's Regulations enables it to hold oral hearings either in connection with a communication alleging human rights violations or "in order to receive information of a general or particular nature related to the situation of human rights in one State or in a group of American states." With respect to states that are parties to the American Convention on Human Rights, Article 48 of the Convention and Article 44 of the Regulations permit the Commission to conduct an on-site investigation "[i]f necessary and advisable . . . for the effective conduct of which it shall request, and the States concerned shall furnish to it, all necessary facilities." Non-parties to the American Convention must give specific permission for an on-site investigation, but, once permission is given, states are subject to the same obligation to furnish "all necessary facilities . . . and not to take any reprisals of any kind" against persons who cooperate with or provide information to the Commission. See Vargas Carreno, Visits on the Spot: The Experience of the Inter-American Commission on Human Rights, in International Law and Fact-Finding in the Field of Human Rights 137 (B. Ramcharan ed. 1982).

The Inter-American Court of Human Rights, created under the American Convention, has interpreted its fact-finding role more broadly than has the European Court of Human Rights. Article 34 of the Inter-American Court's Rules of Procedure permits it to "obtain any evidence which it considers likely to clarify the facts of the case." This includes hearing any witness or expert witness, requesting the production of evidence, authorizing any person or authority to obtain evidence for the Court, and designating one of its members "to conduct an inquiry, carry out an investigation on the spot or take evidence in some other manner." The Court may convene a session in the territory of a state with the state's prior consent.

Finally, the African Charter on Human and Peoples' Rights authorizes the African Commission to "resort to any appropriate method of investigation" and, in general, to "hear from the Secretary General of the Organization of African Unity or any other person capable of enlightening it." The African Commission is authorized to prepare confidential factual reports in response to interstate complaints or, in very restricted circumstances, with respect to "special cases which reveal the existence of a series of serious or massive violations" of rights, but as of mid-1994 there had been no indication that these fact-finding powers had ever been exercised.

Of course, whatever formal fact-finding procedures may be followed, there is no substitute for intelligence and a bit of good luck, as shown by the following experience of a staff member of the Inter-American Commission on Human Rights. The incident occurred while the Commission was preparing its 1980 report on the situation of human rights in Argentina.

T. Buergenthal, R. Norris, and D. Shelton, Protecting Human Rights in the Americas, Selected Problems
299-301 (3d ed. 1990)

According to the Executive Secretary of the Commission, the government of Argentina had declared that there were no political prisoners in Córdoba. Therefore, during the course of the visit, I was not to visit the Cárcel Penitenciaria in that city; however, I had requested by liaison with the Ministry of Foreign Affairs to provide me with a list of all the prisoners held in the provinces of Córdoba and Tucamán.

Upon arriving in Córdoba on September 7, I arranged to speak with the Minister of Government of that Province with regard to my mission and to the plans I would make for the visit of two Members of the Inter-American Commission scheduled to arrive several days later. I explained that we had no plans to visit the penitentiary, but that Commissioners often changed their minds and we should be aware of that possibility. On the basis of previous experience, I described very briefly our normal procedure for visiting jails and other detention centers. The Members would meet with the prison authorities for a briefing, prior to a tour of the locale. They would be interested in interviewing any prisoners who might have a case before the Commission, and they would probably select several prisoners at random for personal interviews with regard to prison conditions. Those interviews would take place in private, and the Members of the Commission might require a temporary office for the purpose. I reminded him that I had requested an alphabetized list of the prisoners in the Province of Córdoba and would need it as soon as possible.

As I conducted interviews with petitioners during the next few days I was informed of the names of several persons who were allegedly being held in the Cárcel Penitenciaria for political reasons. Without mentioning this information, I called the Minister of Government to advise him that the Members would visit the prison and would need the list previously requested.

When the list finally arrived, I carefully went over the names, searching for the "political" cases reportedly detained at the penitentiary. One fact stood out; not one of those names was on the list! I then called a private individual who I knew could make contact with one of the prisoners and asked him to try to obtain a list of all the persons held in the same cellblock. He was only partially successful; he could not get all the names, but he did bring back several, along with the exact number of men and women being held there. Again I checked the list and none of those names were on it. It was an exciting moment; I had a "gut feeling" that some of those people were "disappeared", and the mission had yet to uncover any of the thousands of people who had been abducted and literally dropped from sight. I was afraid at the same time that someone might tip the authorities off and the prisoners would be moved before the visit of the Commissioners.

The prisoners sent word through my contact that they were worried about the confidentiality of the interviews. They were afraid of being overheard, and they were also afraid that the government might take advantage of the announced visit to send a "fake party", as it had allegedly done in that prison some months before under the guise of a Red Cross visit.

I replied, again through the contact, that I would bring plenty of paper and pens in my briefcase so they would not have to talk. They would be sure that it was an official visit by the Commission by asking "Are you Dr. . . . ?" My only reply would be to take out my official OAS passport and show them. Any verbal reply should put them on guard.

When the Members of the Commission did arrive, I briefed them on the situation and provided them with a memorandum on how we should proceed if they wished to visit the penitentiary. They accepted and asked me to finalize the arrangements.

On September 13, I accompanied Professor Carlos Dunshee de Abranches (Brazil) and Dr. Luis Tinoco Castro (Costa Rica) to the penitentiary. In our preliminary briefing by the Director of the prison, Professor Abranches asked for a general explanation of prison rules affecting the inmates. When the Director had finished speaking about visiting rights, Professor Abranches inquired whether all prisoners had the same rights. The reply was affirmative. He then noted that, "according to Dr. . . . [the staff member] there is a sign in one part of the prison which refers to "special prisoners". "We have a complete list of the names of those prisoners, eleven women and thirty-one men, but it is an unofficial list, and we would like to have an official list before we visit that cellblock."

We had no such list, of course, but the fact we knew the exact number must have convinced them that we did. The Director turned to one of his assistants and asked: "Didn't you give them a list of the special prisoners?" "No, sir." "Oh, I see. You didn't give them a list of the special prisoners!"

There followed a long moment of silence. Professor Abranches interrupted: "Since there are only a few names involved, we will simply wait here while the list is prepared." The Director then asked an assistant to bring a list. It only required a few minutes as a list was apparently brought from a file in another room. I could hardly believe my eyes. It was a bonanza, containing not only the names, but under whose disposition. Only seven had been presented before a court of law. Many of the others were at the orders of special councils of war, meaning they were being held indefinitely. Most were held by executive decree, but three were at the orders of the local military commandant. Those three had "disappeared" in the typical fashion just a month before!

When we reached the women's section, we asked to be allowed behind the bars into a large area which served as a dining hall. On the other side of the dining area was a long corridor with tiny cells on either side. We asked that the prisoners be released from their cells, and the Director complied. Not all of the women were accounted for. Professor Abranches shouted down the corridor: "Is anyone else there?" We heard a scream "We're here, we're here" and a hand emerged from a small opening in the door of the very last cell on the right. We had "found" two disappeared persons — Irma Cristina Guillen de Palazzesi and Stella Maria Palazzesi de Cavigliasso. The other women later told us that they had been warned not to mention the presence of the two prisoners being held incommunicado. They were not allowed to talk to them at all.

We left Dr. Tinoco to talk to the women and we continued with the Director to the men's section upstairs. There was another surprise in store. Professor Abranches told the prison officials, "Now that we are here, we'll just stay in the cellblock and interview the prisoners here." "But you can use my office; it's all prepared," blurted the Director. "Tell us who you want to see, and we'll take him to the office where you'll have all the facilities necessary." "No, thank you very much," said Professor Abranches, "we'll stop and see you on the way out!"

Again, we had the prisoners released from their cells, into the dining area, which was also behind bars. The guards withdrew, I brought out the paper and pens and explained what type of information we wanted. When everyone had finished, I took a small tape recorder from my briefcase, chose a cell at random, and interviewed a group of prisoners on general prison conditions.

III.   Evaluating the Facts

A.   *Admissibility of Evidence*

The gathering of facts is an important — and sometimes, as we have seen, controversial — activity. Once it is done, some difficult problems can still remain. How should one evaluate the *significance* of the data that have been obtained?

Lawyers are accustomed to working with rules of evidence, which determine when facts or allegations of facts are admissible in a court of law. In international human rights law, however, the purpose of gathering the evidence is not necessarily to present it to a judicial body. Often the purpose is to disseminate the findings as widely as possible, with a view to rousing public opinion. Is it, then, possible to devise rules as to the admissibility of evidence in the area of human rights fact-finding? If so, then what should they be?

The simple answer seems to be that international human rights bodies are not particularly concerned with formal rules of evidence. Of course, treaties may impose limitations on the kind of evidence that may be considered, for example, by prohibiting the use of information submitted anonymously, but otherwise international bodies enjoy an unfettered right to consider any evidence they consider relevant. The European Court of Human Rights has probably stated the general rule followed by all intergovernmental human rights fact-finding bodies:

> The Court is not bound, under the [European] Convention or under the general principles applicable to international tribunals, by strict rules of evidence. In order to satisfy itself, the Court is entitled to rely on evidence of every kind, including, in so far as it deems them relevant, documents or statements emanating from Governments, be they respondent or applicant, or from their institutions or officials. . . . [T]he Court, being master of its own procedure and of its own rules . . . , has complete freedom in assessing not only the admissibility and the relevance but also the probative value of each item of evidence before it.

Ireland v. United Kingdom, European Court of Human Rights, Judgment of 18 January 1978, Ser. A. No. 25, ¶¶209, 210.

B.   *The Burden of Proof*

One of the most crucial problems of evaluating evidence is determining by what standard the allegations are to be judged as proved? Who has the burden of proof, and what must be done to discharge it? Should proof be required beyond a reasonable doubt, as in the domestic criminal-law system of the United States? Or is proof according to a preponderance of the evidence (i.e., a "more probable than not" standard) sufficient? Or should the burden of proof merely be stated to be whatever the fact-finder finds persuasive under the circumstances? Should the standard of proof be the same for NGOs as for IGOs?

The following readings deal with various aspects of the burden-of-proof question. The first one considers the matter from a general perspective. The next three excerpts offer the views of international bodies on the burdens of proof that they adopt. The final reading discusses the standard of proof applied by NGOs.

It might be noted that Article 42 of the Regulations of the Inter-American Commission on Human Rights provides that "[t]he facts reported in the petition whose pertinent parts have been transmitted to the government of the State in reference shall be presumed to be true if, during the maximum period . . . [provided for the government's reply], the government has not provided the pertinent information, as long as other evidence does not lead to a different conclusion."

Ramcharan, Evidence
in International Law and Fact-Finding in the Field of Human Rights 64, 77-80 (B. Ramcharan ed. 1982)

V.   The Burden and Standard of Proof

The burden of persuasion of a fact means the burden which is discharged when the tribunal which is to determine the existence or non-existence of the fact is persuaded by sufficient evidence to find that the fact exists. The burden of producing evidence of a fact means the burden which is discharged when sufficient evidence is introduced to support a finding that the fact exists. According to one source, fact-finding bodies enjoy considerable flexibility on matters such as the burden and standard of proof: "the question of burden of proof and the degree of probability required to establish facts is obviously of some importance. In some cases the Commission was able to make firm findings on facts . . . ; in others it was only able to form a view on a balance of probabilities . . . ; and in others it was unable to reach a definite conclusion. . . . A court or arbitral tribunal, in considering such points, might well have to decide that the burden of proof lay on one or other party and then decide the issue according to whether the burden of proof so found had been satisfied. A Commission of Inquiry is freer in this respect." The flexible approach here suggested is supported in the practice of the European Court of Human Rights. In its Judgement in the Case of Ireland against the United Kingdom (1978), the Court, dealing directly with 'questions of proof', stated: In order to satisfy itself as to the existence or not in Northern Ireland of practices contrary to Article 3, the

Court will not rely on the concept that the burden of proof is borne by one or other of the two Governments concerned. In the cases referred to it, the Court examines all the material before it, whether originating from the Commission, the Parties or other sources, and if necessary, obtains material *proprio motu*. However, upon the establishment of a *prima facie* case that breaches of human rights have occurred, a burden of proof may rest upon the Government concerned to show that this was not the case. In its views delivered in November 1979, on communication No. 2/9, the Human Rights Committee decided "to base its views on . . . facts which have either been essentially confirmed by the State Party or are unrepudiated or uncontested except for denials of a general character offering no particular information or explanations" and added that "the state party has adduced no evidence that [the complainant's] allegations of ill treatment have been duly investigated in accordance with the laws. . . . A refutation of these allegations in general terms is not enough. The State Party should investigate the allegations in accordance with its laws." Similarly, in its views delivered in May 1980 on communication No. 2/8, the Committee stated that "specific responses and pertinent evidence (including copies of the relevant decisions of the courts and findings of any investigations which have taken place into the validity of the complaints made) in reply to the contentions of the author of a communication are required. The Government did not furnish the Committee with such information. Consequently, the Committee cannot but draw appropriate conclusions on the basis of the information before it."

Turning to the standard of proof, the American Law Institute Model Code of Evidence provided that "wherever 'finds' is used in these rules, it is the equivalent of 'finds by a preponderance of the evidence. . . .' 'Preponderance of evidence' means evidence of greater convincing force. . . . Obviously no trier can know what is the historical fact when there is a dispute about it; all that the trier can do is to find where the preponderance of probability lies." As a general rule the standard of proof applied by fact-finding bodies should be a balance of probabilities. Probability in this sense may be defined as an evaluation of the likelihood of a past event having happened, given the facts and assumptions expected or adopted for the purposes of the evaluation. However, in certain adversarial contexts, the standard "beyond all reasonable doubt may be applied." In the Greek Case as well as in the case of Ireland v. the United Kingdom, the European Commission on Human Rights adopted the standard "beyond reasonable doubt." However, in the latter case, the Irish Government argued before the European Court of Human Rights that this was an excessively rigid standard. The Court agreed with the Commission's approach and adopted the standard "beyond reasonable doubt" but added that "such proof may follow from the co-existence of sufficiently strong, clear and concordant inferences or of similar unrebutted presumptions of fact. In this context, the conduct of the Parties when evidence is being obtained has to be taken into account."

VI. Evaluation

Cogency, according to Nokes, includes the credibility of witnesses, the reliability of documents, the inferences to be drawn from things and the effect of the evidence as to the facts in issue generally. It depends partly on rules of law or practice, but largely upon general considerations of probability. It may be stated as a general principle that the evaluation of evidence is a matter that rests exclusively within the competence of the fact-finding body. . . .

In its comments on the report of the former Ad Hoc Working Group on the Situation of Human Rights in Chile which was submitted to the thirty-first session of the General Assembly the Chilean Government complained among other things that the Working Group had "no criteria for weighing the value of evidence." Replying to this point, the Working Group stated in its next report that it had been following precisely the standard suggested by the Chilean Government, namely, it had been "appraising how much truth there is in information received, so as to discard whatever is false or exaggerated or serves only the special purposes of the person making the statement." The Group recalled that, as a general principle, the probative force of evidence presented is a question for the fact-finding body and referred to the pronouncement of the Permanent Court of International Justice in the case concerning German Interests in Polish Upper Silesia, in which the Permanent Court declared that it was "entirely free to estimate the value of statements made by the Parties."

VII. Conclusions

The conclusions reached in the present chapter may be summarized as follows:

(1) the rules of evidence applicable to any fact-finding exercise depend in the first place upon any relevant provisions in the constitutive instrument initiating the exercise. If the constitutive instrument gives the fact-finding body the power to draw up its own rules of procedure, then the fact-finding exercise will be governed by such rules of evidence as are included in the rules of procedure.

(2) In the absence of any, or sufficiently express, provisions in the constitutive instrument, fact-finding bodies should be guided by the following general principles, both in drawing up their rules of procedure and in their practical operations:

(a) The standard of proof is usually a "balance of probability." Probability in this sense may be defined as an evaluation of the likelihood of a past event having happened, given the facts and assumptions expected or adopted for the purposes of the evaluation. However, in adversarial contexts, the standard "beyond all reasonable doubt" may be applied.

(b) Fact-finding exercises in the field of human rights often being more inquisitorial than adversarial there is usually no onus or burden of proof upon any particular complainant. However, upon the establishment of a *prima facie* case that breaches of human rights have occurred, a burden of proof may rest upon the government concerned to show that this was not the case or that government agents were not responsible for such violations.

(c) Flexible admissibility criteria should be applied. A fact-finding body is free to employ for enlightening itself all the kinds of evidence that it deems necessary. It has the unlimited right of admitting all methods of proof that may be considered in conscience as sufficient and necessary.

(d) As regards the communication of evidence to the government concerned, a fact-finding body should, as a general rule, communicate to the government concerned for its comments such evidence as it may receive. However, it always possesses a discretion as to whether or not to communicate a particular piece of evidence to the government, and may decide not to do so, in order to protect the source of information or to protect other persons from reprisals.

(e) As regards the evaluation of evidence this is a matter that rests exclusively within the competence of the fact-finding body, or after it has submitted its report, upon its parent organ (if any).

Bleier v. Uruguay

Human Rts. Comm., Views of 29 Mar. 1982, Communication
No. 30/1978, Report of the Human Rts. Comm., 37 U.N.
GAOR Supp. (No. 40), Annex X, at 130, 135, U.N. Doc.
A/37/40 (1982), reprinted in 2 Y.B. Human Rts. Comm. 1981-
1982, at 396, 398 (1989)

13.3. With regard to the burden of proof, this cannot rest alone on the author of the communication, especially considering that the author and the State party do not always have equal access to the evidence and that frequently the State party alone has access to relevant information. It is implicit in article 4, paragraph 2, of the Optional Protocol that the State party has the duty to investigate in good faith all allegations of violation of the Covenant made against it and its authorities, especially when such allegations are corroborated by evidence submitted by the author of the communication, and to furnish to the Committee the information available to it. In cases where the author has submitted to the Committee allegations supported by substantial witness testimony, as in this case, and where further clarification of the case depends on information exclusively in the hands of the State party, the Committee may consider such allegations as substantiated in the absence of satisfactory evidence and explanations to the contrary submitted by the State party.

The Velásquez Rodriguez Case
Inter-Am. Ct. Hum. Rts.; Judgment of 29 July 1988, Ser. C
No. 4, at 133-136

122. Before weighing the evidence, the Court must address some questions regarding the burden of proof and the general criteria considered in its evaluation and finding of the facts in the instant proceeding.

123. Because the Commission is accusing the Government of the disappearance of Manfredo Velásquez, it, in principle, should bear the burden of proving the facts underlying its petition.

124. The Commission's argument relies upon the proposition that the policy of disappearances, supported or tolerated by the Government, is designed to conceal and destroy evidence of disappearances. When the existence of such a policy or practice has been shown, the disappearance of a particular individual may be proved through circumstantial or indirect evidence or by logical inference. Otherwise, it would be impossible to prove that an individual has been disappeared.

125. The Government did not object to the Commission's approach. Nevertheless, it argued that neither the existence of a practice of disappearances in Honduras nor the participation of Honduran officials in the alleged disappearance of Manfredo Velásquez had been proven.

126. The Court finds no reason to consider the Commission's argument inadmissible. If it can be shown that there was an official practice of disappearances in Honduras, carried out by the Government or at least tolerated by it, and if the disappearance of Manfredo Velásquez can be linked to that practice, the Commission's allegations will have been proven to the Court's satisfaction, so long as the evidence presented on both points meets the standard of proof required in cases such as this.

127. The Court must determine what the standards of proof should be in the instant case. Neither the Convention, the Statute of the Court nor its Rules of Procedure speak to this matter. Nevertheless, international jurisprudence has recognized the power of the courts to weigh the evidence freely, although it has always avoided a rigid rule regarding the amount of proof necessary to support the judgment (Cfr. Corfu Channel, Merits, Judgment, I.C.J. Reports 1949; Military and Paramilitary Activities in and against Nicaragua (Nicaragua v. United States of America), Merits, Judgment, I.C.J. Reports 1986, paras. 29-30 and 59-60).

128. The standards of proof are less formal in an international legal proceeding than in a domestic one. The latter recognize[s] different burdens of proof, depending upon the nature, character and seriousness of the case.

129. The Court cannot ignore the special seriousness of finding that a State Party to the Convention has carried out or has tolerated a practice of disappearances in its territory. This requires the Court to apply a standard of proof which considers the seriousness of the charge and which, notwith-

standing what has already been said, is capable of establishing the truth of the allegations in a convincing manner.

130. The practice of international and domestic courts shows that direct evidence, whether testimonial or documentary, is not the only type of evidence that may be legitimately considered in a reaching a decision. Circumstantial evidence, indicia, and presumptions may be considered, so long as they lead to conclusions consistent with the facts.

131. Circumstantial or presumptive evidence is especially important in allegations of disappearances, because this type of repression is characterized by an attempt to suppress all information about the kidnapping or the whereabouts and fate of the victim.

132. Since this Court is an international tribunal, it has its own specialized procedures. All the elements of domestic legal procedures are therefore not automatically applicable.

133. The above principle is generally valid in international proceedings, but is particularly applicable in human rights cases.

134. The international protection of human rights should not be confused with criminal justice. States do not appear before the Court as defendants in a criminal action. The objective of international human rights law is not to punish those individuals who are guilty of violations, but rather to protect the victims and to provide for the reparation of damages resulting from the acts of the States responsible.

In a later case, concerned with alleged torture and death in custody rather than with disappearances, the Court seemed somewhat more reluctant to presume too much from unclear facts.

The Gangaram Panday Case
Inter-Am. Ct. Hum. Rts., Judgment of 21 Jan. 1994, Ser. C
No. 16, slip op. at 14-15, 17, 19

49. The Court has maintained that ". . . in proceedings to determine human rights violations the State cannot rely on the defense that the complainant has failed to present evidence when it cannot be obtained without the State's cooperation." In the exercise of its judicial functions and when ascertaining and weighing the evidence necessary to decide the cases before it, the Court may, in certain circumstances, make use of both circumstantial evidence and indications or presumptions on which to base its pronouncements when they lead to consistent conclusions as regards the facts of the case, particularly when the respondent State has assumed an uncooperative stance in its dealings with the Court.

50. The record shows that, by order of the President dated July 10,

1992, the Government was required to provide the official texts of the Constitution and of the substantive and criminal procedure laws governing cases of detention in its territory on the date on which Asok Gangaram Panday was detained. The Government did not produce the texts in question for the record, nor did it give any explanation for the omission."

51. In view of the foregoing, the Court infers from the position taken by the Government that Mr. Asok Gangaram Panday was illegally detained by members of the Military Police of Suriname when he arrived from Holland at Zanderij Airport. . . .

52. As for the torture to which Mr. Asok Gangaram Panday was allegedly subjected during the time he was kept in detention by the Military Police authorities, . . . the Court considers that no conclusive or convincing indications result from the evaluation [of the forensic and other evidence] that would enable it to establish the truth of the charge that Mr. Asok Gangaram Panday was subjected to torture during his detention. . . . Accordingly, the Court cannot conclude . . . that in the instant case there exists a presumption that Article 5(2) of the Convention protecting the right to humane treatment was violated. . . .

62. Nevertheless, [with respect to the cause of the complainant's death in custody] it could be argued that the fact that the Court, by inference, considers that the victim's detention was illegal, should also lead it to conclude that there was a violation of the right to life by Suriname on the grounds that, had Suriname not detained that person, he probably would not have lost his life. However, the Court believes that on the matter of the international responsibility of States for violations of the Convention, "[w]hat is decisive is whether a violation . . . has occurred with the support or the acquiescence of the government, or whether the State has allowed the act to take place without taking measures to prevent it or to punish those responsible. . . ." The circumstances surrounding this case make it impossible to establish the responsibility of the State in the terms described above because, among other things, the Court is fixing responsibility for illegal detention by inference but not because it has been proved that the detention was indeed illegal or arbitrary or that the detainee was tortured. . . .

74. The Court notes that, in principle, the confirmation of a single case of violation of human rights by the authorities of a State is not in itself sufficient ground to presume or infer the existence in that State of widespread, large-scale practices to the detriment of the rights of other citizens.

Weissbrodt, Human Rights Implementation and Fact-Finding by International Organizations
1980 Am. Socy. Intl. L. Proceedings 17, 19-20

There remains a question, however, as to the burden of persuasion which the NGO ought to use in finding either a prima facie case worthy of government response or in establishing the facts on the basis of contradictory evidence. . . .

Amnesty International demanded proof beyond a reasonable doubt on its mission to Israel, but the Amnesty report on its mission to Argentina used a variety of standards of which I will quote a few: "There was strong evidence. . . ." "Amnesty International has received reports that . . . ;" "it is clear that . . . ;" "it is apparent that . . . ;" "There is evidence that . . . ;" "Numerous well substantiated accounts of . . . have been documented . . . ;" "There is no doubt that . . . ;" "Summary executions of political prisoners have occurred . . . ;" "The evidence that . . . is overwhelming."

The disparity among these various measures of proof may be due to different degrees of persuasion on the part of the Amnesty International mission or may only reflect stylistic considerations. A mission may, indeed, discover evidence of varying weight and persuasiveness, but some consistency and care in the formulation of factual findings would appear appropriate in human rights reports. The reader should be informed of the burden or burdens of persuasion which a substantial report generally uses.

NGOs may also use a different burden of proof for taking human rights actions of varying impact. For example, if an NGO proposes only to send a diplomatic letter of inquiry to a government, the NGO may merely need credible secondhand reports of human rights violations. If an NGO is publishing a significant report, however, it may require more substantial evidence of wrongdoing. This distinction is quite similar to that drawn in common law countries between civil and criminal cases, which use different burdens of proof for proceedings of quite distinct consequences. In any case, it is not imperative that any single standard be used in NGO fact-finding, but it is important that the standard for significant determinations be clearly defined.

IV.   Final Comments and Questions

1. The UN General Assembly is a political body. Do you think that it is appropriate for such a body to engage in fact-finding — a process that would seem, by its nature, to demand the highest degree of impartiality? Should one harbor the same misgivings about fact-finding by the Commission on Human Rights, which, after all, consists of member states rather than of neutral human rights experts? The obvious danger is that certain states that are politically unpopular in UN circles will receive a disproportionate share of the attention. How serious do you think this consideration is?

2. Concern over developments in the Israeli-occupied territories in the

Middle East intensified significantly after the commencement of the "uprising" (or intifada, in Arabic) by the populations of the areas in December 1987. In May 1990, a draft resolution was submitted to the UN Security Council that, if adopted, would have led to the sending of a commission to the occupied territories to prepare recommendations on how best to ensure the safety of the Palestinian civilians there. Although the draft resolution was approved by 14 of the 15 Security Council members, it was not adopted because the United States exercised its veto power. The United States explained, after the vote, that it preferred the sending of a special envoy of the UN Secretary-General rather than a commission from the Security Council to study the situation. See UN Press Release DH/652, May 31, 1990, at 2.

What significance, if any, would you attach to the adoption of one of these approaches in preference to the other? More generally, it may be noted that to date the Security Council has not been involved in human rights fact-finding to any significant extent. Is it desirable or feasible for the Security Council to take a higher profile in this area in the future? If so, would it be possible to arrange for Security Council fact-finding in such a way as to minimize the risk of the frustration of the process by vetoes, as in the above-mentioned case? Compare Article 27(2) and Article 27(3) of the UN Charter in this regard.

3. Bayefsky's depressing analysis of the present system of enforcing human rights treaties (see pages 412-417 supra) leads her to conclude that the focus should be shifted from achieving universal membership to preserving the integrity of the treaty regimes. She recommends discontinuing the system of state reporting, appointing country-specific rapporteurs for every states party, and requiring that every party accept the right of individual complaint. Would such a system be likely to lead to greater or lesser compliance with international human rights norms? Would it have a significant impact on fact-finding?

4. To what extent do you think that the fact-finding activities of the UN Commission on Human Rights conform to the Belgrade Rules? The Belgrade Rules appear, on their face, to be oriented toward country, as opposed to thematic, fact-finding. Do you think that it is possible to devise general standards for fact-finding by thematic rapporteurs? If so, what should those standards be? Is the mandate of the thematic rapporteurs to find facts or to resolve a problem on a humanitarian basis? Compare the excerpts, supra at pages 441-443. Might there be a conflict between these two goals?

5. In a certain sense, the system of appointing rapporteurs, of both the country and the thematic variety, is a highly encouraging development. Might it not, however, be an indication of the inadequacy of the basic UN machinery? Rapporteurs always seem to be "special," that is, to have a limited brief. To what extent can it be said that the UN has made progress in the development of a truly *general* system of human rights fact-finding? What steps do you think that the UN should take in this direction?

6. The Belgrade Rules apply to fact-finding by IGOs but not by NGOs.

It might well be argued that it is actually more important that NGOs have a clear set of guidelines in this regard, on the ground that there is more scope for bias on the part of NGOs, many of which are forthrightly "special interest" groups. Would one really have expected objective fact-finding about, say, the situation in South Africa from an anti-apartheid organization? Or about the Soviet Union from an anti-communist organization? It may be contended, of course, that NGOs should have *some* standards but different ones from IGOs. How credible do you find that argument? Is not the process of objective and conscientious fact-finding basically the same, no matter who is doing the investigating?

7. Ramcharan is of the view that human rights fact-finding bodies "may apply flexible admissibility criteria." Does this amount, in effect, to concluding that there should be no rules as to admissibility of evidence? Ramcharan also concludes that "the evaluation of evidence is a matter that rests exclusively within the competence of the fact-finding body." Does not this approach amount to allowing the fact-finder to be judge in his own cause? If so, does this conclusion not violate one of the most fundamental precepts of justice?

8. Weissbrodt contends that "it is not imperative that any single standard [for burden of proof] be used in NGO fact-finding. . . ." See page 483 supra. Do you agree with this conclusion? Is not the question of burden of proof among the most crucial in the whole area of fact-finding? If so, is it not imperative to have uniform as well as relatively clear rules or guidelines on the subject?

9. This Problem has focused on the standards that should be applied to fact-finding, but there are many more practical issues that face NGOs concerned with investigating human rights violations. What substantive, political, financial, or other issues should an NGO consider before embarking on an on-site mission or other fact-finding initiative? See Hannum, Implementing Human Rights: An Overview of Strategies and Procedures, in Guide to International Human Rights Practice 19-38 (2d ed. H. Hannum ed. 1992).

10. In general, which of the various fact-finding strategies identified in this Problem do you think are the most effective? Judging from the extracts from various rapporteurs' reports, which ones do you think are likely to produce the most — and the most reliable — information? Do you think that it is better to have an array of different fact-finding mechanisms and techniques, as we now have at the UN; or would it have been preferable to have adopted the Dutch proposal from the 1960s for a centralized and specialized fact-finding organ of the UN? If you were asked by the Secretary-General of the UN to produce a report on the subject of improvements in UN human rights fact-finding, what kinds of suggestions would you make?

11. In addition to the other sources cited in this Problem, Fact-Finding Before International Tribunals (R. Lillich ed. 1991) contains chapters on fact-finding by the European Commission on Human Rights, Inter-American Commission and Court on Human Rights, and national governments.

Problem VII

Sanctions and Southern Africa

How Effective in Causing
Compliance with Human
Rights Law Are Coercive Measures
That Do Not Involve the Use of
Armed Force?

I.   *Rhodesia: The Factual Context*   489
    A.   The Background   489
    B.   The Prelude to Independence   490
    C.   Unilateral Declaration of Independence   491
    D.   Initial Attempts at Settlement   493
II. *UN Economic Sanctions Against Rhodesia: Their Legality Under the*
    UN Charter   495
        Introductory Note   495
        McDougal and Reisman, Rhodesia and the United Nations:
            The Lawfulness of International Concern   497
        Acheson, The Arrogance of International Lawyers   504
III. *A Brief Overview of Economic Sanctions*   509
    A.   International Sanctions   509
    B.   Regional Sanctions   511
    C.   Unilateral Sanctions   513
    D.   Voluntary Sanctions   514
IV. *U.S. Implementation and Enforcement of UN Sanctions Against*
    Rhodesia   515
    A.   U.S. Implementation of Sanctions   515
        1.   The Legal Framework   515
            Legislative Reference Service, Library of Congress, The
            United Nations Participation Act Sections Relating to Eco-
            nomic and Military Action   515
        2.   Presidential Action: Executive Orders 11,322 and 11,419   517
            U.S. Extends Program Banning Trade with Southern Rhodesia   518
            Executive Order No. 11,419 (Relating to Trade and Other
            Transactions Involving Southern Rhodesia)   518
        3.   The Overlooked (?) Loophole: Rhodesian Sanctions Regula-
            tion 31 C.F.R. §530.307 (1969)   520
    B.   U.S. Enforcement of Sanctions   522
        1.   Introduction   522

2.   Congress Enacts the Byrd Amendment   524
    UN Sanctions Against Rhodesia — Chrome   524
    Hearings on S. 1404, UN Sanctions Against Rhodesia —
      Chrome, Before the Senate Committee on Foreign
      Relations   524
    Note: The Byrd Amendment Becomes Law   531
    Irony in Chrome: The Byrd Amendment Two Years Later   532
3.   Critics Challenge the Byrd Amendment: Diggs v. Shultz
      and the Eventual "Repeal" of the Byrd Amendment   535
    Diggs v. Shultz   536
    The Significance of Diggs v. Shultz   540
    Note: Security Council Resolutions in United States Courts   541
    Congress "Repeals" the Byrd Amendment   542
4.   The Enforcement of UN Sanctions Under U.S. Law: At
      Best, Inconsistent; At Worst, Non-Existent   543
    Carnegie Endowment for International Peace, Business as
      Usual: Transactions Violating Rhodesian Sanctions   544
    Lillich, Examining Mobil's Role as Sanctions-Buster   546
    The Treasury Department Investigations   550
    Note: Sanctions-Breaking Around the World   554
V.   Rhodesia: The Achievement of Majority Rule   561
    A.   The Salisbury Agreement and the Emergence of Zimbabwe
          Rhodesia   561
    B.   The Lancaster House Conference and the Creation of Zimbabwe 562
          Davidow, Dealing with International Crises: Lessons from
            Zimbabwe   563
VI. Viewpoints on International Economic Sanctions: Rhodesia as a
    Case Study   565
    H. Strack, Sanctions: The Case of Rhodesia   565
    D. Losman, International Economic Sanctions   567
    R. Renwick, Economic Sanctions   568
    Auglin, United Nations Sanctions Against South Africa and
      Rhodesia   569
    M. Doxey, International Sanctions in Contemporary Per-
      spective   571
VII. Sanctions Against South Africa   573
    A.   UN Mandatory Sanctions   573
        Security Council Resolution 418   574
        Note: Implementation and Enforcement of Resolution 418   575
        Note: British and U.S. Vetoes Block Further Mandatory
          Sanctions   576
        Statement of Mr. Herbert S. Okun, Acting U.S. Representa-
          tive to United Nations, February 20, 1987   577
    B.   UN Voluntary Sanctions   578
        1.   General Assembly Sanctions   578
        2.   Security Council Sanctions   578
        3.   The Intergovernmental Group to Monitor the Supply and
              Shipping of Oil and Petroleum Products to South Africa:
              A Case Study in Implementing UN Voluntary Sanctions 579

C.   U.S. Sanctions   580
     1.   Introduction   580
     2.   President Reagan's Executive Order: Too Late and Too
          Little   583
          Recent Developments, Economic Sanctions: United States
          Sanctions Against South Africa   583
     3.   The Comprehensive Anti-Apartheid Act of 1986   585
          Note: The Passage of the Federal Anti-Apartheid Act: The
          Culmination of Anti-Apartheid Efforts Within the United
          States   585
          Implementation and Enforcement of the Act   587
     4.   The Rangel Amendment Denies Foreign Tax Credits to
          U.S. Corporations Doing Business in South Africa   588
     5.   The End of Sanctions and an Evaluation of Their Effec-
          tiveness   589
VIII. *Final Comments and Questions*   590

I.   Rhodesia: The Factual Context

A.   *The Background*

In 1888 a British representative persuaded Lobengula, ruler of the Matabele tribe (one of the two principal tribes in the land later to become Southern Rhodesia), to sign an agreement guaranteeing continuous friendship with the United Kingdom and promising not to have dealings with any foreign state without Queen Victoria's consent. Agents of Cecil Rhodes, the personification of nineteenth-century colonialism, obtained from Lobengula exclusive mineral concessions in exchange for £100 per month plus 1,000 rifles and 100,000 rounds of ammunition. In 1889 Rhodes formed the British South Africa Company and received a Royal Charter giving the company authority over the area.

Between 1900 and 1920, the European population of the colony rose from 11,700 to 32,500 while the African population increased from 500,000 to 866,000. Discrimination against the African population had been practiced from the outset: in 1912 the African Labor Regulations laid down jail terms for any African who "without lawful cause deserts or absents himself from his place of employment." Other laws restricting the activities of Africans became commonplace. (Until 1960 Africans were not recognized as "employees" under Southern Rhodesia trade union laws.)

Following a 1922 whites-only referendum, Southern Rhodesia was annexed to the United Kingdom as a "self-governing colony." Certain powers were reserved to the United Kingdom, including the power to reject "any law, save in respect of the supply of arms, ammunition or liquor to Natives, whereby Natives may be subjected or made liable to any liabilities or restrictions to which persons of European descent are not also subjected or made liable." These powers, it should be noted, were not exercised by the United Kingdom in the four decades during which the 1923 Constitution remained in force.

In 1924 Northern Rhodesia chose to become a protectorate of the United Kingdom, eventually to become the independent African republic of Zambia. In 1953 Northern Rhodesia, Nyasaland, and Southern Rhodesia merged into the Federation of Rhodesia and Nyasaland. In 1959 increased nationalist activity heralded a flurry of repressive legislation throughout the Federation. The African National Congress (ANC) of Southern Rhodesia was banned.

B.   The Prelude to Independence

In 1961 a new constitution, approved by Parliament that same year, eliminated the United Kingdom's powers relative to anti-African discriminatory legislation. The 1961 Constitution set up a 65-member Legislative Assembly and a two-roll electoral system with "A-roll" (higher income/property owners) voters and "B-roll" (lower income) voters. As 50 of the 65 representatives were elected by the "A-roll" (European) voters and few Africans could qualify as "B-roll" voters, European supremacy was ensured.

The 1961 Constitution stated that "[n]o written law shall contain any discriminatory provision." It included a Declaration of Rights, but the "rights" could be limited by laws necessary in the interests of "defence, public safety, public order, public morality and public health." The Constitution could be amended only with the approval of the United Kingdom or after separate referenda in which the amendment had been approved by each of the four racial communities (African, European, Asian, and "Coloured").

In 1962 the UN General Assembly affirmed that Southern Rhodesia was a Non-Self-Governing Territory (G.A. Res. 1760, 17 U.N. GAOR Supp. (No. 17) at 3, U.N. Doc. A/5517 (1962)) and requested the United Kingdom:

> (a) to undertake urgently the convening of a constitutional conference, in which there shall be full participation of representatives of all political parties, for the purpose of formulating a constitution for Southern Rhodesia, in place of the Constitution of 6 December 1961, which would ensure the rights of the majority of the people on the basis of "one man, one vote," in conformity with the principles of the Charter of the United Nations and the Declaration on the Granting of Independence to Colonial Countries and Peoples, embodied in General Assembly resolution 1514 (XV);
>
> (b) to take immediate steps to restore all rights of the non-European population and remove all restraints and restrictions in law and in practice on

the exercise of the freedom of political activity including all laws, ordinances, and regulations which directly or indirectly sanction any policy or practice based on racial discrimination;

(c) to grant amnesty to, and ensure the release of, all political prisoners.

In November 1962, elections under the 1961 Constitution took place. A total of 73,349 people voted, about 3,000 being African. The Zimbabwe African Peoples Union (ZAPU), the Zimbabwe National Party (ZANU), and the Pan-African Socialist Union were banned from political activity and, therefore, from election participation. The white electorate ousted the previous government of the United Federal Party and substituted the right-wing Rhodesian Front Party, which remained in power until 1979.

In September 1963, the UN Security Council voted on a draft resolution (18 U.N. SCOR (1068th mtg.) at 2, U.N. Doc. 5/P.V. 1068 (1963)) calling on the United Kingdom not to transfer sovereign powers to Southern Rhodesia until a fully representative government had been established. The United Kingdom vetoed the draft resolution on the grounds that "orderly dissolution" of the Federation of Rhodesia and Nyasaland would be impossible if the United Kingdom prevented such a transfer of sovereignty to Southern Rhodesia. In October 1963, the General Assembly adopted a similar resolution by 90 votes to 2 (South Africa and Portugal) with 13 abstentions, including the United Kingdom (G.A. Res. 1883, 18 U.N. GAOR Supp. (No. 15) at 45, U.N. Doc. A/5515 (1963)). In November 1963, the General Assembly declared that the situation threatened international peace (G.A. Res. 1889, 18 U.N. GAOR Supp. (No. 15) at 46, U.N. Doc. A/5515 (1963)) by 73 votes to 2 with 19 abstentions (several states abstaining indicated that they could not agree that the situation posed a threat to the peace within the meaning of Article 39 of the UN Charter).

C. Unilateral Declaration of Independence

The Federation of Rhodesia and Nyasaland terminated as of 1 January 1964, with Southern Rhodesia reverting to its former status as a self-governing colony. In late 1964 new Rhodesian Prime Minister Ian Smith declared a state of emergency in Salisbury's overpopulated African townships on the grounds that the rival African nationalist organizations ZANU (led by Reverend Ndabaningi Sithole) and ZAPU (led by Joshua Nkomo) had "indulged in intimidation and violence against each other and against law-abiding Africans." By the end of 1964, government figures showed that 1,936 people were restricted or detained under the Law and Order (Maintenance) Act of 1960 or the new emergency regulations.

On 6 May 1965, the Security Council declared itself "deeply disturbed" at the worsening situation and requested the United Kingdom to obtain the release of all political prisoners, repeal all repressive and discriminatory legislation, and remove all restrictions on political activity (S.C. Res. 202, 20 U.N. SCOR, Res. and Dec. at 6 (1965)). One day later Prime Minister Smith's Rhodesian Front Party gained a massive mandate for a unilateral declaration of independence from the white electorate.

On 11 November 1965, the Smith government announced its Unilateral Declaration of Independence (U.D.I.). The following day the Security Council condemned U.D.I. (S.C. Res. 216, 20 U.N. SCOR, Res. and Dec. at 8 (1965)), calling on all states not to recognize the "illegal racist minority regime" and to refrain from rendering it any assistance (10 to 1, with one abstention, France, which considered the matter an internal U.K. problem that the Council should not discuss). Support for military intervention under Article 42 of the Charter was lacking in the Security Council; instead, it adopted a resolution (S.C. Res. 217, 20 U.N. SCOR, Res. and Dec. at 8 (1965)) calling on all states to impose an oil and petroleum embargo and to break all relations with the Smith regime (10 to 0, with France abstaining).

International armed intervention for humanitarian purposes, thus, was ruled out, since the United Kingdom, which had done little enough to prevent the crisis from developing over the years, refused to consider military intervention as a possible policy choice. British Prime Minister Harold Wilson had made this position clear at a press conference that he gave in Salisbury, Rhodesia, on 30 October 1965, less than two weeks before U.D.I., during which he cautioned that no one should expect either that the United Kingdom would use force against Rhodesia or that majority rule would come to Rhodesia any time soon. It would be almost impossible to conceive of a clearer signal to the Smith government that the risks involved in U.D.I. would be substantially less than many of its supporters had feared.

It has been argued that Wilson's decision not to use force in Rhodesia was partly necessitated by doubts about the willingness of the British armed forces to take action against their "kith and kin" in Rhodesia. Persons holding this view doubtless were mindful of the Curragh incident in Ireland in early 1914, when 58 officers in Dublin, including one general, had purported to resign their commissions rather than compel the Ulster Protestants to become part of a united and self-governing Ireland. Other persons would contend that the two situations were not sufficiently comparable to justify fears that there might be a repetition of the Curragh incident in the Rhodesian context.

In any event, instead of invoking the threat or use of force, the United Kingdom adopted, in conjunction with other sympathetic states, including the United States, the policy of voluntary sanctions. At the British Commonwealth conference at Lagos, Nigeria, in January 1966, several black African heads of state vigorously denounced this approach as being too timid. Wilson replied that, on the basis of "expert advice," he expected the sanctions to bring down the rebel regime "within a matter of weeks rather than months." His prediction could not have been wider of the mark.

D. Initial Attempts at Settlement

Even after U.D.I., however, both the United Kingdom and Rhodesia purported to be willing to reach a settlement if the proper terms could be agreed upon. Yet it took 13 years and 6 separate attempts at settlement before Prime Minister Ian Smith and three black nationalist leaders finally were able to reach an accord on the terms of a transition to black majority government, the Salisbury Agreement of 3 March 1978. Ironically, this accord lasted little over a year before it was superseded by the Lancaster House Agreement of 21 December 1979, which led to the creation of the present independent state of Zimbabwe.

The first attempt at settlement came in 1966 when Prime Minister Wilson met with Smith aboard the Royal Navy vessel, the H.M.S. *Tiger*. No agreement was reached. Two years later a second set of negotiations between the same two parties, this time aboard the H.M.S. *Fearless*, also produced no accord, despite a distinct softening of position on the part of the United Kingdom.

Hopes for a settlement were raised sharply in 1971 when the third set of negotiations, this time between Prime Minister Edward Heath's Conservative government and Smith, actually produced an agreement. The concessions that the United Kingdom was willing to make for such a settlement, however, were substantial. The basis for the new arrangement was to be the notorious 1969 Constitution, which had provided for possible black parity in theory, perhaps sometime in the twenty-first century, but had guaranteed against an outright black parliamentary majority ever occurring. In addition to using this Constitution as the basis of the agreement, the settlement contained no guarantees against future retrogressive constitutional amendments. There was to be a bill of civil rights, but it would not invalidate existing discriminatory legislation. In return for these British concessions, the Smith regime agreed to a gradual — almost glacial — increase in black parliamentary representation, even to the point of the ultimate attainment of majority rule. Nonetheless, Smith justifiably could feel proud of his negotiating prowess in the affair, as it was projected that the earliest realistic date for the achievement of even black parity would be 2026.

The United Kingdom had insisted, however, upon one principle: there must be popular acceptance of the settlement within Rhodesia. Pursuant to the terms of the agreement, the United Kingdom appointed a special 24-man commission, chaired by Lord Edward Pearce (a member of the House of Lords Appellate Committee) to ascertain public opinion. The findings of the Pearce Commission, reported in 1972, were that the black community in Rhodesia overwhelmingly opposed the settlement. Thus, the agreement was off, and the impasse continued.

A fourth attempt to resolve the problem came in 1974-1975, after Portugal had announced its withdrawal from its African colonies and after Prime Minister Vorster of South Africa had begun his clandestine campaign of "detente" with black Africa. In December 1974, Smith suddenly announced that a ceasefire had been agreed to in the guerrilla war that had been festering in the countryside since 1972; all black nationalist detainees (about 100, including Nkomo and Sithole) were to be released; and, finally, a constitutional conference was to be held to attempt to reach a solution agreeable to both the black and the white communities. For months thereafter there was a disagreement over where the conference was to take place and under whose chairmanship. In August 1975, when Smith met with Bishop Abel Muzorewa, leader of the ANC, aboard a special South African train on a bridge over the Zambizi River near Victoria Falls, the latter insisted that the former guarantee amnesty to all participants in the coming conference. Without such a guarantee, Sithole in particular would be unable to participate. Smith refused to accede to this request and walked out of the meeting, charging the ANC with sabotaging the conference. Muzorewa made substantially the same charge against Smith.

Smith claimed that a settlement was still possible, and he demonstrated this contention by entering into a fifth round of negotiations, this time with Nkomo alone. The prospects for the success of this effort, however, were not bright, since Nkomo by this time headed only a faction of the ANC. Muzorewa, who had expelled Nkomo from the organization after the collapse of the Victoria Falls talks, announced that any agreement that Nkomo and Smith might reach would be unacceptable to him. Nevertheless, their talks continued, with occasional expressions of optimism, from November 1975 until 19 March 1976, when they, too, broke up.

The sixth attempt at a settlement took place in 1976-1977, at the instigation of then-U.S. Secretary of State Henry Kissinger, who in September 1976 persuaded Smith to agree to grant majority rule to Rhodesia after a transition period of only 18 months. What scuttled the attempt was the inability of the various parties to agree on interim government arrangements during that 18-month period. Smith claimed that the whites were to control the army and the police during the transition period, and that the "Kissinger plan" was a complete package: that is, the meetings with black nationalists were to serve the purpose only of implementing that plan.

The various black factions saw the matter differently, viewing the Kissinger plan as a point of departure for negotiations rather than as a finished product. Also of importance from the black side was the question of which person or persons could speak authoritatively for the black population of Rhodesia. Before the commencement of negotiations in Geneva in October 1976, Nkomo and Robert Mugabe (who had close links with the guerrilla groups operating inside Rhodesia) met to form a union known as the "Patriotic Front." This group was recognized by the presidents of the five "front-line" African states (Botswana, Zambia, Tanzania, and the newly independent states of Mozambique and Angola) as being the official black negotiating group, to the exclusion of Bishop Muzorewa and the Reverend Sithole.

Once in Geneva, the disputes over the transition to black rule, especially as to the form that an interim government should take, proved unresolvable. The five delegations — the Rhodesian government delegation led by Smith and the four black delegations of Nkomo, Mugabe, Muzorewa, and Sithole (the latter two men having received invitations to attend after all) — were unable to find any common ground whatsoever. The conference adjourned just before Christmas until mid-January 1977, but in fact it never reconvened. Both the United Kingdom and the United States, with new governments in office, pressed for its resumption during 1977, but all Anglo-American initiatives came to naught. Thus, a dozen years after U.D.I., resolution of the crisis over Rhodesia remained as elusive as ever.

II. UN Economic Sanctions Against Rhodesia: Their Legality Under the UN Charter

Introductory Note

During the decade after U.D.I., the UN took several important and unprecedented steps to deter the "illegal racist minority regime" in Rhodesia. Against the backdrop of the above section's historical account of settlement negotiations, consider the significance as well as the legality of UN-imposed economic sanctions on the fledgling Rhodesian economy.

After the breakdown of the H.M.S. *Tiger* talks in 1966, the United Kingdom, recognizing that its UN-endorsed policy of voluntary sanctions (page 492 supra) had not brought down the Smith regime "within a matter of weeks," requested a Security Council meeting to propose further action. On 16 December 1966, the latter adopted Resolution 232, imposing mandatory, albeit selective, sanctions against Rhodesia pursuant to Article 41 of the UN Charter (S.C. Res. 232, 21 U.N. SCOR, Res. and Dec. at 7 (1966)). It was the first time that such action had been taken in the UN's history.

Under Resolution 232, the following imports from Rhodesia — its principal exports — were banned: asbestos; iron ore; chrome; pig iron; sugar; tobacco; copper; meat and meat products; and hides, skins, and leather. Also banned was the export to Rhodesia of oil or oil products, arms and military equipment, and aircraft and motor vehicles, as well as equipment or materials for their manufacture, assembly, or maintenance. In June 1968, Secretary-General U Thant informed the Security Council that available data indicated imports into Rhodesia of about $40 million in 1967, compared with $330 million in 1965. South African import figures, however, were not available. Countries accounting for the majority of imports were allegedly the Federal Republic of Germany, the United States, Switzerland, Portugal, the Netherlands, Belgium, Luxembourg, France, and Japan.

On 29 May 1968, the Security Council adopted far more comprehensive mandatory sanctions. Resolution 253 (S.C. Res. 253, 23 U.N. SCOR, Res. and Dec. at 5 (1968)) decided that all member states "shall prevent":

> The import of all commodities and products originating in Southern Rhodesia;
>
> Any activities by their nationals or in their territories which would promote or are calculated to promote the export of any commodities or products from Southern Rhodesia, and any dealings by their nationals or in their territories in any such products, including in particular the transfer of funds for the purpose of such activities;
>
> The shipment in their vessels or aircraft of any Southern Rhodesian commodities;
>
> The sale or supply of any commodities or products to any person or body in Southern Rhodesia, or to any other person or body for the purposes of any business operated from Southern Rhodesia (except for medical and educational material; publications; news material; and, in special humanitarian circumstances, foodstuffs);
>
> The shipment in their vessels or aircraft or the transport across their territories of any commodities consigned to Southern Rhodesia;
>
> The provision of any funds for investment or any other financial or economic resources; or the remitting of any funds except pension payments or funds for strictly medical, humanitarian, or educational purposes, and, in special humanitarian circumstances, foodstuffs;
>
> The entry into their territories, save on exceptional humanitarian grounds, of any person travelling on a Southern Rhodesian passport or any person ordinarily resident in Southern Rhodesia believed to have encouraged the unlawful acts of the illegal regime;
>
> Operation by their airlines to or from Southern Rhodesia.

In 1973 came still further action by the Security Council (S.C. Res. 333, 28 U.N. SCOR, Res. and Dec. at 14 (1973)). Resolution 333 addressed itself to the problem of goods that were being traded in and out of Rhodesia indirectly, through middlemen in neighboring states, both black and white dominated. The resolution called upon states to punish any of their citizens who continued to deal with clients in South Africa, Angola, Mozambique, Portuguese Guinea (as it was then known), and Namibia (formerly South West Africa) after it had become known that such clients were shipping goods either to or from Rhodesia.

The UN tightened sanctions yet again, and for the final time, in 1976, when the Security Council adopted Resolution 388, which forbade the insuring of commodities and products exported from, imported to, or located within Rhodesia (S.C. Res. 388, 31 U.N. SCOR, Res. and Dec. at 6 (1976)).

The significance of these economic sanctions and the role they played in eventually inducing the Smith regime to conclude first the Salisbury Agreement and later the Lancaster House Agreement — which finally led to the establishment of black majority rule in what is now Zimbabwe — is difficult to assess and will be considered later in this Problem. See pages 565-572 infra. Initially, the place of economic sanctions in the scheme of the UN Charter and the question of the legality of their invocation in the Rhodesian context must be considered. These and other related issues are explored in the two readings that follow.

McDougal and Reisman, Rhodesia and the United Nations: The Lawfulness of International Concern
62 Am. J. Intl. L. 1, 1-19 (1968)

I

The basic substantive argument which has been lodged against the legality of the United Nations' Rhodesian action is that the activities of the white regime in Rhodesia cannot be appropriately characterized as constituting "a threat to the peace" within the meaning of the Charter. Hence, no matter how reprehensible white Rhodesian behavior may be, the basic contingency for the United Nations' measures is absent. . . . A careful appraisal of the relevant policies and of the facts of the case will, however, indicate that the Charter provisions have been misunderstood and that, in the absence of an appropriate understanding of the relevant basic policies, the factual elements have not been properly appreciated.

For the better securing of the most fundamental Charter purpose of maintaining "international peace and security," the framers of the United Nations Charter deliberately conferred upon the Security Council, in the provisions of Chapter VII, a very broad competence both to "determine the existence of any threat to the peace, breach of the peace, or act of aggression" and to decide upon what measures should be taken to "maintain or restore international peace and security." . . .

The thought which moved the framers, in rejecting all proposed definitions of the key terms "threat to the peace," "breach of peace" and "act of aggression," was that, for effective discharge of the very difficult and delicate task being imposed upon it, the Security Council should be accorded a large freedom to make ad hoc determinations after a full, contextual examination of the peculiar features of each specific situation of threat or coercion. The facts which might in the future endanger international peace and security could be infinitely various, with the significance of any particular feature of the context being a function of many other features, and the measures which might best promote the establishment and maintenance of peace and security in any specific situation could require careful tailoring to fit the unique requirements of that situation. The course of subsequent events has clearly demonstrated the wisdom of this view, and few voices have been heard to suggest that the broad discretion of the Security Council could rationally be curtailed.

Similarly, it was clearly within the expectations of both the framers and the general community that action by the Security Council might have to be anticipatory and was not required to await the full consummation of disaster. Thus, the competence accorded to the Council in Article 39 relates not merely to perfected "breaches of the peace" and "acts of aggression" but explicitly extends also to the prevention and removal of "threats to the peace." . . . It could not be expected that basic constitutional policies would impose more rigid requirements upon the organized general community as a prerequisite to the employment of a wide range of sanctioning measures. On the contrary, the potentialities that inhere in a "policy of prevention" and of appropriate sanctioning measures to secure such a policy have come to be widely accepted.

It may require emphasis, further, that, as the legislative history of Article 39 anticipates and subsequent practice confirms, the Security Council is authorized to find a "threat to the peace" in a specific situation without an allocation of blame or fault to any of the parties. The finding of a "threat to the peace" is a *factual* determination only, though an indispensable procedure for establishing the authoritative base for sanctioning measures. . . .

It is not intended, however, to suggest that the broad competence accorded the Security Council to make determinations of "threats to the peace" is absolute, without limit or safeguard. The appropriate exercise of such competence must of course require an evaluation of any alleged "threat" in its relevant context and the relation of such challenged activity to the major Charter purpose of maintaining international peace and security; and the Charter, like other constitutions which confer broad competences for action, establishes certain important procedural safeguards against arbitrary and spurious decisions. The expectations of the general community about the requirements and consequences of an appropriate decision by the Security Council are indicated in a dictum of the International Court of Justice in the *Certain Expenses* case:

> The primary place ascribed to international peace and security is natural, since the fulfilment of the other purposes will be dependent upon the attainment of that basic condition. These purposes are broad indeed, but neither they nor the powers conferred to effectuate them are unlimited. Save as they have entrusted the Organization with the attainment of these common ends, the Member States retain their freedom of action. But when the Organization takes action which warrants the assertion that it was appropriate for the fulfilment of one of the stated purposes of the United Nations, the presumption is that such action is not ultra vires the Organization.

The procedural safeguards established by the Charter are incorporated in the voting procedures prescribed for the Security Council, which require the concurring votes of the permanent members and a special majority of all members. The probabilities of arbitrary or spurious decisions escaping these procedures would not appear great.

The important criticisms of the Rhodesian Resolution, as we have noted above, relate more to the relevant substantive criteria than to the procedures by which the decision was taken. Indeed, it would not appear that any plausible question could be raised about the conformity of the decision to the stipulated Charter procedures. . . . [T]he decision is, in its substantive merits, no less in accord with the basic policies established by the Charter. . . .

The first argument against the lawfulness of the decision is that the actions of the white Rhodesians contain no element of aggression: ". . . whatever the Rhodesians have done has been wholly within their own country and contains no element of aggression." Article 39 does not, however, require "aggression" as a constituent element of a threat to the major inclusive concern. This is not to imply that an act of aggression cannot constitute or precipitate a threat to, or breach of, international peace. The point is that it is not necessary, in order to support a finding of a threat to the peace, that some act of overt aggression should have actually been committed. The aggression argument is thus irrelevant to the determination of a "threat" under Article 39 of the Charter.

Yet, it must be added that Rhodesian action does involve elements of aggression in the most comprehensive, relevant sense. The seizure of control of territory which all states of the world recognize to be under the sovereignty of the United Kingdom, accomplished contrary to the desires both of the United Kingdom and the indigenous population of that territory, could be appropriately characterized as an act of aggression against the United Kingdom. Moreover, the promulgation and application of policies of racism in a context as volatile as that of Rhodesia and South Central Africa must give rise to expectations of violence and constitute, if not aggression of the classic type, at least the creation of circumstances under which states have been customarily regarded as justified in unilaterally resorting to the coercive strategies of humanitarian intervention [See Problem VIII on the issues relating to humanitarian intervention.]. . . .

The second argument against the lawfulness of the Security Council decision is that the activities of the Rhodesian elites have been entirely in accord with international law. One compelling answer is that the Charter does not require a violation of international law in any sense other than the constitution of a threat to the peace. In point of fact, however, the list of indictments of Rhodesian transgressions against international law is alarmingly long. As far as conventional international law is concerned, the Rhodesian authorities have repudiated a number of Security Council decisions, which, under Article 25 of the Charter, are binding upon all Member States and which, according to Article 2(6), may be applied to non-members "so far as may be necessary for the maintenance of international peace and security." They have also repudiated the human rights provisions of the Charter, as authoritatively interpreted by the competent U.N. organs, and the prescriptions of the increasingly authoritative Universal Declaration. As far as international customary law is concerned, they have violated the more traditional human rights policies in a degree which, as we have noted, would have in the past served to justify "humanitarian intervention" by individual nation states. It scarcely need be added that circumstances which would justify coercive action undertaken unilaterally by one state must surely be regarded as sufficient to justify organized international action. As far as "general principles" are concerned, the Rhodesian elites have violated the principle of good faith by failing to make effective the assurances which they gave the United Kingdom at various times for just treatment of the African population. The act of unilateral declaration of independence and the subsequent internal legislation violated, as will be documented below, the principle of self-determination in relation to the great bulk of the Rhodesian people, as well as British sovereignty. In the most fundamental sense, the assertion of independence at a time and by means which the authoritative organs of the international community had decided would precipitate a threat to the peace of the surrounding region and the world was an act of irresponsibility in violation of the most basic policies of the Charter for the maintenance of international order.

The final argument of the critics of the Security Council decision is that, even if the acts of the white Rhodesians are unlawful, they are insulated from international concern by virtue of the fact that they occur only within Rhodesia and affect no one else. This bald contention that the actions of the white Rhodesians occur only within the territorial bounds of Rhodesia is factually incorrect. In the contemporary intensely interdependent world, peoples interact not merely through the modalities of collaborative or combative operations but also through shared subjectivities — not merely through the physical movements of goods and services or exercises with armaments, but also through communications in which they simply take each other into account. . . . In the case of Rhodesia, the other peoples of Africa have regarded themselves as affected by the authoritarian and racist policies of the Rhodesian elites. In the context of a world opinion which since World War II has come increasingly to recognize the intimate interdependence of the maintenance of minimum human rights and international peace and security, it would certainly not be easy to demonstrate to these peoples that their expectations of grievous injury from the Rhodesian model are ill-founded. It has been too often confirmed that practices of indignity and strife which begin as internal in physical manifestation in a single community quickly and easily spread to other communities and become international. . . .

II

The arguments relating to basic constitutive limitations which are alleged to preclude the United Nations from lawfully acting in the Rhodesian case invoke the principle of domestic jurisdiction and the right of self-determination. The activities of the white Rhodesian minority are, it is argued, essentially within their domestic jurisdiction and hence insulated from the appraisal and supervision of authoritative international processes. The unilateral declaration of independence by the white elites constitutes, it is claimed, an exercise of self-determination; by seeking to suppress this action, the United Nations is, itself, acting against a fundamental postulate of contemporary international law.

The short and conclusive answer to the argument in terms of domestic jurisdiction is that, once certain activities constitute a threat to international peace and security, they cease to be, if ever they were, "matters essentially within the domestic jurisdiction" of a state. Still further, even if such activities should be thought by some unspecified criteria to remain within the compass of domestic jurisdiction, the very words of the Charter clause, Article 2(7), which created the vague and elusive limitation upon the organization's competence, explicitly provide in a well-known exception that "this principle [that of domestic jurisdiction] shall not prejudice the application of enforcement measures under Chapter VII." The basic constitutional framework of an inclusive organization whose principal purpose is to maintain international peace and security could scarcely prescribe otherwise: if states were to be permitted to impede the organized community's efforts to rectify situations by claims that activities, however threatening, are immune from inclusive concern because they are within domestic jurisdiction, the principal purpose for which the whole constitutive structure is established and maintained could be easily defeated.

The invocation of the principle of domestic jurisdiction in the Rhodesian context is, further, ultimately founded on a serious misunderstanding of the contemporary relation between human rights and matters of "international concern." The point is that, even in the absence of a finding of a threat to the peace, the United Nations could have acquired a considerable competence with respect to Rhodesia because of the systematic suppression of human rights practiced there. The concept of domestic jurisdiction in international law has never been impermeable. Actions occurring within the territorial bounds of one state with palpable deprivatory effects upon others have always been subject to claim and decision on the international plane. There has scarcely ever been a case of major proportions in which the principle of domestic jurisdiction has not been invoked; where transnational effects have been precipitated, the principle has rarely barred effective accommodations in accord with inclusive interest. Hence, domestic jurisdiction means little more than a general community concession of primary, but not exclusive, competence over matters arising and intimately concerned with aspects of the internal public order of states. Where such acts precipitate major inclusive deprivations, jurisdiction is internationalized and inclusive concern and measures become permissible.

The important provision in Article 2(7) of the Charter — that "this

principle shall not prejudice the application of enforcement measures under Chapter VII" — is only the most urgent example of the permeability of
domestic jurisdiction to international supervision. Any matter originating in
one state with deprivatory effects going beyond its borders may become a
matter of international concern. The peoples of the world may regard it as a
matter of international concern and their perspectives may, from the standpoint of an observer, be realistic. Recent decades have witnessed tremendous changes in the perception by peoples of their interdependences with
respect to human rights and in their efforts to clarify and establish appropriate prescriptions and structures to take these interdependences into account. Under Articles 55 and 56 of the Charter, it is made basic constitutive
prescription that the minimum conditions of a dignified human existence
are to be realized and maintained by Member States by "joint and separate
action in cooperation with the Organization." . . .

Thus, even were Rhodesia a state for United Nations purposes, and
even were there no finding of a threat to the peace of major international
proportions, the claim of "domestic jurisdiction" could not be invoked effectively to insulate the systematic deprivation of human rights in Rhodesia
from the scrutiny and rebuke of "international concern."

It may, however, be noted in further demonstration of the irrelevance
of "domestic jurisdiction" that the benefits of this allegedly saving limitation
inhere only to states. The United Nations and its Members have decided,
through authorized procedures, not to recognize the regime in Rhodesia as
a state until it accommodates itself to the internal and external demands for
a genuine sharing of power, majority rule, and conformity to the basic
human rights principles of international law. The Security Council decided
that a unilateral declaration of independence without prior arrangement for
these vital matters would, in the context of South Central Africa, constitute
a threat to the peace.

The recognition of a community as a state for some or all purposes has
long been regarded as largely within the discretionary competence of each
preexisting state, and there are no generally accepted criteria to compel a
recognition which a state wishes to withhold. Competences which individual states may exercise separately, they may of course exercise jointly. Neither the United Nations as a collective organ nor any state of the world has
recognized Rhodesia as a state. To argue, in spite of these facts, that the
white authorities are entitled to the benefit of those international policies
aimed at sustaining the political integrity of bona fide state members of the
world community is at least modestly incongruous.

The unilateral declaration of independence of November 11, 1965, by
the Rhodesian elites was carefully calculated to animate the highly emotive
symbols of self-determination. The right of self-determination is undoubtedly an important feature of contemporary international law, though the
exact content of the right, the criteria for its application, and the procedures
for a contextual examination of situations in which it is claimed have, as yet,

not been carefully delineated. The earlier experience with homogeneous ethnic and cultural groups is not wholly relevant, since recent decades have witnessed a noticeable shift in emphasis from "groups" and "peoples" to individual human rights and notions of democracy. In particular, the precise rôle of the United Nations in supervising the conflicting claims of groups for self-determination and the regulation of minority guarantee provisions remain to be successfully determined. . . .

Whatever the difficulties which continue to inhere in the clarification of appropriate policies about self-determination, the irrelevance of any such policies for protecting the claims of the Rhodesian elites would seem to be clear. Whether one invokes criteria related to the older notions of homogeneous ethnic and cultural groups or to the newer notions of individual human rights and democracy, and whether one investigates sociological, political, psychological or historical factors, by no stretch of the imagination can the actions and avowed and executed political programs of the white Rhodesian minority be characterized as genuine Rhodesian self-determination. It would be a travesty upon the most basic notion of "self-determination" to speak of it, in regard to a claim of 6% of a population against 94% of a population, when the goal of the claim is to gain absolute political control over the majority and to maintain them in a state of secondary and powerless citizenship. . . .

III

It must, accordingly, be concluded that the Security Council decision imposing mandatory sanctions in the Rhodesian situation, contrary to the vigorous criticisms which have been asserted of it, makes an entirely appropriate relation of the facts before the Council to all the relevant basic community policies embodied in the United Nations Charter. In terms of substantive merits, the decision realistically recognizes that in the contemporary world, international peace and security and the protection of human rights are inescapably interdependent and that the impact of the flagrant deprivation of the most basic human rights of the great mass of the people of a community cannot possibly stop short within the territorial boundaries in which the physical manifestations of such deprivations first occur. In terms of the constitutive limitations established by the Charter, the fact that the situation in Rhodesia has been authoritatively found to constitute a threat to international peace makes irrelevant all conceptions of "domestic jurisdiction," and the decision of the Council would not constitute an infringement of the domestic jurisdiction, properly conceived, of Rhodesia, even if Rhodesia were a state entitled to the benefit of the domestic jurisdiction doctrine. Similarly, so far from constituting a violation of the right to self-determination of the great mass of the Rhodesian people, the Security Council resolution is but the most recent expression of a general community concern to preserve that right for them. . . .

Acheson, The Arrogance of International Lawyers
2 Intl. Law. 591, 591-599 (1968)

Five years ago I was bold enough to scold a meeting of this sort about what I call the arrogance that international law seems to instill in its addicts. To be sure, law in general does this to lawyers in general. One can be tolerantly amused at the veneration which craftsmen in any craft have for the materials of their craft. The cobbler, murmurs, "There's nothing like leather!" But he is too modest to envision as man's highest earthly condition the Rule of Leather. Yet the lawyer does not blush to proclaim it to be the Rule of Law. As he describes it, the rule of law seems to be governance by disembodied principle without the intervention of human hand or voice. Even his own not unimportant role at the bar and on the bench the lawyer turns into the mere voice of the oracle inspired by the Law Principle itself. This miracle finds its most mystical expression in the doctrine of Natural Law, which makes it the efflux of the universe, flowing forth from the Godhead. The disciple of Natural Law seemed to Justice Holmes like the knight of romance to whom it was not enough that you agreed that his lady was a very nice girl. If you did not admit that she was the best that God ever made or would make, you must fight. Ordinary lawyers, who work around the temple of Apollo feeding the oracle questions, some of which are loaded, arguing with it and among themselves, "cussing" its pronouncements that go against them, take a more earthy view of law. When former Justice . . . Charles Evans Hughes bluntly — and, perhaps, too "Delphically" — said that the Constitution is what the Supreme Court says it is, the lawyers were not too shocked, although they pretended that they were.

Those who devote themselves to international relations in foreign offices at what is disparagingly called "the working level" are understandably and wisely reticent about the role of law. This, however, is not true of academicians who write about it and teach it. Undeterred by the discipline of adversary procedure or by the test of judgment in contested application, motivated by the highest principles and often spurred by a gift for imaginative rhetoric, some of them recall Disraeli's description of Gladstone as "intoxicated by the exuberance of his own verbosity." I hasten to add that it was the Bar Association en masse, and not the International and Comparative Law Section of it, that voiced the most delusive of all slogans — "World peace through world law."

Those of whom I complain are not the peddlers of spurious panaceas for peace, not those who are overimpressed with the role of international law, but those who would impose upon states in the name of law their own subjective conceptions of justice. As is so often the case with the righteous, deeply convinced of the righteousness of their cause, their impulse is to "snatch the knotted cord from the hand of God and deal out murderous blows." These blows are usually directed against the weak by suborning the subjectivities of the strong. This process also furnishes the fig leaf of legal respectability for otherwise naked aggression.

Such support was given to the action of the United Nations Security Council in calling for economic sanctions against Rhodesia and to the attacks upon the World Court's decision dismissing the complaint in the Southwest Africa case. The viciousness of the substitution of the subjective conception of justice for law in these instances is that in both cases it provides means for collective aggression, in both it degrades international adjudication, and in both it departs from the basic conception of international law. This is that it is inter *national*, between sovereign states, based upon accepted practices and agreements of sovereigns. In this latter respect it differs basically from the law taught by the international lawyers' other academic colleagues. To strike at this concept of agreed limitations on sovereignty is to strike at confidence in judicial honesty and restraint, which alone can lead to the slow development of international law from its primitive state.

It will surprise some of my fellow citizens, though hardly anyone here today, to be told that the United States is engaged in an international conspiracy, instigated by Britain, and blessed by the United Nations, to overthrow the government of a country that has done us no harm and threatens no one. This is barefaced aggression, unprovoked and unjustified by a single legal or moral principle.

The charge that Britain brings against Rhodesians is one that George III once brought against Americans and sought unsuccessfully to enforce by arms. It was that the Colonies felt it necessary, as Mr. Jefferson put it, "to dissolve the political bands which [had] connected them with other [people], and to assume among the powers of the earth, the separate and equal station to which the Laws of Nature and of Nature's God entitle them." However, two academics [McDougal and Reisman] writing in the American Journal of International Law have taken a quite different view. They say:

> . . . In the most fundamental sense, the assertion of independence at a time and by means which the authoritative organs of the international community had decided would precipitate a threat to the peace of the surrounding region and the world was an act of irresponsibility in violation of the most basic policies of the Charter for the maintenance of international order.

Where authorities differ so widely further inquiry and judgment are indicated.

In the first place, was independence so broad a step for Rhodesia to take? While Britain had asserted sovereignty over the Rhodesian countryside since the latter part of the last century when Cecil Rhodes started developing it, Whitehall had never administered government there, nor provided funds or forces for its defense. All this had been done locally, first under the British South Africa Company chartered to Cecil Rhodes and his associates, and after 1923 under the Constitution of that date, established after the electorate had voted for self-government as against incorporation in the Union of South Africa. In fact, so self-governing was Rhodesia that between 1935 and 1953 (the beginning of the Federation) the Rhodesian Prime Minister sat as an equal in the meetings of Prime Ministers, first of the empire and later of the Commonwealth. The Prime Minister of the Federation (with Nyasaland and Northern Rhodesia) took his place until its dissolution in 1964. Thereafter the Prime Ministers of her two associates, now independent states, sat, but Rhodesia's was excluded because of the dispute which then arose.

Turning to this dispute and the circumstances of the Rhodesian assertion of independence, that country had had since the beginning of its history an electorate based on adult male suffrage, later extended to women, with modest literacy and property requirements. These qualifications are those adopted in this and other countries during early stages of representative government by a people among whom education was the exception, and experience, cultural or otherwise, was unequal. When white settlement began in 1890, Rhodesia was sparsely populated by very primitive people. The great bulk of its present population, white and black, has immigrated since then, attracted by opportunity and security of life and property available there. The Rhodesian Constitutional Commission was well aware of this situation:

> . . . the Shona, the Ndebele and the Europeans were all in turn [im]migrants, conquerors and settlers and all now know no other home. Thus they have established for themselves and their successors the right to remain in the country in perpetuity, a right which they have every intention of exercising.
>
> . . . For the[se] reasons . . . Rhodesia is the permanent and rightful home of peoples of different origins and backgrounds, and does not belong to one race or ethnic group alone. . . .

What did the Commission see as the end of the matter? A progressive extension of the franchise, but not majority rule. "For a time which cannot be measured by clock or calendar," Europeans would exercise the more authoritative voice at national government level, and Africans would have a voice that must be allowed increasing, but not limitless, power. The ultimate solution recommended was based on racial parity of representation as most likely to produce immediate and long-term confidence and stability. This was not everyone's cup of tea; neither was it everyone's business; nor was it apartheid. It was a matter relating solely to the internal affairs of Rhodesia — in which the United Nations was forbidden by its Charter to meddle — and to the political relation between Rhodesia and the United Kingdom. When the latter sought to impose a majority rule, in time measured by the calendar, Rhodesia severed the bands that bound them.

It was this act and Rhodesia's assumption, among the powers of the earth, of the separate and equal station to which the Laws of Nature and of Nature's God entitled her which the General Assembly and the Security Council said created a situation that threatened the peace. While Rhodesia threatened no one, the idea was that her independence, "if continued in time," would disturb the peace because, apparently, someone would attempt to terminate it, because of disapproval of Rhodesia's long-established internal legislation on suffrage. The General Assembly spelled this out in its Resolution of November 5, 1965, when it "reaffirm[ed] the right of the people of Southern Rhodesia to freedom and independence [— the very thing which was now threatening the peace —] and recognize[d] the legitimacy of their struggle for the enjoyment of their rights." What sort of rights? Their rights as set forth in the Charter of the United Nations, the Universal Declaration on the Granting of Independence to Colonial Countries and Peoples. [The resolution went on that the United Nations "solemnly warn[ed] the present authorities in Southern Rhodesia and the United Kingdom of Great Britain and Northern Ireland, in its capacity of administering Power, that the United Nations will oppose any declaration of independence which is not based on universal adult suffrage."]

How fortunate were the American colonies to have no United Nations to confront in 1776! I need hardly remind you that our Constitution had nothing to say about adult universal suffrage but did have a few pregnant paragraphs continuing the institution of slavery.

Of course, no one in the United Nations really believed that Britain, which had been handing out independence in wholesale lots, would fight Rhodesia, or that any African state would take on the prickly job.

Perhaps I might pause for a moment to remind you of the present situation. As everybody knew, this blockade of Rhodesia has not worked. Therefore, Her Majesty's government in accordance with that universal principle which seems to instigate all fanatics that one must redouble effort on finding oneself on the wrong road, has asked the United Nations to extend the blockade and our African friends have raised their cry that the British should come out of the bushes and gain enough courage to fight Rhodesia by arms. The point I am making here is that this highly theoretical and imaginative threat was not posed *by* Rhodesia but *against* Rhodesia. From this premise only the most Humpty-Dumpty reasoning could move to the conclusion that Rhodesia should be punished by international action aimed at overthrowing her government and ending her independence. The reasoning provided by academic authority [McDougal and Reisman] is hardly less curious. Here it is:

> . . . In the contemporary intensely interdependent world, peoples interact not merely through the modalities of collaborative or combative operations but also through shared subjectivities — not merely through the physical movements of goods and services or exercises with armaments, but also through communications in which they simply take each other into account. . . . Much more important than the physical movements are the

> communications which people make to each other. In the case of Rhodesia, the other peoples of Africa have regarded themselves as affected by the authoritarian and racist policies of the Rhodesian elites. . . .

In simpler and nonpejorative terms, they do not like Rhodesia's elective system. Subjectivity means the quality or condition of viewing things exclusively through the medium of one's own mind or individuality; the condition of being absorbed in one's personal feelings, thoughts, concerns, etc. The term also means personal bias, emotional predisposition, the substitution of perception for reality, etc. The authors may mean any or all of those senses. But the point is that what we have here is the idea that law is only a mirror of the beholder's emotional condition at the moment.

Consider a situation which wounds shared subjectivities of a wholly different nature and ones with which we may be less in sympathy. Within the month the nations of Eastern Europe have met in Moscow to consider their shared dislike of what they regard as the deviationist, antidemocratic, indeed, bourgeois policies of the Czechoslovakian elites in permitting a modicum of personal liberty in that country. Rumor even carries reports of Soviet troop movements near the Czech border. Suppose that, instead of repeating its armed interventionist tactics in Hungary in 1956, the Soviet Union should appeal to the Security Council to stop this Czech assault on the shared subjectivities of community states. I suppose that the authors would expect it to direct us all to cease building bridges to the East and refurbish our embargoes against trade with a renegade communist state.

Consider, too, our own parlous position in the face of this doctrine. Does any country in the world so widely offend shared subjectivities as we do? Ask General de Gaulle, Mao Tse Tung, Ho Chi Minh, Mrs. Gandhi, Castro, the Arabs. Even the South Vietnamese are not too sure. And what about our own subjectivities should our own brain child, the United Nations, expound on what we have done to theirs. Somehow this romantic interpretation of the Charter does not make it read like the last best hope for peace on earth.

Nevertheless, ridiculous as it appears on analysis, much as it recalls Cicero's observations that there is nothing so absurd but some philosopher has said it, the fact remains that it rationalizes an attempt to overthrow a government that has done us no harm and threatens no harm to any state. Is participation in such an assault desirable foreign policy? Is this cabal what Mr. Hull thought was being prepared at Dumbarton Oaks or what the Senate almost unanimously ratified?

Of course, clever men will attempt to use any instrument to accomplish indirectly what they cannot do directly; but we should have known better than to agree to it had we not been bemused by substituting ideas that appealed to us as ethical for the plain engagements of sovereign states. In the Charter the subscribing sovereigns undertook not to use force as an instrument of policy in their international relations. By a process that cannot be dignified as reasoning, force applied against another state has not been equated with the failure to adopt internally the principle of universal suffrage plus the egalitarian doctrine of equally weighted votes as announced by the Supreme Court of the United States in Baker v. Carr. And this — mark you! — is only the first application of that new doctrine of international lawyers — the sovereign equality of shared subjectivities. . . .

One of the troubles of the troubled age in which we live is that too many people are trying to achieve harmony of interest by forcing everyone to harmonize with them. Conscience used to be an inner voice of self-discipline; now it is a clarion urge to discipline others. It took a long time to develop the international precept that peace would be furthered by governments' having respect for each other's autonomy. That should apply to them when acting in concert. This is the notion embedded in Paragraph 7 of Article 2 of the Charter. Whatever mistakes they may otherwise have made, the draftsmen of the Charter, at least, did not intend to open the way for endless conflict through unbridled impulses to reform. The new romantic impulse is to overthrow that wise inhibition in favor of a compulsion to reshape the world to fit all sorts of shared subjectivities.

Another thought also occurs. Perhaps, if the meek are to inherit the earth, they might consider adding a clause to the litany. It could follow "From all blindness of heart; from pride, vainglory, and hypocrisy; from envy, hatred, and malice, and all uncharitableness" and would add "and from the United Nations Charter as distorted by professors of international law,

Good Lord, deliver us."

III. A Brief Overview of Economic Sanctions

The UN's invocation of economic sanctions against Rhodesia had no close historical precedents. Sanctions had been used, to be sure, on many occasions since the invention of the so-called economic weapon during the Napoleonic Wars. The twentieth century, in particular, contains numerous examples of sanctioning campaigns, but none comparable to the Rhodesian measures in comprehensiveness and universality. Even subsequent efforts to bring similar pressures to bear upon South Africa, as we shall see later in this Problem (see pages 576-577 infra), never were pursued with the enthusiasm of the sanctions imposed against Rhodesia.

A. International Sanctions

The story of the League of Nations' experience with sanctioning is instructive, if hardly dispositive of the question of the effectiveness of sanc-

tions in general. The founders of the League envisioned economic sanctions as the organization's chief peacekeeping tool; military sanctions were
to be of only secondary importance. Accordingly, Article 16 of the League
Covenant provided for immediate and automatic economic sanctions
against a member state that resorted to war. In the fluid world of post-World
War I politics, however, it very soon became apparent that a provision of
that kind was too inflexible to be accommodated realistically within the
traditional framework of politics and diplomacy. Thus, the League decided
in 1921 that the decision as to when the conditions of Article 16 were met
(and, therefore, sanctions were mandatory) was one that each member state
was authorized to make for itself; the article's obligations could not be
activated solely by action of the League Council or Assembly.

The first actual application of Article 16 by the League came in 1935,
when it applied sanctions against Italy for its attempted, and ultimately
successful, conquest of Ethiopia. Not surprisingly, some of the same issues
confronted the League then as confronted the UN 30 years later vis-à-vis
Rhodesia. The League had a serious problem of sanctions-breaking within
its own ranks, particularly by Austria and Hungary; and there was also the
nagging feeling that perhaps the sanctions were in fact harming those persons whom they were intended to aid. Haile Selassie himself brought this
last point poignantly home when he told the League in June 1936 that the
major effect of the sanctions seemed to have been to cause Italy to use
poison gas to hasten the conquest. For a critical assessment of the League's
Italian sanctions, see Taubenfeld and Taubenfeld, The "Economic
Weapon": The League and the United Nations, 1964 Am. Socy. Intl. L.
Proceedings 183.

As discouraging as the failure of sanctions against Italy was, however, it
should be appreciated that there were factors working against their success
that were not present in the Rhodesian situation. First of all, the sanctions
were intended only to prevent the success of the single military adventure at
hand, not to bring about political and social change within Italy itself.
Therefore, they had only a very short time — the time span of the Ethiopian campaign itself — to succeed. Italy had planned the invasion in advance and had simply stockpiled much of the material that was necessary
for that one relatively short war. The Rhodesian sanctions, in contrast, were
open-ended, designed to last until the Smith regime gave way to a truly
representative, black majority government.

A second distinguishing factor in the Italian case was that the League's
limited membership meant that several major states were not legally bound
to comply with the embargo. In particular, the United States and Germany
continued to trade with Italy much as before. Membership in the UN, on
the other hand, is very nearly universal; and, furthermore, Article 2(6) of the
Charter provides that the UN will "ensure" the cooperation of non-member
states "so far as may be necessary for the maintenance of international peace
and security." (Unhappily, a key UN member state — South Africa — failed

to fulfill its legal obligations under the UN Charter to enforce sanctions against Rhodesia.)

Finally, the world political situation in the mid-1930s was such that France and the United Kingdom, neither of which supported sanctions with much enthusiasm, still believed that Italy — a World War I ally — might join them in the coming struggle against Germany. They were, therefore, reluctant to see Italy treated too harshly. No such considerations existed in the case of Rhodesia.

B. Regional Sanctions

There are several instances of sanctioning undertaken on a regional rather than a global basis. Three of these efforts were undertaken by the Organization of American States (OAS). The first was against the Dominican Republic when the Trujillo family controlled the government. The OAS ordered the breaking of diplomatic relations with the Trujillo regime and also the suspension of all trade in arms and war implements with it. Res. I, Sixth Meeting of Consultation of Ministers of Foreign Affairs, San Jose, Costa Rica, August 16-21, 1960, Final Act, OAS Off. Rec. OEA/Ser.C/II.6 (English) at 8 (1960). Within a year Trujillo was toppled by an internal insurrection, allegedly supported by the CIA. While sanctions undoubtedly were a factor in events leading to the end of the Trujillo government, there is little evidence that they were the decisive factor.

The second example of OAS sanctioning is a more interesting one. This effort was the sanctioning of Cuba (Res. I, Ninth Meeting of Consultation of Ministers of Foreign Affairs, Washington, D.C., U.S.A., July 21-26, 1964, Final Act, OAS Off. Rec. OEA/Ser.D/III.15 (English) at 3 (1964)), which consisted of withholding diplomatic recognition of the Castro regime and also of a trade embargo, both measures being a reaction to the Cuban policy of "exporting revolution" to other Latin American states. The sanctions were less than wholly successful for several reasons. First, there was the heavy support provided by the Soviet Union to Cuba, to the extent of $1.5 million per day at its peak. Second was the steep increase in the price of sugar, Cuba's lone cash crop: sugar prices increased sixfold between 1959 and 1974, though prices have since come down considerably from their 1974 peak. A third problem lay in the fact that the sanctions were not applied uniformly, even within the regional framework. Mexico, for instance, was never part of the effort, and Chile withdrew its support after the accession of the Allende government in 1970 (although the junta that overthrew Allende in 1973 reimposed the sanctions). Finally, the general enthusiasm of the Latin American states for the quarantine faded in the late 1960s and early 1970s, when many states came to believe, rightly or wrongly, that Castro no longer sought to foment revolution in the region. Beginning in 1972, one Latin state after another defected from the sanctioning campaign, with the quarantine being formally lifted in 1975 (Res. I, Sixteenth Meeting of Consultation of Ministers of Foreign Affairs, San Jose, Costa Rica, July 29, 1975, Final Act, OAS Off. Rec. OEA/Ser.C/II.16 (English) at 4 (1975)). Although the United States voted for the lifting of the sanctions against Cuba, it has kept its own sanctions in place and, in recent years, actually has strengthened them. See page 593 infra.

The third OAS sanctions effort began as a response to the military coup that overthrew the democratically elected government of President Aristide in Haiti in late September 1991. On 3 October 1991, the OAS Ministers of Foreign Affairs met and adopted Resolution MRE/Res.1/91, OEA/Ser.F/V.1 (1991), which condemned the coup, recognized President Aristide's representatives as the only legitimate representatives of Haiti to the OAS, and recommended that each member state, inter alia, suspend economic, financial, and commercial ties with Haiti. Five days later the Ministers adopted a follow-up resolution urging member states "to proceed immediately to freeze the assets of the Haitian State and to impose a trade embargo on Haiti, except for humanitarian aid." MRE/Res.2/91, OEA/Ser.F/V.1 (1991). Subsequent resolutions sought to expand the sanctions and to achieve greater compliance with the trade embargo. MRE/Res.3/92, OEA/Ser.F/V.1 (1992); MRE/Res.4/92, OEA/Ser.F/V.1 (1992); MRE/Res.5/93, OEA/Ser.F/V.1 (1993). Eventually the UN Security Council, taking note of these resolutions and determining that the Haitian situation threatened international peace and security in the region, invoked Chapter VII of the UN Charter and ordered a limited but mandatory trade embargo (S.C. Res. 841, 48 U.N. SCOR, Res. and Dec. at 119 (1993)), an embargo that it called upon member states to enforce using "such measures commensurate with the specific circumstances as may be necessary. . . ." (S.C. Res. 875, 48 U.N. SCOR, Res. and Dec. at 125 (1993)). Still later, invoking both Chapters VII and VIII, it adopted a near-complete trade embargo and authorized member states, "acting nationally or through regional agencies or arrangements, to use such measures commensurate with the specific circumstances as may be necessary under the authority of the Security Council to ensure strict implementation of the provisions of the present resolution and earlier relevant resolutions. . . ." (S.C. Res. 917, U.N. SCOR, 49th Sess., 3376th mtg. at 4, U.N. Doc. S/RES/917 (1994)).

Another regional — actually subregional — sanctioning effort recently occurred in Africa in connection with the efforts of the Economic Community of West African States (ECOWAS) to achieve a peaceful resolution of the conflict in Liberia. When the NPFL, the principal party opposing the interim government, refused to recognize ECOWAS's peacekeeping force (ECOMOG) as an impartial and neutral force in the conflict, ECOWAS in July 1992 imposed comprehensive economic sanctions against the territory controlled by the NPFL. Report of the Secretary-General on the Question of Liberia at 7, U.N. Doc. S/25402 (1993). Although ECOWAS then sought a Security Council resolution making the sanctions binding on all members of the international community, an idea the Secretary-General thought worth considering, id. at 11, the Council has limited its response to two resolutions establishing an embargo on all deliveries of weapons and military equipment to Liberia (except military equipment and assistance for the sole use of ECOMOG). S.C. Res. 788, 47 U.N. SCOR, Res. and Dec. at 99 (1992); S.C. Res. 813, 48 U.N. SCOR, Res. and Dec. at 108 (1993).

The most notorious and lengthy example of regional sanctioning is the effort of the Arab states against Israel, which began in 1945. The Arab League Boycott Office, which is controlled by the Secretariat of the Arab League (subject to guidance from the League Council and the Economic Council), has attempted over the years to bring pressures of various kinds to bear upon Israel, most controversially in the form of "secondary boycotts," that is, the imposition upon companies working in the Arab states of a requirement not only that they themselves observe the boycott by not having dealings with Israel, but also that they not deal with other companies that do business with Israel.

The United States, which considers this boycott an effort to deny rather than to encourage human rights, has responded to it in a number of ways. The Tax Reform Act of 1976, for instance, cut back on tax advantages available to U.S. firms participating in the boycott. 26 U.S.C. §908 (1988). See Rubenfeld, Legal and Tax Implications of Participation in International Boycotts, 32 Tax L. Rev. 613 (1977). Subsequent legislation also makes illegal certain acts taken in compliance with "any boycott fostered or imposed by a foreign country against a country which is friendly to the United States . . ." (50 U.S.C. App. §2407 (1988)). For a comprehensive survey of the Arab League boycott and the response of the United States and other countries thereto, see A. Lowenfeld, Trade Controls for Political Ends ch. III (2d ed. 1983).

C.   Unilateral Sanctions

The incidence of sanctions imposed unilaterally for human rights purposes was infrequent until relatively recent times. It was not until the mid-1970s that the U.S. Congress enacted legislation on a grand scale to require the President to sanction (primarily by withholding military or economic assistance) states engaging in a consistent pattern of gross violations of human rights. Under the Carter Administration, laws mandating aid cut-offs to recipient countries who violated human rights norms were implemented, and the concept of unilateral economic sanctions for human rights purposes infiltrated almost every aspect of public and private economic policy and trade. One noted example was the successful campaign waged in the Congress to choke the economic lifeline between the United States and Uganda, culminating in the trade embargo of 1978, discussed at pages 73-76 of Problem I. The efforts of the Carter and successive administrations to bring economic pressure to bear to further human rights are considered in more detail in Problem XIII. Other countries increasingly are taking the same approach. See, e.g., the Dutch cut-off of a $1.5 billion aid program to Suriname after the events in that country chronicled at pages 237-239 of Problem III. G. Hufbauer and J. Schott, Economic Sanctions Reconsidered: History and Current Policy 725-729 (1985).

D. Voluntary Sanctions

Finally, what might be termed voluntary sanctions should be considered. Recommendations by the UN General Assembly that member states impose economic sanctions fall readily into this category. Such sanctions are voluntary because the General Assembly only has the power to make recommendations to its members. Decisions that are legally binding must come from the Security Council and, furthermore, must be taken pursuant to a finding of the existence of a threat to or a breach of the peace or an act of aggression under Chapter VII of the Charter.

In at least three instances, the General Assembly has voted for voluntary sanctions. The first instance came in 1949, when the Assembly voted to impose an embargo on war materials against Albania and Bulgaria, which at the time were supporting Communist insurgents in Greece (G.A. Res. 288, U.N. Doc. A/1251, at 9 (1949)). Then, in 1951, came a recommendation for a similar embargo against mainland China (G.A. Res. 498(V), 5 U.N. GAOR Supp. (No. 20A) at 1, U.N. Doc. A/1775/Add.1 (1951)). Out of deference to the Soviet bloc, the General Assembly only included strategic materials in its sanctions; and, even so, the Soviet Union and its allies consistently violated the resolution.

The third example occurred in 1962, when for the first time the General Assembly adopted this tactic against South Africa. States were requested to take the following actions against South Africa: the breaking of diplomatic relations; the closing of their ports to all vessels flying the South African flag; the enacting of domestic legislation to forbid ships flying their flags from entering South African ports; the boycotting of all goods sold by South Africa; and the denial of landing and passage facilities to all aircraft of South African registry (G.A. Res. 1761, 17 U.N. GAOR Supp. (No. 17) at 9, U.N. Doc. A/5217 (1962)). For 15 years this resolution was widely ignored by South Africa's most consistent trading partners: the United Kingdom, the United States, France, West Germany, and Switzerland. Beginning in 1977, however, with the Security Council's adoption of a mandatory arms embargo on South Africa, efforts to impose further sanctions — both mandatory and voluntary — increased. Numerous resolutions recommending voluntary sanctions have been adopted by the General Assembly, as have a few such resolutions by the Security Council. For further discussion of these sanction initiatives against South Africa, see pages 578-580 infra.

IV.   U.S. Implementation and Enforcement of UN Sanctions Against Rhodesia

The brief overview of economic sanctions in the previous section prepares the way for considering some of the domestic, as well as international, aspects of the sanctioning process contemplated by the UN Charter. This process relies primarily, if not exclusively, on the member states of the UN to adopt domestic laws — whether statutes, executive orders, or administrative measures — implementing UN-ordered sanctions and then to monitor and, if need be, enforce compliance with such laws. Thus, Article 48 of the UN Charter provides:

> 1. The action required to carry out the decisions of the Security Council for the maintenance of international peace and security shall be taken by all the Members of the United Nations or by some of them, as the Security Council may determine.
> 2. *Such decisions shall be carried out by the Members of the United Nations directly* and through their action in the appropriate international agencies of which they are members.

(Emphasis added.) To quote Lowenfeld, supra page 513, at 452:

> Though everyone referred to the economic measures against Rhodesia as United Nations sanctions, in fact the United Nations had no enforcement mechanism, no investigative capability, until 1968 not even a coordination facility, and no authority to deal with individuals engaged in trade or other economic activity with Rhodesia. The counterpart of the original understanding that the United Nations deals only with states — often deplored in the context of human rights — was that the United Nations as an organization was wholly dependent on states for implementation of the sanctions program. What [the Security Council resolutions] accomplished was to impose an obligation on states — an obligation that they discharged in quite different ways.

How the United States lived up to its obligation in this regard is the subject of this section.

A.   *U.S. Implementation of Sanctions*

1.   The Legal Framework

Legislative Reference Service, Library of Congress, The United Nations Participation Act Sections Relating to Economic and Military Action
1-4, June 6, 1967

The United Nations Participation Act of 1945 (22 U.S.C. §287 [Supp. V 1975]) was designed to implement United States participation in the

United Nations following Senate ratification of the United Nations Charter. The United Nations Participation Act was amended in 1949 and again in 1965. Sections 5, 6 and 7 (22 U.S.C. §§287c, d, and d-1) of the United Nations Participation Act relate to economic and military sanctions.

Provisions of the United Nations Charter

Before examining Sections 5, 6 and 7 and the effect of subsequent amendments, attention should be given to the pertinent provisions of the United Nations Charter for economic and military sanctions. Article 25 states:

> The Members of the United Nations agree to accept and carry out the decisions of the Security Council in accordance with the present Charter.

Article 25 in effect makes decisions of the Security Council binding upon members of the United Nations. It should be pointed out, however, that the permanent members of the Council, including the United States, can veto its decisions. Article 41 enables the Security Council to call upon members to apply economic sanctions, interruption of communications, and severance of diplomatic relations. Should the measures provided for under Article 41 prove inadequate, the Security Council is given authority under Article 42 to "take such action by air, sea or land forces as may be necessary to maintain or restore international peace and security. . . ."

Provisions of the United Nations Participation Act

Section 5(a) of the United Nations Participation Act [22 U.S.C. §287c (a)] authorizes the President, when called upon pursuant to Article 41 of the Charter by the Security Council, to apply economic sanctions or interruption of communications. Section 5(b) specifies a punishment or a fine of not more than $10,000 or imprisonment of not more than ten years or both to violators or evaders or those who attempt to evade or violate any rule, order, or regulation by the President pursuant to 5(a). Section 5(b) also calls for the forfeit to the United States of "any property, funds, securities, papers, or other articles or documents, or any vessel, together with her tackle, apparel, furniture, and equipment, or vehicle, concerned in such violation." The punishment applies to a natural person, a corporation (with the exception of the ten-year imprisonment), or to the officer, agent, or director of any corporation who knowingly participates in such violation or evasion. Section 5(b) was amended in 1949 to include "aircraft" as being subject to forfeit when concerned in violations of actions taken by the United States in cooperation with the Security Council pursuant to Article 41 of the Charter. This section was not changed by the 1965 amendment.

During the House Foreign Affairs Committee Hearings on the United Nations Participation Act of 1945 it was pointed out by Dean Acheson, then Under Secretary of State, that the effect of section 5 would be to give the President "the authority to do what we have by international treaty agreed to do." Congressman Kee then asked if the President "already has authority to apply other measures, such as severing diplomatic relations." Mr. Acheson responded, "Yes. Under the Constitution the President has that authority. But the interruption of economic relations and communications by rail, sea, radio and telegraph he would not have unless the Congress gave it to him."

The Senate Report on the United Nations Participation Act of 1945 cited precedents in prior legislation delegating to the President the authority to impose embargoes. With reference to Section 5 the following is stated in the Senate Report:

> The committee realizes that the powers proposed to be granted to the President under this section are very great. However, the basic decision in this regard was made when the Charter was ratified and this provision is simply a necessary corollary to our membership in the Organization. The committee also believes that the Security Council must be placed in the most effective position possible to act under article 41 since the prompt and effective application of economic and diplomatic sanctions by all the United Nations (or even the threat or possibility thereof) may avoid the necessity for the use of the armed forces available to the Security Council.

2. Presidential Action: Executive Orders 11,322 and 11,419

When on 16 December 1966 the Security Council adopted Resolution 232, imposing selective mandatory sanctions against Rhodesia (page 495 supra), President Lyndon Johnson moved swiftly pursuant to the authority granted him under the UN Participation Act to ensure U.S. compliance with them. By Executive Order No. 11,322 signed 5 January 1967 he prohibited those transactions proscribed by Resolution 232, including, inter alia, "[a]ny participation in the supply of oil or oil products to Southern Rhodesia (i) by any person subject to the jurisdiction of the United States, or (ii) by vessels or aircraft of United States registration, or (iii) by the use of any land or air transport facility located in the United States." Exec. Order No. 11,322 (Relating to Trade and Other Transactions Involving Southern Rhodesia), 3 C.F.R. §606 (1966-1970 Compilation), reprinted in 22 U.S.C. §287c app. at 5635 (1970) (Section 1(f)). A year and a half later, when the Security Council by Resolution 253 imposed comprehensive mandatory sanctions (page 496 supra), the President moved with equal dispatch. On 29 July 1968, the Department of State issued the following press release announcing the extension of U.S. prohibitions on trade and other transactions with Rhodesia.

U.S. Extends Program Banning Trade
with Southern Rhodesia
59 Dept. State Bull. 199 (1968)

The President on July 29 signed an Executive order [No. 11,419, set out immediately below] implementing United Nations Security Council Resolution No. 253 on May 29, 1968, which extends the program of mandatory economic sanctions against Southern Rhodesia. . . .

The mandatory sanctions imposed by the Security Council's resolution of May 29 supplement the selective mandatory sanctions imposed in December 1966 and the earlier voluntary measures taken by a large majority of the members of the United Nations in response to the Council's appeal of November 20, 1965, just after the Smith regime in Southern Rhodesia had unilaterally declared its independence, that economic relations with Southern Rhodesia be broken. The United States is fully supporting the Security Council Resolutions.

Executive Order No. 11,419 (Relating to Trade and
Other Transactions Involving Southern Rhodesia)
3 C.F.R. §737 (1966-1970 Compilation), reprinted in 22
U.S.C. §287c app. at 5636 (1970)

By virtue of the authority vested in me by the Constitution and laws of the United States, including section 5 of the United Nations Participation Act of 1945 (59 Stat. 620), as amended (22 U.S.C. 287c), and section 301 of Title 3 of the United States Code, and as President of the United States, and considering the measures which the Security Council of the United Nations by Security Council Resolution No. 253 adopted May 29, 1968, has decided upon pursuant to article 41 of the Charter of the United Nations, and which it has called upon all members of the United Nations, including the United States, to apply, it is hereby ordered:

SECTION 1. In addition to the prohibitions of section 1 of Executive Order No. 11322 of January 5, 1967, the following are prohibited effective immediately, notwithstanding any contracts entered into or licenses granted before the date of this Order:

(a) Importation into the United States of any commodities or products originating in Southern Rhodesia and exported therefrom after May 29, 1968.

(b) Any activities by any person subject to the jurisdiction of the United States which promote or are calculated to promote the export from Southern Rhodesia after May 29, 1968, of any commodities or products originating in Southern Rhodesia, and any dealings by any such person in any such commodities or products, including in particular any transfer of funds to Southern Rhodesia for the purposes of such activities or dealings; *Provided*, however, that the prohibition against the dealing in commodities or products exported from Southern Rhodesia shall not apply to any such commodities or products which, prior to the date of this Order, had been lawfully imported into the United States.

(c) Carriage in vessels or aircraft of United States registration or under charter to any person subject to the jurisdiction of the United States of any commodities or products originating in Southern Rhodesia and exported therefrom after May 29, 1968.

(d) Sale or supply by any person subject to the jurisdiction of the United States, or any other activities by any such person which promote or are calculated to promote the sale or supply, to any person or body in Southern Rhodesia or to any person or body for the purposes of any business carried on in or operated from Southern Rhodesia of any commodities or products. Such activities, including carriage in vessels or aircraft, may be authorized with respect to supplies intended strictly for medical purposes, educational equipment and material for use in schools and other educational institutions, publications, news material, and foodstuffs required by special humanitarian circumstances.

(e) Carriage in vessels or aircraft of United States registration or under charter to any person subject to the jurisdiction of the United States of any commodities or products consigned to any person or body in Southern Rhodesia, or to any person or body for the purposes of any business carried on in or operated from Southern Rhodesia.

(f) Transfer by any person subject to the jurisdiction of the United States directly or indirectly to any person or body in Southern Rhodesia of any funds or other financial or economic resources. Payments exclusively for pensions, for strictly medical, humanitarian or educational purposes, for the provision of news material or for foodstuffs required by special humanitarian circumstances may be authorized.

(g) Operation of any United States air carrier or aircraft owned or chartered by any person subject to the jurisdiction of the United States or of United States registration (i) to or from Southern Rhodesia or (ii) in coordination with any airline company constituted or aircraft registered in Southern Rhodesia. . . .

Section 6. Executive Order No. 11322 of January 5, 1967, implementing United Nations Security Council Resolution No. 232 of December 16, 1966, shall continue in effect as modified by sections 2, 3, and 4 of this Order.

/s/ Lyndon B. Johnson

The White House,
July 29, 1968.

3. The Overlooked (?) Loophole: Rhodesian Sanctions Regulation 31 C.F.R. §530.307 (1969)

While considerable attention is paid to Executive Orders initiating sanctions, the various regulations actually implementing them often are ignored. In the first edition of this coursebook, for instance, Executive Order No. 11,419 was set out in full, while the Treasury Department's regulations were not even mentioned. This omission calls for a mea culpa. It also affords the editors an excellent opportunity to show, in the words of Reverend Schulz, who first raised the issue in 1976, how "the U.S. embargo against Rhodesia was designed to be broken." South Africa: Hearings Before the Subcomm. on African Affairs of the Senate Comm. on Foreign Relations, 94th Cong., 2d Sess. 417 (1976).

Insofar as the *content* of the regulations was concerned, no cause for complaint existed, since they scrupulously tracked the provisions of the Executive Order (which in turn mirrored the terms of the Security Council Resolution). With respect to the *reach* of the regulations, however, the latter covered far fewer persons than a reader, especially one familiar with previous U.S. sanctions practice, would have been led to expect after perusing the Executive Order. Why? The reason was the exceptionally restrictive meaning the regulations gave to the phrase "person subject to the jurisdiction of the United States," a phrase that is found six times in the Executive Order and is intended to delimit its coverage.

Before the promulgation of the Rhodesian regulations, this operative phrase uniformly had been defined broadly to reach the activities of foreign branches and subsidiaries of U.S. corporations. For numerous examples of the boilerplate definition of the phrase in use since 1942, see Restatement (Third) of the Foreign Relations Law of the United States §414 Reporters' Note 4 at 277 (1987). Thus, the Cuban Assets Control Regulations read as follows (31 C.F.R. §515.329 (1993)):

§515.329   Person Subject to the Jurisdiction of the United States

The term "person subject to the jurisdiction of the United States" includes:

(a) Any individual, wherever located, who is a citizen or resident of the United States;

(b) Any person within the United States as defined in §515.330;

(c) Any corporation organized under the laws of the United States or of any State, territory, possession, or district of the United States; and

(d) Any corporation, partnership, or association, wherever organized or doing business, that is owned or controlled by persons specified in paragraph (a) or (c) of this section.

Yet in drafting the Rhodesian Sanctions Regulations the Treasury Department redefined the familiar phrase "person subject to the jurisdiction of the United States" to read as follows (31 C.F.R. §530.307 (1969)):

§530.307   Person Subject to the Jurisdiction of the United States

(a) The term "person subject to the jurisdiction of the United States" includes:

(1) Any person, wheresoever located, who is a citizen or resident of the United States;

(2) Any person actually within the United States;

(3) Any corporation organized under the laws of the United States or of any State, territory, possession, or district of the United States; and

(4) Any partnership, association, corporation, or other organization organized under the laws of, or having its principal place of business in, Southern Rhodesia which is owned or controlled by persons specified in subparagraph (1), (2), or (3) of this paragraph.

As the last subparagraph makes crystal clear, the Rhodesian regulations cover only *Rhodesian* branches and subsidiaries of U.S. corporations. Thus, U.S. subsidiaries of Mobil and Caltax in South Africa and (until 1974) Portuguese-ruled Mozambique were able — quite legally — to supply Rhodesia with the oil and petroleum products that enabled the Smith regime to survive for over a decade. See J. Jardim, Sanctions Double Cross: Oil to Rhodesia (1982).

This "glaring deficiency in the coverage of U.S. sanctions against Rhodesia" is difficult, if not impossible, to justify. Butcher, The Unique Nature of Sanctions Against South Africa and Resulting Enforcement Issues, 19 N.Y.U. J. Intl. L. & Pol. 821, 847 (1987). The official explanation attempts to rationalize this loophole by distinguishing UN-initiated from U.S. unilateral sanctions. In the case of Rhodesia, the Treasury Department has stated,

[t]he U.S. sanctions were so limited because, given the multilateral character of the U.N. embargo, it was more appropriate for the other U.N. members states to enforce the embargo in their own territory. For the United States alone to have applied its sanctions extraterritorially would have gone beyond the mandate of the United Nations, and even beyond the level of sanctions imposed by the United Kingdom, which sponsored the embargo.

The Office of Foreign Assets Control: Office of the Assistant Secretary (Enforcement and Operations), Report on Investigation into Alleged Violations of the Rhodesian Sanctions Regulations by the Mobil Oil and Caltex Petroleum Corporations at iv (Oct. 5, 1985).

The Treasury Department explanation is both strained and disingenuous. In the first place, while the UN sanction process obviously contemplated member states implementing and enforcing sanctions within their respective territories, this "more appropriate" approach in no wise precludes other ones. If U.S. unilateral sanctions with extraterritorial reach are legal under general international law, as the United States consistently has maintained, surely such U.S. laws implementing Security Council-mandated sanctions are legal, too, absent a specific limiting provision in the sanction resolution itself. Especially in the case of Rhodesia, where the UN adopted sanctions with full knowledge that South Africa would not implement them, the principle of effectiveness dictates the conclusion that the UN did not rule out the possibility that member states might implement sanctions with extraterritorial reach. Indeed, any other conclusion assumes that the Security Council in adopting Resolution 253 knowingly embarked upon a meaningless exercise.

Second, for the United States to have applied U.S. sanctions extraterritorially would not, as the Treasury Department suggests, "have gone beyond the mandate of the United Nations. . . ." There is nothing in the text of Resolution 253 to support this view. Moreover, an admittedly opaque opinion of the UN's Legal Counsel seems to suggest that, even absent Security Council authorization, nothing in "public international law precludes a State from enacting laws having extraterritorial effect and providing for enforcement within the territory of the legislating State." Sixth Report of the Security Council Committee Established in Pursuance of Resolution 253 (1968) Concerning the Question of Southern Rhodesia, 29 U.N. SCOR Special Supp. (No. 2) at 31, U.N. Doc. S/11178/Rev. 1 (1974).

Finally, the fact that U.S. sanctions having an extraterritorial effect would have gone "even beyond the level of sanctions imposed by the United Kingdom" is true but irrelevant. That the United Kingdom had adopted sanctions "designed to be broken" was no reason for the United States to follow suit. In view of the "Oilgate" scandal that surfaced in the United Kingdom in 1978, moreover, it is passing strange that the Treasury Department in 1985 still should regard that country as a role model insofar as sanctions implementation is concerned. For discussion of the Oilgate scandal involving Shell and BP's violations of U.K. sanctions law, see pages 559-561 infra.

B. U.S. Enforcement of Sanctions

1. Introduction

Although the U.S. regulations implementing UN sanctions against Rhodesia obviously left a lot to be desired, there is little doubt that at least initially the United States made a good faith attempt to enforce the regulations it had adopted. Thus, Lowenfeld, supra page 513, at 467, relates:

In the first five years of the United Nations' embargo program, no country — with the possible exception of Great Britain [?] — enforced the sanctions as effectively as the United States. Even if enforcement was not as zealous — especially with respect to subsidiaries — as in regard to the United States' own economic denial programs, the existence of enforcement staffs at the Commerce and Treasury Departments, a world-wide reporting network, and an experienced customs service resulted in close to air-tight sealing off of prohibited trade between the United States and Rhodesia. None of the cases of sanctions violations reported to the United Nations through 1971 seems to have involved trade to or from the United States.

Some two years after the promulgation of Executive Order No. 11,419, the first fines were levied against violators of the sanctions. In April 1970, William H. Muller & Co., Inc., a New York export-import firm, pleaded guilty to importing $367,782 worth of Rhodesian chrome concentrate and ore into the United States. The company was fined the maximum allowable under the UN Participation Act of 1945: $10,000 (N.Y. Times, Apr. 1, 1970, at 12, col. 1). No corporate officials were fined in connection with the company's breach of the sanctions.

Another instance in which sanctions-breaking was punished by the United States came in April 1972, when two corporations and four individuals pleaded guilty to violating Department of Commerce regulations against trade with Rhodesia (15 C.F.R. §11.2(1975)). The defendants had arranged for the construction of a $50 million chemical fertilizer plant for Sable Chemical Industries in Que Que, Rhodesia, and had contracted with the Rhodesian regime to ship $5 million worth of ammonia to supply the plant. The two companies were Margas Shipping Company of Panama City, Panama, and IDI Management, Inc., of Cincinnati, Ohio. Two of the individuals who were convicted were officials of IDI; a third was a businessman who lived in the Bahamas; and the fourth was the Vermont tax commissioner (N.Y. Times, Apr. 13, 1972, at 5, col. 3).

The very fact that the United States attempted to enforce sanctions, however, ultimately led to trouble. Congress, it will be recalled, never had approved U.S. sanctions against Rhodesia, and some U.S. Congress members believed that, in undertaking prosecutions against corporations such as Muller & Co., the United States was going too far in the direction of sacrificing its own vital interests to vague and even misguided UN concerns. Bills to roll back U.S. implementation of UN sanctions had been introduced in Congress since 1967, but they gained new adherents in 1971 when the issue became linked with supposed national security concerns. Lobbyists for U.S. corporations with substantial interests in Rhodesia — notably Union Carbide Corporation — argued that, notwithstanding Security Council sanctions and the obligation under Article 25 to comply with them, the United States should make an exception in the case of important strategic materials. Senator Harry F. Byrd, Jr., of Virginia, introduced the following bill to this effect.

2.   Congress Enacts the Byrd Amendment

U.N. Sanctions Against Rhodesia — Chrome
Senate Bill S. 1404, 92d Cong., 1st Sess. (1971)

To amend the United Nations Participation Act of 1945 to prevent the imposition thereunder of any prohibition on the importation into the United States of any strategic and critical material from any free world country for so long as the importation of like materials from any Communist country is not prohibited by law.

Be it enacted by the Senate and House of Representatives of the United States of America in Congress assembled, That section 5(a) of the United Nations Participation Act of 1945 (22 U.S.C. §287c (a)) is amended by adding at the end thereof the following new sentence: "On or after the effective date of this sentence, the President may not prohibit or regulate the importation into the United States pursuant to this section of any material determined to be strategic and critical pursuant to section 2 of the Strategic and Critical Materials Stock Piling Act (50 U.S.C. §98a) which is the product of any foreign country or area not listed as a Communist-dominated country or area in general headnote 3(d) of the Tariff Schedules of the United States (19 U.S.C. §1202) for so long as the importation into the United States of material of that kind which is the product of such Communist-dominated countries or areas is not prohibited by any provision of law."

Hearings on S. 1404, U.N. Sanctions Against Rhodesia — Chrome, Before the Senate Committee on Foreign Relations
92d Cong., 1st Sess. 1, 1-7, 11, 19-23, 33-36, 77-78, 82 (1971)

[Senator McGee.] The committee this morning is holding the first of two consecutive public hearings devoted to consideration of a proposal, S. 1404, introduced in the Senate by Senator Harry Byrd, of Virginia. This bill would amend the United Nations Participation Act of 1945 in such a way as to prevent the President having authority to prohibit imports of any strategic material into the United States from a non-Communist country unless that material were also prohibited from importation from a Communist country. . . .

STATEMENT OF HON. HARRY F. BYRD, JR., U.S. SENATOR FROM THE STATE OF VIRGINIA

Senator Byrd. . . . Mr. Chairman and gentlemen of the committee, on March 29 I introduced S. 1404, a bill designed to end the dependence of the United States upon the Soviet Union for chrome ore — a material vital to the defense of this country.

The United States today faces an imminent and serious shortage of chrome. This material is essential in the manufacture of such critical defense items as jet aircraft, missiles and nuclear submarines. . . .

In my view, the imposition of sanctions on Rhodesia by the United Nations Security Council was not justified. The principal reasons given for the sanctions policy were three in number: (1) Rhodesia unilaterally declared her independence from Great Britain; (2) the Rhodesian Government failed to provide for "an orderly transition to majority rule,"; and (3) Rhodesia represents "a threat to international peace and security."

As to the first point, the declaration of independence, that, I feel, is rightly a matter to be settled between Great Britain and Rhodesia. It is not properly the business of the United Nations or the United States.

The second charge is positively ludicrous. If the United Nations Security Council were to impose economic sanctions on every country ruled by a minority, it would have to begin with one of the most prominent members of the Council itself — the Soviet Union, where 240 million people are ruled by a tiny handful of Communist Party leaders.

Recent figures show that 37 members of the United Nations do not have a form of government based on majority rule, and that adherence to the majority rule principle is questionable in 25 other member countries.

Clearly, the existence of minority rule does not justify punitive action by the United Nations against any country.

Turning to the third charge made by the United Nations Security Council, namely, that Rhodesia threatens world peace, this is obviously absurd.

Whom has Rhodesia threatened? What nation has reason to fear an assault by this small African nation?

The answer, of course, is that no one actually believes that Rhodesia threatens the peace.

The policy of the United Nations Security Council toward Rhodesia is rooted, I feel, in falsehood and injustice. Yet, the United States has actively supported this policy.

COMPLIANCE OF U.N. MEMBERSHIP WITH SANCTIONS

It should be noted that the sanctions policy is not only unjust, but is also ineffective. The Secretary General of the United Nations has written to all member states requesting information on actions taken by the several governments to assure compliance with the sanctions against Rhodesia.

As of the latest available Security Council reports, replies had been received from 104 of the 127 members of the United Nations. This means that 23 members have not even answered the inquiry of the Secretary General.

Of the nations which have replied, at least five — Zambia, Botswana, Portugal, Malawi, and Switzerland — have indicated that they are unwilling or unable to comply with the United Nations policy. And of the 95 countries that have definitely indicated compliance, many never had any trade with Rhodesia in the first place. This fact was specifically noted in replies from 13 member countries.

Furthermore, enforcement of the boycott has not been successful. Last year a special United Nations committee on enforcement of the sanctions reported that 60 reports of violations were received during 1969. A total of 21 complaints of violations involving France, Japan, the Netherlands, Italy, Spain, and West Germany were investigated. In addition, the Soviet Union has stated that Communist China, which, of course, is not a member of the United Nations, is not implementing the sanctions.

EFFECT OF TRADE EMBARGO ON RHODESIAN ECONOMY

The effort to destroy the Rhodesian economy by means of trade embargo clearly is a failure. The 1971 economic survey of Rhodesia indicates an increase in the nation's gross national product from $727 million in 1965 to $1,027 million in 1970 — an increase of 41 percent — and despite the sanctions, Rhodesia's export trade rose from $237 million in 1968 to $336 million in 1969. In addition, a record 254,000 tourists visited Salisbury, the capital of Rhodesia, in 1969. . . .

RESTATEMENT OF PROBLEM

[Senator McGEE.] As I see it, as you framed it here, the problem that is raised of whether the specific issue, namely the U.S. need for chrome, should take precedence over a much broader policy position or principle, namely, the role of the United Nations in the sanctions proceedings against Rhodesia. For better or for worse, however complicating this may have been, the whole matter in Africa has assumed not only a proportion, but a dimension that is quite out of balance with the immediacy. The role of our own country, as I see it, is supporting a broad principle to which it seemingly would adhere as a member of the United Nations or at least sustaining a United Nations action, rightfully or wrongfully, as opposed to the country's immediate interest in protecting, as you describe it, a non-Communist source of chrome.

Does that put the problem confrontation fairly? I am not trying to distort what you said, but just simply to rephrase it.

Senator BYRD. Yes; I think the chairman has phrased it quite well; he has phrased it fairly. It is, I recognize, in the context of the times, in the context of the general political situation, should we say, a difficult choice that the committee will need to make.

ACTION AGAINST RHODESIA EXECUTIVE, NOT CONGRESSIONAL

I think it is well perhaps to point out again that the action taken against Rhodesia was a unilateral action on the part of the Chief Executive of our Nation without congressional approval.

Senator PEARSON. Senator Byrd, by what authority does the President take that action?

Senator BYRD. He takes that action under the United Nations Participation Act. I do not charge that he acted illegally. I do suggest, however, that the Congress has a right, as I see it, to review his action, and has a right, as I see it, to adopt legislation such as I am suggesting. . . .

STATEMENT OF DAVID D. NEWSOM, ASSISTANT SECRETARY OF STATE FOR AFRICAN AFFAIRS; ACCOMPANIED BY JOHN A. ARMITAGE, DIRECTOR, OFFICE OF UNITED NATIONS POLITICAL AFFAIRS; AND ROBERT FARRAND, DEPARTMENT OF STATE

. . . What we are dealing with here is essentially an international problem, one involving the highly charged issues of race and colonialism. It is a problem without analogies, either to our history or to other world situations. It is one which must be approached on its merits, with our own national interests in mind, but with the objective of preventing a continuing unresolved and provocative situation in the heart of Africa. Such a situation would not be helpful to us or to our friends. . . .

We have consistently supported British efforts to obtain a satisfactory settlement and none are more anxious than we to see such a settlement reached. We are not now in a position to speculate about either the duration or outcome of these current talks. But, pending their outcome, it is important, and I believe very important, that we in the United States seek to avoid any action which would lessen their chances of success.

And, in our view, a departure by the United States from a complete endorsement of the sanctions policy at this critical juncture could have such an effect.

EFFECTS OF ENACTMENT OF S. 1404

The legislation now under consideration would have exactly this effect. It would encourage the Rhodesian authorities in their determination to maintain a situation which we consider neither practically tenable except in the short-run nor morally defensible at all. Its enactment would make it clear that the United States, in return for better access to chrome ore at lower prices, is prepared formally and unilaterally to renounce a freely assumed treaty obligation; we would be the first nation to do so over the

Rhodesian sanctions issue. We would damage our standing in almost all of Africa and in those other nations of the world that see the Rhodesian issue as a test of our commitment to our international obligations. We would strengthen the arguments of those who maintain that the only possible solution in southern Africa is a violent solution.

We would weaken the hand of the British in their efforts to bring about a negotiated settlement. We would undermine the U.N. effort to enforce sanctions, which we have thus far sought to uphold and, wherever possible, to strengthen. And we would open to question the long-term credibility of the U.S. Government with regard to its treaty obligations and commitments. . . .

EFFECTS OF SANCTIONS ON BLACKS

Senator McGEE. Somewhere in your text you made reference to the fact that there is reason to believe that the U.N. sanctions program has had some impact on the internal economics of Rhodesia. The suggestion sometimes made in that regard is that perhaps its principal effect would be felt by the blacks in Rhodesia. Would that be the case, in your judgment? In other words, are the effects of the sanctions more hurtful to the very people that manifest a source of concern to the U.N.?

Mr. NEWSOM. This is, I know, Mr. Chairman, an argument that is quite often made. In the conversations that I have had with visitors to Rhodesia, both white and black, frequent reference is made to the importance, certainly by many of the educated articulate Africans inside Rhodesia, [of] the maintenance of sanctions as an indication of continued outside support for their goal of an ultimate majority franchise in Rhodesia, whatever the short-term economic consequences for their people may be. . . .

STATUS OF U.N. SECURITY COUNCIL RESOLUTIONS

Senator McGEE. Do United Nations Security Council resolutions which have no terminal date set on them, run on in perpetuity or do they have to be renewed at some predetermined date? What is their status?

Mr. NEWSOM. No; in this case, the action of the Security Council would run on until the Security Council was satisfied that the conditions which have existed in Rhodesia, which brought about their original action, no longer existed.

COMPLIANCE WITH MANDATORY U.N. SECURITY COUNCIL DECISION

Senator McGEE. Has the United States ever refused or failed to comply with a mandatory U.N. Security Council decision?

Mr. NEWSOM. No, Mr. Chairman. I think we have an excellent international record of compliance with those actions in the United Nations which we have supported. Where we have felt that we could not, for one reason or another, support this kind of action we have opposed it in the Security Council itself.

Mr. ARMITAGE. I would like to say this is the only mandatory sanction program that the U.N. has undertaken. . . .

U.S. POSITION TOWARD SOUTH AFRICA

Senator COOPER. What is the position of the United States toward South Africa? How does it compare South Africa with Rhodesia? Were there any mandatory sanctions voted in the Security Council against South Africa?

Mr. NEWSOM. No, Senator, there have been proposals by some of the Africans. But we consider the South African situation quite different from the Rhodesian situation. South Africa has long been a recognized member of the international community, has had diplomatic recognition from a majority of the states of the world. It is recognized even in black Africa as a national entity, a State. The Rhodesian situation is unique in that here there existed in the eyes of the international community in 1966 the possibility of avoiding a continuing unresolved political problem involving both colonialism and the racial situation, and the international community therefore wanted to choose, wanted to take every opportunity to see, if this could not be resolved in a way which would not create the same kind of problems that the situation in South Africa has created.

That opportunity never presented itself to the international community with respect to South Africa.

I would point out . . . we have agreed to and enforced an embargo on any arms deliveries to South Africa. . . .

MAJOR COUNTRIES REFUSING TO SUPPORT SANCTIONS

Senator COOPER. Do any other major countries refuse, have any other major countries refused, to support the sanctions imposed by the Security Council?

Mr. NEWSOM. Only the Republic of South Africa and Portugal have formally refused, Senator. . . .

U.N. WILLINGNESS TO ACT WHEN SMALL, NOT MAJOR, STATES INVOLVED

Senator COOPER. I will just ask one more question which is very general. Looking back of the history of the U.N., would you say that while the United Nations General Assembly and Security Council are quite willing to take action in matters affecting smaller states, that it has shown itself very reluctant to take action where major states were involved or at least, let's say, the United States and the Soviet Union?

Mr. ARMITAGE. Yes, sir; I don't think one can quarrel with that statement. . . .

Senator McGEE. I suppose it would be fair to say that inequitable as it may seem, more of the efforts of the U.N. are addressed to the smaller problems and less to the confrontations between the great powers. I suppose there is a very valid case to be made that you have got to begin where you are and where you can. If you are going to strive to settle the issues between the great powers, the whole system would be blown into smithereens; whereas, if you can build a cumulative history of very modest successes on a very low scale in many instances or isolating smaller crises, I would think at least you are weaving a fabric that could have some subsequent value in the future in the international community. Any contribution we could make in that direction would be generally to the good rather than to the bad.

It is not a matter of saying you shouldn't do it perfectly from the beginning. We don't have perfect people and we don't have a perfect charter and you don't have a perfect climate — you do have a world without law in which you can't just suddenly wave a wand and start all over as though this were a perfect society. I would think there would be much to be said in favor of trying to apply it where you can and make it stick as a precedent for future measures in those circumstances. . . .

[Senator BYRD.] Now, just one other question. Is it your judgment that the United States should involve itself in the internal affairs of other nations?

U.S. INVOLVEMENT IN INTERNATIONAL AFFAIRS
OF OTHER COUNTRIES?

Mr. NEWSOM. It is our policy not to involve ourselves in the internal affairs of other nations, Senator, one that we have reiterated on many occasions.

Senator BYRD. But not adhered to.

Mr. NEWSOM. If I could elaborate both on your earlier comments and on your question, Senator, I think we would find general agreement perhaps with the committee that it is in the interests of the United States to reduce wherever we can the possibilities of continuing unresolved provocative conflicts in the world, particularly those who have the kind of overtones that the situation in Rhodesia does. We feel that we are involved as a member of the Security Council with the United Kingdom in an effort here to help a close ally to bring about a solution to just such a problem, so that we do not have in this critical part of Africa, as we have in so many other places in the world, a problem which continues on year after year without any prospect of solution. . . .

STATEMENT OF HON. CHARLES C. DIGGS, JR., A REPRESENTATIVE
IN CONGRESS FROM THE 13TH CONGRESSIONAL DISTRICT OF THE
STATE OF MICHIGAN . . .

EFFECT ON U.S. RELATIONS WITH BLACK AFRICA

As the sponsor of this measure indicated, the sole effect of this bill
would be to end the so-called embargo against importation of chrome from
Southern Rhodesia, and I am appearing today to emphasize that such an
objective would not only place us in violation of our international obligations under the charter of the United Nations but it would be disastrous to
our foreign policy interests in black Africa.

What is at stake here is our credibility regarding the principles of human rights and self-determination and for all without regard to race and
color. At stake here also is the possibility of our reneging on the one fairly
solid instance where our pronouncements have been accompanied by some
concrete measures toward the demonstration of these principles. And I wish
to underscore that the puzzle of this proposed bill is the unsubstantiated
assertion, which is evidently its foundation, that the United States is facing a
serious shortage of a strategic material. This assumption certainly appears to
be negated by the very fact that the U.S. Government has, upon revision of
chrome ore objectives, an excess in our present stockpile of chrome ore of
some 2,250,000 short dry tons. . . .

OPPOSITION TO S. 1404

In conclusion, Mr. Chairman, I urge that U.S. interests dictate unequivocally that the United States continue to adhere to its international
obligations and its enforcement of U.N. sanctions against Rhodesia and that
for broad policy reasons I have already outlined, on which I was interrogated most ferociously in almost all of the 30-odd countries that I visited
trying to defend the concept of democracy, we must reject any inroad on
our support of the United Nations in its effort to secure for the people of
Rhodesia basic human rights, self-determination, and fundamental freedoms for all without regard to race. . . .

Note: The Byrd Amendment Becomes Law

At the conclusion of the above hearings, the Senate Foreign Relations
Committee declined to report out S. 1404. Senator Byrd then adopted an
alternate strategy: he repackaged his bill as an amendment to the Military
Procurement Authorization Act of 1971, which was approved and reported
out by the more conservative Senate Armed Services Committee. On the

Senate floor, a motion by Senator McGee to delete the amendment lost by 46 votes to 36 (117 Cong. Rec. 33086 (1971)). The House bill contained no equivalent provision, but the Senate-House Conference Committee accepted the Byrd Amendment, and it became Section 503 of the Strategic and Critical Materials Stockpiling Act (50 U.S.C. §98h-4 (1988)). Thus, the United States, along with South Africa and Portugal, became an open and acknowledged violator of UN sanctions against Rhodesia.

Irony in Chrome: The Byrd Amendment Two Years Later, Interim Report of the Special Rhodesia Project of the Carnegie Endowment for International Peace
4-8 (1973)

There were many reasons for the success of this piece of legislation. The parliamentary skill of its supporters, congressional hostility towards the UN after the recent votes on Chinese representation, the ambivalence of the White House, which undercut the efforts of the State Department to defeat the amendment, public apathy, and lack of sustained attention in the press . . . all played a part. Here, we shall look at another key factor — the relative strength of the lobbyists working for and against the Byrd Amendment and the arguments that were made.

In December, 1971, a Christmas party was given by the Rhodesian Information Office in Washington to celebrate the sixth anniversary of Rhodesia's "independence" and the successful passage of Section 503. A song was written for the occasion. As printed in an article by journalist Bruce Oudes in the *Washington Post*, the song provides a *Who's Who* of the anti-sanctions lobbying effort. Sung to the tune of "O Tannenbaum," the "503 Club Marching Song" went like this:

Verse I (To be sung with great joy)
      Oh, 503; oh, 503,
      We gave our very best for thee
      Oh, 503, oh, 503
      We celebrate our victory.
      To Harry Byrd, we'll drink a toast
      And sing his praise from coast to coast
      Jim Collins, too, we'll honor thee
      And hang you on our Christmas tree.
Verse II (To be sung mournfully)
      Oh, 503, oh, 503
      You nearly were the death of me

Oh, 503, oh, 503
The roll call votes were agony.
We very nearly lost our wits;
Fulbright and Fraser gave us fits.
We frown upon you, Gale McGee
And dimly view Ted Kennedy.

Verse III (To be sung with great sincerity)
Oh, 503, oh, 503
Rhodesia's future rode with thee.
Oh, Fulton Lewis Number Three,
We honor your tenacity.
We love the people we are with,
And raise a glass for Ian Smith.
Congratulations, we assume
Are due Lord Goodman, Alec Home.

Verse IV (To be sung with wistful melancholy)
Oh, 503, oh, 503
We faced a mighty enemy
Oh, 503, oh, 503
The State Department thwarted thee.
We ran afoul of David Newsom
Culver and Diggs — an awesome twosome
The UN fought you mightily
And Harold Wilson censured thee.

Verse V (To be sung lovingly)
Oh, 503, we'll blow a kiss
To Margaret S. and Tony Bliss.
And Andy Andrews, you're true blue —
John Donahey, we hail you too.
Hey, Howard Cannon, you're a hit
Sam Ervin — bless you for your wit
Bill Brock, we greet you gratefully —
Defender of the 503.

Verse VI (To be sung bravely, if hoarsely)
Oh, noble House, your Members there
Nailed down the victory with a flair
Let songs of joy ring through the air;
We won the battle fair and square.
And so, tonight let's have some fun;
It's better to have fought and won!
And you'll go down in history,
Our dear, beloved 503.

Verse VII (To be sung diplomatically)
Oh, Kenneth T; oh, Kenneth T.

Ambassador one day you'll be
And may John Hooper follow thee
To posts of great authority.
Next winter may it be your lot
To spend your Christmas where it's hot.
Please raise a toast in Salisbury
In memory of 503.

The first reference to the Rhodesian and chrome lobbies comes in the third verse where Fulton Lewis III is honored for his "tenacity." Lewis is a conservative journalist and radio commentator who worked with the Rhodesian Information Office (the Washington propaganda arm of the Rhodesian regime), spoke out on radio against sanctions, and worked on a number of Members of Congress and officials in the Executive branch. On February 21, 1973, Lewis' credibility may have suffered when he first denied, then admitted before a joint hearing of the House subcommittees on Africa and International Organizations and Movements that in 1972 he had accepted $1,000 from the Rhodesian Information Office to help meet his expenses for a trip to Southern Rhodesia.

It is the fifth verse of the "503 Club Marching Song," however, that most neatly summarizes the lobby at work on the Byrd Amendment. "We'll blow a kiss to Margaret S. and Tony Bliss" refers to Margaret Cox-Sullivan, a consultant to Union Carbide Corporation who was active in late 1970, and to L. G. "Tony" Bliss, the former chairman of the board of the Foote Mineral Company, who began lobbying against the sanctions program almost before it started. Bliss started coming to Washington in early 1967, asking that Foote be allowed to import chrome mined by its Rhodesian subsidiaries before mandatory sanctions took effect. Bliss also put pressure on Representatives from ferroalloy districts to introduce sanctions-busting legislation from 1967 onwards. The same verse of the song mentions John Donahey — the public relations director at Foote — who also did a great deal of lobbying on the amendment.

Verse V thanks "Andy Andrews" as well — E. F. Andrews, a Vice President for Purchases at Allegheny Ludlum Industries — who was another major lobbyist for Section 503. Andrews, as a representative of the stainless steel industry, appeared before Congressional hearings and met with many Members of Congress on the issue. His lobbying and that of other stainless steel companies was coordinated and directed by the Washington law firm of Collier, Shannon, Rill & Edwards. In fact, interviews indicate that it was this law firm, representing the Tool and Stainless Steel Industry Committee, that did the bulk of the lobbying work on the Byrd Amendment. According to an interview with one of the firm's senior partners, Thomas Shannon, he himself introduced the idea of the amendment to Senator Byrd in late 1970. The firm researched the issue thoroughly, sent people to Rhodesia and assigned two lawyers to the effort. In addition, they had all their member companies — like Allegheny Ludlum — lobby representatives in their own districts. Shannon's firm also served as the coordinating point of the lobbying efforts. "We represented Foote Mineral and worked with John Donahey," Shannon says. . . .

Arrayed against this lobbying effort was a disorganized coalition of groups. Strong efforts against the Byrd amendment were made within the Congress by Senator Gale McGee, Congressmen Charles Diggs Jr. and Donald Fraser, and others. But allied groups such as the American Committee on Africa, the United Steelworkers and the Congressional Black Caucus were generally late in getting started, badly coordinated and poorly financed in their lobbying efforts. The most persistent lobbyist against the Byrd amendment was the State Department — and its efforts were vitiated by the refusal of the White House to weigh in with phone calls to wavering Senators.

But a picture of corporate lobbyists blitzing an interested Congress would be inaccurate. The fact is that the Byrd amendment intruded little into the consciousness of most Members of Congress. Absenteeism therefore played a large part in deciding the result. The votes in the Senate were close, and much depended on which Senators happened to be there. In addition, and equally as important, the arguments made by supporters of the Byrd amendment were more likely to appeal to busy and distracted legislators than the less dramatic pleas of its opponents.

3. Critics Challenge the Byrd Amendment: Diggs v. Shultz and the Eventual "Repeal" of the Byrd Amendment

During the 1970s the situation in Southern Africa was challenged in a number of cases in U.S. courts. Several attempts, to be discussed in a Comment to this Problem at pages 595-597 infra, were made to invoke U.S. law as well as international law norms in cases involving South Africa and its activities that had an effect upon or within the United States. These attempts to invoke U.S. domestic law remedies to bring pressure to bear upon the South African government provide an instructive illustration of the range of tactics available to international human rights lawyers. See Lillich, The Role of Domestic Courts in Promoting International Human Rights Norms, 24 N.Y.L. Sch. L. Rev. 153 (1978).

One of the most interesting, and certainly most significant, cases in this regard was the attempt by Congressman Charles Diggs of Michigan to have the Byrd Amendment interpreted in a way that would be consistent with the UN Security Council resolutions on Rhodesia. Mr. Diggs's action sought to take advantage of the fact that, on its face, the Byrd Amendment did not refer either to Rhodesia or to the United States' obligations under the UN

Charter, thus leaving an opening for the argument that it was logically
possible — and therefore legally imperative — for the statute to be interpreted in a fashion consistent with those legal obligations. Relief was being
sought solely on the strength of U.S. law, specifically the well-established
rule that "an Act of Congress ought never to be construed to violate the law
of nations if any other possible construction remains." Murray v. Schooner
Charming Betsy, 6 U.S. (2 Cranch) 64, 118 (1804). See Restatement
(Third) of the Foreign Relations Law of the United States §114 (1987).
In 1972, the year following the enactment of the Byrd Amendment, the
Court of Appeals for the District of Columbia Circuit considered Diggs's
argument.

Diggs v. Shultz
470 F.2d 461 (D.C. Cir. 1972), cert. denied, 411 U.S. 931
(1973)

McGOWAN, J. This is an appeal from the dismissal by the District Court
of a complaint seeking declaratory and injunctive relief in respect of the
importation of metallurgical chromite from Southern Rhodesia. The grava-
men of this action was an asserted conflict between (1) the official authorization of such importation by the United States, and (2) the treaty
obligations of the United States under the United Nations Charter. Plaintiff-
appellants sought summary judgment, as did defendant-appellees alternatively to a motion to dismiss for failure to state a claim upon which relief
could be given.

The District Court's ruling for appellees was grounded primarily upon
lack of standing, but it encompassed as well a concept of the nonjusticiabil-
ity of the issues raised. Although we believe there was standing upon the
part of at least some of the appellants to pursue their cause of action judicially, we think that cause is not one in respect of which relief can be
granted. Accordingly, we affirm the judgment of dismissal.

I

In 1966 the Security Council of the United Nations, with the affirmative vote of the United States, adopted Resolution 232 directing that all
member states impose an embargo on trade with Southern Rhodesia — a
step which was reaffirmed and enlarged in 1968. In compliance with this
resolution, the President of the United States issued Executive Orders
11322 and 11419, 22 U.S.C. §287c, establishing criminal sanctions for
violation of the embargo. In 1971, however, Congress adopted the so-called
Byrd Amendment to the Strategic and Critical Materials Stock Piling Act.
50 U.S.C. §98-98h, which provides in part:

Sec. 10. Notwithstanding any other provision of law . . . the President may not prohibit or regulate the importation into the United States of any material determined to be strategic and critical pursuant to the provisions of this Act, if such material is the product of any foreign country or area not listed as a Communist-dominated country or area . . . for so long as the importation into the United States of material of that kind which is the product of such Communist-dominated countries or areas is not prohibited by any provision of law.

Since Southern Rhodesia is not a Communist-controlled country, and inasmuch as the United States imports from Communist countries substantial quantities of metallurgical chromite and other materials available from Rhodesia, the Byrd Amendment contemplated the resumption of trade by this country with Southern Rhodesia. By direction of the President, the Office of Foreign Assets Control issued to the corporate appellees in this case a General License authorizing the importation of various materials from Southern Rhodesia, and they began importation.

Alleging that the Byrd Amendment did not and could not authorize issuance of such a license contrary to this country's treaty obligations, appellants sought to enjoin further importation, to require official seizure, and to restrain use, of materials already imported under the General License, and to declare the General License null and void.

II

The question of standing turns first on whether the party seeking relief has alleged a sufficient personal interest in the controversy to insure concrete adverseness in the presentation of the issues. Association of Data Processing Service v. Camp, 397 U.S. 150, 152, 90 S. Ct. 827, 25 L. Ed. 2d 184 (1969); Baker v. Carr, 369 U.S. 186, 204, 82 S. Ct. 691, 7 L. Ed. 2d 663 (1962). Appellants allege various personal injuries, and we agree with the District Court that these allegations amply provide the injury in fact element of the standing requirement.

Another requirement of standing is that the complainant be within the zone of interests sought to be protected by the law in question. Association of Data Processing Service v. Camp, 397 U.S. 150, 153, 90 S. Ct. 827, 25 L. Ed. 2d 184 (1969). United Nations Security Council Resolution 232 was — and is — an attempt by means of concerted international pressure to turn the Rhodesian Government away from the course of action which has resulted in the adverse circumstances experienced by appellants. They are unquestionably within the reach of its purpose and among its intended beneficiaries.

. . . [T]he concept of standing has been characterized as contemplating that there be a "logical nexus between the status asserted and the claim sought to be adjudicated," in order to insure that the litigant is the proper party to represent the interests involved. Flast v. Cohen, 392 U.S. 83, 102, 88 S. Ct. 1942, 1953, 20 L. Ed. 2d 947 (1967). The District Court found the causal relationship of appellants' claims to the challenged actions too attenuated to constitute such a nexus. That finding rested largely on the conclusion that appellants' quarrel was really with the Rhodesian Government rather than with appellees. But that view fails to focus on the exact nature of the grievance appearing in the complaint.

Appellants, along with many other persons, have suffered, and continue to suffer, tangible injuries at the hands of Southern Rhodesia. In an attempt to terminate the policies giving rise to those wrongs, the United Nations, with the United States as an assenting member, established the embargo. The precise injury of which appellants complain in this law suit is allegedly illegal present action *by the United States* which tends to limit the effectiveness of the embargo and thereby to deprive appellants of its potential benefits. That quarrel is directly and immediately with this government, and not with Southern Rhodesia.

Appellees suggest that the prospects of significant relief by means of the embargo are so slight that this relationship of intended benefit is too tenuous to support standing. But this strikes us as tantamount to saying that because the performance of the United Nations is not always equal to its promise, the commitments of a member may be disregarded without having to respond in court to a charge of treaty violation. It may be that the particular economic sanctions invoked against Southern Rhodesia in this instance will fall short of their goal, and that appellants will ultimately reap no benefit from them. But, to persons situated as are appellants, United Nations action constitutes the only hope; and they are personally aggrieved and injured by the dereliction of any member state which weakens the capacity of the world organization to make its policies meaningful.

Of course it is true that appellants' plight stems initially from acts done by Southern Rhodesia, and that their primary quarrel is with it. But this does not foreclose the existence of a judicially cognizable dispute between appellants, on the one hand, and appellees, on the other, who are said to be acting in derogation of the solemn treaty obligation of the United States to adhere to the embargo for so long as it is in being.

III

The District Court, in its comments to the effect that non-justiciability would necessitate dismissal of the complaint even if standing be found, reasoned as follows: It is settled constitutional doctrine that Congress may nullify, in whole or in part, a treaty commitment. Congress, by the Byrd Amendment in 1971, acted to abrogate one aspect of our treaty obligations under the U.N. Charter, that is to say, our continued participation in the economic sanctions taken against Southern Rhodesia. The considerations underlying that step by Congress present issues of political policy which courts do not inquire into. Thus, appellants' quarrel is with Congress, and it is a cause which can be pursued only at the polls and not in the courts.

In this court appellants do not seriously contest the first of these propositions, namely, the constitutional power of Congress to set treaty obligations at naught. They seek, rather, to show that, in the Byrd Amendment, Congress did not really intend to compel the Executive to end United States observance of the Security Council's sanctions, and that, therefore, it is the Executive which is, without the essential shield of Congressional dispensation, violating a treaty engagement of this country. Appellants point out in this regard that the Byrd Amendment does not in terms require importation from Southern Rhodesia, but leaves open two alternative courses of action. The statute says the President may not ban importation from Rhodesia of materials classified as critical and strategic unless importation from Communist countries is also prohibited. Instead of permitting resumption of trade with Rhodesia, the President, so it is said, could (1) have banned importation of these materials from Communist nations as well as from Rhodesia, or (2) have taken steps to have these materials declassified, thereby taking them in either case out of the scope of the Byrd Amendment.

Citing the canon of construction that a statute should, if possible, be construed in a manner consistent with treaty obligations, appellants argue that the Byrd Amendment, although discretionary on its face, should be construed to compel the President to take one or the other of these two steps as a means of escape from the necessity of breaching the U.N. Charter. But these alternatives raise questions of foreign policy and national defense as sensitive as those involved in the decision to honor or abrogate our treaty obligations. To attempt to decide whether the President chose properly among the three alternatives confronting him "would be, not to decide a judicial controversy, but to assume a position of authority over the governmental acts of another and coequal department, an authority which plainly we do not possess." Frothingham v. Mellon, 262 U.S. 447, 489, 43 S. Ct. 597, 601, 67 L. Ed. 1078 (1023).

We think that there can be no blinking the purpose and effect of the Byrd Amendment. It was to detach this country from the U.N. boycott of Southern Rhodesia in blatant disregard of our treaty undertakings. The legislative record shows that no member of Congress voting on the measure was under any doubt about what was involved then; and no amount of statutory interpretation now can make the Byrd Amendment other than what it was as presented to the Congress, namely, a measure which would make — and was intended to make — the United States a certain treaty violator. The so-called options given to the President are, in reality, not options at all. In any event, they are in neither case alternatives which are appropriately to be forced upon him by a court. . . .

The Significance of Diggs v. Shultz

The above case was a significant international law decision for several reasons. Not the least important was the court's holding that the intent of Congress could be gleaned from the legislative history of the statute as well as merely from the text. Compare Cook v. United States, 288 U.S. 102, 120 (1932), where the Supreme Court stated that a treaty "will not be deemed to have been abrogated or modified by a later statute unless such purpose on the part of Congress has been clearly expressed." For a recent case where a court examined a statute's legislative history, set a high threshold of congressional intent, and ruled that Congress had not clearly demonstrated sufficient intent to override an international agreement, see United States v. PLO, 695 F. Supp. 1456 (S.D.N.Y. 1988).

One of the critical parts of the court's holding concerned the issue of whether the plaintiffs were asking the judiciary to intervene in a "political question." The very words "political question" have a talismanic ring to them; indeed, the doctrine is probably more frequently invoked than understood. As the Supreme Court observed in Baker v. Carr, 369 U.S. 186, 210 (1962), "[t]he non-justiciability of a political question is primarily a function of the separation of powers." That is to say, courts will sometimes refuse to judge a political question not because the litigants have no right to a resolution of their dispute, but rather because the nature of that dispute is such that organs of government other than the courts are more appropriate places to seek a resolution. "In determining whether a question falls within [the political question] category, the appropriateness under our system of government of attributing finality to the action of the political departments and also the lack of satisfactory criteria for a judicial determination are dominant considerations." Coleman v. Miller, 307 U.S. 433, 454-455 (1939).

The court of appeals held that Diggs v. Shultz presented such a political question.* However, an argument can be made that the Executive Branch of the government, by granting import licenses for Rhodesian goods, was going beyond the scope of its constitutional power entirely. It would appear that such an issue would not be a political question, since the question of whether a given branch of government (here, the Executive Branch) has exceeded its powers is a most inappropriate one to leave to that branch itself. A "political" arm of the government is quite free, concededly, to make political decisions, and anyone objecting to such decisions should seek political and not judicial redress (for example, he should galvanize

---

* 470 F.2d at 466 n.6:

> The Supreme Court in Baker v. Carr was at pains to point out that the so-called "political question doctrine" is an aspect of the separation of powers prescribed by the Federal Constitution; and that, in the intra-federal context, it continues to have meaningful vitality to restrain interference by one branch of the federal establishment with concerns committed to another. The case before us is a classic one for the careful appraisal by a court of the consequences of an exercise of jurisdiction it may technically be thought to have.

Congress into acting, should work to elect a different president, and so on). Yet this conclusion is the same thing as saying that the executive can exceed its lawful powers, free from judicial scrutiny, merely by virtue of the fact that it is a co-equal branch of government with the courts. How the executive behaves when he is acting *within* his authority is a political question, in the legal sense of the term; whether the executive acts *beyond* his authority or not in a given instance is a legal — and, hence, a justiciable — issue.

It should not be thought, however, that Diggs v. Shultz was an unmitigated defeat for the human rights movement, since the plaintiffs did win on the standing issue. The fact that Mr. Diggs was a congressman did not, of course, give him any special or automatic standing to bring lawsuits. In that regard, he stood on precisely the same footing as any individual citizen — that is, he was required to show that he had a "personal stake" in the outcome of the case. Baker v. Carr, 369 U.S. 186, 204 (1962). In fact, several of the original plaintiffs in the action were unable to meet this requirement because their only stake in the issue was the ideological one of sympathy for persons oppressed by the Smith regime. Diggs's own standing to sue, and that of three fellow black Congressmen, Conyers, Rangel, and Stokes, derived from the fact that the four of them had sought to travel to Rhodesia and had been denied permission because of their race. Another plaintiff was M'Babe, a Rhodesian citizen. His injury was the refusal of Rhodesia to allow him back into his country. The Council for Christian Social Action of the United Church of Christ had suffered harassment at the hands of the Smith government. Finally, Gore Vidal derived his standing from the fact that his books had been banned in Rhodesia.

In order to establish standing, however, the plaintiffs had to do more than simply prove tangible personal harm. They also had to prove that a logical nexus existed between the harm done (that is, the repressive acts committed by the Rhodesian regime) and the relief sought (declaratory and injunctive relief against the Executive Branch of the U.S. government). Review the way that the court addressed this issue. For an analysis of the standing aspect of the case, see Note, Standing, 9 Texas Intl. L.J. 114 (1974).

In one other respect, Diggs v. Shultz may presage an advance, albeit a very problematical one, in the incorporation of international human rights law into U.S. domestic law. Consider the following opinion that the case represents a potential breach in the line of argument that the lower courts have followed since *Fujii*, discussed in Problem II at pages 101-120.

Note: Security Council Resolutions in United States Courts
50 Ind. L.J. 83, 92-93 (1974)

The court of appeals in *Diggs* did not question the statement of the district court that the Rhodesian embargo was mandatory, nor the argument in the appellant's brief that it was mandatory under Chapter VII and Article 25 of the Charter. The court focused on whether the resolution created individual rights rather than upon the necessarily anterior question of whether states were bound by the resolution. Prior to *Diggs* a congressional act had had the effect of directing the President to issue import licenses for metallurgical chromite in violation of the Security Council embargo of Rhodesian minerals. The suit challenged the power of the President to violate that embargo resolution (the power of Congress to do so having been admitted). While standing to sue was upheld for those plaintiffs who had either been physically barred from Rhodesia or who had suffered economic damage as a result of the Rhodesian Government's racist policies, the D.C. Court of Appeals ultimately dismissed the case for lack of justiciability in light of the clear intent of the congressional act to direct the President to violate the Charter. However both courts accepted, at least by implication, that the sanctions are binding on U.S. courts unless Congress passes conflicting legislation. It could be argued that resolutions are binding only because they have been implemented by the United Nations Participation Act of 1945 or by Executive orders. Neither court, however, followed this line of reasoning. It is arguable that the courts considered the resolution directly binding. . . .

While it may be "arguable" — indeed, in Diggs v. Richardson (discussed in a Comment to this Problem at pages 595-597 infra), plaintiffs did argue — that another Security Council resolution, without further legislative or executive action, had become part of judicially enforceable U.S. domestic law, it is unlikely that a U.S. court in the near future will hold a UN Security Council resolution to be a self-executing obligation directly enforceable in such fashion. The language in Diggs v. Richardson, in fact, points in the other direction.

Congress "Repeals" the Byrd Amendment

Serious efforts were made in Congress to repeal the Byrd Amendment in the early and mid-1970s, but they were unavailing, and it still is found in the U.S. Code (50 U.S.C. §98h-4 (1988)). It was rendered inapplicable with respect to the U.S. sanctioning effort against Rhodesia, however, by virtue of an amendment in 1977 to the United Nations Participation Act (Pub. L. No. 95-12, 91 Stat. 22 (1977), codified at 22 U.S.C. §287c (1988)). The amendment was one of the first steps taken by the Carter Administration in its attempt to integrate human rights concerns into the foreign policy process. See generally Problem XIII. President Jimmy Carter's speech to the United Nations in March 1977 had committed the United States to rejoining the Rhodesian sanctions effort (57 Dept. State Bull. 329 (1977)), and with active presidential support full U.S. sanctions were reimposed later that month.

In the little over five years that it had applied to Rhodesia, however, the Byrd Amendment had done considerable damage. As shown by the "503 Club Marching Song" (pages 532-534 supra) and later evaluations of the impact of sanctions upon Rhodesia (pages 565-572 infra), it gave the Smith regime an emotional "shot in the arm" as well as some much-needed foreign exchange. It also served to identify the United States as a sanction-breaking state and to cast serious doubts about the strength of the United States' commitment to majority rule in Rhodesia and its respect for the UN and international law in general. See Schwebel, United States Nears Front Ranks of Sanctions Breakers, Wash. Post, Oct. 19, 1971, at 18, col. 3. The UN General Assembly, reacting to the Amendment, annually condemned the United States for its acknowledged sanctions violations from 1971 to 1976. See, e.g., G.A. Res. 2946, 27 U.N. GAOR Supp. (No. 30) at 78, U.N. Doc. A/8730 (1972).

As flagrantly unlawful as the original, undiluted Byrd Amendment had been from the standpoint of international law, however, it should not be thought that chrome importation was the only way U.S. individuals and corporations violated UN sanctions after 1 January 1972, the day it came into force. The materials that follow demonstrate that sanctions-breaking, with or without the knowledge of the U.S. government, was far more widespread from that day through 16 December 1979, when President Carter lifted U.S. sanctions following the reestablishment of U.K. authority over Rhodesia.

4. The Enforcement of UN Sanctions Under U.S. Law: At Best, Inconsistent; At Worst, Non-Existent

Although the United States implemented and initially enforced UN sanctions pursuant to Executive Orders and implementing regulations (pages 517-523 supra), after the enactment of the Byrd Amendment enforcement seems to have become increasingly spotty. An investigation of the extent and overtness of illegal (under U.S. law) sanctions-breaking was undertaken in 1973 by the Carnegie Endowment for International Peace. The excerpt immediately below is taken from their pamphlet, which was incorporated in A. Lake, The "Tar Baby" Option: American Policy Toward Southern Rhodesia (1976). It is followed by a brief article revealing how one major U.S. oil company continued to ship oil and petroleum products to Rhodesia throughout the entire period that sanctions were in place.

Carnegie Endowment for International Peace, Business as Usual: Transactions Violating Rhodesian Sanctions, Interim Report of the Special Rhodesia Project
1, 3-4, 6-9, 12-14 (1973)

Flying to foreign countries can be a trying experience. Visas and shots and tickets, delays and complications . . . all can make travel to most areas of the world something less than an unadulterated pleasure. But if you want to go to Southern Rhodesia, it is a breeze. No visa is required, just one or two inoculations, a passport, and a confirmed onward reservation. And your air travel reservations? Drop by your Pan American ticket counter here in the United States, and in seconds the computer will confirm your space on an Air Rhodesia flight from Johannesburg, South Africa to the Rhodesian capital of Salisbury.

This has been the experience, at least, of many Americans who travelled to Rhodesia during the past few years. It is all very convenient. The trouble is that when Pan American, TWA and perhaps other American carriers help make the going great to Salisbury, they apparently do it illegally. . . .

. . . [T]he [sanction] regulations issued by the American government appear explicit. And, considering the penalties for their violation, they have teeth. But somehow their bite has been less inhibiting than it could be. Despite the fact that Southern Rhodesia has been declared an international outlaw — the only territory in the world against which the United Nations has ordered economic sanctions — if you live in the United States, you can:

— receive mailings about Southern Rhodesia from its information office in Washington, or pick up tourist brochures at the New York office of Air Rhodesia and the Rhodesian National Tourist Board;

— read paid advertisements for Rhodesian firms and investment opportunities printed in an American newspaper;

— make reservations to fly on a Rhodesian airline through airlines registered in the United States;

— make a hotel reservation or reserve a rented car in Rhodesia through a representative of Pan American in the United States;

— reserve a Hertz or Avis rent-a-car there through those companies' offices here;

— pay for your air tickets and rent-a-car with one of a number of American credit cards;

— or visit Rhodesia as part of a package African tour managed by an American travel company. . . .

Flying to Salisbury

On July 15, 1973, we went to the Pan American offices in Washington and made a reservation . . . on Air Rhodesia flight 876 for October 7, 1973, from the Rhodesian capital, Salisbury, to Blantyre, Malawi. (Reservations were also made for other flights in a planned journey from Washington to Salisbury and back.) The reservation was confirmed within seconds by Pan American's computer.

On August 8, a reservation was made . . . at the TWA office in Washington for travel to Africa and back. It included Air Rhodesia flights 873 and 731.

The tickets for all the flights from Washington to Salisbury and back could be paid for here in Washington by major American credit cards.

Pan American also requested a reservation at a hotel in Salisbury, confirmed later, and offered to reserve a Hertz or Avis rent-a-car there.

We asked both Pan American and TWA if there would be problems getting into Southern Rhodesia because of the sanctions program. In neither case did their ticket agents seem particularly aware of the sanctions. Both offices assured us that all that is required to enter Southern Rhodesia is a valid passport, an onward reservation, and a smallpox vaccination (according to Pan American) or a yellow fever inoculation (according to TWA). . . .

According to interviews with sources at Pan American, the airline does hold a block of seats on Air Rhodesia flights that it can sell up to four days before any particular flight. This arrangement, we are informed, is part of an inter-line agreement between Pan American and Air Rhodesia. Thus, Pan American does appear to be acting in violation of the specific provisions of Special Federal Aviation Regulation No. 21. Interviews also indicate that Air Rhodesia acts as Pan American's representative in Rhodesia; since no Pan American office is in operation there, Air Rhodesia provides tickets and reservations for Pan American flights, and represents Pan American in other transactions in Rhodesia.

A source at TWA also stated that it has an inter-line agreement with Air Rhodesia. . . .

. . . [D]irect billing [is] the means by which Pan American and TWA apparently transfer funds to Air Rhodesia. A Pan American official has confirmed in a telephone interview that this is the method used by that airline. It should be noted that neither Pan American nor TWA accept payment for the hotels and rental cars for which it makes reservations; the customer must pay these directly. A "package" can be paid for by credit card, but the airlines receive from the credit card company only that portion of the cost which represents the total air fare. The airlines still pay the connecting air carriers in these cases, however.

According to an interview at Pan American, it transferred to Air Rhodesia in 1972 approximately $200,000, an increase of almost 200% from the previous year. This increase, we were told, cannot be accounted for by higher costs and prices; the increase thus apparently represents an increase in the number of passengers purchasing tickets on Air Rhodesia flights through Pan American. . . .

VISIT SALISBURY, "GARDEN CAPITAL OF RHODESIA"

A visitor to the office of Air Rhodesia and the Rhodesian National Tourist Board in New York can pick up travel brochures advertising package tours to Africa, including Southern Rhodesia, run by Bennet Tours, Percival Tours, Merriman and Finnerty Associates, Orbitair International and United Touring Company. (All but the last are American-based companies. The United Touring Company is a Rhodesian concern.) Included in these brochures are invitations to visit the "garden capital" and Southern Rhodesia's Victoria Falls, "quite likely to be one of the great memories of your life. An indescribable experience. Words fail. . . ." At Gona-re-zhou, "you may decide this is the ultimate experience and the peak of your trip." Or, take a cruise along the Zambezi River — "one of Africa's loveliest rivers."

There is no mention in these brochures, of course, of the fact that the Zambezi flows between territory held by the white minority regime in Southern Rhodesia and the African governments of the North. Nor that there is a United Nations sanctions program against Southern Rhodesia. Nor that Security Council Resolution 253 of May 29, 1968, stated: "4. Decides that all member states of the U.N. shall not make available to the illegal regime in Southern Rhodesia or to any commercial, industrial or public utility undertaking, *including tourist enterprises*, in Southern Rhodesia any funds for investment or any other financial or economic resources and shall prevent their nationals and any persons within their territories from making available to the regime or to any such undertaking any such funds or resources. . . ." (Emphasis added.)

Although official statistics are not available, large numbers of tourists from the United States reportedly visit Southern Rhodesia every year. The American government makes little or no effort to discourage this travel, since it cannot legally invalidate their passports for travel there. The Treasury Department refuses to use financial controls to discourage travel to any embargoed area if passport controls do not apply. It therefore allows American tourists to spend money in Southern Rhodesia for living expenses, in violation of the United Nations resolution, but does not allow them to bring Rhodesian goods back with them to the United States. (Government officials like to recount the fury of a few big game hunters who have been forced to relinquish the heads of the Rhodesian animals they slaughtered.) . . .

Lillich, Examining Mobil's Role as Sanctions-Buster
South, 15 April-May 1981, at 4, 4-6

April is not only the first anniversary of independence of Zimbabwe, but also of Britain's legal amnesty for Rhodesian sanctions-busters, the most prominent of which were Shell and BP. Yet interest in sanctions and their enforcement refuses to subside . . . , kept alive in Britain by Lonrho's £100 million arbitration claim against the two oil companies, issues from which are scheduled to be heard by the House of Lords in early May. Moreover, demands by many African countries for mandatory economic sanctions against South Africa, following the collapse of the recent Geneva talks on Namibia raise questions as to the wisdom and effectiveness of sanctions as a tool of international diplomacy.

Significant new developments in the continuing saga of Rhodesian sanctions-busters have occurred recently in the US, which unlike Britain has not adopted a de jure amnesty and where, therefore, the possibility of legal action against offending US companies (and their officers and directors) still exists. The controversy involves another of the oil multinationals, the US-based Mobil Corporation. It centres around a shareholder proposal to be presented to its annual meeting in May, a US treasury department investigation now underway into Mobil's compliance with Rhodesian sanctions and planned congressional hearings on the subject of sanctions and their enforcement. Since it was allegations against Mobil five years ago that led to the exposure of Shell and BP's sanctions violations, it is only fitting that the spotlight should now come full circle to the activities of the US company.

Evidence of how major international oil companies supplied Rhodesia appeared only in mid-1976, ten years after the UN Security Council had imposed mandatory sanctions against Rhodesia, prohibiting the sale of oil or oil products to its illegal regime. In June 1976 the United Church of Christ (UCC) in the US published a short pamphlet entitled "The Oil Conspiracy." Based upon 95 pages of documents secretly copied from the files of Mobil's Rhodesian subsidiary (MOSR), the pamphlet purported to show how MOSR was obtaining oil from Mobil's South African subsidiary (MOSA) through a series of sales by MOSA to dummy South African companies, which then resold to Genta, a Rhodesian government agency, which in turn supplied MOSR. This "paper chase," as it was described in one document, was allegedly devised to hide the fact that MOSA was furnishing MOSR with oil in contravention of US sanctions regulations, as well as in violation of Mobil's proclaimed company policy that neither it nor any of its subsidiaries was to sell oil to Rhodesia.

The UCC exposé generated both a congressional hearing and an investigation by the Office of Foreign Assets Control (FAC) of the treasury department. At the hearing Mobil's general counsel advanced what has come to be known as the "Mobil Defence." First, US sanctions regulations, he rightly noted, did not apply to third country subsidiaries such as MOSA. Hence, he concluded "even if Mobil South Africa had actually sent products into Rhodesia, that act in itself would not have violated" US sanctions regulations (unless, it should be added, US officers or directors of Mobil, MOSA or another Mobil affiliate actually had been involved). Secondly,

Mobil's efforts to ascertain the authenticity of the documents supplied by the UCC and hence determine whether its company policy — "which goes beyond the prohibitions of those regulations" — had been frustrated by the Official Secrets Acts of South Africa and Rhodesia. Mobil's general counsel related that three Mobil executives sent to South Africa to interview company personnel had been informed by their local lawyers that if they attempted "to carry out any investigation in South Africa, they themselves would be subject to prosecution as foreign agents under the Official Secrets Act." They were given the same advice about Rhodesian law, and without further ado returned home.

The treasury department investigation also purported to be stymied by the Official Secrets Acts. The originals of the documents made available by the UCC could not be obtained from MOSR files, nor could key persons mentioned in them be interviewed as to their authenticity. Two documents, however, were authenticated, and none was proved to be a forgery. Nevertheless, the treasury report issued in May 1977 brushed aside a "clearly incriminating" document on the astonishing ground that it "was signed by a lower level official of Mobil South Africa" and concluded that the evidence of sanctions-busting by Mobil was "inconclusive." Martin Bailey's observation in his book *Oilgate* that "it is now clear that the treasury investigators lacked a certain enthusiasm for discovering the truth" seems to presage what subsequently has come to light.

From 1977 to early 1980 the "Mobil defence" — under which the company argued that its Southern Africa subsidiaries were not covered by the letter of US sanctions regulations and that, despite its best efforts, it was unable to ascertain whether MOSA and MOSR were adhering to company policy — served to insulate the oil giant from extensive criticism in the US. However, starting with the Bingham Report in Britain in August 1978, which while focusing on Shell and BP's violations of sanctions, contained numerous references to Mobil's possible involvement as well, interest in sanctions enforcement in the US slowly revived. In November 1978 the treasury department, acting in response to the Bingham revelations, announced a new investigation into the activities of Mobil and other US oil companies in Southern Africa. Fears that this investigation might be as half-hearted as its predecessor were not lessened when a year later, in October 1979, the US perfunctorily reported to the UN sanctions committee that the investigation was still in progress. The imposition of sanctions against Iran the following month, which fully occupied the attention of the treasury's small FAC staff, brought the investigation to a temporary halt.

At this stage the International Human Rights Law Group of Washington, took up the cause of sanctions enforcement. The Law Group, an arm of the Procedural Aspects of International Law Institute, a nonprofit educational organisation incorporated in New York, provides legal advice on international human rights law matters to other non-governmental organisations and also initiates action itself on behalf of individuals or groups needing such assistance. As part of its Southern Africa Project the Law Group, on behalf of a Mobil shareholder, submitted a resolution to the company's 1980 annual meeting modestly requesting the board of directors to investigate and report to the shareholders on Mobil's compliance with US sanctions regulations. By then the regulations had been lifted prospectively following the Lancaster House settlement and Zimbabwe's independence. Mobil, to the amazement of many corporate observers, opposed the resolution; it again relied on the "Mobil defence" and argued that "no useful purpose (would) be served by a further investigation, (which) would be unlikely to produce any further information."

Although the resolution was ultimately defeated, Mobil's chairman made a significant commitment to the shareholders before the vote on the resolution took place. "I will promise you," he assured them, "that we will go to Zimbabwe Rhodesia. We will take our cue from the government in power. If they want us to be able to open this thing up (by waiving the Official Secrets Act), we will open it up." Not surprisingly, in view of Mobil's track record, scant effort was made to redeem this pledge. Moreover, despite widespread newspaper accounts that Lonrho had secured a waiver of the Official Secrets Act from the Mugabe Government to enable it to collect both documentary evidence and oral testimony for use in its arbitration proceedings against Shell and BP, Mobil never sought a similar waiver. Indeed, in a letter dated 19 December 1980, responding to my request for information about its promised post-independence investigation, Mobil's general counsel ignored his chairman's public commitment and stated — in complete contradiction of the facts — that the "relevant government officials (in Zimbabwe have) declined to respond to Lonrho's request for any information."

Faced with a treasury department investigation "on hold" and Mobil's calculated refusal to conduct its own promised investigation for fear (or perhaps in the knowledge) of what it might uncover, in January the Law Group sent a man to Salisbury. What he discovered underscored previous suspicions that neither the treasury nor Mobil had any intention of carrying out thorough investigations unless prodded into so doing. Interviews with US Embassy officials, for instance, revealed that they had felt "no push" from Washington. "To our surprise," remarked one "we have not been asked by the treasury to request from Zimbabwe a waiver of the Official Secrets Act." A lengthy conversation with the Zimbabwean Minister of Justice, Simbi Mubako, was even more revealing. First, he confirmed public reports that a waiver of the Official Secrets Act had been granted Lonrho, and that, as embassy officials had stated, the US had not requested a similar waiver. More importantly, though, he stated categorically that his government would grant such a waiver if requested either by the US or Mobil. The Law Group promptly transmitted this information to both parties.

At about the same time the Law Group contacted Lonrho headquarters in London and arranged for four large boxes of documents that Lonrho had submitted to the arbitration proceedings to be shipped to the treasury department in Washington. These documents, including customs "bond books" from Mozambique — where the three Mobil officials sent to South Africa in 1976 were careful not to go — show repeated Mobil shipments of oil destined for Rhodesia, clearly a violation of company policy and, depending upon other circumstances, possibly US sanctions regulations as well. The existence of such documents should come as no surprise to the treasury or Mobil, since their availability was widely publicised in Jorge Jardim's Sanctions Double-Cross: Oil to Rhodesia, a revealing and well-documented inside account by a top Portuguese official of how the major international oil companies, including Mobil, supplied Rhodesia with oil through the then Portuguese Mozambique port of Lourenço Marques from 1966 to 1975. Moreover, within recent weeks Lonrho has made available over 8,000 pages of these documents to Mobil. How, prior to receiving them and without any attempt to obtain evidence from Zimbabwe, the company could have contended, as it did, in a 21 January 1981 letter to the Securities and Exchange Commission (SEC), that it had "conducted an extensive investigation to determine whether its policies have been observed" staggers the imagination. . . .

In summation, Mobil's company policy argument is in a shambles, and without the Zimbabwean official Secrets Act to hide behind, the "Mobil Defence" may soon crumble. Only thorough investigations will determine, however, whether enough additional evidence exists to link the parent company, or officers and directors who are US citizens and hence within the reach of the narrowly drawn US sanctions regulations, with actual sanctions violations. At the very least, it seems certain that Mobil will be shown to have violated UN Security Council resolutions on sanctions, if not also US law.

Although the policy of "let bygones be bygones" may be desirable within Zimbabwe, this argument, advanced by a Mobil representative last year, has no place on the international level. Moreover, it would amount to a de facto amnesty to Rhodesian sanctions-busters and signal that sanctions enforcement was not taken any more seriously in the US than in Britain. . . .

The Treasury Department Investigations

The first Treasury report about Mobil's alleged violations of UN sanctions and U.S. law, mentioned in the above reading, was issued on 12 May 1977. Treasury Investigation of Charges Made Against the Mobil Oil Corporation (undated). Framed to assess the charges made by the Reverend Schulz of the United Church of Christ before a subcommittee of the Senate Foreign Relations Committee in 1976, to the effect that Mobil's subsidiary in South Africa (MOSA) was supplying oil and petroleum products to

Mobil's subsidiary in Rhodesia (MOSR), the report correctly concluded that such allegations, which it could neither authenticate nor disprove, in any event would not constitute a violation of the Rhodesian Sanctions Regulations in view of the foreign subsidiaries' loophole (see page 520 supra). The report justified the loophole on the ground that the United States had followed the lead of the United Kingdom when it drafted its regulations implementing UN sanctions, and that the latter "did not apply its sanctions regulations to foreign subsidiaries of British firms, *as a matter of principle."* Id. at 6 (emphasis added). It also noted that

> other major U.N. members also did not control foreign subsidiaries. Since the U.N. sanctions against Rhodesia are a multilateral undertaking, and since many countries object to so-called "extraterritorial" controls over subsidiaries of U.S. firms located in their countries, for the U.S. to unilaterally extend its controls beyond the level of controls adhered to by the sponsor of the sanctions resolutions, and by other major U.N. members did not appear appropriate. If the U.N. sanctions were in fact fully enforced by all U.N. members, U.S. subsidiaries abroad would be prevented from dealing with Rhodesia by the laws of the countries in which they operate. However, this is not uniformly the case and South Africa does not adhere to the embargo at all.

Id. Thus, even if MOSA had been shipping oil to MOSR, no violation of U.S. law (as opposed to UN sanctions) would have occurred. Id. at 7.

Since the Rhodesian Sanctions Regulations did extend "to goods of United States origin, and to United States citizens," id. at 2, the report also addressed allegations that Mobil oil or petroleum products originating in the United States had been shipped to Rhodesia, and that three U.S. citizens who had served on MOSA's board of directors had known of the petroleum importing that MOSR supposedly had carried out in collaboration with MOSA.

Unfortunately, the Official Secrets Act of Rhodesia and South Africa precluded Treasury investigators from obtaining the original documents from Mobil's two subsidiaries that would have proved or disproved the authenticity of copies submitted by the United Church of Christ showing such shipments. However, they were able to interview the three Mobil officials who were U.S. citizens and concluded that they were not aware of, or instrumental in, the alleged scheme to ship Mobil products to MOSR in violation of U.S. law. Thus, as Lowenfeld, supra page 513, at 489, concludes: "The Report of the United Church of Christ was not discredited, but not confirmed; Mobil was not quite exonerated, but was not accused, either of having breached the sanctions or of having known about breaches by its subsidiaries." He adds pointedly: "No changes were made in the Regulations as a result of the investigation." Id.

In late 1978, following the publication in the United Kingdom of the official Bingham Report, which concluded that Shell and British Petroleum had violated UN sanctions along the lines that the United Church of Christ had alleged Mobil had (see pages 559-561 infra), the Treasury Department reopened its investigation of the activities of both Mobil and Caltex subsidiaries in Southern Africa. Before much progress was made, however, the United States imposed sanctions against Iran in response to its seizure of U.S. hostages. Since the responsibility for administering these new sanctions fell on the Treasury Department, it was not until 1982, a year after the termination of Iranian sanctions, that substantial work on the Rhodesian sanction-breaking investigation could be resumed.

Considerable new evidence had emerged in the interval between 1977 and 1982 to establish that MOSA had violated company policy (but not, in view of the foreign subsidiaries' loophole, U.S. law) literally hundreds of times, beginning in August 1966, by shipping substantial quantities of gasoline and other petroleum products through the then-Portuguese port of Lourenço Marques (now Maputo) to Rhodesia. Especially revealing were over 8,000 pages copied from Mozambique Customs bond books covering MOSA's facility in Maputo, made available to the Treasury Department by the U.K. multinational Lonrho through the good offices of the International Human Rights Law Group, a Washington, D.C.-based NGO. That such documentation existed can be credited to the foresight of Portuguese authorities in Mozambique who — anxious not to be called the sole sanctions breakers in 1966 — required MOSA and the other oil companies, when issuing ownership transfer documents to local transit agents in Maputo, to state in writing the final destination of the oil or petroleum products being shipped.

This procedure, which actually was developed in response to Mobil's clumsy attempt to obtain Portugal's collaboration in its efforts to hide the fact that its products were being directly railed to Rhodesia, had been explained as far back as 1978 by Jorge Jardim, Portugal's "economic czar" in Mozambique, who quoted a 10 August 1966 cable from Portugal's Overseas Minister stating that the "operation must be done in such a way that when product is delivered by 'Mobil' to forwarding agent final destination of product will be immediately declared, so that company will not be able to claim ignorance on this subject afterwards." J. Jardim, Sanctions Double-Cross: Oil to Rhodesia 91 (1978) (emphasis deleted). This procedure, confirmed by the Bingham Report, infra page 559, at paras. 7.40-7.41, obviously had been known to Mobil, but not revealed to the Treasury Department during its initial investigation.

Of course, such shipments by MOSA would not have violated U.S. law — absent Mobil's involvement in the procurement process, or the involvement of Mobil itself or any of its officials who were U.S. citizens — unless U.S. oil or petroleum products were involved. That at least in some cases they were seems inescapably clear from 11 bond book entries from 1968 through 1970 showing ships coming from U.S. ports, whose cargoes thereupon were shipped to Rhodesia. Presumably these 11 vessels were carrying special petroleum products, e.g., lubricating oils, not readily available from MOSA's refinery in Durban, South Africa, the port of origin of the overwhelming majority of the ships carrying Mobil cargoes that were found in the bond books.

Details of the 11 U.S. ships, their cargoes, and the fact that such cargoes, in whole or in part, had been consigned to freight forwarders for shipment to Rhodesia are set out in the final report of the Treasury Department. The Office of Foreign Assets Control: Office of the Assistant Secretary (Enforcement and Operations), Report on Investigation into Alleged Violations of the Rhodesian Sanctions Regulations by the Mobil Oil and Caltex Petroleum Corporations 91-93 (Oct. 5, 1985). These 11 instances of possible sanctions-breaking, tracking a legal memorandum furnished the Treasury Department by the International Human Rights Law Group (International Human Rights Law Group, Suggested Lines of Inquiry for the Treasury's Reopened Investigation of Charges of Sanctions Violations Made Against the Mobil Oil Corporation 6 (May 1983)), were not pursued further by the Treasury Department, since its efforts to confirm the authenticity of the bond books were stymied by the Official Secrets Acts of South Africa and (now) Zimbabwe and by the failure of Mozambique, Zimbabwe, the United Kingdom, and other countries to cooperate with its investigation. Treasury Report, supra, at 123. This lack of cooperation, at least on the part of Zimbabwe, is hard to explain in light of previous assurances given to the International Human Rights Law Group. The Treasury Department report makes no attempt at explanation, save for noting in the case of the United Kingdom "that following the establishment of majority rule in Rhodesia, the U.K. Government declined to bring prosecutions against any U.K. citizen as a result of the revelations in the Bingham Report." Id. at 79. Why the United Kingdom's much-criticized failure to enforce its own law should cause it to help block U.S. enforcement of its sanctions laws is hard to understand.

In sum, the Treasury investigations proved "inconclusive." As the Treasury Report, supra, at 124 concludes, its re-opened investigation

> failed to produce any evidence that the Mobil Oil Corporation, the Caltex Petroleum Corporation, or any U.S. national employed by either company participated in the supply or diversion of petroleum or petroleum products to Rhodesia in violation of the Rhodesian Sanctions Regulations. On the other hand, the re-opened investigation also failed to produce evidence demonstrating that Mobil, Caltex, and/or employees of either company did not engage in transactions in violation of the Regulations. It cannot be stated with certainty whether, had the Treasury Department been able to obtain more of the evidence that it sought, its investigation would have ended with more definitive results.

This Scotch verdict — "not proven" rather than "not guilty" — brought the Treasury Department investigations to a close. Several chapters remain to be written, however, before the lessons of sanctions enforcement (and circumvention) are fully learned.

Note: Sanctions-Breaking Around the World

In 1977 the U.S. General Accounting Office (GAO) did a study on the extent to which various federal departments and agencies were implementing the Rhodesian Sanctions Regulations. The following conclusions were reached (Report of the Comptroller General of the United States, Implementation of Sanctions Against Rhodesia 32 (1977)).

> What does appear common among the agencies charged with administering the sanctions is the lack of emphasis on fully enforcing the U.N. sanctions.
>
> For example, . . . compliance activities are limited by the following factors: (1) lack of personnel; (2) Rhodesian sanctions are third in order of priority of workload; (3) mission of the Department of Commerce is to promote rather than control exports; (4) lack of cooperation by allies and other nations who supposedly are supporting the sanctions programs; (5) the inconsistency of allowing the importation of strategic materials from Rhodesia under the provisions of the Byrd Amendment; and (6) lack of authority for cases involving diversion or reexport by foreign firms.

It should not be thought, however, that the United States was alone in its less-than-perfect application of UN sanctions. The United Kingdom, as the Bingham Report testifies and material that follows corroborates (pages 559-561 infra), was a major violator. It has been estimated, in fact, that U.S. violations accounted for only about one-fifth of all the illegal trade with Rhodesia — a substantial share, to be sure, but not even a majority one. Then Ambassador to the United Nations John Scali made this point in the following remarks at the Boston College of Law on 17 May 1973 ([1973] Digest of United States Practice in International Law 413 (1974)):

> I am happy to observe that Delegates in the Security Council have recently paid more attention to covert violations of the sanctions than formerly. I shall continue to demand in the Security Council that those sincerely interested in making sanctions work to bring about justice in Rhodesia look at the whole spectrum of violations and not merely the small fraction of the total for which the United States is responsible.
>
> At the same time, I respectfully invite the Congress to re-examine its position. I ask them to weigh relatively minor domestic considerations against the damage that has been done to America's image and reputation as a law-abiding nation. This damage is not irreparable. I urge them to strengthen the American Delegation to the United Nations as it joins with others in the U.N. to make the sanctions voted by the Security Council an effective and universal reality.

Mr. Scali's advice that the UN and its member states should look to "the whole spectrum of violations" was well taken. A careful look at (or even a casual perusal of) the effectiveness of the sanctions reveals the existence of business dealings both in and with Rhodesia that are of such a scale that they can scarcely even be called covert. See, for example, Figure 7-1, which shows how dramatically Rhodesian exports (and imports) took off after 1971, and also Table 7-1, listing statistics reported to the Sanctions Committee of the UN Security Council.

FIGURE 7-1
Rhodesian Imports and Exports

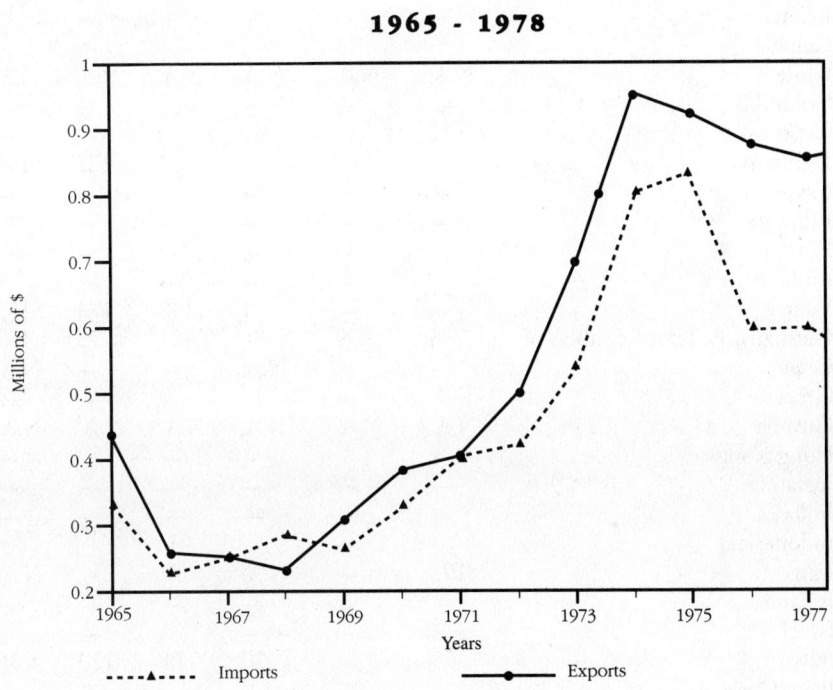

Note: Both exports and imports are valued f.o.b. (free on board, that is, excluding the cost of insurance and freight beyond the border).

Source: Adapted from Yearbook of International Trade Statistics, vol. 1, 1972-1973, and vol. 1, 1984. Graph prepared by Mr. Noel H. Gordon, University of Virginia School of Law, Class of 1990.

TABLE 7-1
Imports and Exports of All Commodities from/to Southern Rhodesia
(As Reported by Countries Listed)*
(in thousands of United States dollars)

Reporting country or area	Imports			Exports		
	1975	1976	1977	1975	1976	1977
Angola	N.A.	N.A.	N.A.	N.A.	N.A.	N.A.
Argentina	—	—	—	—	—	—
Australia	—	—	—	—	—	—
Austria	—	—	65	—	—	—
Bahrain	—	—	—	—	—	—
Barbados	—	—	—	—	—	—
Belgium-Luxembourg	2	—	3	72	110	165
Brazil	—	—	—	—	—	—
Brunei	—	—	—	—	—	—
Canada	3	—	1	3	—	—
Chile	N.A.	N.A.	N.A.	N.A.	N.A.	N.A.
Colombia	—	—	—	—	—	—
Cyprus	2	—	24	3	—	—
Denmark	—	—	—	84	122	190
Egypt	—	—	—	—	—	—
Ethiopia	—	—	—	—	—	—
Fiji	—	—	—	—	—	—
Finland	—	—	—	—	—	4
France	—	—	1	148	174	153
Germany, Federal Republic of	738	499	458	2,481	1,275	1,107
Ghana	—	—	N.A.	—	—	N.A.
Greece	—	—	12	—	—	—
Guyana	N.A.	N.A.	N.A.	N.A.	N.A.	N.A.
Hong Kong	—	—	—	—	—	—
Iceland	—	—	—	—	—	—
India	—	—	—	—	—	—
Indonesia	—	—	—	—	—	—
Iran	192	—	N.A.	10	—	N.A.
Ireland	—	—	—	—	—	—
Israel	—	—	—	—	—	—
Italy	55	—	20	71	120	236
Ivory Coast	—	—	—	—	—	—
Jamaica	—	—	—	—	—	—
Japan	—	—	—	158	68	146
Jordan	—	—	3	—	—	—
Lebanon	N.A.	N.A.	N.A.	N.A.	N.A.	N.A.
Liberia	—	N.A.	N.A.	—	N.A.	N.A.
Libyan Arab Jamahiriya	—	—	—	—	—	—

*Imports from and exports to the countries listed accounted for approximately 86 and 75 per cent, respectively, of the total exports and imports of Southern Rhodesia in 1965.

Reporting country or area	Imports			Exports		
	1975	1976	1977	1975	1976	1977
Malawi	10,602	10,032	6,295	3,496	3,291	2,375
Malaysia	—	—	—	—	—	—
Malta	—	—	—	—	—	—
Mauritius	—	—	—	—	—	—
Mexico	—	—	—	—	—	—
Mozambique	N.A.	N.A.	N.A.	N.A.	N.A.	N.A.
Netherlands	—	—	—	4	—	19
Netherlands Antilles	—	—	—	—	—	—
New Zealand	—	—	—	5	—	—
Nigeria	—	—	—	—	—	—
Norway	—	—	—	—	—	—
Pakistan	—	—	—	—	—	—
Philippines	—	—	—	—	—	—
Portugal	—	—	—	—	—	—
Republic of Korea	—	—	—	—	—	—
Saudi Arabia	—	—	33	—	—	—
Senegal	—	—	—	—	—	—
Singapore	—	—	—	—	—	—
Spain	—	—	—	—	—	—
Sri Lanka	—	—	—	—	—	—
Sweden	—	—	—	1	—	—
Switzerland	7,298	7,644	8,518	2,763	2,001	1,929
Thailand	—	—	—	—	—	—
Trinidad and Tobago	—	—	—	—	—	—
Tunisia	—	—	—	—	—	—
Turkey	—	—	—	—	—	—
Uganda	—	—	—	—	—	—
United Kingdom	334	378	364	2,669	2,463	1,824
United States	59,604	45,829	29,315	1,250	774	834
Samoa	—	—	—	—	—	—
Yugoslavia	—	—	—	—	—	—
Zambia	11	N.A.	N.A.	758	N.A.	N.A.

From the Eleventh Report of the Security Council Committee Established in Pursuance of Resolution 253 (1968) Concerning the Question of Southern Rhodesia [Sanctions Committee], 34 U.N. SCOR Special Supp. (No. 2, Vol. III, App. at 16-17, U.N. Doc. S/13000 (1979).

As interesting as the latter figures are, one can readily see that they conceal at least as much as they disclose. The number of reporting units (not all of the entries in the table are states) for which figures were not available increased dramatically during the years covered in the above report to the point that only 22 out of the 70 entries provided any statistics at all to the Committee. The problem was compounded by the fact that well over one-half of the entire UN membership is not represented in the table. Czechoslovakia is a particularly conspicuous absentee: it was reputed to be one of Rhodesia's foremost clandestine trading partners.

Some of the sanctions-breaking states, to be sure, were victims of economic and geographical circumstance. Two such examples were Zambia and Malawi — both landlocked states, both former U.K. possessions, and both with a long history of economic dependence upon and domination by white-run Rhodesia and South Africa. Zambia, for example, was dependent upon Rhodesian railroads for the carriage of 80 percent of its foreign trade at the time of U.D.I. Full adherence to the sanction program at that point would have been an economic catastrophe. A step-up in guerrilla infiltration from Zambia into Rhodesia in late 1972 brought Smith to close the Rhodesian-Zambian border early in 1973. Zambia responded by doing likewise and even kept its border closed after Smith relented and reversed his position. As a result, the Zambian economy was decidedly weakened, although to be fair one should note that the calamitous decline in world copper prices in 1974-1975 was a substantial contributing factor to this weakness as well.

The UN Charter does take account of situations like this one, in which the burden of forwarding UN policy falls disproportionately and unavoidably onto certain states. Article 49 imposes on states a duty of "mutual assistance" in carrying out Security Council measures. Article 50 gives to states that are "confronted with special economic problems" in adhering to Security Council resolutions "the right to consult the Security Council with regard to a solution of those problems."

Note, however, that Article 50 does not give any state a legal right to receive assistance. Rather, it only confers a right of consultation, leaving any final decision in the matter to the judgment of the Security Council. There still exists the mutual assistance obligation of Article 49, of course, though it is difficult to see how that can be made effective in cases where the Security Council chooses not to make aid assessments against other member states. See L. Goodrich, E. Hambro, and A. Simons, Charter of the United Nations: Commentary and Documents 337-342 (1969). No such assessments were made by the Security Council in the case of the Rhodesian sanctions, so hard-hit states like Zambia and Malawi, dependent upon the generosity of the international community, considered themselves economically unable to implement sanctions fully.

Sanctions-breaking by such small African states, however, dwindles into insignificance when compared with the numerous reported (and often confirmed) violations by major European states. Until the "Oilgate" scandal in 1978, perhaps the most significant exposure of sanctions violations occurred in 1974, when the Sunday Times of London revealed an audacious scheme by the nationalized Austrian steel company, German steel manufacturers, and Swiss trading companies, financed by banks in five different states, to collaborate with Rhodesia in doubling the size of its steel industry. Normally the Sanctions Committee set up by the Security Council, with limited fact-finding resources of its own, had to rely on newspaper reports like that of the Sunday Times and similar information supplied by NGOs.

In doing so, it merely followed the practice of most of the UN's other human rights bodies (see Problem VI). Following the publication of the above story, therefore, it simply requested the governments of the five states named therein to undertake their own investigations and to take appropriate measures against any sanctions violators.

The five states — Austria, the Federal Republic of Germany, Great Britain, Switzerland, and the United States — purported to investigate the companies and banks concerned and reported that they found no evidence of sanctions-breaking. Despite such findings, the Sanctions Committee proceeded to reach its own conclusions, which it issued in a special report to the Security Council in 1975 (30 U.N. SCOR Special Supp. (No. 3), U.N. Doc. S/11597 (1975)). It found that, notwithstanding the results of the individual state investigations, the documentation on "External Participation in the Expansion of the Rhodesian Iron and Steel Company, Ltd." was "the most comprehensive, detailed and technical ever presented to the Committee." It, therefore, deemed the case to be the most serious example of sanctions-breaking to have come to its attention.

By far the major, and certainly the most serious, case of sanctions-breaking, however, involved the conspiracy by Shell and BP to supply Rhodesia with over one-half of its oil and petroleum products needs in the post-U.D.I. period. The conspiracy began to unravel in 1976 when the Sanctions Committee was presented with a copy of the United Church of Christ report. The Committee asked the British and Dutch governments to investigate the report's charges that "the role of Shell in Rhodesia was at least as important as that of Mobil." Ninth Report of the Security Council Committee Established in Pursuance of Resolution 253 (1968) Concerning the Question of Southern Rhodesia, 32 U.N. SCOR Special Supp. (No. 2), Vol. II, at 299, U.N. Doc. S/12265 (1977). Although the British government replied that, after further investigations, it was satisfied that neither Shell nor BP had broken sanctions, pressure on it continued to mount, and on 8 April 1977 a prominent London barrister was named to head an official inquiry.

What became known as the "Bingham Report" was published little over a year later, on 19 September 1978. Foreign and Commonwealth Office, Report on the Supply of Petroleum and Petroleum Products to Rhodesia by T.H. Bingham, Q.C. and S.M. Gray, F.C.A. (1978). Although Martin Bailey, whose award-winning book Oilgate reads like the exciting detective story it is, rightly notes that the report "is a difficult document to digest, written in a dense, legalistic terminology, and displaying great subtlety of language and judgement," M. Bailey, Oilgate 94 (1979), its "bottom line" was clear, and its effect was "devastating." Lowenfeld, supra page 513, at 492. Explains Professor Lowenfeld,

> Despite traditional British understatement and a deliberate avoidance of a quotable "summary of conclusions," the Report set out in close to 300 oversized printed pages a record of continuous supply of petroleum products to

Rhodesia by Shell and BP, not only by their respective South African subsidiaries (generally working together) but with the active collaboration of a [Mozambique] subsidiary incorporated in Britain [and hence subject to U.K. sanctions law] and with the certain knowledge and approval of senior management in London and at least partial knowledge of senior officials of Her Majesty's Government.

Id. Particularly outrageous was the "swap" arrangement, confirmed by the report, pursuant to which, in an effort to avoid technically violating U.K. law, Shell and BP supplied the customers of Total South Africa (the subsidiary of the French company Total) an amount of oil and petroleum products equal in amount to what Total South Africa furnished middlemen in Lourenço Marques for shipment to Rhodesia to fulfill Shell and BP's needs. This arrangement, in operation from 1968 to 1971, actually had the approval of high members in the British government! As the Bingham Report, supra page 559, para. 14.8, forthrightly states,

> The Total exchange arrangement plainly did not have the effect of denying supplies of oil products to Rhodesia. That an arrangement having this deficiency was accepted by HMG had, we think, an important consequence. It induced among those most directly concerned . . . a belief that compliance with the Sanctions Orders was to be regarded as a matter of form rather than of substance, that it was the letter which mattered, not the spirit. . . .

The magnitude of the sanctions violations reported by Bingham caused the then-Prime Minister, James Callaghan, to ask Parliament to establish a Special Commission on Oil Sanctions to pursue the matter. This proposal was approved by the House of Commons but rejected by the House of Lords. As time passed, Oilgate gradually became buried by more immediate political issues, and no further parliamentary action was taken. Annex III of the Bingham Report, on "Evidence of Criminal Prosecutions," while never published, was forwarded to the Director of Public Prosecutions. However, whatever criminal cases might have been brought for the blatant sanctions violations set out in the report became a moot issue when on 21 April 1980, at the time of Zimbabwean Independence, the government of Prime Minister Thatcher issued the Southern Rhodesia (Sanctions) (Amnesty) Order. (1980) 1(2) Stat. Instr. 2056 (No. 565). A charitable assessment is that "let bygones be bygones" had prevailed.

The ironies in the Oilgate revelations are as apparent as the lessons to be learned from them are numerous. As The Economist observed, "While Britain was vigorously pressing economic sanctions against Rhodesia in order to bring down Mr. Ian Smith's regime, BP and Shell were its major oil suppliers. Further, parts of the British government knew this. So an astonishing paradox: British warships blockading the Mozambican port of Beira to prevent oil, always accepted as the key to sanctions, reaching Rhodesia, while British oil companies, with the apparent acquiescence of at least some people in the foreign office, covertly supplying the rebel state." The Economist, Sept. 2, 1978, at 20, col. 1. Small wonder, then, in view of Rhodesia's knowledge that the United Kingdom was undercutting the sanctions program that it had initiated, that Mr. Wilson was unable to negotiate a settlement based upon the principles of majority rule with Mr. Smith!

There are numerous ways in which the above situation can be rationalized. As explained (but not accepted) by The Economist, "Britain [in 1967] had lately devalued and was in the hands of the bailiffs at the time. It was withdrawing from east of Suez. It had neither the economic nor . . . the military capacity to blockade South Africa or force it to cease supplying Rhodesia. To make BP and Shell break their contracts with South African customers would lead to certain legal action against them there and loss of a lucrative oil market plus possible economic retaliation. Besides, was not South Africa a useful intermediary with the Rhodesian rebels?

"No cover up here. The only gentleman not told about this, after all, and thus painlessly bilked of his money, was the British taxpayer. His job was to foot the bill for a revolving naval blockade of Beira which . . . [e]very British minister involved knew . . . to be utterly useless — except as a way of pretending that Mr. Wilson's belief that he would be ending the Rhodesian rebellion 'in weeks rather than months' was still alive." Id., Sept. 9, 1978, at 11, col. 2. Despite such rationalizations, the hypocrisy of the British government's attitude toward sanctions is apparent. Had British oil not flowed into Rhodesia for over a decade, surely the Smith regime would have been brought to its knees far sooner — and over an estimated 10,000 lives saved.

V.   Rhodesia: The Achievement of Majority Rule

A.   *The Salisbury Agreement and the Emergence of Zimbabwe Rhodesia*

Throughout 1977 prospects for a negotiated settlement of the Rhodesian crisis looked bleak. Yet the impact of the world recession of the mid-1970s, the escalating guerrilla war within the country, and pressures brought to bear by the international community (including economic sanctions) all were at work on the Smith regime. By the end of the year, for the first time in years — perhaps ever — he was ready for serious negotiations.

To this end, Smith commenced talks with several black African politicians — principally Bishop Muzorewa, but also the Reverend Sithole and Chief Jeremiah Chirau — looking to an "internal settlement." Finally, after several months of negotiations, Smith and the three black leaders signed the Salisbury Agreement, 17 Intl. Legal Materials 261 (1978), designed to install black majority rule by the end of 1978. Ironically, the signing on 3

March 1978 took place under a large portrait of Cecil Rhodes, the turn-of-the-century colonist who gave his name to the country, now to be renamed Zimbabwe Rhodesia. M. Meredith, The Past Is Another Country: Rhodesia U.D.I. to Zimbabwe 331 (rev. ed. 1980).

The Salisbury Agreement envisaged a transitional government that would draft a new constitution, hold free elections open to all persons over 18, and install a black majority government with an African Prime Minister thereafter. Yet the arrangement was in many ways a Pyrrhic victory for Muzorewa and his colleagues, since it "left the whites in control of the administration, the security forces, the economy and, for the interim period, Parliament; under black rule they were assured of a powerful political voice [28 of the 100 seats in Parliament]; their pensions, property and landholdings were guaranteed; and there was no threat to white jobs." Meredith, supra, at 330-331. A constitution embodying the principles in the Salisbury Agreement was drafted by the transitional government and, on 30 January 1979, approved overwhelmingly by an all-white referendum. In the election, held over a five-day period in April, Muzorewa emerged the clear victor: his party won 67 percent of the total votes cast and 51 of the 72 black seats in Parliament. On 1 June 1979, he took over the reins of government, becoming the first (and, as it turned out, the only) Prime Minister of Zimbabwe Rhodesia.

B. The Lancaster House Conference and the Creation of Zimbabwe

Black majority rule, however, brought neither peace nor recognition to Zimbabwe Rhodesia. "It made little difference when Muzorewa and Sithole argued that, as the cause of majority rule had been won, there was no further justification for the [guerrilla] war to continue," writes Meredith. "For the war was no longer confined to that cause. It involved a black struggle for power." Meredith, supra, at 335. The Patriotic Front, led by Nkomo and Mugabe, had not signed onto the Salisbury Agreement and had denounced the new constitution and the elections thereunder as a fraud. The number of their guerrillas inside Zimbabwe Rhodesia and their disruptive activities and intimidation efforts increased markedly during 1978 and 1979. "Whatever ploy the government tried, it was obvious that the internal settlement was based on a fatal miscalculation: neither Muzorewa nor Sithole had the power or the popularity to undercut the guerrilla campaign." Id. at 340. Nor were they able to obtain the lifting of UN sanctions or recognition from either the United Kingdom or the United States. President Carter, well aware that the Salisbury Agreement had not led to a lasting settlement, rejected the urging of the majority of Congress and refused either to lift U.S. sanctions or extend diplomatic recognition. Violence increased, and a savage civil war grew.

Davidow, Dealing with International Crises: Lessons from Zimbabwe
Occasional Paper 34, The Stanley Foundation, at 9-13 (1983)

NEW NEGOTIATIONS

Not wishing to isolate Britain from her principal ally, newly installed Prime Minister Margaret Thatcher was compelled by the US position and by British self-interest elsewhere in Africa to reinvigorate attempts to negotiate a settlement including all of the parties to the conflict. At the Commonwealth Heads of Government conference in Lusaka, Zambia in early August 1979 Mrs. Thatcher surprised many by entering into serious discussions on Rhodesia with African and other Commonwealth leaders. The result was a British commitment to undertake another negotiating effort. Within a week of the Lusaka conference's close, British Foreign Secretary Lord Peter Carrington invited the leaders of the Patriotic Front and Bishop Muzorewa to a constitutional conference to begin on September 10, 1979, at Lancaster House in London. After some quibbling, all of the parties accepted.

Although not readily apparent at the outset of the conference, Rhodesia had become ripe for settlement. Important pressures weighed heavily on both the Muzorewa delegation, which included Smith and other white cabinet ministers, and on the Patriotic Front. No end was in sight for the vicious, stalemated war. The South African government, less inclined to bankroll the fighting for a black-led government, continually reinforced the Salisbury delegation's inclination to stay in London in the hope that the Patriotic Front would walk out of the conference, or failing that, that Britain would insure Muzorewa's electoral triumph. The parlous state of the Rhodesian economy also greatly influenced the Muzorewa team. The Front Line African states compelled Nkomo and Mugabe to stick with the negotiations. Self-interest motivated Zambia and Mozambique, which were suffering from the economic dislocations of the war and from continued military attacks of their territory. Reinforcing the outside pressures was the belief, which each delegation held, that in a fair election it would emerge victorious over the other.

Even given the above, the conference would have failed if it had not been for the superb management of Lord Peter Carrington. An urbane and skilled diplomat, he effectively manipulated many of the situational factors inherent in the London venue: easy access to the world press, an active intelligence apparatus, the parliamentary forum, and the propinquity of a politically supportive prime minister. More importantly, Carrington tenaciously stuck to a well-planned negotiating strategy based on a strong unwillingness to let either of the other delegations hijack the conference. He insisted on a step by step approach which forced consideration of the thorny issues one at a time rather than as a complete package which might have proven indigestible.

The British realized that their most difficult task would be to convince the Muzorewa delegation, especially its white members, to relinquish their hold over de facto power in Rhodesia. To this end, Carrington presented negotiating positions which spoke to the concerns of the white minority — civil liberties, pension rights, a continuing political presence in parliament — without, however, abandoning the overriding goal of a fully independent, truly African-run Zimbabwe. This relatively sympathetic approach convinced many that the Conservative party's heart remained with Bishop Muzorewa. That impression reinforced Carrington's greatest tactical weapon, his perceived willingness to accept a "second-class" solution, a deal only between Muzorewa and the British. Carrington, by demonstrating his intention at important junctures to negotiate only with the Salisbury delegation in the face of Patriotic Front recalcitrance, was able to keep Muzorewa engaged while compelling Nkomo and Mugabe to buckle on important issues.

Carrington's "second-class" strategy involved considerable risk-taking, the ultimate expression of which was the dispatch of Lord Christopher Soames as governor to Rhodesia on December 11, that is, after Muzorewa had accepted the final Lancaster House agreement document but while Mugabe and Nkomo, particularly the former, still hesitated. Carrington's gamble, abetted by some not so gentle pressure from the Mozambican government on Mugabe, turned the trick. The Patriotic Front finally accepted. On December 21, 1979, the Lancaster House agreement was signed by all of the parties. [19 Intl. Legal Materials 387 (1980).]

The agreement consisted of three main portions. An agreed upon constitution provided for a democratic, parliamentary form of government with a court-protected bill of rights and 20 seats in the 100-member House of Assembly reserved for whites. The constitution's guarantee of individual and property rights and the possibility of a continuing share of political power placated the whites on the Salisbury team. The creation of a democratically elected government with all instruments of authority finally in the hands of blacks appealed to Africans on both the Muzorewa and Patriotic Front delegations. The second major element of the agreement was a plan for a brief transitional period of about ten weeks in which the British governor would exercise all legislative and executive authority and conduct Commonwealth-observed elections. A Commonwealth monitoring military force of 1200 men (900 of them British) would keep the armies apart and under control. As Lancaster House progressed, the British assumed more responsibility for the transition than they had intended, but they found it necessary to do so to allay the Front's fears of continued white Rhodesian control during the electoral period. The third element of the agreement detailed the procedures for the cease-fire and military disengagement.

TRANSITION

The transitional period was touch and go: all parties, but particularly Mugabe's, were guilty of voter intimidation; sporadic violence erupted; and the continuing hostility among the three armies threatened a generalized conflagration. However, with luck and skill the British were able to keep all of the principal actors engaged in the electoral process. Lord Soames's governance echoed Carrington's style at Lancaster House in its firmness, perceived necessity to cajole Muzorewa and the white Rhodesian military leaders, and threats to disqualify all or some of Mugabe's candidates.

In elections held on the last three days of February 1980 almost a million more Africans voted than had cast ballots just eleven months before. Mugabe's party won 57 of the 80 African seats. Nkomo's party took 20, reflecting his strong support among Zimbabwe's Matabele tribe (20 percent of the African population) and little support elsewhere. Muzorewa, whose faith in his own ability to win another election had sustained him through the Lancaster House Conference, was able to garner only three seats for his party. Soames immediately asked Mugabe to form the new state's first government. In the weeks that followed, the relationship between the to-be prime minister and departing governor warmed to one of confidence. Mugabe asked the British to stay on longer than they had intended. Soames extended the period only for a few weeks and the United Kingdom promised to station a military advisory team in independent Zimbabwe to help in the difficult task of integrating the formerly warring armies. On April 18, 1980, the Colony of Southern Rhodesia finally became the state of Zimbabwe.

VI.   Viewpoints on International Economic Sanctions: Rhodesia as a Case Study

H. Strack, Sanctions: The Case of Rhodesia
252-253 (1978)

[The author describes conditions, some unique to Rhodesia, that impeded the sanction effort there and cast doubts about the efficacy of future UN sanctions.]

Yet Rhodesia really has not become more viable in the years that sanctions have been in effect. Initial prosperity after UDI was due in large measure to the basic soundness of the Rhodesian economy at that time and the ability to tap the country's reserves such as excess industrial capacity, import-substitution, increased productivity, and mineral exploitation. But these reserves are not unlimited. A rapidly expanding African population and a marked increase in the guerrilla war dampen optimism about the future of the present political structures in Rhodesia. Sanctions hinder the ability of the Rhodesian government to cope with these two problems — a fact acknowledged by the Rhodesian government. The Rhodesian economy has been remarkably resilient in the face of the enormous costs which must be expended to evade the sanctions, but there is a question as to how long this resiliency can continue in the face of not only the sanctions but the population and guerrilla problems. Prime Minister Ian Smith provided one answer on November 25, 1971, to the House of Assembly: "Things seem to be doing pretty well, and I cannot, by any stretch of the imagination, say that if we had failed to reach agreement this would have prejudiced Rhodesia's position this year, or next year. But, it is our assessment that in ten or twenty years time the position would not be so good for our children." Smith's assessment was correct in the short-term, 1971-74, but was incorrect in the long-term. He could not foresee that Rhodesia's economic viability would be called into question as early as 1976, because of a disintegration of will and determination — not in Salisbury, but rather in Lisbon. The Portuguese coup of April 1974, and all its ramifications for Southern Africa was the single most important factor in persuading Smith to accept the principle of majority rule.

The tenacity with which the idea of Rhodesian sanctions has been maintained — at least on the governmental level — is impressive. As noted above, sanctions have not withered away. For most of the member-states of the United Nations, the effort against Rhodesia is an ideological and symbolic struggle which is not easily forgotten. As the Finnish delegate to the UN noted in the Security Council on June 13, 1969 (S/PV.1476), while the illegal régime continues to survive in an economic sense, it survives as an outcast with no hope of ever gaining recognition. "Thus, what has been achieved so far by the United Nations in the question of Southern Rhodesia is surely an impressive demonstration on behalf of the equality of races and the rights of man." In 1974, UN Secretary-General Kurt Waldheim observed that the question of Southern Rhodesia will go down in history as the first case in which the measures provided for in Article 41 of the UN Charter were implemented. Although the authority was there, practical experience in applying sanctions was completely lacking. It is understandable that it has taken time to develop the sanctions procedure and gradually perfect the machinery by use.

It may be that sanctions are long-term means of influence whose symbolic achievements become apparent before their political achievements. In terms of political achievements, sanctions must be regarded as marginal instruments of influence best employed in conjunction with other means of influence such as armed force — especially if political results are desired in the short-run.

Whether or not the sanctions program against Rhodesia will diminish respect for the United Nations is speculative. But when African majority rule is eventually established in Rhodesia — and even if this is achieved mainly through guerrilla warfare — the United Nations will still be able to claim success for its sanctions program as having been a contributory factor.

D. Losman, International Economic Sanctions
121-123 (1979)

The sanctions promulgated against Rhodesia have, with the exception of 1966, been unable to stop economic growth in that country, although without a doubt they have reduced growth below its potential. At the time sanctions were imposed, the Rhodesian economy had reached a level of sophistication and productive capabilities that allowed successful import substitution and relative ease of adjustment to boycott-induced problems. Three of the four cost categories presented were relevant to the Rhodesian embargo. Direct costs in terms of higher transport and middlemen expenses, lost tobacco revenues, and unemployment in the export sector were abundantly in evidence. Indirect costs, such as unemployment in nontrade sectors resulting from the negative multiplier effects of reduced activity in the export sector, were most visible in 1966 and tended to dissipate fairly quickly after that year. Other costs, such as quality deterioration, have lingered for years. Also included in this category are the storage and warehousing costs involved in stockpiling imported oil and subsidizing the tobacco farmers. Capital effects were only rarely in evidence and presented no serious problems. The import of spare parts and vital raw materials, particularly from South Africa, was made possible by loopholes in sanctions, and thus eliminated this cost category as a problem area. Foregone potential costs are undoubtedly enormous. Growth in tobacco and tourist revenues was assured, as was foreign investment. These potentials have gone unfulfilled, as have economies of scale that were not realized when Rhodesia's markets began to wither.

Sanctions interrupted Rhodesia's economic recovery and delayed the beginning of a period of vigorous and sustained economic growth. The major limiting aspect of sanctions in the Rhodesian case seems to lie in the reduction of export revenues. Imports have been obtainable, despite sanctions, as long as the foreign exchange has been available. It must also be stressed that Rhodesia would have been unable to survive sanctions without enormous gaps in its enforcement. A truly universal embargo, one without loopholes, would have brought quick capitulation. It is, however, unlikely that such a complete isolation can be implemented. . . .

It is also clear that the domestic incidence of sanctions depends not only upon the structure of the target economy but also upon the actions of the domestic political authorities, a variable beyond the control of the boycott initiators. Ian Smith has shown himself to be a skilled politician. By adroitly augmenting and manipulating governmental powers, he disarmed influential sectors that considered capitulation. The domestic impact of sanctions fell upon those with the least political clout.

Negotiations between the Smith government and a number of local African leaders, and between Smith and Anglo-American diplomats and officials of surrounding African nations, became more earnest in 1977-78. The mounting costs of guerrilla warfare, the greater militancy of surrounding states, the increase in Cuban and Soviet influence, and a number of other factors have forced Smith to accept the principle of majority rule. Sanctions continue, but it is these other factors (coupled with pressure from South Africa) that have brought about this dramatic change in the Rhodesian position.

R. Renwick, Economic Sanctions
76-77 (1981)

There is an obvious difficulty in attempting any precise estimate of the effects of sanctions. It is impossible to isolate them from other factors or to judge with any confidence what might have happened if they had not been imposed. It is, however, possible to arrive at certain general conclusions. It is often argued, for instance, that "sanctions have no effect." Yet it is clear that in the main cases considered in this study sanctions did have considerable economic effects. . . .

Rhodesia represents the most ambitious attempt at sanctions enforcement and the only case in which comprehensive mandatory sanctions have been imposed under the appropriate provisions of the U.N. Charter. There can be no doubt that sanctions had a significant economic effect, causing a severe loss of export earnings and foreign exchange difficulties and acting as a constant brake on economic growth. Their effects were very clearly described by Mr. Smith, who was normally in the habit of dismissing them as no more than a "nuisance," in the Rhodesian Parliament in April 1973:

> The imposition of sanctions created many trading problems for us. We find that we are compelled to export at a discount and import at a premium. The result is that we lose out on both transactions. This has the effect of reducing profit margins internally and at the national level it has an adverse effect on our balance of payments and foreign reserves . . . because our foreign reserves are depleted artificially, our natural development is prejudiced. This clearly has a serious inhibiting effect on the creation of job opportunities.

Rhodesia, however, continued to be able to obtain essential imports and to find markets for its exports. The economy was diversified and sustained economic growth was achieved throughout most of the first decade of sanctions enforcement. The subsequent difficulties owed far more to the world economic recession and, increasingly, to the war than to sanctions.

Rhodesia would not have been able to withstand sanctions but for the non-participation of South Africa, leaving a huge gap in their application. . . .

Auglin, United Nations Sanctions Against South Africa and Rhodesia
in the Utility of International Economic Sanctions 34-38
passim (D. Leyton-Brown ed. 1987)

ECONOMIC DEPRIVATION

The capacity of the Rhodesian economy to absorb the shock of sanctions varied over time and from sector to sector. Three phases can be distinguished. . . . Until 1969 exports declined steadily in volume (by 27 per cent) and in value (by 42 per cent), with agricultural products (notably tobacco and sugar) particularly severely hit. On the other hand, manufacturing suffered a less serious slump, and mining was scarcely affected at all. With respect to white employment and incomes, the overall impact was modest and certainly less than had been feared. Moreover, by defaulting on its overseas debts and blocking the payment of dividends owed to overseas investors (but not South Africans), the country ironically actually succeeded in profiting from financial sanctions to improve its balance of payments situation. The government was also able to exploit the valuable breathing space that the leisurely adoption of sanctions provided to devise effective countermeasures and restore business confidence. As a result, by the end of the 1960s, all the economic indicators pointed to the corner having been turned. Between 1968 and 1974, GNP recorded an impressive average annual increase of nearly 9 per cent. Rhodesia, according to one analyst,

> was one of the world's boom economies. . . . The value of mineral production was increasing rapidly. There was a healthy trade surplus and a rapid increase in tourism. By this time a steady increase was also being achieved in overall employment. . . .

The domestic manufacturing sector, in particular, appeared positively to prosper under adversity. Even the depressed tobacco industry continued to account for 10 per cent of the world market, compared with its previous 27 per cent share, with the shortfall more than compensated for by diversification into maize, wheat, cattle and especially cotton.

By the mid-1970s, however, the cumulative strain of a decade or more of economic warfare was beginning to take its toll. The rebel regime's final five-year lease of life saw stagnation set in with per capita incomes falling by 12 percent in real terms, "thus wiping out much of the real improvements in standards of living" made since 1966. Virtually every other indicator of economic performance recorded similar disturbing declines, despite the cushioning effect of South African soft loans.

Only a fraction of this downturn can be attributed to sanctions biting belatedly. More critical, undoubtedly, were the world recession following the escalation in the cost of oil (which led to a reintroduction of gasoline rationing in February 1974 after having been abandoned in 1971) and especially the intensification of the liberation struggle which, among other things, increased defence expenditures "at a rapid annual rate of 35 per cent between 1972 and 1980." Nevertheless, the contribution of sanctions cannot be entirely discounted. While they were not the decisive weapons their authors anticipated, neither was their impact negligible, especially in the long run. It seems likely, however, that it was not so much trade sanctions per se that wore down the Rhodesians, as the shortage of foreign exchange for capital renewal. As The Economist has argued:

> It was Rhodesia's inability to raise long-term credit on the international capital market that put the biggest economic strain on its resources and this, together with the civil war, brought its recalcitrant politicians to the negotiating table. . . .

POLITICAL CHANGE

Measuring the extent of political behaviour modification attributable to sanctions is even more hazardous than calculating their economic impact. Nevertheless, two criteria suggest themselves: the degree of stability of white support for Mr. Smith; and the willingness of the regime to negotiate an end to the impasse.

With respect to the political loyalty of the electorate, the evidence is overwhelming that sanctions proved counterproductive to change — precisely as Galtung predicted. Far from demoralising or dividing white opinion, they encouraged a hardening of hawkish attitudes, a closing of racial ranks and a greater willingness to accept sacrifices. Even the internal business opposition "quickly wilted under pragmatic necessities, compliance requirements under new legislation, and potential or implied threats from the administration." By 1968 the judiciary too had conceded de jure recognition to the illegal regime. The one measure of white morale that did reveal some degree of dissatisfaction, though only during the later years of the rebellion, was the trend of figures on those that voted with their feet. . . . During the first seven years of independence, the rate of emigration actually declined and, except for 1966, immigration numbers increased annually. However, by 1972 emigration figures began to climb, eventually forcing the government to cut back on emigrants' remittances. This was followed, in 1976, by a fall-off in immigration. Since then, the annual net outflow of whites has been substantial. Nevertheless, over a period of UDI, 133,000 settled in Rhodesia — nearly half the white population — compared with only 121,000 who abandoned the country (usually for the security of South Africa).

Almost from the outset of UDI, the United Kingdom sought to coax Ian Smith back to the conference table and, on three occasions — in 1966, 1968 and 1971 — he consented. In each instance, it can be argued, he acted under a certain measure of economic compulsion induced by sanctions. In 1968 Mr. Smith even publicly confessed a willingness to resume negotiations "in order to try and terminate the economic war which is being waged between Britain and Rhodesia to the detriment of both countries." Yet the pressure was never great enough to compel him to qualify his absolute rejection of "unimpeded progress toward majority rule." Rather, it was a case of a confident Smith "talking without negotiating" with the frustrated United Kingdom, in its increasing impatience to disengage, offering successively more retrogressive concessions. Only Mr. Smith's blind intransigence saved the United Kingdom from outright sell-outs in 1966 and 1968, while in 1971 it was the unexpected militancy of the African majority — which for the first time was consulted concerning its fate — that vetoed the notorious Home-Smith agreement to legitimise UDI. Thereafter, other actors entered the arena and negotiations became more complicated. Nevertheless, in the fierce political jockeying that characterised the years 1974 to 1979, the state of the economy was a powerful constraint on Rhodesia's room for manoeuvre. A significant part of the credit for whatever verbal concessions Mr. Smith was forced to voice must go to sanctions. Moreover, the maintenance of sanctions proved a critical ingredient in the success of the final Lancaster House negotiations. Thus, sanctions can claim to have contributed to the defeat of minority rule, but not to have determined the outcome. The decisive factors were undoubtedly the economic impact of the war, the oil price hike and Pretoria's penchant for flexing its economic muscle periodically as a reminder of its regional hegemony.

M. Doxey, International Sanctions in Contemporary Perspective
45-46 (1987)

In seeking to make an overall assessment of the effects of sanctions on the Rhodesian situation, it is hard to disentangle cause and effect. From 1965 first British and then UN sanctions obviously had a direct and generally adverse effect on the economy, particularly by hitting Rhodesia's export trade which brought a serious shortage of foreign exchange. But there was much adaptability and resilience and to the extent that economic sanctions stimulated agriculture and diversification they might possibly have been viewed as useful and certainly not fulfilling the hopes of their backers. Similarly, Rhodesia's greatly enhanced dependence on South Africa which brought close economic integration was not a preferred outcome, and the disposition to negotiate an acceptable settlement may have been lessened by the mood of defiance and by the development of vested interests in the continuation of sanctions which marked the white Rhodesian scene.

But from the mid-1970s the situation in Rhodesia clearly deteriorated steadily. It was not that sanctions per se were more effective, although some of the predicted long-term effects of inability to maintain employment opportunities for increasing numbers of black school-leavers were beginning to be felt in both economic and political terms. Rather, external developments posed new and serious problems.

The first oil shock was followed by an international recession, while changes in the political configuration of the Southern African region were much to the disadvantage of the Smith regime. And all commentators agree that the steadily escalating level of guerrilla warfare inside Rhodesia had a devastating effect on the economy and on white morale. Statistics covering economic performance during the sanctions years are now available from the Zimbabwe Statistical Office. Perhaps the most telling are figures of white migration which still showed a small net gain in 1975 but showed a net loss of 41,246 for the years 1976-9. For a total white population of some 260,000 this was very serious indeed.

Taking the full range of economic restrictions in conjunction with the isolation of Rhodesia from the international community, and the universal non-recognition of its independent status, one must ascribe a cumulatively damaging effect to the overall UN programme. In the early years, the Smith regime hoped for a 'withering away' of isolation; not only would economic sanctions break down (and here the Byrd amendment gave undue grounds for optimism) but international political acceptance would gradually come about. This proved a serious miscalculation of the calibre and tenacity of the forces ranged against Rhodesia, which were to grow stronger, not weaker, in terms both of moral credibility and of the economic strength of many of the third world countries whose goodwill Britain and other western powers could not afford to forfeit. Over fifteen years, the UN norms of non-discrimination and majority rule progressively delegitimised the Rhodesian and South African concepts of white minority rule and apartheid. Sanctions against Rhodesia, while not bringing an immediate result, contributed to the process of undermining white rule there (and in Southern Africa as a whole) but the guerrilla war, the independence of Angola and Mozambique, and pressure from South Africa for a settlement were probably of greater direct significance.

For other authors who characterize the UN sanctions against Rhodesia as a success, see G. Hufbauer and J. Schott, Economic Sanctions Reconsidered: History and Current Policy 409-417 (1985); D. Baldwin, Economic Statecraft 189-204 (1985). For persons who insist on "lessons," the latter suggests the following "less dangerous and misleading ones" (id. at 204):

1. In economic statecraft, as in other spheres of life, perseverance sometimes pays.
2. Economic sanctions may have more of an impact than anyone expects.
3. The "rally round the flag" effect is not an "iron law" of politics.
4. The most important effects of economic sanctions may not be economic. (Economic sanctions may move in mysterious ways.)

VII. Sanctions Against South Africa

Sanctions against Rhodesia, the primary focus of this Problem, always have been linked inextricably to sanctions against South Africa, where the gross and persistent violations of human rights that occurred in the name of apartheid were manifest long before Ian Smith proclaimed U.D.I. Indeed, efforts to have the United Nations adopt sanctions against South Africa began in the early 1960s, several years before the Security Council adopted mandatory economic sanctions against Rhodesia (see pages 495-497 supra). Yet, for a variety of reasons considered later in this section, a decade passed before even a limited sanction — an arms embargo — was adopted by the Council, and thereafter the use or threat of the veto by France, Great Britain, and the United States blocked the extension of sanctions to the general economic area. Nevertheless, building on its experience with Rhodesian and South African sanctions, the United Nations has laid a foundation on which future sanctions efforts against human rights-violating states can be built.

A. UN Mandatory Sanctions

Although the Security Council voted for a voluntary arms embargo against South Africa in 1963 (S.C. Res. 181, 18 U.N. SCOR, Res. and Dec. at 7 (1963)), efforts to make it mandatory or to extend it to the economic area provoked a series of triple vetoes during the 1960s and early 1970s. By late 1977, however, the situation in South Africa had deteriorated to such an extent that the Big Three dramatically reversed their previous position and voted for the following Security Council resolution.

Security Council Resolution 418
32 U.N. SCOR, Res. and Dec. at 5 (1977)

The Security Council,

Recalling its resolution 392 (1976) strongly condemning the South African Government for its resort to massive violence against and killings of the African people, including schoolchildren and students and other opposing racial discrimination, and calling upon that Government urgently to end violence against the African people and take urgent steps to eliminate apartheid and racial discrimination,

Recognizing that the military build-up and persistent acts of aggression by South Africa against the neighbouring States seriously disturb the security of those States,

Further recognizing that the existing arms embargo must be strengthened and universally applied, without any reservations or qualifications whatsoever, in order to prevent a further aggravation of the grave situation in South Africa,

Taking note of the Lagos Declaration for Action against Apartheid (S/12426),

Gravely concerned that South Africa is at the threshold of producing nuclear weapons,

Strongly condemning the South African Government for its acts of repression, its defiant continuance of the system of apartheid and its attacks against neighbouring independent States,

Considering that the policies and acts of the South African Government are fraught with danger to international peace and security,

Recalling its resolution 181 (1963) and other resolutions concerning a voluntary arms embargo against South Africa,

Convinced that a mandatory arms embargo needs to be universally applied against South Africa in the first instance,

Acting therefore under Chapter VII of the Charter of the United Nations,

1. *Determines*, having regard to the policies and acts of the South African Government, that the acquisition by South Africa of arms and related matériel constitutes a threat to the maintenance of international peace and security;

2. *Decides* that all States shall cease forthwith any provision to South Africa of arms and related matériel of all types, including the sale or transfer of weapons and ammunition, military vehicles and equipment, paramilitary police equipment, and spare parts for the aforementioned, and shall cease as well the provision of all types of equipment and supplies, and grants for licensing arrangements, for the manufacture or maintenance of the aforementioned;

3. *Calls* on all States to review, having regard to the objectives of this resolution, all existing contractual arrangements with and licences granted

to South Africa relating to the manufacture and maintenance of arms, ammunition of all types and military equipment and vehicles, with a view to terminating them;

4. *Further decides* that all States shall refrain from any co-operation with South Africa in the manufacture and development of nuclear weapons;

5. *Calls upon* all States, including States non-members of the United Nations, to act strictly in accordance with the provisions of this resolution;

6. *Requests* the Secretary-General to report to the Council on the progress of the implementation of this resolution, the first report to be submitted not later than 1 May 1978;

7. *Decides* to keep this item on its agenda for further action, as appropriate, in the light of developments.

The above resolution represented the second attempt in the UN's history, Rhodesia being the first, to impose mandatory sanctions. More important, it was the first time that the Security Council had adopted mandatory sanctions against a UN member state. The Security Council reaffirmed this resolution in 1984, at the same time requesting states "to refrain from importing arms, ammunition of all types and military vehicles produced in South Africa. . . ." (S.C. Res. 558, 39 U.N. SCOR, Res. and Dec. at 5 (1984).)

Note: *Implementation and Enforcement of Resolution 418*

Implementation of the South African arms embargo, within the United States at least, was accomplished with minimum difficulty. Since the United States already had ceased selling arms to South Africa, pursuant to Resolution 181 adopted by the Security Council in 1963 (see page 573 supra), implementation of Resolution 418 some 14 years later was reduced to an administrative detail; the Department of Commerce merely issued regulations refusing to license the sale of arms and munitions to South Africa. 43 Fed. Reg. 7, 311 (1978), codified at 15 C.F.R. §§771.2(c)(11), 773.1(a) (1994).

Unfortunately, as was pointed out in an excellent article, these regulations, like the Rhodesian Sanctions Regulations (page 521 supra), "do not apply to the activities of foreign subsidiaries of U.S. corporations located either in South Africa or in other foreign countries. . . . Thus, a subsidiary of a U.S. firm located in South Africa or another foreign country could sell the South African military or police an item identical to one the U.S. parent might not be able to sell directly because of Commerce or State Department restrictions." Mehlman, Milch, and Toumanoff, United States Restrictions on Exports to South Africa, 73 Am. J. Intl. L. 581, 596-597 (1979).

The authors recommended that the United States "impose the same export restrictions on foreign subsidiaries that domestic firms are subject to under current regulations." Id. at 600. Three years later, after a revealing report on the shipment of computers to South Africa, the American Friends Service Committee made the same recommendation. NARMIC/American Friends Service Committee, Automating Apartheid: U.S. Computer Exports to South Africa and the Arms Embargo 8-10, 63-65, 73 (1982). It, of course, went unheeded. Comment, The United States Arms Embargo Against South Africa: An Analysis of the Laws, Regulations, and Loopholes, 12 Yale J. Intl. L. 133, 155 (1987).

Enforcement of the regulations implementing Resolution 418 appears to have been lax and ineffective. Prosecutions against Colt Industries and the Olin Corporation occurred early on, but only after newspaper accounts exposed the fact that corporate officials had falsified export documents in order to transship small arms to South Africa. Mehlman, Milch, and Toumanoff, supra, at 594. Olin was convicted, received a suspended sentence, and was put on probation. In an imaginative sentence, Judge Zampano, stating that "[a] financial fine is not enough [since] [t]hese violations could reflect on the credibility of the United States," ordered Olin to donate $500,000 to its home town New Haven charities and pay a $45,000 fine to the United States. N.Y. Times, March 31, 1978, at D1, col. 1; N.Y. Times, June 2, 1978, at D1, col. 3. Several years later, in a "sting" operation, federal authorities in New York, working with two Customs Service agents, obtained the evidence needed to convict three men of attempting to smuggle helicopter gunships to South Africa. They received suspended sentences or were placed on probation. Raab, N.Y. Becoming a Center for Weapons Traffic, Intl. Herald-Tribune, July 22, 1981, at 3, cols. 1-3. Other prosecutions may have occurred, but, if so, they have not been widely reported.

The first prosecution in the United Kingdom for violating the mandatory arms embargo occurred in 1982. Nicholson-Lord, Arms Smugglers Jailed for S. Africa Deals, The Times (London), Oct. 19, 1982, at 1, cols. 7-8. Similar prosecutions may have taken place in other states, but in the absence of effective UN monitoring machinery reliable data about prosecutions are not available.

Note: British and U.S. Vetoes Block Further Mandatory Sanctions

Both before and after the adoption of Security Council Resolution 418 in 1977, the United States, joined by Great Britain and usually France, vetoed proposed resolutions mandating wider sanctions against South Africa. Perhaps the most dramatic (and ironic) veto came in February 1987 when the non-aligned members of the Council introduced a draft resolution (U.N. Doc. No. S/18705 (1987)) that would have imposed mandatory economic sanctions similar to the ones contained in the then-recently-passed Comprehensive Anti-Apartheid Act of 1986 (page 585 infra). The resolution did not seek to go beyond those measures already proscribed by U.S. law, yet the United States, along with Great Britain and West Germany, voted against it (France and Japan abstaining). The United States explained its vote as follows.

Statement of Mr. Herbert S. Okun, Acting U.S. Representative to United Nations, February 20, 1987
42 U.N. SCOR (2738th mtg.) at 64-67 passim, U.N. Doc. S/P.V. 2738 (1987)

. . . [M]y Government is convinced that mandatory sanctions would fail to bring an end to apartheid in a peaceful manner and would make it difficult, if not impossible, to achieve internal reconciliation and regional economic development. My Government believes that mandatory sanctions imposed by the international community at this time would result in the progressive destruction of the South African economy and the heightening of repression in that country as those now in power attempt to consolidate their hold. Who doubts the capacity of the current South African Government to inflict much of the cost of mandatory sanctions on its own black citizens as well as on its immediate neighbours? It is highly unrealistic to believe that aid from the industrialized democracies will be able to cover the costs which mandatory sanctions would inevitably impose upon South Africa's immediate neighbours. . . .

In this connection, both Secretary of State Shultz and Under Secretary of State Armacost recently travelled to Africa. Secretary Shultz's meetings with South Africans across the political spectrum are only the latest example of my Government's continuing efforts to contribute to a positive solution to South Africa's problems.

With a negotiated settlement in mind, the United States is also faithfully enforcing limited, selective measures against South Africa. These measures underscore the seriousness of our rejection of apartheid. Permit me to call it to the Council's attention that these measures include an arms embargo that is stricter than that mandated by this Council.

The United States recognizes that other nations also believe that comprehensive national sanctions may assist in the search for a non-violent solution to South Africa's problems. Yet others believe the best policy is to adopt selective sanctions, or pursue means other than sanctions.

My Government therefore opposes the philosophy underlying the draft resolution before us today. The United States does not believe that the United Nations should mandate to all its Members what their appropriate course of action should be. My Government believes that each nation should be free to determine the form and substance of its measures aimed at eliminating apartheid. My Government also believes that the mandatory sanctions which this draft resolution would impose on all Members of the United Nations would be all but impossible to enforce.

My Government has yet another serious objection to this draft resolution. If it were approved, the Council would find it difficult, if not impossible, to agree subsequently on a yardstick by which to measure whether sufficient progress towards dismantling apartheid had occurred in order to warrant the lifting of the Council's sanctions.

For the reasons I have outlined, my delegation will vote against this draft resolution. In doing so we do not vote in favour of apartheid. My Government will continue to do all in its power to achieve the peaceful elimination of this evil system.

B.   UN *Voluntary Sanctions*

1.   General Assembly Sanctions

As far back as 1962, the General Assembly, in addition to calling on the Security Council to adopt mandatory economic sanctions against South Africa, had urged states to take certain economic measures on a voluntary basis (see page 514 supra). With the Security Council refusing to proceed beyond the arms embargo of 1977, the General Assembly increasingly requested member states to take a variety of steps that would have dampened, if not severely restrained, the South African economy. See, e.g., G.A. Res. 32/105G, 32 U.N. GAOR Supp. (No. 45) at 35, U.N. Doc. A/32/45 (1978). Many of these resolutions reiterated the need for states to enact legislation prohibiting the sale of oil and petroleum products to South Africa. See G.A. Res. 33/183E, 33 U.N. GAOR Supp. (No. 45) at 28, U.N. Doc. A/33/45 (1979); G.A. Res. 41/35F, 41 U.N. GAOR Supp. (No. 53) at 30, U.N. Doc. A/41/53 (1987). Unlike decisions of the Security Council taken under Chapter VII, these resolutions were not binding on member states under Article 25 of the UN Charter, but they constituted an important political statement, increased possible economic pressure on South Africa, and provided a blueprint for future mandatory sanctions had the Security Council been so inclined.

2.   Security Council Sanctions

An interesting development during the 1980s was the adoption by the Security Council of several resolutions urging member states to take certain "voluntary measures" against South Africa. The first such resolution was aimed at ending South Africa's continued illegal occupation of Namibia

(S.C. Res. 566, 40 U.N. SCOR, Res. and Dec. at 11 (1985)). The second such resolution was directed at ending the apartheid system within South Africa itself (S.C. Res. 569, 40 U.N. SCOR, Res. and Dec. at 8 (1985)). Both resolutions were adopted by 13 votes to none, with the United Kingdom and the United States abstaining. A somewhat similar resolution also was adopted clarifying (and perhaps extending) the mandatory arms embargo provisions contained in Resolution 418 and reaffirmed in Resolution 558 (S.C. Res. 591, 41 U.N. SCOR, Res. and Dec. at 17 (1986)). While these resolutions, like their General Assembly counterparts, were not binding on member states, they undoubtedly carried greater weight and certainly alerted South Africa to the possible eventual adoption by the Security Council of limited or even comprehensive mandatory economic sanctions.

3. **The Intergovernmental Group to Monitor the Supply and Shipping of Oil and Petroleum Products to South Africa: A Case Study in Implementing UN Voluntary Sanctions**

General Assembly Resolution 41/35F (supra page 578), which reaffirmed the voluntary oil embargo against South Africa, also established the Intergovernmental Group to Monitor the Supply and Shipping of Oil and Petroleum Products to South Africa. The Group represented the first instance of General Assembly monitoring of voluntary sanctions through an intergovernmental body. Comprised of 11 members from both oil-shipping and oil-exporting states, it issued annual reports describing the legislative and other measures adopted by states to implement the oil embargo and listing individual cases of alleged violations that had come to its attention. Reports of the Intergovernmental Group to Monitor the Supply and Shipping of Oil and Petroleum Products to South Africa, 42 U.N. GAOR Supp. (No. 45), U.N. Doc. A/42/45 (1988); 43 U.N. GAOR Supp. (No. 44), U.N. Doc. A/43/44 (1989); 44 U.N. GAOR Supp. (No. 44), U.N. Doc. A/44/44 (1990); 45 U.N. GAOR Supp. (No. 43), U.N. Doc. A/45/43 (1991); 46 U.N. GAOR Supp. (No. 44), U.N. Doc. A/46/44 (1992); 47 U.N. GAOR Supp. (No. 43), U.N. Doc. A/47/43 (1993); 48 U.N. GAOR Supp. (No. 43), U.N. Doc. A/48/43 (1994).

In April 1989, the Group organized hearings on the voluntary oil embargo at the United Nations in New York, after which it issued a report with a number of recommendations for more effective sanctions enforcement, including the drafting of a proposed model law to be adopted by member states. Such a model law was drafted and considered by a group of legal experts at a meeting of the Group in August 1990. See Lillich, Model Law on the Oil Embargo Against South Africa, UN Centre Against Apartheid, Notes and Documents No. 10/91 (Apr. 1991). The Group decided to commend it to states for their consideration, as did the UN General Assembly by G.A. Res. 45/176F, 45 U.N. GAOR Supp. (No. 49) at 44, U.N. Doc. A/45/49 (1991).

While the Group's mandate expired with the General Assembly's termination of its voluntary sanctions against South Africa, it undoubtedly was more innovative in its enforcement activities than were the sanctions committees established to monitor the UN's sanctions against Rhodesia or its limited arms embargo against South Africa. Thus, it may well become a model for similar committees monitoring other sanctions regimes. See, e.g., Scharf and Dorosin, Interpreting UN Sanctions: The Rulings and Role of the Yugoslavia Sanctions Committee, 19 Brook. J. Intl. L. 772 (1993).

The response of the United States to the Group's monitoring of the voluntary oil embargo against South Africa was predictable, albeit disappointing. "Because the U.S. does not support the idea of a worldwide oil embargo against South Africa, we have made the specific policy decision not to cooperate with the work of the Intergovernmental Group." Letter from E. Gibson Lanpher, Director, Office of Southern African Affairs, U.S. Department of State, to Amy Young, Esq., Executive Director, International Human Rights Law Group (July 11, 1988).

C.   U.S. *Sanctions*

1.   Introduction

Although the U.S. government opposed any additional sanctions against South Africa during the Reagan Administration (see, e.g., U.S. Department of State, South Africa: The Case Against Sanctions, Current Policy No. 686 (Apr. 16, 1985)), pressures for further action — from Congress, from state and local governments, and from the private sector — continued to mount during the 1980s. With respect to taking further economic measures against a regime still committed to apartheid, the body politic seemed well ahead of the Executive Branch.

One of the earliest and initially most promising developments was the Sullivan Principles, originally a voluntary code of conduct for U.S. corporations doing business in South Africa, drafted by the Reverend Leon Sullivan, a director of General Motors, and first accepted by 13 U.S. corporations in 1977. The Principles, amplified over the years and later incorporated into the Comprehensive Anti-Apartheid Act of 1986, 22 U.S.C. §5035(a) (1988), required

> (1) desegregating the races in each employment facility;
> (2) providing equal employment opportunity for all employees without regard to race or ethnic origin;
> (3) assuring that the pay system is applied to all employees without regard to race or ethnic origin;

(4) establishing a minimum wage and salary structure based on the appropriate local minimum economic level which takes into account the needs of employees and their families;

(5) increasing by appropriate means the number of persons in managerial, supervisory, administrative, clerical, and technical jobs who are disadvantaged by the apartheid system for the purpose of significantly increasing their representation in such jobs;

(6) taking reasonable steps to improve the quality of employees' lives outside the work environment with respect to housing, transportation, schooling, recreation, and health; and

(7) implementing fair labor practices by recognizing the right of all employees, regardless of racial or other distinctions, to self-organization and to form, join, or assist labor organizations, freely and without penalty or reprisal, and recognizing the right to refrain from any such activity.

At one time nearly 200 of an estimated 350 U.S. corporations doing business in South Africa had endorsed the Principles, although by late 1987, with many corporations withdrawing from the country, the number was down to 90. Arthur D. Little, Inc., Eleventh Report on the Signatory Companies to the Statement of Principles for South Africa 1 (Nov. 5, 1987).

The Principles, naturally, were not popular with all persons in the business community; nor were they immune from criticism by some human rights activists, who charged that they were "a smoke-screen, allowing corporate signators to say they are fighting racism while reaping profits in a system of institutionalized racism." Gruson, South Africa Job Code Is Fruit of One Man's Battle Against Bias, N.Y. Times, Sept. 9, 1985, at A8, cols. 2, 4. Ultimately, the Reverend Sullivan, perhaps tired of being called a stooge of corporate America, changed his mind and stated that if apartheid were not abolished by 31 May 1987, U.S. corporations should withdraw from South Africa. MacAskill, "Simple Pastor" Raises the Stakes for U.S. Role in S. Africa, Wash. Post, Aug. 15, 1986, at A3, cols. 2-6. In June 1987, he formally disassociated himself from his own Principles, remarking that "something else must be done to bring an end to that despicable system that dehumanizes black people." South Africa Perspectives, No. 1/87, at 4 (July 1987). They lived on in the United States Code, of course, and U.S. corporations doing business in South Africa remained legally obligated to comply with them.

Coincident with the legal adoption of the Sullivan Principles, a grassroots campaign against U.S. corporate involvement in South Africa gained strength throughout much of the United States, as shown by the following extract (South African Project of the Lawyers' Committee for Civil Rights Under Law, Implementation of the Comprehensive Anti-Apartheid Act of 1986, at 111-112 (June 1988)).

One of the most successful aspects of the anti-apartheid movement in the United States has been the campaign to enact state and local laws which govern the enacting jurisdiction's relations with companies doing business in or with South Africa. To date, 23 states and the Virgin Islands,

14 countries, and 75 cities have passed some form of anti-apartheid legislation. There are several typical provisions that have been adopted. Most
frequently the laws mandate that public investment portfolios, such as those
held by state, municipal and county employee pension funds, be sanitized
of investments in companies doing business in South Africa; California and
Massachusetts have statutes with such provisions. Some, like Nebraska,
limit the prohibition to investment in companies not meeting the highest
rating of the Sullivan Principles. Other states, like Tennessee and Louisi-
ana, prohibit the deposit of state funds in banks with loans to the South
African Government or its agencies. A number of jurisdictions have enacted
what is commonly called selective purchasing provisions which prohibit the
procurement of goods and services from South Africa (e.g., Michigan, Boston and Durham) or from companies doing business in South Africa (e.g.,
Los Angeles, Charleston, Newark and San Francisco). Finally, among the
selective purchasing provisions, a number of jurisdictions like New York
City, Washington, D.C., Chicago and Oakland, have established bidding
preferences, ranging from 5 to 8%, for firms not dealing with or in South
Africa.

While there has been some debate over the constitutionality of such state
and local laws (compare Fenton, The Fallacy of Federalism in Foreign
Affairs: State and Local Foreign Policy Trade Restrictions, 13 Nw. J. Intl.
L. & Bus. 563 (1993) with McCardle, In Defense of State and Local
Government Anti-Apartheid Measures: Infusing Democratic Values into
Foreign Policy Making, 62 Temple L. Rev. 813 (1989)), they appear able
to withstand constitutional scrutiny. See Board of Trustees v. Mayor of
Baltimore, 317 Md. 72, 562 A.2d 720 (1989), cert. denied, 493 U.S. 1093
(1990). See also Bilder, The Role of States and Cities in Foreign
Relations, 83 Am. J. Intl. L. 821 (1989), and the cases and writers cited
therein.

    Such legislative steps on the state and local levels not only forced the
hands of the two political branches of the federal government, as the following two sections suggest, but also, together with stockholder resolutions
and consumer boycotts, had an increasing impact on U.S. corporations
with South African connections. Witness the following headlines: Chase
Ends Loans to South Africans, N.Y. Times, Aug. 1, 1985, at A11, cols. 1-4;
Phibro to Pull Out of South Africa, N.Y. Times, Aug. 22, 1985, at D1, cols.
3-5; Bank of America Loan Curb: Borrowers in Pretoria Cut, N.Y. Times,
June 16, 1986, at D3, cols. 4-6; Coke Plans Pretoria Pullout, N.Y. Times,
Sept. 18, 1986, at D1, col. 3; G.M. Plans to Sell South Africa Unit to a
Local Group, N.Y. Times, Oct. 21, at A1, col. 3. Thus, by the mid-1980s,
pressures on the homefront, coupled with political uncertainty and lower
profits in South Africa, were causing many U.S. corporations to pull out.
Ironically, economic pressures were being brought to bear upon Pretoria
even before the President or Congress moved to adopt formal U.S. sanctions.

2. President Reagan's Executive Order: Too Late and Too Little

During the first half of 1985, pressures from the public and Congress for further sanctions against South Africa continued to increase. Finally, with Congress on the verge of passing a rare bill imposing sanctions on a foreign country for human rights purposes, President Ronald Reagan, long an opponent of any sanctions, felt compelled to act himself. The result was Executive Order No. 12,532, 50 Fed. Reg. 36,861 (1985), 3 C.F.R. §387 (1985).

Recent Developments, Economic Sanctions: United States Sanctions Against South Africa
27 Harv. Intl. L.J. 235, 235-242 passim (1986)

The President's Executive Order imposes a series of economic sanctions against South Africa for maintaining its racial system of apartheid. First, the Executive Order bans all computer exports to South African agencies involved in the administration and enforcement of the apartheid system. With certain exceptions, the Order also prohibits exports of nuclear goods or technology to South Africa. Third, the Order forbids loans to the South African government, except those which improve economic opportunities for blacks. Fourth, Reagan's Executive Order bans U.S. importation of South African arms, ammunition or military vehicles. The last major sanction would prohibit importation of Krugerrand gold coins, but only after consultation with other parties to the General Agreement on Tariffs and Trade (GATT). . . .

The new sanctions ostensibly marked a departure from the President's previous policy of "constructive engagement." The failure of constructive engagement to move Pretoria toward a peaceful end to apartheid had become increasingly clear in the face of recently mounting violence in South Africa. After President P.W. Botha introduced a new constitution in 1983 that once again denied blacks political representation, new surges of protest by blacks were met with increasing force and repression. In the ensuing battles between police and protesters, hundreds of blacks were killed. Fervent appeals by moderate black leaders such as Bishop Desmond Tutu for an open dialogue on ending apartheid were ignored. On July 21, the government responded by imposing a state of emergency throughout the country, giving the police and army nearly absolute powers to act against political protesters without fear of legal reprisals.

Even before the state of emergency was declared, both houses in Congress were considering legislation directed against South Africa. [The House had passed a sanctions bill on 5 June 1985, while the Republican-controlled Senate had passed a more modest sanctions bill on 11 July. The compromise conference bill then passed the House by an overwhelming 380-48 vote and was scheduled for a Senate vote on 9 September when the President preempted Congress by issuing his Executive Order.]

The Executive Order enlists the Act's more innocuous sanctions as its central provisions. . . .

The Executive Order, however, cushions the Act's harsher measures, or omits them entirely. Whereas President Reagan merely agreed to discuss with GATT parties the possibility of banning Krugerrand importation, the Act would have imposed an immediate ban. The President could waive this ban only if he determined that the South African government had made at least one of eight specified reforms, such as releasing all political prisoners or negotiating in good faith with representative black leaders. Similarly, the Order does not mention future sanctions. The Act, in contrast, directs the President to choose from among a class of specified sanctions new measures to be imposed should he determine that South Africa had not made "significant progress" toward eliminating apartheid. The stronger sanctions from which the President could choose include: a ban on new commercial investment in South Africa; a denial of most-favored-nation trading status; a prohibition against importation of South African coal or uranium; or any other economic or political sanctions. Finally, the President declined to adopt the Act's provision imposing substantial penalties for sanctions violations. Accordingly, under the President's formulation, officers, directors, or employees in control of an organization in violation of the Act would escape the liability which Congress intended to impose. . . .

The best argument that can be made in favor of the President's sanctions is that they have symbolic importance independent of their marginal economic effects. Proponents point out that even token sanctions distance the United States government from a system of racial subjugation which it finds abhorrent. Moreover, the economic effects of sanctions should not be dismissed altogether. . . .

Yet even though economic sanctions in general inject an important moral component into U.S. foreign policy, the President's Executive Order fails to back anti-apartheid rhetoric with substantive action. It is difficult to determine whether South Africa considers itself censured for its repressive activity, or fortunate to have a friend in President Reagan. While Pretoria arguably has been put on notice that it must implement significant reforms soon or face harsher reprisals in the future, the threat is indeterminate. The Executive Order appears, for the moment, to have disarmed Congress and assuaged the American public without spurring reform. Political unrest continues in South Africa with the President's sanctions offering only the most meager hope for a speedy end to the crisis.

The comparative weakness of the sanctions proclaimed in the Executive Order is made obvious by the following exchange between the President and a reporter at the time of its signing (24 Intl. Legal Materials 1486 (1985)).

Q. Mr. President, why did you change your mind on sanctions?

The President. Helen . . . , I haven't. I thought here I tried to explain. I am opposed and could not sign the bill if it came to me containing the economic sanctions which, as we have repeatedly said, would have harmed the very people we're trying to help.

Q. But much of that's in that — in your order —

The President. But there are — no, there were many things in that bill —

Q. Right.

The President.   — that we could agree with and many of those are incorporated in this Executive order.

Q. But those are basic sanctions, aren't they?

The President. Not in the sense of the economic kind of sanctions that the bill called for and that, as I say, would have hurt the economy there.

Q. And this won't hurt the economy?

The President. No. I don't believe so.

3. The Comprehensive Anti-Apartheid Act of 1986

The hypocrisy of President Reagan's proclamation of toothless sanctions was not lost on Congress; nor was the predictable fact that the President's sanctions were having no effect upon the South African regime. Just a year later, therefore, the Congress overrode a Presidential veto and enacted the Comprehensive Anti-Apartheid Act of 1986, 22 U.S.C. §§5001-5116 (1988). The following extract describes the Act, which from late 1986 through late 1993 was the primary legislative authorization for U.S. sanctions against South Africa.

Note: The Passage of the Federal Anti-Apartheid Act: The Culmination of Anti-Apartheid Efforts Within the United States
11 Suffolk Transnatl. L.J. 387, 409-413 (1987)

The economic impact of the President's sanctions was limited, but there was hope that their symbolic value as an expression of United States disapproval of apartheid might nudge the South African government toward reform. The failure of this attempt became tragically apparent when in June

1986, Botha justified the imposition of another nationwide state of emergency.

As the situation in South Africa deteriorated further, Congress again instituted hearings to consider legislation encompassing more coercive economic measures against Pretoria, which took the form of the Comprehensive Anti-Apartheid Act of 1986. The same arguments thread throughout the debates on the sanctions issue. Those opposed to the 1986 Act denounced sanctions as ineffective and destructive to black South Africans. The majority, in favor of restrictive sanctions, conceded that the sanctions may have no practical impact on dismantling apartheid, but still maintained their position that they represent the only effective non-violent means by which the United States can offer support and at least symbolically express its opposition to apartheid. After highly emotional debates in both houses, Congress passed the 1986 Act by an overwhelming majority. President Reagan subsequently vetoed the bill and the sanctions issue once again became a source of conflict within the Reagan Administration. Upon congressional reconsideration of the Act the vote was lopsidedly in favor of an override, with the House voting 313 to 83 and the Senate voting 78-22. The anti-apartheid movement both internationally and domestically, received a major boost on October 2, 1986 when The Anti-Apartheid Act of 1986 was enacted.

THE COMPREHENSIVE ANTI-APARTHEID ACT OF 1986

The Act echoes other anti-apartheid measures in that its stated purpose is to bring about political, economic and social change within South Africa, leading to the eradication of apartheid and the establishment of a non-racial democratic form of government. The Act's drafters also make clear their underlying purpose to put moral force behind the Administration's anti-apartheid rhetoric, which the President's Executive Order failed to do. The Act does codify the weaker sanctions encompassed by the Order including: a ban on the export of computers and software to agencies enforcing apartheid; a prohibition on loans to South Africa; a ban on the export of nuclear goods and technology, subject to waiver if South Africa should sign the nuclear Non-Proliferation Treaty.

The Act, however, goes much further in its application of extensive punitive sanctions. In addition to banning loans to the South African government and government owned agencies, similar sanctions in the Act bar all new United States loans to South African businesses as well. The broadening of this sanction is significant because it prevents private South African companies that previously enjoyed access to American financial support, from relenting to government entities. The Act does not go so far as to require divestment of existing holdings in businesses with South African contacts, but it does however prohibit United States firms from making any new investments in South Africa, except in those firms owned by black South Africans. Other new sanctions include a prohibition on the importation of uranium, coal, textiles, and agricultural products; a ban on the export of oil and petroleum products; and the cancellation of all landing rights in the United States for South African airlines.

The Act also provides for further sanctions absent significant progress toward the elimination of apartheid policies by the South African government. The Act directs the President to compile an annual report of the progress that South Africa has made. If the report determines that South Africa has not made "substantial progress" toward the elimination of apartheid, then the President must choose from a number of additional punitive sanctions, including a ban on imports of other strategic minerals and diamonds from South Africa, and the cessation of military aid to any country that supplies arms to South Africa. Conversely, the Act allows the President to suspend or modify any of the sanctions if Pretoria actively moves toward the dismantling of the apartheid system.

In contrast to the Executive Order, the Act provides substantial penalties for sanctions' violations. Accordingly, the Act imposes liability on officers, directors or employees of companies who knowingly or willfully violate the statute, where the Order imposed none. This enforcement provision is intended to deter companies from filtering capital, goods, or technology to South Africa through a European subsidiary, and to deter banks from re-routing their loans business with South Africa through a foreign intermediary bank.

Implementation and Enforcement of the Act

A former Department of State official with considerable experience in the sanctions process gave two cheers when the above Act became law. While approving it generally, she noted that "[t]he history of enforcement of previous southern Africa sanctions raises questions concerning the likelihood of rigorous executive enforcement of the CAA sanctions, which were mandated by Congress and enacted over a Presidential veto." Butcher, The Unique Nature of Sanctions Against South Africa, and Resulting Enforcement Issues, 19 N.Y.U. J. Intl. L. & Pol. 821, 843 (1987). An evaluation of the Reagan Administration's enforcement efforts two years later showed that her concern in this regard was not misplaced. South African Project of the Lawyers' Committee for Civil Rights Under Law, Implementation of the Comprehensive Anti-Apartheid Act of 1986 (June 1988).

To take as an example one sanction considered throughout this Problem, the Act provided that "[n]o crude oil or refined petroleum product which is subject to the jurisdiction of the United States may be exported to South Africa, and no crude oil or refined petroleum product may be exported to South Africa by a *person subject to the jurisdiction of the United*

States." 22 U.S.C. §5071(a) (1988) (emphasis added). The Commerce Department regulations implementing this section were drafted specifically to exclude their application to the foreign subsidiaries of U.S. corporations, a loophole identical to the one found in the Rhodesia Sanctions Regulations. 15 C.R.F. §785.4(a)(13) (1990). See South African Project of the Lawyers' Committee for Civil Rights Under Law, supra, at 65-66.

Enforcement of the Act also left much to be desired. For instance, because the U.S. Customs Service had not received additional resources to enforce the Act, it had to rely on existing sources and informants' tips for information regarding possible violations. Id. at 127. Moreover, lack of cooperation by various government departments and agencies added to enforcement problems. McAuliffe, South Africa Sanctions Poorly Enforced, Wash. Post, Aug. 20, 1989, at A12, cols. 1-3.

4. The Rangel Amendment Denies Foreign Tax Credits to U.S. Corporations Doing Business in South Africa

In 1987 Congressman Charles B. Rangel of New York sponsored a change in the U.S. tax law, the effect of which was to deny substantial tax benefits to U.S. corporations on income earned in South Africa. Section 10,231 of the Omnibus Budget Reconciliation Act of 1987, 26 U.S.C. §901(j) (1988). Normally U.S. tax law permits a U.S. corporation to credit its foreign taxes against its U.S. tax liability. Section 10,231 denied this tax break in the case of South Africa. This change in the law "virtually doubles the taxes paid on South African income by a United States corporation investing in South Africa," making "investment in South Africa virtually prohibitive from a business perspective." South African Project of the Lawyers' Committee for Civil Rights Under Law, supra, at 107, 109.

On 28 April 1989, the Rangel Amendment claimed its first major "victim" when the Mobil Corporation announced that it was selling its 12 South African subsidiaries at a net book loss of about $140 million. Kreisler, Mobil Quitting South Africa, Blaming "Foolish" U.S. Laws, N.Y. Times, Apr. 29, 1989, at 1, cols. 4-5. Mobil, which consistently had opposed stockholder resolutions that would have required it to sever or restrict economic ties with South Africa (see, e.g., Mobil Corporation, Notice of 1989 Annual Meeting and Proxy Statement 11-14 (1989)), explained that the loss of foreign tax credits made it difficult to compete with non-U.S. oil companies (especially, one imagines, Shell). Mobil Report 2, at 4-5 (June 1989).

By this time, many other U.S. corporations already had left South Africa. See page 582 supra. "Disinvestment by U.S. companies had accelerated rapidly beginning in 1985. . . . Seven U.S. companies sold or closed down their operations in 1984, 40 followed in 1985, 50 in 1986, and 57 in 1987." Investor Responsibility Research Center, Inc., News Release 1 (Dec.

19, 1988). Twenty-five more withdrew in 1988, the year the Rangel Amendment began to bite. Thus, by mid-1990 only 114 of the 350 U.S. corporations once doing business in South Africa remained there.

5. The End of Sanctions and an Evaluation of Their Effectiveness

Events in South Africa moved swiftly, if not always peacefully, toward the end of minority white rule during the early 1990s. With the assumption of power by President F.W. De Klerk; his bold release of Nelson Mandela, the leader of the African National Congress, and other political prisoners; and the slow but steady progress made during negotiations over a new constitution and free elections, it became only a matter of time before calls for the lifting of sanctions were heard not only in the United States, but also among the black leadership in South Africa. Prematurely, perhaps, President George Bush issued an Executive Order that terminated many of the U.S. sanctions in July 1991. Executive Order No. 12,769, 3 C.F.R. §§342-343 (1992), reprinted in 22 U.S.C.A. §5061, at 61 (Supp. 1994). See Editorial, Bush's Rash Repeal of Sanctions, Boston Globe, July 11, 1991, at 14, cols. 1-2. Less than two years later, however, addressing the United Nations, Mr. Mandela himself called for an end to sanctions. By the end of 1993, Congress had enacted the South African Democratic Transition Support Act of 1993, Pub. L. No. 103-149, 107 Stat. 1503 (1993), 22 U.S.C.A. §5001, at 54 (Supp. 1994), which repealed most of the Comprehensive Anti-Apartheid Act of 1986,[*] as well as other apartheid sanctions laws such as the Rangel Amendment. The Act stated that it should be U.S. policy to continue to respect UN Security Council resolutions on South Africa, such as the mandatory arms embargo (see pages 573-575 supra), and that the General Assembly's voluntary oil embargo (see pages 579-580 supra), to which the United States had paid no legal heed, should not be lifted. Anticipating the adoption of a new constitution; the holding of the first free one-person, one-vote elections; and the installation of a new government with a black majority, the seven-year oil embargo was ended, and the Intergovernmental Group established to monitor it wound up.[†]

Although no definitive studies of the effectiveness of economic sanctions against South Africa have yet appeared, as they have in the case of Rhodesia (see pages 565-573 supra), by common agreement they had a

---

[*] With respect to the code-of-conduct requirements found in the Comprehensive Anti-Apartheid Act of 1986, the South African Democratic Transition Support Act of 1993 provides for their repeal "as of the date on which the President certifies to the Congress that an interim government, elected on a nonracial basis through free and fair elections, has taken office in South Africa." Pub. L. No. 103-149, §4(a)(2), 107 Stat. 1505, 22 U.S.C.A. §5001, at 55 (Supp. 1994). President Bill Clinton did so on 8 June 1994. President's Message to Congress on Elections in South Africa, 30 Weekly Comp. Pres. Doc. 1258 (June 13, 1994).

[†] G.A. Res. 48/1, U.N. Doc. A/RES/48/1 (1993).

substantial impact on the situation there. Even the Reagan Administration's architect of "constructive engagement," who was the leading opponent of sanctions, admitted that "the sanctions of the 80's added an external apart-heid tax to the huge burdens imposed by bureaucrats and ideologues in Pretoria." Crocker, De Klerk, Mandela — and Bush, N.Y. Times, Feb. 14, 1990, at A25, cols. 1-4. The Bush Administration, while opposing any new sanctions, also acknowledged that "[e]xisting U.S. sanctions, the most com-prehensive of any imposed by South Africa's leading trade partners, effec-tively have demonstrated American opposition to apartheid *and have helped stimulate new thinking within South Africa's white power structure.*" U.S. Dept. of State, South Africa: US Policy, Gist 2 (Mar. 1990) (emphasis added). Finally, it should come as no surprise that Congress, which battled the Reagan Administration over sanctions a decade ago, has found in the South African Democratic Transition Support Act of 1993 that "[t]he United States policy of economic sanctions toward the apartheid govern-ment of South Africa, as expressed in the Comprehensive Anti-Apartheid Act of 1986, helped bring about reforms in that system of government and has facilitated the establishment of a nonracial government." Pub. L. No. 103-149, §2(2), 107 Stat. 1503, 22 U.S.C.A. §5001, at 1021 (Supp. V 1993). See Lewis, Congress Was Right, N.Y. Times, June 26, 1990, at A23, col. 1.

VIII.   Final Comments and Questions

1. Before it adopted a policy of sanctions against Rhodesia, the UN Security Council determined the threshold issue, that the Rhodesian situa-tion constituted a "threat to the peace." Was its determination of this issue — which, of course, was non-reviewable — correct, or was former Secretary of State Acheson right when he concluded that the threat "was not posed *by* Rhodesia, but *against* Rhodesia"? Does it matter from whence the threat is coming, as long as the situation itself, in its totality, constitutes a threat? Or is this argument of the "bootstrap" variety? What guidance, if any, does Article 39 of the UN Charter give on this point?

2. Were the sanctions imposed against Rhodesia, in your opinion, a success, a failure, or a mixed bag? What criteria do you use in reaching your opinion: Prime Minister Wilson's, to the effect that sanctions would bring down the Smith regime "within a matter of weeks"? A more realistic expec-tation that, over the years, the pressures of sanctions would either topple the Smith regime or cause it to modify its policies? Some other objective? Does not your answer to the initial question depend upon the criteria you adopt? Was there any consensus as to criteria in the UN Security Council when it voted to adopt sanctions?

3. Professor Lowenfeld observes that "[t]o black Africans, to other countries that had known colonization, and to countries like Britain and the United States that sought friendship with the developing countries and opposed racism, sanctions were a compromise between laissez-faire and war — perhaps just what Article 41 of the United Nations charter was designed for." Lowenfeld, supra page 513, at 477. Do you agree or disagree with this observation, and why?

4. In arguing for the amendment that eventually bore his name, Senator Byrd cited a list of sanctions violations by other states as justification for the United States following suit. (See pages 525-526 supra.) Even assuming the existence of widespread violations elsewhere (a reasonable assumption in view, inter alia, of the Oilgate scandal), did they justify the United States' open flaunting of the UN's sanctions policy, a policy that the United States helped to make legally binding upon all states, including itself, when it voted for Security Council Resolutions 232 and 253?

Similarly, it is well known that the voluntary sanctions that the United States adopted vis-à-vis South Africa were undermined by certain other states that refused to take such action and actually increased their trade with South Africa. Beeston, US Action on Pretoria Opens the Door for British Exports Boost, The Times (London), Oct. 9, 1986, at 8, cols. 1-3; Japan Firms Said to Disguise South Africa Trade, Intl. Herald-Tribune, May 9, 1989, at 12, cols. 5-8. Thus, a 1988 study prepared for the Commonwealth foreign ministers meeting reported that in the two years after the United States enacted the Comprehensive Anti-Apartheid Act of 1986, not only Japan, but also Taiwan, West Germany, Spain, and Turkey dramatically increased their imports from South Africa. Denton, Study Says Japan's South African Imports Undercut Sanctions, Wash. Post, Aug. 4, 1988, at B6, cols. 1-4. Was this fact reason enough for the United States to have repealed the Act in the late 1980s? Do you think it played a major role in President Bush's decision to issue his Executive Order in 1991? (See page 589 supra.) Note that the U.S. veto of the Act in the form of a proposed UN Security Council resolution permitted such trade to continue legally, which, of course, also lessened the impact of U.S. sanctions on South Africa.

Archbishop Desmond Tutu, in a commencement speech to Hunter College on 29 May 1986, addressed in his usual pithy fashion the argument that U.S. sanctions would be ineffective or even counterproductive because other states would move to fill the void.

> There are those who are not ashamed to use the argument that if they pull out others will come in to exploit black South Africa. Now, I must say that the moral turpitude of that argument is quite breathtaking. They are saying we will not do what we know is right because these people will do wrong, and so let us continue to do wrong. My wife does not like this analogy, but I think it is eloquent. They are like someone saying, "If we don't rape you, others will. So we will rape you."

5. Another argument against South African sanctions frequently heard in the United States — and a staple of the Reagan Administration (see page 585 supra) — was that they fell disproportionately on the black population. As Senator John Glenn of Ohio once quipped, "That's a little like saying that the Emancipation Proclamation should have never been issued because it would temporarily put 4 million black Americans out of work. . . ." *Cleveland Plain Dealer*, July 24, 1986, at 7A, col. 1. "Those outside [South Africa] who say that sanctions will 'hurt the blacks' do not know how intense black suffering already is," the Commonwealth Secretary-General has written in his Foreword to the report of the Commonwealth Eminent Persons Group on South Africa. "It is, in any case, a judgment they have no right to make, when the blacks themselves see sanctions, and any additional suffering these involve, as preferable to the far greater tragedy they would otherwise face." Ramphal, Foreword to Mission to South Africa: The Commonwealth Report 15 (1986).

Polls of South African blacks taken throughout the 1980s consistently showed overwhelming support for international sanctions. See, e.g., Poll of South African Blacks Finds Most Favor Sanctions, N.Y. Times, Aug. 26, 1985, at A4, col. 6. Both the African National Congress, the largest black South African party, and its principal spokesman, Nelson Mandela, urged the adoption and strict enforcement of international sanctions. If they were willing to accept short-term economic hardships in the expectation that sanctions ultimately would help produce majority rule in South Africa, as they had in Rhodesia, should not their views have been respected? Is not the UN Security Council in a better position to weigh the costs and benefits of economic sanctions, taking into account the long as well as the short range, than particular governments and multinational enterprises with their own interests — vested and otherwise — in the matter?

6. Do you accept the Treasury Department's explanation about why the Rhodesian Sanctions Regulations were drafted so as to exempt the foreign subsidiaries of U.S. corporations from coverage, contrary to all prior U.S. sanctions practice? Why do you think this loophole was closed in subsequent U.S. sanctions programs, save the one directed against South Africa? Could it be the perceived distinction between sanctions for foreign policy as opposed to national security purposes? Or, more specifically, did the fear that South Africa might take reprisals against the South African subsidiaries of U.S. corporations prevail? Can you think of any reasons why UN-mandated sanctions for human rights purposes should get such second-class treatment insofar as their implementation by the United States is concerned?

7. Security Council Resolutions 232 and 253 mandating sanctions against Southern Rhodesia did not explicitly authorize states to extend their sanction laws to cover foreign subsidiaries. Neither the United States, nor the UN, nor other states apparently thought the resolutions required them to do so. Had the United States wanted to do away with the loophole after it

became widely known in 1976-1977, could it have done so without subjecting itself to charges that its "extraterritorial" assertion of jurisdiction violated international law? See generally Thompson, United States Jurisdiction over Foreign Subsidiaries: Corporate and International Law Aspects, 15 Law & Poly. Intl. Bus. 319 (1983). Or should it have sought the adoption of another UN resolution to bring subsidiaries clearly under the UN's sanctions, thus "legalizing" U.S. moves to cover them? Had the United States, in the absence of a UN resolution specifically authorizing states to adopt sanctions against South Africa on an extraterritorial basis, amended its regulations under the Comprehensive Anti-Apartheid Act to cover U.S.-owned or -controlled foreign subsidiaries, would such an assertion of jurisdiction have violated international law? For arguments that it would not have, see pages 521-522 supra. See also International Law Association, Committee on the Legal Aspects of Extra-Territorial Jurisdiction, Interim Report on Extra-Territorial Jurisdiction in Export Control Law, in International Law Association, Report of the Sixty-Fourth Conference 312, 320 (Queensland 1990).

8. The United States recently reaffirmed and expanded its longstanding unilateral economic sanctions against Cuba. These sanctions, originally adopted in response to Cuba's membership in the former Soviet bloc and its sponsorship of revolutionary movements in Latin America, now are justified on the grounds of the Castro regime's "consistent disregard for internationally accepted standards of human rights and for democratic values." Cuban Democracy Act of 1992, Pub. L. No. 102-484, §1702(1), 106 Stat. 2575, 22 U.S.C.A. §6001(1), at 127 (Supp. 1994). The Act prohibits the foreign subsidiaries or branches of U.S. corporations from doing business with Cuba or Cuban nationals. 22 U.S.C.A. §6005(a), at 132 (Supp. 1994). See United States Economic Measures Against Cuba 90-91 (M. Krinsky and D. Golove eds. 1993). Does this elimination of the loophole found in the Rhodesian and South African sanctions programs indicate that the United States finally has "seen the light," or were other factors at work? If so, what might they have been? Do you think the Act reflects a change of policy with regard to the enforcement of sanctions for human rights purposes? If so, will the policy be extended to UN-mandated as well as U.S. unilateral sanctions programs?

9. Sanctions enforcement by the United States with respect to Rhodesia and South Africa left a lot to be desired. It is hard to take seriously any sanctions regime that permits a major oil company to manipulate other states' Official Secrets Acts to insulate itself from knowledge of possible sanctions violations, while at the same time vigorously enforcing such sanctions against a California professor of anthropology who purchased and brought back to the United States $200 worth of soapstone carvings for scholarly and aesthetic purposes! United States v. Eight (8) Rhodesian Stone Statues, 449 F. Supp. 193 (C.D. Cal. 1978). If you were charged with the overall enforcement of a U.S. sanctions program, what steps would you

recommend be taken to enforce sanctions more effectively? Would they require new laws or regulations? More money for enforcement personnel? What else?

10. The President of Zambia, Dr. Kenneth Kaunda, announced after the Oilgate scandal that his country, which had suffered severe economic hardships as a result of the imposition of UN sanctions against its neighbor Rhodesia, would "sue British oil companies for billions of pounds compensation for damage caused by their failure to honor United Nations sanctions against Rhodesia." The Times (London), Oct. 7, 1978, at 1, col. 3. The case either was not brought or was settled. Do you think Zambia would have been successful in its lawsuit had it gone to trial? What would have been the chances of successfully suing Great Britain, invoking either UN Charter norms or State Responsibility principles, for its condoning Shell's and BP's sanctions violations? Would any other remedies have been available to Zambia?

11. Note that the UN's sanctions against both Rhodesia and South Africa were open-ended and, hence, not subject to periodic renewal. Such sanctions run until the Security Council determines that the conditions that necessitated them no longer exist. In the case of Rhodesia, both the United Kingdom and the United States lifted sanctions before the Security Council did so, thus technically violating their obligations under Article 25 of the UN Charter. For an interesting account of events leading up to President Carter's decision to terminate sanctions a week before the UN did so, see Weissman and Carson, Economic Sanctions Against Rhodesia, in Congress, the Presidency and American Foreign Policy 132 (J. Spanier and J. Nogee eds. 1981). See also Recent Developments, Economic Sanctions: The Lifting of Sanctions Against Zimbabwe-Rhodesia by the United States, 21 Harv. Intl. L.J. 253 (1980).

In the case of South Africa, the open-endedness of draft resolutions that would have imposed mandatory economic sanctions was used by the United States as an additional argument against their adoption (see page 578 supra). To take this U.S. objection into account, draft resolutions were circulated providing that the sanctions would remain in force for 12 months, after which the Security Council would determine whether South Africa had met certain specified requirements. If the Council then decided that it had not, it was to renew or expand the sanctions (such action presumably being subject to veto). See, e.g., U.N. Doc. S/19585 (1988). Although no such resolution was adopted, what are the pros and cons of such a procedural arrangement?

12. The Sullivan Principles, basically a set of fair labor practice guidelines, were intended to appeal to the enlightened self-interest of U.S. corporations doing business or having investments in South Africa in an attempt to induce them to "work from within" to combat apartheid. While the Principles had many of the benefits of the model law approach considered in Problem IV, they, too, suffered, at least initially (see page 580 supra),

from the fact that they were not mandatory in nature. Corporate compliance was spotty, and even when a corporation applied the Principles in good faith, the possibilities of upgrading the status of black workers were circumscribed by the educational deficiencies they suffered under the apartheid system. Thus, many observers regarded them as an exercise in tokenism, and even their drafter, the Reverend Sullivan, moved on to urge far stronger mandatory sanctions. Did they have value — some? substantial? — in the South Africa context? Could they be recycled and used in other contexts, such as China or Northern Ireland? The MacBride Principles, which have been enacted into law in 14 states and 34 cities, are an employers' code of conduct, patterned after the Sullivan Principles, addressing alleged discrimination against Catholics in Northern Ireland. See Fenton, supra page 582, at 568-569. They have not been adopted by the federal government, nor is there any likelihood that they will be. Why not?

13. Also of note is the South African Council of Churches' 1993 Code of Conduct for Businesses Operating in South Africa, an attempt to establish standards for all businesses and investors in post-apartheid South Africa. Interfaith Center on Corporate Responsibility, 22 The Corporate Examiner 4 (No. 4, 1993). These standards concern equal opportunity, training and education, workers' rights, working and living conditions, job creation and security, community relations, consumer protection, environmental protection, and empowerment of black business. The Code, which at present has not been enacted into law by South Africa, has been endorsed by a number of prominent U.S. multinational corporations, who apparently hope that it will be applied "to all multinational companies, creating a more level playing field than existed in the 1980's, when they were under greater pressure from advocacy groups and politicians in the United States to actively fight apartheid than were their European and Japanese competitors." N.Y. Times, Feb. 25, 1994, at A2, cols. 2-3.

14. Diggs v. Shultz, page 536 supra, and several of the cases mentioned in Problem II, represent early attempts to use international human rights law, as well as federal and state statutes, in the struggle to improve human rights conditions in the United States and other countries. A number of these cases, which often ran afoul of the act of state doctrine or were decided on the ground that the state action concerned constituted a prohibited interference in matters of foreign affairs reserved to the federal government, involved Rhodesia or South Africa. They are gathered and critiqued in Lillich, The Role of Domestic Courts in Promoting International Human Rights Norms, 24 N.Y.L. Sch. L. Rev. 153 (1978). See also Reisman, Foreign Affairs and the Several States: Outlines of a Theory for Decision, 1977 Am. Socy. Intl. L. Proceedings 182.

One particularly important case, which raised issues that ultimately will require decision by the Supreme Court, was Diggs v. Richardson, 555 F.2d 838 (D.C. Cir. 1976). The lawsuit, brought by Congressman Diggs, arose out of a visit to Namibia by a Commerce Department mission, undertaken against the explicit advice of the Department of State. The purpose of the mission was to investigate South African fur seal killing policy, with the ultimate goal of granting an import license to the Fouke Company of South Carolina in the event that the South African seal policy measured up to the standards of humaneness set out in the Marine Mammal Protection Act of 1972 (16 U.S.C. §1361 (1988)). After the completion of the mission, Mr. Diggs filed suit against the Secretary of Commerce, seeking (1) a declaration that the mission constituted a violation of U.S. international obligations, and (2) an injunction against any other such missions to Namibia. The basis of Diggs's claim was UN Security Council Resolution 301 (S.C. Res. 301, 26 U.N. SCOR, Res. and Dec. at 7 (1971)), which implemented the finding by the International Court of Justice (Advisory Opinion on the Continued Presence of South Africa in Namibia (South West Africa), 1971 I.C.J. 16) that South Africa's occupation of Namibia was illegal. Diggs asserted that the United States was legally bound by Resolution 301 in view of Article 25 of the UN Charter, under which states "agree to accept and carry out the decisions of the Security Council. . . ."

The district court, in an unreported opinion printed in 14 Intl. Legal Materials 797 (1975), ruled that while the plaintiffs had standing to bring the action it was without subject matter jurisdiction to hear their claim, since the UN Charter was not self-executing and Resolution 301 would not serve as an independent basis of jurisdiction. The court, in dictum, also concluded that the political question doctrine precluded judicial review of the Department of Commerce's challenged actions.

On appeal to the Court of Appeals for the District of Columbia Circuit, that court affirmed "on the ground, related to the issue of standing, but analytically distinct that even assuming there is an international obligation that is binding on the United States — *a point we do not in any way reach on the merits* — the U.N. resolution underlying that obligation does not confer rights on the citizens of the United States that are enforceable in court in the absence of implementing legislation." 555 F.2d at 850 (emphasis added). While seemingly predicated on a holding that Resolution 301 is not self-executing, Judge Levanthal's opinion also contains echoes of the district court's dictum invoking the political question doctrine: "we find that the provisions here in issue were not addressed to the judicial branch of our government. They do not by their terms confer rights upon individual citizens; they call upon governments to take certain action. The provisions deal with the conduct of our foreign relations, an area traditionally left to executive discretion. . . . The Resolution does not provide specific standards. The 'entrenchment' standard of the Resolution, while possibly of such a nature that it might be elaborated by an international tribunal, is essentially the kind of standard that is rooted in diplomacy and its incidents, rather than in conventional adjudication, and is foreign to the general experience and function of American courts." Id. at 851.

This language, with its undue sensitivity to separation of powers considerations, reflects once again the reticence of some courts to play an active role in enforcing domestically any obligations that the United States has undertaken internationally. The court of appeals, with only a modest leap forward, could have enforced effectively, that is, against the United States, internationally agreed-upon human rights norms. Although there was no legislation on the statute books implementing Resolution 301, the United States had voted for the Resolution and had continued to support it by words and deeds thereafter. Consequently, the court should have granted the relief requested by plaintiffs, it being not only consistent with, but also in furtherance of, the thrust of the resolution.

15. Although President Bush's July 1991 Executive Order lifted most U.S. sanctions against South Africa, at least on the federal level, what about the hundreds of state and local laws still in force (see pages 581-582 supra)? (Fenton, supra page 582, at 585, reports that "[o]nly Oregon has responded to events in South Africa by lifting its restrictions.") Congress has not acted to preempt them, although as a policy matter it has urged "all State or local governments and all private entities in the United States that have adopted any restrictions on economic interactions with South Africa, or any policy discouraging such interaction, to rescind such restriction or policy." South Africa Democratic Transition Support Act of 1993, Pub. L. No. 103-149, §4(b)(9), 107 Stat.. 1505, 2 U.S.C.A. §5001, at 56 (Supp. 1994). Since most state and local governments have not, complications can arise. See Hyatt, Apartheid Tangle: State to Penalize Digital for S. Africa Unit, Boston Globe, Aug. 12, 1993, at 1, cols. 3-4 (state pension funds required by governor's executive order to divest themselves of Digital's stock when with ANC's endorsement it opened subsidiary in South Africa).

16. Studies have shown that sanctions must be applied quickly and surgically to have the maximum effect on the government of the target state. "Sanctions imposed slowly or incrementally may simply strengthen the target government at home as it mobilizes the forces of nationalism." G. Hufbauer and J. Schott, Economic Sanctions Reconsidered: History and Current Policy 86 (1985). Their case studies reveal a clear association "between the duration of sanctions and the waning prospects of success." Id. They, therefore, contend that "the inverse relationship between success and sanctions period argues against a strategy of 'turning the screws' on a target country, slowly applying more and more economic pressure over time until the target succumbs." Id.

In the case of both Rhodesia and South Africa, the incremental approach, although ultimately successful, required 14 and 16 years, respectively, to achieve the sanctions' objectives. More recently, the initial June 1993 sanctions against Haiti involved only an oil and arms embargo and the freezing of government funds. S.C. Res. 841, 48 U.N. SCOR, Res. and Dec. at 119 (1993). Not until May 1994 did the Security Council tighten sanctions by prohibiting air travel and imports from Haiti and, specifically targeting the Haitian military, by placing restrictions on their travel and freezing their assets. S.C. Res. 917, U.N. SCOR, 49th Sess., 3376th mtg., U.N. Doc. S/RES/917 (1994). Thus, the military regime hardly noticed the impact of sanctions for nearly a year while much of the general populace — despite exceptions for foodstuffs, medicines, and other essential humanitarian needs — suffered. See French, Study Says Haiti Sanctions Kill Up to 1,000 Children a Month, N.Y. Times, Nov. 9, 1993, at A1, cols. 1-2. But see French, Embargo's Effect on Haiti Debated, N.Y. Times, Nov. 24, 1993, at A12, cols. 3-4 (doctors taking part in study say military rule, as well as shortages, causes high infant mortality). Thus as Hufbauer and Schott (with apologies to the Bard) entitle their discussion on this question, "if it were done, when 'tis done, then 'twere well it were done quickly" — to which one might add: "and, if possible, surgically."

17. Since the end of the Cold War freed up the Security Council, the UN, employing the "threat to the peace" language of Article 39, has invoked Chapter VII of the UN Charter and ordered mandatory economic sanctions for, inter alia, human rights purposes in a growing number of situations. Listed in the order of the first imposition of sanctions, the states against which such sanctions have been invoked are as follows: *Iraq*: S.C. Res. 661, 45 U.N. SCOR, Res. and Dec. at 19 (1990) (general economic and arms embargo); S.C. Res. 687, 46 U.N. SCOR, Res. and Dec. at 11 (1991) (same); S.C. Res. 778, 47 U.N. SCOR, Res. and Dec. at 72 (1992) (transfer of certain Iraqi funds to UN escrow account); *Yugoslavia*: S.C. Res. 713, 46 U.N. SCOR, Res. and Dec. at 42 (1991) (general arms embargo against then-Federal Republic of Yugoslavia); S.C. Res. 757, 47 U.N. SCOR, Res. and Dec. at 13 (1992) (general economic embargo against Federal Republic of Yugoslavia (Serbia and Montenegro)); S.C. Res. 820, 48 U.N. SCOR, Res. and Dec. at 7 (1993) same plus freezing of certain funds of Federal Republic of Yugoslavia (Serbia and Montenegro)); *Somalia*: S.C. Res. 733, 47 U.N. SCOR, Res. and Dec. at 55 (1992) (general arms embargo); *Libya*: S.C. Res. 748, 47 U.N. SCOR, Res. and Dec. at 52 (1992) (general arms embargo, prohibition of sale of aircraft and related services, and denial of aviation rights to any aircraft using Libyan airports); S.C. Res. 883, 48 U.N. SCOR, Res. and Dec. at 113 (1993) (freezing of certain Libyan funds and prohibition of transactions with Libyan Arab Airlines and other aviation arrangements); *Liberia*: S.C. Res. 788, 47 U.N. SCOR, Res. and Dec. at 99 (1992) (general arms embargo); *Angola*: S.C. Res. 864, 48 U.N. SCOR, Res. and Dec. at 59 (1993) (arms and oil embargo against UNITA).

Any evaluation of the effectiveness of sanctions in the above six cases (and consider Haiti, mentioned in Comment 16) most likely would conclude, like The Economist, that they are "seldom decisive, sometimes useful." As that newspaper, speculating about whether sanctions can be "effective," reminds us:

> That judgment inevitably rests upon a view of what constitutes effectiveness. Sanctions have not worked in Iraq, say some, because Mr. Hussein is still there. Yet against that measure the Gulf war too must be judged a failure.

In fact, the postwar sanctions against Iraq have indubitably restrained Mr. Hussein's arms programmes . . . , which was the original intention behind them. Similarly, sanctions against Serbia have not brought an end to the war in Bosnia, yet they cause considerable pain to the Serbs and may represent the world's best weapon for achieving peace. Sanctions against Haiti, now including a ban on commercial flights, have yet to make the country's rulers step down and may do no more than make it harder for their wives to shop in Miami.

The Economist, June 18, 1994, at 19, cols. 1-2. They may, however, accomplish more; and even if they do not, another option exists. Turn now to Problem VIII.

Problem VIII

Bangladesh

When May the UN or Its Member States Use Armed Force for Human Rights Purposes?

I.   Introduction: The Bangladesh Problem   602
         International Commission of Jurists, The Events in East Paki-
         stan, 1971   604
II. Humanitarian Intervention by States   613
     A. Background and Legal Issues   613
         Fonteyne, The Customary International Law Doctrine of Hu-
         manitarian Intervention: Its Current Validity Under the U.N.
         Charter   614
     B. The Debate over Humanitarian Intervention   623
         Brownlie, Humanitarian Intervention   624
         Lillich, Humanitarian Intervention: A Reply to Ian Brownlie
         and a Plea for Constructive Alternatives   631
         Bibliography (Humanitarian Intervention by States)   641
     C. The Aftermath of a Crisis: Bangladesh Since 1971   641
     D. Other Claims of Unilateral Humanitarian Intervention Since the
         Bangladesh Crisis   643
     E. Nicaragua v. United States: Delphic Dicta from the International
         Court of Justice   646
         Nicaragua v. United States, Merits   646
         Rodley, Human Rights and Humanitarian Intervention: The
         Case Law of the World Court   647
         F. Teson, Humanitarian Intervention: An Inquiry into Law and
         Morality   647
         Comments and Questions on the Court's Dicta   649
III. UN Humanitarian Intervention   651
         Lillich, Humanitarian Intervention Through the United Na-
         tions: Towards the Development of Criteria   652
         Security Council Resolution 940 on Haiti   659
         Note: The Significance of Resolution 940   662
         Bibliography (UN Humanitarian Intervention)   663
IV. Forcible Protection of Nationals   664
     A. Contrasting Views Regarding Forcible Protection of Nationals   665
         Letters to the Editor of the New York Times   665

B.   Reading   667
        Lillich, Forcible Protection of Nationals Abroad: The Liberian
            "Incident" of 1990   667
C.   Forcible Protection of Nationals Abroad: Post-Entebbe Case
        Studies   672
V.   *Final Comments and Questions*   675

I.   Introduction: The Bangladesh Problem

Following the passing of the India Independence Act in 1947 by the British Parliament, the two states of India and Pakistan came into existence. Pakistan comprised two separate parts, divided by 1,200 miles of India. West Pakistan (310,000 square miles in area) contained Urdu-speaking people more closely aligned to the countries of the Middle East than to Hindustan. East Pakistan (only 55,000 square miles in area) had Bengali-speaking inhabitants. There were very few links between the two parts, their only real bond being their Muslim faith. Although the majority of Pakistanis actually lived in East Pakistan, West Pakistan was both economically and militarily dominant, and its leaders always had been insensitive to the political aspirations of the Eastern (Bengali) majority.

In 1958, at a time of rising tension between the two parts of Pakistan, the Pakistani army under General Ayub Khan took over. From that time until the fall of President Yahya Khan in 1971 — and despite a new constitution in 1962 — the government remained basically a military dictatorship. Social inequality and disorder grew. In 1969 President (formerly General) Ayub Khan attempted to negotiate with opposition leaders and freed political prisoners (including the former Foreign Minister, Mr. Ali Bhutto, and the Awami League leader, Sheikh Mujibur Rahman). The army, however, refused to yield to democratic pressures demanding direct elections, termination of the emergency regulations, and autonomy for the East. Law and order broke down, and President Ayub Khan ceded power to General Yahya Khan.

Yahya Khan reimposed martial law, but he promised a return to civilian rule. Free elections were set for 5 October 1970; a cataclysmic cyclone in that region postponed them until December. These elections were the first in Pakistan ever to be conducted on a one-man, one-vote basis (thus guaranteeing East Pakistan a majority of votes and of seats in the new constituent assembly). Sheikh Mujibur Rahman's Awami League won 167 out of the 169 East Pakistan seats, and Mr. Bhutto's Pakistan People's Party won 85 of the 144 West Pakistan seats. The two parties were irrevocably split over the principle of economic autonomy for East Pakistan: from their different perspectives, each party regarded this issue as non-negotiable. In February President (formerly General) Yahya Khan, after dismissing his civilian cabinet and returning full control to the army, postponed the assembly indefinitely.

The period from 1 March to 25 March 1971 was punctuated by strikes and sporadic violence. On 23 March ("Pakistan Day," declared in Dacca (East Pakistan) as "Resistance Day"), the new Bangladesh flag was unfurled, and Sheikh Mujibur Rahman issued a "declaration of emancipation." On 25 March, the Pakistani army commenced an orgy of killing, terror, and destruction in East Pakistan. Bengalis were hunted down, prime targets being Awami League politicians, professors, students, and Hindus. Within 48 hours thousands of civilians were killed. The Awami League was banned and all political activity forbidden.

To escape the terror, during the next six months millions of refugees fled over the frontier to neighboring India. Increased guerrilla activity in East Pakistan resulted in increasingly barbarous reprisals. On 25 October 1971, President Yahya Khan, worried about an Indian Army buildup, invited the Secretary-General of the UN to visit India and Pakistan to discuss troop withdrawals from each side of the Indian frontier. Both the Indian and the provisional Bangladesh governments, not surprisingly, opposed this plan.

Border incidents between India and Pakistan (on the East Pakistan border) became more frequent, and on 3 December 1971, Pakistan launched a "pre-emptive air strike" against Indian airfields. Then-Prime Minister of India Indira Ghandi announced that Pakistan had launched a "full-scale war" against India. India invaded Pakistan on both the eastern and western fronts and on 6 December formally recognized Bangladesh. The war, lasting for 12 days, ended when the Pakistani forces surrendered at Dacca on 16 December 1971. Its closing days were marked by atrocities and counter-atrocities.

Except for coping with disaster relief and refugee assistance, the UN said little and did nothing during most of 1971. It was not until December that the veto-blocked Security Council finally passed the matter to the General Assembly, which duly called for an immediate ceasefire and troop withdrawals. India considered this recommendation unrelated to any political solution and, therefore, unacceptable. The Human Rights Commission and the Sub-Commission on Prevention of Discrimination and Protection of Minorities avoided any meaningful role. The Secretary-General, after initially publicizing the gravity of the situation, lapsed into the studied passivity that affected the rest of the organization.

Prompted by the inaction of the UN, an international conference of jurists called upon the International Commission of Jurists (a Geneva-based NGO) in September 1971 to set up a Commission of Enquiry into Events in East Pakistan. The following factual account of the events occurring in East Pakistan from March to December 1971 was undertaken with the cooperation of the Indian Government and the provisional government of Bangladesh. The former government of Pakistan refused to cooperate, arguing that the matter was solely within domestic concern.

International Commission of Jurists, The Events in East Pakistan, 1971
76-96 (1972)

THE ROLE OF THE UNITED NATIONS

The inaction of the United Nations Organization in face of the East Pakistan crisis has been widely commented upon. For some it is proof of the impotence of the organisation. The simple answer to this is that the United Nations cannot, by its nature, be more effective than the members who comprise it. It provides a machinery through which the nations of the world can act, if they have the will to do so. The events in East Pakistan could have been dealt with by the United Nations either as gross violations of human rights, or as a threat to international peace, or both.

VIOLATIONS OF HUMAN RIGHTS

. . . [T]he events in East Pakistan involved gross violations of human rights. These violations began in March 1971 and continued until Pakistan's defeat in December, but the United Nations did not take any action to prevent them. The Secretary-General, on his own initiative, launched a humanitarian relief programme. No United Nations organ would consider the human rights violations in East Pakistan, in spite of appeals by India and by Non-Governmental Organisations. When the Security Council was finally seized of the question in December, it refused to consider the origins of the situation but dealt only with the India-Pakistan conflict. . . .

POSSIBLE ACTION BY THE SECURITY COUNCIL

Pursuant to its primary responsibility under Article 24 for maintaining international peace and security, the Security Council could have investigated the crisis under Article 34 as "a situation which might lead to international friction or give rise to a dispute, in order to determine whether the continuation of the . . . situation is likely to endanger the maintenance of international peace and security."

Equally, any member of the United Nations could have brought the "situation" to the attention of the Security Council under Article 35, or the Secretary-General could have done so under Article 99.

If the Security Council had met to consider the situation, its first duty under Article 39 would have been to determine whether there existed "any threat to the peace, breach of the peace or act of aggression," and if so, determine what recommendations to make or what measures to take to maintain or restore international peace or security.

The Security Council did not, in fact, meet until after international hostilities had broken out in December. Hindsight now establishes that there was a threat to peace, but no great foresight was required in order to recognise this threat at the time. Particularly was this so after the Secretary-General's Note to the Security Council of July 20, 1971, in which he drew attention to three features of the situation which previous experience had shown to present grave dangers to peace, namely:

(1) the violent emotions aroused by the persecution of religious or linguistic groups;
(2) the conflict between the principle of territorial integrity and self-determination of peoples; and
(3) the long-standing tension between India and Pakistan. . . .

It is difficult to resist the conclusion that if the Security Council had met before December 1971 to consider the situation they would have determined that it constituted a threat to the peace. (As no international violence had occurred, it could hardly have determined that there was a "breach of the peace" or an "act of aggression" pace India's contention in a later debate in the Third Committee that the flow of refugees across the border constituted a "civilian invasion.")

If the Security Council had so determined it could, notwithstanding the domestic nature of the dispute, have taken under Chapter VII either non-military measures under Article 41 (including severance of economic relations, of communications, and of diplomatic relations) or "such action by air, sea, or land forces as may be necessary to maintain or restore international peace and security."

Any such decision would, however, have required under Article 27(3) an affirmative vote of seven members * including the concurring vote of the permanent members. It was, of course, the impossibility of reaching agreement among the permanent members which was responsible for the inaction of the Security Council.

Even if agreement had been possible, it must be recognised that measures of the kind envisaged under Articles 41 and 42 are not necessarily best suited to achieving the objects which the situation called for, namely the protection of the different sections of the population of East Pakistan against gross violations of human rights, and the prevention of outside interference in the internal dispute, without supporting or favouring one side or the other to that dispute.

Before taking any action under Articles 41 and 42, the Security Council may also under Article 40 "call upon the parties concerned to comply with such provisional measures as it deems necessary or desirable." These could include such measures as sending a fact-finding committee, or ob-

---

* Since 1963, when the Security Council was enlarged from 11 to 15 members, the vote of 9 members has been required. U.N. Charter art. 27, ¶ 3. — Eds.

server groups, or a peace-keeping force. As this Article is in Chapter VII, such provisional measures could have been taken without the consent of the Pakistan Government, but in practice it is unlikely that any such force would be sent without the consent of the government of the country concerned and, in a case of this kind, of the leaders of the insurgent forces or liberation army.

The Security Council could also, under Article 36, have recommended "appropriate procedures and methods of adjustment" with a view to the pacific settlement of the dispute or situation. The procedures and methods which the Security Council could have recommended under this Article would include procedures for negotiation or mediation as well as the measures open to it under Article 40.

POSSIBLE MEASURES BY THE GENERAL ASSEMBLY

The General Assembly has a general power under Article 10 to discuss any matters within the scope of the Charter and, subject to Article 12, to make recommendations to member states, to the Security Council or both. (Article 12 bars the General Assembly from making any recommendation while the Security Council is exercising its functions in respect of the dispute or the situation; as we have seen, that limitation did not apply.)

There is also a similar power in respect of matters relating to international peace and security under Article 11(2).

Under Article 14 "the General Assembly may recommend measures for the peaceful adjustment of any situation, regardless of origin, which it deems likely to impair the general welfare or friendly relations among nations, including situations resulting from a violation of the provisions of the present Charter setting forth the Purposes and Principles of the United Nations."

These purposes and principles include (Article 1(3)), "to achieve international cooperation . . . in promoting and encouraging respect for human rights and for fundamental freedoms for all without distinction as to race, sex, language or religion."

It may be noted in passing that the fact that Article 14 authorises the General Assembly to act in this way indicates that a situation involving a gross violation of human rights within a state should not be considered one which is "essentially" within the jurisdiction of the state concerned, if it impairs the general welfare or friendly relations among nations. . . .

It may be that the General Assembly could also have acted under Article 55, which provides that:

> With a view to the creation of conditions of stability and well-being which are necessary for peaceful and friendly relations among nations based on respect for the principle of equal rights and self-determination of peoples, the United Nations shall promote: . . .

(c) universal respect for, and observance of, human rights and fundamental freedoms for all without distinction as to race, sex, language or religion.

Under Article 56, "all Members pledge themselves to take joint and separate action in cooperation with the Organisation for the achievement of the purposes set forth in Article 55." . . .

OPPORTUNITIES FOR DISCUSSION OF THE SITUATION IN THE
UNITED NATIONS

Apart from the power of any Member under Article 35 to bring the situation to the attention of the Security Council of the General Assembly or the Committee on the Elimination of Racial Discrimination, ample opportunities in fact arose for discussing it.

The situation was first raised in the Social Committee of ECOSOC in July, and at the 51st Plenary Session of ECOSOC the United Nations High Commissioner for Refugees (UNHCR) reported on the refugee problem. The Council decided to refer the report to the General Assembly without debate.

On August 16, 1971, a representative of the International Commission of Jurists, speaking on their behalf and on behalf of 21 other non-governmental organisations, requested the UN Sub-Commission on the Prevention of Discrimination and Protection of Minorities to examine the situation in East Pakistan and to make recommendations to the Commission on Human Rights on measures to be taken to protect human rights and fundamental freedoms in East Pakistan. After a short debate the matter was closed without any conclusion being reached.

The matter was also raised by India in September 1971, in the Special Committee on Colonialism, but the Committee decided that since the General Assembly had not classified East Pakistan as a colonial territory, it was not authorised to discuss the situation.

In the Introduction to his report to the General Assembly, the Secretary-General stated his belief that the United Nations had to take some action with regard to the situation in East Pakistan, but he did not specifically suggest any action by the General Assembly. . . .

The resolution finally adopted by the General Assembly (Resolution 2790 (XXVI), December 6, 1971) "Urges all Member States in accordance with the purposes and principles of the Charter of the United Nations to intensify their efforts to bring about conditions necessary for the speedy and voluntary repatriation of the refugees to their homes," and notes that the return of the refugees "requires a favourable climate which all persons of goodwill should work to bring about in a spirit of respect for the principles of the Charter of the United Nations."

The wording of this Resolution illustrates the cautious and unrealistic attitude in which most member states viewed the situation in East Pakistan. The discussion in the Third Committee took place just a few weeks before the outbreak of the India-Pakistan war, yet provisions on the political factors were considered too "controversial." Ironically, the General Assembly adopted the Resolution several days after the full-scale war began. Events had overtaken the decision by the General Assembly.

SECURITY COUNCIL AND GENERAL ASSEMBLY ATTEMPT TO STOP
THE INDIA-PAKISTAN WAR

The Security Council finally became seized of the situation in the Indian subcontinent on December 4, when nine members called for a meeting on "the deteriorating situation which has led to armed clashes between India and Pakistan."

In the Security Council Ambassador Y. A. Malik of the Soviet Union vetoed two draft resolutions calling for immediate cease-fire and withdrawal of troops on the grounds that they failed to stress the need for a political settlement in East Pakistan. He criticised members of the Council for viewing the situation as a purely India-Pakistan conflict. . . .

After the Soviet vetoes, the Council referred the matter to the General Assembly under the "Uniting for Peace" resolution.

On December 7, the General Assembly promptly adopted by a vote of 104 in favour, 11 against, with 10 abstentions, a resolution calling for an immediate cease-fire and withdrawal of troops. The overwhelming vote reflected the disapproving attitude by most states to the secession of Bangladesh from Pakistan and India's armed intervention. Many of them were no doubt anxious to discourage dissident minorities in their own states from taking the same course. Certain states, however, criticised the Security Council for not taking action earlier which might have averted the crisis. . . .

The United States on December 12 requested that the Security Council be reconvened due to India's "defiance of world opinion" in not respecting the General Assembly's call for cease-fire and withdrawal of troops. Ambassador George H. Bush stated that Pakistan's use of force in March "does not . . . justify the actions of India in intervening militarily and places in jeopardy the territorial integrity and political independence of its neighbour Pakistan." The draft resolutions at the second series of Council meetings on the whole showed greater attention to the need for a political settlement between Pakistan and the elected leaders of East Pakistan, but India's military success in Bangladesh made these proposals academic. After the surrender of the Pakistan forces in Bangladesh and a de facto cease-fire in both Pakistan and Bangladesh, the Security Council adopted a resolution demanding strict observance of the cease-fire and withdrawal of troops "as soon as practicable." The Council did not insist on India withdrawing its troops from Bangladesh immediately since it recognised its usefulness in protecting from reprisal the persons who collaborated with the Pakistan Government.

THE LESSONS OF EAST PAKISTAN FOR THE UNITED NATIONS

The inability of the United Nations to have any significant impact on the events in East Pakistan suggests that the Organisation should reconsider some of its basic attitudes towards situations of this kind. The most serious omission of the United Nations was its failure to act upon the authenticated reports of massive killings and other gross violations of human rights committed by the Pakistan army in East Pakistan. The United Nations had recognised in the abstract that respect for human rights is an essential condition for the maintenance of international peace and security. As recently as 1970 the General Assembly declared that "universal respect for and full exercise of human rights and fundamental freedoms and the elimination of the violation of those rights are urgent and essential to the strengthening of international security, and hence resolutely condemns all forms of oppression, tyranny and discrimination, particularly racism and racial discrimination, wherever they occur."

It is submitted that the United Nations should act upon this principle in particular situations where governments are conducting massive violations of human rights against their people. The Security Council should be convened immediately to take measures which will persuade the government concerned to discontinue the repression. The Council will be more likely to be able to reduce tensions and create conditions for a pacific settlement of the dispute before neighbouring states have become involved. More speedy procedures are also needed for investigating situations of this kind. On April 5, 1972, a representative of the International Commission of Jurists urged the United Nations Commission on Human Rights to seek the authority to be able to hold emergency sessions to deal with urgent situations involving the imminent threat of wilful destruction of human life on a massive scale.

THE ROLE OF INDIA

. . . This brings us to the traditional doctrine of humanitarian intervention which Sir Hersh Lauterpacht, in the last edition of Oppenheim's International Law defines as follows:

> . . . when a State renders itself guilty of cruelties against and persecution of its nationals in such a way as to deny their fundamental human rights and to shock the conscience of mankind, intervention in the interest of humanity is legally permissible.

And Professor Borchard defines more clearly the form that such intervention may take:

> When these human rights are habitually violated, one or more states may intervene in the name of the society of Nations and may take such measures as to substitute at least temporarily, if not permanently, its own sovereignty for that of the state thus controlled. Whatever the origin, therefore, of the rights of the individual, it seems assured that these essential rights rest upon the ultimate sanction of international law, and will be protected, in the last resort, by the most appropriate organ of the international community.

Humanitarian intervention has been described by Professors McDougal and Reisman as "a venerable institution of customary international law . . . regarded as accepted law by most contemporary international lawyers." It was accepted by both Grotius and Vattel, and it has been invoked many times since. Examples are the armed intervention by Great Britain, France and Russia against Turkey which led to the independence of the Greek nation in 1830, and the Syrian intervention by France in 1860 following the protocol of the Conference of Paris.

The unilateral use of this ancient and respected doctrine, which is the expression of a profound and innate sense of justice corresponding to the natural feelings and reactions of the average person, is nevertheless questionable from two points of view. First of all it may open the door to all sorts of abuses and risks and be used as a pretext for acts of aggression. The justification for it is liable to be subjective, whereas one would wish to see the reasons for a humanitarian intervention established objectively. Secondly, it is reasonable to suggest that as a result of the creation of the United States [sic] Organisation (and possibly of Regional Organisations such as the Council of Europe) there has been a transfer of authority and responsibility and that henceforth humanitarian intervention is a matter to be dealt with by international bodies rather than individual nations. By virtue of Article 39 of the Charter it is in the first instance the responsibility of the Security Council to "determine the existence of any threat to the peace . . . and . . . decide what measures shall be taken." This means that it is for the Security Council to decide whether or not a collective humanitarian intervention is called for or, in certain cases, to authorise action on the part of an individual state, and the Member States are bound to accept this decision and to assist in its implementation. The General Assembly, for its part, may make recommendations in accordance with Article 55 of the Charter concerning the "universal respect for, and observance of, human rights and fundamental freedoms for all," and indeed Article 56 translates this general obligation into a specific duty for each of the Member States, who "pledge themselves to take joint and separate action in cooperation with the Organisation for the achievement of (these) purposes."

Some authorities have argued that the right of unilateral intervention has been completely supplanted by these procedures for collective humanitarian intervention under the United Nations. But what if violations of human rights on a massive scale are not even considered in the United Nations to see whether they constitute a "threat to the peace," and if international organisations offer no redress or hope of redress? Must everyone remain impassive in the face of acts which revolt the human conscience, paralysed by considerations which are primarily of a procedural nature or even — which is worse — by procedural obstruction? When it is clear that the international authorities cannot or will not discharge their responsibilities, it would seem logical to resort again to customary international law, to accept its rules and the validity of the doctrine of humanitarian intervention.

At the same time, to avoid the obvious dangers implicit in this doctrine, it is suggested that before unilateral humanitarian intervention by a single nation can be justified, the following requirements should be satisfied:

1. The state against which measures are to be taken must have shown itself manifestly guilty in respect of its citizens of systematic cruelty and persecution to the point at which
   (a) their fundamental human rights are denied them, and
   (b) the conscience of mankind is shocked and finds that cruelty and persecution intolerable.
2. The circumstances must be such that no practicable peaceful means of resolving the problem is available, such as negotiations with the state which is at fault, intermediation, or submission to a competent international organisation.
3. The international community must have had the opportunity within the limits imposed by the circumstances:
   (a) to ascertain whether the conditions justifying humanitarian intervention do in fact exist, and
   (b) itself to solve the problem and change the situation by applying such measures as it may deem appropriate.
4. If the international community does not avail itself of the opportunities offered and fails to act in order to prevent or put a stop to widespread violations of human rights which have been called to its attention, thereby leaving no choice but intervention, then a state or group of states will be justified in acting in the name of humanity provided that:
   (a) before resorting to force it will deliver a clear ultimatum or "peremptory demand" to the state concerned insisting that positive actions be taken to ameliorate the situation;
   (b) it will resort to force only within the strict limits of what is absolutely necessary in order to prevent further violations of fundamental human rights;

> (c) it will submit reports on its actions to the competent international agency to enable the latter to know what is being done and to intervene if it sees fit to do so;
>
> (d) it will withdraw the troops involved in the intervention as soon as possible.

In our present world it is only in quite exceptional circumstances that unilateral action on the part of a state can be considered as legally justified on the basis of the doctrine of humanitarian intervention, particularly if that action involves the use of force on a scale of some magnitude. Unilateral action is likely to be arbitrary and to lack the disinterested character which humanitarian intervention should possess. In the situation with which we are concerned, and on the basis of the rules we have laid down, India might be accused of not having pursued all possible peaceful means of solving the problem since she did not submit the matter to the Security Council — a step, we may add, which no Member State of the United Nations saw fit to take. Such a reproach may seem somewhat unrealistic, since it was plain to all that there was no prospect of the Members of the Council reaching an agreement capable of offering any possibility of an effective solution, and nothing could have been worse than a show of [in]decision which would have paralysed action without providing a positive solution. In our view the circumstances were wholly exceptional; it was becoming more and more urgent to find a solution, both for humanitarian reasons, and because the refugee burden which India was bearing had become intolerable, with no solution or even any hope of a solution in sight. Events having been allowed to reach this point, it is difficult to see what other choice India could have made.

It must be emphasised that humanitarian intervention is not the ground of justification which India has herself put forward. As we have seen, India claims to have acted first in self-defence, and secondly in giving support to the new Government of Bangladesh which she recognised when the hostilities began. We have given our reasons for not accepting the validity of these claims. If India had wished to justify her action on the principle of humanitarian intervention she should have first made a "peremptory demand" to Pakistan insisting that positive actions be taken to rectify the violations of human rights. As far as we are aware no such demand was made.

In conclusion, therefore, we consider that India's armed intervention would have been justified if she had acted under the doctrine of humanitarian intervention, and further that India would have been entitled to act unilaterally under this doctrine in view of the growing and intolerable burden which the refugees were casting upon India and in view of the inability of international organisations to take any effective action to bring to an end the massive violations of human rights in East Pakistan which were causing the flow of refugees. We also consider that the degree of force used was no greater than was necessary in order to bring to an end these violations of human rights.

II. Humanitarian Intervention by States

A. *Background and Legal Issues*

The issues with which this Problem is concerned involve intervention, specifically intervention for humanitarian purposes, whether those purposes be the protection of individuals from mistreatment at the hands of their own state (humanitarian intervention) or the protection of nationals of one state from mistreatment by another state (forcible protection of nationals). These two doctrines, as we shall see, are governed by different legal norms, just as they apply to different fact patterns. The protection of individuals whose lives and limbs are in jeopardy ex hypothesi is to be applauded. Yet forcible interventions, whether by the UN, regional organizations, groups of states, or an individual state, present problems and always offer possibilities of abuse. Thus, it is well to bear in mind the International Court of Justice's admonition that humanitarian considerations "do not . . . in themselves amount to rules of law." *South West Africa Cases* (Second Phase), 1966 I.C.J. 6, 32 (Judgment of July 18).

The UN Charter mentions intervention only in Article 2(7), which provides that the organization — *not* its member states — shall not "intervene in matters which are essentially within the jurisdiction of any state. . . ." Article 2(4) places analogous but not identical limits on the conduct of member states: they are forbidden to resort to "the threat or use of force against the territorial integrity or political independence of any state. . . ." Intervention itself is not proscribed.

How much latitude do the above provisions leave to the UN and its member states to engage in humanitarian intervention? Conventional wisdom, at least until recently and perhaps even now, had only one clear answer to this question: such an operation would be lawful if carried out by the UN pursuant to a determination by the Security Council that there existed a "threat to the peace, breach of the peace, or act of aggression" under Article 39 of the UN Charter. This conclusion seemed mandated by Article 2(7), which ends with the statement that "this principle [of UN nonintervention] shall not prejudice the application of enforcement measures under Chapter VII."

Beyond this one seemingly clear instance, there is much room for dispute. For example, what is to be done in situations, like that of Bangladesh, where the Security Council is unable or unwilling to act? That the UN remained impotent even in the face of so severe a crisis was a telling indication that international peacekeeping and human rights protection machinery was dangerously inadequate. For additional criticism of the role played — or not played — by the UN in this situation, see Saltzburg, UN Prevention of Human Rights Violations: The Bangladesh Case, 27 Intl. Org. 115 (1973). Consider also a former President of Uganda's criticism of the UN's failure to act during the days of General Amin at pages 72-73 of Problem I.

The question remains, though, whether there exists in international law — or, if not, whether there should exist — a rule authorizing, tolerating, or condoning humanitarian intervention by states, collectively or individually, when the UN fails to act (which, until the 1990s, always had been the case)? Should such interventions be reconciled with or exempted from the normal rules regarding the domestic jurisdiction of states, just as the Charter exempts Security Council actions by means of Article 2(7)? If such a rule exists for human rights interventions, where is its legal justification to be found, and under what circumstances does it come into play? The reading that follows addresses these and other questions.

Fonteyne, The Customary International Law Doctrine of Humanitarian Intervention: Its Current Validity Under the U.N. Charter
4 Cal. W. Intl. L.J. 203, 203-258 passim (1974)

The Indian action in the 1971 Bangladesh crisis has recently revived the debate among scholars on the question of the legality of unilateral humanitarian intervention under the U.N. Charter.

With the exception of some vague and controversial allegations of self-defense by Indian spokesmen, India itself has not tried to justify its intervention in East Pakistan on international legal grounds. Specifically, she has not appealed to the doctrine of humanitarian intervention. Nevertheless, the failure of the Indian government to refer openly to this theory does not alter the fact that its course of action in the Bangladesh situation probably constitutes the clearest case of forceful individual humanitarian intervention in this century. The question which the Indian operation raises is whether the present state of international law, as modified by the U.N. Charter, still permits unilateral resort to force in order to remedy a situation of large-scale deprivation of the most fundamental human rights, committed by a State against its own nationals.

In view of the serious doubts recently expressed by various scholars as to the existence of a "right" to intervene for humanitarian purposes as a generally recognized principle of customary international law (*even in the pre-Charter period*), it will be necessary to analyze this particular contention before assessing the eventual survival of the doctrine in spite of the U.N. Charter prohibition of State-initiated force.

I. THE TRADITIONAL DOCTRINE OF HUMANITARIAN INTERVENTION: STATE PRACTICE

Despite such early precedents as the Crusades, several of which could be considered humanitarian interventions, or the 16th and 17th century religious wars, it seems that the institution of humanitarian intervention is in fact largely a creation of the latter part of the 19th century. This is certainly true so far as State practice *explicitly* referring to this justification is concerned. Earlier instances of humanitarian intervention are too closely tied with a feeling of religious solidarity to allow them to be classified as genuinely humanitarian.

A large number of cases have occurred in which States in the 19th and early 20th century allegedly intervened on behalf of the local populations in other States. Examples include the United States' interventions in Cuba at the end of the 19th century, and the protests by the European Major Powers against the cruel treatment of political prisoners in Morocco in the beginning of the 20th century. These cases seem to lack either a *clear* humanitarian motive or the *highly coercive* character of an armed intervention. Therefore, the analysis of pre-Charter precedents of *forceful* humanitarian intervention must be restricted to the notorious cases in Eastern Europe. . . .

[The author describes and analyzes the interventions in Greece (1827-1830); Syria (1860-1861); the Island of Crete (1866-1868); Bosnia, Herzegovinia, and Bulgaria (1876-1878); and Macedonia (1903-1908, 1912-1913).]

II. THE PRE-CHARTER DOCTRINE

A. THE QUESTION OF PRINCIPLE: IS HUMANITARIAN INTERVENTION PERMISSIBLE UNDER INTERNATIONAL LAW?

While rather vague statements, to the extent that a sovereign is entitled to intervene on the basis of religious solidarity in the internal affairs of another when the latter mistreats his own subjects beyond the limits of what seems acceptable, can be found as early as the writings of St. Thomas Aquinas, it is only later that this doctrine appears to have been secularised in the doctrine of lawful assistance to a people struggling against tyranny.

Albeit in general terms, Grotius accords his support to this view when he declares:

> There is also another question, whether a war for the subjects of another be just, for the purpose of defending them from injuries by their ruler. Certainly it is undoubted that ever since civil societies were formed, the ruler of each

claimed some especial right over his own subjects. . . . [But] . . . [i]f a tyrant . . . practices atrocities towards his subjects, which no just man can approve, the right of human social connexion is not cut off in such case.

Vattel, on the other hand, seems not to have been completely able to resolve what Mosler called "the problem of the friction between Sovereignty and the Law of Nations." First, he observes:

The sovereign is the one to whom the Nation has entrusted the empire and the care of government; it has endowed him with his rights; it alone is directly interested in the manner in which the leader it has chosen for itself uses his power. No foreign power, accordingly, is entitled to take notice of the administration by that sovereign, to stand up in judgment of his conduct and to force him to alter it in any way. If he buries his subjects under taxes, if he treats them harshly, it is the Nation's business; no one else is called upon to admonish him, to force him to apply wiser and more equitable principles.

Vattel immediately qualifies this general statement by the apparently contradictory contention that:

[I]f the prince, attacking the fundamental laws, gives his people a legitimate reason to resist him, if tyranny becomes so unbearable as to cause the Nation to rise, any foreign power is entitled to help an oppressed people that has requested its assistance.

Once the middle of the 19th century is reached, the decline of the Law of Nature and the rising of the contradictory values of nationalism, sovereign independence and nonintervention on the one hand, and humanitarianism on the other hand, influences the thinking on the subject. The statements become clearer; the scholars take positions; and, in general, a dichotomy appears between the champions of an expanding nonintervention norm and those who favor a more flexible rule permitting intervention on various grounds. . . .

. . . [A] substantial body of writers espouse a double-level permissibility by refusing to grant humanitarian motivation the character of a formal *legal* justification of intervention, while at the same time recognizing that a violation of the nonintervention principle, though technically a breach of the law, might in certain circumstances be not only excusable, but even commendable. Bernard, for instance, states: "The law . . . prohibits intervention. . . . Nay, there may even be cases in which it becomes a positive duty to transgress it." Specifically referring to humanitarian considerations, Harcourt argues: "Intervention is a question rather of policy than of law, and when wisely and equitably handled . . . may be the *higher policy* of justice and humanity."

Another tendency in this period is to accept a *limited* right of humanitarian intervention, restricting its lawful application either to very specific circumstances or to situations involving certain categories of States only.

An example of the former type of qualification is provided by Creasy when, acknowledging that "intervention may be justifiable, and even a duty, in certain exceptional cases," he restricts the legality of humanitarian intervention to those cases only:

> [W]here we intervene in behalf of a grievously oppressed people, which has never amalgamated with its oppressors as one nation, and which its oppressors have systematically treated as an alien race, subject to the same imperial authority, but in other respects distinct . . . [or] where the King, or dominant party of a nation keeps up, in defiance of the State's fundamental Laws, a mercenary army of regular troops, especially if carefully organized and officered by men who are of creed, of politics, and of feelings alien from those held by the great majority of the population, and where, by this being done, all effective manifestations of the popular will, and the formation of a truly national force are rendered utterly impossible, . . .

thus requiring a racial element to transgress the *internal matter aspect* of the treatment by a sovereign of his own subjects.

More common, however, was the notion that the *right* to intervene for humanitarian motives was to be restricted to the relations between "civilized" and "non-civilized" nations.

de Martens, for instance, argues that:

> *Vis-a-vis* non-civilized nations . . . intervention by the civilized powers is in principle legitimate, when the Christian population of those countries is exposed to persecutions or massacres. In those circumstances, it is justified by common religious interests and humanitarian considerations. . . . These motives are not applicable to the relations between civilized powers. . . .

By so arguing, he links the notion of humanity with that of religious solidarity and with the existence of different categories of States. Often without the religious connotation, similar opinions can be found in the works of a number of jurists of this period.

Although their pronouncements usually remain vague and are often qualified by considerations of Major Power supremacy and outspoken predilection for collective action, from the 1860's on, writers seem increasingly won to the idea of the lawfulness of humanitarian intervention. . . .

Of particular importance for this development, together with the precedents set by State practice primarily in Eastern Europe, was the fundamental refusal of many authors to allot to State sovereignty the character of an *absolute* principle not susceptible of restrictions or exceptions. Consequently, nonintervention was seen as a flexible notion which could lawfully be disregarded for the defense of higher values in certain circumstances.

In the period immediately preceding the first World War, it seems that the majority of the writers had been won to the idea of the legality of humanitarian intervention, and that only a few scholars, albeit notorious ones, continued to reject the validity of the doctrine. Apparently, most of them did so on the basis of doubts as to the actual integration of the theory in the generally accepted body of customary international law, rather than because of fundamental philosophical, ideological, or political convictions regarding absolute sovereignty and nonintervention. . . .

Nevertheless in 1946, shortly after the United Nations had become a reality, Sir Hartley Shawcross felt entitled to declare at the Nüremberg Trials that:

> [T]he right of humanitarian intervention, in the name of the Rights of Man trampled upon by the State in a manner offensive to the feeling of Humanity, has been recognized long ago *as an integral part of the Law of Nations*. . . .

III. Conclusion as to the Customary Law

Regarding the incorporation of the doctrine of humanitarian intervention as an established principle in customary international law, it has been demonstrated in the preceding analysis that, while historically there has never been unanimity on this point, there has, nevertheless, been some consistency since the latter part of the 19th century. As Lauterpacht points out there has been:

> a substantial body of opinion and practice in support of the view that there are limits to [the] discretion [of states in the treatment of their own nationals] and that when a State renders itself guilty of cruelties against and persecutions of its nationals in such a way as to deny their fundamental human rights and to shock the conscience of mankind, intervention in the interest of humanity is legally permissible. . . .

Turning . . . to the normative problem, it appears that some widely accepted criteria of legality of humanitarian intervention can be distilled from the abundant literature on the subject. This can be done in spite of the overall vagueness and lack of structuration of the pronouncements by pre-Charter scholars:

(1) disinterestedness of the intervening Power(s), in the sense of a nonseeking of particular interests or individual advantages;
(2) restriction of the applicability of the theory to extreme cases of atrocity and breakdown of order;
(3) active participation or passive complicity or condonation of the violations by the sovereign;
(4) general predilection for collective action, by preference at the hands of the Major Powers, who have a particular responsibility for ensuring overall respect of minimal international standards of treatment of local populations.

As the foregoing study has shown, while divergences certainly existed as to the *circumstances* in which resort could be had to the institution of humanitarian intervention, as well as to the *manner* in which such operations were to be conducted, the *principle* itself was widely, if not unanimously, accepted as an integral part of customary international law. Indeed, "the doctrine of humanitarian intervention appears to have been so clearly established under customary international law that only its limits and not its existence is subject to debate."

IV. Present Validity of the Customary Doctrine

A. THE DOMESTIC JURISDICTION LIMITATION AND THE PRINCIPLE OF NONINTERVENTION

The principle of nonintervention, rather surprisingly in view of its wide acceptance at the time of the creation of the United Nations, is not explicitly provided for in the Charter regarding inter-State relations. While article 2(4) specifically prohibits the threat or use of force between *States*, article 2(7) explicitly covers the relations between the United Nations and its Members only. This precludes *the Organization* from intervening in matters essentially within the jurisdiction of any State with the important exception of actions in respect to threats to the peace, breaches of the peace, and acts of aggression. However, this does not affect inter-State relations.

Notwithstanding some sporadic affirmations to the contrary, it seems that the explicit references in articles 1(2) and 2(1) of the Charter and the subsequent interpretation given to the nonintervention principle by a nearly unanimous doctrine and by the United Nations itself, justify the contention that the basic obligation of nonintervention in the domestic affairs of a State is equally, if not more, applicable on the level of inter-State relations.

Today the whole range of activities relating to human rights, both in and outside the United Nations, as exemplified by the large number of declarations and conventions which have in recent years been adopted on the subject, indicate that the scope of domestic jurisdiction is dwindling. Further examples include the almost daily involvement of various U.N. agencies and organs with actual human rights problems; the repeated refusal by the General Assembly and the Security Council to accept article 2(7) of the Charter as preventing consideration by the United Nations of serious cases of human rights violations, particularly in a colonial or para-colonial context; and, the world-wide concern of the public opinion with extreme cases such as Biafra, Southern Africa, Rhodesia or Bangladesh. These developments seem to substantiate Professor Ermacora's conclusion that:

> [T]he right to self-determination and the protection of human rights in matters of discrimination as far as "gross violations" or "consistent patterns of violations" are concerned are no longer essentially within the domestic jurisdiction of States. . . .

Domestic jurisdiction is "an essentially relative question; it depends upon the development of international relations." In view of the variable character of the concept, it appears that the universal attention devoted to the way in which people are treated in their own country, and the practice of the United Nations in this field, must clearly be interpreted as indicating that human rights have finally been removed from the exclusive jurisdiction of States and lifted up into the realm of international concern. As a consequence, human rights have been placed outside the reach of the article 2(7) intervention ban, even in cases not amounting to a threat to the peace. This is true so far as measures by the United Nations are concerned, and probably regarding unilateral State action as well.

B. THE [UN CHARTER'S] PROHIBITION OF THE THREAT OR
     USE OF FORCE

    . . . The approach which [scholars] have taken towards [the] problem [of whether or not the legality accorded to humanitarian intervention by customary international law has survived the advent of the UN Charter] is not uniform and as a result two major strands can be distinguished. They can conveniently be described as the "double-level" and the "legal" approach.

    The proponents of the "double level" approach accept the "classic" view on the Charter prohibition of unilateral use of force as a necessary corollary to the attainment of what they see as the United Nations' primary goal. That is, maintenance of international peace and security through elimination of *all* forceful interactions between States that are not comprised among the legal exceptions expressly mentioned in the Charter; individual and collective self-defense and action in pursuance of a Chapter VII decision. They feel compelled, in view of the already demonstrated inability or unwillingness of the international organizations to cope with such drastic situations as Biafra or Bangladesh, to acknowledge that the absolute interpretation of the Charter prohibition on use of force by States is an unworkable and unacceptable restriction upon last resort unilateral action in case of extreme violation of the most fundamental human rights. Nevertheless, they are not prepared to depart from their allegiance to their basic force-minimalization position and to consider an eventually revived customary doctrine of humanitarian intervention which would fully legalize this kind of action as an additional exception not explicitly provided for in the Charter. On the other hand, they point to the lack of *formal* condemnation or criticism *on principle* in the United Nations and in other international fora in such cases as the Stanleyville operation or the Indian intervention in Bangladesh. From this they conclude that, in circumstances of extreme gravity, the world community, by its lack of adverse reaction, *in practice* condones conduct which, although a *formal* breach of positive legal norms, appears "acceptable" because of higher motives of a moral, political, humanitarian, or other nature. This lack of express condemnation in specific cases, they submit, would in fact confer to such actions the character of some kind of second-tier or sub-legality. . . .

    The main arguments which have been advanced in support of this approach compromise: fear of abusive invocation of a fully legalized doctrine of humanitarian intervention; practical restraints upon the conduct of States due to the necessity of, at least "technical" breach of the law; clarity and simplicity of the general rule of total prohibition of armed intervention, coupled with the fear that recognition of an exception for humanitarian motives might "erode the psychological constraints of the use of force for other purposes;" and, concordance with the present state of the law.

So far as the fear of abuse is concerned, this author must confess that he is unable to see how a "double level" theory, recognizing the permissibility of certain illegalities, would in any respect reduce the opportunities for abusive utilization. It seems likely that a clearly stated rule, restricting by a set of precise criteria the lawfulness of humanitarian intervention to certain well-defined, specific situations, would provide a far stronger incentive for a State to refrain from intervening in a situation or in a manner falling short of the requirements set forth for its legality. This would be much more effective than would a system in which the prospective intervenor knows that, regardless of his motives, he breaches the law, but can hope that the world community will remain silent as a result of apathy or political division, and thus implicitly condone his intervention, however selfish its purposes may have been.

Such a situation would certainly enhance neither clarity nor predictability. An absolute prohibition undermined by creeping exceptions puritanically called "acceptable breaches" seems hardly more straightforward in application than a rule which openly recognizes some limited and strictly defined exceptions, by permitting appraisal and eventual characterization of the conduct of an intervenor as unlawful.

In addition, "[i]t would indeed be wrong to unnecessarily brand conduct unlawful, which is morally justified." This could only encourage States to run the risk, break the law, invoke some vague, plausible higher motive, and hope that the world community will fail to censor their conduct. In the long run such a situation must inevitably lead to an increasing authority deflation of international law in general, and of the Charter in particular. If States can "acceptably" break the law for humanitarian reasons, why should it not be equally tolerable to violate it for other, perhaps morally less commendable motives as well?

Thus it seems that the only real advantage of the "double level" approach is its complete correspondence with the present state of the law, integrating at the same time the strict *theoretical* prohibition of unilateral use of force for any reason not amounting to self-defense, and the *practice* of noncondemnation of at least some types of "technical" violations of this norm. In view of the various disadvantages this theory entails, it might be advisable in assessing what the law *ought* to be, to frame the recommended rule in such a way as to attach the label of lawfulness to what is deemed acceptable.

In view of the highly improbable character of a Charter revision expressly integrating unilateral use of force for humanitarian purposes as an additional exception to the general prohibition of use of force by States, those scholars who want the *legality* of past and future instances of humanitarian operations recognized, have tried to find basis in the Charter, as it presently stands, to support their contention. . . .

The more commonly taken approach combines three main arguments: restrictive interpretation of the article 2(4) prohibition; balancing out of the Charter's major purposes; and limited invocation of the non-realization of the basic expectations of the Members of the United Nations when they renounced their right under customary international law to use force unilaterally.

Article 2(4) of the Charter, it is argued, should be interpreted in accordance with its plain language, so as to prohibit the threat or use of force *only when directed at the territorial integrity or political independence* of a State. . . . Specifically, "[s]ince a humanitarian intervention seeks neither a territorial change nor a challenge to the political independence of the State involved," and particularly in view of the closing words of article 2(4) referring to the purposes of the Charter, this specific modality of the use of force is "not only not inconsistent with the purposes of the United Nations but is rather in conformity with the most fundamental peremptory norms of the Charter." . . .

From the standpoint of text interpretation . . . the argument can be criticized, for this approach takes the words "against the territorial integrity or political independence of any State" to refer to the *motives and goals* of the State resorting to force. Article 2(4), on the other hand, does not indicate that it relates to the intentions of the parties. . . . In most instances of humanitarian intervention on behalf of peoples deprived of their most fundamental human rights by or with the approval of their own government, the infringement upon the State's territorial integrity and political independence will be far more serious. Achievement of a lasting solution in such cases will usually require a change of government or even a secession, so that the foreign intervention will have had to fundamentally influence the domestic political process and organization of the State intervened in.

Considering article 2(4) in the broader perspective of the major purposes of the Charter, and specifically in view of the closing words of paragraph 4, there is clearly a need for balancing the sometimes opposite goals of conflict-minimalization and protection of human rights. Espousing Professor Lillich's view that "a prohibition of violence is not an absolute virtue" and that "it has to be weighed against other values as well," Professors McDougal and Reisman contend that:

> The continuing authority of community expectations about the lawfulness of humanitarian intervention is greatly confirmed by all the contemporary developments associated with the United Nations. The repeated, insistent emphasis upon its underlying policies can only be regarded as strengthening, not weakening, the historic remedy.

Referring in particular to articles 55 and 56 of the Charter, which they interpret as transforming the general commitment of U.N. Members to human rights into "an active obligation for joint and separate action," they submit that:

> [T]he cumulative effect of the Charter in regard to the basic policies of the customary institution of humanitarian intervention is to create a coordinate responsibility for the active protection of human rights: members may act jointly with the Organization in what might be termed a new organized, explicitly conventional humanitarian intervention or singly or collectively in the customary or international common law humanitarian intervention. Any other interpretation would be suicidally destructive of the explicit major purposes for which the United Nations was established.

And conclude that:

> Insofar as it is precipitated by intense human rights deprivations and conforms to the general international legal regulations governing the use of force — economy, timeliness, commensurance, lawfulness of purpose, and so on — [humanitarian intervention] represents a vindication of international law. . . .

Furthermore, since "[the] great expectations of the immediate postwar period have not materialized," in that the machinery for collective security and enforcement envisaged by the States ratifying the Charter has in fact not been established, one might wonder whether a State would not be entitled to challenge the absolute validity of the Charter prohibition of force and fall back upon the traditional doctrine of humanitarian intervention in those exceptional cases of extreme human rights deprivations.

As long as the necessity of strictly defining and limiting the circumstances in which States could rely upon this latitude is kept in mind, would it not be advisable to consider the present potentials of the international organizations? Similarly, it seems reasonable to recognize *legally*, that in certain extreme situations, when neither the United Nations nor the competent regional organization can or wants to assume its responsibilities, a State may be temporarily relieved of its obligation of restraint under article 2(4) so as to provide a form of "substitute or functional enforcement of international human rights." . . .

B. The Debate over Humanitarian Intervention

Although it was the Bangladesh crisis that introduced a sharp note of timeliness into the debates over the legality of humanitarian intervention, legal scholars already had a long history of discussion, and disagreement, behind them. See, for example, E. Stowell, Intervention in International Law (1921); A. Thomas and A. Thomas, Non-Intervention (1956); Wright, The Legality of Intervention Under the United Nations Charter, 1957 Am. Socy. Intl. L. Proceedings 79; M. Ganji, International Protection of Human Rights (1962); and Nanda, The United States' Action in the 1965 Dominican Crisis: Impact on World Order — Part I, 43 Den. L.J. 439 (1966).

One of the principal fora in which the debate took place was the International Law Association (ILA), a non-governmental organization of international law scholars and practitioners from all over the world. In the late 1960s, the ILA's Committee on Human Rights decided to shift its emphasis from the normative to the procedural aspects of human rights protection, on the theory that a sufficiently large body of substantive rights already existed, but that the machinery for their implementation had been left in a fairly primitive state.

Accordingly, the ILA constituted a Subcommittee on the International Protection of Human Rights by General International Law for the purpose of investigating the relevance of various doctrines of customary international law for contemporary human rights protection. This Subcommittee submitted reports to the ILA at each of the latter's biennial conferences from 1970 through 1976. See ILA, Report of the Fifty-Fourth Conference 633 (The Hague 1970); ILA, Report of the Fifty-Fifth Conference 608 (New York 1972); ILA, Report of the Fifty-Sixth Conference 217 (New Delhi 1974); and ILA, Report of the Fifty-Seventh Conference 519 (Madrid 1976). The problem of humanitarian intervention became the major issue studied; in its first report, in 1970, the Subcommittee even envisaged that it would submit a draft Protocol of Procedure for Humanitarian Intervention to the 1972 ILA conference. ILA, Report of the Fifty-Fourth Conference 633, 641 (The Hague 1970).

Between 1970 and 1972, however, occurred the Bangladesh independence struggle. The consequent outpouring of scholarly interest in the international legal community as a whole served greatly to enrich the available literature on the subject, but at the expense of the consensus that the ILA Subcommittee had been seeking so earnestly. By 1976 the Subcommittee concluded that "there appears [to be little] possibility . . . of achieving a consensus on a draft Protocol [on humanitarian intervention] to which all States could adhere." ILA, Report of the Fifty-Seventh Conference 519, 521 (Madrid 1976).

The following exchange of views is illustrative of the debate that then occurred on this subject.

Brownlie, Humanitarian Intervention
in Law and Civil War in the Modern World 217-228 (J.N. Moore ed. 1974)

1. INTRODUCTION

In the recent literature of the law, proposals have been made to the effect that forcible intervention in human rights situations is lawful and, further, that the present need is to clarify the criteria by which the legitimacy of such action may be judged. My purpose is to subject these proposals to a critique. The critique will relate particularly to the views of Richard

Lillich and the Interim Report of the Sub-Committee of the Committee on Human Rights of the International Law Association. The Interim Report was based upon two articles published previously by Lillich.

It is as well if I point out that I share the objectives of the principal Committee in shifting the emphasis from definition to implementation in matters of human rights. . . . The issue, of course, is to discover the best means of implementation acceptable to the majority of states. While publicists and experts can take the initiative in prompting states to action, they cannot afford to ignore the expectations, attitudes and aptitudes of governments when formulating proposals.

Unless the context clearly requires a different interpretation, "humanitarian intervention" in my usage is the threat or use of armed force by a state, a belligerent community, or an international organization, with the object of protecting human rights. It must be emphasized that this usage begs the question of legality and stresses function or objective. In diplomatic usage, the term "humanitarian intervention" has been used more widely to describe diplomatic intervention de bene esse on behalf of non-nationals or on behalf of nationals in matters which are in law within the domestic jurisdiction of the state of their residence or sojourn.

2. The Legal Context

. . . It is clear to the present writer that a jurist asserting a right of forcible humanitarian intervention has a very heavy burden of proof. Few writers familiar with the modern materials of state practice and legal opinion on the use of force would support such a view. In the first place, it is significant that the very small number of writers cited in support of this view by Lillich include two, McDougal and Reisman, who lean heavily on a flexible and teleological interpretation of treaty texts. Leading modern authorities who either make no mention of humanitarian intervention and whose general position militates against its legality, or expressly deny its existence include Brierly, Castrén, Jessup, Jimenez de Arechaga, Briggs, Schwarzenberger, Goodrich, Hambro, and Simons, Skubiszewski, Friedmann, Waldock, Bishop, Sorensen, and Kelsen. In the lengthy discussions over the years in United Nations bodies of the definition of aggression and the principles of international law concerning international relations and cooperation among states, the variety of opinions canvassed has not revealed even a substantial minority in favor of the legality of humanitarian intervention. The Repertory of Practice of United Nations Organs provides no support; nor does the International Law Commission's Draft Declaration of the Rights and Duties of States. The voluminous materials in Whiteman's Digest lack even a passing reference to humanitarian intervention.* Counting heads is not, of course, a sound way of resolving issues of principle. How-

---

* But see 12 M. Whiteman, Digest of International Law 204-215 (1971). — Eds.

ever, quite apart from the weight of the opinion of experts cited above, it is the writer's view that these authorities are reporting and reflecting the universal consensus of government opinion and the practice of states since 1945. Their views thus combine both policy in the sense of the reasonable expectations of states and the normative quality of rules based on *consensus*. With due respect to Lillich, it must be said that, if a new view is to be put forward, either it should be based on a much more substantial exposition of the practice, doctrine, and general development of the law relating to the use of force by states or the view should be offered *tout court* as a proposal to change the existing law. . . . Even those prone to give a broad definition of self-defense do not, in general, support the view that humanitarian intervention is lawful. The minority who would support the legality of intervention to protect the lives of nationals rely significantly on the category of self-defense: and humanitarian intervention is not a form of self-help by definition, whereas self-defense is a legitimate form of self-help. The minority who argue that Article 51 reserves without transformation the right of self-defense in customary law rely on the category of self-defense and do not suggest that the erratic "rights of intervention" variously propounded by pre-1928 writers survive. . . .

3.   STATE PRACTICE

. . . The ILA Report and Lillich's articles on humanitarian intervention are almost entirely devoid of any serious examination of the practice in the period of "customary international law," apparently pre-1945. Reference is made to Turkish treatment of Christians and Russian treatment of Jews — instances of diplomatic intervention. The other pre-1914 references are to the collective intervention in Greece in 1827 and American action in Cuba in 1898. Both these cases can only be recruited as examples by "ex post factoism." The governments of the time did not use a legal justification in the case of the Greek insurgency. Jurists classify the intervention in Cuba in 1898 in various ways, and the Joint Resolution of Congress justified the intervention in terms of American interests. An examination of the practice provides one possibly genuine example of altruistic action, namely, the intervention of 1860 in Syria to prevent the recurrence of massacres of Maronite Christians. The only approximation to use of the justification between 1913 and 1945 was in the Proclamation on the German occupation of Bohemia and Moravia, made by Hitler on March 15, 1939. In this, he referred to "assaults on the life and liberty of minorities, and the purpose of disarming Czech troops and terrorist bands threatening the lives of minorities."

The period of the United Nations Charter is totally lacking in practice on the point. However, the ILA Report holds out the Stanleyville operation of 1964 and the initial introduction of troops into the Dominican Republic as instances of permissible intervention to protect human rights. The

Stanleyville operation took place with the authorization of the Government of the Congo, which, both legally and otherwise, makes a great deal of difference. . . .

4.   THE ARGUMENTS FOR LEGALITY OF INTERVENTION TO PROTECT HUMAN RIGHTS

My examination . . . leads to three conclusions. First, the role of humanitarian intervention, even before the first attempt at regulating resort to war in the League Covenant, was dubious, and the practice probably did not present a constant and uniform usage. Secondly, the practice of the League period cannot be said to assist the somewhat derelict doctrine, although a number of writers, especially prior to the Kellogg-Briand Pact, continued to give it support. Thirdly, the practice in the period of the United Nations Charter is totally inadequate to the task of establishing an interpretation in terms of subsequent conduct of the parties favorable to intervention to protect human rights.

There are two points remaining for consideration. First, how is the "protection of human rights" to be defined? This point will be reserved, partly because the issue of definition is not necessarily identical with the substance of the matter — the existence of the particular legal title to act. Secondly, apart from the subsequent conduct of the parties as a guide to interpretation, what is the proper interpretation of the Charter provisions? The approach to the Charter of the ILA subcommittee is curious to a degree since, in contrast to most lawyers, they place the customary law and Charter in opposition. For most lawyers, the principles of the Charter are the customary law, i.e., general international law, governing use of force by states. This is especially the case after twenty-five years of state practice based upon the Charter.

The ILA subcommittee's remark that the drafters of the Charter "paid no attention to whether these doctrines [of humanitarian intervention] were to survive the Charter" is simply not true. The participating governments took a view of the legal regime as a whole and, because they made no reference to what statesmen would have regarded as a non-issue, it can hardly be said that they were reserving their position on the point.

The ILA subcommittee produced two other points. The first was to cite Professors Reisman and Thomas for the view that intervention which does not impair the "territorial integrity or political independence" of a state is not prohibited by Article 2(4). This argument is used by very few lawyers and has long been discredited. If there is an ambiguity, then, according to ordinary principles of interpretation, one has recourse to the preparatory materials. These make it clear that the phrase "against the territorial integrity" was added at San Francisco at the behest of small states wanting a stronger guarantee against intervention. Of course, the states taking action within the territory of other states commonly attempt to mitigate their policies by assertions that their motives are limited or even benevolent. The other legal argument in the sub-committee's Report is irrelevant to the present issue. This asserts, correctly, that the United Nations can intervene, if the state violating human rights causes an actual threat to peace.

5. Policy Issues

My own assumption is that, basically, Professor Lillich is intent on making lawyers look afresh at humanitarian intervention and that it is constructive to look at his views on their merits as a legislative proposal. A preliminary point to be made is the unprepossessing character of the historical evidence: the near impossibility of discovering an aptitude of governments in general for carefully moderated, altruistic, and genuine interventions to protect human rights. What follows is concerned with humanitarian intervention *as it would be practiced* on the basis of existing evidence of behavior patterns. Naturally, the moral setting, even in genuine cases, is far from simple. There is a moral and legislative problem of the type raised by euthanasia, itself a form of "humanitarian intervention." Euthanasia is unlawful, but doctors on occasion commit technical breaches of the law, for example, by administering massive drug dosages which accelerate coma and death. It is very generally assumed that legalizing euthanasia would alter the moral climate and produce harmful abuse.

Particularly when considering policy issues, attention should be paid to the actual behavior of states. Reference to the behavior of states before 1920, or 1945, on the premise that in the practice of that time one can find models of humanitarian intervention, involves a failure to see the development of the law as a whole. Before 1945, matters of human rights were, apart from treaty, within the domestic jurisdiction of states. When the League Covenant was drafted, modest Japanese proposals concerning racial and religious discrimination received no support. Guarantees concerning minorities were imposed only on defeated states and new states, such as Poland, as the price of recognition. It is surprising to expect a worthwhile doctrine of intervention to protect human rights at a time when the most modest proposals not for implementing but for merely setting of standards were struck down as threats to domestic jurisdiction.

The present writer recognizes that domestic jurisdiction is much less of a shield than it was in 1920 in matters of human rights. The question remains whether state conduct in administering intervention unilaterally has improved since the period before the League and the United Nations. Is it the case that the performance of individual states is and would be better than the centralized enforcement and other measures available to the United Nations? The latter is certainly unreliable, but is the alternative more reliable? I am accused of "throwing the baby out with the bath water" by adopting a cautious attitude to intervention to protect human rights, but my view is that those making novel proposals need to produce more evidence. What is the price *in human terms* of intervention? What were the casualty ratios in the Stanleyville operation in 1964, the Dominican Republic in 1965, and other possible examples? How many were killed in order to "save lives"? To what extent does the typical intervention cause collateral harms by exacerbating a civil war, introducing indiscriminate use of air power in support operations, and so on? Was there a policy of pacification and general involvement, together with extraction of concessions by treaty or otherwise as the price of withdrawal?

Since a part of Lillich's argument is based on the *essence* of state practice, i.e., on what it was really about, aside from the existence of some formal title to intervention, one can also look at the evidence in this way. The *general* picture, as others may see it, is not encouraging. In the years of Stanleyville and the landings in the Dominican Republic, there were far more serious and persistent threats to human rights which were ignored. In 1965, not less than 300,000 persons of Chinese origin were murdered in Indonesia. The facts were well reported in the world press. The regime responsible received massive material support from several governments, including a million-pound-sterling credit from the United Kingdom. The whole field is riven by political expediency and capriciousness. One area of human rights in which there is a strong consensus in the United Nations is racial discrimination and especially the practice of apartheid. The United States has shown caution in supporting even mandatory economic sanctions against South Africa through the Security Council. Moreover, human rights is a category which can provide good public relations for national policies. In the Western hemisphere, concern for human rights sharpened considerably after the change of regime in Cuba in 1959.

There are other, more precise, considerations of policy. A major issue, unexplored by the ILA subcommittee, is the whole question of the use of force in community relations. The situation in Ulster, the desegregation issue in the United States, and comparable problems in many countries cannot be "solved" by a use of force. Community relations can be policed in a crude sense; massacres can be prevented. The wrong kind of intervention and the drawing of police lines, however, may increase alienation, worsen communal relations, and produce new problems. A further point of great importance is the extent to which the position of minorities is hazarded by foreign protection or sponsorship. There is a good deal of literature, ignored by the ILA subcommittee, on the working of the League of Nations machinery for the protection of minorities. Even when the supervision was through international machinery and was not very demanding, it was felt by many commentators that the position of "minority" groups within the state was invidious by reason of their partly externalized status.

6. The Value of Proto-Legal Guidelines

The ILA subcommittee's Report recapitulates five standards formulated by Professor John Norton Moore which can be used in evaluating the legitimacy of a putative humanitarian intervention. They are as follows: "(1) An immediate and extensive threat to fundamental human rights, particularly a threat of widespread loss of human life; (2) A proportional use of force which does not threaten greater destruction of values than the human rights at stake; (3) A minimal effect on authority structures; (4) A prompt disengagement, consistent with the purpose of the action; and (5) Immediate full reporting to the Security Council and appropriate regional organizations." Nanda and Lillich have offered criteria which are similar but include the existence of an invitation by the recognized government and the relative disinterestedness of the intervening state or states. If an invitation to intervene has been made, then the action would be lawful on any view. Apart from that and consistent with my own view of the law, I would regard such criteria as of value, as providing (a) good criteria should humanitarian intervention become a part of the law, and (b) a fine basis for a political plea in mitigation in parliaments, U.N. organs, and regional organizations. My euthanasia parallel applies here: a defense lawyer and a court still need to distinguish the false from the genuine case, as a matter of mitigation.

7. Definition of Intervention to Protect Human Rights

A subject not taken up by the ILA subcommittee is the isolation of "intervention situations." Obviously, they do not extend to all violations. Professor Moore refers to "an immediate and extensive threat to fundamental human rights, particularly a widespread loss of human life." Oppenheim (edited by Hersch Lauterpacht) gives apparent approbation to intervention "when a state renders itself guilty of cruelties against and persecution of its nationals in such a way as to deny their fundamental human rights and to shock the conscience of mankind." Since a good number of states qualify in this way every decade, the opportunities for intervention will be very many. It is also the case that only a few powerful states will have a choice of voluntary intervention of this kind. Nearly every legal issue may raise a problem of definition, but few are on this scale. It is significant that governments are commonly more cautious than writers in giving currency to vaguely formulated and easily abused excuses for unilateral action. In the Cuban missile crisis, the United States Department of State avoided reference to the somewhat fugitive concept of anticipatory self-defense and chose to use a justification related to the Organization of American States as a regional arrangement. Various states have neighbors playing host to intermediate-range ballistic missiles, just as they may have neighbors guilty of cruelties which may shock the conscience of mankind. "Realism" in the sphere of policy includes restraint and caution in state policy. . . .

9.   CONCLUDING REMARKS

My general position is clear and general recapitulation is unhelpful. But a few points may be made by way of emphasis. The position taken up by Lillich is completely outside the general consensus of state practice and the opinion of experts of various nationalities. In the Sixth Committee of the General Assembly, when Spiropoulos once stated that intervention to prevent genocide against a racially related minority in a neighboring state should be lawful, the reaction from other delegates, including those of Israel, Nationalist China, and Panama was unfavorable. A development proximate to a concept of humanitarian intervention is the support by some members of the United Nations, including most members of the O.A.U., for the view that intervention against a liberation movement is unlawful and assistance to such a movement is lawful. It is common knowledge that there is no consensus on this as yet in the United Nations.

I am in favor of humanitarian intervention, i.e., effective implementation of human rights, in conditions in which this can occur within the law and when the methods and circumstances of the operation do not lead to results which bear no positive relation to the original objective, even assuming it to be genuine. What I find depressing is the absence of evidence that proponents of humanitarian intervention and other very plastic doctrines have spent much time examining state practice in detail. This should be essential for those concerned with policy. . . .

Lillich, Humanitarian Intervention: A Reply to Ian Brownlie and a Plea for Constructive Alternatives
in Law and Civil War in the Modern World 229-233, 235-251
(J.N. Moore ed. 1974)

The preceding [essay] by Ian Brownlie represents another welcome contribution to the current debate on the contemporary relevance of the doctrine of humanitarian intervention. As could be expected of one of the leading advocates of the view that Article 2(4) of the United Nations Charter absolutely prohibits forcible self-help by States, save in cases of individual or collective self-defense against armed attack authorized by Article 51, [he] . . . reaches the categorical conclusion that "unilateral action by a State in the territory of another State on the ground that human rights require protection, or a threat of force against a State for this reason, is unlawful." Somewhat unexpectedly, however, he finds the present writer's criteria for judging the legitimacy of a state's use of forcible self-help for humanitarian purposes of some value, if only "as providing a fine basis for a political plea in mitigation in parliaments, U.N. organs and regional organizations." Indeed, by twice citing a supposed parallel between euthanasia and humanitarian intervention, a parallel one hopes he will develop more fully in his subsequent writings, Brownlie seems to suggest that some such interventions, while technically breaches of Article 2(4), might be condoned, if not actually approved, by the world community.

. . . In the opinion of the present writer, the actual course events took during 1971 in Bangladesh (formerly East Pakistan) should put an end once and for all to the doctrinal argument that "action in part concerned with the protection of human rights and the prevention of genocide may be lawful" when, and only when, undertaken by international institutions. Surely the abject inability of the United Nations to take effective action to terminate the genocidal conduct and alleviate the mass suffering in Bangladesh necessitates a fundamental reassessment by Brownlie and like-minded authorities of the role of self-help, and especially of humanitarian intervention, in international affairs today. Pending such a reassessment, many of the specific arguments made in the preceding [essay] require "prompt, adequate and effective" rebuttal, if only for the record, while Brownlie's general attitude toward humanitarian intervention, including his suggested euthanasia approach, warrants a more extensive critique.

I.   PRE-CHARTER PRACTICE

One interested in the doctrine of humanitarian intervention and its contemporary relevance approaches the subject cautiously. On the one hand, some scholars, including a friendly critic of the present writer (and, incidentally, of Brownlie too), consider "that past law relating to humanitarian intervention has little relevance to the present system." On the other hand, numerous authorities, including Brownlie, "place special emphasis on the relevant State practice and diplomatic materials." Rightly noting that "a policy-oriented view, as well as concern for State practice as such, requires such an emphasis," Dr. Brownlie finds this writer's prior studies "almost wholly devoid of any serious examination of the practice in the period of 'customary international law,' apparently pre-1945." While the present writer admittedly has yet to essay an extensive examination of pre-Charter humanitarian intervention claims, in the words of McDougal and Reisman, responding to a similar indictment by Marshall, "the raw materials for such a survey are readily accessible in many sources." Reiteration of the numerous instances where humanitarian interventions occurred during the nineteenth and early twentieth centuries previously had been considered superfluous.

A cursory perusal of Chapter I ("Humanitarian Intervention") of Dean Ganji's International Protection of Human Rights, a standard work not included in Brownlie's references, reveals many cases where interventions occurred for humanitarian purposes. In addition to the intervention of 1860 by Austria, France, Great Britain, Prussia, and Russia in Syria, acknowledged somewhat grudgingly by Brownlie as "one possibly genuine example of altruistic action," Ganji lists the following instances:

> 1. The intervention of France, Great Britain, and Russia against the Turkish massacres and suppression of the Greeks, which resulted in the independence of Greece in 1830;
> 2. The peremptory demands of Austria, France, Italy, Prussia, and Russia (during the years 1866-68) on the Ottoman Empire for the institution of positive action leading to the betterment of the lot of the persecuted Christian population of Crete;
> 3. The Russian intervention against Turkey (1877-78) on the occasion of insurrections resulting from Turkish misrule and from the outrageous persecutions of the Christian populations of Bosnia, Herzegovina, and Bulgaria; and
> 4. The intervention of Austria, Russia, Great Britain, Italy, and France in Turkey as a result of insurrections and misrule in Macedonia (1903-8).

Moreover, to these cases of humanitarian intervention he adds "many instances of humanitarian protest and representation by one or more states on behalf of the citizens of other states." While, apparently ignoring the implications of his own investigations, Ganji surprisingly concludes that "the doctrine of humanitarian intervention *does not seem* to claim the authority of a customary rule of international law," he frankly concedes that this view is a minority one by acknowledging that the doctrine "claims the authority of such jurists as Grotius, Vattel, Wheaton, Heiberg, Woolsey, Bluntschli, Westlake, Rougier, Arntz, Winfield, Stowell, Borchard and many others."

Since Brownlie himself once asserted that "[b]y the end of the nineteenth century the majority of publicists admitted that a right of humanitarian intervention (*l'intervention d'humanité*) existed," citing nine of the above twelve authorities, his complaint that the present writer has failed to examine pre-Charter practice adequately, a failure perhaps excused by the writer's reliance upon the authoritativeness of Brownlie's own treatise, is somewhat puzzling. After devoting a single paragraph in his treatise to an examination of state practice, Brownlie does reach the conclusion, repeated in [his essay above], that contrary to the views of the above authorities, "no genuine case of humanitarian intervention has occurred, with the possible exception of the occupation of Syria in 1860 and 1861." Yet this lame attempt to discredit the very authorities he otherwise relies upon produces the opposite effect in the reader. True, "[t]he doctrine was inherently vague and its protagonists gave it a variety of forms," but it was acknowledged by scholars and invoked by governments, and no contemporary reassessment can deprive it retroactively of its pre-Charter impact.

. . . This traditional doctrine obviously should not be "superimposed on the present international legal order without regard to the criteria which formed the basis of past decisions," but since a careful examination of the criteria invoked in the humanitarian interventions mentioned above reveals so many similarities to contemporary claims to use force for humanitarian objectives, neither should its importance be dismissed out of hand.

II.   POST-CHARTER PRACTICE

. . . While the Charter contains no provision authorizing unilateral or collective humanitarian intervention by States, neither does it specifically abolish the traditional doctrine. Actually, despite Dr. Brownlie's vigorous objection, it warrants reiteration that "[t]he drafters of the Charter . . . paid no attention to whether these doctrines [of protection of nationals and humanitarian intervention] were to survive the *Charter.* . . ." One therefore may accept as common ground Brownlie's contention "that it is impossible to place any form of intervention in the context of the law without examining the legal regime *as a whole*," while rejecting his conclusion that the Charter and subsequent practice thereunder absolutely forbids intervention for humanitarian purposes by a state or a group of states.

Examining the United Nations Charter "as a whole," it is apparent that its two major purposes are the maintenance of peace and the protection of human rights. Article 2(4), the Charter provision relevant to both these purposes prohibits "the threat or use of force against the territorial integrity or political independence of any State, or in any other manner inconsistent with the Purposes of the United Nations." Since humanitarian interventions by states, far from being inconsistent with Charter purposes, actually may further one of the world organization's major objectives in many situations, such interventions run afoul of Article 2(4) only if they are thought to affect the "territorial integrity" or "political independence" of the state against which they are directed. Brownlie, adopting what one commentator has called "an arid textualist approach," considers all humanitarian interventions by States to have such an effect and hence to violate the Charter. Taking what Professor Stone has labeled "the extreme view" of Article 2(4), he rejects out-of-hand Stone's argument that what the article prohibits is not all threats or uses of force, but only those actions specifically directed against "the territorial integrity" or "political independence" of a state. "This argument," Brownlie states, "is used by very few lawyers and has long been discredited."

Stone's view is a minority one, admittedly, but, far from being "discredited," it seems to be gaining new recruits annually, at least insofar as humanitarian intervention is concerned. While the present writer agrees with Brownlie that "[c]ounting heads is not, of course, a sound way of resolving issues of principle," in view of the thirteen authorities Brownlie cites in his attempt to demonstrate that humanitarian intervention by states violates the

United Nations Charter, a few contrary authorities should be mentioned here. First and foremost among these scholars is McDougal, who, several years ago, reassessing his earlier position, acknowledged that

> I'm ashamed to confess that at one time I lent my support to the suggestion that article 2(4) and the related articles did preclude the use of self-help less than self-defense. On reflection, I think this was a very grave mistake, that article 2(4) and article 51 must be interpreted differently. . . . In the absence of collective machinery to protect against attack and deprivation, I would suggest that the principle of major purposes requires an interpretation which would honor self-help against prior unlawfulness. The principle of subsequent conduct certainly confirms this. Many states of the world have used force in situations short of the requirements of self-defense to protect their national interests.

In collaboration with Reisman, he subsequently utilized this revised approach to justify non-United Nations intervention to prevent serious human rights deprivations. Brownlie casually dismisses their conclusions on the ground that McDougal and Reisman "lean heavily on a flexible and teleological interpretation of treaty texts," but surely the convincing arguments they marshall, and which Brownlie in large measure chooses to ignore, deserve consideration.

   In the first place, it should be noted that the above approach to humanitarian intervention is conditioned upon "the absence of collective machinery" to protect human rights, not upon a preference for unilateral over collective intervention. Effective United Nations action remains everyone's goal. The real issue, which Brownlie largely ignores, and which is made especially poignant by events in Bangladesh, is whether, absent such action in serious human-rights deprivation cases, states today must sit by and do nothing merely because Article 2(4) arguably was intended by its drafters in 1945 to preclude unilateral humanitarian interventions. Doctrinal analysis of Article 2(4), much of it written shortly after the Charter's adoption or based upon attitudes and expectations formed during the immediate post-war period, frequently fails to mention that, to the extent that states consciously relinquished the right to use forcible self-help, they took such action under the assumption that the collective implementation measures envisaged by Chapter VII soon would be available. Yet even staunch supporters of the collective approach, such as Judge Jessup, admitted that unilateral humanitarian interventions might be permissible if the United Nations lacked the capacity to act speedily. . . .

   Reisman, who accepts the . . . thesis that the United Nations Charter does not absolutely rule out forcible self-help, acknowledges that, as a historical interpretation, the contrary view espoused by Brownlie and other writers is "quite accurate."

> From the standpoint of the contemporary needs of the international community however, it is clearly outmoded. Only in the most exceptional cases will

the United Nations be capable of functioning as an international enforcer; in the vast majority of cases, the conflicting interests of diverse public order systems will block any action. A rational and contemporary interpretation of the Charter must conclude that article 2(4) suppresses self-help insofar as the organization can assume the role of enforcer. When it cannot, self-help prerogatives revive.

As the above extract reveals . . . Reisman regards the right as conditional. Hence his statement that, given the present status of the United Nations, "self-help prerogatives revive," and his correlative comment elsewhere about "the partial suspension of the full thrust of Article 2(4)." . . . Reisman's approach . . . clearly contemplates the gradual phasing out of the doctrine as the United Nations develops the capacity and the will to act in such situations.

In addition to being conditional, the McDougal-Reisman approach to humanitarian intervention relies upon a major-purposes construction of the Charter, under which the protection of human rights is accorded equal weight with the maintenance of peace. As mentioned above, this construction would permit humanitarian intervention by states despite Article 2(4) when such intervention [was] consistent with human rights objectives. "A close reading of [Article 2(4)] will indicate that the prohibition is not against the use of coercion per se," Reisman . . . has observed, "but rather the use of force for specified unlawful means. . . ." He continues:

> Since a humanitarian intervention seeks neither a territorial change nor a challenge to the political independence of the state involved and is not only not inconsistent with the Purposes of the United Nations but is rather in conformity with the most fundamental peremptory norms of the Charter, it is distortion to argue that it is precluded by Article 2(4). Insofar as it is precipitated by intense human rights deprivations and conforms to the general international legal regulations governing the use of force — economy, timeliness, commensurance, lawfulness of purpose and so on — it represents a vindication of international law, and is, in fact, substitute or functional enforcement.

Although this construction of Article 2(4) has been called an exercise in "doctrinal manipulation" by Farer, it at least merits more examination than it has received from Brownlie.

The latter . . . adopts a rather fatalistic attitude toward the human-rights deprivations his rigid construction of Article 2(4) tolerates. . . . Unlike Friedmann, who comes to the same result but finds it "a painful conclusion to reach," there is little evidence that Brownlie has contemplated the costs in terms of human life and dignity his construction of the Charter demands. Other authorities, including several cited by Brownlie to support his absolute view of Article 2(4), have made careful cost-benefit analyses and have concluded that Article 2(4) does not constitute an absolute prohibition against all unilateral humanitarian interventions. Among the contemporary commentators taking the position, in addition to

McDougal, Reisman, Stone, and the present writer, are the following: Alford, Goldie, Lauterpacht, J. N. Moore, Nanda, Perez-Vera, Röling, Thapa, and Verzijl.

Finally, the McDougal-Reisman approach to humanitarian intervention, conditioned upon the absence of collective action and otherwise consistent with the major purposes of the Charter, receives substantial support from the conduct of states and the response of the United Nations itself during the post-Charter period. Granted that this pattern of conduct falls far short of a consensus approving the doctrine, neither is it "totally inadequate to the task of establishing an interpretation in terms of subsequent conduct of the parties favourable to intervention to protect human rights." Indeed, only one holding an exceptionally narrow view of international law and relations would conclude, as Brownlie does, that "[t]he period of the United Nations Charter is totally lacking in practice on the point." By ruling arbitrarily that certain state conduct does not constitute practice, and by ignoring completely the implications to be drawn from certain decisions (or non-decisions) of the United Nations during the past decade, he adopts the posture commonly attributed to the ostrich.

Without examining once again the Stanleyville rescue operation . . . it is worth considering what that operation and the ensuing United Nations debate generated by it reveal about the world community's attitude toward humanitarian intervention claims twenty years after the Charter's enactment. While African accusations in the United Nations against the intervening states — Belgium, Great Britain, and the United States — occasionally bordered on the slanderous, they generally were grounded upon the political rather than the legal aspects of the case. Thus even the Sudanese representative observed that "[i]n normal circumstances, it would be difficult to oppose a rescue operation for humanitarian purposes." The debate does show, as Higgins concludes, that "the international community is reluctant to approve such interventions," but it also should be noted that, in the vague Resolution finally adopted by the Security Council, "[d]eploring the recent events in [the Democratic Republic of the Congo]," "[t]he concept of humanitarian intervention was not mentioned, and Belgium and the United States received no official condemnation." Indeed, a recent student notewriter suggests that the Resolution constitutes an implied if not an express approval of the operation: "After the Congo debates, the legal principle of Article 2(4) remains, but what that Article means has been altered by political evolution. There is now an unwillingness on the part of the world community to read Article 2(4) as an absolute prohibition on the use of force in humanitarian intervention."

One must be careful, of course, not to overclarify the outcome of the above decision (or non-decision) of the United Nations. Moreover, other actions of the United Nations, such as the adoption of a broad non-intervention principle in the recently-adopted Declaration on Principles of International Law Concerning Friendly Relations and Co-Operation

Among States in Accordance with the Charter of the United Nations, cut against the implied approval thesis advanced by the above notewriter. Nevertheless, the fact that neither the Stanleyville rescue operation nor any other claimed humanitarian intervention has been condemned by the United Nations as a violation of Article 2(4), in marked contrast to its repeated condemnation of claims to use forcible self-help by way of reprisals, throws considerable light upon the world community's attitude toward humanitarian interventions today. At the very least, this practice shows that such interventions might be considered condonable in appropriate instances, a view kited by Brownlie that warrants serious study.

III. A Plea for Constructive Alternatives

It is common ground between Brownlie and most authorities, including the present writer, that humanitarian interventions by the United Nations are preferable to such interventions by individual states. As he rightly observes, "[u]nder Chapter VII of the Charter, action may be taken in instances of violations of human rights which give rise to a threat to the peace." Moreover, other authorities, such as Ermacora, contend that, under recent United Nations resolutions, gross or consistent patterns of violations of human rights "are no longer essentially within the domestic jurisdiction of States, and therefore the principle of non-intervention is not applicable." Unfortunately, despite the fact that these jurisdictional bases for remedial action by the world organization exist, "[a] model which accords primary competence to the United Nations to intervene for humanitarian purposes does not . . . reflect the present conditions of the [international] system." A combination of the failure to establish a permanent international military force and the existence of the veto power, records Friedmann, has "effectively destroyed the power of the United Nations to act as an organ of enforcement of international law against a potential lawbreaker." He thus reaches the pessimistic conclusion that, like it or not, in the immediate future "the effective power of using military or lesser forms of coercion in international affairs essentially remains with the nation States."

Brownlie, apparently living in what Reisman has dubbed "the paper world of the Charter," considers humanitarian interventions by the United Nations to be more reliable than such interventions by individual states. It is difficult, if not impossible, to find support for this view in the events of the past decade. In the case of the Stanleyville rescue operation, for example, the United Nations failed to take effective action during a four-month period between the seizure of the hostages and the airdrop by the intervening states. At about the same time, as Brownlie himself points out, "there were far more serious and persistent threats to human rights which were ignored. In 1965, not less than 300,000 persons of Chinese origin were murdered in Indonesia." Yet the United Nations and its Member States, supporting his

[handwritten marginal notes at top: × not to act by them. × not act alone × sh, Reach extn - all 1-organization]

observation that "[t]he whole field is riven by political expediency and capriciousness," did nothing. The dismal failure of the United Nations with
respect to Bangladesh is too recent to need recounting. From these instances and others one is compelled to conclude that, at the very least, "the
prospects for effective United Nations actions are presently weak." Indeed,
without overstatement, they may be said to be almost nonexistent.

Given this bleak outlook, one would have thought that Brownlie and
other proponents of the view that humanitarian interventions are permissible only when undertaken by the United Nations would have turned their
attention to strengthening its capacity to respond in such situations. At the
very least, one would have expected from them a body of literature canvassing the difficulties and suggesting possible solutions to the obvious procedural defects, such as the absence of a standby international expeditionary
force and the presence of the veto power, both of which must be remedied
before effective and uniform humanitarian interventions by the United Nations can become a reality. One especially would have welcomed serious
examination of the conventional wisdom which places collective interventions in a preferred position over unilateral ones. Yet the writings of Brownlie and like-minded authorities make no mention of these problems.
Likewise, they are wholly devoid of constructive alternatives to the admittedly "unreliable" response by the United Nations. Brownlie's message in
the preceding chapter, for instance, amounts to no more than a plea to keep
the "faith in collective action. . . ."

If, as Falk has remarked, "the renunciation of intervention does not
substitute a policy of nonintervention; it involves the development of some
form of collective intervention," then concomitantly the failure to develop
effective international machinery to facilitate humanitarian interventions
arguably permits a state to intervene unilaterally in appropriate situations.
Writing a decade ago, Ronning wisely observed that "it is useless to outlaw
intervention without providing a satisfactory substitute as it was to outlaw
war when no satisfactory substitute was available." . . .

If, as seems to be the case, "a simple prohibition to intervene is unable
to cope with the problem of intervention," then surely, as the present writer
noted some years ago, the most important task confronting international
lawyers is "to clarify the various criteria by which the legitimacy of a state's
use of forcible self-help in human rights situations can be judged." Nanda,
taking this approach, has suggested five such criteria: (1) a specific limited
purpose; (2) an invitation by the recognized government; (3) a limited
duration of the mission; (4) a limited use of coercive measures; and (5) a
lack of any other recourse. Occasionally overlapping these criteria but also
including several additional ones, the present writer has recommended elsewhere his own five tests by which a unilateral humanitarian intervention
should be judged: (1) the immediacy of the violation of human rights; (2)
the extent of the violation of human rights; (3) the existence of an invitation
by appropriate authorities; (4) the degree of coercive measures employed;

[handwritten marginal notes right side: ness propo not the invitation by com- to interven | uni or colle- interv | humanitarian]

[handwritten at bottom: Root Beer]

and (5) the relative disinterestedness of the state invoking the coercive measures. Moreover, Moore has suggested three further criteria: "a minimal effect on authority structures, a prompt disengagement consistent with the purpose of the action, and immediate full reporting to the Security Council and appropriate regional organizations."

Brownlie, invoking an analogy to euthanasia, the legalizing of which he assumes "would alter the moral climate and produce harmful abuse," rejects the above criteria as determinants of legitimacy, but accepts them as

> a fine basis for a political plea in mitigation in parliaments, U.N. organs and regional organizations. My euthanasia parallel applies here: a defence lawyer and a court still need to distinguish the false from the genuine case, as a matter of mitigation.

. . . Brownlie [thus] seems to have reached the camp of those authors who . . . "deny the legality of humanitarian intervention in law, but who condone it to a greater or less degree in practice."

Whether one regards humanitarian interventions as legal if they meet the various criteria recommended above, or whether one considers them illegal de jure, yet condonable de facto, if they satisfy the selfsame criteria, seems to the present writer of more jurisprudential than practical importance. Like Falk, who while condemning reprisals nevertheless has worked out a systematic framework for the assessment of claims to use retaliatory force, Brownlie apparently believes that the above criteria, largely based upon the traditional doctrine of humanitarian intervention, are acceptable illustrations of "a kind of second-order level of legal inquiry that is guided by the more permissive attitudes toward the use of force to uphold national interests that is contained in customary international law." . . . Under this highly sophisticated approach, subsequently adopted and developed by Bowett, numerous criteria are formulated which, when met by a state taking unilateral action, may prevent its running afoul of the United Nations Security Council. The Security Council's recent resolution which avoids condemning India for its invasion of East Pakistan (now Bangladesh) might be considered an example of this "second-order legality" approach. The parallel to Brownlie's euthanasia analogy is obvious.

If the present writer has not overclarified Brownlie's position, it would appear that, at least as to outcome, there is actually little difference between their views. While this writer prefers a doctrinal approach which forthrightly sanctions unilateral humanitarian interventions when they meet detailed criteria to one which unqualifiedly proscribes such interventions but condones them when compatible with the selfsame criteria, he nevertheless welcomes Brownlie's tentative contribution to the current debate on humanitarian intervention. Hopefully, in his subsequent writings, Brownlie will give serious consideration not only to refining the above criteria, for whatever purposes they may be of use, but also to establishing procedures under which humanitarian interventions through the United Nations someday may take place. Both Reisman's Protocol of Procedure for Humanitarian Intervention and Senator Edward Kennedy's proposal for an Emergency Relief Force may be too ambitious for today's fragmented world community, but these and other innovative recommendations certainly deserve more attention than they have received to date. Granted that most international lawyers have been remiss in their failure to address such procedural problems, Brownlie and other authorities critical of unilateral humanitarian intervention have a special obligation to respond to this plea for constructive alternatives.

Bibliography (Humanitarian Intervention by States)

There has been much commentary on the doctrine of humanitarian intervention by states in the post-Bangladesh era. A number of books, in whole or in part, consider the topic. See Intervention in World Politics (H. Bull ed. 1984); The Current Legal Regulation of the Use of Force (A. Cassesse ed. 1986); Humanitarian Intervention and the United Nations (R. Lillich ed. 1973); Law and Civil War in the Modern World (J.N. Moore ed. 1974); N. Ronzitti, Rescuing Nationals Abroad Through Military Coercion and Intervention on Grounds of Humanity (1985); F. Teson, Humanitarian Intervention: An Inquiry into Law and Morality (1987). For over 30 articles on the topic, see R. Lillich, International Human Rights: Problems of Law, Policy, and Practice 604-606 (2d ed. 1991).

Although most recent writing has focused primarily, if not exclusively, on UN humanitarian intervention (see Bibliography (UN Humanitarian Intervention) at pages 663-664 infra), the contemporary status of the legal doctrine of humanitarian intervention by states continues to draw commentary. See, e.g., Nanda, Tragedies in Northern Iraq, Liberia, Yugoslavia, and Haiti — Revisiting the Validity of Humanitarian Intervention Under International Law — Part I, 20 Denv. J. Intl. L. & Poly. 205 (1992); Note, The Contemporary Legality of Unilateral Humanitarian Intervention, 24 Cal. W. Intl. L.J. 117 (1993); Note, Unilateral Humanitarian Intervention Legalizing the Use of Force to Prevent Human Rights Atrocities, 16 Fordham Intl. L.J. 120 (1992-1993).

C. The Aftermath of a Crisis: Bangladesh Since 1971

That the achievement of statehood by a politically oppressed people is far from being a panacea for the other ills — generally economic ones — that afflict them has been nowhere better demonstrated than by the case of Bangladesh. Seldom if ever has a new state been faced with such staggering problems as confronted this one in 1971 and the years that followed. In its three decades of independence, it has been plagued by low administrative and governmental capacity, political instability, endemic corruption, widespread poverty (an estimated 40 percent of the population subsist *below* the absolute poverty level), a pitifully inadequate natural resource base, rapid population growth in a country of over 118 million people packed into an area about the size of Wisconsin, and a vulnerability to a variety of natural disasters. The country remains the recipient of some of the largest amounts of international aid in the world, but these billions of dollars seem to have accomplished little save to multiply opportunities for corruption and black marketeering.

It, therefore, should come as little surprise that democratic institutions have found Bangladesh to be a forbidding place in which to take root. Over the years, attempts have been made to establish a genuine parliamentary system. However, Bangladesh's first two popularly chosen Presidents were assasinated in office. The country has alternated between civil and military rule, spending about one-half of its years since independence under martial law administrations. For over two decades, groups of tribal insurgents, some allegedly supported by India, have been fighting for autonomy in the Chittigong Hills Tracts. This situation reflects the staggering magnitude of Bangladesh's economic and social problems, coupled with a belief among the military that they should always be prepared to assume authority and responsibility for the country's affairs. Consequently, Bangladesh has continued to face many problems in the area of human rights.

Sheikh Mujibur Rahman became both the first President and Premier of Bangladesh after independence, announcing that socialism would be introduced by democratic means. However, it soon became clear that the reality would prove more difficult than the promise. In January 1975, he assumed dictatorial powers and converted Bangladesh into a one-party state. In August 1975, a military coup took place, overthrowing and killing him. After two coups within the space of a week, Major General Zia ur-Rahman emerged in November 1975 as "martial law administrator." He abolished both the Parliament and the Council of Ministers.

Zia assumed the presidency in 1977 and presided over a reform of the constitution that led to some strengthening of the country's political institutions, as well as relief from the martial law court system, which had been the cause of various human rights abuses. However, he, too, was assassinated on 30 May 1981 by a small group of dissident army officers. The constitutional machinery survived the coup and provided for a relatively fair election in November 1981, but the elected government of Abdus Sattar failed to establish any kind of power base or to reach an accommodation with the military. On 24 March 1982, in a bloodless coup, the military leaders again proclaimed martial law, suspending the constitution and granting the new administration draconian powers. Most basic human rights were left unprotected, and fears of government violations of these rights dramatically increased.

The military rulers, however, were relatively restrained in exercising their theoretically unlimited powers. Led by General H.M. Ershad, who proclaimed himself President in December 1983, they held the first parliamentary elections in seven years in May 1986. In October of that year, Ershad, who had retired from the army, was elected to a five-year term as President. On 10 November 1986, he officially lifted martial law.

The revised constitution was in operation for most of 1987, though parliamentary proceedings were marred by opposition walkouts. In November 1987, Ershad declared a state of emergency and dissolved Parliament after street protests and a general strike, caused at least in part by distress over serious flooding that occurred in August and September. On 12 April 1988, the state of emergency was lifted and a new Parliament elected, with Ershad's Jatiya Party winning 252 of the 300 seats. The election was heavily boycotted and did little to solve the conflicts between Ershad and opposition leaders. Eventually, on 6 December 1990, Ershad again dissolved Parliament. Later that same day he swore in Chief Justice Shahabuddin Ahmen as Vice President, after which he resigned, permitting Ahmen to become Acting President of an interim government.

Countrywide parliamentary elections were held on 27 February 1991 under the scrutiny of international observers. The elections were widely regarded as free, fair, and unprecedented in the history of Bangladesh. After the National Assembly unanimously voted to amend the constitution to reintroduce a parliamentary form of government, an action endorsed by the electorate in a referendum held on 15 September 1991, Bangladesh again became a parliamentary democracy led by Prime Minister Begum Khaleda Zia. Her ruling Bangladesh Nationalist Party now has a parliamentary majority. The leading opposition party, the Awami League, is headed by Sheikh Hasina Wajed. The two leaders are bitter political enemies, and the opposition's call for early elections, backed up by street demonstrations, has caused some uncertainty in the country. Burns, "The 2 Women" of Bangladesh: At the Top, at Odds, N.Y. Times, July 28, 1994, at A4, cols. 3-6. Since the human rights situation seems to be improving slightly, one can only hope that democracy will take root at long last. U.S. Dept. of State, Country Reports on Human Rights Practices for 1993, at 1319 (1994); Amnesty International, 1994 Ann. Rep. 67 (1994).

D.   *Other Claims of Unilateral Humanitarian Intervention Since the Bangladesh Crisis*

The Indian intervention in the Bangladesh war for independence may have been the most spectacular intervention of the 1970s, but it was not the only one. During the past two decades, several such uses of force by individual states have been justified, at least in some quarters, by invoking the doctrine of humanitarian intervention. A brief list of these interventions includes the following:

Syrian Occupation(s) of Lebanon, 1976. In April 1976, Syrian troops, acting in concert with other Arab League forces, intervened in the bloody civil war that has ravaged Lebanon from 1975 until the present. This intervention helped bring the bloodshed to a temporary halt, but continuing political factionalism saw a renewal of the conflict throughout most of the 1980s. Thus, evaluating this episode is difficult. That Syria initially performed a humanitarian task in helping to bring the war to a halt cannot be denied. However, some of its actions since that time, especially its outright rejection of the Lebanese-Israeli Withdrawal Agreement of 17 May 1982, suggest that its primary interest is to maintain a sphere of influence over the region, even to the point of inhibiting efforts to settle the conflict. See McDowall, Lebanon: A Conflict of Minorities 18 (Minority Rights Group Report No. 61, 1986).

Vietnamese Invasion of Kampuchea, 1978-1979. On 25 December 1978, the Vietnamese armed forces, accompanied by Cambodian rebels, invaded Kampuchea, eventually occupying the country and bringing to an end the genocidal Khmer Rouge regime headed by Pol Pot. Vietnam claimed that it was exercising its right of self-defense in response to Kampuchean armed attacks, and that in any event the Khmer Rouge government was overthrown by the rebels. As was the case with the Syrian intervention in Lebanon, the Vietnamese invasion brought to an end the slaughter of Kampuchean innocent civilians, thus achieving a humanitarian result. The extent to which Vietnam's actions were motivated by other factors remains unclear, although by the end of 1989 Vietnamese troops had ended their occupation of Kampuchea. See Bazyler, Reexamining the Doctrine of Humanitarian Intervention in Light of the Atrocities in Kampuchea and Ethiopia, 23 Stan. J. Intl. L. 547, 607-611 (1987).

Tanzanian Intervention in Uganda, 1979. This case, which is probably the most likely candidate for legitimate humanitarian intervention status, is considered at pages 76-78 of Problem I.

French Intervention in Central Africa, 1979. On 20-21 September 1979, the dictator Jean-Bedel Bokassa, self-proclaimed emperor of the Central African Empire, was overthrown by local opposition supported by 1,800 French troops. The rebellion and intervention were sparked by verified reports of atrocities committed by Bokassa's regime, especially the massacre of schoolchildren. This case, too, is a likely candidate for legitimate humanitarian intervention status, since "[t]he humanitarian motives of France can hardly be doubted." F. Teson, Humanitarian Intervention: An Inquiry into Law and Morality 177 (1987).

U.S. Operation in Grenada, 1983. On 25-28 October 1983, United States troops landed in and took control of Grenada, overthrowing that country's Marxist government. The United States did not invoke the doctrine of humanitarian intervention, relying instead on a request from the Governor-General, an invitation from the Organization of Eastern Caribbean States, and the doctrine of forcible self-help to protect nationals abroad (on this latter rationale, see page 673 infra). However, some commentators have examined the operation from the perspective of humanitarian intervention principles. See, e.g., F. Teson, supra, at 188-200; Riggs, The Grenada Intervention: A Legal Analysis, 109 Mil. L. Rev. 1, 36-43 (1985); Note, The Grenada Invasion: Expanding the Scope of Humanitarian Intervention, 8 B. C. Intl. & Comp. L. Rev. 413 (1985).

U.S. Invasion of Panama, 1989. In the early morning of 20 December 1989, United States troops stationed in the Canal Zone, aided by an equal number deployed from the United States, invaded Panama in a successful, albeit costly, effort to topple the regime of General Manuel Noriega. While the United States justified its action on the ground, inter alia, of the need "to protect the lives of American citizens in Panama," Leich, Contemporary Practice of the United States Relating to International Law, 84 Am. J. Intl. L. 536, 546 (1990), as in the case of Grenada it did not invoke the doctrine of humanitarian intervention. For an unconvincing attempt to justify the invasion on this basis, see D'Amato, The Invasion of Panama Was a Lawful Response to Tyranny, 84 id. 516 (1990).

Note that none of the states in the above six cases relied upon the doctrine of humanitarian intervention to justify its actions. Thus, whatever states have done in fact, their legal arguments provide scant support for the doctrine. Even when dealing in abstracto with the question, state practice has not been supportive, at least until relatively recently.

One marked exception is Great Britain, which has gone on record twice during the past decade, first rejecting, then endorsing, unilateral humanitarian intervention. In 1984 the British Foreign and Commonwealth Office (FCO) produced a paper for internal use, later extracted in United Kingdom Materials on International Law 1986, 57 Brit. Y.B. Intl. L. 614 (1986), in which it noted that "[a] substantial body of opinion and of practice [supports] the view that when a state commits cruelties against and persecution of its nationals in such a way as to deny their fundamental human rights and to shock the conscience of mankind, intervention in the interest of humanity is legally permissible." Id. at 618. It concluded, however, that:

> the overwhelming majority of contemporary legal opinion comes down against the existence of a right of humanitarian intervention, for three main reasons: first, the UN Charter and the corpus of modern international law do not seem specifically to incorporate such a right; secondly, state practice in the past two centuries, and especially since 1945, at best provides only a handful of genuine cases of humanitarian intervention, and, on most assessments, none at all; and finally, on prudential grounds, that the scope for abusing such a right argues strongly against its creation. . . . In essence, therefore, the case against making humanitarian intervention an exception to the principle of non-intervention is that its doubtful benefits would be heavily outweighed by its costs in terms of respect for international law.

Id. at 619.

More recently, however, in giving evidence before the House of Commons, the FCO's Legal Counsellor, during a colloquy over UN humanitarian intervention, took the position that "the intervention in northern Iraq 'Provide Comfort' was in fact, not specifically mandated by the United Nations, but the states taking action in northern Iraq did so in exercise of the customary international law principle of humanitarian intervention." Foreign Affairs Comm., H.C., The Expanding Role of the United Nations and Its Implications for UK Policy, Minutes of Evidence 85 (Dec. 2, 1992). Thus, it would appear that at least one of the permanent members of the Security Council now accepts that, where there is "a severe human rights and humanitarian situation," unilateral humanitarian intervention may be legally justified under contemporary international law. See also id. at 92.

E.   *Nicaragua v. United States: Delphic Dicta from the International Court of Justice*

As the above readings on the doctrine of humanitarian intervention indicate (see pages 614-641 supra), state practice, not arbitral or judicial decisions, has been the grist for the scholarly mills in this area of international law. In its 1986 Judgment in the Case Concerning Military and Paramilitary Activities in and Against Nicaragua, however, the International Court of Justice uttered some dicta that seem to suggest that the use of force to protect human rights, at least under the facts of that case, cannot be justified under customary international law (or, by analogy, under the UN Charter). Extracts from the Judgment and two views of its impact upon the doctrine of humanitarian intervention follow.

Nicaragua v. United States, Merits
1986 I.C.J. 14, 134-135

The Court also notes that Nicaragua is accused by the 1985 findings of the United States Congress of violating human rights. . . .
. . . [W]hile the United States might form its own appraisal of the situation as to respect for human rights in Nicaragua, the use of force could not be the appropriate method to monitor or ensure such respect. With regard to the steps actually taken, the protection of human rights, a strictly humanitarian objective, cannot be compatible with the mining of ports, the destruction of oil installations, or again with the training, arming and equipping of the *contras*. The Court concludes that the argument derived from the preservation of human rights in Nicaragua cannot afford a legal justification for the conduct of the United States, and cannot in any event be reconciled with the legal strategy of the respondent State, which is based on the right of collective self-defence.

Rodley, Human Rights and Humanitarian Intervention: The Case Law of the World Court
38 Intl. & Comp. L.Q. 321, 332 (1989)

This language unmistakably places the Court in the camp of those who claim that the doctrine of humanitarian intervention is without validity. Under that doctrine a State could rely on an alleged exception to the principle prohibiting unilateral resort to armed force by one State against another, where the purpose of its intervention was to protect persons (other than its own citizens) from serious and widespread violations of their human rights. It has been a doctrine defended in recent years by commentators, rather than by States. The States that might have been expected to invoke it (India, in respect of Bangladesh; Vietnam, in respect of Kampuchea; Tanzania, in respect of Uganda; and the United States itself, in respect of Grenada) have been notably hesitant to do so, at least in their formal legal justifications for their actions.

The Court's confirmation of the inapplicability of the doctrine should not be seen as a setback for human rights. There is nothing in its history to suggest that it was ever more than a rare and arbitrary alleviation of the hapless plight of those who happened to be suffering in a small country where the political interests of a militarily more powerful country conduced to the intervention. The ruling is more a clarification aimed at preventing breaches of international peace and security.

F. Teson, Humanitarian Intervention: An Inquiry into Law and Morality
241-244 passim (1987)

The Court's holding on humanitarian intervention must be construed in the light of the Nicaraguan reality. Indeed, although at the time of this writing the human rights situation in Nicaragua is a matter of serious concern, it has not reached the grave proportions that would authorize other states to seek forcible remedies. . . . The United States forcible intervention, to meet the test of legality suggested in this book, must be genuinely aimed at effectively restoring human rights (even if it entertains additional objectives). The intervention must also be necessary, proportionate, and welcomed by the victims themselves.

Those acts of the United States in support of the *contras* that involve the *direct* use of force do not seem to withstand scrutiny under those standards. . . . [A]s the Court correctly points out, acts like the mining of harbors are incompatible with a humanitarian objective. Such an action sheds doubt on the presence of the first requirement, that the intervention has to have chiefly humanitarian objectives.

The *indirect* use of force, that is, what the Court describes as "arming, training" of the Nicaraguan rebels does not fare very well under the humanitarian intervention test either. To be sure, the Court's assertion that arming and training rebels is *incompatible* with humanitarian objectives is mistaken. Again, if the *contras* were the pro-human rights forces fighting against an oppressive regime, one that would extensively and gravely violate human rights, foreign support for them would amount to humanitarian intervention par excellence. Still, it is not possible to say that the United States has met the first requirement of humanitarian intervention — that the intervention must be genuinely aimed at restoring human rights — in its support for the Nicaraguan rebels. . . .

. . . [T]he United States efforts in Nicaragua do not seem to meet the other requirements either: necessity, proportionality and welcome by the local population. As to necessity, the United States should have used less intrusive means first. For example, the United States could have appeared before the Court and perhaps could have even countersued Nicaragua for human rights violations. Or the United States could have ratified the human rights conventions and resorted to those mechanisms to force the Sandinistas to keep their human rights promises. Nor do the United States actions in Nicaragua . . . seem to meet the proportionality test. While the violations of human rights in Nicaragua are a reality, it is doubtful that they have reached proportions that would justify the forcible actions that the United States was accused of performing. The human rights situation in Nicaragua does not seem so grave, in terms of what I have called disrespectful human rights violations, as to justify departure from the prohibition against the use of force. The final requirement, that the oppressed population must welcome the intervention, does not seem to have been met either. Most of the population, while not enthusiastically pro-Sandinista, would most probably oppose United States intervention. Because humanitarian intervention is defined as support for victims of oppression, the whole enterprise fails even if the United States envisions democracy and respect for human rights as a legitimate objective.

To conclude: The *Nicaragua* ruling must be read narrowly, as bearing only on these particular facts. Because the rebels are not clearly pro-human rights forces, and because the human rights violations do not seem grave enough, forcible methods to protect those rights are not justified *in this specific case*. The Court's ruling should not affect:

(a)   The right of states to use proportionate non-forcible means, such as diplomatic pressure, economic sanctions and non-military help to pro-human rights opposition in dictatorial states. In Central America, this entails the right of American states to hold Nicaragua to its commitment to democracy and human rights and thus prevent the Sandinistas from imposing a totalitarian dictatorship on the Nicaraguan people.

(b) The right of coercive intervention, including direct and indirect military action, to stop actual or potential serious and widespread violations of human rights, whenever such action may be undertaken with reasonable chance of success and with the support of the population.

The Court's discussion of human rights and humanitarian intervention is unsatisfactory. Its reasoning is overly pro-governmental and insufficiently concerned with human dignity. One cannot avoid the impression that the Court has missed a unique opportunity to develop the law in the sense of reinforcement of human rights. The main effect of the Court's endorsement of the sacredness of national borders will be to reassure tyrants from the right and the left against legitimate demands for freedom and human rights. Yet I fear that the Court did no more than reflect the moral impotence of international law as conventionally understood. If so, it is time to . . . start rethinking the law of nations in a fundamentally different way. International law must be wed to notions of legitimacy associated with human rights and political consent.

Comments and Questions on the Court's Dicta

1. Contrary to Teson's suggestion, the ICJ issued no "holding on humanitarian intervention." Its two-paragraph essay on the "use of force" to protect human rights (it did not employ the term "humanitarian intervention") was pure dictum, albeit dictum that undoubtedly will have an impact upon the doctrine of humanitarian intervention. Teson, supra, at 201. Since the United States had not relied upon humanitarian intervention arguments during the jurisdictional phase of the hearings, it is surprising that the Court raised them sua sponte at the merits stage after the United States had withdrawn from the proceedings. Admittedly, "the Court is not solely dependent on the argument of the parties before it with respect to the applicable law," 1986 I.C.J. at 24, but one can only speculate why the Court set up a "straw man" argument — for, as Teson correctly concludes, the doctrine of humanitarian intervention obviously did not justify the use of force by the United States — only to attempt to knock it down. As the Court itself stated, "the legal strategy of the [United States] is based on the right of collective self-defence," id. at 135, and having disposed of the case by ruling against the United States' arguments on this score, the Court's comments with respect to the use of force to protect human rights were unnecessary dicta.

2. Rodley asserts that the Court "unmistakably" ruled that the doctrine of humanitarian intervention has no legal validity. Elsewhere in his article he reiterates that the ICJ laid down a "clear prohibition of humanitarian intervention," and that "[o]n this issue, the Court could not have been

clearer." Rodley, supra, at 330, 332. Is the Court's Judgment in this respect so crystal clear? What about Teson's argument that the Judgment should be read narrowly, as bearing only upon the specific fact pattern of the case and, thus, not affecting the validity of a humanitarian intervention to remedy truly egregious human rights violations? Cf. Teson, Le Peuple, C'est Moi! The World Court and Human Rights, 81 Am. J. Intl. L. 173, 178 n.28 (1987): "The humanitarian intervention argument was expressly rejected by the Court in unduly broad terms."

3. Immediately preceding its discussion of the right to use force to protect human rights, the Court raised (and rejected) what it characterized as "a supposed rule of 'ideological intervention.'" It acknowledged that this "new principle" had been advanced solely in a political context and not as a legal argument by the United States. 1986 I.C.J. at 133-134. Apparently the concept would have justified discretionary interventions by states for a variety of foreign policy reasons.

Once again, one can only speculate why the ICJ elevated and then leveled this patently "straw man" argument. Perhaps it represents a "preemptive strike" against more focused arguments in favor of coercive measures to promote self-determination and prevent gross human rights abuses that had just appeared in the American Journal of International Law in the wake of the Grenada operation. Compare Reisman, Coercion and Self-Determination: Construing Charter Article 2(4), 78 Am. J. Intl. L. 642 (1984) with Schachter, The Legality of Pro-Democratic Invasion, 78 id. 645 (1984). Cf. D'Amato, Nicaragua and International Law: The "Academic" and the "Real," 79 id. 657, 659-661 (1985). In any event, it, too, constitutes unnecessary dicta.

4. It should be noted that Rodley, who reads the Nicaragua case as standing for the proposition "that individual States may not use armed force to intervene against other States on the ground of the latter's human rights record," Rodley, supra, at 333, recognizes the need for the United Nations and regional international organizations to develop the machinery to be able to act expeditiously in situations where gross violations of fundamental human rights are occurring.

> The need for increasingly effective measures, within the framework of competent inter-governmental organisations, to protect against grave and systematic human rights violations remains and is indeed underlined by the Nicaragua judgment. In recent years there has been an impressive development in the array of inter-governmental machinery available to investigate alleged human rights violations and even intercede on behalf of victims. However, criminal violations of human rights, such as torture, murder and prolonged or permanent abduction (the so-called "disappearance"), continue to be widely reported. If the ban on unilateral humanitarian intervention is to be politically credible, it should be accompanied by more determined inter-governmental action, not necessarily excluding coercive measures, to eliminate such practices.

Rodley, supra, at 332-333. See generally, Rodley, Collective Intervention to Protect Human Rights and Civilian Populations: The Legal Framework, in To Loose the Bands of Wickedness: International Intervention in Defence of Human Rights 14 (N. Rodley ed. 1992). For an earlier argument along similar lines, see Lillich, pages 638-641 supra.

III.   UN Humanitarian Intervention

In the preceding Section, both advocates and opponents of unilateral humanitarian intervention accept — generally without question, almost like a given — that "humanitarian interventions by the United Nations are preferable to such interventions by individual states." Lillich, page 638 supra. The underlying assumption of almost all commentators, too, drawing upon Rhodesia and South Africa as precedents, was that the UN possessed such powers, at least when the situation could be characterized as a "threat to the peace" within the meaning of Article 39 of the Charter. See page 613 supra. How the Security Council, should it have the opportunity, would apply its rather notional "threat to the peace" approach taken in the case of Rhodesia and South Africa — where systematic racial discrimination and self-determination issues were involved — to other human rights situations with less of an international profile was at the time so unlikely a possibility that it was not contemplated, albeit widely assumed. Also, few observers addressed the question of whether, absent such a determination by the Security Council, the UN had the power to take or authorize humanitarian interventions. One who did, the late Judge Baxter, found it difficult to locate Charter provisions that gave the Security Council the power, in his pithy phrase, to authorize "Swedes descending by parachute to keep the local populace from massacring itself." Baxter, Remarks, in Humanitarian Intervention and the United Nations 110 (R. Lillich ed. 1973).

Since the end of the Cold War, as we have seen in Problem VII (see Comment 17 at pages 598-599 supra), the Security Council has found a "threat to the peace" in at least seven situations and has ordered differing degrees of economic sanctions applied in all of them. In four cases — Iraq, Yugoslavia, Somalia, and, most recently, Haiti — it also has authorized, to one extent or another, forcible coercive measures. To what extent do these operations constitute "UN humanitarian intervention," and under what legal rationale can they be justified? What has been the reaction of UN member states, both in the Security Council and in the General Assembly, to these Security Council decisions and the precedents, no matter how circumscribed, they have been setting? The extract that follows chronicles developments from the end of the Gulf War through 1993, after which Security Council Resolution 940 of 31 July 1994 on Haiti and its impact and aftermath will be taken up.

Lillich, Humanitarian Intervention Through the United Nations: Towards the Development of Criteria
53 ZaoRV (Heidelberg J. Intl. L.) 557, 563-573 (1993)

II.   CONSTITUTIONAL UNDERPINNINGS OF UN
      HUMANITARIAN INTERVENTION

UN humanitarian interventions, to be justified on legal grounds, presumably must be authorized by the Security Council under Art. 42 after a finding, pursuant to Art. 39, that there exists a "threat to the peace, breach of the peace, or act of aggression. . . ." Absent such authorization, some observers have postulated that the General Assembly might be seised with the power to intervene pursuant to its Uniting-for-Peace Resolution or, *de lege ferenda*, proposed Uniting-Against-Genocide or Uniting-Against-Crimes-Against-Humanity resolutions. While the possible future role of the General Assembly in this regard is worthy of far more consideration than it has received to date, until now attention has been focused almost exclusively upon the Security Council. For this reason, it is the focus adopted for the balance of this Article.

One must begin a parsing of the authority granted the Council by Art. 39 by acknowledging the fact that, just as the Charter's drafters did not expressly address the doctrine of unilateral humanitarian intervention, so too "[n]othing in the *travaux* suggests that the parties envisioned a government's treatment of its own nationals as likely to catalyze a threat or breach" triggering potential Security Council action under Chapter VII. Subsequent Council practice, however, has put a gloss on the phrase "threat to the peace" and, especially during the past three years, has changed the attitudes and expectations of UN Member States with respect to the legitimacy, if not the likelihood, of UN humanitarian interventions. While these changes, following the end of the Cold War and the break-up of the former Soviet Union, may have come as a surprise, the Security Council's *de facto* amendment of the Charter to permit humanitarian intervention by the organization, regional organizations and Member States is in keeping with the constitutional law of the Charter. For, to paraphrase Chief Justice Hughes' remarks about the U.S. Constitution and the Supreme Court, the international community is bound by the UN Charter, but the Charter is what (in this case) the Security Council says it is.

The Security Council first interpreted a State's human rights violations to constitute a "threat to the peace" in 1968 when it adopted comprehensive mandatory economic sanctions in the case of Southern Rhodesia. Nine years later it used the same rationale when it imposed a mandatory arms embargo upon South Africa. These resolutions, while precedent-setting, nevertheless were so entwined with the issues of self-determination and apartheid that their value in situations involving other internal human rights deprivations is somewhat problematic.

The same cannot be said with respect to a Gulf War follow-up resolution designed to protect Iraqi nationals, primarily Kurds, from further repression by their Government. Security Council Resolution 688, adopted on 5 April 1991, noted the Council's responsibilities for the maintenance of international peace and security — an implied reference to Chapter VII — and expressed its concern that Iraq's actions had "led to a massive flow of refugees towards and across international frontiers and to cross border incursions, which threaten international peace and security." The resolution, which demanded that Iraq immediately end its repression and allow immediate access by international humanitarian organizations to all persons in need of assistance, contained no express reference to Chapter VII, however, nor did it specifically authorize the allied military intervention to create "safe havens" that subsequently took place.

Pease and Forsythe maintain that by adopting Resolution 688 "[t]he Security Council for the first time in its history stated a clear and explicit linkage between human rights violations materially within a state (although there were indeed international repercussions) and a threat to international security." They conclude, therefore, that "the Council clearly has the legal authority to authorize [*in futuro*] armed action, or lesser coercive measures, to correct human rights violations materially within a territorial state." Malanczuk, on the other hand, believes that "the resolution cannot be cited as precedent for the proposition that the Security Council views massive, but purely internal human rights violations as such, without transboundary effects, as a direct threat to international peace and security." Nor does he regard the resolution as precedent "for the authorization of the use of force by the Security Council to protect human rights in such circumstances." His more guarded conclusions seem persuasive. Nevertheless, the resolution remains a pathbreaking one insofar as it characterizes internal human rights deprivations having external effects as constituting a threat to international peace and security.

The most recent and striking "normative landmark of genuine Security Council practice of humanitarian intervention," however, is Resolution 794, adopted on 3 December 1992, concerning Somalia. After first determining that "the magnitude of the human tragedy caused by the conflict in Somalia, further exacerbated by the obstacles being created to the distribution of humanitarian assistance, constitutes a threat to international peace and security," the Council further determined "to restore peace, stability and law and order with a view to facilitating the process of a political settlement under the auspices of the United Nations, aimed at national reconciliation in Somalia. . . ." To achieve these objectives the Council, invoking Chapter VII, authorized the Secretary-General and cooperating Member States "to use all necessary means to establish as soon as possible a secure environment for humanitarian relief operations in Somalia. . . ."

It is noteworthy that this resolution, while invoking Chapter VII, makes no mention whatsoever of the effects, real or notional, of the Somalia crisis on neighboring States, specifically the flow of refugees. Likewise, in the debate leading up to Resolution 794, the principal focus was on the violence and vandalism occurring within Somalia, not on the actual or possible flow of refugees to neighboring States. Although the participants in the debate clearly recognized that the situation in Somalia had external repercussions, the sense of the Security Council was that the internal situation, in and of itself, warranted action and would anywhere that it might be replicated.

While the Somalian situation was very different from that which had presented itself in Iraq, the Security Council clearly saw common ground between Resolutions 688 and 794, namely, that internal disorders of such magnitude were a proper concern of the Council wherever they may occur. Thus, in voting for the resolution, the U.S. representative noted that, while the Council's immediate objective was to resolve the Somalia crisis, "the international community is also taking an important step in developing a strategy for dealing with the potential disorder and conflicts of the post-Cold War world." He added that "in the case of Somalia, and in other cases we are sure to face in the future, it is important that we send this unambiguous message: the international community has the intent and will to act decisively regarding peace-keeping problems that threaten international stability."

Heartening as it is to see the Security Council, freed from its Cold War shackles, move towards the recognition and clarification of a doctrine of UN-sanctioned humanitarian intervention, it should not be overlooked that the Council, the key player in this area, is not necessarily reflective of the views of many UN Member States. As Reisman reminds us, "[t]he United Nations system was essentially designed to enable the Permanent Five, if all agree, to use Charter obligations and the symbolic authority of the organization as they think appropriate to maintain or restore international peace, as they define it." A decision by the Security Council that a threat to the peace sufficient to warrant UN humanitarian intervention exists, according to Reisman,

> expands the Charter's contingencies for action under Art. 39 and engages the full authority of the United Nations, yet it need not be financed through the general budget and, hence, is not subject to control by the General Assembly. As such, [it] may aggravate certain latent tensions between the Permanent Five and the rest of the United Nations.

These tensions have surfaced recently in several contexts. In the *Lockerbie* case,* for instance, where Libya challenged as *ultra vires* a Security Council resolution — based upon a threat to the peace rationale — ordering it to surrender two of its nationals accused of bombing Pan Am 103, the International Court of Justice held that the resolution, taken under Chapter VII, preempted its jurisdiction under the Montreal Convention. Franck, likening the case to *Marbury* v. *Madison*, believes that "the Court has carefully, and quietly, marked its role as the ultimate arbiter of institutional legitimacy." "As in *Marbury*," he argues,

> the Court superficially appears to accede to the broad discretionary power of the system's political "branch." But, as in *Marbury*, it accedes not by refusing to decide, but by exercising its power of decision. The Security Council's action in imposing sanctions is adjudged *intra vires* precisely because the majority of judges seems to agree that, for purposes of interim measures, Art. 103 of the Charter "trumps" any rights Libya might have under the Montreal Convention, and thus frees the Security Council to apply sanctions as a suitable remedy in exercise of its powers under Chapter VII.

One need not share Franck's enthusiasm for this reading of *Lockerbie* to agree that the case raises the fundamental question of whether the Court, under the UN Charter, possesses the competence to review decisions of the Security Council taken under Chapter VII. Certainly, as Reisman has recently pointed out, "several judges in *Lockerbie* indicated, some more tentatively than others, that, under certain circumstances, a decision by the Security Council might be viewed as invalid by the Court." However, he finds it difficult to locate limitations in the Charter on the Security Council's actions taken when it is operating under Chapter VII, noting particularly that the term "threat to the peace" "has proved to be quite elastic in the hands of the Council." The very absence of limiting standards, he concludes, "in a context where so much power is assigned to the Council, is telling. A judicial review function, viewed in the formal Charter regime, seems somewhat difficult." The real significance of *Lockerbie*, therefore, may be less in the case itself than in the fact that it is the judicial manifestation of "an international constitutional struggle on many fronts, as the governments of the majority of small states seek some checks and balances on unrestrained Security Council action, just as they sought to impose them, without significant success, in San Francisco in the spring of 1945."

The political counterpart to the legal debate in and over *Lockerbie* is reflected throughout various UN fora. At the Security Council summit meeting in January 1992, Zimbabwe's Foreign Minister Shamuyarira, focusing upon UN humanitarian intervention, posed the issue with especial cogency and caution:

---

* Questions of Interpretation and Application of the 1971 Montreal Convention Arising from the Aerial Incident at Lockerbie (*Libya* v. *U.K.*; *Libya* v. *U.S.*), Provisional Measures, 1992 ICJ Rep. 3, 114 (Orders of Apr. 14).

In the era we are entering, the Council will be called upon to deal more and more with conflicts and humanitarian situations of a domestic nature that could pose threats to international peace and stability. However, great care has to be taken to see that these domestic conflicts are not used as a pretext for the intervention of big Powers in the legitimate domestic affairs of small States, or that human rights issues are not used for totally different purposes of destabilizing other Governments. There is, therefore, the need to strike a delicate balance between the rights of States, as enshrined in the Charter, and the rights of individuals, as enshrined in the Universal Declaration of Human Rights.

Zimbabwe supports very strongly both the Universal Declaration of Human Rights and the Charter on these issues. Zimbabwe is a firm subscriber to the principles in the United Nations Declaration on Human Rights. However, we cannot but express our apprehension about who will decide when to get the Security Council involved in an internal matter and in what matter. In other words, who will judge when a threshold is passed that calls for international action? Who will decide what should be done, how it will be done, and by whom? This clearly calls for a careful drawing up and drafting of general principles and guidelines that would guide decisions on when a domestic situation warrants international action, by the Security Council or by regional organizations.

Shamuyarira's two rhetorical questions pose no particular problem and call for the same answer: the Security Council. His final point, the major purpose of this Article, is addressed in the next Section.

Conventional wisdom calls for the elaboration of criteria by which the legitimacy of UN humanitarian intervention may be judged. Since . . . most States can be expected to show little interest in such an exercise (pace the Zimbabwean Foreign Minister), the academic community and NGOs must take the initiative. As the former Secretary General of Amnesty International remarked in a recent lecture, "[t]he human rights movement has the principles and the impartiality to contribute to the definition of criteria for legitimate intervention, and it must work to develop the effectiveness of the UN and regional organizations in mounting and fully controlling such interventions." Until such criteria have been agreed upon, he observed, the movement "must remain inhibited in calling for armed intervention, even though only armed intervention can prevent the continued perpetration of mass violations."

Nevertheless, a cautionary word may be in order. Given the lack of prior precedent, criteria necessarily must be fashioned primarily from earlier ones developed to govern unilateral or collective humanitarian intervention or otherwise derived from principles of general international law. In either case, what is their juridical status: potential legal norms or merely policy recommendations? Since they obviously are not to be found in the text of the UN Charter, what is the impact of proposed criteria upon the Security Council's decision-making process under Chapter VII? Furthermore, is it even desirable to establish criteria during a time of rapid change, or is it not preferable to handle each situation, as Malanczuk has suggested, on a case-by-case basis? Schachter, a seasoned UN veteran, has warned against "a tendency on the part of those seeking to improve the United Nations to prescribe sets of rules for future cases, usually over-generalizing from past cases. Each crisis has its own configuration. Governments will always take account of their particular interests and the unique features of the case. While they can learn from the past, it is idle — and often counter-productive — to expect them to follow 'codified' rules for new cases."

Nevertheless, the greatly increased activity of the United Nations in the humanitarian intervention and assistance areas warrants fresh study and constructive criticism to ensure that the organization — primarily the Security Council — is not proceeding down a path that may damage its future capabilities and credibility. Categorizing actual or even likely massive human rights deprivations as threats to international peace and security has a compelling moral quality to it. Yet, unless the Security Council shows itself ready, willing and able to act effectively to address such situations without in fact contributing to their exacerbation, the new opportunities that the Council certainly will face could have adverse consequences not only for its capabilities to cope with massive human rights deprivation cases, but also to resolve other, more traditional threats to the peace.

At present, the Security Council's credibility as a protector and enforcer of human rights surely is at stake. The use of limited military force in Iraq and, more recently, in Somalia, has given credibility to the Council's decisions because it has demonstrated a resolve to enforce them effectively; earlier UN actions in Somalia and, lamentably to this day, its decisions with respect to the former Yugoslavia, were not backstopped by a credible authorization or even a reasonable threat to use force if Council demands were not met. Another aspect of the credibility problem concerns the Council's willingness to act consistently in the face of widespread human rights deprivations. While it has focused its attention on Iraq, the former Yugoslavia and Somalia, equally severe deprivations have occurred in numerous other countries — Angola, Haiti and Liberia have been mentioned — without provoking significant Council action.

To ensure even-handed treatment of roughly similar human rights situations and to guarantee wider acceptance of the legitimacy of future UN humanitarian interventions, it is recommended that the Security Council consider the following criteria in determining whether and how to intervene in a Member State for human rights purposes. This tentative list is not necessarily complete, and it is not closed: it is offered in the hope that it will provoke debate and, in the meantime, perhaps provide some useful guidance to decisionmakers in Government and at the United Nations. Presumably it will be generally acceptable to most such persons, since the list is derived not only from a revision and modification of the criteria developed to govern unilateral and collective humanitarian interventions, but also from statements made by the intervening States in the cases of Iraq and Somalia.

1. UN humanitarian intervention must be based on the actual existence or pending likelihood of gross and persistent human rights violations that shock the world's conscience. (Such violations occur, *inter alia*, from systematic and indiscriminate attacks on civilians by a central government, or a system breakdown in law and order producing the dislocation and starvation of the civilian population.)

2. The intervention should be authorized, except in rare cases, only after all reasonable diplomatic efforts on the international and regional level have been exhausted and have failed to bring about the cessation of such human rights violations.

3. The intervention must be strictly limited in scope to actions necessary and proportionate to bring about the cessation of such human rights violations.

4. The intervening forces must begin their withdrawal as soon as reasonably possible, and in any event complete such withdrawal within a reasonable period after the cessation of such human rights violations. (If a lengthy presence is necessary, the intervening forces, if possible, should be under the direct command and control of the United Nations.)

5. The intervention should preserve the territorial integrity of the target State, by which is meant that the State's boundaries, except in rare cases, should not be redrawn.

6. The intervention should not interfere with the authority structure of the target State, except where the cessation of human rights violations clearly is dependent upon the removal of the central government. (In the case of "failed States", e.g., Somalia, the intervening authorities should seek through UN auspices a national reconciliation based on the will of the people.)

The likelihood of prompt and impartial application of these criteria to situations involving actual or impending gross and persistent human rights violations obviously would be enhanced if the UN Security Council had its own capabilities to act and was no longer dependent upon the *ad hoc* initiatives of member States. In both Iraq and Somalia, the initiatives were taken and the military assets provided by major Western powers. The possibility of more, prompt and effective UN-authorized humanitarian interventions exists if the United Nations itself is provided greater capabilities to organize and command on short notice sufficient forces to carry out at least small or perhaps even mid-scale interventions. In such a case, charges that UN humanitarian interventions were Western-driven would lose much, if not all, of their validity.

Negotiation and conclusion of Art. 43 agreements between the United Nations and Member States for the provision of military forces, assistance and facilities to the organization on its call would expedite its ability to deploy "UN" forces promptly in humanitarian situations. The Secretary-General actually considered the option of a country-wide enforcement operation in Somalia to be carried out under UN command and control.

However, he concluded that the Secretariat did not "at present have the capability to command and control an enforcement operation of the size and urgency required by the present crisis in Somalia." Concluding Art. 43 agreements would allow for coordination and training of a truly multinational force in advance of a humanitarian crisis, along with resolving in advance any humanitarian intervention command and control issues and questions as to rules of engagement. While such agreements have not been thought achievable in the past, in today's post-Cold War climate States may find them more politically acceptable, especially if limited to humanitarian interventions rather than traditional actions to repel aggression or maintain the peace.*

Security Council Resolution 940 on Haiti
S.C. Res. 940, U.N. SCOR, 49th Sess., 3413th mtg., U.N. Doc. S/RES/940 (1994)

The Security Council,

Reaffirming its resolutions 841 (1993) of 16 June 1993, 861 (1993) of 27 August 1993, 862 (1993) of 31 August 1993, 867 (1993) of 23 September 1993, 873 (1993) of 13 October 1993, 875 (1993) of 16 October 1993, 905 (1994) of 23 March 1994, 917 (1994) of 6 May 1994 and 933 (1994) of 30 June 1994,

Recalling the terms of the Governors Island Agreement (S/26063) and the related Pact of New York (S/26297),

Condemning the continuing disregard of those agreements by the illegal de facto regime, and the regime's refusal to cooperate with efforts by the United Nations and the Organization of American States (OAS) to bring about their implementation,

Gravely concerned by the significant further deterioration of the humanitarian situation of Haiti, in particular the continuing escalation by the illegal de facto regime of systematic violations of civil liberties, the desperate plight of Haitian refugees and the recent expulsion of the staff of the International Civilian Mission (MICIVIH), which was condemned in its Presidential statement of 12 July 1994 (S/PRST/1994/32),

Having considered the reports of the Secretary-General of 15 July 1994 (S/1994/828 and Add.1) and 26 July 1994 (S/1994/871),

---

* In addition to Art. 43 agreements the suggestion has been made that the United Nations establish a small international volunteer force under the exclusive authority of the Security Council and the day-to-day direction of the Secretary-General. See Urquhart, For a UN Volunteer Military Force, 40 N.Y. Rev. Books No. 11, at 3 (June 10, 1993). Commentary on this proposal, generally favorable, may be found in A UN Volunteer Force — Four Views, 40 id. No. 12, at 58 (June 24, 1993); A UN Volunteer Force, 40 id. No. 13, at 52 (July 15, 1993). The likelihood of such a force being established by the United Nations in the near future seems remote.

Taking note of the letter dated 29 July 1994 from the legitimately elected President of Haiti (S/1994/905, annex) and the letter dated 30 July 1994 from the Permanent Representative of Haiti to the United Nations (S/1994/910),

Reiterating its commitment for the international community to assist and support the economic, social and institutional development of Haiti,

Reaffirming that the goal of the international community remains the restoration of democracy in Haiti and the prompt return of the legitimately elected President, Jean-Bertrand Aristide, within the framework of the Governors Island Agreement,

Recalling that in resolution 873 (1993) the Council confirmed its readiness to consider the imposition of additional measures if the military authorities in Haiti continued to impede the activities of the United Nations Mission in Haiti (UNMIH) or failed to comply in full with its relevant resolutions and the provisions of the Governors Island Agreement,

Determining that the situation in Haiti continues to constitute a threat to peace and security in the region,

1. Welcomes the report of the Secretary-General of 15 July 1994 (S/1994/828) and takes note of his support for action under Chapter VII of the Charter of the United Nations in order to assist the legitimate Government of Haiti in the maintenance of public order;

2. Recognizes the unique character of the present situation in Haiti and its deteriorating, complex and extraordinary nature, requiring an exceptional response;

3. Determines that the illegal de facto regime in Haiti has failed to comply with the Governors Island Agreement and is in breach of its obligations under the relevant resolutions of the Security Council;

4. Acting under Chapter VII of the Charter of the United Nations, authorizes Member States to form a multinational force under unified command and control and, in this framework, to use all necessary means to facilitate the departure from Haiti of the military leadership, consistent with the Governors Island Agreement, the prompt return of the legitimately elected President and the restoration of the legitimate authorities of the Government of Haiti, and to establish and maintain a secure and stable environment that will permit implementation of the Governors Island Agreement, on the understanding that the cost of implementing this temporary operation will be borne by the participating Member States;

5. Approves the establishment, upon adoption of this resolution, of an advance team of UNMIH of not more than sixty personnel, including a group of observers, to establish the appropriate means of coordination with the multinational force, to carry out the monitoring of the operations of the multinational force and other functions described in paragraph 23 of the report of the Secretary-General of 15 July 1994 (S/1994/828), and to assess requirements and to prepare for the deployment of UNMIH upon completion of the mission of the multinational force;

6. Requests the Secretary-General to report on the activities of the team within thirty days of the date of deployment of the multinational force;

7. Decides that the tasks of the advance team as defined in paragraph 5 above will expire on the date of termination of the mission of the multinational force;

8. Decides that the multinational force will terminate its mission and UNMIH will assume the full range of its functions described in paragraph 9 below when a secure and stable environment has been established and UNMIH has adequate force capability and structure to assume the full range of its functions; the determination will be made by the Security Council, taking into account recommendations from the Member States of the multinational force, which are based on the assessment of the commander of the multinational force, and from the Secretary-General;

9. Decides to revise and extend the mandate of the United Nations Mission in Haiti (UNMIH) for a period of six months to assist the democratic Government of Haiti in fulfilling its responsibilities in connection with:

(a) sustaining the secure and stable environment established during the multinational phase and protecting international personnel and key installations; and

(b) the professionalization of the Haitian armed forces and the creation of a separate police force;

10. Requests also that UNMIH assist the legitimate constitutional authorities of Haiti in establishing an environment conducive to the organization of free and fair legislative elections to be called by those authorities and, when requested by them, monitored by the United Nations, in cooperation with the Organization of American States (OAS);

11. Decides to increase the troop level of UNMIH to 6,000 and establishes the objective of completing UNMIH's mission, in cooperation with the constitutional Government of Haiti, not later than February 1996;

12. Invites all States, in particular those in the region, to provide appropriate support for the actions undertaken by the United Nations and by Member States pursuant to this and other relevant Security Council resolutions;

13. Requests the Member States acting in accordance with paragraph 4 above to report to the Council at regular intervals, the first such report to be made not later than seven days following the deployment of the multinational force;

14. Requests the Secretary-General to report on the implementation of this resolution at sixty-day intervals starting from the date of deployment of the multinational force;

15. Demands strict respect for the persons and premises of the United Nations, the Organization of American States, other international and humanitarian organizations and diplomatic missions in Haiti, and that no acts of intimidation or violence be directed against personnel engaged in humanitarian or peace-keeping work;

16. Emphasizes the necessity that, inter alia:

(a) All appropriate steps be taken to ensure the security and safety of the operations and personnel engaged in such operations; and

(b) The security and safety arrangements undertaken extend to all persons engaged in the operations;

17. Affirms that the Council will review the measures imposed pursuant to resolutions 841 (1993), 873 (1993) and 917 (1994), with a view to lifting them in their entirety, immediately following the return to Haiti of President Jean-Bertrand Aristide;

18. Decides to remain actively seized of the matter.

Note: The Significance of Resolution 940

The military junta that ousted Haiti's freely elected President, Jean-Bertrand Aristide, from office in 1991 ruled that impoverished country with the proverbial iron fist, relying upon murder, disappearances, torture, and intimidation to maintain itself in power. OAS efforts and UN sanctions relatively had little effect upon the military and business establishment. See pages 512 and 597-598 of Problem VII. Thus, it was argued for some time that "only a surgical lancing of the Haitian military carbuncle has a reasonable chance of breaking the army's hold and, simultaneously, of restoring the democratic initiative. An intervention could also bring to an end the massive suffering of the Haitian people." Rotberg, What Now in Haiti?, Boston Globe, Dec. 29, 1993, at 15, cols. 4-6. By mid-1994, the question of whether a humanitarian intervention should be mounted and, if so, what type — UN, OAS, or U.S. unilateral — was much debated. Compare Trainor, Clinton Should Send in the Troops to Haiti, Boston Globe, May 16, 1994, at 11, cols. 2-4 with Editorial, No Good Reason to Invade Haiti, N.Y. Times, July 13, 1994, at A18, cols. 1-2.

Eventually, the Clinton Administration took the matter to the UN Security Council and secured the adoption of Resolution 940, a far-reaching one that pushed past the Council's previous "normative landmark" (see page 653 supra) — Resolution 794 on Somalia (S.C. Res. 794, 47 U.N. SCOR, Res. and Dec. at 63 (1992)) — to authorize what arguably is the "purest" UN humanitarian intervention to date. In Resolution 940, the Council, after expressing its grave concern with "the significant further deterioration of the humanitarian situation in Haiti, in particular the continuing escalation by the illegal de facto regime of systematic violations of civil liberties," determined that "the situation in Haiti continue[d] to constitute a threat to peace and security in the region" and, invoking Chapter VII of the Charter,

> authorize[d] Member States to form a multinational force under unified command and control and, in this framework, to use all necessary means to facilitate the departure from Haiti of the military leadership, consistent with

the Governors Island Agreement, the prompt return of the legitimately elected President and the restoration of the legitimate authorities of the Government of Haiti. . . .

The code phrase "all necessary means," taken from Paragraph 2 of the Gulf War Resolution (S.C. Res. 678, 45 U.N. SCOR, Res. and Dec. at 27 (1990)) and Paragraph 10 of Resolution 794 on Somalia, supra, constituted an authorization by the UN of forcible intervention, if it was needed, to put an end to the gross human rights violations going on in Haiti. While there is a passing reference in the third preambular paragraph to "the desperate plight of Haitian refugees" — a nod in the direction of an international element to support the finding of "a threat to peace and security in the region" — the reference to "systematic violations of civil liberties," the operative language quoted above, the overall structure and phrasing of the Resolution, and the context in which it was adopted all combine to suggest that the Council was concerned almost exclusively with the worsening human rights situation within the country. Although it contains the by now obligatory references to "the unique character of the present situation" and to its "complex and extraordinary nature, requiring an exceptional response," Resolution 940 may be considered an important general precedent for UN-authorized humanitarian intervention,* especially if the September 1994 occupation of Haiti by U.S. forces turns out to be a success and, therefore, a model for future such UN-authorized actions. See generally Jackson, America's Long, Slow, "Rush" to Invade Haiti, Boston Globe, Sept. 14, 1994, at 15, cols. 1-3; Lewis, Question of Power, N.Y. Times, Sept. 24, 1994, at A35, cols. 5-6.

Bibliography (UN Humanitarian Intervention)

The activism of the Security Council since the end of the Cold War has spawned many books and articles concerned, in whole or in part, with what may be called UN humanitarian intervention. Among the legal works not quoted or cited elsewhere in this Problem, see R. Haas, Intervention: The Use of Force in the Post-Cold War World (Carnegie Endowment 1994); P. Malanczuk, Humanitarian Intervention and the Legitimacy of the Use of Force (1993); Law and Force in the New World Order (L. Damrosch and D. Scheffer eds. 1991); To Loose the Bonds of Wickedness: International Intervention in Defence of Human Rights (N. Rodley ed. 1992); U.S. Intervention for the Post-Cold War World: New Challenges and New Re-

---

* Persons wishing to limit the precedential value of Resolution 940 may choose to emphasize the sixth preambular paragraph, which refers to two letters from the recognized Haitian government of President Aristide. They requested the UN "to take prompt and decisive action" to implement the so-called Governors Island Agreement and specifically noted the "agreement" of President Aristide with the draft text that was adopted as Resolution 940. Thus, in the minds of some observers, "intervention" may be too strong a description of an action based upon at least the tacit consent, if not the express invitation, of the de jure government concerned.

sponses (L. Brooks and A. Kanter eds. 1994); Adelman, Humanitarian Intervention: The Case of the Kurds, 4 Intl. J. Refugee L. 4 (1992); Alston, The Security Council and Human Rights: Lessons to Be Learned from the Iraq-Kuwait Crisis and Its Aftermath, 13 Austl. Y.B. Intl. L. 107 (1992); Arnison, International Law and Non-Intervention: When Do Humanitarian Concerns Supersede Sovereignty?, 17 Fletcher Forum 199 (1993); Comment, On Humanitarian Intervention: The New World Order and Wars to Preserve Human Rights, 1994 Utah L. Rev. 269; Comment, UN Intervention After the Cold War: Political Will and the United States, 29 Tex. Intl. L.J. 231 (1994); Delbruck, A Fresh Look at Humanitarian Intervention Under the Authority of the United Nations, 67 Ind. L.J. 887 (1992); Gordon, United Nations Intervention in Internal Conflicts: Iraq, Somalia and Beyond, 15 Mich. J. Intl. L. 519 (1994); Haass, Military Force: A User's Guide, 96 Foreign Policy 21 (1994); Kresock, "Ethnic Cleansing" in the Balkans: The Legal Foundations for Foreign Intervention, 27 Cornell Intl. L.J. 203 (1994); Mandelbaum, The Reluctance to Intervene, 95 Foreign Policy 3 (1994); Martin, Haiti: Mangled Multilateralism, 95 id. 72 (1994); Nafziger, Self-Determination and Humanitarian Intervention in a Community of Power, 20 Denv. J. Intl. L. & Poly. 9 (1991); Note, Command of Sovereignty Gives Way to Concern for Humanity, 26 Vand. J. Transnatl. L. 141 (1993); Pease and Forsythe, Human Rights, Humanitarian Intervention, and World Politics, 15 Hum. Rts. Q. 290 (1993); Recent Developments, Restoring Hope: U.N. Security Council Resolutions for Somalia and an Expanded Doctrine of Humanitarian Intervention, 34 Harv. Intl. L.J. 624 (1993); Scheffer, Toward a Modern Doctrine of Humanitarian Intervention, 23 U. Tol. L. Rev. 253 (1992).

IV. Forcible Protection of Nationals

Earlier in this Problem (see page 613 supra), the distinction between humanitarian intervention and forcible protection of nationals was explained. While the former, as we have seen, may involve states, regional organizations, and the UN, the latter is of interest primarily to states alone. Neither the UN nor the OAS, for instance, has evinced much interest in the protection of nationals problem, and while UN or unilateral humanitarian interventions may benefit foreigners in, as well as nationals of, a state, such benefits are a by-product of rather than even a minor factor in decisions to intervene.

The legal issues behind the forcible protection of nationals doctrine are, if anything, even more complex than the considerations behind the various types of humanitarian intervention. Not only is there strong disagreement between persons who believe that forcible protection still is permissible under the UN Charter and persons who believe it now is unlawful, but also there is much debate among members of the former group as to what is the preferable legal justification for a state's use of force to protect its nationals abroad.

A. Contrasting Views Regarding Forcible Protection of Nationals

Letter to the Editor
N.Y. Times, July 16, 1976, at 30, col. 3

To the Editor:

There is a bizarre Newspeak quality to the denunciations, in terms of asserted international law, of the Israeli rescue of hijacked passengers from the Entebbe airport in Uganda on July 4.

The initial act of air piracy at Athens was a violation of international law, as was the holding of the hostages for political purposes thereafter. At least one of these acts, piracy, is an international crime subject to universal jurisdiction.

The Israeli action would appear justified as a humanitarian intervention, a doctrine whose roots go back, at least, to Hugo Grotius. Where gross violations of human rights are taking place within a state whose government will not or cannot prevent them, the organs of the international community, or in exigent circumstances a single state, may enter the territory of the defaulting state for the sole purpose of terminating the outrage.

This act is recognized as a lawful humanitarian intervention. . . .

Another hallowed doctrine of international law, availing Israel in this case and expressing in many forms the common interests of all peoples, is that of "self-help." The forms of this doctrine include self-defense, reprisals, retaliation, impact territoriality, contiguous zones and other equivalents. The core meaning is that if a state is grievously injured but the organized international community is incapable of affording timely redress, the injured party may take necessary and proportionate measures to protect itself and its nationals.

In a context of the most inhumane deprivations and the failure of the Ugandan Government to give protection, it can only be Opposite-speak to describe the rescue operation as an act of aggression against Uganda. The action of the Israelis could not possibly have had the effect of threatening the territorial integrity or political independence of Uganda. This action, on the contrary, was entirely necessary and proportionate to the lawful purposes of the rescue.

The suggestion that, under the circumstances, Israel's action was an invasion of the sovereignty of Uganda involves a complete misunderstanding of sovereignty. Sovereignty even in its most comprehensive conception refers only to that competence of states which international law confers. States are not accorded a competence to exclude themselves from the operative provisions of international law.

It is regrettable that states and international organizations fail to censure the Amin regime. One can only wonder at the Security Council's strange strabismus in focusing righteously on the wrong problem.

MYRES S. McDOUGAL
MICHAEL REISMAN
New Haven, July 9, 1976

Letter to the Editor
N.Y. Times, July 27, 1976, at 28, col. 3

To the Editor:

The letter of Professors McDougal and Reisman on the Entebbe rescue illustrates what many skeptics have long maintained: that international law and the smugness with which it is often cited by academicians is part of the problem, not part of the solution.

The overwhelming evil of the Uganda regime and the indifference to human life of the hijackers must be denounced. But the enormity of their deeds should not be used for draping an academic fig leaf over the modern equivalent of gunboat diplomacy.

"Humanitarian intervention" obviously is a doctrine only for the powerful nations. Moreover, if Cuba were able to send an armada of planes to rescue abused nationals in Uruguay and if more and more nations got into the act, the professors would undoubtedly conclude that things had gone too far.

If every nation is to be its own judge of the justification for "humanitarian intervention," the result will be chaos. Yet if a principle cannot be applied generally, what is it worth as "law"?

The concept is derived from colonialism and is a kind of "law" that has no future, if indeed it has any present.

WILLIAM B. LLOYD, JR.
Rochester, July 19, 1976

Note the use made in both letters of the "humanitarian intervention" doctrine. Have the letter-writers got it right? Return to this question after having read the rest of the materials in this Section.

B. Reading

Lillich, Forcible Protection of Nationals Abroad: The Liberian "Incident" of 1990
35 German Y.B. Intl. L. 205, 213-221 (1993)

III. INTERNATIONAL LAW NORMS GOVERNING THE FORCIBLE
PROTECTION OF NATIONALS ABROAD

Traditionally international law sanctioned a State's use of force to protect the lives as well as the property of its nationals abroad. According to Professor *Bowett,*

> [t]there is ample evidence that, prior to 1945, States assumed the right to use force abroad for the protection of their nationals when their lives or their property were in imminent danger, and whether this danger emanated from the acts of mobs or of the authorities of the States in which these nations resided. Moreover, there is also ample evidence to show that States regarded this right of protection as being essentially part of the more general right of self-defence.

Professor *Brownlie,* after a similar survey of doctrine and practice, reaches the same conclusion.

> The jurists of the nineteenth century universally considered as lawful the use of force to protect the lives and property of nationals. The generous doctrines of the time accommodated such a right. Thus it could be regarded as the exercise of the right of self-preservation, the right of self-defence, as one of several justifiable forms of intervention, or as action justified in terms of necessity.

Numerous other publicists, among them *Borchard, Dunn, Hyde, Jessup, Oppenheim, O'Connell,* the *Thomases,* and *Waldock,* also agree that traditional international law, under one or more theories, sanctioned a State's forcible protection of its nationals abroad.

The adoption of the United Nations Charter in 1945, however, ushered in a new and supposedly comprehensive international legal regime governing the use of force. In this connection, two provisions in the Charter made it "very doubtful," at least in the opinion of a considerable number of early commentators, whether a State still was entitled to resort to forcible action to protect its nationals at risk in other countries. First, under Article 2(4), all States that are UN members renounce "the threat or use of force against the territorial integrity or political independence of any State, or in any other manner inconsistent with the Purposes of the United Nations." Secondly, although Article 51 provides that "[n]othing in the present Charter shall impair the inherent right of individual or collective self-defence," suggesting that States may retain the right of forcible protection of their nationals abroad, it restricts such right to situations where "an armed attack occurs against a Member of the United Nations. . . ." These provisions, it was argued, preempted the traditional international law rule permitting a State to use force to protect its nationals abroad.

Shortly after the establishment of the United Nations, the late Judge *Jessup* articulated this view of the Charter provisions, concluding that the forcible protection of nationals was inconsistent with the organization's purpose of promoting collective measures:

> The landing of armed forces of one state in another state is a "breach of the peace" or "threat to the peace" [in violation of Article 39] even though under traditional international law it is a lawful act. It is a measure of forcible self-help, legalized by international law because there has been no international organization competent to act in an emergency. The organizational defect has now been at least partially remedied through the adoption of the Charter, and a modernized law of nations should insist that the collective measures envisaged by Article 1 of the Charter shall supplant the individual measures approved by traditional international law.

Nevertheless, while positing a new rule of international law banning the unilateral or collective use of force for such purposes, he prophetically recognized that the old norms might survive (or be revived) if the Charter system failed to function as planned.

> It would seem that the only possible argument against the substitution of collective measures under the Security Council for individual measures by a single state would be the inability of the international organization to act with the speed requisite to preserve life. If may take some time before the Security Council, with its Military Staff Committee, and the pledged national contingents are in a state of readiness to act in such cases, but the Charter contemplates that international actions shall be timely as well as powerful.

Obviously, these great expectations of the immediate postwar period never materialized. Specifically, for a variety of political and logistical reasons the United Nations had neither the will nor the capacity to act with the requisite speed needed to protect the lives of U.S. and foreign nationals in any of the six cases mentioned above.* Hence, the "only possible argument" for unilateral (or collective) forcible protection mentioned by *Jessup* can be raised with considerable justification today. Otherwise, as the Professors *Thomas* observed in their now-neglected study entitled *Non-Intervention*, "it would seem that the Charter encumbers rather than advances the human rights and fundamental freedoms involved in the protection of aliens abroad."

Two principal arguments interpreting the Charter provisions to permit the forcible protection of nationals abroad have been made. The first,

---

* Lebanon in 1958, the Congo in 1964, the Dominican Republic in 1965, Iran in 1980, Grenada in 1983, and Panama in 1989. — Eds.

which the present writer endorsed a quarter of a century ago,† maintains that forcible protection does not run afoul of Article 2(4) since "such emergency action does not impair the territorial integrity or political independence of a state; it merely rescues nationals from a danger which the territorial state cannot or will not prevent." As explained by Professor *Paust*, in the course of justifying the Israeli rescue operation at Entebbe,

> Article 2 (4) of the Charter does *not* prohibit all forms of transnational coercion. . . . An evacuation mission designed to assure fundamental human rights would not appear to be inconsistent with the purposes of the Charter nor the employment of force against territorial integrity or political independence. A reasonably necessary and proportionate evacuation mission then should be permissible under the Charter since it is *not* prohibited by Article 2 (4).

Many other commentators, primarily Anglo-American, consider this argument the principal (if not necessarily exclusive) justification of forcible protection of nationals today.

The second argument for permitting the forcible protection of nationals abroad rests not upon a restrictive reading of Article 2 (4), but upon a broad interpretation of the words found in Article 51, which preserves to UN Member States the inherent right of self-defense in the event of an armed attack. The leading proponent of this justification of forcible protection, a justification that the present writer once considered "less satisfactory than the first argument" but now regards as being of equal if not greater weight, is Professor *Bowett*, who in his seminal monograph on the subject acknowledged the contention that "an injury to the nationals of a state constitutes an injury to the state itself, and that the protection of nationals is an essential function of the state. On this reasoning it is feasible to argue that the defence of nationals, whether within or without the territorial jurisdiction of the state, is in effect the defence of the state itself." The learned author not only adopted this argument in his monograph, but he has reiterated it repeatedly in his subsequent writings. So too have a goodly number of the other international lawyers who have recognized a right of forcible protection of nationals abroad. Moreover, a survey of those States that have advanced legal arguments in forcible protection of nationals cases — the United States, Great Britain and Israel — reveals an almost uniform reliance on the self-defense argument.

In the event, as Professor *Moore* recently remarked, the conceptual argument as to whether the forcible protection of nationals abroad is "simply not inconsistent with Article 2 (4)" or, if it is, whether it still can be justified as being "consistent with Article 51," while of great interest to legal scholars, may be relatively unimportant. Indeed, many U.S. commentators, including three welcome if somewhat grudging converts to the cause of

† See Lillich, Forcible Self-Help to Protect Human Rights, 53 Iowa L. Rev. 325, 334-351 (1967). — Eds.

forcible protection, leave their readers in the twilight, if not the dark, as to their exact legal position. Professor *Farer*, for instance, formerly a fearsome critic of forcible protection proponents, now is "prepared to argue that practice and expectations have reached a point where there is sufficient expectation that powers will rescue their citizens and that we should probably regard this as a gloss on the Charter." Professor *Henkin*, long an opponent of forcible coercion for human rights purposes, now apparently regards the forcible protection of nationals abroad "as an exception to Article 2 (4)'s prohibition on the use of force . . . under 'the *Entebbe* principle'." Professor *Schachter*, on the other hand, who once concluded that, "as a matter of law, an armed rescue action to save lives of nationals . . . is not prohibited by article 2 (4)", now appears to justify forcible protection by means of an "expanded" conception of self-defense under Article 51. The recently-published Ninth Edition of Oppenheim's International Law, edited by Judge *Jennings* and Sir *Arthur Watts*, which treats the forcible protection of nationals abroad under the heading "Circumstances which may justify intervention", concludes without explanation that "there has been little disposition on the part of states to deny that intervention properly restricted to the protection of nationals is, in emergencies, justified."

Moreover, even among European scholars who read Articles 2 (4) and 51 to prohibit the forcible protection of nationals abroad, such as *Brownlie*, *Ronzitti* and *Schweisfurth*, there appears a willingness — even, in some cases, an anxiousness — to condone or rationalize a State's use of force to protect its nationals in an appropriate case. Professor *Brownlie*, for instance, recognizes "that the protection of nationals presents particular difficulties and that a government faced with a deliberate massacre of a considerable number of nationals in a foreign state would have cogent reasons of humanity for acting, and would also be under very great political pressure." Thus, while denying the legality of forcible action in such a case, he is willing to condone it. Professor *Ronzitti*, recognizing that "the [state] practice which has grown up gives rise to a claim which does not have an entirely wrongful basis," devotes five pages to expounding "the main features of what — *de lege ferenda* — could be a modern right of intervention for protecting nationals abroad." Finally, Dr. *Schweisfurth*, advocating a "human rights approach" under which States have an *erga omnes* obligation to ensure the human rights of their nationals, believes that under this approach "unilateral actions to rescue nationals abroad should be . . . tolerated although they include a temporary breach of the law." His view, which is interesting but to date has attracted no academic or government support, is that "[i]t is more convincing when the state of nationality bases its rescue action on an *obligation* which aims at the protection of high values such as human rights than when it bases it on a *right* so widely contested, thereby invoking the protection of human rights only as a (usually undiscussed) background consideration."

The consensus that emerges from most contemporary scholarly comment — backed by a respectable if limited amount of State practice — is that at present the forcible protection of nationals abroad, if not actually permissible pursuant to what is now a gloss on the UN Charter, at least will be tolerated or condoned in an appropriate case. If this conclusion is correct, then it behooves both academic and government lawyers to renew their efforts to develop and refine the various criteria by which a State's forcible protection claim may be judged. The seminal formulation of the principles to be applied to such claims is that of the late Judge *Waldock*, who 40 years ago laid down the following test:

> There must be (1) an imminent threat of injury to nationals, (2) a failure or inability on the part of the territorial sovereign to protect them and (3) measures of protection strictly confined to the object of protecting them against injury.

Other and more elaborate criteria subsequently have been developed by U.S. commentators, including the present writer. They have been helpfully synthesized by Professor *Farer* as follows:

(1)   that there be an immediate and extensive threat to fundamental human rights;
(2)   that all other remedies for the protection of those rights have been exhausted to the extent possible within the time constraints posed by the threat;
(3)   that an attempt has been made to secure the approval of appropriate authorities in the target State;
(4)   That there is a minimal effect on the extant structure of authority (*e.g.*, that the intervention not be used to impose or preserve a preferred régime);
(5)   that the minimal requisite force be employed and/or that the intervention is not likely to cause greater injury to innocent persons and their property than would result if the threatened violation actually occurred;
(6)   that the intervention be of limited duration; and
(7)   that a report of the intervention be filed immediately with the Security Council and where relevant, regional organizations.

For further readings, see D. Bowett, Self-Defence in International Law 87-105 (1958); N. Ronzitti, Rescuing Nationals Abroad (1985); O. Schachter, International Law in Theory and Practice 117-199, 123-126 (1991).

C. Forcible Protection of Nationals Abroad: Post-Entebbe Case Studies

Instances of forcible protection have continued to occur with reasonable regularity since the Entebbe raid (see pages 665-666 supra). The following instances have fueled the debate over the legality of such uses of force by states.

French Intervention in Zaire, 1978. On 19 May 1978, French and Belgian parachutists, with logistical support from the United States, successfully evacuated more than 2,000 Europeans in danger of their lives during civil war hostilities in the province of Shaba. Most observers viewed the action as a restrained use of force dictated by humanitarian motives, although some commentators remarked that the intervention helped the French-supported Mobutu regime to survive and also gain control of the valuable copper industry in the area. See Verwey, Humanitarian Intervention Under International law, 32 Neth. Intl. L. Rev. 357, 403 (1985); Schweisfurth, Operations to Rescue Nationals in Third States Involving the Use of Force in Relation to the Protection of Human Rights, 23 German Y.B. Intl. L. 159, 159-160 (1980).

U.S. Attempt to Rescue Its Hostages in Iran, 1980. After the 4 November 1979 seizure of hostages from its embassy in Iran by Muslim fundamentalist students supporting and eventually supported by the regime of the Ayatollah Khomenei, the United States employed various peaceful means to secure their release, including invoking economic sanctions, taking the matter to the UN Security Council, and initiating proceedings in the International Court of Justice (ICJ). When the ICJ's Interim Order to release the hostages went unheeded by Iran, on 24-25 April 1980 U.S. commandos landed in the Iranian desert to begin military operations to free them. After several helicopters malfunctioned, the mission commander determined that the operation should be aborted. During the withdrawal, a helicopter collided with a C-130 refueling aircraft, and eight crew members died. The force then withdrew on board the remaining aircraft.

In its Judgment of 24 May 1980, the ICJ expressly noted that it was not passing on the question of the legality of the rescue attempt. Case Concerning United States Diplomatic and Consular Staff in Tehran (U.S. v. Iran), 1980 I.C.J. 3, 43-44. Commentary on the operation generally considered it consistent with U.S. obligations under the UN Charter. See, e.g., Schachter, International Law in the Hostage Crisis: Implications for Future Cases, in American Hostages in Iran 325 (P. Kreisberg ed. 1985). For other commentary, see N. Ronzitti, Rescuing Nationals Abroad 41-49, 57, 61-62 (1985); The Iran Crisis and International Law, Proceedings of the John Bassett Moore Society for International Law (R. Steel ed. 1981); D'Angelo, Resort to Force by States to Protect Nationals: The U.S. Rescue Mission to Iran and Its Legality Under International Law, 21 Va. J. Intl. L. 485 (1981);

Fisher, Iranian Crisis: Who Should Do What?, 14 Akron L. Rev. 1 (1980); Jeffery, The American Hostages in Tehran: The I.C.J. and the Legality of Rescue Missions, 30 Intl. & Comp. L.Q. 717 (1981); Riggs, The Grenada Intervention: A Legal Analysis, 109 Mil. L. Rev. 1, 19-21 (1985); Rubin, the Hostages Incident: The United States in Iran, 36 Y.B. World Aff. 213 (1982); Schachter, Self-Help in International Law: U.S. Action in the Iranian Hostages Crisis, 37 J. Intl. Aff. 231 (1984); Schachter, The Right of States to Use Armed Force, 82 Mich. L. Rev. 1620 (1984); Schweisfurth, Operations to Protect Nationals in Third States Involving the Use of Force in Relation to the Protection of Human Rights, 23 German Y.B. Intl. L. 159 (1980); Schweppe, Iran: World Court Rulings of December 15, 1979 and May 24, 1980, 14 Intl. Law. 529 (1980); Terry, The Iranian Hostages Crisis: International Law and United States Policy, 32 JAG J. 31 (1982).

U.S. Operation in Grenada, 1983. This operation has been mentioned previously in connection with the doctrine of humanitarian intervention. See page 644 supra. While occupying the island, U.S. forces secured the St. George's Medical School, which housed 350 U.S. students. These students, plus approximately 650 other U.S. nationals who were in Grenada, were said to have been in danger following violent political unrest on the island. Reports of such danger may have been greatly exaggerated, but the United States, four years after the seizure of the hostages in Iran in the wake of similar political unrest, was unwilling to risk another hostage crisis. The opportunity to overthrow Grenada's Marxist government, thus insulating the island from increasing Cuban influence, certainly was a more significant factor in the U.S. decision to intervene.

For a wide variety of views as to the operation's legality, see A. Francis, Legal Implications of United States Intervention in Grenada (1984); W. Gilmore, The Grenada Intervention: Analysis and Documentation (1984); J.N. Moore, Law and the Grenada Mission (1984); M. Shahabuddeen, The Conquest of Grenada: Sovereignty in the Periphery (1986); Beck, International Law and the Decision to Invade Grenada: A Ten-Year Retrospective, 33 Va. J. Intl. L. 765 (1993); Committee on Grenada, Section on International Law and Practice, American Bar Association, International Law and the United States Action in Grenada: A Report, 18 Intl. Law. 331 (1984); Dore, The U.S. Invasion of Grenada: Resurrection of the Johnson Doctrine?, 20 Stan. J. Intl. L. 175 (1984); Doswald-Beck, The Legality of the U.S. Intervention in Grenada, 31 Neth. Intl. L. Rev. 355 (1984); Fraser, Grenada: The Sovereignty of a People, 7 West Indiana L.J. 205 (1983); Joyner, The United States Action in Grenada: Reflections on the Lawfulness of Invasion, 78 Am. J. Intl. L. 131 (1984); Levitin, The Law of Force and the Force of Law: Grenada, the Falklands and Humanitarian Intervention, 27 Harv. Intl. L.J. 621 (1986); Moore, Grenada and the International Double Standard, 78 Am. J. Intl. L. 145 (1984); Nanda, The United States Armed Intervention in Grenada — Impact on World Order, 14 Cal. W. Intl. L.J. 395 (1984); Note, The Grenada Intervention: "Illegal" in Form, Sound as Policy, 16 N.Y.U. J. Intl. L. & Pol. 1167 (1984); Riggs, The Grenada Intervention: A Legal Analysis, 109 Mil. L. Rev. 1 (1985); Schachter, The Legality of Pro-Democratic Invasion, 78 Am. J. Intl. L. 645 (1984); Vagts, International Law Under Time Pressure: Grading the Grenada Take-Home Examination, 78 Am. J. Intl. L. 169 (1984).

U.S. Invasion of Panama, 1989.   This military action has been mentioned previously in connection with the doctrine of humanitarian intervention. See page 645 supra. The objectives of the United States, according to the Department of State, were "(1) to protect American lives; (2) to assist the lawful and democratically elected government in Panama in fulfilling its international obligations; (3) to seize and arrest General Noriega, an indicted drug trafficker; and (4) to defend the integrity of United States rights under the Panama Canal treaties." Leich, supra page 645, at 547.

Although the protection of U.S. lives was the first legal principle advanced by the Department to justify the invasion, and despite the fact that President George Bush in announcing it declared that his decision had been made in response to "General Noriega's reckless threats and attacks upon Americans [that] created an imminent danger to the 35,000 American citizens in Panama," id. at 546, the factual basis to support a protection of nationals argument appears slim at best. Id. For commentary supporting this conclusion, see Nanda, The Validity of United States Intervention in Panama Under International Law, 84 Am. J. Intl. L. 494, 496-497 (1990). See also Farer, Panama: Beyond the Charter Paradigm, 84 id. 503 (1990).

U.S. Rescue Operation in Liberia, 1990.   During a civil war in Liberia, one of the rebel leaders, whose troops occupied a part of Monrovia, threatened to arrest U.S. citizens and other foreigners in an apparent attempt to provoke foreign intervention. On 5 August 1990, U.S. troops were deployed from offshore ships to rescue civilians and secure the embassy. The evacuation extracted 74 people, including U.S. embassy officials, their dependents, and U.S. citizens from two other sites in Liberia.

United States forces continued to evacuate U.S. and foreign nationals over the next two weeks, eventually bringing 1,640 civilian men, women, and children to safety. All told, U.S. troops evacuated 166 U.S. citizens from Liberia during the operation. Among foreign nationals evacuated were persons from Canada, France, Great Britain, Ireland, Italy, Liberia, the Philippines, Portugal, Singapore, and Spain, with over 300 from India and nearly 600 from Lebanon. No lives were lost, nor were there any U.S. military casualties or civilian injuries.

Since the operation took place soon after Iraq's invasion of Kuwait, little notice was taken of it, and no protests were made. The United States justified the operation by referring to the threats that had been made against U.S. citizens and the general deterioration of security in Liberia. From the facts on record, it would appear that the introduction of U.S. troops in this case constituted a classic case of forcible protection. See Lillich, Forcible Protection of Nationals Abroad: The Liberian "Incident" of 1990, 35 German Y.B. Intl. L. 205 (1993).

U.S. Rescue Operation in Somalia, 1991.   In late 1990 rebel groups in Somalia intensified their efforts to overthrow the government of President Siad Barre. Fighting was fierce in the capital city of Mogadishu, with an estimated 1,500 people killed and 4,500 wounded during the first week of 1991. The U.S. Ambassador, considering the situation unacceptably dangerous, requested military assistance to evacuate the embassy staff and other U.S. citizens and foreigners who had sought refuge there.

United States helicopters, launched from ships fortuitously stationed in the Indian Ocean as part of the Gulf War buildup, ferried out 281 persons over a two-day period, 5-6 January 1991. In addition to 66 U.S. citizens, among the evacuees were nations of 29 other countries, including the ambassadors or chargés d'affaires of Germany, Great Britain, Kenya, Nigeria, Oman, Qatar, the Soviet Union, Sudan, and Turkey. Since preparations for the Gulf War completely overshadowed the evacuation mission, there was no discussion of it in the UN and little public comment by the diplomatic or the legal community. Since there had been a complete breakdown of law and order in Mogadishu, including fighting immediately outside the walls of the U.S. embassy, the threat to U.S. citizens and other foreigners was clear. Thus, as in the case of Liberia the previous year, it would seem that the Somalia rescue operation was a textbook case of forcible protection.

V.   Final Comments and Questions

1. UN humanitarian intervention is the "new child on the block," so to speak, and its parameters and impact upon traditional intervention doctrines are uncertain at present. From the materials in this Problem, what are your views on the following questions:

(a) May the UN intervene in a member state for human rights purposes only if it finds an Article 39 "threat to the peace"?

(b) If your answer is no, what other basis is there under the Charter to justify UN intervention for humanitarian purposes?

(c) Regardless of whether your answer is yes or no, do you agree or disagree with the approach the Security Council has taken in determining whether a "threat to the peace" exists? Is it all in the eye of the beholder, or are there some objective criteria being applied? If so, what are they? What (additional or alternative) ones would you recommend the Council adopt?

2. One of the principal arguments for unilateral humanitarian intervention advanced by Lillich, Reisman, and Moore has been that states should be free to act when the UN cannot or will not. Now that the UN has demonstrated an ability to act — if only occasionally and not always effectively — how does that weigh in the scales? Is unilateral humanitarian intervention, always questionable, now definitely illegal? Or unneeded?

3. Consider the contention of Professor Reisman that "[f]rom the standpoint of the contemporary needs of the international community [the view that the UN Charter rules out self-help measures] is clearly outmoded. Only in the most exceptional cases will the United Nations be capable of functioning as an international enforcer; in the vast majority of cases, the conflicting interests of diverse public order systems will block any action. A rational and contemporary interpretation of the Charter must conclude that Article 2(4) suppresses self-help insofar as the organization can assume the role of enforcer. When it cannot, self-help prerogatives revive." W. Reisman, Nullity and Revision 850 (1971). For a more recent restatement of his views, see Reisman, Coercion and Self-Determination: Construing Charter Article 2(4), 78 Am. J. Intl. L. 642 (1984). Is this line of argument, applied to unilateral humanitarian intervention, still valid? Was it ever?

4. Many Third World states seem uncomfortable with the Security Council's new role as human rights enforcer in crisis situations. Indications of this unease may be found in the speech by Zimbabwe's Foreign Minister (see page 656 supra), in the insistence that Security Council resolutions authorizing intervention for humanitarian purposes reference the supposed uniqueness of the situation (see page 663 supra), and in calls for the restructuring of the Security Council or for limitations on its newly flexed powers. See Franck, The "Powers of Appreciation": Who Is the Ultimate Guardian of UN Legality?, 86 Am. J. Intl. L. 519, 523 (1992). One German scholar gives the following explanation of some of this growing uneasiness with the Security Council's new activism:

> Some of the beneficiaries of the paralyzing conflict between the United States and the late Soviet Union now find themselves uprooted from the cozy shelter of client-state status and exposed to the new reality of a world lacking the counterbalancing forces of bipolarism. The first signs of a forceful, albeit incoherent, enforcement of widely shared values have spurred a growing choir of scholars to voice concern about the paramount influence of the only remaining superpower within the United Nations, the Security Council, and to express doubts about the legitimacy of this body's potential for intervention.

Herdegen, The "Constitutionalization" of the UN Security System, 27 Vand. J. Intl. L. 135, 137 (1994). Will the "growing choir" increase more rapidly now that the Security Council, in Resolution 940, has laid the legal groundwork for a genuine doctrine of UN humanitarian intervention? Or might it not shrink, since, as the former Secretary General of Amnesty International rightly noted, "Haiti is surely the clearest case today where multilateral armed intervention would be justified, to remove a military almost devoid of support and capable only of repressing its own people." Martin, Haiti: Mangled Multilateralism, 95 Foreign Policy 72, 89 (1994).

5. For the people of many Third World states, as opposed to their governments, the possibility of UN humanitarian intervention in extreme

cases may not be unattractive. Yet, as the record indicates, it is highly unlikely to occur, despite the perception in some quarters that the Security
Council is overly eager and overly zealous. Indeed, critics of the Council
often make the point that it is highly selective in its concerns, overlooking
or ignoring many situations where gross human rights violations are taking
place. On this score they surely are right, since, while there now is the
opportunity for the UN to act, the traditional reasons for intervention —
economic gain, glory and altruism, and national security, real or perceived
— rarely exist to motivate the major powers, who realistically remain the
linchpins of any successful intervention. See Mandelbaum, The Reluctance to Intervene, 95 Foreign Policy 3 (1994). As Professor Mandelbaum
rightly observes, with the end of the Cold War "the forces that have historically driven the governments of the powerful to intervene beyond their
borders have all but vanished." Id. at 16. Moreover, reinforcing this reluctance — and even driving policy in this CNN era — is the reluctance of
many governments, especially that of the United States, to take or even risk
the casualties associated with any intervention labeled "humanitarian."
Ryan, The Casualty Risk, Boston Globe, Oct. 9, 1993, at 13, cols. 1-2;
Lewis, World Without Power, N.Y. Times, July 25, 1994, at A15, cols. 5-6.
Opponents of UN humanitarian intervention, whether on legal or other
grounds, thus may have a stronger hand to play than they once perceived.

6. Conventional wisdom has it that economic sanctions are preferable
to military intervention in that they cause less hardship to civilians in the
country concerned. True in Iraq? True in Haiti? Consider the views of
Professor Schachter, no supporter of indiscriminate military action:

> [T]he preference for economic sanctions rather than military action is under-
> standable. However, situations vary. Prolonged economic boycotts are likely
> to exact heavy costs upon the general population, especially the poor, infirm
> and usually the vulnerable minorities, without decisively affecting the tar-
> geted states' rulers. Military action, in contrast, may be decisive with far less
> destructive impact on people. Context is crucial, and it is doubtful that eco-
> nomic sanctions are always preferable to the use of armed force.

Schachter, Remarks, 1992 Am. Socy. Intl. L. Proceedings 320.

7. In a perceptive essay several years ago, Professor Farer made the
following provocative suggestion:

> Concede that certain deeply-embedded parasitic governments in the
> Third World have so debilitated the society on which they respectively feed
> that it seems incapable of removing them without external assistance. Then
> ponder these questions. Where . . . the United States has protected the para-
> site, should we undertake to remove it as an alternative to removing the
> protection? And assuming that we should act at all, should the United States
> ever act unilaterally when it cannot induce support from other democracies?
> Can unilateral or multilateral action be justified morally unless the actors are
> willing to accept the cost and responsibility of serving as trustees of the liber-
> ated people until institutions of self-government can be consolidated and

years of damage repaired? If accepting a trustee's responsibilities is a moral condition for action, can action be squared with traditional conceptions of national interest?

Farer, Defending Human Rights in the Post-Reagan Era: Candor and Competence, 28 Va. J. Intl. L. 854, 859 (1988). How would you answer these questions?

8. Reread Resolution 940 (see pages 659-662 supra). Note how many of Professor Farer's suggestions have been built into this decision to authorize UN humanitarian intervention. Clearly the Security Council was not content with the "in-and-out" approach that President Bush first took with respect to Somalia, for the Resolution speaks not only to the ousting of the military dictatorship, but also to the establishment of "a secure and stable environment," the restoration of the "legitimately elected President," "the professionalization of the Haitian armed forces and the creation of a separate police force," "the organization of free and fair legislative elections," and the monitoring thereof by the UN in cooperation with the Organization of American States (OAS). The Resolution, in sum, reads like a list of steps to be taken in the process of "nation building." Note also that, while the cost of the initial military operation is to be borne by the participating member states, there is no mention of the source of the much more substantial funding that eventually will be required.

9. That the United States still recognizes the right of forcible protection when its citizens are in peril overseas was made clear after the failed rescue operation in Iran, when in justifying it President Carter observed that "the United States was acting wholly within its right, in accordance with Article 51 of the United Nations Charter, to protect and rescue its citizens where the government of the territory in which they are located is unable or unwilling to protect them." 1980 Digest of United States Practice in International Law 323 (1986). The Department of State's Legal Adviser advanced the same argument in the case of Grenada. Robinson, Letter from the Legal Adviser, United States Department of State, 18 Intl. Law. 381, 385 (1984). The Department again advanced the argument after the Panama Invasion. Leich, supra page 645, at 548.

10. This Problem has considered the Charter provisions and other legal norms governing the use of force by the UN, regional organizations, and nation states to protect the human rights of persons in states where those rights are being severely abused. This focus on the legal norms and the evolution of what one might term "true" UN humanitarian intervention is appropriate for a course on International Human Rights Law, but as some of the above Comments suggest it is not enough. Consider the following peroration by Professor Reisman, directed to UN "peacemaking" but applicable to UN humanitarian intervention as well.

The reason we do not have peacemaking in Somalia, in Bosnia, in the Sudan, or in Haiti has little to do with defects in the normative arrangements of the

Charter. Much could be done within the existing regime. The real obstacles lie in features of international politics, and they must be overcome politically, whatever the changes in the U.N. system. As the Secretary-General has said, the real issue is, indeed, political will.

Alas, that will has been absent. The leadership of the great democracies have behaved pusillanimously in the face of horrors that the international community should never have allowed to occur. No leader has emerged as a world voice of conscience to mobilize his or her own nation and others to remedy what is remediable. Regional organizations, whose members are most acutely aware of and will bear the burden of most of the refugee outflows from the internal chaos of a neighboring state, always have the greatest incentive to stop carnage and make peace. When the world community was inactive with respect to Liberia's agony, Nigeria, leading an ad hoc coalition of states who happened to be members of a sub-regional economic group, was not. By contrast, no regional leader has come forward in Europe to provide a balm for Bosnia. No regional leader in East Africa or in the Arab League has come forward to succor Somalia or the Sudan. Trying to justify inaction on the ground that the situation is "complicated" is contemptible. All situations are complicated. Life is complicated. Trying to justify inaction on the pretense of respect for sovereignty and domestic jurisdiction is no less contemptible. These are legal concepts designed to protect people, not to protect their oppressors.

Fiddling endlessly with legal arrangements can become an excuse for inaction. Supposedly inadequate legal arrangements can even become a type of scapegoat. Let us not kid ourselves. Legal arrangements by themselves can no more create power than alchemy can create gold. No legal arrangements has ever or will ever work by itself. A legal arrangement will only work with courageous leadership. The reasons for the failure of international peacemaking are to be found in the failure of that leadership at every level of the world community.

Reisman, Peacekeeping, 18 Yale J. Intl. L. 415, 422-423 (1993). Accord, Lillich, supra page 652, at 573-575.

Problem IX

The European Regime for the Protection of Human Rights

Can Regional Systems to Protect Human Rights Be More Effective Than UN Mechanisms?

682 – 708

I. The Regional Approach to Human Rights   682
    Weston, Lukes, and Hnatt, Regional Human Rights Regimes: A
    Comparison and Appraisal   682
II. The Council of Europe   684
  A. The European Convention for the Protection of Human Rights
     and Fundamental Freedoms   684
     Council of Europe, Protocol No. 11 to the Convention for the
      Protection of Human Rights and Fundamental Freedoms and
      Explanatory Report   687
     Note: Interstate Complaints   692
     Ireland v. United Kingdom   693
     Note: "Degrading Treatment or Punishment" vs. "Cruel and
      Unusual Punishment"   715
     Letters to the Editor   719
     Not Sparing the Rod; How Cruel, How Unusual?   721
     Soering v. United Kingdom   724
     Note: The "Death Row Phenomenon"   760
  B. The European Social Charter   760
  C. The European Convention for the Prevention of Torture and
     Inhuman or Degrading Treatment or Punishment   762
     Evans and Morgan, The European Convention for the Preven-
      tion of Torture: Operational Practice   762
     Comments and Questions   765
III. The Organization on Security and Cooperation in Europe   769
    Commission on Security and Cooperation in Europe, Beyond
     Process: The CSCE's Institutional Development, 1990-92   769
    Helsinki Document 1992, The Challenges of Change   772
IV. The European Community   775
    Boyle, Europe: The Council of Europe, the CSCE, and the
     European Community   775
    Comments and Questions   777

681

I.   The Regional Approach to Human Rights

Thus far our concern has been almost exclusively with issues relating to the promotion and protection of human rights by the United Nations. This and the next Problem move outside the UN framework to examine human rights protection at the regional level, which occurs primarily through treaty-based mechanisms. This Problem considers the extensive jurisprudence developed under the European Convention for the Protection of Human Rights and Fundamental Freedoms (hereinafter the European Convention or simply the Convention), as well as other human rights activities at the European regional level.

The jurisprudential and practical reasons for regional human rights regimes and their origins are set out in the following reading.

Weston, Lukes, and Hnatt, Regional Human Rights Regimes: A Comparison and Appraisal
20 Vand. J. Transnatl. L. 585, 588-592 (1987)

[The authors begin by listing the various regional human rights instruments.]

From a progressive point of view, this proliferation of human rights activity from the global to the regional plane must be seen as salutary. The greater the dispersion of human rights initiatives, after all, the greater the likelihood that international human rights and their challenge to traditional notions of state sovereignty will be taken seriously. Yet, because the world community has seen fit to arrange for the advancement of human rights through the United Nations and its allied agencies virtually from the United Nations' founding, and because the United Nations system has worldwide competence, one may legitimately ask why it has been deemed necessary or even desirable to arrange for the advancement of human rights on a regional basis as well. It is, indeed, precisely this question that arose at the United Nations' beginning. Because many believed regional approaches to human rights might detract from the perceived universality of human rights, the wisdom of encouraging the creation of regional human rights systems was to some extent doubted.

At least three interrelated responses to this doubt have influenced the development of regional human rights systems, however. Each explains, at any rate, why the idea of regional human rights regimes is no longer a matter of real controversy.

First, regions (by which we mean geographic areas or units marked by relatively high socioeconomic, cultural, political and juridical commonalities) tend toward homogeneity. While by no means guaranteeing unanimity of viewpoint, this fact appears nonetheless to facilitate debate over the substance of the rights to be protected, to assist in the development of more or less familiar systems of redress and, consequently, to enhance the actual promotion and protection of human rights.

Second, geographic proximity, like cultural propinquity, generally leads to socioeconomic, environmental and security interdependence — which in turn helps to breed a reciprocal tolerance and mutual forbearance (or, in any event, less concern over alliance conflict and power balances) that can secure the cooperative transformation of universal proclamations of human rights into more-or-less concrete realities. The development of human rights instruments and mechanisms among states generally is facilitated when alliances based on common interests are in place, and this circumstance not infrequently occurs at the regional level more than it does at the global.

Finally, both geographic proximity and cultural propinquity make more probable the investigation and remedying of violations. The proverbial "bottom line" to the promotion and protection of human rights is, as with other kinds of legal claims, not merely the intention but also the capacity to apply some sort of pressure on states on redress violations. Regional human rights regimes are more likely than global ones to manifest this competence and, hence, are more likely to be effective in applying diplomatic, economic, and other sanctions in defense of human rights.

In any event, recognizing the advantages of a regional approach to human rights and stirred by World War II Axis Power atrocities, both the European and the American communities set out to create their own human rights systems. Indeed, influenced by United Nations efforts to articulate an "international bill of rights" (begun in 1946 and culminating in the 1948 Universal Declaration of Human Rights, the 1966 International Covenant on Economic, Social and Cultural Rights and the 1966 International Covenant on Civil and Political Rights), the regionalization of human rights norms, institutions and procedures began even before the United Nations adopted the Universal Declaration in December 1948. Meeting in Bogotá in spring 1948, the Ninth International Conference of American states proclaimed the American Declaration of the Rights and Duties of Man; meeting in The Hague in May 1948, the Congress of the European Movement announced that is would receive proposals for a European Charter of Human Rights.

As the European and Inter-American systems evolved, United Nations resistance to the idea of regional human rights regimes waned. In fact, through an ad hoc study group, the United Nations actually considered creating regional human rights regimes of its own. It ultimately concluded, however, that the Member States themselves bore the responsibility for forming regional human rights systems. Thus, in 1977, via Resolution 32/127, the General Assembly asked states not belonging to regional human rights regimes "to consider agreements with a view to the establishment within their respective regions of suitable regional machinery for the promotion and protection of human rights." Shortly thereafter, in 1979, the Assembly of Heads of State and Government of the Organization of African Unity (OAU) called on the Secretary General of the OAU to draft an "African Charter on Human and Peoples' Rights."

Thus began the regionalization of regimes designed to promote and protect international human rights. . . .

II.   The Council of Europe

A.   The European Convention for the Protection of Human Rights and Fundamental Freedoms

The Council of Europe is an intergovernmental body created in 1949 to promote cultural, social, and political cooperation in (originally) Western Europe. It has been extremely active in the area of human rights, and in 1950 it adopted the European Convention for the Protection of Human Rights and Fundamental Freedoms (see the Documentary Supplement), which entered into force in 1953. Ten Protocols to the Convention have been adopted subsequently, several of which expand the rather limited range of substantive rights included in the 1950 Convention. (Protocols Nos. 1, 4, 6, and 7 are found in the Documentary Supplement.)

Although the Convention entered into force relatively quickly, its acceptance was neither immediate nor unanimous. France and Greece, for example, did not ratify the Convention until 1974, and many parties did not initially accept the optional right of individual petition (Article 25 of the Convention) or the jurisdiction of the European Court of Human Rights (Article 46).

By the 1980s, however, the acceptance of basic human rights norms and the legitimacy of the European Convention machinery was so widespread that ratification of the Convention had become a de facto political condition for membership in the Council of Europe itself. With the end of Soviet domination of Eastern Europe in the late 1980s, membership in the Council of Europe expanded dramatically, as did the number of ratifications of the Convention. As of May 1994, 29 of the 32 members of the Council had ratified the Convention, and the three remaining members (Estonia, Lithuania, and Slovenia) are likely to have submitted their ratifications by the time the present book is published. All parties to the Convention have accepted both the right of individual petition and the jurisdiction of the European Court.

The principal enforcement bodies are the European Commission of

Human Rights and the European Court of Human Rights, together with the Committee of Ministers of the Council of Europe. The Commission is composed of members equal in number to the parties to the Convention who sit in their individual capacities, not as representatives of states. Judges of the Court also serve in their individual capacities; the Court consists of a number of judges equal to the number of members of the Council of Europe.

The jurisdiction of the Commission and the Court originally extended automatically only to cases brought by one state against another state party (Article 24); complaints from individual petitioners could be considered only if the state concerned had declared its acceptance of this optional jurisdiction. As noted above, however, the theoretically "optional" jurisdiction over individual cases has now been unanimously accepted by the parties. If the Commission determines that a case is admissible (according to the criteria set forth in Articles 25 and 26), it then conducts an investigation to determine the facts. This investigation may include on-site visits or the hearing of witnesses, and it is likely to include an oral hearing at which both sides (the individual and the state, or both states if it is an interstate complaint) are represented. The Commission also is charged with attempting to find a "friendly settlement" to the case (Articles 28 and 30).

If no settlement is reached, the Commission draws up a report in which it reaches conclusions as to the facts and "state[s] its opinion as to whether the facts found disclose a breach by the State concerned of its obligations under the Convention" (Article 31). If the case is not referred to the Court, the report theoretically need be transmitted only to the state concerned and the Committee of Ministers; the latter decides whether there has been a violation of the Convention and whether the report should be published. In practice, however, the individual applicant also is sent a copy of the report, and publication is more or less automatic.

Prior to the entry into force of Protocol No. 9 to the Convention, which was adopted in 1990, only the Commission or a concerned state could refer a case to the European Court; Protocol No. 9 grants this right to individual petitioners as well. Despite the fact that the individual had no formal standing before the Court, it has become the practice of the Commission to invite the applicant or the applicant's lawyer to assist it in preparing and presenting a case to the Court. In addition, the Court has since 1983 permitted NGOs and others to file amicus curiae briefs.

The Court functions primarily as an appellate tribunal that reviews questions of law, but is also may engage in additional fact-finding. It has the Commission's report before it and normally gives it great weight, but it is not bound by the Commission in reaching its judgment on either the law or the facts (as demonstrated by the Court's unanimous reversal of the Commission's 6-5 vote on the key legal question in the *Soering* case, pages 724-759 infra). The Court's judgment is final and binding on the state concerned, and it may include the awarding of monetary damages. The Committee of Ministers is responsible for supervising execution of the judgment.

In effect, the European Court of Human Rights has become a constitutional rights court for Europe, and its decisions deal with both the mundane and the highly political. Extensive jurisprudence has been developed in the area of criminal procedure, particularly with respect to Article 6's guarantee of "a fair and public hearing within a reasonable time by an independent and impartial tribunal." Other cases have dealt with matters ranging from privacy issues, such as homosexuality and abortion, to freedom of expression, the legality of "closed shop" employment arrangements, expropriation, and government wiretapping. A vast body of literature now exists that considers the substantive impact of the European Convention. See, e.g., M. Delmas-Marty, The European Convention for the Protection of Human Rights: International Protection Versus National Restrictions (1992); P. van Dijk and G.J.H. van Hoof, Theory and Practice of the European Convention on Human Rights (1990); A. Drzemczewski, European Human Rights Convention in Domestic Law (1983); The European System for the Protection of Human Rights (R. Macdonald, F. Matcher, and H. Petzold eds. 1993); J. Fawcett, The Application of the European Convention on Human Rights (2d ed. 1987); M. Janis and R. Kay, European Human Rights Law (1990); J.G. Merrills, The Development of International Law by the European Court of Human Rights (2d ed. 1993); Monitoring Human Rights in Europe, Comparing International Procedures and Mechanisms (A. Bloed et al. eds. 1993).

As the Council of Europe itself has stated, the procedures described briefly above are "somewhat complicated," and they also have led to a system that can be frustratingly slow. The procedural distinctions between individual and interstate cases have disappeared in practice (although there remain important differences in the criteria for admissibility and the substantive scope of complaints that may be filed by individuals and states, respectively), and the rapid expansion of the Council's membership and the number of ratifications of the Convention have subjected the present system to increasing stress. Despite the fact that the vast majority of individual petitions are declared to be inadmissible, the caseload of the Commission and the Court has grown considerably.

Various proposals for reforming the enforcement system for the Convention have been discussed in the past decade, and a wholesale revision of the present system was finally approved by the Council of Europe as Protocol No. 11 in May 1994. The Protocol will not enter into force until all parties to the Convention have ratified it, which will probably not occur until the late 1990s. The following excerpt from a Council of Europe publication explains the reasons for the reform and summarizes the new machinery, which will, inter alia, create the first permanent international human rights court to replace the present part-time European Commission and Court.

Council of Europe, Protocol No. 11 to the Convention for the Protection of Human Rights and Fundamental Freedoms and Explanatory Report
(1994)

19. Although the question of a reform of the supervisory machinery has been discussed since the beginning of the 1980s, the need for a reform is considered increasingly urgent as a growing number of complaints has been lodged with the Commission; in addition, new States have joined the system. The increasing workload of the Commission has also resulted in more cases being referred to the Court in the last few years.

20. The number of applications registered with the Commission has increased from 404 in 1981 to 2,037 in 1993. This figure can be expected to increase significantly in view of the fact that the system has become better known to individuals in member States, and in view of the fact that new States have and will become Parties to the Convention. By the year 2000, there may well be 35-40 States Parties to the Convention. The number of judges and members of the Commission will increase in a corresponding manner.

21. The backlog of cases before the Commission is considerable. At the end of the Commission's session in January 1994, the number of pending cases stood at 2,672, more than 1,487 of which had not yet been looked at by the Commission. It takes an average over 5 years for a case to be finally determined by the Court or the Committee of Ministers.

Also, whereas up to 1988 there were never more than 25 cases referred to the Court in one year, 31 were referred in 1989, 61 in 1990, 93 in 1991, 50 in 1992 and 52 in 1993, and it is probable that the number will increase even more in the next few years when the full effects will be felt of Protocol No. 8 regarding the Commission. Likewise at the end of 1992 the Committee of Ministers had before it 15 cases for examination under Article 32 of the Convention; the figure was 189 at the end of 1993. . . .

23. The reform proposed is thus principally aimed at restructuring the system, so as to shorten the length of Strasbourg proceedings. There is need for a supervising machinery that can work efficiently and at acceptable costs even with forty member States and which can maintain the authority and quality of the case-law in the future. . . .

IV.   Main Features of the Single Court System

26. The new single Court will replace two of the existing supervisory organs created by the European Convention on Human Rights and will perform the functions carried out by these organs. The Committee of Ministers will retain its competence [to supervise execution of the Court's judgments] under former Article 54; its competence [in the event a case is not referred to the Court] under former Article 32 of the Convention will be abolished.

COMPETENCE OF THE NEW COURT

27. The Court will have jurisdiction in all matters concerning the interpretation and application of the Convention including inter-State cases as well as individual applications. In addition, the Court will, as at present, be able to give advisory opinions when so requested by the Committee of Ministers.

28. The Court will function on a permanent basis.

COMPOSITION OF THE COURT

29. The Court will consist of a number of judges equal to that of the State Parties to the Convention, elected, as at present, by the Parliamentary Assembly with respect to each State Party. The members of the Court will be elected for a period of six years; they can be re-elected.

30. The Court will have a registry.

31. Judges may be assisted by legal secretaries (law clerks), i.e. assistants appointed for a specific period of time to work on case-files.

ORGANISATION OF THE COURT

32. When deciding cases the Court will sit in committees, Chambers and in a Grand Chamber. The judge elected in respect of the State concerned will always sit in the Chambers and Grand Chamber. Organisational matters will be dealt with by the Court in plenary, comprising all judges.

33. Committees will consist of three judges, Chambers of seven judges and the Grand Chamber of seventeen judges. There will be no quorum. The Court will appoint substitute members so that committees and Chambers can sit with the required composition of judges.

34. Committees will be set up by Chambers for a fixed period of time. Chambers will themselves determine the judges and substitute judges who are to sit in the committees. Committees will only have the power to declare cases inadmissible or strike them from the list.

35. Chambers will also be set up by the Court for a fixed period of time. The Court will designate the seven judges who will sit in a Chamber. The Court will appoint the judges and substitute judges in a way which may be specified in its rules. The possibility that a judge may be a member of two Chambers is not excluded.

36. There will be a Grand Chamber of seventeen judges to decide on individual as well as inter-State applications referred to it and to consider requests for advisory opinions. The President of the Court, the Vice-Presidents, the Presidents of the Chambers and the judge elected in respect of the State against which the application is lodged, will be *ex officio* members of the Grand Chamber. The other judges will be appointed by the Court in a way specified in the rules. When the Grand Chamber examines

cases referred to it under Article 43, of the Chamber concerned only the judge elected in respect of the State and the President of the Chamber which rendered the judgment may sit in the Grand Chamber. . . .

PROCEDURE BEFORE THE COURT

38. The Court will receive applications from:

a. any person, non-governmental organisation or group of individuals claiming to be the victim of a violation of the Convention by one of the States Parties; or

b. a State Party in the case of inter-State applications.

39. As the Secretariat of the Commission does at present, the registry of the new Court will communicate with applicants in order to deal with any matters requiring clarification before registration of an application.

40. As soon as an application is registered, a judge rapporteur will be designated by a Chamber. The individual application will normally be examined by a committee, including the judge rapporteur. The committee will have the power, exercisable by unanimous vote, to declare an application inadmissible or strike it from its list of cases if such a decision can be taken without further examination. If an application is not considered inadmissible by the committee, the case will be transferred to a Chamber, which will examine both the admissibility as well as the merits of the case. Details concerning the procedure may be dealt with in the rules of the Court. The rules of the Court may provide for the immediate transfer of applications to the Chamber, when appropriate.

41. The admissibility criteria remain unchanged. Thus the intention is that the Court will continue to exercise an effective filter function, as presently performed by the Commission.

42. Subject to powers specifically attributed to committees and the Grand Chamber, Chambers will have inherent competence to examine the admissibility and the merits of all individual and inter-State applications (for inter-State cases see also paragraph 54 below).

43. As already indicated, every application registered will be allocated to a judge rapporteur. With the help of the registry of the Court, the judge rapporteur will, under the authority of the Court, prepare the case, communicate as appropriate with the parties for that purpose and may, after the case has been declared admissible, take steps with a view to a friendly settlement.

44. The procedure will be written and oral, unless otherwise decided by the Court after consultation with the parties. Subject to powers delegated to committees, the admissibility of applications will be examined by the Chambers or the Grand Chamber. The Chamber's decisions on admissibility will, in principle, be taken separately from the merits.

The facts will be established by the Court, with the co-operation of the parties. The Court will be at the disposal of the parties in order to secure a friendly settlement on the basis of respect for human rights.

45. The merits of an application will be examined by a Chamber and, exceptionally, by the Grand Chamber. The parties will present their submissions by means of a written procedure. Oral procedure will consist of a hearing at which the applicant, or a State Party in an inter-State case, and the respondent State will have the right to speak.

46. In cases with specified serious implications, a Chamber will be able to relinquish jurisdiction *proprio motu* in favour of the Grand Chamber at any time, as long as it has not yet rendered judgment, unless one of the parties to the case objects. Such relinquishment should also speed up proceedings. Once a judgment has been rendered by a Chamber, only the parties may request that the case be referred to the Grand Chamber for a rehearing.

47. Following the judgment delivered by a Chamber of the Court, the Grand Chamber, at the request of one of the parties to the case and in exceptional cases, will be competent to re-examine a case if the case raises serious questions concerning the interpretation or application of the Convention or its protocols, or if the case raises an issue of general importance. The purpose is to ensure the quality and consistency of the Court's case-law by allowing for a re-examination of the most important cases if the above-mentioned conditions are met. A panel of five judges of the Grand Chamber will decide on whether a case is to be accepted for re-examination.

48. The provisions of the Protocol also provide for the participation of third parties in proceedings before the Court. In cases declared admissible, States whose nationals have lodged applications against other States Parties to the Convention, will have the possibility to submit written comments and take part in hearings.

Likewise, the President of the Court will be able to invite or authorise any Contracting State which is not Party to proceedings and any person establishing an interest in the result of any case brought before it to submit observations.

49. The Court will determine the question of just satisfaction, including that of costs and expenses.

50. The judgment of the Grand Chamber will be final. The judgment of the Chamber will become final in accordance with the new Article 44, paragraph 2, if the case in which it has been rendered is not brought before the Grand Chamber. Final judgments of the Court will be binding. The Committee of Ministers will, as at present, supervise their execution. . . .

OUTLINE OF THE PROCEDURE

52. The basic order of procedure in a case which proceeds to judgment on the merits will be, in most cases, as follows:

- lodging of application;
- preliminary contacts with Court's registry;
- registration of application;
- assignment of application to a Chamber;
- appointment of judge rapporteur by the Chamber;
- examination by a three-member committee;
- communication of the application to the Government;
- filing of observations and establishment of facts;
- oral hearing;
- admissibility decision by Chamber;
- possibility of friendly settlement negotiations;
- judgment by the Chamber.

53. In exceptional cases an application may be referred to the Grand Chamber which will render judgment after written and, if the Court so decides, oral proceedings.

PROCEDURE APPLICABLE TO INTER-STATE APPLICATIONS

54. Any State Party will be able to refer to the Court any alleged breach of the provision of the Convention by another State Party; a Chamber will have jurisdiction.

V. The Choice of an Amending Rather Than
   an Optional Protocol

55. The fundamental character of the reform of the control mechanism necessitates approval by all States Parties to the Convention. Therefore, Protocol No. 11 is conceived in the form of an amending protocol, in respect of which all States Parties must express their consent to be bound in order for it to enter into force.

56. Only an amending protocol can prevent two different mechanisms of control from existing side by side. Such a parallelism would not be desirable because a homogeneous and clearly consistent development of case-law constitutes an important basis of human rights protection under the Convention. Furthermore, the existence of two groups of States subject to two different supervisory mechanisms would invariably cause considerable procedural complications, e.g. for the registry and for judges sitting in both the old and the new Courts. This would run counter to the aim of the reform to increase efficiency. Finally, the parallelism of two mechanisms of supervision could cause confusion for individual applicants, a result contrary to the aim of creating a more transparent system.

Note: Interstate Complaints

In Problem III it was noted that the state-to-state complaint procedure provided for by the Civil and Political Covenant never has produced a single such case. The record under the European Convention is a bit better. As of 1 July 1994, the Commission had registered 18 cases brought by one member state against another member state. The perpetual tension in Cyprus has been the most fruitful source of interstate complaints: even before Cyprus achieved its independence in 1960, Greece had lodged two complaints against the United Kingdom for its activities there. In the 1970s, Cyprus itself, now a party to the Convention, lodged three complaints against Turkey. Austria has complained against Italy regarding the latter's treatment of German-speaking Italian nationals from the South Tyrol. A total of five complaints against Greece for conditions there under the military regime were filed in the early 1970s, as were five complaints against Turkey in 1983. The disturbances in Northern Ireland also produced two complaints by Ireland against the United Kingdom, one of which is considered below.

The Greek and Irish cases have been the most interesting. The first four complaints against Greece, brought in 1967 by Norway, Sweden, Denmark, and The Netherlands, alleged violations of Articles 5, 6, 8, 9, 10, 11, 13, and 14 of the Convention. Later, in 1970, an additional complaint was lodged by the three Scandinavian states. At the same time, the political organs of the Council of Europe were investigating conditions in Greece. Speculation as to the result of either procedure was abruptly reduced to an academic question on 12 December 1969, when Greece withdrew from the Council of Europe and renounced the Convention. (See [1971] Eur. Y.B. 273-335.) Greece rejoined the Council and Convention on 28 February 1974 after the return of parliamentary government to Greece.

The Irish complaint against the United Kingdom, brought in 1971, alleged that the latter had resorted to torture and degrading treatment in breach of Article 3 of the Convention when interrogating detainees in Northern Ireland. Although the United Kingdom had announced, pursuant to Article 15, that it was derogating from certain of the rights guaranteed by the Convention, that Article also forbids any derogation whatever from the prohibition of torture and degrading treatment. In 1976 the Commission completed and published its conclusions in the matter, conclusions that largely were favorable to the Irish position. See [1976] Y.B. Eur. Conv. on Human Rights 512-949 (Eur. Commn. on Human Rights). It was Ireland, however, and not the United Kingdom, that appealed the case to the Court pursuant to Article 48. The case is of interest not only for its holding about what constitutes torture as opposed to inhuman or degrading treatment, but also because it is the only case that the Court has decided that has not originated through the individual petition route.

Ireland v. United Kingdom
European Ct. Hum. Rts., Judgment of 13 Dec. 1977, Ser. A
No. 25, 2 Eur. Hum. Rts. Rep. 25

[The Court's judgment opens with a lengthy history of the conflict in Northern Ireland, ending with the United Kingdom's introduction in 1971 of internment without trial of IRA suspects and its imposition in 1972 of direct rule by the United Kingdom. It then proceeds to examine in great detail the two principal claims by the Irish government: (1) that various persons taken into custody on or after 9 August 1971 by British authorities (including the British Army and the Royal Ulster Constabulary or RUC) under the Special Powers Act had been subjected to treatment that constituted torture and inhuman and degrading treatment contrary to Article 3 of the European Convention; (2) that in any event internment without trial, as carried out in Northern Ireland subsequent to 9 August 1971, constituted a violation of Article 5 of the European Convention (which guarantees the right to liberty and security of person).]

III. ALLEGATIONS OF ILL-TREATMENT

A. INTRODUCTION

92. . . . [O]n 9 August 1971 and thereafter numerous persons in Northern Ireland were arrested and taken into custody by the security forces acting in pursuance of the emergency powers. The persons arrested were interrogated, usually by members of the RUC, in order to determine whether they should be interned and/or to compile information about the IRA. In all, about 3,276 persons were processed by the police at various holding centres from August 1971 until June 1972. The holding centres were replaced in July 1972 by police offices in Belfast and at Ballykelly Military Barracks.

93. Allegations of ill-treatment have been made by the applicant Government in relation both to the initial arrests and to the subsequent interrogations. The applicant Government submitted written evidence to the Commission in respect of 228 cases concerning incidents between 9 August 1971 and 1974.

The procedure followed for the purposes of ascertaining the facts (Article 28, sub-paragraph (a), of the Convention) was one decided upon by the Commission and accepted by the Parties. The Commission examined in detail with medical reports and oral evidence 16 "illustrative" cases selected at its request by the applicant Government. The Commission considered a further 41 cases (the so-called "41 cases") on which it had received medical reports and invited written comments; it referred to the remaining cases.

The nature of the evidence submitted by the two Governments and the procedure followed by the Commission in its investigation of such evidence are set out in some detail in the Commission's report. The Commission came to the view that neither the witnesses from the security forces nor the case-witnesses put forward by the applicant Government had given accurate and complete accounts of what had happened. Consequently, where the allegations of ill-treatment were in dispute, the Commission treated as "the most important objective evidence" the medical findings which were not contested as such.

The following account of events is based on the information set out in the Commission's report and in the other documents before the Court.

94. In order to protect the identity of certain persons, notably witnesses, the published version of the Commission's report . . . incorporated changes to the original text; these changes mainly took the form of designating such persons by letters and/or figures. . . .

B.   THE UNIDENTIFIED INTERROGATION CENTRE OR CENTRES

96. Twelve persons arrested on 9 August 1971 and two persons arrested in October 1971 were singled out and taken to one or more unidentified centres. There, between 11 to 17 August and 11 to 18 October respectively, they were submitted to a form of "interrogation in depth" which involved the combined application of five particular techniques.

These methods, sometimes termed "disorientation" or "sensory deprivation" techniques, . . . consisted of:

(a) *wall-standing*: forcing the detainees to remain for periods of some hours in a "stress position," described by those who underwent it as being "spreadeagled against the wall, with their fingers put high above the head against the wall, the legs spread apart and the feet back, causing them to stand on their toes with the weight of the body mainly on the fingers";

(b) *hooding*: putting a black or navy coloured bag over the detainees' heads and, at least initially, keeping it there all the time except during interrogation;

(c) *subjection to noise*: pending their interrogations, holding the detainees in a room where there was a continuous loud and hissing noise;

(d) *deprivation of sleep*: pending their interrogations, depriving the detainees of sleep;

(e) *deprivation of food and drink*: subjecting the detainees to a reduced diet during their stay at the centre and pending interrogations. . . .

97. From the start, it has been conceded by the respondent Government that the use of the five techniques was authorised at "high level." Although never committed to writing or authorised in any official docu-

ment, the techniques had been orally taught to members of the RUC by the English Intelligence Centre at a seminar held in April 1971.

98. The two operations of interrogation in depth by means of the five techniques led to the obtaining of a considerable quantity of intelligence information, including the identification of 700 members of both IRA factions and the discovery of individual responsibility for about 85 previously unexplained criminal incidents.

99. Reports alleging physical brutality and ill-treatment by the security forces were made public within a few days. . . . A committee of enquiry under the chairmanship of Sir Edmund Compton was appointed by the United Kingdom Government on 31 August 1971 to investigate such allegations. Among the 40 cases this Committee examined were 11 cases of persons subjected to the five techniques in August 1971; its findings were that interrogation in depth by means of the techniques constituted physical ill-treatment but not physical brutality as it understood that term. The Committee's report, adopted on 3 November 1971, was made public, as was a supplemental report of 14 November by Sir Edmund Compton in relation to 3 further cases occurring in September and October, one of which involved the techniques.

100. The Compton reports came under considerable criticism in the United Kingdom. On 16 November 1971, the British Home Secretary announced that a further Committee had been set up under the chairmanship of Lord Parker of Waddington to consider "whether, and if so in what respects, the procedures currently authorised for interrogation of persons suspected of terrorism and for their custody while subject to interrogation require amendment."

The Parker report, which was adopted on 31 January 1972, contained a majority and a minority opinion. The majority report concluded that the application of the techniques, subject to recommended safeguards against excessive use, need not be ruled out on moral grounds. On the other hand, the minority report by Lord Gardiner disagreed that such interrogation procedures were morally justifiable, even in emergency terrorist conditions. Both the majority and the minority considered the methods to be illegal under domestic law, although the majority confined their view to English law and to "some if not all the techniques."

101. The Parker report was published on 2 March 1972. On the same day, the United Kingdom Prime Minister stated in Parliament:

> [The] Government, having reviewed the whole matter with great care and with reference to any future operations, have decided that the techniques . . . will not be used in future as an aid to interrogation.

. . . As foreshadowed in the Prime Minister's statement, directives expressly prohibiting the use of the techniques, whether singly or in combination, were then issued to the security forces by the Government (see paragraph 135 below).

102. At the hearing before the Court on 8 February 1977, the United Kingdom Attorney-General made the following declaration:

> The Government of the United Kingdom have considered the question of the use of the "five techniques" with very great care and with particular regard to Article 3 of the Convention. They now give this unqualified undertaking, that the "five techniques" will not in any circumstances be reintroduced as an aid to interrogation. . . .

G. MEASURES CONCERNING THE TREATMENT OF PERSONS ARRESTED OR HELD BY THE SECURITY FORCES

. . . 2. Provisions Designed to Prevent Ill-Treatment

134. It would appear that at the beginning of the internment operation reliance was simply placed on the normal regulations requiring humane treatment and forbidding the use of violence.

135. Following the Parker report and the Prime Minister's statement to Parliament (see paragraph 101 above), a directive on interrogation was issued prohibiting the use of coercion and, in particular, of the five techniques. In addition, it made mandatory medical examination, the keeping of comprehensive records and the immediate reporting of any complaints of ill-treatment. In April 1972, army instructions and the RUC Force Order 64/72, concerning respectively arrests under the Special Powers Regulations and the treatment of prisoners, directed that excessive force should never be used. Shortly after the introduction of direct rule, the United Kingdom Attorney-General gave a ministerial directive on the proper treatment of persons in custody, making it clear that where any form of ill-treatment was reported the Director of Public Prosecutions would prosecute. Further army and RUC instructions of August 1972 in respect of arrest and interrogation enjoined the proper and humane treatment of prisoners; they strictly forbade resort to violence, the five techniques, threats or insults and concluded with a prohibition similar to Article 3 of the Convention. In August 1973 new instructions with regard to arrests by the army re-emphasised the need for correct behaviour.

The respondent Government submitted that steps had been taken for the diffusion and enforcement at all levels of these orders and directives. However, both the Commission and the applicant Government considered that there was a lack of satisfactory evidence as to how the regulations were implemented and obeyed in practice.

136. Section 6 of the Emergency Provisions Act . . . contained provisions designed to exclude as evidence before an ordinary criminal court statements by an accused obtained by torture or inhuman or degrading treatment; the section did not apply to the extrajudicial procedures or to statements by third parties.

3. Complaints Procedures and Criminal Prosecutions

(a) The police

137. Under the Police Act (Northern Ireland) 1970, an investigation department within the RUC had been set up to report to the Chief Constable on all complaints against the police whatever their source. An official committee of five members of the Police Authority of Northern Ireland, including two Catholics and two Protestants, examined each month the records of complaints kept by the Chief Constable.

Where a serious criminal offence was disclosed, reports were submitted to the Attorney-General for Northern Ireland or, after the introduction of direct rule, to the Director of Public Prosecutions in Northern Ireland, a newly-created office for decisions whether to prosecute. On 15 June 1972, the United Kingdom Attorney-General instructed the Director of Public Prosecutions to direct the RUC to investigate and report on any circumstances which might involve the commission of a criminal offence by a member of the security forces. From November 1972 onwards, all completed investigations of both police officers and army personnel had to be sent to the Director of Public Prosecutions.

In September 1973, new disciplinary regulations brought the arrangements for the investigation of complaints against the RUC into line with the arrangements existing elsewhere in the United Kingdom. In 1975, a fresh unit was established within the RUC under the direct control of the Deputy Chief Constable to be responsible for the investigation of complaints.

138. The Gardiner Committee in its report of January 1975 . . . , while expressing itself satisfied that full investigations were made, nevertheless found a widespread belief in Northern Ireland that complaints against members of the security forces were not taken seriously. It therefore recommended the setting up of an independent means of investigating complaints.

The Police (Northern Ireland) Order 1977 established a completely independent Police Complaints Board for Northern Ireland with supervisory functions in the matter.

(b) The army

139. The policy of the General Officer Commanding, as stated in the evidence before the Commission, was that every complaint should be investigated. An investigator was automatically appointed as soon as an incident was reported, even before a formal complaint had been made. As with the RUC, notice was also taken of allegations in the press or from third parties.

It would seem that in the early stages of the emergency complaints against soldiers were handled by the army authorities themselves; later on, two RUC officers were appointed to oversee army enquiries and subsequently investigations were actually carried out by the RUC, at least where there appeared to be a serious criminal offence. In addition, complainants were encouraged to channel their complaints through the police. On 20 January 1972 a joint army/RUC investigation team was created.

Complaints against the army were referred to an outside authority — the Director of Public Prosecutions as from April 1972 — for direction whether to prosecute.

(c) Statistics relating to complaints and prosecutions

140. Between 9 August 1971 and 30 November 1974, 2,615 complaints against the police were made, 1,105 alleging ill-treatment or assault; the 23 prosecutions for assault resulted in 6 convictions leading to fines and, in one case, a conditional discharge.

As regards the army, from 31 March 1972 to 30 November 1974, 1,268 complaints in respect of assaults or shootings had been received and 1,078 cases of alleged assault were submitted to the Director of Public Prosecutions. By January 1975, directions to prosecute had been given in 86 out of the 1,038 cases then dealt with.

Overall, between April 1972 and the end of January 1977, 218 members of the security forces were prosecuted for assault at the direction of the Director of Public Prosecutions and 155 were convicted.

(d) Particular instances of investigation, disciplinary action or prosecution

141. Soon after complaints relating to the arrests carried out on 9 August 1971 became known, nearly 1,800 soldiers, including 300 or so who had left Northern Ireland, were interviewed in order to determine their rôle in the arrest operation. The Commission's report also mentions a few other specific examples of members of the security forces being investigated or disciplined, but these examples are not connected with the cases submitted by the applicant Government. No information of any investigation into the submitted cases was vouchsafed to the Commission by the respondent Government except in relation to the illustrative cases. Even as regards the illustrative cases, the Commission had before it just one item of direct evidence — the Compton reports, filed by the applicant government — and it noted that in none of them had the authorities carried out a thorough investigation of the allegations of ill-treatment; evidence as to disciplinary action or prosecution was furnished to the Commission in one case alone, that of T7. . . .

4. Compensation

142. Procedures to obtain compensation were available before the domestic courts to all persons who considered themselves to have been ill-treated by the security forces. There is no suggestion that the domestic courts were or are anything other than independent, fair and impartial. The

respondent Government have emphasised the difference between domestic civil and criminal law. Under the former the authorities are liable for any wrongful act, established on the balance of probabilities, committed in the course of their duty by soldiers or policemen, whether individually identified or not. The criminal law, in contrast, requires proof beyond reasonable doubt of the guilt of an indentified individual. Like any plaintiff in a civil action, a plaintiff alleging ill-treatment by the security forces was entitled to obtain disclosure of relevant documents, for example medical reports, in the possession of the defendant authorities.

143. Between 9 August 1971 and 31 January 1975, compensation totalling £302,043 had been paid in settlement of 473 civil claims for wrongful arrest, false imprisonment, assault and battery, leaving 1,193 actions still outstanding. At the time of the Commission's report, compensation, ranging from about £200 to £25,000, had been paid in settlement of 45 of 228 cases submitted by the applicant Government. In the only case of alleged physical ill-treatment which seems to have been fought, namely the case of Moore v. Shillington . . . , the judge disbelieved the evidence of the security forces.

PROCEEDINGS BEFORE THE COMMISSION

144. In their original application, lodged with the Commission on 16 December 1971, and later supplemented, the Irish Government made various allegations of violations by the United Kingdom of Articles 1, 2, 3, 5, 6 and 14 of the Convention.

145. On 1 October 1972, the Commission declared the application inadmissible as regards Article 2 but accepted the allegations that:
— the treatment of persons in custody, in particular the methods of interrogation of such persons, constituted an administrative practice in breach of Article 3;
— internment without trial and detention under the Special Powers Act and the Special Powers Regulations constituted an administrative practice in breach of Articles 5 and 6 in connection with Article 15;
'— the exercise by the respondent Government of their power to detain and intern persons was being carried out with discrimination on the grounds of political opinion and thus constituted a breach of Article 14 with respect to the rights and freedoms guaranteed in Articles 5 and 6 in conjunction with Article 15;
— the administrative practices complained of also constituted a breach of Article 1.

146. In addition to receiving written observations and evidence from the two Governments concerned and to hearing their oral submissions, the Commission also heard — through delegates and in the circumstances

more particularly detailed in its report — a total of 119 witnesses. One hundred gave evidence in relation to the issues under Article 3 and nineteen in relation to those under Article 14; of the latter, three were witnesses proposed by the respondent Government who were heard by the delegates in London in the absence of representatives of the Parties and without being subjected to cross-examination.

147. In its report, the Commission expressed the opinion:

    (i)   unanimously, that the powers of detention and internment without trial as exercised during the relevant periods were not in conformity with Article 5, §§1 to 4, but were "strictly required by the exigencies of the situation" in Northern Ireland, within the meaning of Article 15 §1;

    (ii) unanimously, that Article 6 did not apply to the said powers;

    (iii) unanimously, that the facts found in relation to the relevant periods did not disclose any discrimination contrary to Article 14 in the exercise of the said powers;

    (iv) unanimously, that the combined use of the five techniques in the cases before it constituted a practice of inhuman treatment and of torture in breach of Article 3;

    (v) unanimously, that violation of Article 3 occurred by inhuman, and in two cases degrading, treatment of
       — T6, in an unidentified interrogation centre in August 1971,
       — T2, T8, T12, T15, T9, T14, and T10 at Palace Barracks, Holywood, in September, October and November 1971,
       — T16, T7 and T11, at various places in August, October and December 1971;

    (vi) unanimously, that there had been at Palace Barracks, Holywood, in the autumn of 1971, a practice in connection with the interrogation of prisoners by members of the RUC which was inhuman treatment in breach of Article 3 of the Convention;

    (vii) unanimously, that no practice in breach of Article 3 had been found to exist in relation to the cases of T16, T7 and T11, including the general conditions at Girdwood Park in August 1971;

    (viii) unanimously, that the conditions of detention at Ballykinler in August 1971 did not disclose a violation of Article 3;

    (ix) by twelve votes to one, that Article 1, not granting any rights in addition to those mentioned in Section 1 of the Convention, cannot be the subject of a separate breach.

The report contains various separate opinions.

As to the Law

. . . In their written and oral pleadings before the Court, the Irish Government allege breaches of Article 1, 3, 5 (taken together with Article 15), 6 (taken together with Article 15) and 14 (taken together with Articles 5 and 6). . . .

149. The Court notes first of all that it is not called upon to take cognisance of every single aspect of the tragic situation prevailing in Northern Ireland. For example, it is not required to rule on the terrorist activities in the six counties of individuals or of groups, activities that are in clear disregard of human rights. The Court has only to give a decision on the claims made before it by the Irish Republic against the United Kingdom. However, in so doing, the Court cannot lose sight of the events that form the background to this case.

I.   On Article 3

150. Article 3 provides that "no one shall be subjected to torture or to inhuman or degrading treatment or punishment." . . .

C.   QUESTIONS CONCERNING THE MERITS

162. As was emphasised by the Commission, ill-treatment must attain a minimum level of severity if it is to fall within the scope of Article 3. The assessment of this minimum is, in the nature of things, relative; it depends on all the circumstances of the case, such as the duration of the treatment, its physical or mental effects and, in some cases, the sex, age and state of health of the victim, etc.

163. The Convention prohibits in absolute terms torture and inhuman or degrading treatment or punishment, irrespective of the victim's conduct. Unlike most of the substantive clauses of the Convention and of Protocols Nos. 1 and 4, Article 3 makes no provision for exceptions and, under Article 15 §2, there can be no derogation therefrom even in the event of a public emergency threatening the life of the nation.

164. In the instant case, the only relevant concepts are "torture" and "inhuman or degrading treatment," to the exclusion of "inhuman or degrading punishment."

1.   The Unidentified Interrogation Centre or Centres

(a)   The "five techniques"

165. The facts concerning the five techniques are summarised . . . above. In the Commission's estimation, those facts constituted a practice

not only of inhuman and degrading treatment but also of torture. The applicant Government ask for confirmation of this opinion which is not contested before the Court by the respondent Government. . . .

167. The five techniques were applied in combination, with premeditation and for hours at a stretch; they caused, if not actual bodily injury, at least intense physical and mental suffering to the persons subjected thereto and also led to acute psychiatric disturbances during interrogation. They accordingly fell into the category of inhuman treatment within the meaning of Article 3. The techniques were also degrading since they were such as to arouse in their victims feelings of fear, anguish and inferiority capable of humiliating and debasing them and possibly breaking their physical or moral resistance.

On these two points, the Court is of the same view as the Commission.

In order to determine whether the five techniques should also be qualified as torture, the Court must have regard to the distinction, embodied in Article 3, between this notion and that of inhuman or degrading treatment.

In the Court's view, this distinction derives principally from a difference in the intensity of the suffering inflicted.

The Court considers in fact that, whilst there exists on the one hand violence which is to be condemned both on moral grounds and also in most cases under the domestic law of the Contacting States but which does not fall within Article 3 of the Convention, it appears on the other hand that it was the intention that the Convention, with its distinction between "torture" and "inhuman or degrading treatment," should by the first of these terms attach a special stigma to deliberate inhuman treatment causing very serious and cruel suffering.

Moreover, this seems to be the thinking lying behind Article 1 *in fine* of Resolution 3452 (XXX) adopted by the General Assembly of the United Nations on 9 December 1975, which declares; "Torture constitutes an *aggravated* and deliberate form of cruel, inhuman or degrading treatment or punishment."

Although the five techniques, as applied in combination, undoubtedly amounted to inhuman and degrading treatment, although their object was the extraction of confessions, the naming of others and/or information and although they were used systematically, they did not occasion suffering of the particular intensity and cruelty implied by the word torture as so understood.

168. The Court concludes that recourse to the five techniques amounted to a practice of inhuman and degrading treatment, which practice was in breach of Article 3. . . .

II.   On Article 5

188. The substance of the Irish Government's allegations is that

— the various powers relating to extrajudicial deprivation of liberty which were used in the six counties from 9 August 1971 to March 1975 did not satisfy the conditions prescribed by Article 5;

— those powers violated Article 5 since they failed to meet in full the requirements of Article 15;

— those powers were furthermore exercised with discrimination and consequently also violated Article 14 taken together with Article 5. . . .

191. It will, of course, be necessary to have regard to Article 15 in deciding whether any derogations from Article 5 were, in the circumstances of the case, compatible with the convention, but the Court considers that it should ascertain in what respects the measures complained of derogated from Article 5 before assessing them under Article 15.

A.   PARAGRAPHS 1 TO 4 OF ARTICLE 5, TAKEN ALONE

192. Paragraphs 1 to 4 of Article 5 read as follows:

1. Everyone has the right to liberty and security of person. No one shall be deprived of his liberty save in the following cases and in accordance with a procedure prescribed by law:

(a)   the lawful detention of a person after conviction by a competent court;

(b)   the lawful arrest or detention of a person for non-compliance with the lawful order of a court or in order to secure the fulfilment of any obligation prescribed by law;

(c)   the lawful arrest or detention of a person affected for the purpose of bringing him before the competent legal authority on reasonable suspicion of having committed an offence or when it is reasonably considered necessary to prevent his committing an offence or fleeing after having done so;

(d)   the detention of a minor by lawful order for the purpose of educational supervision or his lawful detention for the purpose of bringing him before the competent legal authority;

(e)   the lawful detention of persons for the prevention of the spreading of infectious diseases, of persons of unsound mind, alcoholics or drug addicts or vagrants;

(f)   the lawful arrest or detention of a person to prevent his effecting an unauthorised entry into the country or of a person against whom action is being taken with a view to deportation or extradition.

2. Everyone who is arrested shall be informed promptly, in a language which he understands, of the reasons for his arrest and of any charge against him.

3. Everyone arrested or detained in accordance with the provisions of paragraph 1(c) of this Article shall be brought promptly before a judge or other officer authorised by law to exercise judicial power and shall be entitled to trial within a reasonable time or to release pending trial. Release may be conditioned by guarantees to appear for trial.

4. Everyone who is deprived of his liberty by arrest or detention shall be entitled to take proceedings by which the lawfulness of his detention shall be

decided speedily by a court and his release ordered if the detention is not lawful.

193. In the Commission's opinion, the powers at issue — as exercised by the competent authorities — did not comply with paragraphs 1 to 4 of Article 5 on a number of points.

The applicant Government agree with this conclusion; the respondent Government do not contest it but indicate that they do not necessarily accept all of the reasons.

1. Paragraph 1

194. *Paragraph 1* of Article 5 contains a list of the cases in which it is permissible under the Convention to deprive someone of his liberty. Subject to Article 15 — and without prejudice to Article 1 or Protocol No. 4 which the United Kingdom has not ratified — , that list is exhaustive: this appears from the words "save in the following cases" and is confirmed by Article 17.

195. The different forms of deprivation of liberty in this case clearly did not fall under sub-paragraphs (a), (d), (e) and (f) of paragraph 1.

Neither were such deprivations covered by *sub-paragraph (b)*, since they had no connection whatsoever with a "non-compliance with the . . . order of a court" and were not designed to "secure the fulfilment of any obligation prescribed by law" (Lawless judgment of 1 July 1961, Series A no. 3, p. 51, §12; Engel and others judgment of 8 June 1976, Series A no. 22, p. 28, §69, third sub-paragraph).

196. At first sight, the different forms of deprivation of liberty may appear to bear some resemblance to the cases contemplated by *sub-paragraph (c)*.

However, a "suspicion" of an "offence" was not required before a person could be arrested under Regulation 10, nor did it have to be "considered necessary to prevent his committing an offence or fleeing after having done so"; arrest had merely to be "for the preservation of the peace and maintenance of order" and was sometimes used to interrogate the person concerned about the activities of others. . . .

On the other hand, the other three Regulations complained of by the Irish Government did require a suspicion. While Regulations 11(1) (arrest) and 11(2) (detention) spoke both of an "offence" and of activity "prejudicial to the preservation of the peace or maintenance of order" . . . , and while this latter concept alone appeared in Regulation 12(1) . . . , section 2(4) of the Special Powers Act made such activity an offence.

The Terrorists Order (interim custody and detention) and the Emergency Provisions Act (arrest, interim custody and detention), for their part, were applicable only to individuals suspected of having been concerned in the commission or attempted commission of any act of terrorism, that is the use of violence for political ends, or in the organisation of persons for the purpose of terrorism; these criteria were well in keeping with the idea of an offence. . . .

Irrespective of whether extrajudicial deprivation of liberty was or was not founded in the majority of cases on suspicions of a kind that would render detention on remand justifiable under the Convention, such detention is permissible under Article 5 §1(c) only if it is "effected for the purpose of bringing [the detainee] before the competent legal authority." Yet this condition — if interpreted, as must be done, in the light of paragraph 3 of Article 5 (Lawless judgment of 1 July 1961, Series A no. 3, pp. 51-53, §14) — was not fulfilled; the Court refers, in this connection, to paragraph 199 below.

2.   Paragraphs 2 to 4

197. Paragraphs 2 to 4 of Article 5 place the Contracting States under an obligation to provide several guarantees in cases where someone is deprived to his liberty.

198. Under *paragraph 2*, "everyone who is arrested shall be informed promptly . . . of the reasons for his arrest and of any charge against him." However, there was no such provision either in Regulations 10 and 11(1) or in section 10 of the Emergency Provisions Act. In point of fact, the persons concerned were not normally informed why they were being arrested; in general, they were simply told that the arrest was made pursuant to the emergency legislation and they were given no further details. . . . This practice originated in instructions issued to the military police in May 1970 and it continued at least until it was declared unlawful by the courts (see the *McElduff* case, judgment of 12 October 1971, and the *Kelly* case, judgment of 11 January 1973, on Regulation 11(1); the *Moore* case, judgment of 18 February 1972, on Regulation 10).

199. As for *paragraph 3*, taken together with paragraph 1(c) (see paragraph 196 above), the Court finds that the impugned measures were not effected for the purpose of bringing the persons concerned "promptly" before "the competent legal authority," namely "a judge or other officer authorised by law to exercise judicial power."

Persons originally detained under, for example, Regulation 11(2) were, in fact, sometimes brought before the ordinary courts . . . , but paragraphs 1(c) and 3 of Article 5 of the Convention are not satisfied by an appearance "before the competent legal authority" in some cases since such appearance is obligatory in every single case governed by those paragraphs. For its part, the advisory committee before which were brought — on the occasions when they so consented — individuals interned under Regulation 12(1) did not have power to order their release and accordingly did not constitute a "competent legal authority." . . .

On the other hand, such a power was vested by the Terrorists Order and, subsequently, by the Emergency Provisions Act in the commissioners who adjudicated on cases of persons subjected to interim custody orders made by the Secretary of State for Northern Ireland. However, even if such a commissioner is regarded as a judicial authority ("officer," "magistrat"), appearance before him did not take place "aussitôt," or even "promptly." . . .

A person "arrested or detained" pursuant to one of the provisions complained of was even less entitled to "trial within a reasonable time" or to "release pending trial" conditioned, if need be, by "guarantees to appear for trial," within the meaning of Article 5 §3. Quite the contrary: the reason for the existence of those provisions and of the related practice was the fact that the circumstances prevailing at the time made it difficult, subject to exceptions, to institute criminal proceedings which would in principle have led to a judicial hearing ("audience") and to a "[decision] on the merits" (Lawless judgment of 1 July 1961, Series A no. 3, p. 52, first sub-paragraph).

200. There remains *paragraph 4* which is applicable to "everyone who is deprived of his liberty," whether lawfully or not (De Wilde, Ooms and Versyp judgment of 18 June 1971, Series A no. 12, pp. 39-40, §73).

Under Regulations 10, 11(1) and 11(2) there was no entitlement to "take proceedings by which the lawfulness of [the] detention [would] be decided speedily by a court" and "release ordered if the detention" proved to be "not lawful. . . ." As regards Regulation 12(1), the advisory committee to which internees had the possibility of making representations could at most recommend, as opposed to order, release, as the Court has already noted (see paragraph . . . 199 above). Moreover, the committee's procedure did not afford the fundamental guarantees inherent in the notion of "court" as used in Article 5 §4 (De Wilde, Ooms and Verysp judgment of 18 June 1971, Series A no. 12, pp. 40-42, §76, second and third sub-paragraphs, and §78). . . .

The last remark also applies, mutatis mutandis, to the commissioners and to the appeal tribunal entrusted with supervisory functions by the Terrorists Order and, subsequently, by the Emergency Provisions Act. . . . Here again, the Court does not consider it indispensable to enquire further into the matter. In fact, only the Chief Constable and, in certain circumstances, the Secretary of State were empowered to refer to a commissioner the case of a person detained under an interim custody order. . . . The detainee himself was not entitled to "take proceedings" in respect of an interim custody order; he had no means of contesting the "lawfulness" of his detention, either during its initial twenty-eight day period or during its extension pending the commissioner's adjudication. . . . When that adjudication resulted in a detention order, the individual could challenge the order before the appeal tribunal; in general, however, that tribunal did not give its decision "speedily," at least if, as must be done, the length of the earlier proceedings before the commissioner is also taken into account. . . . Accordingly, the commissioners and the appeal tribunal did not meet each of the requirements of Article 5 §4.

The respondent Government maintain that habeas corpus proceedings, on the other hand, fully satisfied those requirements. The Court has, in fact, cognisance of a judgment delivered by a court before whom an individual had challenged under common law his deprivation of liberty pursuant to Regulations 11(1) and 11(2) (the *McElduff* case, judgment of 12 October 1971). However, the courts considered that their powers did not go beyond the limits indicated . . . above [in omitted portions]. The judicial review of the lawfulness of the measures in issue was thus not sufficiently wide in scope, taking into account the purpose and object of Article 5 §4 of the Convention.

201. On paragraphs 1 to 4 of Article 5, taken alone, the Court therefore arrives at conclusions in line with those of the Commission.

B. ON ARTICLE 5 TAKEN TOGETHER WITH ARTICLE 15

202. The applicant Government maintain that the powers relating to extrajudicial deprivation of liberty which were applied in Northern Ireland from 9 August 1971 to March 1975 were not in complete conformity with Article 15 and, accordingly, violated Article 5.

The Commission is unanimous in not accepting this claim and it is disputed by the respondent Government.

203. Article 15 provides:

> 1. In time of war or other public emergency threatening the life of the nation any High Contracting Party may take measures derogating from its obligations under this Convention to the extent strictly required by the exigencies of the situation, provided that such measures are not inconsistent with its other obligations under international law.
>
> 2. No derogation from Article 2, except in respect of deaths resulting from lawful acts of war, or from Articles 3, 4 (paragraph 1) and 7 shall be made under this provision.
>
> 3. Any High Contracting Party availing itself of this right of derogation shall keep the Secretary-General of the Council of Europe fully informed of the measures which it has taken and the reasons therefore. It shall also inform the Secretary-General of the Council of Europe when such measures have ceased to operate and the provisions of the Convention are again being fully executed.

204. Article 5 does not appear amongst the entrenched provisions listed in paragraph 2 of Article 15 and is therefore one of the Articles subject to the "right of derogation" reserved by the Contracting States, the exercise of which is regulated by paragraphs 1 and 3.

1. On the "Public Emergency Threatening the Life of the Nation"

205. Article 15 comes into play only "in time of war or other public emergency threatening the life of the nation." The existence of such an emergency is perfectly clear from the facts summarised . . . and was not

questioned by anyone before either the Commission or the Court. The crisis experienced at the time by the six counties therefore comes within the ambit of Article 15.

2.   On the "Extent Strictly Required"

206. The Contracting States may make use of their right of derogation only "to the extent strictly required by the exigencies of the situation." The Irish Government consider the "extent strictly required" to have been exceeded, whereas the British Government and the Commission assert the contrary. . . .

[The Court then went on to consider the proper scope of its role in reviewing the United Kingdom's declaration of a state of emergency and the weight it should give to various kinds of evidence. Excerpts from these paragraphs are set out at page 475 of Problem VI and pages 926-927 of Problem XI.]

(c)   Questions concerning the merits

211. The Court has to decide whether the United Kingdom went beyond the "extent strictly required." For this purpose the Court must, as in the Lawless case (judgment of 1 July 1961, Series A no. 3, pp. 57-59, §§36 - 37), enquire into the necessity for, on the one hand, deprivation of liberty contrary to paragraph 1 of Article 5 and, on the other hand, the failure of guarantees to attain the level fixed by paragraphs 2 to 4.

(i)   On the necessity for derogation from paragraph 1 of Article 5 by extrajudicial deprivation of liberty

212. Unquestionably, the exercise of the special powers was mainly, and before 5 February 1973 even exclusively, directed against the IRA as an underground military force. The intention was to combat an organisation which had played a considerable subversive rôle throughout the recent history of Ireland and which was creating, in August 1971 and thereafter, a particularly far-reaching and acute danger for the territorial integrity of the United Kingdom, the institutions of the six counties and the lives of the province's inhabitants. . . . Being confronted with a massive wave of violence and intimidation, the Northern Ireland Government and then, after the introduction of direct rule (30 March 1972), the British Government were reasonably entitled to consider that normal legislation offered insufficient resources for the campaign against terrorism and that recourse to measures outside the scope of the ordinary law, in the shape of extrajudicial deprivation of liberty, was called for. When the Irish Republic was faced with a serious crisis in 1957, it adopted the same approach and the Court did not conclude that the "extent strictly required" had been exceeded (Lawless judgment of 1 July 1961, Series A no. 3, pp. 35-36, §14, and pp. 57-58, §36).

However, under one of the provisions complained of, namely Regulation 10, a person who was in no way suspected of a crime or offence or of activities prejudicial to peace and order could be arrested for the sole purpose of obtaining from him information about others — and this sometimes occurred. . . . This sort of arrest can be justifiable only in a very exceptional situation, but the circumstances prevailing in Northern Ireland did fall into such a category. Many witnesses could not give evidence freely without running the greatest risks. . . . [T]he competent authorities were entitled to take the view, without exceeding their margin of appreciation, that it was indispensable to arrest such witnesses so that they could be questioned in conditions of relative security and not be exposed to reprisals. Moreover and above all, Regulation 10 authorised deprivation of liberty only for a maximum of forty-eight hours.

213. From 9 August 1971 to 5 February 1973, the measures involving deprivation of liberty taken by the respondent State were used only against Republican terrorism even though as early as this period outrages, at first sporadic but later constantly more numerous, were attributable to Loyalist terrorism; even after 5 February 1973, the measures were applied against Republican terrorism to a much greater extent than against Loyalist terrorism despite the latter's organisation and extensive development shortly after 30 March 1972.

The Court will examine below (paragraphs 228-232) whether the difference of treatment between the two types of terrorism was such as to violate Article 14 of the Convention.

The issue apart, it appears to the Court that the extrajudicial measures brought into operation could, in the situation described above, reasonably have been considered strictly required for the protection of public security and that, in the context of Article 15, their intrinsic necessity, once recognised, could not be affected by the restriction of their field of application.

214. The Irish Government submit that experience shows extrajudicial deprivation of liberty to have been ineffectual. They contend that the policy introduced on 9 August 1971 not only failed to put a brake on terrorism but also had the result of increasing it. . . . Consequently, the British Government, after attenuating the policy in varying degrees following the introduction of direct rule . . . , abandoned it on 5 December 1975: since then, it appears that no one has been detained in the six counties under the emergency legislation, despite the persistence of an intense campaign of violence and even though the Emergency Provisions Amendment Act has remained in force. . . . This, claim the applicant Government, confirms that extrajudicial deprivation of liberty was not an absolute necessity.

The Court cannot accept this argument.

It is certainly not the Court's function to substitute for the British Government's assessment any other assessment of what might be the most prudent or most expedient policy to combat terrorism. The Court must do no more than review the lawfulness, under the Convention, of the measures

adopted by that Government from 9 August 1971 onwards. For this purpose
the Court must arrive at its decision in the light, not of a purely retrospective examination of the efficacy of those measures, but of the conditions and
circumstances reigning when they were originally taken and subsequently
applied.

Adopting, as it must, this approach, the Court accepts that the limits of
the margin of appreciation left to the Contracting States by Article 15 §1
were not overstepped by the United Kingdom when it formed the opinion
that extrajudicial deprivation of liberty was necessary from August 1971 to
March 1975.

   (ii)   On the necessity for derogation from the guarantees under
          paragraphs 2 to 4 of Article 5 . . .

220. An overall examination of the legislation and practice at issue
reveals that they evolved in the direction of increasing respect for individual
liberty. The incorporation right from the start of more satisfactory judicial,
or at least administrative, guarantees would certainly have been desirable,
especially as Regulations 10 to 12(1) dated back to 1956-1957 and were
made under an Act of 1922, but it would be unrealistic to isolate the first
from the later phases. When a State is struggling against a public emergency threatening the life of the nation, it would be rendered defenceless if
it were required to accomplish everything at once, to furnish from the outset
each of its chosen means of action with each of the safeguards reconcilable
with the priority requirements for the proper functioning of the authorities
and for restoring peace within the community. The interpretation of Article
15 must leave a place for progressive adaptations.

The Northern Ireland Government sought in the first place — unsuccessfully — to meet the most pressing problem, to stem the wave of violence that was sweeping the region. After assuming direct responsibility for
the future of the province, the British Government and Parliament lost little
time in moderating in certain respects the severity of the laws applied in the
early days. The Court asked itself whether those laws should not have been
attenuated even more, especially as regards interim custody (see paragraph
217 above), but does not consider that it can give an affirmative answer. It
must not be forgotten that the crisis experienced at the time by the six
counties was serious and, hence, of a kind that justified far-reaching derogations from paragraphs 2 to 4 of Article 5. In view of the Contracting States'
margin of appreciation, the Court does not find it established that the
United Kingdom exceeded in this respect the "extent strictly required" referred to in Article 15 §1.

221. According to the applicant Government, the non-contested violations of Article 3 are relevant under Articles 5 and 15 taken together. They
claim that deprivation of liberty was sometimes imposed on the strength of
information extracted in conditions contrary to Article 3 and was thereby

rendered unlawful under Article 15. The Irish argument is also said to be confirmed by the existence of those violations since they would probably have been prevented by the impugned legislation if it had afforded genuine guarantees to the persons concerned.

The Court emphasizes, as do the respondent Government and the Commission, that Articles 3 and 5 embody quite separate obligations. Moreover, the violations of Article 3 found in the present judgment fail to show that it was not necessary to apply the extrajudicial powers in force. . . .

5. Conclusion

224. The Court has accordingly come to the conclusion that, since the requirements of Article 15 were met, the derogations from Article 5 were not, in the circumstances of the case, in breach of the Convention.

C. ON ARTICLE 14 TAKEN TOGETHER WITH ARTICLE 5

225. Article 14 provides

> The enjoyment of the rights and freedoms set forth in [the] Convention shall be secured without discrimination on any ground such as sex, race, colour, language, religion, political or other opinion, national or social origin, association with a national minority, property, birth or other status.

Before 5 February 1973, the extrajudicial powers were employed only against persons suspected of engaging in, or of possessing information about, IRA terrorism; later on, they were also utilised, but to a far lesser extent, against supposed Loyalist terrorists. According to the applicant Government, the circumstances of the case show that the United Kingdom thereby followed a policy or practice of discrimination.

226. The principle [sic] submission of the Irish Government is that it would not be correct to apply here the criteria used by the Court in the field of Article 14 since its judgment of 23 July 1968 on the merits of the "Belgian Linguistic" case (Series A no. 5, pp. 34-35, §10). The Government's argument runs as follows: those criteria are applicable only where a respondent State admits having introduced a difference of treatment and where that difference is expressly permitted by legislation; however, the British Government pleaded before the Commission not the existence of an "objective and reasonable justification" but rather the complete absence of such a difference, and the inequalities found in the report of 25 January 1976 arose from the mere application of laws which themselves created no inequalities; therefore the Commission was in error in applying those criteria; the Court should depart therefrom and rely on a number of inferences which, in the applicant Government's view, indicate that those inequalities were discriminatory. . . .

227. The applicant Government submit, in the alternative, that the

difference of treatment in question lacked an "objective and reasonable justification."

228. Before ruling on this submission, the Court must examine why, as early as 1971, Loyalist terrorism was not fought with the same weapons as Republican terrorism. . . .

The Court finds that there were profound differences between Loyalist and Republican terrorism.

At the time in question, the vast majority of murders, explosions and other outrages were attributable to Republicans. Although Loyalists had begun towards 1963 to perpetrate acts of violence, reaching a high level in 1969 when the IRA was scarcely in evidence, . . . since 1970 the scale of their activities had been minute in comparison with those of the IRA. . . .

In the second place, the IRA, with its far more structured organisation, constituted a far more serious menace than the Loyalist terrorists. In 1970 and 1971 the Protestant community included political pressure groups with extremist tendencies, but apparently concealed within its ranks no under-ground military force akin to the IRA. At that time Loyalist terrorism was seen by the authorities as the sporadic work of individuals or isolated factions. . . .

Lastly, it was as a general rule easier to institute criminal proceedings against Loyalist terrorists than against their Republican counterparts and the former were frequently brought before the courts. Accordingly, although Loyalist terrorists were not extrajudicially deprived of their liberty, they do not seem to have been able to act with impunity.

229. The later period (30 March 1972-4 February 1973) gives rise to delicate questions.

When assuming direct rule of the province (30 March 1972), the United Kingdom Government and Parliament wished, amongst other things, to combat the discrimination long prevalent there in the area of electoral rights, employment, housing, etc., in the hope of reaching an equitable solution to the Northern Ireland problem. . . .

However, this approach did not have a consequence which might have been expected, namely a complete equality of treatment between the two categories of terrorists in the exercise of special powers. Shortly after 30 March 1972, there was a spectacular increase in Loyalist terrorism. Furthermore, the UVF proved to have increased its membership, expanded its holding of arms and improved its organisation. Towards the middle of the year, the police as a general rule had reasonably good intelligence as to the identity of violent elements on the Protestant side but there were cases in which it was impossible to procure sufficient evidence to bring them before the courts. Nevertheless, about ten months elapsed before the first two Loyalists were extrajudicially deprived of their liberty. . . .

Several explanations for what is at first sight a surprising time-lag are advanced by the respondent Government and the Commission, for example the three combined facts that it had been decided to attempt the phasing-out of internment, that the IRA were still responsible for the great majority of serious acts of terrorism and that, broadly speaking, the ordinary criminal processes remained far more suited to the campaign against the Loyalist terrorists than to that against their Republican opponents. . . .

The cause or causes behind the conduct of the Government and the security forces at the time cannot be determined with certainty from the evidence, but it seems beyond doubt that the reasons that had been influential before 30 March 1972 became less and less valid as time went on.

However, the Court considers it unrealistic to carve into clear-cut phases a situation that was inherently changing and constantly evolving. The Court can understand the authorities' hesitating about the course to take, feeling their way and needing a certain time to try to adapt themselves to the successive demands of an ugly crisis. On the basis of the data before it, and bearing in mind the limits on its powers of review, the court cannot affirm that, during the period under consideration, the United Kingdom violated Article 14, taken together with Article 5, by employing the emergency powers against the IRA alone.

230. To sum up, the aim pursued until 5 February 1973 — the elimination of the most formidable organisation first of all — could be regarded as legitimate and the means employed do not appear disproportionate.

231. 5 February 1973 marked a turning-point. Thereafter, extrajudicial deprivation of liberty was used to combat terrorism as such, as defined a few months previously by the 1972 Order, and no longer just a given organisation. In point of fact, the measures were not applied against Loyalist terrorists to anything like the same extent as against the IRA . . . , but the IRA were still committing the majority of the acts of terrorism. . . . Furthermore, Loyalist terrorists could still be brought before the courts more easily than their Republican counterparts. Criminal proceedings were opened against many of the former and often led to convictions, above all in one particular field — sectarian assassinations. . . . The Court cannot reproach the United Kingdom for having attempted to avail itself as far as possible of this procedure under the ordinary law. Taking into account, as it must, the full range of the processes of the law applied in the campaign against the two categories of terrorists, the Court finds that the initial difference of treatment did not continue during the last period considered.

232. Accordingly, no discrimination contrary to Articles 14 and 5 taken together is established. . . .

V. On Article 50

244. Under Article 50 of the Convention, if the Court finds, as in the present case, "that a decision or a measure taken" by an authority of a Contracting State "is completely or partially in conflict with the obligations arising from the . . . Convention, and if the internal law of the said [State]

allows only partial reparation to be made for the consequences of this decision or measure," the Court "shall, if necessary, afford just satisfaction to the injured party." . . .

On 14 October 1977, the Agent of the applicant Government replied as follows:

> . . . the applicant Government, while not wishing to interfere with the de bene esse jurisdiction of the Court, have not as an object the obtaining of compensation for any individual person and do not invite the Court to afford just satisfaction under Article 50, of the nature of monetary compensation, to any individual victim of a breach of the Convention. . . .

246. The Court accordingly considers that it is not necessary to apply Article 50 in the present case. . . .

For these reasons, the court

I. On Article 3

1. *holds* unanimously that, although certain violations of Article 3 were not contested, a ruling should nevertheless be given thereon;

2. *holds* unanimously that it has jurisdiction to take cognisance of the cases of alleged violation of Article 3 to the extent that the applicant Government put them forward as establishing the existence of a practice;

3. *holds* by sixteen votes to one that the use of the five techniques in August and October 1971 constituted a practice of inhuman and degrading treatment, which practice was in breach of Article 3;

4. *holds* by thirteen votes to four that the said use of the five techniques did not constitute a practice of torture within the meaning of Article 3;

5. *holds* by sixteen votes to one that no other practice of ill-treatment is established for the unidentified interrogation centres;

6. *holds* unanimously that there existed at Palace Barracks in the autumn of 1971 a practice of inhuman treatment, which practice was in breach of Article 3;

7. *holds* by fourteen votes to three that the last-mentioned practice was not one of torture within the meaning of Article 3;

8. *holds* unanimously that it is not established that the practice in question continued beyond the autumn of 1971;

9. *holds* by fifteen votes to two that no practice in breach of Article 3 is established as regards other places;

10. *holds* unanimously that it cannot direct the respondent State to institute criminal or disciplinary proceedings against those members of the security forces who have committed the breaches of Article 3 found by the Court and against those who condoned or tolerated such breaches.

II. ON ARTICLE 5

11. *holds* unanimously that at the relevant time there existed in Northern Ireland a public emergency threatening the life of the nation, within the meaning of Article 15 §1;

12. *holds* unanimously that the British notices of derogation dated 20 August 1971, 23 January 1973 and 16 August 1973 fulfilled the requirements of Article 15 §3;

13. *holds* by sixteen votes to one that, although the practice followed in Northern Ireland from 9 August 1971 to March 1975 in the application of the legislation providing for extrajudicial deprivation of liberty entailed derogations from paragraphs 1 to 4 of Article 5, it is not established that the said derogations exceeded the extent strictly required by the exigencies of the situation, within the meaning of Article 15 §1;

14. *holds* unanimously that the United Kingdom has not disregarded in the present case other obligations under international law, within the meaning of Article 15 §1;

15. *holds* by fifteen votes to two that no discrimination contrary to Articles 14 and 5 taken together is established. . . .

IV. ON ARTICLE 50

18. *holds* unanimously that it is not necessary to apply Article 50 in the present case. . . .

[Separate opinions were filed by Judges Zekia, O'Donoghue, Fitzmaurice, Eurigenis, and Matscher.]

Note: *"Degrading Treatment or Punishment"* vs. *"Cruel and Unusual Punishment"*

The concept of degrading treatment, discussed at length in the *Irish Case*, received further attention from the Court in the so-called *Isle of Man Case* (Tyrer v. United Kingdom, Judgment of 25 April 1978, Series A No. 26 (1978), reprinted in 2 Eur. Hum. Rts. Rep. 1 (1979)). In that case the Court held that the "birching" (i.e., caning) of a 15-year-old boy following his conviction for assault constituted degrading punishment in violation of Article 3 of the Convention. The judgment, which provoked a strong dissent by Judge Fitzmaurice, proved to be quite controversial in Great Britain, to say the least, and served to keep the debate over the status of the European Convention in British law going. A sampling of immediate reactions follows.

Letters to the Editor, The Verdict Against Birching
The Times (London), Apr. 28, 1978, at 17, col. 5

From Mr. Ronald M. Bell, QC, MP for Beaconsfield (Conservative)

Sir, You rightly refer (April 26) to the "great issue" raised by the Manx birching case, but have you identified it correctly? No high sounding convention or declaration is too absurd for there to be pressure from "liberal" quarters for us to join it, nor, since Western countries are increasingly influenced by pressure groups, too absurd to be joined. If we join these things lightly, and then take them as seriously as your leading article suggests, we shall find that we are largely governed from outside, and by the strangest people.

The European "Court" of Human Rights is not really a court: it has no powers, and what it utters is no judicial decision, but a political opinion. What is degrading? The British member of the team said what he thought, and that it might well be based on his experience at school, where beatings went down well. The majority said what they thought, and that they were influenced by movements in penal thinking. And these were all subjective opinions on something about which diverse views are widely held, and anybody's view could be as good as anybody else's.

In fact, the majority's view in this panel game was a far out one. That the punishment was awarded for a violent attack they thought irrelevant; that it might be acceptable to Manx public opinion was also irrelevant. Even if, they said, it could be shown that law and order could not be maintained in the Isle of Man without it, that still would not affect their opinion. Nor did the privacy: the youth might still be humiliated in his own eyes, if not in the eyes of others. The physical assault injured his human dignity . . . and so on. His own physical assault on his victim, causing actual bodily harm, was apparently an unrelated matter, nothing to do with human dignity. Has there ever been a better example of using strict legal interpretation as a foundation for dogmatic political waffle? As far as these mandarins were concerned, public order could go to pot, and public opinion could take a running jump.

Thus we have the remarkable spectacle of an Italian lecturing the Manx people on the right way to deal with violent crime. It is like the grasshopper reading a homily on industry to the ant.

I have been opposed in the past both to capital and to corporal punishment. But it is all a question of degree, and of the state of society in which you live. As I see violent crime spiralling up even in Britain until the streets, buses and underground trains are no longer safe places at night, I am certainly prepared to reverse my earlier views about birching or about any other system of punishment if I should come to the conclusion that its adoption was the only way of maintaining the safety of streets and homes in

Britain. And I shall not be influenced by the cloudy transcendentalism on the subject of distant and somewhat introverted foreign functionaries. Salus populi surpema lex.

> I have the houour to be, Sir
> Your obedient servant,
> RONALD M. BELL,
> House of Commons.

From Mr. Ian Harvey

Sir, When you state (April 26), concerning birching and the people of the Isle of Man, that "morally they have a good case, constitutionally they have not" you touch on the most sensitive and controversial aspect of the argument. It raises the question — is the constitution made for man or man for the constitution?

I myself concur with the view of Sir Gerald Fitzmaurice that birching or caning is not degrading. I add the proviso that it must be carried out for just or lawful reasons and by legitimate and authorized persons. The caning of boys at school by other boys, which is a practice which has now largely ceased, is undesirable and can have sadistic undertones.

Mr. Tyrer was birched for committing assault with violence which the Court judged not to be relevant. The act must have been extremely degrading for the victim. This too appears not to have been relevant.

In an age of vandalism, mugging, hijacking and kidnapping the absence of an effective deterrent is becoming more and more obvious. It would seem to me that in cases of this sort each community should be entitled to make the punishment fit the crime by such methods as it believes to be appropriate to its own local conditions.

> Yours faithfully,
> IAN HARVEY,
> 28A Star Street, W2.

Verdict Against Birching
The Times (London), Apr. 29, 1978, at 17, col. 4

From Mr. Colin Bagnall

Sir, The verdict of the European Court that birching is illegal as a degrading punishment under Article Three of the Convention of Human Rights has implications which go beyond the Isle of Man.

Our recent survey of local education authorities' regulations shows that corporal punishment in schools, even if it is not as severe as birching, can be just as degrading and is less rigidly controlled in its application.

Only 19 out of 104 education authorities, for example, require corporal punishment to be in private, as birching has always been; in the rest pupils can be beaten in front of their class or the whole school. Only two authorities have banned the corporal punishment of girls, who were never subject to the birch, and in nearly a third they can be corporally punished by male teachers. The whole ritual of the two punishments may be equally degrading in law in view of the fact that the judges did not consider the state of undress of the offender being birched to be a decisive factor.

The judges' references to the potential adverse psychological effects of birching, the assault on dignity and physical integrity, the anguish of anticipation and the fact that it is not necessary for the maintenance of law and order apply equally to caning.

Four cases concerning corporal punishment in schools have already been brought against the British government under Article Three, and are awaiting consideration at Strasbourg. We have asked the Secretary of State to introduce the legislation necessary to abolish the whole barbarous business if only to save Britain further embarrassment at the bar of Europe.

COLIN BAGNALL,
Honorary Secretary,
Society of Teachers Opposed
    to Physical Punishment,
10 Lennox Gardens,
Croydon, Surrey.
April 27.

From Mr. Nicholas Bourne
Sir, The judgment of the European Court of Human Rights sitting at Strasbourg in the birching case given on Tuesday, April 25, will have come as a surprise to few.

The use of the birch as a judicial punishment is confined to the Isle of Man, Jersey and Guernsey amongst those territories covered by the Court's compulsory jurisdiction and the Court was guided by the practice of other states which accept its jurisdiction.

However, I think two features of the case merit discussion.

Firstly, the court held that the punishment was an assault on one of the main purposes of Article Three — to protect a person's dignity and physical integrity. Now presumably applying this test borstal, imprisonment and even probation would be in contravention of the Convention. Such a position would be absurd as the Court recognized, and some guidance as to what aggravating features take birching into the "degrading" category would have been useful.

The other feature of the case that is of some importance is that the Court expressly countenanced that the punishment was an effective deterrent or aide to crime control. This did not affect the Court's finding, nor under the wording of the Convention should it do so.

However, it is surely desirable that the Convention should be modified to take express account of the position of the victim of the crime.

Perhaps this seeming lack of concern with the position of the victim of the crime (and of the potential victim) is why the Court's judgment is so obviously at odds with opinion on the Isle of Man and probably throughout the United Kingdom as a whole, too.

This is not to suggest that birching is desirable, defensible or necessary, but simply to wonder whether the court in seeking to divorce questions of individual freedom and human dignity from questions of security and law and order will lead similarly to a division of opinion according to whether one considers law and order or individual freedom to be under greater threat.

Yours faithfully,
Nicholas Bourne,
Department of Law,
Brunel University,
Uxbridge, Middlesex.
April 27.

Of Birching and Human Rights
N.Y. Times, May 3, 1978, at 32, col. 4

To the Editor:

The ordering or priorities of the European Court of Human Rights makes a travesty of serious concerns for improvement of the condition of peoples throughout the world. Its formal trial and condemnation of the innocuous Isle of Man . . . for applying the branches of a birch to the posteriors of youthful male offenders convicted of crimes of violence ignores the serious questions of human degradation and genocide practiced by totalitarian regimes.

No doubt the tiny island maintained the paddling in lieu of confinement as an accepted community standard, else they would have done away with it. And, who would disagree that the three swats — though painful for a moment — may be a far less painful administration of justice in the long run when compared with the handling of juvenile cases elsewhere in the European community?

Birching as corporal punishment is certainly no mini-holocaust, and is an unworthy target of the European tribunal when the pages of The Times report daily the sufferings of the persecuted in dictator states. Great Britain and the Isle of Man should throw the decision back to the Euro-

Culver Pictures, Inc.

pean Court of Human Rights with a demand that the continent first put its own house in order and face up to the real priorities of the human rights movement.

WILLIAM R. VANNIN
Washington, April 26, 1978

To the Editor:
    Instead of waxing indignant over three strokes of the birch in the Isle of Man, a sentence that would have been scoffed at by any English schoolboy of my own generation, human rights courts might consider the new third world, where something akin to "whipping" actually exists, and is not a matter of choice.
    Both Nigeria and Uganda employ it, the former at roadside for traffic offenders. Pakistan administers the cane to rapists in public sports arenas, to the cheers of assembled schoolchildren, and doesn't worry overmuch about the culprit's "mental anguish" beforehand, either. From Jamaica to Guyana "strokes" are ordered by local magistrates, generally for violent assault against women, as the ex-British Caribbean island restores what the liberal colonists outlawed. Perhaps in this, as in other matters, our black brothers know best.

GEOFFREY WAGNER
New York, April 28, 1978

Mr. Wagner's letter, in which he waxes enthusiastic about the use of the cane in various Commonwealth countries that once were British colonies before concluding that "our black brothers know best," should be reread after studying the recent case of State v. Ncube, [1987] 2 Zimb. L. Rep. 246, [1988] L.R.C. (Const.) 442 (Sup. Ct. of Zimbabwe), where the highest court of that former British colony actually went further than the European Court in the *Isle of Man Case* by holding that whipping an adult male offender constituted *both* inhuman and degrading punishment in violation of Section 15(1) of the Declaration of Rights contained in the Constitution of Zimbabwe, a provision that closely tracks Article 3 of the European Convention. See Lillich, The Constitution and International Human Rights, 83 Am. J. Intl. L. 851, 854-855 (1989). Accord, International Decisions, Juvenile v. State, 84 Am. J. Intl. L. 742, 768 (1990) (juvenile offender).

Of course, caning as a punishment is not restricted to British public schools. The caning by Singapore of an 18-year-old U.S. student in 1994, after his conviction for vandalism, caused diplomatic protests — but it also apparently was supported by a majority of persons canvassed in U.S. opinion polls and led to initiatives in the United States to introduce caning and other forms of corporal punishment on the local level. See, e.g., Gross, California Contemplates Paddling Graffiti Vandals, N.Y. Times, Aug. 7, 1994, at 22, col. 5; Canings for Vandals Proposed in St. Louis, N.Y. Times, May 21, 1994, at 8, col. 6. In addition to Singapore, caning or other forms of corporal punishment are practiced in Afghanistan, Antigua and Barbuda, Bahamas, Bangladesh, Brunei, Iran, Libya, Malaysia, Pakistan, Qatar, Saudi Arabia, South Africa, Sudan, Swaziland, Trinidad and Tobago, United Arab Emirates, United States (27 states permit corporal punishment in schools), Yemen, and Zimbabwe. Kuntz, Beyond Singapore: Corporal Punishment, A to Z, N.Y. Times, June 26, 1994, §4, at 5, col. 1.

Not Sparing the Rod; How Cruel, How Unusual?
Boston Globe, Apr. 10, 1994, at 69

Last month, Singapore's Supreme Court rejected the appeal of Michael Fay, an American found guilty of vandalism for stealing signs and spray-painting automobiles. Fay, 18, was sentenced to four months in jail, a fine of $2,230 and six lashes with a rotan, a 4-foot-long palm rod.

This last item has attracted international attention. Caning is not a ruler on the knuckles. A martial arts specialist is to administer six lashes across Fay's buttocks. The rotan invariably draws blood. The victim often passes out and is usually scarred for life. President Clinton has called the punishment "extreme" and appealed to President Ong Teng Cheong for clemency, as have 34 US senators.

Francis Seow was Singapore's solicitor general in 1966, when vandalism was made a corporal offense. Later, he served as president of the Law

Society, Singapore's equivalent of the American Bar Association. Forced into exile in 1988, he is currently a fellow in Harvard Law School's East Asian Legal Studies Program. This spring will see publication of his memoirs, "To Catch a Tartar: A Dissident in Lee Kuan Yew's Prison." Last week, Seow discussed the Fay case with Focus editor Mark Feeney.

Q. Are you surprised this case has become such a cause celebre?
A. It has been fanned by the media — or, as I've said to a few people, it's been flogged to death by the media. You know, I've asked the people who've been interviewing me that same question, and they say, "No, this is like another Kerrigan-Harding case." As long as there's interest, the media will continue to exploit the news.
Q. Would you say, then, in the larger view, this is as essentially trivial as the Kerrigan-Harding case [which involved an alleged assault on one Olympic figure skater by another]?
A. There's very little to it, really. I'm sure the average Singaporean is wondering what's going on, what is making the Americans all worked up. There are canings every now and again in Singapore, and nobody seems very excited about it when it's Singaporeans or Malaysians involved.
Q. Do you think, then, there's an element of racism involved: that it's because an Asian country is practicing this on an American that has people so exercised here?
A. No, absolutely none. That is a slant some of the media are taking, but it's absolutely unjustified.
Q. Might you describe how caning came to be used in Singapore?
A. We have a penal code which we inherited from India — through the British, of course. In the code, there were provisions for whipping by the cat-o'-nine-tails. That was introduced by the British as part of the colonial penal code. Then in the late '40s, the British eliminated many offenses for which the whip was prescribed, retaining whipping in the statute book only for crimes of violence, like robbery or rape. The maximum allowable number was 24 strokes. Also at that time, the rotan (which is a Malay word — you use "rattan") was substituted for the whip.

The law continued in that form until 1966, when the prime minister, Lee Kuan Yew, decided to introduce a bill to provide that punishment for acts of vandalism. It came about in this way: The opposition party, Barisan Sosialis, which in English means "Socialist Front," was so outmaneuvered by Lee that they abandoned Parliament and took their struggle to the streets. Among their most ardent supporters were high school students, who in the middle of the night would go out with tins of paint to deface walls with political graffiti, slogans or logos. This became a daily, or nightly, affair.

So the prime minister was rather frustrated at this form of defiance of law and order. What annoyed him was the political aspect of the case, and he hit upon this idea of having a law to provide for the punishment of acts of vandalism.

Q.   So previously, where caning had been restricted to acts of violence, the punishment was now used for nonviolent crimes?

A.   Yes. Now he decided to introduce this law. . . . This was Lee Kuan Yew's brainchild, no getting around it. When this came to my attention, in my capacity as solicitor general, I thought it was a rather retrogressive step; in introducing caning for acts of vandalism, we were stepping back to the Middle Ages. . . . Be that as it may, the bill was passed. And, as the proof of the pudding lies in the eating, the proof of the caning lies in the cleanliness and orderliness of the city. Overnight, acts of vandalism dropped — a dramatic drop. Even I had to concede that it worked to all intents and purposes.

Q.   Would you then characterize caning in such circumstances as cruel and unusual punishment?

A.   Let me put it this way: I personally am not in favor of corporal punishment. Still, it is clear that Singapore is the green and lovely city it is, in part, because of the severity of punishment we're talking about here. But the question is: at what price?

The punishment meted out to Tyrer and Fay may be of a different order of magnitude than the paddling or other forms of corporal punishment traditionally utilized in some schools, but the latter have been frequently challenged as violating Article 3. For an examination of these cases, and a suggestion that they might be more appropriately considered under the rubric of violations of the right to privacy rather than under the absolute prohibition of Article 3, see Phillips, The Case for Corporal Punishment in the United Kingdom: Beaten into Submission in Europe?, 43 Intl. & Comp. L.Q. 153 (1994).

Finally, it should be noted that the European Convention has far greater breadth of protection than the U.S. Constitution. Article 3 of the Convention prohibits, in addition to torture, "inhuman or degrading treatment or punishment." The Eighth Amendment speaks only to "cruel and unusual punishments." Not only does the addition of the adjective "degrading" expand the list of potentially proscribed acts, but also the insertion of the term "treatment" before "punishment" must be viewed to expand the thrust of the prohibition beyond the field of criminal law and prisons into the area of the civil law and all state-sponsored facilities — hospitals, mental treatment centers, foster homes, old age residences, and the like. Thus, the potential impact of Article 3 on the domestic law of the European Convention states is tremendous.

The potential impact in the United States of Article 7 of the Civil and Political Covenant and Article 16 of the Torture Convention — both of which contain language tracking that of Article 3 of the European Convention — might have been considerable had not the United States in both instances attached a reservation to its ratification limiting the proscribed conduct, insofar as the United States is concerned, to what the Supreme Court has deemed cruel and unusual treatment or punishment under the Fifth, Eighth, and Fourteenth Amendments to the U.S. Constitution. (A similar reservation can be expected to be made to Article 5(2) of the American Convention, should the United States eventually ratify it.) This approach means that, with respect to ill-treatment, persons in the United States have less protection than persons in Europe. The U.S. reservations were adopted at least in part in response to the European Court case that follows.

Soering v. United Kingdom
European Ct. Hum. Rts., Judgment of 7 July 1989, Ser. A No. 161, 11 Eur. Hum. Rts. Rep. 439

[As previously mentioned, the *Irish* case is the only case decided by the Court that originated as an interstate complaint. The vast majority of cases are instituted by individual petitions under Article 25 of the Convention and follow the course ably described in Boyle, Europe: The Council of Europe, the CSCE, and the European Community, in Guide to International Human Rights Practice (2d ed. H. Hannum ed. 1992). The *Soering* case is one example of such a case. Moreover, the Court's judgment dramatically illustrates the possible impact of the Convention upon states not even party to it.]

As to the Facts

I.   Particular Circumstances of the Case

11. The applicant, Mr Jens Soering, was born on 1 August 1966 and is a German national. He is currently detained in prison in England pending extradition to the United States of America to face charges of murder in the Commonwealth of Virginia.

12. The homicides in question were committed in Bedford County, Virginia, in March 1985. The victims, William Reginald Haysom (aged 72) and Nancy Astor Haysom (aged 53), were the parents of the applicant's girlfriend, Elizabeth Haysom, who is a Canadian national. Death in each case was the result of multiple and massive stab and slash wounds to the neck, throat and body. At the time the applicant and Elizabeth Haysom,

aged 18 and 20 respectively, were students at the University of Virginia. They disappeared together from Virginia in October 1985, but were arrested in England in April 1986 in connection with cheque fraud.

13. The applicant was interviewed in England between 5 and 8 June 1986 by a police investigator from the Sheriff's Department of Bedford County. In a sworn affidavit dated 24 July 1986 the investigator recorded the applicant as having admitted the killings in his presence and in that of two United Kingdom police officers. The applicant had stated that he was in love with Miss Haysom but that her parents were opposed to the relationship. He and Miss Haysom had therefore planned to kill them. They rented a car in Charlottesville and travelled to Washington where they set up an alibi. The applicant then went to the parents' house, discussed the relationship with them and, when they told him they would do anything to prevent it, a row developed during which he killed them with a knife.

On 13 June 1986 a grand jury of the Circuit Court of Bedford County indicted him on charges of murdering the Haysom parents. The charges alleged capital murder of both of them and the separate non-capital murders of each.

14. On 11 August 1986 the Government of the United States of America requested the applicant's and Miss Haysom's extradition under the terms of the Extradition Treaty of 1972 between the United States and the United Kingdom (see paragraph 30 below). On 12 September a Magistrate at Bow Street Magistrates' Court was required by the Secretary of State for Home Affairs to issue a warrant for the applicant's arrest under the provisions of section 8 of the Extradition Act 1870 (see paragraph 32 below). The applicant was subsequently arrested on 30 December at HM Prison Chelmsford after serving a prison sentence for cheque fraud.

15. On 29 October 1986 the British Embassy in Washington addressed a request to the United States' authorities in the following terms:

> Because the death penalty has been abolished in Great Britain, the Embassy has been instructed to seek an assurance, in accordance with the terms of . . . the Extradition Treaty, that, in the event of Mr Soering being surrendered and being convicted of the crimes for which he has been indicted . . . , the death penalty, if imposed, will not be carried out.
>
> Should it not be possible on constitutional grounds for the United States Government to give such as assurance, the United Kingdom authorities ask that the United States Government undertake to recommend to the appropriate authorities that the death penalty should not be imposed or, if imposed, should not be executed.

16. On 30 December 1986 the applicant was interviewed in prison by a German prosecutor (*Staatsanwalt*) from Bonn. In a sworn witness statement the prosecutor recorded the applicant as having said, inter alia, that "he had never had the intention of killing Mr and Mrs Haysom and . . . he could only remember having inflicted wounds at the neck on Mr and Mrs Haysom which must have had something to do with their dying later"; and

that in the immediately preceding days "there had been no talk whatsoever [between him and Elizabeth Haysom] about killing Elizabeth's parents." The prosecutor also referred to documents which had been put at his disposal, for example the statements made by the applicant to the American police investigator, the autopsy reports and two psychiatric reports on the applicant (see paragraph 21 below).

On 11 February 1987 the local court in Bonn issued a warrant for the applicant's arrest in respect of the alleged murders. On 11 March the Government of the Federal Republic of Germany requested his extradition to the Federal Republic under the Extradition Treaty of 1872 between the Federal Republic and the United Kingdom (see paragraph 31 below). The Secretary of State was then advised by the Director of Public Prosecutions that, although the German request contained proof that German courts had jurisdiction to try the applicant, the evidence submitted, since it consisted solely of the admissions made by the applicant to the Bonn prosecutor in the absence of a caution, did not amount to a prima facie case against him and that a magistrate would not be able under the Extradition Act 1870 (see paragraph 32 below) to commit him to await extradition to Germany on the strength of admissions obtained in such circumstances.

17. In a letter dated 20 April 1987 to the Director of the Office of International Affairs, Criminal Division, United States Department of Justice, the Attorney for Bedford County, Virginia (Mr James W. Updike Jr.) stated that, on the assumption that the applicant could not be tried in Germany on the basis of admissions alone, there was no means of compelling witnesses from the United States to appear in a criminal court in Germany. On 23 April the United States, by diplomatic note, requested the applicant's extradition to the United States in preference to the Federal Republic of Germany.

18. On 8 May Elizabeth Haysom was surrendered for extradition to the United States. After pleading guilty on 22 August as an accessory to the murder of her parents, she was sentenced on 6 October to 90 years' imprisonment (45 years on each count of murder).

19. On 20 May 1987 the government of the United Kingdom informed the Federal Republic of Germany that the United States had earlier "submitted a request, supported by prima facie evidence, for the extradition of Mr Soering." The United Kingdom Government notified the Federal Republic that they had "concluded that, having regard to all the circumstances of the case, the court should continue to consider in the normal way the United States' request." They further indicated that they had sought an assurance from the United States' authorities on the question of the death penalty and that "in the event that the court commits Mr Soering, his surrender to the United States' authorities would be subject to the receipt of satisfactory assurances on this matter."

20. On 1 June 1987 Mr Updike swore an affidavit in his capacity as Attorney for Bedford County, in which he certified as follows:

> I hereby certify that should Jens Soering be convicted of the offence of capital murder as charged in Bedford County, Virginia . . . a representation will be made in the name of the United Kingdom to the judge at the time of sentencing that it is the wish of the United Kingdom that the death penalty should not be imposed or carried out.

This assurance was transmitted to the United Kingdom Government under cover of a diplomatic note on 8 June. It was repeated in the same terms in a further affidavit from Mr Updike sworn on 16 February 1988 and forwarded to the United Kingdom by diplomatic note on 17 May 1988. In the same note the Federal Government of the United States undertook to ensure that the commitment of the appropriate authorities of the Commonwealth of Virginia to make representations on behalf of the United Kingdom would be honoured.

During the course of the present proceedings the Virginia authorities have informed the United Kingdom Government that Mr Updike was not planning to provide any further assurances and intended to seek the death penalty in Mr Soering's case because the evidence, in his determination, supported such action.

21. On 16 June 1987 at the Bow Street Magistrates' Court committal proceedings took place before the Chief Stipendiary Magistrate.

The Government of the United States adduced evidence that on the night of 30 March 1985 the applicant killed William and Nancy Haysom at their home in Bedford County, Virginia. In particular, evidence was given of the applicant's own admissions as recorded in the affidavit of the Bedford County police investigator (see paragraph 13 above).

On behalf of the applicant psychiatric evidence was adduced from a consultant forensic psychiatrist (report dated 15 December 1986 by Dr Henrietta Bullard) that he was immature and inexperienced and had lost his personal identity in a symbiotic relationship with his girlfriend — a powerful, persuasive and disturbed young woman. The psychiatric report concluded:

> There existed between Miss Haysom and Soering a 'folie à deux,' in which the most disturbed partner was Miss Haysom. . . .
> At the time of the offence, it is my opinion that Jens Soering was suffering from [such] an abnormality of mind due to inherent causes as substantially impaired his mental responsibility for his acts. The psychiatric syndrome referred to as 'folie à deux' is a well-recognised state of mind where one partner is suggestible to the extent that he or she believes in the psychotic delusions of the other. The degree of disturbance of Miss Haysom borders on the psychotic and, over the course of many months, she was able to persuade Soering that he might have to kill her parents for she and him to survive as a couple. . . . Miss Haysom had a stupefying and mesmeric effect on Soering which led to an abnormal psychological state in which he became unable to think rationally or question the absurdities in Miss Haysom's view of her life and the influence of her parents. . . .

In conclusion, it is my opinion that, at the time of the offences, Soering was suffering from an abnormality of mind which, in this country, would constitute a defence of 'not guilty to murder but guilty of manslaughter.'

. . . The Chief Magistrate found that the evidence of Dr Bullard was not relevant to any issue that he had to decide and committed the applicant to await the Secretary of State's order for his return to the United States.

22. On 29 June 1987 Mr Soering applied to the Divisional Court for a writ of habeas corpus in respect of his committal and for leave to apply for judicial review. On 11 December both applications were refused by the Divisional Court (Lord Justice Lloyd and Mr Justice Macpherson).

In support of his application for leave to apply for judicial review, Mr Soering had submitted that the assurance received from the United States' authorities was so worthless that no reasonable Secretary of State could regard it as satisfactory under Article IV of the Extradition Treaty between the United Kingdom and the United States (see paragraph 36 below). In his judgment Lord Justice Lloyd agreed that "the assurance leaves something to be desired":

> Article IV of the Treaty contemplates an assurance that the death penalty will not be carried out. That must presumably mean an assurance by or on behalf of the Executive Branch of Government, which in this case would be the Governor of the Commonwealth of Virginia. The certificate sworn by Mr Updike, far from being an assurance on behalf of the Executive, is nothing more than an undertaking to make representations on behalf of the United Kingdom to the judge. I cannot believe that this is what was intended when the Treaty was signed. But I can understand that there may well be difficulties in obtaining more by way of assurance in view of the federal nature of the United States Constitution.

Leave to apply for judicial review was refused because the claim was premature. . . .

23. On 30 June 1988 the House of Lords rejected the applicant's petition for leave to appeal against the decision of the Divisional Court.

24. On 14 July 1988 the applicant petitioned the Secretary of State, requesting him to exercise his discretion not to make an order for the applicant's surrender under section 11 of the Extradition Act 1870 (see paragraph 34 below).

This request was rejected, and on 3 August 1988 the Secretary of State signed a warrant ordering the applicant's surrender to the United States' authorities. However, the applicant has not been transferred to the United States by virtue of the interim measures indicated in the present proceedings firstly by the European Commission and then by the European Court. . . .

25. On 5 August 1988 the applicant was transferred to a prison hospital where he remained until early November 1988 under the special regime applied to suicide-risk prisoners.

According to psychiatric evidence adduced on behalf of the applicant (report dated 16 March 1989 of Dr D. Somekh), the applicant's dread of extreme physical violence and homosexual abuse from other inmates in death row in Virginia is in particular having a profound psychiatric effect on him. The psychiatrist's report records a mounting desperation in the applicant, together with objective fears that he may seek to take his own life.

26. By a declaration dated 20 March 1989 submitted to this Court, the applicant stated that should the United Kingdom government require that he be deported to the Federal Republic of Germany he would consent to such requirement and would present no factual or legal opposition against the making or execution of an order to that effect.

II. RELEVANT DOMESTIC LAW AND PRACTICE IN THE UNITED KINGDOM

A. CRIMINAL LAW

27. In England murder is defined as the unlawful killing of a human being with malice aforethought. The penalty is life imprisonment. The death penalty cannot be imposed for murder (Murder (Abolition of the Death Penalty) Act 1965, section 1). Section 2 of the Homicide Act 1957 provides that where a person kills another, he shall not be convicted of murder if he was suffering from such abnormality of mind (whether arising from a condition of arrested development of mind or any inherent causes or induced by disease or injury) as substantially impaired his mental responsibility for his acts in doing the killing. A person who but for the section would be liable to be convicted of murder shall be liable to be convicted of manslaughter.

28. English courts do not exercise criminal jurisdiction in respect of acts of foreigners abroad except in certain cases immaterial to the present proceedings. Consequently, neither the applicant, as a German citizen, nor Elizabeth Haysom, a Canadian citizen, was or is amenable to criminal trial in the United Kingdom.

B. EXTRADITION

29. The relevant general law on extradition is contained in the Extradition Acts 1870-1935.

30. The extradition arrangements between the United Kingdom and the United States of America are governed by the Extradition Treaty signed by the two Governments on 8 June 1972, a Supplementary Treaty signed on 25 June 1982, and an Exchange of Notes dated 19 and 20 August 1986 amending the Supplementary Treaty. These arrangements have been incorporated into the law of the United Kingdom by Orders in Council (the

United States of America (Extradition) Order 1976, S.I. 1976/2144 and the United States of America (Extradition) (Amendment) Order 1986, S.I. 1986/2020).

By virtue of Article I of the Extradition Treaty, "each Contracting Party undertakes to extradite to the other, in the circumstances and subject to the conditions specified in this Treaty, any person found in its territory who has been accused or convicted of any offence [specified in the Treaty and including murder], committed within the jurisdiction of the other Party."

31. Extradition between the United Kingdom and the Federal Republic of Germany is governed by the Treaty of 14 May 1872 between the United Kingdom and Germany for the Mutual Surrender of Fugitive Criminals, as reapplied with amendments by an Agreement signed at Bonn on 23 February 1960 and as further amended by an Exchange of Notes dated 25 and 27 September 1978. These agreements have been incorporated into the law of the United Kingdom by Orders in Council (the Federal Republic of Germany (Extradition) Order 1960, S.I. 1960/1375 and the Federal Republic of Germany (Extradition) (Amendment) Order 1978, S.I. 1978/1403).

32. After receipt of an extradition request, the Secretary of State may, by order, require a magistrate to issue a warrant for the arrest of the fugitive criminal (Extradition Act 1870, sections 7 and 8).

Extradition proceedings in the United Kingdom consist of an extradition hearing before a magistrate. Section 10 of the Extradition Act 1870 provides that if "such evidence is produced as (subject to the provisions of this Act) would, according to the law of England, justify the committal for trial of the prisoner if the crime of which he is accused had been committed in England . . . the . . . magistrate shall commit him to prison but otherwise he shall order him to be discharged." A magistrate must be satisfied that there is sufficient evidence to put the accused on trial; before committing him a prima facie case must be made out against him. "The test is whether, if the evidence before the Magistrate stood alone at the trial, a reasonable jury properly directed could accept it and find a verdict of guilty" (Schtraks v. Government of Israel [1964] Appeal Cases 556).

33. Section 11 of the Extradition Act 1870 provides that decisions taken in committal proceedings may be challenged by way of application for habeas corpus. In practice, such application is made to a Divisional Court and, with leave, to the House of Lords. Habeas corpus proceedings are primarily concerned with checking that the magistrate had jurisdiction to hear the case; that there was evidence before him which could justify the committal; that the offence is an extradition crime which is not of a political character; and that there is no bar on other grounds to surrender. Section 12 of the 1870 Act provides for the release of a prisoner, if not surrendered, at the conclusion of such proceedings or within two months of committal unless sufficient cause is shown to the contrary.

34. Furthermore, under section 11 of the 1870 Act the Secretary of State enjoys a discretion not to sign the surrender warrant (Atkinson v. United States [1971] Appeal Cases 197). This discretion may override a

decision of the courts that a fugitive should be surrendered, and it is open to every prisoner who has exhausted his remedies by way of application for habeas corpus to petition the Secretary of State for that purpose. In considering whether to order the fugitive's surrender, the Secretary of State is bound to take account of fresh evidence which had not been before the magistrate (Schtraks v. Government of Israel, loc. cit.).

35. In addition, it is open to the prisoner to challenge both the decision of the Secretary of State rejecting his petition and the decision to sign the warrant in judicial review proceedings. In such proceedings the court may review the exercise of the Secretary of State's discretion on the basis that it is tainted with illegality, irrationality or procedural impropriety (Council of Civil Service Unions and Others v. Minister for the Civil Service [1984] 3 All England Law Reports 935). . . .

However, the courts will not review any decision of the Secretary of State by reason of the fact only that he failed to consider whether or not there was a breach of the European Convention on Human Rights (R v. Secretary of State, ex parte Kirkwood [1984] 1 Weekly Law Reports 913). . . .

36. There is no provision in the Extradition Acts relating to the death penalty, but Article IV of the United Kingdom-United States Treaty provides:

> If the offence for which extradition is requested is punishable by death under the relevant law of the requesting Party, but the relevant law of the requested Party does not provide for the death penalty in a similar case, extradition may be refused unless the requesting Party gives assurances satisfactory to the requested Party that the death penalty will not be carried out.

37. In the case of a fugitive requested by the United States who faces a charge carrying the death penalty, it is the Secretary of State's practice, pursuant to Article IV of the United Kingdom-United States Extradition Treaty, to accept an assurance from the prosecuting authorities of the relevant State that a representation will be made to the judge at the time of sentencing that it is the wish of the United Kingdom that the death penalty should be neither imposed nor carried out. This practice has been described by Mr David Mellor, then Minister of State at the Home Office, in the following terms:

> The written undertakings about the death penalty that the Secretary of State obtains from the federal authorities amount to an undertaking that the views of the United Kingdom will be represented to the judge. At the time of sentencing he will be informed that the United Kingdom does not wish the death penalty to be imposed or carried out. That means that the United Kingdom authorities render up a fugitive or are prepared to send a citizen to face an American court on the clear understanding that the death penalty will not be carried out — it has never been carried out in such cases. It would be a fundamental blow to the extradition arrangements between our two countries if the death penalty were carried out on an individual who had been returned under those circumstances. (Hansard, 10 March 1987, Col. 955)

There has, however, never been a case in which the effectiveness of such an undertaking has been tested.

38. Concurrent requests for extradition in respect of the same crime from two different States are not a common occurrence. If both requests are received at the same time, the Secretary of State decides which request is to be proceeded with, having regard to all the facts of the case, including the nationality of the fugitive and the place of commission of the offence.

In this respect Article X of the Extradition Treaty between the United Kingdom and the United States provides as follows:

> If the extradition of a person is requested concurrently by one of the Contracting Parties and by another State or States, either for the same offence or for different offences, the requested Party shall make its decision, in so far as its law allows, having regard to all the circumstances, including the provisions in this regard in any Agreements in force between the requested Party and the requesting State, the relative seriousness and place of commission of the offences, the respective dates of the requests, the nationality of the person sought and the possibility of subsequent extradition to another State.

III.   Relevant Domestic Law in the Commonwealth of Virginia

A.   THE LAW RELATING TO MURDER

39. The relevant definition and classification of murder and sentencing for murder are governed by the Code of Virginia of 1950, as amended, and the decided cases in the State and Federal courts.

40. Section 18.2-31 of the Virginia Code provides that eight types of homicide constitute capital murder, punishable as a Class 1 felony, including "the wilful, deliberate and premeditated killing of more than one person as a part of the same act or transaction" (sub-section (g)). The punishment for a Class 1 felony is "death or imprisonment for life" (Virginia Code, section 18.2-10(a)). Except in the case of murder for hire, only the "triggerman," that is the actual perpetrator of the killing, may be charged with capital murder (Johnston v. Commonwealth, 220 Va. 146, 255 S.E.2d 525 (1979)).

Murder other than capital murder is classified as murder in the first degree or murder in the second degree and is punishable by varying terms of imprisonment (Virginia Code, sections 18.2-10(b), (c) and 18.2-32).

41. In most felony trials, including trials for capital murder, the defendant is guaranteed trial by jury. The defendant may waive this right but does not often do so.

B.   SENTENCING PROCEDURE

42. The sentencing procedure in a capital murder case in Virginia is a separate proceeding from the determination of guilt. Following a determina-

tion of guilt of capital murder, the same jury, or judge sitting without a jury, will forthwith proceed to hear evidence regarding punishment. All relevant evidence concerning the offence and the defendant is admissible. Evidence in mitigation is subject to almost no limitation, while evidence of aggravation is restricted by statute (Virginia Code, section 19.1-264.4).

43. Unless the prosecution proves beyond a reasonable doubt the existence of at least one of two statutory aggravating circumstances — future dangerousness or vileness — the sentencer may not return a death sentence.

"Future dangerousness" exists where there is a probability that the defendant would commit "criminal acts of violence" in the future such as would constitute a "continuing serious threat to society" (Virginia Code, section 19.2-264.2).

"Vileness" exists when the crime was "outrageously or wantonly vile, horrible or inhuman in that it involved torture, depravity of mind or an aggravated battery to the victim" (Virginia Code, ibid.). The words "depravity of mind" mean "a degree of moral turpitude and physical debasement surpassing that inherent in the definition of ordinary legal malice and premeditation." The words "aggravated battery" mean a battery which, "qualitatively and quantitatively, is more culpable than the minimum necessary to accomplish an act of murder" (Smith v. Commonwealth, 219 Va. 455, 248 S.E.2d 135 (1978), certiorari denied, 441 U.S. 967 (1979)). Proof of multiple wounds sustained by the victim, particularly a neck wound, which even considered alone, constituted an aggravated battery in the light of the savage, methodical manner in which it was inflicted, leaving the victim to suffer an interval of agony awaiting death, has been held to satisfy the test of "vileness" under this section (Edmonds v. Commonwealth, 229 Va. 303, 329 S.E.2d 807, certiorari denied, 106 S. Ct. 339, 88 L. Ed. 2d 324 (1985)).

44. The imposition of the death penalty on a young person who has reached the age of majority — which is 18 years (Virginia Code, section 1.13.42) — is not precluded under Virginia law. Age is a fact to be weighed by the jury (Peterson v. Commonwealth, 225 Va. 289, 302 S.E.2d 520, certiorari denied, 464 U.S. 865, 104 S. Ct. 202, 78 L. Ed. 2d 176 (1983)).

45. Facts in mitigation are specified by statute as including but not being limited to the following:

> (i) the defendant has no significant history of prior criminal activity, or (ii) the capital felony was committed while the defendant was under the influence of extreme mental or emotional disturbance, or (iii) the victim was a participant in the defendant's conduct or consented to the act, or (iv) at the time of the commission of the capital felony, the capacity of the defendant to appreciate the criminality of his conduct or to conform his conduct to the requirements of law was significantly impaired, or (v) the age of the defendant at the time of the commission of the capital offence [Virginia Code, section 19.2.264.4B].

46. In a case of trial by jury, the jury in a capital murder case has the duty to consider all evidence relevant to sentencing, both favourable and

unfavourable, before fixing punishment. In particular, a jury may sentence a defendant to death only after having considered the evidence in mitigation of the offence (Watkins v. Commonwealth, 229 Va. 469, 331 S.E.2d 422 (1985), certiorari denied, 475 U.S. 1099, 106 S. Ct. 1503, 89 L. Ed. 2d 903 (1986)). Furthermore, unless the jury is unanimous the sentence cannot be death but must be life imprisonment (Virginia Code, section 19.2-264.4). Even if one or more of the statutory aggravating circumstances are shown, the sentencer still remains at liberty to fix a life sentence instead of death in the light of the mitigating circumstances and even for no reason other than mercy (Smith v. Commonwealth, loc. cit.).

47. Following a sentence of death, the trial judge must order the preparation of an investigative report detailing the defendant's history and "any and all other relevant facts, to the end that the court may be fully advised as to whether the penalty of death is appropriate and just"; after consideration of the report, and upon good cause shown, the judge may set aside the sentence of death and impose a life sentence (Virginia Code, section 19.2-264.5).

48. Following a moratorium consequent upon a decision of the United States Supreme Court (Furman v. Georgia, 92 S. Ct. 2726 (1972)), imposition of the death penalty was resumed in Virginia in 1977, since which date seven persons have been executed. The means of execution used is electrocution.

The Virginia death penalty statutory scheme, including the provision on mandatory review of sentence (see paragraph 52 below), has been judicially determined to be constitutional. It was considered to prevent the arbitrary or capricious imposition of the death penalty and narrowly to channel the sentencer's discretion (Smith v. Commonwealth, loc. cit.; Turnver v. Bass, 753 F.2d 342 (4th Cir. 1984); Briley v. Bass, 750 F.2d 1238 (4th Cir. 1984)). The death penalty under the Virginia capital murder statute has also been held not to constitute cruel and unusual punishment or to deny a defendant due process or equal protection (Stamper v. Commonwealth, 220 Va. 260, 257 S.E.2d 808 (1979), certiorari denied, 445 U.S. 972, 100 S. Ct. 1666, 64 L. Ed. 2d 249 (1980)). The Supreme Court of Virginia rejected the submission that death by electrocution would cause "the needless imposition of pain before death and emotional suffering while awaiting execution of sentence" (ibid.).

C.   INSANITY, MENTAL DISORDERS AND DIMINISHED
     RESPONSIBILITY

49. The law of Virginia generally does not recognise a defence of diminished capacity (Stamper v. Commonwealth, 228 Va. 707, 324 S.E.2d 682 (1985)).

50. A plea of insanity at the time of the offence is recognised as a defence in Virginia and, if successful, is a bar to conviction. Such a plea

will apply where the defendant knows that the act is wrong but is driven by an irresistible impulse, induced by some mental disease affecting the volitive powers, to commit it (Thompson v. Commonwealth, 193 Va. 704, 70 S.E.2d 284 (1952) and Godley v. Commonwealth, 2 Va. App. 249 (1986)) or where he does not understand the nature, character and consequences of his act or is unable to distinguish right from wrong (Price v. Commonwealth, 228 Va. 452, 323 S.E.2d 106 (1984)). Where no insanity defence is interposed, the defendant's mental condition is only relevant at the guilt stage in so far as it might be probative of a fact in issue, for example premeditation at the time of the killing (Le Vasseur v. Commonwealth, 225 Va. 564, 304 S.E.2d 644 (1983), certiorari denied, 464 U.S. 1063, 104 S. Ct 744, 79 L. Ed. 2d 202 (1984)).

51. In a capital murder trial, the defendant's mental condition at the time of the offence, including any level of mental illness, may be pleaded as a mitigating factor at the sentencing stage. Evidence on this may include, but is not limited to, showing that the defendant was under the influence of extreme mental or emotional disturbance or that at the time of the offence his capacity to appreciate the criminality of his conduct was significantly impaired (Virginia Code, section 19.2-264.4B — see paragraph 45 above). . . .

Upon presentation of evidence of the defendant's mental state, the sentencer may elect to impose life imprisonment rather than the death penalty.

D.   APPEALS IN CAPITAL CASES

52. The Supreme Court of Virginia reviews automatically every case in which a capital sentence has been passed, regardless of the plea entered by the defendant at his trial. In addition to consideration of "any errors in the trial" alleged by the defendant on appeal, the Supreme Court reviews the death sentence to determine whether it was imposed "under the influence of passion, prejudice or any other arbitrary factor" and whether it is excessive or disproportionate "to the penalty imposed in similar cases" (Virginia Code, section 17-110.1). . . .

After this appeal process is completed, the sentence of death will be executed unless a stay of execution is entered. As a practical matter, a stay will be entered when the prisoner initiates further proceedings.

There has apparently been only one case since 1977 where the Virginia Supreme Court has itself reduced a death sentence to life imprisonment.

53. The prisoner may apply to the United States Supreme Court for certiorari review of the decision of the Supreme Court of Virginia. If unsuccessful, he may begin collateral attacks upon the conviction and sentence in habeas corpus proceedings in both State and Federal courts.

The prisoner may file a habeas corpus petition either in the Supreme Court of Virginia or in the trial court, with appeal to the Supreme Court of

Virginia. Thereafter he may once more apply to the United States Supreme Court for certiorari review of the State's habeas corpus decision.

He may then file a petition for a writ of habeas corpus in the Federal District Court. The decision of the District Court may be appealed to the Federal Circuit Court of Appeals, followed, if no relief is obtained, by a petition for certiorari review in the United States Supreme Court.

At each stage of his collateral attacks, the prisoner may seek a stay of execution pending final determination of his applications.

54. The Virginia and Federal statutes and rules of court set time-limits for the presentation of appeals following conviction or appeals against the decisions in habeas corpus proceedings. There are, however, no time-limits for filing the initial State and Federal habeas corpus petitions.

55. The grounds which may be presented and argued on appeal and in habeas corpus proceedings are restricted by the "contemporaneous objections rule" to those which have been raised in the course of the trial (see Rule 5.25 of the Rules of the Supreme Court of Virginia). . . .

By way of exception to the rule, errors to which no objections were made at the trial may be objected to on appeal where this is necessary to attain the ends of justice or where good cause is shown. This exception has been applied by the Supreme Court of Virginia to overturn a capital murder conviction (Ball v. Commonwealth, 221 Va. 754, 273 S.E.2d 790 (1981)). In death penalty cases, the proportionality of the sentence and the issue of whether the sentence was imposed under the influence of passion, prejudice or other arbitrary factor (see paragraph 52 above) is reviewed without regard to whether objection was made at trial (see Briley v. Bass, loc. cit.).

56. The average time between trial and execution in Virginia, calculated on the basis of the seven executions which have taken place since 1977, is six to eight years. The delays are primarily due to a strategy by convicted prisoners to prolong the appeal proceedings as much as possible. The United States Supreme Court has not as yet considered or ruled on the "death row phenomenon" and in particular whether it falls foul of the prohibition of "cruel and unusual punishment" under the Eighth Amendment to the Constitution of the United States. . . .

60. The Governor of the Commonwealth of Virginia has an unrestricted power "to commute capital punishment" (Article V, section 12, of the Constitution of Virginia). As a matter of policy, the Governor does not promise, before a conviction and sentence, that he will later exercise his commutation power. Since 1977 there has been no case in which the Governor has commuted a death sentence. . . .

G.   PRISON CONDITIONS IN MECKLENBURG CORRECTIONAL
     CENTER

61. There are currently 40 people under sentence of death in Virginia. The majority are detained in Mecklenburg Correctional Center, which is a modern maximum security institution with a total capacity of 335 inmates.

Institutional Operating Procedures (IOP 821.1) establish uniform operating procedures for the administration, security, control and delivery of necessary services to death row inmates in Mecklenburg. In addition conditions of confinement are governed by a comprehensive consent decree handed down by the United States District Court in Richmond in the case of Alan Brown et al. v. Allyn R. Sielaff et al. (5 April 1985). Both the Virginia Department of Corrections and the American Civil Liberties Union monitor compliance with the terms of the consent decree. The United States District Court also retains jurisdiction to enforce compliance with the decree. . . .

63. The size of a death row inmate's cell is 3m by 2.2m. Prisoners have an opportunity for approximately 7½ hours' recreation per week in summer and approximately 6 hours' per week, weather permitting, in winter. The death row area has two recreation yards, both of which are equipped with basketball courts and one of which is equipped with weights and weight benches. Inmates are also permitted to leave their cells on other occasions, such as to receive visits, to visit the law library or to attend the prison infirmary. In addition, death row inmates are given one hour out-of-cell time in the morning in a common area. Each death row inmate is eligible for work assignments, such as cleaning duties. When prisoners move around the prison they are handcuffed with special shackles around the waist. . . .

64. The applicant adduced much evidence of extreme stress, psychological deterioration and risk of homosexual abuse and physical attack undergone by prisoners on death row, including Mecklenburg Correctional Center. This evidence was strongly contested by the United Kingdom government on the basis of affidavits sworn by administrators from the Virginia Department of Corrections.

65. Death row inmates receive the same medical service as inmates in the general population. An infirmary equipped with adequate supplies, equipment and staff provides for 24-hour in-patient care, and emergency facilities are provided in each building. Mecklenburg also provides psychological and psychiatric services to death row inmates. The United States District Court (Eastern District of Virginia) has recently upheld the adequacy of mental health treatment available to death row inmates in Mecklenburg (Stamper et al. v. Blair et al., decision of 14 July 1988).

66. Inmates are allowed non-contact visits in a visiting room on Saturdays, Sundays and holidays between 8.30am and 3.30pm. Attorneys have access to their clients during normal working hours on request as well as during the scheduled visiting hours. Death row inmates who have a record of good behaviour are eligible for contact visits with members of their immediate family two days per week. Outgoing correspondence from inmates is picked up daily and all incoming correspondence is delivered each evening. . . .

68. A death row prisoner is moved to the death house 15 days before he is due to be executed. The death house is next to the death chamber where the electric chair is situated. Whilst a prisoner is in the death house he is watched 24 hours a day. He is isolated and has no light in his cell. The

lights outside are permanently lit. A prisoner who utilises the appeals process can be placed in the death house several times.

69. Relations between the United Kingdom and the United States of America on matters concerning extradition are conducted by and with the Federal and not the State authorities. However, in respect of offences against State laws the Federal authorities have no legally binding power to provide, in an appropriate extradition case, an assurance that the death penalty will not be imposed or carried out. In such cases the power rests with the State. If a State does decide to give a promise in relation to the death penalty, the United States Government would have the power to give an assurance to the extraditing Government that the State's promise will be honoured.

According to evidence from the Virginia authorities, Virginia's capital sentencing procedure and notably the provision on post-sentencing reports (see paragraph 47 above) would allow the sentencing judge to consider the representation to be made on behalf of the United Kingdom Government pursuant to the assurance given by the Attorney for Bedford County (see paragraph 20 above). In addition, it would be open to the Governor to take into account the wishes of the United Kingdom Government in any application for clemency (see paragraph 60 above).

I.   MUTUAL ASSISTANCE IN CRIMINAL MATTERS

70. There is no way of compelling American witnesses to give evidence at a trial in the Federal Republic of Germany. However, such witnesses would normally, unless imprisoned, be free to appear voluntarily before a German court and the German authorities would pay their expenses. Furthermore, a United States Federal court may, pursuant to a letter rogatory or a request from a foreign tribunal, order a person to give testimony or a statement or to produce a document or other thing for use in a proceeding in a foreign tribunal (28 United States Code, section 1782). In addition, public documents, for example the transcript of a criminal trial, are available to foreign prosecuting authorities.

IV.   RELEVANT LAW AND PRACTICE OF THE FEDERAL
REPUBLIC OF GERMANY

71. German criminal law applies to acts committed abroad by a German national if the act is liable to punishment at the place where the offence is committed (Criminal Code, section 7(2)).

72. Murder is defined as follows in section 211(2) of the Criminal Code:

> He is deemed a murderer who because of murderous lust, to satisfy his sexual instinct, for reasons of covetousness or for otherwise base motives, insidiously or cruelly or by means constituting a public danger or in order to render another crime possible or to conceal another crime kills a person.

Murder is punishable with life imprisonment (Criminal Code, section 211(1)), the death penalty having been abolished under the Constitution (Article 102 of the Basic Law, 1949).

73. Under the terms of the Juvenile Court Act (1953) as amended, if a young adult — defined as a person who is 18 but not yet 21 years of age at the time of the criminal act (section 1(3)) — commits an offence, the judge will apply the provisions applicable to a juvenile — defined as a person who is at least 14 but not yet 18 years of age (ibid.) — if, inter alia, "the overall assessment of the offender's personality, having regard also to the circumstances of his environment, reveals that, according to his moral and mental development, he was still equal to a juvenile at the time of committing the offence" (section 105(1)). The sentence for young adults who come within this section is youth imprisonment of 6 months to 10 years or, under certain conditions, of indeterminate duration (sections 18, 19 and 105(3)).

Where, on the other hand, the young adult offender's personal development corresponds to his age, the general criminal law applies but the judge may pass a sentence of 10 to 15 years' imprisonment instead of a life sentence (section 106(1)).

74. Where an offender, at the time of commission of the offence, was incapable of appreciating the wrongfulness of the offence or of acting in accordance with such appreciation by reason of a morbid mental or emotional disturbance, by reason of a profound disturbance of consciousness or by reason of mental deficiency or some other serious mental or emotional abnormality, there can be no culpability on his part and he may not be punished (Criminal Code, section 20). In such a case, however, it is possible for an order to be made placing the offender in a psychiatric hospital indefinitely (Criminal Code, section 63).

In a case of diminished responsibility, namely where there is substantial impairment of the offender's ability to appreciate the wrongfulness of the offence or to act in accordance with such appreciation at the time of commission of the offence for one of the reasons set out in section 20 (Criminal Code, section 21), punishment may be reduced and, in particular, in homicide cases imprisonment of not less than 3 years shall be substituted for life imprisonment (Criminal Code, section 49(1)(2)). Alternatively, the court may order placement in a psychiatric hospital.

75. Where a death sentence is risked, the Federal Government will

grant extradition only if there is an unequivocal assurance by the requesting State that the death penalty will not be imposed or that it will not be carried out. The German-United States Extradition Treaty of 20 June 1978, in force since 29 August 1980, contains a provision (Article 12) corresponding, in its essentials, to Article IV of the United Kingdom-United States Extradition Treaty (see paragraph 36 above). The Government of the Federal Republic of Germany stated in evidence that they would not have deemed an assurance of the kind given by the United States Government in the present case to be adequate and would have refused extradition. In accordance with recent judicial decisions, the question whether an adequate assurance has been given is subject to examination in proceedings before the higher regional court.

PROCEEDINGS BEFORE THE COMMISSION

76. Mr Soering's application (no. 14038/88) was lodged with the Commission on 8 July 1988. In his application Mr Soering stated his belief that, notwithstanding the assurance given to the United Kingdom Government, there was a serious likelihood that he would be sentenced to death if extradited to the United States of America. He maintained that in the circumstances and, in particular, having regard to the "death row phenomenon" he would thereby be subjected to inhuman and degrading treatment and punishment contrary to Article 3 of the Convention. In his further submission his extradition to the United States would constitute a violation of Article 6 §3 (c) because of the absence of legal aid in the State of Virginia to pursue various appeals. Finally, he claimed that, in breach of Article 13, he had no effective remedy under United Kingdom law in respect of his complaint under Article 3.

77. On 11 August 1988 the President of the Commission indicated to the United Kingdom Government, in accordance with Rule 36 of the Commission's Rules of Procedure, that it was desirable, in the interests of the parties and the proper conduct of the proceedings, not to extradite the applicant to the United States until the Commission had had an opportunity to examine the application. This indication was subsequently prolonged by the Commission on several occasions until the reference of the case to the Court.

78. The Commission declared the application admissible on 10 November 1988.

In its report adopted on 19 January 1989 (Article 31) the Commission expressed the opinion that there had been a breach of Article 13 (seven votes to four) but no breach of either Article 3 (six votes to five) or Article 6 §3 (c) (unanimously). . . .

FINAL SUBMISSIONS TO THE COURT BY THE UNITED KINGDOM
GOVERNMENT

79. At the public hearing on 24 April 1989 the United Kingdom Government maintained the concluding submissions set out in their memorial, whereby they requested the Court to hold

1. that neither the extradition of the applicant nor any act or decision of the United Kingdom Government in relation thereto constitutes a breach of Article 3 of the Convention;
2. that neither the extradition of the applicant nor any act or decision of the United Kingdom Government in relation thereto constitutes a breach of Article 6 §3 (c) of the Convention;
3. that there has been no violation of Article 13 of the Convention;
4. that no issues arise under Article 50 of the Convention which call for consideration by the Court.

. . . AS TO THE LAW

I.   ALLEGED BREACH OF ARTICLE 3

80. The applicant alleged that the decision by the Secretary of State for the Home Department to surrender him to the authorities of the United States of America would, if implemented, give rise to a breach by the United Kingdom of Article 3 of the Convention, which provides: "No one shall be subjected to torture or to inhuman or degrading treatment or punishment."

APPLICABILITY OF ARTICLE 3 IN CASES
OF EXTRADITION

81. The alleged breach derives from the applicant's exposure to the so-called "death row phenomenon." This phenomenon may be described as consisting in a combination of circumstances to which the applicant would be exposed if, after having been extradited to Virginia to face a capital murder charge, he were sentenced to death.

82. In its report (at paragraph 94) the Commission reaffirmed "its case-law that a person's deportation or extradition may give rise to an issue under Article 3 of the Convention where there are serious reasons to believe that the individual will be subjected, in the receiving State, to treatment contrary to that Article."

The Government of the Federal Republic of Germany supported the approach of the Commission, pointing to a similar approach in the case-law of the German courts.

The applicant likewise submitted that Article 3 not only prohibits the Contracting States from causing inhuman or degrading treatment or punishment to occur within their jurisdiction but also embodies an associated obligation not to put a person in a position where he will or may suffer such treatment or punishment at the hands of other States. For the applicant, at least as far as Article 3 is concerned, an individual may not be surrendered out of the protective zone of the Convention without the certainty that the safeguards which he would enjoy are as effective as the Convention standard.

83. The United Kingdom Government, on the other hand, contended that Article 3 should not be interpreted so as to impose responsibility on a Contracting State for acts which occur outside its jurisdiction. In particular, in their submission, extradition does not involve the responsibility of the extraditing State for inhuman or degrading treatment or punishment which the extradited person may suffer outside the State's jurisdiction. To begin with, they maintained, it would be straining the language of Article 3 intolerably to hold that by surrendering a fugitive criminal the extraditing State has "subjected" him to any treatment or punishment that he will receive following conviction and sentence in the receiving State. Further arguments advanced against the approach of the Commission were that it interferes with international treaty rights; it leads to a conflict with the norms of international judicial process, in that it in effect involves adjudication on the internal affairs of foreign States not Parties to the Convention or to the proceedings before the Convention institutions; it entails grave difficulties of evaluation and proof in requiring the examination of alien systems of law and of conditions in foreign States; the practice of national courts and the international community cannot reasonably be invoked to support it; it causes a serious risk of harm in the Contracting State which is obliged to harbour the protected person, and leaves criminals untried, at large and unpunished.

In the alternative, the United Kingdom Government submitted that the application of Article 3 in extradition cases should be limited to those occasions in which the treatment or punishment abroad is certain, imminent and serious. In their view, the fact that by definition the matters complained of are only anticipated, together with the common and legitimate interest of all States in bringing fugitive criminals to justice, requires a very high degree of risk, proved beyond reasonable doubt, that ill-treatment will actually occur.

84. The Court will approach the matter on the basis of the following considerations.

85. As results from article 5 §1 (f), which permits "the lawful . . . detention of a person against whom action is being taken with a view to . . . extradition", no right not to be extradited is as such protected by the Convention. Nevertheless, in so far as a measure of extradition has consequences adversely affecting the enjoyment of a Convention right, it may,

assuming that the consequences are not too remote, attract the obligations of a Contracting State under the relevant Convention guarantee (see, mutatis mutandis, the Abdulaziz, Cabales and Balkandali judgment of 25 May 1985, Series A no. 94, pp. 31-32, §§59-60 — in relation to rights in the field of immigration). What is at issue in the present case is whether Article 3 can be applicable when the adverse consequences of extradition are, or may be, suffered outside the jurisdiction of the extraditing State as a result of treatment or punishment administered in the receiving State.

86. Article 1 of the Convention, which provides that "the High Contracting Parties shall secure to everyone within their jurisdiction the rights and freedoms defined in Section I," sets a limit, notably territorial, on the reach of the Convention. In particular, the engagement undertaken by a Contracting State is confined to "securing" ("reconnaître" in the French text) the listed rights and freedoms to persons within its own "jurisdiction." Further, the Convention does not govern the actions of States not Parties to it, nor does it purport to be a means of requiring the Contracting States to impose Convention standards on other States. Article 1 cannot be read as justifying a general principle to the effect that, notwithstanding its extradition obligations, a Contracting State may not surrender an individual unless satisfied that the conditions awaiting him in the country of destination are in full accord with each of the safeguards of the Convention. Indeed, as the United Kingdom Government stressed, the beneficial purpose of extradition in preventing fugitive offenders from evading justice cannot be ignored in determining the scope of application of the Convention and of Article 3 in particular.

In the instant case it is common ground that the United Kingdom has no power over the practices and arrangements of the Virginia authorities which are the subject of the applicant's complaints. It is also true that in other international instruments cited by the United Kingdom Government — for example the 1951 United Nations Convention relating to the Status of Refugees (Article 33), the 1957 European Convention on Extradition (Article 11) and the 1984 United Nations Convention against Torture and Other Cruel, Inhuman and Degrading Treatment or Punishment (Article 3) — the problems of removing a person to another jurisdiction where unwanted consequences may follow are addressed expressly and specifically.

These considerations cannot, however, absolve the Contracting Parties from responsibility under Article 3 for all and any foreseeable consequences of extradition suffered outside their jurisdiction.

87. In interpreting the Convention regard must be had to its special character as a treaty for the collective enforcement of human rights and fundamental freedoms (see the Ireland v. the United Kingdom judgment of 18 January 1978, Series A no. 25, p. 90, §239). Thus, the object and purpose of the Convention as an instrument for the protection of individual human beings require that its provisions be interpreted and applied so as to make its safeguards practical and effective (see, inter alia, the Artico

judgment of 13 May 1980, Series A no. 37, p. 16, §33). In addition, any interpretation of the rights and freedoms guaranteed has to be consistent with "the general spirit of the Convention, an instrument designed to maintain and promote the ideals and values of a democratic society" (see the Kjeldsen, Busk Madsen and Pedersen judgment of 7 December 1976, Series A no. 23, p. 27, §53).

88. Article 3 makes no provision for exceptions, and no derogation from it is permissible under Article 15 in time of war or other national emergency. This absolute prohibition of torture and of inhuman or degrading treatment or punishment under the terms of the Convention shows that Article 3 enshrines one of the fundamental values of the democratic societies making up the Council of Europe. It is also to be found in similar terms in other international instruments such as the 1966 International Covenant on Civil and Political Rights and the 1969 American Convention on Human Rights and is generally recognised as an internationally accepted standard.

The question remains whether the extradition of a fugitive to another State where he would be subjected or be likely to be subjected to torture or to inhuman or degrading treatment or punishment would itself engage the responsibility of a Contracting State under Article 3. That the abhorrence of torture has such implications is recognised in Article 3 of the United Nations Convention Against Torture and Other Cruel, Inhuman or Degrading Treatment or Punishment, which provides that "no State Party shall . . . extradite a person where there are substantial grounds for believing that he would be in danger of being subjected to torture." The fact that a specialised treaty should spell out in detail a specific obligation attaching to the prohibition of torture does not mean that an essentially similar obligation is not already inherent in the general terms of Article 3 of the European Convention. It would hardly be compatible with the underlying values of the Convention, that "common heritage of political traditions, ideals, freedom and the rule of law" to which the Preamble refers, were a Contracting State knowingly to surrender a fugitive to another State where there were substantial grounds for believing that he would be in danger of being subjected to torture, however heinous the crime allegedly committed. Extradition in such circumstances, while not explicitly referred to in the brief and general wording of Article 3, would plainly be contrary to the spirit and intendment of the Article, and in the Court's view this inherent obligation not to extradite also extends to cases in which the fugitive would be faced in the receiving State by a real risk of exposure to inhuman or degrading treatment or punishment proscribed by that Article.

89. What amounts to "inhuman or degrading treatment or punishment" depends on all the circumstances of the case (see paragraph 100 below). Furthermore, inherent in the whole of the Convention is a search for a fair balance between the demands of the general interest of the community and the requirements of the protection of the individual's funda-

mental rights. As movement about the world becomes easier and crime takes on a larger international dimension, it is increasingly in the interest of all nations that suspected offenders who flee abroad should be brought to justice. Conversely, the establishment of safe havens for fugitives would not only result in danger for the State obliged to harbour the protected person but also tend to undermine the foundations of extradition. These considerations must also be included among the factors to be taken into account in the interpretation and application of the notions of inhuman and degrading treatment or punishment in extradition cases.

90. It is not normal for the Convention institutions to pronounce on the existence or otherwise of potential violations of the Convention. However, where an applicant claims that a decision to extradite him would, if implemented, be contrary to Article 3 by reason of its foreseeable consequences in the requesting country, a departure from this principle is necessary, in view of the serious and irreparable nature of the alleged suffering risked, in order to ensure the effectiveness of the safeguard provided by that Article (see paragraph 87 above).

91. In sum, the decision by a Contracting State to extradite a fugitive may give rise to an issue under Article 3, and hence engage the responsibility of that State under the Convention, where substantial grounds have been shown for believing that the person concerned, if extradited, faces a real risk of being subjected to torture or to inhuman or degrading treatment or punishment in the requesting country. The establishment of such responsibility inevitably involves an assessment of conditions in the requesting country against the standards of Article 3 of the Convention. Nonetheless, there is no question of adjudicating on or establishing the responsibility of the receiving country, whether under general international law, under the Convention or otherwise. In so far as any liability under the Convention is or may be incurred, it is liability incurred by the extraditing Contracting State by reason of its having taken action which has as a direct consequence the exposure of an individual to proscribed ill-treatment.

B.   APPLICATION OF ARTICLE 3 IN THE PARTICULAR
      CIRCUMSTANCES OF THE PRESENT CASE

92. The extradition procedure against the applicant in the United Kingdom has been completed, the Secretary of State having signed a warrant ordering his surrender to the United States' authorities (see paragraph 24 above); this decision, albeit as yet not implemented, directly affects him. It therefore has to be determined on the above principles whether the foreseeable consequences of Mr Soering's return to the United States are such as to attract the application of Article 3. This inquiry must concentrate firstly on whether Mr Soering runs a real risk of being sentenced to death in Virginia, since the source of the alleged inhuman and degrading treatment

or punishment, namely the "death row phenomenon," lies in the imposition of the death penalty. Only in the event of an affirmative answer to this question need the Court examine whether exposure to the "death row phenomenon" in the circumstances of the applicant's case would involve treatment or punishment imcompatible with Article 3.

1. Whether the Applicant Runs a Real Risk of a Death Sentence and Hence of Exposure to the "Death Row Phenomenon"

93. The United Kingdom Government, contrary to the Government of the Federal Republic of Germany, the Commission and the applicant, did not accept that the risk of a death sentence attains a sufficient level of likelihood to bring Article 3 into play. Their reasons were fourfold.

Firstly, as illustrated by his interview with the German prosecutor where he appeared to deny any intention to kill (see paragraph 16 above), the applicant has not acknowledged his guilt of capital murder as such.

Secondly, only a prima facie case has so far been made out against him. In particular, in the United Kingdom Government's view the psychiatric evidence (see paragraph 21 above) is equivocal as to whether Mr Soering was suffering from a disease of the mind sufficient to amount to a defence of insanity under Virginia law (as to which, see paragraph 50 above).

Thirdly, even if Mr Soering is convicted of capital murder, it cannot be assumed that in the general exercise of their discretion the jury will recommend, the judge will confirm and the Supreme Court of Virginia will uphold the imposition of the death penalty (see paragraphs 42-47 and 52 above). The United Kingdom Government referred to the presence of important mitigating factors, such as the applicant's age and mental condition at the time of commission of the offence and his lack of previous criminal activity, which would have to be taken into account by the jury and then by the judge in the separate sentencing proceedings (see paragraphs 44-47 and 51 above).

Fourthly, the assurance received from the United States must at the very least significantly reduce the risk of a capital sentence either being imposed or carried out (see paragraphs 20, 37 and 69 above).

At the public hearing the Attorney General nevertheless made clear his Government's understanding that if Mr Soering were extradited to the United States there was "some risk," which was "more than merely negligible," that the death penalty would be imposed.

94. As the applicant himself pointed out, he has made to American and British police officers and to two psychiatrists admissions of his participation in the killings of the Haysom parents, although he appeared to retract those admissions somewhat when questioned by the German prosecutor (see paragraphs 13, 16 and 21 above). It is not for the European Court to usurp

the function of the Virginia courts by ruling that a defence of insanity would or would not be available on the psychiatric evidence as it stands. The United Kingdom Government are justified in their assertion that no assumption can be made that Mr Soering would certainly or even probably be convicted of capital murder as charged (see paragraphs 13 *in fine* and 40 above). Nevertheless, as the Attorney General conceded on their behalf at the public hearing, there is "a significant risk" that the applicant would be so convicted.

95. Under Virginia law, before a death sentence can be returned the prosecution must prove beyond reasonable doubt the existence of at least one of the two statutory aggravating circumstances, namely future dangerousness or vileness (see paragraph 43 above). In this connection, the horrible and brutal circumstances of the killings (see paragraph 12 above) would presumably tell against the applicant, regard being had to the case-law on the grounds for establishing the "vileness" of the crime (see paragraph 43 above).

Admittedly, taken on their own the mitigating factors do reduce the likelihood of the death sentence being imposed. No less than four of the five facts in mitigation expressly mentioned in the Code of Virginia could arguably apply to Mr Soering's case. These are a defendant's lack of any previous criminal history, the fact that the offence was committed while a defendant was under extreme mental or emotional disturbance, the fact that at the time of commission of the offence the capacity of a defendant to appreciate the criminality of his conduct or to conform his conduct to the requirements of the law was significantly diminished, and a defendant's age (see paragraph 45 above).

96. These various elements arguing for or against the imposition of a death sentence have to be viewed in the light of the attitude of the prosecuting authorities.

97. The Commonwealth's Attorney for Bedford County, Mr Updike, who is responsible for conducting the prosecution against the applicant, has certified that "should Jens Soering be convicted of the offence of capital murder as charged . . . a representation will be made in the name of the United Kingdom to the judge at the time of sentencing that it is the wish of the United Kingdom that the death penalty should not be imposed or carried out" (see paragraph 20 above). The Court notes, like Lord Justice Lloyd in the Divisional Court (see paragraph 22 above), that this undertaking is far from reflecting the wording of Article IV of the 1972 Extradition Treaty between the United Kingdom and the United States, which speaks of "assurances satisfactory to the requested Party that the death penalty will not be carried out" (see paragraph 36 above). However, the offence charged, being a State and not a Federal offence, comes within the jurisdiction of the Commonwealth of Virginia; it appears as a consequence that no direction could or can be given to the Commonwealth's Attorney by any State or Federal authority to promise more; the Virginia courts as judicial bodies

cannot bind themselves in advance as to what decisions they may arrive at on the evidence; and the Governor of Virginia does not, as a matter of policy, promise that he will later exercise his executive power to commute a death penalty (see paragraphs 58-60 and 69 above).

This being so, Mr Updike's undertaking may well have been the best "assurance" that the United Kingdom could have obtained from the United States Federal Government in the particular circumstances. According to the statement made to Parliament in 1987 by a Home Office Minister, acceptance of undertakings in such terms "means that the United Kingdom authorities render up a fugitive or are prepared to send citizen to face an American court on the clear understanding that the death penalty will not be carried out. . . . It would be a fundamental blow to the extradition arrangements between our two countries if the death penalty were carried out on an individual who had been returned under those circumstances" (see paragraph 37 above). Nonetheless, the effectiveness of such an undertaking has not yet been put to the test.

98. The applicant contended that representations concerning the wishes of a foreign government would not be admissible as a matter of law under the Virginia Code or, if admissible, of any influence on the sentencing judge.

Whatever the position under Virginia law and practice (as to which, see paragraphs 42, 46, 47 and 69 above), and notwithstanding the diplomatic context of the extradition relations between the United Kingdom and the United States, objectively it cannot be said that the undertaking to inform the judge at the sentencing stage of the wishes of the United Kingdom eliminates the risk of the death penalty being imposed. In the independent exercise of his discretion the Commonwealth's Attorney has himself decided to seek and to persist in seeking the death penalty because the evidence, in his determination, supports such action (see paragraph 20 *in fine* above). If the national authority with responsibility for prosecuting the offence takes such a firm stance, it is hardly open to the Court to hold that there are no substantial grounds for believing that the applicant faces a real risk of being sentenced to death and hence experiencing the "death row phenomenon."

99. The Court's conclusion is therefore that the likelihood of the feared exposure of the applicant to the "death row phenomenon" has been shown to be such as to bring Article 3 into play.

2. Whether in the Circumstances the Risk of Exposure to the "Death Row Phenomenon" Would Make Extradition a Breach of Article 3

(a) General considerations

100. As is established in the Court's case-law, ill-treatment, including punishment, must attain a minimum level of severity if it is to fall within the scope of Article 3. The assessment of this minimum is, in the nature of

things, relative; it depends on all the circumstances of the case, such as the nature and context of the treatment or punishment, the manner and method of its execution, its duration, its physical or mental effects and, in some instances, the sex, age and state of health of the victim (see the above-mentioned Ireland v. the United Kingdom judgment, Series A no. 25, p. 65, §162; and the Tyrer judgment of 25 April 1978, Series A no. 26, pp. 14-15, §§29 and 30).

Treatment has been held by the Court to be both "inhuman" because it was premeditated, was applied for hours at a stretch and "caused, if not actual bodily injury, at least intense physical and mental suffering," and also "degrading" because it was "such as to arouse in [its] victims feelings of fear, anguish and inferiority capable of humiliating and debasing them and possibly breaking their physical or moral resistance" (see the above-mentioned Ireland v. the United Kingdom judgment, p. 66, §167). In order for a punishment or treatment associated with it to be "inhuman" or "degrading," the suffering or humiliation involved must in any event go beyond that inevitable element of suffering or humiliation connected with a given form of legitimate punishment (see the Tyrer judgment, loc. cit.). In this connection, account is to be taken not only of the physical pain experienced but also, where there is a considerable delay before execution of the punishment, of the sentenced person's mental anguish of anticipating the violence he is to have inflicted on him.

101. Capital punishment is permitted under certain conditions by Article 2 §1 of the Convention, which reads:

> Everyone's right to life shall be protected by law. No one shall be deprived of his life intentionally save in the execution of a sentence of a court following his conviction of a crime for which this penalty is provided by law.

In view of this wording, the applicant did not suggest that the death penalty per se violated Article 3. He, like the two Government Parties, agreed with the Commission that the extradition of a person to a country where he risks the death penalty does not in itself raise an issue under either Article 2 or Article 3. On the other hand, Amnesty International in their written comments . . . argued that the evolving standards in Western Europe regarding the existence and use of the death penalty required that the death penalty should now be considered as an inhuman and degrading punishment within the meaning of Article 3.

102. Certainly, "the Convention is a living instrument which . . . must be interpreted in the light of present-day conditions"; and, in assessing whether a given treatment or punishment is to be regarded as inhuman or degrading for the purposes of Article 3, "the Court cannot but be influenced by the developments and commonly accepted standards in the penal policy of the member States of the Council of Europe in this field" (see the above-mentioned Tyrer judgment, Series A no. 26, pp. 15-16, §31). De facto the death penalty no longer exists in time of peace in the Contracting

States to the Convention. In the few Contracting States which retain the death penalty in law for some peacetime offences, death sentences, if ever imposed, are nowadays not carried out. This "virtual consensus in Western European legal systems that the death penalty is, under current circumstances, no longer consistent with regional standards of justice," to use the words of Amnesty International, is reflected in Protocol No. 6 to the Convention, which provides for the abolition of the death penalty in time of peace. Protocol No. 6 was opened for signature in April 1983, which in the practice of the Council of Europe indicates the absence of objection on the part of any of the Member States of the Organisation; it came into force in March 1985 and to date has been ratified by thirteen Contracting States to the Convention, not however including the United Kingdom.

Whether these marked changes have the effect of bringing the death penalty per se within the prohibition of ill-treatment under Article 3 must be determined on the principles governing the interpretation of the Convention.

103. The Convention is to be read as a whole and Article 3 should therefore be construed in harmony with the provisions of Article 2 (see, mutatis mutandis, the Klass and Others judgment of 6 September 1978, Series A no. 28, p. 31, §68). On this basis Article 3 evidently cannot have been intended by the drafters of the Convention to include a general prohibition of the death penalty since that would nullify the clear wording of Article 2 §1.

Subsequent practice in national penal policy, in the form of a generalised abolition of capital punishment, could be taken as establishing the agreement of the Contracting States to abrogate the exception provided for under Article 2§1 and hence to remove a textual limit on the scope for evolutive interpretation of Article 3. However, Protocol No. 6, as a subsequent written agreement, shows that the intention of the Contracting Parties as recently as 1983 was to adopt the normal method of amendment of the text in order to introduce a new obligation to abolish capital punishment in time of peace and, what is more, to do so by an optional instrument allowing each State to choose the moment when to undertake such an engagement. In these conditions, notwithstanding the special character of the Convention (see paragraph 87 above), Article 3 cannot be interpreted as generally prohibiting the death penalty.

104. That does not mean however that circumstances relating to a death sentence can never give rise to an issue under Article 3. The manner in which it is imposed or executed, the personal circumstances of the condemned person and a disproportionality to the gravity of the crime committed, as well as the conditions of detention awaiting execution, are examples of factors capable of bringing the treatment or punishment received by the condemned person within the proscription under Article 3. Present-day attitudes in the Contracting States to capital punishment are relevant for the assessment whether the acceptable threshold of suffering or degradation has been exceeded.

(b)   The particular circumstances

105. The applicant submitted that the circumstances to which he would be exposed as a consequence of the implementation of the Secretary of State's decision to return him to the United States, namely the "death row phenomenon," cumulatively constitute such serious treatment that his extradition would be contrary to Article 3. He cited in particular the delays in the appeal and review procedures following a death sentence, during which time he would be subject to increasing tension and psychological trauma; the fact, so he said, that the judge or jury in determining sentence is not obliged to take into account the defendant's age and mental state at the time of the offence; the extreme conditions of his future detention on "death row" in Mecklenburg Correctional Center, where he expects to be the victim of violence and sexual abuse because of his age, colour and nationality; and the constant spectre of the execution itself, including the ritual of execution. He also relied on the possibility of extradition or deportation, which he would not oppose, to the Federal Republic of Germany as accentuating the disproportionality of the Secretary of State's decision.

The Government of the Federal Republic of Germany took the view that, taking all the circumstances together, the treatment awaiting the applicant in Virginia would go so far beyond treatment inevitably connected with the imposition and execution of a death penalty as to be "inhuman" within the meaning of Article 3.

On the other hand, the conclusion expressed by the Commission was that the degree of severity contemplated by Article 3 would not be attained.

The United Kingdom government shared this opinion. In particular, they disputed many of the applicant's factual allegations as to the conditions on death row in Mecklenburg and his expected fate there.

i.   Length of Detention Prior to Execution

106. The period that a condemned prisoner can expect to spend on death row in Virginia before being executed is on average six to eight years (see paragraph 56 above). This length of time awaiting death is, as the Commission and the United Kingdom Government noted, in a sense largely of the prisoner's own making in that he takes advantage of all avenues of appeal which are offered to him by Virginia law. The automatic appeal to the Supreme Court of Virginia normally takes no more than six months (see paragraph 52 above). The remaining time is accounted for by collateral attacks mounted by the prisoner himself in habeas corpus proceedings before both the State and Federal courts and in applications to the Supreme Court of the United States for certiorari review, the prisoner at each stage being able to seek a stay of execution (see paragraphs 53-54 above). The remedies available under Virginia law serve the purpose of ensuring that the ultimate sanction of death is not unlawfully or arbitrarily imposed.

Nevertheless, just as some lapse of time between sentence and execution is inevitable if appeal safeguards are to be provided to the condemned person, so it is equally part of human nature that the person will cling to life by exploiting those safeguards to the full. However well-intentioned and even potentially beneficial is the provision of the complex of post-sentence procedures in Virginia, the consequence is that the condemned prisoner has to endure for many years the conditions on death row and the anguish and mounting tension of living in the ever-present shadow of death.

   ii.   Conditions on Death Row

107. As to conditions in Mecklenburg Correctional Center, where the applicant could expect to be held if sentenced to death, the Court bases itself on the facts which were uncontested by the United Kingdom Government, without finding it necessary to determine the reliability of the additional evidence adduced by the applicant, notably as to the risk of homosexual abuse and physical attack undergone by prisoners on death row (see paragraph 64 above).

   The stringency of the custodial regime in Mecklenburg, as well as the services (medical, legal and social) and the controls (legislative, judicial and administrative) provided for inmates, are described in some detail above (see paragraphs 61-63 and 65-68). In this connection, the United Kingdom Government drew attention to the necessary requirement of extra security for the safe custody of prisoners condemned to death for murder. Whilst it might thus well be justifiable in principle, the severity of a special regime such as that operated on death row in Mecklenburg is compounded by the fact of inmates being subject to it for a protracted period lasting on average six to eight years.

   iii.   The Applicant's Age and Mental State

108. At the time of the killings, the applicant was only 18 years old and there is some psychiatric evidence, which was not contested as such, that he "was suffering from [such] an abnormality of mind . . . as substantially impaired his mental responsibility for his acts" (see paragraphs 11, 12 and 21 above).

   Unlike Article 2 of the Convention, Article 6 of the 1966 International Covenant on Civil and Political Rights and Article 4 of the 1969 American Convention on Human Rights expressly prohibit the death penalty from being imposed on persons aged less than 18 at the time of commission of the offence. Whether or not such a prohibition be inherent in the brief and general language of Article 2 of the European Convention, its explicit enunciation in other, later international instruments, the former of which has been ratified by a large number of States Parties to the European Convention, at the very least indicates that as a general principle the youth of the person concerned is a circumstance which is liable, with others, to put in question the compatibility with Article 3 of measures connected with a death sentence.

It is in line with the Court's case-law (as summarised above at paragraph 100) to treat disturbed mental health as having the same effect for the application of Article 3.

109. Virginia law, as the United Kingdom Government and the Commission emphasised, certainly does not ignore these two factors. Under the Virginia Code account has to be taken of mental disturbance in a defendant, either as an absolute bar to conviction if it is judged to be sufficient to amount to insanity or, like age, as a fact in mitigation at the sentencing stage (see paragraphs 44-47 and 50-51 above). Additionally, indigent capital murder defendants are entitled to the appointment of a qualified mental health expert to assist in the preparation of their submissions at the separate sentencing proceedings (see paragraph 51 above). These provisions in the Virginia Code undoubtedly serve, as the American courts have stated, to prevent the arbitrary or capricious imposition of the death penalty and narrowly to channel the sentencer's discretion (see paragraph 48 above). They do not however remove the relevance of age and mental condition in relation to the acceptability, under Article 3, of the "death row phenomenon" for a given individual once condemned to death.

Although it is not for this Court to prejudge issues of criminal responsibility and appropriate sentence, the applicant's youth at the time of the offence and his then mental state, on the psychiatric evidence as it stands, are therefore to be taken into consideration as contributory factors tending, in his case, to bring the treatment on death row within the terms of Article 3.

iv.   Possibility of Extradition to the Federal Republic of Germany

110. For the United Kingdom Government and the majority of the Commission, the possibility of extraditing or deporting the applicant to face trial in the Federal Republic of Germany (see paragraphs 16, 19, 26, 38 and 71-74 above), where the death penalty has been abolished under the Constitution (see paragraph 72 above), is not material for the present purposes. Any other approach, the United Kingdom Government submitted, would lead to a "dual standard" affording the protection of the Convention to extraditable persons fortunate enough to have such an alternative destination available but refusing it to others not so fortunate.

This argument is not without weight. Furthermore, the Court cannot overlook either the horrible nature of the murders with which Mr Soering is charged or the legitimate and beneficial role of extradition arrangements in combating crime. The purpose for which his removal to the United States was sought, in accordance with the Extradition Treaty between the United Kingdom and the United States, is undoubtedly a legitimate one. However, sending Mr Soering to be tried in his own country would remove the danger of a fugitive criminal going unpunished as well as the risk of intense and protracted suffering on death row. It is therefore a circumstance of relevance for the overall assessment under Article 3 in that it goes to the search for the requisite fair balance of interests and to the proportionality of the contested extradition decision in the particular case (see paragraphs 89 and 104 above).

(c)   Conclusion

111. For any prisoner condemned to death, some element of delay between imposition and execution of the sentence and the experience of severe stress in conditions necessary for strict incarceration are inevitable. The democratic character of the Virginia legal system in general and the positive features of Virginia trial, sentencing and appeal procedures in particular are beyond doubt. The Court agrees with the Commission that the machinery of justice to which the applicant would be subject in the United States is in itself neither arbitrary nor unreasonable, but, rather, respects the rule of law and affords not inconsiderable procedural safeguards to the defendant in a capital trial. Facilities are available on death row for the assistance of inmates, notably through provision of psychological and psychiatric services (see paragraph 65 above).

However, in the Court's view, having regard to the very long period of time spent on death row in such extreme conditions, with the ever present and mounting anguish of awaiting execution of the death penalty, and to the personal circumstances of the applicant, especially his age and mental state at the time of the offence, the applicant's extradition to the United States would expose him to a real risk of treatment going beyond the threshold set by Article 3. A further consideration of relevance is that in the particular instance the legitimate purpose of extradition could be achieved by another means which would not involve suffering of such exceptional intensity or duration.

Accordingly, the Secretary of State's decision to extradite the applicant to the United States would, if implemented, give rise to a breach of Article 3.

This finding in no way puts in question the good faith of the United Kingdom Government, who have from the outset of the present proceedings demonstrated their desire to abide by their Convention obligations, firstly by staying the applicant's surrender to the United States authorities in accord with the interim measures indicated by the Convention institutions and secondly by themselves referring the case to the Court for a judicial ruling (see paragraphs 1, 4, 24 and 77 above).

II.   Alleged Breach of Article 6

A.   THE UNITED STATES CRIMINAL PROCEEDINGS

112. The applicant submitted that, because of the absence of legal aid in Virginia to fund collateral challenges before the Federal courts . . . , on

his return to the United States he would not be able to secure his legal representation as required by Article 6 §3 (c), which reads:

> Everyone charged with a criminal offence has the following minimum rights:
> . . . (c) to defend himself in person or through legal assistance of his own choosing or, if he has not sufficient means to pay for legal assistance, to be given it free when the interests of justice so require;

The Commission expressed the opinion that the proposed extradition of the applicant could not give rise to the responsibility of the United Kingdom Government under Article 6 §3 (c). The United Kingdom Government concurred with this analysis and, in the alternative, submitted that the applicant's allegations were ill-founded.

113. The right to a fair trial in criminal proceedings, as embodied in Article 6, holds a prominent place in a democratic society (see, inter alia, the Colozza judgment of 12 February 1985, Series A no. 89, p. 16 §32). The Court does not exclude that an issue might exceptionally be raised under Article 6 by an extradition decision in circumstances where the fugitive has suffered or risks suffering a flagrant denial of a fair trial in the requesting country. However, the facts of the present case do not disclose such a risk.

Accordingly, no issue arises under Article 6 §3 (c) in this respect.

B.   THE EXTRADITION PROCEEDINGS IN ENGLAND

114. The applicant further contended that the refusal of the Magistrates' Court in the extradition proceedings to consider evidence as to his psychiatric condition (see paragraph 21 above) violated paragraphs 1 and 3 (d) of Article 6, which respectively provide:

> 1. In the determination . . . of any criminal charge against him, everyone is entitled to a fair . . . hearing. . . .
> 3. Everyone charged with a criminal offence has the following minimum rights:
> . . . (d) to examine or have examined witnesses against him and to obtain the attendance and examination of witnesses on his behalf under the same conditions as witnesses against him. . . .

115. As the Delegate of the Commission pointed out, this complaint was not pleaded before the Commission. Such claims as the applicant then made of a failure to take proper account of the psychiatric evidence were in relation to Article 3 and limited to the Secretary of State's ultimate decision to extradite him to the United States. He did not formulate any grievances, whether under Article 6, Article 3 or Article 13, regarding the scope or conduct of the Magistrates' Court proceedings as such. This being so, the new allegation of a breach of Article 6 constitutes not merely a further legal submission or argument but a fresh and separate complaint falling outside

the compass of the case, which is delimited by the Commission's decision on admissibility (see, inter alia, the Schiesser judgment of 4 December 1979, Series A no. 34, p. 17, §41, and the Johnston and Others judgment of 18 December 1986, Series A no. 112, p. 23, §48).

Accordingly, the Court has no jurisdiction to entertain the matter.

III. ALLEGED BREACH OF ARTICLE 13

116. Finally, the applicant alleged a breach of Article 13, which provides:

> Everyone whose rights and freedoms as set forth in [the] Convention are violated shall have an effective remedy before a national authority notwithstanding that the violation has been committed by persons acting in an official capacity.

In his submission, he had no effective remedy in the United Kingdom in respect of his complaint under Article 3. The majority of the Commission arrived at the same conclusion. The United Kingdom Government however disagreed, arguing that Article 13 had no application in the circumstances of the present case or, in the alternative, that the aggregate of remedies provided for under domestic law was adequate.

117. In view of the Court's finding regarding Article 3 (see paragraph 111 above), the applicant's claim under that Article cannot be regarded either as incompatible with the provisions of the Convention or as not "arguable" on its merits (see, inter alia, the Boyle and Rice judgment of 27 April 1988, Series A no. 131, p. 23, §52).

The United Kingdom Government contended, however, that Article 13 can have no application in the circumstances of the case, because the challenge is in effect to the terms of a treaty between the United Kingdom and the United States and also because the alleged violation of the substantive provision is of an anticipatory nature.

The Court does not consider it necessary to rule specifically on these two objections to applicability since it has come to the conclusion that in any event the requirements of Article 13 were not violated.

118. The United Kingdom Government relied on the aggregate of remedies provided by the Magistrates' Court proceedings, an application for habeas corpus and an application for judicial review (see paragraphs 21-23, 32-33 and 35 above).

119. The Court will commence its examination with judicial review proceedings since they constitute the principal means for challenging a decision to extradite once it has been taken.

Both the applicant and the Commission were of the opinion that the scope of judicial review was too narrow to allow the courts to consider the subject matter of the complaint which the applicant has made in the context of Article 3. The applicant further contended that the courts' lack of jurisdiction to issue interim injunctions against the Crown was an additional reason rendering judicial review an ineffective remedy.

120. Article 13 guarantees the availability of a remedy at national level to enforce the substance of the Convention rights and freedoms in whatever form they may happen to be secured in the domestic legal order (see the above-mentioned Boyle and Rice judgment, Series A no. 131, p. 23, §52). The effect of Article 13 is thus to require the provision of a domestic remedy allowing the competent "national authority" both to deal with the substance of the relevant Convention complaint and to grant appropriate relief (see, inter alia, the Silver and Others judgment of 25 March 1983, Series A no. 61, p. 42, §113 (a)).

121. In judicial review proceedings the court may rule the exercise of executive discretion unlawful on the ground that it is tainted with illegality, irrationality or procedural impropriety (see paragraph 35 above). In an extradition case the test of "irrationality", on the basis of the so-called "Wednesbury principles", would be that no reasonable Secretary of State could have made an order for surrender in the circumstances (ibid.). According to the United Kingdom government, a court would have jurisdiction to quash a challenged decision to send a fugitive to a country where it was established that there was a serious risk of inhuman or degrading treatment, on the ground that in all the circumstances of the case the decision was one that no reasonable Secretary of State could take. Although the Convention is not considered to be part of United Kingdom law (ibid.), the Court is satisfied that the English courts can review the "reasonableness" of an extradition decision in the light of the kind of factors relied on by Mr Soering before the Convention institutions in the context of Article 3.

122. Mr Soering did admittedly make an application for judicial review together with his application for habeas corpus and was met with an unfavourable response from Lord Justice Lloyd on the issue of "irrationality" (see paragraph 22 above). However, as Lord Justice Lloyd explained, the claim failed because it was premature, the courts only having jurisdiction once the Minister has actually taken his decision (ibid.). Furthermore, the arguments adduced by Mr Soering were by no means the same as those relied on when justifying his complaint under Article 3 before the Convention institutions. His counsel before the Divisional Court limited himself to submitting that the assurance by the United States' authorities was so worthless that no reasonable Secretary of State could regard it as satisfactory under the Treaty. This is an argument going to the likelihood of the death penalty being imposed but says nothing about the quality of the treatment awaiting Mr Soering after sentence to death, this being the substance of his allegation of inhuman and degrading treatment.

There was nothing to have stopped Mr Soering bringing an application for judicial review at the appropriate moment and arguing "Wednesbury unreasonableness" on the basis of much the same material that he adduced

before the Convention institutions in relation to the death row phenomenon. Such a claim would have been given "the most anxious scrutiny" in
view of the fundamental nature of the human right at stake (see paragraph
35 above). The effectiveness of the remedy, for the purposes of Article 13,
does not depend on the certainty of a favourable outcome for Mr Soering
(see the Swedish Engine Drivers' Union judgment of 6 February 1976,
Series A no. 20, p. 18, §50), and in any event it is not for this Court to
speculate as to what would have been the decision of the English courts.

123. The English courts' lack of jurisdiction to grant interim injunctions against the Crown (see paragraph 35 *in fine* above) does not, in the
Court's opinion, detract from the effectiveness of judicial review in the
present connection, since there is no suggestion that in practice a fugitive
would ever be surrendered before his application to the Divisional Court
and any eventual appeal therefrom had been determined.

124. The Court concludes that Mr Soering did have available to him
under English law an effective remedy in relation to his complaint under
Article 3. This being so, there is no need to inquire into the other two
remedies referred to by the United Kingdom Government.

There is accordingly no breach of Article 13.

IV. APPLICATION OF ARTICLE 50

125. Under the terms of Article 50,

> If the Court finds that a decision or a measure taken by a legal authority or
> any other authority of a High Contracting Party is completely or partially in
> conflict with the obligations arising from the . . . Convention, and if the
> internal law of the said Party allows only partial reparation to be made for the
> consequences of this decision or measure, the decision of the Court shall, if
> necessary, afford just satisfaction to the injured party.

126. No breach of Article 3 has as yet occurred. Nevertheless, the Court
having found that the Secretary of State's decision to extradite to the United
States of America would, if implemented, give rise to a breach of Article 3,
Article 50 must be taken as applying to the facts of the present case.

127. The Court considers that its finding regarding Article 3 of itself
amounts to adequate just satisfaction for the purposes of Article 50. The
Court is not empowered under the Convention to make accessory direc-
tions of the kind requested by the applicant (see, mutatis mutandis, the
Dudgeon judgment of 24 February 1983, Series A no. 59, p. 8, §15). By
virtue of Article 54, the responsibility for supervising execution of the
Court's judgment rests with the Committee of Ministers of the Council of
Europe.

128. The United Kingdom Government did not in principle contest
the claim for reimbursement of costs and expenses, but suggested that, in

the event that the Court should find one or more of the applicant's complaints of violation of the Convention to be unfounded, it would be appropriate for the Court, deciding on an equitable basis as required by Article 50, to reduce the amount awarded accordingly (see the Le Compte, Van Leuven and De Meyere judgment of 18 October 1982, Series A no. 54, p. 10, §21).

The applicant's essential concern, and the bulk of the argument on all sides, focused on the complaint under Article 3, and on that issue the applicant has been successful. The Court therefore considers that in equity the applicant should recover his costs and expenses in full.

For These Reasons, the Court Unanimously

1. *Holds* that, in the event of the Secretary of State's decision to extradite the applicant to the United States of America being implemented, there would be a violation of Article 3;
2. *Holds* that, in the same event, there would be no violation of Article 6 §3 (c);
3. *Holds* that it has no jurisdiction to entertain the complaint under Article 6 §§1 and 3 (d);
4. *Holds* that there is no violation of Article 13;
5. *Holds* that the United Kingdom is to pay to the applicant, in respect of legal costs and expenses, the sum of £26,752.80 (twenty-six thousand seven hundred and fifty-two pounds sterling and eighty pence) and 5,030.60 FF (five thousand and thirty French francs and sixty centimes), together with any value added tax that may be chargeable;
6. *Rejects* the remainder of the claim for just satisfaction.

The underlying principle in *Soering* — that the European Convention prohibits extradition or expulsion of any person to a country where he or she might be subject to treatment contrary to Article 3 — has been upheld in a long line of decisions by the Commission and the Court. See the cases collected in Council of Europe, 1 Digest of Strasbourg Case-Law Relating to the European Convention on Human Rights 117-155 (1984); id., Supplement to Volume 1, §3.0.3.4, at 1-18 (1988); Cruz Varas and others v. Sweden, Eur. Ct. Human Rts., Judgment of 20 Mar. 1991, Ser. A No. 201, 14 Eur. Hum. Rts. Rep. 1. The same principle has been applied in cases where expulsion and consequent separation from close relatives might violate the right to family life set forth in Article 8, although few such arguments have been successful. One of the exceptions is Berrehab v. Netherlands, Eur. Ct. Human Rts., Judgment of 21 June 1988, Ser. A No. 138, 11 Eur. Hum. Rts. Rep. 322, in which deportation of a divorced husband who had maintained close ties with his young daughter was found to be disproportionate and, therefore, to violate Article 8. See generally J. Fawcett, The Application of the European Convention on Human Rights 223-225 (2d ed. 1987). Is a state permitted to deport or expel a person while that person's application under the European Convention is still pending? See Cruz Varas and others v. Sweden, supra.

Note: The "Death Row Phenomenon"

The substantive issue discussed in *Soering* — whether the combined effects of the so-called "death row phenomenon" violate the prohibition against inhuman or degrading punishment — has been the subject of a "rich chaos" of jurisprudence before at least three national courts and the Human Rights Committee. See Lillich, Towards the Harmonization of International Human Rights Law, in Festschrift für Rudolf Bernhardt (M. Bothe ed. 1995).

The Human Rights Committee has considered the issue in several cases from Jamaica and one from Canada, holding in each instance that the treatment complained of (in one case, 13 years on death row) did not amount to punishment in violation of the Civil and Political Covenant. See, e.g., Kindler v. Canada, Communication No. 470/1991, Views of July 30, 1993, reprinted in 14 Hum. Rts. L.J. 307 (1993); Barrett and Sutcliffe v. Jamaica, Communications Nos. 270/1988 and 271/1988, Hum. Rts. Comm. Annual Report, 47 U.N GAOR Supp. (No. 40) at 254, 258, U.N. Doc. A/47/40 (1993); Pratt and Morgan v. Jamaica, Communications Nos. 210/1986 and 225/1987, Hum. Rts. Comm. Annual Report, 44 U.N. GAOR Supp. (No. 40) at 222, U.N. Doc. A/44/40 (1989). The highest national courts in the United Kingdom and Zimbabwe, on the other hand, have recently found that delays in execution of several years violated prohibitions against inhuman or degrading treatment and, thus, required that the sentences be commuted to life imprisonment. See Pratt & Morgan v. Attorney-General (Privy Council 1993), reprinted in 14 Hum. Rts. L.J. 338 (1993); Catholic Commn. for Justice & Peace v. Attorney-General, Judgment No. S.C. 73/93 (Zimbabwe S. Ct. June 24, 1993), reprinted in 14 Hum. Rts. L.J. 323 (1993).

B.   The European Social Charter

"The European Social Charter is the regional counterpart of the International Covenant on Economic, Social and Cultural Rights. It was conceived as the 'pendant' of the European Convention on Human Rights: the Convention guarantees civil and political rights, the Charter protects economic and social rights. But there the parallel ends. Whereas the Convention is firmly established as the jewel in the Council of Europe crown, the Charter has led a twilight existence." Harris, A Fresh Impetus for the European Social Charter, 41 Intl. & Comp. L.Q. 659 (1992).

The European Social Charter (not to be confused with the Charter of the Fundamental Social Rights of Workers, adopted in 1989 under the auspices of the European Community), 529 U.N.T.S. 89, Europ. T.S. No. 35, entered into force in 1965 and had 20 parties as of 1 March 1994. Designed as a tool to encourage the progressive implementation of various social and economic (particularly labor) rights, the Charter includes a set of principles to which all parties agree as a matter of policy and a number of specific rights which parties have the option to accept in whole or in part. Parties must accept a minimum of five of the seven basic articles, which respectively guarantee the right to work; the right to organize; the right to bargain collectively; the right to social security; the right to social and medical assistance; the right of the family to social, legal, and economic protection; and the rights of migrant workers. An Additional Protocol to the Charter, Europ. T.S. No. 128, expanded some of the substantive rights guaranteed therein and entered into force in 1992, although only a few states have thus far ratified it.

If some of the Charter's rights may be said to have a "twilight existence," in Harris's words, the provisions for its implementation create a system that might best be described as murky. States are required to submit biennial reports on the manner in which they are implementing the obligations they have accepted; these reports are then reviewed by no fewer than four expert or governmental bodies. There is no oral hearing or dialogue between the supervisory bodies and the reporting states (unlike the reporting procedures under the UN treaty bodies, discussed at pages 211-214 of Problem III). The reports are confidential, although copies must be sent to national organizations of employers and trade unions, which may submit comments on them to the Council of Europe, via the reporting state. The ultimate supervisory body is the Committee of Ministers of the Council of Europe, but the Committee has never exercised its power under Article 29 of the Charter to make "any necessary recommendations" to a party that may be found to be in breach of its obligations. See generally D. Harris, The European Social Charter (1984); 25 Years: European Social Charter (T. Jaspers and L. Betten eds. 1987).

In order to remedy some of the widely criticized defects of the supervisory system, a second Protocol amending the Charter was adopted in 1991, Europ. T.S. No. 142, reprinted in 31 Intl. Legal Materials 155 (1992), although it will not enter into force until accepted by all of the parties to the Charter. The amendments will generally strengthen the role of the Committee of Independent Experts, which initially examines state reports, giving the Committee the authority to request additional information from states and, "if necessary," to invite a party to attend a meeting to provide additional information or clarify a report. The role of the Governmental Committee, which now reviews reports after the Committee of Independent Experts, will be somewhat diminished and altered; it will be easier for the Committee of Ministers to adopt recommendations to states; employers' organizations and trade unions will have a modestly increased role to play; and state reports will be public (although not automatically published). See Harris, A Fresh Impetus for the European Social Charter, supra. However, proposals to institute a complaint procedure, which could be initiated by an employers' organization or a trade union, have not yet been acted upon.

C.   The European Convention for the Prevention of Torture and Inhuman or Degrading Treatment or Punishment

The European Convention for the Prevention of Torture and Inhuman or Degrading Treatment or Punishment (European Torture Convention), Europ. T.S. No. 126, entered into force in 1989 and had 24 parties as of 1 March 1994. The following excerpt offers an early appraisal of this innovative mechanism, which aims more at preventing human rights abuses than at identifying and condemning violations after they have occurred.

Evans and Morgan, The European Convention for the Prevention of Torture: Operational Practice
41 Intl. & Comp. L.Q. 590, 591, 598-599, 601-602, 606, 608-609 (1992)

On 1 February 1989 the European Convention for the Prevention of Torture and Inhuman or Degrading Treatment or Punishment ("the Torture Convention") came into force. Unlike other human rights instruments, this Convention does not seek to establish any new norms, but is designed to introduce a procedure which will "strengthen by non-judicial means of a preventive nature" the realisation of the obligation contained in Article 3 of the European Convention for the Protection of Fundamental Human Rights and Freedoms — that is, "No one shall be subjected to torture or to inhuman or degrading treatment or punishment."

The procedure adopted by the Torture Convention is based on a system of visits. Article 2 provides that "Each Party shall permit visits, in accordance with this Convention, to any place within its jurisdiction where persons are deprived of their liberty by a public authority." These visits are to be organised by the European Committee for the Prevention of Torture and Inhuman or Degrading Treatment or Punishment ("the Torture Committee"), a body established under the Convention, whose function is, "by means of visits, [to] examine the treatment of persons deprived of their liberty with a view to strengthening, if necessary, the protection of such persons from torture and from inhuman or degrading treatment or punishment". . . .

It has been suggested that the Torture Convention is unnecessary, since the European Convention on Human Rights ("ECHR") itself makes provision for fact-finding visits in Article 28.1(a) and thus there is an unnecessary duplication. This criticism is ill founded since a fact-finding visit under the ECHR can take place only in the context of the examination of an application. The scope of the Torture Convention is wider, embracing regular visits of inspection forming the basis for general recommendations that would fall beyond the remit of an ECHR fact-finding visit. In short, the focus of the Torture Convention is upon the institution, rather than upon the individual detained. A further consequence of this is that an investigation of a particular situation in the course of a visit by the Torture Committee will not act as a bar to an application by an individual under the ECHR, or, indeed, to the Human Rights Committee under the First Optional Protocol to the UN Civil and Political Covenant. . . .

The Torture Convention envisages that the Torture Committee will organise periodic visits to places of detention, in accordance with Article 2. There are no explicit provisions in the Convention itself which require the Committee to ensure that such periodic visits are made to *all* State parties, although it is unlikely that State parties — or the Committee itself — would countenance anything less than an even-handed approach in this matter. In addition to periodic visits, the Committee "*may* organise such other visits as appear to it to be required in the circumstances". Just what circumstances would require other visits above and beyond those provided for by the system of periodic visits is not spelt out by the Convention, and thus a considerable degree of leeway is given to the Committee in deciding how to fulfil its obligation under Article 1. . . .

Striking a balance between the need to allow a country to prepare for a visit and the need to visit before abuses can be "covered up" is a delicate matter. The Torture Committee has devised a threefold procedure which goes a long way to meeting the practical problems presented.

Those countries which have been selected for a visit in the following year are notified of this fact. Shortly after this has happened, a press release is issued indicating the countries concerned. About two weeks before a visit is to take place, the country is informed of the proposed dates and duration as well as the names of the Committee members, experts and interpreters. Finally, a few days before the visit commences, a provisional list of places to be visited is sent. This procedure should give the country the time it needs to make the necessary practical preparations and arrange for meetings with officials, without allowing time to effect significant changes of condition or regime at the places to be visited.

An important aspect of this system is that, by giving public notice that a visit is to take place, interested pressure groups will be able to forward information to the Torture Committee, thus helping it formulate a plan of visits. Without this information, the Committee might be working in the dark. Clearly, when an *ad hoc* visit is being undertaken this will not be a problem because it is likely that the decision to undertake such a visit will have been based upon some such evidence already submitted to the Committee.

Exceptionally, a State may argue for the postponement of a visit on specified grounds, namely national defence, public safety, serious disorder in places where persons are deprived of their liberty, the medical condition of the person, or that an urgent interrogation relating to a serious crime is in progress. This clearly gives a wide — though not unfettered — margin of appreciation to the State concerned. It may be that the application of Article 9(1) is intended to operate in the context of visits arranged in the light of special circumstances. Periodic visits will tend to focus upon general conditions in places of detention, and it is unlikely that the factors listed in Article 9(1) could justifiably be invoked. Particular circumstances giving rise to the need to arrange a special visit are more likely to arise in the context of the type of extenuating circumstances outlined in Article 9(1). In addition, it is not unreasonable to suppose that particular, as opposed to periodic, visits may also be made with reference to particular individuals. It is noteworthy that Article 9(2) envisages that any such particular person to whom access is denied under the provisions of Article 9(1) is placed under a form of protected status pending the ultimate access of the Torture Committee. . . .

Article 2 of the Torture Convention obliges a State to permit visits "to any place within its jurisdiction where persons are deprived of their liberty by a public authority". . . .

A key aspect of the Torture Convention is its granting the Torture Committee the facility to interview in private persons deprived of their liberty and granting the Committee the freedom to communicate with any person whom it believes can supply relevant information. . . .

Once it has been adopted, the report is to be sent to the State party concerned, along with any recommendations the Torture Committee considers necessary. Because of its sensitive nature, the Committee's work is confidential. That confidentiality may, however, be avoided in one of two ways, each fulfilling a very different purpose.

1.   AT THE REQUEST OF THE STATE INVOLVED

It is only when the State party visited wishes a report to be published that it passes into the public domain. Indeed, the Torture Committee has an obligation to publish not only the report if it is requested to do so, but must also publish with the report any comments that the State party involved wishes to make. . . .

2.   By Decision of the Torture Committee

If the State party fails to co-operate or refuses to improve the situation in the light of the Torture Committee's recommendations, the Committee may decide to make a public statement on the matter, but only if there is a two-thirds majority on the Committee in favour of doing so. It should be noted that it is not the report itself which is to be made public, but a statement concerning the matter. The report itself remains confidential. This, then, is the "sanction" that the Committee wields.

The Committee has made an average of eight regular visits to institutions in various states parties annually, and most of its reports, along with comments by the state, have been published at the request of the state concerned. Most visits have been to police stations and prisons, although mental hospitals and refugee camps also have been the subject of committee visits.

Comments and Questions

1. Note that in the *Soering* case, the applicant was not a U.K. national. Nationality of the state against which an individual petition is filed, or indeed nationality of any of the states parties to the Convention, is not required for its invocation. See Article 1 of the Convention, which provides that states parties "secure to everyone within their jurisdiction the rights and freedoms" it guarantees. Moreover, unlike other petition processes, the European one is available to legal as well as natural persons. Thus, the locally incorporated subsidiary of a U.S. multinational corporation nationalized by a state party could petition the Commission if it regarded the preferred compensation inadequate under the standards laid down in Article 1 of Protocol No. 1. Cf. Lithgow and Others v. United Kingdom, Eur. Ct. Hum. Rts., Judgment of 8 July 1986, Ser. A No. 102, reprinted in 8 Eur. Hum. Rts. Rep. 329 (1986).

2. The Court in the *Irish* case held that, while the "five techniques" did not amount to "torture," they did constitute "inhuman and degrading treatment" in violation of Article 3. Thus, the Court rightly recognized that two analytically distinct alleged violations of international human rights law were involved. Recall that the district court in *Forti* (see pages 152-154 of Problem II) held that "torture" was proscribed by customary international law, but "cruel, inhuman or degrading treatment" was not. How does one rationalize these different holdings? If, as Judge Jensen in *Forti* concludes, there is nothing "even remotely approaching universal consensus as to what constitutes 'cruel, inhuman or degrading treatment,' " how can the European Court's decision in the *Irish* case be justified?

3. The Irish government filed its case against the United Kingdom in December 1971, but both governments and the Court discussed subsequent UK actions in some detail (see pages 695-699 and 708-713 supra). Of what relevance were these subsequent acts to the question of whether or not the United Kingdom had violated the Convention at the time the case was filed in 1971?

4. Numerous cases arising out of the continuing conflict in Northern Ireland have been filed in the two decades since the decision in Ireland v. United Kingdom. Two knowledgeable observers have described the response of the Convention organs during this process as "somewhat equivocal."

> Decisions have been made against the United Kingdom in respect of the ill-treatment of suspects during interrogation in 1971 and the operation of seven-day detention for interrogation in 1987. But in many other cases the complaints have been rejected and the authorities have been at least partially vindicated. The use of internment without trial in 1971, a killing by the use of plastic bullets for riot control in 1976, the refusal of concessions to convicted IRA prisoners demanding special status in prison in 1980, the use of lethal force against suspected terrorists attempting to drive through a roadblock in 1985 and the entry of a derogation to legitimize the continuation of seven-day detention following the previous Court decision against it have all been approved by the Commission or the Court at Strasbourg. In all these cases both the Commission and the Court have in practice been ready to grant the government a wide "margin of appreciation" — i.e. to give the government the benefit of any doubt — in adopting the special measures it thinks appropriate in dealing with terrorism and associated disorders.

K. Boyle and T. Hadden, Northern Ireland: The Choice 101-102 (1994).

Compare the way in which the European system deals with widespread human rights violations in a particular country with the methods available to the Inter-American Commission on Human Rights. See pages 787-792 of Problem X.

5. Article 26 of the Convention, which applies to both individual and interstate applications, requires that "all domestic remedies" be exhausted, "according to the generally recognized rules of international law." Did the Irish government attempt to exhaust the domestic remedies available in Northern Ireland? Could it have done so? Compare the substantive scope of an interstate case filed under Article 24 ("any alleged breach") with that of an individual case filed under Article 25 (from any organization or individual "claiming to be the victim of a violation").

6. Following a two-week spree of minor thefts by her seven-year-old son, a woman in Alameda County, California, punished the boy by forcing him "to wear a fake pig's snout and sit, hands tied and face painted blue, in front of their apartment, where neighbors could see him. . . . As she explained to police investigators, summoned by neighbors, she wanted the youngster to understand, 'if only for 30 minutes, that lying and stealing

make you ugly like Pinocchio.' " William Raspberry, The Case of the Fake Pig's Snout, Wash. Post, Aug. 31, 1988, at A25, col. 2. Should the county welfare authorities have taken the boy into temporary custody to protect him from abuse? If the punishment had been imposed by a public school teacher, would it constitute "degrading punishment" in violation of the European Convention?

7. The Court's unanimous holding in the *Soering* case raises a host of interesting and difficult questions. Consider:

(a) Does the decision not, in effect, constitute an "extraterritorial" application of the European Convention? Even if technically it does not, will it not have an impact on the law and practice of U.S. states in mandating and carrying out the death penalty?

(b) Will the decision be limited to its facts, or will it be argued to bar extradition in non-capital cases where, absent the "death row phenomenon," inhuman and degrading treatment and punishment of prisoners can be shown to exist?

(c) Are Council of Europe countries now prohibited from extraditing persons to the United States for crimes that carry the death penalty? If so, what steps can the United States take to plug this European Convention-produced hole in the law of extradition? Should it protest Great Britain's Court-mandated violation of the bilateral extradition treaty? Should it consider (an unlikely prospect) a constitutional amendment prohibiting the death penalty? What other steps should it consider taking?

(d) If the "death row phenomenon" constitutes "inhuman or degrading treatment or punishment" under Article 3, is that not further support for the proposition that "cruel, inhuman, or degrading treatment or punishment" violates the customary international law of human rights? See Section 702(d) of the Restatement (Third) of the Foreign Relations Law of the United States (1987) at page 162 of Problem II. If so, then cannot it be used by U.S. lawyers? How would you structure such an argument? See Hartman, "Unusual" Punishment: The Domestic Effects of International Norms Restricting the Application of the Death Penalty, 52 U. Cin. L. Rev. 655 (1983); Note, Thompson v. Oklahoma: The Role of International Law in Juvenile Death Penalty Litigation, 8 Wis. Intl. L.J. 165 (1989).

(e) Since Soering was a German national and Germany, which also sought his extradition, applies its criminal law to acts committed by German nationals in other states, Soering, if found guilty of the murder of his girlfriend's parents, would not have gone unpunished even if he had not been extradited to the United States, which he eventually was (see (f) below). Suppose, however, he had been a national of a state (like the United States) that did not apply its criminal law extraterritorially on the basis of nationality. Would such a defendant go untried? If so, will not Council of Europe states become a haven for many criminals who have committed offenses that carry the death penalty? The fear that Canada would become such a "safe haven" was mentioned by the Canadian Supreme Court as one reason for granting extradition to the United States in a "death row phenomenon" case. See Kindler v. Minister of Justice, [1991] 2 R.C.S. 779.

(f) Soering was extradited to the United States in early 1990 after the federal government assured the United Kingdom that he would not be tried in Virginia for a crime for which, if convicted, he could be sentenced to death. (This commitment bound the United States internationally, but domestically presented some troublesome federal-state constitutional questions that ultimately were mooted.) He was tried and convicted on 22 June 1990 on two counts of first-degree murder. The jury recommended that he be sentenced to serve two life terms. Daily Progress (Charlottesville, Va.), June 23, 1990, at A1, cols. 3-4.

8. Article 50 of the European Convention permits the Court, if necessary, to "afford just satisfaction to the injured party." When the Court has awarded monetary damages, they always have been paid, but if they were not, how would a judgment be enforced? Compare Article 63(1) of the American Convention, which permits the Inter-American Court to rule "that fair compensation be paid to the injured party," and especially Article 68(2) thereof, providing that "[t]hat part of a judgment that stipulates compensatory damages may be executed in the country concerned in accordance with domestic procedure governing the execution of judgments against the state." What explains this potentially effective enforcement provision in the American Convention? Should the European Convention be amended to insert in its Article 50 a counterpart of the American Convention's Article 68(2)? For monetary damages awarded by the Inter-American Court, see page 799 of Problem X infra.

9. What is the situation with respect to judgments of the Court that require a non-monetary response? Article 53 of the Convention provides that "[t]he High Contracting Parties undertake to abide by the decision of the Court in any case to which they are parties." The decision, moreover, is to "be transmitted to the Committee of Ministers which shall supervise its execution" (Article 54). The compliance record of the European Convention states is remarkably good. Thus, in each of the eight occasions between 1979 and 1986 when the Court rendered judgments against Great Britain, new primary legislation, or amendments to existing regulations or administrative practice, were introduced.

10. Given the ineffective supervisory mechanism of the European Social Charter, the obvious lack of enthusiasm for its provisions on the part of

both trade unions and employers' organizations, the increasing significance of the European Union, and the entry into force of the Covenant on Economic, Social, and Cultural Rights, why not just scrap the whole treaty and recognize that it has been overtaken by other events? Does Europe really need another system for implementing human rights?

III. The Organization on Security and Cooperation in Europe

Commission on Security and Cooperation in Europe, Beyond Process: The CSCE's Institutional Development, 1990-92
1-2 (1992)

Although some early proposals conceived of the Conference on Security and Cooperation in Europe as an international institution with headquarters, secretariat, and treaty, the CSCE emerged from Helsinki in 1975 as an amorphous process, moving from conference to conference with no fixed address or schedule. For fifteen years, its review conferences and experts meetings succeeded in focusing attention on a range of inter-related problems from human rights to the environment to threatening military maneuvers, operating on the principle that these and other elements of security could not be treated separately. However, the end of the bipolar security "system" that had characterized the Europe in which CSCE was created led many of its participants to look to the CSCE as a new over-arching "system" within which its members could improve both their security and cooperation. As such, they pleaded for more structure and permanence for its activities, as well as a larger role for it in addressing the challenges of the time.

The Paris Summit of November 1990 endowed the CSCE with its first permanent institutions: the CSCE Secretariat, Conflict Prevention Center, and Office of Free Elections, later expanded to the Office for Democratic Institutions and Human Rights. These three institutions, minimally funded and staffed, were created to give the CSCE process some visible permanence and to assist the regular political consultations set up at the same time. The consultations process envisioned meetings of CSCE heads of state or government every two years; foreign ministers annually, plus possible meetings of other ministers; and senior officials three to four times per year. The CSCE Secretariat was set up in Prague to organize these meetings; the Conflict Prevention Center in Vienna to give institutional support to risk reduction efforts; and the Office of Free Elections in Warsaw to assist the transition to democracy across the continent. In April 1991, parliamentarians from the participating States took up proposals from the summit and formed a CSCE Parliamentary Assembly, to meet once a year to further security and cooperation in Europe, reviewing CSCE implementation and activities.

As the disintegration and unrest which were byproducts of the end of totalitarian rule in East-Central Europe continued to develop after 1990, states turned more and more to the CSCE. At the same time, CSCE took in new states emerging from the collapse of the communist order bringing its membership up to 52 states in 1992. Instead of the theoretical plans for collective security systems and talk of integrating the East into Europe that had sparked the small-scale, sometimes grudging institutionalization of 1990, states looked to the CSCE in 1991 and 1992 as a source of solutions for the broad and deep European problems that had emerged. More extensive procedures were developed, allowing CSCE bodies to send missions to a state without its participation in the decision; engage in conciliation or other forms of peaceful settlements of disputes through CSCE; exclude one participating State from decision-making; and even to establish and deploy CSCE peacekeeping forces. And, CSCE plunged into the major disputes threatening peace and stability among its members, sponsoring a conference on the conflict in and around Nagorno-Karabakh and working with the EC and UN on various initiatives relating to the Yugoslav crisis.

However, a lack of willingness among participating States to maximize the procedures and bodies they have created, and to revise them as necessary to solve problems, has brought CSCE up short time after time. None of the more complex CSCE mechanisms has yet been used; and the steps that have been taken, such as the development of the Minsk Conference on Nagorno-Karabakh, have not led to resolutions.

Thus left without political imperative, the CSCE institutions have remained small and weak. Situated in three cities in order to send signals of inclusion to emerging democracies (two of which host the Secretariat and Office of Democratic Institutions and Human Rights), the institutions are isolated. Staffed by seconded diplomats for cost-saving purposes, they are inexpert. Responsible to committees of representatives of all participating States, they are unable to take independent or immediate action. They are small executive organs for the participating States' consultations, and as such scarcely have a record of their own to judge. On the other hand, this is precisely what most CSCE states want at this stage — institutions without significant independent power.

This somewhat depressing evaluation of the CSCE accurately describes its minimal institutional structure and essentially political character. Nevertheless, the human rights principles set forth in the 1975 Helsinki Final Act, adopted Aug. 1, 1975, reprinted in 14 Intl. Legal Materials 1292 (1975), were significant in encouraging human rights activists in Eastern Europe and the Soviet Union throughout the 1970s and 1980s. The numerous "review" meetings from 1975 to 1990 provided the opportunity for direct criticisms of human rights violations in communist bloc countries, even if such criticisms were often motivated by Cold War politics. The CSCE also has been regularly concerned with security and conflict resolution issues.

The CSCE process was never intended to create binding *legal* obligations, and neither the Helsinki Final Act nor subsequent texts are considered to be treaties by any of the now 53 "participating states," which stretch from North America through Western and Eastern Europe, central Asia, and Russia. However, since all CSCE decisions are adopted by consensus (with a few recent exceptions), no state could claim that it had not accepted the political principles set forth in CSCE texts, which are variously denominated as final documents, principles, declarations, or decisions. See the discussion of "soft law" in Problem IV.

As communism crumbled in the late 1980s, the all-encompassing CSCE process became the focus of many of the newly installed governments, which wished to align themselves politically with the West and reinforce the human rights obligations set forth in the Helsinki Final Act. The breakthrough meeting was held in 1990, when the CSCE adopted the Document of the Copenhagen Meeting of the Conference on the Human Dimension of the CSCE, adopted June 29, 1990, reprinted in 29 Intl. Legal Materials 1305 (1990). The Copenhagen Document contained a broad commitment to "full respect for human rights and fundamental freedoms and the development of societies based on pluralistic democracy and the rule of law." Id., Preamble. It went on to outline in considerable detail rights related to democracy, free elections, constitutionalism, national minorities, and other issues.

During roughly the same period, the CSCE adopted a series of "mechanisms" to enable states, or groups of states, to place potential interstate conflicts on the CSCE agenda or to request the dispatch of human rights fact-finding missions. In practice, missions have been sent on an ad hoc basis after decisions by the Committee of Senior Officials, the de facto governing body of CSCE, which normally meets several times a year. In 1994 the small CSCE secretariat and the Conflict Prevention Center were consolidated in Vienna; a small office remains in Prague, while the Office for Democratic Institutions and Human Rights (ODIHR) continues its activities from Warsaw. The latter is supposed to "assist the monitoring of implementation of commitments in the Human Dimension [the CSCE's code word for human rights]," but its practical impact seems to be minimal. It does convene a three-week review meeting of experts every other year, but increased activism and impact will depend on financial resources as well as political will. In 1995, the CSCE was renamed the "Organization" on Security and Cooperation in Europe.

The most significant CSCE innovation since 1990 has been the appointment in 1992 of a High Commissioner on National Minorities. The High Commissioner's functions and authority are set forth in the following excerpt.

Helsinki Document 1992, The Challenges of Change
Conference on Security and Cooperation in Europe, Helsinki
Decisions, Annex II, at 7-13 (1992)

CSCE HIGH COMMISSIONER ON NATIONAL MINORITIES

(1) The participating States decide to establish a High Commissioner
on National Minorities.

MANDATE

(2) The High Commissioner will act under the aegis of the CSO [Com-
mittee of Senior Officials] and will thus be an instrument of conflict prevention at the earliest possible stage.

(3) The High Commissioner will provide "early warning" and, as appropriate, "early action" at the earliest possible stage in regard to tensions
involving national minority issues which have not yet developed beyond an
early warning stage, but, in the judgement of the High Commissioner, have
the potential to develop into a conflict within the CSCE area, affecting
peace, stability or relations between participating States, requiring the attention of and action by the Council or the CSO.

(4) Within the mandate, based on CSCE principles and commitments,
the High Commissioner will work in confidence and will act independently
of all parties directly involved in the tensions.

(5a) The High Commissioner will consider national minority issues
occurring in the State of which the High Commissioner is a national or a
resident, or involving a national minority to which the High Commissioner
belongs, only if all parties directly involved agree, including the State concerned.

(5b) The High Commissioner will not consider national minority issues in situations involving organized acts of terrorism.

(5c) Nor will the High Commissioner consider violations of CSCE
commitments with regard to an individual person belonging to a national
minority.

(6) In considering a situation, the High Commissioner will take fully
into account the availability of democratic means and international instruments to respond to it, and their utilization by the parties involved.

(7) When a particular national minority issue has been brought to the
attention of the CSO, the involvement of the High Commissioner will
require a request and a specific mandate from the CSO. . . .

EARLY WARNING

(11) The High Commissioner will:

(11a) collect and receive information regarding national minority issues from sources described below (see Supplement paragraphs (23)-(25));

(11b) assess at the earliest possible stage the role of the parties directly concerned, the nature of the tensions and recent developments therein and, where possible, the potential consequences for peace and stability within the CSCE area;

(11c) to this end, be able to pay a visit, in accordance with paragraph (17) and Supplement paragraphs (27)-(30), to any participating State and communicate in person, subject to the provisions of paragraph (25), with parties directly concerned to obtain first-hand information about the situation of national minorities.

(12) The High Commissioner may during a visit to a participating State, while obtaining first-hand information from all parties directly involved, discuss the questions with the parties, and where appropriate promote dialogue, confidence and co-operation between them.

PROVISION OF EARLY WARNING

(13) If, on the basis of exchanges of communications and contacts with relevant parties, the High Commissioner concludes that there is a *prima facie* risk of potential conflict (as set out in paragraph (3)) he/she may issue an early warning, which will be communicated promptly by the Chairman-in-Office to the CSO. . . .

ACCOUNTABILITY

(17) The High Commissioner will consult the Chairman-in-Office prior to a departure for a participating State to address a tension involving national minorities. The Chairman-in-Office will consult, in confidence, the participating State(s) concerned and may consult more widely.

(18) After a visit to a participating State, the High Commissioner will provide strictly confidential reports to the Chairman-in-Office on the findings and progress of the High Commissioner's involvement in a particular question. . . .

SOURCES OF INFORMATION ABOUT NATIONAL MINORITY ISSUES

(23) The High Commissioner may:

(23a) collect and receive information regarding the situation of national minorities and the role of parties involved therein from any source, including the media and non-governmental organizations with the exception referred to in paragraph (25);

(23b) receive specific reports from parties directly involved regarding developments concerning national minority issues. These may include reports on violations of CSCE commitments with respect to national minorities as well as other violations in the context of national minority issues.

(24) Such specific reports to the High Commissioner should meet the following requirements:

— they should be in writing, addressed to the High Commissioner as such and signed with full names and addresses;
— they should contain a factual account of the developments which are relevant to the situation of persons belonging to national minorities and the role of the parties involved therein, and which have taken place recently, in principle not more than 12 months previously. The reports should contain information which can be sufficiently substantiated.

(25) The High Commissioner will not communicate with and will not acknowledge communications from any person or organization which practises or publicly condones terrorism or violence.

PARTIES DIRECTLY CONCERNED

(26) Parties directly concerned in tensions who can provide specific reports to the High Commissioner and with whom the High Commissioner will seek to communicate in person during a visit to a participating State are the following:

(26a) governments of participating States, including, if appropriate, regional and local authorities in areas in which national minorities reside;

(26b) representatives of associations, non-governmental organizations, religious and other groups of national minorities directly concerned and in the area of tension, which are authorized by the persons belonging to those national minorities to represent them.

CONDITIONS FOR TRAVEL BY THE HIGH COMMISSIONER

(27) Prior to an intended visit, the High Commissioner will submit to the participating State concerned specific information regarding the intended purpose of that visit. Within two weeks the State(s) concerned will consult with the High Commissioner on the objectives of the visit, which may include the promotion of dialogue, confidence and co-operation between the parties. After entry the State concerned will facilitate free travel and communication of the High Commissioner subject to the provisions of paragraph (25) above.

(28) If the State concerned does not allow the High Commissioner to enter the country and to travel and communicate freely, the High Commissioner will so inform the CSO.

(29) In the course of such a visit, subject to the provision of paragraph (25) the High Commissioner may consult the parties involved, and may

receive information in confidence from any individual, group or organization directly concerned on questions the High Commissioner is addressing. The High Commissioner will respect the confidential nature of the information.

(30) The participating States will refrain from taking any action against persons, organizations or institutions on account of their contact with the High Commissioner.

————————

Although the High Commissioner's mandate is clearly subordinated to the political control of the Committee of Senior Officials, the first High Commissioner (former Dutch Foreign Minister Max van der Stoel) has exercised a great deal of independence and conducted several on-site missions to states in which minority problems were apparent. His recommendations or reports, which often take the form of relatively short letters to relevant government officials, are generally made public; as of mid-1994, they concerned national minorities in Albania, the former Yugoslav Republic of Macedonia (which is only an observer at the CSCE, not a full member), Estonia, Hungary, Latvia, Lithuania, Romania, and Slovakia and also the situation of the Roma (gypsies) throughout the CSCE region. Although it is too early to draw definitive conclusions, the High Commissioner appears thus far to be fulfilling his mandate to provide "early warning" of potential conflicts and may be contributing to their peaceful resolution.

IV.   The European Community

Boyle, Europe: The Council of Europe, the CSCE, and the European Community
in Guide to International Human Rights Practice 133, 153-155 (H. Hannum ed. 2d ed. 1992)

The 1957 Treaty of Rome, the foundation of the European Community (EC), dealt only in a limited way with human rights. Article 7 prohibits discrimination between EC citizens; article 48 establishes the right to freedom of movement for workers in the Community; and article 119 provides that men and women should receive equal pay for equal work. As the Community has developed, however, human rights have become a more important concern of its institutions. For example, the . . . Treaty of European Union . . . expands the rights of free movement and residence to all EC citizens and would create a Community Ombudsman to redress individual complaints about maladministration by EC institutions.

The twelve [soon to be 15] members of the EC are all parties to the

European Convention on Human Rights, and it has been proposed that the Community as an institution accede to the European Convention on Human Rights. The European Court of Justice, which has jurisdiction to decide disputes and interpret Community law, has frequently referred to the rights and freedoms protected under the Convention as sources for that interpretation. In a 1970 case, for example, the Court said, "International treaties for the protection of human rights on which the member states have collaborated or to which they are signatories, can supply guide-lines which should be followed within the framework of Community law." This and subsequent jurisprudence confirms that human rights principles have been incorporated into the legal order of the Community.

European Community law is extremely complex and cannot be developed here. It is nevertheless important to note that EC law, unlike the European Convention on Human Rights and most international law, has direct effect in EC member states and prevails over any inconsistent domestic law. In general, individuals cannot bring an action directly in the European Court of Justice but must commence proceedings in a national court. If a human rights issue arises in domestic proceedings concerning the interpretation of the Treaty of Rome, it can be referred to the European Court of Justice for a preliminary ruling under article 177 of the Treaty of Rome.

In 1989, the EC Council of Ministers adopted a Community Charter of the Fundamental Social Rights of Workers; only the United Kingdom voted against its adoption. The Charter was incorporated as a protocol to the Treaty on European Union proposed following the December 1991 Maastricht summit meeting, although the United Kingdom maintained its objection. This new set of guarantees will therefore be implemented through EC institutions for eleven states and reflects an increasing commitment to social rights in the Community.

THE EUROPEAN PARLIAMENT

The European Parliament is the directly elected "legislature" of the EC, although its powers are more properly described as advisory and supervisory rather than legislative. In 1989, it adopted a non-binding Declaration of Fundamental Rights for EC citizens, which includes civil, political, social, and economic rights. The Declaration does not provide for any enforcement mechanism.

The Parliament does have a Human Rights Sub-Committee, whose mandate is to consider human rights concerns globally. It is an important forum for NGOs to consider as a channel for communicating reports and concerns about violation of human rights anywhere in the world. The Sub-Committee adopts resolutions and can contribute to other pressures on non-EC governments to cease human rights abuses. It also produces an annual report on human rights in the world, limited to the right to life, the right to respect for the physical and moral integrity of the person, and the right to a fair trail.

In 1987, the Parliament established a Petition Committee which gave every EC citizen the right to submit written petitions to Parliament concerning any matter within the sphere of activity of the Community. The proposed Treaty on European Union formally recognizes this right of petition. In 1988-89, 692 petitions were admitted, of which 212 concerned human rights. There is no requirement to exhaust domestic remedies, and there is no procedure to determine admissibility. The Committee can act by requesting information or it can send a representative to investigate the facts of a case. It can prepare a report for the plenary Parliament, conduct an investigation, or ask questions of other institutions, such as national authorities, through Members of Parliament. It has also the competence to request the Commission of the European Community to bring an action against an offending member state under article 169 of the Treaty of Rome.

The Petition Committee has examined cases concerning, inter alia, denial of access to a lawyer, detention without charge, the right to a fair hearing, and conscientious objection to military service, and there is undoubted overlap with the individual petition procedure under the European Convention on Human Rights. Cases which concern rights protected under the European Convention should probably be dealt with under that machinery. Nevertheless, for rights that fall outside the scope of the European Convention, the potential of the European Parliament's petition procedure should not be ignored.

The full range of human rights affected by the acts of the European Community (EC) and European Union is considered in a recent three-volume work, European Union: The Human Rights Challenge (A. Cassese, A. Clapham, and J. Weiler eds. 1992). Most works on EC law address briefly the relationship between EC law and fundamental rights protected under national law. See, e.g., P. Kapteyn and P. Verloren van Themaat, Introduction to the Law of the European Communities 165-169 (2d ed. L. Gormley ed. 1989); T. Hartley, The Foundations of European Community Law 132-139 (2d ed. 1988).

Comments and Questions

1. Compare the mandate of the CSCE High Commissioner on National Minorities with the mandates of the thematic rapporteurs of the UN Commission on Human Rights, pages 394-395 of Problem V. Can the early warning and potential mediation/conciliation functions of the former be likened to the humanitarian concerns of the latter? Which enjoys greater flexibility in the performance of its mandate?

2. The European Community was profoundly transformed by the 1992 Treaty on European Union, signed at Maastricht, which identifies as Union objectives, inter alia, establishment of a full economic and monetary union, introduction of a single currency and a common European citizenship, and implementation of a common foreign, security, and defense policy. The treaty also commits the Union to "respect fundamental rights, as guaranteed by the European Convention for the Protection of Human Rights . . . and as they result from the constitutional traditions common to the Member States, as general principles of Community law." Does this language mean that the European Court of Justice (the judicial body of the Community/ Union) should interpret the European Convention? Could the EC or the Union itself become a party to the European Convention on Human Rights?

Problem X

The Protection of
Human Rights in the
Americas and Africa

Can Regional Systems to Protect Human Rights Be More Effective Than UN Mechanisms?

I.   Introduction   782
II. The Inter-American System   782
     A. The Inter-American Commission and Court   782
         Medina, The Inter-American Commission on Human Rights
         and the Inter-American Court of Human Rights: Reflections
         on a Joint Venture   782
         1. Country-Specific Reports   787
         Inter-American Commission on Human Rights, Report on the
         Situation of Human Rights in Haiti   788
         2. Individual Complaints   793
         Association of the Bar of the City of New York, Committee on
         International Human Rights, The Inter-American Commis-
         sion: A Promise Unfulfilled   793
         Note: The Role of the Court   799
         The Velásquez Rodríguez Case   799
         Note: The United States Before the Inter-American Commis-
         sion   802
         Inter-American Commission on Human Rights Resolution
         3/87, Case 9647 (United States)   803
         3. Advisory Opinions of the Court   804
         Compulsory Membership in an Association Prescribed by Law
         for the Practice of Journalism   805
         Note: The U.S. Position on Ratification of the American Con-
         vention on Human Rights   820
         Message of the President Transmitting Four Treaties Pertaining
         to Human Rights   820
     B. Other Initiatives   826
III. The African Charter on Human and Peoples' Rights   827
         Welch, The African Commission on Human and Peoples'
         Rights: A Five-Year Report and Assessment   827
         International Commission of Jurists, Background Paper   830
IV. Final Comments and Questions   833

I. Introduction

Recall the article by Weston, Lukes, and Hnatt at pages 682-684 of Problem IX. One of the virtues of regional regimes to protect human rights is that they can be fashioned to accommodate local political conditions. While the machinery created under the auspices of the Council of Europe is clearly the most legalistic of the three existing regional systems — and it will become even more so with the establishment of the first permanent international human rights court later this decade — this is not necessarily the only approach.

As will be seen in the present Problem, the Americas and Africa have developed less formal mechanisms, which have strong promotional as well as protective functions. It was only in 1978, with the entry into force of the American Convention on Human Rights, that the Inter-American Court of Human Rights was created; no court is even envisaged under the African system. Nonetheless, the activities of the Inter-American Commission on Human Rights, in particular, may be better suited to address widespread violations of human rights in a particular country than are the European procedures, although such initiatives obviously depend to a large extent on the political will of the states in the region and the dedication and competence of the regional human rights bodies.

In every region, of course, the ultimate goal must be to protect the human rights of all individuals within the region, not merely to create international machinery to issue unheeded reports. As you read this Problem, try to determine the extent to which the European, American, and African human rights regimes have contributed effectively to developing a regional legal and political order in which promoting and protecting human rights has come to be seen as an essential function of government.

II. The Inter-American System

A. The Inter-American Commission and Court

Medina, The Inter-American Commission on Human Rights and the Inter-American Court of Human Rights: Reflections on a Joint Venture
12 Hum. Rts. Q. 439, 440-447 (1990)

II. THE DEVELOPMENT OF THE INTER-AMERICAN SYSTEM

The Inter-American Commission on Human Rights was established as an autonomous entity of the OAS by a resolution of the Fifth Meeting of

Consultation of Ministers of Foreign Affairs in 1959. The Commission was originally conceived as a study group concerned with abstract investigations in the field of human rights. However, the creators of the Commission did not foresee the appeal this organ would have for the individual victims of human rights violations. As soon as it was known that the Commission had been created, individuals began to send complaints about human rights problems in their countries. Prompted by these complaints, the Commission started its activities with the conviction that in order to promote human rights it had to protect them.

A significant part of the Commission's work was addressing the problem of countries with gross, systematic violations of human rights, characterized by an absence or a lack of effective national mechanisms for the protection of human rights and a lack of cooperation on the part of the governments concerned. The main objective of the Commission was not to investigate isolated violations but to document the existence of these gross, systematic violations and to exercise pressure to improve the general condition of human rights in the country concerned. For this purpose, and by means of its regulatory powers, the Commission created a procedure to "take cognizance" of individual complaints and use them as a source of information about gross, systematic violations of human rights in the territories of the OAS member states.

The Commission's competence to handle individual communications was formalized in 1965, after the OAS reviewed and was satisfied with the Commission's work. The OAS passed Resolution XXII, which allowed the Commission to "examine" isolated human rights violations, with a particular focus on certain rights. This procedure, however, provided many obstacles for the Commission. Complaints could be handled only if domestic remedies had been exhausted, a requirement that prevented swift reactions to violations. Also, the procedure made the Commission more dependent on the governments for information. This resulted in the governments' either not answering the Commission's requests for information or answering with a blanket denial that did not contribute to a satisfactory solution of the problem.

Furthermore, once the Commission had given its opinion on the case, there was nothing else to be done; the Commission would declare that a government had violated the American Declaration of the Rights and Duties of Man and recommend the government take certain measures, knowing that this was unlikely to resolve the situation. The fact that some of the Commission's opinions could reach the political bodies of the OAS did not solve the problem, because the Commission's opinions on individual cases were never discussed at that level. Consequently, in order not to lose the flexibility it had, the Commission interpreted Resolution XXII as granting the Commission power to "examine" communications concerning individual violations of certain rights specified in the resolution without diminishing its power to "take cognizance" of communications concerning the rest of the human rights protected by the American Declaration. The Commission preserved this broader power for the purposes of identifying gross, systematic human rights violations.

The procedure to "take cognizance" of communications evolved and became the general case procedure and was later used in examining the general human rights situation in a country. This procedure, maturing with the Commission's practice, had several positive characteristics in view of the Commission's purposes. First, it could be started without checking whether the communications met any admissibility requirements or even in the absence of any communication. All that was necessary was for news to reach the Commission that serious violations were taking place in the territory of an OAS member state. Second, the Commission assumed a very active role by requesting and gathering information by telegram and telephone from witnesses, newspapers, and experts, and also requesting consent to visit the country at the Commission's convenience. Third, the Commission could publicize its findings in order to put pressure upon the governments. Finally, the report resulting from the investigation could be sent to the political bodies of the OAS, thereby allowing for a political discussion of the problem which, at least theoretically, could be followed by political measures against the governments involved.

Since financial and human resources were limited, the Commission concentrated all its efforts on the examination of the general situation of human rights in each country. The examination of individual cases clearly took a secondary place. The Commission appeared to process them only because it had a duty to do so and not because of a conviction that its intervention would be helpful. After all, the special procedure for individual cases did not improve the victims' possibilities for redress, and the Commission could attempt to solve the cases through an examination of the general human rights situation in the country.

In short, the Commission was the sole guarantor of human rights in a continent plagued with gross, systematic violations, and the Commission was part of an international organization for which human rights were definitely not the first priority, and these facts made an imprint on the way the Commission looked upon its task. Apparently, the Commission viewed itself more as an international organ with a highly political task to perform than as a technical body whose main task was to participate in the first phase of a quasi-judicial supervision of the observance of human rights. The Commission's past made it ill-prepared to efficiently utilize the additional powers the Convention subsequently granted it.

A.   THE SYSTEM UNDER THE AMERICAN CONVENTION ON
     HUMAN RIGHTS

The Convention [see the Documentary Supplement] vested the authority to supervise its observance in two organs: the Inter-American Commission, which pre-existed the Convention, and Inter-American Court of Human Rights, which was created by the Convention.

The Inter-American Commission is composed of seven members elected in a nongovernmental capacity by the OAS General Assembly and represents all the OAS member states. The entry into force of the Convention in 1978 invested the Commission with a dual role. It has retained its status as an organ of the OAS, thereby maintaining its powers to promote and protect human rights in the territories of all OAS member states. In addition, it is now an organ of the Convention, and in that capacity it supervises human rights in the territories of the states parties to the Convention.

The Commission's functions include: (1) promoting human rights in all OAS member states; (2) assisting in the drafting of human rights documents; (3) advising member states of the OAS; (4) preparing country reports, which usually include visits to the territories of these states; (5) mediating disputes over serious human rights problems; (6) handling individual complaints and initiating individual cases on its own motion, both with regard to states parties and states not parties to the Convention; and (7) participating in the handling of cases and advisory opinions before the Court.

The Inter-American Court consists of seven judges irrespective of the number of states that have recognized the jurisdiction of the Court. Although the Court is formally an organ of the Convention and not of the OAS, its judges may be nationals of any member state of the OAS whether or not they are parties to the Convention.

The Court has contentious and advisory jurisdiction. In exercising its contentious jurisdiction, the Court settles controversies about the interpretation and application of the provisions of the American Convention through a special procedure designed to handle individual or state complaints against states parties to the Convention. Under its advisory jurisdiction, the Court may interpret not only the Convention but also any other treaty concerning the protection of human rights in the American states. The Court may also give its opinion regarding the compatibility of the domestic laws of any OAS member state with the requirements of the Convention or any human rights treaties to which the Convention refers. In addition, the Court is not prevented from giving its opinion regarding any question relating to the content or scope of the rights defined in the Convention or any question that might have to be considered by the Court in the exercise of its contentious jurisdiction or by the Commission's supervision of human rights. The advisory jurisdiction of the Court may be set in motion by any OAS member state, whether or not it is a party to the Convention, or by any OAS organ listed in Chapter X of the OAS Charter, which includes the Commission.

The procedure for handling individual or state complaints begins before the Commission. The procedure resembles those set forth in the European Convention and in the Additional Protocol to the International

Covenant on Civil and Political Rights. It is a quasi-judicial mechanism which may be started by any person, group of persons, or nongovernmental entity legally recognized in one or more of the OAS member states, regardless of whether the complainant is the victim of a human rights violation. This right of individual petition is a mandatory provision in the Convention, binding on all states parties. Inter-state communications, however, are dependent upon an explicit recognition of the competence of the Commission to receive and examine them. In addition, the Commission may begin processing a case on its own motion.

After receiving the communication, the Commission determines the admissibility of the complaint. The Commission will judge any communication admissible if all of the following requirements are met: (1) the communication alleges a violation of a right or rights protected by the Convention; (2) a communication on the same subject is not pending or has not previously been studied by the Commission or any other international organization; (3) the remedies under the state's domestic laws have been exhausted or the state does not respect the due process of law for the alleged violation; and (4) the communication is brought in a timely manner.

The Commission has powers to request information from the government concerned and, with the consent of the government, to investigate the facts in the complaint at the location of the alleged violation. If the government does not cooperate in the proceedings by providing the requested information within the time limit set by the Commission, Article 42 of the Commission's Regulations allows the Commission to presume that the facts in the petition are true, "as long as other evidence does not lead to a different conclusion." Following this, the Commission need investigate the case no further.

Before ending its consideration of a case, the Commission "shall place itself at the disposal of the parties with a view to reaching a friendly settlement of the matter on the basis of respect for the human rights recognized in the Convention." In following the regulations, the Commission attempts a friendly settlement only when (1) both parties to the dispute expressly agree to cooperate in this effort; (2) the positions and allegations of the parties are sufficiently precise; and (3) in the judgment of the Commission, the dispute is susceptible to this settlement procedure.

If no friendly settlement is reached, Article 50 of the Convention directs the Commission to draw up a draft report setting forth the facts and stating the Commission's conclusions. This first report is not published but is transmitted only to the state concerned so the state's officials may respond. When the Commission transmits the report, it may also make proposals or recommendations to the state. Under Article 51 of the Convention, the Commission may write a second report if, within the period prescribed in that article, the matter has not been submitted to the Court by the Commission or by the state concerned, or it has not been settled by other means. This second report will contain the Commission's opinion and conclusions regarding the case, the measures the Commission recommends, and a time limit for the state to comply with these measures. When the time limit has expired, the Commission decides whether the state has responded with adequate measures and whether to publish the report.

The Court may consider a case that is brought either by the Commission or by a state party to the Convention. For the Commission to refer a case to the Court, the case must have been admitted for investigation and the Commission's draft report sent to the state party. In addition, the state must recognize the Court's general contentious jurisdiction or a limited jurisdiction specified by a time period or case. For a state party to be able to place a case before the Court, the only requirement is that both states must have recognized the Court's contentious jurisdiction.

During the proceedings, the Court has powers to investigate the facts as it deems necessary. The Court ordinarily concludes its consideration of a case by issuing a judgment. If the Court finds that there has been a violation of a right or freedom protected by the Convention, it shall rule "that the injured party be ensured the enjoyment of his right or freedom that was violated." If appropriate, it may also rule that "the consequences of the measure or situation that constituted the breach of such a right or freedom be remedied and that fair compensation be paid to the injured party." States are under the international obligation to comply with the judgment of the Court in any case to which they are parties. The part of the judgment that stipulates compensatory damages has executory force in the state concerned.

If a state does not comply with the decision of the Court, the Court may inform and make recommendations to the OAS General Assembly. There is no reference in the Convention to any action that the General Assembly might take; the assembly, being a political body, may take any political action it deems necessary to persuade the state to comply with its international obligations.

1. Country-Specific Reports

As noted by Medina, the Inter-American Commission on Human Rights has a number of quite separate functions, unlike the more restricted mandate of the European Commission on Human Rights. In addition to its ability to "take cognizance" of communications, it may "prepare such studies or reports as it considers advisable for the performance of its duties" (Art. 12, American Convention; Art. 18, Statute of the Commission (Documentary Supplement)). This authority has been utilized to prepare a relatively large number of reports on "the situation of human rights" in particular countries. The reports may be inspired by a series of individual complaints, by NGO reports or requests, or at the Commission's own initiative.

Unless the human rights situation in a country improves dramatically, the Commission normally follows up an initial report with subsequent reports. These later reports may focus on particular aspects of human rights, or they may simply update information previously reported. For example, the Commission issued seven reports on Cuba between 1962 and 1983, four reports on Chile between 1975 and 1985, and seven reports on Haiti since 1979. Shorter observations (perhaps 10-30 pages long) may be included in the Commission's annual report to the OAS General Assembly under the heading "status of human rights in several countries."

The country reports normally include an analysis of the political and legal framework in the country, reports on specific human rights violations, and the Commission's conclusions and recommendations. They are frequently based on on-site investigations by the Commission and its staff, although such visits require the consent of the country concerned. (For an account of some of the difficulties encountered in fact-finding missions, see pages 472-474 of Problem VI.) The reports are published and presented to the OAS General Assembly for the latter's information.

The following excerpts from the introduction and conclusions of the Commission's 1994 report on Haiti give a flavor of the range of issues considered and the Commission's general approach to country reports.

Inter-American Commission on Human Rights, Report on the Situation of Human Rights in Haiti
O.A.S. Doc. OEA/Ser.L/V/II.85, Doc. 9 rev., at 1-3, 149-152
(1994)

INTRODUCTION

1. Given the critical situation of human rights persisting in Haiti, aggravated by the military coup of September 29, 1991, the Inter-American Commission on Human Rights (IACHR) has continued to assign priority to the country, and has been presenting a report on the situation of human rights in Haiti every year.

2. During this period, the Commission has repeatedly been asked by the Permanent Council and the Ad Hoc Meeting of Ministers of Foreign Affairs of the Organization of American States to conduct on-site visits to Haiti. It has also received requests from President Jean-Bertrand Aristide to visit the country. Unfortunately, each attempt taken by the Commission to organize such a visit to Haiti was either ignored or rejected by those who exercise power in Haiti. Finally, after President Aristide asked the Commission on July 6, 1993 to conduct an on-site investigation, on July 19, 1993, the Ministry of Foreign Affairs indicated a willingness to allow the Commission to visit the country.

3. The Commission conducted the visit from August 23 to 27, 1993. All of the information compiled by the Special Delegation pointed to a systematic pattern of human rights violations lodged against supporters of President Aristide by the military, the police and their collaborators. Most of the reported cases of extrajudicial executions and arbitrary, unlawful detention, (which were always accompanied by beatings and mistreatment), took place in the poor neighborhoods of Port-au-Prince, where the vast majority of President Aristide's supporters live.

4. The Commission also observed that the number of human rights violations in rural areas had increased, especially in the Artibonite region and the Central Plateau. Witnesses interviewed by the IACHR Delegation testified to the repression they were suffering at the hands of the military, including the destruction of their homes. This has led to a mass displacement of people constantly fleeing the violence.

5. During the period covered by this report, human rights violations increased in Haiti, despite the signing of the Governors Island and New York Agreements. Such violations, which include extra-judicial executions; disappearances; arbitrary detention; torture; mistreatment; extortion; prohibition of the right of assembly and repression of the media, increased greatly in number. In the capital, violence by gunmen operating on the instructions of the Army has escalated. Assaults by *zenglendos* — gangs of gunmen trained by former members of the military — have contributed towards heightening the atmosphere of fear and insecurity among the population. Paramilitary groups called *attachés*, as well as the *zenglendos*, operate with full impunity. In the provinces, violations are being committed not only by section chiefs and their associates, but also by new "militia" recently created by the Army to continue the repression. Most of the violations have occurred in a political climate promoted by the armed forces in their efforts to remain in power.

6. In Chapter I, this report describes the activities carried out by the Commission as of December 1991 and its most recent visit to Haiti in August 1993. Chapter II reviews the political and legal system in Haiti, as established by the 1987 Constitution. Chapter III provides background information on the political developments in Haiti after the 1991 coup d'etat, and on the steps taken by the Organization of American States and the United Nations to facilitate a political dialogue between the parties concerned so as to bring about the return of President Aristide and the restoration of democracy to Haiti.

7. Chapter IV of the report analyzes the current human rights situation in Haiti. This report is based mainly on the testimony given by either the victims of human rights violations themselves or their family members during the last visit conducted by the Commission. Claims of violations of individual rights received at IACHR headquarters are similarly considered. Also included in this Chapter is the information presented by the OAS/UN Civilian Mission and documentation provided by a number of human

rights groups working both inside and outside Haiti. Chapter IV additionally gives a brief description of the military structure in Haiti as background
to the subsequent analysis of the various institutional factors contributing to
the aggravation of the human rights situation in the country. In addition, a
few of the many claims of human rights violations received by the Commission are illustrated. The last chapter of the report, Chapter 5, discusses the
issue of Haitian refugees, the vast majority of whom seek asylum in the
United States because of the critical situation they face in Haiti today. . . .

CONCLUSIONS AND RECOMMENDATIONS

309. From the presentation made on the political and human rights
situation in Haiti the Inter-American Commission on Human Rights has
drawn conclusions and made recommendations. Firstly, the Commission
wishes to note that the human rights situation in Haiti has continued to
deteriorate severely despite the many efforts made by the international community to find a solution to the Haitian crisis.

310. The Commission has observed that most of the complaints of
human rights violations received, have sprung from attempts at political
expression among supporters of a return to democracy. Emboldened by the
signing of the Governors Island Agreement made by President Jean-
Bertrand Aristide and the Chief of the Armed Forces, General Raoul
Cedras, and additionally, by the acceptance of the Pact of New York, the
supporters have publicly expressed their support for the constitutional President. This reaction has provoked a wave of repression on the part of the
Armed Forces to prevent fulfillment of these Agreements reached in July
1993.

311. Violations of human rights, including executions without benefit
of trial, disappearances, arbitrary arrests normally accompanied by mistreatment, torture, and extortion, of which members of the Armed Forces are
regularly accused, are proof of the corruption that exists in that military
institution and of its domination over the system of justice in Haiti. Most of
these violations have been committed by the Army for the purpose of repressing and frightening the Haitian population and thereby maintaining
themselves in power.

312. In particular, the charge of "lavalassien" [being an Aristide supporter] has been used by the military to justify arbitrary seizures and violent
surprise searches. Demonstrations and meetings have been broken up and
their participants severely punished. Restrictions on the right to free speech
and threats to members of the press and owners of radio stations have
continued, as have physical attacks on persons distributing newspapers.

313. The Commission has observed that violations of human rights
have increased particularly in rural areas, where the peasant population is
bereft of any legal recourse for the assertion of its rights. Most of these

violations are committed by Section Heads and their assistants, who are appointed by the Armed Forces and are members thereof. This has given rise to the institutionalized practice of violence.

314. Following Mr. Robert Malval's confirmation as Prime Minister and the lifting of the embargo imposed by the United Nations and the Organization of American States, acts of violence increased and were directed at hindering the installation and operation of the new government and at preventing the functioning of the OAS-UN Civilian Mission, which for its own safety had to leave the country. Also, the violence unleashed by extreme-right groups, supported by paramilitary groups, resulted in the withdrawal of the United Nations Mission (MINUHA) before its arrival.

315. The present climate in Haiti is still characterized by the repression practiced by the military and collaborating armed groups. They, as demonstrated by the murders of Antoine Izméry and Guy-François Malary by "attaches" in September and October 1993, are becoming more brazen and are committing crimes in the full light of day against political activists who have openly supported the regime of deposed President Jean-Bertrand Aristide. During the period in question, the Commission recorded many deaths whose political connections were fully demonstrated by the fact that the military could instigate or stop them. Further more, as in the present situation, not only did it provoke and sponsor them, but the military also failed to investigate and punish the perpetrators of these murders, who operated in death-squad like fashion. This prompts the conclusion that they operate because they are granted impunity by the military.

316. Despite the undertaking in the Governors Island Agreement to generate a climate of pacification throughout the country so that President Aristide could return and its reaffirmation by the Chief of the Armed Forces and his General Staff in their talks with the Commission in August 1993, the resurgence of violence and the Army's indifference to combatting it demonstrate the lack of any intention or disposition to lead Haiti to democracy. Indeed, the military appears to see no inconsistency between their military regime and democracy, and disregards the fact that the assumption of power through a coup d'état is inherently anti-democratic, especially in light of Article 3(d) of the Charter of the Organization of American States and Article 23 of the American Convention on Human Rights.

317. By the coup d'état, the military regime has attempted to nullify the Haitian Constitution of 1987, which the population had sweepingly approved. The use of violence by the military to foil the popular will has repeatedly been condemned by the Commission and democratic nations. The Constitution of 1987 is the standard by which the legitimacy of the Haitian government must be measured. Today, all guarantees contained in that Constitution are direly threatened by the Armed Force's monopoly on force. They operate as a police force that does not protect security in the country but instead, represses those who try to change the wretched conditions in which the Haitian people live.

318. The Commission has previously stated that, regardless of the current political situation in Haiti, the American Convention on Human Rights continues in effect, and those who hold power are under the obligation to respect the rights contained in that international instrument.

319. Moreover, the Commission acknowledges that the Governors Island Agreement and Pact of New York are threatened by the repression and violence carried out by the Armed Forces. In effect, while the critical steps called for to secure the transition to constitutional democracy in Haiti are consolidated in those instruments, the obligation of all parties to commit to action to ensure the fulfillment of those steps remains. The Commission is convinced that the member states of the United Nations and the Organisation of American States must go on acting with increased boldness, using every possible means to prevent the further loss of countless lives in flight from repression. As part of these efforts, the UN and OAS should authorize the return of the OAS-UN Civilian Mission to Haiti, whose presence has proved to have a dampening effect on many tense situations. Similarly, the introduction of a UN force of technical training personnel for the police, and an international training program for the military should be carried out.

320. The Commission calls upon member states to comply with their obligations under international conventions and instruments, including the American Declaration of the Rights and Duties of Man, to ensure that persons who flee their countries from political persecution are afforded the right to determine their claims for asylum or refugee status.

321. The Commission is convinced that the essential requirement to remedy the grave human rights situation in Haiti is quick re-establishment of the constitutional democratic regime elected at the polls on December 16, 1990, and deposed in the coup d'état of September 29, 1991. This restoration should be accompanied by fundamental changes such as separation of the Army and the police as provided in the Constitution of 1987. At the same time, the necessary steps should be taken to professionalize an independent police force.

322. The Commission is convinced that in order to safeguard the personal rights and liberties of Haitians and to protect the population from abuses by the military, there must be:

a. a substantial reform of the legal system to ensure that the perpetrators of criminal acts are brought to justice and that persons who are arrested are brought to trial in as short a time as possible, and

b. an immediate disarming and disbanding of the paramilitary forces and sections chiefs who commit indiscriminate acts of violence with impunity.

323. Conscious of the gravity of the present situation in Haiti, the Commission is considering the possibility of making another *in loco* visit as soon as possible, in order to observe the human rights situation in that country and to maintain a continuing presence in Haiti.

2. Individual Complaints

Of course, the Commission and the Court (the latter only with respect to countries that have ratified the American Convention and accepted the optional jurisdiction of the Court) also deal with complaints by individuals that their rights have been violated. As suggested by Medina, page 784 supra, the Commission, in particular, seems to have treated individual cases with less rigor than one might wish. The following report by a New York City lawyers group offers particularly harsh criticisms of the Commission's effectiveness — or lack thereof — in redressing individual human rights violations.

Association of the Bar of the City of New York, Committee on International Human Rights, The Inter-American Commission: A Promise Unfulfilled
48 The Record 589, 598-602, 603-604, 606-608, 611-613
(1993)

The current functions of the Commission include making recommendations to member states of the OAS about measures in aid of human rights, requesting the states to prepare reports, responding to inquiries made by states concerning human rights, preparing reports, making on-site visits, and preparing protocols and amendments to the American Convention on Human Rights. The Commission thus has administrative, drafting, and even diplomatic functions, in addition to the quasi-judicial function of examining and deciding upon individual petitions. Everyone interviewed about the work of the Commission, those who are its most enthusiastic supporters, as well as its critics, agreed that many of the problems with the work of the Commission concerning individual petitions grow out of this profusion which tends to lead to a confusion of functions.

As a practical matter, the largest part of the Commission's work involves monitoring human rights, conducting on-site investigations, writing country reports, and handling individual petitions. The Commission has broad power to receive a petition, from an individual directly or from a human rights organization on the individual's behalf. The Commission can seek provisional remedies from the state to protect the petitioner, or it can ask the Court in a proper case to provide such protection. After the Commission has forwarded the petition to the member state, the petition passes through an initial procedure in which the government answers, then the petitioner may comment, and then the government responds again. If the state does not respond, as frequently happens, the Commission has the power to treat the allegations in the petition as presumptively true. This procedure, which we in the United States might call a "sanctions procedure," is called an Article 42 procedure under the Commission's regulations.

After this pleading stage, the case may pass to an investigative phase, in which the Commission can conduct a hearing or an on-site investigation. Very rarely, the parties may seek a friendly settlement. After the investigative phase, the Commission will prepare a decision, which is sent to the parties. The state has a period set by the Commission, usually sixty days, to comply with the decision, after which the Commission may publish its decision, or, when the state has accepted the Court's jurisdiction, the case may be referred to the Court within ninety days of the time the decision was transmitted to the state. . . .

The problems that confront the Inter-American Commission in cases of individual complaints alleging human rights violations, moreover, are especially difficult. Just investigating such a case can be daunting, according to accounts from Commission staff and consultants, because of threats to the lives of witnesses, as well as the difficulties of travel and communication over large distances. Further, the Commission's powers under the American Convention, much less its residual jurisdiction under the OAS Charter, do not give it enough authority to obtain redress from a recalcitrant government without strong support from the OAS itself.

Nevertheless, the inadequacies of the Commission's work on individual complaints cannot be explained fully by the intractability of the cases or the obstruction by governments. Those causes will not explain the Commission's reluctance, still persisting in some instances, to prepare and refer cases to the Court. Because the Commission's charter-based jurisdiction long antedated the emergence of the Inter-American Court, the Commission became accustomed to resolving its cases without the aid of the Court. After the creation of the Court, the custom continued; the Commission feared, for example, that resort to the Court might prolong the already protracted resolution of complaints. Whatever the reason, it is a habit that never completely changed. This created tension between the Commission and the Court, which appears, according to Court opinions and other cases described below, not entirely to have dissipated.

Nor is the difficulty of the cases or the obstruction of governments alone sufficient to explain why the Commission's decisions are often not persuasive or well-reasoned, nor why they are so long delayed. According to the Commission, it "opened" 181 individual cases in 1991, reporting to the OAS in 19, leaving a backlog of 978 cases pending. The Commission does not report how many complaints it receives each year, nor the current status of them.

To some extent, the shortcomings of the Commission can be explained by pressures from the OAS, either exerted directly through intervention at the Commission, or through budget decisions and control of staffing. It is also true, however, as will appear more fully in the sections that follow, that they result from working methods of the Commission and its staff that can and should be changed.

The Politics and Law of Individual Petitions

Critics described the problems with the Commission's treatment of individual petitions in several ways. It was said that the Commission does not follow its own regulations, that it is confused about its functions, and, most bluntly, that its decisions are politicized. The Committee has concluded that all of these are aspects of one problem: the Commission does not function well as a neutral, quasi-judicial adjudicative body for individual cases.

Some of the functions assigned to the Commission are diplomatic and political. Thus, advising member states about human rights matters, or drafting proposed new human rights instruments, call for political and diplomatic skills. Even preparing a report concerning the overall human rights situation in an entire country doubtless involves political decisions. But in the individual cases, the Commission has an adjudicative function — to determine and state the law and the facts with respect to an individual or group. The Commission, however, often confuses its other functions with its adjudicative role, treating individual complaints as diplomatic and political as much as legal problems. . . .

The manipulation of the Commission's regulations for political and negotiation purposes, with its attendant delays, finally provoked sharp criticism from the Inter-American Court in an opinion [Advisory Opinion OC-12/91 of 6 Dec. 1991] at the end of 1991 that undoubtedly did not improve the already strained relations between the Court and the Commission. In that case, the government of Costa Rica sought the advice of the Court concerning whether proposed Costa Rican laws would infringe upon the right to appeal in criminal cases established by the American Convention. The Court declined to give the advice, because there were individual complaints pending before the Commission, never decided or sent to the Court, which might have resolved the question of law through a contentious case. Some of those complaints had been pending since before 1986, during which time the Commission had given Costa Rica repeated opportunities, extending over five years, to resolve the question of law through legislation, while delaying the resolution of the individual cases. The Commission's strategy of delay had denied the complainants the opportunity to determine their rights through individual cases, without yielding any result through the negotiation process. . . .

PROBLEMS IN LAWMAKING

The habit of bargaining extends even to the Commission's reporting and lawmaking functions. The Commission took this path in the case of complaints filed against Uruguay and Argentina for having granted impunity to military and police personnel for liability for disappearances and other crimes during the recent dictatorships. The petitions were based in part on the theory that putting an end to the investigations of the crimes in these cases deprived each of the petitioners of his right under the American Convention to a "simple and prompt recourse . . . to a competent court or tribunal for protection against acts that violate his fundamental rights. . . ." They presented a question of central importance to the administration of human rights in the Americas.

According to word received later by the lawyers for the petitioners, the Commission decided these extraordinary cases favorably to the petitioners in the fall of 1991, and sent the decision to the governments, without then notifying or sending a copy to the petitioners, as the Commission was supposed to do under its own regulation. The Commission ignored its regulation, apparently hoping to obtain some diplomatic leverage — a private admission of liability or an offer of compensation, perhaps — by issuing the decision only to the state, while keeping it from the petitioners. Instead, Uruguay's foreign minister took advantage of the situation to denounce the decision against Uruguay as an infringement of sovereignty and "a slap in the face to the Uruguayan people," without having to explain the substance of the decision. Late in 1992, after a year's delay, the Commission finally did send the decisions to the petitioners. The matter has not been referred to the Court, even though Uruguay and Argentina had accepted its jurisdiction.

The process in the Argentina-Uruguay cases forms part of a pattern in which the Commission does not seem to take seriously its power — potentially very great — to make law in the Inter-American system. Its opinions have been criticized for being poorly reasoned; indeed, an examination of decisions in the annual reports shows that sometimes they are little more than collections of events, dates, and conclusions. It is clear that the situation is in part a result of the poor record of obedience to decisions from the respondent states, the failure of the OAS to insist on compliance, and the pressure from some member states to be even more lenient in enforcement. It is doubtless difficult to take decision-making seriously when important decisions result in verbal abuse amounting almost to threats; Uruguay, for example, was most vociferous at the spring, 1992, meeting of the OAS in advocating restrictions on the Commission's work. It is equally clear that the pressures in the OAS can be countered chiefly by the leadership of those states, including the United States, that claim to be committed to the enforcement of international human rights. And the Commission itself could relieve some of the pressure by referring more cases to the Inter-American Court.

PROCEDURAL ERRORS

Nevertheless, most sources interviewed by the Committee agreed that the results of cases could be better if a more nearly judicial attitude were taken toward them. The manipulation and disregard of regulations has led to slipshod handling of cases, with results that encourage disrespect and create legal difficulties for the Commission. The important case concerning the massacre by the army, using axes, machetes and knives, of at least twenty-nine villagers at Cayara in the Ayacucho region of Peru in 1988, gave rise to a grim comedy of errors. The Commission submitted the case to the Court at the end of May 1991, only to be informed by Peru that the Commission had failed to forward to the government some of the petitioners' responses to the government's arguments, as the Commission was required to do under its regulations. The Commission staff chose to withdraw the case from the Court — an act for which there is no specific provision in the law — and to send the missing papers to the government. When the Commission then re-submitted the case to the Court in 1992, Peru made preliminary objections in effect that the Commission had no power to withdraw and re-submit the case. . . . [The Court agreed with Peru and consequently dismissed the case.]

BUDGET

The budgetary situation of the Inter-American Commission on Human Rights is, in a word, a scandal. The budget is much too small, viewed either as a percentage of the OAS budget, or from the point of view of the work to be done by the Commission. In addition, the Commission has too little control over the allocation and expenditure of its budget.

Although human rights have been designated a priority for the OAS, the funds for the Commission are an extremely small percentage of the OAS budget, as the figures below (in U.S. dollars) demonstrate:

	OAS	Inter-American Commission	Percentage
1991	$60,060,100	$1,337,000	2.2
1990	60,060,100	1,305,000	2.1
1989	66,054,500	1,168,900	1.8
1988	66,054,500	1,083,700	1.6
1987	64,980,100	1,074,200	1.6

All sources agreed that while the members of the OAS give lip-service to human rights, many of them who are in fact offended by the attentions of the Commission, [and] work to keep it starved for funds so that it will not be able to function as effectively as it could. . . .

PERSONNEL AND STAFF

The election process in the OAS has not always produced Commissioners with a strong commitment to human rights; moreover, the Commission is not getting the full benefit of the talents of its present Commissioners. Although the Commission's statute authorizes them to meet for up to eight weeks, in 1991 they met for only four weeks; it seems doubtful that there is budget available for them to meet more than that. . . . [The Commission continued to meet for only four weeks annually through 1994.]

Furthermore, the present Commission staff of seven human rights specialists, together with the Executive Secretary and the support staff, is far too small to investigate and prepare cases in a region as vast as the Americas. Each lawyer is potentially responsible for complaints from as many as six countries, a situation that verges on the absurd. All sources interviewed by the Committee thought that the legal staff ought to be at least twice as large as it is, and probably larger.

As the preceding excerpt indicates, compliance with decisions of the Inter-American Commission on Human Rights has been less than satisfactory. However, this conclusion should come as no surprise when one considers that many of the governments to whom the Commission's recommendations are directed have been military or otherwise authoritarian regimes with little to gain (or apparently to lose — see Problem XIII) by respecting human rights.

However, the impact of politics on the Commission may be even more obvious when it is dealing with a government that is not unrelievedly repressive. This situation is illustrated by an individual case that challenged the legality of certain Mexican elections held in 1990. The Commission first adopted Report No. 7/93 "on a provisional basis," which was sent to the Mexican government (not to the complainant) and never published. Following the Mexican government's response, the Commission adopted and published a second report, noting, inter alia, that "progress has been made at the legislative level, a fact which is important to note . . . ; some of the new provisions are in response to the recommendations issued by the Commission, and some others, independently of those recommendations, further the aim of ensuring free and genuine elections. . . .

"The Inter-American Commission on Human Rights hopes that, as it was told by the authorities of that country, these amendments will effectively allow greater 'authenticity, equality, and transparency' in current and future electoral processes, and trusts that the recommendations this Commission has been making for some time to the Mexican authorities will be carried out . . . legislatively and operationally by the competent authorities." Rep. No. 14/93, Case 10.956 (Mexico), reprinted in Annual Report of the Inter-American Commission on Human Rights 1993, at 259, 291, 292, O.A.S. Doc. OEA/Ser.L/V/II.85, Doc. 9 rev. (1993). No finding was ever made publicly on the allegations of fraud raised by the complainant.

Note: The Role of the Court

The Inter-American Court of Human Rights has been in existence for less than 20 years; as of December 1993, its jurisdiction had been accepted by 16 of the 25 parties to the American Convention. Its advisory opinions and judgments have been generally more legalistic than the opinions of the Commission, and compliance with the Court's legally binding judgments seems to be good. The Court has awarded monetary damages to the relatives of victims in cases involving Honduras and Suriname. See Godinez Cruz Case, Judgment of 21 July 1989, reprinted in Annual Report of the Inter-American Court of Human Rights 141, O.A.S. Doc. OEA/Ser.L/V/III.21, doc. 14 (1989); Velásquez Rodríguez Case, Judgment of 21 July 1989, reprinted in id. at 123; Aloeboetoe et al. Case, described at page 238 of Problem III.

The first contentious case submitted to the Court originated in an individual petition against Honduras that the Commission received on 7 October 1981. In brief, it alleged that Angel Manfredo Velásquez Rodríguez, a student at the National Autonomous University of Honduras, had been violently detained without a warrant for his arrest by Honduran security and military personnel on the afternoon of 12 September 1981, in Tegucigalpa, Honduras. According to eyewitnesses, Velásquez Rodríguez was taken to the cells of Public Security Forces Station No. 2, where he was "accused of alleged political crimes and subjected to harsh interrogation and cruel torture." On 17 September 1981, he was moved to the First Infantry Battalion, where the interrogation continued. The police and security forces, however, denied that he had been detained. He has been missing since the events described above.

The Court, after a lengthy recitation of the facts and a weighing of the evidence (see pages 480-481 of Problem VI supra), concluded that Velásquez Rodríguez's "disappearance" was attributable to Honduras and constituted a violation of Articles 7, 5, and 4 of the American Convention. The Court summarized its reasoning as follows.

The Velásquez Rodríguez Case
Inter-Am. Ct. Hum. Rts., Judgment of 29 July 1988, Ser. C: Decisions and Judgments, No. 4, at 159-163

186. As a result of the disappearance, Manfredo Velásquez was the victim of an arbitrary detention, which deprived him of his physical liberty without legal cause and without a determination of the lawfulness of his detention by a judge or competent tribunal. Those acts directly violate the right to personal liberty recognized by Article 7 of the Convention . . . and are a violation imputable to Honduras of the duties to respect and ensure that right under Article 1(1).

187. The disappearance of Manfredo Velásquez violates the right to

personal integrity recognized by Article 5 of the Convention. . . . First, the mere subjection of an individual to prolonged isolation and deprivation of communication is in itself cruel and inhuman treatment which harms the psychological and moral integrity of the person, and violates the right of every detainee under Article 5(1) and 5(2) to treatment respectful of his dignity. Second, although it has not been directly shown that Manfredo Velásquez was physically tortured, his kidnapping and imprisonment by governmental authorities, who have been shown to subject detainees to indignities, cruelty and torture, constitute a failure of Honduras to fulfill the duty imposed by Article 1(1) to ensure the rights under Article 5(1) and 5(2) of the Convention. The guarantee of physical integrity and the right of detainees to treatment respectful of their human dignity require States Parties to take reasonable steps to prevent situations which are truly harmful to the rights protected.

188. The above reasoning is applicable to the right to life recognized by Article 4 of the Convention. . . . The context in which the disappearance of Manfredo Velásquez occurred and the lack of knowledge seven years later about his fate create a reasonable presumption that he was killed. Even if there is a minimal margin of doubt in this respect, it must be presumed that his fate was decided by authorities who systematically executed detainees without trial and concealed their bodies in order to avoid punishment. This, together with the failure to investigate, is a violation by Honduras of a legal duty under Article 1(1) of the Convention to ensure the rights recognized by Article 4(1). That duty is to ensure to every person subject to its jurisdiction the inviolability of the right to life and the right not to have one's life taken arbitrarily. These rights imply an obligation on the part of States Parties to take reasonable steps to prevent situations that could result in the violation of that right.

XII

189. Article 63(1) of the Convention provides:

> If the Court finds that there has been a violation of a right or freedom protected by this Convention, the Court shall rule that the injured party be ensured the enjoyment of his right or freedom that was violated. It shall also rule, if appropriate, that the consequences of the measure or situation that constituted the breach of such right or freedom be remedied and that fair compensation be paid to the injured party.

Clearly, in the instant case the Court cannot order that the victim be guaranteed the enjoyment of the rights or freedoms violated. The Court, however, can rule that the consequences of the breach of the rights be remedied and that just compensation be paid.

190. During this proceeding the Commission requested the payment of compensation, but did not offer evidence regarding the amount of damages or the manner of payment. Neither did the parties discuss these matters.

191. The Court believes that the parties can agree on the damages. If an agreement cannot be reached, the Court shall award an amount. The case shall, therefore, remain open for that purpose. The Court reserves the right to approve the agreement and, in the event no agreement is reached, to set the amount and order the manner of payment.

192. The Rules of Procedure establish the legal procedural relations among the Commission, the State or States Parties in the case and the Court itself, which continue in effect until the case is no longer before the Court. As the case is still before the Court, the Government and the Commission should negotiate the agreement referred to in the preceding paragraph. The recipients of the award of damages will be the next-of-kin of the victim. This does not in any way imply a ruling on the meaning of the word "parties" in any other context under the Convention or the rules pursuant thereto.

XIII

193. With no pleading to support an award of costs, it is not proper for the Court to rule on them (Art. 45(1), Rules of Procedure).

XIV

194. THEREFORE,

THE COURT:

Unanimously

1. Rejects the preliminary objection interposed by the Government of Honduras alleging the inadmissibility of the case for the failure to exhaust domestic legal remedies.

Unanimously

2. Declares that Honduras has violated, in the case of Angel Manfredo Velásquez Rodríguez, its obligations to respect and to ensure the right to personal liberty set forth in Article 7 of the Convention, read in conjunction with Article 1(1) thereof.

Unanimously

3. Declares that Honduras has violated, in the case of Angel Manfredo Velásquez Rodríguez, its obligations to respect and to ensure the right to humane treatment set forth in Article 5 of the convention, read in conjunction with Article 1(1) thereof.

Unanimously

4. Declares that Honduras has violated, in the case of Angel Manfredo Velásquez Rodríguez, its obligation to ensure the right to life as set forth in Article 4 of the Convention, read in conjunction with Article 1(1) thereof.

Unanimously

5. Decides that Honduras is hereby required to pay fair compensation to the next-of-kin of the victim.

By six votes to one

6. Decides that the form and amount of such compensation, failing agreement between Honduras and the Commission within six months of the date of this judgment, shall be settled by the Court and, for that purpose, retains jurisdiction of the case.

JUDGE RODOLFO E. PIZA E. dissenting.

Unanimously

7. Decides that the agreement on the form and amount of the compensation shall be approved by the Court.

Unanimously

8. Does not find it necessary to render a decision concerning costs.

[The Court subsequently awarded 750,000 lempiras (approximately $250,000) to the family of Velásquez Rodríguez, although the full amount was not paid by Honduras until 1995.]

Note: The United States Before the Inter-American Commission

Although the United States has not ratified the American Convention on Human Rights, see pages 820-826 infra, as a party to the OAS Charter it remains subject to the jurisdiction of the Commission, which is an organ of the OAS. In that capacity, the Commission interprets and applies to all OAS member states the rights set forth in the American Declaration on the Rights and Duties of Man (see Documentary Supplement), pursuant to Article 1 of its Statute.

The Commission remains the only international governmental body to have conducted a formal on-site investigation of human rights in the United States, which it did when it visited Haitian refugee camps in Florida and Puerto Rico in 1982. See Annual Report of the Inter-American Commission on Human Rights 1981-1982, at 17-18, O.A.S. Doc. OEA/Ser.L/V/II.57,

Doc. 6 rev. 1 (1982). The situation of Haitians seeking to apply for asylum in the United States has been the subject of numerous complaints to the Commission, many of which have foundered on the rock of non-exhaustion of domestic remedies.

Other complaints that have led to formal decisions by the Commission on allegations of human rights violations in the United States include a challenge to legalized abortion, Res. No. 23/81, Case 2141 (United States), reprinted in Annual Report of the Inter-American Commission on Human Rights 1980-1981, at 25, O.A.S. Doc. OEA/Ser.L/V/II.54, Doc. 9 rev. 1 (1981) (the so-called "Baby Boy" case); allegations that the death penalty is imposed in a racially discriminatory manner, Res. No. 23/89, Case 10.031 (United States), reprinted in Annual Report of the Inter-American Commission on Human Rights 1989-1990, at 62, O.A.S. Doc. OEA/Ser.L/V/II.77, Doc. 7 rev. 1 (1990); and a complaint concerning police misconduct and alleged murder of members of the Move Organization in Philadelphia, which was declared inadmissible for failure to exhaust domestic remedies, Rep. No. 19/92, Case 10.865 (United States), reprinted in Annual Report of the Inter-American Commission on Human Rights 1992-1993, at 142, O.A.S. Doc. OEA/Ser.L/V/II.83, Doc. 14 corr. 1 (1993).

The only case in which the Commission has found a violation of the American Declaration by the United States involved imposition of the death penalty on persons who were under 18 years of age at the time they committed the crime for which they were convicted. Although the Commission found that "in the Member States of the OAS there is recognized a norm of *jus cogens* which prohibits the State execution of children," it agreed with the United States that there was no consensus as to the minimum age for imposition of the death penalty. It nevertheless continued:

Inter-American Commission on Human Rights Resolution 3/87, Case 9647 (United States)
Annual Report of the Inter-American Commission on Human Rights 1986-1987, at 148, 172-173, O.A.S. Doc. OEA/Ser.L/V/II.71, Doc. 9 rev. 1 (1987)

The Commission, however, does not find the age question dispositive of the issue before it, which is whether the absence of a federal prohibition within U.S. domestic law on the execution of juveniles, who committed serious crimes under the age of 18, is in violation of the American Declaration.

The Commission finds that the diversity of state practice in the U.S. — reflected in the fact that some states have abolished the death penalty, while others allow a potential threshold limit of applicability as low as 10 years of age — results in very different sentences for the commission of the same crime. The deprivation by the State of an offender's life should not be made subject to the fortuitous element of where the crime took place. . . .

The failure of the federal government to preempt the states as regards this most fundamental right — the right to life — results in a pattern of legislative arbitrariness throughout the United States which results in the arbitrary deprivation of life and inequality before the law, contrary to Articles I and II of the American Declaration of the Rights and Duties of Man, respectively.

_____

The two applicants on whose behalf the case was brought were executed while proceedings were pending before the Commission, despite requests from the OAS that the executions be stayed. The governor of South Carolina refused to stay the execution of one of the applicants, and the governor of Texas did not bother to reply to the OAS request. See Fox, Current Development: Inter-American Commission on Human Rights Finds United States in Violation, 82 Am. J. Intl. L. 601 (1988).

In 1993 the Commission decided to admit two additional cases filed against the United States. The first alleged human rights violations during the U.S. invasion of Panama in 1989, Rep. No. 31/93, Case 10.573 (United States), reprinted in Annual Report of the Inter-American Commission on Human Rights 1993, at 312, O.A.S. Doc. OEA/Ser.L/V/II.85, Doc. 9 rev. (1993), while the second challenged the U.S. practice of interdicting Haitians on the high seas in order to prevent them from seeking asylum in the United States, Rep. No. 28/93, Case 10.675 (United States), reprinted in id. at 334. A third case, concerning U.S. actions during the 1983 invasion of Grenada, was admitted in spring 1994, Rep. No. 14/94, Case 10.951 (United States), O.A.S. Doc. OEA/Ser.L/V/II.85, Doc. 25 (1994).

3.   Advisory Opinions of the Court

Protocol No. 2 to the European Convention on Human Rights gives the European Court the authority to issue "advisory opinions on legal questions concerning the interpretation of the Convention," upon the request of the Committee of Ministers of the Council of Europe. No such request has ever been made, and, although the power to issue advisory opinions is retained in the comprehensive amendment to the European system adopted in 1994, there seems to be little interest within Europe in utilizing this possibility of expanding the Court's activities.

The Inter-American Court of Human Rights, on the other hand, spent most of its time during its first decade of existence issuing advisory opinions, which are authorized by Article 64 of the American Convention. One reason for this difference may be the initial reluctance of the Commission to refer contentious cases to the Court (discussed in Medina, supra page 782, at 448-456); another is the much broader range of entities authorized to request advisory opinions, which includes all OAS member states, the Commission, and other OAS organs. Of course, states also accepted the

Court's contentious jurisdiction only gradually, and advisory opinions were thus the only "business" the Court could conduct.

It should be noted that the Court's advisory jurisdiction extends to interpreting not only the American Convention, but also "other treaties concerning the protection of human rights in the American states." Despite the potential for conflicting interpretations were the Court to consider non-American instruments, the Court has adopted a broad view of this provision that encompasses not only "any international treaty applicable in the American States," whether or not OAS members are parties to it, but also the American Declaration of the Rights and Duties of Man, even though the latter is not a treaty. See Inter-American Court of Human Rights, Advisory Opinion OC-1/82 of 24 Sept. 1982, reprinted in Annual Report of the Inter-American Court of Human Rights 1983, at 12, O.A.S. Doc. OEA/Ser.L/V/III.9, Doc. 13 (1983); id., Advisory Opinion OC-10/89 of 14 July 1989, reprinted in Annual Report 1989, at 109, O.A.S. Doc. OEA/Ser.L/V/III.21, Doc. 14 (1989).

Two advisory opinions, in particular, have made a significant contribution to protecting rights during states of emergency by expanding the scope of non-derogable due process rights, such as habeas corpus and amparo (see pages 927-928 of Problem XI).

A state may request an advisory opinion in order to test the compatibility of its own law with the American Convention, while avoiding the legally binding result that would follow from a judgment by the Court in a contentious case. Costa Rica, where the Court is based, was the earliest and most vocal supporter of an increased role for the Court, and the following opinion is but one of several based on requests from Costa Rica. The opinion is interesting not only for its substantive discussion of freedom of expression, but also for some of the jurisdictional issues it addresses.

Compulsory Membership in an Association Prescribed by Law for the Practice of Journalism
Inter-Am. Ct. Hum. Rts., Advisory Opinion OC-5/85 of 13 Nov. 1985, Ser. A No. 5, at 19, 20-21, 22-25, 26, 27-29, 30-32, 34, 35, 36-38, 39-43, 44

1. By note of July 8, 1985, the Government of Costa Rica (hereinafter "the Government") submitted to the Inter-American Court of Human Rights (hereinafter "the Court") an advisory opinion request relating to the interpretation of Articles 13 and 29 of the American Convention on Human Rights (hereinafter "the Convention" or "the American Convention") as they affect the compulsory membership in an association prescribed by law for the practice of journalism (hereinafter "compulsory licensing"). The request also sought the Court's interpretation relating to the compatibility of Law No. 4420 of September 22, 1969, Organic Law of the Colegio de

Periodistas (Association of Journalists) of Costa Rica (hereinafter "Law No. 4420" and "the Colegio," respectively), with the provisions of the aforementioned articles. According to the express declaration of the Government, its request was formulated in fulfillment of a commitment it had made to the Inter-American Press Association (hereinafter "the IAPA").

2. In a note of July 12, 1985, the Secretariat of the Court, acting pursuant to Article 52 of the Rules of Procedure of the Court, requested written observations on the issues involved in the instant proceeding from the Member States of the Organization of American States (hereinafter "the OAS") as well as, through the Secretary General, from the organs listed in Chapter X of the Charter of the OAS.

3. The Court, by note of September 10, 1985, extended, until October 25, 1985, the date for the submission of written observations or other relevant documents.

4. Responses to the Secretariat's communication were received from the Government of Costa Rica, the Inter-American Commission on Human Rights (hereinafter "the Commission") and the Inter-American Juridical Committee.

5. Furthermore, the following non-governmental organizations submitted amici curiae briefs: the Inter-American Press Association; the Colegio de Periodistas of Costa Rica; the World Press Freedom Committee, the International Press Institute, the Newspaper Guild and the International Association of Broadcasting; the American Newspaper Publishers Association, the American Society of Newspaper Editors and the Associated Press; the Federación Latinoamericana de Periodistas; the International League for Human Rights; and the Lawyers Committee for Human Rights, the Americas Watch Committee and the Committee to Protect Journalists. . . .

STATEMENT OF THE ISSUES

11. Invoking Article 64 of the Convention, the Government requested the Court to render an advisory opinion on the interpretation of Articles 13 and 29 of the Convention with respect to the compulsory licensing of journalists, and on the compatibility of Law No. 4420, which establishes such licensing requirements in Costa Rica, with the aforementioned articles of the Convention. The communication presented the request in the following manner:

> The request that is presented to the Inter-American Court, therefore, also includes a specific request for an advisory opinion as to whether there is a conflict or contradiction between the compulsory membership in a professional association as a necessary requirement to practice journalism, in general, and reporting, in particular — according to the aforementioned articles of Law No. 4420 — and the international norms (Articles 13 and 29 of the American Convention on Human Rights). In this respect, it is necessary to

have the opinion of the Inter-American Court regarding the scope and limitations on the right to freedom of expression, of thought and of information and the only permissible limitations contained in Articles 13 and 29 of the American Convention, with an indication as to whether the domestic norms contained in the Organic Law of the Colegio de Periodistas (Law No. 4420) and Articles 13 and 29 are compatible.

Is the compulsory membership of journalists and reporters in an association prescribed by law for the practice of journalism permitted or included among the restrictions or limitations authorized by Articles 13 and 29 of the American Convention on Human Rights? Is there any incompatibility, conflict or disagreement between those domestic norms and the aforementioned articles of the American Convention?

12. Both the briefs and the oral arguments of the Government and the other participants in the proceedings clearly indicate that the Court is not being asked to define in the abstract the reach and the limitations permitted on the right of freedom of expression. Instead, the request seeks an opinion, under Article 64(1) of the Convention, concerning the legality, in general, of the requirement of compulsory licensing. It also seeks a ruling under Article 64(2) of the Convention on the compatibility of Law No. 4420, which establishes such compulsory licensing in Costa Rica, with the Convention. . . .

ADMISSIBILITY

16. As has already been observed, the advisory jurisdiction of the Court has been invoked with respect to Article 64(1) of the Convention with regard to the general question and with respect to Article 64(2) concerning the compatibility of Law. No. 4420 and the Convention. Since Costa Rica is a Member State of the OAS, it has standing to request advisory opinions under either provision, and no legal argument suggests itself that could prevent a state from invoking both provisions in one request. Hence, the fact that both provisions were invoked does not make the petition of Costa Rica inadmissible.

17. It is now necessary to ask whether that part of the request of Costa Rica which refers to the compatibility of Law No. 4420 with the Convention is inadmissible because it is a matter that was considered in a proceeding before the Commission (Schmidt case, . . .), and to which the Government made specific reference in its request.

18. Under the protective system established by the Convention, the instant application and the Schmidt case are two entirely distinct legal proceedings, even though the latter case dealt with some of the same questions that are before the Court in this advisory opinion request.

19. The Schmidt case grew out of an individual petition filed with the Commission pursuant to Article 44 of the Convention. There Mr. Schmidt charged the Government of Costa Rica with a violation of Article 13 of the Convention, which he alleged resulted from his conviction in Costa Rica for violating the provisions of Law No. 4420. After ruling the petition admissible, the Commission examined it in accordance with the procedures set out in Article 48 of the Convention and, in due course, adopted a Resolution in which it concluded that Law No. 4420 did not violate the Convention and that Mr. Schmidt's conviction did not violate Article 13. . . .

20. Costa Rica has accepted the contentious jurisdiction of the Court (Art. 62 of the Convention). However, neither the Government nor the Commission exercised its right to bring the case to the Court before the proceedings in the Schmidt case had run their full course, thereby depriving the individual applicant of the possibility of having his petition adjudicated by the Court. This result did not divest the Government of the right to seek an advisory opinion from the Court under Article 64 of the Convention with regard to certain legal issues, even though some of them are similar to those dealt with in the Schmidt case. . . .

25. Although the Convention does not specify under what circumstances a case should be referred to the Court by the Commission, it is implicit in the functions that the Convention assigns to the Commission and to the Court that certain cases should be referred by the former to the Court, provided they have not been the subject of a friendly settlement, notwithstanding the fact that there is no legal obligation to do so. The Schmidt case clearly falls into this category. The controversial legal issues it raised had not been previously considered by the Court; the domestic proceedings in Costa Rica produced conflicting judicial decisions; the Commission itself was not able to arrive at a unanimous decision on the relevant legal issues; and its subject is a matter of special importance to the hemisphere because several states have adopted laws similar to that of Costa Rica.

26. Considering that individuals do not have standing to take their case to the Court and that a Government that has won a proceeding in the Commission would have no incentive to do so, in these circumstances the Commission alone is in a position, by referring the case to the Court, to ensure the effective functioning of the protective system established by the Convention. In such a context, the Commission has a special duty to consider the advisability of coming to the Court. Where the Commission has not referred the case to the Court and where, for that reason, the delicate balance of the protective system established by the Convention has been impaired, the Court should not refuse to consider the subject when it is presented in the form of an advisory opinion. . . .

FREEDOM OF THOUGHT AND EXPRESSION

29. Article 13 of the Convention reads as follows:

Article 13.   Freedom of Thought and Expression

1. Everyone has the right to freedom of thought and expression. This right includes freedom to seek, receive, and impart information and ideas of all kinds, regardless of frontiers, either orally, in writing, in print, in the form of art, or through any other medium of one's choice.

2. The exercise of the right provided for in the foregoing paragraph shall not be subject to prior censorship but shall be subject to subsequent imposition of liability, which shall be expressly established by law to the extent necessary to ensure:

   a.   respect for the rights or reputations of others; or
   b.   the protection of national security, public order, or public health or morals.

3. The right of expression may not be restricted by indirect methods or means, such as the abuse of government or private controls over newsprint, radio broadcasting frequencies, or equipment used in the dissemination of information, or by any other means tending to impede the communication and circulation of ideas and opinions.

4. Notwithstanding the provisions of paragraph 2 above, public entertainments may be subject by law to prior censorship for the sole purpose of regulating access to them for the moral protection of childhood and adolescence.

5. Any propaganda for war and any advocacy of national, racial, or religious hatred that constitute incitements to lawless violence or to any other similar illegal action against any person or group of persons on any grounds including those of race, color, religion, language, or national origin shall be considered as offenses punishable by law.

Article 29 establishes the following rules for the interpretation of the Convention:

Article 29.   Restrictions Regarding Interpretation

No provision of this Convention shall be interpreted as:

   a.   permitting any State Party, group, or person to suppress the enjoyment or exercise of the rights and freedoms recognized in this Convention or to restrict them to a greater extent than is provided for herein;
   b.   restricting the enjoyment or exercise of any right or freedom recognized by virtue of the laws of any State Party or by virtue of another convention to which one of the said states is a party;

    c.   precluding other rights or guarantees that are inherent in the human personality or derived from representative democracy as a form of government; or

    d.   excluding or limiting the effect that the American Declaration of the Rights and Duties of Man and other international acts of the same nature may have.

30. Article 13 indicates that freedom of thought and expression "includes freedom to seek, receive, and impart information and ideas of all kinds. . . ." This language establishes that those to whom the Constitution applies not only have the right and freedom to express their own thoughts but also the right and freedom to seek, receive and impart information and ideas of all kinds. Hence, when an individual's freedom of expression is unlawfully restricted, it is not only the right of that individual that is being violated, but also the right of all others to "receive" information and ideas. The right protected by Article 13 consequently has a special scope and character, which are evidenced by the dual aspect of freedom of expression. It requires, on the one hand, that no one be arbitrarily limited or impeded in expressing his own thoughts. In that sense, it is a right that belongs to each individual. Its second aspect, on the other hand, implies a collective right to receive any information whatsoever and to have access to the thoughts expressed by others.

31. In its individual dimension, freedom of expression goes further than the theoretical recognition of the right to speak or to write. It also includes and cannot be separated from the right to use whatever medium is deemed appropriate to impart ideas and to have them reach as wide an audience as possible. When the Convention proclaims that freedom of thought and expression includes the right to impart information and ideas through "any . . . medium," it emphasizes the fact that the expression and dissemination of ideas and information are indivisible concepts. This means that restrictions that are imposed on dissemination represent, in equal measure, a direct limitation on the right to express oneself freely. The importance of the legal rules applicable to the press and to the status of those who dedicate themselves professionally to it derives from this concept.

32. In its social dimension, freedom of expression is a means for the interchange of ideas and information among human beings and for mass communication. It includes the right of each person to seek to communicate his own views to others, as well as the right to receive opinions and news from others. For the average citizen it is just as important to know the opinions of others or to have access to information generally as is the very right to impart his own opinions.

33. The two dimensions mentioned (supra 30) of the right to freedom of expression must be guaranteed simultaneously. One cannot legitimately rely on the right of a society to be honestly informed in order to put in place a regime of prior censorship for the alleged purpose of eliminating informa-

tion deemed to be untrue in the eyes of the censor. It is equally true that the right to impart information and ideas cannot be invoked to justify the establishment of private or public monopolies of the communications media designed to mold public opinion by giving expression to only one point of view.

34. If freedom of expression requires, in principle, that the communication media are potentially open to all without discrimination or, more precisely, that there be no individuals or groups that are excluded from access to such media, it must be recognized also that such media should, in practice, be true instruments of that freedom and not vehicles for its restriction. It is the mass media that make the exercise of freedom of expression a reality. This means that the conditions of its use must conform to the requirements of this freedom, with the result that there must be, inter alia, a plurality of means of communication, the barring of all monopolies thereof, in whatever form, and guarantees for the protection of the freedom and independence of journalists. . . .

38. Article 13(2) of the Convention defines the means by which permissible limitations to freedom of expression may be established. It stipulates, in the first place, that prior censorship is always incompatible with the full enjoyment of the rights listed in Article 13, but for the exception provided for in subparagraph 4 dealing with public entertainments, even if the alleged purpose of such prior censorship is to prevent abuses of freedom of expression. In this area any preventive measure inevitably amounts to an infringement of the freedom guaranteed by the Convention.

39. Abuse of freedom of information thus cannot be controlled by preventive measures but only through the subsequent imposition of sanctions on those who are guilty of the abuses. But even here, in order for the imposition of such liability to be valid under the Convention, the following requirements must be met:

a) the existence of previously established grounds for liability;
b) the express and precise definition of these grounds by law;
c) the legitimacy of the ends sought to be achieved;
d) a showing that these grounds of liability are "necessary to ensure" the aforementioned ends.

All of these requirements must be complied with in order to give effect to Article 13(2).

40. Article 13(2) is very precise in specifying that the restrictions on freedom of information must be established by law and only in order to achieve the ends that the Convention itself enumerates. Because the provision deals with restrictions as that concept has been used by the Court . . . , the legal definition of the liability must be express and precise.

41. Before analyzing subparagraphs (a) and (b) of Article 13(2) of the Convention, as they relate to the instant request, the Court will now con-

sider the meaning of the expression "necessary to ensure," found in the same provision. To do this, the Court must take account of the object and purpose of the treaty, keeping in mind the criteria for its interpretation found in Articles 29(c) and (d), and 32(2), which read as follows:

Article 29.   Restrictions Regarding Interpretation

No provision of this Convention shall be interpreted as:

. . .

    c. precluding other rights or guarantees that are inherent in the human personality or derived from representative democracy as a form of government; or

    d. excluding or limiting the effect that the American Declaration of the Rights and Duties of Man and other international acts of the same nature may have.

Article 32.   Relationship Between Duties and Rights

. . .

    2. The rights of each person are limited by the rights of others, by the security of all, and by the just demands of the general welfare, in a democratic society.

The Court must also take account of the Preamble of the Convention in which the signatory states reaffirm "their intention to consolidate in this hemisphere, within the framework of democratic institutions, a system of personal liberty and social justice based on respect for the essential rights of man."

42. These articles define the context within which the restrictions permitted under Article 13(2) must be interpreted. It follows from the repeated reference to "democratic institutions," "representative democracy" and "democratic society" that the question whether a restriction on freedom of expression imposed by a state is "necessary to ensure" one of the objectives listed in subparagraphs (a) or (b) must be judged by reference to the legitimate needs of democratic societies and institutions. . . .

[The Court then analyzed comparable provisions regarding freedom of expression in the European Convention on Human Rights and the UN Covenant on Civil and Political Rights.]

47. Article 13(2) must also be interpreted by reference to the provisions of Article 13(3), which is most explicit in prohibiting restrictions on freedom of expression by "indirect methods and means . . . tending to impede the communication and circulation of ideas and opinions." Neither the European Convention nor the Covenant contains a comparable clause. It is significant that Article 13(3) was placed immediately after a provision —

Article 13(2) — which deals with permissible restrictions on the exercise of freedom of expression. This circumstance suggests a desire to ensure that the language of Article 13(2) not be misinterpreted in a way that would limit, except to the extent strictly necessary, the full scope of the right to freedom of expression.

48. Article 13(3) does not only deal with indirect governmental restrictions, it also expressly prohibits "private controls" producing the same result. This provision must be read together with the language of Article 1 of the Convention wherein the States Parties "undertake to respect the rights and freedoms recognized (in the Convention) . . . and to ensure to all persons subject to their jurisdiction the free and full exercise of those rights and freedoms. . . ." Hence, a violation of the Convention in this area can be the product not only of the fact that the State itself imposes restrictions of an indirect character which tend to impede "the communication and circulation of ideas and opinions," but the State also has an obligation to ensure that the violation does not result from the "private controls" referred to in paragraph 3 of Article 13. . . .

50. The foregoing analysis of Article 13 shows the extremely high value that the Convention places on freedom of expression. A comparison of Article 13 with the relevant provisions of the European Convention (Article 10) and the Covenant (Article 19) indicates clearly that the guarantees contained in the American Convention regarding freedom of expression were designed to be more generous and to reduce to a bare minimum restrictions impeding the free circulation of ideas. . . .

Possible Violations of the American Convention

53. Article 13 may be violated under two different circumstances, depending on whether the violation results in the denial of freedom of expression or whether it results from the imposition of restrictions that are not authorized or legitimate.

54. In truth, not every breach of Article 13 of the Convention constitutes an extreme violation of the right to freedom of expression, which occurs when governmental power is used for the express purpose of impeding the free circulation of information, ideas, opinions or news. Examples of this type of violation are prior censorship, the seizing or barring of publications and, generally, any procedure that subjects the expression or dissemination of information to governmental control. Here the violation is extreme not only in that it violates the right of each individual to express himself, but also because it impairs the right of each person to be well informed, and thus affects one of the fundamental prerequisites of a democratic society. The Court believes that the compulsory licensing of journalists, as that issue is presented in the instant request, does not fall into this category.

55. Suppression of freedom of expression as described in the preceding paragraph, even though it constitutes the most serious violation possible of Article 13, is not the only way in which that provision can be violated. In effect, any governmental action that involves a restriction of the right to seek, receive and impart information and ideas to a greater extent or by means other than those authorized by the Convention, would also be contrary to it. This is true whether or not such restrictions benefit the government.

56. Furthermore, given the broad scope of the language of the Convention, freedom of expression can also be affected without the direct intervention of the State. This might be the case, for example, when due to the existence of monopolies or oligopolies in the ownership of communications media, there are established in practice "means tending to impede the communication and circulation of ideas and opinions."

57. As has been indicated in the preceding paragraphs, a restriction of the right to freedom of expression may or may not be a violation of the Convention, depending upon whether it conforms to the terms in which such restrictions are authorized by Article 13(2). It is consequently necessary to analyze the question relating to the compulsory licensing of journalists in light of this provision of the Convention.

58. The compulsory licensing of journalists can result in the imposition of liability, including penal, for those who are not members of the "colegio" if, by imparting "information and ideas of all kinds . . . through any . . . medium of one's choice" they intrude on what, according to the law, is defined as the professional practice of journalism. It follows that this licensing requirement constitutes a restriction on the right of expression for those who are not members of the "colegio." This conclusion makes it necessary for the Court to determine whether the law is based on considerations that are legitimate under the Constitution and, consequently, compatible with it.

59. Accordingly, the question is whether the ends sought to be achieved fall within those authorized by the Convention, that is, whether they are "necessary to ensure: a) respect for the rights or reputations of others; or b) the protection of national security, public order, or public health or morals" (Art. 13(2)).

60. The Court observes that the arguments employed to defend the legitimacy of the compulsory licensing of journalists are linked to only some, but not all, of the concepts mentioned in the preceding paragraph. It has been asserted, in the first place, that compulsory licensing is the normal way to organize the practice of the professions in the different countries that have subjected journalism to the same regime. Thus, the Government has pointed out that in Costa Rica

there exists an unwritten rule of law, of a structural and constitutive nature, regarding the professions. This rule can be stated in the following terms: each profession must organize itself, by law, into a public corporation called a "colegio."

Similarly, the Commission has indicated that

> There is no opposition to the supervision and control of the exercise of the professions, either directly by government agencies, or indirectly through an authorization or delegation made for that purpose by a corresponding statute to a professional organization or association, under the vigilance and control of the state, since the former, in performing its mission, must always be subject to the law. Membership in a professional association or the requirement of a card for the exercise of the profession of journalists does not imply restriction of the freedoms of thought and expression, but rather a regulation that the Executive Branch may make on the validation of academic degrees, as well as the inspection of their exercise, as an imperative of social order and a guarantee of a better protection of human rights (Schmidt Case, supra 15).

The Colegio de Periodistas of Costa Rica also pointed out that "this same requirement (licensing) exists in the organic laws of all professional 'colegios.'" For its part, the Federación Lationoamericana de Periodistas, in the observations that it submitted to the Court as amicus curiae, stated that some Latin American constitutions stipulate the compulsory licensing for the professions in a manner similar to that prescribed by the here relevant law, and that this stipulation has the same normative rank as does freedom of expression.

61. Second, it has been argued that compulsory licensing seeks to achieve goals, linked with professional ethics and responsibility, that are useful to the community at large. . . .

62. It has also been argued that licensing is a means of guaranteeing the independence of journalists in relation to their employers. . . .

63. The Court, in relating these arguments to the restrictions provided for in Article 13(2) of the Convention, observes that they do not directly involve the idea of justifying the compulsory licensing of journalists as a means of guaranteeing "respect for the rights or reputations of others" or "the protection of national security" or "public health or morals" (Art. 13(2)). Rather, these arguments seek to justify compulsory licensing as a way to ensure public order (Art. 13(2)(b)) as a just demand of the general welfare in a democratic society (Art. 32(2)).

64. In fact it is possible, within the framework of the Convention, to understand the meaning of public order as a reference to the conditions that assure the normal and harmonious functioning of institutions based on a coherent system of values and principles. In that sense, restrictions on the exercise of certain rights and freedoms can be justified on the ground that they assure public order. The Court interprets the argument to be that compulsory licensing can be seen, structurally, as the way to organize the exercise of the professions in general. This contention would justify the

submission of journalists to such a licensing regime on the theory that it is compelled by public order.

65. The concept of general welfare, as articulated in Article 32(2) of the Convention, has been directly invoked to justify the compulsory licensing of journalists. The Court must address this argument since it believes that, even without relying on Article 32(2), it can be said that, in general, the exercise of the rights guaranteed by the Convention must take the general welfare into account. In the opinion of the Court that does not mean, however, that Article 32(2) is automatically and equally applicable to all the rights which the Convention protects, including especially those rights in which the restrictions or limitations that may be legitimately imposed on the exercise of a certain right are specified in the provision itself. Article 32(2) contains a general statement that is designed for those cases in particular in which the Convention, in proclaiming a right, makes no special reference to possible legitimate restrictions.

66. Within the framework of the Convention, it is possible to understand the concept of general welfare as referring to the conditions of social life that allow members of society to reach the highest level of personal development and the optimum achievement of democratic values. In that sense, it is possible to conceive of the organization of society in a manner that strengthens the functioning of democratic institutions and preserves and promotes the full realization of the rights of the individual as an imperative of the general welfare. It follows therefrom that the arguments that view compulsory licensing as a means of assuring professional responsibility and ethics and, moreover, as a guarantee of the freedom and independence of journalists in relation to their employers, appear to be based on the idea that such licensing is compelled by the demands of the general welfare.

67. The Courts must recognize, nevertheless, the difficulty inherent in the attempt of defining with precision the concepts of "public order" and "general welfare." It also recognizes that both concepts can be used as much to affirm the rights of the individual against the exercise of governmental power as to justify the imposition of limitations on the exercise of those rights in the name of collective interests. In this respect, the Court wishes to emphasize that "public order" or "general welfare" may under no circumstances be invoked as a means of denying a right guaranteed by the Convention or to impair or deprive it of its true content. (See Art. 29(a) of the Convention.) Those concepts, when they are invoked as a ground for limiting human rights, must be subjected to an interpretation that is strictly limited to the "just demands" of "a democratic society," which takes account of the need to balance the competing interests involved and the need to preserve the object and purpose of the Convention.

68. The Court observes that the organization of professions in general, by means of professional "colegios," is not per se contrary to the Convention, but that it is a method for regulation and control to ensure that they act in good faith and in accordance with the ethical demands of the profes-

sion. If the notion of public order, therefore, is thought of in that sense, that is to say, as the conditions that assure the normal and harmonious functioning of the institutions on the basis of a coherent system of values and principles, it is possible to conclude that the organization of the practice of professions is included in that order.

69. The Court also believes, however, that that same concept of public order in a democratic society requires the guarantee of the widest possible circulation of news, ideas and opinions as well as the widest access to information by society as a whole. Freedom of expression constitutes the primary and basic element of the public order of a democratic society, which is not conceivable without free debate and the possibility that dissenting voices be fully heard. . . .

70. Freedom of expression is a cornerstone upon which the very existence of a democratic society rests. It is indispensable for the formation of public opinion. It is also a *conditio sine qua non* for the development of political parties, trade unions, scientific and cultural societies and, in general, those who wish to influence the public. It represents, in short, the means that enable the community, when exercising its options, to be sufficiently informed. Consequently, it can be said that a society that is not well informed is not a society that is truly free.

71. Within this context, journalism is the primary and principal manifestation of freedom of expression of thought. For that reason, because it is linked with freedom of expression, which is an inherent right of each individual, journalism cannot be equated to a profession that is merely granting a service to the public through the application of some knowledge or training acquired in a university or through those who are enrolled in a certain professional "colegio."

72. The argument that a law on the compulsory licensing of journalists does not differ from similar legislation applicable to other professions does not take into account the basic problem that is presented with respect to the compatibility between such a law and the Convention. The problem results from the fact that Article 13 expressly protects freedom "to seek, receive, and impart information and ideas of all kinds . . . either orally, in writing, in print. . . ." The profession of journalism — the thing journalists do — involves, precisely, the seeking, receiving and imparting of information. The practice of journalism consequently requires a person to engage in activities that define or embrace the freedom of expression which the Convention guarantees.

73. This is not true of the practice of law or medicine, for example. Unlike journalism, the practice of law and medicine — that is to say, the things that lawyers or physicians do — is not an activity specifically guaranteed by the Convention. It is true that the imposition of certain restrictions on the practice of law would be incompatible with the enjoyment of various rights that the Convention guarantees. For example, a law that prohibited all lawyers from acting as defense counsel in cases involving anti-state activi-

ties might be deemed to violate the accused's rights to counsel under Article 8 of the Convention and, hence, be incompatible with it. But no one right guaranteed in the Convention exhaustively embraces or defines the practice of law as does Article 13 when it refers to the exercise of a freedom that encompasses the activity of journalism. The same is true of medicine.

74. It has been argued that what the compulsory licensing of journalists seeks to achieve is to protect a paid occupation and that it is not directed against the exercise of freedom of expression as long as it does not involve remuneration and that, in that sense, it deals with a subject other than that dealt with by Article 13 of the Convention. This argument is based on a distinction between professional journalism and the exercise of freedom of expression that the Court cannot accept. This argument assumes that it is possible to distinguish freedom of expression from the professional practice of journalism, which is not possible. Moreover, it implies serious dangers if carried to its logical conclusion. The practice of professional journalism cannot be differentiated from freedom of expression. On the contrary, both are obviously intertwined, for the professional journalist is not, nor can he be, anything but someone who has decided to exercise freedom of expression in a continuous, regular and paid manner. It should also be noted that the argument that the differentiation is possible could lead to the conclusion the guarantees contained in Article 13 of the Convention do not apply to professional journalists.

75. The argument advanced in the preceding paragraph does not take into account, furthermore, that freedom of expression includes imparting and receiving information and has a double dimension, individual and collective. This fact indicates that the circumstance whether or not that right is exercised as a paid profession cannot be deemed legitimate in determining whether the restriction is contemplated in Article 13(2) of the Convention because, without ignoring the fact that a guild has the right to seek the best working conditions for its members, that is not a good enough reason to deprive society of possible sources of information.

76. The Court concludes, therefore, that reasons of public order that may be valid to justify compulsory licensing of other professions cannot be invoked in the case of journalism because they would have the effect of permanently depriving those who are not members of the right to make full use of the rights that Article 13 of the Convention grants to each individual. Hence, it would violate the basic principles of a democratic public order on which the Convention itself is based.

77. The argument that licensing is a way to guarantee society objective and truthful information by means of codes of professional responsibility and ethics, is based on considerations of general welfare. But, in truth, as has been shown, general welfare requires the greatest possible amount of information, and it is the full exercise of the right of expression that benefits this general welfare. In principle, it would be a contradiction to invoke a restriction to freedom of expression as a means of guaranteeing it. Such an

approach would ignore the primary and fundamental character of that right, which belongs to each and every individual as well as the public at large. A system that controls the right of expression in the name of a supposed guarantee of the correctness and truthfulness of the information that society receives can be the source of great abuse and, ultimately, violates the right to information that this same society has. . . .

79. The Court believes, therefore, that the freedom and independence of journalists is an asset that must be protected and guaranteed. In the terms of the Convention, however, the restrictions authorized on freedom of expression must be "necessary to ensure" certain legitimate goals, that is to say, it is not enough that the restriction be useful (supra 46) to achieve a goal, that is, that it can be achieved through it. Rather, it must be necessary, which means that it must be shown that it cannot reasonably be achieved through a means less restrictive of a right protected by the Convention. In this sense, the compulsory licensing of journalists does not comply with the requirements of Article 13(2) of the Convention because the establishment of a law that protects the freedom and independence of anyone who practices journalism is perfectly conceivable without the necessity of restricting that practice only to a limited group of the community.

80. The Court also recognizes the need for the establishment of a code that would assure the professional responsibility and ethics of journalists and impose penalties for infringements of such a code. The Court also believes that it may be entirely proper for a State to delegate, by law, authority to impose sanctions for infringements of the code of professional responsibility and ethics. But, when dealing with journalists, the restrictions contained in Article 13(2) and the character of the profession, to which reference has been made (supra 72-75), must be taken into account.

81. It follows from what has been said that a law licensing journalists, which does not allow those who are not members of the "colegio" to practice journalism and limits access to the "colegio" to university graduates who have specialized in certain fields, is not compatible with the Convention. Such a law would contain restrictions to freedom of expression that are not authorized by Article 13(2) of the Convention and would consequently be in violation not only [of] the right of each individual to seek and impart information and ideas through any means of his choice, but also the right of the public at large to receive information without any interference.

[Following this reasoning, the Court proceeded to find the specific Costa Rican licensing law incompatible with the Convention. The Court's opinion was unanimous, although separate opinions or declarations were filed by four of the seven judges.]

On the Court's advisory jurisdiction, see generally Buergenthal, The OAS and the Protection of Rights, 3 Emory J. Intl. Dispute Res. 1, 19-23

(1988); Buergenthal, The Advisory Practice of the Inter-American Court of Human Rights, 79 Am. J. Intl. L. 1 (1985).

Note: *The U.S. Position on Ratification of the American Convention on Human Rights*

As noted in Problem III, the American Convention is one of several human rights treaties that have been pending before the U.S. Senate since the Carter Administration. As of late 1994, there seemed little likelihood that the American Convention would be ratified in the near future, and the only official U.S. government position on its ratification remains that articulated in 1977. Many of the Carter Administration's objections to substantive provisions of the Convention are similar to those it made with respect to the Civil and Political Covenant, discussed at pages 240-246 of Problem III.

Message of the President Transmitting Four Treaties Pertaining to Human Rights
S. Exec. Doc. Nos. 95-C, D, E, and F, 95th Cong. 2d Sess.
XVII-XXIII (Feb. 23, 1978)

Department of State
Washington, December 17, 1977.

The PRESIDENT,
The White House.
The PRESIDENT: I have the honor to submit to you, with a view to its transmission to the Senate for advice and consent to ratification subject to specified reservations, understandings and declarations, the American Convention on Human Rights, signed by you and by Ambassador Gale McGee on June 1, 1977. . . .
Along with the United Nations Covenants on Human Rights and the United Nations Convention on the Elimination of All Forms of Racial Discrimination, the American Convention on Human Rights constitutes a significant contribution to the developing international law of human rights. The American Convention, like the United Nations treaties, gives legally binding expression to human rights that are, for the most part, accepted in United States law and practice. The Convention provides for extensive protection of personal liberty, preserves the right to a fair trial, to freedom of assembly, and to participation in government, and protects many other rights of great significance to Americans. In addition, the Convention includes provisions which recognize certain rights that are not protected by the United Nations human rights treaties. Among the most

important of these are the provision protecting the right to privacy (Article 11), and the provision concerning territorial application (Article 28), which takes account of the federal structure of many countries in the Western Hemisphere, including the United States.

The large number of States concerned and the disparity of views on certain questions made it impossible to negotiate a convention that was in every respect consonant with United States law. The small number of provisions not in accord with United States law requires reservations which, along with a number of interpretive understandings and declarations, will permit United States ratification of the Convention should the Senate give its approval. The Department of Justice is of the view that, with the reservations, understandings and declarations recommended below, there are no constitutional or other legal objections to United States ratification of the Convention.

The following is a summary of the provisions of the Convention, with the reservations, understandings and declarations to them recommended to the Senate by the Department of State.

The Convention begins with a general provision on nondiscrimination (Article 1), and follows with an obligation to adopt legislative or other measures as may be necessary to give effect to the rights and freedoms protected by the Convention (Article 2). While the latter provision thus indicates that the substantive provisions of the Convention are not self-executing, in order to avoid possible discrepancies in wording and to leave the implementation of all substantive provisions to the domestic legislative and judicial process, the following declaration is recommended:

> The United States declares that the provisions of Articles 1 through 32 of this Convention are not self-executing.

This declaration will ensure that no substantive provisions of the Convention will operate as domestic law except insofar as they may be reflected in existing law or future legislation.

Articles 3 through 25 of the Convention set forth the fundamental civil and political rights protected by the Convention. Article 3, on juridical personality, states that every person has the right to recognition as a person before the law. Article 4 deals with the right to life generally, and includes provisions on capital punishment. Many of the provisions of Article 4 are not in accord with United States law and policy, or deal with matters in which the law is unsettled. The Senate may wish to enter a reservation as follows:

> United States adherence to Article 4 is subject to the constitution and other law of the United States.

Article 5, on the right to humane treatment, bans cruel, inhuman or degrading punishment, and requires that persons deprived of their liberty be treated with respect for the dignity of the human person.

Paragraph (4) of Article 5 provides that accused persons, except in unusual circumstances, are to be segregated from convicted persons. Paragraph (5) requires that minors subject to criminal proceedings are to be separated from adults and brought before specialized tribunals as speedily as possible. Paragraph (6) stipulates that punishment constituting of deprivation of liberty shall have as an essential aim the reform and social readaptation of prisoners.

Paragraphs (4) and (6) of Article 5 set forth standards of treatment for prisoners not yet met in United States practice. With respect to paragraph (5), the law reserves the right to try minors as adults in certain cases and there is no present intent to revise these laws. The following statement is recommended:

> The United States considers the provisions of paragraphs (4) and (6) of Article 5 as goals to be achieved progressively rather than through immediate implementation, and, with respect to paragraph (5), reserves the right in appropriate cases to subject minors to procedures and penalties applicable to adults. . . .

Article 8 sets forth the several procedural and other requirements necessary for a fair trial, including an independent and impartial tribunal, a presumption of innocence, language assistance if necessary, prior notification in detail of charges, adequate time and means for the preparation of a defense, the right to counsel of the defendant's own choosing, the right to counsel provided by the State, the right to examine witnesses in court and to obtain their appearance, the right not to be compelled to be a witness against oneself, and the right of appeal. Confessions of guilt are valid only if made without coercion of any kind. A statement of understanding is recommended as follows:

> The United States understands that subparagraph (2)(e) of Article 8 does not require the provision of court-appointed counsel for petty offenses for which imprisonment will not be imposed or when the defendant is financially able to retain counsel; it further understands that subparagraph (2)(f) does not forbid requiring an indigent defendant to make a showing that the witness is necessary in order for his attendance to be compelled by the court. The United States understands that the prohibition on double jeopardy contained in paragraph (4) is applicable only when the judgment of acquittal has been rendered by a court of the same governmental unit, whether the Federal Government or a constituent unit, which is seeking a new trial for the same cause.

Article 9 prohibits ex post facto criminal laws, and requires as well that the benefit of any statutory reductions in the penalty for crimes be applied retroactively. The later provision, which goes beyond existing United States law, necessitates a reservation as follows:

> The United States does not adhere to the third sentence of Article 9.

Article 10 provides for the right to compensation in the event of a sentence imposed through "a miscarriage of justice." United States law provides only a limited right to recovery, available to innocent persons who have been unjustly convicted and imprisoned, and not to those whose improper conviction was due to procedural errors alone. The Senate may wish to record its understanding that the United States Code, Title 28, §§1495 and 2513, meets the requirements of Article 10.

Article 11 protects the right to privacy. Article 12 provides for freedom of conscience and religion, subject to legal limitations "necessary to protect public safety, health, or morals, or the rights or freedom of others."

Article 13 protects freedom of thought and expression, including the right to seek, receive, and impart information and ideas of all kinds, regardless of frontiers. Paragraph (2) of Article 13 states that these rights "shall not be subject to prior censorship" but shall be subject to subsequent imposition of liability in order to ensure respect for the rights or reputation of others, or the protection of national security, public order, health or morals. . . .

Paragraph (5) of Article 13 stipulates that "any propaganda for war and any advocacy of national, racial, or religious hatred that constitute incitements to lawless violence or to any other similar illegal action against any person or group of persons on any grounds including those of race, color, religion, language, or national origin shall be considered as offenses punishable by law."

Both paragraph (2) and paragraph (5) of Article 13 raise questions under the First Amendment and of consistency with United States law. The following reservation is recommended:

> The United States reserves the right to permit prior restraints in strictly defined circumstances where the right to judicial review is immediately available; the United States does not adhere to paragraph (5) of Article 13.

Article 14, on the right of reply, provides:

> 1. Anyone injured by inaccurate or offensive statements or ideas disseminated to the public in general by a legally regulated medium of communication has the right to reply or make a correction using the same communications outlet, under such conditions as the law may establish.
> 2. The correction or reply shall not in any case remit other legal liabilities that may have been incurred.
> 3. For the effective protection of honor and reputation, every publisher, and every newspaper, motion picture, radio, and television company, shall have a person responsible, who is not protected by immunities or other privileges.

Under United States law the "fairness doctrine," applicable to radio and television, is narrower than the right provided by paragraph (1) of Article 14. Further, paragraph (3) does not reflect the sovereign immunity granted government publishers under United States law. The following reservation and understanding are recommended:

> The United States does not adhere to paragraph (1) of Article 14, and understands that paragraph (3) of that Article applies only to non-governmental entities. . . .

Article 17, on the rights of the family, requires that the family unit be protected by society and the State. No marriage is to be entered into without the free and full consent of the intending spouses. Paragraphs (4) and (5) forbid discrimination against illegitimate children and obligate States to take steps to eliminate discrimination between spouses during marriage and in the event of its dissolution. Both paragraphs state goals towards which United States law is moving, but neither goal has been fully achieved. The following statement is recommended:

> The United States considers the provisions of paragraphs (4) and (5) of Article 17 as goals to be achieved progressively rather than through immediate implementation. . . .

Paragraph (8) of Article 22 states that in no case may an alien be deported or returned to a country in which his life or freedom would be endangered because of his race, nationality, religion, social status or political opinions. United States law and the Protocol Relating to the Status of Refugees, to which the United States is party, permit immigration officers, in their discretion, to deport persons even to countries in which their lives or freedom are so threatened if such persons have committed a serious crime or are considered a danger to the security of this country. The following statement is recommended:

> The United States considers that its adherence to the Protocol Relating to the Status of Refugees constitutes compliance with the obligation set forth in paragraph (8) of Article 22. . . .

Article 26 is the only provision in the American Convention devoted to economic, social, and cultural rights. It requires States Parties to adopt measures, particularly those of an economic and technical nature, "with a view to achieving progressively, by legislation or other appropriate means, the full realization of the rights implicit in the economic, social, educational, scientific, and cultural standards set forth in the Charter of the Organization of American States as amended by the Protocol of Buenos Aires."* . . .

Article 28 is the federal State clause, which takes account of and is in the interest of federal systems such as the United States. It provides that the

---

* An additional protocol, which would expand the protections of the American Convention in the area of economic, social, and cultural rights, was adopted by the OAS in 1988, O.A.S.T.S. No. 69, but it had been ratified by only three states (Ecuador, Panama, and Suriname) by the end of 1994. (See the Documentary Supplement.) The protocol will enter into force when 11 ratifications have been received. — EDS.

national government is to implement those provisions of the Convention over whose subject matter it exercises legislative and judicial jurisdiction. Where the several states have jurisdiction, the national government is to take "suitable measures" in accordance with its constitution and laws, to the end that the state authorities "may adopt appropriate provisions" for the fulfillment of the terms of the Convention.

The second half of the American Convention, including Articles 33 through 82, establishes machinery for monitoring compliance. The Inter-American Commission on Human Rights is empowered to receive complaints from individuals or groups or upon appropriate declaration, from States regarding violations of the rights protected by the Convention.

Petitions or communications are not admissible unless domestic law remedies have been exhausted. The Commission's powers are limited to requesting information from the State whose compliance with the Convention is in question, requesting assistance for the carrying out of any necessary investigation, and making recommendations and releasing to the public reports on unresolved cases.

Should the Senate give its advice and consent to ratification of the Convention, it is contemplated that the United States will make a declaration pursuant to Article 45, which permits, but does not require, a declaration recognizing the competence of the Commission "to receive and examine communications in which a State Party alleges that another State Party has committed a violation of a human right set forth in this Convention." As with the United Nations Covenant on Civil and Political Rights, it is in the interest of the United States to participate in and influence the State-to-State complaint procedure.

The enforcement machinery of the Convention includes as well an Inter-American Court of Human Rights which gains jurisdiction over cases by the voluntary declaration of States. Cases may also be submitted by special agreement between the parties to a dispute. Acceptance by the United States of the Court's jurisdiction, whether by means of a voluntary declaration or by a special agreement, would of course require separate Senate advice and consent. The Court, which votes by majority, has power to require that the injured party be ensured the enjoyment of the freedom violated, and, if appropriate, it may require the payment of compensation. It may issue temporary or permanent injunctions in all cases concerning the interpretation and application of the provisions of the Convention. States Parties to the Convention undertake to obey the judgments of the Court in cases to which they are parties.

The American Convention on Human Rights is a significant advance in the development of the international law of human rights and in the development of human rights law among the American States. United States ratification of the Convention is likely to spur interest in this important document among other American States. United States adherence is in the national interest and in that of the world community. It is our hope that the Senate, after full consideration, will give prompt approval to the Convention, and that the United States will become a party to it.

Respectfully submitted.

WARREN CHRISTOPHER

B. Other Initiatives

Within the past decade, the Organization of American States has addressed several human rights issues, including torture, indigenous peoples, violence against women, and disappearances, in three new instruments. Three of these initiatives have led to the adoption of new multilateral treaties.

The Inter-American Convention to Prevent and Punish Torture, signed Dec. 9, 1985, entered into force Feb. 28, 1987, O.A.S.T.S. No. 67, O.A.S. Doc. OEA/SER.A/42, does not create a separate body to visit places of detention or otherwise take an active role to prevent torture from occurring, unlike its European counterpart (see pages 762-765 of Problem IX). Instead, the Convention obliges parties, inter alia, to prevent and punish torture within their jurisdiction and to consider torture to be an extraditable crime. The minimal implementation machinery, found in Article 17, merely provides that parties "undertake to inform the Inter-American Commission . . . of any legislative, judicial, administrative, or other measures they adopt" to implement the convention and that the Commission "endeavor in its annual report to analyze the existing situation . . . in regard to the prevention and elimination of torture" in O.A.S. member states.

On the initiative of the Inter-American Commission of Women, an O.A.S. specialized agency not heretofore noted for its activity in the human rights field, the O.A.S. adopted in 1994 the Inter-American Convention on the Prevention, Punishment and Eradication of Violence against Women ("Convention of Belem do Para"), adopted June 9, 1994, entered into force March 6, 1995, 33 Intl. Legal Materials 1534 (1995). The convention, which required only two ratifications to enter into force, obliges states "to pursue, by all appropriate means and without delay, policies to prevent, punish and eradicate" violence against women, whether committed by private persons or state agents. State parties are to report to the Commission of Women on measures they have taken to implement the Convention, and Article 12 authorizes the Inter-American Commission on Human Rights to consider petitions from any person, group, or NGO alleging violations of the Convention, under the same rules applicable to other petitions.

Finally, the O.A.S. also has adopted and opened for ratification the Inter-American Convention on Forced Disappearance of Persons, adopted June 9, 1994, 33 Intl. Legal Materials 1529 (1995) which had not entered into force by early 1995.

Given the fact that none of these treaties create new enforcement mechanisms, and bearing in mind the financial and other difficulties of the Commission raised in the report of the Association of the Bar of the City of

New York, pages 793–798 supra, the impact of these new instruments may be somewhat problematic.

III. The African Charter on Human and Peoples' Rights

Welch, The African Commission on Human and Peoples' Rights: A Five-Year Report and Assessment
14 Human Rts. Q. 43, 45-49, 53-57 (1992)

The Organization of African States (OAU) was conceived and born in 1963 in a context of nearly untrammeled state sovereignty, in which heads of states sought sedulously to safeguard the independence so recently won. Only passing mention was made in the OAU Charter of human rights. Eighteen years later, however, following a period of widely decried abuses of basic liberties in several member states, the OAU's policy-making body adopted the African Charter on Human and Peoples' Rights (the Banjul Charter). In late 1987 the African Commission on Human and Peoples' Rights, created by the Banjul Charter, started to function. As the body nears its fifth anniversary, a preliminary report and assessment are in order. . . .

In content, language, and organization, the Banjul Charter owes much to prior international human rights documents, notably the Universal Declaration of Human Rights and the two International Covenants, on Civil and Political Rights and on Economic, Social and Cultural Rights. On the other hand, its drafters, headed by the noted Sengalese jurist Keba Mbaye, sought to infuse a distinctly African character into the document. While most of the twenty-nine articles in the Charter that specify rights and freedoms apply to individuals, a good number involve collective rights of "peoples." The Banjul Charter begins with a statement of nondiscrimination (i.e., no differentiation on the basis of "race, ethnic group, color, sex, language, religion, political or any other opinion, national and social origin, fortune, birth or other status"). It lists a variety of civil and political ("first generation") rights in Articles 3 through 14 and economic, social, and cultural ("second generation") rights in Articles 15 through 18. The Charter blazes some new ground by including rights of peoples ("third generation") in Articles 19 through 24 and "duties" in Articles 25 through 29. Duties apply both to states parties (including the responsibility "to promote and ensure through teaching, education and publication the respect of the rights and freedoms contained in the present Charter") and to individuals. As A.H. Robertson observed: "[T]he States concerned wished to put forward a distinctive conception of human rights in which civil and political rights were seen to be counter-balanced by duties of social solidarity, just as they are complemented by economic and social rights and supplemented by peoples' rights."

Commentators on the Banjul Charter have tended to stress its short-comings. Perhaps the mildest rebuke comes from B. Obinna Okere, who deems the document "modest in its objectives and flexible in its means." One of the strongest comes from the respected weekly *West Africa*, which noted that "congenital defects [in the Banjul Charter] in no small way account for the near irrelevance of the Charter and its institutions to Africa's political life." Criticism is levelled particularly at "claw back" clauses that essentially confine the Charter's protections to rights as they are defined in national law. Rights are qualified, but no reference is made to the circumstances that may lead to their limitation. For example, Article 6 provides that "[e]very individual shall have the right to liberty and to the security of his person," but with the proviso that "[n]o one may be deprived of his freedom *except for reasons and conditions previously laid down by law.*" Nowhere does the Charter define these "reasons and conditions," nor does it subject them to any test of conformity with standards such as those in the International Covenant on Civil and Political Rights. . . .

The major OAU instrument for ensuring the observance of the rights in the Charter is the African Commission on Human and Peoples' Rights. As much of the text of the Charter is devoted to the Commission's organization, mandate, and procedure as to the rights and duties just mentioned. Politically, the African Commission is subordinate to the OAU Assembly of Heads of State and Government, to which it reports. The Commission's members are elected by the Assembly; publication of its reports comes only after Assembly consideration; and the OAU provides financial and staff support.

Of the three functioning regional systems for protection of human rights (Africa, the Americas, and Western Europe), the African system is the only one lacking a court to complement the Commission. Like the other protective regimes, however, it relies on an essentially political body (the OAU) for enforcement of its decisions.

Apart from stipulating the means of electing members and its reporting relationship to the Assembly of Heads of State and Government, the Banjul Charter offers only general guidance about what the Commission should do and how it should do it. According to Article 45, the Commission's functions are largely promotional:

The functions of the Commission shall be:

1. To promote Human and Peoples' Rights and in particular:

a. To collect documents, undertake studies and researches on African problems in the field of human and peoples' rights, organize seminars, symposia and conferences, disseminate information, encourage national and local institutions concerned with human and peoples' rights and should the case arise, give its views or make recommendations to Governments.

b. to formulate and lay down, principles and rules aimed at solving legal problems relating to human and peoples' rights and fundamental freedoms upon which African Governments may base their legislations.

c. to co-operate with other African and international institutions concerned with the promotion and protection of human and peoples' rights.

2. Ensure the protection of human and peoples' rights under conditions laid down by the present Charter.

3. Interpret all the provisions of the present Charter at the request of a State Party, an institution of the OAU or an African organization recognized by the OAU.

4. Perform any other tasks which may be entrusted to it by the Assembly of Heads of State and Government.

The Commission "may resort to any appropriate method of investigation," and may hear from the OAU Secretary-General "or any other person capable of enlightening it." In common with the American and European Conventions, the Banjul Charter provides that the African Commission may deal with a matter only after "local remedies, if they exist, have been exhausted," unless "achieving these remedies would be unduly prolonged." In instances of communications from one state party involving actions of another, the Commission shall attempt "to reach an amicable solution"; its report of "facts and . . . findings" shall be sent to the Assembly, and may include recommendations. "Other" communications may be considered by vote of a majority of Commission members, though only if several conditions are met: authors must be indicated; communications must be "compatible" with the OAU and Banjul Charters; communications must "not [be] written in disparaging or insulting language directed against" the state or the OAU; communications must not be based exclusively on media reports; local remedies must have been exhausted (unless such procedure is "unduly prolonged"); communications must be submitted within a reasonable period; and communications must not deal with cases already settled by the states involved. If communications, in the Commission's judgment, "reveal the existence of a series of serious or massive violations of human and peoples' rights, the Commission shall draw the attention of the Assembly . . . to these special cases"; the Assembly, in turn, may request an "in-depth study . . . and . . . factual report, accompanied by its findings and recommendations." All matters considered by the Commission remain confidential until the Assembly decides otherwise, at which point its report shall be published. The Charter lists sources from which the Commission can "draw inspiration" or which it may "take into consideration." . . .

. . . [T]he current situation of the Commission is far from satisfactory — though not as serious as its most severe critics allege. Several factors account for the weaknesses the Commission has shown to date.

First, the obligation to submit detailed reports has not been taken seriously by most states. . . .

Second, . . . the African Commission has "lacked adequate equipment, resources and support to make it truly operational." . . .

Third, confidentiality of proceedings remains a sore point. . . .

Finally, perhaps the greatest problem for the Commission lies outside its control. Human rights NGOs have yet to take root in much of Africa. . . .

The result of the dearth of NGOs is that the Commission lacks both independent, Africa-based sources of information about human rights abuses and domestic advocacy groups for its activities. Effective protection of human rights within individual countries depends not only on government institutions and policies, but also on citizen awareness and participation, in which human rights NGOs play a central role. . . .

As of late 1990 the Commission had received more than 100 petitions, which it examined in confidential sessions, but had yet either to make public any steps taken relative to them or to name the states from which they had come. . . .

As a general observation, the African Commission on Human and Peoples' Rights is reformist in nature, not revolutionary. Many factors interact to ensure that the Commission will play a relatively quiet role in African politics in the near future: the state-centric, conservative natures of the Banjul and OAU Charters; the relatively legalistic outlook of the individuals selected to the Commission; the direct links of some Commission members to discredited governments or leaders; the limited support provided by the OAU; the nonincorporation of Charter norms into domestic law; and the relative impotence of human rights NGOs in Africa. Those who expect the African Commission rapidly to ameliorate human rights conditions within ratifying states do not understand current political realities in Africa.

More recent evaluations are no more positive than the preceding excerpt, although there is evidence of an increasing willingness on the part of the African Commission and the Organization of African Unity (OAU) to consider possible reforms. The Geneva-based International Commission of Jurists and other NGOs have been actively seeking to galvanize the Commission into greater action, as suggested by the recommendations in the following paper.

International Commission of Jurists, Background Paper
Brain-Storming Session on the African Charter on Human and Peoples' Rights, Dakar, Senegal, Jan. 13-15, 1993

The crucial question is: Where do we go from here?

Recent commentaries on the African Charter would seem to indicate two schools of thought on the subject. These are the "rejectionists" and the "revisionists."

The rejectionists argue that having regard to the ineffectiveness, inefficiency and incoherence of the African Charter, it is to be properly regarded as a model of *Lex imperfecta and simulata.* (*Lex imperfecta* is the epitome of a legal instrument which prescribes norms but whose framers deliberately guarantee that it is a "law without teeth"; *lex simulata,* the cognate instrument of *lex imperfecta,* represents law which generate[s] a mirage of legal change which is consciously designed to merely enact a simulation and thus prove to be either inoperable or unenforceable.) What [it] was intended to achieve was the generation of an innocuous instrument which would do no more than provide public catharsis. The OAU [is] consistently risk averse in matters regarding sovereignty and power, and was merely responding to the unprecedented moral demands of the late 1970s that something ought to be done about human rights violations in Africa. The goal, the argument concludes, was not enforceability but rather to "steal the opposition's thunder." Consequently, the African Charter is a non-starter and should be replaced by a more effective instrument.

The revisionists are more optimistic about the African Charter's efficacy than the rejectionists. The former subscribe to the view that it is not possible to produce a perfect human rights instrument in matters relating to the balance between individual rights and state power. The practical drafting problem is how to maintain the delicate balance between these two competing interests. The relatively more conservative political environment in which the African Charter was drafted and approved explains the inherent weaknesses of the instrument. In recognition of changing circumstances, the African Charter allows for revision through amendments and protocols. Rather than advocating an outright rejection of the instrument, revisionists urge that serious attention be paid to formal and less formal methods of strengthening the human rights regime established by the African Charter. They regard the African Charter as a useful tool for further elaboration and improvement.

The position of the revisionist school raises the question as to whether or not the African Charter should be subjected to revision. The affirmative response of this school is based on three grounds: In the first place, the changing circumstances of Africa of the 90s, as reflected in the attempts to establish and consolidate democratic institutions, provide a unique opportunity to strengthen the weaknesses of the African Charter and its implementation machinery. Secondly, the role of non-governmental organizations (NGOs) in exerting moral pressure on their governments for change is likely to be intensified in a manner that would provide the catalyst for the African Charter's revision to meet the challenges of the 21st century. Finally, as the African Commission's work becomes better known in Africa, the sheer volume of demands for protection would inevitably necessitate the establishment of other protective institutions such as a human rights court.

STAGES OF REVISION

If one accepts that it is justifiable to begin the processes of the African Charter's revision, two stages may be posited.

— The first stage involves the further strengthening of the role of the African Commission. The promotional activities of the African Commission must be diversified and fully supported by NGOs. As already mentioned, to deal effectively with the problems of the African Commission's wide mandate and constituency, it is proposed that the first stage of amendment should begin with a revision of the composition of the African Commission. This should aim at increasing the membership to 15 to include women commissioners and representatives of Portuguese and Spanish-speaking African states. . . .
Another pressing amendment is the deletion of clawback clauses and the substitution of a general derogation clause. Some basic rights should remain non-derogable.

— The second stage of the revision process should focus upon further amendments and the introduction of protocols. In particular, the splitting of the African Commission's broad mandate to accommodate the establishment of an African Human Rights Court to focus upon the protective functions.

By the end of the African Commission's 14th session in December 1993, 48 of the 52 members of the OAU were parties to the African Charter, and 129 NGOs had been given observer status with the Commission. However, no information has yet been published by the African Commission giving details of either individual or interstate communications that it has considered. Despite the ending of apartheid in South Africa and some evidence of increasing democratization in other African countries, there appears to be little likelihood that the African Charter will be of more than theoretical assistance to those seeking to promote and protect human rights in Africa in the near future. In fairness, however, one should at least recall the faltering steps of other regional human rights bodies in the first few years of their existence.

On the African Charter and the Commission generally, see Flinterman and Ankumah, The African Charter on Human and Peoples' Rights, in Guide to International Human Rights Practice 159-169 (2d ed. H. Hannum ed. 1992); Gittleman, The African Charter on Human and Peoples' Rights: A Legal Analysis, 22 Va. J. Intl. L. 667 (1982). The African Commission's annual activity reports are generally reprinted in the Human Rights Law Journal.

IV.   Final Comments and Questions

1. Note that under the Inter-American system, as opposed to the European, persons filing petitions need not be victims of the alleged human rights violations. NGOs, therefore, may file petitions on behalf of other persons, which they cannot do in Europe. On the other hand, juridical persons cannot petition in the Americas, whereas in Europe they can (see the *Lithgow* case, referred to at page 765 of Problem IX supra). Which system, or blend of systems, seems preferable? Why?

2. The Inter-American Commission's country reports have been rightly praised for their quality and usefulness. However, the Commission, in the absence of specific authorizing language, has not attempted to establish a systematic reporting process *by states* along the lines of the one found in the UN Covenant on Civil and Political Rights (see pages 211-214 of Problem III). Article 43 of the American Convention permits the Commission to request information from states parties "as to the manner in which their domestic law insures the effective application of any provision of this Convention." Could an innovative Commission seize upon this language to develop an effective reporting process?

3. The Inter-American Court's decision in the Velásquez Rodríguez case that a "disappearance" constitutes a violation of the American Convention came in the same year as Judge Jensen's decision in Forti v. Suarez-Mason (see pages 148-152 of Problem II) that a "disappearance" constitutes a violation of customary international law. Certainly the respective decisions are mutually reinforcing and support the Restatement (Third) of the Foreign Relations Law of the United States' position that this norm has achieved jus cogens status (see pages 164-165 of Problem II). If the Court continues to have contentious cases referred to it, its jurisprudence may prove just as helpful as that of the European Court in establishing customary international norms in Alien Tort Statute and other cases in the United States.

4. The Inter-American Commission on Human Rights has often been criticized for the fact that it is less legalistic than its European counterpart. Given the very different political contexts in which the two bodies operate, is this a fair criticism? Is it significant that the Inter-American Commission's competence has always extended to all OAS members, while that of the European Commission is restricted to those states that have ratified the European Convention?

5. Compare the substantive rights protected under the American Convention with those protected under the European Convention. Would it still be correct to conclude that "some of the provisions of the American Convention are so advanced that it may be doubted whether there is a country in the Americas that is in full compliance with all of them," as a

former president of the Inter-American Court remarked in 1984? See Buergenthal, The Inter-American System for the Protection of Human Rights, in 2 Human Rights in International Law: Legal and Policy Issues 439, 442 (T. Meron ed. 1984).

6. A growing body of literature now exists, much of it descriptive in nature, on the Inter-American system. Among the better analytical works are T. Buergenthal, R. Norris, and D. Shelton, Protecting Human Rights in the Americas: Selected Problems (3d rev. ed. 1990); C. Medina Quiroga, The Battle of Human Rights: Gross, Systematic Violations and the Inter-American System (1988); Farer, Collectively Defending Democracy in a World of Sovereign States: The Western Hemisphere's Prospect, 15 Hum. Rts. Q. 716 (1993); Grossman, Proposals to Strengthen the Inter-American System of Protection of Human Rights, 32 German Y.B. Intl. L. 264 (1990); Shelton, The Inter-American Human Rights System, in Guide to International Human Rights Practice 119-132 (2d ed. H. Hannum ed. 1992).

7. Re-read the Background Paper from the International Commission of Jurists (ICJ), pages 830-832 supra. Is there really any difference between the "rejectionists" and the "revisionists," except for the tactical issue of how best to proceed to make the system more effective? Is there another school of thought that the ICJ neglects to mention? Another section of the ICJ paper notes that "[f]inancial matters of the African Commission are subject to the principle of confidentiality, and as such they are not publicly discussed." Is money the real problem and the real means of control exercised by the OAU?

8. The OAU Charter has never been amended to reflect the existence of the African Commission. What is the legal effect of Article 30 of the African Charter, which provides that the African Commission "shall be established within the Organization of African Unity"?

Problem XI

Human Rights in Extremis

How Can Human Rights Be
Protected in Armed Conflict, Civil
Strife, and States of Emergency?

I. Human Rights in International Armed Conflict: The Traditional Law
   of War   839
   A. An Eventful Day in My Lai Hamlet, South Vietnam, March 1968   839
   B. The Development of the Law of War   844
      Note: Historical Roots of the Concern for Human Rights in the
         Law of War   844
      Draper, Human Rights and the Law of War   844
      Note: The Law Protecting Civilians in Time of War — Interna-
         tional and Domestic   848
   C. Where Does Responsibility Lie for Violations of the Law of War?   853
      In re Yamashita   855
      Note: The Treatment of Command Responsibility in U.S.
         Domestic Law   858
   D. Prosecuting Those Persons Responsible for My Lai   859
      1. The Legal Framework and the Dramatis Personae   859
      2. The Calley Court-Martial   861
      Extracts from the Original Transcript of the Court-Martial of
         Lieutenant William Calley   862
      3. Lieutenant Calley's Conviction and the Public's Response   872
      4. The Subsequent Fate of Lieutenant Calley   873
      5. The Courts-Martial of Captain Medina and the Other My Lai
         Defendants   874
      6. "Orders" from Above: The Experience of Lieutenant James
         Duffy   875
      Lieutenant Duffy's Statement   876
      Note: The Gulf War   879
   E. Recent Developments in the Law of War   879
      Baxter, Modernizing the Law of War   880
      Note: Relevant Articles of Protocol I   884
      Roberts, The New Rules for Waging War: The Case Against
         Ratification of Additional Protocol I   888
      Aldrich, Progressive Development of the Laws of War: A Reply
         to Criticisms of the 1977 Geneva Protocol I   891

Message from the President Transmitting Protocol II Additional
to the 1949 Geneva Conventions   894
Comments and Questions   896
II. Human Rights in Internal Armed Conflict: The Developing Norms   900
A. Background   900
B. Common Article 3: Its Status and Content   901
Smith, New Protections for Victims of International Armed
Conflicts   901
Case Concerning Military and Paramilitary Activities in and
Against Nicaragua (Nicaragua v. United States)   903
C. Protocol II: Its Scope and Content   904
Smith, New Protections for Victims of International Armed
Conflicts   904
Note: The Content of Protocol II   905
Junod, Additional Protocol II: History and Scope   906
U.S. Position on Protocol II   908
D. Invoking Common Article 3 and Protocol II in Internal Armed
Conflicts   908
Weissbrodt, The Role of International Organizations in the Im-
plementation of Human Rights and Humanitarian Law in
Situations of Armed Conflict   909
Comments and Questions   912
III. Human Rights in Civil Strife and States of Emergency   914
J. Fitzpatrick, Human Rights in Crisis, The International Sys-
tem for Protecting Rights During States of Emergency   915
Note: Humanitarian Law as a Limitation on the Right of
Derogation: Internal Armed Conflict and Civil Strife Con-
trasted   922
Note: Monitoring States of Emergency   924
Habeas Corpus in Emergency Situations   927
Note: Limitation Clauses   928
IV. Final Comments and Questions   929

Traditional international law made sharp distinctions between peace
and war, between civil war and international conflict, between civilians and
soldiers. In a law that was based on the rights and duties of states as such,
that approach may have made sense. For contemporary international human rights law, however, whose fundamental task is the protection of the
rights of individuals, these distinctions often seem woefully artificial. Previous Problems have shown that a substantial body of international law, both
conventional and customary, has been developed for times of peace. This
Problem demonstrates that much the same is true for times of war. These
two bodies of international law, however, have different historical origins,
and they have operated in quite different institutional settings. As a result,

they have tended to go their own separate ways. Until the last decade or so, even practitioners in the two areas have had surprisingly little contact with one another. International human rights lawyers, with a few notable exceptions, rarely have taken full advantage of the "law of war" or "humanitarian law" in formulating and presenting complaints against states. It is important, however, in the interest of a coherent, comprehensive, and effective body of international human rights law that these barriers be broken down, that these two traditions take more notice of one another, and that a systematic body of international human rights law be developed that will protect innocent persons not only in times of armed conflict, but also during times of civil strife and states of emergency. This Problem provides some of the raw materials for that effort.

I. Human Rights in International Armed Conflict: The Traditional Law of War

A. An Eventful Day in My Lai Hamlet, South Vietnam, March 1968

Readers of the official newsletter of the United States Americal Division in Vietnam found the following report in their copy for 17 March 1968 (N.Y. Times, Nov. 26, 1969, at 10, col. 7).

> Jungle warriors together with artillery and helicopter support hit the village of My Lai early yesterday morning. Contacts [i.e., with the enemy] throughout the morning and early afternoon resulted in 128 enemy killed, 13 suspects detained and 3 weapons captured.

The "jungle warriors" referred to were Company C, 1st Battalion, 20th Infantry of the 11th Infantry Brigade, commanded by Captain Ernest R. Medina. However much difference of opinion there may be about precisely what happened at My Lai on the morning in question and about what the consequences of those occurrences should have been, there is at least widespread consensus that the terse report quoted above did far less than justice to the activities of Company C that day.

It is now common knowledge that the Army very soon had reason to know that something seriously wrong had happened at My Lai, although the now-notorious "cover-up" ensured that this knowledge did not go up too high. Civilian officials of the U.S. government had no inkling of the events at My Lai until nearly a year later. In March 1969, one Ronald Ridenhour, who had not himself been present that day but who had pieced the story together from various first-hand reports, wrote 25 letters on the subject — to the President, to the Secretary of Defense, and to 23 congressmen. At that point, the Army began looking into the affair and subsequently mounted a full-fledged investigation in the spring of 1969. In September of that year, this investigation led to the indictment of one of the platoon commanders of Company C, Lieutenant William F. Calley, on four counts of murder. The indictment was made public, but the general public took no special notice.

It was only on 24 November 1969 that the events at My Lai became common knowledge. On that day journalist Seymour Hersh brought a man named Paul Meadlo, who had been a member of Calley's platoon, to CBS for a nationally televised interview. Meadlo proceeded to stun his audience by his account of what really had happened at My Lai hamlet Number 4 that day: he told of a whole village — including old men, women, children, and babies — systematically murdered by C Company soldiers. He claimed that some 370 villagers had been killed and admitted to having been responsible himself for some 35 to 40 of those deaths. He told of one incident in which 70-odd people had been pushed into a ditch and shot en masse (an incident for which Calley later was to be indicted); some of these victims were mothers clutching children and begging for mercy.

In the course of the next few months, Mr. Hersh set about piecing together the tale of what had happened in My Lai that day, the results of which he published in 1970 in the book My Lai 4: A Report on the Massacre and Its Aftermath. The following brief account is based on these findings.

C Company, new to Vietnam in December 1967, had been in the field for some 40 days in a grueling, frustrating search and destroy operation in Quang Ngai Province. They encountered few enemy troops face to face, but they did acquire a deep-seated contempt for the Vietnamese people, which manifested itself in a systematic policy of beating any civilian prisoners who came into their custody. At first, the beatings were irregular, until officers Medina and Calley convinced the company that most of the suspects in the area were Viet Cong.

In the course of its missions, C Company encountered several booby traps. On 25 February 1968, it stumbled into a well-laid minefield, which killed 6 and seriously wounded 12. For his efforts in rescuing the wounded, Medina was awarded the Silver Star, the Army's third highest medal.

On 15 March 1968, the eve of the My Lai operation, the company held a funeral for one of their number who had been killed by a booby trap. It was a highly emotional moment, and it was on this occasion that Medina stood up to tell his assembled troops about the next day's mission. He claimed that they would be outnumbered at least 2-1 in My Lai but added that he did not expect heavy casualties. Much of what happened at My Lai stemmed from what Medina said that preceding day, but the facts are in sharp dispute. Medina later said that he gave no instructions on what to do with the women and children. One soldier disputed this assertion during the subsequent Army investigation, claiming that Medina ordered the men to kill everyone in the village. Other soldiers recalled that Medina ordered the destruction of the village itself, but gave no explicit orders regarding the inhabitants.

In any case, C Company started toward My Lai the following morning at 7:30 A.M. Two platoons swept into the village — Lieutenant Calley's to the south, and Lieutenant Stephen Brooks's to the north. A third platoon, with which Medina himself traveled, was held in reserve.

The target hamlet had a population of about 700 people. It long since had become known that U.S. soldiers assumed that anyone taking flight was a member of the Viet Cong, so the villagers stayed calm. Senseless brutality began almost immediately: a man taken into custody after routine searches of the huts was bayonetted in the back; a middle-aged man was thrown down a well, and a hand grenade was dropped in after him. Such isolated events were only the beginning.

Shooting then began to break out all over the village. One enlisted man later described his version of the scene to the Army's criminal investigation division (C.I.D.): "We were all psyched up, and as a result, when we got there the shooting started, almost as a chain reaction. The majority of us had expected us to meet VC combat troops, but this did not turn out to be so. . . . Everybody was just firing. After they got in the village, I guess that you could say that the men were out of control." Men walked up to huts, blindly pouring rifle and machine gun fire inside.

The Brooks platoon entered its part of the hamlet with guns blazing but upon finding only women and children became uncertain what to do. One soldier stated that the platoon then radioed Medina about the situation, Medina replying that they were to "just keep going."

Serious uncertainty now begins as to Medina's activity. He himself claimed that he did not enter the hamlet until well after 10:00 A.M. One soldier from the Brooks platoon reported that Medina was "right behind" as that unit entered My Lai. Another reported that Medina shot several civilians as he entered the hamlet. One soldier made a detailed allegation of Medina's personally shooting one woman and one teen-aged boy and also of his ordering everyone to be killed. On the other hand, Medina's own radio operator doubted that he ever entered the hamlet.

Most people were being shot inside their houses or just outside their doorways. Villagers who tried to flee were herded into bunkers or drainage ditches and hand grenaded.

Several soldiers later had vivid recollections of Lieutenant Calley's activities that morning. One report was that he found an old lady in bed, with a white robed man (probably a Buddhist monk) praying over her. Calley reportedly asked the man about the Viet Cong (through an interpreter). After the monk denied being a Viet Cong, Calley took him outside, pushed him into a rice paddy, and shot him. As we shall see below, Calley later was to be convicted of murder for this incident.

In the meantime, about 70 people had been herded together near a ditch and left by Calley under the charge of Meadlo and several other soldiers. "You know what I want you to do with them," Meadlo later reported Calley as saying. Ten minutes later, Calley returned, this time being more explicit. "Haven't you got rid of them yet?" he asked. "I want them dead." Calley then began shooting them, ordering Meadlo to do likewise. Meadlo at first followed orders, killing 20 to 25 by his own estimate. He then refused to do any more killing, at which point Calley ordered one Robert Maples to load his gun and begin firing. Maples refused. Seconds after this shooting stopped, a two-year-old boy crawled out of the ditch crying and began to run back toward the hamlet. After a long pause, Calley ran after the child, threw him back in the ditch, and shot him. This incident, too, was to figure prominently in Calley's court-martial.

There were some isolated acts of sanity that day. Chief Warrant Officer Hugh Thompson, a helicopter pilot, had been witnessing the carnage from overhead. Appalled by what he observed, Thompson landed his craft to rescue the civilians from Calley's troops. Before leaving his helicopter, Thompson had ordered his subordinates that if the Americans fired again at the Vietnamese, then they were to open fire on the Americans. Calley angrily told Thompson that the only way to get the women and children out of the ditch was with hand grenades. Thompson stood his ground between Calley's men and the ditch while the helicopters rescued 9 people (5 of them children). After the helicopter flew off, Calley ordered one of his soldiers, Ron Grzesik, to kill the remaining survivors. Grzesik refused, twice. In another part of the hamlet, one soldier who came upon a group of children asked for and received permission from an officer to let them go unharmed.

Such actions, though, were all too few on that macabre day. The third platoon, which had been in reserve earlier in the morning, entered the

Photograph of My Lai

village and promptly joined the slaughter. Several soldiers began molesting a 15-year-old Vietnamese girl, an incident that caused several villagers to begin fighting the soldiers. At the approach of a photographer, a burst of automatic fire put a stop to the fracas. A small child who had chanced to survive the burst was then shot. Platoon leader West was annoyed that a photographer had been present: "I thought it was wrong for him to stand up and take pictures of these things. Even though we had to do it, I thought, we didn't have to take pictures of it."

By 10:30 A.M., the worst was over. A large part of the village was in flames. One soldier was so appalled by the cruelty about him that he shot himself in the foot in order to be evacuated. Medina by this time was giving orders that the shooting stop. Lieutenant Brooks radioed Medina for instructions about what to do with three men who were found still alive. "Don't kill them," Medina is said to have replied. "There's been too much of that already." One soldier recalled that Medina dashed frantically about the hamlet telling his troops to start moving out. There was a halt for lunch shortly after 11:00; then the systematic destruction of the hamlet continued to completion. Shortly after noon, C Company left My Lai.

The official body count, as noted above, was 128, although it is difficult to see how such a figure was reached: the actual death toll was by all accounts far higher. The official brigade account of the action was wildly inaccurate. It credited C Company with only 15 of the 128 kills (the rest supposedly having been accounted for by a preliminary artillery barrage). The official report even claimed that none of these 15 victims was killed inside the hamlet itself.

This Problem introduces the student to that body of international law — technically not "international human rights law," but rather the "law of war" or "humanitarian law" — that governed the activities of C Company (and supposedly protected the rights of the Vietnamese inhabitants) in My Lai that day. It focuses primarily upon the legal consequences of the appalling activities that took place — what happened to those soldiers who participated in the carnage, to those officers who ordered it (if, indeed, anyone did), and to those persons higher up in the chain of command under whose general authority the massacre took place. Specifically, are the procedures designed to ensure compliance with the law of war effective, and did the United States live up to its obligations to prosecute those persons responsible for breaches thereof?

In considering these questions, it is first necessary to explore how the law of war developed and, at least generally, what its substantive provisions require today. Also, what does the law of war have to say about the interrelated key issues of superior orders and command responsibility? Under precisely what circumstances can — or must — a soldier refuse to obey an order given to him by a superior? Under what circumstances is a commander legally responsible for activities performed by his troops with or without his explicit knowledge? Before proceeding further, some background information is essential.

B.   The Development of the Law of War

Note: *Historical Roots of the Concern for Human Rights in the Law of War*

Beginning at least as far back as the Middle Ages (and probably a good deal further), people have thought about the association between justice and warfare from two basic perspectives: from the standpoint of the decision to resort to war (jus ad bellum) and from the standpoint of the actual conduct of the war once hostilities had begun (jus in bello). By the nineteenth century, international lawyers had more or less abandoned questions of jus ad bellum — of the just war — to philosophers and theologians. Lawyers by then had accepted the view that states had the sovereign right to settle their differences by resort to arms if they so chose. Instead, they concentrated their energies on the questions of jus in bello, on right and wrong ways of making war.

For a long time, little attention was accorded to the development of detailed rules for the protection of civilians. The assumption behind this inattention was that the best way of protecting civilians was by ensuring that the horrors of battle affected only the military forces of the participating states. Civilians were sought (and thought) to be protected by the sharp distinction drawn between them and combatants. If civilians could be kept out of the fray altogether, the reasoning ran, then a detailed body of rules for their protection would be unnecessary. On that supposition, the nineteenth-century pioneers of the modern law of war (or humanitarian law, as it is often termed) devoted their attention to developing rules for the humane treatment of soldiers — for the wounded and sick, for prisoners of war, for the banning of particularly inhumane types of weapons, and so forth. Only during the course of the twentieth century, however, did it become apparent that it would be necessary for the law of the war to broaden its concerns in certain important ways.

Draper, Human Rights and the Law of War
12 Va. J. Intl. L. 326, 326-333 (1972)

I.   Human Development: Human Rights and the Law of War

The Law of War in its historical development ingested humanitarian restraints and prohibitions relatively late in its long history. At some time in history, probably in the 18th century, the Law of War began to pay some attention to humanitarian considerations. The matter needs careful investigation, but I suspect that the writings of Rousseau, though much maligned, form some clues to the process. In the Contrat Social, published in 1762 and subsequently condemned and publicly burnt in Geneva, Rousseau gave expression to certain ideas which have had considerable ethical, juridical, and political consequences. One such statement was:

> War is not, therefore, any relation between man and man, but a relation between state and state in which individuals are enemies only accidentally, not as men, or even as citizens, but as soldiers. . . .

By the mid-19th century, the humanitarian movement gathered force under the impact of a number of diverse, social, moral, political, scientific, military and economic factors. Religious considerations, so decisive in the early formation of the old Law of Arms, the precursor of our Law of War, were not controlling in the infusion of humanitarian considerations into the 19th century Law of War. It will be recalled that the Red Cross emblem has no Christian connotation, but is merely the heraldic arms of the Swiss Confederation, a white cross on a red background, reversed, as tribute to the origin of the Red Cross movement in that country inspired by Henry Dunnant.

The ideas lying behind the first Geneva Convention of 1864, the direct outcome of the appalling suffering on the battlefield of Solferino in 1859, dealing exclusively with the treatment of the sick and wounded as well as medical services and installations, and the powerful de Martens preamble to the Hague Convention No. IV of 1907 on the Law of War on Land, both give us the climate of humanitarian sentiment of the second half of the 19th century. De Martens, a Lutheran by religion, and a German-Balt by parentage, was converted to the Russian Orthodox faith. He became Professor of International Law at the Imperial University of St. Petersburg and held a senior position in the Imperial Foreign Ministry as well as his Chair at the University. He published his main work, in two volumes entitled International Law of Civilized Nations in 1882. He was one of the moving forces at the First Hague Peace Conference of 1899, convened by his master, Czar Nicholas II. In particular he was the draftsman of the famous Preamble to the Hague Convention No. IV, of 1907, which, in part, reads thus:

> Being animated by the desire to serve, even in this extreme case (the resort to armed conflict), the interest of humanity and the ever progressive needs of civilization; . . . Until a more complete code of the laws of war can be drawn up, the High Contracting Parties deem it expedient to declare that, in cases not covered by the rules adopted by them, the inhabitants and the belligerents remain under the protection and governance of the principles of the law of nations, derived from the usages established among civilized peoples, from the laws of humanity and from the dictates of the public conscience.

This basic formula is today repeated and inserted in each of the four Geneva Conventions of 1949 for the Protection of War Victims.

The ideas reflected in this formula are still a long way from our modern ideas of Human Rights, but the parentage is surely there. Yet, as one can see in the debates surrounding the establishment of the criteria for lawful belligerency in articles 1 and 2 of the Hague Regulations appended to the Hague Convention No. IV of 1907, the powerful thrust of military considerations is apparent. The position of the individual in the Law of War was still that of an object of the Law and not that of a legal persona endowed with rights under the Law of Nations. However, it was true that the individual, whether a regular soldier, a volunteer or a marauder, was subjected to sharp legal duties deriving from the Law of Nations. The consequence of the breach of such duties was drastic. Perhaps the basis of their limited legal persona was to enable their trial, conviction and execution for violations of the Law of War. However, before we mount too stringent a criticism of our forbears on this account we would do well to remember that in our own time it has not yet been agreed among jurists that the individual enjoys legal rights under the modern Law of Armed Conflicts. States may be enjoined by that Law to ensure certain humanitarian standards of treatment to war victims such as prisoners of war, civilians in occupied territory, the sick and wounded in the armed forces. But that is not the same thing as conferring rights to such treatment directly upon individuals, flowing from the Law of Nations. Indeed, it is much to be hoped that in this direction will lie one of the main influences of our contemporary Law of Human Rights upon the Law of Armed Conflicts, as we style it today. . . .

II.   POST WAR DEVELOPMENTS

A.   HUMAN RIGHTS

In the main it can be said that in the League of Nations era the direct nexus between the idea of Human Rights and the existing Law of War was not envisaged. No doubt, the great improvement made by the International Committee of the Red Cross and the League of Nations in the establishment of the two Geneva Conventions of 1929, dealing with the better treatment of the Sick and Wounded in the Armed Forces and of Prisoners of War, respectively, and the Geneva Gas Protocol of 1925, a very relevant instrument of law today, furthered the humanitarian endeavor. As yet, however, the idea that individuals should receive specified human rights, simply as human beings and determined by that nature of that central entity, at the hands of International Law, was substantially something for the future. The critical period in this development arrived with the nightmare experiences of World War II and the establishment of the Charter of the United Nations in 1945. It is that appalling experience and that basic instrument of International Law which brings effectively into juxtaposition Human Rights and the Law of War. Both the preamble and article 1 of the U.N. Charter make crystal clear that the framers were under the impression that the unleashing of aggressive war occurred at the hands of those States in which the denial of the value and dignity of the individual human being, of whatever race, color or creed, was most evident. The nexus that the framers of the U.N. Charter saw between the gross criminality of State aggression by armed forces and the no less gross denial of human worth within the frontiers of such States rammed home in a way that mankind was not likely to forget the connection between aggressive war and the total disregard of the individual. As we know, the culmination of that lesson was seen in the genocide activities of the Third Reich and the many labor or "work education camps" where genocide was achieved more slowly and with almost worse suffering. In that experience, the juxtaposition between the process of war and the position of the human being stood for all mankind to see and reflect upon. The culmination of the War in the Far East by the new weapon of mass and indiscriminate destruction of human life, and all that it had achieved, was a fitting culmination to the period of barbarity the world had experienced for 6 years.

It was therefore not surprising that the conception of "Crimes against Humanity" found in [sic] a place in the Charter annexed to the London Agreement of August, 1945, establishing the International Military Tribunal at Nuremberg and delineating the substantive law to be applied by it. The idea of crimes against humanity, though playing a marginal role in the final estimate of the guilt of the accused, affirmed the existence of certain fundamental human rights superior to the law of the State and protected by international criminal sanction even if violated in pursuance of the law of the State. Such ideas are of considerable importance in the story of the emergence of the concept of Human Rights protected by international law. States might still remain the primary right holders under that system of law but individuals, acting as the organs of State power, might, within International Law, be criminally answerable for grave denials of those essential rights inhering in all human beings just by virtue of that quality of existence. Prominent among such essential rights was the right to life and the prohibition of its arbitrary extinction. The Genocide Convention of 1948 filled out this idea in specific legal prohibitions attached to specific definitions of what constitutes genocide, rightly considered as the supreme denial of human rights. The Convention also marked in a way not shared with the Geneva War Victims Conventions the important departure point that the regime of human rights would apply in time of peace as well as in war, for one is no less a human being in the one than in the other. At that time, it was thought a strange thing that an international crime was so defined that it extended to commission in peace and war, so ingrained was the idea of a dichotomy between the international Law of Peace and of War, the traditional and classical legal distinction. It is a measure of the progress that we have made in our thinking since 1948 that this writer attended a Conference of 40 odd States in Geneva this year in which there was a strong move to obtain acceptance of the idea that the Law of Human Rights should operate full boom in time of war as in time of peace. Things are indeed changing and at great speed.

The Charter of the United Nations puts the scourge of war and the faith in fundamental human rights for all in the forefront of its preamble and thereby colors and informs the content of all that follows in the Charter. Gross disregard of Human Rights was for all time allied in the minds of men and women everywhere with the scourge of War. Article 2(4) of the Charter has established a prohibition of the threat or use of force by one State against another, a considerable extension of any idea implicit in the old idea of the "just war." Further, the equal application of the Law governing the conduct of armed conflicts to those illegally resorting to armed forces and those lawfully resorting thereto is accepted as axiomatic in modern International Law. It may not be without importance to point out that this is the first time in the long history of the Law about armed force that we have reached a point where there is a major legal limitation upon resort to armed force and an extensive body of law governing the manner of using armed force applicable irrespective of the legality or otherwise of the initial resort to armed force, existing at one and the same time within the system of International Law. This is achievement indeed.

Note: The Law Protecting Civilians in Time of War — International and Domestic

The defendants at Nuremberg, as Draper indicates, were charged not only with violations of the law of war — "war crimes" — but also with two new crimes under international law: "crimes against peace," a concept that provoked much controversy but is beyond the scope of this Problem; and "crimes against humanity," defined by Article 6(c) of the Charter of the International Military Tribunal (the body set up to conduct the Nuremberg Trials) to consist of "murder, extermination, enslavement, deportation, and other inhumane acts committed against *any* civilian population, . . . or persecutions on political, racial, or religious grounds . . . , whether or not in violation of the domestic law of the country where perpetrated." 82 U.N.T.S. 279, 288 (emphasis added). Designed to criminalize severe human rights deprivations that otherwise would have gone unpunished, e.g., Nazi Germany's attempt to exterminate its own Jewish population, crimes against humanity, "though playing a marginal role in the final estimate of the guilt of the accused, affirmed the existence of certain fundamental human rights superior to the law of the State and protected by international criminal sanction even if violated in pursuance of the law of the State." Draper, page 847 supra.

Not only was the focus at Nuremberg principally upon war crimes — crimes in violation of the law of war — but it has remained so thereafter. See U.S. Army, The Law of Land Warfare 178 (Field Manual 27-10, 1956): "members of the armed forces will normally be concerned only with those offenses constituting 'war crimes.' " Such crimes, it should be noted though, may be committed by any person or persons, civilian as well as military. Id. Since "[e]very violation of the law of war is a war crime," id., just what constitutes the law of war becomes exceptionally important. Although some of it is customary international law, by far the vast bulk of the law of war is derived from law-making treaties, especially the Hague and Geneva Conventions. Id. at 4.

The Geneva Conventions, the focus of this Problem, were adopted in 1949, three years after the completion of the Nuremberg Trials. Three of these Conventions replaced earlier instruments dealing with (1) Wounded and Sick in the Armed Forces in the Field; (2) Wounded, Sick and Shipwrecked Members of the Armed Forces at Sea; and (3) Prisoners of War. The Fourth Convention, on the Protection of Civilian Persons in Time of War, was new.

The heart of this Fourth Convention, at least for present purposes, may be found in the following five articles, which are important enough to be set out in full (75 U.N.T.S. 287, 306, 308-309).

Article 27

Protected persons are entitled, in all circumstances, to respect for their persons, their honour, their family rights, their religious convictions and practices, and their manners and customs. They shall at all times be humanely treated, and shall be protected especially against all acts of violence or threats thereof and against insults and public curiosity.

Women shall be especially protected against any attack on their honour, in particular against rape, enforced prostitution, or any form of indecent assault.

Without prejudice to the provisions relating to their state of health, age and sex, all protected persons shall be treated with the same consideration by the Party to the conflict in whose power they are, without any adverse distinction based, in particular, on race, religion or political opinion.

However, the Parties to the conflict may take such measures of control and security in regard to protected persons as may be necessary as a result of the war.

Article 31

No physical or moral coercion shall be exercised against protected persons, in particular to obtain information from them or from third parties.

Article 32

The High Contracting Parties specifically agree that each of them is prohibited from taking any measure of such a character as to cause the physical suffering or extermination of protected persons in their hands. This prohibition applies not only to murder, torture, corporal punishment, mutilation and medical or scientific experiments not necessitated by the medical treatment of a protected person, but also to any other measures of brutality whether applied by civilian or military agents.

Article 33

No protected person may be punished for an offence he or she has not personally committed. Collective penalties and likewise all measures of intimidation or of terrorism are prohibited.

Pillage is prohibited.

Reprisals against protected persons and their property are prohibited.

Article 34

The taking of hostages is prohibited.

The rest of the Convention may be summarized briefly. It provides for the protection of wounded and sick civilians, with particular provision for expectant mothers (Article 14). It encourages opposing armed forces to reach local agreements for the evacuation of civilian populations from zones of combat (Article 17). It contains provisions for the protection of civilian hospitals from attack (Articles 18 to 20) and for the protection of civilian evacuees (Articles 21 and 22). Free passage is to be guaranteed for hospital and medical stores for civilians, together with articles for religious worship (Article 23). There is a specific provision for care of orphans (Article 24). Communications between family members is to be guaranteed (Article 25), and armed forces are to take steps to assist with the reunion of dispersed families (Article 26). Articles 35 to 46 concern aliens found in the territory of parties to an armed conflict. The administration of occupied territories is covered by Articles 47 to 78. Finally, provisions relating to civilian internees are contained in Articles 79 to 135.

The 177 states parties to the Convention (including the United States, which became a party in 1956) are under a general obligation, set forth in Article 1, "to ensure respect for the present Convention in all circumstances." More specifically, states parties are obligated, under Article 146, to enact legislation providing "effective penal sanctions" for persons committing certain specified "grave breaches" of the Convention. Article 147 states these grave breaches to be "wilful killing, torture or inhuman treatment, including biological experiments, wilfully causing great suffering or serious bodily injury to body or health, unlawful deportation or transfer or unlawful confinement of a protected person, compelling a protected person to serve in the forces of a hostile Power, or wilfully depriving a protected person of the rights of fair and regular trial . . . , taking of hostages and extensive destruction and appropriation of property, not justified by military necessity and carried out unlawfully and wantonly."

Since the United States has provided, in what is now Article 18 of the Uniform Code of Military Justice, 70A Stat. 43, 10 U.S.C. §818 (1994), that "[g]eneral courts-martial also have jurisdiction to try any person who by the law of war is subject to trial by a military tribunal and may adjudge any punishment permitted by the law of war," the law of war — much like the other international criminal laws considered in Problem XII — in effect has become part of U.S. domestic law (in this case without the necessity of additional federal legislation). Indeed, at the time the Senate gave its advice and consent to the Geneva Conventions, the Department of Justice stated that "[a] review of existing legislation reveals no need to enact further legislation in order to provide effective penal sanctions for those violations of the Geneva Convention which are designated as grave breaches." Hearing on the Geneva Conventions for the Protection of War Victims Before the Senate Comm. on Foreign Relations, 84th Cong., 1st Sess. 58 (1955). Subsequently, in a 1967 communication to the UN Secretary-General, the United States, citing Article 18, acknowledged that "[t]hus, the law of war is incorporated into United States military law." Quoted from Paust, My Lai and Vietnam: Norms, Myths and Leader Responsibility, 57 Mil. L. Rev. 99, 124 (1972). See Ex parte Quirin, 317 U.S. 1, 28 (1942). As Paust points out, "prosecutions of U.S. troops for violations of the law of war have been in military fora and generally for violations of our domestic law as in prosecutions for military offenses under the present Uniform Code of Military Justice." Id. at 117. The My Lai defendants, for example, were prosecuted under the Uniform Code of Military Justice (UCM).

The law of war relevant to this section of the Problem is summarized conveniently in the following eight paragraphs from the U.S. Army's publication The Law of Land Warfare (Field Manual 27-10, 1956), whose purpose is "to provide authoritative guidance to military personnel on the customary and treaty law applicable to the conduct of warfare on land. . . ." Id. at 3.

85. Killing of Prisoners

A commander may not put his prisoners to death because their presence retards his movements or diminishes his power of resistance by necessitating a large guard, or by reason of their consuming supplies, or because it appears certain that they will regain their liberty through the impending success of their forces. It is likewise unlawful for a commander to kill his prisoners on grounds of self-preservation, even in the case of airborne or commando operations, although the circumstances of the operation may make necessary rigorous supervision of and restraint upon the movement of prisoners of war.

498. Crimes Under International Law

Any person, whether a member of the armed forces or a civilian, who commits an act which constitutes a crime under international law is responsible therefor and liable to punishment. Such offenses in connection with war comprise:

    a.   Crimes against peace.
    b.   Crimes against humanity.
    c.   War crimes.

Although this manual recognizes the criminal responsibility of individuals for those offenses which may comprise any of the foregoing types of crimes, members of the armed forces will normally be concerned only with those offenses constituting "war crimes."

499.   War Crimes

The term "war crime" is the technical expression for a violation of the law of war by any person or persons, military or civilian. Every violation of the law of war is a war crime.

500.   Conspiracy, Incitement, Attempts, and Complicity

Conspiracy, direct incitement, and attempts to commit, as well as complicity in the commission of, crimes against peace, crimes against humanity, and war crimes are punishable.

501.   Responsibility for Acts of Subordinates

In some cases, military commanders may be responsible for war crimes committed by subordinate members of the armed forces, or other persons subject to their control. Thus, for instance, when troops commit massacres and atrocities against the civilian population of occupied territory or against prisoners of war, the responsibility may rest not only with the actual perpetrators but also with the commander. Such a responsibility arises directly when the acts in question have been committed in pursuance of an order of the commander concerned. The commander is also responsible if he has actual knowledge, or should have knowledge, through reports received by him or through other means, that troops or other persons subject to his control are about to commit or have committed a war crime and he fails to take the necessary and reasonable steps to insure compliance with the law of war or to punish violators thereof.

507.   UNIVERSALITY OF JURISDICTION

   a.   Victims of War Crimes.   The jurisdiction of United States military tribunals in connection with war crimes is not limited to offenses committed against nationals of the United States but extends also to all offenses of this nature committed against nationals of allies and of cobelligerents and stateless persons.
   b.   Persons Charged with War Crimes.   The United States normally punishes war crimes as such only if they are committed by enemy nationals or by persons serving the interests of the enemy State. Violations of the law of war committed by persons subject to the military law of the United States will usually constitute violations of the Uniform Code of Military Justice and, if so, will be prosecuted under that Code. Violations of the law of war committed within the United States by other persons will usually constitute violations of federal or state criminal law and preferably will be prosecuted under such law. . . . Commanding officers of United States troops must insure that war crimes committed by members of their forces against enemy personnel are promptly and adequately punished.

508.   PENAL SANCTIONS

   The punishment imposed for a violation of the law of war must be proportionate to the gravity of the offense. The death penalty may be imposed for grave breaches of the law. Corporal punishment is excluded. Punishments should be deterrent, and in imposing a sentence of imprisonment it is not necessary to take into consideration the end of the war, which does not of itself limit the imprisonment to be imposed.

510.   GOVERNMENT OFFICIALS

   The fact that a person who committed an act which constitutes a war crime acted as the head of State or as a responsible government official does not relieve him from responsibility for his act.

C.   Where Does Responsibility Lie for Violations of the Law of War?

   Since compliance with the law of war is considered the responsibility of individuals, it is hardly surprising that there have been many attempts by military personnel accused of such violations to shift responsibility onto the shoulders of persons either above or below them in the chain of command.

Sometimes the attempt is made to shift the blame upward by contending that the acts in question were ordered by superiors, and that, therefore, the actual perpetrator of the violations should be exonerated and his superior punished instead. See generally L. Green, Superior Orders in National and International Law (1976). Conversely, there have been occasions where commanding officers prosecuted for violations of the law of war have attempted to shift the responsibility downwards by arguing that the acts in question had been committed by troops in the field without the commander's knowledge or consent. See, e.g., the *Yamashita* case, page 855 infra.

The first of these issues, the question of the defense of superior orders, received attention at the time of the Nuremberg Trials of the leaders of Nazi Germany after World War II. To a great extent, the Charter that established the International Military Tribunal (IMT) foreclosed the issue by expressly providing in Article 8 that "[t]he fact that the defendant acted pursuant to order of his Government or of a superior shall not free him from responsibility, but may be considered in mitigation of punishment if the Tribunal determines that justice so requires." 82 U.N.T.S. 279, 288. Nevertheless, the IMT did elaborate on the question of superior orders several times in its Judgment, most notably when it commented that the rule found in Article 8 was "in conformity with the law of nations. That a soldier was ordered to kill or torture in violation of the international law of war has never been recognized as a defense to such acts of brutality, though, as the Charter here provides, the order may be urged in mitigation of the punishment." The Nuremberg Trial, 6 F.R.D. 69, 111 (1946). Later in its Judgment the IMT added that "[s]uperior orders, even to a soldier, cannot be considered in mitigation where crimes as shocking and extensive [as the crimes involved] have been committed consciously, ruthlessly and without military excuse or justification." Id. at 154. "Participation in such crimes," it concluded, "has never been required of any soldier and he cannot now shield himself behind a mythical requirement of soldierly obedience at all costs as his excuse for commission of these crimes." Id. at 177.

This approach to the defense of superior orders has been incorporated into U.S. domestic law. The U.S. Army's The Law of Land Warfare (Field Manual 27-10, 1956), previously mentioned at page 851 supra, provides as follows:

509. Defense of Superior Orders

a. The fact that the law of war has been violated pursuant to an order of superior authority, whether military or civil, does not deprive the act in question of its character of a war crime, nor does it constitute a defense in the trial of an accused individual, unless he did not know and could not reasonably have been expected to know that the act ordered was unlawful. In all cases where the order is held not to constitute a defense to an allegation of war crime, the fact that the individual was acting pursuant to orders may be considered in mitigation of punishment.

    b. In considering the question whether a superior order constitutes a valid defense, the court shall take into consideration the fact that obedience to lawful military orders is the duty of every member of the armed forces; that the latter cannot be expected, in conditions of war discipline, to weigh scrupulously the legal merits of the orders received; that certain rules of warfare may be controversial; or that an act otherwise amounting to a war crime may be done in obedience to orders conceived as a measure of reprisal. At the same time it must be borne in mind that members of the armed forces are bound to obey only lawful orders. . . .

The defense of superior orders, as embodied in the above paragraph, was at issue in the court-martial of Lieutenant Calley for his activities at My Lai, taken up later in this Problem.

The issue of whether a commanding officer can absolve himself from blame for violations of the law of war committed by his troops, on the ground that he did not authorize or even know of such violations, involves the concept of "command responsibility." See Note, Command Responsibility for War Crimes, 82 Yale L.J. 1274 (1973). The issue received an authoritative airing in the U.S. Supreme Court case that follows.

In re Yamashita
327 U.S. 1, 5-6, 13-18 (1946)

CHIEF JUSTICE STONE delivered the opinion of the Court. . . .

From the petitions and the supporting papers it appears that prior to September 3, 1945, petitioner was the Commanding General of the Fourteenth Army Group of the Imperial Japanese Army in the Philippine Islands. On that date he surrendered to and became a prisoner of war of the United States Army forces in Baguio, Philippine Islands. . . . [P]etitioner was served with a charge prepared by the Judge Advocate General's Department of the Army, purporting to charge petitioner with a violation of the law of war. On October 8, 1945, petitioner, after pleading not guilty to the charge, was held for trial. . . .

On the same date a bill of particulars was filed by the prosecution, and the commission heard a motion made in petitioner's behalf to dismiss the charge on the ground that it failed to state a violation of the law of war. . . . [T]he motion to dismiss was denied. The trial then proceeded until its conclusion on December 7, 1945. . . . On that date petitioner was found guilty of the offense as charged and sentenced to death by hanging.

The petitions for habeas corpus set up that the detention of petitioner for the purpose of the trial was unlawful for reasons which are now urged as showing that the military commission was without lawful authority or jurisdiction to place petitioner on trial, as follows: . . .

(b) That the charge preferred against petitioner fails to charge him with a violation of the law of war; . . .

The Supreme Court of the Philippine Islands, after hearing argument, denied the petition for habeas corpus. . . .

The charge. Neither congressional action nor the military orders constituting the commission authorized it to place petitioner on trial unless the charge preferred against him is of a violation of the law of war. The charge, so far as now relevant, is that petitioner, between October 9, 1944 and September 2, 1945, in the Philippine Islands, "while commander of armed forces of Japan at war with the United States of America and its allies unlawfully disregarded and failed to discharge his duty as commander to control the operations of the members of his command permitting them to commit brutal atrocities and other high crimes against people of the United States and of its allies and dependencies, particularly the Philippines; and he . . . thereby violated the laws of war."

Bills of particulars, filed by the prosecution by order of the commission, allege a series of acts, one hundred and twenty-three in number, committed by members of the forces under petitioner's command during the period mentioned. The first item specifies the execution of "a deliberate plan and purpose to massacre and exterminate a large part of the civilian population of Batangas Province, and to devastate and destroy public, private and religious property therein, as a result of which more than 25,000 men, women and children, all unarmed noncombatant civilians, were brutally mistreated and killed, without cause or trial, and entire settlements were devastated and destroyed wantonly and without military necessity." Other items specify acts of violence, cruelty and homicide inflicted upon the civilian population and prisoners of war, acts of wholesale pillage and the wanton destruction of religious monuments.

It is not denied that such acts directed against the civilian population of an occupied country and against prisoners of war are recognized in international law as violations of the law of war. Articles 4, 28, 46, and 47, Annex to the Fourth Hague Convention, 1907, 36 Stat. 2277, 2296, 2303, 2306-7. But it is urged that the charge does not allege that petitioner has either committed or directed the commission of such acts, and consequently that no violation is charged as against him. But this overlooks the fact that the gist of the charge is an unlawful breach of duty by petitioner as an army commander to control the operations of the members of his command by "permitting them to commit" the extensive and widespread atrocities specified. The question then is whether the law of war imposes on an army commander a duty to take such appropriate measures as are within his power to control the troops under his command for the prevention of the specified acts which are violations of the law of war and which are likely to attend the occupation of hostile territory by an uncontrolled soldiery, and whether he may be charged with personal responsibility for his failure to take such measures when violations result. That this was the precise issue to be tried was made clear by the statement of the prosecution at the opening of the trial.

It is evident that the conduct of military operations by troops whose excesses are unrestrained by the orders or efforts of their commander would almost certainly result in violations which it is the purpose of the law of war to prevent. Its purpose to protect civilian populations and prisoners of war from brutality would largely be defeated if the commander of an invading army could with impunity neglect to take reasonable measures for their protection. Hence the law of war presupposes that its violation is to be avoided through the control of the operations of war by commanders who are to some extent responsible for their subordinates.

This is recognized by the Annex to the Fourth Hague Convention of 1907, respecting the laws and customs of war on land. Article I lays down as a condition which an armed force must fulfill in order to be accorded the rights of lawful belligerents, that it must be "commanded by a person responsible for his subordinates." 36 Stat. 2295. Similarly Article 19 of the Tenth Hague Convention, relating to bombardment by naval vessels, provides that commanders in chief of the belligerent vessels "must see that the above Articles are properly carried out." 36 Stat. 2389. And Article 26 of the Geneva Red Cross Convention of 1929, 47 Stat. 2047, 2092, for the amelioration of the condition of the wounded and sick in armies in the field, makes it "the duty of the commander-in-chief of the belligerent armies to provide for the details of execution of the foregoing articles, [of the convention] as well as for unforeseen cases. . . ." And finally, Article 43 of the Annex of the Fourth Hague Convention, 36 Stat. 2306, requires that the commander of a force occupying enemy territory, as was petitioner, "shall take all the measures in his power to restore, and ensure, as far as possible, public order and safety, while respecting, unless absolutely prevented, the laws in force in the country."

These provisions plainly imposed on petitioner, who at the time specified was military governor of the Philippines, as well as commander of the Japanese forces, an affirmative duty to take such measures as were within his power and appropriate in the circumstances to protect prisoners of war and the civilian population. This duty of a commanding officer has heretofore been recognized, and its breach penalized by our own military tribunals. . . .

We do not make the laws of war but we respect them so far as they do not conflict with the commands of Congress or the Constitution. There is no contention that the present charge, thus read, is without the support of evidence, or that the commission held petitioner responsible for failing to take measures which were beyond his control or inappropriate for a commanding officer to take in the circumstances. We do not here appraise the evidence on which petitioner was convicted. We do not consider what measures, if any, petitioner took to prevent the commission, by the troops under his command, of the plain violations of the law of war detailed in the bill of particulars, or whether such measures as he may have taken were appropriate and sufficient to discharge the duty imposed upon him. These are questions within the peculiar competence of the military officers composing the commission and were for it to decide. See Smith v. Whitney, 116 U.S. 167, 178. It is plain that the charge on which petitioner was tried charged him with a breach of his duty to control the operations of the members of his command, by permitting them to commit the specified atrocities. This was enough to require the commission to hear evidence tending to establish the culpable failure of petitioners to perform the duty imposed on him by the law of war and to pass upon its sufficiency to establish guilt.

Obviously charges of violations of the law of war triable before a military tribunal need not be stated with the precision of a common law indictment. Cf. Collins v. McDonald, [258 U.S. 416, 420 (1922)]. But we conclude that the allegations of the charge, tested by any reasonable standard, adequately allege a violation of the law of war and that the commission had authority to try and decide the issue which it raised. . . .

For a lively exchange on the applicability of the above case and the Nuremberg Principles to the Vietnam War, compare T. Taylor, Nuremberg and Vietnam: An American Tragedy 42-43, 159-182 (1970) with Solf, A Response to Telford Taylor's "Nuremberg and Vietnam: An American Tragedy," in 4 The Vietnam War and International Law 421, 433-446 (R. Falk ed. 1976).

Note: The Treatment of Command Responsibility in U.S. Domestic Law

Paragraph 501 of the U.S. Army's Law of Land Warfare (Field Manual 27-10, 1956), page 852 supra, basically tracks the *Yamashita* case in its treatment of command responsibility. The UCMJ itself, however, does not contain a section specifically dealing with the question. This omission causes some complications, as indicated by the following extract from Note, Command Responsibility for War Crimes, 82 Yale L.J. 1274 (1973).

> Despite Article 18's incorporation of international law, American war crimes are customarily tried as violations of specific criminal provisions in the UCMJ. Apparently, the prosecution has unfettered discretion to proceed either under these provisions or under Article 18's international law.
>
> While the UCMJ's articles do not expressly mention command responsibility, the offense might conceivably be charged as a form of complicity in the subordinate's crime, as an inferior grade of homicide, or as the inchoate offense of "dereliction of duty." Only complicity would, like Article 18, involve the possibility of capital punishment or life imprisonment. Inferior grades of homicide and "dereliction" carry much lower maximum penalties.
>
> Complicity-through-omission requires that the defendant have had a "duty to interfere" with the crime. While the command relationship does

apparently raise this duty, the alleged accomplice must have been at the scene of the crime, must have approved of the crime's perpetration, and must have, through this approval, provided "encouragement" for the perpetration. As for involuntary manslaughter, the Manual for Courts-Martial's broad definition might be read as requiring a commander to eliminate a high risk that his subordinates will commit murder, but the Manual's illustrative examples of the offense do not even hint at such an interpretation. An officer has been convicted of negligent homicide for failing to stop a subordinate's crime, but the Board of Review, in reversing, indicated that an officer must have actual knowledge of the subordinate's crime before incurring a duty to intervene against it. Assimilating command responsibility to traditional notions of homicide is obviously a troublesome project. Officers have quite frequently been convicted of "dereliction of duty" concerning subordinate crimes. While typically the officer was present during the crimes and "did nothing," breach of general supervisory duties has occasionally been punished where subordinate crimes followed, and the Code criminalizes dereliction of any duty created by "custom of the service," an obviously elastic concept.

In short, rather than resolving the conflicts in international law, the UCMJ supplements them with additional theories of command responsibility, also poorly formulated, and fails to indicate which provisions apply in which circumstances.

Id. at 1289-1291. Since higher officers were never tried for offenses arising out of the My Lai massacre (see pages 860-861 and 874-875 infra), the questions raised in the above extract remain unresolved.

D. Prosecuting Those Persons Responsible for My Lai

1. The Legal Framework and the Dramatis Personae

Given that massive violations of the law of war (incorporated into U.S. domestic law) had been committed by U.S. soldiers, and that the violations at last had come to the attention of the Executive Branch of the U.S. government, the next step was to put those persons responsible on trial. The question was, in what forum? There was little problem in the case of those potential defendants who were still in the service: they would be tried by courts-martial.

The term "court-martial" is somewhat misleading, since the tribunal in question is not really a "court" in the sense in which that word is used in Article III of the U.S. Constitution (which concerns the Judicial Branch of the government). Courts-martial are the creatures of Congress; they are part of the disciplinary machinery of the armed forces and not part of an independent, co-equal branch of the government, as is the case with Article III courts. They are not permanent, independent institutions; rather, they are limited, temporary tribunals meeting at the behest of and constituted by the "convening authority," who is usually the person of highest military rank available.

These differences between civilian and military justice have generated much criticism of the fairness of the court-martial process. See, for example, R. Sherrill, Military Justice Is to Justice As Military Music Is to Music (1969). The differences, moreover, have caused the U.S. Supreme Court to hold that courts-martial do not have jurisdiction over ex-servicemen, United States ex rel. Toth v. Quarles, 350 U.S. 111 (1955), or those persons accompanying servicemen, Reid v. Covert, 354 U.S. 1 (1952). That rule presented the U.S. government with the problem of whether such persons could be tried at all. Some argued that they could not, since they were not subject to civilian law at the time of the alleged offenses. See Note, Judicial Problems Related to the Prosecution of Former Servicemen for Violations of the Law of War, 56 Va. L. Rev. 947 (1970). Another possibility was to convene special military commissions for the purpose. Other commentators believed that the ordinary federal district courts had the jurisdiction to try such men. On this last position, see Paust, After My Lai: The Case for War Crime Jurisdiction over Civilians in Federal District Courts, 50 Tex. L. Rev. 6 (1971). Unfortunately (or fortunately, from the standpoint of the soldiers in this amorphous category), the issue became an academic one. In April 1971, immediately after the conviction of Lieutenant Calley, the United States declared that it would not prosecute ex-servicemen for violations of the law of war in Vietnam.

Whether this stance placed the United States in violation of international law is an interesting issue. The legality (under international law) of the United States non-prosecution of certain of the My Lai troops had arisen already in a slightly different context — the granting of immunity to former soldier Paul Meadlo, who had been subpoenaed by the prosecution in the Calley court-martial after admitting on national television to having participated in the massacre. When subpoenaed, Meadlo invoked the Fifth Amendment for fear of being prosecuted himself for his testimony. A grant of military immunity did not budge him. In fact, even after civil immunity had been granted, it took the threat of an arrest for contempt to get him to take the witness stand. In a comment on these proceedings, then-Assistant Attorney General William Rehnquist made the statement that he thought that the United States may have placed itself in violation of its international commitments by this immunity grant. Wall St. J., Jan. 21, 1971, at 1, col. 3. See Comment, Punishment for War Crimes: Duty — or Discretion?, 69 Mich. L. Rev. 1312 (1971). See also Paust, supra page 851, at 121 n.84.

At any rate, there were a number of men not so fortunate as to have left the service before the story broke. Eventually, 25 officers and enlisted men were charged with My Lai-related offenses under the UCMJ. The original indictments were no respecters of rank — two generals were among those charged. Major General Samuel W. Koster, commander of the Americal

Division in Vietnam, was accused of failure to obey lawful regulations and
dereliction of duty (in connection with the cover-up); Brigadier General
George H. Young, the assistant division commander, had the same charges
brought against him. Neither, however, was ever tried. The charges against
Young were dropped in June 1970 on the ground that they were "unsup-
ported by the evidence" as the Army put it, while the charges against Koster
were dropped in January 1971 on the ground that he "did not show any
intentional abrogation of responsibilities."

All told, charges against 19 of 25 were dropped. The Army, however,
did take disciplinary action in five cases. Koster was demoted to brigadier
general, stripped of his distinguished service medals, and issued a letter of
censure. Young also was stripped of his distinguished service medals and
given a letter of censure. Colonel N.A. Parson was stripped of his Legion of
Merit and issued a letter of censure. Captain D.H. Johnson received a letter
of reprimand. Sergeant K.L. Hodges was discharged from the service.

The six men not so fortunate as to escape prosecution were:

Colonel Oran K. Henderson (the brigade commander) — charged
with failure to obey lawful regulations, dereliction of duty, making
of a false official statement, and false swearing.
Captain Ernest R. Medina (the company commander) — charged with
failure to report a felony (later dropped), three counts of murder,
and two counts of assault.
Captain Eugene M. Kotouc (an intelligence officer) — charged with
maiming and assault.
Lieutenant William Calley (platoon commander) — charged with four
counts of murder: (1) the murder of at least 30 people along a trail
at the south end of the village; (2) the murder of at least 70 people
in a ditch outside of My Lai; (3) the premeditated murder of a
South Vietnamese man in white robes; and (4) the murder of a
small child.
Sergeant Charles E. Hutto — charged with assault with intent to commit murder.
Staff Sergeant David Mitchell — charged with assault with intent to
commit murder.

The courts-martial began against the lowest ranks and worked their way
upward. Mitchell came first and was acquitted in November 1970. Next
came Hutto, who was acquitted in January 1971. Then it was Calley's turn.

2. The Calley Court-Martial

Calley's court-martial was the longest in U.S. military history up to that
time. Like all the men accused, he was charged with violations of the
UCMJ: specifically, violations of Articles 118 (Murder) and 134 (General

Article) of the Uniform Code of Military Justice (70A Stat. 72, 76, 10 U.S.C. §§918, 934 (1994)). The court-martial was convened by the commanding general of Fort Benning, Georgia; it took place in late 1970 and early 1971 before a jury of six officers, all of whom had served in Vietnam.

Calley's defense was based essentially on three strategies. First was the possibility that the deaths at My Lai were caused either by artillery or helicopter fire or by soldiers not under Calley's control. When Calley admitted on the witness stand that he had fired into a ditch full of villagers, however, this line of defense became untenable. A second strategy was to contend that Calley's mental processes were so impaired that day that he was incapable of forming the requisite intention and premeditation necessary to support the charges. There was a month-long interruption in the trial while Calley went to Walter Reed Hospital in Washington for a psychiatric examination by a three-man Army board. Testimony then was taken on the subject at the trial, and the issue was left to the jury. The third defense strategy was that Calley was only following Medina's orders.

On this issue, Medina took the witness stand for the prosecution and testified that he had ordered only the destruction of the village itself: the huts, the livestock, the wells, and the crops. He denied ever having received word from Calley that large numbers of civilians had been encountered. Various C Company veterans were called to the stand who testified that, on the contrary, Medina had ordered them to "kill everything that breathed." Calley, in his own turn on the witness stand, made the following summation of his activities that day: "I felt then and I still do that when I acted as I was directed, and I carried out the orders I was given, and I do not feel wrong in so doing. . . ." This and other possible defenses are raised in the edited original transcript of his court-martial that follows.

Extracts from the Original Transcript of the Court-Martial of Lieutenant William Calley
Vol. 3, Bk. 9, at 3769-3772, 3990-3991, 3868-3870, 3896-3899, 3924-3930, 3950-3952, 3967-3969, 3983-3985 (on file in Library of Judge Advocate General's School, Charlottesville, Virginia)

[The direct examination of Lieutenant Calley began with an attempt to establish his lack of training in the law of war — save for the principle of following orders — before he was sent to Vietnam.]

Q: Now I will ask you if, during those three periods of instruction and training, were you instructed by anybody in connection with the Geneva Conference [sic]?

A: Yes, sir, I was.

Q: What was — if you have a recollection — what was the extent and nature of that tutoring or training?

A: I know there was classes. I can't remember any of the classes. Nothing stands out in my mind as to what was covered in the classes, sir.

Q: Did you learn anything in those classes of what actually the Geneva Conference [sic] covers with respect to the rules of warfare?

A: Not in the laws and rules of warfare, sir.

Q: Did you receive any training in any of those places which had to do with the obedience to orders?

A: Yes, sir.

Q: And what was the nature of the training, and what were you informed was the principles involved in that field?

A: That all orders were to be assumed legal, that it was a soldier's job to carry out any order given to him to the best of his ability.

Q: Did it tell you or talk to you or inform you anything about what occurred if you disobeyed an order by a senior officer?

A: You could be court-martialed for refusing an order, and if you refused an order in the face of the enemy, you could be sentenced to death, sir.

Q: Did they tell you anything about — did you ever hear a philosophy which might have involved the legality or illegality of orders?

A: I'm not sure I understand your question except that all orders are to be presumed legal and that all orders are to be obeyed.

Q: Well, let me ask you this. What I'm talking about and asking you about is whether or not you were given any instructions on the necessity for or whether you are required in any way, shape, or form to make a determination of the legality or illegality of an order?

A: No, sir, I was never told that I had a choice, sir. . . .

Q: If you had a doubt about an order, what were you supposed to do?

A: If I questioned the order, I was to carry it out and come back and make my complaint. That is generally what I was told. If you were given a mission to attack, you would carry it out immediately. If you had a discrepancy with the order, you reported it after you carried it out.

Q: Was it a training of do first and ask later?

A: Yes, sir.

Q: Now when you went to Vietnam, was there any variation in the nature of the training or in the requirements of you to obey or permission to disobey orders given to you there in Vietnam that was different than what you had received?

A: I'm not sure if I understand exactly what you are asking for, other than nothing had changed except you were in the face of the enemy which could be considered a capital offense.

Q: Was anything said to you about the duty in combat of obeying orders?

A: Yes, sir. It was an officer's job to carry out the orders to the best of his ability and not to question them, sir.

[The direct examination continued in an effort to show that, far from receiving more adequate training in the law of war after he reached Vietnam, Calley had been instructed that all Vietnamese — men, women and children — were potential enemies.]

Q: Now when you were in Vietnam early in your period of service there, were you given any instructions or any advice or training in connection with characteristics or things connected with the enemy that you might be expected to engage?

A: We had a series of classes while at Duc Pho. I don't — They are partially sponsored by the 2d ARVN division, their cadre, and another element in classroom speaking. I don't know who they were if that's what your question was.

Q: I am talking to you about the training that you received — I don't know who would give it to you. It had to do with the enemy you would face and what you could expect, who they might be and information in that general area?

A: Well, there was never any word of exactly who the enemy was, but to suspect everyone, that everyone was a potential enemy and that men and women were equally as dangerous and because of the unsuspectedness of children, they were even more dangerous. . . .

Q: Was there any information given to you about the manner which men, women, and children might fight or annoy you or kill you or information such as that?

A: Yes, sir, there was.

Q: What were your teachings in that field?

A: I believe — I don't know if we got it out of that class — but the Vietnamese women for some reason were better shots than the men are. They fight equally the same. Men and women can both be armed. Children can be used in a multitude of facets from warning signals, being used as warning signals, also at the same time inflict casualties. One of the first ways to warn the VC in the area that an American unit has come in is to give a small child a hand grenade and let them throw it at the area. It might kill one GI and alert the enemy in the area to get out of it. They also use children to collect and distribute booby-traps and mines. Children are very good at planting mines, and, well, just basically they are very dangerous.

Q: Let me ask you this, Lieutenant Calley. Was there any change in your feelings or attitudes from when you changed from the OCS in garrison to the area of actual combat?

A: Yes, sir. Of course, in OCS and garrison everybody got the school solution. Everybody had all the answers, completely, and there was no doubt in anybody's mind the tactics that we used and the way we practiced tactics to do the job. When we got to Vietnam, it was very frustrating because it wasn't true.

[The cross-examination of Calley began with his entry into My Lai, at which time he ordered one or more of his sergeants "[t]o hang on to some of the people to clear the mine field." One of the military judges returned to this point later in the trial.]

Q: Let me ask you this, where did you get the information about using civilians to clear these mine fields?
A: I don't know where that originally came from. The first time we hit some mines —
Q: I am talking about now the operation of 16 March?
A: The morning before we lifted off I got that information from Captain Medina. He told me to hang on to a few people in case we hit the mine fields, sir.
Q: Did he elaborate as to what you were to do with these people? Was that understood by you?
A: Yes, sir, just have them go ahead of you. That was understood. He didn't have to go into detail.

[After the mention of the contemplated use of Vietnamese civilians "to clear the mine field," the cross-examination continued as follows.]

Q: When is the first time you encountered a live Vietnamese inside the village?
A: That time when I shot one. . . .
Q: Where did you see him?
A: He was inside of a brick house, sir. . . .
Q: What was the circumstances under which you saw this individual?
A: I stepped up and looked into the house, and one man was fleeing out a back window and another man was standing in the fireplace, sir.
Q: So what did you do?
A: I shot them, sir.
Q: Which did you shoot first?
A: The one going out the window or running for the window. . . .
Q: What was the other man doing while you shot him?
A: He was coming down out of the chimney, sir. . . .
Q: What did you do?
A: I shot him, sir. . . .
Q: Did you look for weapons on these two individuals? . . .
A: They weren't carrying a weapon. I didn't go up and search them.
Q: Did you search the house?
A: No, sir.

[The cross-examination then proceeded to the infamous incident involving a large number of Vietnamese civilians who had been rounded up and herded into a rice paddy near a ditch.]

Q: Did you have to pass back the location where you had left Meadlo with the group?

A: Yes, sir, I did.

Q: What did you find there?

A: Meadlo was still there.

Q: What were the people doing?

A: Still standing there, sir. . . .

Q: Did you say anything to him back on this pass?

A: Yes, I did.

Q: What?

A: I told him to "waste them," sir.

Q: So he had not moved the people, is that correct, and they were still there?

A: That's the way I felt about it, yes, sir. . . .

Q: Were you angry when he didn't move the group?

A: I don't think a violent anger, no, sir. It was distressing. It was slowing me down, but it wasn't actually Meadlo's fault. I mean I didn't take it personally out on him.

Q: You don't feel he disobeyed your order?

A: He had basically disobeyed my order, but I didn't know what his problem was. I didn't take out a resentment on him. As far as I know, he couldn't move the people.

Q: He disobeyed your order?

A: Yes, sir.

Q: This didn't upset you in combat for a subordinate to disobey your order?

A: It would — not that order, no, sir. I felt that the man was trying to do the job the best he could.

Q: It depends on the type of order?

A: Yes, sir.

Q: What did you say to him then on this occasion?

A: If he couldn't move the people, to "waste them."

Q: What did he say?

A: He said, "Roger." . . .

[Having left Meadlo to carry out his order to "waste them," Calley was talking with Sergeant Mitchell when he heard semiautomatic firing from the direction from whence he had come. The cross-examination continued as follows.]

Q: Then what did you do?

A: Sergeant Mitchell moved away to comply with what I had told him. I moved in that direction toward the firing, sir.

Q: Then what happened?

A: Then I came out of the wood line and saw my troops shooting the people in the ditch there.

Q: You moved up the ditch?

A: Yes, sir, moved north along the side of the ditch. . . .

Q: What did you find when you got there?

A: The men were shooting in a ditch, sir.

Q: [Who were they shooting?]

A: Vietnamese men.

Q: They were all men?

A: I don't know sir.

Q: Did you look?

A: I looked into the ditch, yes, sir.

Q: What did you do when you got there?

A: I fired into the ditch and told my men to hurry up and get down the other side and get into position, sir.

Q: Who of your men were there?

A: I spoke — I recognized Meadlo being there and I recognized Dursi being there, sir. There was other men there but I can't relate who they were. . . .

Q: What did you say to Meadlo?

A: Hurry up and get on the other side of the ditch.

Q: What did he say to you?

A: He moved out and got on the other side of the ditch.

Q: Did you shake him?

A: Yes, sir.

Q: When?

A: Well, I didn't stand there — I grabbed him by the arm and pointed him in the direction.

Q: What did he do?

A: Moved out across the ditch.

Q: Was he crying?

A: I don't know, sir.

Q: Did you ever see Meadlo cry that day? . . .

A: I don't know if I did or not, sir.

Q: Would you say you did not?

A: No sir, I wouldn't.

Q: You don't remember him crying?

A: No, sir.

Q: How long did you fire into the ditch?

A: I have no idea, sir.

Q: How many shots did you fire?

A: Six to eight, sir. . . .

Q: What did you fire at?

A: Into the ditch, sir. . . .

Q: What at in the ditch?

A: At the people in the ditch, sir.

Q: How many people were in the ditch?

A: I don't know, sir. . . .

Q: What were these people doing as they were being fired upon?
A: Nothing, sir.
Q: Were they being hit?
A: I would imagine so, sir.
Q: Well, do you know?
A: I don't know if they were being hit when I saw them.
Q: Do you know if you hit any of them?
A: No sir, I don't.
Q: How far away from them were you when you fired?
A: Muzzle would have been five feet, sir.
Q: You didn't see the bullets impact?
A: No, not that I recall, no sir.
Q: How do you know these people weren't dead when you left the ditch?
A: I don't know that they were, sir.
Q: Didn't you say they were apparently all dead?
A: I said they were apparently all dead. I don't know exactly if they were dead.
Q: Why were they apparently dead?
A: They were lying still.
Q: Was there blood on them?
A: Yes, sir.
Q: Where?
A: I don't know exactly where the blood was on them in that ditch, sir.
Q: Was Meadlo firing automatic when you arrived? . . .
A: I don't know exactly, sir. I remember everybody firing semi-automatic. I don't believe anybody would have been firing automatic at that time.
Q: Was Dursi firing when you arrived?
A: I don't know, sir.
Q: Do you know if he did or did not fire?
A: No, I do not, sir.
Q: Do you know if Meadlo did or did not fire?
A: No, sir.
Q: You don't know when any of your men fired into the ditch?
A: I wasn't paying attention to when they were firing, if they were, how they were firing, how they were holding their weapons. My main thing was go on, finish off those people as fast as possible and get my people out into position, sir.
Q: Why?
A: Because that was what I was instructed to do, sir, and I had been delayed long enough and I was trying to get out there before I got criticized again, sir. . . .

[After the Vietnamese in the ditch had been "wasted" and the hamlet completely "pacified," a platoon leaders' meeting occurred at which Calley reported on the day's events to Medina. The cross-examination follows.]

Q: Did you tell Captain Medina you had shot the people in the ditch?
A: Yes sir, I did.
Q: Did he ask you any facts about that?
A: No, sir.
Q: How did you tell him that?
A: He asked — well, after the higher called back and asked — said it had been reported that a lot of civilians were killed in the area, he wanted to know what the percentage of civilians was.
Q: What did you tell him?
A: I told him he would have to make that decision, sir.
Q: Is that what you told him, those were your exact words to Captain Medina?
A: Yes, sir.
Q: Did he then ask you to describe the people you shot?
A: No, sir.
Q: Did you offer any description of them?
A: No, sir.
Q: Did you give him any estimate?
A: No, sir.
Q: Did you tell him which of your men had been involved?
A: Involved with what, sir?
Q: Shooting at the ditch.
A: It wasn't any big deal, no sir.
Q: You told Captain Medina that you rounded these people up, put them in a ditch, and shot them?
A: No sir, I didn't.
Q: What did you tell him?
A: I told him there was people over there shot in the ditch and people shot in the village.
Q: You didn't tell him the circumstances under which they were shot?
A: No, sir. Why should I? He knew what circumstances they were shot under.
Q: How did he know?
A: Because he had told me to shoot them, sir.
Q: When?
A: The day before, that day.
Q: The day before or that day?
A: Both, sir.
Q: He never made any further inquiry of you as to the details?
A: No, sir. . . .

[The cross-examination concluded with a discussion of why Calley had not "saved" any Vietnamese for the mine field operation and an explanation of the "body count" policy of Company C.]

Q: The group of Vietnamese that your platoon had, were all of them killed in the ditch?

A: I don't know, sir.

Q: Let me ask you this, did you have any saved up for the mine field?

A: No, I did not.

Q: You testified that you received an order before to save some up for the mine field?

A: Yes sir, I did.

Q: Why didn't you save some up for the mine field?

A: Captain Medina rescinded that order and told me to waste them, sir.

Q: When did he rescind the order?

A: When he called me on the radio when I was on the eastern part of the village, sir.

Q: Did he specifically tell you "disregard the previous order?"

A: No, sir. He said if those people were slowing me down "waste them," sir. . . .

Q: You interpreted that as save none for the mine fields?

A: The second time he told me, yes sir.

Q: Were you concerned about utilizing people for the mind field?

A: Yes sir, I was.

Q: Did you ask him if it might not be advisable to save people for the mine fields?

A: Not after he told me the second time, sir.

Q: After he told you the second time to waste them?

A: Yes, sir.

Q: How many people would you normally use to take through the mine field?

A: Never any larger than the front I was covering, sir. If I had five men on the front, I wouldn't use no more than five. If I had a 20-man front, I would use no more than 20.

Q: One per man?

A: Yes, sir. . . .

Q: You testified previously concerning the body count policy within your company. Would you explain what that was? . . .

A: The body count you was to push for and try to get as much body count that you possibly could.

Q: Could you tell us where you first learned this?

A: My first impression of it was when I first got to Vietnam and all of the units talked about and every briefing I went to there were charts on body count. Every unit had a body count. That was the general topic of conversation when you got to Vietnam — what everybody's body count was, sir.

Q: How about with your company?

A: When we got there we didn't have one.

Q: What was the general topic of conversation then regarding body count?

A: Try to catch up with everybody else.

Q: Could you tell us some particular situation in which you heard that statement made and by whom?

A: I was told sometimes on patrol to go out and don't come back or don't come back — when you come back today, you had better have some body count.

Q: Who told you that?

A: Captain Medina, sir. . . .

[On redirect examination, Calley stated that Medina had "chewed me out a couple of times" when he had failed to follow up Medina's orders promptly in the past. The questioning then turned to just what Medina had ordered Calley to do during the course of several conversations they had over the radio on 16 March 1968.]

Q: . . . [I]n connection with the message that involved orders, would you state in substance and effect your recollection of what Captain Medina told you on the first order in connection with the tactical situation aside from the contingency plan? . . .

A: He called me and basically asked me where I was or what I was doing and I told him I was still in the eastern edge of the village because I still had some bunkers to check out and had a group of Vietnamese there and I still had another part of the hamlet to check out. He told me to hurry up and get rid of the people and get into the position I was supposed to be in, sir.

Q: All right now, let's go to the next one. I want the substance and effect of the conversation that you had between Captain Medina and yourself on that occasion on the 16th day of March, that would be the one — I want you to piece it in — that would be the one you had in connection with your failure to move?

A: Well, I was still in the basic location and Captain Medina more or less called me and well, he called me and asked me why I had disobeyed his orders and hadn't moved out as he had directed me to and I told him again that I was moving as fast as I possibly could and I was checking these bunkers in this other part of the village and that I still had the Vietnamese people there that were slowing me down.

Q: What did Captain Medina tell you?

A: Basically "the hell with the bunkers. Waste the people and get your people out of there where I told you to and I don't want to hear any more about it." That was it, sir. . . .

Q: At any time did you stop and consider the legality or the illegality of those orders?

A: No, sir. Sir, excuse me. Could we take a recess at this time?

3. Lieutenant Calley's Conviction and the Public's Response

The jury in Lieutenant Calley's court-martial deliberated for 79 hours and 58 minutes over a period of 13 days. Their verdict, report on 29 March 1971, was as follows:

(1) On the charge of the murder of 30 persons along the trail: guilty of the murder of "an unknown number, not less than 1";

(2) On the charge of the murder of 70 people in the ditch: guilty of murder of "an unknown number, not less than 20";

(3) On the charge of the premeditated murder of the white-robed man: guilty;

(4) On the charge of the murder of the child: not guilty of murder, but guilty of assault with intent to commit murder.

On the following day, Calley received his sentence: dismissal from the service, forfeiture of all pay and allowances, and confinement for life at hard labor.

Calley's conviction evoked one of the greatest outpourings of public sympathy in memory. Within days the White House reported receiving over 5,000 telegrams on the subject, running (it was said) about 100 to 1 in favor of clemency for Calley. The governor of Indiana ordered all flags in his state to be flown at half mast. Several state assemblies passed resolutions asking for clemency for Calley. Governor George Wallace of Alabama paid a much-publicized personal call on the convicted man at his quarters in Fort Benning. Then-Governor Jimmy Carter of Georgia, in whose state the court-martial had taken place, proclaimed 5 April 1971 to be "American Fighting Men's Day"; he urged state residents to fly the flag that day and to drive with their headlights on. N.Y. Times, Apr. 2, 1971, at 16, col. 3. A Nashville, Tennessee, record company reported that "The Battle Hymn of Lieutenant Calley" (sung to the tune of "The Battle Hymn of the Republic") had become an overnight best seller. A Gallup poll reported that 79 percent of the American public disapproved of the verdict while only 9 percent approved (the remaining 12 percent had no opinion).

The reaction of particular persons is of some interest. President Richard Nixon announced on 3 April 1971 that he personally would ultimately review the decision to ensure that the case got "more than the technical review" provided by the UCMJ. N.Y. Times, Apr. 4, 1971, at 1, col. 8. He also ordered Calley removed from the Fort Benning stockade and placed instead under house arrest.

Professor Telford Taylor, who had been the chief prosecutor at the Nuremberg Trials after World War II, remarked that the verdict was "opaque as well as harsh," although he acknowledged that an acquittal would have been a disaster. He said the trial pointed up the need for "a dispassionate, thorough inquiry into our conduct of the war." N.Y. Times, Apr. 5, 1971, at 12, col. 6.

Then-Army Chief of Staff General William Westmoreland, who had been the commander in Vietnam at the time of the My Lai massacre, was asked whether he felt any guilt. He replied:

> No, I feel no guilt, not in the least. It is an absurd allegation.
>
> It was clearly known by our troops in Vietnam that they were to avoid civilian casualties at all costs.
>
> My orders were that all atrocities were to be reported and investigated according to the rules of the Geneva Convention, and it is our obligation to follow through and punish those atrocities.

General Westmoreland admitted that many civilians had been killed in the course of the war, but he said that the cause of such deaths had been troops "led by inexperienced lieutenants and sergeants." N.Y. Times, Apr. 3, 1971, at 14, col. 8.

4. The Subsequent Fate of Lieutenant Calley

Calley's conviction was only the beginning of a tortuous maze of legal proceedings, which were to last for fully five years before the case of United States v. Calley could be considered closed. The first official review of the conviction was by the convening authority of the court-martial, the commanding general of Fort Benning. In August 1971, he approved the finding of guilty but reduced the sentence to 20 years' confinement. Next came the Court of Military Review, to which Calley had an automatic right to appeal under Article 66 of the UCMJ (70A Stat. 59, 10 U.S.C. §866 (1994)); it affirmed both the conviction and the sentence in February 1973. United States v. Calley, 46 C.M.R. 1131 (1973). The Court of Military Appeal, the highest court in the military system, then granted a limited review and affirmed by a split decision in December 1973. United States v. Calley, 22 C.M.A. 534, 48 C.M.R. 19 (1973). Next the Secretary of the Army reviewed the case, as required by Article 71(b) of the UCMJ (70A Stat. 62, 10 U.S.C. §871(b) 1994)). He also approved both the finding of guilty and the sentence, but in a separate clemency action, he further reduced the confinement period from 20 to 10 years. On 3 May 1974, President Nixon notified the Secretary that he had reviewed the case, as promised, and had no changes to recommend.

The case, however, was hardly over yet. In February 1974, Calley had begun habeas corpus proceedings in the civil courts in Georgia with a view to gaining his freedom. On 25 September 1974, Federal District Judge J. Robert Elliott overturned the conviction on four grounds (382 F. Supp. 650 (M.D. Ga. 1974)): first, prejudicial pre-trial publicity; second, the failure of the court-martial judge to subpoena certain witnesses for Calley; third, the failure of the House of Representatives to grant Calley access to certain information that it had discovered in the course of its own investigation of the My Lai affair; and fourth, the inadequacy of the descriptions of the crimes that Calley was alleged to have committed (specifically, the lack of names or descriptions of the "at least 30" and the "at least 70" alleged victims).

The government appealed the district court decision to the Fifth Circuit Court of Appeals. In a decision reached en banc in September 1975, the court decided, 8 to 5, to reverse Judge Elliott and to reinstate the conviction. 519 F.2d 184 (5th Cir. 1975). The Supreme Court denied certiorari on 5 April 1976. 425 U.S. 911 (1976). The legal procedures over at last, Calley remained a convicted criminal.

The Army then decided, however, that so little time remained of the 3⅓ years that Calley actually had to serve before his parole that he should be immediately released. "No purpose would be served by returning Mr. Calley to formal military custody for so short a period" was the official reason given for the decision. N.Y. Times, Apr. 6, 1976, at 1, col. 5. Former Lieutenant Calley is a free man today, running a jewelry store in Columbus, Georgia.

5. The Courts-Martial of Captain Medina and the Other My Lai Defendants

Lieutenant Calley's court-martial, for all of the controversy that it engendered, was not the last one to result from the My Lai massacre. Immediately after Calley's conviction came the fourth of the courts-martial, that of Captain Eugene Kotouc, an intelligence officer charged with maiming and assault. He was acquitted in April 1971. Next came C Company Commander Captain Ernest R. Medina.

There were three counts of murder and two of assault against Medina. The former consisted of allegations of the premeditated murder of one Vietnamese woman, the murder of not less than 100 Vietnamese civilians, and the murder of a child. The assault charges resulted from Medina's having shot twice over the head of a prisoner. In the course of the court-martial, which began in July 1971, the judge dismissed the charge as to the murder of the child; he also reduced the charge as to the murder of the civilians to involuntary manslaughter. Medina argued strenuously that the death of the woman was a "justifiable battlefield homicide." As to the assault charges, he contended, quite erroneously, that the Field Manual 27-10 permitted "threats of violence" against prisoners who refuse to talk.

As the trial developed, it became apparent that the command responsibility issue was critical. To what extent, and under what circumstances, was Medina to be held accountable for the actions of his troops? It is important to realize that the Field Manual is quite clear on this issue: it makes the commander responsible for the acts of his troops "if he has actual knowledge, *or should have knowledge*, through reports received by him or through other means, that troops . . . subject to his control . . . have committed a war crime. . . ." (Emphasis added.) See the complete text of this provision at page 852 supra. The military judge's instruction to the jury, however, was significantly different. He instructed them that Medina was to be held responsible for the acts of his troops *only if he had actual knowledge of their war crimes* (the presence or absence of such knowledge being an issue of fact left solely to the jury to decide). The prosecution strangely enough made no objection to this erroneous instruction, and Medina was acquitted of all charges on 22 September 1971.

The only court-martial then remaining was that of Colonel Henderson, the brigade commander, who was charged with failure to obey a lawful instruction, dereliction of duty, the making of a false official statement, and false swearing. His court-martial, which equalled Calley's in length, ended in December 1971 in an acquittal. Thus, Calley was left as the only man to be convicted for his activities at My Lai.

6. "Orders" from Above: The Experience of Lieutenant James Duffy

One of the most disturbing aspects of warfare in general is that sometimes the most important decisions of all — whether particular persons are to live or die — must be made on the spot by the lowest ranking and least trained personnel in the armed services. Is it really fair to assume that when war crimes occur in such a context they are attributable only to the individual soldiers involved? It is true that soldiers often receive no formal, direct orders on what to do about, say, prisoners taken during a search and destroy mission. It is also true, however, that more subtle — though none the less effective — messages do filter down from above that can get translated into war crimes in the field. One officer explained the problem this way (The Interrogation of Captain Howard Turner at the Trial of Lieutenant James Duffy, 1970, in Crimes of War: A Legal, Political-Documentary, and Psychological Inquiry into the Responsibility of Leaders, Citizens, and Soldiers for Criminal Acts in Wars 239, 246 (R. Falk, G. Kolko, and R. Lifton eds. 1971)):

> "Go out and kill the gooks" is the word they use around here. This comes down from Brigade, this comes down from two field forces, the 25th Division and the whole works. There is nothing written, nothing I could point out and show you. . . . The more you kill, the more efficient you are.

This problem of the filtering downward of an ethos of killing, as distinct from any formal orders to kill indiscriminately, can leave the soldier in the field in a nearly hopeless dilemma. He is quite consciously acting to further his superiors' policy. Yet he is not acting under direct orders; so the responsibility for any wrong doing — or excessive zeal, if you will — stays on his shoulders.

The case of Lieutenant James Duffy, the holder of two Bronze Stars, the Purple Heart, and seven other honorable citations, is a case in point. Duffy was a squad commander, like Lieutenant Calley. He was court-martialed in 1970 for ordering a prisoner to be shot in cold blood. At his trial, Duffy made the following observations.

Lieutenant Duffy's Statement
in Crimes of War: A Legal, Political-Documentary, and Psychological Inquiry into the Responsibility of Leaders, Citizens, and Soldiers for Criminal Acts in Wars 248, 249-254 (R. Falk, G. Kolko, and R. Lifton eds. 1971)

There was only one thing that really upset me (and many other people in the platoon too). That was taking prisoners that we knew were VC and having them released by Brigade as innocent civilians. It's not hard to spot a VC after you've spent some time in the field. The only people who live out there are farmers and the VC. The farmers are only women and children and old men. They were always very friendly toward us. We would stop in a house for lunch or dinner and share our food with them, talk, play with the children and really have a good time. I almost never saw any young men in the rice paddies. Whenever we found any young men we immediately questioned them. I can think of only two young men that I ever found in the field and they were just 15 years old and still going to school. The only other young men I ever found in the field were VC who were shooting at us.

Once we ambushed a sampan in the Plain of Reeds, which is a free-fire zone and anybody who moves is fair game. This sampan came down a canal at about 2100 hours. When we opened up, two men were killed and two women were injured. The women were yelling, "Don't shoot, don't shoot, we are VC!" Sergeant Lanasa swam out and rescued the two women and brought them back to shore. The next morning he carried one of them three-quarters of a mile through swamps to an area where we dusted them off for medical treatment and interrogation. We found out two days later that both women had been released by Brigade as innocent civilians. This really upset me and many others in the platoon. . . . It's hard enough to find the enemy, but to catch and just let them go is ridiculous.

After that incident I decided I was not going to take any more prisoners. If at all possible I was not going to let the situation arise where a prisoner might be taken. I told all my squad leaders and my company commander of this. I told all my men that if they were going to engage someone, not to stop shooting until everyone was dead. I told them if they were going to shoot at somebody, they had better kill him. Nobody ever said anything against this policy and I think most of the men agreed to it. My company commander felt the same way I did about it. . . .

Sometimes innocent civilians are killed out there, but it just can't be helped. We were always careful not to shoot towards any populated areas when we prepped a woodline, and even in a contact we would try not to shoot towards civilians if at all possible. But still you would hit a few, especially at night. Many of the farmers would be out after curfew wandering around, or going over to a friend's house.

They just sort of disregarded the curfew and we have no choice but to engage them, since anybody moving after curfew is supposed to be considered VC. When we kill a man after curfew and he has a valid ID or he is an old man, etc., you can pretty well guess that he was just an innocent civilian out after the curfew (but, of course, you never know for sure because anybody can be a VC, valid ID card or not). . . .

Whenever we did take prisoners, they were always roughed up and then questioned. When we worked with ARVN's or national police, we found that they were excellent interrogators. You could tell that they really hated the VC by the way they beat them when they caught one. They do not mess around at all. I once had a national policeman with me when we chased a VC through a house. The VC got away but the national policemen wanted to take one of the women in the house with us for questioning. That night he beat and kicked that woman for about two hours while he questioned her. When he was finished he came over and told me she was okay, not a VC, and to let her go in the morning. I went along with his decision. I always listened to my Tiger Scouts, ARVN's or national police and would do what they say. They always seem to know who is a VC and who isn't. . . .

I know in my case, platoon leaders never got any guidance on treatment of prisoners. Battalion HQS never said anything about them. There was no SOP [Standard Operating Procedure], there was never a request that we take any prisoners. The only thing we ever heard was to get more body count, kill more VC! We heard that all the time; it was really stressed. My squad leader told me that in his old unit they couldn't come in from the field unless they turned in a body count. Many units "pad" their body count so they can say they killed more than anybody else. The only way anybody judged a unit's effectiveness was by the number of body counts they had. If you had a lot of body counts, everybody would think you were really good. If you didn't have a lot of body counts, they would think you were a poor unit.

I know I was always conscious of how many body counts my platoon had. I keep a record on the wall of my room and had a record painted on the side of my APC. I was always proud of the fact that my platoon had more kills than any other platoon in the company and that our company led the battalion in kills. The men in the platoon were aware of all this, too, and they were proud of their record. They considered themselves to be the best platoon around. It kept our morale very high when we were leading everyone else for the month.

Some people might have thought it was wrong to judge a unit just by the number of kills they get. I think it is the only way a unit should be judged. That is really the only mission we have in the field, to kill the enemy. As far as I'm concerned that's why we were sent over here and that's what our job is. The only way to see how well a unit is performing its job is to see how many body counts they have. My platoon killed, found or captured about 50 enemy from mid-July to mid-September and I only had one man killed and only two seriously wounded. I always thought that was a pretty good record.

I'm out of the field now and I thank God I made it in one piece. I am not sorry at all that I came over here. I didn't mind all that humping through the mud — I didn't even mind being wounded. That's all part of war; you can't do anything about it. Over-all, I have really enjoyed my tour over here in Vietnam and I'm glad I came over. I had a lot of good times in the field, made many friends and have learned an awful lot. I know now just how much we have back in America when I see how hard a life the Vietnamese people live here. Most have known war all their lives. It has killed their sons, even their women and children, and has destroyed their land. They must be very tired of this war. I am glad, though, that we are fighting over here and not in the United States.

I feel that by coming over here I have accomplished a great deal. I feel that I helped a few dozen GI's make it through their tour without being killed and that I was able to help the Vietnamese people, as well as our allied friends, in their fight against Communism. I am only sorry that more Americans back home do not support our efforts over here. I don't think that they really know what it's all about, especially what a soldier has to go through in the field. They do not know what it's like to see Communism face to face. They think we can fight a "moral" war over here. It seems to me that only the bad guys are supposed to get killed, and even then they have to be killed in a nice way. It just doesn't work that way, everything is not black and white, and all the killing is not nice by any means. I always felt that I was living close to death while I was in the field. It was something you had to get used to, seeing dead men, killing some myself and knowing I could be killed in a minute. It became so commonplace that I never worried about it really. That doesn't mean I enjoyed all killing and brutality — I just got used to it.

It's something you have to experience to understand. I think the only ones who really know what's going on in the battlefield are the soldiers who have to go out and kill the enemy to stay alive. They are the ones who know war best. . . .

[Do you think Duffy was convicted? Should he have been? See United States v. Duffy, 47 C.M.R. 658 (1973).]

Note: The Gulf War

The issue of war crimes remains with us, as evidenced by the widespread calls for individual prosecution for alleged crimes committed by both sides during the 1991 Gulf War, which followed Iraq's invasion of Kuwait. Interestingly, most public condemnation was directed against the political and military leaders of the operations rather than individual soldiers — perhaps because the ground phase of the war lasted only 100 hours. However, no prosecutions appear to have been brought by any side to the conflict, and there was no effort to establish a war crimes tribunal, despite early expressions of interest. See pages 968-978 of Problem XII.

Most of the alleged crimes were committed by Iraqi forces and might include the uncontroverted fact of the invasion of Kuwait (perhaps more accurately termed a crime against peace) and the firing of Scud missiles at cities in Israel, a state not otherwise involved in the conflict. Other allegations concerned the taking of diplomatic hostages and the treatment of Kuwaitis during the Iraqi occupation, including killing, rape, looting, and destruction of property. See Kahn, Lessons for International Law from the Gulf War, 45 Stan. L. Rev. 425 (1993); Robbins, War Crimes: The Case of Iraq, 18 Fletcher F. World Aff. 45 (No. 2, 1994).

The "coalition forces," led by the United States, were accused of targeting civilian installations (including Iraq's water supply, a "munitions" factory that purportedly produced milk powder, and an air raid shelter in which hundreds of civilians were killed) and of unnecessarily massacring Iraqi soldiers at the end of the brief ground war. The United States also was accused of having encouraged Saddam Hussein's attack on Kuwait and, thus, sharing in guilt for the invasion itself. See Clark, Complaint to the Commission of Inquiry for the International War Crimes Tribunal, 48 Guild Prac. 33 (1991); Heidenrich, The Gulf War: How Many Iraqis Died?, 90 Foreign Policy 108 (1993); Kamen, Iraqi Factory's Product: Germ Warfare or Milk?, Wash. Post, Feb. 8, 1991, at Al; Madigan, In War, the Bottom Line Is Death, Chi. Trib., Feb 15, 1991, at 1.

Among the many readings on war crimes and the Gulf War, see also R. Clark, The Fire This Time: U.S. War Crimes in the Gulf (1992); Baker, Legal Protections for the Environment in Times of Armed Conflict, 33 Va. J. Intl. L. 351 (1993); Gardam, Proportionality and Force in International Law, 87 Am. J. Intl. L. 391 (1993).

E.   Recent Developments in the Law of War

Lieutenant Duffy's testimony provides a poignant reminder of one of the most difficult problems in the modern law of war. That law is premised on the possibility and the necessity of distinguishing between combatants and civilians, between military targets and civilian habitats. Certainly nothing is more important insofar as the protection of the human rights of civilians is concerned. At the same time, nothing is more difficult. Moreover, the problem has become increasingly serious in the decades since the adoption of the Fourth Geneva Convention in 1949. The Vietnam War was only the most vivid illustration of the fact that the traditional law of war — designed to regulate international armed conflicts — was inadequate to handle the complex issues arising during the course of wars of "national liberation," situations of civil strife, and states of emergency.

During the early 1970s, the International Committee of the Red Cross, (ICRC) convened a diplomatic conference to reaffirm and develop the international humanitarian law applicable in armed conflicts. The result, in 1977, was the adoption of two protocols to the four Geneva Conventions. Protocol I is concerned with international armed conflicts, the traditional subject matter of the law of war, but it defines such conflicts to include ones "in which peoples are fighting against colonial domination and alien occupation and against racial regimes in the exercise of their right of self-determination," that is, wars of "national liberation." Protocol Additional to the Geneva Conventions of 12 August 1949, and Relating to the Protection of Victims of International Armed Conflicts (Protocol I), art. 1(4), opened for signature Dec. 12, 1977, U.N. Doc. A/32/144, Annex I (1977), reprinted in 16 Intl. Legal Materials 1391 (1977). Protocol II, which will be taken up in the next section, is concerned with internal armed conflicts (i.e., conflicts that take place within the confines of a single country) and, thus, potentially breaks even more new ground. Protocol Additional to the Geneva Conventions of 12 August 1949, and Relating to the Protection of Victims of Non-International Armed Conflicts (Protocol II), opened for signature Dec. 12, 1977, U.N. Doc. A/32/144, Annex II (1977), reprinted in 16 Intl. Legal Materials 1442 (1977).

To place these Protocols in context, extracts from an article by the late Judge Baxter, a rapporteur at the conference that drafted them, follow. Thereafter the key relevant articles of Protocol I are set out and an exchange of views on the merits of the Protocol given. Finally, President Ronald Reagan's reasons for recommending that the United States not ratify Protocol I are included. Despite criticisms, this recommendation has been followed by both his successors in office.

Baxter, Modernizing the Law of War
78 Mil. L. Rev. 165, 168-173 (1978)

One can understand the work of the Conference on International Humanitarian Law only in the setting of human rights law and humanitarian law in general. Until comparatively recently, the general perception was that there were two separate bodies of law — human rights law applicable to one's own nationals in time of peace and the law with respect to the protection of war victims, incorporated in the Geneva Conventions of 1949 and other treaties and applicable for the most part to individuals depending in one way or another on the adversary. The two bodies of law went their own ways and were supported by quite separate interest groups.

In the last ten years or so, it has come to be realized that human rights are as much at peril in time of war as they are in time of peace and that the law of human rights and the humanitarian law of war are actually closely related. In addition, the humanitarian law of war, which up till now has been applied to "all cases of declared war or of any other armed conflict which may arise between two or more of the High Contracting Parties," has not been brought to bear on two important forms of contemporary conflict.

With the exception of common Article 3 of the Geneva Conventions of 1949, the Geneva law applies only to conflicts between states. Article 3 contains the short bill of rights for noninternational armed conflicts and was thought to be a radical transformation of the law when it was incorporated in the Conventions in 1949. But since that time, a large number of internal conflicts have reached a scale akin to that of international armed conflicts whether measured in terms of the number of persons involved or the degree and kinds of force employed. Moreover, a number of international armed conflicts have an important noninternational element. The conflict in Vietnam, for example, had both international and noninternational elements, and a strict distinction between the two aspects of the conflict in terms of the law applied proved to be out of the question.

The period since the adoption of the Geneva Conventions of 1949 has also seen the emergence of a new kind of conflict — the war of national liberation. In essence, this is an anticolonial war, which, under the traditional law of war, was governed by whatever law there might be concerning noninternational armed conflicts. When the colony achieved independence, was recognized as a state, and became a party to the Geneva Conventions, then any conflict with the former colonial power was an international armed conflict governed by the totality of the Geneva Conventions. The case for saying that such an anticolonial war is from the outset a conflict that should be governed by the whole of the international law of war is that, if a colony or dependent territory is entitled to independence as a matter of international law, the law should treat such a colony or dependent territory as if it were independent and give it all the benefits of the law governing international armed conflicts. Otherwise the colonial power would profit by its own wrong in refusing to recognize the independence of the colony and in refusing to apply to it the law governing conflicts between two independent states. This is a simplified approach to a complex problem, and there are obvious difficulties that lie in the way of applying the whole corpus of the law of war to conflicts of this character. The developing countries, particularly those that had recently secured their independence, regarded the application of the whole of the law of war to wars of national liberation as the most important reform that ought to be made in the humanitarian law of war.

The situation when the Diplomatic Conference began its deliberations was thus that there were four different types of situations to be taken account of: peacetime (to which the law of human rights applies); internal armed conflicts (to which only Article 3 of the Geneva Conventions applied); international or interstate armed conflicts (to which all of the rest of the Geneva Conventions of 1949 applied); and wars of national liberation (which had not previously been dealt with by the humanitarian law of war). The case can be made, in theory at least, that the same body of law should govern the protection of human rights in all four types of situations and that the war-peace distinction reflected an oversimplified and outmoded view of the world. Nevertheless, the situations are different. Even a human rights convention, such as the European Convention, may be suspended in time of war. The guarantee of the basic rights of one's own nationals in time of peace and the safeguarding of enemy personnel in time of war belong to two different spheres of state action and interests. As a matter of history the development of the law of war has taken a quite different path from that newly laid out for the legal protection of human rights in time of peace. The law of war had developed its own institutions, such as the status of a prisoner of war or the role of the protecting power. And finally, the scale of violence employed in the torture of an individual and in the nuclear bombing of the enemy are so vastly different that they cannot be thought of within the same legal framework.

When the I.C.R.C. began its work on the development of the humanitarian law of war, there were high hopes for a separate new Protocol (or convention) on noninternational armed conflicts. . . . This proved to be too much for the majority of the states participating in the Conference. Opposition to the Protocol first took the form of raising the threshold of violence to which the Protocol would apply. Common Article 3 of the Geneva Conventions simply applies to "armed conflict not of an international character," but the new Protocol II was made to apply to

> all armed conflicts . . . which take place in the territory of a High Contracting Party between its armed forces and dissident armed forces or other organized armed groups which, under responsible command, exercise such control over a part of its territory as to enable them to carry out sustained and concerted military operations and to implement this Protocol.

What was obviously in the minds of the draftsmen was a conflict resembling the Civil War in Spain rather than the civil wars in Nigeria or the Congo. Through this definition two levels of internal armed conflicts were created, even as to parties to both the Conventions of 1949 and Protocol II — the lower level, governed by Article 3, and the higher level, governed by Protocol II. Such nice legal distinctions do not make the correct application of the law any easier.

The second limitation on the scope of the Protocol came in the fourth session of the Conference when, at the initiative of Pakistan, the drafting of provisions was changed from the form "The parties to the conflict shall . . ."

to statements of the protections which are to be extended to the participants and nonparticipants in the conflict. A number of provisions already adopted were simply dropped, and the simplified Protocol II was adopted in its reduced scale. There was some danger that the Protocol would not have survived at all if this radical surgery had not be employed.

The legal protection of persons affected by noninternational armed conflicts was seen by the developing and newly independent countries forming a majority of the Conference as much less consequential than the protection of belligerents and civilians in wars of national liberation. In this case, the law swung to the opposite extreme. A new article was steamrollered through the first session of the Conference, which provided in its most significant paragraph that:

> The situations referred to [in Article 2 common to the Geneva Conventions of 1949, namely interstate armed conflicts] . . . included armed conflicts in which peoples are fighting against colonial domination and alien occupation and against racist regimes in the exercise of their right of self-determination, as enshrined in the Charter of the United Nations and the Declaration on Principles of International Law concerning Friendly Relations and Cooperation among States in accordance with the Charter of the United Nations.

By this provision not only Protocol I on International Armed Conflicts itself but also the totality of the Geneva Conventions of 1949 are made applicable to wars of national liberation.

The various types of conflicts which constitute wars of national liberation deserve some further explanation. The conflicts in which peoples fight against "colonial domination" are those in which a colony or dependent territory rebels, as was the case, for example, when the Portuguese colonies in Africa rebelled and became independent. "Alien occupation" may seem an unnecessary provision, because belligerent occupation by one state of the territory of another is already governed by the Hague Regulations of 1907 and by the Geneva Civilians Convention of 1949. Presumably these two words were inserted to catch the votes of the Arab States; the territory under "alien occupation" is that claimed by the Arab States but under Israeli occupation. Hostilities in Rhodesia (Zimbabwe) and South Africa against the dominant white administrations are instances of fight[s] against a "racist regime." The United States was concerned that a provision on wars of national liberation might introduce a subjective and judgmental element into the law of war, which had hitherto rested on a foundation of neutrality and equality of application to all belligerents, without regard to the legality of their resort to hostilities. However, the pressure in favor of the application of the whole of the law of war to wars of national liberation was such that it could not be resisted, and the United States and its NATO allies simply accepted the provision in silence.

One of the procedural complications occasioned by the provision on wars of national liberation was that a national liberation movement or any other entity or authority constituting the moving party in a war of national liberation would not be a party to the Geneva Conventions of 1949 or to Protocol I. To deal with this difficulty, a clause [Article 96(3)] was inserted whereby an "authority representing a people" engaged in a war of national liberation would undertake to apply the Protocol and the Conventions by a unilateral declaration addressed to Switzerland, the depositary of the Protocol. This declaration would bring the Protocol and Conventions into force between the "authority" and the other party to the conflict.

Political forces dominated the consideration of "noninternational armed conflicts" and "wars of national liberation." Developing countries, led by those who had experienced civil wars, succeeded in blunting the edge of the movement for a much more ample protection of the victims of civil wars. It was that same bloc of developing countries, supported by the U.S.S.R. and its allies, that succeeded in giving special status to wars of national liberation. . . .

Note: Relevant Articles of Protocol I

Part IV of Protocol I (Articles 48 to 79) deals with the protection of civilians and contains much of interest. Article 48 sets forth a "basic rule" that the parties to the conflict "shall at all times distinguish between the civilian population and combatants and between civilian objects and military objectives and accordingly shall direct their operations only against military objectives." Article 51, concerning "protection of the civilian population" generally, is of especial importance.

Article 51 — Protection of the Civilian Population

1. The civilian population and individual civilians shall enjoy general protection against dangers arising from military operations. To give effect to this protection, the following rules, which are additional to other applicable rules of international law, shall be observed in all circumstances.

2. The civilian population as such, as well as individual civilians, shall not be the object of attack. Acts or threats of violence the primary purpose of which is to spread terror among the civilian population are prohibited.

3. Civilians shall enjoy the protection afforded by this Section, unless and for such time as they take a direct part in hostilities.

4. Indiscriminate attacks are prohibited. Indiscriminate attacks are:

    (a) those which are not directed at a specific military objective;

    (b) those which employ a method or means of combat which cannot be directed at a specific military objective; or

    (c) those which employ a method or means of combat the effects of which cannot be limited as required by this Protocol;

and consequently, in each such case, are of a nature to strike military objectives and civilians or civilian objects without distinction.

5. Among others, the following types of attacks are to be considered as indiscriminate:

(a) an attack by bombardment by any methods or means which treats as a single military objective a number of clearly separated and distinct military objectives located in a city, town, village or other area containing a similar concentration of civilians or civilian objects; and

(b) an attack which may be expected to cause incidental loss of civilian life, injury to civilians, damage to civilian objects, or a combination thereof, which would be excessive in relation to the concrete and direct military advantage anticipated.

6. Attacks against the civilian population or civilians by way of reprisals are prohibited.

7. The presence or movements of the civilian population or individual civilians shall not be used to render certain points or areas immune from military operations, in particular in attempts to shield military objectives from attacks or to shield, favour or impede military operations. The Parties to the conflict shall not direct the movement of the civilian population or individual civilians in order to attempt to shield military objectives from attacks or to shield military operations.

8. Any violation of these prohibitions shall not release the Parties to the conflict from their legal obligations with respect to the civilian population and civilians, including the obligations to take the precautionary measures provided for in Article 57.

Also of major importance is Article 57, which sets forth the precautions that must be taken when mounting attacks to minimize injuries to the civilian population:

Article 57 — Precautions in Attack

1. In the conduct of military operations, constant care shall be taken to spare the civilian population, civilians and civilian objects.

2. With respect to attacks, the following precautions shall be taken:

(a) those who plan or decide upon an attack shall:

(i) do everything feasible to verify that the objectives to be attacked are neither civilians nor civilian objects and are not subject to special protection but are military objectives within the meaning of paragraph 2 of Article 52 and that it is not prohibited by the provisions of this Protocol to attack them;

(ii) take all feasible precautions in the choice of means and methods of attack with a view to avoiding, and in any event to minimizing, incidental loss of civilian life, injury to civilians and damage to civilian objects;

(iii) refrain from deciding to launch any attack which may be expected to cause incidental loss of civilian life, injury to civilians, damage to civilian objects, or a combination thereof, which would be excessive in relation to the concrete and direct military advantage anticipated;

(b) an attack shall be canceled or suspended if it becomes apparent that the objective is not a military one or is subject to special protection or that the attack may be expected to cause incidental loss of civilian life, injury to civilians, damage to civilian objects, or a combination thereof, which would be excessive in relation to the concrete and direct military advantage anticipated;

(c) effective advance warning shall be given of attacks which may affect the civilian population, unless circumstances do not permit.

3. When a choice is possible between several military objectives for obtaining a similar military advantage, the objective to be selected shall be that the attack on which may be expected to cause the least danger to civilian lives and to civilian objects.

4. In the conduct of military operations at sea or in the air, each Party to the conflict shall, in conformity with its rights and duties under the rules of international law applicable in armed conflict, take all reasonable precautions to avoid losses of civilian lives and damage to civilian objects.

5. No provision of this Article may be construed as authorizing any attacks against the civilian population, civilians or civilian objects.

Finally, Article 75 elaborates an impressive number of "fundamental guarantees" — in addition to the rules contained in the Fourth Geneva Convention, as well as to other international law rules relating to the protection of fundamental human rights during international armed conflicts (Article 72) — to which persons in the power of a party to a conflict are entitled.

Article 75 — Fundamental Guarantees

1. In so far as they are affected by a situation referred to in Article 1 of this Protocol, persons who are in the power of a Party to the conflict and who do not benefit from more favourable treatment under the Conventions or under this Protocol shall be treated humanely in all circumstances and shall enjoy, as a minimum, the protection provided by this Article without any adverse distinction based upon race, colour, sex, language, religion or belief, political or other opinion, national or social origin, wealth, birth or other status, or on any other similar criteria. Each Party shall respect the person, honour, convictions and religious practice of all such persons.

2. The following acts are and shall remain prohibited at any time and in any place whatsoever, whether committed by civilian or by military agents:

(a) violence to the life, health, or physical or mental well-being of persons, in particular:

(i) murder;

(ii) torture of all kinds, whether physical or mental;

(iii) corporal punishment; and

(iv) mutilation;

(b) outrages upon personal dignity, in particular humiliating and degrading treatment, enforced prostitution and any form of indecent assault;

(c) the taking of hostages;

(d) collective punishments; and

(e) threats to commit any of the foregoing acts.

3. Any person arrested, detained or interned for actions related to the armed conflict shall be informed promptly, in a language he understands, of the reasons why these measures have been taken. Except in cases of arrest or

detention for penal offences, such persons shall be released with the minimum delay possible and in any event as soon as the circumstances justifying the arrest, detention or internment have ceased to exist.

4. No sentence may be passed and no penalty may be executed on a person found guilty of a penal offence related to the armed conflict except pursuant to a conviction pronounced by an impartial and regularly constituted court respecting the generally recognized principles of regular judicial procedure, which include the following:

(a) the procedure shall provide for an accused to be informed without delay of the particulars of the offence alleged against him and shall afford the accused before and during his trial all necessary rights and means of defence;

(b) no one shall be convicted of an offence except on the basis of individual penal responsibility;

(c) no one shall be accused or convicted of a criminal offence on account of any act or omission which did not constitute a criminal offence under the national or international law to which he was subject at the time when it was committed; nor shall a heavier penalty be imposed than that which was applicable at the time when the criminal offense was committed; if after the commission of the offence, provision is made by law for the imposition of a lighter penalty, the offender shall benefit thereby;

(d) anyone charged with an offence is presumed innocent until proved guilty according to law;

(e) anyone charged with an offence shall have the right to be tried in his presence;

(f) no one shall be compelled to testify against himself or to confess guilt;

(g) anyone charged with an offence shall have the right to examine, or have examined, the witnesses against him and to obtain the attendance and examination of witnesses on his behalf under the same conditions as witnesses against him;

(h) no one shall be prosecuted or punished by the same Party for an offence in respect of which a final judgment acquitting or convicting that person has been previously pronounced under the same law and judicial procedure;

(i) anyone prosecuted for an offence shall have the right to have the judgment pronounced publicly; and

(j) a convicted person shall be advised on conviction of his judicial and other remedies and of the time limits within which they may be exercised.

5. Women whose liberty has been restricted for reasons related to the armed conflict shall be held in quarters separated from men's quarters. They shall be under the immediate supervision of women. Nevertheless, in cases where families are detained or interned, they shall, whenever possible, be held in the same place and accommodated as family units.

6. Persons who are arrested, detained or interned for reasons related to the armed conflict shall enjoy the protection provided by this Article until their final release, repatriation or re-establishment, even after the end of the armed conflict.

7. In order to avoid any doubt concerning the prosecution and trial of persons accused of war crimes or crimes against humanity, the following principles shall apply;

(a) persons who are accused of such crimes should be submitted for the purpose of prosecution and trial in accordance with the applicable rules of international law; and

(b) any such persons who do not benefit from more favourable treatment under the Conventions or this Protocol shall be accorded the treatment provided by this Article, whether or not the crimes of which they are accused constitute grave breaches of the Conventions or of this Protocol.

8. No provision of this Article may be construed as limiting or infringing any other more favourable provision granting greater protection, under any applicable rules of international law, to persons covered by paragraph 1.

Roberts, The New Rules for Waging War: The Case Against Ratification of Additional Protocol I
26 Va. J. Intl. L. 109, 124-127, 150-152 (1985)

V. CRITIQUE OF THE MAJOR PROVISIONS OF PROTOCOL I

A.   NATIONAL LIBERATION MOVEMENTS: A NEW CATEGORY FOR
THE LAW OF WAR COVERING INTERNATIONAL CONFLICTS

A major aim of the Third World countries and the eleven participating national liberation movements (NLM's) at the Diplomatic Conference was to achieve recognition of the international character of wars of national liberation. Their goal was to see such wars elevated to the status of armed conflicts between sovereign states so that the Geneva Conventions would apply in those conflicts. Article 1(4) of Protocol I accomplishes this purpose by declaring that the Protocol applies, inter alia, to armed conflicts

> in which peoples are fighting against colonial domination and alien occupation and against racist regimes in the exercise of their right of self-determination, as enshrined in the Charter of the United Nations and the Declaration on Principles of International Law concerning Friendly Relations and Co-operation among States in accordance with the Charter of the United Nations.

Traditionally, these types of struggles were commonly characterized as internal or non-international matters. Proponents of "internationalizing" such conflicts contended that Protocol I should affirm "the right of self-determination," and recognized the "lawfulness" and "justness" of such wars. With article 1(4), Protocol I incorporates these beliefs and affords international status to NLM's thereby legitimizing foreign intervention in wars of national liberation.

Resistance to article 1(4) was initially quite strong. First, some states pointed out that the terms were vague and subject to political interpretation. For example, what constitutes a "racist regime"? What is "alien occupation"? How is a discrete "people" to be defined? Many delegates felt the terms were not sufficiently precise to identify with certainty the situations to which the article would apply.

The practicality of the article was also called into question at the Conference. As the U.S. representative noted:

> Liberation movements could not fulfil all their obligations under the Conventions and would thus be branded as being in violation of those Conventions. The only benefit which those movements would receive from labeling their struggle as international would be enhanced political status, but nothing on the humanitarian plane. Protocol II [concerning non-international conflicts] was the instrument best suited to afford those movements the degree of humanitarian protection required, without imposing on them obligations which they could not accept.

Furthermore, states would be unlikely to accept the "racist," "alien" or "colonial" labels necessary for triggering the provisions of Protocol I. As the Israeli delegate noted, "[Article 1(4)] had within it a built-in non-applicability clause, since a party would have to admit that it was either racist, alien or colonial . . . ensur[ing] that no State by its own volition would ever apply that article." Essentially, the main argument of the Western states against incorporating article 1(4) was that "the proposed national-liberation-war language would [legitimize] certain types of war, license belligerent foreign meddling in the sovereign domain of certain states, politicize humanitarian law, and thereby render humanitarian law even less sturdy a shield for its intended beneficiaries."

Despite the strong reasons against approving the article, the Western states did not resist the demands of the NLM's. The United States and most other Western nations abstained when a final vote was taken on the article, and only Israel voted against it. Exactly why the West failed to resist more rigorously the adoption of the article is unclear. As one noted expert proclaimed:

> The damage to Humanitarian Law, the benefit of which [national liberation movements] have claimed, is apparent because discrimination has been imported into it. It does violence to the facts, including the political and military facts of the situation. Even with the palliatives of Protocol I, Article 96(3), the declaration of intent made during the conflict, and the interpretative statements made by certain states before the signing of the Final Act of the Conference as to the minimum level of intensity of the conflict being determined by reference to the scope provisions [article 1] of Protocol 2, the international community is likely to be confronted with entities bound by a body of humanitarian law that they are unable to apply, even if they had the will to do so. The net effect of the "political coup" obtained by the adoption of the N.L.M. insertion . . . is to weaken the delicate network of humanitarian rules established for the conduct of international armed conflicts and at the same time to diminish confidence in Protocol 2 governing internal disputes.

In view of the subjective judgment required to apply article 1(4), the great potential for inconsistent interpretation, and the blatant politicization of the law of war indicated by the reintroduction of the "just war" concept, ratification of Protocol I without reserving this article would significantly set back efforts to create concrete and workable rules of war. . . .

E.   THE IMPACT OF PROTOCOL I ON MILITARY OPERATIONS

. . . 3. Articles 50-54: Protection of Civilian Population and Objects

Articles 50(1) and 52(3) require that "in cases of doubt" as to whether a person or object is a legitimate military target, such doubts must be resolved by assuming the person or object has non-combatant status. Although on its face this provision seems laudable and reasonable, an all-encompassing presumption of this nature is not operationally practicable and likely to be ignored. First, the "in cases of doubt" language is sufficiently vague as to make possible political rather than objective evaluations of the facts. Although one can argue that "the practical impact of this rule is to require that persons responsible for an attack act honestly on the basis of information available to them at the time they take their actions and not on the basis of mere speculation," what represents one commander's doubt under cool reflection may be another's certainty in the heat of battle.

On the modern battlefield, hesitation over the legitimacy of a military target or objective may have dire consequences for the military commander. The mere fact that an individual or an object is in a location that poses danger to military forces may be sufficient to warrant an attack, for the primary duty of a commander, apart from accomplishing his mission, is the protection of his soldiers and equipment. The rules contained in articles 50(1) and 52(3) require all unidentifiable individuals and objects to be treated as civilian and thus immune from attack — an impossible requirement given the exigencies of modern warfare and weaponry.

Article 51(5) prohibits states from carrying out indiscriminate attacks. . . . [See page 885 supra for text.] Paragraph (b) does little more than restate in somewhat vague terms the principle of proportionality; it requires that military necessity outweigh the incidental damage to civilians and civilian objects expected in any given attack. Paragraph (a), on the other hand, poses significant practical problems for the military commander. First, it fails to define what is meant by "clearly separated and distinct military objectives." How far apart must objectives be in order to be considered "separate and distinct"? Of what significance is the method of weapons delivery and type of weapons used on the target? The U.S. delegation and others understood the words "clearly separated" to refer not only to an observable separation of two or more military objectives but to a separation over a significant distance. Even under this interpretation, the article remains difficult to apply and ambiguous, susceptible to be invoked in any case where civilians or civilian objects are unintentionally damaged.

Aldrich, Progressive Development of the Laws of War: A Reply to Criticisms of the 1977 Geneva Protocol I
26 Va. J. Intl. L. 693, 700-703, 712-714 (1986)

I. Wars of National Liberation

Article 1 of the Protocol provides, in paragraph 3, that the Protocol, which supplements the 1949 Geneva Conventions, "shall apply in the situations referred to in article 2 common to those Conventions," that is to all armed conflicts between two or more of the Parties to the Conventions. In paragraph 4 of article 1, the Protocol adds the following:

> The situations referred to in the preceding paragraph include armed conflicts in which peoples are fighting against colonial domination and alien occupation and against racist regimes in the exercise of their right of self-determination, as enshrined in the Charter of the United Nations and the Declaration on Principles of International Law concerning Friendly Relations and Co-operation among States in accordance with the Charter of the United Nations.

. . . Most Western States, including the United States, reacted negatively to the inclusion of paragraph 4 in article 1 primarily out of a concern that it imported into humanitarian law the dangerous concept of the just war and might thus lead to other provisions limiting protections of law to those engaged in "just wars." As noted above, however, we were successful in our efforts to include in the preamble a provision that prohibits the denial of protections accorded by the Conventions and the Protocol on such grounds. Moreover, the Conference also adopted article 96, paragraph 3, which provides as follows:

> The authority representing a people engaged against a High Contracting Party in an armed conflict of the type referred to in article 1, paragraph 4, may undertake to apply the Conventions and this Protocol in relation to that conflict by means of a unilateral declaration addressed to the depositary. Such declaration shall, upon its receipt by the depositary, have in relation to that conflict the following effects:
>
> (a) The Conventions and this Protocol are brought into force for the said authority as a Party to the conflict with immediate effect;
>
> (b) the said authority assumes the same rights and obligations as those which have been assumed by a High Contracting Party to the Conventions and this Protocol; and
>
> (c) the Conventions and this Protocol are equally binding upon all Parties to the conflict.

As a result of that provision, the Conventions and Protocol have, by their terms, no application to wars of national liberation. Members of the armed forces of a national liberation movement do not therefore enjoy the protections of those treaties unless the Movement formally accepts all the obligations of the Conventions and the Protocol in the same way as the States Parties. Few, if any, liberation movements could expect to be in a position to carry out such obligations unless and until they are about to succeed in becoming the government of the State. In any event, members of armed forces of liberation movements are not granted protections simply because they may be deemed to be fighting for a just cause; the Protocol and the Conventions must apply equally to both sides if they are to apply to the conflict at all.

Article 1, paragraph 4 was designed with certain conflicts in mind, specifically those in Palestine and southern Africa and was drafted in terms fashioned to exclude its application to civil wars within existing States. That is why it uses emotionally loaded terms like "colonial domination," "alien occupation," and "racist regimes;" indeed, the use of these terms goes far to ensure that the provision will never be applied. First, the language by itself may deter the main target states (Israel and South Africa) from acceding to the Protocol. Second, if a State Party to the Protocol should find itself suppressing a rebellion, it is not likely to agree that it is a "colonial" power or is engaged in "alien occupation" or is a "racist regime;" and, if it does not agree that it fits within those categories, the provision simply will not be applied. Third, as noted above, liberation movements are unlikely to even file declarations under article 96, in which case the State involved need not address the question at all.

Finally, in the more than eight years since the signing of Protocol I, not a single declaration has been filed under article 96. . . .

In sum, article 1, paragraph 4 poses no threat to the United States and needs no reservation. If it were feasible to apply the Geneva Conventions and Protocol I to the armed conflicts to which that provision is intended to apply, compliance with these treaties could bring significant humanitarian benefits. Such application and compliance have not been and seem unlikely to become feasible for a multitude of reasons, both political and practical. In effect, the provision is a dead letter. . . .

VII.   PROTECTION OF CIVILIANS

Major Roberts raises several objections to some of the provisions of the Protocol designed to protect civilians and the civilian population. First, he objects to the provisions in articles 50 and 52 requiring that, in case of doubt as to whether a person is a civilian or a certain object is a military objective, the person shall be considered a civilian and the object shall not be considered a military objective. He says that such a provision "is not operationally practicable and likely to be ignored," and he construes these rules as requiring "all unidentifiable individuals and objects to be treated as civilian and thus immune from attack." But there is no reason to interpret these provisions in such a distorted way. The reasons why Roberts thinks they are likely to be ignored are reasons why I think they will be interpreted in practice as directing commanders not to make decisions about civilian character irresponsibly or without taking into account all relevant information reasonably available to them.

Thus, it was the view of the American negotiators of these provisions, which has been endorsed by the most comprehensive scholarly study of the Protocol, that:

> The person's behavior, location and appearance in relation to other circumstances known to the decision maker are relevant factors in deciding whether such person is a civilian. Such decisions must not be judged on the basis of hindsight.

With respect to civilian objects, Major Roberts fails to point out that only certain types of objects enjoy, in case of doubt, the benefit of any presumption that they are not being used to make an effective contribution to military action. Moreover, these are objects normally used only for civilian purposes, such as churches, houses or schools.

Second, Major Roberts objects to article 51, paragraph 5, subparagraph (a), which is one of two examples in the article of prohibited indiscriminate attacks. That example is defined as:

> an attack by bombardment by any methods or means which treats as a single military objective a number of clearly separated and distinct military objectives located in a city, town, village or other area containing a similar concentration of civilians or civilian objects.

Major Roberts is troubled by the phrase "clearly separated and distinct" which is undefined and which he believes makes the article susceptible to being invoked whenever civilians or civilian objects suffer injury. The provision was intended to prohibit target-area bombardment in cities as practiced during the Second World War, and is surely a worthy goal. It was not intended to immunize military objectives from attack simply because they are located within urban areas. In context, the provision unavoidably means that an attacker is not to attack an area within a concentration of civilians, even if the military objectives entitle such an attack. The military objectives must be sufficiently separated so as to be capable of being attacked individually by the weapons available. As so understood, the rule is practical, desirable, and no more subject to abuse than most other protective measures.

Message from the President Transmitting Protocol II
Additional to the 1949 Geneva Conventions, and
Relating to the Protection of Victims of
Noninternational Armed Conflicts
S. Treaty Doc. No. 2, 100th Cong., 1st Sess. III-V (1987)

LETTER OF TRANSMITTAL

THE WHITE HOUSE, *January 29, 1987.*
To the Senate of the United States:

I transmit herewith, for the advice and consent of the Senate to ratification, Protocol II Additional to the Geneva Conventions of 12 August 1949,
concluded at Geneva on June 10, 1977. I also enclose for the information of
the Senate the report of the Department of State on the Protocol.

The United States has traditionally been in the forefront of efforts to
codify and improve the international rules of humanitarian law in armed
conflict, with the objective of giving the greatest possible protection to victims of such conflicts, consistent with legitimate military requirements. The
agreement that I am transmitting today is, with certain exceptions, a positive
step toward this goal. Its ratification by the United States will assist us in
continuing to exercise leadership in the international community in these
matters.

The Protocol is described in detail in the attached report of the Department of State. Protocol II to the 1949 Geneva Conventions is essentially
an expansion of the fundamental humanitarian provisions contained in the
1949 Geneva Conventions with respect to non-international armed conflicts, including humane treatment and basic due process for detained persons, protection of the wounded, sick and medical units, and protection of
noncombatants from attack and deliberate starvation. If these fundamental
rules were observed, many of the worst human tragedies of current internal
armed conflicts could be avoided. In particular, among other things, the
mass murder of civilians is made illegal, even if such killings would not
amount to genocide because they lacked racial or religious motives. Several
Senators asked me to keep this objective in mind when adopting the Genocide Convention. I remember my commitment to them. This Protocol
makes clear that any deliberate killing of a noncombatant in the course of a
non-international armed conflict is a violation of the laws of war and a
crime against humanity, and is therefore also punishable as murder.

While I recommend that the Senate grant advice and consent to this
agreement, I have at the same time concluded that the United States
cannot ratify a second agreement on the law of armed conflict negotiated
during the same period. I am referring to Protocol I additional to the 1949
Geneva Conventions, which would revise the rules applicable to interna-

tional armed conflicts. Like all other efforts associated with the International Committee of the Red Cross, this agreement has certain meritorious elements. But Protocol I is fundamentally and irreconcilably flawed. It contains provisions that would undermine humanitarian law and endanger civilians in war. One of its provisions, for example, would automatically treat as an international conflict any so-called "war of national liberation." Whether such wars are international or non-international should turn exclusively on objective reality, not on one's view of the moral qualities of each conflict. To rest on such subjective distinctions based on a war's alleged purposes would politicize humanitarian law and eliminate the distinction between international and non-international conflicts. It would give special status to "wars of national liberation," an ill-defined concept expressed in vague, subjective, politicized terminology. Another provision would grant combatant status to irregular forces even if they do not satisfy the traditional requirements to distinguish themselves from the civilian population and otherwise comply with the laws of war. This would endanger civilians among whom terrorists and other irregulars attempt to conceal themselves. These problems are so fundamental in character that they cannot be remedied through reservations, and I therefore have decided not to submit the Protocol to the Senate in any form, and I would invite an expression of the sense of the Senate that it shares this view. Finally, the Joint Chiefs of Staff have also concluded that a number of the provisions of the Protocol are militarily unacceptable.

It is unfortunate that Protocol I must be rejected. We would have preferred to ratify such a convention, which as I said contains certain sound elements. but we cannot allow other nations of the world, however numerous, to impose upon us and our allies and friends an unacceptable and thoroughly distasteful price for joining a convention drawn to advance the laws of war. In fact, we must not, and need not, give recognition and protection to terrorist groups as a price for progress in humanitarian law.

The time has come for us to devise a solution for this problem, with which the United States is from time to time confronted. In this case, for example, we can reject Protocol I as a reference for humanitarian law, and at the same time devise an alternative reference for the positive provisions of Protocol I that could be the real humanitarian benefit if generally observed by parties to international armed conflicts. We are therefore in the process of consulting with our allies to develop appropriate methods for incorporating these positive provisions into the rules that govern our military operations, and as customary international law. I will advise the Senate of the results of this initiative as soon as it is possible to do so.

I believe that these actions are a significant step in defense of traditional humanitarian law and in opposition to the intense efforts of terrorist organizations and their supporters to promote the legitimacy of their aims and practices. The repudiation of Protocol I is one additional step, at the ideological level so important to terrorist organizations, to deny these groups legitimacy as international actors.

Therefore, I request that the Senate act promptly to give advice and consent to the ratification of the agreement I am transmitting today, subject to the understandings and reservations that are described more fully in the attached report. I would also invite an expression of the sense of the Senate that it shares the view that the United States should not ratify Protocol I, thereby reaffirming its support for traditional humanitarian law, and its opposition to the politicization of that law by groups that employ terrorist practices.

RONALD REAGAN

As of mid-1994, Protocol II remained pending before the U.S. Senate for its advice and consent. Neither President George Bush nor President Bill Clinton had recommended U.S. ratification of Protocol I, despite the optimism expressed in Aldrich, Prospects for United States Ratification of Additional Protocol I to the 1949 Geneva Conventions, 85 Am. J. Intl. L. 1 (1991).

Comments and Questions

1. The law of war, while violated at My Lai and on countless other occasions during the Vietnam War, nevertheless had a restraining effect on both sides during the conflict. Recall, for instance, that while the North Vietnamese committed numerous atrocities during the Tet offensive, they previously had backed down from their announced plans to try U.S. airmen as "war criminals" when the United States was able to demonstrate conclusively, within and without the UN, that a serviceman's participation in a war — even arguendo an aggressive one — did not render him criminally responsible. Thus, despite the inhumane treatment many airmen received at the hands of their North Vietnamese captors, they did receive some protection from the law of war — protection that in some instances may have made the difference between life and death.

2. The traditional law of war depends for its enforcement upon the knowledge of the ordinary soldier and his willingness to disobey superior orders when such orders clearly are illegal. Is this approach to achieving compliance with the law of war a realistic one? Does it not place the greatest burden upon the weakest link in the chain of command? Consider your response to these questions taking into account:

(a)   Calley's statement that, while he received some instructions in the Geneva Conventions, he actually learned nothing about "the laws and rules of warfare" and, indeed, had been told that "all orders were to be assumed legal. . . ."

(b)   Duffy's statement that "platoon leaders never got any guidance on treatment of prisoners. Battalion HQS never said anything about them."

(c)   Professor Wasserstrom's observation that "the doctrine of military necessity (conceived of as a general justifying condition) makes it virtually impossible for the soldier to determine from this limited perspective whether an ostensible war crime in fact comes under this exemption. It is, in short, often a fiction that the soldier in the field is in any position to ascertain to which situations the laws of war apply and to which they do not." Wasserstrom, Contribution to "Individual Responsibility in Warfare," in Law and Responsibility in Warfare: The Vietnam Experience 194, 202 (P. Trooboff ed. 1975).

3. Mrs. Anthony Meadlo, the mother of Paul Meadlo, who admitted to killing 35-40 villagers at My Lai and ultimately was granted immunity in return for his testimony at the Calley trial, remarked of her son: "I sent them a good boy, and they made him a murderer." N.Y. Times, Nov. 30, 1969, §4, at 1, col. 5. Obviously, learning how to kill is part of any soldier's training, but so should be the distinction between fixing one's sights on an armed enemy as opposed to a defenseless civilian.

Aside from the moral dimensions of the law of war, considerations of self-interest and concerns for reciprocal treatment are good reasons for instructing soldiers to comply with it. Contemplate the example related in the following Letter to the Editor in The Independent (London), Mar. 2, 1988, at 21, cols. 1-2.

The Ethics of War

Dear Sir,

Mark Urban writes convincingly about the difficulties of soldiers who are given orders to shoot prisoners ("The dilemma posed by 'total warfare' ", 29 February). What about the less publicised casual shooting of prisoners in or near the front line? The British are not blameless: see Keegan, *The Face of Battle*, and Max Hasting's *Overlord*.

In March 1943 in northern Tunisia, my sergeant wanted to shoot two unarmed stretcher bearers picking up wounded in front of our position — they had shouted their purpose as a warning to us. Fortunately, I managed to restrain him: fortunately, because the following day, together with three others, I was captured some 200 yards behind the first position. My captors, who behaved in an exemplary way, would have certainly come across the bodies of the stretcher bearers.

I had some sympathy with my sergeant. We had been well-drilled in what to do if we were captured and we had endured a lot of gung-ho nonsense about bringing back Hun scalps. As far as I can remember, we were told nothing specific about a code for taking and treating prisoners. It was certainly not a significant part of our training. Maybe things are different now.

I believe that societies laying claim to fair play and humanity need clearly defined codes of conduct for their soldiers — and need to enforce them vigorously *all the way down the line of command*. Only then is there any hope that 18-year-old conscripts can be trained when to take off their safety catches.

> Yours faithfully,
> KEN CLARK
> Bedford

4. Calley's statement that he sometimes was told not to come back from patrol without "some body count," as well as Duffy's similar complaint that "[t]he only thing we ever heard was to get more body count, kill more VC! . . . My squad leader told me that in his old unit they couldn't come in from the field until they turned in a body count," reveals rather starkly that the My Lai massacre was nothing more that the logical extension of the body count approach to "pacification." Consider here:

(a) Taylor's contention (T. Taylor, supra page 858, at 161-163) that the body count emphasis came close to being an illegal superior order, and that as a practical matter it, therefore, was taken into account in mitigation in the Duffy court-martial.

(b) Wasserstrom's arguments (Wasserstrom, supra page 897, at 209) to the effect that leaders who knowingly encouraged or permitted the body count emphasis, especially if they knew or should have known that it led to the killing rather than the capture of enemy soldiers who wished to surrender (as well as to the death of innocent civilians), could have been held liable for the ensuing war crimes.

(c) Westmoreland's denial of any feeling of guilt over My Lai, calling it a product of "inexperienced lieutenants and sergeants" and relying upon what Taylor (T. Taylor, supra page 858, at 168) calls "virtually impeccable" paper directives to limit the application of the command responsibility principle to a relatively low level of officers.

5. As we have seen (page 861 supra), the highest ranking officer charged after My Lai was a colonel, and most Americans undoubtedly agreed with former government official Townsend Hoopes when he observed that it would have been "absurd" to contemplate trying high civilian officials as war criminals. Hoopes, The Nuremberg Suggestion, in Crimes of War: A Legal, Political-Documentary, and Psychological Inquiry into the Responsibility of Leaders, Citizens, and Soldiers for Criminal Acts in Wars 233, 236 (R. Falk, G. Kolko, and R. Lifton eds. 1971). Even if this conclusion is correct as a practical matter, however, should not more thought have been given to the potential responsibility of U.S. leaders, rather than focusing nearly exclusively upon that of "inexperienced lieutenants and sergeants . . ."? Are not such leaders "persons to whom many principles of responsibility most obviously and plausibly apply, and to whom culpability most fairly and appropriately appears to attach"? Wasserstrom, supra page 897, at 204. Do not the Nuremberg Principles and *Yamashita* support his contention that "actual knowledge" was not required to hold both civilian and military leaders criminally responsible for acts of subordinates of the type committed at My Lai? Id. at 210.

Re-read paragraphs 498, 501, and 510 of The Law of Land Warfare (Field Manual 27-10, 1956), found at pages 851-853 supra. Then recall the remarks of Justice Jackson, the chief prosecutor for the United States at the Nuremberg Trials: "[i]f certain acts in violation of treaties are crimes, they are crimes whether the United States does them or whether Germany does them, and we are not prepared to lay down a rule of criminal conduct against others which we would not be willing to have invoked against us." Report of Robert H. Jackson, United States Representative to the International Conference on Military Trials, U.S. Dept. of State Pub. No. 3080, at 330 (1949).

6. Many commentators have cited statistics about the number of courts-martial conducted by the United States in Vietnam in an effort to show that the United States, unlike North Vietnam or many other states, has made a good faith effort to enforce the law of war in armed conflicts. See, e.g., Bishop, The Question of War Crimes, 54 Commentary 85, 88 (Dec. 1972). While this enforcement effort is commendable, did it fully satisfy the international obligations of the United States in this regard? Consider:

(a) The fact that the United States failed to prosecute ex-servicemen for war crimes (see text at pages 859-860 supra).

(b) The fact that, despite the injunction in Paragraph 508 of Field Manual 27-10 that "[t]he punishment imposed for a violation of law of war must be proportionate to the gravity of the offense," the sentence imposed upon Calley for the premeditated murder of at least 22 unarmed civilians was so short in length as to be derisory and was not fully imposed to boot.

7. On 28 October 1975, the Senate, by a 49-43 vote, confirmed the promotion to Lieutenant General in the U.S. Air Force of Alton D. Slay, who during the Vietnam War knowingly and unquestioningly received and carried out orders to conduct air strikes on North Vietnam in early 1972 in violation of the Air Force's written rules of engagement, later concealing these violations by the falsification of reports (itself a violation of Article 107 of the UCMJ). Slay's only excuse was that he had been carrying out the orders of his superior officer, Major General John D. Lavelle, commander of the U.S. Seventh Air Force in Vietnam.

During the Senate debate, Senator Strom Thurmond argued that Slay had done no wrong, since he "was merely executing the orders issued to him by a superior officer," 121 Cong. Rec. 33993 (1975), while Senator Barry Goldwater asserted that "when one is in combat or even when he is just in the military, he obeys orders and that is all that General Slay has done." Id. at 34000. What do these comments, and the Senate's vote, reveal about the level of understanding of the defense of superior orders? Have the lessons of the Vietnam War — especially the Calley court-martial — been learned?

8. Perhaps understandably, My Lai has been the subject of little writing in the United States during the last two decades. For a vivid account of the massacre and the effect it has had on the lives of its U.S. "survivors," see My Lai: A Half-Told Story, The Sunday Times Magazine (London), Apr. 23, 1989, at 24-35.

II. Human Rights in Internal Armed Conflict: The Developing Norms

A. Background

The traditional law of war has always governed international armed conflicts. Since international law was considered to be a body of rules that applied only to states in their conduct with one another, by definition internal armed conflicts — civil wars and civil strife — fell outside its ambit. Both combatants and civilians in such "non-international conflicts" drew no protection from it. Specifically, with one exception that has become increasingly important, the four Geneva Conventions covered only international armed conflicts.

That one exception is Article 3 (common to all four Geneva Conventions), an innovative provision applicable to non-international conflicts that seeks to "humanize" them for the benefit of both combatants and civilians. More recently, many articles in Protocol Additional to the Geneva Conventions of 12 August 1949, and Relating to the Protection of Victims of

Non-International Armed Conflicts (Protocol II), opened for signature Dec. 12, 1977, U.N. Doc. A/32/144, Annex II (1977), reprinted in 16 Intl. Legal Materials 1442 (1977) (see the Documentary Supplement), attempt to achieve the same objective.

B. Common Article 3: Its Status and Content

Smith, New Protections for Victims of International Armed Conflicts: The Proposed Ratification of Protocol II by the United States
120 Mil. L. Rev. 59, 63-65 (1988)

III. THE DEVELOPMENT OF INTERNATIONAL STANDARDS GOVERNING NONINTERNATIONAL ARMED CONFLICTS

The events of World War II led to the four Geneva Conventions of August 12, 1949 for the Protection of Victims of War. At the 1949 Diplomatic Conference, the delegates of many states believed the Geneva Conventions should apply to both civil and international armed conflicts. This position was certainly influenced by Lieber, who believed that rules of warfare could be observed during internal conflicts without giving recognition to the rebel forces. The initial proposal by the International Committee of the Red Cross (ICRC) incorporated this view, and explicitly provided that the application of the Geneva Conventions to internal armed conflicts would not affect the status of the parties. The proposal, however, met stiff resistance from a considerable number of delegates. Many states feared unqualified application of the Conventions to an internal armed conflict would give rebels de facto status as belligerents and possibly even de jure legal recognition. They believed observance of the Conventions would hamper the legitimate repression of rebellions and wanted to limit the laws of war to traditional armed conflicts between states. These states particularly did not want to give rebels prisoner of war status, with its attendant immunity for lawful actions on the battlefield.

Common Article 3 was the compromise between these two views; it provides some minimum protections for victims of internal armed conflicts, while avoiding any recognition of the rebel forces or any rebel entitlement to prisoner of war status. It states:

> In the case of armed conflict not of an international character occurring in the territory of one of the High Contracting Parties, each Party to the conflict shall be bound to apply, as a minimum, the following provisions:
> (1) Persons taking no active part in the hostilities, including members

of armed forces who have laid down their arms and those placed *hors de combat* by sickness, wounds, detention, or any other cause, shall in all circumstances be treated humanely, without any adverse distinction founded on race, colour, religion or faith, sex, birth or wealth, or any other similar criteria.

To this end, the following acts are and shall remain prohibited at any time and in any place whatsoever with respect to the above-mentioned persons:

> (a) violence to life and person, in particular murder of all kinds, mutilation, cruel treatment and torture;
>
> (b) taking of hostages;
>
> (c) outrages upon personal dignity, in particular humiliating and degrading treatment;
>
> (d) the passing of sentences and the carrying out of executions without previous judgment pronounced by a regularly constituted court, affording all the judicial guarantees which are recognized as indispensable by civilized peoples.

(2) The wounded and sick shall be collected and cared for.

An impartial humanitarian body, such as the International Committee of the Red Cross, may offer its services to the Parties to the conflict.

The Parties to the conflict should further endeavor to bring into force, by means of special agreements, all or part of the other provisions of the present Convention.

The application of the preceding provisions shall not affect the legal status of the Parties to the conflict.

Common Article 3 was a major step toward recognizing the need for basic humanitarian protections for non-combatants in internal armed conflicts. It represented the first internationally accepted law that regulated a state's treatment of its own nationals in internal armed conflicts. The articles also established that the laws governing internal armed conflict were of legitimate international concern.

Although Common Article 3 advanced the laws governing internal armed conflicts, it has not been very effective from a practical standpoint. Some governments have explicitly accepted the applicability of Common Article 3 and have attempted to comply with it, but these have been the exception rather than the general rule. Most governments have been reluctant to admit the existence of "armed conflicts" within their states. They still fear the rebels will gain international legal status as insurgents or belligerents if Common Article 3 is applied to the internal strife. To compound this problem the text of Common Article 3 and its drafting history do not clearly define the term "non-international armed conflict." This has made it easier for states to deny that the provision applies. Finally, Common Article 3 sets forth very general principles rather than the precise standards of conduct necessary to regulate the conduct of states effectively.

Case Concerning Military and Paramilitary Activities in and Against Nicaragua
(Nicaragua v. United States)
1986 I.C.J. 14, 66-69, 113-114, 129-130 (Judgment of 27 June)
(Merits)

[Among the many questions raised in this complicated case was whether the United States incurred legal responsibility for the CIA's preparation and dissemination to the *contras* in 1983 of a publication, in Spanish, entitled *Operaciones sicologicas en guerra de guerillas* (Psychological Operations in Guerrilla Warfare).]

122. The Court concludes that in 1983 an agency of the United States Government supplied to the FDN a manual on psychological guerrilla warfare which, while expressly discouraging indiscriminate violence against civilians, considered the possible necessity of shooting civilians who were attempting to leave a town; and advised the "neutralization" for propaganda purposes of local judges, officials or notables after the semblance of trial in the presence of the population. The text supplied to the *contras* also advised the use of professional criminals to perform unspecified "jobs," and the use of provocation at mass demonstrations to produce violence on the part of the authorities so as to make "martyrs." . . .

218. The court [finds it unnecessary to decide whether common Article 3 applies under the facts of this case,] since in its view the conduct of the United States may be judged according to the fundamental general principles of humanitarian law; in its view, the Geneva Conventions are in some respects a development, and in other respects no more than the expression, of such principles. . . . Article 3 which is common to all four Geneva Conventions of 12 August 1949 defines certain rules to be applied in the armed conflicts of a noninternational character. There is no doubt that, in the event of international armed conflicts, these rules also constitute a minimum yardstick, in addition to the more elaborate rules which are also to apply to international conflicts; and they are rules which, in the Court's opinion, reflect what the Court in 1949 called "elementary considerations of humanity" (Corfu Channel, Merits, I.C.J. Reports 1949, p. 22 . . .). The Court may therefore find them applicable to the present dispute, and is thus not required to decide what role the United States multilateral treaty reservation might otherwise play in regard to the treaties in question.

219. The conflict between the *contras*' forces and those of the Government of Nicaragua is an armed conflict which is "not of an international character." The acts of the *contras* towards the Nicaraguan Government are therefore governed by the law applicable to conflicts of that character; whereas the actions of the United States in and against Nicaragua fall under the legal rules relating to international conflicts. Because the minimum rules applicable to international and to non-international conflicts are iden-

tical, there is no need to address the question whether those actions must be looked at in the context of the rules which operate for the one or for the other category of conflict. The relevant principles are to be looked for in the provisions of Article 3 of each of the four Conventions of 12 August 1949, the text of which, identical in each Convention, expressly refers to conflicts not having an international character.

220. The Court considers that there is an obligation on the United States Government, in the terms of Article 1 of the Geneva Conventions, to "respect" the Conventions and even "to ensure respect" for them "in all circumstances," since such an obligation does not derive only from the Conventions themselves, but from the general principles of humanitarian law to which the Conventions merely give specific expression. The United States is thus under an obligation not to encourage persons or groups engaged in the conflict in Nicaragua to act in violation of the provisions of Article 3 common to the four 1949 Geneva Conventions. . . .

[The Court held, 14 votes to 1 (Judge Oda dissenting), that the United States, by producing the manual and disseminating it to the *contras*, had "encouraged the commission by them of acts contrary to general principles of humanitarian law; but does not find a basis for concluding that any such acts which may have been committed are imputable to the United States of America. . . ." 1986 I.C.J. at 148.]

C. Protocol II: Its Scope and Content

Protocol II, which supplements Common Article 3, emerged from the same Diplomatic Conference of 1974-1977 as did Protocol I. The following brief extract describes the background of the Protocol and its "main weakness," which without doubt will work to limit its applicability. The Note and reading that follow summarize its contents and compare it with Common Article 3 and other international human rights instruments.

Smith, New Protections for Victims of International Armed Conflicts: The Proposed Ratification of Protocol II by the United States
120 Mil. L. Rev. 59, 66-67 (1988)

Protocol II sets forth, with more specificity than Common Article 3, the fundamental rights of noncombatants, that is, people who are not involved in the conflict, or who have ceased to take part in the hostilities. Protocol II provides greater protection for civilians, children, and medical and religious personnel. It also articulates more specific due process guarantees and standards for treatment of persons deprived of their liberty. Despite these improvements in humanitarian protections for noncombatants in internal armed conflicts, many delegates were disappointed with Protocol II. The main weakness is the high threshold of armed conflict necessary before Protocol II applies. At the Diplomatic Conference in 1973, the International Committee of the Red Cross (ICRC), as well as many delegates, wanted Protocol II to cover all conflicts covered by Common Article 3 of the Geneva Conventions. This position met strong opposition from states that preferred to handle internal matters without incurring any international obligations. These states believed that such an application of Protocol II would endanger their sovereignty. As a result of this dispute, the threshold for Protocol II to apply is higher than that of Common Article 3. For Protocol II to apply to an internal armed conflict, the dissident armed forces must be under responsible command; they must exercise control over a part of the state's territory so as to enable them to carry out sustained and concerted military operations; and they must be able to implement Protocol II. Most internal conflicts take many years to reach this level, and, even if the threshold is crossed, governments are not likely to admit it except in the most obvious situations.

Note: The Content of Protocol II

Many states, particularly Third World ones, opposed efforts to regulate internal armed conflicts by international norms. While this position did not prevail at the Diplomatic Conference, Protocol II emerged therefrom a much weaker instrument than the ICRC and most human rights activists had hoped to see drafted. As the above extract indicates, one major concession made to states reluctant to develop a legal regime to govern internal wars and civil strife concerned the "threshold" of the Protocol's application. In the first place, Article 1(2) provides that it shall *not* apply "to situations of internal disturbances and tensions, such as riots, isolated and sporadic acts of violence and other acts of a similar nature, as not being armed conflicts." Secondly, the situations to which it *shall* apply, according to Article 1(1), are those armed conflicts "which take place in the territory of a High Contracting Party between its armed forces and dissident armed forces or other organized armed groups which, under responsible command, exercise such control over a part of its territory as to enable them to carry out sustained and concerted military operations and to implement this Protocol." Thus, as Professor Goldman correctly concludes, "the objective conditions that must be satisfied to trigger Protocol II's application contemplate a situation of civil war essentially comparable to a state of belligerency under customary international law." Goldman, International Humanitarian Law and the Armed Conflicts in El Salvador and Nicaragua, 2 Am. U.J. Intl. L. & Poly.

539, 549 (1987). These conditions effectively bar the Protocol's application to many internal armed conflicts.

Assuming that the Protocol's conditions are met, its core protective provisions are contained in Article 4, which provides, inter alia, as follows:

Article 4 — Fundamental Guarantees

1. All persons who do not take a direct part or who have ceased to take part in hostilities, whether or not their liberty has been restricted, are entitled to respect for their person, honour and convictions and religious practices. They shall in all circumstances be treated humanely, without any adverse distinction. It is prohibited to order that there shall be no survivors.

2. Without prejudice to the generality of the foregoing, the following acts against the persons referred to in paragraph 1 are and shall remain prohibited at any time and in any place whatsoever:

(a) violence to the life, health and physical or mental well-being of persons, in particular murder as well as cruel treatment such as torture, mutilation or any form of corporal punishment;

(b) collective punishments;

(c) taking of hostages;

(d) acts of terrorism;

(e) outrages upon personal dignity, in particular humiliating and degrading treatment, rape, enforced prostitution and any form of indecent assault;

(f) slavery and the slave trade in all their forms;

(g) pillage;

(h) threats to commit any of the foregoing acts.

Numerous other articles also extend protection to the civilian population, either generally or specifically. The full text of Protocol II is contained in the Documentary Supplement. See Lysaght, The Scope of Protocol II and Its Relation to Common Article 3 of the Geneva Conventions of 1949 and Other Human Rights Instruments, 33 Am. U. L. Rev. 9, 24 (1983).

Junod, Additional Protocol II: History and Scope
33 Am. U.L. Rev. 29, 34-37 passim (1983)

Protocol II [incorporates] several important features [not found in Common Article 3]. It substantially develops, for example, modalities of care for the sick and wounded. Persons engaged in medical activities are awarded special protection, and the Red Cross emblem is specifically protected.

Furthermore, the guarantees of humane treatment and the judicial guarantees mentioned very succinctly in common article 3 have been developed and completed. It must be noted that the fundamental guarantees that cannot be suspended in any circumstances, the "hard core" of the 1966

International Covenant on Civil and Political Rights, have been inserted almost completely into the Protocol. The existence of an "overlapping zone" of situations in which international humanitarian law and human rights are applicable simultaneously contributes to the reinforcement of protection because the means of implementation of the Protocol and of the Covenant are different.

In addition, Article 3 and Protocol II are binding not only on the established government, but also on the insurgent party. They bind all parties to the conflict in their relation to each other. How an opposition party, which is not a High Contracting Party, can be bound by an international treaty, is a question that must be considered. In theory, the ratification of or adherence to an international treaty creates rights and obligations not only for the authorities in place, but also for the entire population of the territory of that state. Although this explanation, which is followed by the ICRC, has not always been considered doctrinally satisfactory, it has never really been formally contested.

Finally, Protocol II contains a clause on conditions of detention for persons deprived of their liberty, and adopts the principle of the protection of the civilian population as such, setting forth certain rules to that effect. In particular, article 14 prohibits the use of starvation as a method of warfare, and article 17 prohibits the forced displacement of civilians. Relief actions are explicitly included, but they are subject to the consent of the High Contracting Party under Article 18. . . .

A.   THE LINK WITH COMMON ARTICLE 3

Protocol II develops and supplements article 3 common to the Geneva Conventions "without modifying its existing conditions of application." The Diplomatic Conference chose to adapt the scope of protection of Protocol II to the degree of intensity of the conflict. Thus, in those situations in which the conditions for the application of Protocol II are fulfilled, both Protocol II and common article 3 apply simultaneously, because the scope of Protocol II is included in the wider scope of common article 3. On the other hand, in a low-intensity conflict, which does not fulfill the conditions for the application of Protocol II, only common article 3 applies. In fact, article 3 retains an autonomous existence; its applicability is neither restricted nor subjected to the scope of Protocol II. This legally rather complex situation has the advantage of assuring that there can be no regression of the long-standing protection granted by common article 3. The specific mention of article 3 in the Protocol was one of the key elements that permitted agreement on the scope of the Protocol.

Protocol II completes and develops common article 3; it is an extension of article 3, and it is based on the same structural concept.

U.S. Position on Protocol II

Despite concerns about the high threshold of armed conflict necessary to trigger Protocol II, President Jimmy Carter signed it in 1977, and 10 years later President Reagan submitted it to the Senate for its advice and consent to ratification with one reservation, two understandings, and one declaration. See Message from the President, page 894 supra. Only the last is of major importance. It declares that the United States will apply Protocol II to all armed conflicts covered by Common Article 3 (and only such conflicts), which will include all non-international armed conflicts as traditionally defined (but not internal disturbances, riots, and sporadic acts of violence), and that it will encourage all other states to do likewise. Message from the President, supra page 894, at 7. The Legal Adviser to the Directorate, ICRC, has called the proposed declaration "a positive step forward that should set an example for other states." Gasser, An Appeal for Ratification by the United States, 81 Am. J. Intl. L. 912 (1987). If the declaration sets a trend, Protocol II's area of application will be broadened considerably. Compare Smith, page 901 supra.

D. Invoking Common Article 3 and Protocol II in Internal Armed Conflicts

The traditional law of war, considered in the first section of this Problem, depends on states, "protecting powers," and the ICRC for its enforcement. Insofar as internal or non-international armed conflicts are concerned, Common Article 3 singles out the ICRC among impartial humanitarian bodies that may offer their services to the parties to the conflict. See Veuthey, Implementation and Enforcement of Humanitarian Law and Human Rights Law in Non-International Armed Conflicts: The Role of the International Committee of the Red Cross, 33 Am. U. L. Rev. 83 (1983). Increasingly, other international non-governmental organizations are seeking to play a role in the enforcement process by invoking what Professor Draper has called "meta-legal forces such as reciprocity, external opinion of the community of the States and the desire to obtain the support of the bulk of the population of the State in which the conflict has arisen." Draper, The Implementation and Enforcement of the Geneva Conventions of 1949 and the Two Additional Protocols, 164 Recueil des Cours (Hague Academy of International Law) 9, 50 (1979-III). In so doing, international human rights lawyers, many for the first time, are going beyond international human rights law and taking the law of armed conflict into account.

The desirability and problems of this approach are reviewed in the following reading.

Weissbrodt, The Role of International Organizations in the Implementation of Human Rights and Humanitarian Law in Situations of Armed Conflict
21 Vand. J. Transnatl. L. 313, 315-317, 331-337, 343-345 (1988)

Governments are principally responsible for the implementation of human rights law and humanitarian law during periods of international armed conflict. During periods of noninternational armed conflict, governments and armed opposition groups each bear responsibility for their obedience to human rights law and humanitarian law.

International human rights organizations can only encourage participants in armed conflicts to respect human rights law and humanitarian law. Several human rights organizations have attempted to do so. For many years the International Committee of the Red Cross (ICRC) has taken a leading role in encouraging the application of humanitarian law during periods of international armed conflict; recently it has also begun referring to human rights law in situations of domestic strife or tension that international humanitarian law does not cover.

Intergovernmental organizations such as the United Nations General Assembly (General Assembly), the United Nations Commission on Human Rights, the International Court of Justice, the Inter-American Commission on Human Rights and several others have occasionally attempted to use their influence to seek the protection of human rights law during armed conflicts, and they have referred irregularly to humanitarian law in such endeavors. These intergovernmental organizations have attempted to fill the vacuum left by the failure of the United Nations Security Council and other international mechanisms to cope successfully with violations of human rights law during periods of armed conflict.

International nongovernmental organizations . . . have also recognized that human rights need protection during periods of armed conflict. In addressing human rights violations, these organizations and the United Nations have relied principally on the Universal Declaration of Human Rights and the International Covenant on Civil and Political Rights. These organizations have begun to refer more frequently, however, to principles of humanitarian law applicable to armed conflict. . . .

[The writer proceeds to review how NGOs have attempted to apply human rights law and humanitarian law during periods of armed conflict, using as examples reports issued by Americas Watch, Amnesty International, and the International Commission of Jurists. He then examines the practice of the UN General Assembly in citing humanitarian law. He finds the references to humanitarian law by both NGOs and the General Assembly to have been inconsistent and often inaccurate. He then addresses the question posed by the following heading.]

SHOULD NONGOVERNMENTAL ORGANIZATIONS AND THE UNITED
NATIONS CITE INTERNATIONAL HUMANITARIAN LAW IN SUPPORT OF
THEIR HUMAN RIGHTS CONCERNS?

International human rights organizations and the General Assembly
ordinarily refer in their actions, reports, and resolutions to the Universal
Declaration of Human Rights, the International Covenant on Civil and
Political Rights, and occasionally, for the principle of nonrefoulement, to
the Convention and Protocol Relating to the Status of Refugees.

When the United Nations and nongovernment organizations confront
human rights violations in the context of armed conflicts, international
humanitarian law often provides an additional legal foundation for their
concerns. In some cases, international humanitarian law may even offer a
stronger basis for human rights work than the Universal Declaration of
Human Rights or the International Covenant on Civil and Political Rights.

[The writer points out that the multilateral treaties that make up international humanitarian law apply more broadly than the principal human
rights treaties. As of 31 March 1993, 177 states had ratified the Geneva
Conventions; 121 states had ratified Protocol I; and 112 states had ratified
Protocol II. In contrast, at a slightly later date (1 July 1994), 127 states had
ratified the Covenant on Civil and Political Rights, with 76 having accepted
its Optional Protocol.]

Some principles of international humanitarian law are more specific or
more exacting than the provisions of international human rights law. Humanitarian law applies specifically to emergency situations; international
human rights permits significant derogations during these same periods.
. . . [See the discussion of derogations at pages 914-922 infra.]

In any case, neither the International Covenant on Civil and Political
Rights nor the Universal Declaration of Human Rights constitutes a completely satisfactory legal basis for the human rights concerns of nongovernmental organizations and the United Nations, particularly when these
concerns arise during armed conflicts or other public emergencies. At a
minimum, humanitarian legal principles constitute an important body of
international law that human rights organizations have used and can continue to use in appropriate situations.

Several impediments to the use of international humanitarian law exist.
First, international humanitarian law includes a relatively unfamiliar body
of principles. Human rights organizations must communicate their concerns in a sufficiently simplistic fashion in order to attract media attention
and to benefit from the pressure of public opinion. Humanitarian law adds
to the complexity of the legal principles that human rights organizations
must communicate to the media, the public, and human rights activists.
The staff and members of human rights organizations have only begun to
understand humanitarian law norms sufficiently to use these norms in their

reports and campaign work. At first glance, international humanitarian law may appear dauntingly complex and, therefore, difficult for human rights organizations to use. Most of the articles of the Geneva Conventions are not directly relevant to the principal concerns of human rights organizations, but a few provisions, such as common article 3, are quite brief, straightforward, easily explained, and directly applicable to the concerns of most human rights organizations.

The second obstacle to the use of international humanitarian law is the most problematic: to apply humanitarian law, one must ordinarily determine what sort of armed conflict is occurring and, thus, which set of humanitarian principles is relevant. This determination is often difficult, involving issues that are politically sensitive, facts that are outside the normal research competence of human rights organizations, and decisions that may conflict with ICRC judgments.

[The writer notes that international humanitarian law applies different legal principles and instruments to each type of armed conflict. While analytically NGOs should distinguish the type of situation and resultant legal regime involved, there may be practical reasons for not making public legal assessments of the precise sort of armed conflict that might be occurring.]

For example, a human rights organization might simply observe that the Government of Country A has, by torturing prisoners, violated article 5 of the Universal Declaration of Human Rights, article 7 of the International Covenant on Civil and Political Rights, and common article 3. The human rights organization might amplify this observation by stating that Country A had ratified the International Covenant on Civil and Political Rights in 1974 and the Geneva Conventions in 1964. It would not be necessary to state further that the human rights organization had concluded that common article 3 applied because an armed conflict not of an international character was occurring in Country A. . . .

It should be clear that intergovernmental and nongovernmental organizations are not required to cite provisions of humanitarian law except where such citation would appear useful in protecting human rights. In addition, consideration should be given to the use of humanitarian law not as a primary source of applicable norms but as a point of reference. For example, a human rights organization should not say: "These trial procedures violated common article 3." Instead, the report might observe: "Such trial procedures are forbidden even in periods of civil war under common article 3." Such a use of humanitarian law would obviate the need to characterize a situation as a certain type of armed conflict, or to state that humanitarian law applied. Rather, this more subtle way of citing humanitarian law would make use of the public perception that the Geneva Conventions and Additional Protocols establish the most basic, minimum standard of conduct for governments.

Comments and Questions

1. Why did so many states attending the Diplomatic Conference, especially Third World states, oppose or seek to weaken (in this case successfully) Protocol II? What can be done to counteract and possibly remedy the effects of such opposition at this late date? Is President Reagan's proposed declaration (see page 908 supra) a step in the right direction? Does it go far enough? What other steps might be taken, by the United States or the international community? What are their chances of success?

2. How much of humanitarian law is customary international law? All of the Geneva Conventions? Certain articles thereof? Only Common Article 3? What guidance can be obtained from the ICJ's Judgment in the *Nicaragua* case? Compare the following views of the customary international law status of the Geneva Conventions in the wake of that decision.

> I believe that the norms stated in Article 3(1)(a)-(c) are of such an elementary, ethical character, and echo so many provisions in other humanitarian and human rights treaties, that they must be regarded as embodying minimum standards of customary law also applicable to non-international armed conflicts. This is also true for the obligation to treat humanely persons who are *hors de combat*, which is rooted in Hague Regulations 23(c)-(d), which undoubtedly reflect customary law, and in the customary obligation contained in the law of human rights to treat with humanity all persons deprived of their liberty. I consider at least the core due process principle stated in Article 3(1)(d) . . . to embody customary law, notwithstanding a recent authoritative enumeration of customary human rights which does not list due process of law.

T. Meron, Human Rights and Humanitarian Norms as Customary Law 34-35 (1989).

> [T]here must be at least very serious doubts whether those conventions could be regarded as embodying customary law. Even the Court's view that the [C]ommon Article 3, laying down a "minimum yardstick" (para. 218) for armed conflicts of non-international character, are applicable as "elementary considerations of humanity" is not a matter free from difficulty.

1986 I.C.J. at 537 (Judge Sir Robert Jennings, Dissenting Opinion).

3. One objection to Protocol II is that its application might give greater credibility to insurgent or guerrilla forces engaged in a civil war, despite Article 3(1)'s injunction that "[n]othing in this Protocol shall be invoked for the purpose of affecting the sovereignty of a State or the responsibility of the government, by all legitimate means, to maintain or reestablish law and order in the State or to defend the national unity and territorial integrity of the State." Is this a legitimate concern? Is a state prohibited from treating terrorists as common criminals if Protocol II is applicable?

4. Article 3(2) of Protocol II provides, "Nothing in this Protocol shall be invoked as a justification for intervening, directly or indirectly, for any reason whatever, in the armed conflict or in the internal or external affairs of the High Contracting Party in the territory of which that conflict occurs." Nonetheless, multinational "peacekeeping" forces are now present in many countries, not always with the consent of the government concerned (if any).

> Everyone and no one is responsible for controlling the UN forces. There is no common code of military discipline within the UN, no military police with responsibility for investigating abuses by military personnel, no authority to punish the guilty and compensate their victims. Self-criticism goes no further than expressions of regret at abuses committed by some less well-organized contingents. But there is very limited respect for authority and discipline in the national contingents, since in any case the orders come from the UN.
>
> Today, the UN goes on the military offensive, but without accepting its status as a belligerent subject to the laws of war. Does it regard itself as above the law? Are no holds barred as long as one's purpose is to restore peace, to overthrow oppressors and cut the cost to the international tax-payer? . . .
>
> It is no exaggeration to say that international policing operations are in a dangerous state of flux. Their legality must be strengthened and anchored in humanitarian law, which applies to all and which it is their function to uphold.

Bouchet-Saulnier, Peacekeeping Operations Above Humanitarian Law, in Life, Death and Aid, The Médecins Sans Frontières Report on World Crisis Intervention 125, 130 (F. Jean ed. 1993). Also see Amnesty International, Peace Keeping and Human Rights (1994); Human Rights Watch, The Lost Agenda, Human Rights and U.N. Field Operations (1993). Are UN and similar forces (see the discussion of UN humanitarian intervention at pages 651-664 of Problem VIII) "above the law," or are they bound in the conduct of military operations by the Geneva Conventions? By Protocol II? By customary international law?

5. Protocol II, although ratified by 112 states, is presumably not part of customary international law. Why not? What will have to occur before it, or any of its articles, achieves such status? Does the ICJ Judgment in the *Nicaragua* case help answer any of these questions?

6. Weissbrodt recommends that NGOs consider using humanitarian law "not as a primary source of applicable norms but as a point of reference." Re-read the example he posits (page 911 supra) and consider whether this "more subtle way of citing humanitarian law" is a good idea. Whatever its effectiveness when used in an NGO report, would you consider such a use before the ICJ or the European or American courts and commissions? Why or why not?

III. Human Rights in Civil Strife and States of Emergency

The prior two sections have explored the law of war (or humanitarian law) applicable during international and non-international armed conflict. Its applicability, however, depends on the existence of an armed conflict. As already noted (see page 905 supra), Article 1(2) of Protocol II makes it inapplicable "to situations of internal disturbances and tensions, such as riots, isolated and sporadic acts of violence and other acts of a similar nature," and many states deny the applicability of Common Article 3 to such situations, too. Nevertheless, situations of civil strife can be serious enough to cause governments to assume drastic emergency powers. Whenever they do, there is always danger that the human rights of individuals may be abused. Indeed, one UN human rights expert states:

> It has been demonstrated repeatedly that some of the worst violations of human rights and humanitarian law occur during periods of emergency. Protective systems often break down; governments may wage war on their own subjects; countries, to use the words of Leopoldo Benitez, former President of the United Nations General Assembly and Chairman of the United Nations Commission on Human Rights, are occupied by their own armies; and extremist groups of varying political complexions dispense terror with impunity.

Ramcharan, The Role of International Bodies in the Implementation and Enforcement of Humanitarian Law and Human Rights in Non-International Armed Conflicts, 33 Am. U. L. Rev. 99, 105 (1983).

While international human rights law is basic and, thus, applies (*concurrently with the relevant humanitarian law*) in times of both international and non-international armed conflict, it is the only legal regime applicable during civil strife and states of emergency, which states may declare either during "peacetime" or during situations in which tensions and disturbances within the state fall short of actual armed conflict. Thus, human rights law is important to study and apply not only for the additional protection it may afford during armed conflicts, but also for its role during internal disturbances that may lead to a declaration of a state of emergency.

The drafters of the International Covenant on Civil and Political Rights (as well as the European and American Conventions) were well aware of the dangers that such states of emergency could pose to human rights. Thus, while Article 4 of the Covenant concedes the necessity of permitting states to derogate from their normal human rights obligations in times of genuine public emergency, it seeks to ensure that the most basic human rights remain respected by listing certain core rights from which no derogation, even in times of emergency, is permitted. The following reading compares the derogation provisions of the major international instruments.

J. Fitzpatrick, Human Rights in Crisis, The International System for Protecting Rights During States of Emergency
36-38, 52-66 (1994)

There is nothing remarkable about the fact that substantial restrictions are placed on other human rights during states of emergency. Indeed, the whole point of recognizing a concept of public emergencies in international human rights law was to provide reasonable limits upon the antici-pated restrictions of rights that emergencies would entail. These restrictions were expected to go further than those permitted under ordinary circum-stances for purposes such as the maintenance of public order. Much of the work of treaty-based human rights monitors with respect to states of emer-gency has involved setting the contours for emergency derogations from such rights.

In a United Nations survey of governments the rights most often men-tioned as having been the subject of derogations during emergencies were liberty and security of the person, liberty of movement, protection of pri-vacy, freedom of expression and opinion, and the right of peaceful assembly. Many monitors have noted that excessive invasions of these and other rights have occurred during many emergencies, often in association with depriva-tions of non-derogable rights, such as the right to life and the prohibition on torture. But, as the International Commission of Jurists observed:

> Some writers have emphasized the effects of states of emergency on individ-ual rights, particularly the right to be free from arbitrary deprivation of free-dom and the right to a fair trial. This tends to create a somewhat false image of states of emergency, for one of their most fundamental characteristics is precisely the breadth of their impact on a society. They typically affect trade union rights, freedom of opinion, freedom of expression, freedom of associa-tion, the right of access to information and ideas, the right to an education, the right to participate in public affairs . . . not only individual rights but also collective rights and rights of peoples, such as the right to development and the right to self-determination.

The scope of these effects naturally results in a potential concern with states of emergency by all the monitoring bodies with an interest in any of this wide range of rights. These potentially extensive effects have also influenced the debate over the drafting of non-treaty-based substantive standards for government behavior during states of emergency. . . .

Two crucial sets of treaty standards were also drafted at approximately the same time as Common Article 3. Article 15 of the European Conven-tion was drafted primarily during early 1950 with the benefit of almost three years of discussion by drafters of the Covenant on Civil and Political Rights within the United Nations. The derogation article of the European Convention served as a focal point for the debate between two alternate approaches to treaty drafting, which might be called "general enumeration" and "precise definition." The proponents of general enumeration favored drafting a document with positive definitions of rights and no exceptions or restrictions other than a single general limitations clause, similar to Article 29 of the Universal Declaration. The proponents of precise definition, on the other hand, wanted not only specific limitations clauses in many provisions defining particular rights but also a derogation article for emergencies, arguing that these clauses would actually prevent abusive suspension or denial of rights. During the final stages of the drafting process, the attraction of entrenching a list of non-derogable rights swayed a majority to favor inclusion of the derogation article.

Whereas the drafting of the Covenant on Civil and Political Rights dragged on until 1966, debate on the advisability and specific terms of a derogation article occurred during the relatively compressed period between 1947 and 1952. Article 4 became the focus of the division of opinion between the general-enumeration and precise-definition camps, as had Article 15 in the case of the European Convention. Another key division, leading to an awkward compromise, developed on the question whether the clause on non-derogable rights should include only those rights most important and central to human dignity and most at risk during typical emergencies, or should be expanded to include all rights that no reasonable government would need to limit substantially in any conceivable emergency.

The drafters of the American Convention on Human Rights, who began work in earnest in the 1960s, had the benefit of earlier-drafted human rights treaties as a model and began with an apparent consensus on the precise-definition approach. Moreover, the OAS had the benefit of a specific study of the problem of the protection of human rights during states of emergency, conducted by the Inter-American Commission on Human Rights. This study was undertaken with three aims, which sound rather familiar to anyone who has worked in this field: (1) to examine the history of states of siege in the Americas to see how human rights had been violated; (2) to determine if it would be possible to articulate general principles that could be binding on all countries in the region and that might be incorporated into the internal laws of those countries; and (3) to determine if there might be international organs that could control the juridical and practical regimes of states of siege. The special interest developed with the OAS on protecting human rights during states of emergency may help explain the rather different form the derogation article takes in the American Convention, as compared to those in the European Convention and the Covenant.

A brief comparison of the three derogation articles in the human rights treaties to the relevant portions of the major humanitarian law instruments reveals some interesting similarities and differences, as well as "lacunae," that have attracted ongoing efforts to formulate additional, more complete standards. Discussion will be limited to the substantive aspects of these emergency provisions, since the ensuing chapters will focus upon measures for their implementation. Certain basic principles are embodied in each of the three derogation articles: a threshold of severity of cause, requirements of notification and/or proclamation, good faith motivation, consistency with other international obligations of the derogating state, proportionality between cause and measures taken, non-discrimination in the application of emergency measures, and entrenchment of a core of non-derogable rights.

1. SEVERITY

While the threshold for a legitimate derogation under the three human rights treaties is largely similar, there are interesting variations in terminology. The Covenant offers the simplest formulation: a public emergency threatening the life of the nation. The European Convention in addition makes explicit reference to "war," but the inclusion of war as a ground for derogation is implicit in the Covenant. The text of Article 27 of the American Convention differs strikingly: "war, public danger, or other emergency that threatens the independence or security of a State Party." On the surface, the American Convention might appear to set a lower threshold than the two earlier treaties, but the drafting history of the provision suggests the contrary.

While "the life of the nation" is clearly intended to have a restrictive meaning, its scope is not self-evident. An emergency that threatens the life of the nation must imperil some fundamental element of statehood or survival of the population — for example, the functioning of a major constitutional organ, such as the judiciary or legislature, or the flow of vital supplies. Threats to a discrete segment of the national territory are particularly problematic, although a risk of detachment or loss of control over an important region, which would have a significant impact on central institutions and the general population, would appear to be sufficient. Though not arising out of political causes, certain natural disasters might meet the criteria for derogation.

War presents its own special problems. As a textual matter, it has been suggested that a reference to "war" in a derogation clause encompasses only external war and not internal armed conflict, though the latter would fit under the general term "emergency." Satisfaction of technical criteria for the existence of a state of war is neither necessary nor sufficient for derogation from human rights treaties, though it bears obvious importance with respect to the applicability of international humanitarian law. Derogation would not be permissible in the case of a war that did not threaten the "life of the nation" or "the independence or security" of the derogating state. For example, involvement in foreign hostilities that did not threaten attack or have a significant impact on domestic institutions, or the mere existence of a state of war without active hostilities, would not meet the threshold of severity to justify substantial restrictions on the domestic enjoyment of fundamental rights.

Despite the benefit of the high threshold set in the earlier two human rights treaties and significant experience within the region of problems arising out of states of emergency, initial proposed drafts of the American Convention would have set a very low threshold of severity for derogation. The version prepared by the Inter-American Council of Jurists (IACJ) permitted derogation in undefined "exceptional situations"; the proposals of Chile and Uruguay also adopted this formula, while making it explicit that each state could define such "exceptional situations" for itself. The IACHR, with the benefit of the Martins study, criticized this terminology and adopted a resolution in 1968 stating that suspension of guarantees should be permissible only "when adopted in case of war or other serious public emergency threatening the life of the nation or the security of the State." The IACHR draft submitted to the Conference of San José offered the formula "[i]n time of war or other emergency which threatens the independence or security of a State Party or Parties."

During the Conference, the term "public danger" was inserted. Norris and Reiton explain that while this phrase may seem "strikingly broad," it was intended to cover "public calamity" that was "not necessarily a threat to internal or external security." They question the need for this provision, suggesting that the limitations clauses in particular treaty articles would be adequate to permit governments to deal with such natural disasters.

2.   Notification and Proclamation

. . . For the present, it is sufficient to note that all three treaties require formal notification, though the details vary in three respects: (1) while the Covenant and the American Convention require that the other states parties be notified through the intermediary of the secretaries-general of the United Nations and the Organization of American States, respectively, the European Convention simply requires notification to the Secretary-General of the Council of Europe, without mentioning the states parties; (2) the Covenant and the American Convention require that this notice be supplied "immediately," while the European Convention is silent as to timing; and (3) the Covenant requires information concerning the provisions from which the state has derogated, the European Convention demands an explanation of the "measures which it has taken," and the American Convention requires information concerning "the provisions the application of which it has suspended, the reasons that gave rise to the suspension, and the date set for the termination of such suspension."

The Covenant is unique among the three in also requiring proclamation of a public emergency. The aim of this provision was to ensure that derogating states also complied with domestic legal requirements for states of emergency.

3. GOOD FAITH MOTIVATION

This requirement is merely implicit in the derogation articles themselves, though it is express in certain other clauses of the three treaties, which provide that no state party may perform any act aimed at the destruction or undue limitation of rights and freedoms protected by the treaties. Thus, a state of emergency declared in order to destroy a democratic system of government would arguably be invalid.

4. OTHER INTERNATIONAL OBLIGATIONS

Each of the three human rights treaties specifically forbids derogations that are inconsistent with the state's other obligations under international law. Chief among these obligations in relevance would be non-derogable rights in customary and conventional international humanitarian law, as well as the more restrictive or demanding provisions of other human rights treaties and customary human rights law (*e.g.*, any human rights that are *jus cogens* and thus not subject to suspension or denial under any circumstances). An intriguing question is whether these other international obligations are thereby substantively incorporated into the derogation articles and thus subject to the treaty-based monitoring mechanisms.

5. PROPORTIONALITY

Along with the threshold of severity, the principle of proportionality is the most important and yet most elusive of the substantive limits imposed on the privilege of derogation. The three treaties impose a similar standard — measures in derogation of treaty rights are permitted only to the extent "strictly required by the exigencies of the situation," although the American Convention also makes explicit the preeminently important requirement that such measures may be imposed only "for the period of time strictly required." The principle of proportionality embodied in the derogation clauses has its roots in the principle of necessity, which also forms one of the key pillars of international humanitarian law. The existence of competent, active, and informed organs of supervision, both at the national as well as at the international level, is vital if the proportionality principle is to have meaning in practice. . . . [B]oth logistical (access to information and ability to act promptly) and attitudinal (deference to national authorities, *e.g.*, by extension of a "margin of appreciation") factors affect the functioning of the various treaty implementation organs.

6. NON-DISCRIMINATION

The Covenant and the American Convention include clauses specifying
that derogation measures may not be imposed in a manner that discriminates on the grounds of race, color, sex, language, religion, or social origin.
Three interesting issues are raised by these clauses: (1) why no similar
provision exists in the European Convention, and whether its absence denotes a real substantive difference among the treaties; (2) what the term
"discrimination" is intended to mean; and (3) whether this meaning is
affected by the further inclusion of the qualifying term "solely" in the Covenant.

Article 15 of the European Convention is silent on the issue of discrimination in the application of emergency measures. Of course the European
Convention, like the other two treaties, elsewhere prohibits discrimination
on the grounds listed. But these various non-discrimination provisions outside the derogation articles are generally subject to derogation. The issue of
discriminatory treatment of minorities in the application of emergency measures was touched on during the drafting of the European Convention, but
it never achieved prominence in the discussions, and no concrete proposals
for a non-discrimination clause were made. Nevertheless, arbitrary discrimination against disfavored groups of various types would be difficult to justify
as being "strictly required." Thus, there may be no substantive difference
between the silence of the European Convention and the explicit non-
discrimination clauses of the other two treaties, if only arbitrary distinctions
are outlawed by the latter.

Draft non-discrimination provisos to the Covenant's derogation article
were proposed by the United States (in 1948) and by France (in 1949), but
adding the element of non-discrimination was not easily accomplished. The
Commission on Human Rights voted in May 1950, on the basis of an oral
amendment during debate, to add Article 20, the non-discrimination article, to the list of non-derogable rights in Article 4. Objections were immediately raised that disparate treatment of enemy aliens would be necessary
during wartime, and the decision was reversed the following day. A way
around this impasse was found in 1952 when a non-discrimination clause,
not including the classification of national origin, was added to the draft
derogation article.

The idea that only arbitrary discrimination is outlawed by Article 4(1) is
underlined by the deliberate inclusion of the word "solely" in its text. Even
without this term, however, the reference to discrimination in Article 4
conveys the implication that only arbitrary and unjustifiable distinctions in
the application of emergency measures would be outlawed. Thus, where an
identifiable racial or religious group poses a distinct security threat not
posed by other members of the community, presumably, emergency measures could be deliberately targeted against the group, despite the non-
discrimination clause.

The absence of the word "solely" from the non-discrimination clause in Article 27(1) of the American Convention on Human Rights apparently has no intended significance. The word was included in the draft prepared by the IACHR but "disappeared from the final text, and the records of the conference provide no clue as to the reason." Thus, the three treaties would seem to impose a virtually identical non-discrimination obligation, despite disparate phraseology.

7. NON-DEROGABLE RIGHTS

The three treaties diverge dramatically with respect to defining absolute rights never subject to suspension. The process of defining non-derogable rights has been a markedly progressive one, with each later-drafted instrument expanding the core of non-derogable rights. The European Convention begins with just four, sparely defined: the right to life, excepting deaths resulting from lawful acts of war (Article 2); the ban on torture or inhuman or degrading treatment or punishment (Article 3); the prohibition on slavery or servitude (Article 4(1)); and the prohibition on retroactive criminal penalties (Article 7).

The United Kingdom's initial proposal for a clause on non-derogable rights in the Covenant tracked this list closely, but suggestions were immediately made for extensive expansion of the catalogue of non-derogable rights. When the blank space for the list of non-derogable rights was filled in by the United Nations Commission on Human Rights in 1950, the additional provisions included the ban on imprisonment for failure to fulfill a contractual obligation, right to juridical personality, and freedom of thought, conscience and religion.

The drafters of the Covenant touched on the basic issue whether defining non-derogable rights should proceed from the perspective of identifying those rights most vital to human integrity and most likely at risk during abusive emergencies, or whether those rights should include all provisions whose suspension could not conceivably be necessary during times of public emergency. Article 4(2) appears to be an uneasy compromise between these two camps, especially with respect to the anomalous inclusion of the ban on imprisonment for contractual debt and the provision on freedom of religion, which has the distinction of being non-derogable, yet subject to limitation at all times.

The American Convention is somewhat more consistent in its approach and includes many rights that are not as central as the right to life or the protection against torture, but whose suspension would not be justifiable in an imaginable emergency. The 1966 study by IACHR member Martins favored the approach of listing rights subject to derogation and suggested making suspendable only the provisions on arbitrary detention and prompt notice of charges, interference with private life and correspondence, and prior restraint on publication; the rights of assembly, association, and movement would not need to be included because they would be subject to limitation even under ordinary circumstances. The IACHR draft presented to the Conference of San José did not follow this recommendation, but offered instead a list of non-derogable rights only slightly more expansive than that of the Covenant.

During Conference debate, the suggestion was made that the IACHR draft was too vague, and a working group was appointed to redraft the clause. Their product was a major transformation of the IACHR draft, adding not just numerical references to particular treaty articles that would be non-derogable, but deleting three rights and including five new rights. The handiwork of the working group was later modified by the addition to Article 27(2) of the key phrase "the judicial guarantees essential for the protection of such rights," which includes at least some aspects of the protections against arbitrary detention and for due process of law that would have been nonsuspendable under the original IACHR proposal.

The gradual expansion of the list of non-derogable rights in the three major human rights treaties and, particularly, the recognition of a core of fundamental process rights for detainees in the American Convention have stimulated non-treaty-based efforts to articulate standards for protection of human rights during states of emergency. Efforts to refine and perfect these standards continue to the present. An awareness that, in some respects, the principles of international humanitarian law are more advanced than those of the human rights treaties has been an especially important factor in stimulating some of these standard-drafting efforts.

Note: *Humanitarian Law as a Limitation on the
         Right of Derogation: Internal Armed Conflict
         and Civil Strife Contrasted*

When a state is involved in an internal armed conflict, Article 4 of the Covenant permits it to declare a state of emergency and derogate from many of its conventional international human rights obligations. On the other hand, the Geneva Conventions and their two Protocols are not subject to derogation on grounds of public emergency, since the very purpose of their adoption was to provide rules to govern situations of armed conflict. The question raised is thus: "in what way do common article 3 and Protocol II limit the power of a state to suspend its international human rights obligations during the existence of an exceptional danger caused by an internal armed conflict?" Montealegre, The Compatibility of a State Party's Derogation Under Human Rights Conventions with Its Obligations Under Protocol II and Common Article 3, 33 Am. U. L. Rev. 41, 44 (1983).

The answer to this question is that the humanitarian law instruments have great potential for limiting a state's right of derogation. An example of this potential is found in the following extract.

> Among the normative rules subject to . . . derogation are the fair trial guarantees of article 14 of the Covenant on Civil and Political Rights, article 6 of the European Convention, and article 8 of the American Convention.
>
> On the other hand, the norms of article 3 common to the 1949 Geneva Conventions and those of 1977 Protocol II are not subject to derogation. Indeed, they were formulated to be applied in armed conflict — obviously a situation of grave public emergency which threatens the life of the nation. With respect to procedural due process, article 3 prohibits "the passing of sentences and carrying out of executions without previous judgment pronounced by a regularly constituted court, affording all the judicial guarantees which are recognized as indispensable by civilized peoples." Therefore, for the [177] nations bound by common article 3, their right to derogate from some of the judicial guarantees of the human rights treaties is inconsistent with their non-derogable obligation under article 3. But, as Colonel Draper pointed out, common article 3 is only a statement of general principles. It does not spell out categorically what judicial guarantees are deemed indispensable by all the peoples of the West, the communist countries, and the third world.
>
> A solution to the conflict between the right to derogate and the non-derogable obligations of common article 3 is suggested by article 6 of Protocol II, which was adopted by the consensus of the western, communist, and third world states represented at the 1974-1977 Diplomatic Conference. Article 6 provides a respectable catalogue of what these indispensable guarantees are, including an independent and impartial tribunal, a continuing opportunity to exercise all necessary rights and means of defense, notice of charges, conviction only on the basis of individual penal responsibility, protection against ex post facto legislation, presumption of innocence, and the privilege against compulsory self-incrimination. I doubt that there were many military lawyers present when the human rights treaties were drafted, but military lawyers were represented on most delegations at the 1949 and 1977 diplomatic conferences on the Law of Armed Conflict and they did not seem to think that there was any reason to dispense with fair trial standards, even in the heat of a civil war.
>
> Presently, only [112] states are bound by Protocol II, and it may be a long time before it attains the same universal acceptance as common article 3. Article 6 of Protocol II serves as an authoritative declaration of the judicial guarantees deemed indispensable by civilized peoples. Therefore, derogations from fair trial guarantees under the human rights instruments are effectively precluded by common article 3 as interpreted by article 6 of Protocol II, and as a result, the parallel norms of the human rights treaties are strengthened and reinforced.

Solf, infra page 929, at 295-296. Other humanitarian law authorities have taken the same approach. See, e.g., Goldman, International Legal Standards Concerning the Independence of Judges and Lawyers, 1982 Am. Socy. Intl. L. Proceedings 307, 310-312. It also has been used by NGOs.

See, e.g., Americas Watch, Human Rights in Guatemala: No Neutrals Allowed 89-91 (Nov. 1982).

The legal position is different, of course, where a state of emergency is declared in response to civil strife not rising to the level of a non-international armed conflict. Neither Common Article 3 nor Protocol II being applicable in such a situation, a state's derogation could not easily be said to conflict with any obligation under them per se, except to the extent that these humanitarian instruments now reflect customary international law.

Finally, in both internal armed conflict and civil strife situations, what is the impact of humanitarian law upon derogations by states not parties to the Covenant? Consider the following extract (Meron, On the Inadequate Reach of Humanitarian and Human Rights Law and the Need for a New Instrument, 77 Am. J. Intl. L. 589, 601-602 (1983)).

> It can hardly be argued that the enumeration contained in Article 4 of that Covenant is to be regarded, per se, as binding erga omnes. It is significant that the European Convention for the Protection of Human Rights and Fundamental Freedoms and the American Convention on Human Rights contain different lists of nonderogable rights. It must also be noted that the enumeration of customary human rights in the draft Restatement* is different from that given in Article 4. Some of the nonderogable rights under the latter article, such as those stated in Articles 11 and 16 of the Political Covenant, are not even mentioned in the draft Restatement. It may thus be argued that the enumeration given in Article 4 is to be considered only as a treaty provision. States that are not parties to the Covenant may not derogate from human rights that are categorical or absolute (their determination in concreto is difficult). Neither can derogations be made that are in conflict with other international obligations of the derogating state or are clearly excessive or arbitrary. This still leaves a large and fertile field for violations of human rights.

Note: Monitoring States of Emergency

Merely determining whether or not a state of emergency exists in a particular state is often a difficult task, as evidenced by the work of a special rapporteur of the UN Sub-Commission on the Prevention of Discrimination and the Protection of Minorities since 1985. The rapporteur is to draw up and update annually a list of countries that proclaim or terminate a state of emergency, as well as to study the legality of such declarations and their impact on human rights and to recommend "concrete measures" that would guarantee respect for human rights during emergencies. Between 1985 and late 1993, the rapporteur identified 85 states or territories in

---

* The language of the draft Restatement was incorporated in haec verba into Section 702 of the Restatement (Third), found at page 162 of Problem II. — Eds.

which de facto or de jure emergencies were declared, extended, maintained, or terminated. See Sixth Revised Annual Report and List of States Which, Since 1 January 1985, Have Proclaimed, Extended or Terminated a State of Emergency, U.N. Doc. E/CN.4/Sub.2/1993/23/Rev.1 (1993). Some of the problems faced by the rapporteur are discussed in Fitzpatrick, supra page 915, at 168-173.

As discussed in Problem III, the Human Rights Committee fulfills its supervisory role with respect to the Covenant on Civil and Political Rights through reviewing state reports and, for those states that have accepted it, examining individual complaints filed under the Optional Protocol. The Committee also has issued a General Comment concerning derogations; unfortunately, the Comment does little more than paraphrase the Covenant by noting that "measures taken under article 4 are of an exceptional and temporary nature and may only last as long as the life of the nation concerned is threatened and that, in times of emergency, the protection of human rights becomes all the more important, particularly those rights from which no derogations can be made." General Comment 5/13, Report of the Hum. Rts. Comm., 36 U.N. GAOR Supp. (No. 40), Annex VII at 107, 110, U.N. Doc. A/36/40 (1981).

Although the Committee has addressed critical remarks to states during its examination of their reports, no observer seems to conclude that such examinations constitute an effective means of determining the legitimacy of derogations. "The widespread failure to comply with the notification requirement according to article 4(3), the exclusively legalistic approach which is often unrealistic, and the unwillingness of some States fully to cooperate with the Committee are among the main setbacks of the reporting procedure." J. Oraá, Human Rights in States of Emergency in International Law 50 (1992). "The article 40 report process fails as a device for fact-finding in derogation situations because it is unfocused, subject to substantial delays, and unequipped either to produce or to test the veracity of relevant information." Fitzpatrick, supra page 915, at 84. More recently, however, the Committee has begun to take "special decisions" and to request that states in which de facto or de jure emergencies exist provide the Committee with supplemental information. See id. at 94-95. In 1993 the Committee amended its rules of procedure to permit its chairman, after consulting other members, to request such additional reports from states.

The Committee at least has established the principle that the mere declaration of a state of emergency is insufficient to justify it without further details. In a case filed against Uruguay under the Optional Protocol, for example, the Committee declared:

> 8.3 Although the sovereign right of a State party to declare a state of emergency is not questioned, yet, in the specific context of the present communication, the Human Rights Committee is of the opinion that a State, by merely invoking the existence of exceptional circumstances, cannot evade the

obligations which it has undertaken by ratifying the Covenant. Although the substantive right to take derogatory measures may not depend on a formal notification being made pursuant to article 4, paragraph 3, of the Covenant, the State party concerned is duty-bound to give a sufficiently detailed account of the relevant facts when it invokes article 4, paragraph 1, of the Covenant in proceedings under the Optional Protocol. It is the function of the Human Rights Committee, acting under the Optional Protocol, to see to it that States parties live up to their commitments under the Covenant. In order to discharge this function and to assess whether a situation of the kind described in article 4, paragraph 1, of the Covenant exists in the country concerned, it needs full and comprehensive information. If the respondent Government does not furnish the required justification itself, as it is required to do under article 4, paragraph 2, of the Optional Protocol and article 4, paragraph 3, of the Covenant, the Human Rights Committee cannot conclude that valid reasons exist to legitimize a departure from the normal legal régime prescribed by the Covenant.

Landinelli Silva v. Uruguay, Communication No. 34/1978, Report of the Hum. Rts. Comm., 36 U.N. GAOR Supp. (No. 40), Annex XII at 130, 132-133, U.N. Doc. A/36/40 (1981), reprinted in 2 Y.B. Human Rts. Comm. 1981-1982, at 307, 308 (1989).

The European Commission and Court of Human Rights may only address the legitimacy of a derogation in the context of a specific case, which may be brought by an individual or another state. One commentator observes that "[t]he Commission has taken the lead among intergovernmental bodies in developing the formal jurisprudence of states of emergency and has made invaluable contributions to the definition of the elements of permissible and impermissible emergencies. Nevertheless, it also has been cautious and somewhat deferential to governments." Fitzpatrick, supra page 915, at 194. An example of that caution is reflected in the following excerpt from the European Court of Human Rights, which is consistent with the Commission's jurisprudence.

> It falls in the first place to each Contracting State, with its responsibility for 'the life of [its] nation', to determine whether that life is threatened by a 'public emergency' and, if so, how far it is necessary to go in attempting to overcome the emergency. By reason of their direct and continuous contact with the pressing needs of the moment, the national authorities are in principle in a better position than the international judge to decide both on the presence of such an emergency and on the nature and scope of derogations necessary to avert it. In this matter Article 15(1) [of the European Convention] leaves those authorities a wide margin of appreciation.
>
> Nevertheless, the States do not enjoy an unlimited power in this respect. The Court, which, with the Commission, is responsible for ensuring the observance of the States' engagements, is empowered to rule on whether the States have gone beyond the 'extent strictly required by the exigencies' of the crisis. The domestic margin of appreciation is thus accompanied by a European supervision.

Ireland v. United Kingdom, European Ct. Hum. Rts., Judgment of 18 Jan. 1978, Ser. A No. 25, at 78-79 (citations omitted).

In contrast to the Human Rights Committee and the European system, the Inter-American Commission on Human Rights has the authority to examine states of emergency on its own initiative, and it has frequently done so. It has also addressed derogations in the context of individual complaints. See generally Fitzpatrick, supra page 915, at 178-189; Oraá, supra page 925, at 51-55.

The Inter-American Court of Human Rights significantly expanded the scope of non-derogable rights that must be protected, even in emergencies, in two advisory opinions it delivered in 1987. The opinions responded to separate requests from the Inter-American Commission and the government of Uruguay to clarify the prohibition in the American Convention on Human Rights against suspending "the judicial guarantees essential for the protection" of the non-derogable rights set forth in Article 27(2) of the Convention.

Habeas Corpus in Emergency Situations
Inter-Am. Ct. Hum. Rts., Advisory Opinion OC-8/87 of
30 Jan. 1987, Ser. A No. 8, at 38, 41-42, 48 (1987)

20. It cannot be denied that under certain circumstances the suspension of guarantees may be the only way to deal with emergency situations and, thereby, to preserve the highest values of a democratic society. The Court cannot, however, ignore the fact that abuses may result from the application of emergency measures not objectively justified in the light of the requirements prescribed in Article 27 and the principles contained in other here relevant international instruments. This has, in fact, been the experience of our hemisphere. . . .

27. As the Court has already noted, in serious emergency situations it is lawful to temporarily suspend certain rights and freedoms whose free exercise must, under normal circumstances, be respected and guaranteed by the State. However, since not all of these rights and freedoms may be suspended even temporarily, it is imperative that "the judicial guarantees essential for (their) protection" remain in force. Article 27(2) does not link these judicial guarantees to any specific provision of the Convention, which indicates that what is important is that these judicial remedies have the character of being essential to ensure the protection of those rights.

28. The determination as to what judicial remedies are "essential" for the protection of the rights which may not be suspended will differ depending upon the rights that are at stake. The "essential" judicial guarantees necessary to guarantee the rights that deal with the physical integrity of the human person must of necessity differ from those that seek to protect the right to a name, for example, which is also non-derogable.

29. It follows from what has been said above that the judicial remedies that must be considered to be essential within the meaning of Article 27(2) are those that ordinarily will effectively guarantee the full exercise of the rights and freedoms protected by that provision and whose denial or restriction would endanger their full enjoyment.

30. The guarantees must be not only essential but also judicial. The expression "judicial" can only refer to those judicial remedies that are truly capable of protecting these rights. Implicit in this conception is the active involvement of an independent and impartial judicial body having the power to pass on the lawfulness of measures adopted in a state of emergency. . . .

42. From what has been said before, it follows that writs of habeas corpus and of "amparo" are among those judicial remedies that are essential for the protection of various rights whose derogation is prohibited by Article 27(2) and that serve, moreover, to preserve legality in a democratic society.

43. The Court must also observe that the Constitutions and legal systems of the States Parties that authorize, expressly or by implication, the suspension of the legal remedies of habeas corpus or of "amparo" in emergency situations cannot be deemed to be compatible with the international obligations imposed on these States by the Convention.

In the second opinion, the Court held that the "essential" judicial guarantees not subject to derogation included, in addition to amparo and habeas corpus, "any other effective remedy before judges or competent tribunals, which is designed to guarantee the respect of the rights and freedoms whose suspension is not authorized by the [American] Convention . . . [and which] should be exercised within the framework and the principles of due process of law." Inter-Am. Ct. Hum. Rts., Advisory Opinion OC-9/87 of 6 Oct. 1987, Judicial Guarantees in States of Emergency, Ser. A No. 9, at 48 (1987).

Note: Limitation Clauses

The focus on derogations sometimes obscures the fact that numerous articles of the Civil and Political Covenant, while guaranteeing rights, simultaneously permit states parties to limit or restrict those rights for various reasons, even absent the existence of a public emergency. Limitation clauses found in the Covenant permit the restriction of human rights for purposes of the protection of the rights of others (Arts. 12(3), 18(3), 19(3)(a), 21, and 22(2)), national security (Arts. 12(3), 14(1), 19(3), 21, and 22(2)), public safety (Arts. 18(3), 21, and 22(2)), public order (*ordre public*) (Arts. 12(3), 14(1), 18(3), 19(3), 21, and 22(2)), public health (Arts. 12(3), 18(3), 19(3), 21, and 22(2)), and public morals (Arts. 12(3), 14(1), 18(3), 19(3), 21, and 22(2)). See Kiss, Permissible Limitations on Rights, in The International Bill of Rights: The Covenant on Civil and Political Rights 290, 293 (L. Henkin ed. 1981). Similar provisions are found in the regional human rights treaties.

As Professor Kiss notes,

> It is important to distinguish between derogation from rights in time of public emergency . . . and the permissible limitations on rights [authorized by the Covenant]. Although the circumstance permitting derogations, "public emergency which threatens the life of the nation," resembles one of the grounds for possible limitations, "national security," derogations and limitations differ in character and scope, in the circumstances in which they may be imposed, and in the methods by which they may be effected. Derogations in time of emergency are clearly intended to have only a temporary character; limitations, in contrast, can be permanent. Limitations on guaranteed rights must be provided by law but there is no such requirement for temporary derogations. Certain articles of the Covenant are not subject to derogations, for example Article 18 which provides for freedom of thought, conscience and religion, yet such rights are expressly made subject to possible limitations.

Id. at 290. See generally Symposium: Limitation and Derogation Provisions in the International Covenant on Civil and Political Rights, 7 Hum. Rts. Q. 1 (1985), which includes the text of the Siracusa Principles on the Limitation and Derogation Provisions in the International Covenant on Civil and Political Rights, which was adopted by 31 international law experts in 1984.

IV. Final Comments and Questions

1. As noted above, over 100 states have ratified Protocol II to the 1949 Geneva Conventions, dealing with non-international armed conflicts. Have combatants in Angola, Liberia, Mozambique, Rwanda, Somalia, Sri Lanka, Sudan, and the former Yugoslavia — to mention only a few recent civil wars that may meet the threshold requirements of Protocol II — abided by its proscriptions? Does it matter that, out of this list, only Rwanda and Yugoslavia have ratified Protocol II? If the other states are not bound, is there no international legal protection for civilians caught up in widespread brutality? See Problem VIII.

2. Review the four pre-Protocol law of war categories outlined by Professor Baxter on pages 881-882 supra. Compare them with the four "separate but overlapping regimes" that Professor Solf concludes now exist to govern non-international armed conflict. Solf, Problems with the Application of Norms Governing Interstate Armed Conflict to Non-International Armed Conflict, 13 Ga. J. Intl. & Comp. L. 291 (1983). They are:

1. In situations in which tensions and disturbances within the state fall short of actual armed conflict, domestic law and international human rights principles are applicable.

2. In situations severe enough to constitute an armed conflict, but falling short of being a civil war, article 3 common to the 1949 Geneva Conventions, domestic law, and international human rights principles are all applicable. However, since common article 3 does not define "armed conflict," the determination of the threshold for the application of common article 3 is left to the government of the affected state.

3. A third stage of conflict is high intensity civil war in which the rebels have organized armed groups under a responsible command, and they have exercised control over a part of the national territory sufficient to enable them to carry out sustained and concerted military operations, and therefore sufficient to implement Protocol II. In such situations, 1977 Protocol II is applicable in addition to the norms applicable in situation number 2 above. Despite the high threshold, which approaches the threshold for the application of the nineteenth century doctrine of recognized belligerency, there is no requirement for granting prisoner of war status.

4. In select struggles for self-determination, article 1(4) and 96(3) of Protocol I operate to make most of the rules governing international armed conflict applicable. The parties to a conflict may also agree, expressly or impliedly, to make the rules of international armed conflict applicable.

Id. at 294-295.

4. Not long ago it was observed that "[t]he juridical nexus between the humanitarian law of internal armed conflict and regimes of human rights is still an uncharted area of law." Draper, Humanitarian Law and Internal Armed Conflicts, 13. Ga. J. Intl. & Comp. L. 253, 276 (1983). More recently, a leading humanitarian/human rights expert has written the following:

> The convergence between humanitarian and human rights law is progressing rapidly. Although these systems of protection continue to have different institutional "umbrellas" (for the humanitarian law, the ICRC and the Red Cross movement; for human rights, the United Nations and various specialized and regional organizations), a strict separation between the two is artificial and hinders efforts to maximize the effective protection of the human person.

T. Meron, Human Rights in Internal Strife: Their International Protection 28 (1987). Yet despite the many pluses the Geneva Conventions possess — their nearly universal ratification, their emerging status as part of customary international law, their comprehensiveness and specificity, their application to governments and insurgents, and their non-derogability — they do not provide an overarching regime to govern armed conflicts, especially situations of civil strife where states have declared states of emergency and derogated from their human rights obligations. For an examination of some recent attempts to enforce humanitarian law at the international level, see Problem XII.

Do you agree with Meron that a better approach would be to create "a continuum of norms protecting human rights in all situations, from international armed conflicts at one end of the spectrum to situations of non-armed internal conflicts at the other"? See Meron, supra page 924. Cf. the Code of Conduct in the Event of Internal Disturbances and Tensions contained in Gasser, A Measure of Humanity in Internal Disturbances and Tensions: Proposal for a Code of Conduct, Intl. Rev. Red Cross, No. 262, at 38, 51 (Jan.-Feb. 1988).

For additional views on the convergence of humanitarian and human rights law, see, e.g., The New Humanitarian Law of Armed Conflict (A. Cassese ed. 1979); Dinstein, Human Rights in Armed Conflict: International Humanitarian Law, in 2 Human Rights in International Law 345 (T. Meron ed. 1984); Draper, Human Rights and the Law of War, 12 Va. J. Intl. L. 326 (1972); Marks, Principles and Norms of Human Rights Applicable in Emergency Situations: Underdevelopment, Catastrophes and Armed Conflicts, in 1 The International Dimension of Human Rights 175, 193-94 (K. Vasak ed. 1982); Meron, Human Rights in Time of Peace and in Time of Armed Conflict, in Contemporary Issues in International Law (T. Buergenthal ed. 1984); Paust and Blaustein, War Crimes Jurisdiction and Due Process: The Bangladesh Experience, 11 Vand. J. Transnatl. L. 1, 15-18 (1978); Robertson, Humanitarian Law and Human Rights, in Studies and Essays on International Humanitarian Law and Red Cross Principles in Honour of Jean Pictet 793 (C. Swinarski ed. 1984); Schindler, Human Rights and Humanitarian Law: The Interrelationship of the Laws, 31 Am. U. L. Rev. 935 (1982); L. Sohn, Fundamental Guarantees, Human Rights, Seminario Interamericano Sobre Seguridad del Estado, Derechos Humanos y Derecho Huamnitario, San Jose, Costa Rica, 27 September-2 October 1982. See also M. El Kouhene, Les Garanties Fondamentales de la Personne en Droit Humanitaire et Droits de L'Homme 8-12 (1986); Independent Commission on International Humanitarian Issues, Modern Wars: The Humanitarian Challenge 143 (1986); Les Dimensions Internationales du Droit Humanitaire 345 (1986); T. Meron, Human Rights in International Strife: Their International Protection 3-17 (1987). At the same time, many scholars and significant actors in the field of human rights have ignored humanitarian law. See, e.g., Human Dignity, The Internationalization of Human Rights (A. Henkin ed. 1978).

4. The International Law Association's Committee on the Enforcement of Human Rights Law produced a lengthy report on Minimum Standards of Human Rights Norms in a State of Exception. ILA, Report of the Sixty-First Conference 56 (Paris 1984). Based upon this report, the ILA adopted the Paris Minimum Standards of Human Rights Norms in a State of Emergency. Id. at 1, reprinted in Lillich, The Paris Minimum Standards of Human Rights Norms in a State of Emergency, 79 Am. J. Intl. L. 1072, 1073 (1985). For an extensive commentary on the Paris Minimum Standards, see S. Chowdhury, Rule of Law in a State of Emergency (1989).

5. One of the first steps in monitoring is simply to gather information on emergencies. In addition to the work of the Sub-Commission's special rapporteur, supra pages 924-925, data bases on states of emergency have been or are being created by the UN High Commissioner for Refugees, the International Labor Organization, the Council of Europe, the Human Rights Information and Documentation System (HURIDOCS, an NGO based in Norway), and the Center for International and Comparative Human Rights at Queen's University, Belfast.

Problem XII

International Criminal Law and Procedure and the Domestic Enforcement of "Piecemeal" Conventions

Can the Criminal Process Be Used to Help Enforce Human Rights Law?

I. Past Efforts to Bring the Criminal Process to Bear upon Human Rights
    Violators   936
    A. Introduction   936
    B. Background and Legal Issues   938
        Bridge, The Case for an International Court of Criminal Justice
            and the Formulation of International Criminal Law   938
        Wise, Codification: Perspectives and Approaches   952
    C. The International Criminalization of Human Rights Violations   954
        M. Bassiouni, International Criminal Law: A Draft Interna-
            tional Criminal Code   954
        Bassiouni, The Proscribing Function of International Criminal
            Law in the Processes of International Protection of Human
            Rights   954
        Mueller, Four Decades After Nuremberg: The Prospect of an
            International Criminal Code   957
II. Current Efforts to Draft a Code of Crimes Against the Peace and Se-
     curity of Mankind   959
     A. Introductory Note   959
     B. Readings on the ILC's 1991 Draft Code of Crimes Against the
         Peace and Security of Mankind   961
         Ferencz, An International Criminal Code and Court: Where
             They Stand and Where They're Going   961
         Bassiouni, "Crimes Against Humanity": The Need for a Spe-
             cialized Convention   963
         Note: The ILC's Draft Code: A Prognosis   965
         Note: NGO Efforts to Draft an International Criminal Code   966
III. Toward an International Criminal Court   968
      A. An Iraqi War Crimes Tribunal: Proposed But Rejected   968
          Moore, War Crimes and the Rule of Law in the Gulf Crisis   968
          O'Brien, The Nuremberg Precedent and the Gulf War   973
      B. The Yugoslav War Crimes Tribunal: The Security Council Estab-
          lishes an Ad Hoc International Criminal Court   978
          Orentlicher, Yugoslavia War Crimes Tribunal   978

Zagaris, Introductory Note: International Tribunal for the Pros-
ecution of Persons Responsible for Serious Violations of In-
ternational Humanitarian Law Committed in the Territory of
the Former Yugoslavia Since 1991: Rules of Procedure and
Evidence   985
Comments and Questions   989
C. The ILC Draft Statute for an International Criminal Court   993
D. NGO Efforts to Draft a Statute for an International Criminal
Court   1001
E. U.S. Attitudes Toward an International Criminal Court   1002
IV. *The Progressive Development of International Criminal Law: The
"Piecemeal" Convention Approach Coupled with Domestic Enforce-
ment*   1005
A. Transnational Terrorism   1005
Gross, International Terrorism and International Criminal Juris-
diction   1005
Murphy, Woetzel, and Lador-Lederer, Correspondence [About
Professor Gross's Comments]   1006
B. Apartheid, Torture, Hostage-Taking   1011
V. *Other Suggested Uses of the International Criminal Process*   1013
Mueller, Two Enforcement Models for International Criminal
Justice   1013
J. Carey, UN Protection of Civil and Political Rights   1018
VI. *Final Comments and Questions*   1022

I. Past Efforts to Bring the Criminal Process to Bear upon Human Rights Violators

A. *Introduction*

The criminal process has been used to punish human rights violators only sporadically. True, the commission of a traditional international crime — such as piracy on the high seas — subjected the offending individual to the criminal sanction of any state able to bring him to justice, since (the offense being international) jurisdiction was universal. 1 Oppenheim's International Law 503 n.3, 746 (9th ed. R. Jennings and A. Watts eds. 1992). Moreover, as Problem XI has shown, persons committing war crimes frequently have been brought to book before domestic courts — generally courts-martial established by their own states. At the end of World War II, an ad hoc international tribunal sitting at Nuremberg applied legal standards set out in a special charter during the trials of the Nazi war criminals for crimes against peace, war crimes, and crimes against humanity. (See page 848 of Problem XI.) In many ways, Nuremberg was and remains the highwater mark insofar as the use of the international criminal process is concerned (although the recently established Yugoslav War Crimes Tribunal (see pages 978-992 supra) may become an equally important precedent in this regard).

Immediately after Nuremberg, efforts were made to codify certain large-scale or particularly grave human rights violations as international crimes, the commission of which would render the offender subject to trial in various domestic, or perhaps even international, courts. This period saw the UN General Assembly's adoption of the Genocide Convention (see the Documentary Supplement), followed by the International Law Commission's formulation of the Nuremberg Principles (5 U.N. GAOR Supp. (No. 12) at 11-14, U.N. Doc. A/1316 (1950)) and the Draft Code of Offenses Against the Peace and Security of Mankind (9 U.N. GAOR Supp. (No. 9) at 11-12, U.N. Doc. A/2693 (1954)). Simultaneously, the UN was considering the possible establishment of a related international criminal court (Report of 1953 Committee on International Criminal Jurisdiction, 9 U.N. GAOR Supp. (No. 12) at 23-26, U.N. Doc. A/2645 (1954)). In 1957, however, the General Assembly decided to defer consideration of the court until it had completed the Draft Code and also a definition of aggression (G.A. Res. 1187, 12 U.N. GAOR Supp. (No. 18) at 52, U.N. Doc. A/3805 (1957)). This decision effectively "pigeonholed" the court for nearly two decades, since the General Assembly took until 1974 to agree on an official definition of aggression (G.A. Res. 3314, 29 U.N. GAOR Supp. (No. 31) at 142, U.N. Doc. A/9631 (1974)). See generally B. Ferencz, Defining International Aggression (1975) (2 vols.).

Even then, however, efforts to revive the idea of an international criminal court met with considerable resistance: the General Assembly did refer the Draft Code back to the International Law Commission in 1981 (G.A. Res. 31/106, 36 U.N. GAOR Supp. (No. 51) at 239, U.N. Doc. A/36/51 (1981)), but it took the Commission 10 years to adopt provisionally 26 articles of a renamed Draft Code of Crimes Against the Peace and Security of Mankind. Report of the International Law Commission to the General Assembly, 46 U.N. GAOR Supp. (No. 10) at 238-250, U.N. Doc. A/46/10 (1991). Moreover, in 1991 the Commission failed to adopt draft articles for an international criminal court, contenting itself with yet another general debate on whether to establish such a court. Id. at 214-235. Thus, as of the end of 1991, little progress had been made toward the adoption of a Draft Code, while efforts to establish an international criminal court seemed to have stalled.

While the United Nations was proceeding with something less than deliberate speed in its effort to draft an international criminal code and establish an international criminal court, an interesting and perhaps more significant phenomenon developed, namely, the international criminalization of certain specific acts, such as aerial hijacking, attacks on internationally protected persons, and the taking of hostages. These acts have been labeled international crimes in various multilateral conventions, to be considered later in this Problem, and all states that are parties to them are given universal jurisdiction over alleged offenders. The latter are prosecuted, therefore, in domestic courts under domestic law (enacted by states to implement their obligations under the conventions). The parallel to the normal enforcement of the law of war (see pages 850-851 of Problem XI) is obvious.

Whether such "piecemeal" conventions, coupled with domestic enforcement, are the "wave of the future" will be discussed later in this Problem. Initially, however, a general overview of past attempts to apply the criminal process to individuals who violate the human rights of other individuals is needed.

B. Background and Legal Issues

Bridge, The Case for an International Court of Criminal Justice and the Formulation of International Criminal Law
13 Intl. & Comp. L.Q. 1255, 1255-1281 passim (1964)

INTRODUCTION

The problem of an international criminal court has been the subject of more or less continuous discussion since the end of the First World War. The problem still awaits solution; the world is still without an international criminal court. Today the problem is as pressing as it has ever been and the reasons for the creation of such a court are equally compelling.

The problem may be stated in a few words: before what court and according to what law should an individual who has committed an international crime be tried? At present there are two possibilities. An international criminal may remain at large and unpunished. The case of Eichmann (and of how many others?) shows how an international criminal can remain at large and evade justice for a considerable period. On the other hand an international criminal may be tried by the court of any State which can bring him physically within its jurisdiction. In Germany, where German nationals are being tried for offences of an international character committed against other German nationals during the Nazi regime, such trials are perhaps less obviously open to objection. But the case of Eichmann may again be cited to illustrate what can happen. The abduction of Eichmann from Argentina by Israel contrary to well-established rules of international law and Eichmann's trial before an Israeli court for international crimes have established a dangerous precedent. * The dangers and disadvantages of

---

* One followed by the United States in its recent orchestration of the forcible kidnapping and abduction of a Mexican national to stand trial for violations of U.S. criminal laws. Alvarez-Machain v. United States, 112 S. Ct. 2188 (1992). The Supreme Court's decision,

individual States resorting to such illegal means of self-help or acting as what have been described as international "vigilantes" are patently obvious.

It is proposed . . . to deal with the problem in two stages. First, to make a critical assessment of the existing procedure whereby international criminals may only be tried, if at all, by municipal courts. Secondly, to state the case for the formulation of international criminal law and the establishment of an international criminal court with jurisdiction to try individuals charged with offences against that law.

1. The Trial of International Criminals by Municipal Courts

(A) THE PROBLEM OF JURISDICTION

"With regard to crimes as defined by international law, that law has no means of trying or punishing them. The recognition of them as constituting crimes and the trial and punishment of the criminals are left to the municipal courts of each country." This statement by Lord Sankey still represents the present position.

When an individual commits an international crime today before what municipal court will he be tried? The answer appears to depend on the nature of the crime and the circumstances of its commission. For example, the Genocide Convention of 1948, which declares genocide, as defined in the Convention, to be a crime under international law, directs that persons charged with genocide shall be tried "by a competent tribunal of the State in the territory of which the act was committed, or by such international penal tribunal as may have jurisdiction." The Geneva Convention on the High Seas of 1958, which defines piracy, provides that any State may seize a pirate vessel, in any place outside the jurisdiction of any other State, and the courts of the State carrying out the seizure may decide upon the penalties to be imposed.

In the case of war crimes it is a settled principle of international law that a belligerent has the right to punish such war criminals as fall into its hands during the war. Upon the cessation of hostilities the victorious belligerents may continue to try nationals of the defeated belligerents who are charged with war crimes. They may do this by setting up their own individual courts and/or by acting in concert with other victorious States after the examples of Nuremberg and Tokyo.

A State may also acquire jurisdiction over an international criminal by such legal means as extradition or a special agreement with the State in

which amounts to an endorsement of state-sponsored abductions, has been widely criticized for its blatant disregard of fundamental principles of international law. See, e.g., Rayfuse, International Abduction and the United States Supreme Court: The Law of the Jungle Reigns, 42 Intl. & Comp. L.Q. 882 (1993). — Eds.

which the criminal has sought refuge or, in the light of recent events, by illegal abduction.

Thus there is no one test whereby we may discover whether a State will have jurisdiction over a given international criminal. Nor is there any certainty from the criminal's point of view. If he commits genocide in State A only the courts of that State may try him, in the absence of a competent international penal tribunal. If he commits piracy there is no way of knowing what State will try him. In the case of war crimes it will depend very much whether he is on the winning side or having, as he thinks, escaped justice he may be spirited away years later to be tried before the courts of a country which may not have been in existence at the time he committed the crimes alleged against him.

The question of what municipal court will have jurisdiction over a given international criminal cannot be given a certain answer. This uncertainty of necessity perpetuates uncertainty in international criminal law itself and militates against the development of a unified international criminal jurisprudence.

(B)   THE PROBLEM OF APPREHENSION

If the courts of a State claim jurisdiction over a particular international criminal by what means can that State cause the criminal to appear before its courts to stand trial? If the criminal is found on the territory of that State there is no problem.

But suppose X has incited the inhabitants of State A to commit genocide, which is an offence punishable under the Genocide Convention to which State A is a contracting party. If X flees to State B how can he be made to appear before the courts of State A which have jurisdiction over him? If State B is itself a contracting party to the Genocide Convention, genocide will probably be an extraditable crime under the terms of an extradition treaty between States A and B. The Genocide Convention provides that genocide shall not be considered as a political crime for the purposes of extradition and it imposes a duty on contracting parties to grant extradition in such cases in accordance with their laws and treaties in force. Indeed, it would appear that contracting parties are bound to provide for the extradition of persons charged with genocide, since they are obliged to enact the necessary legislation to give effect to the provisions of the Convention.

If X flees to State C which is not a contracting party to the Genocide Convention, State A could ask for X to be surrendered. But international law imposes no obligation on State C to comply with this request. If the request is refused the only course open to State A would be to resort to illegality in order to implement international law.

A similar choice will face a State who wishes to apprehend a war criminal over whom it has jurisdiction. If the offence is not covered by an extradition treaty and negotiations for the criminal's surrender are unsuccessful the State wishing to try him will have to resort to self-help or allow him to evade justice.

In the case of piracy it is a case of first come, first served. Any State can take action to restrain piracy, arrest the pirates and try them before its courts.

It is patently obvious that the present arrangements for the apprehension of international criminals are far from satisfactory. Some form of permanent machinery is required: one answer to the problem would be to establish an international police force. But such a force is unlikely either to be acceptable or reasonably effective until some sort of world State has come into being.

A more practical solution would be an international convention dealing with the apprehension of international criminals. Contracting parties to the Convention would be obliged to arrest international criminals found on their territory, whether they were aliens or their own nationals, and to surrender them to the appropriate court for trial. The appropriate court should be an international criminal court.

It is not suggested that such a convention would ensure that every international criminal would stand trial. Some would still manage to seek refuge in a State which had not accepted the convention. But it would be a progressive step; the machinery would have been set up and with goodwill it could become very effective.

(C) THE PROBLEM OF THE INCORPORATION OF CRIMES "JURE GENTIUM" INTO MUNICIPAL LAW

Once a municipal court, which has jurisdiction over a particular international criminal, has that criminal before it, by what law will he be tried? The State concerned may regard international law as part of the law of the land. If it does not adopt this view, since the accused is charged with the commission of an international crime, that offence will have to be incorporated into its municipal law.

One instance of the incorporation of international crimes into municipal law is the Nazi Collaborators (Punishment) Law, 1950, enacted by the Israeli Parliament, which makes crimes against the Jewish people, crimes against humanity, and war crimes part of Israeli criminal law. But this is far from being an isolated example. [The author gives examples of the incorporation of international crimes into the criminal codes of Hungary, Yugoslavia, and the Soviet Union.]

Among Western States Holland, in addition to Israel, has incorporated some international crimes into its municipal law. Article 8 of the Dutch law of May 18, 1952, provides, inter alia, that breaches of the laws of warfare, inhuman treatment and systematic terrorising of civilians in time of war shall be crimes visited with various penalties.

This practice of incorporating international crimes into municipal law is open to serious objection. When a State sets out to do this it is faced with two alternatives: the crimes may be defined in general terms or they may be defined by enumeration. Definition in general terms is objectionable since it would express criminal liability in terms too vague to satisfy the principle of legality. Thus Article 8(1) of the Dutch law cited above provides generally that anyone who commits a breach of the laws of warfare shall be punished by a term of imprisonment up to a maximum of ten years. . . .

Definition by enumeration is equally unacceptable. There is an intrinsic danger of distortion in a subjective concept of international crime. Interpretations of international law differ. As one commentator puts it: "The position of a country determines the outlook of its lawyers and of its judges, their evaluation of values of interests, their opinion about the meaning of treaty texts and their appreciation of specific custom." A clear example is provided by the Dutch Special Court of Cassation set up in 1949 as the Supreme Court for War Criminals in Holland. One of the members of this court records that it sometimes adopted standards applied by courts exercising similar jurisdiction, both national and international, and sometimes dissented from opinions widely accepted in other countries. Yet at the same time that court claimed that when trying war criminals it has "the object of giving expression to the sense of justice of the community of nations." . . .

When States incorporate international crimes into their municipal criminal law, whatever drafting technique they adopt, whether general definition, enumeration, or a mixture of both, in no case will this produce the uniformity of formulation and the similarity of interpretation which are essential if a rule of law is to be universally accepted as a rule of international law. The only conclusion is that municipal law cannot be regarded as a satisfactory instrument whereby international criminal law may be implemented.

2. TRIAL OF INTERNATIONAL CRIMINALS BY AN INTERNATIONAL TRIBUNAL IN ACCORDANCE WITH INTERNATIONAL LAW

(A) INTERNATIONAL CRIMINAL LAW

(i) The Concept of Crime "Jure Gentium"

Nicholas Politis has pointed out that the concept of international crime is one of considerable antiquity. Indeed it has been the practice throughout most of the history of international law to speak of certain acts as delicta juris gentium. Piracy is perhaps the most familiar example of such an offence. Customary international law has also long recognised war crimes of various description, of which espionage and war treason are probably the oldest examples. . . .

Thus the concept of crime jure gentium is firmly established in international law. The work of the Nuremberg Tribunal and the affirmation by the United Nations of the principles of international law recognised by the

Nuremberg judgment have reaffirmed this concept and it has been supported to some extent by the formulation of the Genocide Convention and the drafting of a code of offences against the peace and security of mankind.

The offences mentioned above have been variously described as internationally authorised and prescribed municipal criminal law and as crimes *under* international law. The originators of these terms put forward the view that these offences are not international crimes in any true sense of the term but are merely offences which international law prescribes or authorises municipal courts to try on a universal international plane. The soundness of this view is apparent. The implication of the description of such offences as international crimes has always been "that in relation to their trial and punishment there is permissible some departure from the normal principles upon which national criminal jurisdiction is exercised — and particularly from the alleged principle of the territoriality of crimes." As Professor Schwarzenberger has pointed out, the argument that municipal courts in implementing so-called international criminal law are acting as the agents of international law merely gives added force to the conclusion that there is as yet no such thing as international criminal law in the true sense of the term.

Professor Schwarzenberger describes international crimes in the material sense of the word as acts which "strike at the very roots of international society"; these acts being of a prohibitive nature and backed by penal sanctions. Genocide, war crimes and piracy for that matter are clearly offences which "strike at the very roots of international society."

All that is necessary in order to make them international crimes in the material sense of the word is that they be expressed in clearly prohibitive terms and be supported by penal sanctions. Thus, these offences could be described as international crimes in embryo, potential international crimes which by means of conventions or wholesale codification could become true and international crimes.

The concept of crime jure gentium has been long established. A number of offences exist which await transformation into true international crimes. Whatever casuistry is employed to describe these offences it is beyond dispute that they are offences of an international character recognised by international law. Nor can it be denied that because of their international character the trial and punishment of these offences should be harmonised and unified. . . .

(iii)   The Formulation of International Criminal Law and Its Acceptance by States

The problems of the manner in which international criminal law should be formulated and its acceptance by States are naturally germane. The manner of formulation has a direct bearing on the possibility of acceptance. The purpose of formulation is to achieve harmonisation and unification. There are three possible means by which this purpose may be fulfilled:

a code of international criminal law; a number of international conventions enshrining international crimes; or the incorporation of international criminal law into municipal laws.

Something has already been said about the incorporation of international criminal law into municipal law as it is practised at present. The present practice may be faulted on the ground that there is no likelihood that the texts of international criminal law will be uniform, nor is there any hope of certainty in its interpretation and application. Certainty of interpretation and application will only be attained when international criminal law is administered by one international court and not by a host of municipal courts. Uniformity of formulation could perhaps be achieved if States followed an agreed authoritative text when incorporating international criminal law into their municipal systems. But this would be a rather devious means of formulating international criminal law. If States accept a certain text as a model, why not make that text, depending on its contents, either an international convention or a code of international criminal law? The incorporation of international criminal law into municipal law is inappropriate as a direct means of formulating international criminal law. It merely acts as the means by which States express their willingness to be bound by the international criminal law set out in a code or in a particular convention and to cause such law to be binding on their nationals.

This leads to the conclusion that international criminal law should be formulated either in a code or in a series of international conventions. A code of international criminal law has obvious attraction. A comprehensive code setting out in one document an authoritative statement of international criminal law has overwhelming advantages over the present amorphous state of international criminal law. But such a code must by definition be of universal application if it is to have any meaning and it also follows that it must be accepted in its entirety or not at all. A piecemeal acceptance of such a code subject to a variety of reservations would damn it before it became operative.

It is unthinkable to suggest that anything approaching a majority of States would be willing to accept and be bound by the terms of such a code. Further, if the code is to work effectively exclusive jurisdiction over the offences set out in it would have to be conferred upon an international criminal court. States would thus be asked to accept unconditionally an international criminal code which would be applied by a newly created and untried international court. States will obviously be unwilling to do this. They will naturally wish to be shown evidence that the court works in a satisfactory manner before binding themselves so completely.

How can this evidence be produced? In the writer's opinion the answer lies in international conventions setting out particular international crimes. Although unwilling to be bound by a comprehensive code States would perhaps confer jurisdiction more readily upon an international criminal court in a limited field of international crime. This could be achieved by drawing up international conventions setting out single or perhaps closely allied groups of international crimes. There could, for example, be such a convention on war crimes. The various crimes would be defined in prohibitive terms and adherents to the Convention would accept the exclusive jurisdiction of an international criminal court over such crimes. Signatories would also pledge themselves to honour and enforce the sanctions set out in the convention. Similar conventions dealing with other international crimes or categories of international crimes could be made in the course of time.

Thus once an international criminal court has been set up its impartiality and efficiency could be tested by one of these conventions. The activity of such a court in trying cases submitted to it under the terms of one of these conventions would, in the course of time, produce sufficient evidence that the court was working in a satisfactory manner. Once the court has proved itself in this way it should be possible to widen its jurisdiction by concluding further international conventions setting out other international crimes. This process would, of course, be spread over a long period. The eventual result could be the existence of an international criminal court with universal and exclusive jurisdiction over international crimes. The series of conventions on international criminal law could, as a series of related enactments, be regarded as an international criminal code. . . .

(B)   AN INTERNATIONAL CRIMINAL COURT

(i)   The Need for an International Criminal Court

The lack of an international tribunal to try individuals charged with the commission of international crimes is one of the most serious defects in the existing machinery for the administration of international justice. The need for such a court has been long recognised by international lawyers.

[The author traces the origins of the movement for an international criminal court back to World War I and describes unsuccessful efforts by the League of Nations and NGOs to establish such a court.]

During the Second World War the idea of an international criminal court gained increasing significance and it is often not realised how much effort was devoted to the practicalities of the creation and organisation of such a court. The work of a number of official and unofficial bodies paved the way for the deliberations of the International Conference on Military Trials which resulted in the establishment of the International Military Tribunal at Nuremberg.

Although the International Military Tribunal, functus officio, ceased to exist, the question of the creation of an international criminal court was actively taken up by the United Nations. [The author relates the events set out at page 937 supra.]

Certain arguments have already been put forward . . . which have criticised the present arrangements for the trial of international criminals and have suggested that this jurisdiction be transferred to a newly created international criminal court through the agency of international conventions on international criminal law. It is now proposed to deal with further aspects of the case for an international criminal court.

The contention that individuals whether personally or as the agents of States cannot be criminally liable for violations of international criminal law is no longer tenable. The judges at Nuremberg declared that "crimes against international law are committed by men, not by abstract entities, and only by punishing individuals who commit such crimes can the provisions of international law be enforced." Man's potentialities as an offender against international law have been immeasurably increased since modern weapons have been placed in his hands. Today it is even more important that individuals who commit crimes against international law should be tried and punished by an international criminal court whether, in the words of the Genocide Convention, they are constitutionally responsible rulers, public officials or private individuals.

The existence of international crimes and the recognition of individual responsibility for such crimes logically suggests that there should be an international tribunal with power to try individuals for the commission of international crimes. It is just as important to have an international criminal court to administer international criminal law as it is to have national criminal courts to administer national criminal law. For however objective and impartial national courts may in fact be, because they are the courts of particular States there will inevitably be a suspicion of bias when a national court tries an international criminal. . . .

A more practical objection to allowing national courts to exercise jurisdiction over international crimes is that different national courts would tend to hand down conflicting decisions and impose varying penalties for offences against international criminal law. Two cases tried by national war crimes tribunals after the Second World War will serve as an illustration. In 1946 a British military court tried three members of a German firm of chemical manufacturers for supplying the poison gas Zyklon B which was used to exterminate allied nationals in German concentration camps. Two of the accused were found to have supplied the gas knowing for what purpose it was to be used. They were found guilty and condemned to death. In an almost identical case before a German court the manager of a chemical firm was found guilty of supplying Zyklon B knowing that it was to be used at Auschwitz for the extermination of inmates of the camp. He was sentenced to penal servitude for five years and to loss of civil rights for three years.

That two such inequable penalties should have been imposed in these cases is manifestly unjust. The severity of the punishment obviously depends on the court before which an accused is tried. Such a situation hinders the harmonious development of international criminal law. One permanent international criminal court is needed, which, over a period, could develop a unified and universal international criminal law. This argument has received strong support from Hans Kelsen, who has written: "The objective examination and unbiassed decision of the question whether or not the law has been violated is the most important, the essential stage in any legal procedure. As long as it is not possible to remove from the interested states the prerogative to answer the question of law and transfer it once and for all to an impartial authority, namely, an international court, any further progress on the way to the pacification of the world is absolutely excluded." . . .

Perhaps the major obstacle which stands in the way of the creation of an international criminal court is the objection that its jurisdiction would violate the doctrine of State sovereignty. States of the Soviet bloc, for example, base their objections on this doctrine. In particular they claim that the right to try crimes committed on a State's territory belongs exclusively to that State. Thus, they argue, an international criminal court would violate the principle of the sovereign equality of members of the United Nations and would amount to an intervention in matters essentially within the domestic jurisdiction of States.

This latter objection is not valid. Although international crimes may be committed on the territory of a State they cannot be said to be subject to the exclusive jurisdiction of courts of that State. International crimes, by definition, are crimes against mankind, crimes which endanger the peace and security of the world. In the words of Professor Schwarzenberger they are acts which strike at the very roots of international society. Thus the prime right to try and punish international criminals does not belong to one State or to any group of States but to international society. This right should be exercised through an international criminal court which would represent the entire international community.

Objections on the basis of State sovereignty are similarly suspect. The absolute doctrine that a State is supreme and does not accept orders from any other authority is no longer tenable. States today are not in the position to invoke their sovereignty in order to restrict or avoid the operation of international law. States can be said to be still sovereign only in the sense that they are subject only to the authority of international law and not to that of any other State. Thus in reality the concept of sovereignty has been replaced by independence under international law.

Those States who still cling to the doctrine of absolute sovereignty may be answered in their own terms: absolute sovereignty implies absolute power which includes the power to join the United Nations or to accept the jurisdiction of an international criminal court. There can be no question of the violation of State sovereignty if a State voluntarily submits to the jurisdiction of an international criminal court. By limiting its sovereignty a State proves that it is sovereign.

(ii) Some Characteristics of an International Criminal Court

In the short space of this article it is impossible to consider in detail the host of problems connected with the organisation and procedure of an international criminal court. But having argued the case for the establishment of such a court something must be said about what this would mean in practice.

It may be asked whether it is indeed advisable to set up an international criminal court at the present time. It has rightly been observed that international criminal law "pierces national sovereignty and presupposes that statesmen of the several States have a responsibility for international peace and order as well as their responsibilities to their own States." The problem is whether we should wait until this responsibility is generally recognised or should make a start now in the belief that a universal international criminal jurisdiction will develop.

One of the arguments adduced in support of the former point of view is that it is not possible to devise a court and procedure which would be both effective and acceptable to States. This has been disproved by the creation and comparative success of the International Court of Justice and its predecessor. A further point has been made, however, that there are inherent differences between civil and criminal courts. Because of these differences and the intensely national character of criminal law it has been concluded that the use of criminal process in the international sphere is strictly limited. The successful functioning of the Nuremberg Tribunal has shown this view to be erroneous. The fact that the Nuremberg Charter was the product of particular circumstances does not lessen its importance. It cannot be denied that at Nuremberg agreement was reached by lawyers from nations whose legal systems, philosophies and traditions differ widely. This agreement did not merely amount to a theoretical reconciliation but was proved to work in practice. Thus with "a minimum of goodwill and commonsense" technical difficulties may be overcome.

Many aspects of the composition, organisation and procedure of an international criminal court could be dealt with according to the tried procedures of the International Court of Justice. These matters include the qualification, terms of office and election of the judges and the organisation and functions of the registry of the court. But criminal courts have important characteristics which are not possessed by civil courts and it is now proposed to consider some of these.

One vital problem concerns the introduction of cases before the court and the conduct of the prosecution. There are three possible answers to the question of who shall undertake the prosecution of someone accused of an international crime: prosecution by the party bringing the charge; prosecution by the appropriate organ of the United Nations; prosecution by a newly created international public prosecutor's department.

The first possibility must be rejected on the ground that the prosecution of international criminals should be undertaken not only on behalf of the individual prosecutor but also on behalf of the international community as a whole. It has already been argued that international crimes are crimes against international society and so the prosecution should be conducted by an international organ. Moreover the prosecuting authority would thus be distinct from the individual prosecutor and this would help to ensure that the prosecution was conducted in a non-partisan spirit.

The question remains whether this international prosecuting authority should be either an organ of the United Nations or a specially devised body. It has been suggested that the appropriate organ of the United Nations should be entrusted with the conduct of the prosecution: the Security Council would be the appropriate organ for crimes endangering peace and the Economic and Social Council for crimes against humanity. But apart from the practical problem of how these United Nations organs could take over such additional activities, there is surely much danger inherent in the suggestion that an international criminal court should be brought into close contact with such a politically centered body as the Security Council.

In order to ensure that persons accused of international crimes should have as fair a trial as possible it is surely essential that there should be a permanent international public prosecutor's department, in no way connected with the parties to the action, which would prepare and conduct prosecutions on behalf of the international community. Such a department would be a specialised extension of the international civil service. It could be established either as an independent international organ or possibly by developing the Legal Department of the United Nations Secretariat.

Another problem concerns the cases to be tried by the court: should all cases that are brought be tried or only those which have successfully satisfied a preliminary inquiry?

The very nature of international criminal jurisdiction makes it probable that attempts would be made to use the court as a political weapon. Thus it will be necessary to provide some sort of screening device to ensure that the cases which are eventually tried by the court have not been brought from purely political motives nor are of a trifling nature. Some preliminary examination of the evidence against the accused to determine whether it warrants a prosecution is an essential feature of a just procedure. Only those cases concerning the alleged commission of recognised international crimes within the jurisdiction of the court which are substantiated by a prima facie case should be tried by the international criminal court.

It is suggested that the body charged with the conduct of such preliminary inquiries should be made up of a number of the judges of the international criminal court, chosen periodically for the purpose, who would take no part in the subsequent trial proper. This special chamber of the court would exercise a function similar to that of examining magistrates in England and the *chambre de mise en accusation* on the Continent. It is preferable for the preliminary inquiry to be undertaken by members of the court itself rather than by a specially created body. The establishment of yet another international organ, which might be regarded as of a political nature, would unnecessarily complicate the procedure of bringing cases before the court.

If the Committing Chamber is satisfied that there is a reasonable case against a given accused then it would certify to that effect and the trial would follow.

As far as the form of trial and rules of procedure are concerned, a clear distinction can be made between what may be called the fundamental principles of criminal procedure, which are largely designed to ensure that the accused has a fair trial, and other rules concerned with more detailed aspects of procedure. The statute of an international criminal court should contain a statement of these fundamental principles which would, in brief, guarantee that every person charged with an international crime before the international criminal court would "be presumed innocent until proved guilty according to law in a public trial at which he has had all the guarantees necessary to his defence." It should be left to the court itself, however, to decide what detailed rules of procedure should be adopted and in this it would of course be guided by experience.

Another matter which requires mention is the provision of machinery for the custody of the accused pending trial and for the execution of sentences. It has already been suggested that the apprehension of international criminals should be the subject of an international convention. Contracting parties to this convention would guarantee to arrest international criminals found on their territory and deliver them up for trial before the international criminal court.

There are two possible means of providing for the custody of accused pending trial: an international prison service could be established or arrangements for custody could be made with the State on whose territory the court has its seat. Ideally an international body should be set up but from a practical point of view, bearing in mind the small amount of business with which the court would be for some time concerned, the simplest remedy would be to arrange with the prison authorities of the State in which the court has its seat to take custody of [the] accused pending and during trial. The decision whether an accused is to be kept in custody or is to be given his freedom by a system of bail would rest with the court itself.

The question of the machinery to be used to execute sentences is of a similar nature: should there be a detention centre under the control of either the court or the United Nations or should individual States be asked to undertake the execution of sentences on behalf of the international community. Again, for the time being, the practical answer must be that the services of States should be employed for this purpose. A panel of States willing to provide this service could be drawn up and the court could select a State from this panel to execute the sentence imposed on a given international criminal. There is an important caveat to this suggestion: in a given case neither the State initiating the prosecution nor the State of which the criminal is a national should be asked to execute the sentence. A further guarantee of the humane treatment of persons convicted of international crimes would be to make the prisons of States providing this service subject to inspection by impartial United Nations officials.

(iii) The Means of Creating an International Criminal Court

[The author sets out to examine three means of creating an international criminal court, namely, by amending the UN Charter, by a General Assembly resolution, or by an international convention. He concludes that the first is impracticable and the second unwise.]

The third possibility, which appears most feasible, is to establish an international criminal court by means of an international convention. This is in fact the means adopted by the drafters of a number of proposals including the 1951 and 1953 Committees on International Criminal Jurisdiction.

There have been criticisms of this mode of creation largely on the grounds that a court created in this way would lack prestige in that it would not be supported by the United Nations and the probable delay in bringing the convention into force because of the diverse constitutional procedures of States for ratifying international conventions. But despite these criticisms the establishment of the court by an international convention has one overriding advantage in that only those States seriously interested in the creation of the court would take part in negotiations leading to the convention and so any adverse effect derived from the participation of antagonistic States would be avoided.

The 1953 Committee in particular was in favour of creating the court by international convention. It suggested that the Secretary-General be empowered to convene a diplomatic conference which would consider the draft statute and any other recommendations. It was also suggested that the convention should not become effective unless a predetermined number of States were in favour of it.

At present this seems to be the most practicable means of establishing an international criminal court. . . .

CONCLUSION

The case for the establishment of an international criminal court and the formulation of international criminal law may be summed up in the following way. The concept of crime has long been recognised by international law. The present means of trying international criminals before municipal courts is haphazard, unjust and militates against the development of a universal international criminal law. The administration of international criminal law will only become systematic, just and universal when the organ of its administration is a permanent international criminal court. Further, while international criminality is recognised, international criminal law does not exist in any material sense. Authoritative texts of international crimes backed by sanctions are needed for the proposed international criminal court to apply. An international criminal code, although a desirable goal, is not a sine qua non for the establishment of an international criminal court. The gradual formulation of crimes in international conventions is the only practicable way in which progress may be made.

The existence of international crimes, even in their present amorphous state, logically suggests that there should be an international criminal court. It is obvious that at the present time such a court would be far from perfect. For the time being jurisdiction would have to be on a voluntary basis; compulsory jurisdiction would only be possible if and when we have some sort of world State. But it is surely not too much to expect that if adequate judicial machinery were set up, it would in time so commend itself to world opinion that its jurisdiction would come to be automatically accepted by States.

Thus it would be worth while to set up an international criminal court at the present time even on this imperfect, voluntary basis. Legal institutions need time to grow. It is too much to expect that an international criminal court could be created at once in a perfect form. This imperfect beginning is unavoidable. It would be wrong to wait until a more perfect form could be established, since this would exclude the possibility of gradual development.

Wise, Codification: Perspectives and Approaches
in 1 M. Bassiouni, International Criminal Law 101, 106-107 (1986)

The existing law on international crimes can be roughly divided into perhaps three general heads.

1) First, its "classical domain" — that more or less covered by the International Law Commission's 1951 Draft Code of Offenses Against the Peace and Security of Mankind. Conventional war crimes — violations of the laws and customs of war — are the prototypical offenses under this head. It also includes, by extension, the two analogous categories of crime prosecuted at Nuremberg: crimes against peace and crimes against humanity; then, by further extension, genocide (under the 1948 Genocide Convention) and, if one likes, "aggression" (under the General Assembly's so-called definition of 1974) and apartheid (under the 1973 Apartheid Convention). The systemic use of torture by governments [also should be included now that it is proscribed by the 1984 Torture Convention].

2) Second, crimes associated with terroristic activities that have been the subject of relatively recent conventions, although the prototype here is in some ways the old offense of piracy. This head includes offenses involving interference with civil aviation (under the 1963 Tokyo, 1970 Hague, and 1971 Montreal Conventions), with diplomatically protected persons (under the 1973 convention on Crimes Against Internationally Protected Persons), and the taking of hostages (under the 1979 Hostages Convention). Unlike the first class of international crimes, these are not offenses commit-

ted directly by state authorities, but the actual reason for international concern with them largely has been a lax attitude sometimes seeming to amount to complicity on the part of states in which such offenders have taken refuge.

3) Third, acts which have been subjected to treaty prohibition because they involve either international traffic in noxious commodities (narcotics, slaves, women and children, and, at one time, obscene publications), or harm to certain common or mutual interests of states (through overfishing, pollution of the sea by oil, interference with submarine cables, unlawful use of the mails, or counterfeiting of currency).

This all adds up to a sizeable body of law. But is it an unmanageable mass in urgent need of formal systematization? The point of having an international criminal code surely lies elsewhere.

Historically, the idea of codifying international criminal law is bound up with the idea of establishing an international criminal court. There is no necessary connection between the two ideas. One could have an international criminal court whose jurisdiction is defined simply through reference to existing treaties; this has been proposed most recently by the International Criminal Law Committee of the International Law Association. One could have a code without a court, relying instead on "indirect enforcement" through interstate cooperation, or on an international investigating commission to focus public outrage on those to whom prima facie violations can be attributed. Still, there seems little point to trying to get up a code unless one can count on some kind of enforcement mechanism.

Enforcement, of course, it not an end in itself, any more than a code should be. The chief reason for wanting a code and a court — or some workable alternative — always has been that crimes deserving not only condemnation but damnation are neither condemned nor punished because they are committed by rulers of states and miscreants in their employ, and no ready mechanism exists for bringing these offenders to book or even officially exposing their conduct to public indignation.

It may be prudent to begin with third-class international offenses, which are relatively free from political implications: to create an undisputed international criminal law strictissimo sensu, as a preliminary to bringing graver crimes within its sphere of operation. Sir Henry Maine once suggested that enactment of a penal code was relatively easier to achieve than enactment of a civil code since "nobody cares about criminal law except theorists and habitual criminals." This suggestion may not be invariably valid; there are counter-examples. In any event, it obviously does not hold where the lawmakers themselves are the "habitual criminals." Adoption of a code that meaningfully condemns conduct by those in high places faces formidable obstacles. Nonetheless, the primary function of any international criminal code must be to serve as a propaedeutic to a system in which "over-mighty" official offenders are stamped with infamy in proportion to their misdeeds. That, it seems to me, is the main motive, if not the only worthy motive, for trying to draft an international criminal code.

C. The International Criminalization of Human Rights Violations

The extract by Professor Wise immediately above shows how the international community increasingly has applied the criminal process to individuals who violate the human rights of other individuals, at least when those violations are gross in character. The next three readings explain the object of international criminal law in general, point out how it contributes to the protection of human rights specifically, and speculate about whether the United States would adopt, either by legislation or by treaty, the Draft Code of Crimes Against the Peace and Security of Mankind were it ever officially promulgated by the UN General Assembly.

M. Bassiouni, International Criminal Law: A Draft International Criminal Code
1 (1980)

. . . [I]nternational criminal law is that branch of the international legal system which represents one of the strategies employed to achieve, in respect to certain world social interests, [a] greater degree of compliance and conformity with the goals of the world community of prevention, preservation, and rehabilitation. These world social interests have emerged from common experience in the course of time and reflect certain shared values which the world community has come to recognize as requiring collective coercive or cooperative efforts to their protection. Thus, the object of the normative proscription of international criminal law is to specify conduct identified as harmful to a given world social interest whose protection is deemed to require the imposition of criminal sanctions on violators and which sanctions are enforced by the member states of the world community through international collective, cooperative or national action.

Bassiouni, The Proscribing Function of International Criminal Law in the Processes of International Protection of Human Rights
9 Yale J. World Pub. Ord. 193, 193-197 (1982)

It may appear upon initial examination that international criminal law has little to contribute to the development and protection of international human rights. Close analysis demonstrates, however, that the international protection of human rights can be viewed as a continuum along which criminal proscription has become the ultima ratio modality of protection. Resort to criminal proscription is compelled when a given right encounters an "enforcement crisis" in which other modalities of protection appear inadequate. Yet, the need to find an international or transnational element in human rights violations together with the need to rely on national courts to implement international penal proscriptions present impediments to scrutiny of violations committed by officials of sovereign states. This paper describes how international criminal law facilitates the proscribing function and initiates an inquiry as to its role in a comprehensive system of international protections.

I. A THEORY OF HUMAN RIGHTS DEVELOPMENT

The twentieth century has witnessed an unprecedented expansion in the international protection of human rights. This expansion can be attributed to an ever-increasing sharing of fundamental values and expectations among nations. As a result, the world community now acknowledges the need to protect the individual from a variety of human depredations.

Depredations, while sometimes the result of private conduct, are most frequently committed by persons acting in a pubic or quasi-public capacity. Governmental policies are thus the primary cause of human rights violations today. Fortunately, the claim that sovereignty prevents scrutiny of a state's human rights practices has been at least partially overcome. This development presents the opportunity to adopt modalities of protection that can directly influence a state's human rights practices.

The rationale for international protection of human rights is that certain forms of depredations become matters of international concern when committed under the aegis of state policy because of the presumed international impact of such behavior. Thus, the rationale posits that collective effort is required to protect against policies that may ultimately affect the entire world community.

Concepts upon which a comprehensive framework for development and enforcement of human rights can be based are as yet poorly defined. Indeed, international human rights are themselves inadequately defined and inconsistently enforced. There is no classification of rights according to the values sought to be advanced or effective enforcement modalities. Proceeding from this observation, natural rights thinkers simply might conclude that human rights are divinely endowed. Nevertheless, despite the dearth of scholarly analysis, human rights do emerge and develop as part of a coherent process.

The immediate task is to chart and differentiate the stages through which human rights evolve. The degree to which a given right has attained international acceptance can be assessed by considering the following pattern of emergence and development.

Stage 1 — *The Enunciative Stage* — The emergence and shaping of internationally perceived shared values through intellectual and social processes.

Stage 2 — *The Declarative Stage* — The declaration of certain identified human interests or rights in an international document or instrument.

Stage 3 — *The Prescriptive Stage* — The articulation of these human rights in some prescriptive form in an international instrument (general or specific) generated by an international body; or the elaboration of specific normative prescriptions in binding international conventions.

Stage 4 — *The Enforcement Stage* — The search for, or the development of, modalities of enforcement.

Stage 5 — *The Criminalization Stage* — The development of international penal proscriptions.

Rights in the declarative stage (Stage 2) frequently are framed in general terms. In the prescriptive stage (Stage 3), rights are more specifically articulated in general international instruments having some legally binding effect. In the final stage, international criminalization, rights are always expressed in specific international conventions which deal exclusively with the rights and proscribe violation of them.

A particular human right may not necessarily evolve through each of these stages in the order listed above. Nevertheless, there is sufficient similarity in the pattern of development of most international human rights to validate the categorization. Perhaps positioning a right at a given stage is a function of the perception of the significance of the interest protected through the articulation of the right and of the appraisal of the degree of protection that the interest requires. Although it is less structured in the international context, the process of evolutionary development can be analogized to the evolution of social values and the development of civil prescription and penal proscriptions in any organized society.

Throughout the evolutionary process, the enactment of international criminal proscriptions invariably has followed an implementation crisis. Nevertheless, the adoption of criminal proscriptions has not derived from an appraisal of the significance of the right sought to be preserved and protected; rather, it has been caused by the inadequacy of modalities of protection in the first four stages. Thus, the inadequacy of these modalities has compelled the transformation of the protected right into a prohibited crime. Therefore, international criminal proscriptions are the ultima ratio modality of enforcing internationally protected human rights.

II.   AN ILLUSTRATION OF THE THEORY

Demonstrating the existence of the pattern of development described above requires the selection of a substantive premise and a functional starting point. This paper adopts the existing international instruments as the substantial premise and the evolution of those protected rights contained in such instruments as the functional starting point. On this basis, the evolutionary development of a given human right can be traced from the enunciative stage (Stage 1) to the criminalization stage (Stage 5). Reversing the analysis, from the criminalization stage to the enunciative stage, is equally valid. The outcome of the analysis should be identical regardless of methodology.

For example, a number of declared protected human rights with respect to physical integrity, contained in the Universal Declaration of Human Rights, can be traced through succeeding international instruments to their inclusion in international penal proscriptions. This observation reveals that these declared rights which were first enunciated in the Universal Declaration were then reiterated more specifically, or more emphatically, in the International Covenant on Civil and Political Rights. They later became the subject of specialized conventions, and finally the subject of specialized international penal protections (e.g., genocide and apartheid). With this framework established, the discussion turns to more specific applications based on existing international proscriptions.

The proscriptions which are contained in multilateral conventions of a penal nature can be topically categorized as follows: (1) crimes against peace; (2) war crimes; (3) crimes against humanity; (4) genocide; (5) apartheid; (6) slavery and slave-related practices; (7) torture; (8) unlawful human experimentation; (9) piracy; (10) hijacking; (11) kidnapping of diplomats and the taking of civilian hostages; and (12) unlawful use of the mails. These topical subject matters share the following characteristics. Each is predicated on one or more international conventions which either explicitly declare the conduct in question to be an international crime or require the contracting parties to do so in their national laws, and frequently obligate the parties to prosecute or extradite the offender. Each substantive area and its related conventions seek to preserve and protect certain human interests which have been enunciated in one or more preceding human rights instruments. Each of the enumerated international penal proscriptions is the product of an evolutionary and progressive development through which an international instrument, relying on its predecessor, adds a new dimension to the definition, content, implementation or enforcement of the right sought to be preserved and protected.

Mueller, Four Decades After Nuremberg: The Prospect of an International Criminal Code
2 Conn. J. Intl. L. 499, 501-506 (1987)

[The author notes that any discussion of international criminal law must begin by examining the Nuremberg Principles, which he proceeds to do in succinct fashion. He then describes how the international community has gone beyond Nuremberg in its attempt to "draft an international criminal code which would be administered both nationally and internationally through an international criminal court." Next he surveys the work of the International Law Commission through the mid-1980s on the Draft Code and concludes that, despite drafting problems, "the General Assembly debates evidence a willingness to complete the task and resolve the remaining disagreements."]

Assuming that work on the Code will be completed in the foreseeable future, what obstacles to ratification can be expected? Twenty one years ago, I discerned four types of objections to the then fledgling draft of the Code: the emotional, the juridical, the practical, and the jurisprudential. The emotional objection is rooted in the old American belief in the superiority of the American due process model of criminal justice. As Senator Jesse Helms said in opposing approval of the Genocide Convention: "I do not want to see the United States submit itself to any international regime of law which is enforced by a group of nations which do not have our legislative history and goals, and perhaps no understanding of those principles of our nation."

This view, however, fails to differentiate between government policies with which other nations may not agree and mankind's collective views regarding the administration of justice as expressed in the Universal Declaration of Human Rights, the Covenants, and the Draft Code. By participating in the creation of a system of international criminal justice, the United States is not subjecting itself to the will of alien systems. Rather, it is joining in a system which incorporates common values. The emotional argument, therefore, is devoid of merit. If anything, it simply reflects the ancient bias of lawyers of the common law system against the continental law system, a bias which evidences scant understanding of continental law.

The juridical objections, too, are but an extension of emotional bias, centering on such issues of substantive criminal law as ex post facto or the congressional prerogative to enact penal laws at the federal level. Nuremberg has earlier laid to rest the ex post facto issue. And it will, of course, be the prerogative of Congress to enact the Code of Offences Against the Peace and Security of Mankind, thereby making it American law, as other nations would use their legislative processes to make it the law of their lands.

Another major juridical objection concerns the fear that a defendant charged and tried before an international criminal court might not enjoy the usual due process guaranteed in American courts, including the right to trial by jury. This argument erroneously assumes that violations of the Code *must* be tried before the prospective international criminal court. No one demands that this court have exclusive jurisdiction. Rather, the principle aut dedere-aut judicare would apply. An American court with jurisdiction over such a defendant would thus have three options: to try him in the United States with all American due process guarantees; to surrender him for trial by the courts of a requesting country with jurisdiction (a practice our courts have long followed); or to surrender him to the international criminal court for trial.

The practical or political obstacles were succinctly described by Professor Schwarzenberger thirty-five years ago:

> [A]n international criminal law that is meant to be applied to the world powers is a contradiction in terms. It presupposes an international authority which is superior to these states. In reality, however, any attempt to enforce an international criminal code against either the Soviet Union or the United States would be war under another name.

I have had considerable sympathy for the view, which simply recognizes that the Nuremberg Tribunal succeeded due to a completely defeated enemy, prostrate and thus prone to prosecution. Since these objections were first made, however, a number of changes have taken place in the international community. The United Nations has become a universal organization. Moreover, nations large and small have demonstrated that they can condemn their own past actions and even bring national leaders to trial. More and more dictators who have been ousted and have fled to other countries will be tried for offenses such as those to be included in the Code. Of course, it may take years of world peace, disarmament and increased trust among nations before the Code can become truly operative. However, that should not stop us from preparing this Code now, as yet another step on the long road toward the establishment of a system of universal justice.

The jurisprudential objections remain. Though the 1954 version of the Code was a statement of deeply felt convictions, it was rightly attacked as naive and devoid of any of the adjuncts that mark a true penal code at the national level. What were to be the penal aims of the Code? Deterrence, retribution, or rehabilitation? What was to be the delimitation of the scope of the topic ratione materiae? What of concursus plurium ad delictum and all the other general principles necessary if an international, rather than a national, court were to try a defendant? The jurisprudential objections were well taken, and the International Law Commission, the Special Rapporteur, and the Drafting Committee have set about rectifying these substantial shortcomings. In a few years, assuming their work succeeds, the jurisprudential objections will no longer hold.

Some may see in America's accession to the Genocide Convention the triumph of decency over the horrors of the holocausts witnessed by several ethnic groups and peoples, particularly the Jewish people. But surely this accession evidences more than the success of lobbying on Capitol Hill. Within the context of the gradual creation of an international criminal law with universal jurisdiction, the American ratification of the Genocide Convention, forty years after Nuremberg, is evidence of an inevitable evolution toward the recognition of a civitas maxima, the ultimate community. . . .

II. Current Efforts to Draft a Code of Crimes Against the Peace and Security of Mankind

A. Introductory Note

As mentioned at the outset of this Problem, the UN General Assembly, to which the International Law Commission forwarded its Draft Code of Offences Against the Peace and Security of Mankind in 1954, took 27 years to refer the Draft Code back to the Commission for further elaboration. Now renamed, perhaps tentatively and certainly inaccurately, the Draft Code of Crimes Against the Peace and Security of Mankind, it has been an item on the Commission's agenda at each of its sessions since 1983. For reports of the progress the Commission is making, see the annual Current Developments survey by the U.S. member of the Commission in 78 Am. J. Intl. L. 457, 472-475 (1984); 79 id. 755, 755-757 (1985); 80 id. 185, 186-188 (1986); 81 id. 668, 680-681 (1987); 82 id. 144, 144-147 (1988); 83 id. 153, 154-160 (1989); 84 id. 930, 930-936 (1990); 85 id. 703, 706-707 (1991); 87 id. 138 (1993); 88 id. 134 (1994). At its 1991 session, the ILC provisionally adopted 26 articles of the Draft Code, which it asked the Secretary-General to transmit to governments for their comments and observations before it undertook revisions during the course of a second reading. (See pages 965-966 infra.)

In its recent drafting efforts, the Commission has proceeded on the assumption that its revised Draft Code should cover only such offenses "whose characterization as crimes against the peace and security of mankind was hard to challenge." Thus, the ILC's 1991 Draft Code includes the offenses found in its 1954 Draft Code — for example, crimes against the peace, war crimes, and (to some extent) crimes against humanity* — plus acts such as genocide, apartheid, and other systematic or mass violations of human rights. Traditional international crimes like piracy and newer international crimes like the taking of hostages are not included. Yet the 1991 Draft Code does cover colonial and alien domination, international terrorism, illicit traffic in narcotic drugs, and willful and severe damage to the environment, all offenses not necessarily a threat to peace and security. Report of the International Law Commission to the General Assembly, 46 U.N. GAOR Supp. (No. 10) at 238-250, U.N. Doc. A/46/10 (1991). Whatever one thinks of this approach (two views follow this Note), clearly the Commission does not view its task as one of drafting a comprehensive international criminal code.

Finally, it should be noted that the Draft Code applies to individuals, not states. Id. at 239 (Article 3(1)). Whatever the ultimate fate of Article 19 of the Draft Articles on State Responsibility, also pending before the Commission (Report of the International Law Commission to the General Assembly, 35 U.N. GAOR Supp. (No. 10) at 64, U.N. Doc. A/35/10 (1980)), which provides that certain acts of a state may constitute international crimes, the Draft Code clearly criminalizes only the acts of individuals. The Draft Code explains the relationship between an individual's crime against the peace and security of mankind and a state's internationally wrongful act constituting an international crime under the Draft Articles on State Re-

---

* The Draft Code fails to cover adequately and define precisely "crimes against humanity." See Bassiouni, "Crimes Against Humanity": The Need for a Specialized Convention, 31 Colum. J. Transnatl. L. 457, 483-486 (1994).

sponsibility as follows: "Prosecution of an individual for a crime against the peace and security of mankind does not relieve a State of any responsibility under international law for an act or omission attributable to it." Article 5. See Spinedi, International Crimes of State: The Legislative History in International Crimes of State: A Critical Analysis of the ILC's Draft Article 19 on State Responsibility 7, 110-112 (J. Weiler, A. Cassese, and M. Spinedi eds. 1989).

B. Readings on the ILC's 1991 Draft Code of Crimes Against the Peace and Security of Mankind

Ferencz, An International Criminal Code and Court: Where They Stand and Where They're Going
30 Colum. J. Transnatl. L. 375, 379-382 (1992)

[The author observes that until 1991 "the Code was going practically nowhere"; he attributes this situation to opposition in the UN's Sixth (Legal) Committee and a "somnolent ILC."]

When, in 1990, Iraq invaded Kuwait and claimed Kuwait's territory as its own, the Security Council was able for the first time to act collectively in an effort to stop aggression. After diplomatic efforts failed, coalition armies, led by the United States, used devastating military power and drove Iraq out of Kuwait. World leaders began to speak about a "New World Order" where the rule of law would replace the law of the jungle. The new political atmosphere made it easier to approach the problems of a draft code of crimes and an international criminal court in a more rational and objective way. Hopes were aroused that the law of force might be replaced by the force of law.

By July 1991, the ILC, under pressure to produce something, succeeded in completing a first reading of a draft code of crimes against the peace and security of mankind. It was, admittedly, an imperfect instrument, but it was intended to enable states to focus more clearly on the many issues that would have to be resolved before the code could become an accepted reality.

The draft of the twenty-six articles was divided into two parts. Part I defined and characterized the crimes and enunciated certain general principles. Stated offenses were all crimes against the peace and security of mankind even if not punishable under the internal law of a state (Articles 1, 2). Individuals, including those who aided, abetted or attempted the crime, would be held responsible (Article 3). The general principles stipulated that virtuous motives would not excuse an offense; states would be responsible for their acts and for their omissions; and states would be obliged to either try or extradite the accused (Articles 4, 5, and 6). No statute of limitations would apply; fair trial would be mandatory; as further protection, there would be no double jeopardy or retroactive application of the code except for deeds which were previously recognized as international crimes (Articles 8, 9, and 10). The order of a superior would not excuse the crime, nor would the superior be relieved of responsibility — regardless of official position (Articles 11, 12, and 13). Finally, the hearing court would decide about permissible defenses and extenuating circumstances (Article 14).

Part II of the ILC's draft code enumerated the specific crimes covered by the code: an act or threat of aggression "by a State"; intervention in the internal affairs of a state; colonial or alien domination; genocide; apartheid; systematic or mass violations of human rights; "exceptionally serious" war crimes; recruitment, use, financing and training of mercenaries; international terrorism; illicit traffic in narcotic drugs; and willful and severe damage to the environment (Articles 15 through 26).

To be sure, the ILC code was far from complete or free of ambiguity. When these proposals came before the Sixth Committee, the delegates heaped their customary praise on the Special Rapporteur for his skill in making such remarkable progress but then proceeded to point out the many shortcomings in the draft.

Some of the clauses were too broad or too vague. For example, a State is said to be the "main victim" of the crimes covered (Art. 9); superior orders are no excuse if it was possible for the perpetrator "not to comply" (Article 11); a threat of aggression is a crime only if there was "good reason" to believe that aggression was "being seriously contemplated" (Article 16). There are vague references to "any other form of alien domination" (Article 18), "exploitation" of labor of "members of a racial group" (Article 20), violating human rights "in a systematic manner or on a mass scale" (Article 21), "exceptionally serious" war crimes, and "use of unlawful weapons" (Article 22). These references are not specific enough to be useful in a criminal code. Crimes such as "tolerating acts" of a nature "to create a state of terror in the minds of public figures, groups of persons or the general public" (Article 24), "encouraging illicit traffic in narcotic drugs on a large scale" (Article 25), or doing "long-term and severe damage to the natural environment" (Article 26) and others are not defined at all.

Many of these vague or ambiguous expressions derived from political declarations or conventions with terminology dictated by the drive for consensus but totally inadequate to meet the standards of precision and clarity required by a penal statute designed for the fair trial and conviction of individual malefactors. How were the prior instruments, and their definitions, to be related to the code? On some issues, bilateral and multilateral treaties already in existence would also have to be taken into account.

One of the problems that would certainly have to be clarified related to the role of the Security Council in dealing with the prosecution of the crime of aggression. Article 39 of the U.N. Charter assigns to the Security Council the responsibility for determining the existence of any act of aggression. The consensus definition of aggression, following the Charter, did the same. Yet the Council was not a judicial but a political body some of whose members, indeed those most capable of committing aggression, held a veto power. How could the veto power and the prosecutorial role of the Security Council be reconciled with a fair and impartial trial? This question was raised by the ILC, but no answers were offered.

In the rather understated words of the ILC itself, the draft was "still open to some improvements, which can be made on second reading, with the benefit of further points made in the comments and observations of Governments." Despite severe infirmities, no one suggested that the draft was dead on arrival and could not be resuscitated. It would be fair to conclude that most nations regarded the 1991 first draft of a code of crimes against the peace and security of mankind as an encouraging, if faltering, step in the right direction.

Bassiouni, "Crimes Against Humanity": The Need for a Specialized Convention
31 Colum. J. Transnatl. L. 457, 484-486 (1994)

[The author briefly describes the history of the Draft Code, concluding with the ILC's first reading of the text, a text that he believes "leaves a great deal to be desired."]

The 1991 Draft Code does not contain a general definition of "Crimes Against Humanity." Some of the specific crimes contained in the ILC's formulation correspond in part to the Nuremberg Charter's Article 6(c), * while others do not. The range of crimes listed in the Draft Code covers less than does Article 6(c) of the Charter. At the same time that the Draft Code fails adequately to cover analogous conduct and harmful results, it adds a number of new crimes that were not included in the Charter's Article 6(c), and which cannot reasonably be analogized to the core conduct hitherto sought to be prohibited. Some of the crimes enunciated by the ILC have only a tenuous connection to the original meaning of "Crimes Against Humanity."

---

* The London (or Nuremberg) Charter, appended to the Agreement for the Prosecution and Punishment of the Major War Criminals of the European Axis, Aug. 8, 1945, 59 Stat. 1544, 82 U.N.T.S. 279 (entered into force Aug. 8, 1945), established the basis and structure for the prosecution of the major war criminals before the International Military Tribunal at Nuremberg. Crimes coming within the Tribunal's jurisdiction included "crimes against peace" (Article 6(a)), "war crimes" (Article 6(b)), and "crimes against humanity" (Article 6(3)). The last were defined to include:

> murder, extermination, enslavement, deportation, and other inhumane acts committed against any civilian population, before or during the war, or persecutions on political, racial or religious grounds in execution of or in connection with any crime within the jurisdiction of the Tribunal, whether or not in violation of the domestic law of the country where perpetrated.

The 1991 Draft Code lists the following as "Crimes Against the Peace and Security of Mankind": "Aggression"; "Threat of Aggression"; "Intervention"; "Colonial Domination and Other Forms of Alien Domination"; "Genocide"; "Apartheid"; "Systematic or Mass Violations of Human Rights"; "Exceptionally Serious War Crimes"; "Recruitment, Use, Financing and Training of Mercenaries"; "International Terrorism"; "Illicit Traffic in Narcotic Drugs"; and "Wilful and Severe Damage to the Environment."

The first three of these crimes — "Aggression," "Threat of Aggression," and "Intervention" — are essentially "Crimes Against Peace." Others, such as "Colonial Domination and Other Forms of Alien Domination," "Genocide," "Apartheid," and "Systematic or Mass Violations of Human Rights," fall within the category of "Crimes Against the Security of Mankind." With the exception of "Colonial Domination and Other Forms of Alien Domination," which has never been internationally criminalized, the other listed crimes are encompassed by the conventional and customary scope of "Crimes Against Humanity."

The other crimes listed in the 1991 Draft Code either restate existing international crimes or have been heretofore entirely unknown to international criminal law. As to the redundant crimes like "Exceptionally Serious War Crimes," "International Terrorism," and "Illicit Traffic in Narcotic Drugs," there is no valid reason or justification for their inclusion in the Draft Code since their scant definition there does not include any new elements which would distinguish them from their otherwise established meaning in other international instruments. Then there is "Wilful and Severe Damage to the Environment," a crime newly developed by the ILC which, so far, has no basis in conventional or customary international criminal law. Furthermore, it is so vaguely defined that it fails any reasonable test of the "principles of legality" under any of the world's major criminal justice systems. As to "Recruitment, Use, Financing and Training of Mercenaries," it is embodied in a recent convention that has attracted few ratifications.

The provisions of the Draft Code concerning "Crimes Against Humanity" are insufficiently defined and fail adequately to describe the necessary legal elements by which to determine individual criminal responsibility. The provision on genocide, for example, simply duplicates the text of the Genocide Convention, preserving its weaknesses as well. Among these weaknesses, the Genocide Convention does not criminalize mass killings conducted without the intent to "eliminate the group in whole or in part," thus excluding mass killings where this requisite intent is not present. Furthermore, it does not cover collective victimization of social and political groups. Presumably these gaps in the Genocide Convention are intended to be covered by the ILC's Article 21 on "Systematic or Mass Violations of Human Rights." But there is no definition of this category of international crimes and none of the specifics are set forth in the Draft Code, thus leaving in place the same weaknesses which plagued the earlier definition in Article 6(c) of the Charter.

For these and other reasons, the 1991 version of the Draft Code fails adequately to codify "Crimes Against Humanity," to cure the weaknesses of Article 6(c), and to cover the type of human rights depredations which have occurred since World War II. Furthermore, it fails even to codify adequately post-World War II instruments related to "Crimes Against Humanity." *

Note: The ILC's Draft Code: A Prognosis

The International Law Commission, after a first reading and adoption of a 26-article Draft Code of Crimes Against the Peace and Security of Mankind in 1991, has devoted most of its time and efforts to drafting a statute for an international criminal court. With that task, somewhat surprisingly, now completed (see pages 993-1001 infra), the Commission intends to turn its attention to the Draft Code. It began a second reading of the draft code in 1994 (Report of the International Law Commission to the General Assembly, 49 U.N. GAOR Supp. (No. 10) at 161-194, U.N. Doc. A/49/10 (1994)), plans to finish this second reading in 1995 (Report of the International Law Commission, Topical Summary of the Discussion Held in the Sixth Committee of the General Assembly During Its Forty-Eighth Session Prepared by the Secretariat, U.N. Doc. A/CN. 4/457, at 97 (1994)), and hopes to complete its consideration of the Draft Code in 1996 (id. at 96). Whether it can adhere to this schedule and also produce a quality product that will win the approval of the Sixth Committee and the General Assembly is problematic.

As the two readings in the previous section make clear, the 1991 Draft Code is an "imperfect instrument" (Ferencz) that "leaves a great deal to be desired" (Bassiouni). These views find support in the views of governments and the critical comments of legal writers, especially ones with expertise in international criminal law. As the Introduction to a volume of comprehensive commentaries on the Draft Code by a distinguished group of scholars concludes:

> [T]he 1991 Draft Code is, by the consensus of most international criminal law experts, insufficient as it now stands. If it were not to be a Code of Crimes under which individuals could be judged before an international or national criminal court, this text would adequately represent the general expectations of what the world community has and should criminalize. But it is not. The most serious concern is with the principles of legality which the ILC drafters have acknowledged in their work, but which are not satisfied. Thus, what most experts question are not the values sought to be protected but the techni-

---

* The author concludes that, "[f]or these reasons, a specialized convention on 'Crimes Against Humanity' is needed." An alternative solution, and certainly one more likely to marshall political support, simply would be to clarify or if need be amend the Draft Code. This process already is under way, as the Note that follows demonstrates. — Eds.

cal legal means by which this was accomplished by the ILC. However, since technical defects can be cured, there is hope yet for a new and improved version to be elaborated in the near future.

Bassiouni, Introduction to Commentaries on the International Law Commission's 1991 Draft Code of Crimes Against the Peace and Security of Mankind, 11 Nouvelles Etudes Penales viii (1993).

At the ILC's session in 1994, the special rapporteur on the topic, during the course of the second reading of Part I of the Draft Code, submitted drafting changes to three articles (Articles 1, 3, and 9), proposed two new articles (Articles 14 and 15), and recommended the deletion of one article (Article 4). Overall, however, the Commission's narrow and non-technical approach to the drafting of an international criminal code — criticized in the above readings and commentaries — remains the same. Since it did not approve the 15 articles that now make up Part I, much less address the 12 articles in Part II that spell out the international crimes to be covered, the Commission obviously will be hard pressed to complete its second reading in 1995, much less a final Draft Code by 1996. In view of the fact that the Commission has had the topic on its agenda for over four decades, however, it would seem prudent to rethink and revise the Draft Code, even if it takes the balance of this decade, rather than adhere to an arbitrary, somewhat procrustean schedule that well might produce a fatally flawed document.

Note: NGO Efforts to Draft an International Criminal Code

Several years ago a leading international criminal lawyer remarked that the International Law Commission's long and laborious effort to produce a Draft Code, "which started with the expectation by the world community that it would be the beginning of the codification of international criminal law, has become nothing more than a frustrated attempt, with many technical flaws, at codifying only a limited number of international crimes." M. Bassiouni, A Draft International Criminal Code and Draft Statute for an International Criminal Court 10 (1987). Moreover, he realistically added that "[t]here are few encouraging signs *at present* that the International Law Commission will produce a legally enforceable Draft Code. . . ." Id. at 11 (emphasis added). This skepticism, as the previous Note suggests, still seems warranted.

Over the years, however, efforts to draft a comprehensive international criminal code outside the United Nations have been made by a small number of specialized non-governmental organizations. Thus, the Foundation for the Establishment of an International Criminal Court 25 years ago produced a useful "laundry list" of crimes that might be included in any such code. Stone, Range of Crimes for a Feasible International Jurisdiction, in Toward a Feasible International Criminal Court 315, 337-339 (J. Stone and R. Woetzel eds. 1970). More recently, as Professor Wise has pointed out (see page 953 supra), the International Law Association's proposed Statute for an International Criminal Court has defined its jurisdiction by reference to over two dozen conventions already making certain acts criminal. International Criminal Law Committee, Sixth Interim Report, in International Law Association, Report of the Sixty-First Conference 252, 257 (Paris 1984). Finally, in 1992 the Center for U.N. Reform Education recommended the establishment by convention of an international criminal court with jurisdiction over war crimes, broadly defined, as well as other international crimes included in a special protocol. B. MacPhearson, An International Criminal Court: Applying World Law to Individuals (C.U.R.E. Monograph No. 10, Apr. 1992).

By far the most significant effort in this area, however, has come from the International Association of Penal Law, whose current president, Professor Bassiouni, has produced a steady stream of books and articles advocating both an international criminal code and an international criminal court. See, e.g., M. Bassiouni, supra; 1 M. Bassiouni, International Criminal Law (1986); M. Bassiouni, International Criminal Law: A Draft International Criminal Code (1980). His systematic analysis of the history and development of international offenses has led to a suggested list of 24 crimes, delicts, and infractions — admittedly a judgmental categorization — that he has incorporated into a Draft International Criminal Code. M. Bassiouni, Draft Statute International Criminal Tribunal, 9 Nouvelles Etudes Penales 174 (1992); M. Bassiouni, supra, at 79, 115-117. Many of these offenses — war crimes, crimes against humanity, genocide, racial discrimination and apartheid, slavery, torture, unlawful human experimentation, and hostage-taking — are taken directly from one or more international human rights instruments for criminalization purposes.

Efforts to use this process to protect the human rights of individuals, whether made within or without the UN context, will be aided by the various publications of Professor Bassiouni and the International Association of Penal Law. Moreover, international human rights lawyers should pay special heed to his recommendation that "[e]xperts in the fields of international criminal law and internationally protected human rights should focus their attention on the interrelationship of the two disciplines. Such a collaborative effort will lead to a better understanding of the role of international criminal law and a comprehensive system of international protections." Bassiouni, The Proscribing Function of International Criminal Law in the Processes of International Protection of Human Rights, 9 Yale J. World Pub. Ord. 193, 214 (1982). The International Law Commission, especially, would be well advised to take into account the above studies and, since its members are public international lawyers generally unfamiliar with international penal law, to avail itself of the expertise of the growing number of specialists on interstate cooperation in penal matters.

III. Toward an International Criminal Court

Historically, an international criminal code and an international criminal court have been viewed as a "package deal." The Gulf War and the events in the former Yugoslavia and Rwanda, however, have generated widespread support for ad hoc international criminal courts and have caused the International Law Commission to decouple the Draft Code from the permanent court and give priority to the latter. This section describes how the international community has sought to invoke the international criminal process during the 1990s.

A. An Iraqi War Crimes Tribunal: Proposed But Rejected

In the run-up to the Gulf War, the UN Security Council repeatedly warned Iraq that it would be held responsible for grave breaches of the laws of war. S.C. Res. 664, 45 U.N. SCOR, Res. and Dec. at 21 (1990); S.C. Res. 666, 45 U.N. SCOR, Res. and Dec. at 22 (1990); S.C. Res. 667, 45 U.N. SCOR, Res. and Dec. at 23 (1990); S.C. Res. 670, 45 U.N. SCOR, Res. and Dec. at 24 (1990). One resolution expressly called upon UN member states "to collate substantiated information in their possession or submitted to them on the grave breaches by Iraq . . . and to make this information available to the [Security] Council. . . ." S.C. Res. 674, 45 U.N. SCOR, Res. and Dec. at 25, 26 (1990). The Office of the Judge Advocate General of the U.S. Army began collecting information on Iraqi war crimes on 3 August 1990 and continued to do so throughout the Gulf War and its aftermath. See War Crimes Documentation Center of the Department of the Army, Report on Iraqi War Crimes (Desert Shield/Desert Storm) [Unclassified Version] (Jan. 8, 1992). At the end of hostilities, the United States had documented the commission by Iraq and its nationals of hundreds of war crimes under 16 headings. Id. at 11-13. The question then became what to do with these data.

Moore, War Crimes and the Rule of Law in the Gulf Crisis
31 Va. J. Intl. L. 403, 404-409 (1991)

Conventional wisdom, which has a strong intellectual grip on our thinking about international relations, is leery of war crimes trials. Indeed, there have been no major war crimes trials since World War II. This conventional wisdom, or "old thinking," however, is wrong. The Gulf crisis teaches us that what we need "new thinking" if we are seriously to move forward with a new world order based on the rule of law.

I. Reasons for War Crimes Trials in the Gulf Crisis

I believe that there are at least five reasons why it is of *great* importance that there be war crimes trials in the Gulf crisis for Iraqi violations of the basic norms of civilized behavior. . . . These reasons are:

1. Holding such trials is a moral imperative in view of the scale, brutality, and depravity of Iraq's violations of the Third and Fourth Geneva Conventions, Iraq's deliberate instigation of a new form of environmental terrorism, and Iraq's ballistic missile terror attacks against civilian populations. To sweep these actions under the rug is to diminish ourselves.

2. The United States, and all other nations bound by the 1949 Geneva Conventions, are required by existing international treaty obligations to search out and prosecute or extradite persons alleged to have committed "grave breaches" of these Conventions. In this respect, article 146 of the Fourth Geneva Convention (Relative to the Protection of Civilian Persons in Time of War) is representative as it provides: "Each High Contracting Party shall be under the obligation to search for persons alleged to have committed, or to have ordered to be committed, such grave breaches, and shall bring such persons, regardless of their nationality, before its own courts. It may also, if it prefers, and in accordance with the provisions of its own legislation, hand such persons over for trial to another High Contracting Party concerned, provided such High Contracting Party has made out a *prima facie* case." *

   This obligation is the heart of measures for implementation of the important human rights standards of these Conventions. Arguments against enforcing these human rights Conventions because to do so would somehow interfere with foreign relations are based on "old thinking" long ago rejected in our general human rights policy. Moreover, they fail to recognize the importance of the nation's existing legal obligations.

3. The United Nations Security Council warned Iraq that individuals, as well as the Government of Iraq, would be liable for the commission of grave breaches of the Fourth Geneva Convention. To permit flagrant violations of the Fourth Geneva Convention to go unpunished when brazenly committed *after* such a Security

---

* Fourth Geneva Convention, art. 146, 6 U.S.T. 3516, T.I.A.S. No. 3365, 75 U.N.T.S. 287.

Council warning would be to doom the Council to irrelevance in enforcing the humanitarian laws of war during ongoing hostilities.

4. We have every reason to seek vigorously to apply the rule of law to Saddam Hussein. Although the allied coalition has chosen to let the people of Iraq struggle for the leadership of their country, we certainly have no interest in sheltering the world class evil of Saddam from the rule of law. Indeed, the core principle of Watergate (a setting which is not even remotely comparable in the extent of its lawlessness) is that even the position of President of the United States is subject to the rule of law.

5. Perhaps the most important reason for holding war crimes trials in the Gulf crisis is that we must bring deterrence home to totalitarian elites if we are to be most effective in avoiding aggressive war and human rights violations. The sad reality is that these elites, including Saddam Hussein by his demonstrated behavior, are prepared to sacrifice thousands of their own people in pursuit of their vile aggression. Deterrence, even if at the margin, must begin work directly on these regime elites as they make decisions to commit aggression and human rights violations. In my judgment, this point is of far greater importance in creating a structure for peace than has been generally understood.

II.   RESPONDING TO ARGUMENTS AGAINST HOLDING WAR CRIMES TRIALS

At a time during the Gulf crisis when it was still possible to obtain Iraqi acceptance of Security Council resolutions without the sacrifice of coalition force men and women, an argument could be made with some strength that war crimes trials might inhibit the chances for a peaceful settlement. Because coalition forces were required to physically evict Saddam Hussein and his forces from Kuwait, however, there would no longer seem to be any merit in such an argument. Indeed, perhaps it is a good message for future aggressors that if they force a military defeat as the only means for reversing their aggression, then they can expect war crimes trials.

At the time of the Nuremberg trials, a plausible (although incorrect) argument was made that planning and ordering an aggressive war were not offenses giving rise to personal criminal accountability. Since Nuremberg, and the International Law Commission adoption of the Nuremberg principles, this argument has no merit whatever. Moreover, this argument certainly has no merit with respect to trials for grave breaches of the Third and Fourth Geneva Conventions, which have been settled law for over forty years. In this respect, it might be noted that if Saddam Hussein ordered the kidnapping of thousands of Kuwaiti hostages or the torching of 600 to 700 Kuwaiti oil wells, then he committed grave breaches of the Fourth Geneva

Convention, just to select two visible grave breaches of the Geneva Conventions. As such, *all* of the States bound by the Geneva Convention are *now* legally bound to search him out and either try him or extradite him for trial.

A third concern with war crimes trials is that they may interfere with international relations or exacerbate regional tensions. But such arguments were also made against taking any military action in the Gulf crisis. The real cost in settings as outrageous as the Gulf crisis may be in giving an impression for the future that such depraved actions are acceptable and will incur no responsibility. Moreover, even if this argument that international relations may be affected were correct, is not the rule of law worth even considerable costs? Did we not just fight and win a major conflict for this principle?

A fourth concern is that war crimes trials could become a loose cannon on the deck — aimed in every direction including the United States and its allies. The answer to this objection, however, is obvious. Major war crimes trials should be seriously entertained only in settings of substantial clarity that aggression has been committed or that violations of the laws of war have been committed. In this respect, there are few clearer settings in modern international law than the aggression and human rights violations of Saddam Hussein in the Gulf crisis. The United States need not fear the rule of law; it is a major objective of our foreign policy. Efforts to carry out politicized war crimes trials — which have been frequent in recent years against the United States and its allies — should be rejected, as they have been, for the politicized exhibitions that they are.

Finally, there has been a general misunderstanding that war crimes trials necessarily require the presence of the accused. Normally, of course, that would be strongly preferable, but it would not be impossible to try persons accused of war crimes even in absentia. Any such accused persons should, of course, be offered an opportunity to participate, and such trials should be scrupulously honest and fair — but it is not an absolute bar to war crimes trials that a nation refrains from taking steps to topple a government militarily and seize its leaders for trial. The results of any such trials carried out against an accused in absentia could be made binding on all nations in the world through Security Council action, thus affecting the future freedom of movement of those convicted. Indeed, even indictments based on probable cause and filed with Interpol would seem to give rise to an obligation by 166 nations adhering to the Geneva Conventions either to try or extradite such accused persons found within their jurisdiction at any time in the future.

III. Some Procedural Points

A number of procedural points are also worth noting in connection with violations of the laws of war in the Gulf crisis. These are:

- In addition to, or even in the absence of war crimes trials, the Government of Iraq is liable in state-to-state damages for reparations for such violations of the laws of war, and it is possible that individual Iraqis who have committed grave breaches of the laws of war may be liable for civil damages in national courts around the world.

- Whether or not war crimes trials are held, an important step that should be taken is that one or more commissions of impeccable international credentials and ability should begin work at an early time to document fully the Iraqi violations of the laws of war. The work of such commissions is as important for history as it is to lay the groundwork for possible war crimes trials. It is essential that future generations in Iraq, and indeed in the whole world, understand the reality and the extent of the Iraqi atrocities. In the Gulf crisis, I would prefer to see prestigious commissions established independently by both the United Nations Security Council and the Gulf Co-Operation Council. . . .

- With respect to the auspices of any such trials, there are a number of possibilities: Security Council authorization of an ad hoc international tribunal; authorization of such an ad hoc international tribunal by the allied coalition (as at Nuremberg and the Military Tribunal for the Far East); or by the Gulf Co-operation Council; or by the Arab League; or trials by individual nations in their own tribunal, such as by the State of Kuwait for violations of the Third and Fourth Geneva Conventions with respect to citizens and nationals of Kuwait, and possibly by the United States for violations of the Third Geneva Convention with respect to former United States prisoners of war. I believe that the best option would be a Security Council authorized ad hoc international tribunal that would try for crimes against peace as well as for war crimes. Another important option would be such a tribunal established by either the coalition or the Gulf Co-operation Council.

IV. CONCLUSION

. . . [T]he aftermath of the Gulf crisis is an important crossroads. The world community can respond to one of the truly outrageous atrocities in human history by vigorously insisting on a meaningful rule of law as it seeks a new world order, or it can succumb to "old thinking" and sweep war crimes violations under the rug. I would like to say in this connection that as a practical matter the allies accepted such "old thinking" after World War I. Perhaps the horror of World War II might at least have been lessened if the allies had stuck with the Versailles Treaty and their convictions and insisted that those who committed war crimes were criminals to be placed meaningfully on trial rather than to become celebrated as national heroes.

In considering this choice, I would particularly urge reflection on the following three points. If we are serious about the important humanitarian and environmental standards embodied in the laws of war, do we not have a responsibility to hold accountable those who commit grave breaches of these laws? Is it not important to live up to our existing international legal obligations under the Third and Fourth Geneva Conventions to seek out and either try or extradite those alleged to have committed grave breaches of these important Conventions? And if we seek peace more broadly, is it not important that we seek to add deterrence at a more personal level to the regime elites actually engaged in planning and ordering aggressive war and brutal war crimes?

O'Brien, The Nuremberg Precedent and the Gulf War
31 Va. J. Intl. L. 391, 391-392, 397-401 (1991)

From the first day of Iraq's aggression against Kuwait, the United States government charged Saddam Hussein's government and military forces with violations of international law reminiscent of the charges in the Nuremberg trials of the major war criminals: namely, crimes against peace, war crimes and crimes against humanity. At the conclusion of the swift and successful ground war against Iraq, President Bush reiterated the proposition that Saddam Hussein and his forces were responsible for their numerous and heinous violations of international law. There is no doubt that Iraq is guilty of crimes against peace, war crimes and crimes against humanity. There is no doubt that Iraq, as an international person, is responsible for these crimes committed by its government and its armed forces. Moreover, in the light of the precedent established by the trials at Nuremberg, there is no doubt that Saddam Hussein, his civilian officials, military officers and enlisted personnel are personally liable to trial and punishment if they ordered or participated in the commission of these crimes. Under the principle of command responsibility, commanders are subject to trial for crimes committed by their units or in their areas of jurisdiction even if it cannot be proven that they ordered such crimes. All that is required is that a responsible commander knew or should have known of the illegal behavior and did not take reasonable actions to prevent, suppress and punish it.

The foregoing propositions assume the validity of what is broadly known as the Nuremberg Precedent. Given the current interest in the possibility of war crimes proceedings against Saddam Hussein and members of his government and armed forces, it is appropriate to review that precedent and to reflect on the extent of its relevance to the aftermath of the 1990-91 Gulf War.

I. THE ESTABLISHMENT OF THE NUREMBERG PRECEDENT

[The author relates how the Nuremberg Charter established the International Military Tribunal to try German and Japanese political and military leaders responsible for waging aggressive war and war crimes and crimes against humanity. He notes that in 1946 the UN General Assembly unanimously adopted Resolution 95(I) affirming "the principles of international law recognized by the Charter of the Nuremberg Tribunal and the judgment of the Tribunal."]

Thus, as of 1946, the Nuremberg Precedent, embracing the concepts of an international military tribunal, the substantive categories of crimes against peace, war crimes, crimes against humanity and conspiracy to commit these crimes, and the denial of the defenses of act of state and superior orders, was clearly established in international law. What was the status of the Nuremberg Precedent when Saddam Hussein invaded Kuwait on August 2, 1990?

II. THE DORMANT NUREMBERG PRECEDENT, 1946-1991

There have been no successors to the Nuremberg and Tokyo trials of major war criminals. The reason is obvious. There have been no wars in which a coalition broadly supported by other members of the international legal system has defeated an obvious aggressor and violator of the laws of war and humanity so decisively as to place it in a state of *debellatio*. Moreover, as early as the Korean War it became clear that the concepts of the Nuremberg Precedent could be abused and exploited to justify grave violations of the rights of prisoners of war (POWs) and to give inspiration to propaganda.

In both the Korean and Vietnam Wars, the communist belligerents accused all prisoners of crimes against the peace, war crimes and crimes against humanity. They used these charges to justify denial of minimal POW protection, including exclusion of the International Committee of the Red Cross. Because repatriation of POWs was a critical issue at the end of both wars and there was no clear victory in either conflict, there was no possibility of war crimes proceedings being brought by any of the parties involved.

A further development has lessened the utility and relevance of the Nuremberg Precedent. The Nuremberg concepts lend themselves to the propaganda not only of belligerents but of political groups, including anti-military or anti-war factions within countries. Thus, for example, the solemn term "genocide" has been so degraded by misuse that the terrible events that gave birth to it are mocked. The result is that the law of Nuremberg remains valid but that part of it relating to the trial of war criminals —

as distinguished from the substantive war-decision (*jus ad bellum*) and war-conduct (*jus in bello*) law — has been almost entirely irrelevant to the practical enforcement of international law.

III.   NUREMBERG AND THE 1990-91 GULF WAR

The events of the 1990-91 Gulf War have forced us to reconsider the question of trying persons charged with violations of crimes against peace, war crimes and crimes against humanity. The legal and moral justifications for such trials are clear. However, a number of considerations may render them infeasible. Although Iraq has been badly defeated, it is not in a state of *debellatio*: only a part of its territory is occupied; its armed forces have not totally surrendered; and, although beset by pockets of rebellion (as of March, 1991), its government still functions. True, tens of thousands of its soldiers are POWs and alleged war criminals among them could be tried. However, Saddam Hussein and the top civilian and military personnel responsible for Iraq's aggression and grave violations of the laws of war are not in the custody of the coalition forces. The situation, therefore, is quite different from Germany and Japan in 1945.

If there were a revolutionary change of regimes in Iraq and the successor government were willing to turn over Saddam Hussein and other alleged war criminals, trials might then be possible. The trials could be held in Kuwaiti courts or, failing that, special tribunals might be established, preferably consisting of judges from the Arab members of the coalition.

Despite the warnings from the U.S. government and military that war crimes would be punished, it seems unlikely that the United States would participate directly in war crimes proceedings. The risk of fueling accusations of American imperialism, Western triumphalism and oppression of Muslims by infidels seem too great. Additionally, it seems that the warnings about responsibility for war crimes were not intended to lead to U.S.-initiated trials, but were mainly designed to discourage Iraq's use of chemical warfare, continuation of the indiscriminate Scud missile attacks, and the scorched earth and genocidal policies in Kuwait.

Thus, while Saddam Hussein and large numbers of his political and military decision-makers, as well as thousands of his lawless and vicious troops, thoroughly deserve trial and punishment as war criminals, the odds are rather against a large number of them being brought to trial.

Beyond this estimate of the situation there is a further point to be made, one of prudence. As remarked above, anyone can play the game of accusations of crimes against the peace, war crimes and crimes against humanity. Moreover, we live in age of cultural relativism in which there is a great reluctance to admit that evil is done by one party without balancing the judgment with condemnations of supposedly equivalent evils committed by another party. If there are extensive war crimes trials of Iraqis, the charges and trials will not end there. The first victim will be Israel. There will be widespread demands to punish the Israelis for violation of UN resolutions and for their conduct in wars and occupations of the West Bank and Gaza. The difference between Israeli actions in literal defense of their national existence and Iraqi actions of gratuitous aggression and cruelty against a peaceful Arab neighbor will not be recognized by the majority of the world community.

Close behind the demands for trials of Israelis will be demands for trials of Americans. There will be calls for trials of Reagan, for his role in Grenada and for the 1982-83 intervention in Lebanon, and Bush, for his role in the 1989 invasion of Panama, as well as of U.S. military personnel for their participation in the actions. Such demands will not, of course, lead to actual trials — except for trials conducted by self-appointed private tribunals such as those of Bertrand Russell during the Vietnam War. They will, however, be extremely divisive and injurious to efforts to create an atmosphere in which peace negotiations in the Middle East might have some prospects for progress.

A return to the Nuremberg Precedent, in short, may be opening a Pandora's Box. Where would it end? It is not only Israelis and Americans that might be accused as war criminals. There are charges of acts of aggression, war crimes and crimes against humanity in most modern conflicts — and they are still bitterly remembered. Indeed, the quest for punishment of war criminals could easily move into internal revolutionary wars, with Sikhs charging Indians, southern Sudanese blacks charging northern Sudanese Muslims, Salvadorans and Nicaraguans of all persuasions charging each other.

To be sure, an epidemic of demands for war crimes trials will not have created the grievances and animosities alluded to, but they might encourage and escalate them. The question is whether the perfectly valid desire to punish Saddam Hussein and his henchmen for an extraordinarily illegal, immoral and destructive war should prevail over prudential caution in the use of the institution of war crimes trials. It may well turn out that the Nuremberg and Tokyo trials were unique, *sui generis*. They contributed greatly to the substance of international war-decision and war-conduct law and, beyond that, they called attention, dramatically, both to the need for international law and the devastating effects of its violation in war. I have grave doubts, however, that Nuremberg and Tokyo have established for us a political-legal institution for the adjudication of alleged violations of international law.

Over the years, the U.S. attitude toward the establishment of an international criminal court with jurisdiction over, inter alia, war crimes and crimes against humanity has been lukewarm at best. See Ferencz, supra page 961, at 385-390. Cf. Scharf, The Jury Is Still Out on the Need for an

International Criminal Court, 1991 Duke J. Comp. & Intl. L. 135, 159-168. Following the Gulf War, the Senate unanimously passed a resolution urging President George Bush to confer with the UN and other states "to establish an International Criminal Court or an International Military Tribunal to try and punish all individuals involved in the planning or execution of the above referenced crimes, including Saddam Hussein." S. Res. 76, 101st Cong., 1st Sess., 137 Cong. Rec. S3345, S3346 (daily ed. Mar. 14, 1991). The President, however, did not follow through, although his press secretary, Mr. Fitzwater, remarked that, while the United States would not take the lead in bringing charges against the President and senior officials of Iraq, or against officers and men of the Iraqi army, it would cooperate in such efforts if Kuwait and Saudi Arabia pursued the matter.

In any event, they did not, and, thus, no war crimes trials were held. The reasons for President Bush's reticence, or at least the primary ones, are set out in the following exchange (1993 Am. Socy. Intl. L. Proceedings 241-242).

> Professor *Buergenthal:* When I ended my talk, I pointed out that a great deal of law still needs to be developed in order to make individual responsibility a reality, and I think this is certainly true of the procedural area. Let me follow up in this connection. I have come to the conclusion, after years and years in the human rights area, and after sitting on the Inter-American Court of Human Rights, that unless you go after individuals, governments are subject to being blackmailed by certain powerful groups. They are forced to pardon them, absolving them of responsibility; thus, there is no incentive to stop violations. The only way to deal with that issue is to let potential rights abusers know ahead of time that they will be held criminally responsible for large-scale violations of human rights on the international level.
>
> Mr. *Bolton:* * In the case of Iraq, although the Security Council authorized the collection of information about human rights abuses, we took a very explicit decision then not to set up a war crimes tribunal, for two reasons: (1) We were hoping the Iraqi top military officials would have the sense to stage a coup and get rid of Saddam, and we didn't want them on trial at the very time we were hoping they would do so, because if they were tried *in absentia* and convicted, what incentive would they have? (2) The second reason was that we didn't know how trying them in absentia would fly in many parts of the world where people would be convinced that, absent the defendants themselves, they couldn't possibly receive a fair trial.
>
> Professor *D'Amato:* I think there was a third reason too — the allegations of war crimes committed by the allies.
>
> Mr. *Bolton:* That had nothing to do with it.

Thus, as Professor Meron has concluded, "[an] historic opportunity was missed to breathe new life into the critically important concept of individual criminal responsibility for the laws of war violations. At the very least, the Security Council should have issued a warning that Saddam and other

---

* Former Assistant Secretary of State for International Organizations. — EDS.

responsible Iraqis would be subject to arrest and prosecution under the grave breaches provisions of the Geneva conventions whenever they set foot abroad." Meron, The Case for War Crimes Trials in Yugoslavia, 72 Foreign Aff. 122, 124-125 (1993).

B. The Yugoslav War Crimes Tribunal: The Security Council Establishes an Ad Hoc International Criminal Court

Although the Security Council failed to establish an Iraqi War Crimes Tribunal and efforts by the International Law Commission to draft a statute for an international criminal court were proceeding at a snail's pace, by 1992 the situation in the former Yugoslavia, especially in Bosnia and Herzegovina, had produced a strong demand within and without the UN for the creation of a Yugoslav War Crimes Tribunal to hold criminally responsible those persons involved in "ethnic cleansing," war crimes, and numerous other human rights violations. As Professor Meron persuasively argued,

> [r]eaffirming the Nuremberg tenets and the principle of accountability should deter those in Yugoslavia and elsewhere who envisage "final solutions" to their conflicts with ethnic and religious minorities. A war crimes tribunal could also educate the general public not to accept egregious violations of human rights and humanitarian norms. Above all, there is a moral imperative to rigorously prosecute the offenders, given the deliberate, systematic and outrageous nature of the violations in the former Yugoslavia.

Meron, The Case for War Crimes Trials in Yugoslavia, 72 Foreign Aff. 122 (1993). See also Szasz, The Proposed War Crimes Tribunal for Ex-Yugoslavia, 25 N.Y.U. J. Intl. L. & Pol. 405 (1993). How the International Tribunal for the Prosecution of Persons Responsible for Serious Violations of International Humanitarian Law Committed in the Territory of the Former Yugoslavia Since 1991 was established, the international crimes over which it has jurisdiction, and the rules of procedure and evidence that will guide its operations are described and explained in the two summary extracts that follow.

Orentlicher, Yugoslavia War Crimes Tribunal
ASIL Focus 1-4 (No. 1 1993)

Almost a half century after the Allied powers established an International Military Tribunal (IMT) to punish major Nazi war criminals, the United Nations Security Council has breathed new life into the law enforced at Nuremberg. Building on the foundation of Nuremberg law and the related work of the Tokyo war crimes tribunal, the Security Council recently decided to establish an International Tribunal (IT) with jurisdiction over international crimes committed during the continuing conflict in the territory of the former Yugoslavia.

While the IT's work is firmly anchored in the law of Nuremberg, the decision establishing the Tribunal raises novel questions of international law, and the IT itself will consider a raft of complex legal issues. But the most significant challenges will be eminently pragmatic. How, with a three-sided war still underway in Bosnia-Herzegovina, can the prosecution gather sufficient evidence to convict those responsible for war-related atrocities? Will the prosecution be able to persuade survivors of rape, a war crime committed on a massive scale during the conflict, to testify? Above all, will the Tribunal be able to arrest those who bear primary responsibility for crimes committed during the conflict? Ultimately, the credibility and effectiveness of the Tribunal will turn on its success in addressing these challenges.

Security Council Action

On May 25, 1993 the Security Council unanimously adopted Resolution 827. Acting under Chapter VII of the UN Charter, the Council decided "to establish an international tribunal for the sole purpose of prosecuting persons responsible for serious violations of international humanitarian law committed in the territory of the former Yugoslavia between 1 January 1991 and a date to be determined by the Security Council upon the restoration of peace . . . ," and also adopted the Statute of the Tribunal. *

Earlier resolutions had laid the foundation for this historic step. The Security Council had, for example, repeatedly reaffirmed that those who commit or order others to commit "grave breaches" of the Geneva Conventions of 1949 during the Balkan conflict are individually responsible for these war crimes. † In October 1992, the Secretary-General announced the appointment, pursuant to a Security Council resolution, of a Commission of Experts that would document violations of humanitarian law committed in the former Yugoslavia. **

---

* S.C. Res. 827, U.N. SCOR, 48th Sess., 3217th Mtg. at 2, U.N. Doc. S/RES/827 (1993), reprinted in 32 Intl. Legal Materials 1203 (1993). The Statute of the Tribunal may be found in the Documentary Supplement. — Eds.

† See, e.g., S.C. Res. 764, 47 U.N. SCOR, Res. and Dec. at 19 (1992). — Eds.

** S.C. Res. 780, 47 U.N. SCOR, Res. and Dec. at 36 (1992). By Resolution 771, the Security Council already had requested states and international humanitarian organizations "to collate substantiated information in their possession or submitted to them relating to the violations of humanitarian law, including gross breaches of the Geneva Conventions, being committed in the territory of the former Yugoslavia and to make this information available to the Council. . . ." S.C. Res. 771, 47 U.N. SCOR, Res. and Dec. at 25-26 (1992). Governments that subsequently submitted evidence to the Committee of Experts included Austria, Germany, the Netherlands, Norway, and the United States. See, e.g., Eighth Report on War Crimes in the Former Yugoslavia, 4 U.S. Dept. State Dispatch 537 (July 26, 1993). In

Then, in Resolution 808 of February 22, 1993, the Council decided
that an international tribunal should be established "for the prosecution of
persons responsible for serious violations of international humanitarian law
committed in the territory of the former Yugoslavia since 1991[.]" †† Pursuant to that resolution, on May 3, 1993 the Secretary-General submitted to
the Security Council a report setting forth recommendations for the establishment of a tribunal. Annexed to the report was a proposed statute for the
Tribunal, which the Security Council adopted in Resolution 827. ***

LEGAL BASIS OF TRIBUNAL

The first substantial issue raised by Resolution 808 was whether the *ad
hoc* tribunal should be established by treaty or, instead, through a Security
Council resolution. Following the recommendation of the Secretary-
General, the Security Council established the IT as an enforcement measure under Chapter VII of the UN Charter. As such, the decision had to be
(and was) predicated on a Security Council determination that the situation
giving rise to its action constituted a threat to the peace, breach of the
peace, or an act of aggression.

Although the Council had previously determined that the situation in
the former Yugoslavia constitutes a threat to international peace and security, its decision to establish a tribunal under Chapter VII was not without
controversy. Some States, including China, feared that this represented an
unwarranted intrusion on sovereignty. Others, such as Brazil, suggested that
the establishment of an international tribunal might exceed the Security
Council's competence, and took pains to insist that Resolution 827 and the
Statute for the IT "are . . . not meant to establish new norms or precedents
of international law," a "legislative" act thought to be beyond the Council's
competence. Instead, the IT would only apply "existing norms of international humanitarian law."

Any concern that the Security Council could, by acting under Chapter
VII, create a criminal tribunal that would not be constrained by existing
principles of international law seems unwarranted. The Security Council is
bound, when exercising its responsibilities for maintaining international
peace and security, to "act in accordance with the Purposes and Principles
of the United Nations." (UN Charter, art. 24(2).) In promoting the primary
purpose of the UN — to maintain international peace and security — the

---

addition to receiving state reports, Resolution 780 authorized the Commission to obtain
further information through its own investigations. For its Final Report, see page 991 infra. —
EDS.

†† S.C. Res. 808, U.N. SCOR, 48th Sess., 3175th Mtg. at 2, U.N. Doc. S/RES/808
(1993). — EDS.

*** Report of the Secretary-General Pursuant to Paragraph 2 of Security Council Resolution 808 (1993), U.N. Doc. S/25704 (1993), reprinted in 32 Intl. Legal Materials 1163
(1993). — EDS.

Organization is to take collective measures "in conformity with the principles of justice and international law." (*Id.*, art. 1(1).)

The Secretary-General's report to the Security Council makes clear that, whatever theoretical issues the Security Council's action might raise, the decision was driven by pragmatic concerns. Noting that an international tribunal would ordinarily be established by treaty, the Secretary-General observed that this approach would require "considerable time," and "there could be no guarantee that ratifications will be received from those States which should be parties to the treaty if it is to be truly effective."

The most significant consequence of the Security Council's approach will likewise be practical: Member States of the United Nations are legally required to comply with the decision establishing the IT. (This, of course, is a key reason why some countries thought establishment of the IT by any route other than treaty an undue infringement on sovereignty.) This obligation may prove to be critical in addressing one of the most daunting challenges that the prosecution will face — obtaining jurisdiction over indicted suspects. Among the obligations that the IT Statute imposes on Member States is a duty to comply with any others of the Tribunal relating to the arrest or detention of persons. That obligation may help assure, at the very least, that suspected war criminals effectively become prisoners in their own countries, lest they risk arrest abroad. In this respect, the Security Council's action may help mitigate the risk that the IT will appear ineffectual by virtue of its inability to obtain personal jurisdiction over key defendants.

Jurisdiction Ratione Materiae

Nowhere is the IT's debt to Nuremberg more apparent than in the statutory provisions establishing the Tribunal's subject matter jurisdiction. Each of the crimes subject to the IT's jurisdiction was encompassed in the jurisdictional provisions of the Nuremberg and Tokyo tribunals, although in several respects the Statute of the IT reflects contemporary definitions of those crimes. (The most controversial crime subject to the jurisdiction of the IMT — crimes against peace — has no analogue in the IT Statute.)

The Statue of the IT confers jurisdiction over three categories of crime:

1) VIOLATIONS OF HUMANITARIAN LAW, COMPRISING BOTH
   GRAVE BREACHES OF THE GENEVA CONVENTIONS OF 1949
   AND VIOLATIONS OF THE LAWS OR CUSTOMS OF WAR

Together these categories constitute a modern analogue to the "war crimes" subject to the jurisdiction of the Nuremberg and Tokyo tribunals. While this area of law is firmly established, its application to the situation in the former Yugoslavia will likely raise several complex issues. For example it is not yet clear whether all crimes encompassed by the temporal jurisdiction of the IT will be governed by provisions of the Geneva Conventions of 1949 applicable only to international armed conflicts. As noted above, the IT will have jurisdiction over designated crimes committed between January 1, 1991 and a yet-to-be-determined date. Since none of the States that were formerly republics of Yugoslavia was recognized as a sovereign state before June 25, 1991, it is unclear whether crimes committed before then will be governed by the "grave breaches" provisions of the Geneva Conventions, which apply only in situations of international armed conflict. Begging this question, the Secretary-General's report to the Security Council describes the choice of January 1, 1991 as "a neutral date which is not tied to any specific event and is clearly intended to convey the notion that no judgement as to the international or internal character of the conflict is being exercised."

2)   CRIMES AGAINST HUMANITY

"Crimes against humanity" were explicitly designated in the jurisdictional provisions of the Nuremberg and Tokyo Charters, as well as in Control Council Law No. 10, which established the jurisdiction of military tribunals of the Allied Powers in their respective zones of occupation. The United Nations ratified the principle that crimes against humanity are an international crime in the post-War period, but crimes against humanity as such have not been codified in a widely accepted treaty. Thus the IT's assertion of jurisdiction over crimes against humanity should afford an opportunity to revitalize an international crime that is in principle well established, if rarely punished.

But the Statute may, however inadvertently, introduce some ambiguity into the definition of crimes against humanity. The Secretary-General's report asserts the accepted view that crimes against humanity do not require a nexus to armed conflict, yet the provision of the Statute governing crimes against humanity, Article 5, provides that the IT "shall have the power to prosecute persons responsible for the following crimes *when committed in armed conflict, whether international or internal in character . . .*" (emphasis added). Read in light of the Secretary-General's accompanying observation, the italicized language should be understood as a jurisdictional limitation on the IT, and not as a codification of the international law of crimes against humanity.

This interpretation is also consistent with the fact that the IT was established as a Chapter VII enforcement action, tying the Security Council's action to the threat to international peace posed by the conflict in the former Yugoslavia. Moreover, any suggestion that crimes against humanity require a nexus to war would narrow the widely accepted definition of the crime under international law. Although crimes against humanity were punished at Nuremberg only if they were linked to crimes against peace or war crimes, effectively requiring a nexus to war, that requirement was a jurisdictional limitation of the Nuremberg tribunal, and not part of the definition of crimes against humanity under international law.

The phrase "when committed in armed conflict" introduced another potential ambiguity, which representatives to the Security Council effectively addressed by making clarifying statements when Resolution 827 was adopted. To remove any possibility that the phrase might be thought to cover only acts committed in the middle of an armed encounter, the United States Ambassador observed that Article 5 "applies to all acts listed in that article, when committed . . . *during a period of* armed conflict in the territory of the former Yugoslavia . . ." (emphasis added), and several other representatives made similar statements.

3)   GENOCIDE

Although the word "genocide" was not used in the Charter or judgment of the IMT, it appeared in the Indictment of Major War Criminals and was considered the quintessential crime against humanity by various U.S. Military Tribunals operating under Control Council Law No. 10. But unlike crimes against humanity generally, the international crime of genocide has been codified in a widely ratified convention. The IT Statute adopts the definition of genocide set forth in the 1948 Convention on the Prevention of Punishment of the Crime of Genocide, which has become part of customary law.

JURISDICTION *RATIONE PERSONAE*

Consistent with the Nuremberg principles, the Statute of the IT assures that those who have ordered or instigated crimes, or who knew or had reason to know about crimes by subordinates and failed to take necessary and reasonable steps to prevent or punish them, are criminally liable. The Statute also incorporates the Nuremberg principle that a person generally is not relieved of criminal responsibility for a crime because it was committed pursuant to superior orders, though such orders can be considered in mitigation of punishment. In these and other respects, the Statute reaffirms the principle of individual responsibility — the bedrock concept underlying international criminal law.

One respect in which the Statute of the IT departs from the Nuremberg precedent is its provision for jurisdiction over natural persons only. The Nuremberg Charter, in contrast, provided that membership in certain criminal organizations, such as the SS, could be considered criminal.

CHALLENGES

Other advances since Nuremberg include the IT Statute's provision
that no defendant may be tried *in absentia,* and the fact that available
penalties do not include the death penalty. In contrast, the IMT sentenced
Martin Bormann to death *in absentia.*

But for all its improvements over Nuremberg, the circumstances of the
IT's creation imperil its effective operation. While the Nuremberg trial was
widely faulted as "victors' justice," the circumstances of that prosecution
assured that individuals bearing substantial responsibility for Nazi crimes
could be arrested and brought to trial. In striking contrast, those who are
most responsible for war crimes committed in the former Yugoslavia may
insist on impunity as a condition for ending the war. Even if the UN resists
the temptation to capitulate to such demands, it will be hard-pressed to
obtain personal jurisdiction over those individuals.

Prosecutions before the IT will also face substantial evidentiary challenges. While Nazi criminals left a staggering paper trail, it is generally
believed that those responsible for atrocities in the former Yugoslavia have
not created significant documentary evidence of their crimes, and in any
event will surely block UN access to such documentary evidence as may
exist. The case against potential defendants will, then, be based largely on
testimonial evidence.

Such evidence can, in fact, be very compelling, even when used cir-
cumstantially, and advances in the use of computer technology as a tool of
human rights research will aid the prosecution's efforts to build a persuasive
record in which testimonial evidence plays a central part. Still, with the war
continuing, many potential witnesses are inaccessible, while others are in
flux — an intended consequence of "ethnic cleansing." The location of the
IT — its seat will be in The Hague — will compound the logistical hurdles
relating to eyewitness testimony. More generally, the process of developing
a testimonial record is both labor-intensive and costly, and the UN's failure
to provide adequate staff and funding for the Commission of Experts points
up the risk of similar problems with respect to the IT.

Resources aside, the prosecution will face formidable challenges in its
efforts to persuade victims of rape and other traumatic war crimes to provide
testimony. The special trauma associated with mass rapes committed during
the conflict in the former Yugoslavia compounds rape survivors' general
reluctance to testify about their experience, and few have been willing to
speak to human rights investigators. Many have received credible threats of
retaliation from the perpetrators if they talk of their experience. Thus the
UN's success in prosecuting rape will require special attention to the needs
of the survivors. During the investigation phase, the office of the prosecutor
should, for example, assure that testimony of rape survivors is taken by
persons of the same gender (although not widely reported or documented,
there is evidence that men have also been subjected to sexual assault on a

significant scale during the conflict in Bosnia-Herzegovina). Further, special procedures will have to be established to protect potential witnesses at trial, consistent with the defendants' due process rights. While the IT Statute generally provides for protective measures, including *in camera* testimony, procedures implementing this mandate have not yet been adopted.

CONCLUSION

Resolution 827 represents an historic step, a watershed in international law and policy. If successful, the Tribunal that it authorizes will add new impetus to long-standing proposals for a permanent international criminal court. Perhaps of more lasting consequence, the work of the Tribunal will reaffirm a principle that has been deeply compromised by the unchecked sweep of "ethnic cleansing" in the former Yugoslavia: there can be no impunity for crimes against humanity.

Zagaris, Introductory Note: International Tribunal for the Prosecution of Persons Responsible for Serious Violations of International Humanitarian Law Committed in the Territory of the Former Yugoslavia Since 1991: Rules of Procedure and Evidence
33 Intl. Legal Materials 484, 484-490 (1994)

On February 11, 1994, the International Tribunal for the Prosecution of Persons Responsible for Serious Violations of International Humanitarian Law Committed in the Territory of Former Yugoslavia since 1991 adopted Rules of Procedure and Evidence, under which the Tribunal will operate. The Rules came into force on March 14, 1994. . . . [Rule 1]

The Rules of Procedure and Evidence have historical significance for public international law in part because of the relative novelty of the Tribunal for War Crimes in Former Yugoslavia and perhaps, even more importantly, for the precedent they set for the establishment of a permanent International Criminal Court. For many years the establishment of the latter Tribunal has been hindered by the perception that it would be impossible if not difficult [sic] to elaborate workable rules of procedure and evidence in view of the many legal systems of the world and the political issues of such a Tribunal.

The Rules complement the Statute establishing the Tribunal and provide for the operation of the Tribunal. They contain nine Parts as follows: 1) General Provisions; 2) Primacy of the Tribunal; 3) Organization of the Tribunal; 4) Investigations and Rights of Suspects; 5) Pre-Trial Proceedings;

6) Proceedings Before Trial Chambers; 7) Appellate Proceedings; 8) Review Proceedings; and 9) Pardon and Commutation of Sentence.

Part One, "General Provisions," provides that the working language of the Tribunal will be English and French although an accused has the right to use his own language or by leave of the Chamber a language other than the two working languages or his own. [Rule 3] A Chamber may exercise its functions at a place other than the Hague, which is the seat of the Tribunal, if the Tribunal's President authorizes it in the interests of justice. [Rule 4]

The Rules may be amended, provided they are unanimously approved by the Judges. [Rule 6] The ability to amend the Rules provides an internal dynamic that will facilitate the need to accommodate unforseen demands on the Tribunal.

Part Two provides for the operation of the principle of primacy of the Tribunal's concurrent jurisdiction with national courts under certain circumstances. For instance, the Prosecutor can propose to the Trial Chamber designated by the President that a formal request be made to the national court to defer to the competence of the Tribunal where it appears to the Prosecutor that in any such investigations or criminal proceedings instituted in the national courts of any state:

(i) the national court characterizes the act under investigation as an ordinary crime;

(ii) a lack of impartiality or independence exists, or the investigations or proceedings are designed to shield the accused from international criminal responsibility, or the case is not diligently prosecuted; or

(iii) the proceeding concerns matters closely related to significant factual or legal questions that may have implications for investigations or prosecutions before the Tribunal. [Rule 9]

The Tribunal may also request a national court to defer to the competence of the Tribunal [Rule 10] and, if within 60 days after a request for deferral has been made the national state fails to respond satisfactorily, the Tribunal may request the Tribunal's President to report the matter to the Security Council which can take whatever action it deems appropriate. [Rules 11 & 13] The ability of the Tribunal to have competence over national courts and to enforce its right of having national courts defer proceedings is designed to ensure fairness, integrity, and efficiency. Already, the Bosnian courts have tried war crimes and the German Government has arrested and is considering prosecuting a Serb for war crimes in the former Yugoslavia.

Part Three, "Organization of the Tribunal," provides for Judges, the Tribunal's Presidency, the Registry, the Prosecutor, and the Bureau. The latter is composed of the President, Vice-President and the Presiding Judges of the Trial Chambers, and is to consider all major questions relating to the functioning of the Tribunal. [Rule 13]

The judges will rotate on a regular basis between the Trial Chambers and the Appeals Chamber. [Rule 27]

A critical organ will be a Victims and Witnesses Unit that will be established under the authority of the Registrar and will have as its obligations to: recommend protective measures for victims and witnesses in accordance with Article 22 of the Statute; and provide counselling and support for them, especially in cases of rape and sexual assault.

Under Part Four "Investigations and Rights of Suspects," a prosecutor may request any State to take provisional measures, such as arresting a suspect provisionally, seizing physical evidence, and taking all necessary measures to prevent the escape of a suspect or an accused, injury to or intimidation of a victim or witness, or the destruction of evidence. [Rule 40]

The rights of suspects are set forth, including the right to the assistance of counsel, including the appointment of counsel and interpreters for indigents. No defendant or suspect can be questioned without the presence of counsel unless the defendant or suspect has voluntarily waived his right to counsel.

Part Five, "Pre-Trial Proceedings," sets forth procedure for indictments. [Rules 47-53] When the Prosecutor is satisfied that sufficient evidence exists to provide reasonable grounds for believing that a suspect has committed a crime within the jurisdiction of the Tribunal, he must prepare and forward to the Registrar an indictment for confirmation by a Judge, together with supporting material. Upon receipt of the material from the Registrar, the judge will review the indictment and, after hearing from the Prosecutor, may confirm or dismiss each count or may adjourn the review. [Rule 47]

A Prosecutor may amend an indictment, without leave, at any time before its confirmation, and thereafter with leave of the Judge who confirmed it or, if at trial, with leave of the Trial Chamber. [Rule 50]

Although indictments are to be made public, the judge may delay public disclosure of the indictment until it is served on the accused, if satisfied that the making of such an order is in the interest of justice. [Rule 53]

A judge or a Trial Chamber can issue such orders, summonses and warrants as may be necessary for the purposes of investigation or for the preparation or conduct of the trial. [Rule 54]

The procedure for issuing and executing arrest warrants is set forth. [Rule 55] A State must arrest and transfer the accused to the Tribunal. [Rules 56-58] If it is unable to execute an arrest warrant, a State must transmit the reasons therefor. If it does not, the Tribunal may notify the Security Council accordingly. [Rule 59]

If a warrant of arrest has not been executed and the Prosecutor satisfies a judge that all reasonable steps have been taken to effect personal service and inform the accused of the indictment, including publication of newspaper advertisements, the Trial Chamber may hear evidence and, if there exist reasonable grounds for believing the accused has committed all or any of the crimes charged in the indictment, it will so determine. [Rule 61]

Once detained, an accused may not be released except by order of a Trial Chamber, only in exceptional circumstances, and only if it is satisfied that the accused will appear for trial and, if released, will not pose a danger to any victim, witness or other person. [Rule 65]

Three rules make specific provision for disclosure of evidence by the prosecutor to the defense, for reciprocal disclosure, and disclosure of exculpatory evidence. [Rules 66-68]

In exceptional circumstances the Prosecutor can apply to a Trial Chamber to order the non-disclosure of the identity of a victim or witness who may be in danger or at risk until such person is brought under the protection of the Tribunal. Subject to measures that can be taken for the protection of victims or witnesses, their identity must be disclosed in sufficient time prior to the trial to permit adequate time for preparation of the defense. [Rule 69]

In Part Six, "Proceedings Before Trial Chambers," a Chamber can, if it considers it desirable for the proper determination of the case, invite or grant leave to a State, organization or person to appear before it and make submissions on any issue the Chamber specifies. [Rule 74] Human rights organizations can be expected to try actively to participate.

A Judge or Chamber can order appropriate measures for privacy and protection of victims, provided that the measures are consistent with the rights of the accused. [Rule 75 (A)] A Chamber can hold an *ex parte* proceeding to determine whether to order measures to prevent disclosure to the public or the media of the identity or location of a victim or a witness, or of persons related to or associated with him through various means. [Rule 75 (B)]

A criticism of the Tribunal's Statute and the Rules is that they do not grant victims the right to plead and be represented by counsel. . . . Perhaps, the Tribunal's ability to invite or grant leave to an organization to appear before it will be creatively used to enable victims to have appropriate representation throughout the proceedings.

In the rules for case presentation the Trial Chamber, if it finds the accused guilty of a crime and concludes from the evidence that unlawful taking of property by the accused was associated with it, it must make a specific finding to that effect in its judgement and may order restitution. [Rule 88 (B)] Dissenting opinions are permitted. [Rule 88 (C)]

Within Part Six, the Section on "Rules of Evidence" sets forth general rules [Rule 89] and also detailed ones. For instance, evidence obtained directly or indirectly by means which constitute a serious violation of internationally protected human rights will not be admissible. [Rule 95] In cases of sexual assault, three specific rules apply: no corroboration of the victim's testimony is required; consent will not be permitted as a defense; and prior sexual conduct of the victim will not be admitted in evidence. [Rule 96]

The Section on "Sentencing Procedure," provides that a convicted person may be sentenced to imprisonment for a term up to and including life, taking into account the factors mentioned in Article 24(2) of the Statute. [Rule 101] The place of imprisonment will be served in a State designated by the Tribunal from a list of States which have indicated their willingness to accept convicted persons. [Rule 103]

After a judgement of conviction, the Prosecutor can convene a special hearing of the Trial Chamber to determine the restitution of the property or the proceeds thereof. The Chamber may order such provisional measures for the preservation and protection of the property or proceeds as it considers appropriate. [Rule 105]

A victim or persons claiming through him can bring an action in a national court or other competent body to obtain compensation pursuant to relevant national legislation. [Rule 106]

Part Seven, "Appellate Proceedings," allows for and sets forth procedure for appeals, including briefs, timing, and the status of the accused following appeal.

Part Eight sets forth "Review Proceedings," which may occur where a new fact has been discovered which was not known to the moving party at the time of the proceedings before a Trial Chamber or the Appeals Chamber, and could not have been discovered through the exercise of due diligence. [Rules 119-122]

Part 9, "Pardon and Commutation of Sentence," allows a State in which a convicted person is imprisoned to notify the Tribunal of eligibility of the person for pardon or commutation of sentence, which ultimately, the Tribunal's President determines, in consultation with the judges under the standards set forth in Rule 125. [Rules 123-125]

The Rules of Procedure and Evidence will play a critical role in achieving success for the Tribunal. Indeed the Tribunal confronts formidable financial, legal, and political obstacles to success. The Rules are endeavoring to pioneer a path through the forest of impediments. Professionals, scholars, and policymakers should scrutinize the operation of the entire effort, as well as the component parts, since enforcement of international humanitarian law is an imperative which mankind no longer has the luxury to consider only for its academic interest.

Comments and Questions

1. While the major reason for the establishment of the Yugoslav War Crimes Tribunal surely was "a reaction to the bankruptcy of the legal, political, moral and military commitment of the world community to intervene for the prevention of significant human rights violations . . . in the former Yugoslavia," Bassiouni, Remarks, Panel on the United Nations Ad Hoc Tribunal for the Former Yugoslavia, 1993 Am. Socy. Intl. L. Proceedings 20, 22, its genesis in no way lessens its importance. The Security Council's decision to create it, as Mr. Greenwood has observed,

> breaks new ground, both for the Council and for the international community as a whole. Not since the Nuremberg and Tokyo trials has an international criminal tribunal been created to try individuals charged with violations of international law. The international military tribunals which sat

at Nuremberg and Tokyo, however, were the creation of the victorious allies of the Second World War. The tribunal for former Yugoslavia, by contrast, has been established by the Security Council, acting on behalf of the entire international community, in the exercise of its responsibility for the maintenance of international peace and security.

Greenwood, The International Tribunal for Former Yugoslavia, 69 Intl. Aff. 641, 641 (1993). For other informed commentary on the Tribunal, see O'Brien, The International Tribunal for Violations of International Humanitarian Law in the Former Yugoslavia, 87 Am. J. Intl. L. 639 (1993); Task Force on War Crimes in the Former Yugoslavia of the ABA Section of International Law and Practice, Report on the International Tribunal to Adjudicate War Crimes Committed in the Former Yugoslavia (July 8, 1993).

2. Read the Statute of the International Tribunal found in the Documentary Supplement. Note that the Tribunal's jurisdiction is limited in time (crimes committed since 1991 — Art. 1), in space (crimes committed in the territory of the former Yugoslavia — id.), and in the nature of the offenses proscribed: grave breaches of the Geneva Conventions (Art. 2); violations of the laws and customs of war (Art. 3); genocide (Art. 4); and crimes against humanity (Art. 5). Cf. Paust, Applicability of International Criminal Laws to Events in the Former Yugoslavia, 9 Am. U. J. Intl. L. & Poly. 499 (1994). Obviously these limitations, plus the fact that the Tribunal was established by a Security Council resolution rather than a General Assembly-sponsored or approved treaty, made it much easier to obtain the necessary state support for the Tribunal. Does that lessen its precedential value? If so, in what ways? Note that the Secretary-General, in his report on the proposed tribunal, mentions its circumscribed scope and purpose ordained by the Security Council's decision in Resolution 808: "[t]he decision does not relate to the establishment of an international criminal jurisdiction in general nor to the creation of an international criminal court of a permanent nature, issues which are and remain under active consideration by the International Law Commission and the General Assembly." Report of the Secretary-General Pursuant to Paragraph 2 of Security Council Resolution 808 (1993), U.N. Doc. S/25704, at 5 (1993), reprinted in 32 Intl. Legal Materials 1166 (1993).

3. The Secretary-General's report on the proposed tribunal contained an annex with a 34-article draft statute that the Security Council approved in haec verba when it adopted Resolution 827. In addition to creating a tribunal of limited jurisdiction, as pointed out in Comment 2, the Statute of the International Tribunal deals with a number of key and long-debated issues that any international criminal court would face, e.g., command responsibility (Art. 7 (3)); superior orders (Art. 7 (4)); concurrent jurisdiction (with the International Tribunal having "primacy" over national courts) (Art. 9); non-bis-in-idem (double jeopardy) (Art. 10); conduct of trial (Art. 20); rights of accused (Art. 21); pronouncement of judgments (no jury trials) (Art. 23); penalties (no death penalty) (Art. 24); appeals (by convicted

persons and prosecutor) (Art. 25); enforcement of sentences (Art. 28); and cooperation and judicial assistance by states (Art. 29).

Review the text of the above articles in the Documentary Supplement to see how these issues have been resolved and whether, in your opinion, they have been resolved satisfactorily. See also the ABA Task Force report, supra page 990, for an in-depth analysis of the Tribunal's Statute containing a number of recommendations concerning due process considerations, protection for victims and witnesses, structure of the Tribunal, and appropriate U.S. implementing legislation. The Task Force urged the UN to take needed remedial measures through implementing directives, interpretative statements, or, if necessary, supplementary decisions of the Security Council.

4. The five-member Commission of Experts established to gather evidence of grave breaches of the Geneva Conventions and other violations of international humanitarian law in the territory of the former Yugoslavia commenced its activities in November 1992 and concluded its work with the submission of its Final Report in April 1994. See Final Report of the Commission of Experts Established Pursuant to Security Council Resolution 780 (1992), U.N. Doc. S/1994/674 Annex (1994). During this period it held 12 sessions, conducted a series of studies and on-site investigations, and established a data base designed to provide a comprehensive record of all reported violations within its mandate. The Final Report, with which the Secretary-General fully concurred, concluded that:

> grave breaches of the Geneva Conventions and other violations of international humanitarian law have been committed in the territory of the former Yugoslavia on a large scale, and were particularly brutal and ferocious in their execution. The practice of so-called "ethnic cleansing" and rape and sexual assault, in particular, have been carried out by some of the parties so systematically that they strongly appear to be the product of a policy, which may also be inferred from the consistent failure to prevent the commission of such crimes and to prosecute and punish their perpetrators.

Id. at 1-2. The Commission's findings, of course, have been communicated to the Office of the Prosecutor of the International Tribunal. Id. at 71.

5. The Final Report of the Commission, chaired by Professor Bassiouni, contains a succinct but thorough survey of selected legal issues raised by the violations of international humanitarian law in the former Yugoslavia. Id. at 13-29. Its detailed substantive findings about the nature, extent, and severity of the violations make shocking reading. Id. at 37-70. The Final Report concludes by noting "the victims' high expectations that this Commission will establish the truth and that the International Tribunal will provide justice. All sides expect this. Thus, the conclusion is inescapable that peace in the future requires justice, and that justice starts with establishing the truth." Id. at 72. *

---

* "Establishing the truth is the best method of enhancing deterrence. In fact, early investigation of the facts, in any context of criminal activity, increases the effectiveness of future prosecution. The combination of investigation and prosecution makes deterrence more

6. The Commission of Experts operated on an extremely tight budget, with most of its expenses paid from a trust fund of $1.3 million contributed by 17 UN member states. (Canada, the Netherlands, and the United States contributed 75 percent.) Id. at 73 n.4. The Commission's data base was financed exclusively from funds provided by DePaul University and two foundations. Id. at 73 n.2. Both states and NGOs contributed personnel and logistical support. Future war crimes investigations, it is hoped, will be adequately funded and not have to rely on "pro bono" contributions. Specifically, as the Commission observed in its Final Report, "the International Tribunal must be given the necessary resources and support to . . . accomplish its task." Id. at 72. Accord, Orentlicher, supra page 984; O'Brien, supra page 990, at 658; Greenwood, supra page 990, at 655. For a somewhat pessimistic assessment that by disbanding the Commission the UN already has gutted the International Tribunal, see Aga Khan, War Crimes Without Punishment, N.Y. Times, Feb. 8, 1994, at A15, cols. 2-5.

7. After getting off to a troubled start, the International Tribunal of 11 judges is now sitting; Rules of Procedure and Evidence and Rules Governing the Detention of Prisoners have been adopted; a Prosecutor and Deputy Prosecutor have been appointed (a South African Supreme Court judge and the former Director of the Australian War Crimes Prosecution unit, respectively); a Registrar has been named; Denmark and Germany have arrested persons suspected of committing war crimes, crimes against humanity, or genocide in the former Yugoslavia; the initial indictments have been issued; and the first trials are scheduled to be held in 1995. See generally Lynch, UN Crimes Bid Against Serbs Gains in Force, Boston Globe, Aug. 15, 1994, at 2, cols. 5-6.

8. The massacres that took place in Rwanda in 1994 also spurred calls for international trials of Hutu perpetrators. See The Economist, July 30, 1994, at 16-17, cols. 2-3. But see Binaisa, Letter to the Editor, N.Y. Times, Aug. 22, 1994, at A12, cols. 3-4 (urging reconciliation rather than resort to an international criminal court). The Security Council responded by creating a second ad hoc tribunal — the International Tribunal for Rwanda — with "the power to prosecute persons responsible for serious violations of international humanitarian law committed in the territory of Rwanda and Rwandan citizens responsible for such violations committed in the territory of neighbouring States, between 1 January 1994 and 31 December 1994. . . ." S.C. Res. 955, U.N. SCOR, 49th Sess., 3453rd mtg. at 3, U.N. Doc. S/RES/ 955 (1994). While most of the provisions in the Tribunal's 32-article Statute are taken in haec verba from the Statute of the Yugoslav War Crimes Tribunal, the Rwandan War Crimes Tribunal is an independent body, although the former's Prosecutor also will serve as Prosecutor for the latter. Id. at 9.

---

effective, thereby reducing possible violations in the future. Without effective investigations and prosecutions, the converse is true." Id. at 84 n.88.

C. The ILC Draft Statute for an International Criminal Court

After noting that, "[h]istorically, the idea of codifying international criminal law is bound up with the idea of establishing an international criminal court." Wise points out that "[t]here is no necessary connection between the two ideas." See page 953 supra. Yet the perceived linkage caused the General Assembly to decide in 1957 to postpone consideration of a court until it had completed a Draft Code, which as we have seen (see page 937 supra) effectively delayed serious work on the former for well over three decades. The nexus between the two projects finally was broken in 1992 when the General Assembly, responding to the ILC's Forty-Fourth Report (Report of the International Law Commission to the General Assembly, 47 U.N. GAOR Supp. (No. 10) at 143, U.N. Doc. A/47/10 (1992)) and undoubtedly influenced by the massive international humanitarian law violations coming to light in the former Yugoslavia, instructed the Commission to undertake "the project for an international criminal court as a matter of priority as from its next session," separate and distinct in principle from its Draft Code project, "with a view to drafting a statute on the basis of the report of [its] Working Group, taking into account the views expressed during the debate in the Sixth Committee as well as any written comments received from States. . . ." G.A. Res. 47/33, 47 U.N. GAOR Supp. (No. 49) at 287, U.N. Doc. A/47/49 (1992).

The main features of the Working Group's model were summarized by the U.S. member on the Commission, "albeit somewhat simplistically," as follows (Rosenstock, The Forty-Fourth Session of the International Law Commission, 87 Am. J. Intl. L. 138, 140 (1993)).

(1) the court should be established by a statute in the form of multilateral treaty;

(2) it should have jurisdiction over individuals and not states;

(3) while the court would exist pursuant to the statute, and thus not be subject to the charge of being created *post facto*, it would not be a standing or full-time body but, rather, a structure to be activated when required — a facility for states;

(4) states that become party to the statute of the court would not *ipso facto* accept the jurisdiction of the court over particular crimes;

(5) the subject matter jurisdiction would consist of offenses contained in specified international treaties in force (e.g., aircraft hijacking, hostage taking, genocide, grave breaches of the Geneva Conventions on the protection of victims of armed conflict, large-scale drug trafficking) and not include the notion of common law crimes;

(6) states would be free to accept the jurisdiction of the court with regard to none, some or all of the listed offenses;

(7) the statute and structure of the court would guarantee due process, independence and impartiality in its procedures; and

(8) while the handing over or rendition of an accused to the court would not be regarded as extradition to a foreign state, the protections afforded by standard extradition-type provisions and the assistance provided by traditional mutual legal assistance provisions would be an integral part of the recommended total package.

These features all were reflected in the Working Group's Draft Statute for an International Criminal Tribunal, which the ILC took note of at its 1993 session and transmitted to the General Assembly for its comments. Report of the International Law Commission to the General Assembly, 48 U.N. GAOR Supp. (No. 10) at 255-335, U.N. Doc. A/48/10 (1993) (report of Working Group containing Draft Statute and commentaries thereto). The Draft Statute is reprinted in 33 Intl. Legal Materials 253 (1994) and as an appendix to the Final Report of the ABA's Task Force on an International Criminal Court, 28 Intl. Law. 475, 510 (1994). For an excellent summary of the Draft Statute by a member of the Working Group, see Crawford, The ILC's Draft Statute for an International Criminal Tribunal, 88 Am. J. Intl. L. 140 (1994).

The Draft Statute was the subject of extensive debate by the Sixth Committee of the General Assembly during its session in the fall of 1993. Report of the International Law Commission, Topical Summary of the Discussion Held in the Sixth Committee of the General Assembly During Its Forty-Eighth Session Prepared by the Secretariat, U.N. Doc. A/CN.4/457, at 6-47 (1994). For a concise summary of this debate, see Morris and Bourloyannis-Vrailas, The Work of the Sixth Committee at the Forty-Eighth Session of the UN General Assembly, 88 Am. J. Intl. L. 343, 349-351 (1994). For further commentary on the Draft Statute, see the Final Report of the ABA's Task Force on an International Criminal Court, supra. Thus, the International Law Commission (taking into account comments received from governments, the Statute and Rules of Procedure and Evidence of the Yugoslav War Crimes Tribunal, and a compilation of earlier draft statutes for an international criminal court elaborated within the framework of the UN or by other public or private bodies) was well prepared for its task of completing its drafting labors when it met in 1994 and reconvened the Working Group to review and revise the latter's 1993 Draft Statute. The Working Group explained its work plan as follows (Working Group on a Draft Statute for an International Criminal Court, Report of the Working Group, U.N. Doc. A/CN.4/L.491/Rev. 2, at 3 (1994)).

The Working Group proceeded to a re-examination [of the Draft Statue] bearing in mind, *inter alia*, (a) the need to streamline and simplify the articles concerning the subject matter jurisdiction of the Court, while better determining the extent of such jurisdiction; (b) the fact that the Court's system should be conceived as complementary with national systems which function on the basis of existing mechanisms for international cooperation and judicial assistance and (c) the need for coordinating the common articles to be found in the draft statute for an international criminal court and in the draft code of crimes against the peace and security of mankind.

In revising the articles concerning subject matter jurisdiction, the Working Group abandoned its previous "two-strand" approach contained in Articles 22 and 26 of its 1993 Draft Statute (which attempted to distinguish treaties that define crimes as international crimes from treaties that merely provide for the suppression of undesirable conduct constituting crimes under national law) and instead specifically spelled out in new Article 20 a number of crimes under general international law over which the Court has jurisdiction; in addition, Article 20 gives the Court jurisdiction over certain crimes arising from or pursuant to a number of multilateral treaties listed in an annex. Article 20 and the annex are set out immediately below (id. at 16, 35-36).

Article 20.   Crimes within the Jurisdiction of the Court

The Court has jurisdiction in accordance with this Statute with respect to the following crimes:

(a) the crime of genocide;

(b) the crime of aggression;

(c) serious violations of the laws and customs applicable in armed conflict;

(d) crimes against humanity;

(e) crimes, established under or pursuant to the treaty provisions listed in the Annex, which, having regard to the conduct alleged, constitute exceptionally serious crimes of international concern.

Annex.   *Crimes Pursuant to Treaties* (see Art. 20 (e))

1. Grave breaches of:

  (i) the Geneva Convention for the Amelioration of the Condition of the Wounded and Sick in Armed Forces in the Field of 12 August 1949, as defined by Article 50 of that Convention;

  (ii) the Geneva Convention for the Amelioration of the Condition of Wounded, Sick and Shipwrecked Members of Armed Forces at Sea of 12 August 1949, as defined by Article 51 of that Convention;

  (iii) the Geneva Convention relative to the Treatment of Prisoners of War of 12 August 1949, as defined by Article 130 of that Convention;

  (iv) the Geneva Convention relative to the Protection of Civilian Persons in Time of War of 12 August 1949, as defined by Article 147 of that Convention;

  (v) Protocol I Additional to the Geneva Conventions of 12 August 1949 and relating to the Protection of Victims of International Armed Conflicts of 8 June 1977, as defined by Article 85 of that Protocol.

2. The unlawful seizure of aircraft as defined by Article 1 of the Hague Convention for the Suppression of Unlawful Seizure of Aircraft of 16 December 1970.

3. The crimes defined by Article 1 of the Montreal Convention for the Suppression of Unlawful Acts against the Safety of Civil Aviation of 23 September 1971.

4. Apartheid and related crimes as defined by Article II of the International Convention on the Suppression and Punishment of the Crime of Apartheid of 30 November 1973.

5. The crimes defined by Article 2 of the Convention on the Prevention and Punishment of Crimes against Internationally Protected Persons, including Diplomatic Agents of 14 December 1973.

6. Hostage-taking and related crimes as defined by Article 1 of the International Convention against the Taking of Hostages of 17 December 1979.

7. The crime of torture made punishable pursuant to Article 4 of the Convention against Torture and Other Cruel, Inhuman or Degrading Treatment or Punishment of 10 December 1984.

8. The crimes defined by Article 3 of the Convention for the Suppression of Unlawful Acts against the Safety of Maritime Navigation of 10 March 1988 and by Article 2 of the Protocol for the Suppression of Unlawful Acts against the Safety of Fixed Platforms Located on the Continental Shelf of 10 March 1988.

9. Crimes involving illicit traffic in narcotic drugs and psychotropic substances as envisaged by Article 3 (1) of the United Nations Convention against Illicit Traffic in Narcotic Drugs and Psychotropic Substances of 20 December 1988 which, having regard to Article 2 of the Convention, are crimes with an international dimension.

As a reading of Article 20 and the annex reveals, the Court's jurisdiction under its latest Draft Statute extends to two types of international crimes: crimes under general international law (Art. 20(a)-(d)) * and crimes of international concern as defined by 11 treaties (Art. 20(e) and Annex). Under the "opt-in" approach adopted by the ILC, moreover, a state's acceptance of the Statute of the Court does not, except for the crime of genocide (Art. 21(1)(a); Art. 25(1)), constitute an automatic acceptance of the Court's jurisdiction over all the other crimes listed in Article 20; any acceptance, which is optional, occurs only with respect to those crimes specified by a state in a declaration made pursuant to Article 22(1).

Even when a state that has made a declaration with respect to a particu-

---

* Article 20(a)-(d) is not (and was not intended to be) an exhaustive list of crimes under general international law. As the ILC notes, "[i]t is limited to those crimes under general international law which the Commission believes should be within the jurisdiction of the Court *at this stage*, whether by reason of their magnitude, the continuing reality of their occurrence or their inevitable international consequences." Report of the International Law Commission to the General Assembly, 49 U.N. GAOR Supp. (No. 10) at 77-78, U.N. Doc. A/49/10 (1994) (emphasis added).

lar crime brings a complaint alleging that such a crime has been committed (Art. 25(2)),† the Court may not exercise jurisdiction over a person with respect to the crime unless the state that has custody of the suspect *and* the state where the act occurred also have accepted the Court's jurisdiction with respect to that crime (Art. 21(1)(b)). Thus, while Article 20 and the annex grant the Court jurisdiction over a wide range of international crimes, as a practical matter it will take some time and numerous declarations before the Court is in a position to exercise much of its potential jurisdiction.

Furthermore, contrary to the Statute of the International Tribunal for the Former Yugoslavia, Article 9(2) of which proclaims the Tribunal's "primacy over national courts," the ILC's Draft Statute operates in principle on the basis of concurrent jurisdiction. The somewhat complex relationship between the Court and national courts is the subject of Articles 53 and 54 of the Draft Statute set out below, both of which are followed by the Commission's accompanying commentary (Report of the International Law Commission to the General Assembly, 49 U.N. GAOR Supp. (No. 10) at 131-136, U.N. Doc. A/49/10 (1994)).

Article 53.   Transfer of an Accused to the Court

1. The Registrar shall transmit to any State on the territory of which the accused may be found a warrant for the arrest and transfer of an accused issued under article 28, and shall request the cooperation of the State in the arrest and transfer of the accused.

2. Upon receipt of a request under paragraph 1:

(a) all States parties:

(i) in a case covered by article 21(1)(a) [genocide], or

(ii) which have accepted the jurisdiction of the Court with respect to the crime in question;

shall, subject to paragraphs 5 and 6, take immediate steps to arrest and transfer the accused to the Court;

(b) in the case of a crime to which article 20 (e) applies, a State party which is a party to the treaty in question but which has not accepted the Court's jurisdiction with respect to that crime shall, if it decides not to transfer the accused to the Court, forthwith take all necessary steps to extradite the accused to a requesting State or refer the case to its competent authorities for the purpose of prosecution;

(c) in any other case, a State party shall consider whether it can, in accordance with its legal procedures, take steps to arrest and transfer the accused to the Court, or whether it should take steps to extradite the accused to a requesting State or refer the case to its competent authorities for the purpose of prosecution.

† Only a state that has made such a declaration may lodge a complaint (Art. 25(2)). In the case of genocide, however, where the Court has inherent jurisdiction and, hence, no declaration is necessary, any state party to the Statute that is also a party to the Genocide Convention may lodge a complaint (Art. 25(1)).

3. The transfer of an accused to the Court constitutes, as between States parties which accept the jurisdiction of the Court with respect to the crime, sufficient compliance with a provision of any treaty requiring that a suspect be extradited or the case referred to the competent authorities of the requested State for the purpose of prosecution.

4. A State party which accepts the jurisdiction of the Court with respect to the crime shall, as far as possible, give priority to a request under paragraph 1 over requests for extradition from other States.

5. A State party may delay complying with paragraph 2 if the accused is in its custody or control and is being proceeded against for a serious crime, or serving a sentence imposed by a court for a crime. It shall within 45 days of receiving the request inform the Registrar of the reasons for the delay. In such cases, the requested State:

(a) may agree to the temporary transfer of the accused for the purpose of standing trial under this Statute; or

(c) shall comply with paragraph 2 after the prosecution has been completed or abandoned or the sentence has been served, as the case may be.

6. A State party may, within 45 days of receiving a request under paragraph 1, file a written application with the Registrar requesting the Court to set aside the request on specified grounds. Pending a decision of the Court on the application, the State concerned may delay complying with paragraph 2, but shall take any provisional measures requested by the Court.

Commentary

(1) Having regard . . . to the need to establish a clear relationship between existing obligations to try or extradite and the Statute, article 53 is a crucial provision. . . . [I]t is necessary to distinguish between the various levels of obligation States parties to the Statute may have accepted, which can range from not being a party to the relevant treaty defining a crime, on the one hand, to having accepted the jurisdiction of the Court over such crimes in all cases, on the other hand. Article 53 is drafted accordingly. . . .

(2) In the first place, the Registrar may request any State to cooperate in the arrest and transfer of an accused pursuant to a warrant issued under article 28. As to States not parties to the Statute, no obligation of transfer can be imposed, but cooperation can be sought in accordance with article 56. . . .

(3) Paragraph 2 spells out the extent of the obligation of a State party to respond to a transfer request. Four different situations have to be considered, as follows:

(a) All States parties to the Statute will have accepted the Court's "inherent" jurisdiction over genocide under articles 20(a) and 21(1)(a). In that case, subject to the other safeguards and guarantees in the Statute, the transfer obligation in article 53(2)(a) will apply.

(b) The same obligation should apply to States parties which have accepted the jurisdiction of the Court with respect to the crime in question; they must take immediate steps to arrest and surrender the accused person to the Court under paragraph 2(a).

(c) In the case of crimes defined by the annexed treaties, a State party which is also a party to the relevant treaty defining the crime in question but which has not accepted the Court's jurisdiction must arrest and either transfer, extradite or prosecute the accused.

(d) In any other case, a State party must consider whether its own law permits the arrest and transfer of the accused. As to other crimes under general international law, some States may not have some of these crimes (e.g. aggression) as part of their own criminal code; it was thought that the only obligation that could be imposed in such cases, if a State does not accept the jurisdiction of the Court in relation to the crimes, was that spelt out in paragraph 2(c).

(4) As to the relationship between extradition and transfer, several provisions of article 53 are relevant. Under paragraph 2(b), a State which is a party to the relevant treaty defining the crime but which has not accepted the jurisdiction of the Court with respect to a crime is under an *aut dedere aut judicare* obligation, and thus has the option of extraditing the accused to a requesting State. . . . Under paragraph 4, a State party which accepts the Court's jurisdiction over the crime must, as far as possible, give priority to a transfer request from the Court, bearing in mind that such a request will not have been made before the confirmation of the indictment and an opportunity on the part of the interested States to challenge the Court's jurisdiction or the admissibility of the particular case, which is provided for under articles 34 or 35. The words "as far as possible" inserted in paragraph 4 reflect, on the one hand, the inability of the Statute to affect the legal position of non-parties, and, on the other hand, the difficulties of imposing a completely homogeneous obligation on States parties to the Statute given the wide range of situations covered.

(5) Transfer to the Court is to be taken, as between parties to the Statute which accept the jurisdiction of the Court with respect to the crime, to constitute compliance with *aut dedere aut judicare* provisions in extradition treaties: paragraph 3. In other cases it is recognized that the decision as between transfer or extradition must rest with the requested State, in particular so far as requests from non-parties to the Statute are concerned, and this being so there is no reason to disadvantage requesting States that have become parties to the Statute but have not accepted the Court's jurisdiction in a given case.

(6) Taking these various provisions together, it is the view of the Commission that these provisions provide adequate guarantees that the Statute will not undermine existing and functional extradition arrangements. Some members, however, felt that paragraph 4 went too far in the direction of giving priority to the Court's jurisdiction as compared with that of a State requesting extradition: they stressed that the Court should in no case interfere with existing and functioning extradition agreements. . . .

Article 54. Obligation to Extradite or Prosecute

In a case of a crime referred to in article 20 (e), a custodial State party to this Statute which is a party to the treaty in question but which has not accepted the Court's jurisdiction with respect to the crime for the purposes of article 21 (1) (b) (i) shall either take all necessary steps to extradite the suspect to a requesting State for the purpose of prosecution or refer the case to its competent authorities for that purpose.

Commentary

(1) . . . Article 54 is, in effect, a corollary for States parties to the Statute of unwillingness to accept the Court's jurisdiction in respect of apparently well-founded charges of treaty crimes.

(2) Thus, a State party whose acceptance of the Court's jurisdiction is necessary, but does not accept the jurisdiction, is under an *aut dedere aut judicare* obligation, equivalent to the obligation included in most of the treaties listed in the Annex. As between parties to the Statute this in effect integrates the International Criminal Court into the existing system of international criminal jurisdiction and cooperation in respect of treaty crimes. It should avoid the situation of a State party in effect giving asylum to an accused person in relation to prima facie justified charges of crimes which have been accepted as such by that State. On the other hand it gives States parties the same range of options when confronted with a request for transfer of an accused that they have now under the listed treaties, unless the State in question has expressly accepted the jurisdiction of the Court in relation to the crime: see article 53(2(a).

(3) The Commission gave careful consideration to the question whether an equivalent obligation should be imposed on States parties generally with respect to the crimes under general international law referred to in article 20(b)-(d). On balance it decided that this was difficult to achieve with respect to such crimes in the absence of a secure jurisdictional basis or a widely accepted extradition regime. The problem is most acute with respect to article 20(d) (crimes against humanity), but many States do not have as part of their criminal law a provision specifically dealing with such crimes.

From a careful study of the above two articles and the Commission's commentary thereto, one may conclude that in reexamining its 1993 Draft Statute the ILC made considerable progress in achieving the three goals set by its Working Group (see pages 994-995 supra). First, it not only simplified, but also helpfully clarified the provisions concerning the proposed Court's subject matter jurisdiction (Article 20 and the annex). Moreover, by taking an "opt-in" approach, the Commission obviously hopes to obtain greater state support for its 1994 Draft Statute. Second, by establishing a system of concurrent jurisdiction — one which in some ways tilts toward the Court (e.g., Article 53(2)(a)) but simultaneously envisages a major role for national courts, especially when a state has ratified the Court's Statute but not accepted its jurisdiction with respect to a certain crime (e.g., Article 54) — the Commission has struck what appears to be a sensible balance between the need for an active Court and the desire not to undermine existing treaty and extradition arrangements. In view of the relative success of the "piecemeal" treaty approach, to be considered in the next section, plus the concern in some quarters that granting the Court substantial compulsory jurisdiction would disrupt the existing system of international law enforcement (see, e.g., Scharf, supra page 976, at 164-166, reflecting the views of previous U.S. administrations), the balance struck in the 1994 Draft Statute seems just about right. Third, the Commission has paid some —

albeit relatively little — attention to coordinating its catalogue of crimes found in Article 20 and the annex of the Draft Statute with the crimes contained in Articles 12-26 of its 1991 Draft Code of Crimes Against the Peace and Security of Mankind (see page 960 supra). True, it tipped its hat to the Draft Code by inserting "the crime of aggression" into Article 20, but it ignored such Draft Code staples as "colonial domination and other forms of alien domination"; "recruitment, use, financing and training of merce-naries"; and "wilful and severe damage to the environment." Having severed the cord between the Draft Code and the Draft Statute, the Commission seemed content to ignore the former, leaving its much-needed revision to another day.

It should be noted that the ILC's Working Group viewed the Draft Statute as an attachment to a future international convention and drafted the Statute's provisions accordingly. Thus, it comes as no surprise that, after adopting the 1994 Draft Statute and its commentaries, the Commission recommended to the General Assembly that it convene an international conference to study its work product and conclude a convention on the establishment of an international criminal court. Report of the International Law Commission to the General Assembly, 49 U.N. GAOR Supp. (No. 10) at 43, U.N. Doc. A/49/10 (1994). Whether the General Assembly accepts this recommendation or decides to undertake the task itself, prospects for an international criminal court at long last seem to be looking up.

Yet, as the above materials reveal, many issues in connection with the Court still remain controversial, and considerable revisions may have to be made to accommodate political as well as legal concerns. Many "technical" issues of the kind mentioned in connection with the Yugoslav War Crimes Tribunal (see pages 978-992 supra) will need review and refining. Indeed, the experience of that Tribunal and the Rwandan War Crimes Tribunal may necessitate remedial revisions of the ILC's Draft Statute. Nevertheless, much progress has been made in the past few years toward the establish-ment of an international criminal court. Since the prime purpose of this exercise has been to create an institution to help protect the human rights that individuals already are guaranteed by general international law or mul-tilateral treaties, it is to be hoped that more progress will be made in the near future and that this 40-year endeavor will be brought to a successful conclusion.

D. NGO Efforts to Draft a Statute for an International Criminal Court

In the absence of UN initiatives to establish an international criminal court after the 1950s, non-governmental organizations took the lead in pro-moting the idea and eventually produced a number of draft statutes for such a court. See generally B. Ferencz, An International Criminal Court (1980) (2 vols.). Among them are the Foundation for the Establishment of an International Criminal Court (see Toward a Feasible International Criminal Court (J. Stone and R. Woetzel eds. 1970)), the International Law Association (see International Criminal Law Committee, Sixth Interim Report, in International Law Association, Report of the Sixty-First Conference 252, 257 (Paris 1984)), and the International Association of Penal Law (see M. Bassiouni, A Draft International Criminal Code and Draft Statute for an International Criminal Tribunal 215 (1987)).

These efforts were inspired, at least in part, by Article 6 of the Genocide Convention (see the Documentary Supplement) and Article V of the International Convention on the Suppression and Punishment of the Crime of Apartheid, Nov. 30, 1973, G.A. Res. 3068, 28 U.N. GAOR Supp. (No. 30) at 75, 76, U.N. Doc. A/9030 (1974), both of which permit the trial of persons charged with convention violations by an international penal tribunal having jurisdiction with respect to those states parties that have accepted its jurisdiction. Indeed, pursuant to a 1979 request from the United Nations, Professor Bassiouni, the current president of the International Association of Penal Law, prepared a lengthy report for circulation to member states that included a Draft Convention on the Establishment of an International Penal Tribunal for the Suppression and Punishment of the Crime of Apartheid and Other International Crimes. See Bassiouni and Derby, Final Report on the Establishment of an International Criminal Court for the Implementation of the Apartheid Convention and Other Relevant International Instruments, 9 Hofstra L. Rev. 523, 547 (1981).

Professor Bassiouni later used the above Draft Convention as a model for his draft statute for an international criminal court, which was submitted to the Eighth UN Congress on the Prevention of Crime and the Treatment of Offenders in 1990 (U.N. Doc. A/CONF.144/NGO7 (1990), reprinted in 15 Nova L. Rev. 353 (1991)). He subsequently revised and published it in M. Bassiouni, Draft Statute International Tribunal, 10 Nouvelles Etudes Pénales (1993). Without doubt it was one of the draft statutes that the ILC's Working Group had in mind when it acknowledged taking NGO studies into account while preparing its 1994 Draft Statute. See Working Group on a Draft Statute for an International Criminal Court, Report of the Working Group, U.N. Doc. A/CN.4/L.491/Rev. 2, at 3 (1994).

E. U.S. Attitudes Toward an International Criminal Court

One of the arguments against U.S. ratification of the Genocide Convention, first raised during the early 1950s, was that U.S. citizens conceivably could be tried for the crime in foreign courts where they would not have the benefit of U.S. constitutional safeguards. Compare Parker, An International Criminal Court: The Case for Its Adoption, 38 A.B.A. J. 641 (1952) with Finch, An International Criminal Court: The Case Against Its Adoption, 38 A.B.A. J. 644 (1952). Article 6 of the Convention raises this possibility by providing that "[p]ersons charged with genocide . . . shall be tried by a competent tribunal of the State in the territory of which the act was committed, or by such international penal tribunal as may have jurisdiction with respect to those Contracting Parties which shall have accepted its jurisdiction."

The likelihood of a U.S. citizen being tried abroad is sought to be reduced by the following understanding that the Senate attached to its advice and consent to the Convention's ratification: "nothing in Article VI affects the right of any state to bring to trial before its own tribunals any of its nationals for acts committed outside a state." Senate Comm. on Foreign Relations, Report on the International Convention on the Prevention and Punishment of the Crime of Genocide, S. Exec. Rep. 2, 99th Cong., 1st Sess. 23 (1985). This understanding makes it clear that the United States reserves the right to try "its nationals for acts of genocide regardless of where the acts took place. Were, for example, a United States citizen accused of genocidal acts abroad, the United States could meet its obligations under Article VI by prosecuting him under United States law." Id. at 24. Of course, the U.S. citizen alleged to have committed genocide abroad can count on a U.S. trial only if he is physically within the jurisdiction of the United States; if he is physically within the state where the conduct allegedly occurred, that state would have jurisdiction to try him for the crime under its criminal justice system.

This reluctance to allow U.S. citizens to be tried by foreign courts pales into utter insignificance when compared to the unwillingness of the Senate even to contemplate such trials by an international criminal court. This unwillingness, repeatedly reflected in the record over the years, finds legal expression in another understanding that the Senate attached to its advice and consent to the ratification of the Genocide Convention: "with regard to the reference to an international penal tribunal in Article VI of the Convention, the United States declares that it reserves the right to effect its participation in any such tribunal only by a treaty entered into specifically for that purpose with the advice and consent of the Senate." Id. at 25. The Senate report explained the rationale behind the understanding as follows:

> The international penal tribunal contemplated by Article VI represents a sharp departure from the concepts contained in the Genocide Convention. The Convention is an agreement among the parties to make certain acts criminal under their municipal laws and to prosecute individuals accused of violating them. The notion of an international penal tribunal suggests the existence of a body of law separate from the municipal laws of the contracting parties. What this law would be and what procedures would govern in proceedings before the tribunal remain to be determined.

From time to time different organs of the United Nations have considered draft conventions establishing such a tribunal. The Committee is extremely skeptical of these efforts. It notes, among other things, that serious Constitutional objections to U.S. participation have been raised. Given the novelty of the concept and the fact that U.S. adherence would raise many legal and policy issues, U.S. agreement to a convention creating a penal tribunal should only be effected with the advice and consent of the Senate.

Id. at 25-26.

Nevertheless, there are some indications that at least on the congressional front the concept of an international criminal court is no longer always an anathema. Section 1201(c) of the Omnibus Diplomatic and Antiterrorism Act of 1986, Pub. L. No. 99-399, 100 Stat. 853, 896 (1986), a "sense of the Congress" provision, urges the President to consider the negotiation of "an international criminal tribunal for prosecuting terrorists." Similarly, Section 4108 of the Anti-Drug Abuse Act of 1988, Pub. L. No. 100-690, 102 Stat. 4181, 4267 (1988), provides as follows:

Sec. 4108. International Criminal Court

(a) IN GENERAL. — It is the sense of the Senate that the President should begin discussions with foreign governments to investigate the feasibility and advisability of establishing an international criminal court to expedite cases regarding the prosecution of persons accused of having engaged in international drug trafficking or having committed international crimes.

(b) UNITED STATES CITIZENS. — Such discussions shall not include any commitment that such court shall have jurisdiction over the extradition of United States citizens and shall assure that any international agreement shall recognize the rights and privileges guaranteed to United States citizens under the United States Constitution.

Thereafter, both Congressmen Leach and Senator Specter wrote op-ed pieces urging the establishment of such a court. Leach, Don't Help Pol Pot. Try Him, N.Y. Times, Sept. 27, 1989, at A29, cols. 2-5; Specter, A World Court for Terrorists, N.Y. Times, July 9, 1989, §4, at 27, cols. 1-3. Thereafter, the Foreign Operations Appropriations Act of 1991 contained a request that the President "explore the need for the establishment of an International Criminal Court on a universal or regional basis to assist the International Community in dealing more effectively with criminal acts defined in international conventions. . . ." Foreign Operations, Export Financing, and Related Programs Appropriations Act of 1991, Pub. L. No. 101-513, §599E(b)(1), 104 Stat. 1979, 2066 (1991).

At present, it is impossible to say whether the above episodic expression of support for some sort of international criminal court ever will materialize into a serious congressional, or even Executive Branch, commitment to the idea. According to two Sixth Committee observers, in 1993 "[t]he United States described the report of the ILC working group as excellent, thoughtful, serious and deserving of attention by member states and indicated a somewhat more favorable position toward the court than in previous years,"

Morris and Bourloyannis-Vrailas, supra page 994, at 350, and the adoption of the Commission's 1994 Draft Code, which appears to take into account most U.S. concerns, may mark a turning point toward active support of the UN's international criminal court initiative.

IV.   The Progressive Development of International Criminal Law: The "Piecemeal" Convention Approach Coupled with Domestic Enforcement

On page 942 supra of this Problem, it is suggested that "municipal law cannot be regarded as a satisfactory instrument whereby international criminal law may be implemented," a point made directly or indirectly in several other readings. Yet, as the materials in the prior sections suggest and in this section demonstrate, in the area of transnational terrorism, as well as apartheid, torture, and hostage-taking, this approach is increasingly being followed, in "piecemeal" fashion. Indeed, at present it may be the most realistic way to both develop progressively and enforce effectively international criminal law. Consider the arguments for and against this approach in the readings below.

A.   Transnational Terrorism

Gross, International Terrorism and International Criminal Jurisdiction
67 Am. J. Intl. L. 508, 509-511 (1973)

Since the elaboration of the Draft Code [by the ILC in 1953], the work of United Nations on terrorism in its various manifestations has been in response to events and consequently piecemeal. This has been so whether one considers the three hijacking conventions or the draft articles on the Prevention and Punishment of Crimes against Diplomatic Agents and other Internationally Protected Persons prepared by the International Law Commission, or the U.S. Draft Convention for the Prevention and Punishment of Certain Acts of International Terrorism, submitted to the 1972 session of the General Assembly. This latter project fared very badly in the Sixth Committee where it was submerged in the boundless problem of the underlying causes of terrorism and never surfaced again.

In any event, it is doubtful whether this piecemeal approach will add up to a comprehensive system for the prevention and punishment of terrorist activities. Certainly without a tribunal to give a degree of coherence and consistency to the several international instruments, their application by national tribunals may well fall short of the objectives of certainty and impartiality.

It is gratifying, therefore, to note that an unofficial organization, The Foundation for the Establishment of an International Criminal Court, is devoted to the study of the problem of terrorism in the broad framework of the League and the Draft Code of Offences against the Peace and Security of Mankind rather than in the current response-to-events manner of the United Nations. Under the direction of its President, Professor Robert K. Woetzel, the Foundation continued work on drafting a convention on international crimes and a statute for an international court. . . .

The draft on international crimes has been made more comprehensive than the 1953 Draft Code by the inclusion of hijacking, kidnapping of public officials, acts of violence against internationally protected persons, international acts of terrorism, illicit traffic in drugs, and finally international pollution of the environment "causing substantial harm to the health, safety and welfare of mankind." The substantive convention is linked to the proposed criminal court in the same fashion in which the League of Nations linked the International Criminal Court to its Convention on Terrorism: each party undertakes to prosecute the alleged offender or to extradite him or to surrender him to the International Criminal Court. . . .

The former Secretary-General of the United Nations, U Thant, was reported to have suggested the creation of an international tribunal to deal with hijacking of airplanes because such crimes were "directed against an international service affecting a diversity of nations, men and interests." They were in a different category from other crimes and therefore "could not be dealt with by national courts defending the interests of one particular people or nation." The Foundation, like the League of Nations and the United Nations in its earlier phase, is concerned with at least offering the possibility of an international proceeding for what are substantially international crimes, that is, crimes affecting more than one state or an international service. The Foundation has performed and it will continue to perform a useful function in educating jurists of different countries in a vital problem area of an evolving body of international law, in both its substantive and procedural aspects.

Murphy, Woetzel, and Lador-Lederer, Correspondence [About Professor Gross's Comments]
68 Am. J. Intl. L. 306-308, 717-719 (1974)

By way of editorial comment in the July 1973 issue of the Journal, Professor Leo Gross, in his usual thoughtful and scholarly manner, takes note . . . that, in its early efforts, the United Nations followed the "comprehensive" approach of the League in preparing the Draft Code of Offences against the Peace and Security of Mankind and a statute for an International Criminal Court. In contrasting these efforts with recent UN work on terrorism, Professor Gross expresses doubt that the present "piecemeal" approach "will add up to a comprehensive system for the prevention and punishment of terrorist activities." In any event, he believes, "without a tribunal to give a degree of coherence and consistency to the several international instruments, their application by national tribunals may well fall short of the objectives of certainty and impartiality."

It is not my purpose to deprecate Professor Gross's well-taken comments concerning the quality of the work of the Foundation for the Establishment of an International Criminal Court. On the contrary, I agree that the Foundation has made a commendable contribution to international jurisprudence, which may well serve as a model for official action. More troubling, however, are Professor Gross's negative description of the recent work of the United Nations on terrorism as "piecemeal" and "in response to events" and the implication in his remarks that a return to the more "comprehensive" approach of the League is needed.

In his comments to the Sixth Committee concerning the U.S. Draft Convention for the Prevention and Punishment of Certain Acts of International Terrorism, the U.S. representative referred to the broad approach taken by the League in its conventions on terrorism and an international criminal court, and suggested, correctly in my opinion, that the League's ambitious approach was a primary reason for the refusal of member states to accept the conventions. (Statement of Ambassador W. Tapley Bennett, Jr., to the Sixth Committee, Nov. 13, 1972, 68 Dept. State Bull. 85 (1973).) Professor Gross's answer to this contention is that the failure of member states to ratify the conventions is not a conclusive argument against the soundness of the League approach, in light of the high craftsmanship reflected in these documents and of the need for comprehensive coverage of the substantive law and its impartial and uniform application by an international tribunal. But it may be questioned whether the crucial issue is the quality of the League's work product or the need for an impartial international criminal court. The crucial issue would seem rather to be what approach will most effectively prevent and punish acts of international terrorism, given that these acts have greatly increased in number and pose an immediate threat of the greatest magnitude to minimal world order.

As noted by Professor Gross, the U.S. Draft Convention did not meet with a favorable reception at the 27th General Assembly. Instead of adopting the Convention, the Assembly decided to establish an ad hoc committee to study the problem and make recommendations for action. A primary reason for this unfavorable reception, inter alia, was that, in spite of the efforts of the U.S. delegation, the discussion in the Sixth Committee on the Draft Convention did not focus on the specific acts sought to be covered but rather went into almost all areas that arguably have involved or might involve terrorist activities.

Two areas into which discussion wandered in the Sixth Committee were so-called state terrorism — i.e., illegal threats or use of force by states, in particular the use of force to deny the right to self-determination — and the underlying causes of terrorism. With respect to state terrorism, in a recent statement to the United Nations Ad Hoc Committee on International Terrorism, the United States representative pointed out that "[t]he Declaration of Principles of International Law Concerning Friendly Relations has covered most aspects of interstate violence and has affirmed such fundamental principles as the prohibition of the threat or use of force, equal rights and self-determination, and the good-faith fulfillment obligations. . . ." He suggested that the Ad Hoc Committee should not "rework" this area and should instead "concentrate on those acts of violence by individuals or groups which do not involve, directly or indirectly, state action." As to the question of the causes underlying acts of terrorism, the U.S. representative was of the opinion that consideration of this "long range effort" should not interfere with the adoption on an urgent basis of measures to prevent and punish individual acts of international terrorism. Rather, in his view, it was necessary to "adopt means to deal with present violence while we devote parallel efforts to the study of its causes and ways to bring about its elimination." (Statement of Ambassador W. Tapley Bennett, Jr., to the UN Ad Hoc Committee on International Terrorism, July 24, 1973, 69 Dept. State Bull. 85 (1973).)

These remarks on the causes of terrorism are apposite to Professor Gross's call for a return to a more comprehensive approach on international terrorism. Such an approach could divert attention away from efforts to prevent and punish such individual acts of international terrorism as hijacking of airplanes, attacks on diplomats, the sending of letter bombs through the mails, and the murder of innocent civilians. This is not to say that the adoption of a comprehensive convention on all forms of terrorism and the establishment of an international criminal court are unworthy goals. It is to say that they are goals that, in the present world atmosphere of hostility and tension, must be regarded as of a long range nature. . . .

There is a compelling need for worldwide agreement on measures to combat the rash of individual acts of international terrorism endangering innocent citizens. To this end the United Nations should adopt, and member states should ratify, a convention dealing with the most serious individual acts of international terrorism, either the U.S. draft or another containing effective measures. The recently adopted UN Convention on the Prevention and Punishment of Crimes against Diplomatic Agents and other Internationally protected Persons should be widely ratified by member states. For its part ICAO should continue to seek wide ratification of the Tokyo, Hague, and Montreal Conventions dealing with interference with civil aviation, and should reach agreement on a system of sanctions, such as suspension of all air service, to be applied against states which have not ratified these conventions and which allow hijackers to use their territories as sanctuaries. Adoption of these measures would not only constitute an effective response to the urgent problems of international terrorism, but also might create an atmosphere allowing diplomats and international lawyers to turn again to the important task of drafting a comprehensive convention on international terrorism and a statute for an international criminal court.

JOHN F. MURPHY

With due appreciation of Professor Murphy's kudos regarding "the quality of the work of the Foundation for the Establishment of an International Criminal Court" and our "commendable contribution to international jurisprudence which may well serve as a model for official action," it appears necessary to us to clarify our approach in the light of other statements of Professor Murphy regarding Professor Gross's comments. The Foundation's draft Convention on International Crimes and draft Statute for an International Criminal Court do not envisage an obligatory comprehensive approach. Quite the contrary, in ratifying or acceding to the Convention on International Crimes each party shall make a declaration with respect to those acts for which it accepts the obligations under the Convention, e.g. crimes against peace, war crimes, crimes against humanity, slavery, piracy, hijacking, terrorism, international traffic in illicit drugs, etc. (Article 3). This allows states "freedom of choice" and could not possibly "direct attention away from efforts to prevent and punish such individual acts of international terrorism as hijacking of airplanes. . . ."

Furthermore, the draft Statute for an International Criminal Court does not rule out alternate jurisdiction of states, nor is the jurisdiction of the proposed Court obligatory unless specified by a state. Once the Court exists any state, whether a party to the Convention creating the Court or not, could by its unilateral decision deliver suspects (submit cases) to the Court. The Court could be seized without the requirement of consent of the state of which the suspect is a citizen or of any other state or states, which is significantly different from the Nuremberg scheme. This would be equitable because all parties would have the right to deliver each other's citizens to the Court. Such delivery to an outside, impartial Court could not be criticized because the Court would be expected to be, if anything, fairer than domestic courts of an opposing party. At present three highly unsatisfactory choices are frequently resorted to, namely trial of defeated opponents by victors, or indefinite incarceration without trial, or elimination without due process.

The Court would also deal with cases of a nonpolitical character, such as narcotic smugglers, and cases of a nongovernmental character such as hijackers. The draft Statute envisages solutions other than criminal adjudication; it would facilitate and institutionalize machinery for compromises such as those negotiated between Bangladesh, India, and Pakistan concerning war crimes suspects and exchange of populations. It would be empowered to render advisory opinions. In short, the plan would create new methods to debrutalize and depoliticize the international scene and contribute to international and domestic morality without interfering with the sovereignty of states. Nor would there be any imputation of collective guilt, since the Court would deal with individuals, which incidentally the International Court of Justice at The Hague is not empowered to do. The proposed International Criminal Court would assist states in cases which they are either unable or unwilling to try themselves.

[Finally, the Foundation for the Establishment of an International Criminal Court] will continue in accordance with Professor Gross's comments to fulfill the function of educating jurists of different countries in this vital problem area both in and outside of the world body. To this end Rules of Procedure have now been drafted for the institution of a Commission of Inquiry as a first step in the establishment of a reliable system of world criminal justice based on the principle of impartiality and due process of law. This should fulfill the prerequisites for practicality as stated by Professor Murphy in his letter.

ROBERT K. WOETZEL

. . . Professor Gross is certainly in no need of my support for his thesis; but having reached, independently, the same conclusions, I hope I may be permitted to refer to a paper I recently published "A Legal Approach to International Terrorism" [9 Israel L. Rev. 194 (1974)]. In that article I argued that outlawry of both genocide and terrorism follows the same humanitarian, philosophical, and moral guidance; that they must also follow the same legal methods; that they are interdependent and complementary; and that the postwar affluent societies are prepared to give preference to any pragmatic compromise in order to avoid the risk of having to fight blackmail.

That said, I certainly agree with Professor Murphy that "the crucial issue" is "what approach will most effectively prevent and punish acts of international terrorism"; but I do not agree with him that the last General Assembly would have succeeded had it "focus[ed] on the specific acts sought to be covered." If I understood Professor Gross correctly, he also disagrees with this view. I would therefore also not agree that the statements made by Ambassador Bennett were "apposite to Professor Gross's call for a return to a more comprehensive approach" (which, incidentally, is also mine).

What I deplore in this case is not the clash of philosophies but that this difference of approach alone made it possible for the debate in the Assembly's Sixth Committee to be cynical and desultory. What was important was the apparent impression given by the U.S. approach that it was intended (I repeat the quotation and add emphasis) to "focus on the *specific acts sought to be covered.*" Indeed, half measures are half persecution and half release; they are half respect of the law and half a snubbing of it. And in this case, as

I have tried to show, the law is the norm postulating genocide to be an international crime, and terrorism to be "bit-by-bit" genocide.

To prove this point, I refer to: (a) figures which Professor Quintana has published — originating with ICAO and according to which out of 134 cases (120 hijackings and 14 acts of sabotage) only 72 hijackers were apprehended (figures up to July 1970); and (b) a schedule drawn up by one of my colleagues [not here included] which shows that out of 161 terrorists the world over, which one could not help but arrest, less than ten are positively known to have remained in prison to expiate their crime, 50 more are perhaps being held for trial, but a full hundred are positively known to have been released under conditions (blackmail) which themselves are crimes.

I must add a caveat to this list: it makes no claim to be exhaustive; it is a "minimum list" for illustration purposes only. It excludes not a few more cases where foreign administrations found it expedient not to divulge facts because they took no action lest they might invite further terrorist acts designed to liberate terrorists in detention (as happened with the murders of the Israeli participants in the Munich Olympics, and, more recently, at Karachi). Add thereto the playing-down of preparatory terrorist acts: conspiracy and part execution. (Compare the approach by the League of Nations with the latest draft!) Those are failures (and Professor Murphy too makes the point) in contemporary attempts at international regulation. But, as I hope I may be allowed to point out, the failure of these efforts was made possible because of the justified anticipation by those concerned of the strictly controlled, lukewarm support of the Great Powers for any such measure. . . .

J. LADOR-LEDERER

B. Apartheid, Torture, Hostage-Taking

The "piecemeal" convention approach to combating transnational terrorism, as the above readings make clear, relies upon the domestic enforcement of domestic criminal law, the latter enacted to fulfill a state's obligation to "domesticate" the offense criminalized by the particular convention. To date this approach has been taken in the Hague Convention for the Suppression of Unlawful Seizure of Aircraft, Dec. 16, 1970, arts. 2, 4, 7, & 8, [1971] 22 U.S.T. 1641, T.I.A.S. No. 7192; the Montreal Convention for the Suppression of Unlawful Acts Against the Safety of Civil Aviation, Sept. 23, 1971, arts. 3, 5, 7, & 8, [1973] 24 U.S.T. 565, T.I.A.S. No. 7570; and the UN Convention on the Prevention and Punishment of Crimes Against Internationally Protected Persons, Including Diplomatic Agents, Dec. 14, 1973, arts. 2, 3, 7, & 8, [1977] 28 U.S.T. 1975, T.I.A.S. No. 8532.

In addition to its use in the transnational terrorism context, the "piecemeal" approach to international criminal law has been tried in the apartheid, torture, and hostage-taking areas. The International Convention on the Suppression and Punishment of the Crime of Apartheid, Nov. 30, 1973, arts. I, IV, & V, G.A. Res. 3068, 28 U.N. GAOR Supp. (No. 30) at 75, U.N. Doc. A/9030 (1974), which, unlike the transnational terrorism conventions, the United States has not ratified, actually goes beyond its terrorism counterparts and contains several provisions compatible with the Gross-Woetzel approach. Article I, for instance, declares that apartheid is "a crime against humanity," and that inhuman acts resulting from it are "crimes violating the principles of international law," while Article V, in addition to providing more explicitly that domestic courts may try offenders under the principle of universal jurisdiction, adds the provision (nearly identical with the one found in Article 6 of the Genocide Convention, page 1002 supra) that trial also may occur before "an international penal tribunal having jurisdiction with respect to those States Parties which shall have accepted its jurisdiction." This latter option, of course, is a purely theoretical one at this time.

The Convention Against Torture and Other Cruel, Inhuman or Degrading Treatment or Punishment, Dec. 10, 1984, arts. 1, 4, 7, & 8, G.A. Res. 39/46, 39 U.N. GAOR Supp. (No. 51) at 197, U.N. Doc. A/39/51 (1984), which the United States ratified in 1994, closely tracks the language of the three transnational terrorism conventions, as does the International Convention Against the Taking of Hostages, Dec. 17, 1979, arts. 1, 2, 6, & 8, G.A. Res. 34/146, 34 U.N. GAOR Supp. (No. 46) at 245, U.N. Doc. A/34/46 (1980), which the United States ratified in 1985. Under the Hostage Taking Act, 18 U.S.C. §1203 (1994), enacted to implement its Convention obligations, the United States has successfully prosecuted a Lebanese resident-citizen for the hijacking of a Jordanian civilian aircraft in the Middle East with three U.S. nationals aboard. United States v. Yunis, 681 F. Supp. 896, 904-905 (D.D.C. 1988). The district court held, inter alia, that aircraft piracy and hostage-taking were international crimes justifying the assertion of universal jurisdiction. Id. at 900-901.

An even more recent example of the "piecemeal" convention approach is the Convention for the Suppression of Unlawful Acts Against the Safety of Maritime Navigation, with Related Protocol, Mar. 10, 1988, arts. 3, 5, 10, & 11, I.M.O. Doc. SUA/CON/15 (1988), reprinted in 27 Intl. Legal Materials 668 (1988), which the United States has yet to ratify. Message of the President Transmitting the Convention for the Suppression of Unlawful Acts Against the Safety of Maritime Navigation, with Related Protocol, S. Treaty Doc. No. 1, 101st Cong., 1st Sess. (1989). See generally Halberstam, Terrorism on the High Seas: The Achille Lauro, Piracy and the IMO Convention on Maritime Safety, 82 Am. J. Intl. L. 269 (1988). Thus, the trend toward what Professor Bassiouni has called the "indirect enforcement system" of international criminal law continues apace. See Bassiouni, The Penal Characteristics of Conventional International Criminal Law, 15 Case W. Res. J. Intl. L. 27, 29-37 passim (1983).

For arguments supporting the right of non-parties to the "piecemeal" conventions to exercise universal jurisdiction over proscribed offenses with which they have no connection, see Randall, Universal Jurisdiction Under International Law, 66 Tex. L. Rev. 785, 815-841 (1988). The American Law Institute has taken the position that "piracy, slave trade, attacks on or hijacking of aircraft, genocide, war crimes, and perhaps certain acts of terrorism" are offenses subject to universal jurisdiction as a matter of customary international law. Restatement (Third) of the Foreign Relations Law of the United States §404 (1987). "Universal jurisdiction for additional offenses is provided by international agreements, but it remains to be determined whether universal jurisdiction over a particular offense has become customary law for states not party to such an agreement." Id., §404, comment at 255.

V. Other Suggested Uses of the International Criminal Process

Domestically, a criminal justice system involves far more than just the trial of individual offenders. Indeed, such trials, while the focal point of the system, are a relatively minor part of it. Grand juries, indictments, and plea bargaining all play an important part in punishing offenders and, notionally, deterring future criminal behavior. While most of the literature on international criminal law also focuses upon bringing the individual offender to trial, a small number of scholars have begun to suggest other ways in which the emerging international criminal justice system can play a role in curtailing human rights violations. Extracts from the works of two such scholars follow.

Mueller, Two Enforcement Models for International Criminal Justice
in Etudes en l'honneur de Jean Graven 107, 107-115 (1969)

[The author states that past efforts to hold persons criminally responsible for starting and conducting wars have been futile.]

The past efforts to which I refer are, of course, the United Nations Draft Statute for an International Criminal Court, and its Draft Code of Offenses Against the Peace and Security of Mankind. The latter, sometimes referred to as the Substantive International Criminal Code, was a fantastically simplistic document, drafted by well-meaning international lawyers and international politicians, but utterly lacking the sophistication of the specialists in criminal law and criminology. For the last decade it has lingered in the International Law Commission of the United Nations. . . .

Work on the creation of an international criminal court, under the Draft Statute for an International Criminal Court, has been totally in abeyance, for if there be no substantive international criminal law, under a substantive code, there need be no court and no procedure. . . .

In reviewing the past efforts, it seems to me that the proponents have been too naively optimistic. When Germany, the aggressor of World War II, had been fully defeated, it was an all too simple fallacy to construct an international criminal justice model on the idea of an easy application of a redistributive sanction on defendants in the custody of the judging part of mankind. Two decades later it seems unlikely that total defeats with consequent easy imposition of retributive sanctions will be the rule. On the contrary, the model of the late 1940s and early 1950s contains two fallacies: that of the defeated and prostrate, easily available defendant, and that of retributive justice.

The model of international criminal justice of the future must contain two changes: it must be directed to a relatively powerful, not easily available defendant, and it should aim at preventive — or deterrent — sanctions.

Implicitly, I am sure, it is generally recognized that such an attitudinal change in our approach must take place, for reasons of political reality as well as to reflect the progress in penological thinking. Perhaps it is this recognition which has created the current frustration and stalemate in the development. It must be our task to find a way out of the impasse: Heads of state of powerful nations could wage aggressive wars, in hopes of winning them, for whatever reasons of prestige, honor, glory, or principle, because abject defeat and consequent Nuremberg-style justice seem virtually impossible. Heads of state of small nations could wage aggressive wars, whether on their own or some other nation's account, for they, too, fear no retributive justice. Moreover, little nations are much more certain to obtain the sympathy of the rest of the world in any such conflict than big nations, simply because they are small. World opinion plays a major, perhaps a decisive role, in international conflicts today. Might it not be possible to put such world opinion into the service of international criminal law, by channelizing it from the present political arenas into those of an international penal tribunal?

The past model relied absolutely on the jurisdictional and enforcement power of an international criminal court, and an execution arm of that court. It is clear now that the powerful nations of this world are not about to commit themselves now to a surrender of their heads of state and cabinet ministers for trial before an international criminal court — though they might be willing to conceive of the creation of such a court! And even if they were to bind themselves *now* to surrender their heads of state and cabinet officers when summoned, they might have second thoughts when such summonses are issued. In short, the old model stood and fell with the idea of a prostrate, defeated nation, with no power to resist the jurisdiction of a court.

The new model must rest on the idea that unwilling heads of state must be coerced by an international judicial apparatus, without their consent, and perhaps not even through trial. The solution would center on the problems of (1) subjecting non-consenting, uncooperative third parties to the powers of an international judicial apparatus, and (2) using sanctions short of physical constraint, but powerful in terms of psychological force. Let us begin with the consideration of criminal jurisdiction over a non-consenting uncooperative defendant.

Let it be assumed that one hundred and ten smaller member nations of the United Nations were to agree on the establishment of an International Criminal Court with jurisdiction over crimes as envisaged under the Draft Code of Offenses against the Peace and Security of Mankind. Let it be assumed also that the remaining major powers would not ratify such a convention. It can no longer be doubted that international law would have come into effect which would bind even the non-consenting U.N. members — and non-members of the U.N. — if they were to become aggressors, and would thus seem to fall under the jurisdiction of the court in question.

A majority of nations of this world may indeed legislate for a dissenting minority and bind that minority. But the matter does not end there. For even if the few hypothetical non-consenting major powers would be bound de jure by the jurisdiction of such a newly to be created international criminal court, would they not refuse de facto to accept the jurisdiction of such a court?

It might be argued that trials for waging aggressive war or for other offenses against the peace and security of mankind could be statutorily authorized against absent parties. But trials in absentia are unknown in Anglo-American countries, are regarded as distasteful, and unjust, and have limited effect even in civil law jurisdictions.

However, proceedings for the finding of indictments, informations or accusatory pleadings, are ex parte in most nations of the world, and the testing of such accusations for their legal sufficiency for purposes of a potential trial thereunder likewise may be had without the defendant's presence in virtually all countries. It is, in effect, only the trial at which the defendant enjoys a universally recognized right to presence. While it is true that without recourse to ultimate trial in at least some cases, no system of criminal justice would seem viable, it is also true that in many nations of the world an incredibly large number of criminal cases are brought to conclusion without a trial, and many of these end at the stage of finding and testing an indictment. The number of cases effectively terminated without trial is unquestionably greater in the common law countries, because of the institution of the guilty plea. But it is believed that in the civil law countries, too, a great number of cases are terminated by the indictment chamber (chambre d'accusation) or comparable institution, when the facts would not support a conviction. Moreover, a pretesting of the accusation, even in a civil law country, will make the trial of the case more efficient and effective.

Thus, much can be said for the institution of an indictment or committing chamber, not just as a regular conduit, but as a potential independent institution, with ex parte jurisdiction, and thus capable of receiving facts pertaining to charges of international crime, even as against third parties who have not consented to the jurisdiction of the court and its chamber, and who are *not* cooperative. There may be little hope of ever bringing a head of state or other person charged with a crime against the peace and security of mankind before the court itself for trial. But there is no reason not to inquire into charges brought against him and determining whether to officially file an accusation for possible trial thereunder, just in case the party ultimately were to consent or become available. Article 33 of the existing U.N. Draft Statute provides for such a "Committing Chamber," but does not sufficiently cater to the potential use of such a chamber as *a possible terminal point* of an international criminal proceeding. It would require the power to hold its inquiry publicly and to release its report and accusation publicly, thus subjecting the defendant to the spotlight of world opinion, the coercive psychological pressure of a respected juridical organ of organized mankind.

It might be asked how such a commitment chamber would differ from existing institutions in which charges of aggression are aired and condemnatory resolutions are voted upon, e.g., the U.N. General Assembly or the Security Council. The answer is threefold: (1) The proceedings in the political organ of the United Nations are truly political, the charges are loose, the debates are heated and emotional, and the proceedings are formless. In the envisaged Committing Chamber, the proceedings would be formal and strictly regulated by rules of procedure. Factual allegations would have to be substantiated instantly before they could be inserted into any accusatory document. The personnel of the Chamber would be composed of jurists of highest ability, achievement and respect, whether they be committing magistrates, prosecutors or — when appearing — defense counsel. The difference between the U.N. General Assembly with its political charges on the one hand, and the Committing Chamber of an International Criminal Court, on the other, would indeed be the difference between the parliament of France, or the Congress of the United States, on the one hand, and the chambre d'accusation, or a pretrial hearing in a U.S. Federal Court, on the other.

Why do I expect proceedings before such a committing chamber, with release of a well-documented accusation, to be effective, even though there be little or no chance of an ultimate trial before the International Criminal Court itself, — usually for want of an appearance?

The experience in enforcing the European [Convention] of Human Rights, I believe, has taught us this lesson: The European scheme envisages trial before the European Court of Human Rights in any dispute involving a charge of violation of one of the provisions of the [Convention] by a member nation. Prior to submission of the complaint to the Court itself, it is tested for sufficiency before the European Commission of Human Rights — a veritable parallel to a chambre d'accusation or Committing Chamber. While only a consenting nation could be cited before the court, experience has taught that the *pressure* generated before the Commission has generally been sufficient to bring the matter to successful termination. No nation relishes the thought of being adjudicated as violating the European [Convention] of Human Rights. Thus, actually existing shortcomings in national systems of justice have usually been corrected when the spotlight of a proceeding before the *Commission* was turned on them, so that adjudication was not necessary. If the Commission declares an application wholly or partially admissible, a subcommission is usually set up in order to fully ascertain the facts and attempt to reach a solution as between the parties.

The experience with orderly procedure, diligent and unbiased fact finding, and use of the concentrated power of publicity, especially when representing world-opinion, has been encouraging in many differing settings, apart from the experience of the Council of Europe. The International Labor Organization has effectively used its power to report infringements of the right of freedom of association. Allegations of violations of various provisions of the Universal Declaration of Human Rights may be addressed to organs of the United Nations, which have their own fact-finding apparatus, and which use the power of the international public opinion in efforts of terminating abuses. While these precedents lack the precision, neutrality and orderliness of a judicial inquiry, they nevertheless go far to demonstrate my point. Judge Golt of Canada recently put the point well when he said: "Far from taking advantage of the absence of any coercive method of enforcing obedience to the principles of international law, states actually compete with each other in asserting their strict fidelity to such principles. . . . [P]ublic opinion of the civilized world plays in an ever increasing degree the part of a sanctioning authority."

But publicity and shaming a national pride are not the only purposes and justified expectations for a Committing Chamber. If compliance is not brought about, an indictment against a head of state or other powerful figure may indeed be handed down. A summons or warrant of arrest could be issued, which any nation that had signed the convention creating the court and chamber could execute at any time, whenever the person subject to arrest might appear in its jurisdiction, for surrender to the International Criminal Court. If the hypothetical one hundred and ten nations, signatory to the convention, really are serious about their obligations, that would rather seriously hamper the freedom to travel of aggressive heads of state — for all future, whether in office or after retirement!

The old model of international criminal justice looked primarily to an international criminal court, with the power to dispense retributive justice. This model cannot succeed. The new model of international criminal justice, while still aiming at a universal criminal jurisdiction inherent in an International Criminal Court, should look primarily to the potential of obtaining preventive effect through proceedings before a Committing Chamber which — if need be, in an ex parte proceeding — will direct the coercive effect of a frightened yet determined mankind's public opinion on an aggressor. While no one can guarantee such a system, I should think we citizens of the world would be fools not to try it. We might not live to regret it!

J. Carey, UN Protection of Civil and Political Rights
63-69 (1970)

[The author's chapter on Protection by Criminal Adjudication begins with a description of the growing trend to define certain acts as international crimes. He then proceeds to set out various ideas that have been presented for improving and developing procedures of enforcement.]
. . . In 1967 Sean MacBride, Secretary-General of the International Commission of Jurists, speaking for his own and other non-governmental organizations, proposed at the UN Seminar in Zambia on apartheid, racial discrimination and colonialism in southern Africa

> that a register or record office be established at United Nations Headquarters for the purpose of registering all complaints of acts of brutality and other acts amounting to crimes against humanity committed in South Africa, South West Africa, Southern Rhodesia, Angola and Mozambique . . . by anyone in these territories purporting to act in pursuance of the racial or colonial laws or practices being applied in those areas.

The British author Colin Legum proposed that Mr. MacBride's own organization

> open a register of people accused of committing atrocities in defiance of [a Convention on Crimes Against Humanity]. Men like Inspector Lambron, head of the Greek security police, Asphalia, and the torturers in South Africa, Portugal and other countries, should have dossiers on them prepared against the day when conditions change and they become available for prosecution. The mere threat of such a possibility might make torturers think twice before they commit their loathsome brutalities.

Mr. MacBride later proposed a Universal Court of Human Rights to deal with crimes against humanity.

> For a start, violations of the United Nations and the Red Cross Conventions could be made indictable offences before an International Tribunal to punish crimes against humanity. Such a Tribunal could, in addition, be given general power to pass judgment on crimes that violate ". . . the law of nations, the laws of humanity and the dictates of the public conscience." Gradually,

later, a code of Crimes against Humanity could be evolved and embodied in an international convention, but the Tribunal with the jurisdiction indicated would be set up now.

A geographically narrower proposal appeared in the Montreal Statement of the Assembly for Human Rights on March 22-27, 1968, which concluded that "criminal courts and procedures might be established for dealing with gross violations of human rights" in South West Africa, whose "unique status provides a special opportunity to experiment with further implementation procedures."

The pace for proposals for criminal jurisdiction was escalated when the UN Human Rights Commission's Special Rapporteur on apartheid and racial discrimination suggested to the Commission in early 1968 that it recommend to the Assembly asking the South African Government to repeal its discriminatory laws:

> In case the present situation continued to prevail, the General Assembly would declare the leaders and responsible officials of the South African Government criminals at large who could be apprehended and tried by the courts of any State under the charge of the commission of crimes against humanity. In case of conviction the penalty would be the severest (penalty) which could be imposed under the laws of the country concerned.

This proposal was not dealt with explicitly by the Commission. The Special Rapporteur went further with his proposal for a Grand Jury of Legal Experts for South West Africa:

> The Commission could recommend to the General Assembly that it establish, in connection with the Assembly's decisions to administer South West Africa (Resolutions 2145 (XXI) and 2248 (SV)), a Grand Jury of Legal Experts for South West Africa for the protection of the life, personal safety and rights of the inhabitants of the Territory. Such a body of legal experts would determine prima facie violations of international law, crimes against humanity and other serious offenses committed by individual South African Government officials against the inhabitants of the territory for which the Assembly has assumed special responsibility. It could be given a variety of police powers including the powers to issue arrest warrants, lists of wanted men and requests that they be brought to justice by Member States of the United Nations. By acting in personam it could have some deterrent effect on South African officialdom in so far as torture, brutality and the execution of death sentences are concerned. Later the terms of reference of this same body may be extended to cover Southern Rhodesia and South Africa as well, in case the Assembly's call for repeal, amendment and replacement of legislation is not heeded.

An American viewpoint on the usefulness of international criminal proceedings was expressed by the Human Rights Committee of the American Branch of the International Law Association, which reached the following conclusions:

Prima Facie Findings Without Trial

Grand-jury-type proceedings might be useful in cases where the accused were not available to be tried. The spotlight of public opinion could be focused sharply through orderly measures taken in the drastic context of criminality. Those accused might feel compelled to respond, with public statements if not formal appearance, where the spotlight shone from an impartial source, depoliticized as far as possible.

Criminal "Trials" Without Presence of Defendants

The reasons for prima facie findings apply even more strongly in favor of proceedings in which such findings are subjected to "trial." A greater impact on public opinion should result from facts found after hearing both sides. If the accused neither appeared nor submitted statements, a hearing of sorts for both sides could be obtained through an active tribunal seeking evidence on its own, on the order of an American administrative body or European "juge d'instruction." . . .

While international criminal jurisdiction lagged, the practice of national prosecution of crimes of "universal jurisdiction" was used occasionally to fill the gap. Building on the long-standing precedent subjecting pirates to punishment by any state, other serious wrongs have been made universally punishable by convention. Chief among these are the four 1949 Geneva Conventions for the protection of war victims, to which the United States is one of many parties. Typical of the universal jurisdiction provisions in the 1949 Geneva Conventions is that in the Convention for the Protection of Civilian Persons in Time of War, not only authorizing but actually obligating "each High Contracting Party . . . to search for persons alleged to have committed, or to have ordered to be committed, such grave offenses [as defined therein], and [to] bring such persons, regardless of their nationality, before its own courts." . . .

With respect to the relative merits of international and national courts for prosecution of international crimes, the Human Rights Committee of the International Law Association's American Branch concluded that

> while universal criminal jurisdiction has been widely accepted, not only in the four 1949 Geneva Conventions but also in the 1958 Convention on the High Seas (for piracy), its lack of use causes concern. Like state vs. state complaints, found in I.L.O. experience to be seldom used and then most likely for political purposes, universal criminal jurisdiction may be a rusty tool, seized at times in haste and crudely wielded. Unilateral prosecution of offenses against the whole international community would seem less desirable than machinery whose guidance is multilateral. Politically motivated prosecutions could then be better controlled. Political prevention of otherwise desirable prosecutions, which might occur, would be a lesser evil than uncontrolled political prosecution.

The growing interest in criminal process to protect basic rights, matched in the United States by concern over personal accountability for international crimes connected with the Viet Nam conflict, is not difficult to comprehend. Frustration at the impregnability of white supremacy bastions like South Africa . . . is bound to add appeal to the notion of punishing apartheid's individual practitioners who, though presently immune through safe location, would, if ever caught, be as subject to punishment as are their own present victims. The actual capture of Adolph Eichmann encourages speculation about others accused of human rights crimes. . . .

Can it be wrong, in the light of Nuremberg, to plan for prosecution on international authority of today's oppressors? The answer is not categorical but qualified. The qualifications concern geographical jurisdiction, the nature of the tribunal, the type of findings made, and the consequence for the accused.

Geographical jurisdiction is better founded in Namibia (South West Africa) than it would be for South Africa itself. As mentioned, a special rapporteur of the UN Human Rights Commission has argued for UN criminal accusation based on jurisdiction gained by General Assembly action in 1967 declaring South Africa's Mandate ended and the UN responsible. While one may differ with the Assembly's right to end the Mandate, its end is hardly disputed, leaving a jurisdictional vacuum in which the UN's authority can be disputed only by South Africa, based on its having conquered the area fifty years before. In its own territory, however, South Africa could assert its lack of consent to international prosecution, a far more potent objection not available at Nuremberg where the Allied Powers spoke as successor sovereigns to the beaten Reich.

The nature of the tribunal, as between the national type of court which sentenced Eichmann and the jointly formed Nuremberg tribunal, should be determined — apart from the legal requirement of an injured sovereign — by the test of wide acceptability. The Nuremberg Tribunal would have been less acceptable if constituted by but one of the victorious states. The injured sovereign requirement would loom less large if, for the normal arrest-trial-punishment sequence, there were substituted less complete criminal proceedings. Prima facie findings like indictments could be made without arrest and with far lighter legal foundation. The body making the findings would rely on public opinion, not on legal jurisdiction to punish, for its sanction. Trial of indictments could be held, again without arrest so long as punishment was not the goal, and the truth-seeking machinery of the normal trial could be supplied through an official designated either to cross examine and argue the accused's case or, alternatively, to interrogate all witnesses like a European juge d'instruction.

In short, criminal-type proceedings can be conceived of in forms suitable for UN protection of civil and political rights today and tomorrow.

VI.   Final Comments and Questions

1. Bridge states that "[i]nternational crimes are not frequently committed, at least not in peace time." While this observation may be valid with respect to traditional international crimes, does it not need revision in view of the many new international crimes created by the "piecemeal" convention approach since he wrote his article? Do these recent developments strengthen or weaken his argument that a permanent international criminal court is preferable to ad hoc tribunals?

2. Bridge's conclusion that a Code of International Criminal Law would not be accepted by states without "a variety of reservations [that] would damn it before it became operative" leads him to suggest, as an alternative route, the adoption of "international conventions setting out particular international crimes." Thus, he presages the "piecemeal" approach recommended by Murphy. Note, however, that even 20 years ago Woetzel (see page 1009 supra) was recommending an international criminal court with opt-in ("freedom of choice") jurisdiction, to coexist with "piecemeal" conventions in much the same fashion that the ILC's proposed Court will interact with the international regimes established pursuant to the treaties mentioned in Article 20(e) and listed in the Annex of its 1994 Draft Statute. Is this arrangement, which in essence requires a state holding an alleged offender to prosecute or extradite him if it has not accepted the Court's jurisdiction with respect to crimes under a particular treaty, a satisfactory compromise? Are there loopholes in the bargain struck? If so, what are they, and can they be plugged during the drafting of the international convention?

3. Mueller speaks of the need for an "indictment" or "committing" chamber, and Carey quotes the American Branch of the ILA's proposal for "grand-jury-type proceedings" that might hand down prima facie findings. The idea behind such suggestions is to depoliticize the prosecution process and at the same time make a record for future use when the jurisdiction over accused persons might be obtained. The Prosecutor for the Yugoslav War Crimes Tribunal, who under Article 16(2) of its statute acts "independently as a separate organ of the International Tribunal," and the Procuracy of the ILC's proposed international criminal court, which under Article 12(1) of the Commission's 1994 Draft Statute is "an independent organ of the Court responsible [inter alia] for the investigation of complaints," both seem to possess sufficient independence of office to guarantee depoliticized investigations and prosecutions.

One interesting possibility is to establish independent, fact-gathering bodies, international and perhaps regional, to seek out and disseminate information about serious international crimes to assist governments in bringing alleged perpetrators before the fledgling international criminal court or national courts. For an interesting proposal along these lines, following in the footsteps of Mueller and Carey, see International Criminal Law Committee, Fifth Interim Report, in International Law Association, Report of the Sixtieth Conference 377, 424 (Montreal 1982), containing a Draft Statute for an International Commission of Criminal Inquiry. Recall also the work of the Commission of Experts established to gather evidence of international humanitarian law violations in the former Yugoslavia, which conducted extensive investigations and accumulated a massive record of gross human rights violations that it turned over to the Yugoslav War Crimes Tribunal. It would serve as an excellent model for future investigatory bodies, whether ad hoc or permanent. See Comments 4 and 5 at page 991 supra.

4. Along the above lines, what do you think of Carey's imaginative suggestion to register human rights violations, to compile dossiers on human rights violators, and even possibly to try such violators in absentia (recall that Martin Bormann was tried and convicted at Nuremberg in absentia)? As for the registration of violations and violators, why has the UN not moved to implement this idea? Should not the Inter-American Commission on Human Rights consider doing so? What might be the role of NGO's in this regard?

5. Discussing the UN efforts, Mueller makes the surprising statement that "[a] majority of the nations of this world may indeed legislate for a dissenting minority and bind that minority." Is Libya really bound by the international law norms of the Hague Convention, to which it is not a party? Is the United States bound by the Apartheid Convention, which it has not even signed? At what number of ratifications or point of universal acceptance of its norms does a multilateral convention become binding upon non-parties? Is aerial hijacking, for instance, now truly an "international crime," so that a state not a party to the Hague and Montreal Conventions nevertheless could assert jurisdiction, under the universal principle, over a non-national for acts committed outside its territory? For arguments that it and other "piecemeal" convention crimes are just that, see pages 1012-1013 supra.

6. What do you think of the ILC's attempt, in its 1991 Draft Code of Crimes Against the Peace and Security of Mankind, to make international crimes out of "threat of aggression," "colonial domination and other forms of alien domination," and "wilful and severe damage to the environment"? What are your views on the Commission's present exclusion of many new crimes — like hostage-taking — from its Draft Code? Did not Iran's seizure of the U.S. hostages in 1979 constitute a threat to the peace and security of the international community? If so, should not hostage-taking be proscribed by the Draft Code, despite the narrow terms of reference under which the Commission is operating? For that matter, should not the Commission's mandate be widened somewhat? If so, in what way? To include more offenses? To embrace the criminal responsibility of states as well as individuals?

7. As was apparent from the speedy and efficient creation of the Yugoslav War Crimes Tribunal and, more recently, its Rwandan counterpart, the Security Council acting under Chapter VII can impose an international criminal court upon a state or situation without endless debate; moreover, it can do so without having to obtain the consent of each and every state needed to make it truly effective. As Rosenstock points out, "the mode of creation of the tribunal, with its consequent automatic application of Articles 2(5), 25, 48 and 49 of the United Nations Charter, accounts for almost all the differences between the institution created by Security Council Resolution 827 (1993) and the [1993] draft proposed by the working group of the Commission." Rosenstock, The Forty-Fifth Session of the International Law Commission, 88 Am. J. Intl. L. 134, 135 (1994). Review the above articles of the UN Charter, found in the Documentary Supplement, and consider how they simplify the Security Council's task of creating effective international criminal courts (e.g., mandating primacy of jurisdiction).

8. The question of in absentia trials, permitted at Nuremberg and certainly not prohibited by international law, remains an issue open to debate. When jurisdiction cannot be obtained over individuals wanted for trial for the commission of international law crimes, as in the case of Iraq and the former Yugoslavia, in absentia trials establish a record, generate a judgment, and, as Moore remarks, at the very least may affect the movement of those persons convicted. Note, however, that the Yugoslavia War Crimes Tribunal and its Rwandan counterpart will not be holding in absentia trials, a development that Orentlicher considers one of their "advances" (see page 984 supra), and that Article 37 of the ILC's Draft Statute for an international criminal court requires that the accused be present at his trial except where for reasons of security or his ill health that is undesirable or where he has escaped from custody or has broken bail. Where a trial cannot be held because of "the deliberate absence" of the accused, the Court may establish an "Indictment Chamber" to record the evidence, determine whether it establishes a prima facie case, and, if so, issue a warrant of arrest. Is this procedure, along the lines of suggestions made in Comment 3, a satisfactory alternative to in absentia trials? If not, what other arrangements might be devised? How do you stand, indeed, on the question of in absentia trials, which after all are not uncommon in European civil law countries? Are they a violation of the defendant's right to a fair trial guaranteed by Articles 10 and 11 of the Universal Declaration and Article 14 of the Civil and Political Covenant?

9. Bassiouni, Mueller, and other international criminal law scholars frequently have remarked that many of the deficiencies found in the ILC's Draft Code of Crimes Against the Peace and Security of Mankind could have been avoided if the public international lawyers and government officials involved in its drafting had possessed or had availed themselves of international criminal law expertise. Presumably this problem will not arise during the course of turning the ILC's 1994 Draft Statute into an inter-

national convention. Nor should it be a problem for the 18-judge Court that will be established pursuant to Article 6 of the Draft Statute, since in setting out the qualifications of judges that article requires that 10 possess "criminal trial experience" and 8 have "recognized competence in international law."

10. Why have most international human rights lawyers not used the possibilities of international criminal law more often in their efforts to promote and protect the rights of individuals? As was the case in the areas covered in Problems IV and XI, here, too, relevant norms of international law and institutional bodies developing and applying them have been overlooked and ignored. Re-read Professor Bassiouni's essay about the relevancy of international criminal law to the international protection of human rights. Why have so few international human rights lawyers seen and taken advantage of the connection? In view of the widespread publicity given to the Yugoslav War Crimes Tribunal and, more recently, the Rwandan War Crimes Tribunal, do you think things will change?

Problem XIII

The Carter Administration's Human Rights Initiatives and Its Legacy

How Relevant Are Human Rights Concerns to the Foreign Policy Process?

I. Human Rights Factors in the Foreign Policy Process: A Brief Overview
    from a Pre-Carter Perspective   1029
    A. Lawyers, Human Rights, and the Foreign Policy Process   1029
    B. Human Rights and U.S. Foreign Policy   1030
        Bilder, Human Rights and U.S. Foreign Policy: Short-Term
        Prospects   1031
II. The Carter Administration's Attitude Toward Human Rights Concerns
    in the Foreign Policy Process   1039
    A. The Congressional Backdrop: Giving Credit Where Credit Is Due 1039
        Lillich, U.S. Foreign Policy, Human Rights, and Foreign Trade
        and Investment   1039
    B. Defining the Carter Administration's Human Rights Policy   1041
        Introduction   1041
        Vance, Human Rights and Foreign Policy   1042
        Carter, Humane Purpose in Foreign Policy   1047
    C. Criticism of the Carter Administration's Human Rights Policy and
        Its Response   1048
        1. Criticism   1048
        Panel, Human Rights: A New Policy by a New Administration   1048
        Hoffman, The Hell of Good Intentions   1052
        Kissinger, Continuity and Change in American Foreign Policy   1053
        2. Response   1059
        Derian, Human Rights in American Foreign Policy   1059
    D. Human Rights and U.S. Foreign Policy: Argentina as a Case
        Study: Part I   1064
        de Onis, U.S. Denial of Loan Angers Argentines   1065
        Evans and Novak, Human-Rights Zeal That Costs U.S. Jobs   1066
        Reagan, Argentina's View on Human Rights   1068
        DeYoung and Krause, Our Mixed Signals on Human Rights in
        Argentina   1069
        Letters to the Editor, When Morality Interferes with Exports-as-
        Usual   1075
III. The Reagan Administration's Attitude Toward Human Rights Concerns
    in the Foreign Policy Process   1077

A. The Initial Reagan Reaction to the Carter Administration's Hu-
    man Rights Policy   1077
    1. David Rockefeller: Advance Man in Latin America   1077
        Schumacher, Latins Welcome Word on Reagan by Rockefeller   1077
        Lewis, On Lending Comfort to Evil in Argentina   1079
    2. President-Elect Reagan Adopts the Totalitarian/Authoritarian
        Distinction   1081
        Rosenblum, Reagan and Human Rights: Beyond Classic Ex-
        amples   1081
        Buchwald, Moderate Repression   1083
    3. Downgrading Human Rights: The Reagan Administration
        Takes Office   1084
        International Commission of Jurists, Human Rights and U.S.
        Foreign Policy   1084
        Baker, A Meddling Muddle   1087
    4. Human Rights and U.S. Foreign Policy: Argentina as a Case
        Study: Part II   1088
        de Onis, U.S. Acts to Improve Its Ties with Rightist Latin
        Governments   1088
        Editorial, Doing Favors for Argentina   1089
        Lewis, U.S. and Argentina: Question of the Soul   1090
        Editorial, Semantics and Human Rights   1093
B. The Reagan Administration's Human Rights Policy Falls into
    Place   1095
        International Commission of Jurists, Human Rights and U.S.
        Foreign Policy   1095
        U.S. Department of State, Country Reports on Human Rights
        Practices for 1982   1097
        U.S. Department of State, Country Reports on Human Rights
        Practices for 1983   1101
        Note: Two Key Differences in the Reagan Administration's Hu-
        man Rights Policy   1103
C. Criticism of the Reagan Administration's Human Rights Policy
    and Its Response   1105
        Shestack, An Unsteady Focus: The Vulnerabilities of the Rea-
        gan Administration's Human Rights Policy   1106
        El Salvador: "The Certification Joke"   1107
        Editorial, The Certification Joke   1108
        Response   1110
        Abrams, Latin America in the Time of Reagan   1110
        Schifter, Building Firm Foundations: The Institutionalization
        of United States Human Rights Policy in the Reagan Years   1113
        Human Rights and U.S. Foreign Policy: Argentina as a Case
        Study: Part III   1119
        Editorial, A Toast to Argentina   1120
        Lewis, Lessons from Argentina   1120
        Schell, Carter on Rights — a Re-Evaluation   1122
IV. The Bush Administration's Attitude Toward Human Rights Concerns
     in the Foreign Policy Process   1124

V.   *The Clinton Administration's Attitude Toward Human Rights Concerns
        in the Foreign Policy Process*   *1126*
            A Vision for Democracy (Remarks by Governor Bill Clinton) 1127
            Statement of the Honorable Timothy E. Wirth, Counselor,
                U.S. Department of State   1128
            Shattuck, Human Rights and Democracy in Asia   1131
            President's News Conference (May 26, 1994)   1135
            McGrory, Human Rights Retreat   1139
            Editorial, Speak Louder on Rights in China   1141
VI.   *Comments and Questions*   *1143*

I.   Human Rights Factors in the Foreign Policy Process: A Brief Overview from a Pre-Carter Perspective

A.   *Lawyers, Human Rights, and the Foreign Policy Process*

The preceding Problems in this coursebook have focused primarily on "legal" issues: the countless regimes, institutions, procedures, and practices that comprise what has come to be known as international human rights law. Lawyers, of course, have played a major role in the creation and clarification of this body of law and its slow but increasingly effective application in recent years. Human rights, however, also can be furthered through the foreign policy process. Indeed, in many instances it is the most promising way to improve the lives of individuals in a given country. With all due respect, the attitude that the United States takes toward a repressive regime in, say, Central America, can have far more impact upon the lives of people living under that regime than, for example, numerous petitions filed with the United Nations or the Inter-American Commission on Human Rights.

The role of lawyers in the foreign policy process can take many forms. A select few participate as government officials, perhaps as Secretary of State, often as Assistant Secretary of State for Democracy, Human Rights, and Labor, and always as Assistant Legal Adviser, Office of the Legal Adviser. In addition to the lawyers with human rights responsibilities sprinkled throughout the Executive Branch, numerous lawyers serve as members of Congress, often sitting on key committees such as the Subcommittee on International Security, International Organizations, and Human Rights of the House Committee on International Relations. Many Foreign Service officers are lawyers, too, monitoring human rights conditions in various countries and reporting thereon. Far more international human rights lawyers, however, are found outside government, either participating (sometimes on a full-time basis, more often as pro bono counsel) in the related work of non-governmental organizations or representing clients affected by U.S. human rights policies, whether codified in statutes or Executive Orders or just flowing from the ordinary course of diplomatic relations. Additionally, many lawyers act as independent experts by, say, testifying before congressional committees or consulting with members of the Executive Branch or act as interested observers by corresponding with government officials here and abroad or writing letters to the editor or "op-ed" articles. A small but growing number of international human rights lawyers even teach the subject.

The role that lawyers (and other concerned citizens) can play in promoting and protecting human rights by means of the foreign policy process thus needs consideration. Naturally, the success of such efforts depends in large measure on the receptiveness of the U.S. government of the day to human rights concerns and its willingness to take them into account in making and implementing foreign policy. The following subsection and reading outline the evolution of the role human rights factors have played in the U.S. foreign policy process over the years and describe and assess the situation in this regard as of the mid-1970s.

B. Human Rights and U.S. Foreign Policy

Human rights factors always have loomed large in the U.S. foreign policy process. In 1787 Thomas Jefferson wrote James Madison that "a bill of rights is what the people are entitled to against every government on earth." During the late nineteenth century, several U.S. Presidents spoke out strongly against Czarist oppression of Russian Jews. The genocide committed by the Ottoman Empire against the Armenians early in this century prompted President Woodrow Wilson to condemn the Turks, and his call to Congress to declare war on Germany in 1917 was that "the world must be made safe for democracy." President Franklin Roosevelt, shortly before World War II, restated the United States' commitment to human rights in the famous Four Freedoms address — freedom of speech, freedom of worship, freedom from want, and freedom from fear. Thus, it was only natural that when the UN was formed in the aftermath of that war and the horrors of the Holocaust, the United States took the lead in an attempt to create an international structure to promote and protect human rights.

Unhappily, as it has all so often during the Republic's history, this "idealist" approach to the international community ran up against the arguments of the "realists," who invoked the dangers of the Cold War to bring U.S. foreign policy more into line with the dictates of realpolitik. During the 1950s the United States effectively abdicated its leadership role in the international human rights movement, and this lack of concern carried over into the 1960s as the United States became increasingly preoccupied with its domestic civil rights problems and its deepening involvement in Vietnam. Vice Presidents calling on Greek colonels and Secretaries of State embracing Brazilian dictators were the order of the day. By the early 1970s, international human rights considerations had become, in Professor Farer's apt phrase, "the stepchildren of United States foreign policy." Farer, United States Foreign Policy and the Protection of Human Rights, 14 Va. J. Intl. L. 623 (1974). (Farer added that "[t]here is nothing particularly American about this attitude. It appears to characterize foreign policy elites in most states." Id.)

In the immediate post-Vietnam, post-Watergate period, however, a new and renewed interest in international human rights appeared in the United States. This interest found expression in the seminal hearings held in 1973 by Congressman Fraser's House Subcommittee on International Organizations (International Protection of Human Rights: Hearings Before the Subcomm. on International Organizations and Movements of the House Comm. on Foreign Affairs, 93d Cong., 1st Sess. (1973)) and in that Subcommittee's remarkable report the following year (Human Rights in the World Community: A Call for U.S. Leadership, Report of the Subcomm. on International Organizations and Movements of the 93d Cong., 2d Sess. (Comm. Print 1974)). The above hearings and report had their counterpart in the academic world, where in 1974 the Virginia Journal of International Law published a Symposium on Human Rights and United States Foreign Policy, 14 Va J. Intl. L. 591-701 (1974). The following reading, taken from that Symposium, reflects the situation in the pre-Carter period and raises numerous issues still relevant to the subject of this Problem.

Bilder, Human Rights and U.S. Foreign Policy: Short-Term Prospects
14 Va. J. Intl. L. 597, 597-609 passim (1974)

It is difficult to conceive of the development of an effective human rights system without the active and affirmative participation of the United States. Consequently, to those involved in international human rights efforts, the future attitude of the United States toward international human rights issues is of great concern. How important a role are human rights considerations likely to play in U.S. foreign policy during the next few years? Will Vietnam, Watergate and the growing list of other problems the American people are experiencing have the effect of increasing United States support for international human rights efforts, decreasing it, or will they leave the U.S. posture essentially unchanged? This essay will note some of the problems in forecasting the input of human rights in the future foreign policy of the United States and suggest some answers to these questions.

I

An attempt to assess or predict the role of human rights in U.S. foreign policy involves a number of conceptual and empirical problems which deserve at least brief comment.

First, it is questionable whether the U.S. Government has any unified attitude with respect to the appropriate significance of international human rights considerations in foreign policy matters. "Foreign policy" is a broad abstraction, comprising many separate policies, decisions, actions and reactions. In certain areas of concern, such as national security, U.S. foreign policy may follow a relatively clearly defined and consistent pattern. But in other areas, policy decisions may be ad hoc and sometimes inconsistent, and thus difficult to fit into a single pattern. U.S. international human rights decisions seem to fall principally into the latter category. Decisions relating to general participation in institutional aspects of international human rights activities, such as U.N. or inter-American programs, will involve different considerations than decisions concerning human rights issues potentially relevant to relations with a particular foreign country. The United States may have one stance with respect to ratification of Human Rights Conventions, another towards the establishment of the position of U.N. Human Rights Commissioner, and still others regarding human rights problems in a variety of different countries such as the Soviet Union, Greece, Vietnam, the Dominican Republic, or Rhodesia. We may therefore have to phrase our enquiry in terms of the significance of human rights concerns in different kinds of foreign policy decisions rather than in foreign policy as a whole.

Second, even if we surmise that human rights considerations may have been relevant to a particular foreign policy decision, it may prove very difficult to isolate and measure empirically the particular "role" or "input" of these considerations in that decision. Foreign policy decisions are frequently the result of a complex interaction of many diverse domestic, international and bureaucratic interests and pressures. It may not be easy for the involved officials themselves to assess or articulate accurately all the reasons why they reached their decision. Moreover, due to bureaucratic inaccessibility, diplomatic reticence or government secrecy, evidence indicating the actual influence of various factors may be hard to obtain. Where we are seeking to determine the influence of what are likely to be relatively secondary factors, such as human rights considerations, these problems may be magnified. In many instances, the best we may be able to say is that, in the broadest terms, human rights considerations seem to have had a relatively "major," "significant," or "negligible" role in the relevant decision.

Third, even if we are able to make a rough assessment of the relative role of human rights in a particular decision, this may furnish only limited guidance as to official attitudes towards human rights generally. The role played by human rights considerations in any single decision will be a function of their influence relative to the influence of all of the other interests and pressures involved in the decision. Thus, to make any useful general judgment, we have to look at the decisional matrix as a whole. There may be contexts in which even the most oppressive government, evincing little concern for human rights objectives, may find it expedient to make decisions supporting these objectives. This would be the case, for example, where strong political interests happen to coincide with what purport to be human rights aims, or if (as in the case of voting for a U.N. human rights decision irrelevant to that country's own situation) there are virtually no costs or countervailing reasons for not supporting such aims. Thus, U.S. condemnation of apartheid in Rhodesia may be a relatively weak test of real U.S. human rights attitudes, since the political costs of such condemnation are comparatively minor and the political gains of currying favor with Black African countries are thought to be high. Conversely, even a genuine and deeply-held official commitment to international human rights objectives may on occasion be submerged by exceptionally strong countervailing interests and pressures. For example, U.S. failure to condemn Soviet repressive policies may not in itself be conclusive evidence of overall U.S. attitudes, since the Administration clearly views the potential costs of any such condemnation, in terms of its overriding objective of detente, as extremely high.

Fourth, there is considerable ambiguity as to what we mean by human rights considerations. In recent years, the term "human rights" has been used to describe a variety of very different goals and values. These include not only the civil and political liberties embraced in traditional Western human rights concepts, but also other economic, social, and cultural rights, including the right of self-determination, the right to a decent environment, and so forth. As the definition of human rights considerations is broadened to include at least quasi-political state interests, the apparent role played by such considerations will, of course, broaden accordingly. For example, many American citizens and officials undoubtedly see anti-Communism as essentially a human rights position. In this view, the United States must oppose Communism in order to save foreign peoples and ultimately our own country from domination by an ideology which represents tyranny and denial of all basic liberties. If anti-Communism may properly be characterized in this way, one might conclude that human rights considerations have been extremely influential in post-World War II U.S. foreign policy. On the other hand, if the influence of human rights considerations is judged by more traditional criteria, such as participation in U.N. Human Rights Conventions, support for U.N. efforts against racial discrimination, or a willingness to condemn oppression in anti-Communist or Third World dictatorships, one might reach a different conclusion as to their role in U.S. policy. The analysis is further complicated by the fact that different human rights values may conflict. Some countries justify suppression of civil and political liberties as necessary to the achievement of economic and social liberties. Similarly, U.S. accommodation with oppressive foreign dictatorships is sometimes justified as necessary to fight the greater human rights threat of Communism, or as a necessary compromise to the achievement of peace, which is described in this context as the "highest human right." Can we say that human rights considerations played no role in these decisions?

Fifth, the historic character of American foreign policy makes generalization and prediction as to the role of human rights particularly uncertain. U.S. foreign policy has long embodied various coexisting themes. It seems undeniable that one of these themes has been moralism and humanitarianism: a desire to do good in the world by spreading the blessings of the American way of life and its concept of civil and political liberties. It is clear that, for many Americans, U.S. involvement in Vietnam had such a moral and human rights basis. But another theme has been pragmatism, a businessman's sense of the world's harsh realities. Sometimes one theme has clearly dominated our foreign policies, sometimes the other. There is some evidence to suggest that, as American power is perceived as relatively more limited, our foreign policy has tended to shift towards the more pragmatic side of the spectrum. More frequently, however, our policy has represented an uneasy compromise between these two. Even where pragmatism and *realpolitik* are clearly at the center of the stage, the theme of moralism often lurks in the wings, pressing to get into the act and make its presence felt.

Finally, it is difficult to predict the role of human rights in U.S. foreign policy without knowing who will be the officials making relevant decisions. Our foreign policy will be more or less responsive to human rights considerations depending upon whether the President is Wilson, Kennedy, or Nixon; whether the Secretary of State is Dulles, Rusk, or Kissinger; whether the U.S. Representative to the United Nations who deals with human rights matters is Eleanor Roosevelt or perhaps a less committed or influential person. Even relatively low-ranking officials — a Deputy Assistant Secretary of State, for example, or an individual Senator or Congressman — may by virtue of particular interest, energy, persuasive ability or strategic position, exert a significant influence either for or against U.S. involvement in international human rights efforts.

In summary, we can generalize about the role of human rights in U.S. foreign policy only with caution. There are inherent difficulties both in deciding what constitutes human rights considerations and in measuring the influence of such considerations in particular decisions. Human rights considerations may play different or even inconsistent roles in different aspects of our foreign policy depending upon the total configuration of relevant interests and the personalities of the individuals involved. Further, the tension between the moral and humanitarian theme and the pragmatic theme in American foreign policy is a continuing one, and neither can be ignored if our policy is to be understood. Perhaps the most that we may be able to say is that human rights considerations frequently play at least some role in U.S. foreign policy, though rarely a determinative one. What this "some role" is likely to mean will depend upon the circumstances.

II

There are a number of reasons why human rights considerations seem likely to play only a relatively limited role in U.S. foreign policy during the next few years.

First, foreign policy officials have in the past apparently accorded human rights a relatively low priority in their decisions, and there is little indication that they will soon change their attitude. Officials must typically justify their actions in practical terms, closely related to immediate and obvious national interests. They tend to be skeptical that efforts to promote the human rights of foreigners have much relevance to these practical national interests. Of course, on occasion support for human rights objectives may coincide with immediate political goals. Support for U.N. anti-apartheid policies may help our relations with Black African countries. Mild statements condemning Soviet treatment of Jews or dissidents may appease domestic political interests. A general posture of support for innocuous human rights activities may reinforce our national moral posture at little risk. But, by and large, officials tend to see any potential national gains from U.S. participation in international human rights efforts as, at best, indirect, speculative, and long-term, and therefore not worth substantial political costs or risks. . . .

Second, there has been a long series of recent U.S. actions and decisions which appear to accord a relatively low priority to human rights considerations. The continued failure of the United States to ratify human rights conventions, reaffirmed only this February in the Senate's refusal to override a filibuster against ratification of the Genocide Convention, is one part of this picture. Moreover, in the past few years the government has, at least on a public and official level, largely ignored substantial human rights issues in such countries as Vietnam, Cambodia, Spain, Portugal, Greece, Biafra, Indonesia, Burundi, Brazil, Chile, Bangladesh, a variety of Arab states, and others. Even where the presence of special domestic or international pressures have resulted in some action, as in the case of the Soviet Union and South Africa, our condemnation has been relatively muted. In each of these cases, pragmatic considerations — the high risk of antagonizing the foreign governments concerned or their friends, the likelihood that protests or other actions would have little practical effect, and the limited approval we could expect from other states for a moral stance — were deemed by the United States to outweigh any human rights or humanitarian considerations. At least in terms of short-run national interest, there seemed little to be gained and much to be lost from concerning ourselves with mistreatment of foreign citizens by their own governments. These attitudes are well-described in the Carnegie Endowment's excellent recent study of U.S. policy with respect to the 1972 massacres by the Tutsi-controlled Government of Burundi of an estimated several hundred thousand Hutu citizens. The study, which attempts to explain why the United

States failed to take any meaningful action, is appropriately entitled *Passing By*. . . .

Third, the U.S. government appears to have become increasingly disillusioned both with the United Nations, as an institution, long the focus of international human rights activities, and with U.N. human rights activities in particular. In recent years, the most significant aspects of U.S. foreign relations have taken place outside of the U.N. context. Much of current U.S. policy in the U.N. appears to be in the nature of a holding action, an attempt to keep anything too harmful from occurring. If the U.N. continues to play a subsidiary role in U.S. policy, it may be expected that U.N. international human rights efforts are likely also to play a subsidiary role in U.S. policy. . . .

Fourth, it seems unlikely that any strong public pressures will develop in the near future for the U.S. government to act more affirmatively to promote international human rights. With the exception of special groups of Americans who have felt a special racial, religious, or ethnic tie with victims of foreign oppression, public concern for the human rights problems of people in other countries has probably never been very widespread or intense. Most Americans are not aware of these problems. Of those that do know, it seems realistic to say that most probably do not really care. The probability that these public attitudes toward international human rights will markedly change or become politically significant seems at present especially low. A depressingly long list of other problems with a more immediate impact on the average American citizen's life — inflation, the energy crisis, political corruption, environmental deterioration, crime, drugs, consumer problems — are absorbing an increasing share of his attention and concern. The Vietnam experience probably further diminished potential public support for increased United States involvement in international human rights issues. For the many Americans who accepted successive Administrations' claims that the war was justified by moral and human rights considerations, the course of events may have produced a profound disillusionment. Certainly, Vietnam has left us all more skeptical as to our capacity to influence deep-seated foreign problems, more aware that even our well-meaning intervention may cause more harm than good, less confident of our ability to judge the rights and wrongs of foreign internal conflicts, and therefore less willing to get involved in other people's domestic troubles.

Finally, even if the U.S. government wishes to adopt a more affirmative posture on international human rights issues, its past policies may for some time prove embarrassing and thus impede its efforts. Countries whose domestic policies raise human rights issues, their friends, or other unfriendly countries may attack such a change in U.S. policy as insincere or hypocritical. They may cite our actions in Vietnam, our failure to ratify human rights conventions, our continuing domestic racial and other civil liberties problems, or our long record of support for oppressive dictatorships. Thus, even if the United States chooses to resume a position of leadership in international human rights, it may have to proceed very slowly since its credibility in this field will need careful rebuilding.

III

There are, of course, certain countervailing factors which might suggest a less pessimistic view of the influence of human rights considerations on U.S. foreign policy in the near future.

Human rights influences are clearly not irrelevant to American foreign policy. One can assume that neither Secretary Kissinger nor other U.S. foreign policy officials are indifferent to moral and humanitarian issues, and they can be expected at least to take human rights considerations into account when such action in their view advances or is not inconsistent with national interests. Congress has frequently shown a concern for international human rights considerations. . . . American nongovernmental and professional organizations continue to be concerned with international human rights issues and to press the government for more meaningful efforts in this field. Recent developments such as the Carnegie Endowment's Burundi study, the debate over Soviet MFN treatment, and the Vietnam and Watergate issues more generally, may make the public and governmental officials, both in Congress and in the State Department, more conscious of human rights issues. Changing national leadership could bring individuals more sensitive and committed to human rights objectives into positions of responsibility.

Moreover, as the international political scene changes, practical American foreign policy interests might require a greater American involvement in international human rights efforts. For example, if other nations generally became more active in international human rights efforts, U.S. officials may consider it appropriate and expedient to keep in step. Certainly, as more nations join in such activities, the political risks to the United States of participation will tend to decrease. More likely, particular groups of nations, such as the African or Arab states, may place increasing pressure on the United States and other nations to become involved in human rights issues concerning, for example, the apartheid and Palestine refugee problems. Indeed, successful use of the oil boycott by the Arabs to coerce third states to support their anti-Israel policy could establish a precedent for attempts to use such techniques for other policy purposes, including objectives related to human rights. U.S. foreign policy would obviously have to take such developments into account.

Finally, it is at least conceivable that the American people, in the aftermath of Vietnam and Watergate, may prove more, rather than less, inclined to demand a foreign policy responsive to international human rights ideals. Contemporary social comment suggests that Americans today want very much to find a sense of national purpose, that they want their country to stand for things in which they can take pride. Whatever the practical virtues of *realpolitik*, it may do little to fulfill these needs.

IV

It seems clear that international human rights considerations will not play a major role in U.S. foreign policy until government officials are persuaded that pursuit of these goals serves major national interests. As previously suggested, whatever their personal preferences as to the role of human rights, officials feel compelled to justify their decisions by practical criteria related to immediate and significant state interests. If the reasons that can be given for supporting human rights efforts are solely moral and humanitarian, one cannot expect officials to give these efforts high priority. . . .

Thus, the problem of finding "selfish" national interest reasons why governments such as the United States should be concerned with denials of human rights in other countries remains a basic one. It can be argued that such denials may threaten world peace and security, may spread to other countries, or may produce adverse economic consequences. But these arguments are hard to prove and not fully persuasive. Despite considerable effort, it has been difficult to construct a wholly convincing "selfish" rationale for major U.S. national commitments to promote the human rights of foreigners. Until we do so, the prospects for any substantial increase in the role of human rights in U.S. foreign policy seem limited.

It is possible to argue, however, that the dichotomy between moral concerns and selfish national interests is not as rigid as foreign policy officials have tended to see it. Moral compromises, or "passing by," may have real costs in terms of the way Americans view their own country and its role in the world. We are coming to see that national pride, self-respect, cohesion, and purpose are meaningful elements of both national power and domestic tranquility. It is true that there are practical limits to what the United States can reasonably attempt to accomplish in promoting the human rights of other peoples. But, in a period following Vietnam and Watergate, it may be worth some foreign policy risks to reassert historic American commitments to human worth and dignity.

II. The Carter Administration's Attitude Toward Human Rights Concerns in the Foreign Policy Process

In the above reading, Professor Bilder pessimistically predicted that "human rights considerations seem likely to play only a relatively limited role in U.S. foreign policy during the next few years." Professor Henkin, writing in the same Symposium, also concluded that "[r]adical transformations in U.S. attitudes are not in sight." Henkin, The United States and the Crisis in Human Rights, 14 Va. J. Intl. L. 653, 666 (1974). He added, however, that "[m]uch that I have described might change dramatically," and with the election in 1976 of Jimmy Carter to the presidency, change it did. Before turning to the dramatic changes wrought during the first two years of his Administration, however, attention should be drawn to the important legislative groundwork laid by Congress in the final years of the Nixon/Ford period.

A. The Congressional Backdrop: Giving Credit Where Credit Is Due

Lillich, U.S. Foreign Policy, Human Rights, and Foreign Trade and Investment
in Private Investors Abroad — Problems and Solutions in International Business in 1979, at 281, 288-291 (Southwestern Legal Foundation 1979)

With the withdrawal of U.S. troops from South Vietnam in 1973 came a reassessment of the underpinnings of U.S. foreign policy. The realpolitik of the Kissinger era, in the view of the distinguished historian and former foreign policy adviser Arthur Schlesinger, Jr.,

> frustrated those in the Wilsonian tradition who felt that American foreign policy should be founded on ideals. It frustrated equally those in the school of FDR who did not doubt that foreign policy must be founded on national interest but considered ideals an indispensable constituent of American power. Official indifference to the Soviet dissidents [who, Schlesinger maintains, "forced the human rights issue on the world"], symbolized by President Ford's refusal in mid-1975 to receive Solzhenitsyn, seemed to reveal a vacuum at the center of American foreign policy.

Nature, it is said, abhors a vacuum, and in this instance it was Congress that proceeded to fill it. Beginning with a "sense-of-the-Congress" provision in 1973 to the effect that "the President should deny any economic or military assistance to the government of any foreign country which practices the internment or imprisonment of that country's citizens for political purposes," it enacted a series of statutes linking foreign assistance or trade benefits to the status of human rights in foreign countries. One of the earliest and most controversial instances was the Jackson-Vanik Amendment to the Trade Reform Act of 1974, which prohibits, inter alia, the granting of most-favored-nation treatment to nonmarket economy countries that deny or restrict the right of their citizens to emigrate. Designed to place economic pressure upon the Soviet Union and other Communist countries to secure their compliance with Article 13(2) of the Universal Declaration and Article 12(2) of the U.N. Covenant on Civil and Political Rights, which guarantee the right to emigrate, this amendment initially was relatively successful in the case of Rumania and recently has had an impact upon Soviet emigration patterns as well.

Also enacted in 1974 was a new Section 502B to the Foreign Assistance Act of 1961, a "sense-of-the-Congress" provision stating that "except in extraordinary circumstances, the President shall substantially reduce or terminate security assistance to any government which engages in a consistent pattern of gross violations of human rights." Two years later, Congress eliminated the "sense-of-the-Congress" language and mandated the President to terminate military assistance to countries so violating human rights unless "extraordinary circumstances" exist which make it in the "national interest" to continue such aid. This national security exception, first invoked by President Ford in late 1976, may be . . . overridden by a joint resolution of Congress. *

Having taken up military assistance in 1974, Congress tackled economic aid the following year by adding Section 116[b] to the Foreign Assistance Act of 1961, which requires the President to terminate such assistance to recipient countries, under criteria roughly similar to the ones contained in Section 502B, "unless such assistance will directly benefit the needy people in such country." Again, this "needy people" exception, often relied upon by the President, is subject to Congress's override, this time by concurrent resolution. †

The policy of seeking compliance with internationally recognized human rights norms by the use of economic levers gained momentum in 1976 when Congress enacted several other related statutes. . . . [Thus,] at the end of 1976, a substantial amount of legislation, all initiated by Congress in the face of outright opposition by, or at best tepid approval of, the Nixon-Ford administrations was in place and ready for the Carter administration's use.

---

* Section 502B may be found in the Documentary Supplement. As of December 1994, Congress has made no attempt to override a President's invocation of the exception. — Eds.

† Section 116b may be found in the Documentary Supplement. As of December 1994, Congress has made no attempt to override a President's invocation of the exception. — Eds.

B.   Defining the Carter Administration's Human Rights Policy

Introduction

President Carter was something of a "Johnny-come-lately" to the cause of international human rights. "It is not altogether clear how Carter personally came to human rights," Professor Schlesinger has written. "The phrase does not appear in the chapter on foreign policy in his memoir, *Why Not the Best?* (1975). Nor was the issue prominent in his presidential campaign." Schlesinger, Human Rights and the American Tradition, 57 Foreign Aff. 503, 513 (1978). Suffice to say that between the election and inauguration day, he and his advisers concluded that human rights was "the perfect unifying principle" needed to give U.S. foreign policy the moral thrust that it had lacked during the Nixon-Ford period. Id. at 514. Thus, in his inaugural address, the President singled out human rights as a key element in his proposed new foreign policy, declaring that "our commitment to human rights must be absolute. . . . Because we are free, we can never be indifferent to the fate of freedom elsewhere. Our moral sense dictates a clearcut preference for those societies who share with us an abiding respect for individual human rights." 1 Pub. Papers of the Presidents 2, 3 (1977). He developed this theme in his 17 March 1977 address to the United Nations (76 Dept. State Bull. 329, 332-333 (1977)).

> The search for peace and justice means also respect for human dignity. All the signatories of the UN Charter have pledged themselves to observe and to respect basic human rights. Thus, no member of the United Nations can claim that mistreatment of its citizens is solely its own business. Equally, no member can avoid its responsibilities to review and to speak when torture or unwarranted deprivation occurs in any part of the world.
>
> The basic thrust of human affairs points toward a more universal demand for fundamental human rights. The United States has a historical birthright to be associated with this process.
>
> We in the United States accept this responsibility in the fullest and the most constructive sense. Ours is a commitment and not just a political posture. I know perhaps as well as anyone that our own ideals in the area of human rights have not always been attained in the United States, but the American people have an abiding commitment to the full realization of these ideals. And we are determined, therefore, to deal with our deficiencies quickly and openly. We have nothing to conceal. . . .
>
> This issue is important in itself. It should not block progress on other important matters affecting the security and well-being of our people and of world peace. It is obvious that the reduction of tensions, the control of nuclear arms, the achievement of harmony in the troubled areas of the world, and the provision of food, good health, and education will independently contribute to advancing the human condition.

In our relationships with other countries, these mutual concerns will be reflected in our political, our cultural, and our economic attitudes. . . .

I believe that this is a foreign policy that is consistent with my own Nation's historic values and commitments. And I believe that it is a foreign policy that is consonant with the ideals of the United Nations.

The theme was developed further by Secretary of State Vance and the President in the two major addresses that follow.

Vance, Human Rights and Foreign Policy
76 Dept. State Bull. 505, 505-508 (1977)

. . . I speak today about the resolve of this Administration to make the advancement of human rights a central part of our foreign policy.

Many here today have long been advocates of human rights within our own society. And throughout our Nation that struggle for civil rights continues.

In the early years of our civil rights movement, many Americans treated the issue as a "Southern" problem. They were wrong. It was and is a problem for all of us. Now, as a Nation, we must not make a comparable mistake. Protection of human rights is a challenge for all countries, not just for a few.

Our human rights policy must be understood in order to be effective. So today I want to set forth the substance of that policy and the results we hope to achieve.

Our concern for human rights is built upon ancient values. It looks with hope to a world in which liberty is not just a great cause but the common condition. In the past it may have seemed sufficient to put our name in international documents that spoke loftily of human rights. That is not enough. We will go to work, alongside other people and governments, to protect and enhance the dignity of the individual.

Let me define what we mean by "human rights."

First, there is the right to be free from governmental violation of the integrity of the person. Such violations include torture; cruel, inhuman, or degrading treatment or punishment; and arbitrary arrest or imprisonment. And they include denial of fair public trial, and invasion of the home.

Second, there is the right to the fulfillment of such vital needs as food, shelter, health care, and education. We recognize that the fulfillment of this right will depend, in part, upon the stage of the nation's economic development. But we also know that this right can be violated by a Government's action or inaction — for example, through corrupt official processes which divert resources to an elite at the expense of the needy, or through indifference to the plight of the poor.

Third, there is the right to enjoy civil and political liberties — freedom of thought, of religion, of assembly; freedom of speech; freedom of the press; freedom of movement both within and outside one's own country; freedom to take part in government.

Our policy is to promote all these rights. They are all recognized in the Universal Declaration of Human Rights, a basic document which the United States helped fashion and which the United Nations approved in 1948. There may be a disagreement on the priorities these rights deserve, but I believe that, with work, all these rights can become complementary and mutually reinforcing.

The philosophy of our human rights policy is revolutionary in the intellectual sense, reflecting our Nation's origin and progressive values. As Archibald MacLeish wrote during our Bicentennial a year ago, "The cause of human liberty is now the one great revolutionary cause. . . ."

President Carter put it this way in his speech before the United Nations:

> . . . All the signatories of the United Nations Charter have pledged themselves to observe and to respect basic human rights. Thus, no member of the United Nations can claim that mistreatment of its citizens is solely its own business. Equally, no member can avoid its responsibilities to review and to speak when torture or unwarranted deprivation occurs in any part of the world. . . .

Since 1945 international practice has confirmed that a nation's obligations to respect human rights is a matter of concern in international law.

Our obligation under the UN Charter is written into our legislation. For example, our Foreign Assistance Act now reads: "A principal goal of the foreign policy of the United States is to promote the increased observance of internationally recognized human rights by all countries." In these ways our policy is in keeping with our tradition, our international obligations, and our laws.

In pursuing a human rights policy, we must always keep in mind the limits of our power and of our wisdom. A sure formula for defeat of our goals would be a rigid, hubristic attempt to impose our values on others. A doctrinaire plan of action would be as damaging as indifference.

We must be realistic. Our country can only achieve our objectives if we shape what we do to the case at hand. In each instance we will consider these questions as we determine whether and how to act:

1. First, we will ask ourselves, what is the nature of the case that confronts us? For example, what kind of violations or deprivations are there? What is their extent? Is there a pattern to the violations? If so, is the trend toward concern for human rights or away from it? What is the degree of control and responsibility of the Government involved? And, finally, is the Government willing to permit independent, outside investigation?

2. A second set of questions concerns the prospects for effective action. Will our action be useful in promoting the overall cause of human rights? Will it actually improve the specific conditions at hand? Or will it be likely to make things worse instead? Is the country involved receptive to our interest and efforts? Will others work with us, including official and private international organizations dedicated to furthering human rights? Finally, does our sense of values and decency demand that we speak out or take action anyway, even though there is only a remote chance of making our influence felt?

3. We will ask a third set of questions in order to maintain a sense of perspective. Have we steered away from the self-righteous and strident, remembering that our own record is not unblemished? Have we been sensitive to genuine security interests, realizing that outbreak of armed conflict or terrorism could in itself pose a serious threat to human rights? Have we considered all the rights at stake? If, for instance, we reduce aid to a Government which violates the political rights of its citizens, do we not risk penalizing the hungry and poor who bear no responsibility for the abuses of their Government?

If we are determined to act, the means available range from quiet diplomacy in its many forms through public pronouncements to withholding of assistance. Whenever possible, we will use positive steps of encouragement and inducement. Our strong support will go to countries that are working to improve the human condition. We will always try to act in concert with other countries through international bodies.

In the end a decision whether and how to act in the case of human rights is a matter for informed and careful judgment. No mechanistic formula produces an automatic answer.

It is not our purpose to intervene in the internal affairs of other countries, but as the President has emphasized, no member of the United Nations can claim that violation of internationally protected human rights is solely its own affair. It is our purpose to shape our policies in accord with our beliefs and to state them without stridency or apology when we think it is desirable to do so.

Our policy is to be applied within our own society as well as abroad. We welcome constructive criticism at the same time as we offer it.

No one should suppose that we are working in a vacuum. We place great weight on joining others in the cause of human rights.

The UN system is central to this cooperative endeavor. That is why the President stressed the pursuit of human rights in his speech before the General Assembly last month. That is why he is calling for U.S. ratification of four important human rights covenants and conventions, and why we are trying to strengthen the human rights machinery within the United Nations.

And that is an important reason why we have moved to comply with UN sanctions against Rhodesia. In one of our first acts, this Administration sought and achieved repeal of the Byrd amendment, which had placed us in violation of these sanctions and thus in violation of international law. We are supporting other diplomatic efforts within the United Nations to promote basic civil and political rights in Namibia and throughout southern Africa.

Regional organizations also play a central role in promoting human rights. The President has announced that the United States will sign and seek Senate approval of the American Convention on Human Rights. We will continue to work to strengthen the machinery of the Inter-American Commission on Human Rights. This will include efforts to schedule regular visits to all members of the Organization of American States, annual debates on human rights conditions, and the expansion of the inter-American educational program on human rights.

The United States is seeking increased consultation with other nations for joint programs on economic assistance and more general efforts to promote human rights. We are working to assure that our efforts reach out to all, with particular sensitivity to the problems of women. . . .

The United States looks to use of economic assistance — whether bilateral or through international financial institutions — as a means to foster basic human rights. . . .

This Administration's human rights policy has been framed in collaboration and consultation with Congress and private organizations. We have taken steps to assure firsthand contact, consultation, and observation when members of Congress travel abroad to review human rights conditions.

We are implementing current laws that bring human rights considerations directly into our decisions in several international financial institutions. At the same time, we are working with the Congress to find the most effective way to fulfill our parallel commitment to international cooperation in economic development.

In accordance with human rights provisions of legislation governing our security assistance programs, we recently announced cuts in military aid to several countries.

Outside the government, there is much that can be done. We welcome the efforts of individual American citizens and private organizations — such as religious, humanitarian, and professional groups — to work for human rights with commitments of time, money, and compassion.

All these initiatives to further human rights abroad would have a hollow ring if we were not prepared to improve our own performance at home. So we have removed all restrictions on our citizens' travel abroad and are proceeding with plans to liberalize our visa policies.

We support legislation and administrative action to expand our refugee and asylum policies and to permit more victims of repressive regimes to enter the United States. . . .

What results can we expect from all these efforts?

We may justifiably seek a rapid end to such gross violations as those cited in our law: ". . . torture, or cruel, inhuman or degrading treatment or punishment, or prolonged detention without charges. . . ." Just last week our Ambassador at the United Nations, Andrew Young, suggested a series of new ways to confront the practice of torture around the world.

The promotion of other human rights is a broader challenge. The results may be slower in coming but are no less worth pursuing, and we intend to let other countries know where we stand.

We recognize that many nations of the world are organized on authoritarian rather than democratic principles — some large and powerful, others struggling to raise the lives of their people above bare subsistence levels. We can nourish no illusions that a call to the banner of human rights will bring sudden transformations in authoritarian societies.

We are embarked on a long journey. But our faith in the dignity of the individual encourages us to believe that people in every society, according to their own traditions, will in time give their own expression to this fundamental aspiration.

Our belief is strengthened by the way the Helsinki principles and the UN Declaration of Human Rights have found resonance in the hearts of people of many countries. Our task is to sustain this faith by our example and our encouragement.

In his inaugural address, three months ago, President Carter said; "Because we are free, we can never be indifferent to the fate of freedom elsewhere." Again, at a meeting of the Organization of American States two weeks ago, he said: "You will find this country . . . eager to stand beside those nations which respect human rights and which promote democratic ideals."

We seek these goals because they are right, and because we too will benefit. Our own well-being, and even our security, are enhanced in a world that shares common freedoms and in which prosperity and economic justice create the conditions for peace. And let us remember that we always risk paying a serious price when we become identified with repression.

Nations, like individuals, limit their potential when they limit their goals. The American people understand this. I am confident they will support foreign policies that reflect our traditional values. To offer less is to define America in ways we should not accept.

America fought for freedom in 1776 and in two World Wars. We have offered haven to the oppressed. Millions have come to our shores in times of trouble. In times of devastation abroad, we have shared our resources.

Our encouragement and inspiration to other nations and other peoples have never been limited to the power of our military or the bounty of our economy. They have been lifted up by the message of our Revolution, the message of individual human freedom. That message has been our great national asset in times past. So it should be again.

Carter, Humane Purpose in Foreign Policy
76 Dept. State Bull. 621, 621-623 (1977)

[The President began his remarks by stating that the United States needed a foreign policy "that is democratic, that is based on fundamental values, and that uses power and influence . . . for humane purposes." He then proceeded to review his Administration's early record in and renew its commitment to the human rights area.]

First, we have reaffirmed America's commitment to human rights as a fundamental tenet of our foreign policy. In ancestry, religion, color, place of origin, and cultural background, we Americans are as diverse a nation as the world has ever seen. No common mystique of blood or soil unites us. What draws us together, perhaps more than anything else, is a belief in human freedom. We want the world to know that our Nation stands for more than financial prosperity.

This does not mean that we can conduct our foreign policy by rigid moral maxims. We live in a world that is imperfect and which will always be imperfect — a world that is complex and confused, and which will always be complex and confused.

I understand fully the limits of moral suasion. We have no illusion that changes will come easily or soon. But I also believe that it is a mistake to undervalue the power of words and of the ideas that words embody. In our own history, that power has ranged from Thomas Paine's "Common Sense" to Martin Luther King, Jr.'s "I Have a Dream."

In the life of the human spirit, words are action, much more so than many of us may realize who live in countries where freedom of expression is taken for granted. The leaders of totalitarian nations understand this very well. The proof is that words are precisely the action for which dissidents in those countries are being persecuted.

Nonetheless, we can already see dramatic worldwide advances in the protection of the individual from the arbitrary power of the state. For us to ignore this trend would be to lose influence and moral authority in the world. To lead it will be to regain the moral stature that we once had.

The great democracies are not free because we are strong and prosperous. I believe we are strong and influential and prosperous because we are free.

Throughout the world today in free nations and in totalitarian countries as well, there is a preoccupation with the subject of human freedom, human rights, and I believe it is incumbent on us in this country to keep that discussion, that debate, that contention alive. No other country is as well qualified as we to set an example. We have our own shortcomings and faults, and we should strive constantly and with courage to make sure that we are legitimately proud of what we have. . . .

C. Criticism of the Carter Administration's Human Rights Policy and Its Response

1. Criticism

Panel, Human Rights: A New Policy by a New Administration
1977 Am. Socy. Intl. L. Proceedings 68, 72-76

[The panel, under the chairmanship of Professor Henkin, first heard a speech by an Assistant Legal Adviser of the Department of State urging U.S. ratification of the Genocide Convention and other human rights instruments. After further remarks by two additional speakers, the panel continued as follows.]

REMARKS BY ERNEST HAAS

I will proceed on four premises:

— The United States has embarked on the most naive and moralistic campaign since Woodrow Wilson.
— This rhetoric is immoral if it misleads foreign citizens into thinking that the United States will help them significantly to change national repressive policies.
— Most of the world today is primarily interested in collective rights, and success in the field of collective human rights implies a weakening of human rights of individuals.
— International law is rigged in favor of collective rights and against individual rights, as a matter of principle.

As to the naive character of the current campaign for human rights, only about 35% of the 145 sovereign states are committed to protecting the human rights of their citizens. Human rights are no more important than, for example, disarmament and the improvement of the world's food supply, and there are trade-offs to be considered between human rights and these objectives. Moreover, the cementing of the international order can only be accomplished by taking important matters up one at a time; human rights should not be tied to other issues if more important objectives are thus jeopardized. The failure of recent SALT deliberations is an example of what happens when human rights are tied to other issues.

As to the danger of current rhetoric on the advancement of human rights, their international protection is a task which cannot be accomplished. Self-confident totalitarian regimes will not take seriously a symbolic American protest of its violations of human rights. Symbolic protest can only help occasional individuals and only if the matters are worked out quietly.

As to the third point, developing countries are predominantly interested in the development of collective rights such as systematic economic growth. In order to achieve these collective rights, we may expect that harsh official measures will continue to be taken, often requiring a suppression of individual rights.

As to the fourth point, the rigging of international law against individual rights is enshrined in the double standard, practiced by a large majority in the United Nations hostile to the United States, that "rights are for me, obligations are for you." Official positions on human rights will broaden U.S. exposure to this hostile majority which will act as both judge and jury against the interests of this country.

The United States is not omnipotent and should, therefore, refrain from projecting its values into a heterogeneous world without qualification for time and place. The current human rights campaign will be victimized by the UN's double standard and fool this country into thinking that it is able to change the world by moral precept.

REMARKS BY ALEXANDER DALLIN

The Administration's policy of supporting human rights abroad may be viewed in the light of three issues: morality, legality, and practicality.

On the issue of morality, we may welcome the tone of the new U.S. policy, providing it is not grandstanding. We need also to be reminded of the tragic example of Woodrow Wilson. On the issue of legality, existing international law is both vague and self-contradictory. Many troublesome federal issues, such as the standing of individuals, are frequent obstacles. The third issue, practicality, is as yet inconclusive. Thus far, the new policy has not helped human rights anywhere and, in fact, on balance may have been counterproductive. We might note four examples of problems in this connection.

There is, first, an inconsistency in implementing the U.S. positions — for example, there has been no condemnation of China, Taiwan, Korea, Iran, Philippines, and Romania. These failures suggest that the policy is being manipulated politically. Second, the policy unwittingly contributes to the incitement of dissidents and militants all over the world. Third, it has a disadvantageous impact on the international atmosphere and helps provoke hostility — for example, the Soviets in the SALT negotiations and hostile reactions of countries which have declined to accept aid. Fourth, the new policy derogates from the record of previous accomplishment by quiet diplomacy in obtaining release or emigration for individuals without loss of face by their governments.

Another problem is the uncertainty of the rights themselves. Our definition of them is culturebound and, even within this country, it has changed with the passage of time. Suppose that another country insisted that freedom from unemployment was a human right. What would be the response of this country?

The history of recent U.S. foreign policy would have been written differently had human rights been given the priority then that they are now ostensibly being accorded. This country might not have supported Yugoslavia in 1948, nor a range of World War II allies from Greece to China, nor might it have attempted to normalize relations with mainland China. The biggest question is how and at what cost we can realistically help foreign nationals to secure their human rights.

Discussion

Comments and questions from the audience began by considering the scope of human rights. One emigré from the Soviet Union suggested that the most basic human right was the right to leave a country. Two members of the audience suggested that U.S. human rights policy was an exercise in self-indulgence and that President Carter would be as content with the maintenance of the status quo on this issue as had previous Administrations. An emigré from the Philippines challenged the statement made by Professor Haas that advancement of human rights was not possible in face of the desire of the Third World for economic advancement. This assertion, he submitted, was contradicted by the recent Indian experience in which Prime Minister Indira Ghandi, pushing economic advance by suppressing civil rights, was turned out of office. He added that Filipinos are disappointed by the U.S. reticence toward the military rule in the Philippines. He pointed out that the value of political and civil rights had been taught by U.S. citizens to the Filipinos.

Another member of the audience commented that it is unrealistic to say that a choice must be made between collective rights, for example, economic progress, and human rights. Human rights have been suppressed in the Soviet Union for 60 years in order to achieve collective rights, and the Soviet citizens today have neither collective nor human rights. Several comments recalled the rebellions in Hungary and Czechoslovakia and wondered how the United States would respond today to a coup in Eastern Europe.

Professor Dallin reemphasized that the nature of human rights is subjective. He said that he had no quarrel with the therapeutic uses of human rights policy, but he wondered if there might be better uses for it. He added his fear that the new emphasis might get out of hand. Politics is the art of the possible, and it is not possible for the United States systematically to influence human rights abroad except at an unreasonable price to itself.

Professor HAAS cautioned that executive actions to promote human rights abroad are very dangerous; more good would be wrought by the use of a more attenuated human rights policy. He questioned whether there was any real consensus, even within the United States, on a definition of protected rights and whether the ratification of the international conventions will have any effect in promoting human rights.

Mr. ROVINE replied that the differences between himself and Professors Haas and Dallin reflected a difference in personal philosophy and differences in view as to the power of ideas to influence people's thinking and their behavior. The treaties on human rights can actually affect the way people think and behave. The current human rights policy warrants further implementation and further experimentation, and certainly the United States should adhere to the human rights treaties.

Professor HENKIN summed up the meeting. He concluded that there are no good reasons for the United States to refrain from adhering to human rights conventions and many good reasons for doing so. The suggestion that they would subject us to criticism, he thought unreal and ignoble. We are subject to criticism, warranted and unwarranted, even without being party to the conventions. Our record on human rights is quite good; when it is not we ought to be criticized. He saw no reason either for failing to take other actions in regard to human rights, for example, opening our doors wider to refugees or to Communist visitors.

The original subject of the panel had not been fully developed at this meeting. Congress and the executive are no longer sharply divided. The executive now recognizes that some congressional intervention, even some legislative "rigidity," is useful to the executive. Some observers might add that such congressional limitations might be necessary to keep the executive from backsliding. Some might insist also that the executive must recognize that Congress is more representative and more responsible to citizen interests and opinion. But Congress should recognize that the executive is better able to see the national interest as a whole and is closer to what goes on abroad day to day. Ideally, we might hope to combine the common sense of a practical, responsive Congress with the perspective and expertise of the executive branch.

The discussion, Professor HENKIN thought, revealed the need to explore some of the assumptions, as well as expose some fallacies, reflected in the discussion now going on around the world. It is assumed that economic-social rights must come first and that they will lead to civil and political rights. Economic and social improvements have not in fact led to civil-political rights anywhere. Is there any evidence to support the view that one must sacrifice political-civil rights to make economic-social progress? There is also a tendency to lump together all rights without distinction. Perhaps one cannot expect advanced representative government in new states, and perhaps some degree of "regimentation" will contribute to economic development. But what excuse is there for torture, detention, and other repressions?

There is also room for disagreement as to what the United States should do, as was clearly heard here. For himself, Professor HENKIN submitted that we need more rhetoric not less, and if Professor Haas asks what will we do for an encore, Professor HENKIN would say, "Play it again, Sam." We should not underestimate the power of ideas. Ideas ended colonialism, and they will end racism in Southern Africa. In the Covenant on Civil and Political Rights the world accepted our ideas; we need not hesitate to remind them, to see to it that those ideas are not distorted or diluted for narrow political ends.

The real issue is what the United States should do beyond rhetoric. No one suggests that the United States send troops to liberate people or otherwise improve human rights. There is no serious danger that anyone hearing our rhetoric will count on that. But some "linkages" do have some affect. At Helsinki, the USSR in effect agreed to a linkage of human rights to trade and security. Professor HENKIN saw no objection to using U.S. influence where it is likely to work. Some "linkage," moreover, is inevitable and inherent in the system. Whether we like it or not, our interests are affected by what we do or do not do in Southern Africa or Chile. Our alliances and friendships can be firm only with those more or less like minded. Surely we do not have to identify ourselves too closely with gross violators, nor do we owe them largesse or warm friendship.

Hoffman, The Hell of Good Intentions
29 Foreign Policy 3, 7-9 (1977)

[The following extract comes from a tentative examination of the Carter Administration's foreign policy during its first year in office.]

Finally, there is a contradiction between both the traditional state-of-war aspects of international relations and the run-of-the-mill world order concerns, on one hand, and the ethical emphasis on human rights, on the other. The quest for human rights and the quest for world order are not identical. Ordinary world order issues may foster conflict, yet the ultimate objective is accommodation — compromise for survival and progress. The issue of human rights, however, by definition, breeds confrontation. Raising the issue touches on the very foundations of a regime, on its sources and exercise of power, on its links to its citizens or subjects. It is a dangerous issue — a difficult one to manipulate, because if the Carter administration does mean what it says it means, many other nations may take this as an assertion of American hubris, of an old fondness for telling others how to run their affairs. The subject of human rights almost inevitably increases tensions with our enemies. If it is pursued very avidly it diminishes the chances of cooperation on a number of other world order issues.

Any human rights policy is also constantly complicated by the problem of consistency. It is very difficult to assess exactly what other nations do to their own people, and what the trend may be. Furthermore, even if that information is available, treating human rights separately from all other issues may distort foreign policy; if it is weighed against other American interests and other aspects of a foreign nation's conduct, that may result either in rubbery criteria or in a rapidly shrinking concern for human rights. The choices are in some ways all unpleasant: If the United States is too selective about which countries to denounce, it risks becoming hypocritical (for instance, if it singles out only its foes and spares its friends). If it pursues the cause of human rights everywhere, in an almost crusading manner, that is likely to be a highly self-destructive ordeal. But if the policy becomes merely verbal, it will be a splendid demonstration of impotence.

These contradictions may never be entirely eliminated. Still, it is the problem of strategy to try to manage them. But the Carter administration does not even give the impression of being systematically aware of these contradictions, or of trying to cope with them at the levels where strategy is shaped.

Kissinger, Continuity and Change in American Foreign Policy
15 Society 97, 99-102 (1977)

Morality and Pragmatism

. . . I would now like to turn to one of the basic challenges of foreign policy, the perennial tension between morality and pragmatism. Whenever it has been forced to wield its great power, the United States has also been driven to search its conscience. How does our foreign policy serve moral ends? How can the United States carry out its role as humane example and champion of justice in a world in which power is still often the final arbiter? How do we reconcile ends and means, principle and survival? How do we keep secure both our existence *and* our values? These have been the moral and intellectual dilemmas of the United States for two hundred years.

From the time of the Declaration of our Independence, Americans have believed that this country has a moral significance for the world. The United States was created as a conscious act by men and women dedicated to a set of political and ethical principles they held to be of universal meaning. Small wonder, then, that Santayana declared that "being an American is, of itself, almost a moral condition."

At the same time, since Tocqueville it has been observed that we are a pragmatic people, commonsensical, undogmatic, undoctrinaire — a nation with a permanent bent to the practical and an instinct for what works. We have defined our basic goals — justice, freedom, equality, and progress — in open and libertarian terms, seeking to enlarge opportunity and the human spirit rather than to coerce a uniform standard of behavior or a common code of doctrine and belief.

This duality of nature is *not* at war with reality. For in international politics our morality and power should not be antithetical. Any serious foreign policy must begin with need for survival. And survival has its practical necessities. A nation does not willingly delegate control over its future. For a great power to remit its security to the mercy of others is an abdication of foreign policy. All serious foreign policy therefore begins with maintaining a balance of power — a scope for action, a capacity to affect events and conditions. Without that capacity a nation is reduced to striking empty poses.

But, equally, our nation cannot rest its policy on power alone. Our tradition and the values of our people ensure that a policy that seeks only to manipulate force would lack all conviction, consistency, and public support. This is why the United States has been most successful in our relations with the world when we combined our idealism and our pragmatism — from the days when our Founding Fathers manipulated the monarchical rivalries of Europe to secure our independence and launch the great democratic experiment to the creative American initiatives after the Second World War such as the Marshall Plan. Our modern efforts to achieve strategic arms limitation, peace in the Middle East and southern Africa, the opening to China, recasting international economic relations based on the principle of interdependence — these have also served both moral and practical ends and can be sustained only by a combination of moral conviction and practical wisdom.

Enhancing Human Rights

These considerations come to bear powerfully on the question of the relationship between human rights and foreign policy. The world needs to know what this country stands for. But we cannot rest on this; we must know how to implement our convictions and achieve an enhancement of human rights *together* with other national objectives. Neither the issue nor the concern are new:

— It was under the two previous administrations that Jewish emigration from the Soviet Union was raised from 400 a year in 1968 to 35,000 by 1973. This resulted from a deliberate policy, as a concomitant to the process of improving American-Soviet relations.

— The release of the courageous Soviet dissident Bukovsky in exchange for the Chilean Communist leader imprisoned in Chile was arranged in 1976 through American intercession. It was but one of many such acts which were not publicized in order to be able to continue to assist hardship cases.

— American diplomatic action in the same period brought about the release of hundreds of prisoners from jails all over the world.

— American foreign policy of the past decade helped enshrine basic principles of human rights in the Final Act of the Helsinki Conference on Security and Cooperation in Europe — providing the indispensable political and legal basis for pursuing the issue of human rights in East-West relations.

— We also worked to improve the efforts of the United Nations Human Rights Commission and to upgrade the Commission on Human Rights of the Organization of American States. Common human rights policies were forged with the other democracies, and steps were taken to improve the institutional response of the international system to the challenge of human rights.

The accomplishment of the new administration is not that it originated the concern with human rights, but that free of the legacy of Vietnam and Watergate it has seized the opportunity to endow the policy with a more explicit formulation. The aim of the Carter administration has been to give the American people, after the traumas of Vietnam and Watergate, a renewed sense of the basic decency of this country, so that they may continue to have pride and self-confidence to remain actively involved in the world.

Having had to conduct American foreign policy in a period of national division and self-flagellation, I applaud and support this objective. The president has tapped a wellspring of American patriotism, idealism, unity, and commitment which are vital to our country and to the world. He has focused public concern on one of the greatest blights of our time.

The modern age has brought undreamt-of benefits to mankind — in medicine, in scientific and technological advance, and in communication. But the modern age has also spawned new tools of oppression and of civil strife. Terrorism and bitter ideological contention have weakened bonds of social cohesion; the yearning for order even at the expense of liberty has resulted all too often in the violation of fundamental standards of human decency.

The central moral problem of government has always been to strike a just and effective balance between freedom and authority. When freedom degenerates into anarchy, the human personality becomes subject to arbitrary, brutal, and capricious forces — witness aberrations of terrorism in even the most humane societies. Yet when the demand for order overrides all other considerations, man becomes a means and not an end, a tool of impersonal machinery. Human rights are the very essence of a meaningful life, and human dignity is the ultimate purpose of civil governments. Respect for the rights of man is written into the founding documents of almost every nation of the world. It has long been part of the common speech and daily lives of our citizens.

The obscene and atrocious acts systematically employed to devalue, debase, and destroy man during World War II vividly and ineradicably impressed on the world the enormity of the challenge to human rights. It was to end such abuses and provide moral authority in international affairs that new institutions and legal standards were forged after that war — globally in the United Nations and in this hemisphere in a strengthened inter-American system.

The fact remains that continuing practices of intimidation, terror, and brutality, fostered sometimes from outside national territories and sometimes from inside, mark the distance yet to be traveled before the community of nations can claim that it is truly civilized. This is why the distinguished junior senator from New York, Senator Moynihan, is surely right in stressing that human rights should be not simply a humanitarian program but a *political* component of American foreign policy.

For the difference between freedom and totalitarianism is not transient or incidental; it is a moral conflict, of fundamental historical proportions, which gives the modern age its special meaning and peril. Our defense of human rights reminds us of the fundamental reason that our competition with totalitarian systems is vital to the cause of mankind. There is no reason for us to accept the hypocritical double standard increasingly prevalent in the United Nations where petty tyrannies berate us for our alleged moral shortcomings. On this issue we are not — and have no reason to be — on the defensive. "The cause of human liberty," the poet Archibald MacLeish has written, "is now the one great revolutionary cause."

And yet, while human rights must be an essential component of our foreign policy, to pursue it effectively over the long term we must take the measure of the dangers and dilemmas along the way. First, any foreign policy must ultimately be judged by its operational results. "In foreign relations," Walter Lippmann once wrote, "as in all other relations, a policy has been formed only when commitments and power have been brought into balance."

To be sure, the advocacy of human rights has in itself a political and even strategic significance. But in the final reckoning more than advocacy will be counted. If we universalize our human rights policy, applying it indiscriminately and literally to all countries, we run the risk of becoming the world's policeman — an objective the American people may not support. At a minimum we will have to answer what may be the question for several friendly governments: how and to what extent we will support them if they get into difficulties by following our maxims. And we will have to indicate what sanctions we will apply to less well-disposed governments which challenge the very precepts of our policy.

If, on the other hand, we confine ourselves to proclaiming objectives that are not translated into concrete actions and specific results, we run the risk of demonstrating that we are impotent and of evoking a sense of betrayal among those our human rights policy seeks to help. Such a course could tempt unfriendly governments to crack down all the harder on their dissidents, in order to demonstrate the futility of our proclamations — this indeed has already happened to some extent in the Soviet Union.

Nor can we escape from the dilemma by asserting that there is no connection between human rights behavior and our attitude on other foreign policy problems — by "unlinking," as the technical phrase goes, human rights from other issues. For this implies that there is no cost or consequence to the violation of human rights, turning our proclamation of human rights into a liturgical theme — decoupled, unenforced, and compromised. Or else we will insist on our values only against weaker countries, in Latin America or Asia, many of which may even be conducting foreign policies supportive of our own. This would lead to the paradox that the weaker the nation and the less its importance on the international scene, the firmer and more uncompromising would be our human rights posture.

Second, precisely because human rights advocacy is a powerful political weapon, we must be careful that in its application we do not erode all moral dividing lines. We must understand the difference between governments making universal ideological claims and countries which do not observe all democratic practices — either because of domestic turmoil, foreign danger, or national traditions — but which make no claim to historical permanence or universal relevance. In the contemporary world it is the totalitarian systems which have managed the most systematic and massive repression of human rights.

In recent decades no totalitarian regime has ever evolved into a democracy. Several authoritarian regimes — such as Spain, Greece, and Portugal — have done so. We must therefore maintain the moral distinction between aggressive totalitarianism and other governments which with all their imperfections are trying to resist foreign pressures or subversion and which thereby help preserve the balance of power in behalf of all free peoples. Our human rights policy owes special consideration to the particular international and domestic setting of governments important to our security and supportive of free world security interests.

There are, of course, some transgressions of human rights which no necessity — real or imagined — can justify. But there are also realities in the threats nations face, either from terrorism at home such as in Argentina or aggression across borders such as Iran or Korea. And we must keep in mind that the alternative to some governments that resist totalitarianism with authoritarian methods may not be greater democracy and an enhancement of human rights but the advent of even more repression, more brutality, more suffering. The ultimate irony would be a posture of resignation toward totalitarian states and harassment of those who would be our friends and who have every prospect of evolving in a more humane direction.

We must take care, finally, that our affirmation of human rights is not manipulated by our political adversaries to isolate countries whose security is important for the future of freedom, even if their domestic practices fall short of our maxims. The membership of the UN Human Rights Commission, composed as it is of a number of nations with extremely dubious human rights practices, does not augur well for an objective approach to this issue in the United Nations. Cuba and other Communist governments, as well as the more repressive regimes of the less developed world, have no moral standing to bring other nations to international account. We should not hesitate to say so.

Third, there is the ominous prospect that the issue of human rights if not handled with great wisdom could unleash new forces of American isolationism. This could defeat the administration's goal of using it to mobilize support for continued American involvement in world affairs. That the human rights issue could develop a life of its own, regardless of the administration's prudent sense of its aims and limits, is already evident from some developments in Congress.

A distorted or misunderstood human rights policy can become the basis and justification of a modern isolationism. What appeals to many as a useful impetus to resistance to the Communist challenge can be used by others to erase all the distinctions between totalitarians and those that resist them, to induce indifference to European Communist parties' accession to power, or to disrupt security relationships which are essential to maintaining the geopolitical balance. Excuses can be found to deny help to almost any friendly country at the precise moment when it faces it most serious external challenge. If conservatives succeed in unravelling ties with nations on the Left and liberals block relations with nations on the Right, we could find ourselves with no constructive foreign relations at all, except with a handful of industrial democracies. The end result ironically could be the irrelevance of the United States to other nations of the world. A policy of moral advocacy that led to American abdication would surely condemn countless millions to greater suffering, danger, or despair.

Fourth and most fundamentally, we should never forget that the key to successful foreign policy is a sense of proportion. Some of the most serious errors of our foreign policy, both of overcommitment and withdrawal, have occurred when we lost the sense of balance between our interests and our ideals. It was under the banners of moralistic slogans a decade and a half ago that we launched adventures that divided our country and undermined our international position. A few years later young people were parading in front of the White House carrying coffins and candles and accusing their government of loving war; the national leadership was denounced as excessively, indeed imperialistically, involved in the internal affairs of other nations. A few years later still, the government was attacked for sacrificing our ethical values on the altar of détente and being *insufficiently* concerned with the domestic behavior of other nations. Neither we nor the rest of the world can any longer afford such extreme fluctuations.

Human rights policy in this period of American responsibility must strengthen the steady purpose and responsible involvement of the American People. It can do so only if it is presented in the context of a realistic assessment of world affairs and not as the magic cure for the difficulties and shortcomings of mankind's contemporary experience.

The administration is surely right in insisting that human rights is a legitimate and recognized subject of international discourse; it is an object of international legal standards — importantly as a result of American initiatives by administrations of both parties. At the same time, we must recognize that we serve the cause of freedom also by strengthening international security and maintaining ties with other countries defending their independence against external aggressions and struggling to overcome poverty, even if their internal structures differ from ours.

We cannot afford to subordinate either concern to the other. Morality without security is ineffectual; security without morality is empty. To establish the relationship and proportion between these goals is perhaps the most profound challenge before our government and our nation. . . .

2. Response

Derian, Human Rights in American Foreign Policy
55 Notre Dame Law. 264, 271-280 passim (1979)

[The author, then Assistant Secretary of State for Human Rights and Humanitarian Affairs, after describing "the modern international law of human rights" and the three-part formulation thereof set out by Secretary Vance, pages 1042-1043 supra, proceeds to explain how the United States implemented its human rights policy during the Carter Administration.]

The first tool of implementation is steady, quiet diplomacy. It is more effective than many people realize. Perhaps quiet diplomacy got a bad name in earlier years when officials sometimes claimed to be working for human rights through quiet diplomacy and in reality they were saying virtually nothing to representatives from other governments. Quiet diplomacy is not silent diplomacy. In fact it may seem quite noisy to the government with whom we engage in dialogue. It is quiet only in the sense that it does not reach the public. Another government may then find it easier to make changes in its practices without seeming to be knuckling under to outside pressures. For this reason, quiet diplomacy is our preferred approach. A concern for human rights is now a consistent part of our official contacts with other governments. Human rights issues also find their way into the briefing books and talking points prepared for high level meetings between our government and any other. Other governments know we will keep the matter on the agenda. As Dr. Brzezinski has put it, "there is today not a government in the world that does not know that how it behaves in regard to human rights will affect its relationship with the U.S." This awareness inevitably affects government leaders' thinking whenever they are tempted to restrict political rights or crack down on the opposition.

Quiet diplomacy is, however, not always sufficient. We may also use carefully selected public statements, to bring the focus of world opinion to bear on the violating country.

When high U.S. officials visit countries with serious human rights problems, they frequently meet with opposition figures or with the families of victims of government repression. Such visits afford a tangible symbol of American concern for conditions in that country. Not only do they reinforce our message to the government, in some instances they can boost the morale of democratic forces.

There are also efforts that we can undertake in international fora, such as the U.N. Human Rights Commission, the Inter-American Human Rights Commission, the biennial sessions held under the Helsinki Final Act, or conclaves on particular crises like the Geneva conference on Indochinese refugees held last July. Indeed, new international machinery has been developed in recent years, and this affords promise for long-run observance of human rights. It is not widely known that UNESCO has recently adopted a new complaint procedure under which individuals can file complaints of violations of their rights in the areas under UNESCO's jurisdiction. Governments are then called upon to respond. In addition, a new Inter-American Court of Human Rights is being constituted under the American Convention on Human Rights. And a resolution passed last July by the Organization of African Unity has moved a long way toward setting up a regional human rights commission for Africa. Meanwhile, the U.N. Human Rights Commission has finally become more active than before in pursuing the complaints of gross violations lodged with it. In 1978, inquiries were pressed into gross violations by the governments of Uganda, Cambodia, and Equatorial Guinea. And for the first time, there was consensus to take action under procedures providing for confidential review of complaints alleging systematic violations. Ten countries were affected, spanning the ideological spectrum. We have played an important role in developing some of this machinery and in encouraging its use.

In addition to this role, we also encourage other democratic countries, which may enjoy better standing with a particular government, to join in efforts to foster greater respect for human rights. There are signs that other countries are increasingly willing to undertake such efforts. The United Kingdom's work to settle the Zimbabwe-Rhodesia problem clearly reflects that government's concern for human rights. And this year the French government explicitly cited human rights factors in explaining its decision to cut the aid France provided to the regime of the now-deposed Emperor Bokassa of the Central African Empire. Significantly, this decision was reached after a fact-finding mission documented widespread killings of schoolchildren by Bokassa's forces.

Finally, in this list of available implementation methods, there is the heavy artillery of the diplomatic arsenal: decisions on the level and types of economic and military assistance. Congress has taken a major role in shaping the context for these decisions. During the early 1970s and largely in reaction to inattention by the Executive Branch to human rights values, the Congress passed a number of statutes establishing explicit human rights criteria for decisions on military and economic assistance. Section 502B of the Foreign Assistance Act forbids military assistance or arms sales or the transfer of crime control and police equipment to governments that engage in a consistent pattern of gross violations of internationally recognized human rights, unless "extraordinary circumstances" justify such a step. Section 116[e] of the same Act forbids economic assistance to such countries, unless the aid will directly benefit needy people. We have also gone beyond the strict requirements of this legislation. Some countries with serious human rights problems might not technically fall within the language "consistent pattern of gross violations." Nevertheless, we have tried to make sure that our assistance levels reflect their human rights performance. By the same token, we strive to increase assistance to countries with especially good human rights records, such as Botswana or the Dominican Republic.

The State Department is often pressed to describe in detail specific examples where U.S. action has led to human rights improvements in other countries. Such a description is usually not appropriate because of the confidential nature of our contacts with the other government. Moreover, the United States is really not in a position to claim credit for such human rights improvements as do occur. They are not our doing; they result from choices made by the people of the particular country involved. Our role is to encourage progress by creating a climate that may make it easier for the government to improve its observance of internationally recognized human rights, or easier for democratic forces within the country to push success-fully for such progress. . . .

DILEMMAS AND OPPORTUNITIES

Looking to the future, I see a number of dilemmas that must be confronted as our human rights work continues. The first involves consistency. When there are two countries with roughly the same human rights conditions, the same tactics are rarely adopted for both. For that reason, the charge might be made that the United States ignores the sins of one regime while taking visible steps against another whose behavior is equivalent.

The choice of tactics, however, rests on three considerations which are basic elements of the policy. First, we do what we can, given the state of our relations with another government, to improve the quality of human rights observance in that country. Sometimes the public is not aware of the strengths or limitations in that relationship that dictate the choice of certain tactics. Second, it must be remembered that human rights is not our only foreign policy priority. We do have other interests: fostering national security, avoiding nuclear war, promoting trade. In every case we weigh the importance of those interests and the effect a particular human rights initiative may have upon them before deciding any course of action. We have consciously determined to give a higher priority to human rights concerns in that process. We have, for the first time, allowed human rights a seat at the table of traditional foreign policy objectives. That seat, however, can be accurately compared to the one occupied by the youngest member of the family at a dinner: sometimes when the big decisions are made, the youngest is excused. Third, we look to the historical and cultural differences among nations, as well as a given country's present conditions, in deciding what specific actions to take.

There is no universal grid to be applied automatically to each situation. Even though these elements of our human rights diplomacy may lend themselves to rather economical summary, those formulations describe a policy that is complex and ambitious. It deliberately forsakes simple formulae and single-factor decisions. As a result, the charge of inconsistency will no doubt persist. I wish it were otherwise. But the fundamental design of the policy, despite its complexity, is sound and must be maintained.

It would be less than candid to suggest that only the public impression of inconsistency constitutes a potential problem. One of the dangers of complexity is that it may be used to mask genuine inconsistency. Opponents of vigorous action to promote human rights — and there are some within the Department — can often frame their opposition to sound as if it were premised on the human rights policy itself. The only way to guard against this danger is to examine the arguments against a particular human rights initiative very carefully. The mere possibility of some negative impact on trade or national security is not enough. The risk must be so serious that it truly outweighs the expected human rights improvement. The burden of proof must remain on those who oppose a human rights initiative. If that standard is kept firmly in mind, then the problem becomes one of artful application of a policy that, for all its complexity, is fundamentally sound.

A second dilemma arises in those countries where, because of overriding security interests, the United States must continue to provide military assistance despite serious human rights problems. That assistance strengthens the recipient government and makes it a more effective bulwark against a common adversary. But at the same time, it obviously makes it easier for the regime in power to repress its own people. The dilemma then is this: What can we do, within the constraints placed by our security interests, to pursue our human rights goals effectively? A few things are obvious: we can still make *demarches*, we can still review other forms of assistance, we can still engage in symbolic acts. And I want to emphasize that, even with countries in this category, we do take all available steps to press human rights concerns. It is nevertheless undeniable that in some countries the human rights message risks being drowned out by the size and nature of the military assistance. To this problem there are no easy answers.

A third dilemma involves raising human rights concerns without imposing too great a strain on America's bilateral relations. This seems especially urgent in the early days of the policy. When our concerns were first voiced, they were often met with a confused, hurt, or irritated reaction. But the record of the past two and a half years shows that our ties with other countries are not so fragile that we must ignore human rights abuses. In particular, the Philippines, Thailand, and Brazil come to mind as instances where the United States raises human rights issues and also pursues other interests. With the Soviets too, after early difficulties, we have been able to pursue serious arms control negotiations and, at the same time, register our concern over the treatment of political dissidents and emigration. We will continue to press for implementation in Eastern Europe of the human rights provisions of the Helsinki Final Act, without unduly jeopardizing our pursuit of our other objectives.

I turn now from real dilemmas to a false issue. If a country develops internal instability at any time after we have brought human rights pressure on the governing regime, blame is often laid at the feet of the human rights policy. Critics then charge that our policy weakened security measures, fomented unrest, encouraged violent opposition. Some of this criticism has come recently from very distinguished figures in foreign policy circles.

This criticism is wrong. Our policy is designed to prevent abuses of human dignity, not to foster turmoil. It is applied, as previously emphasized, with a careful awareness of the practical limits the government may be operating under. We are not so naive as to rush in expecting full implementation of the U.S. Bill of Rights on the next Fourth of July. As the recent history of Spain attests, moving from authoritarian government to genuine respect for human rights is a delicate process demanding skill and statesmanship. But having said that, I should stress that it is no less urgent to start the process and keep it moving — carefully, but meaningfully and persistently.

When our human rights policy is blamed for instability, I would turn this criticism around and point it back at those who make it. In the long run, it is not human rights policy, but the absence of a human rights policy, that poses the greatest risk. Genuine observance of human rights affords the best hope for stability — stability that can be sustained because it rests on mutual respect between government and governed, rather than on a temporary quiet enforced by security police and the torture cell.

Now, what about the opportunities the human rights policy represents? In some sense the goals of the policy are opportunities enough — the opportunity for the United States to play a role in reducing human suffering by careful use of all the diplomatic tools at our command. But there is another fundamental way in which the human rights policy poses a vital opportunity for us. This policy has opened the way to regaining the esteem America lost over the last two decades, the period of Vietnam and Watergate. It helps reestablish our sense as a nation of being true to our own highest ideals. . . .

When I speak for a foreign policy built on certain fundamental values, it may sound as though I am coming down hard on one side of the old dichotomy pitting pragmatism against principle. Realpolitik against moral ideal. I am not. In this instance that stark difference does not hold. What used to be presented to us as Realpolitik was too often empty — indistinguishable from infatuation with the status quo, bound to a view of the world as a global chessboard whose only players were nations, a conception in which flesh-and-blood people disappeared from view. America became identified as dedicated to little more than military power and economic might. And I do not need to tell you that this image of our country has had little magnetism.

In addition, even the central objectives of the old Realpolitik were not well served. That approach failed to recognize that identification with repressive regimes undermines us seriously when the inevitable reaction sets in. Our experience with the Greek junta or the Salazar regime in Portugal should be instructive. Crucially, the old Realpolitik took too little account of some of the deepest stirrings of our time. The human rights idea is one of these. It has taken on a momentum worldwide that none of us could have predicted two years ago. It has found its way into wall posters in Peking. It has become an obligatory part of the vocabulary of world leaders, even those whose observance in practice is at best grudging. Its importance as an issue with young people in Western Europe and elsewhere has enhanced U.S. standing with those groups, now that we have an active human rights policy.

In ruthlessly pragmatic political terms, then, this nation's leadership in the human rights field means a great deal for our prestige, our domestic support, and ultimately for our long-term strength on the world scene. Here pragmatism and principle to a large extent coincide. That in itself constitutes a tremendously significant opportunity. We must not allow the lingering dilemmas confronting our policy — however knotty — to sap our energy or our dedication, lest this opportunity slip away. We have made a start. We must do more.

D.   Human Rights and U.S. Foreign Policy: Argentina as a Case Study: Part I

In the mid-1970s Argentina was the scene of much violence, initially by left-wing terrorist groups and, after the military coup of 24 March 1976 that ousted Mrs. Peron from the presidency, by the state security apparatus itself. Hundreds of persons died and thousands "disappeared" as the military junta pursued its "campaign against subversion," in the words of the Inter-American Commission on Human Rights, "by dispensing with all moral and legal considerations" (Inter-American Commn. on Human Rights, Report on the Situation of Human Rights in Argentina, OEA/Ser.L./V/II.49, doc. 19 corr. 1, at 134 (1980)). Shortly after it took office, in what the New York Times called "the first time in memory that any administration had publicly announced a reduction in foreign aid because of human rights considerations" (N.Y. Times, Feb. 25, 1977, at A1, col. 6), the Carter Administration announced that it was reducing aid to Argentina, whereupon the latter declared that it wished to receive no further U.S. assistance whatsoever. See also the Department of State's highly critical report on Argentina later that winter (Human Rights Practices in Countries Receiving U.S. Security Assistance, Report to the House Comm. on International Relations, 95th Cong., 1st Sess. 101-103 (1977)). The imposition of unilateral economic sanctions has been considered at pages 513-514 of Problem VII. What is raised at this juncture is not only the use of such sanctions for human rights purposes, but also the domestic backlash that the imposition of sanctions may produce.

de Onis, U.S. Denial of Loan Angers Argentines
N.Y. Times, July 21, 1978, at A4, col. 3

BUENOS AIRES, July 20 — A decision by the United States Export-Import Bank to withhold a $270 million loan from Argentina because of human rights violations produced an angry reaction today from Argentine officials and American businessmen here.

The Export-Import Bank's decision came yesterday after Allis Chalmers, a Milwaukee-based manufacturer of electrical equipment, had sought the loan for Argentina. The money would have been used to buy electrical equipment from the company for a hydroelectrical project on the upper Paraná River at Yaciretá-Apipé.

The bank's board, after consulting with the State Department, said that the financing could not be authorized until the Administration reported an improvement in the human rights situation in Argentina. The bank, a Government agency, finances American sales abroad on terms that are usually more favorable than those offered by private banks.

Alexander Perry, a representative in Argentina of the St. Joe mining company, led a delegation of American businessmen today in protesting the decision at a meeting with Ambassador Raul Castro, who returned from Washington last week after a review of the human rights situation here.

'LACK OF UNDERSTANDING' NOTED

Jorge Wehbe, a former Minister of Economy, expressed a widespread feeling in the Argentina business community when he said that the action reflected "a lack of understanding of the Argentine situation and an unfair discrimination by President Carter."

"When President Carter went to Poland, did he find respect for human rights there?" he asked. "Why didn't the Export-Import Bank suspend credits to Poland?"

Since 1974, when left-wing guerrillas began a full-scale insurgency against Argentina's elected government, about 4,000 people have been killed here. Most have been killed since the armed forces seized power in March 1976.

More than 3,000 people are in jail for security reasons and human rights groups have made up lists of missing people with numbers ranging from 1,600 to 3,000.

The American Embassy has been urging President Jorge Rafael Videla to release prisoners held without charges. The Carter Administration also wants Argentina to accept an inspection visit from the Human Rights Commission of the Organization of American States.

Evans and Novak, Human-Rights Zeal That Costs U.S. Jobs
Wash. Post, Sept. 18, 1978, at 23, col. 1

Administration policy makers alarmed over loss of American export business are moving against human-rights vetoes of commercial sales abroad with help from a most surprising source: U.N. Ambassador Andrew Young.

As a result, barriers to foreign trade imposed by Assistant Secretary of State Patt Derian's Human Affairs Bureau will soon be lowered. These changes will remove some of the restrictions on Export-Import Bank credits for foreign sales, and assure foreign nations of new efforts to protect their traditional trade patterns with the United States.

The intervention of Andy Young, a potent human-rights disciple, came in a secret diplomatic cable Aug. 22 to National Security Adviser Zbigniew Brzezinski. Young warned that rigid application of Derian's human-rights standards was "denying jobs to U.S. workers" and "weakening" the U.S. economy. Young's unexpected missive also went to Deputy Secretary of State Warren Christopher, the administration's top human-rights strategist, and Secretary of Commerce Juanita Kreps.

Its timing gives special significance to the warning from Young, who has frequently embarrassed the White House with rhetorical hip-shooting. It coincided with the arrival on the president's desk of Kreps's proposals for beefing up U.S. exports — essential to strengthening the dollar and reducing the trade deficit. These proposals have been in the drafting stages for months.

One key part of the Kreps plan argues along the lines laid out in Young's cable to the White House. Without quite demanding detailed studies on the cost-benefit ratio of foreign-trade deals rejected by Derian's human-rights office, the Commerce document argues cogently as follows: U.S. exports are depressed by human-rights vigilance as well as regulations restricting under-the-table payments to middle-men and dealing with the Arab boycott against Israel.

The implication is strong: Benefits to American foreign policy of these restrictive measures must be weighed against their cost in terms of U.S. jobs and the U.S. competitive position in world trade.

Young posed the issue this way in his diplomatic cable to the White House: "We should avoid using our economic power in a way that impedes [economic] development in the recipient countries while denying jobs to U.S. workers and weakening our economy and our balance-of-payments situation."

Many examples of such "denying" worry State Department economic officials, the Commerce Department and — most directly — American manufacturers and exporters. One conspicuous case is the Export-Import Bank's denial of credit, at the order of Derian's office, for the $270-million sale of turbines produced by Allis-Chalmers for the new hydroelectric dam on the Paraná River between Argentina and Paraguay. The two countries have just given an additional 30-day grace period to Allis-Chalmers, rather than order turbines elsewhere, in hopes that the Ex-Im Bank decision will be reversed.

A less publicized case involved a hydroelectric project called the Itaipu Dam between Brazil and Paraguay. With both Westinghouse and subsidiaries of General Electric as principal bidders for 18 large turbine generators valued at $700 million, the contract went to foreign producers, including Switzerland's Brown-Boveri.

Administration officials told us several factors were involved in losing that award, including Brazilian anger at President Carter's campaign against a nuclear reprocessing plant. But they also said human rights was a factor.

That was made clear in a brief aside to a U.S. diplomat by President Alfredo Stroessner of Paraguay shortly after the award was made. Stroessner commented icily that Derian ought to be informed that the contract had not gone to a U.S. source. The State Department was promptly informed.

One problem has been Derian's passionate conviction that the U.S. must use its economic power as a lever to pry concessions out of states guilty of human-rights violations — many of which are right-wing dictatorships in Latin America. Until now, her zeal has carried the day within the bureaucracy. She has unquestionably caused some improvements, but at heavy cost. Now the tide is turning.

Economic officials at State and Commerce are joining forces in the campaign to dull her human-rights sword without impairing its ideological sheen. One high State Department official told us privately that Derian "is now acknowledging that on occasion she herself may have overstated the human-rights case."

The result of excess zeal: overstress on human rights at the cost of U.S. jobs during high unemployment and record trade deficits.

Reagan, Argentina's View on Human Rights
Miami News, Oct. 20, 1978, at 13, col. 1

There is an old Indian proverb: "Before I criticize a man, may I walk a mile in his moccasins." Patricia Derian and her minions at Mr. Carter's Human Rights office apparently have never heard of it. If they had, they might not be making such a mess of our relations with the planet's seventh largest country, Argentina, a nation with which we should be close friends.

No sooner had President Carter made his early and strong statement on human rights than born-again McGovernites began infesting various foreign policy-making levels, with an eye toward forcing any nation they could to toe the mark — and they defined the mark.

Nearly any charge made against nations such as Argentina, Brazil and Chile was assumed to be true. Worse, the Carter Human Rights office has managed to hold up important sales to these and other nations.

Now comes a man whose moccasins Ms. Derian & Co. should try: Dr. Jose A. Martinez de Hoz, Argentina's minister of economy, came to the United States recently, and he put Argentina's story in perspective.

Martinez de Hoz is the architect of what may turn out to be one of the most remarkable economic recoveries in modern history. By March of 1976, Argentina's people were being crushed by a 920 per cent inflation rate; and the government was falling toward chaos. Leftist terrorists worked day and night to tear the country apart. American businessmen were favorite targets of kidnappers. In Rosario, the U.S. consul was kidnapped and riddled with bullets.

The armed forced stepped in, as Martinez de Hoz explained, to bring continuity and to keep the country together.

Amnesty International estimated early last year that about 15,000 persons had disappeared under the new government. Martinez de Hoz said he thought the figure was "grossly exaggerated." He said that Argentina had faced a well-equipped, disciplined force of 15,000 terrorists who were "destroying the social fabric" of the country. "What the government had to do was to protect the human rights of 25 million people against a minority of people who had gone ideologically haywire," he said.

In this civil war atmosphere, "no quarter was asked and no quarter was given," he said. He did not deny that some innocents may have been caught up in the crossfire between leftist terrorists, right-wing vigilantes and government forces. Though the situation is virtually under control today, Martinez de Hoz says "it is a sad reality that there will be a certain number of people that the government will never be able to account for."

When this slight, quiet, Cambridge-educated man speaks about a return to democracy he speaks with a conviction.

Argentina's economic recovery shows every sign of making that day come sooner, not later. Inflation, though still sky-high by our standards, is down from that 920 per cent to 102 per cent. Tax collections have doubled, the deficit has been systematically forced down almost to zero and no more printing press money is needed.

Ms. Derian, would you care to try on a new pair of moccasins?

DeYoung and Krause, Our Mixed Signals on Human Rights in Argentina
Wash. Post, Oct. 29, 1978, at C1, col. 5

On the afternoon of Friday, Sept. 29, military attachés representing the army, navy and air force of Argentina were called to the Pentagon and given a piece of bad news. Because of the Argentine government's dismal human rights record, the State Department had decided to turn down 212 pending license requests for the sale of nearly $100 million worth of U.S. military equipment to Argentina's armed forces.

The massive turndown came one day before the Oct. 1 deadline for the complete cutoff of all such sales to Argentina's ruling military junta. Originally scheduled to take effect one year earlier, in 1977, the cutoff had been postponed when the administration persuaded its sponsor, Sen. Edward M. Kennedy (D-Mass.), to amend the deadline to give the State Department a year of "maneuvering room" to try a carrot-and-stick approach in persuading the junta to change its repressive ways.

Few such changes had been forthcoming over the year. More than 15,000 Argentines, according to Amnesty International, are still among the missing, with many presumed dead, after allegedly being kidnapped or arrested by government security forces. "We see nothing," Assistant Secretary of State for Human Rights Patricia Derian said in congressional testimony last August, "to indicate there is a genuine trend toward human rights in Argentina."

Accordingly, what one State Department official involved in the decision called the "vast majority" of munitions license requests still pending as the deadline approached were turned down. The denials, the official said, "send an unmistakable message to the Argentines" of U.S. disapproval.

A Series of Exceptions

But did they? In the months preceding the deadline, when Derian had seen "nothing" to indicate human rights improvement, the State Department had authorized nearly $120 million in military sales to the junta, including five Chinook helicopters, two C130 military transports and 15 Beechcraft trainer aircraft.

In fact, on the same day the State Department was "messaging" the Argentines with the 212 denials, it approved more than 30 training slots for Argentine officers at U.S. military installations.

Even the department itself did not seem sure if its message was one of encouraging carrots or punishing sticks. While Washington officials touted the denials as evidence the administration was fed up with the junta, U.S. Ambassador to Argentina Raul Castro, in a recent interview in Buenos Aires, didn't even mention them.

Instead, Castro announced that the Carter administration had decided to suspend its policy of imposing largely ineffective and often counter-productive sanctions against the junta in favor of incentives to encourage human rights improvement. As evidence of the new incentives policy, Castro pointed to several "overt acts," including the training, the helicopters and what another embassy official called lots of "other stuff" sold to Argentina.

Regardless of the interpretation the junta puts on this somewhat confusing set of circumstances, the fact is that the sale of major defense items to Argentina over the past year has had little to do with human rights. In many cases, the sales have been "exceptions" to legislative restrictions, licensed by virtue of State Department discretionary authority, because of pressure by a U.S. company or its representative in Congress.

The government's human rights watch-dogs have consistently condemned the junta, and repeatedly deemed it ineligible for such sales, as well as for U.S. government-guaranteed and multilateral loans. But those concerned with problems closer to home, such as domestic employment, the balance of payments, profits and military security — including the Commerce and Treasury departments, the Pentagon and private industry — have argued, in many cases successfully, that human rights sanctions are costing an exorbitant price in U.S. jobs, trade and overseas allies.

PRACTICE AND PRINCIPLE

The conflict between U.S. moral, economic and security priorities is not a new one. But beginning perhaps with the 1971 passage and subsequent repeal of the Byrd Amendment exempting vital chrome imports from United Nations trade sanctions against Rhodesia's white minority government, it has grown to the point of outright war under the human rights-conscious Carter administration. With a focus on rights violations in Argentina — and what the United States can and should do about them — the battle between domestic and foreign policy interests is threatening the entire foundation of the administration's human rights campaign.

While the conflict certainly did not begin with Carter, and he was not the first candidate or president to set human rights as a policy priority, by the time he had been in office barely a month it seemed he had invented the concept.

He spoke about it at every opportunity, repeatedly defining the concept and his concern about it. On various occasions, Carter has defined human rights as "free speech . . . respect for the individuality of persons . . . the chance to express one's political beliefs . . . freedom to speak and think as one pleases . . . to participate in the determination of [one's] destiny . . . freedom from torture . . . from prolonged imprisonment without charge."

Those concepts, Carter has said, are "an expression of the most deeply felt values of the American people." His stand on them "is compatible with the consciousness of this country" and "almost overwhelmingly supported by the American people."

The immediate question was what to do about human rights violators. On March 16, 1977, Carter told a town meeting in Clinton, Mass., that the United States "ought to have a right to express displeasure and to do something about" violations. Two days later, he said the administration was "reforming the policies which have, on occasion, awarded liberal grants and loans to repressive regimes."

Later, Carter noted that he had "reduced military relationships which in some countries in the past have seemed to support repressive regimes. . . . Our foreign assistance programs will now reflect more clearly our concern about human rights."

The problem quickly became which countries would be the recipients of "expressed displeasure" and which would suffer "reformed policies." Clearly, the Soviet Union, to which the United States neither sold arms nor gave aid, could not be deprived of such assistance. At the same time, national security interests prevented Carter from doing much more than expressing severe displeasure, as in the case of Anatoly Scharansky, often and loudly in the early months of his administration.

Repressive but friendly governments in strategically important countries like Iran and South Korea were similarly exempted from reformed U.S. policy. What was left was a group of Third World, primarily Latin American, countries, which met the triple criteria of having repressive governments, little economic or strategic importance, and either an embarrassing previous connection with the United States or evidence of Soviet support.

Thus, in early March last year, Carter announced cuts in military assistance to Argentina, Uruguay and Ethiopia. Although a number of other Latin American countries, including Brazil and El Salvador, angrily cancelled their own bilateral military aid agreements with the United States, none of the cutbacks provoked much domestic outcry.

As the human rights situation in Argentina grew worse, however, Congress began legislating more severe sanctions, first prohibiting all military assistance, and finally, with the Kennedy proposal, cancelling even private sales to the junta by U.S. defense contractors. That action had previously been applied only to Chile, whose military regime was so notorious that the bad publicity to be gained by trading with it outweighed economic gains for most U.S. exporters.

The Junta's PR Campaign

The fact that economic interests in the United States chose to challenge the human rights sanctions over the case of Argentina is due not only to the severity of the sanctions, but also to the U.S. unemployment rate, last year's $31 billion balance of trade deficit and, perhaps most importantly, to a multi-million-dollar junta public relations and lobbying campaign that both attempted to justify repression and showed U.S. exporters what they were missing.

The campaign was spelled out in a proposal to the junta by Burson-Marsteller, a New York public relations agency it now employs. Rather than implementing and publicizing human rights improvements, the agency proposed in a mid-1977 memo, Argentina should "project a new, progressive and stable image throughout the world."

The campaign was targeted at three main audiences: "those who influence thinking, which includes the press, government functionaries and educators . . . those who influence investments . . . and those who influence travel, which includes travel agents, travel writers, airline personnel and tour operators."

In addition to government-organized tours for journalists, businessmen and members of Congress, the campaign included pages of advertising in a number of U.S. magazines and newspapers, most running along the lines of a four-page New York Times supplement last June that told "the whole truth" about Argentina, the leftist terrorism that had provoked repression and the Marxist propaganda about the junta spread abroad.

A 17-page supplement in Nation's Business called Argentina "the best location in today's world for *private* investments, production facilities and United States exports." Economy Minister Jose Martinez de Hoz made several trips to the United States in which he spoke primarily to bankers and businessmen and, according to a lengthy article in the Buenos Aires magazine Siete Dias, "broke the trap" of sanctions by assuring investors of "the degree of institutional stability" in Argentina.

Armed with evidence that the Argentine violations case had been overstated, and assurances of sales, U.S. business began to take issue with the human rights sanctions policy.

At the same time, the State Department carrot-and-stick policy, in the absence of substantial junta rights improvements, began to appear confused, and there followed a series of seemingly contradictory decisions.

Protests and Pressure

In late October 1977, House Speaker Thomas P. O'Neill and Rep. Silvio Conte, both of Massachusetts, protested in a letter to Secretary of State Cyrus Vance that his human rights bureau was unnecessarily delaying license approval for an order of periscopes, made by Kollmorgen Co., of Northampton, Mass., for Argentina's German-built submarine fleet. Apparently the threat of lost Massachusetts jobs and income, combined with the fact that most Kollmorgen periscopes are sold to the U.S. Navy, whose costs go down the more are sold abroad, brought results. On Nov. 3, despite the fact that the periscopes were among controlled munitions items, not to be released unless rights improvements could be shown, the approval came through.

Perhaps the most propitious time for license approvals over the past year has been whenever a high-level U.S. mission has traveled to Argentina hoping for what one State Department official called "a big breakthrough" in human rights improvements in response to U.S. prodding. Just prior to those trips, the State Department normally tries, the official said, "to create a climate" for Argentine concessions.

An application for the sale of Boeing-Vertol helicopters to the junta arrived at the State Department just before Vance's trip to Argentina last November. Accordingly, Boeing was given an "advisory" opinion stating that the license was likely to be approved and signed a contract. Although Vance came home with virtually no Argentina rights concessions, and State cautioned that the "advisory" in no way guaranteed license approval, the sale of five helicopters was eventually approved.

"You have no idea of the pressure" Boeing exerted, said another State Department source. Without the Argentine order, the company warned it would have to close an assembly line and lay off workers. At the same time, the junta pointedly told Boeing it might buy its helicopters elsewhere and might place all future orders with a European competitor.

A department spokesman defended the helicopter approval by saying that three of the five requested were outfitted for operation in Argentina's Antarctic naval bases, where it was felt they would not be involved in repressive military operations.

Other licenses, the official said, were for even more innocuous items. In one case, Argentina and the seller of a previously purchased C130 troop transport requested and received a license to fly it back to the United States for a new paint job.

"The Argentines were going to sue" the seller for the initial faulty painting, the official said, "so we let him bring it back in."

"We get into the ridicule factor here," the official said. "It's hard to tell a guy that our human rights policy doesn't permit us to allow him" to paint an airplane.

"PLAYING POLITICS WITH U.S. EXPORTS"

The department came in for more than ridicule, however, with last summer's denial of a $270 million Export-Import Bank loan for the Argentine purchase of turbine generators from Allis-Chalmers Corp. "From an economic and financial point of view," bank chairman John Moore said, "the proposed transaction is clearly the kind of project in Argentina which we would be prepared to consider favorably for financial assistance."

Yet Moore noted that, under law, he was forced to "take into account the observance and respect for human rights in countries receiving exports we support with loans or financial guarantees."

The denial, one of the biggest nommilitary projects ever turned down on human rights grounds, was the catalyst for cries of outrage against Derian's office.

In testimony July 19 before the House Inter-American Affairs subcommittee, defense industry spokesman Joseph E. Karth protested that sanctions against Argentina had cost an estimated "$813.5 million . . . lost jobs to American workers . . . loss of American influence on the behavior of other nations."

"The administration and Congress often cannot resist the attempt to impose our moral and political values on someone else, and the weapon closest at hand is often economic sanctions," Karth said. "But playing politics with U.S. exports, playing politics with the American economy, has become increasingly risky."

Commerce Secretary Juanita Kreps opposed the use of U.S. trade as a "political gesture" in a pointed reference to rights sanctions and another high-level Commerce official accused the administration of "tilting the balance" toward human rights sanctions and away from balance of payments problems.

Beech Aircraft, with a $10 million Argentine order worth 10 per cent of its total 1978 export volume on the line, protested that "human rights policies are administered without a balanced approach . . . sometimes according to the personal prejudices of State Department officials" who make the policy decisions. Besides, Beech echoed the Argentina advertisements, "in Argentina, human rights violations are reactions by the [junta] to attempts at violent overthrow by terrorists. . . . The Argentine government is gradually restoring stability."

During the last week in September, at the same time the 212 munitions licenses were turned down, the State Department reversed its denial of the Allis-Chalmers Export-Import Bank loan. While no one pointed to human rights improvements as a reason for the reversal, a State Department spokesman said the administration had "expectations" of improvement.

The expectations were based on a private promise made to the U.S. government by Argentine President Jorge Rafael Videla in August that the junta would allow an inspection of its prisons by the Organization of American States Human Rights Commission. The same promise, informed sources said, had been made without results to Vance last November, and to Undersecretary of State David Newsom in a visit to Argentina last spring.

Last week, the junta publicly invited such OAS inspection. While the

State Department has called the invitation a clear indication that the carrots worked, sources in the Bureau of Human Rights say it was the sticks. "It's more a case of economics than human rights," one source said. With continued high inflation and restricted imports, the junta "has not been able to meet the needs of the middle class. It has nothing to do with human rights; it's a problem of not being creditworthy."

In other words, what may eventually end human rights violations in Argentina is the same thing that may eventually end the administration's human rights policy. It's just too expensive.

"According to Washington sources, President Carter personally ordered the reversal of the Export-Import Bank's decision, and Mr. Scott, the chief Allis-Chalmers executive, met with President Videla and Minister of Economy José Martinez de Hoz this week, bringing assurances of U.S. backing. He offered to set up a factory here to provide the electrical equipment if Allis-Chalmers won the contract." de Onis, U.S. Reverses a Ban on Argentina Loan, N.Y. Times, Nov. 11, 1978, at 1, col. 1

Letters to the Editor, When Morality Interferes with Exports-as-Usual
N.Y. Times, June 24, 1980, at A14, cols. 3-5

To the Editor:

Your June 9 "Washington Watch" column, describing current efforts to "clarify and define" the Foreign Corrupt Practices Act because it is having "a 'chilling' effect on American international trade," concludes with the observation that "Congress now has something new: an export lobby." Whether it is new is doubtful, but the appearance of Alexander Perry's Op-Ed article "On 'Exporting Morality' " on the same day is proof indeed that it is actively preaching its standard message: business-as-usual.

Stripped of its rhetorical flourishes (one wonders why Mr. Perry needs to inveigh against "post-Vietnam" morality three times in one essay), the author's principal argument is that the U.S. is losing foreign exports and domestic jobs because of "crippling" trade restrictions designed, among other things, "to enforce the observance of human rights." While he may be right in the Argentine case he cites, he greatly exaggerates the effect human-rights concerns have had on U.S. trade. Moreover, despite the standard disclaimer that he rejects and resents "any implication that [businessmen] don't share common-sense concerns about human rights," he ignores the moral dimension of the problem.

His one example is a perfect case in point. Argentina, as he must know, has been run since 1976 by a brutal and repressive military junta. Many thousands of persons have been arrested, tortured and killed. The State

Department's Country Reports on Human Rights Practices for 1979 mentions up to 20,000 "disappeared" persons and states that "there is substantial evidence that most of these persons were abducted by the security forces and interrogated under torture; as most have not reappeared, many observers believed that they were summarily executed."

If Mr. Perry regards these continuing violations of international human rights law (which he demeaningly labels "ethnocentric political fashions") as unproved assertions, he should consult the recent report of the Inter-American Commission of Human Rights, a distinguished seven-man body headed by an American law professor, which after a visit to Argentina last fall reached similar conclusions. They are confirmed by numerous nongovernmental organizations, such as the Washington Office on Latin America, and by such prestigious bar groups as the Association of the Bar of the City of New York.

Mr. Perry, applying the businessman's version of "situation ethics," ignores all such evidence. Exports and jobs are all he sees. If they are hurt by a U.S. trade policy sensitive to human-rights concerns — and there is little hard evidence to show that they are in a substantial way — then he is correct in asserting that a price is being paid for the U.S. adherence to international human-rights law. That, however, just raises the question, avoided by Mr. Perry but the title of Sandra Vogelgesang's perceptive article in the July 1978 issue of Foreign Affairs: "What Price Principle?" In a democratic society, answers to this question may vary, but ultimately it must be addressed.

RICHARD B. LILLICH
Charlottesville, Va., June 9, 1980

ALLIS-CHALMERS DIDN'T LOSE

To the Editor:

Alexander Perry's Op-Ed article deals head-on with the failure of a policy that tries to export morality through aid and trade restrictions and comes out right on target.

There is one point, however, that needs clarification. Perry's article discusses the matter of U.S. exports lost because of human rights restrictions and gives as one example the denial of Allis-Chalmer's request for an Export-Import Bank letter of interest for the sale of turbines to Argentina two years ago. While it is true that the letter of interest was initially denied and later approved and issued, no loss of exports resulted in that case.

In fact, the project involving these turbines is still very much alive, and in March 1980 the U.S. Government sent a delegation, headed by Deputy Secretary of Commerce Luther Hodges and including a director of the Export-Import Bank and a representative of the Department of State, to call on officials in Argentina and Paraguay to promote the interests of potential American suppliers (including Allis-Chalmers) in this project.

R. A. EDWARDS JR.
Regional Vice President, Allis-Chalmers
Washington, June 12, 1980

III. The Reagan Administration's Attitude Toward Human Rights Concerns in the Foreign Policy Process

A. *The Initial Reagan Reaction to the Carter Administration's Human Rights Policy*

1. David Rockefeller: Advance Man in Latin America

In view of his earlier attacks on the Carter Administration's human rights policy (see pages 1068-1069 supra), it came as no surprise that, even before his inauguration, President-Elect Reagan began staking out the new approach that his Administration intended to follow in the human rights area. What confounded many observers at the time was the radical nature of this new approach. Henceforth, adopting the distinction between totalitarian and authoritarian regimes initially suggested by former Secretary of State Kissinger (see page 1057 supra) and subsequently popularized by Professor (later Ambassador) Jeane Kirkpatrick (see pages 1084-1085 infra), the United States was to play down its criticism of the human rights records of the latter and avoid cutting off military and economic aid to them. The first signal of this new policy approach came from David Rockefeller, the Chairman of Chase Manhattan Bank, during a Latin American trip made a week after the 1980 presidential election. The following two readings describe and critique the Rockefeller trip.

Schumacher, Latins Welcome Word on Reagan by Rockefeller
N.Y. Times, Nov. 11, 1980, at A10, col. 1

BUENOS AIRES, Nov. 10 — Government and business leaders in several Latin American countries have been turning out in droves for the last week to listen to David Rockefeller, chairman of Chase Manhattan Bank, tell them what they want to hear: The election of Ronald Reagan will likely lead to a lessening of human rights restrictions on their countries.

"In the campaign Mr. Reagan made it clear that he will deal with the world as it is," Mr. Rockefeller told 100 government and business leaders at a private luncheon at a yacht club here today. "He is not going to try to change the world in his own image."

It is a message that Mr. Rockefeller has spread while traveling from Panama to Chile, Paraguay and now Argentina and that he will carry with him to Brazil tomorrow.

Mr. Rockefeller, in Latin America to attend a meeting of the Chase board of directors, stresses that he does not speak for Mr. Reagan. He originally supported George Bush, now the Vice President-elect, in the Republican primaries for President, and later transferred his support to Mr. Reagan.

FAVORED BY BUSINESS LEADERS

Nonetheless, local business and government leaders and the press are eager to hear his message one week after the election of Mr. Reagan, the heavy favorite among businessmen in military-ruled countries in the region. These countries have borne much of the brunt of Mr. Carter's human rights policies, including the cutting of military and economic aid.

The military governments in such countries as Argentina, Chile, Paraguay and Brazil have in the past resorted to assassination and torture in the fight against leftist terrorism and opposition. Much of the official violence has abated, though only limited freedom of expression is allowed and security forces still use broad powers, including torture.

Mr. Rockefeller criticized Mr. Carter for basing American foreign policy too much on human rights while failing to recognize the chaos and terrorism many of the countries faced.

"I don't think anyone in this room opposes the promotion of the application of human rights," he told the Argentine group today. But, he added, "I hope that Mr. Reagan, while in no sense abandoning the objectives, will pursue a different approach."

"I think Mr. Reagan," he said, "will base his foreign policy on U.S. national interest," such as trade and natural resources.

Not all Argentines welcomed Mr. Rockefeller's visit. The National Labor Commission, the country's largest coalition of unions, called for a go-slow job action, though few workers appeared to respond. The Committee of 25, a competing labor coalition, declared Mr. Rockefeller "persona non grata."

The unions charged that the visit by Mr. Rockefeller and the Chase board was an attempt to intervene in Argentine politics to back the military Government's economic policies drawn by Martínez de Hoz, the Minister of Economy. Mr. Martínez de Hoz has opened the economy to competition from imports, which has caused some industries to go bankrupt.

Both Mr. Rockefeller and Mr. Martínez de Hoz denied that the board's visit had a political intent. "This Government," said the minister in an interview, "does not need the open support of Chase to survive."

Lewis, On Lending Comfort to Evil in Argentina
Intl. Herald-Tribune, Nov. 25, 1980, at 4, cols. 6-7

BOSTON — At a press conference in Buenos Aires the other day, David Rockefeller, chairman of the Chase Manhattan Bank, praised the Argentine military government for having "stabilized" the country. Life in Argentina, he said, was "much better than before."

In Argentina and other countries on a Latin American tour, Mr. Rockefeller signaled a change in U.S. human rights policy. He told a group of Argentine government and business leaders that President-elect Reagan "will deal with the world as it is. He is not going to try to change the world in his image."

Reading reports of those remarks, I thought about Jacob Timerman, who was Argentina's leading newspaper editor until he was kidnapped by an army unit, tortured, imprisoned, held under house arrest and finally expelled. No charges were ever brought, but the reasons for his brutal treatment were clear enough: He had spoken out for human rights, and he was a Jew.

FIRST QUESTIONS

Mr. Timerman was in New York recently, on a visit from his new home in Israel, and he spoke quietly about what had happened to him. He remembered the first three questions put to him when the interrogation started:

"Are you a Jew?"

"Are you a Zionist?"

"Is your newspaper Zionist?"

He answered yes to all three questions — the last falsely, because his newspaper was not "Zionist," but Mr. Timerman thinks the answers saved his life. His interrogators had told him he was going to be killed. Instead, they thought they could use him in a show trial to prove the existence of a worldwide Jewish conspiracy. In time, protests from the outside world led Argentine authorities to release him.

FASCIST CHARACTER

The Argentine government is one of the few in the world today that includes elements of unmistakably, unashamedly fascist character. They have not only used violence and murder to force conformity with extreme right-wing views; they are openly anti-Semitic. Many who survived time in jails and interrogation centers report seeing the swastika on display.

Right-wing repression in Argentina followed years of left-wing terrorism. The terrorists carried out political assassinations and kidnappings on a scale that traumatized the country. Outsiders do not always appreciate that Argentine society came near to crumbling under that assault.

But the violence by agents of the state in the last four years has been condemned by international bodies as going beyond any justified response. More than 7,000 Argentinians, among them children, have been taken away from their homes and have simply disappeared. A recent report to the Organization of American States said Argentine government tactics amounted to "state terrorism."

Widespread Torture

Widespread torture has been documented. Among its victims was Adolfo Perez Esquivel, the Argentine sculptor who was just awarded the Nobel Peace Prize for his activities on behalf of human rights.

All this makes one wonder why Mr. Rockefeller chose to go to Argentina at this time and say the things he did. For the effect could only be to lend legitimacy to a system that allows the use of bestial methods for political ends.

Mr. Rockefeller told the meeting of Argentine businessmen and government officials: "I don't think anyone in this room opposes the promotion of the application of human rights." But he said he hoped that Mr. Reagan, "while in no sense abandoning the objectives, will pursue a different approach" — one based on U.S. national interests, such as trade and natural resources.

His listeners had no doubt of his meaning. A New York Times correspondent, Edward Schumacher, wrote that they and others who met Mr. Rockefeller in nearby countries heard what they wanted to hear: that the election of Mr. Reagan will likely lead to a lessening of human rights restrictions on them.

Real Danger

President Carter's human rights policy, with all its imperfections, has saved lives and helped to relax repression in some places, such as Brazil. It is not the only way to advance U.S. ideas of human decency. But if Washington is going to try new policies in the field, surely prominent individual Americans should avoid gestures of accommodation with evil.

Mr. Rockefeller has the burden of living with lunatic conspiracy theories — about his bank, his family, the Trilateral Commission. But he is a man of unusual prominence, whose example matters. The next time he considers such a gesture to Argentina, he might think of something said by Mr. Timerman — said of Argentines, but applicable to all of us:

"It is very easy to hate a Nazi, a guardian in the Gulag. But the real danger is not them. It is the decent people who compromise with evil."

2. President-Elect Reagan Adopts the Totalitarian/ Authoritarian Distinction

Shortly after the Rockefeller trip, the head of President-Elect Reagan's Department of State transition team told Foreign Service officers to expect "a fundamental change of course" in U.S. foreign policy. The new policy, he was reported to have said, was to be "avowedly nationalistic," one that would avoid "the abstractions," such as undue emphasis on human rights, that supposedly characterized President Carter's foreign policy. See Goshko, Foreign Policy Shift Seen by Reagan Aide, Intl. Herald-Tribune, Dec. 19, 1980, at 3, col. 1. Contemporaneously, the President-Elect himself served notice that his Administration would apply the totalitarian/authoritarian distinction when deciding whether to speak out against repressive regimes. The following reading describes and critiques Mr. Reagan's views in this regard. The column by Art Buchwald thereafter makes fun of them.

Rosenblum, Reagan and Human Rights: Beyond Classic Examples
Intl. Herald-Tribune, Dec. 30, 1980, at 4, cols. 3-6

PARIS — Those who had hoped that an election would somehow elevate Ronald Reagan above simplistic, from-the-hip analysis of vital problems are hardly comforted by some of the president-elect's recent observations.

For example, when asked recently by Newsweek how he felt about pressure for him to deplore "political oppression," Mr. Reagan said: ". . . In the name of human rights we have found ourselves [intervening] in a civil dispute in a smaller country, ending up with a totally totalitarian government taking over. And the people end up with less human rights than they had before. . . .

"The classic example," he said, "is Cuba. Sure, Batista was more autocratic than we believe in. And there were things being done to the people that we did not think were right. But, good Lord, I don't know of any Cuban who wouldn't say today that what he had was heaven compared to what Castro has given them. There wouldn't have been a Castro had we not interfered."

Never mind that Mr. Reagan's limited circle of Cuban acquaintances is a thin basis for his absurd generality; Fidel Castro is no Thomas Jefferson, but Cubans who prefer him to Batista can be produced by the carload. Never mind that the Republican administration then in Washington backed Batista, not Mr. Castro, in that civil dispute.

But it is profoundly disturbing that the case of Cuba — or any particular case — should be used as an excuse to back away from a fundamental issue. President Carter's policy on human rights has been flawed and unevenly applied. Nevertheless, under Mr. Carter, the United States has demonstrated its willingness to make sacrifices to protect victims of gross injustice. And that policy, according to people who were directly concerned, saved lives.

ENCOURAGING ABUSES

In contrast, Mr. Reagan's vague and derisive remarks about a U.S. role in persuading repressive governments not to murder and torture their people have already encouraged the sort of abuses that the Carter policy helped to diminish.

In El Salvador, a variety of sources, including a former junta member, report that government agents have killed thousands of suspected leftist activists without arrest or trial. The rationale is that the other side does not use the courts either. Fire, the argument runs, must be fought with fire.

Mr. Carter's approach has been that governments cannot ignore their own systems of justice, that their function is to protect people and their institutions. If terrorists attack the government, they are outlaws and must be eliminated. But if the government itself responds with terrorism, the entire society suffers.

In a Christmas vigil in Paris, a group of Argentines offered a stark reminder of what can happen when governments embrace methods that are outside the law. They recalled the thousands of *desaparecidos*, persons who vanished in Argentina after the military leaders turned loose death squads to impose what dissidents call "the order of the cemetery."

Of the thousands killed in Argentina's official terror, some undoubtedly were guerrillas. Some, just as certainly, were innocent victims who happened to be in the wrong place. In either case, families have spent years searching for signs that their "disappeared" loved ones might still be alive. Official terrorists keep few records, and most families will never know for sure.

The activities of Argentina's death squads diminished considerably in recent years and, according to the testimony of those affected, this is attributable in large measure to U.S. pressure. Now, it is already clear, ranking Argentine officers are among the authoritarians who are cheered by the arrival of a "more realistic" administration in Washington.

Cuba is a valid example of a Communist country where rights abuses require U.S. attention. But as other Latin American governments have demonstrated, it is not axiomatic that leftist governments violate human rights more flagrantly than rightist governments. In the Soviet system, a dissident might face a rigged trial and be sent to prison where he is allowed only occasional contact with his aggrieved family. This is bad enough, but at least the dissident's case is known and he has a chance of emerging alive. When punishment is left to a death squad, reporting to no one, the victim simply disappears without a trace, along with anyone who might be with him at the time of his abduction.

The situation is different in every country, and situations change from month to month. U.S. leverage varies widely, and other American interests inevitably come into the balance. There is no "classic example" for human rights or for any other fundamental issue that a world leader must face. . . .

Buchwald, Moderate Repression
Intl. Herald-Tribune, Dec. 20-21, 1980, at 16, cols. 1-2

WASHINGTON — The Reagan administration has a new approach to human rights which, while it won't affect anyone in the United States, may have some important ramifications for political prisoners around the world. The philosophy of the new approach was expressed recently by Prof. Jeane Kirkpatrick of Georgetown University, who is a very influential Reagan adviser.

"If we are confronted with the choice between offering assistance to a moderately repressive autocratic government, which is also friendly to the United States, and permitting it to be overrun by a Cuban-trained, Cuban-armed, Cuban-sponsored insurgency, we would assist the moderate autocracy," Ms. Kirkpatrick was quoted as saying.

Nobody in his or her right mind would argue with that. The big question is, how far a moderately repressive autocratic government (MRAG) can go to keep the opposition down? New human rights guidelines will have to be written for the MRAG countries.

Right now the ambassadors of moderately repressive autocratic governments are being called home for Christmas to advise their juntas on what the new U.S. administration will expect of them in the human rights field.

"Colonels, I am happy to report that we can expect all the support we need from the United States to put down the political opposition, providing we can prove our repressive government is being threatened by Cuban intervention."

"Suppose we can't prove it?"

"They'll take our word for it, if we can produce confessions from our political opponents."

"Does that mean we can still resort to torture to exact the confessions?"

"In moderation. Obviously, a certain amount of torture has to be used but we can't overdo it."

"Can we still beat political prisoners with truncheons?"

"Of course that is acceptable. But attaching electrical wires to a person's intimate parts can only be done under the supervision of a doctor."

"What about dunking them in water until they almost drown?"

"If it's done with compassion. But I think we better stay away from pulling out the fingernails, at least at the beginning of the Reagan term."

"Can we continue summary executions without trials?"

"Nobody in the Reagan transition team has spoken out against them. From all I can gather, the U.S. will no longer interfere in our justice system."

"Thank God. Does that mean we can still throw writers, editors and students into prison without have our military aid cut off?"

"I believe that the U.S. would encourage it as long as we can prove they are a threat to the regime."

"Will the secret police be able to get the latest equipment to put down terrorism in our country?"

"That goes without saying. If the United States wants to keep us as a friend, they're going to give us the tools to keep another regime from taking over."

"They're finally making some sense in Washington. As I see it, as long as we torture our opponents in moderation and repress our people for their own good, and only shoot the people who deserve it, we can have good relations with the United States again."

"Colonels, I don't know about the rest of you, but as head of the Moderate Repressive Junta I recommend we give human rights a try."

3. Downgrading Human Rights: The Reagan Administration Takes Office

International Commission of Jurists, Human Rights and U.S. Foreign Policy
32-35 (1984)

In a much noted article, which brought her views on distinctions between "authoritarian" and "totalitarian" regimes to Ronald Reagan's attention, Professor Kirkpatrick wrote:

> The failure of the Carter administration's foreign policy is now clear to everyone except its architects. . . . [In] Iran and Nicaragua, the Carter administration . . . actively collaborated in the replacement of moderate autocrats friendly to American interests by less friendly autocrats of extremist persuasion. . . .

> The [Carter] administration's conception of national interest borders on doublethink . . . [Its] foreign policy fails . . . for lack of realism about the nature of traditional versus revolutionary autocrats. . . . Only intellectual fashion and the tyranny of Right/Left thinking prevent intelligent men of goodwill from perceiving the *facts* that traditional authoritarian governments are less repressive than revolutionary autocracies, that they are more suscepti- ble of liberalization, and they are more compatible with U.S. interest.

Professor Kirkpatrick's . . . opinions, endorsed by other neo-conserva- tive intellectuals in the Reagan camp, profoundly influenced the new Ad- ministration's international stance. Tough-minded firmness toward totalitarian adversaries and a more conciliatory approach to authoritarian allies, it was indicated, would rectify the Carter vacillations that had encour- aged Soviet aggression and tilted the balance of global power against the United States.

Early Reagan Administration Position

The new policy-makers lost little time in announcing their position. At his confirmation hearing, Secretary of State-designate Alexander Haig de- clared, "International terrorism will take the place of human rights in our [foreign policy] concern." National security adviser Richard Allen asserted that the new Administration would "not place as much ideological empha- sis on human rights."

Professor Kirkpatrick, appointed U.S. Permanent Representative to the United Nations, reiterated her opposition to the Carter human rights pro- gram "Because it was utopian, because it was conducted outside of the political and historical context, and because it didn't work. . . . Our posi- tion in the Western Hemisphere has deteriorated to the point where we must now defend ourselves against the threat of a ring of Soviet bases being established on and around our borders. I'm not saying that the Carter hu- man rights policy was the only factor in bringing this about, but it certainly played a role. . . . The central goal of our foreign policy should not be the moral elevation of other nations, but the preservation of a civilized concep- tion of our own national interest."

Even President Reagan's instinctual reactions were repudiated by his policy-makers. On April 30, 1981, at a "Day of Remembrance" ceremony for Holocaust victims, the President departed from his prepared speech with the improvised pledge, "I intend that [the Presidency] shall be used on every occasion . . . to point a finger of shame . . . wherever it takes place in the world against the act of violence or terrorism . . . [and] the persecution of people for whatever reason . . . — that it is a matter to be on the negoti- ating table or the United States will not belong at that table."

The next day the Washington press reported, "President Reagan yester- day raised the previously downgraded banner of human rights, only to have his spokesman lower it." The President, a White House spokesman hastily announced, had "not meant to alter his policy of playing down the human rights issue in foreign relations."

The changes in administration tone and verbiage were matched by changes in substance and policy. The high-level Inter-Agency Committee, created to consider human rights factors in foreign economic policy, was disbanded. The administration urged that Argentina, Chile, Guatemala and Uruguay, all previously denied military and economic aid because of human rights violations, should have such assistance reinstated. U.S. delegates at the international development banks were directed not only to reverse the U.S. opposition to loans for authoritarian Latin American governments, but also for the Philippines and South Korea. In the United Nations and other international agencies, U.S. representatives emphasized Soviet human rights violations while largely ignoring comparably repressive actions by friendly authoritarian regimes; at the 37th session of The Commission on Human Rights in February, 1981, the United States voted with Argentina, Brazil and Ethiopia in an unsuccessful attempt to abolish the United Nations Working Group on Enforced or Involuntary Disappearances established the previous year. And the strategic post of Assistant Secretary of State for Human Rights remained conspicuously empty amid mounting rumors that the Human Rights Bureau would be either discarded or left to wither on the State Department vine.

Finally, in the late spring of 1981, Ernest Lefever was proposed by the White House as the new Assistant Secretary of State for Human Rights and Humanitarian Affairs. The American human rights community, normally a loose assembly of discrepant and even vying organizations, joined in a rare display of unity to mobilize Congressional and public opinion against the nomination. Despite overt Presidential endorsement, the Senate Foreign Relations Committee on June 5th voted 13-4 to reject the Lefever appointment and to provide the President with his first major defeat on a foreign policy issue.

The Congressional Quarterly, in reporting the situation, noted:

> Lefever's nomination generated controversy on two counts. First, because of the man himself, who proclaimed his devotion to human rights but whose sincerity was questioned by his opponents; secondly, because of rancor of the human rights debate. . . .
>
> For all the criticisms of Lefever personally, the root issue was the Reagan human rights policy in general. Lefever and other critics of the Carter policy complained that it alienated friendly authoritarian regimes, such as Argentina's, while overlooking greater human rights abuses by totalitarian communist nations such as the Soviet Union. His supporters, including Reagan, said abuses in anti-communist authoritarian regimes could be reduced most readily by offering their leaders the security of U.S. friendship, quietly using the influence thus gained. . . . Advocates of the Carter policy contended that . . . "quiet diplomacy" would mean ignoring human rights abuses by anti-communist U.S. allies while publicly condemning abuses only in Marxist nations.

Commenting on this period, Representative Jim Leach, ranking Republican on the Subcommittee on Human Rights and International Organizations, concluded, "The inauguration of Ronald Reagan as the 40th President of the United States marked the inauguration as well of a new approach to human rights policy — an approach motivated . . . more by an intense desire to repudiate the tactics of the preceding Administration than by a willful design to establish a vision for the future. . . . The Lefever nomination was an unambiguous signal of the administration's rejection of the Carter human rights approach [and] implied an abandonment not only of the methodology but of the substance of American human rights concern."

Baker, A Meddling Muddle
Intl. Herald-Tribune, June 5, 1981, at 24, cols. 1-2

NEW YORK — As the Minister of Clarification, sir, will you spare me a moment?

A. Delighted, my muddled friend. Always delighted to clarify the waters. Out with it.

Q. My question goes back to 1977 when Moscow criticized President Carter's human rights policy as mistaken and obnoxious. Remember that?

A. Of course not. How can anything be clarified if people are going to go around remembering the past? Next question.

Q. To refresh your memory, the Soviets said our human rights policy amounted to meddling in the international affairs of other countries. If I have it right, the Reagan people are now saying the same thing. What are we to conclude from this?

A. That it's a mistake to read four-year-old newspapers. If you don't want to get confused, don't fool around with history.

Q. Isn't it encouraging to discover that there's at least one thing on which the most conservative capitalists can see eye-to-eye with the godless Communists?

A. Nonsense. There is absolutely no agreement between the Soviet and American attitudes on human rights. The Soviets trample on human rights. The Americans have always stood for human rights.

Q. Everybody knows Americans stand for human rights, but why do the Reagan folks take the Soviet line by refusing to meddle for them?

A. You misstate the case. The Reagan administration is perfectly willing to meddle for human rights and will never cease meddling so long as human rights continue to be violated in totalitarian states.

Q. What are totalitarian states?

A. States that follow the Moscow line.

Q. What about violations in states that follow the Washington line?

A. Those are not totalitarian states. They are partners in the free world. It is wrong to meddle in the internal affairs of our free-world partners. Meddling must be confined to totalitarian states.

Q. What is the policy on free-world partners who violate human rights?

A. The Reagan people are not fooled. They know that certain free-world partners maintain prisons with torture facilities. The policy on such free-world partners is simple: Don't call them totalitarian states.

Q. What should we call them?

A. Authoritarian states.

Q. What's the difference between totalitarian and authoritarian?

A. If you are totalitarian the United States will meddle with you. If you are authoritarian, it won't.

Q. Say I am suspended by the thumbs in a dungeon. A government employee is approaching me with red-hot tongs. From Washington's point of view, am I better off in a totalitarian dungeon or in an authoritarian dungeon?

A. It depends on what you want. If it's a totalitarian dungeon, we have a right to meddle but no power to help you. But there's a chance the president will mention your name in a speech as evidence that the Russians treat civil rights with contempt. That could get you an awful lot of publicity.

Q. Then I'd be better off in an authoritarian dungeon, unless I was a publicity hound?

A. Well, if it's authoritarian, Washington has the leverage to get you out, but that would be meddling. The policy does, however, allow for applying discreet pressures without publicity.

Q. You mean the president might send a note to the dictator's mother saying she ought to be ashamed of what her son is doing?

A. From the president, a note to the mother would probably constitute meddling. I'd think the note would have to come from somebody in the civil service.

Q. What kind of policy is that for a man hanging by his thumbs?

A. A simple policy. If Washington can't help you, it will meddle; if it can help you, it won't.

Q. I've had policies like that myself. Was it written by an insurance salesman?

A. This is, after all, a businessman's administration.

4. Human Rights and U.S. Foreign Policy: Argentina as a Case Study: Part II

de Onis, U.S. Acts to Improve Its Ties with Rightist Latin Governments
Intl. Herald-Tribune, Mar. 9, 1981, at 2, cols. 1-2

WASHINGTON — The Reagan administration is moving rapidly to improve U.S. relations with South America's rightist military regimes through invitations to military leaders from Chile, Brazil, Bolivia and Argentina for talks here.

State Department officials confirmed that Lt. Gen. Roberto C. Viola, designated by Argentina's military junta to assume the country's presidency March 29, will make a private visit here starting March 15. Argentine diplomatic sources said Gen. Viola will be received by President Reagan and other high officials.

Gen. Viola's visit will follow the little-publicized visits here by Gen. Fernando Matthei, Chile's air force commander and member of the junta headed by President Augusto Pinochet; by a Brazilian delegation led by Gen. Jose Ferraz da Rocha, chairman of Brazil's Joint Chiefs of Staff, and by Gen. Hugo Banzer, former president of Bolivia, who is trying to make a political comeback. . . .

Through its human rights policy, the Carter Administration came into serious diplomatic confrontation with these South American countries. Under President Jimmy Carter, the United States publicly condemned political killings and torture in these countries and suspended military aid to them. Pentagon sources said that the Reagan administration has shifted priorities in relations with the South American military regimes from human rights to hemispheric security, particularly in Argentina and Brazil, which command the South Atlantic coast of South America.

Brazilian diplomatic sources said that, in meetings with the Brazilian chiefs of staff, U.S. military officials proposed cooperation to strengthen naval and air control of South Atlantic sea lanes, where oil tankers travel from the Gulf to supply South America and the United States.

Brazil rejected in 1977 any military aid from the United States and terminated joint military planning agreements that had been in effect since 1950 — a reaction to criticism by the State Department of human rights violations in Brazil.

Argentina, viewed by Pentagon planners as a key to South Atlantic naval security, cannot be given any military aid under an amendment to the Foreign Assistance Act of 1978 sponsored by Sen. Edward M. Kennedy and the late Sen. Hubert H. Humphrey.

The human rights record of the Argentine military regime that took power in 1976 was condemned in a report last year by the Inter-American Human Rights Commission that documents the disappearance of more than 6,000 persons known to have been arrested or abducted by security forces. . . .

Editorial, Doing Favors for Argentina
Intl. Herald-Tribune, Apr. 28, 1981, at 4, cols. 1-2

Earlier this month, Argentina's foreign minister said that his country's top foreign policy priority was to improve its relations with Western Europe and the United States. But he also said that Argentina would not change its human rights policy to achieve that goal. And he reaffirmed that Argentina would not sign the Nuclear Nonproliferation Treaty or a regional treaty banning nuclear weapons. He also made it clear that Argentina would reject Western pressure not to sell grain to the Soviet Union should another embargo be imposed. Because Western Europe has sharply cut back on purchases of Argentine wheat, he argued, the sales to the Soviet Union are an economic necessity. Argentina also maintains strong links with the Third World, despite the fact that it has the highest standard of living in Latin America. That means it frequently votes counter to Western interests in the United Nations and other international forums. With friends like that, as the old adage goes, who needs enemies?

Nevertheless, the Reagan administration is courting the Argentines. The United States argues that the human rights situation has improved; that people aren't "being disappeared" anymore. It's true about the disappearances, but torture is common, all political activity is illegal, the press is controlled, more than 900 are in jail for more than five years without being charged and the government refuses to say anything about the thousands of Argentines who have disappeared since the military took over. The U.S. military contends that the Argentines are an important hemispheric ally. The new Argentine president, Roberto Viola, a general, has visited President Reagan, and the U.S. Army Chief of Staff, Gen. Edward Meyer, has visited Argentina. It is not quite clear what new threat in the South Atlantic has upgraded Argentina's strategic significance, but the Argentine junta is apparently delighted with the Reagan administration's show of interest.

Argentina, like Saudi Arabia in its pursuit of AWACS, is acting as if it holds all the cards. And the Reagan administration, as in the case of the AWACS, is responding like a pussycat. If a rationale can be invented that contains the words strategic or tactical, the collection of tough guys in the White House seem to fall all over themselves in an effort to please. Obviously, Argentina doesn't plan to give them much in return. Instead, the Reaganites might listen more attentively to voices like those of Jose Federico Westerkamp, whose son has been in prison for five years without being charged. "The case of Argentina is very similar to the Russian one," he said. "One is far right, the other is far left, but they use the same methods." Mr. Westerkamp is properly unimpressed by Secretary of State Alexander M. Haig's distinction between friendly authoritarian (rightist) dictatorships and totalitarian (leftist) dictatorships. Before the United States does any more favors for Argentina, it should at least ascertain that the junta is prepared to act like a friendly dictatorship.

Lewis, U.S. and Argentina: Question of the Soul
Intl. Herald-Tribune, May 22, 1981, at 6, cols. 6-7

NEW YORK — Secretary of State Alexander M. Haig Jr. had a closed meeting last week with the House Foreign Affairs Committee, a general discussion of policy. In the course of it there was an extraordinarily revealing exchange.

Mr. Haig was explaining the Reagan administration's plan to resume arms aid to the rightist military government of Argentina. The United States, he said, had shared values with Argentina: a compatibility of views.

Sometime later Rep. Gerry E. Studds, Democrat of Massachusetts, asked the secretary what values he thought the United States shared with the Argentine regime except for opposition to Communism. For several minutes, in emotional tones, Mr. Haig denounced those — presumably including Rep. Studds — who did not understand how Communism was advancing in our hemisphere.

The congressman said he noted the comments but still would like an answer to his question: What values does the United States share with the Argentine government? According to two persons who were present, Mr. Haig replied: "A belief in God."

Torquemada's God?

Could he have meant the God of Torquemada? Of the Cossacks who terrorized Jews? Of Julius Streicher? For in the last five years Argentina, under its military regime, has experienced anti-Semitism so widespread and brutal that it cannot be a secret to anyone who cares. In the words of Jacobo Timerman, "nothing equal to it has taken place in the Western world since 1945."

Mr. Timerman, who was a leading Buenos Aires editor and publisher until his detention and torture by Argentine military units, describes in his just-published book what it was like to be a Jew in those circumstances. He heard the Nazi talk, the theories of Jewish conspiracy. He was taunted as a Jew. He felt in his torturers "a gut excitement, the sense of one's entire being abandoned to hatred."

And Mr. Timerman is not the only first-hand witness who has described the anti-Semitism at work in Argentina. In a country where most political expression is banned, anti-Semitic magazines are freely sold. The swastika appears on the walls of prison interrogation rooms.

It is possible that Mr. Haig is unaware of those facts? After Mr. Haig's answer about a shared belief in God, Rep. Studds said he thought Mr. Timerman would be surprised. Mr. Haig replied that Mr. Timerman was not the only expert on the subject.

Mr. Haig's remarks showed at the least an incredible insensitivity to the fact and meaning of anti-Semitism — and to the terrible danger for everyone, Jew and non-Jew, when it appears in so morbid a form in a supposedly civilized country.

There is a question here, too, for the American Jewish community. Is it going to sit quietly by while a high official of the government says the

Timerman as he was arrested
in Argentina in 1978.

country shares values — "a belief in God" — with a regime under which violent anti-Semitism has been practiced?

In Argentina many Jewish community leaders thought it best not to protest too loudly, not to rock the boat. That troubled Mr. Timerman more than anything else. When he was visited by Yigal Allon of Israel, he writes, "I told him that I had not been humiliated by torture, by electric shocks on my genitals, but had been profoundly humiliated by the silent complicity of Jewish leaders."

Guatemala, Too

The undersecretary of state for security assistance, former Sen. James Buckley, urged the Foreign Affairs Committee successfully not to demand some Argentine steps toward decency before resuming arms aid. He assured the committee that the Argentine government was not involved in anti-Semitic acts. Is the American Jewish community going to accept such statements, such insults to common intelligence, in silence?

But of course it is not just a Jewish question. Over the last five years thousands of Argentines of all faiths — the estimates run from 5,000 to 15,000 and more — have "disappeared." They were kidnapped by armed military men. Sometimes their bodies turned up, hacked to pieces or burned. More often they were simply never seen again. And no one with the least knowledge of the situation doubts that official military units were responsible.

Nor is it by any means a question limited to Argentina. The Reagan administration is now considering the resumption of arms sales to the government of Guatemala, which in some ways makes Argentina's look moderate. Amnesty International estimates that murder squads under direct Guatemalan government control have carried out more than 3,000 political killings in the last two years. The Christian Democratic Party has had 76 of its leaders assassinated in the last 10 months.

The question is one of America's soul. Are things at such a point that Americans must enlist torturers and murderers as allies and proclaim their values, their God, as America's own? Can Americans conceivably believe that embracing these people will strengthen U.S. influence in this hemisphere? How must the United States appear to its most important Latin neighbors, Mexico and Venezuela? How must Americans appear to themselves? What kind of country is the United States?

Editorial, Semantics and Human Rights
Intl. Herald-Tribune, May 25, 1981, at 6, cols. 1-2

If you can't argue the law, argue the evidence, and if that won't work, invoke God and motherhood. That old legal adage describes the Reagan administration's shameful squirming on human rights. Facing a law it dislikes and evidence it finds embarrassing, it is reduced to arguing that torture in Christian societies is less dreadful than in Marxist lands.

But the human rights argument turns not on religious doctrine, free elections or political liberties. It turns on a transcendent regard for human life. The point needs stressing, because it is being insistently distorted by Ernest Lefever, the president's unworthy nominee to run human rights policy. His grudging testimony implies that Jimmy Carter somehow lost ground to the Russians by trying to foist the U.S. Constitution on friendly countries with different traditions.

Concern for basic human rights is a global cause. There is nothing uniquely American or Western in denouncing imprisonment without trial, government-sponsored torture and political, religious or ethnic massacres. Abhorrence for these outrages is so widespread that even governments that permit them are ashamed to confess it.

To its lasting credit, the Carter administration reaffirmed America's dedication to human rights. Even before Mr. Carter came to office, Congress ordered annual evaluations of human rights conditions abroad from the State Department. What Congress intended was accurately expressed by Secretary of State Haig in January: "I do not believe we should, other than in the most exceptional circumstances, provide aid to any country which consistently and in the harshest manner violates the human rights of its citizens."

Mr. Haig also held that public censure of offending regimes was often unproductive. He said he preferred quiet but firm diplomacy on the issue. But what might have been a prudent and quietly effective diplomacy now bodes to be neither.

The nomination of Mr. Lefever was the worst possible signal. He is much too worshipful of governments that profess anti-Communism and clearly intends to acquiesce in their abuses of human rights. Now the administration wants to sell arms to Argentina and Guatemala, the hemisphere's main delinquents in respect for human rights.

Unmistakably, the Reagan team aims to remove the restraints of conscience from collaborations with "friendly" dictatorships. Favored tyrannies are thus described as merely "authoritarian" whereas Marxist ones are branded "totalitarian." But however much national security requries collaborating with tyranny, this distinction obscures the essence of human rights.

The real world is not neatly divided into free-market or God-fearing friends and Marxist enemies. There is more respect for human life in Communist Yugoslavia than in Christian Argentina. And why is Poland's externally imposed totalitarianism more hateful than South Korea's home-bred authoritarianism?

As the Carter team discovered, the United States will occasionally find itself sacrificing concern for human rights to some overriding strategic ambition. But inconstancy does not invalidate the cause or diminish its achievements.

For the Reagan administration to excuse the abuse of basic human rights — in merely "authoritarian" societies — violates a cherished American faith. Not so incidentally, it also weakens the effort to counter Soviet influence. President Reagan needs urgently to reassert the nation's ideals and to prove he means it by withdrawing the Lefever nomination.

President Reagan never withdrew the Lefever nomination. Indeed, even after the Senate Foreign Relations Committee overwhelmingly rejected his nomination, the White House continued to insist that he was "the man for the job." See Shestack, The Rise and Decline of Human Rights in United States Foreign Policy, 15 Colum. Human Rts. L. Rev. 19, 32-33 (1984). The candidate himself withdrew his name on 5 June 1981. 37 Cong. Q. Almanac 153, 18-A (1981).

B.   The Reagan Administration's Human Rights Policy Falls into Place

International Commission of Jurists, Human Rights and U.S. Foreign Policy
35-38 (1984)

CHANGE IN THE ADMINISTRATION POSTURE

The strong opposition to the Lefever nomination from diverse sources — Congressional, public interest, academic and religious — precipitated a clamorous public debate. It revealed that the issue of human rights had a vocal constituency within and outside the Congress far deeper and wider than the new Washington policy-makers had anticipated. The Carter program against which they had leveled their most scathing criticisms had proven to have generated extensive support at home and abroad which could not be casually disregarded. A decided moderation in the tone and nature of official rhetoric ensued which amounted to a virtual repudiation of earlier policy declarations.

In June, soon after the Lefever rejection, Secretary of State Haig delivered a major address in Washington entitled "Human Rights and American Interests" to the Trilateral Commission. "Human rights are not only compatible with our national interests," he informed his audience, "they are the major focus of our foreign policy."

That same month, national security adviser Richard Allen assured a New York rally protesting the treatment of Jews in the Soviet Union that the Reagan foreign policy was "inescapably linked to human rights."

In July, testifying before a Congressional Foreign Affairs Subcommittee, Under Secretary of State Walter J. Stoessel stressed, "Ours is not a policy of selective indignation," but of opposition to human rights violations "whether by ally or adversary, friend or foe. . . . The overall thrust of our policy is to be even-handed."

In August, in a New Delhi speech on American foreign policy to an audience of Indian diplomats and scholars, Ambassador Kirkpatrick attacked what she described as the "myth" that the Reagan Administration was unconcerned about human rights.

The task of fashioning new directions in a complex international society had turned out to be neither so simple nor so easy as had been anticipated by the Reagan policy-makers. Academic abstractions conceived in secluded study centers were proving oddly discordant with the harsh realities of an untidy world. Emergent developments in disparate parts of the world were already impinging on U.S. foreign policy that gave pause to those who had once advanced sweeping ideological generalizations on categoric differences between authoritarian and totalitarian regimes as final policy truths. . . .

NEW DIRECTIVES FOR HUMAN RIGHTS

But, nine months after the Reagan Administration had taken office, the symbolically important post of Assistant Secretary for Human Rights was still unfilled and the Bureau of Human Rights was virtually inoperative. By this time, however, a few intermediate-level Reagan appointees, supported by some career State Department officials, were urging reconsideration of the policy that denigrated human rights. They found an unexpected ally in the arrival of an inexperienced new Deputy Secretary of State, Judge William P. Clark, a trusted California political associate of the President.

A memorandum dated October 27, 1981, written by Assistant Secretary for International Organization Affairs Elliott Abrams for Deputy Secretary Clark and Richard T. Kennedy, Under Secretary of State for Management, was sent to Secretary Haig which recommended a basic administration policy revision. The memorandum, Assistant Secretary Abrams later said, "crystallized recognition of a growing realization of the need for change. A consensus in key policy-making circles was built to introduce a revised approach and develop a more positive acceptance of human rights." The document, approved by Secretary Haig, affirmed:

> Human rights is at the core of our foreign policy because it is central to what America is and stands for. . . . Congressional belief that we have no consistent human rights policy threatens to disrupt important policy initiatives. . . . Our human rights policy must be at the center of our response. Overall foreign policy, based on a strong human rights policy, will be perceived as a positive force for freedom and decency. This policy must be applied even-handedly. If a nation, friendly or not, abridges freedom, we should acknowledge it. . . . Human rights is not advanced by replacing a bad regime with a worse one, or a corrupt dictator with a zealous communist politburo.
>
> A human rights policy means trouble, for it means hard choices which may adversely affect certain bilateral relations. At the very least, we will have to speak honestly about our friends' human rights violations and justify any decisions wherein other considerations (economic, military, etc.) are determinative. There is no escaping this without destroying credibility of our policy, or otherwise we would simply be coddling friends and criticizing foes.
>
> Despite the cost of such a human rights policy, it is essential. . . . While we need a military response to the Soviets to reassure our friends and allies, we also need an ideological response. . . . We seek to improve human rights performance wherever we reasonably can. We desire to demonstrate, by acting to defend liberty and identifying its enemies, that the difference between East and West is a crucial policy distinction of our times.

The memorandum recommended the appointment of Elliott Abrams as Assistant Secretary of State for Human Rights and Humanitarian Affairs, and noted that "H.A. [Humanitarian Affairs] should be designated the lead agency on human rights, not only for the Department but also for the Government, with a specific role providing policy guidance on human rights [to other relevant agencies]."

The Abrams nomination was reinforced by an unusual White House disclaimer which denied charges that human rights had been derogated in the Administration's foreign policy. "The promotion of liberty," President Reagan asserted, "has always been a central element of our nation's foreign policy. In my administration, human rights considerations are important in all aspects of our foreign policy." Then, in sharp contrast to the acrimonious debate that enveloped the Lefever nomination, the Senate Foreign Relations Committee on November 17 unanimously approved the Abrams appointment.

A revised public style was rapidly evident in the operations of the revived Human Rights Bureau. Human rights leaders were no longer ignored; some were even courted. The new Administration approach was actively proselytized among public opinion groups. Officials insisted that an "even-handed" approach to human rights would be pursued; at the same time, the actions of the Soviet Union and its surrogates continued to be emphasized as the primary threat to international peace and stability.

U.S. Department of State, Country Reports on Human Rights Practices for 1982*
1-8 passim (1983)

Human rights can be grouped into broad categories:
— first, the right to be free from governmental violations of the integrity of the person — violations such as killings, torture, cruel, inhuman, or degrading treatment or punishment; arbitrary arrest or imprisonment; denial of fair public trial; and invasion of the home;
— second, the right to enjoy civil and political liberties, including freedom of speech, press, religion, and assembly; the right of citizens to participate in governing themselves; the right to travel freely within and outside one's own country; the right to be free from discrimination based on race or sex. . . .

* The Country Reports, which for two decades Congress has required the Secretaries of State to transmit to it annually pursuant to Section 116b of the Foreign Assistance Act of 1961 (see the Documentary Supplement), describe the status of certain internationally recognized human rights in all UN member states. This extract and the one that follows are taken from the Introductions to the 1982 and 1983 Reports, prepared under the supervision of and probably written by the Assistant Secretary of State for Human Rights and Humanitarian Affairs, Elliott Abrams. — EDS.

The Problems of Human Rights

. . . The original understanding of the meaning of human rights was clearly expressed in the American Declaraton of Independence. The Declaration asserted that human rights could not be created or abrogated by any human enactment, whether of one government or of an international body, because they were based on "the laws of nature and of nature's God," on truths which are "self-evident." Thus it was confidently stated that "all men are created equal, that they are endowed by their creator with certain inalienable rights."

When the authors of the Declaration called these rights "inalienable," they implied that rights should not depend upon the prior performance of certain duties by the citizen or be postponed until any other group of "rights" was achieved. The original enumeration of human rights in the Declaration of Independence thus did not include anything that could only be gained gradually, such as economic development.

The rights the Declaration asserted covered only part of justice as it was understood in earlier moral codes, and supplied only some of the goods men normally desired. As examples of inalienable rights, the Declaration gave "life, liberty, and the pursuit of happiness." Rights were considered to enable individuals to pursue happiness freely, but not to supply happiness itself. The human rights activists of the eighteenth century would thus have said there was a right of individuals to develop, but no right to development. For a government to insist it could define and supply happiness itself would take away men's right to liberty.

The intention of the originators of human rights, then, seems to have been to select from the vast range of things that men need or want, certain crucial things that they are entitled to by their very nature — human rights — which, when fulfilled, will create the preconditions for the satisfaction of other needs. These preconditions are created, in this understanding, by a political system of choosing the laws and the officials that govern men, and by an economic system that enables individuals to engage freely in various approaches to the "pursuit of happiness." . . .

Unfortunately, the widespread longing for rights in the contemporary world confronts a real lack of consensus on these rights. Many governments fear individual liberty; many others do not accept the original and distinctive intellectual foundations of the belief in human rights. Those opposing the human rights movement find themselves in a world already shaped by it, and they are compelled to fight on its ground, using the terminology of democracy. Thus there arise the many "peoples' democracies" of today that are not democratic in any normal sense. In 1776 those who practiced slavery or absolute monarchy admitted it openly; now they draw around themselves the name of freedom. A nominal consensus on human rights thus hides the reservations of leaders who remain more comfortable with the ancient priority of duties over rights, and of rulers who simply find it inconvenient or threatening to respect their subjects' rights. For such people there is a great temptation to legitimize their own interests by broadening the basic concept of rights to include these interests — thus allowing some to claim, for example, that duty to authority is a special kind of right and others to claim that certain theoretically desirable rights cannot be afforded at their country's stage of development.

This leads to increasing uncertainty as to what desirable things really are rights. This uncertainty has been encouraged by some new interpretations of social and economic rights, such as the newly minted concept of the "right to development." The urgency and moral seriousness of the need to eliminate starvation and poverty from the world are unquestionable, and continue to motivate large American foreign aid efforts. However, the idea of economic and social rights is easily abused by repressive governments which claim that they promote human rights even though they deny their citizens the basic rights to the integrity of the person, as well as civil and political rights. This justification for repression has in fact been extensively used. No category of rights should be allowed to become an excuse for the denial of other rights. For this reason, the term economic and social rights is not used in this year's reports. . . .

HUMAN RIGHTS IN INTERNATIONAL RELATIONS

How to embody the fundamental principles of democratic societies — human rights — in foreign policy has become an especially pressing question for the United States. Because Americans are of many faiths and ethnic heritages, the national identity of the United States is more constituted by its political principles than is that of any other powerful nation. The United States fought its bloodiest war not for territory but to free the slaves. In fact the United States, protected from the harsh necessities of foreign policy by two great oceans only entered world politics in a serious way when impelled to do so by its sense that freedom was threatened. The three times when the United States recommitted itself to active involvement with the outside world — whether in wars for the liberty of Europe or in the Marshall Plan — it has done so because it felt called to the defense of human rights.

The attempt to make foreign policy serve human rights confronts several specific problems that must be faced in developing a policy.

A continuing problem for human rights policy is the fact that it traditionally aims at affecting the domestic behavior of other countries, while governments are reluctant to alter their nation's political system for foreign policy reasons. The leverage that the United States does have is strongest in friendly countries, where we have more access and more influence. Such influence is an important resource in pursuing human rights, but its concentration in friendly countries creates a danger; human rights policy might highlight and punish human rights violations in friendly countries, while giving unfriendly countries immunity. If this took place it would blind men to the complex geography of human rights abuses in the world. Moreover, a nation that came to display a general pattern of undermining or estranging friendly governments would obviously limit its future influence over them, including its influence over their human rights behavior. This is a second problem of human rights — the need to avoid pressing only where our influence is greatest rather than where the abuses are greatest.

There is a danger that human rights policy will become like the labor of Sisyphus because it deals only with effects and not their causes. To take an example, it is important not only to free political prisoners, but also to encourage conditions in which new political prisoners are not taken. Many, although not all, of the things we consider rights are difficult to implant in adverse conditions. This fact creates the danger that by aiming at too much we will not get what is really possible. The founders of the Weimar Republic, by aiming at a democracy stripped of all the authoritarian features of imperial Germany, created a system so fragile that it was overwhelmed by something wholly barbaric in only fourteen years. On the other hand, there still exist in many areas of the world indigenous traditions of decency that coincide in part with the human rights tradition. The best hope for creating the preconditions of effective human rights observance may sometimes lie in working on the basis of these traditions.

For all these reasons, a human rights policy, unless it is very carefully constructed, runs the danger of being ineffective. And if it is ineffective it can also be counterproductive, creating additional resistance to improvement in human rights. It can embitter bilateral relations with other countries, increasing international tension. . . .

United States Human Rights Policy

Human rights is at the core of American foreign policy because it is central to America's conception of itself. This nation did not "develop." It was *created* in order to make real a specific political vision. It follows that "human rights" is not something added on to our foreign policy, but its ultimate purpose: the preservation and promotion of liberty in the world. Freedom is the issue that separates us from the Soviet bloc and embodies America's claim on the imagination of people all over the world.

Our human rights policy has two goals. First, we seek to improve human rights practices in numerous countries — to eliminate torture or brutality, to secure religious freedom, to promote free elections, and the like. A foreign policy indifferent to these issues would not appeal to the idealism of Americans, would be amoral, and would lack public support. Moreover, these are pragmatic, not utopian, actions for the United States. Our most stable, reliable allies are democracies. Our reputation among the people in important countries that are dictatorships will suffer if we come to be associated not with liberty, but with despotism. Often the people whose rights we are defending are the national leaders of future years.

As to the question of tactics, the Reagan Administration's test is effectiveness. With friendly countries, we prefer to use diplomacy, not public pronouncements. We seek not to isolate them for their injustices and thereby render ourselves ineffective, but to use our influence to effect desirable change. Our aim is to achieve results, not to make self-satisfying but ineffective gestures.

But the second goal of our human rights policy sometimes can conflict with this search for effectiveness: we seek also a public association of the United States with the cause of liberty. This is an eminently practical goal: our ability to win international cooperation and defeat anti-American propaganda will be harmed if we seem indifferent to the fate of liberty. Friendly governments are often susceptible to quiet diplomacy, and we therefore use it rather than public denunciations. But if we never appear seriously concerned about human rights in friendly countries, our policy will seem one-sided and cynical. Thus, while the Soviet bloc presents the most serious long-term human rights problem, we cannot let it falsely appear that this is our only human rights concern. So a human rights policy does inescapably mean trouble — for example, from friendly governments if the United States Government places pressure upon them, or from the American people if their government appears not to be doing so. Yet a human rights policy embodies our deepest convictions about political life, and our interests: the defense and expansion of liberty.

Our human rights policy also has two sides, the negative and the positive. The negative side is embodied in the way we oppose (through act or word) specific human rights violations in the short term. The positive side is strongly emphasized by the Reagan Administration in which we seek over the long term to help democracy, the surest safeguard of human rights. It is a fact that most democracies have excellent human rights records; nothing is as likely as democracy to produce this result.

U.S. Department of State, Country Reports on Human Rights Practices for 1983
4-5, 10-11 (1984)

The Experience of Human Rights Work

Over the past three years, the United States Government has employed a broad range of instruments and techniques in responding to specific cases of human rights violations. In dealing with friendly governments, we have engaged in the kind of frank diplomatic exchanges often referred to as "quiet diplomacy." Where diplomatic approaches have not availed, or where our influence with a foreign government is minimal, we have dissociated ourselves from odious human rights practices by denying economic and military assistance, voting against multilateral loans, and denying diplomatic support. Where appropriate, we have distanced ourselves from human rights violators by public pressures and statements denouncing their actions. In most cases, we have employed a mixture of traditional diplomacy and public affirmation of American interest in the issue.

The success of these efforts has varied with the degree of leverage we have in a given country, the political environment, and the energy and skill of our diplomatic representatives.

Diplomatic exchanges on behalf of dissidents, and other victims of human rights abuse, are by their very nature confidential. Although we cannot publicly claim credit, American representations have often been instrumental in halting human rights violations against dissidents by governments with whom we enjoy some common interests. Perhaps the phrase "quiet diplomacy" does not fully convey either the intensity of American efforts, or the depth of our concern, on behalf of human rights victims, yet in many cases, this kind of intercession has proven an effective response to human rights violations. Let us be clear that "quiet" diplomacy refers only to the confidentiality of the diplomatic channels we use, *not* to the intensity of our representations.

Compassion requires us to intervene in specific cases. When we have done so, we have often had successes. Such successes are important because they relieve suffering; in a few cases they can also have a major symbolic impact on a country and serve as a precedent for future improvements. But it is important to acknowledge the frustrations of this kind of work. All too often, the best efforts of any government can secure the release of a political prisoner only to see another political prisoner arrested; they can persuade a government to suspend the practice of torture only to see it renewed later on; they can secure permission for someone to leave his country only to see the next citizen who seeks to leave denied this right. We intervene, knowing very well that our interventions may fail to prevent new violations of the same type.

In this regard, the human rights work traditionally done by the State Department differs from most other kind of work undertaken in foreign policy. In other areas, diplomatic effort frequently culminates in major transformations: an arms control treaty, a treaty resolving a major conflict, an alliance between ourselves and another country, a diplomatic opening to a heretofore hostile country, a successful military action in defense of our friends, a new aid program. These are actions that may change the international system. Our case-by-case human rights work, in its very specific nature, cannot effect such changes. Of all the areas of traditional human rights work it is perhaps only in the international organizations, where we can sometimes obtain a vote publicly identifying a major human rights violation, that our work is most marked by spectacular events similar to those that can take place in other areas of foreign policy. Thus, the criteria of success in human rights work are inherently less clear, and human rights work is inherently more frustrating for those doing it than other branches of diplomacy.

DEMOCRACY AND HUMAN RIGHTS

For this reason, the Reagan administration has developed a two-track human rights policy. The first track is embodied in the way we oppose specific human rights violations over the short term. Thus, to take only public activities, we have spoken out against such gross affronts to human rights as the incarceration of Soviet dissidents in psychiatric wards and the resurgence of officially sponsored anti-Semitism in the Soviet Union; the barbaric persecution of adherents of the Baha'i faith in Iran; the institutionalization of racial injustice by the apartheid system in South Africa; the destruction of the free trade union movement, Solidarity, in Poland; the activities of the "death squads" in El Salvador; the persecution of the Miskito Indians in Nicaragua; and the use of outlawed toxic weapons by Soviet forces in Afghanistan, and Vietnamese forces in Kampuchea. In these and other cases of human rights abuse, we have made use of such influence as we possess to help individual victims.

At the same time, we have addressed the long range need to create a system of government which institutionalizes the protection of human rights. For just as the creation of an economic system which promotes growth and prosperity is a better long term solution to the problem of poverty than repeated acts of charity, so, too, the creation of a system of government which safeguards human rights is a better long range response to the problem of human rights abuse than repeated, case-by-case diplomatic representations.

This, then, is the second track of United States human rights policy: the long-term development of democratic governments, which are the surest safeguard of human rights. President Reagan has made the encouragement of democracy throughout the world a central goal. Too often our human rights policy has been simply reactive, responding to violations after they have occurred rather than working to prevent them. The President has sought to go beyond this to an active, positive human rights policy. . . .

Note: Two Key Differences in the Reagan Administration's Human Rights Policy

The above readings provide ample ammunition for arguments pro and con the Reagan Administration's human rights policy, which subsequent readings will bring out. This Note seeks simply to highlight (and criticize) two key differences between the Reagan and Carter approaches to international human rights and their invocation in the foreign policy process.

In the first place, the Reagan Administration, in sharp contrast to its predecessor (see page 1042 supra), redefined international human rights specifically to exclude economic and social rights. Ambassador Kirkpatrick launched a scathing attack on such rights, which are mentioned in the Universal Declaration and set out in great detail in the International Covenant on Economic, Social, and Cultural Rights (signed by President Carter on 5 October 1977 and still awaiting Senate advice and consent), claiming somewhat patronizingly that "no great reflection produced them," and that they were no more than a "letter to Santa Claus," based upon "a vague sense that Utopia is one's due." Kirkpatrick, Establishing a Viable Human Rights Policy, 143 World Aff. 323, 332 (1981). While these rights may partake of the aspirational, they have been deemed rights by the international community in numerous norm-setting international human rights instruments and, hence, are part of the international law of human rights. Economic and social rights cannot be unilaterally "derecognized" by the United States, although, of course, they can be downplayed or, in the case of the Reagan Administration, actually ignored. A foreign policy that ignores rights embraced by a vast majority of the states that comprise the international community, however, is not a very appealing or effective foreign policy. Attempts to justify the elimination of economic and social rights from the Reagan human rights agenda have not been persuasive. (For criticism of such attempts, see Shestack, An Unsteady Focus: The Vulnerabilities of the Reagan Administration's Human Rights Policy, 2 Harv. Hum. Rts. Y.B. 25, 39-45 (1989).) Few observers would disagree with his conclusion that "[t]he Reagan Administration's failure to address economic and social rights either in its own or multilateral initiatives was a serious deficiency in its human rights record." Id. at 44.

Secondly, although the Reagan Administration sought to soft-pedal Ambassador Kirkpatrick's totalitarian/authoritarian distinction after the severe criticism it received during the first half of 1981, the Administration never really backed away from it. Indeed, it continued to endorse and apply it. Surveying the Administration's human rights performance in 1984, three leading NGOs noted critically that

> the Administration was vigorous in denouncing abuses in countries aligned with the Soviet Union or otherwise considered to be hostile by the United States. For the most part, those denunciations were well-deserved. Our only complaint about them is that they were not as effective as they might have been had they been part of an even-handed effort to promote human rights worldwide. Accordingly, the moral force of the U.S. denunciation was sharply reduced. This lack of evenhandedness made it possible for the countries criticized by the U.S. to respond by pointing to human rights abuses in countries defended by the United States. In addition, the U.S. was frequently ineffectual in enlisting support from other governments in denouncing

abuses because those governments perceived the U.S. as using human rights as a way of pursuing other agendas.

In the case of governments aligned with the United States, the Administration's policy and practice were entirely different. In general, the Administration avoided denunciations of even the grossest abuses. . . .

Americas Watch, Helsinki Watch, and the Lawyers Committee for Human Rights, The Reagan Administration's Human Rights Record in 1984, at 1-2 (Jan. 1985). This double standard approach did little to enhance the credibility of the Reagan Administration's human rights policy. In the waning days of the President's second term, he explicitly repudiated this approach, thus rejecting (once and for all, one hopes) the totalitarian/authoritarian distinction that had driven over seven years of his Administration's human rights policy. Gelb, U.S. Vows to Resist Despots of Right as Well as of Left, N.Y. Times, Mar. 14, 1988, at A1, col. 6.

C. Criticism of the Reagan Administration's Human Rights Policy and Its Response

Over the years, beginning in the mid-1970s, Congress has crafted a number of laws designed to restrict the flow of U.S. economic and military assistance to states that are gross human rights violators. See generally International Human Rights Law Group, U.S. Legislation Relating Human Rights to U.S. Foreign Policy (4th ed. 1991). The purpose of such laws is to encourage the Executive Branch to put pressure on such states to improve their human rights records or, at the very least, to distance the United States from their human rights violations. The earliest and most comprehensive of such statutes, discussed above in connection with congressional initiatives in the human rights/foreign policy area (see pages 1039-1040 supra), are Sections 116b and 502B of the Foreign Assistance Act of 1961, dealing with economic and military assistance, respectively, found in the Documentary Supplement.

Even under the Carter Administration, these attempts to influence U.S. human rights policy had relatively little effect. See Lillich, supra page 1039, at 299-303. In an insightful first-hand study, a former (1978-1980) Deputy Assistant Secretary of State for Human Rights and Security Assistance observed that "[t]he history of section 502B is a case study of executive frustration of congressionally mandated foreign policy and underlines the need, particularly with this kind of legislation, for clearer directives, less discretion, and more assiduous congressional oversight." Cohen, Conditioning U.S. Security Assistance on Human Rights Practices, 76 Am. J. Intl. L. 246, 277 (1982). However, under the Reagan Administration these laws and other "country-specific" legislation were ignored or misapplied so frequently that the will of Congress was completely thwarted. The following reading, by a U.S. representative to the Commission on Human Rights during the Carter Administration, considers this frequent criticism of the Reagan Administration's human rights policy.

Shestack, An Unsteady Focus: The Vulnerabilities of the Reagan Administration's Human Rights Policy
2 Harv. Hum. Rts. Y.B. 25, 36-39 (1989)

[The author first points out that human rights activists quarreled not with the Administration's increasingly (after mid-1981) eloquent public pronouncements on human rights, but with the fact that too often they were not converted into practice in an even-handed way.]

The gap between pronouncement and performance created suspicion, not just among human rights activists, but also in Congress. In Congress, the Reagan Administration's lack of credibility was highlighted by its resistance to . . . laws linking United States security and economic aid to a nation's human rights policy. . . .

Neither the Carter Administration nor the Reagan Administration invoked the provisions of section 502B. But there were differences. The Carter Administration did not cut off security assistance under section 502B; however, without formally invoking section 502B, it used executive authority to deny security assistance to a number of nations. The Reagan Administration, however, did not follow section 502B, nor did it independently withhold security assistance to various right-wing governments engaged in patterns of human rights violations. . . . *

The Carter Administration tried to comply with section 116 and reduced some aid levels because of human rights violations. The Reagan Administration, however, declined to implement section 116. In 1983, Assistant Secretary for Human Rights and Humanitarian Affairs Elliott Abrams said, "We are reluctant to use economic aid as a tool for our [human rights] policy." This reluctance became the policy. Except in a few cases involving leftist regimes, the Reagan Administration did not restrict aid because of human rights violations. . . .

Frustrated by the Reagan Administration's use of specious arguments to bypass general human rights legislation, Congress resorted to country-

---

* As Professor Forsythe has observed, the Reagan Administration used interpretive techniques and manipulative statistics to avoid section 502B. In noncommunist regimes, "any statistic or event would be cited to show that a pattern of human rights violations [was] not completely consistent. No matter how poor the human rights record, there was always the interpretation of improvement. It followed for the administration that if anything positive occurred in a right-wing country, Section 502B did not apply." D. Forsythe, Human Rights and U.S. Foreign Policy 54-55 (1988).

specific legislation. Such legislation addressed specific countries and established certain human rights conditions as the qualifications for security assistance. For example, the International Security and Development Cooperation Act of 1981 required the President regularly to certify that the Government of El Salvador had met four conditions: concerted and significant efforts to protect human rights; improved prevention of serious human rights abuses by the army; economic and political reforms; and progress towards free elections. However, in 1981, despite reports that Salvadoran forces murdered thousands of civilians, Reagan certified that El Salvador had met the four conditions. Congress was skeptical. Successive certifications were somewhat more forthcoming about human rights conditions but still were far from candid. Misuse of the certification process undermined the credibility of State Department witnesses before congressional committees.

Frustrated once again, Congress turned to "action-specific" legislation which responded to specific occurrences. For example, in November 1983, the Specter Amendment provided for a partial withholding of aid to El Salvador until the verdict was obtained (in May 1984) in the trial of the 1980 murder of four churchwomen from the United States. Congress found these action-specific measures easier to monitor than the more general certification procedures.

The point of this review is not to assess the pros and cons of the congressional limitations or of the certification process. The point is that Congress regarded the Administration's certifications as evasions of human rights legislation. Congress enacted a plethora of "country-specific" and "action-specific" statutes conditioning foreign aid on the satisfaction of human rights objectives because the Administration appeared unwilling to follow more general congressional directives. The Administration regularly complained about congressional interference in the specifics of foreign policy. But it was the Administration's blatant bypass of human rights legislation properly within the congressional prerogative that compelled these congressional directives.

El Salvador: "The Certification Joke"

Shestack's comments and Oliphant's cartoon reveal the inadequacy of even "country-specific" legislation, at least when it is coupled with a certification process that a President is willing and able to abuse. See Editorial, A Certificate Is Not a Policy, N.Y. Times, Jan. 30, 1982, at A24, cols. 1-2; Editorial, Decertify Hypocrisy on Salvador, N.Y. Times, Jan. 24, 1983, at A18, cols. 1-2. Further evidence supporting this conclusion is found in the following editorial and cartoon.

"AH, NOT TOO MANY, AT ALL! THAT SHOWS A DISTINCT IMPROVEMENT IN HUMAN RIGHTS, MR. SHULTZ."

Editorial, The Certification Joke
Cleveland Plain Dealer, Jan. 28, 1983, at 2-B, cols. 1-2

We suspect Salvadoran government and military officials must get a good laugh from the numerous delegations from the United States that spend a few days touring El Salvador before returning home to decry human rights abuses in that Central American nation. For, after all the bellowing, just like clockwork, the Reagan administration certifies human rights progress in El Salvador and keeps the arms flowing to the war-torn nation.

Forget that U.S.-backed land reform is at a standstill. Forget that suspected guerrillas or leftist sympathizers are indiscriminately imprisoned, if they are fortunate, or found slaughtered alongside some roadway if they are not. Forget that the inept Salvadoran justice system is so bogged down in a political quagmire that it has been unable to bring to justice the murderers of six Americans, including two churchwomen from Cleveland. As Washington sees it, communism must be stopped before it spreads to other regions of Central America and these numerous abuses are costs the Reagan administration is willing to accept to do so.

But the delegations to El Salvador continue, as does the criticism of the certification formalities, because the American public, for the most part, is uncomfortable with Washington's support of right-wing hoodlums who are no less brutal — perhaps even more so — than the leftists they resist. Sup-

port for such thugs runs contrary to the ideals of democracy many Americans find supportable.

Historically, following the president's certification, talk ensues in Congress of bills to suspend all military aid to El Salvador. We hope some action takes the place of rhetoric.

There is little reason to believe that a military victory is possible in El Salvador. Government forces cannot achieve one without American aid, and U.S. citizens will never tolerate the military and monetary commitment necessary to bring such a victory about.

Thus far, Congress has given Washington and San Salvador little cause to pursue any serious negotiations with leftist leaders that might lead to a cessation of the fighting and bloodshed. Since all other forms of reason have failed, perhaps a congressional bill barring military aid to El Salvador will bring the administration and Salvadoran officials to their senses.

Ultimately, the Administration found its position unsupportable, and the President sought to end the problem, as he saw it, by vetoing a bill that would have extended the legislation (with its certification procedure). According to a prominent columnist (Lewis, On the Side of Death, N.Y. Times, Dec. 5, 1983, at A19, cols. 5-6):

The immediate reason for Mr. Reagan's veto was plain. He has certified human rights progress in El Salvador four times in the last two years, despite continuing death squad activity. This time the activity was so flagrant, the facts so overwhelming, that his own people would not have held their noses for another certification.

"In the present circumstances," Secretary of State Shultz told reporters after the veto, "unless there were a change between now and the middle of January, I think it would be very difficult to sign a certification." The next one would have been due in mid-January.

The veto sent a signal that could not be missed. Ronald Reagan is not going to let anything that happens in El Salvador stand in the way of aid for its armed forces — not even terrorism that is supported by elements in those forces and that is tearing the society apart.

That message destroys the hope that the United States could bring effective pressure on El Salvador to end the death squad activity. For the only practical form of pressure was the threat to cut off military aid unless the murders stopped.

Although, as Shestack notes (see page 1107 supra), "action-specific" legislation enacted in 1983 produced results in one particular situation, after President Reagan's veto of the above-mentioned bill Congress tacitly acquiesced in his Administration's policy in El Salvador by continuing to appropriate money for both military and economic assistance. Indeed, well over $3 billion was pumped into the country during the 1980s. Yet political violence — including killings, torture, and disappearances — continued unabated while "many U.S. policymakers seem[ed] unwilling to acknowledge the dimensions of the . . . human rights crisis." Lawyers Committee for Human Rights, Underwriting Injustice 9 (1989). Thus, it was and remains difficult to perceive the democratic gains in El Salvador that the former Assistant Secretary of State for Human Rights and Humanitarian Affairs, in the article immediately below, purported to see.

Response

Abrams,* Latin America in the Time of Reagan
N.Y. Times, July 27, 1988, at A25, cols. 2-6

WASHINGTON — Magical realism — that unique Latin invocation of literary fantasy amid factual description — characterizes not only much of

---

* The author was Assistant Secretary of State for Human Rights and Humanitarian Affairs (1981-1985) and later Assistant Secretary of State for Inter-American Affairs (1985-1989) during the Reagan Administration. He subsequently pleaded guilty to two misdemeanor counts of withholding information from House and Senate committees about secret Executive Branch efforts to aid the contras in Nicaragua, despite a ban on military assistance in existence at the time, and about his own role in soliciting a $10 million contribution to the contras from the Sultan of Brunei. On 15 November 1991, he was sentenced to two years'

Latin American literature, but also much of our own debate about Latin American life.

Throughout Latin America, astonishing political and intellectual change is under way. The historical pendulum that should have returned new Latin democracies to army control, has been suspended for all seven and a half of the Reagan years. Though still fragile, the civilian governments have introduced and preserved great human rights gains. Traditional Marxist orientations among intellectuals are growing weaker as Cuba stagnates and the Soviets reach for market mechanisms.

The American role in all this has been to urge, promote, assist. We have resisted domestic protectionism and kept our huge market open to Latin exports, thus helping to alleviate the debt crisis. We have managed extremely sensitive trade problems with Brazil when most observers thought a trade war was inevitable. Despite many foreign policy disagreements with Mexico, we have cooperated steadily on border, financial, immigration, environmental and trade issues.

Relations with Argentina, once said to have been ruined by the war over the Malvinas or Falkland Islands, are better than ever. We have helped in the political changes in Guyana and Suriname. We have helped stop coup attempts, most recently in Guatemala; supported reform in the administration of justice throughout Central America; and worked hard to support the Human Rights Commission of the Organization of American States.

Cuba has truly been put on the defensive on human rights, and forced to accept both the International Red Cross and United Nations Human Rights Commission presence there. Latin governments now dedicate many more of their own resources to the struggle against drug trafficking, and they have become convinced that drugs are a Latin problem and not simply a United States crisis. Legislation for the Caribbean basin has led to more jobs in the Dominican Republic.

One of the most extraordinary aspects of this astonishing chain of events is the unwillingness of the American left to accept this democratic progress. Instead, the left has been blinded by a fixation on two factors in United States policy: the struggle against Communist advances and the willingness to countenance the use of force against them.

The achievement and survival of democracy in Latin America is still profoundly threatened by Communist or Communist-run groups willing to use force. Guerrilla groups in Chile, Colombia and El Salvador, as well as the Sandinista Front in Nicaragua, are among the more visible examples.

Opposition to Communist violence and dictatorship is fundamental to our political and diplomatic efforts to help democrats in the region. Our tactics, developed in concert with what local democratic forces think most useful to gain or preserve democracy, have involved efforts at the United

---

probation and 100 hours of community service. Johnston, Poindexter Wins Iran-Contra Case in Appeals Court, N.Y. Times, Nov. 16, 1991, at A1, col. 5. — EDS.

Nations Human Rights Commission, private pressures on military leaders, security assistance for governments fighting Communist insurgencies, and aid to the resistance forces fighting the Communist regime in Nicaragua.

This policy has met with extraordinary success in building democracy, except of course in Nicaragua. Just when resistance strength had forced the Communists to the table, Congress cut off military support for the fighters. Since then, the predictable has happened: The Communists have increased repression and mocked the promises they made at Esquipulas, San José and Sapoá. And why not, when our military support for the fighters has been halted while Soviet arms deliveries continue?

While we use American power to fight hard for democracy against extremism on both left and right, our critics seem suspicious of any asser-tion of United States power or influence against any government or group that claims to be on the left. In response to all tough questions they wave a magic wand: multilateralism.

It is simply not the case that these critics on the left really mean what they say about multilateralism: I have never once heard them say that we should back off in Chile or Paraguay, where tough United States pressure for democratization is quite unmatched by any similar pressure from the new Latin democracies or the Europeans.

The fiercest critics of our role in Nicaragua call for a much greater intervention in Panama. Some even urge that the United States invade Haiti. Multilateralism is less a positive policy choice than a rallying cry against the Administration.

This Administration has proved that it knows how to use multilateral diplomacy: witness, for example, the dual-track NATO decisions on me-dium-range nuclear arms, and the success in the United Nations Human Rights Commission regarding Cuba. But the struggle for democracy in this region will not succeed if run by committee.

For one thing, many Latin democracies have too much trouble strug-gling for survival to use scarce human and political resources fighting some-one else's battle. For another, the Communist left remains powerful enough to exact a very high price from the Latin democratic leader who decides to take on Fidel Castro or Daniel Ortega Saavedra; solidarity among Commu-nists is far more active than that among democrats. Moreover, the weight of history is great, and no Latin leader wants to assume it by publicly espous-ing a large role for the United States in the region even as part of multilat-eral efforts. Our interventions to help stop coups are very thankfully acknowledged — if mainly in private.

Multilateralism is always desirable, but the real question is what we do when an immediate and forceful multilateral effort is not possible. Is multi-lateralism nothing more than a dodge for simple inaction? Is it a form of magical realism at variance with the realities of Latin life, an incantation offered in the hope that it will make hard choices go away?

Critics have the luxury of invoking whatever concept they find useful in the struggle to resist a vigorous United States foreign policy, but policy makers live a tougher life. How do we stabilize democratic gains in El Salvador, Guatemala, Honduras? How do we end brutal human rights violations in Cuba? How can we provide effective help to democratic governments resisting the attacks of guerrillas in Peru, Colombia and elsewhere?

In 1980, no one predicted that President Reagan's Latin policy would be an extraordinary success. Nor did anyone predict that his Administration would come to be a more effective advocate and supporter of democracy in the region than any of its predecessors. Yet the key ingredients were there: strong belief in individual freedom in all parts of life, and a willingness to use America's influence in this region as throughout the world.

Those ingredients have combined to associate our country with the greatest expansion of democracy in Latin history. But the gains are unconsolidated and in danger. Violent Communist groups and far-right extremists remain implacably opposed to democracy; poverty and injustice are still the lot of millions of Latin Americans. American leadership has meant democratic progress. If we refuse to lead the struggle for democracy — including the struggle against its enemies — will we put all those gains at risk?

Schifter,* Building Firm Foundations: The Institutionalization of United States Human Rights Policy in the Reagan Years
2 Harv. Hum. Rts. Y.B. 3, 17-24 (1989)

INTRODUCTION

Few predictions as to the dire consequences of Ronald Reagan's election to the presidency were repeated quite as often and with as much fervor as those which foretold the "dismantling" of United States human rights policy. However, a close analysis of the early Reagan years reveals that the Administration not only avoided dismantlement, but moved beyond policy pronouncements to the institutionalization of mechanisms for developing and enforcing a comprehensive human rights policy. This Article focuses on the internal bureaucratic development of the Administration's human rights policy. . . .

I. GENESIS OF THE HUMAN RIGHTS POLICY

[The author discusses the framing of the Reagan Administration's human rights policy despite the bureaucratic vacuum that existed during 1981.]

---

* The author succeeded Mr. Abrams as Assistant Secretary of State for Human Rights and Humanitarian Affairs in the Reagan Administration and continued in that position throughout the Bush Administration. — EDS.

II. INSTITUTIONALIZATION OF THE POLICY

[The 1980s] saw the institutionalization of human rights as a significant element in U.S. foreign policy. In particular, the Bureau of Human Rights and Humanitarian Affairs ("HA") enhanced its ability to promote human rights in foreign policy by improving coordination of human rights policy in Washington and obtaining the support of the State Department's regional bureaus.

A. LAYING AN OPERATIONAL FOUNDATION

. . . [A]lthough the highest levels of government appeared to agree that the Reagan Administration would be committed to a vigorous human rights policy, human rights concerns in the State Department continued to be operationally adrift as late as the summer of 1981. And in the absence of an Assistant Secretary for Human Rights and Humanitarian Affairs appointed by the new Administration, bureaus other than HA, with geopolitical or economic concerns and with Reagan-appointed leadership, dominated decisionmaking.

Initially, Secretary of State Alexander Haig had asked Deputy Secretary of State William Clark to look into this problem. Clark, in turn, had assigned the Director of Policy Planning, Paul Wolfowitz, to study the issue. Wolfowitz had undertaken that task together with Charles Fairbanks, a staff member. Wolfowitz engaged his close friend Elliott Abrams, then Assistant Secretary for International Organizations, in discussions of this assignment. As Abrams began to work with Wolfowitz on human rights policy, he became increasingly intrigued by the challenge of the human rights job and decided to tell Clark that he would be interested in switching from International Organizations to HA. Clark agreed and the process for Abrams' nomination got underway in the fall of 1981.

In October 1981, Abrams prepared a memorandum clarifying the Administration's principles regarding human rights and spelling out in concrete terms how these principles could best be carried out:

> A *human rights policy means trouble,* for it means hard choices which may adversely affect certain bilateral relations. At the very least, we will have to speak honestly about our friends' human rights violations and justify any decision that other considerations (economic, military, etc.) are determinative. There is no escaping this without destroying the policy, for otherwise what would be left is simply coddling friends and criticizing foes. Despite the costs of such a real human rights policy, *it is worth doing and indeed it is essential.* We need not only a military response to the Soviets, which can reassure European and Asian allies and various friends around the world. We also need an ideological response, which reminds our citizens and theirs what the game is all about and why it is worth the effort. We aren't struggling for oil or wheat or territory but for political liberty. The goal of human rights policy

is to improve human rights performance whenever we sensibly can; and to demonstrate, by acting to defend liberty and speaking honestly about its enemies, that the difference between East and West is the crucial political distinction of our times.

Abrams thus emerged as the leader of an in-house effort to develop an operational policy directive for the execution of the Reagan Administration's stated policy objectives. This team framed this directive in light of the experience of their predecessors. They viewed themselves as differing from Carter Administration human rights officials in substance (by paying greater attention to long-range results and to geopolitical concerns) and in form (by greater use of quiet diplomacy to solve human rights problems). But more importantly, they believed that bureaucratic failure had caused the Carter Administration to be long on words but short on achievements in the field of human rights. Carter Administration Assistant Secretary of State for Human Rights and Humanitarian Affairs Patricia Derian had been engaged in a lonely crusade without support from other parts of the State Department bureaucracy. The new policymakers wanted to avoid this bureaucratic isolation.

Abrams was nominated Assistant Secretary of State for Human Rights and Humanitarian Affairs on October 30, 1981 and was confirmed by the Senate on November 20, 1981. Once in office, he saw to it that his ideas on Reagan Administration human rights policy were properly endorsed and communicated to his colleagues.

For example, in January 1982, Secretary of State Haig circulated a directive drafted by Abrams to eighteen top officials of the State Department, calling for their cooperation with Abrams:

> I have asked Assistant Secretary Elliott Abrams to ensure that human rights and humanitarian affairs occupy a prominent place in the formulation of conduct of our foreign policy. Assistant Secretary Abrams and the HA Bureau will be working closely with all regional and functional bureaus. The promotion of political freedom should not be considered only as an afterthought. Rather, it should be integral to our work and we should give careful thought to means to advance this goal in our day-to-day diplomacy. Quiet diplomacy, public statements, and economic and security assistance policies should all be given close scrutiny for the impact they can have on expanding civil liberties and political rights.
>
> I count on you and HA to work together in this effort, and want you to instruct your staffs to pay close attention to these issues in discussions you and our Embassies have with foreign government officials here and abroad. I particularly want you to include background and talking points on these considerations, whenever relevant, in the briefing papers you do for me and department principals for our meetings with foreign officials. We must be sure to convey to these officials the continuing interest of Congress, the American people, and the Administration in the expansion of personal and political freedom.

Thus, after a hiatus of one year, an Assistant Secretary of State for Human Rights and Humanitarian Affairs who represented the Administration held office and a policy commitment to give weight to human rights concerns in the formulation of United States foreign policy had been made.

B. ENLISTING BUREAUCRATIC SUPPORT IN THE
   STATE DEPARTMENT

To translate the generalized human rights ideals of the Reagan Administration into potentials for concrete policy initiatives had taken an entire year. In 1982 the principal architect of the new approach to human rights, Abrams, faced the job of carrying it out.

The idea that human rights should be considered in the formulation of United States foreign policy had been endorsed by the President and by the Secretary of State and incorporated into Administration policy statements. This idea also had strong bipartisan support in Congress. However, the State Department bureaucracy had only recently been instructed as to the relevance of human rights to foreign policy. After all, human rights dealt with the relationship between governments and their citizens and, according to hoary diplomatic tradition, a government's actions toward its citizens was not a matter of concern for other governments. Although the United Nations Charter and the Universal Declaration of Human Rights had elevated human rights to the international diplomatic plane, many diplomats insisted that this meant merely that human rights questions could and should be debated in United Nations fora, preferably in the abstract. State Department officials for many years had not wanted official representatives of the United States to engage in lengthy discussions of human rights abuses by foreign governments.

By late 1981, this problem of United States bureaucratic opposition to public human rights dialogues had been substantially overcome. Statements by Max Kampelman, leader of the United States delegation to the second review meeting to the Helsinki Final Act at Madrid (1980-1983), Kirkpatrick in the United Nations General Assembly and United States representatives in other international fora all reflected the United States' deepening commitment to human rights as a major element of foreign policy.

Nevertheless, in 1981 HA and Assistant Secretary Abrams still confronted several problems in fulfilling this responsibility of incorporating human rights into foreign policy. The nearly year-long hiatus in which HA had been without a leader appointed by the new Administration had diminished the little power HA had had. In addition, HA, as a recent arrival on the bureaucratic scene, often sought to cause foreign policy formulation to deviate from tradition and, to accomplish that result, necessarily impinged on the jurisdiction of other long-established bureaus. These bureaus did not yield without a struggle. However, eventually HA activities — information gathering through embassies and convincing regional bureaus and embassies to conduct quiet diplomacy about human rights — strengthened HA's position.

A 1976 amendment to sections 116(d) and 502B(b) of the Foreign Assistance Act of 1961 required the State Department to submit annually to the Congress a report on human rights conditions throughout the world, broken down on a country-by-country basis — the United States Department of State Country Reports on Human Rights Practices ("Country Reports"). The reports were intended to enable the Congress to review a country's human rights record when voting on a proposal to provide foreign assistance to that country.

But the amendment had a far more profound effect inside and outside the State Department. Over time, the coverage and quality of the Country Reports improved significantly. Moreover, the preparation of the Country Reports increased human rights awareness at all levels of the bureaucracy. The task of writing initial drafts of the country reports on human rights was assigned to the United States embassies. Each chief of mission appointed a member of his staff as "human rights officer" with the responsibility to prepare the embassy's annual report. In some countries, such as Switzerland, the lack of human rights violations made the task simple. In other countries, producing the report became a difficult but challenging job.

In those countries with serious human rights problems, the new law had its most significant impact. In most instances, the designated human rights officers took their duties seriously. To fulfill their responsibilities they could not rely on easily obtained information — the normal and traditional diplomatic routine of talking with host government officials, reading the press or following accounts in the electronic media. Instead, they sought out citizens who did not share the official views — who would shed a different light on current events from that of governmental circles. In addition, they read underground publications which reported developments ignored by the official press. Thus, in countries in which human rights problems seemed endemic, United States embassy personnel routinely contacted citizens who held no official position and many who opposed the country's government. These unofficial contacts provided an untraditional dimension to the work of United States diplomatic posts abroad. But this new role fit the representatives of a country breaking ground in human rights advocacy.

Moreover, the human rights officers did not keep their notes to themselves, to be used only once a year to prepare their human rights reports. As events with human rights implications occurred, these officers would report to Washington their observations and information. Human rights reporting became routine. The arrival in Washington of a gradually swelling stream of messages about human rights violations in various parts of the world in turn made the regional bureaus of the State Department increasingly aware of these problems and caused them to effect appropriate United States reactions.

Thus the annual country reports on human rights and the continuing flow of human rights information from all parts of the world came to enable the HA Assistant Secretary to perceive and to think about human rights in a global context. The reporting process also continued to sensitize embassies and other bureaus in the State Department to the human rights issue. A new generation of foreign service officers increasingly became attuned to the State Department's concerns regarding human rights and responded sympathetically to appeals from HA.

In addition, Abrams strengthened HA's position by convincing his colleagues in the regional bureaus of the State Department and elsewhere in the bureaucracy to cooperate with him. This institutionalization of human rights also occurred as HA tried to carry out the operational guidelines to which the Administration had pledged itself: (a) to apply a uniform standard in the advocacy of human rights throughout the world, (b) to focus on efforts to improve human rights conditions rather than merely to condemn human rights abusers and (c) to accomplish that result through the use of quiet diplomacy — speaking out only when quiet diplomacy would not yield results.

All these guidelines necessitate the cooperation of all members of the bureaucracy: HA, regional bureaus and embassies. For example, using quiet diplomacy requires United States embassies to make representations to the governments to which they are accredited. Embassies take their guidance from their regional bureaus at the State Department. Therefore, in order to effectuate human rights policy through quiet diplomacy, the regional bureaus had to become an integral part of the policy. Equipped with Haig's January 1982 memorandum, Abrams began to alert the regional bureaus to human rights concerns. Abrams succeeded: the increasing receptivity of the State Department's regional bureaus to human rights issues has been one of the major human rights achievements of the Reagan Administration.

This receptivity in turn helped quiet diplomacy to work. During the Reagan years, Washington routinely instructed embassies to raise human rights matters with their host governments. Less public castigation occurred than before, and only occasionally was there heavy reliance on the cutoff of assistance. Instead, the emphasis shifted to problem-solving through dialogue. First, regional bureau officials identified a human rights issue and made a decision to instruct the United States embassy in the country in question to make representations. Then, officials focused on who would express the United States government's concern, to whom it would be expressed and precisely what words would be used. As the years passed and this procedure was perfected, the success rate increased.

By raising human rights issues frequently in bilateral contexts, the Reagan Administration expressed its views of various countries' human rights records, not only in isolated cases, but across the board. A number of the countries affected have become accustomed to the idea and at least some of the Western democracies have begun to follow the United States' example.

HA's policy recommendations were not always accepted unquestioningly. Both substantive and bureaucratic problems persisted. Some embassies wished to shy away from engaging in discussions with host governments which could adversely affect United States bilateral relations. Also, regional bureaus tended to view human rights as an integral part of the political agenda for which *they* had responsibility. They resented the newly-arrived "interloper," HA, for trying to intrude.

But as the years passed, these obstacles were encountered less and less frequently. Human rights had become an accepted element in foreign policy formulation. In fact, the human rights factor had become so embedded in the structure of United States foreign policy that any future administration will find it difficult to reverse the course.

CONCLUSION

As the contribution to this volume by Jerome J. Shestack indicates, a substantial policy consensus among advocates of human rights has yet to be reached. However, many differences among human rights advocates seem more semantic and procedural than substantive, the product of misunderstandings and personality disputes or the result of the assumption that a government can and should act as a nongovernmental organization would. In the Reagan years, United States human rights policy came of age — mechanisms for its application were developed, strengthened and tested. Much remains to be done. In particular, many individual country situations need to be analyzed with care to determine how the United States government can best advance the cause of human rights. But the new Administration stands on the firm foundation of an institutionalized human rights policy. Its beacon can bring hope to the suffering and guidance to the concerned.

Human Rights and U.S. Foreign Policy: Argentina as a Case Study: Part III

As we saw in Problem V, the Greek junta was toppled in 1974 when it precipitated the Cyprus crisis that almost plunged it into a full-scale war with Turkey. Nearly a decade later, in 1983, the Argentine junta was driven from power after it launched an adventurous and needless war with Great Britain over the Falkland Islands. Democracy returned to Argentina, appropriately enough, on 10 December 1983, when a newly elected President, Raul Alfonsin, assumed office. The United States had little to do with this return to civilian rule, and in view of President Reagan's past support of the generals and criticism of the Carter Administration's policies with respect to Argentina (see pages 1068-1069 supra), it is somewhat surprising, to say the least, to see his Administration attempt to claim credit for this human rights victory (see page 1111 supra). The following articles suggest that in Argentina, as elsewhere in Latin America, the Carter human rights policy and its effects are not forgotten.

Editorial, A Toast to Argentina
N.Y. Times, Dec. 10, 1983, at 22 cols. 1-2

Break out the champagne for Argentina. A great country, blessed with human and natural riches, returns today to the democratic fold after eight ruinous years of military dictatorships. But credit the departing generals with a sense of drama. Perhaps by inspired design, they chose to have the elected President, Raúl Alfonsin, inaugurated on Dec. 10: Human Rights Day.

Alas, this symbolism escaped the Reagan Administration. Its inaugural gift to a democratic and civilian Government was the end of America's arms embargo, which Mr. Alfonsin did not request. A better gift would have been a belated confession that Jimmy Carter's human rights policy made a crucial difference in Argentina. Principles are practical: they kept alive the promise now realized in Buenos Aires.

There is no better witness than Mr. Alfonsin. When a repressive junta resorted to terrorism in the name of battling terrorism, its "dirty war" claimed at least 6,000 lives. The press was mostly silenced and among political leaders only Mr. Alfonsin dared to join a small human rights commission that protested the official barbarism.

The rampage reached its peak in 1976, the year in which Congress for the first time tied human rights strings to America's military and economic aid. It was a risky and disputed attempt to harness principle to diplomacy. But would it work? As administered by President Carter in important cases, it plainly did.

According to Mr. Alfonsin, thousands were saved in Argentina because the United States openly expressed its concern. Patricia Derian, the State Department's first human rights monitor, encouraged the United States Embassy in Buenos Aires to become an information center for the families of the "disappeared." She was denounced as a meddler by the junta and its American friends, but she and all America are remembered by the democrats who now govern as gallant allies.

Lewis, Lessons from Argentina
N.Y. Times, Jan. 26, 1984, at A23, cols. 1-3

BOSTON, Jan. 25 — In a bleak world there is one place to look these days for good news of freedom and human decency. That is to Argentina, where years of mass torture and murder under a military junta have given way to a regime of democracy and law.

The new Argentine President, Raul Alfonsin, has transformed the mood of that tormented country, whose great potential has been dissipated over the decades by political folly. He is undoing the cover-up of official crimes and prosecuting the generals responsible for them. The press is free, and people need no longer fear the knock at the door — and disappearance into secret prisons and death.

In all this there is a bitter reproach to the Government of the United States, and especially to its neo-conservative ideologists. For they gave sympathy and support to the Argentine gangsters in uniform. It was a sordid policy and a stupid one.

One of the very first foreign dignitaries invited to Washington by the Reagan Administration after it took office was the general about to assume the presidency of Argentina. Secretary of State Alexander Haig told Congress that the Administration favored the resumption of arms sales, which had been cut off because of Argentine human rights atrocities. He explained that Argentina shared our values.

Jeane Kirkpatrick, the U.S. representative at the United Nations, went down to meet the military leaders of Argentina. That was an appropriate symbol, because the policy of smiling upon them represented perfectly her doctrine that America should be more tolerant of "authoritarian" regimes than of "totalitarian," meaning Communist.

Then came an amazing episode, still hard to believe. On April 2, 1982, the evening after Argentina invaded the Falkland Islands, Ambassador Kirkpatrick attended a dinner in her honor at the Argentine Embassy in Washington. Not even naked external aggression stopped her smiling at the men responsible for so much butchery inside Argentina.

Fortunately, Margaret Thatcher took a different view. She sent British forces to the Falklands. The Reagan Administration came down on the British side, albeit rather lamely and, reportedly, over Mrs. Kirkpatrick's objection. With courage and the help of Argentine military ineptitude, Britain won the war. The Argentine junta, its prestige shattered, slunk out of power.

To the end the Reagan Administration displayed its insensitivity to human rights in Argentina. Last April, in a final effort to avoid responsibility, the junta issued a document saying that all the kidnappings and killings had been "acts of service" against subversion. America's European allies deplored the outrageous statement; the Pope spoke out. The State Department waited nearly three weeks and then issued a whimpering paragraph of "disappointment."

The depressing record of Reagan policy is not just history. It is a present obstacle to the United States doing what it ought to be doing in relation to Argentina — and other countries.

President Alfonsin, for all his political success so far, is hardly secure. There is danger that Argentines, who have lurched so often from one political extreme to another, may overdo their zeal to punish all who were involved in the thousands of "disappearances" and deaths. If the process goes far below the responsible military and police chiefs, to ordinary soldiers, chaos and another coup are possible.

In the circumstances it would be helpful if President Alfonsin could rely on a close and understanding relationship with the United States. But how can he rely on a Government that dealt so benignly with the savagers of his country?

Washington should, too, be helping transitions to democracy in Chile and Uruguay, whose military tyrants are quaking at the Alfonsin example. But who could expect leadership of that kind from the Reagan Administration?

One of the electrifying events in the new Argentine democracy has been the return of Jacobo Timerman, the editor who was tortured and held in secret prisons. Reading about him, I thought of what may have been the single most disgusting act of the American right in recent years: the campaign, led by the guru of the neo-conservatives, Irvin Kristol, to smear this victim of the Argentine fascists.

Jacobo Timerman is alive today only because Jimmy Carter and his Assistant Secretary of State for Human Rights, Patt Derian, intervened strongly to save him. The Carter policy on human rights saved others, too, and Argentines have not forgotten.

The Argentine story has a straightforward moral for the United States. This country is at its most effective abroad when its diplomacy coincides with its ideals. Of all people, we should be arguing for the values that President Alfonsin embraces: freedom under law.

Schell, Carter on Rights — A Re-Evaluation
N.Y. Times, Oct. 25, 1984, at A27, cols. 3-4

The hero's welcome accorded to former President Jimmy Carter when he visited South America this month was a tribute to his identification with human rights. It is also an opportunity to re-evaluate the complaint, still heard with some frequency, that the human rights policies of his Administration damaged the strategic interests of the United States by alienating the military governments of otherwise friendly and important allies. In fact, as Mr. Carter's visit showed, nothing could be further from the truth.

Jeane J. Kirkpatrick, whose writings on this subject earned her appointment by President Reagan as chief delegate to the United Nations, focused her arguments on Latin America and cited Bolivia as an example. In the last month of the Carter Administration, she criticized the preoccupation with human rights that led President Carter to take steps to undo a military coup in that country.

Detecting "a significant Communist/Castroite component" in the co-alition supporting the elected President, Hernán Siles Zuazo, she criticized Mr. Carter's intensity in opposing the coup and asserted that five years earlier "the U.S. would have welcomed a coup," 10 years earlier "the U.S. would have sponsored it," and 15 years earlier, "we would have conducted it." The Carter Administration's effort to throw its weight behind Mr. Siles Zuazo, and against a coup, showed its "indifference to strategic concerns."

As it happens, Mr. Siles Zuazo has served as President of Bolivia for the last three years, and by now not even the Reagan Administration believes that his democratic government threatens United States strategic interests. In fact, much in keeping with the approach charted by the Carter Adminis-tration, the Reagan Administration acted a few months ago to help head off a military coup in Bolivia. Sadly, but not surprisingly, no one in Washing-ton gave any credit to the Carter human rights policy.

Bolivia was not on Mr. Carter's itinerary on this trip. His stops did, however, include the two most strategically significant countries in South America, Brazil and Argentina. Among those who greeted him in Brazil was Leonel Brizola, now Governor of Rio de Janeiro, who credited Mr. Carter with saving his life. Among those who greeted him in Argentina was Jacobo Timerman, who has returned from exile and has become editor of the country's largest circulation evening newspaper. He also credited Mr. Carter with saving his life. The Argentine President, Raul Alfonsin, though not so vitally affected by Mr. Carter's human rights policy, made clear by his welcome how much he believed the Carter policy did for Argentina.

It now seems evident that, although the Carter Administration may have alienated repressive military regimes by criticizing their human rights abuses, it produced long-lasting friendships in countries where successor governments are restoring democracy and respect for human rights. That is hardly a disservice to our strategic interests. Indeed, if the Reagan Adminis-tration is right that the trend in Latin America is toward democratic devel-opment, speaking out against human rights abuses may even be considered a way to promote the long term strategic interests of the United States.

Postscript: After serving one term, President Alfonsin was succeeded by President Carlos Saul Menem, who proceeded to pardon scores of military officers convicted or facing trial in connection with acts of tor-ture, abduction, and murder committed during the so-called "dirty war" of 1976-1983. Christian, Pardoned Argentine Officers Out of Jail, N.Y. Times, Oct. 10, 1989, at A3, cols. 4-6. Among the officers reported par-doned was General Carlos Guillermo Suarez-Mason of Forti v. Suarez-Mason "fame" (see pages 148-154 of Problem II). Neier, Menem's Pardons and Purges, N.Y. Times, Oct. 2, 1989, at A19, cols. 1-2. This attempt at "reconciliation" has been severely criticized by President

Menem's political opponents and by human rights groups. A physics professor who was kidnapped by security forces and held in secret jails has charged that "[t]he pardons take us a step closer to vindicating the repression, and vindication will lead to repetition of what happened last decade. . . ." Pardon of Argentine Officers Angers Critics of the Military, N.Y. Times, Oct. 9, 1989, at A3, cols. 1-3.

The pardons granted to gross human rights violators in Argentina and the amnesties adopted in other countries have been the subject of much recent debate and criticism. See, e.g., Artucio, Impunity of Perpetrators, in Seminar on the Right to Restitution, Compensation and Rehabilitation for Victims of Gross Violations of Human Rights and Fundamental Freedoms 182 (SIM Special No. 12, 1992); Garro and Dahl, Legal Accountability for Human Rights Violations in Argentina: One Step Forward and Two Steps Backward, 8 Hum. Rts. L.J. 283 (1987); Malamud-Goti, Transitional Governments in the Breach: Why Punish State Criminals?, 12 Hum. Rts. Q. 1 (1990); J. Mendez, Truth and Partial Justice in Argentina: An Update (Americas Watch 1991); Orentlicher, Settling Accounts: The Duty to Prosecute Human Rights Violations of a Prior Regime, 100 Yale L.J. 2537 (1991); Pion-Berlin, To Prosecute or to Pardon? Human Rights Decisions in the Latin American Southern Cone, 16 Hum. Rts. Q. 105 (1994).

IV. The Bush Administration's Attitude Toward Human Rights Concerns in the Foreign Policy Process

No discernable pattern emerged with respect to the role of human rights in the foreign policy process during President George Bush's four years in office. Unlike the Carter Administration, where both the President and his Secretary of State spoke out forcefully for human rights shortly after assuming office, the Bush Administration's principal officials made no major speeches and adopted no new or innovative policies. Perhaps no more could have been expected from a man who, as Vice President, once toasted President Ferdinand Marcos of the Philippines for his adherence to democratic principles and processes. Bush Pledges U.S. Support for the Philippines, N.Y. Times, July 1, 1981, at A13, cols. 3-6.

That President Bush would continue the status quo of the last years of the Reagan Administration could be gleaned from his reappointment of Ambassador Richard Schifter as Assistant Secretary of State for Human Rights and Humanitarian Affairs. His views on the role of human rights in the foreign policy process had been widely publicized (Schifter, Building

Firm Foundations: The Institutionalization of United States Human Rights Policy in the Reagan Years, 2 Harv. Human Rts. Y.B. 3 (1989), and apparently the President felt comfortable with them. "Fine tuning" rather than striking new policies was the order of the day.

Although there were exceptions — the successful effort to achieve ratification of the Civil and Political Covenant, ironically long opposed by Ambassador Schifter, was one — the Bush Administration pursued few new initiatives in the human rights area and responded in languid fashion to one of the major human rights crises during its four years in office: Tiananmen Square. President Bush's patently inadequate response to the massacre is confirmed by the remarkably candid account of none other than Ambassador Schifter, given at a recent symposium at the Harvard Law School (East Asian Legal Studies, Human Rights and Foreign Policy 13-15 (1994) (emphasis added)).

> During the late 1970s, the United States government largely ignored China's human rights problems. Throughout the Reagan Administration, "our expectation was that China was on a course that would inevitably result in a loosening of restrictions and compel increased adherence to human rights. Together with our concern to maintain the PRC's goodwill during the Cold War, that caused us not to let human rights concerns intrude into our relations with China." In essence, through both the Carter and Reagan years, "we did try to report accurately on human rights in China, but we did nothing about them."
>
> "Then came Tiananmen Square." The initial response of the American government suggested that human rights concerns had become "sufficiently infused into U.S. policy for the bureaucracy to respond effectively." Various statutorily required measures, including an end to the sale of military equipment and a curtailment of most World Bank lending to China, went into effect. "From the general behavior of my colleagues, including those in the State Department's East Asian Bureau, I had the distinct impression in early June 1989 that we were going to pursue human rights concerns regarding China as we had regarding the Soviet Union."
>
> Mr. Schifter, in what he characterized as the first public description of his thoughts about the "evolution of China policy under the Bush Administration," underscored that this new, more vigorous policy did not come about for the reason that "the China desk officer sat in the Oval Office." President Bush "most assuredly found the arrest and torture of students for the advocacy of democracy to be abhorrent, but he simply did not believe that it was sound policy for the United States to risk its relationship with the leaders of China. He never fully realized that the schoolboys and schoolgirls of the years that he had spent in Beijing had become adults, that many of them had been exposed to the ideas of democracy and respect for human rights, and that they had come to believe in and fight for them." *Both the President and his National Security Advisor, Brent Scowcroft, "were sympathetic to the Kissinger approach to foreign policy, one that simply did not factor human rights considerations in policy formulation."*
>
> The result, continued Mr. Schifter, "was that we sent mixed signals to China. We did what the law required, but we made no effort to coordinate a

comprehensive China human rights policy with our allies as we had through the CSCE process with regard to the Soviet Union." Most-favored-nation (MFN) status was not suspended. "But let us keep in mind that the law, under its terms at that time, was directed purely to emigration policy." US-led efforts on the multilateral front produced the initial restrictions on World Bank lending, but "after a while that unravelled. Whether we fought hard to prevent it from unravelling, I do not know for sure. I doubt that we did."

What was striking in the midst of this approach was that the "basic commitment to a human rights policy had by then sufficiently imbued the Foreign Service to keep alive a concern in spite of the clear lack of interest at high levels." The concern about China was further nourished by members of Congress from both parties, as well as the general public. "I do want to say that Asia Watch did a very good job in that regard, so that the Administration could not simply shrug off the human rights problems of China."

As a consequence, the idea of sending a "message to Beijing that we cared" did not fade away. The ongoing Congressional concern about renewal of MFN status "began after a time to have its impact on the Chinese," given how important the American market is for China's exports. The Chinese therefore agreed to receive Mr. Schifter in December of 1990 and again in November of 1991 for serious talks, as well as to continue these discussions in Washington through their embassy. Due to this, Mr. Schifter believes, "the number of people convicted was smaller and the sentences were shorter than they would have been without expressions of concern from the United States." Nevertheless, more could have been accomplished if we "had pressed harder and particularly if our allies had joined us in our protestations."

The lesson of the above tale is twofold: first, the human rights concerns initially pressed by President Carter have become institutionalized by the U.S. foreign policy bureaucracy; and second, despite this fact, little can be achieved in the way of pressuring a human rights violator to improve its record if there is "a clear lack of interest at high levels." That there appears to have been during the Bush Administration.

V. The Clinton Administration's Attitude Toward Human Rights Concerns in the Foreign Policy Process

During the 1992 presidential campaign, candidate Bill Clinton never really addressed the role of human rights in the foreign policy process. Indeed, he rarely used the phrase "human rights" in his major foreign policy speeches. Rather, he spoke of the need for a "pro-democracy foreign policy" that would foster democratic regimes (always with "market econo-mies") abroad. It was in this context, moreover, that he criticized the per-ceived failings of the Bush Administration, especially its response, or lack thereof, to the Tiananmen Square massacre. Consider the following passage from his Milwaukee speech of 1 October 1992.

A Vision for Democracy (Remarks by Governor Bill Clinton)
Milwaukee, Wis., Oct. 1, 1992

. . . [T]here is no more striking example of President Bush's indifference to democracy than his policy toward China. None of us will ever forget the images of millions of Chinese people demonstrating peacefully for democracy; the solitary young man staring down a tank; or the students raising a model of our Statue of Liberty in Tiananmen Square. Neither will we ever forget the horror of seeing hundreds of innocent people mowed down for their belief in freedom.

But instead of allying himself with the democratic movement in China, George Bush sent secret emissaries to raise a toast with those who crushed it.

The stakes in China's future are very high. For the course taken by that great nation will help shape the future of Asia and the world. Three years after the Tiananmen Square tragedy, the tremors of change continue to shake China. We do not want China to fall apart or descend into chaos. Rather, we should use our relationship and influence to work with the Chinese for a peaceful transition to democracy and the spread of free markets.

But today, we must ask ourselves, what has President Bush's China policy really achieved? The Chinese leadership still sells missiles and nuclear technology to Middle Eastern dictators who threaten us and our friends. They still arrest and hold in prison leaders of the pro-democracy movement. They restrict American access to their markets, while our trade deficit with China will reach $15 billion this year. The Chinese now have the second biggest trade surplus of any nation in the world. Yet, just a few days ago, President Bush vetoed legislation passed with bipartisan Congressional majorities that would place conditions on most-favored nation trade status for China's state-owned enterprises. And just today, the Senate failed by a vote of 59-40 to override that veto.

I do not want to isolate China. But I believe our nation has a higher purpose than to coddle dictators and stand aside from the global movement toward democracy. For the greatest strength America can count on in today's world is not our personal relations with foreign dignitaries. Individual leaders come and go — even in the United States, I hope. Rather, it is the powerful appeal of our democratic values and our enduring political institutions to people around the world that make us special.

This does not mean embarking on a reckless crusade. Every ideal, including the promotion of democracy, must be tempered with prudence and common sense. We know that ballot boxes alone do not solve every world problem, and that some countries and cultures are many steps away from democratic institutions. We know there may be times when other security needs or economic interests will diverge from our commitment to democracy and human rights. . . .

Today, however, the danger that we will get carried away with ideals does not loom large. That has not been our problem in the last four years. The real danger in this time of sweeping change is that, under President Bush, we will cling to tired and outdated notions that do not work and cannot inspire.

We shall return later in this section to the question of democracy and human rights in China and how President Clinton's views thereon have shifted dramatically during his term in office. Before addressing this question, however, let us consider how the President's campaign rhetoric has been transformed into official policy and the effect, if any, this transformation has had on human rights issues stricto sensu.

Initially, the new (or renewed) focus on democratization and its link to human rights drove a reorganization at the Department of State, which saw the old Bureau of Human Rights and Humanitarian Affairs transformed into the Bureau of Democracy, Human Rights, and Labor, one of four offices under the direction of a new Undersecretary of State for Global Affairs. Institutionally as well as symbolically, this change of names and commingling of duties caused some concern among the international human rights community, which feared that the focus on democratization might come at the expense of human rights. While neither President Clinton nor Secretary of State Warren Christopher nor any other government official has provided an authoritative elaboration of the link between democracy and human rights, the following two readings — testimony by Undersecretary of State Wirth and a speech by Assistant Secretary of State Shattuck — give the best guidance available as to the Administration's thinking in this regard and the role it considers human rights concerns should have in the foreign policy process.

Statement of the Honorable Timothy E. Wirth, Counselor, U.S. Department of State
in Human Rights Policy Under the New Administration:
Hearing and Markup of H. Res. 188 and H. Con. Res. 106
Before the Subcomm. on International Security, International
Organizations and Human Rights of the House Comm. on
Foreign Affairs, 103d Cong., 1st Sess. 6-8 (1993)

I am delighted to be here and have a chance to talk to you about the administration's human rights policy. . . . Promoting respect for human rights worldwide is one of the pillars of this administration's foreign policy.

By fostering pluralism and democracy around the world, we also lay the foundation for stability and economic progress that benefits us as well as others. By working to ensure that other governments respect the rights of their citizens, we create a safeguard against threats to international peace and security. . . .

We are fortunate to live in a country expressly founded on human rights principles. Our ideals have inspired people around the world. In recent years, we have witnessed the flourishing of democracy as well. Elections in recent weeks in Burundi, Cambodia, Paraguay, and Yemen, and the referendum on democracy and economic reform in Russia are just the most recent examples of a worldwide trend away from authoritarianism and toward representative government.

The desire to enjoy the full range of human rights is universal. We respect the national ethnic, religious, and cultural differences that make countries unique. However, where you live should not determine whether you will be imprisoned, tortured, or killed merely for expressing your beliefs.

While a growing number of countries do respect these rights, they continue to be under severe challenge in many other countries, including Bosnia, Burma, China, Cuba, Iran, Iraq, North Korea, and Sudan.

The U.N. World Conference on Human Rights, which . . . will take place over the next 2 weeks, June 14 to 25, represents an important opportunity for the Clinton administration and for the U.S. Government to show U.S. support for the popular movements for freedom and democracy that are emerging all over the world in this post-cold war era.

The conference represents an opportunity to reaffirm the universality of those rights, which are enshrined in the United Nations charter and in the 1948 Universal Declaration of Human Rights.

We cannot afford to take a business as usual approach to human rights. The administration has made human rights a key component of its foreign policy. And we intend to follow up that policy with activism to advance the cause of human rights. And one of the most important ways that we can do this is to strengthen the U.N. systems for dealing with human rights.

We have worked closely with nongovernmental human rights organizations to develop an action plan to improve the United Nation's effectiveness in addressing and resolving human rights problems. And that draft action plan has been made available to members of the committee.

This plan figures prominently in our strategy for the conference next week in Vienna. And I would like to summarize briefly for you some of the components of that plan.

First, we want to ensure greater effectiveness of the U.N. Human Rights Center, and its advisory services and reporting activities.

Second, we hope to better target U.N. assistance toward helping nations establish the rule of law, eliminate torture, and resolve ethnic, religious, and racial conflict.

Third, we believe that we must integrate more fully the rights of women and children system-wide throughout the United Nations, and support the appointment of a Special Rapporteur on Violence Against Women.

Fourth, we believe that the capacity of the United Nations to promote democracy will be increased by assisting in the conduct of elections and improving the administration of justice.

Fifth, we believe that human rights considerations should be integrated in the U.N. activities, such as peacekeeping, refugee protection, conflict resolution, and development of humanitarian programs.

And finally, we believe that an office of a U.N. High Commissioner for Human Rights should be created as a means of improving the effectiveness of the United Nations in implementing human rights standards.

These are the highlights of the action plan which we have developed, Mr. Chairman, in cooperation with a very broad and inclusive group of nongovernmental organizations with the help of the staff of the CSCE Commission and with broad consultations, which will be the basis of the position which we take in Vienna.

Throughout much of our history, the United States has provided moral leadership in our foreign policy. We must now be in the forefront of those members of the international community who are supporting international human rights standards.

As Members of Congress, you have already done a great deal and can do more to help achieve that goal. For example, we believe that it is necessary as soon as possible to pass the implementing legislation necessary to complete ratification of the U.N. convention against torture.

In addition, the administration is considering ratification of the four international human rights treaties that are pending before the Senate Foreign Relations Committee. The convention to eliminate racial discrimination. The convention to eliminate all forms of discrimination against women. The American convention on human rights. And the International Covenant on Economic, Social and Cultural Rights.

We must, of course, look beyond the world conference to the longer term. The ambitious American agenda will not be completed in Vienna, nor should we expect it to be. However, we can work with other nations to reaffirm our commitment to those fundamental principles; to implement them around the world; and to isolate, Mr. Chairman, those renegade countries who are backsliding and who are using this conference and using other discussions of national sovereignty as a way of covering up and hiding their own egregious human rights abuses.

Mr. Chairman, and members of the committee, I thank you very much for the opportunity to be with you today. As I pointed out, our full statement, I hope, will be included in the record, along with the draft U.S. Action Plan, which lays out in great detail the position taken by this administration broadly embraced, I believe, by NGO's of all stripes across the country.

Shattuck, Human Rights and Democracy in Asia
5 U.S. Dept. State Dispatch 480, 480-481 (July 18, 1994)

U.S. POLICY ON HUMAN RIGHTS AND DEMOCRACY

Protecting human rights and promoting democracy are integral elements of U.S. foreign policy for two distinct but closely related reasons. First, respect for human rights in the processes of government and law reflects fundamental values, which not only have played a major role in shaping America's world view but also represent binding and universal principles as expressed in the Universal Declaration of Human Rights and, more recently, at last year's Vienna conference. Second, human rights protection serves far-reaching, long-term interests of the U.S., its trading partners and allies, and, indeed, the entire international community.

We know from historical experience that democracies are more likely than other forms of government to respect human rights; to settle conflicts peacefully; to observe international law and honor agreements; to go to war with great reluctance and rarely against other democracies; to respect the rights of ethnic, racial, and religious minorities; and to provide the social and political basis for free market economies.

Open societies make for better and more stable trading partners because they tend to honor agreements and provide reliable systems of justice. By contrast, repressive regimes foster instability in the long run and put investment at great risk of expropriation or loss.

By contrast, the costs to the world of repression and authoritarianism are painfully clear. In the 20th century, the number of people killed by their own governments under authoritarian regimes is four times the number killed in all this century's wars combined. Repression pushes refugees across borders and triggers wars, and unaccountable governments are heedless of environmental destruction.

We do not seek to replicate America's unique society around the world. Rather, we promote accountable government, a free press, effective judiciaries, and the rule of law. We encourage the development of civil society — of civic, religious, trade, and social groups — that creates breathing room for society to develop apart from the state and affords individuals and communities the greatest opportunity for growth.

The Clinton Administration is incorporating human rights and democracy into the mainstream of our foreign policy. We encourage institutions of accountability that will hold violators to account. Examples include the UN War Crimes Tribunal for the former Yugoslavia, the Truth Commission in El Salvador, and administration of justice programs in many countries, including in Latin America, Russia, and other states of the former Eastern bloc.

We are working to build new multilateral institutions to address racial, ethnic, and religious conflict — institutions that can work to defuse conflicts before they lead to gross violations of human rights. We are especially involved in pursuing cooperation with regional groups to create mechanisms of conflict resolution and are actively engaged in supporting initiatives by the OAU, OAS, and the CSCE. We are integrating, for the first time, women's rights into all aspects of our human rights policy.

We are working to meet U.S. international human rights obligations by pressing for the ratification of a number of pending international treaties and conventions. Thanks to our efforts, the Senate recently ratified the convention on the elimination of race discrimination, which had been languishing for years.

We led the effort in the UN to create a UN High Commissioner for Human Rights, and we are working with other states to improve the functioning of the UN Human Rights Commission. Finally, and perhaps above all, we are strengthening our relationship with non-governmental organizations striving to promote democracy and human rights around the globe.

While the above two readings rightly stress the importance of promoting democracy and protecting human rights, they are less than crystal clear about the relationship between and relative importance of the two concepts. Thus, many members of the human rights community, it has been reported, "are uncomfortable with a dual approach and argue that human rights alone, not democracy promotion, should be the centerpiece of the Clinton administration's foreign policy." Carothers, Democracy and Human Rights: Policy Allies or Rivals?, 17 Wash. Q. 109, 110 (1994). The prime point of difference, these human rights advocates point out, is one of law versus politics.

> For many in the human rights movement there is a very significant difference in formal status between human rights and democracy: human rights are international legal norms whereas democracy is a political ideology. In their view, U.S. government pressure on a foreign government to improve its human rights behavior is a form of entirely legitimate intervention in the internal affairs of that country because human rights norms are binding under international law on all states. By contrast, they consider that U.S. pressure on a foreign government to become democratic is of questionable legitimacy because democracy is just one of a number of competing political ideologies, not a binding obligation. Democracy promotion by the U.S. government, they hold, constantly runs the risk of veering off into neo-imperialism.

Id. at 111.

Moreover, according to the former executive director of Human Rights Watch, to international human rights lawyers "the Reagan-Bush emphasis on democracy often seemed not only a means of manipulating human rights for political purposes, . . . but also a pretext for not taking a strong stand on systematic violations of core human rights in countries identified [often too optimistically] as democratic." Neier, Asia's Unacceptable Standard, Foreign Pol'y 42, 48 (No. 92, Fall 1993). Whether the Clinton

Administration would manipulate human rights in such fashion remains problematic. Yet even if it does not, the human rights camp will remain split as to whether to embrace pro-democracy initiatives in addition to traditional human rights concerns. As Neier maintains:

> The Universal Declaration of Human Rights does commit the countries of the world to representative government, and the International Covenant on Civil and Political Rights commits the 120 countries that are party to it to periodic free and fair elections. Nevertheless, there is division within the movement about whether human rights organizations should promote democracy. Some fear that associating themselves with the espousal of democracy would align them with the political opponents of nondemocratic governments and, thereby, diminish their credibility in criticizing violations of core human rights. Others consider that support for the right of citizens to take part in self-government is legitimate in that it is analogous to, and an extension of, their efforts on behalf of the freedom of expression recognized in international law. Even those within the movement who fall into the latter camp readily agree, however, that promoting democracy is far less central than stopping torture, murder, and disappearances.

Id.

Whatever the attitude of U.S. NGOs, pushing both democracy and human rights would seem to be a wise choice politically, despite the problems inherent in this dual-track approach, for it permits the Clinton Administration to justify its actions on both fronts on national security grounds. See Carothers, The Democracy Nostrum, 11 World Poly. J. 47, 47-48 (No. 3, 1994):

> In the early 1990s, President George Bush and Secretary of State James Baker began to include references to the concept of a democratic peace in their foreign policy addresses. But the Clinton administration has embraced it wholeheartedly, elevating it to the status of a controlling credo. Hardly a foreign policy speech goes by these days without a reference to the proposition that democracies do not make war with each other (the more cautious academic conclusion that democracies *rarely* make war with each other is sacrificed for the simplicity and absoluteness of the flat assertion). President Clinton and his advisers go beyond simply proclaiming that democracies do not make war with each other; they have converted that proposition into a security policy manifesto. Given that democracies do not make war with each other, they contend, the United States should seek to guarantee its security by promoting democracy abroad. As President Clinton declared in his 1994 State of the Union address, "the best strategy to ensure our security and to build a durable peace is to support the advance of democracy elsewhere."
>
> The notion of democracy promotion as security policy is of particular appeal to the Clinton team as a quintessential "New Democrat" idea. New Democrats are drawn to democracy promotion by their liberal instinct to do good in the world. Yet tempered by the experiences of the Carter human rights policies of the late 1970s, they want their do-good, moralistic instincts to withstand the judgmental fires of hardheaded realism. Casting democracy

promotion as a form of war prevention, as a security enhancement, neatly squares this circle. Democracy promotion becomes a bridge spanning the traditional divide between liberal moralism and conservative realism.

While waiting to see how the Clinton Administration's pro-democracy and pro-human rights policies play out, one can rest assured that there is little likelihood of it (or subsequent administrations) abandoning human rights as an element of foreign policy; rather, the issue is one of good faith, sound judgment, and effectiveness. Here President Clinton has taken a number of steps in the right direction that clearly differentiate his Administration from those of his immediate predecessors: (1) he has appointed a Secretary of State, an Undersecretary of State, and an Assistant Secretary of State all committed to an active and aggressive human rights policy; (2) he has reversed the Reagan-Bush attitude toward economic, social, and cultural rights, once again recognizing that such rights are an integral part of the corpus of international human rights law; (3) he has continued the process, initiated by President Bush when he asked the Senate to give its advice and consent to the Civil and Political Covenant, of seeking ratification of the backlog of human rights treaties pending for nearly 20 years; (4) he has demonstrated a willingness to work with the United Nations in achieving human rights objectives, the establishment of the Yugoslav War Crimes Tribunal and the UN-authorized humanitarian intervention in Haiti being examples; and (5) he has encouraged the Department of State, after a 12-year hiatus, to reestablish good working relationships with the principal U.S. NGOs.

Earlier in this section there appeared an extract from a 1992 campaign speech of then-Governor Clinton severely criticizing President Bush for unconditionally renewing China's MFN trade status (see page 1127 supra). In another statement made during the campaign, he labelled his predecessor's decision "yet another sad chapter in this administration's history of putting America on the wrong side of human rights and democracy." Clinton Criticizes Bush Decision to Renew China's Most Favored Nation Status, U.S. Newswire, June 3, 1992, available in LEXIS, News Library, Wire File. Yet even before his inauguration the President-Elect started shifting ground. On 14 December 1992, he announced that he favored retaining China's MFN trade status, although he would condition it upon progress in human rights and other areas. President-Elect Clinton Supports Renewing MFN Trade Status for China, 9 Intl. Trade Rep. (BNA) 2124 (1992). Once in office, moreover, the President actually issued an Executive Order unconditionally extending MFN until 3 July 1994, but conditioning subsequent extensions upon China's fulfillment, inter alia, of several human rights criteria. Exec. Order No. 12,850, 3 C.F.R. §606 (1994). As the end of the year approached, he came full circle and then some, using language strikingly similar to that employed by President Bush when he justified his unconditional extension of MFN to China in 1990 (President's News Conference (May 24, 1990), 1990-I George Bush Pub. Papers 707 (1991).

President's News Conference (May 26, 1994)
30 Weekly Comp. Pres. Doc. 1166, 1166-1169 (May 30, 1994)

The President.   Good afternoon. Today I would like to announce a series of important decisions regarding United States policy toward China.

Our relationship with China is important to all Americans. We have significant interests in what happens there and what happens between us. China has an atomic arsenal and a vote and a veto in the U.N. Security Council. It is a major factor in Asian and global security. We share important interests, such as in a nuclear-free Korean Peninsula and in sustaining the global environment. China is also the world's fastest growing economy. Over $8 billion of United States exports to China last year supported over 150,000 American jobs.

I have received Secretary Christopher's letter recommending, as required by last year's Executive order, reporting to me on the conditions in that Executive order. He has reached a conclusion with which I agree, that the Chinese did not achieve overall significant progress in all the areas outlined in the Executive order relating to human rights, even though clearly there was progress made in important areas, including the resolution of all emigration cases, the establishment of a memorandum of understanding with regard to how prison labor issues would be resolved, the adherence to the Universal Declaration of Human Rights and other issues.

Nevertheless, serious human rights abuses continue in China, including the arrest and detention of those who peacefully voice their opinions and the repression of Tibet's religious and cultural traditions.

The question for us now is, given the fact that there has been some progress but that not all the requirements of the Executive order were met, how can we best advance the cause of human rights and the other profound interests the United States has in our relationship with China?

I have decided that the United States should renew most-favored-nation trading status toward China. This decision, I believe, offers us the best opportunity to lay the basis for long-term sustainable progress in human rights and for the advancement of our other interests with China. Extending MFN will avoid isolating China and instead will permit us to engage the Chinese with not only economic contacts but with cultural, educational, and other contacts and with a continuing aggressive effort in human rights, an approach that I believe will make it more likely that China will play a responsible role, both at home and abroad.

I am moving, therefore, to delink human rights from the annual extension of most-favored-nation trading status for China. That linkage has been constructive during the past year. But I believe, based on our aggressive contacts with the Chinese in the past several months, that we have reached the end of the usefulness of that policy and it is time to take a new path toward the achievement of our constant objectives. We need to place our relationship into a larger and more productive framework.

In view of the continuing human rights abuses, I am extending the sanctions imposed by the United States as a result of the events in Tiananmen Square, and I am also banning the import of munitions, principally guns and ammunition from China. I am also pursuing a new and vigorous American program to support those in China working to advance the cause of human rights and democracy. This program will include increased broadcasts for Radio Free Asia and the Voice of America, increased support for nongovernmental organizations working on human rights in China, and the development with American business leaders of a voluntary set of principles for business activity in China.

I don't want to be misunderstood about this: China continues to commit very serious human rights abuses. Even as we engage the Chinese on military, political, and economic issues, we intend to stay engaged with those in China who suffer from human rights abuses. The United States must remain a champion of their liberties.

I believe the question, therefore, is not whether we continue to support human rights in China but how we can best support human rights in China and advance our other very significant issues and interests. I believe we can do it by engaging the Chinese. I believe the course I have chosen gives us the best chance of success on all fronts. We will have more contacts. We will have more trade. We will have more international cooperation. We will have more intense and constant dialog on human rights issues. We will have that in an atmosphere which gives us the chance to see China evolve as a responsible power, ever-growing not only economically but growing in political maturity so that human rights can be observed.

To those who argue that in view of China's human rights abuses we should revoke MFN status, let me ask you the same question that I have asked myself over and over these last few weeks as I have studied this issue and consulted people of both parties who have had experience with China over many decades.

Will we do more to advance the cause of human rights if China is isolated or if our nations are engaged in a growing web of political and economic cooperation and contacts? I am persuaded that the best path for advancing freedom in China is for the United States to intensify and broaden its engagement with that nation.

I think we have to see our relations with China within the broader context of our policies in the Asian-Pacific region, a region that, after all, includes our own Nation. This week, we've seen encouraging developments, progress on resolving trade frictions with the Japanese, and possible progress towards stopping North Korea's nuclear program.

I am determined to see that we maintain an active role in this region in both its dynamic economic growth and in its security. In three decades and three wars during this century, Americans have fought and died in the Asian-Pacific to advance our ideals and our security. Our destiny demands that we continue to play an active role in this region. The actions I have taken today to advance our security, to advance our prosperity, to advance our ideals I believe are the important and appropriate ones. I believe, in other words, this is in the strategic, economic, and political interests of both the United States and China, and I am confident that over the long run this decision will prove to be the correct one.

Q.   Mr. President, most of the conditions, the aspects of this problem were prevalent last year when you made very strong threats of a cutoff of human rights. Aren't you really bowing to big business and backing off of human rights in terms of the world perception?

The President.   No. No, I don't think so. And if you've seen the statements of recent days by many others — Senator Bradley and many other Members of the Senate, other members of the American political community who have also evolved in their view, I think most people believe, number one, that conditions have changed.

I think it's very important to say that under the terms of this agreement some progress has been made. Some important political dissidents have been released. We've gotten information on Tibetan prisoners for the first time. We have a process now with operable deadlines for looking into these disputes over prison labor matters. We have at least an adherence, an explicit adherence by the Chinese to the Universal Declaration of Human Rights. We have an ongoing set of negotiations now on how to deal with the jamming we've suffered on our Voice of America broadcast. So there have been some changes.

And interestingly enough, many of the most vocal human rights advocates have argued that — not that we should lift MFN status but that instead we should have some intermediate sanctions which cover a bigger section of the economy. But things have changed to the point, both in terms of what has gone on in China and in terms of the other strategic issues — the situation in Korea, for example, I think everyone would admit is somewhat different than it was a year ago — that I believe, that everybody believes we should do something differently.

The question is, should we delink, or should we continue to do this on an annual basis? I believe the answer to that is no. And I believe the answer to what we should do is to pursue a broader strategy of engagement. I think that is where we are now. And I think that it is far more likely to produce advances in human rights as well as to support our strategic and economic interests.

Q.   Mr. President, how do you answer those who say you are — using your own words now — coddling tyrants? And with the leverage of linkage now moved away, what incentive is there for China to improve human rights?

The President.   Well, let me turn it on its head, first of all. China is a very great and important nation. What gave rise to this MFN in the first place, this issue? Why did anyone believe human rights should be tied to MFN in China as opposed to other nations in the world? The MFN law basically is tied to emigration, and we have — I haven't said that, I don't think, today — we have successfully resolved all outstanding emigration cases with the Chinese. Why was it extended to involve human rights here? Because of the frustration in the Congress that the previous administration had reestablished relationships too quickly after Tiananmen Square, and there seemed to be no other aggressive human rights strategy.

The United States has pursued the cause of human rights around the world in many, many ways without tying it to MFN with those countries. I have had, for example, several conversations on this subject with one of our Nation's most dedicated human rights advocates, President Carter, who strongly believes that the decision I have taken today is the right one and more likely to produce human rights progress. Because, let me answer your question precisely, every nation, every great nation makes some decisions and perhaps most decisions based on what is in the interest of the nation at that moment in time internally. But no nation likes to feel that every decision it makes for the good, to do something that's right, that makes progress, is being made not because it's the right thing to do but only because of external pressure from someone else.

And I believe, based on my — and this is the root of this judgment, and all of you and all of the American people will have to draw your own conclusions about whether I'm right or wrong, but I'm prepared to fight for my position in the Congress and elsewhere, because I believe it's right. I believe, based on intensive efforts over the last few weeks, that we are far more likely to have human rights advances when it is not under the cloud of the annual question of review of MFN. That is what I believe.

That is not to say that there will not continue to be human rights abuses in China, that there won't be ups and downs in this. But I believe that over the long run we're more likely to make advances if there's more contact with the Chinese, not less; if there's more economic growth, not less — we saw that in Taiwan and Korea — and if we are free to explicitly and aggressively pursue our human rights agenda, as we would with any other country. That is the conclusion I have drawn. I think it's the correct one.

Q. On the first question, aren't you coddling tyrants just as you accuse —

The President. No, because I do believe what happened — what has happened since then? Has there been any progress? There's been so much progress that even the people who have supported these strong resolutions, the legislation in the past, are now arguing for a different course. I'm not the only person arguing that the time has come to take a different path. It's that they will say, well, I should have done something else. But virtually everyone says the time has come to move out of the framework now.

We obviously have something going on in this relationship now. We obviously have a broader and deeper relationship, and we obviously are going to see some changes here. So I think everybody acknowledges that there is some dynamism in this relationship now which warrants a change. The question is what tactical path should we take. And I expect that many people who criticize my decision will say, "Well, he should have put stiffer tariffs on something or another or should have had a bigger section of the economy affected or gone after the military enterprises or something like that." But I think nearly everybody recognizes that there has been some real change in this and that we have the chance to move it to a different and better plane. And I think what I'm doing is the right thing to do.

McGrory, Human Rights Retreat
Wash. Post, July 7, 1994, at A1, cols. 4-5

In ways both great and small, the Clinton administration is signaling its retreat from human rights. When our "putting people first" president renewed most favored nation standing for China and practically apologized to Beijing for ever tying trade to human rights, he all but announced that the Republicans were right about human rights: It is a drag, it is inconvenient, it costs money.

Last week the Senate gave human rights the death of a thousand cuts, or to be more precise, a vote of 59 to 35 against a practical application in East Timor. The case is minuscule compared to China. Sen. Patrick J. Leahy (D-Vt.) offered a modest proposal that the United States specifically prohibit the use of U.S.-provided arms in East Timor, the wretched island where Indonesia is diligently practicing ethnic cleansing in the hope of eliminating local resistance to an Indonesian takeover.

It figured that an administration that had swallowed the China camel was not about to strain over the gnat of East Timor.

Sen. J. Bennett Johnston (D-La.) led the victory against human rights. He got a notable assist from Deputy Secretary of Defense John M. Deutch and a last-minute letter from Secretary of State Warren Christopher, who called the Leahy initiative "unnecessary and inconsistent."

"We have raised our human rights concerns at the highest levels in meetings with Indonesia," wrote Christopher. Does it sound familiar? Yes, it is the "quiet diplomacy" that was so popular, and so ineffectual, during the Reagan-Bush years.

Johnston made the also familiar argument about size. Indonesia is big. It is the fourth-largest nation on Earth, he pointed out, the largest Muslim nation in the world. It has a correspondingly large market. Its feelings would be hurt if we indicated we disapproved of its bloody suppression of an island people.

Sen. Alan K. Simpson (Wyo.), the Republican whip, called Leahy's suggestion "arrogant intrusion." Of course, any attempts at behavior modification are invasions of sovereignty, and advocates of human rights don't deny it. The point of the policy was that the world's leading democracy feels that "a decent respect for the opinions of mankind," as it says in the Declaration of Independence, is a transcendent foreign policy consideration.

As the senators were busy proving the opposite, the Indonesian government was demonstrating the shortcomings of quiet diplomacy. Three periodicals were closed, and in the wake of the action, peaceful demonstrators were attacked by riot police and more than 50 people were arrested.

Johnston conceded that "not everything taking place in Indonesia is encouraging . . . but Indonesia has made huge steps forward in human rights" without saying what they were.

He also said that "if we are going to take sanctions against every country in the world that is criticized by Amnesty International . . . the list of our friends will be short indeed."

Another country severely criticized by Amnesty International as an egregious violator of human rights is being smiled upon by the Clinton administration. Turkey, which is abusing Kurds within its borders and building up an appalling record of death-by-torture — 24 last year — is being reprimanded only by human rights groups.

"The bottom lines are very similar to the Reagan and Bush years," says James O'Dea, director of Amnesty International's Washington office. "What Clinton is doing with Turkey is what Ronald Reagan did when he stepped up security assistance to El Salvador in the face of death squad killings."

In a five-page letter to Turkish Prime Minister Tansu Ciller, the president devoted one-half sentence to human rights. The House suggested cutting security assistance to Turkey by 25 percent; the president called the prime minister and bade her not to worry.

Turkey, like Indonesia, is considered in Clinton realpolitik a valuable ally in a strategic location.

Kerry Kennedy Cuomo, director of the Kennedy Human Rights Foundation, calls the action on Indonesia "a disaster — I don't see how it promotes democracy."

The president seems determined to exhibit hardheadedness in foreign policy, to put trade and "democracy-building" as top priorities. He rarely discusses human rights and with good reason. The evidence is building that if you don't put human rights at the top, it slides right off the screen.

Yet, when challenged, the administration people say they do too advocate human rights and a source on the National Security Council suggests that the decision on Indonesia, at least, will be revisited.

If it isn't, the cynicism the president so deeply deplores will be on the rise again.

President Clinton's decision to delink trade and human rights in the case of China was for most purposes merely a replay of the Carter Administration's decision to permit Allis-Chalmers to sell turbine generators to Argentina discussed earlier in this Problem (see pages 1065-1077 supra). In both cases the desire to protect U.S. jobs and increase corporate profits prevailed over demonstrable human rights concerns, and in both instances the country concerned skillfully orchestrated U.S. business and congressional interests to bring pressure to bear upon the President involved. See, e.g., Brown, Rights Issues Aside, Asia Deals Rise, N.Y. Times, Aug. 1, 1994, at D1, cols. 3-5 & D2, cols. 3-4 ("Nearly 800 big American companies wrote to President Clinton supporting China, a tactic crucial to China's success in the trade decision."). Moreover, as countries like Indonesia and India have seen, their own quickly growing markets are a key to muting U.S. criticism of their human rights records. As reported in the New York Times:

> After years of trying unsuccessfully to quiet criticism of human-rights records, Asian nations have found powerful allies: American businesses eager to invest in their growing markets and the Clinton Administration, with its emphasis on economic interests in the post-cold-war foreign policy.
>
> The Clinton Administration's spring decision to continue China's favorable trade status gave some of the largest and fastest growing countries new confidence that their influence is now strong enough to have an effect on American policy. And from India and Indonesia to smaller nations like Singapore, Vietnam, Thailand and Malaysia, they are showing it.
>
> "It seems to me the message is loud and clear: if American business gets strongly involved in a country, human rights takes second place or even less than that," Ashutosh Varshney, an India expert at Harvard, said of the China decision.

Id. Moreover, in the case of China, it would appear that "the Chinese leadership has shown little good will in return for the political risks Mr. Clinton took in separating rights from China's trade status." Tyler, Abuses of Rights Persist in China Despite U.S. Pleas, N.Y. Times, Aug. 29, 1994, at A1, col. 6 (reporting that China has refused to permit ICRC inspection of its prisons to check reports of torture, political detention, and other abuses and has continued or increased the arrests of religious, labor, and democracy advocates). Nor apparently are the Chinese being pressured greatly to improve their human rights record. When Secretary of Commerce Ron Brown made a much-publicized, week-long trip to Beijing to promote trade ties with China, he "barely mentioned human rights issues at his public appearances and did not publicly address the 12-hour detention of leading dissident Wang Dan just before his weekend arrival here." Mufson, U.S., China Act to Boost Trade Ties, Wash. Post, Aug. 30, 1994, at A1, col. 1. Suggestions about what the United States might do to recover a portion of its human rights credibility vis-à-vis China and similarly situated countries may be found in the following editorial.

Editorial, Speak Louder on Rights in China
N.Y. Times, Aug. 29, 1994, at A14, cols. 1-2

Commerce Secretary Ron Brown, now in China with an entourage of U.S. executives, is being spared the personal humiliations showered on his

Cabinet colleague, Warren Christopher, last March. Those spring tantrums achieved their goal of convincing the Clinton Administration to drop all human rights conditions for China's tariff privileges. Though Mr. Brown yesterday promised to raise human rights concerns with his hosts, he has made it clear that commerce is his priority.

Beijing is showing its appreciation by upgrading the Commerce Secretary's protocol status to "Presidential envoy." But on matters of substance, China has given the Administration little to show for its human rights retreat.

Mr. Brown arrived amid reports that Qin Yongmin, who protested against China hosting the 2000 Olympic Games, has been beaten and mutilated in a prison labor camp. Wang Dan, a student leader in the Tiananmen Square movement, was briefly detained Saturday after weeks of surveillance. Wei Jingsheng, China's leading democracy activist, who was harassed during Mr. Christopher's visit, soon after disappeared into the labyrinth of China's penal system and has not been heard from since.

As for Mr. Clinton's original human rights conditions, progress went into reverse the day the President changed his policy. As The Times's Patrick Tyler reports, China has continued to round up democracy, labor and religious activists, including some it had previously released, like Mr. Wei. It has broken off talks with the Voice of America over jamming of its broadcasts and dropped discussions with the Red Cross about humanitarian visits to prisons. China has also toughened its terms for talking to Washington about proliferation issues.

This tough-minded behavior should come as no surprise. While Beijing always reacts badly to public pressure, it never concedes anything when it believes there is no penalty for refusing.

How can the United States now recover its human rights credibility? One way would be for Mr. Brown to persuade American businessmen to adopt a voluntary code of conduct, which would assure minimal labor standards, restrict business cooperation with political surveillance activities and prohibit dealing with suppliers that use prison labor.

Another would be to begin loosely linking progress on particular U.S. grievances to relevant aspects of the official U.S.-China relationship. For example, progress on Voice of America broadcasts could be linked to the frequency of ceremonial visits by high U.S. officials, progress on proliferation to military cooperation and progress on prison labor exports to Chinese membership in the World Trade Organization. Perhaps other links could be found that would make Beijing more eager to permit Red Cross visits and release prominent dissidents.

These loose linkages need not insist on perfect performance, merely good-faith efforts measurable by results. Meanwhile, none of the new links should be interpreted to preclude actions that directly serve obvious American interests, such as holding high-level talks on North Korea.

If Mr. Clinton is at all serious about defending human rights in China, Cabinet officers like Mr. Brown need to use their private meetings to convince Chinese leaders that the quality of their relations with the United States will in part depend on how they treat their own people.

Whether, having been given the green light to do business with China, U.S. corporations voluntarily will adopt a code of conduct à la the Sullivan Principles (see pages 580-581 of Problem VII) is highly problematic. However, with China having replaced the Soviet Union and South Africa as the world's leading human rights violator, it would seem high time for the United States to take on, not retreat from, the human rights issues posed by its aberrant behavior. President Clinton's decision to de-link trade from these human rights concerns, a stance that he strongly opposed in the past, arguably may produce results over the long haul, but to date it has not paid tangible dividends (except, perhaps, to corporate shareholders). What is more troubling is that the China decision suggests that, despite his rhetoric about democracy and human rights, the latter certainly are not at the top of his priority list and, indeed, as the McGrory column suggests, even have slid right off his screen.

VI. Comments and Questions

1. Bilder, writing in 1974, predicted that "international human rights considerations will not play a major role in U.S. foreign policy until government officials are persuaded that pursuit of these goals serves major national interests." Reviewing the "practical" reasons for supporting a human rights-oriented foreign policy, he concluded that "the problem of finding 'selfish' national interest reasons why governments such as the United States should be concerned with denials of human rights in other countries remains a basic one." See page 1038 supra. Clearly President Carter, Secretary of State Vance, and other key government officials in that Administration were convinced that their human rights initiatives were in the national interest, but did they ever identify and adequately explain their reasons for such belief? Have the explanations of the Clinton Administration, more recently, been any more enlightening or convincing? Review the justifications of both Administrations for "selfish" national interest reasons. What other reasons — "selfish" or otherwise — also might be advanced? Can a convincing argument be constructed to persuade the U.S. and other governments, and their bodies politic, that "peoples and governments . . . had [a] stake in international human rights. . . ."?

2. Bilder also observed that (as of 1974) human rights considerations were "relatively secondary factors" in the making of foreign policy decisions.

See page 1032 supra. Has that situation changed, and if so, to what extent, during the past two decades? Note that President Clinton, in his Milwaukee campaign speech, cautioned that "there may be times when other security needs or economic interests will diverge from our commitment to democracy and human rights. . . ." See page 1128 supra. Does this caveat perhaps explain his decision to de-link trade and human rights insofar as China is concerned? Will a "waiver" of human rights principles in one instance not spark demands for similar "waivers" in other situations? If so, what should be the U.S. response?

3. As the title of Schifter's article indicates, U.S. human rights policy, in principle if not always in content, has been institutionalized during the past decade. However, the costs of such a policy and its necessarily slow and episodic payoffs may cause future administrations, as well as the body politic, to lose interest in such concerns. Consider the following extract from a perceptive article by Vogelgesang, who correctly anticipated the demise of the Carter Administration.

> The "hell of good intentions" described by Stanley Hoffman [see pages 1052-1053 supra] is often due to the time it takes to achieve them. Americans are notoriously impatient with long-term crusades. Just as most turned against the Vietnam War because they were tired and saw no "light at the end of the tunnel," so might they turn on the policy envisaged as the moral antidote to the war. If stress on human rights provides few quick fixes, as seems likely, or costs too much, as seem possible, it could boomerang by 1980. Human rights might then, for that and other reasons, lose one of its most influential spokesmen.

Vogelgesang, What Price Principle? U.S. Policy on Human Rights, 56 Foreign Aff. 819, 829-830 (1978).

If you were a political adviser to President Clinton, how would you recommend that he articulate and justify his human rights concerns to the U.S. electorate over the short run? What educational efforts would you suggest that he undertake in order to convince the general public that human rights factors should continue to be taken into account in foreign policy-making over the long haul? Do the break-up of the Soviet Union, the liberation of Eastern Europe and the Baltic states, and the end of the white apartheid regime in South Africa not provide arguments for an active U.S. human rights policy? In this era of deficit spending and fiscal restraint, what arguments can be marshalled to persuade U.S. voters that they should pay the economic price — in tax hikes for foreign assistance or in lost jobs for the sake of trade restrictions against China — that a truly effective human rights policy would require? Draft an outline of the principal points to be covered should the President decide to have a politically courageous "fireside chat" on the importance of human rights concerns in the foreign policy process.

4. The totalitarian/authoritarian distinction that held sway during most

of the Reagan Administration was seen by many observers to reflect a double standard approach insofar as applying diplomatic and other pressures to states violating basic human rights. Even before its adoption, however, arguments were heard that the United States applied at least a double standard in judging the human rights records of other states, coming down hard on certain African countries (say, Uganda) or Latin American countries (say, Paraguay), but ignoring or soft-pedaling the records of certain communist states (say, China) with which it hoped to have better relations and various right-wing allies (say, Indonesia) with which it maintained military ties. Can this obvious inconsistency, implicitly written into sections 502B and 116b of the Foreign Assistance Act of 1961 and other such legislation (see page 1040 supra), be justified? Consider, for example, the following comments by Vogelgesang:

> Concentration on consistency . . . misses the point. There can and should be consistent determination to take human rights into serious account for U.S. foreign policy. Yet stress on human rights must at all times be weighed against other factors. A rigid rubric for human rights can obscure the importance of other goals, some of which may have overarching global significance.

Vogelgesang, supra, at 828. Do you agree with the author? Is she attempting to find consistency in inconsistency? Could not her argument be used as a rationalization for doing nothing? For not doing more? Would President Clinton agree (or disagree) with her conclusion? What are your views, and would they change were you to become a government official?

5. As Vogelgesang also notes, "The executive branch has yet to address the long-run implications of existing and proposed congressional attempts to expand human rights restrictions on international business transactions." Id. at 837. While the 1978-1979 ban on trade with Uganda created little popular stir or business community reaction — that state being considered beyond the pale and few U.S. firms doing business there — attempts to apply economic sanctions to Argentina for human rights purposes, as we have seen, produced a substantial backlash. So, too, did attempts to apply sanctions to South Africa, which culminated in the Comprehensive Anti-Apartheid Act of 1986 (see pages 585-588 of Problem VII). Yet, given the nature of the U.S. free enterprise system, can any human rights policy that contemplates the possible tightening of economic screws be successful if it concerns itself exclusively, as do Sections 502B and 116b, with the public sector? To take one example, did not the Chilean junta laugh all the way to the bank — perhaps literally — when, after Congress placed a $27.5 million ceiling on economic aid to Chile in 1975, that country was able to turn immediately to private banks in the United States to satisfy all its pressing financial needs? If the United States genuinely wishes to put pressure upon China to improve its human rights record, should U.S. corporations with branches or subsidiaries there not be required, at the very least, to adhere to

a strict code of conduct in their dealings with the Chinese government and their own workers?

6. Note that the Reagan Administration's representative at the 1981 session of the Commission on Human Rights voted to abolish the Working Group on Enforced and Involuntary Disappearances (page 1086 supra). Fortunately, the effort to eliminate what has become one of the UN's most important non-petition procedures (see pages 390-392 of Problem V) failed. Why do you think the representative was instructed to vote the way he did? Had you been the representative of a Western European state at the session, what would your reaction have been to such a vote? What reasons can be advanced to justify it? Are they persuasive ones?

7. Recall that one critic of the Carter Administration's human rights policy complained (see page 1049 supra) that the policy "unwittingly contributes to the incitement of dissidents and militants all over the world." He feared, he said (see page 1050 supra), that it "might get out of hand." In view of recent events in the former Soviet Union, the Eastern European and Baltic states, and South Africa, what do you think of this criticism? Indeed, is it not an argument for, rather than against, an active human rights policy? When the status quo is that of Pinochet's Chile, Marcos's Philippines, or Mobutu's Zaire, is keeping things under control necessarily the great virtue that the above remarks seem to suggest it is?

8. The originator of the totalitarian/authoritarian distinction, former Secretary of State Kissinger, observed in 1977 that "[i]n recent decades no totalitarian regime has ever evolved into a democracy." The Introduction to the Department of State's Country Reports in 1983 also noted that "the world has yet to witness the peaceful transformation of a single communist dictatorship into a democracy." Obviously events in the former Soviet Union, the Eastern European and the Baltic states, and South Africa undercut the credibility of arguments based on the totalitarian/authoritarian distinction. Freedom, and perhaps democracy, has come to many of the above countries because their peoples, aided and abetted by the human rights policies of the United States and other Western nations, finally prevailed in their demands to live under legal regimes that respected basic human rights. Yet, ironically, while authoritarian regimes, too, have crumbled (Greece, Spain, Portugal, Argentina, and Chile being examples), it is regimes of this nature that present the major human rights problems today (China, of course, excepted). What does that tell us about the validity of the totalitarian/authoritarian distinction?

9. Now that Professor Kirkpatrick's fears of "a ring of Soviet bases being established on and around our borders" (see page 1085 supra) have been eased, does not that necessitate a rethinking of her position that condoned the coddling of numerous Central and Latin American repressive regimes in the name of U.S. national security? Now that entrenched dictatorships are no longer able to play the "Communist card," are they not more susceptible than ever to a vigorous and far-sighted U.S. human rights policy? Does

not the same hold true for repressive regimes, whether authoritarian or totalitarian, wherever they may be? If so, does not the United States, no longer transfixed by real or imagined fears of the "Evil Empire," have a splendid opportunity to pursue, one hopes in collaboration with other like-minded countries, a foreign policy far more compatible with human rights concerns than it has had for most of the Cold War period? Or have the "jobs card" and the "markets card" now replaced the "Communist card" in the hands of repressive regimes?

10. The readings and discussion in this Problem have focused on the role human rights concerns have played in the U.S. foreign policy process over the past two decades. It should not be thought, however, that other countries, not only in Western Europe, but also in other parts of the globe, have not taken such concerns into account in forging and applying their own foreign policies. While data are scarce and much more comparative information is needed, several other states have sought to incorporate human rights factors into their foreign policy processes in an institutionalized way. See, e.g., the First Report of the Provisional Human Rights and Foreign Policy Advisory Committee (The Netherlands), On an Equal Footing: Foreign Affairs and Human Rights (Apr. 1985), reprinted in 7 Hum. Rts. Q. 451 (1985); Mathews and Pratt, Human Rights and Foreign Policy: Principles and Canadian Practice, 7 id. 159 (1985); Maruyama, Japan's Role in the Global Debate on Human Rights, in Carnegie Council on Ethics and International Affairs, Japan Programs Occasional Papers (No. 3, 1993). Moreover, the well-attended Vienna Conference of 1993 may have raised the collective consciences of many government representatives engaged in shaping policy for their respective states. If you are a non-U.S. reader, consider what steps your country has taken to address the issues raised in this Problem. If you are a U.S. reader, how should the United States proceed to encourage its friends and allies, in Europe and elsewhere, to collaborate on common initiatives in the human rights area?

11. Although technically beyond the scope of this Problem, it should be noted that various international financial institutions such as the World Bank and the International Monetary Fund (IMF), as well as various international organizations such as the European Union, increasingly have taken a country's human rights record into account when making decisions about financial and developmental assistance. See, e.g., K. Tomasevski, Development Aid and Human Rights Revisited (1993); Marantis, Human Rights, Democracy, and Development: The European Community Model, 7 Harv. Hum. Rts. J. 1 (1994); Rajagopal, Crossing the Rubicon: Synthesizing the Soft International Law of the IMF and Human Rights, 11 Bost. U. Intl. L.J. 81 (1993); Shihata, Human Rights, Development, and International Financial Institutions, 8 Am. U. J. Intl. L. & Pol. 27 (1992). Obviously these decisions reflect the human rights policies of the participating states.

12. Consider the following views (Reisman, Through or Despite Governments: Differentiated Responsibilities in Human Rights Programs, 72 Iowa L. Rev. 391, 398 (1987)):

> What do we really want when we encounter a cancerous social situation in which there is a serious rights violation? It is not enough to terminate or stop one particular practice. We want to make sure that the situation after intervention — after pulling one strand out of a complex social fabric — is better in terms of all the human values we cherish. . . . There are circumstances that are so comprehensively evil that only a complete revolution may make sense. In other situations, sober appraisal may suggest that pressure for organic and incremental rather than radical change may be more appropriate. A single strategy must be evaluated prospectively, not in terms of its consequences for one clause of one article of the Universal Declaration of Human Rights, but in terms of its consequences for all of them.

(a) Assume that you are named Assistant Secretary of State for Democracy, Human Rights, and Labor at the start of a hypothetical new administration. In light of the above comments, examine the recent history of human rights problems in one of the countries mentioned in the next paragraph and develop a long-term strategy (i.e., until the next U.S. presidential election in four years) for U.S. efforts to promote human rights in that country. Pay careful attention to the indigenous footholds, if any, available for human rights progress in the country (such as recent elections, a relatively independent judiciary, or strong non-governmental institutions such as labor unions or church groups) and to the particular points of leverage the United States may have (such as aid and trade relationships). Attend as well to the other U.S. interests in the country that may make it difficult to adopt certain human rights measures.

Countries that you might consider are Algeria, Brazil, Guatemala, Indonesia, Mexico, Nigeria, the Philippines, Turkey, and Vietnam. Or you may wish to select another country to take advantage of recent developments.

(b) Assume now that you are a member of the U.S. Congress at the time of this hypothetical change in administrations. You are aware of the ways in which the Executive Branch in the past has circumvented international human rights legislation. What modifications would you make to general legislation such as Sections 116b and 502B of the Foreign Assistance Act (see the Documentary Supplement) to provide a better and less easily evaded statutory framework? Would such changes unduly limit an administration's flexibility if the new administration in fact turned out to be genuinely committed to a vigorous but also pragmatic human rights policy? Consider also what country-specific legislation you might propose and how exactly you would frame it with regard to the countries listed in the above paragraph. Bear in mind the lessons learned from the history of the legislation in the early 1980s requiring presidential certification as a condition for continued aid to El Salvador.

13. The resistance to the ratification of the human rights treaties is but one example of the United States' reluctance to be judged by the same standards it uses to judge other nations. Nor is this attitude limited to Congress. At a Department of State-sponsored National Foreign Policy Conference on Human Rights in the late 1970s, some officials were "stunned" by "the proposal that U.S. victims of human rights violations establish their own Helsinki monitoring group." Vogelgesang, supra, at 832. Why should they have been? More recently, this fear of examining the human rights situation in the United States has manifested itself in the refusal of the Reagan, Bush, and Clinton Administrations to recommend acceptance of the right of individual petition by U.S. citizens to the Committee Against Torture, the Human Rights Committee, and the Committee on the Elimination of Racial Discrimination.

The assertion of a vigorous human rights policy internationally naturally encourages expectations internally. There is nothing to fear about this development — if one is concerned with civil rights and social justice — but its full ramifications for U.S. society have not been fully appreciated (or, as we have seen from pages 239-272 of Problem III, fully understood), resulting in some cases in opposition to the international human rights movement. To construct a foreign policy with human rights as its keystone, therefore, one must be very much concerned with domestic social justice and the political process necessary to make advances in that direction. When human rights are concerned, as Problem I demonstrated, there is no longer an artificial wall separating the international arena from "domestic jurisdiction."

Finally, "plus ça change, plus c'est la même chose." Notwithstanding some of his follow-up actions, consider the wise counsel contained in President Teddy Roosevelt's Message to Congress in 1904 ((1904) Foreign Relations of the United States XLII (1905)).

> Ordinarily it is very much wiser and more useful for us to concern ourselves with striving for our own moral and material betterment here at home than to concern ourselves with trying to better the conditions of things in other nations. We have plenty of sins of our own to war against, and under ordinary circumstances we can do more for the general uplifting of humanity by striving with heart and soul to put a stop to civic corruption, to brutal lawlessness and violent race prejudices here at home than by passing resolutions about wrongdoing elsewhere. Nevertheless there are occasional crimes committed on so vast a scale and of such peculiar horror as to make us doubt whether it is not our manifest duty to endeavor at least to show our disapproval of the deed and our sympathy with those who have suffered by it. The cases must be extreme in which such a cause is justifiable. There must be no effort made to remove the mote from our brother's eye if we refuse to remove the beam from our own.

Index

Aboriginal peoples, 332-337
Acheson, Dean, 517
Act of state doctrine, 159, 595
"Action-specific" legislation, 1107, 1110
African Charter on Human and People's
    Rights, 826-832
Alien Land Law, 101, 102
Alien Tort Statute, 157, 159, 160, 272
Allis-Chambers, 1065-1077
American Convention on Human Rights,
    240, 820-826, 920, 921, 927
American Declaration on Rights and Duties
    of Man, 805
American Federation of Labor v. American
    Sash and Door Company, 130
American Law Institute (ALI), 163, 164
Amin, Idi, 18, 19, 56, 60, 62, 67-69, 75-77,
    83, 84, 87, 366, 373
Anti-Drug Abuse Act of 1988, 1004
Apartheid, 418, 1011, 1012. See also South
    Africa
Arab League Boycott Office, 513
Arbitrary detention
    appointment of working group, 394
    Philippines, 396
    response to inquiry from Cuba, 311-313
    revised methods of work, 441-443
Argentina
    Carter Administration, 1064-1077, 1122,
    1123
    Reagan Administration, 1088-1093,
    1199-1124
Aristide, Jean-Bertrand, 662, 788
Armitage, John A., 527
Asakura v. Seattle, 118, 119
Attica uprising
    overview, 278-281
    relevance of Standard Minimum Rules,
    285-296

Baboeram Communication, 228, 229
Bagaya, Elizabeth, 69
Baker v. Carr, 540, 541
Bangladesh
    aftermath, 641-643

background, 602, 603
commission of enquiry report, 604-612
Belgrade Rules, 449-451, 484
Bell v. Wolfish, 315
Berrehab v. Netherlands, 759
Binaisa, Godfrey, 72
Bingham Report, 559
Birching/caning, 715-724
Bleier v. Uruguay, 479
Bosnia-Herzegovina. See Yugoslav War
    Crimes Tribunal
Buckley, James, 1092
Bush, George, 248, 250, 589, 597, 896,
    976, 977, 1124, 1125
Bush Administration
    approach to economic/social/cultural
    rights, 199, 200
    ratification of Civil and Political
    Covenant, 260
    ratification process, and, 246-248, 260
    response to Tiananmen Square massacre,
    1124-1126
    sanctions against South Africa, 590
Byrd, Harry F., Jr., 524, 531
Byrd Amendment
    challenges to, 535-541
    effect of, 543
    passage of, 531, 532
    "repeal" of, 542, 543

California Alien Land Law, 101, 102
Calley, William F., 840-843, 855, 861, 874
Calley Court-Martial. See also My Lai
    massacre
    extracts from original transcript, 862-871
    overview, 861, 862
    public response, 872, 873
    subsequent fate of Calley, 873, 874
    verdict, 872
Caning/birching, 715-724
Carter, Jimmy, 48, 75, 197, 248, 542, 543,
    562, 594, 678, 820-826, 872, 908,
    1039, 1041, 1047, 1089, 1094, 1122
Carter Administration. See also U.S. foreign
    policy

aid cut-offs to countries violating norms, 513
amendment to Byrd Amendment, 542
American Convention on Human Rights, and, 820-826
human rights policy, 240
ratification process, and, 245, 250
Reagan Administration, and, contrasted, 1103-1105
trade embargo against Uganda, and, 73-75
Case of the Fake Pig's Snout, 766, 767
Certain Expenses case, 498
Charter of the Fundamental Social Rights of Workers, 761
Chevreau case, 56
Children's Rights Convention, 193
Chile, 427-429, 788
China, 1126-1143
Christopher, Warren, 200, 826
Churchill, Winston, 16
Civil and Political Covenant, 191, 192
date when ratified by U.S., 187
example of use of complaint procedure, 228-237
general comments (Human Rights Committee), 224-226
individual communications/petitions, 214-222
interstate complaints, 222, 223
limitation clauses, 928, 929
prisoners, treatment of, 283, 284
ratification by U.S.
reaction of NGO community, 261-268
reaction of Senate Committee, 260, 261
reservations/understandings debate, 250-260
state reporting, 211-214
states of emergency, 914, 920, 921
substantive provisions, 209, 210
U.S. Constitution/laws, and, contrasted, 248
where to find text, 187
Civil strife. *See* States of emergency
Civil wars. *See* Internal armed conflict
Clinton, Bill, 269, 896, 1126, 1127, 1134, 1135, 1140
Clinton Administration
approach to economic/social/cultural rights, 200, 201
China, and, 1126-1143
humanitarian intervention in Haiti, 662
ratification of Racial Discrimination Convention, 268, 269
Codes of ethics, 301-304
Command responsibility, 855-859

Commission on Status of Women, 343, 398
Committee against Apartheid, 418
Committee against Torture, 414-416
Committee of Ministers of the Council of Europe, 685, 686
Committee of 24, 417, 418
Common Article 3, 907-911
Complaints. *See also* Non-petition procedures, Petition procedures
Civil and Political Covenant, 222, 223, 228-237
European Convention, 692
Inter-American system, 793-804
overview, 214-222
Comprehensive Anti-Apartheid Act of 1986, 580, 585-588
Compulsory licensing, 805
Conference on Security and Cooperation in Europe (CSCE), 769-775
Confidential review. *See* Resolution 1503
Convention against Torture and Other Cruel, Inhuman, or Degrading Treatment of Punishment. *See* Torture Convention
Convention for Suppression of Unlawful Acts against Safety of Maritime Navigation, 1012
Convention on Elimination of All Forms of Discrimination Against Women (CEDAW), 193
Convention on Elimination of All Forms of Racial Discrimination. *See* Racial Discrimination Convention
Convention on Prevention and Punishment of Crime of Genocide. *See* Genocide Convention
Convention on Rights of the Child. *See* Children's Rights Convention
Conventional international law, 93
Cook v. United States, 540
Corporal punishment, 715-724
Costa Rica, 805-819
Council of Europe, 684
Country Reports, 1097
Courts-martial, 859, 860
Covenant on Civil and Political Rights. *See* Civil and Political Covenant
Covenant on Economic, Social and Cultural Rights
overview, 191, 192
U.S. reaction to, 195-201, 239
Crimes against humanity, 847, 848
Criminal justice. *See* Prisoners, treatment of
Criminals, international. *See also* International criminal law
apprehension, 940, 941
crimes jure gentium, 941-943
jurisdiction, 939, 940

trial in accordance with international law, 942-951
trial in municipal courts, 939-942
Cruz Varas and others v. Sweden, 759, 760
CSCE High Commissioner on National Minorities, 771-775
Cuba
    report by IACHR, 788
    report of rapporteur, 424-427
    sanctions against, 511, 593
Cuban Assets Control Regulations, 520
Customary international law, 93
Cyprus, 692

De Klerk, F.W., 589
"Death Row Phenomenon," 746, 760
Declaration of Santiago, 342
Declaration on Human Rights of Individuals Who Are Not Citizens of the Country in Which They Live, 84, 85
Defense of superior orders, 855
Derian, Patricia, 1059, 1122
Diggs v. Richardson, 542, 595-597
Diggs v. Schultz, 535-541, 595
Diggs, Charles C., Jr., 531, 535
Disappearances Working Group, 390-392
Discrimination
    education, in, 10
    religion/belief, based on, 439-440
Dobriansky, Paula, 200
"Double-bunking," 315, 316
Douglas-Home, Sir Alec, 26, 27, 29
Draft Code of Crimes against Peace and Security of Mankind
    historical review, 959-961
    NGO efforts, 966, 967
    prognosis, 965, 966
    prospects for, 957-959
    second reading, 965
    viewpoints, 961-965
Dreyfus v. Von Finck, 95
Duffy, James, 875-879
Duvalier, Jean-Claude, 366

East Pakistan. See Bangladesh
Economic Community of West African States (ECOWAS), 512, 513
Economic rights, 195-201
Economic sanctions. See Sanctions
ECOSOC Resolution 1503. See Resolution 1503
ECOSOC Resolution 1235. See Resolution 1235
El Salvador, 1107-1109
Elles Declaration, 84, 85
European Commission of Human Rights, 684, 685

European Community, 775-778
European Convention for Protection of Human Rights and Fundamental Freedoms
    breadth of protection, 723
    enforcement bodies, 684, 685
    further readings, 686
    interstate complaints, 692
    reform, 686-691
    states of emergency, 920, 921, 926
    terminology, 682
European Court of Human Rights, 684-686, 724, 926
European Parliament, 776, 777
European Social Charter, 760, 761
European Torture Convention, 762-765
"Evolving standards of decency" test, 175

Fact-finding
    admissibility of evidence, 475
    African Charter on Human and People's Rights, by, 472
    burden of proof, 475-483
    Committee against Torture, by, 470
    country-specific rapporteurs, 423-431
    European Court of Human Rights, by, 470, 471
    final comments/questions, 483-485
    general standards, 448-451
    Inter-American Commission on Human Rights, by, 471-474, 476
    Inter-American Court of Human Rights, by, 471, 472
    International Court of Justice, by, 470
    international human rights bodies, by, 470
    non-governmental organizations, 452-469
    oversight committee for protection of detainees, by, 471
    overview, 410, 411
    South Africa, in, 418, 419
    South Vietnam, in, 418
    state reporting, 411-417
    thematic mechanisms, 431-448
    UN Center for Human Rights, role of, 444
    UN Commission on Human Rights, by, 422
    UN General Assembly, by, 417-422
    UN Secretariat, role of, 444, 445
Farband, Robert, 527
Fay, Michael, 721
Federal-state clause, 243
Fernandez v. Wilkinson, 143-147, 161, 162
Filartiga v. Pena-Irala, 137-143, 154-160
503 Club Marching Song, 532-534
Forcible protection of nationals
    contrasting views, 665, 666
    defined, 613

Forcible protection of nationals (*continued*)
humanitarian intervention, and,
contrasted, 613
legal validity, 667-671
post-Entebbe incidents, 672-675
Foreign Sovereign Immunities Act (FSIA),
157, 158
Forti v. Suarez-Mason, 148-154, 157-160,
765
Foster v. Nielson, 95, 96, 106, 109
Four Freedoms, 36, 1030
Frankel, Marvin E., 263, 268
Fraser, Donald, 535
French intervention in Central Africa,
644
French invasion in Zaire, 672
Fujii case
background, 101, 102
commentary, 104-115, 118-120
decision of District Court of Appeal,
102-104
decision of Supreme Court, 115-118

Gangaram Panday case, 481, 482
General comments
derogations, 925
minorities, 327, 328
self-determination, 335
summary (1981-1994), 224-226
"General principles," 93
Geneva Conventions, 901. *See also*
Common Article 3, Protocol I,
Protocol II
customary international law, status of,
912
first three conventions, 849
fourth convention, 849-851
ratification process, 910
Genocide Convention, 193, 273, 847
Glenn, John, 592
Goldwater, Barry, 900
Greece, 692
aftermath (overthrow of regime), 361,
362
background, 344-348
communication alleging violations,
348-354
reaction of Greek regime, 357-361
response of Amnesty International, 362,
363
UN response to allegations, 354-357
Grenada, U.S. operation in, 644, 645, 673
Gulf War, 879, 968-978

Habana. See Paquete Habana, The
Haig, Alexander M., Jr., 1085, 1090, 1094,
1095, 1121

Haiti
humanitarian intervention (Resolution
940), 659-663, 678
report by IACHR, 788-792
sanctions against, 512, 597, 598
Head-of-state immunity, 158, 160
Henderson, Oran K., 861, 875
Hostage-taking, 1012
Hostages case, 48, 136, 169, 173
Human rights
complaints, 214-222
denial, effect of, 79-83
enforcement, methods of, 342
factor in financial/development
assistance, as, 1147
historical review, 32-41
Human rights clauses
background and description, 36-41
interpretation, 39, 40, 45
invocation of, on international level,
48-55
legal status, 41-48
present status, 121
relevance to expulsion of Asians from
Uganda, 55-66
status in domestic law, 92-176
statutory construction cases, and, 175
Human Rights Committee, 925
Human rights treaties. *See also* Treaties
impact of, 275
list of treaties in force, 185-187
overview, 183-189
ratification by U.S. *See* United States
specific treaties (overview), 193, 194
Humanitarian intervention. *See* UN
humanitarian intervention
Humanitarian intervention by states
bibliography, 641
debate over, 623-641
defined, 613
dicta of International Court of Justice,
646-651
doctrine of, 614-623
incidents of, 643-646
Humanitarian law. *See* Law of war
Humphrey, Hubert H., 1089
Hussein, Saddam, 879, 977
Hutto, Charles E., 861

In absentia trials, 1020, 1024
Indians, 332-337
Indigenous peoples, 332-337
Inter-American Commission on Human
Rights (IACHR)
country-specific reports, 787-792, 833
criticism of, 833
fact-finding role, 471, 472
impact of politics, 798
overview, 782-787

report on U.S. practice (executions), 803, 804
states of emergency, 918, 921, 922, 927
Inter-American Convention to Prevent and Punish Torture, 826
Inter-American Court of Human Rights
  advisory opinions, 804-820, 927, 928
  burden of proof, 480-482
  fact-finding role, 471, 472
  overview, 782-787, 798, 799
Inter-American system, 782-826
  country-specific reports, 787-792, 833
  filing of petitions, 832
  further readings, 833, 834
  individual complaints, 793-804
  torture convention, 826
Intergovernmental Group to Monitor Supply and Shipping of Oil and Petroleum Products to South Africa, 418, 419, 579, 580
Internal armed conflict, 900-913
  background, 900, 901
  civil strife, and, contrasted, 922, 923
  four "separate but overlapping regimes," 929, 930
  invocation of Article 3/Protocol II, 908-911
International armed conflict. See Law of war
International Bill of Human Rights, 7, 190
International Committee of the Red Cross (ICRC), 880, 901, 905, 908, 909
International Convention against Taking of Hostages, 1012
International Convention on Suppression and Punishment of Crime of Apartheid, 1012
International conventions, 93
International Court of Justice
  fact-finding role, 470
  Namibia case, 49-55
International criminal code. See Draft Code of Crimes against Peace and Security of Mankind
International criminal court. See also Iraqi War Crimes Tribunal, Rwandan War Crimes Tribunal, Yugoslav War Crimes Tribunal
  draft statute, 993-1001
  imposition of, without endless debate, 1024
  jurisdiction, 995, 996
  means of creating, 951
  NGO efforts, 1001, 1002
  relationship to national courts, 997-1000
  U.S. attitudes, 976, 1002-1005
International criminal law
  draft code. See Draft Code of Crimes against Peace and Security of Mankind

object of, 954-957
past efforts to use, to punish human rights violators, 936-959
"piecemeal convention" approach, 1005-1013
protection of civil and political rights, 1018-1021
two enforcement models, 1013-1018
International custom, 93
International human rights
  "first generation," 194
  implementation measures, 210
  post-World War II movement, 94
  "second generation," 195-201
  "third generation," 201-206
International Labor Organization (ILO)
  adoption of conventions/recommendations to protect human rights, 184
  indigenous workers, 333
  overview, 4, 5
  petition procedures, 381
International law
  conventional, 93
  customary, 93
  defined, 32
  domestic law, and, contrasted, 92-94
  norms of, 93
  peremptory norms, 165
  sources of, 92, 93
  unwritten rules, 93
  written rules, 93
International Law Association (ILA)
  humanitarian intervention, 624
  relationship to human rights, 1
  rules of fact-finding, 449
  states of emergency, 931, 932
  status of Universal Declaration, 135, 166-171
International law of human rights
  basic assumption, 79, 80
  development of covenants and declaration, 191, 192
  historical review, 1-13
Investigations
  fact-finding. See Fact-finding
  future prospects, 400-404
  non-petition procedures, 382-400
  petition procedures, 342, 343, 380-382
  Resolution 1503 procedure. See Resolution 1503
Iran
  attempted rescue of hostages, 672, 673
  fact-finding in, 430, 431
Iraq
  execution of Israeli spies, 46
  repression of Kurds, 653
Iraqi War Crimes Tribunal, 968-978
Ireland v. United Kingdom, 475, 693-715, 765, 926, 927

Isle of Man Case, 715-721
Israel
  developments in Israeli-occupied
      territories, 483, 484
  fact-finding in, 418-422
  rescue operation at Entebbe, 669
  sanctions against, 513
Italy, sanctions against, 510, 511

Jefferson, Thomas, 1030
Johnson, Lyndon, 240, 517, 519
Jus cogen norm/exception, 158, 165, 803
Juvenile offenders, 305, 306

Kennedy, Edward M., 1089
Kennedy, John, 79
Kirkpatrick, Jeane J., 1077, 1084, 1085,
    1095, 1104, 1121, 1122
Kissinger, Henry, 1053, 1146
Koster, Samuel W., 860, 861
Kotouc, Eugene M., 861, 874

Lancaster House Conference, 562-565
Law of war. *See also* My Lai massacre
  comments/questions, 896-900
  convergence of humanitarian and human
      rights laws, 931
  development of, 844-851
  "orders" from above, 875-878
  recent developments, 879-896
  summary of relevant law, 851-853
  who bears responsibility for violations of,
      853-859
Lawyers, role of, 1029, 1030
League of Nations, 2-5, 509, 510
Lefever, Ernest, 1093, 1094
Lockerbie case, 655

Maastricht Treaty, 778
Madison, James, 1030
Mandela, Nelson, 589
Marcos, Ferdinand, 1124
Mass expulsion, 59, 60
McGee, Gale, 526, 528, 530, 532, 535, 820
Meadlo, Paul, 840, 860, 897
Medina, Ernest R., 840, 841, 861, 862,
    874, 875
Mexico, 798
Military intervention. *See* Humanitarian
      intervention by states
Minorities, 324-332, 336, 337
Mitchell, David, 861
Model laws. *See* Soft laws
Monetary damages, 768
Montreal Statement, 132, 133

My Lai massacre. *See also* Calley
      Court-Martial
  further reading, 900
  prosecution of those responsible, 859-879
  what happened, 839-843

Namibia case, 48-55, 119, 134
Neier, Aryeh, 265, 266
New international economic order (NIEO),
    203, 206
New Mexico prison uprising, 281
Newsom, David D., 527
Nicaragua, 458-464
Nicaragua v. United States, 646-651, 903,
    904
Nigeria, expulsion of Ghanian migrant
      workers, 85, 86
Nixon, Richard, 872, 873
Nixon Administration, 74
Non-international armed conflict. *See*
      Internal armed conflict
Non-petition procedures, 382-400. *See also*
      Resolution 1503
Nuremberg Trials, 848, 849, 899, 936, 937,
    1021

Obote, Milton, 17, 18, 87
Oilgate, 546-553
Okun, Herbert S., 577
Optional Protocol to International
      Covenant on Civil and Political
      Rights, 214-222
Organization of African Unity (OAU),
    826-830
Organization of American States (OAS),
    511, 512, 678
Owen, Roberts, 246
Oyama v. California, 102

Paquete Habana, The, 138, 161, 162
Panama, U.S. invasion of, 645, 674
Peacekeeping, 913
Peacemaking, 678, 679
Pell, Clairborne, 246, 248, 261, 268
Peron, Eva, 1064
Personal sovereignty, 33
Petition procedures, 342, 343, 380-382
Principle of domestic jurisdiction, 501
Principle of "equality," 62
Principle of nonintervention, 619
Principle of proportionality, 919
Prisoners, treatment of
  arbitrary detention. *See* Arbitrary
      detention
  basic international regulations. *See*
      Standard Minimum Rules for
      Treatment of Prisoners

European rules, 313, 314
NGO response, 317, 318
purpose of incarceration, 282
United States
   Attica uprising. *See* Attica uprising
   comments by prison officials, 319-321
   federal/state standards, 314-317
   "maxi-maxi" prison, 283
   New Mexico prison uprising, 281
Proclamation of Tehran, 132, 133
Professional behavior, 302-304
Protocol I
   overview, 880-884
   ratification process, 910
   relevant articles, 884-888
   U.S. position, 894-896
   viewpoints, 888-893
Protocol II
   applicability to states of emergency, 914
   content, 905-907
   customary international law, as part of,
      913
   objection to, 912
   overview, 880-884
   ratification process, 910, 913, 929
   U.S. position, 894-896, 908

Racial Discrimination Convention, 193,
   240, 268, 269, 343
   state reporting, and, 414-416
Rangel Amendment, 588, 589
Rapporteurs. *See* Country-specific
   rapporteurs, Thematic rapporteurs
Reagan, Ronald, 247, 583, 880, 894-896,
   908, 976, 1094
Reagan Administration. *See also* U.S.
   foreign policy
   approach to economic/social/cultural
      rights, 199, 200
   Carter Administration, and, contrasted,
      1103-1105
   position on Protocols to Geneva
      Convention, 894-896
   ratification process, and, 246-248
   sanctions against South Africa, 580, 590
Regional regimes, 682-684, 782
Rehnquist, William, 860
Reports. *See also* Country-specific
   rapporteurs, State reporting,
   Thematic rapporteurs
   country reports (U.S.), 1097
   country-specific reports (IACHR),
      787-792, 833
Resolution 1235, 385-390, 393, 401, 402
Resolution 1503
   evaluation of, 379, 380, 401, 402
   historical review, 366-378
   limited success, as, 405
   outline of procedure, 354, 355, 365, 366

procedural problems, 363-365
situations referred to Commission
   (1973-1979), 369
situations referred to Commission
   (1978-1986), 374
when adopted, 344, 354
Resolutions
   ECOSOC Resolution 1235. *See*
      Resolution 1235
   ECOSOC Resolution 1503. *See*
      Resolution 1503
   Resolution 41/120, 207, 208
   Resolution 47/135, 329, 330
   Resolution 232, 495
   Resolution 253, 496
   Resolution 940, 659-663, 678
Restatement (Third) of Foreign Relations
   Law of the United States, 162-166,
   248-250
Rhodes, Cecil, 489
Rhodes v. Chapman, 316
Rhodesia
   achievement of Black majority rule,
      561-565
   background, 489, 490
   initial attempts at settlement, 493-495
   prelude to independence, 490, 491
   UN sanctions
      legality of, 497-509
      Resolution 232, 495
      Resolution 253, 496
      viewpoints on effect of, 565-573
      violations of, 543-561
   unilateral declaration of independence,
      491, 492
   U.S. enforcement of sanctions
      Byrd Amendment. *See* Byrd
         Amendment
      introduction, 522-524
      Senate hearings, 524-531
   U.S. implementation of UN sanctions
      Executive Order 11,322, 517
      Executive Order 11,419, 518, 519
      implementing regulations, 520-522
      introduction, 515-517
Rhodesian Sanctions Regulations, 521
Rice v. Sioux City Cemetery, Inc., 171
Rockefeller trip to Latin America,
   1077-1080
Roosevelt, Eleanor, 7, 107, 126, 134, 144
Roosevelt, Franklin D., 5, 36, 196, 197, 1030
Roosevelt, Theodore, 1149
Rwandan War Crimes Tribunal, 992

Safety of maritime navigation, 1012
Salisbury Agreement, 562
Sanctions. *See also* Rhodesia, South Africa
   Albania/Bulgaria, against, 514
   Argentina, against, 1064-1077

Sanctions (*continued*)
  China, against, 514
  Cuba, against, 511, 593
  Dominican Republic, against, 511
  Haiti, against, 512, 597, 598
  international, 509-511
  Israel, against, 513
  Italy, against, 510, 511
  Liberia, against, 512, 513
  list of, since end of Cold War, 598
  mandatory, 573, 575
  regional, 511-513
  unilateral, 513, 514
  voluntary, 514
  when most effective, 597
  whether preferable to military
    intervention, 677
Scali, John, 554
Sei Fujii v. State. *See Fujii* case
Self-determination, 334-337
"Sense-of-the-Congress" provision, 1039,
  1040
SIM Fact-Finding Conference, 467
Slavery, 1, 4, 184
Slay, Alton D., 900
Smith, Ian, 491, 561
Soering v. United Kingdom
  applicant not UK national, 765
  court reversal of Commission, 685
  final outcome for applicant, 768
  questions raised by, 767, 768
  substantive issue, 760
  text of decision, 724-759
  underlying principle, 759
Soft laws, 277-338
  defined, 284
  juvenile offenders, 305, 306
  standards of administration of justice,
    306
  treatment of prisoners, 305
Solidarity rights, 201
Somalia, 653, 654, 675
South Africa
  fact-finding in, 418, 419
  Namibia, and, 48-55, 578, 579
    Security Council sanctions, 578, 579
  UN mandatory sanctions (arms embargo)
    implementation/enforcement, 575,
      576
    text of Resolution 418, 534, 535
    vetoes of further sanctions, 576-578
  UN voluntary sanctions
    General Assembly sanctions, 578, 579
    monitoring group, 418, 419, 579, 580
    oil embargo, 578

U.S. sanctions
  Comprehensive Anti-Apartheid Act,
    580, 585-588
  end of sanctions, 589, 590
  introduction, 580-582
  Rangel Amendment, 588, 589
  Reagan's Executive Order, 583-585
South African Council of Churches' 1993
    Code of Conduct for Business
    Operating in South Africa, 595
South African Democratic Transition
    Support Act of 1993, 589
South Vietnam. *See also* My Lai massacre
  fact-finding, in, 418
Sovereign immunity, 158
Standard Minimum Rules for Treatment of
    Prisoners
  implementation, 306-310
  legal status of, 296-300
  overview, 284
  relevance to Attica uprising, 285-296
State reporting
  Civil and Political Covenant, 211-214
  fact-finding, 411-417
States of emergency
  applicability of conventions, 914
  data bases, 932
  derogation provisions, 914-929
  determining existence of, 924-927
  habeas corpus, 927, 928
  internal armed conflict/civil strife,
    contrasted, 922, 923
  position of ILA, 931, 932
Sub-Commission on Prevention of
    Discrimination and Protection of
    Minorities, 344, 400, 924
Sullivan Principles, 580, 581, 594
Summary/arbitrary executions, 431-436,
  445-448
Suriname
  aftermath, 237-239
  background, 181-183
  letter alleging violations, 228, 229
  report of rapporteur, 445-448
  response of Human Rights Committee,
    229-237
  violation of Civil and Political Covenant,
    224-226
Syrian occupation of Lebanon, 644

Tanzanian intervention in Uganda, 644
Taylor, Telford, 872
Territorial sovereignty, 33
Terrorism, 1005-1011
Thatcher, Margaret, 563
Thematic procedures, 390-398
Thematic rapporteurs, 393-398, 431-448
Thurmond, Strom, 900
Timerman, Jacobo, 1081, 1091, 1092, 1122

Torture, 141, 142, 158
  Argentina, in, 1080
  "piecemeal" approach to international
    criminal law, 1011, 1012
  report of special rapporteur, 436-439
  what constitutes, 692-715, 762
Torture Convention, 193, 343, 1012
  fact-finding, 470
Torture Victim Protection Act (TVPA),
  160
Transnational terrorism, 1005-1011
Treaties. See also Human rights treaties
  binding effect of, 93
  clauses authorizing petitions, 343
  non-self-executing, 110
  self-executing, 96, 120-122, 172
Truman, Harry, 6
Tutu, Desmond, 591
Tyrer v. United Kingdom, 715-721

Uganda
  demise of Amin, 75-78
  expulsion of Asians
    compensatory payments, 83, 84
    overview, 19-25
    relevance of UN Charter, 55-66
    response of world community, 26-32,
      70-73
  history, 16-19
  situation today, 87, 88
  subsequent abuses, 66-78
  U.S. trade embargo, 73-76
UNESCO, petition procedures, 343, 381
Uniform Code of Military Justice (UCMJ),
  851
United Nations, 5-11
  bodies dealing with human rights issues,
    398-400
  human rights treaties, listed, 185-187
  legal force of decisions, 92
  means of achieving respect for human
    rights, 183
  quality control/standard setting, 206-208
  South Africa, and, 50
  Uganda, and, 28-32, 70-73
UN Charter. See also Human rights clauses
  Article 25, 516
  Article 48, 515
  Article 56, 110-114
  humanitarian intervention, 613, 614
UN Commission on Human Rights
  fact-finding, 422
  historical review of activities, 382-390
UN High Commissioner for Human Rights,
  445
UN humanitarian intervention
  bibliography, 663, 664
  Haiti, in, 659-663

  overview, 651, 652
  recent developments, 652-659
UN instruments/resolutions. See General
  comments, Resolutions, Vulnerable
  groups
United Nations Participation Act, 515-517
UN sanctions. See Sanctions
UN Secretary-General, 445
United States. See also U.S. foreign policy
  attitude toward establishment of
    international criminal court, 976,
    1002-1005
  Covenant on Economic, Social and
    Cultural Rights, 195-201, 239
  cruel and unusual punishment, 723, 724
  double standard on human rights issues,
    1145, 1149
  Economic Bill of Rights, 196
  execution of juveniles, 803, 804
  Grenada, operation in, 644, 645, 673
  impact on development of "first
    generation" of human rights, 195,
    196
  Iran, attempted rescue of hostages, 672,
    673
  Israel, and, 484, 513
  legal effect of UN Charter domestically,
    92-176
  legal status of human rights clauses, 46
  Liberia, rescue operation, 674
  Panama, invasion of, 645, 674
  ratification of American Convention, 820
  ratification of Civil and Political
    Covenant. See Civil and Political
    Covenant
  ratification of human rights treaties
    Carter Administration initiatives,
      240-246, 250
    conditions for ratification of future
      treaties, 269
    introduction, 239, 240
    Reagan/Bush Administration
      developments, 246-248
  ratification of Racial Discrimination
    Convention, 268, 269
  resolutions, legal effect of, 541, 542
  restatement, 162-166, 248-250
  sanctions, legal effect of, 541, 542
  Somalia, rescue operation, 653, 654, 675
  trade embargo against Uganda, 73-76
  treatment of prisoners. See Prisoners,
    treatment of
U.S. Army's The Law of Land Warfare,
  851-855, 858, 859
U.S. foreign policy. See also Bush
  Administration, Carter Administration,
  Clinton Administration, Nixon
  Administration, Reagan
  Administration
  Bush Administration, 1124-1126

U.S. foreign policy (*continued*)
  Carter Administration
    Argentina, sanctions against,
      1064-1077, 1122, 1123
    criticism and response, 1048-1064
    defining the policy, 1041-1047
  Clinton Administration, 1126-1143
  congressional influence in Nixon/Ford
      period, 1039, 1040
  evolution, 1030-1038
  Reagan Administration
    Argentina, and, 1088-1093, 1119-1124
    change in administration posture,
      1095-1105
    criticism and response, 1105-1119
    El Salvador and, 1107-1109
    initial reaction to policies of Carter
      Administration, 1077-1095
  totalitarian/authoritarian distinction,
      1081-1084, 1144, 1145
United States v. Percheman, 109
Universal Declaration of Human Rights, 3,
    4, 11-13, 39, 55, 65, 94, 106, 107,
    190, 283
  analysis of, 166-171
  historical perspective, 122-126
  impact on international/national law,
      127-131
  normative impact of its standards, 134,
      135
  overview, 133

Uruguay, 925, 926

Vance, Cyrus, 1042
Velásquez Rodríguez case, 480, 481,
    799-803, 833
Vidal, Gore, 541
Vietnamese invasion of Kampuchea, 644
Vulnerable groups, 322-324

Wallace, George, 872
War crimes, 848, 849, 852
Westmoreland, William, 873, 898
Wilson v. Seiter, 316
Wilson, Woodrow, 2, 3, 80, 1030
World War II, 5

Yamashita case, 854-858, 899
Yost, Charles, 46
Young, George H., 861
Yugoslav War Crimes Tribunal
  current status, 992
  jurisdiction, 978-985, 990
  rules of procedure and evidence,
      985-989

Zaire, 404
Zimbabwe. *See* Rhodesia